# Social Beings
## Core Motives in Social Psychology

Second Edition

**Susan T. Fiske**
*Princeton University*

www.wiley.com/college/fiske

Vice President & Executive Publisher  *Jay O'Callaghan*
Executive Editor  *Christopher Johnson*
Associate Editor  *Eileen McKeever*
Production Manager  *Dorothy Sinclair*
Senior Production Editor  *Valerie A. Vargas*
Marketing Manager  *Danielle Torio*
Creative Director  *Harry Nolan*
Senior Designer  *Madelyn Lesure*
Production Management Services  *Laserwords Maine*
Editorial Assistant  *Mariah Maguire-Fong*
Media Editor  *Bridget O'Lavin*
Cover Design  *Madelyn Lesure*

This book was set in Times by Laserwords Private Limited and printed and bound by Courier-Westford. The cover was printed by Phoenix Color Group.

*Library of Congress Cataloging in Publication Data:*
Fiske, Susan T.
 Social beings: core motives in social psychology / Susan Fiske.
  p. cm.

Includes bibliographical references and index.
ISBN 0-471-14529-7 (pbk. : acid-free paper)
1. Social psychology. 2. Motivation (Psychology) I. Title.

HM1033.F57 2004
302-dc22

USA ISBN 13: 978-0-470-12911-1
WIE ISBN: 0-471-45151-7

Printed in the United States of America

10 9 8 7 6 5 4 3 2 1

**Soci**

**Core** **y**

*Dedicated to the memories of my mother, Barbara Page Fiske,
and my father, Donald W. Fiske,
with love and respect.*

# Brief Contents

# Contents

**Chapter 2**

## SCIENTIFIC METHODS FOR STUDYING PEOPLE IN INTERACTION   37

**Chapter 3**

## ORDINARY PERSONOLOGY: FIGURING OUT WHY PEOPLE DO WHAT THEY DO   81

Chapter 4
# SOCIAL COGNITION: MAKING SENSE OF OTHERS   127

Chapter 11

# STEREOTYPING, PREJUDICE, AND DISCRIMINATION: SOCIAL BIASES   427

# Preface to First Edition

Social psychology professors and students are stuck. They have the most wonderful material to teach and learn, all about people and why we do what we do. Undergraduates love social psychology, if the material is selected right. Graduate students stake their careers on it. So why must we choose between, on one side, same-old texts and, on the other side, a couple of outliers, brilliant but dated and idiosyncratic. Some of my best friends have authored each kind of textbook, but the problems remain. This book proposes to remove social psychologists from the horns of their dilemma by presenting familiar topics in a novel way. My preferred mode of operation is synthesis, so in this book I twist the dilemma's horns around each other, making something new, while preserving the best of the traditional.

I have written a social psychology text using standard chapter topics; it's too much trouble for most faculty to rewrite their syllabi and lecture notes to fit some totally new parsing of the field, idiosyncratic to one senior name. Besides, the standard parsing of the field has some internal logic; it typically moves from within the individual (attribution, social cognition, self, attitudes) to between individuals (attraction, relationships, helping, aggression) to groups (prejudice, groups, influence). What's more, the standard parsing has the merits of familiarity. But my allegiance to standard texts stops there, for several good reasons.

Here are some goals I've had:

- Use the standard chapter headings
- Keep to five main points; too many principles bore and overwhelm, and too few principles explain everything and therefore nothing
- Focus on an emphatically social approach to adaptation
- Integrate culture throughout, not as a separate topic
- Communicate social psychology as a friendly and personal field
- Strive to be accurate and even-handed
- Avoid self-promotion and self-indulgence
- Mix materials that are classic—ones that got us all into the field in the first place—with the contemporary, cutting edge—ones that make social psychology a topic for today
- Cover European and Asian authors, younger and older authors, as well as current American authors
- Demonstrate our field's good instincts on gender and ethnicity, integral to the weave of the book, not politically correct add-ons
- Use absorbing anecdotes from classic and contemporary fiction

- Provide examples from students themselves
- Keep applications integral to the chapters (health, law, organizations, politics, and marketing appear throughout)
- Create a narrative flow
- Not be too idiosyncratic
- Provide separate chapters on liking and loving, a division that reflects the recent explosion of research in this area as well as students' main preoccupations
- Attend to aesthetic appeal, from the cover inward
- Write from the heart

In the realm of textbook writing, what lies between the dull clones and the brilliant outliers? Into this vast space, I am launching a book that retains the familiar, safe outward structure of the standard texts, allowing professors to keep their hard-won lecture preps and retaining social psychology's intrinsic logic of intra-individual to inter-individual to group analyses. Simultaneously, I want to import a point of view, a narrative flow, both across chapters and within each chapter.

Across chapters, the linkages are core social motives repeatedly identified by personality and social psychologists over the decades, so they are not idiosyncratic to this author. Granted, listing and parsing motives are risky, but this strategy buys a manageable number of organizing themes: fewer than a dozen and more than one. In any one chapter, perhaps three motives are highlighted, given the emphasis of the theories and research in a given area. The five motives overall appear and reappear throughout the book, making both intuitive and theoretical sense.

The book starts from the premise that people are adapted to live with other people and that social relations are the most relevant adaptation environment. This focuses, then, on the social psychology of people's adaptive, functional motives and goals. From a pragmatic point of view, people need other people to survive, and a few core social motives follow logically from that basic premise.

As a foundation, people first and foremost need to *belong* (to relationships and groups) in order to survive; the environment to which people adapt is the social group, and culture codifies survival rules in different groups. Thus, nature and nurture interact, and this theme underlies the other four core motives. Belonging particularly explains some kinds of self-presentation, identity-related attitudes, prejudices, and social influence, but of course belonging especially explains principles of close relationships, altruism, and groups.

Two more "cognitive" motives follow from the basic need to belong. *Understanding* aims at knowing quickly and predicting well enough to function in ordinary life. People's motive to understand adapts them to group life and its shared construction of reality. Understanding also describes why people bother to make sense of each other (attribution and social cognition), themselves, and various attitude objects in the social environment. Easy understanding and prediction also drive some of the attraction to similar others and the distance from dissimilar others (outgroups).

A related motive with a cognitive flavor, *controlling*, encourages people to feel competent and effective at dealing with their social environment and themselves.

The belief in control describes how people make sense of each other (e.g., personality attributions), how certain attitudes are retained, how people feel initially attracted, and how relationships cause emotions. Control also enters into aggression and prejudice, as well as maintaining the ingroup and social influence within it.

The two more solidly "affective" motives likewise follow from the basic need to belong and likewise describe various social phenomena.

People need to feel special; *enhancing self* comprises self-esteem, self-improvement, and self-sympathy. Some people and some cultures emphasize putting oneself first and viewing oneself in a positive light, but others emphasize the humble self: always striving to improve, putting others first, but sympathetic to one's own failings. The term *self-enhancing* captures both senses, which of course explains many aspects of the social self. Self-enhancing also explains some aspects of attribution, attitudes, attraction, helping, aggression, and social influence.

*Trusting*—feeling good about the world—makes people more adaptable, open, and cooperative in interaction, but also hypersensitive to negative information from others. The predisposition to expect pretty good things from most people (until or unless proven otherwise) enables people to adapt to their ingroups, perceiving others as basically good (person perception), encouraging mutual altruism, and building group loyalty.

These five motives go by the mnemonic BUCET, pronounced "bucket," as in a bucket of motives. As indicated in every chapter, they provide unity and continuity throughout the book, intellectual themes taken seriously, not merely as add-on boxes. Certainly the particular motives are debatable, but that makes them interesting to read, consider, and teach as they appear and reappear across chapters.

Within chapters, the book's aim is, first, to capture the imagination of students by relating social psychology to everyday life. Having taught introductory social psychology in large and small lectures, to honors and average students, in public and private institutions, for more than two decades, I have a sense of what engages students (and the rest of us as students for life). They care about their own lives, their relationships, and their futures, but they also care about making the world a better place. Social psychology provides a perfect forum for all these concerns. To this end, the book selectively covers the most intriguing theories within traditional chapter topics. It's easier to write enthusiastic prose when the author thinks the ideas are nifty, and I do.

My stylistic goals are to provide a readable, informal style; to illustrate scientific methods and results; and to provide some intellectual tidbits for the professor and the more motivated students. Overall, the book integrates material showing how applicable the research is to human problems and brings in motivation, social evolution, and culture as intrinsic features of the project. The book is produced without cartoons, photos, boxes, bells, or whistles. It has summaries at the ends of sections and chapters, as well as outlines in the table of contents.

This book has benefited enormously from comments on one or more chapters by the following, mostly masked, reviewers, now unmasked as a group: Daniel Batson, University of Kansas; Ellen Berscheid, University of Minnesota; Fletcher Blanchard, Smith College; Galen Bodenhausen, Northwestern University; Kelly Brennan, State University of New York at Stony Brook; Jeff Bryson, San Diego State University;

Brad Bushman, Iowa State University; Michael Caruso, University of Toledo; Jerome Chertkoff, Indiana University; Diana Cordova, Yale University; John Darley, Princeton University; Kari Edwards, Brown University; Allan Fenigstein, Kenyon College; Randy Fisher, University of Central Florida; Barry Gillen, Old Dominion University; Stephanie Goodwin, Purdue University; Melanie Green, University of Pennsylvania; Anthony Greenwald, University of Washington; Monica Harris, University of Kentucky; James Hilton, University of Michigan; Dacher Keltner, University of California–Berkeley; Joachim Krueger, Brown University; David Kuhlman, University of Delaware; G. Daniel Lassiter, Ohio University; John Levine, University of Pittsburgh; Helen Linky, Marshall University; Angela Lipsitz, Northern Kentucky University; René Martin, University of Iowa; Kristin Mickelson, Kent State University; Rick Miller, University of Nebraska–Kearney; Beth Morling, Muhlenberg College; Carolyn Murray, University of California–Riverside; Sidney Perloe, Haverford College; Vaida Thompson, University of North Carolina at Chapel Hill; and Luis Vega, California State University–Bakersfield. I am deeply grateful for their thoughtful comments.

This book has also benefited from the masked feedback of students in two classes: Kenworthey Bilz, Amy Cuddy, Karla Evans, Morgan Flusser, Michelle Garretson, Amir Goren, Uri Hasson, Linda Kochman, Yevgenia Kozorovitskiy, Elli Maria Lavidas, Ngar Yin Louis Lee, Agatha Lenartowtiz, Anesu Mandisodza, Aviva Meerschwam, Kimberly Montgomery, Evan Morrison, Ehrin Newman, Michael Norton, Lauren Rigney, Jessica Salvatore, Rebecca Stewart, and Cara Talaska. They kept me believing in the project, at the same time that they told me what needed fixing. My parents, Donald W. Fiske and Barbara Page Fiske, provided many wise words regarding early drafts. Of course, none of the reviewers is responsible for any remaining problems.

I also want to thank my staff of helpers over the many years this book has required. Most recently, Vera Sohl has been a great help with permissions and bibliography. Special thanks go to Chris Rogers, the editor who originally signed and believed in this book; to Anne Smith, who stayed with me when the going got tough; to Tim Vertovec, who saw it through to completion; and to Kris Pauls, for her patience and speed. Previously, library research and general facilitation have been aided by Christine McGroarty, Geoff Emery, Stephanie Strebel, Mona Mody, Lisa Leslie, and Lisa Taylor. Finally, and most importantly, loving gratitude to my children, who have patiently supported the long hours and years this book has required, especially Lydia, who can't remember a time when Mom wasn't working on The Book, but also Geoff, and more recently Vanessa. To Doug, I can only say how lucky I feel. And thanks to the cats, who have sat on many a manuscript page.

# Preface to Second Edition

Some things change, and others remain the same. The First Preface still describes this book's goals, and the second edition aims to do all that, and more. Here are some of the new features:

- Social neuroscience appears, throughout the topics, just as it's been appearing in the field, lately.
- Cutting-edge topics—embodied cognition, mind perception, emotion, terrorism, and homosexual close relationships—join the relevant chapters.
- New research updates every topic in every chapter.

Among the features that remain are the core social motives, creating themes that unify social psychology; applications to real-world experiences and social issues; scientific summaries; and everyday and literary examples. A word on the use of fiction here: these are anecdotal evidence at best, and some writer's fevered imagination at worst, so they do not provide scientific evidence. But they also provide windows into human nature, allowing each of us to simulate the experience of others who may differ from us; fiction is the original immersive environment (Mar & Oatley, 2008). The literary examples—like the entire book—aim to communicate the impact of social situations.

All books require a village. Thanks to Wiley editors Chris Johnson and Eileen McKeever, as well as reviewers Randolph Cornelius, Wendy Harrod, Brian Armenta, Alexis Franzese, Curtis Haugvedt, and Christy Porter.

Dear reader (as writers used to say), this book is for you. Thank you for attending, thinking, and engaging. And I thank my students, who provide feedback every year; my family, who were patient again this time, and now even read the book for their own respective purposes. The cats no longer sit on manuscript pages, which appear on-screen only. But they do their best to sit on the keyboard.

STF

# About the Author

**Susan T. Fiske** is Eugene Higgins Professor of Psychology, Princeton University. A Harvard Ph.D., she has honorary doctorates from the Université catholique de Louvain-la-Neuve, Belgium, and Universiteit Leiden, Netherlands. She has just finished a third edition of *Social Cognition* (1984, 1991, 2008, each with Shelley Taylor) on how people make sense of each other. She has written more than 200 articles and chapters, as well as editing many books and journal special issues. Notably, as part of her effort to keep up with the field she loves, she edits the *Annual Review of Psychology* (with Daniel Schacter and Robert Sternberg) and the *Handbook of Social Psychology* (5th edition, 2010, with Daniel Gilbert and Gardner Lindzey).

Her social cognition research has focused on how people choose between category-based and individuating impressions of other people. She emphasizes the role of interdependence and power in stereotyping. Her current research shows that social structure (status, interdependence) predicts distinct kinds of bias against different groups in society, focusing on disrespecting versus disliking.

Her research has sparked opportunities for real-world impact. Her expert testimony in discrimination cases includes some cited by the U.S. Supreme Court in a 1989 landmark case on gender bias. In 1998, she also testified before President Clinton's Race Initiative Advisory Board, and in 2001–2003, she coauthored a National Academy of Science report on Methods for Measuring Discrimination. Fiske won the 1991 American Psychological Association Award for Distinguished Contributions to Psychology in the Public Interest, Early Career, in part for the expert testimony. Fiske also won, with Peter Glick, the 1995 Gordon Allport Intergroup Relations Award from the Society for the Psychological Study of Social Issues for work on ambivalent sexism. Bringing together some of these practical applications, she edited *Beyond Common Sense: Psychological Science in the Courtroom* (2008, with Eugene Borgida).

Recent recipient of a Guggenheim Award, Fiske was elected to the American Academy of Arts and Sciences. She is currently President of the Foundation for the Advancement of Brain and Behavioral Sciences, seeking to educate the public about the importance of our research, and she previously served as President of the Association for Psychological Science in 2002–2003. She was 1994 President of the Society for Personality and Social Psychology and served on the executive committee of the Society for Experimental Social Psychology. She has served on the boards of Scientific Affairs for the American Psychological Association, the Association for Psychological Science, Annual Reviews Inc., the Social Science Research Council, and the Common School in Amherst.

On campus, she teaches graduate and undergraduate courses in social psychology, social cognition, and racism, and has chaired both departmental and college personnel committees, as well as diversity and multiculturalism committees. She lives in Prince-ton, Philadelphia, and Vermont, with her sociologist husband, with frequent visits from her college-aged daughter and stepdaughter, and her stepson's new family. She grew up in a stable, racially integrated neighborhood and still wonders why more of the world isn't like that.

# Chapter 1

# Introduction: Adaptive Motives for Social Situations, via Cultures and Brains

What are your major concerns? What do you think about in the shower, discuss with friends after midnight, or ponder on the way to school? If you are like many students, various thoughts, both trivial and life-shaping, come to mind: Who am I, and who will I become? Do I look better in a sweater or a sweatshirt? How will I get that reading done in time? Should I go into clinical psychology, teaching, law, business, or some other field? How can I support myself in a career that makes sense to me? Who loves me, and whom do I love? Will that attractive person in my social psychology class be there today? What groups do I like, and what groups like me? Should I join the campus drama club or do some community service? Am I safe here? Why do people hurt and kill each other? Are people basically loving, good, and helpful? How can we make the world a better place? Although social psychology won't tell you whether you look good in a sweatshirt, it can help you answer some of these questions about your life and the world around you.

To introduce social psychology, this chapter tackles five issues. First, what is social psychology all about, and how does it relate to everyday concerns? Second, what is social psychology's main intellectual contribution? Third, what core social motives help people adapt to living with other people? Fourth, how does culture shape these general motives? Fifth, how does the brain influence our social motives and interactions? And finally, what key features characterize social psychology's scientific approach?

## WHAT IS SOCIAL PSYCHOLOGY?

To illustrate social psychology at work, try this exercise. Take a clean sheet of paper, and fold it in half the long way. Now open it up, and fold one top corner down to meet the center crease. Then fold down the other top corner the same way. Now fold the paper in half again along the center crease. Fold one of the long sides backward to the outside of the crease, making another fold parallel to the central one. Flip the paper over and repeat this last step on the other side. What is this shape? What does it look like?

If you are like most readers, you have probably read this far and not done what I just asked you to do; you are reading on ahead to see if it is really necessary to put the book down, find a piece of paper, think through each instruction, fold the paper, and so on. No one will know whether you do it or not, so why bother until you find out if you really have to? You are especially unlikely to have followed these instructions if you are sitting someplace where other people can see you.

Now, try a thought experiment: Compare your reactions to those of students in my social psychology classes. In large and small classes alike, to a person, they all obediently take their pristine course syllabus, fold it in half, fold down the top corners, and construct... what? A paper airplane.

I never quite have the nerve to ask my students to take off their shoes and put them on their desks, or to stand up and face the back of the classroom and wave at the projection booth, but I suspect that if I did, they would probably comply. Why? Would they normally take off their shoes and put them on the desk in front of them? Would they normally fold their syllabus into a paper airplane? Then, why do they do it, semester after semester, year after year? Because I ask them to. But that's not the only reason. They comply because everyone else does. And why did you *not* fold the paper airplane when I asked you to? Because your professor is not standing over you, in person and in authority. Because you are not sitting in a classroom full of other students doing the same thing. (If you did do it, you are a remarkably cooperative and active learner; congratulations!) In the classroom—as opposed to your room, the library, the lounge, the café, or wherever you are reading this—two simultaneous forms of social pressure occur: the professor's request and other people going along with it.

Consider a second example. Eight male college students participate in a perception experiment, in which they judge one standard line against three comparison lines (see Figure 1.1). Given a standard line of 10″, they choose the comparison line that is closest in length, stating their choice aloud, each in turn. The task is easy, and the first two judgments are unanimous. On the third trial, a 3″ standard appears beside comparison lines of 3 3/4″, 4 1/4″, and 3″. Seven participants all choose the first comparison line as equivalent to the standard, and the eighth student finds himself a minority of one in the midst of a unanimous and erroneous majority. This experience is repeated in 11 of the remaining 15 trials.

This strange circumstance occurs because seven members of the group are confederates of the experimenter, who is studying group pressure on judgments (Asch, 1956). And indeed, three-quarters of the participants go along at least once with the conspirators' mistakes, blatant errors of 1/2″ to 1 3/4″ on lines ranging from 2″ to 10″. Conversely, no participant making private judgments in a control condition makes any mistakes. On average, a third of the trial judgments are erroneous, with no other cause than conformity to the group, in direct violation of the participants' senses.

Consider a third and final example. Jennifer King, a student at a small private college, wanted to make the world a better place. Along with many other students, she joined an organization called Western Massachusetts Labor Action. This group

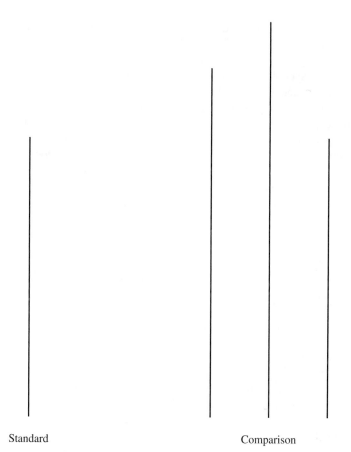

Standard                                    Comparison

**Figure 1.1**   Sample Standard Line and Comparison Lines Judged in Asch Study of Group
Conformity (as described by Asch, 1956)

recruited students to chop wood for the poor, attend educational meetings, and canvass
for new members; the group was known on campus as "a sort of Salvation Army with
a political edge" (Rabinovitz, 1996). Indeed, lots of students participated as a way to
fulfill a community service requirement for one particular course. Jennifer soon left
college to become a full-time volunteer at the group's Brooklyn office, the National
Labor Federation. She had a dream of organizing the poor to create a more just world,
and she was willing to work hard toward her vision.

Instead, she spent all her time confined inside a cramped apartment building,
filing and telephoning; every minute was scheduled. Each evening, everyone in the
group had to attend political lectures, which would sometimes last until 4:00 or 5:00
a.m. Jennifer and about 50 other recruits would stagger off to bed, only to wake up
to commands from a loudspeaker six hours later. She was exhausted and had no time
to think. Also, she was not allowed to chat with other recruits; she was isolated from
family and friends; and she was not allowed outside. The group's stated goal was
mobilizing the poor to challenge the economic system, but they never seemed to get

around to it, although they did collect a supply of rifles, shotguns, ammunition, and explosives. Jennifer became terrified, and after a few weeks, she escaped. Many other people never did.

The social-psychological question is this: Why did someone with such ideals choose to stay in such a useless, dangerous psychological prison? Some people would call this a cult, especially as its charismatic founder, Eugenio Perente-Ramos, had kept many people enthralled until his death a few years before. But why were people trapped by this group even now? Why were they afraid to leave the building? Most people never knew about the guns, so they were not physically coerced. The simple answer is the same one that causes my students, year after year, to fold their syllabi into paper airplanes and the same one that caused the experiment's participants to conform in violation of their senses: People influence other people.

## A Classic Definition

Social psychology is all about people influencing other people. **Social psychology** is the scientific attempt to explain how the thoughts, feelings, and behaviors of individuals are influenced by the actual, imagined, or implied presence of other human beings. This is a classic definition of social psychology; it dates back decades to Gordon Allport (1954a, p. 5), one of the field's pioneers. This definition describes social psychology as the study of social influence: all the ways that people have an impact on one another. Social influence affects not only trivial behavior, such as making paper airplanes in class. It also affects important behavior, such as yielding to majority opinion over one's own judgment, as the research participants did; allowing oneself to be imprisoned doing useless paperwork, as Jennifer did; or torturing innocent people, as soldiers sometimes have done (Fiske, Harris, & Cuddy, 2004). These behaviors have one feature in common: people doing what others around them are doing.

If we unpack the classic definition of social psychology, we can overview the key elements of this science. First, people are influenced by *other people's* presence to do something that they would not have done otherwise. As noted earlier, students in my classes are influenced both by my presence making a request and by the presence of other students complying. The experiment's participants were primarily influenced by their peers' erroneous but unanimous public judgments. Jennifer was influenced both by the leaders of the group who were telling her what to do and by the unquestioning cooperation of the other recruits.

Second, the terms *actual, imagined*, and *implied* differentiate among three degrees of perceived human presence. In the situation with the paper airplanes, students are influenced by the *actual* presence of other people making airplanes. Ditto for the conforming participants in the experiment, Jennifer and the other volunteers, and the soldiers just following orders. Other people's actual presence is enormously powerful, as anyone knows who has consumed too much alcohol by just going along with the crowd.

The *imagined* presence of others also matters: When you show up for class on time, you are influenced by your imagination. As you are running to class, you envision walking in late, which can be a little or a lot embarrassing, depending on the door's location relative to the teacher and the eyes of the class. As another example, you may imagine other people's reactions when you get dressed in the morning. What are other people going to think of you in sweats? Most people don't attend class in a business suit, a bathing suit, or their birthday suit. Why not? Because people monitor their own behavior against the imagined reactions of other people: You do not have to have first-hand experience to avoid showing up in a clown suit.

The *implied* presence of others refers, for example, to the ways that social artifacts (human-made objects) in the environment imply the interests and presence of other people. Upon driving up to a red light at 3:00 a.m., most people stop. Even if no one else is coming—not for miles—people wait for it to turn green. Why is that? The light is a social artifact implying that people should obey traffic signals even when nobody is monitoring them. Of course, natural objects endowed with social meaning (a solar eclipse, a black cat crossing your path) can elicit socially learned behavior, implying the presence of others. But artifacts more directly imply other people's shared intentions.

Unlike the imagined presence of others, the implied presence of others does not require that you think about the other people, just as you might be socially trained to stop at a red light without explicitly thinking about specific people. However, the traffic light also raises the imagined possibility that a police officer might suddenly materialize. Whatever the specific circumstances, we are social creatures even when alone.

In the classic definition, another cluster of words—*thought, feeling*, and *behavior*—distinguishes respectively among cognition, affect, and behavior. **Cognition** is thought, **affect** (note well, with an "a") is feeling, and **behavior** is action. This tripod underlies many phenomena in social psychology. To be able to separate them affords a more complete view of all the facets of social behavior.

Finally, notice how the definition divides up into a cause (the actual, imagined, or implied presence of other human beings), a verb (influence), and an effect (note well, with an "e") or result (the thought, feeling, and behavior of individuals). Think of it as an equation:

$$\text{actual, imagined, or implied presence of others} \rightarrow$$
$$\text{individual thought, feeling, and behavior}$$

Or, for short,

$$\text{other people} \rightarrow \text{individual}$$

Alternatively, consider it a fill-in-the-blank template, as in the party game Mad Libs: _____ [something about other people] influences _____ [something about an individual]. The next chapter will come back to this cause-effect template, but for now the point is that the definition has a causal side (other people) and an effect side (the individual).

## Levels of Analysis

Notice that individuals are on the effect side of the classic definition. Social psychology primarily analyzes what happens to people as individuals. When social scientists investigate the behavior of groups of people, they move toward the sociological end of social psychology; indeed, some social psychologists work in sociology departments.

Scientific explanations operate at different levels of analysis (see Table 1.1). For example, one can analyze the fine-grained level of neurons or neural systems; move up a level to individual thought, feeling, and behavior; move up to face-to-face pairs; or move up further to entire groups. Each approach constitutes a different level of analysis, from **micro** (small-scale) to **macro** (large-scale). Trying to explain neurons is neuroscience's typical level of analysis; trying to explain larger groups is sociology's typical level of analysis. Social psychology borders at one end on the social sciences, which tend toward macro levels of analysis. Sociology examines society, at levels from small groups, families, neighborhoods, institutions, cities, to nations. Other social sciences focus respectively on political institutions or political behavior, economic institutions or economic behavior, but all typically at a more macro level than psychology. Social psychology borders, at its other end, on psychology's other subfields, which tend to look at an individual (or parts of an individual) in isolation.

Of all psychology's subfields—clinical psychology, social psychology, developmental psychology, cognitive psychology, and neuroscience—social psychology most concerns interaction among people. Social psychology lies at the more sociological end of psychology, going from micro to macro. Thus, social psychology does not usually try to explain the individual completely alone without examining other people (actual, imagined, or implied). Research in other subfields, such as cognitive psychology, does not usually examine thought in the context of social interactions. For instance, measuring someone's memory for nonsense words or geometric shapes does not directly implicate other people. Social psychologists are concerned primarily with the individual (affect, behavior, and cognition), as influenced by interactions with others.

**Table 1.1**   Social Psychology's Level of Analysis, Relative to Other Psychological and Social Sciences, from Relatively Macro Disciplines to Relatively Micro Disciplines

| Field | Level of Causes | Level of Effects |
|---|---|---|
| Sociology | Social structure, groups | Groups, neighborhoods, institutions |
| Social psychology | Groups, individuals | Individual affect, cognition, behavior |
| Clinical psychology | Individual disorders | Individual emotional distress |
| Developmental psychology | Age, stage | Individual life-cycle change |
| Cognitive psychology | Mental structure | Individual thinking, deciding |
| Neuroscience | Brain systems | Individuals' neural responses |

On the causal side of the definition of social psychology, other human beings constitute the **social situation** that influences the individual. Sometimes the relevant social situation might be the artifacts or traces of other people (a trash barrel, a shortcut worn in the grass); sometimes the situation might consist of a single other person (a bystander glaring after you drop some litter or trample the grass), and sometimes the situation consists of several other people (police officers beckoning you).

Social psychology is the psychology of the individual, as influenced by one or more other people, who make up the social situation. Let's examine the social situation more closely.

## SITUATIONISM

Social psychology argues for the often-unappreciated importance of the social situation. This section first addresses the concept of **situationism**—scientific belief in the significance of context. Then, the section describes the surprising influence of situations, compared to laypeople's reliance on personality explanations. Finally, the section explores precisely why the social situation is so psychologically important, given people's evolutionary history as adapting social creatures.

### The Major Intellectual Contribution of Social Psychology

Let's begin with a formal statement of situationism: Social behavior is, to a larger extent than people commonly realize, a response to people's social context, not a function of individual personality. This concept comes from Kurt Lewin (1951), one of the founders of the field, and has been elaborated by Lee Ross and Richard Nisbett (1991), two major thinkers in social psychology. Situationism, a remarkably simple premise, opens up a number of ideas that people commonly take for granted. It contrasts insights gained from social psychology with the ways people ordinarily explain their own and other people's behavior.

People usually explain other people's behavior in terms of personality. "Why did he do that?" "Well, he's just that kind of person."... "Why did she turn her paper in late?" "You know, she's a procrastinator."... "Why would he choose to live alone for the third year in a row?" "He just isn't very social." People credit (or blame) other people's personalities all the time, especially when talking to others. Yet, social psychology shows, over and over, that the social situation, not just unique personality, dramatically controls people's behavior.

Lewin and his students designed compelling experiments showing the power of the situation. For example, during World War II, ordinary kinds of meat were scarce, and persuading people to eat unusual kinds of meat would stretch the nation's supply of protein more efficiently. Lewin tackled the problem of persuading people to consume organ meats (beef hearts, tripe, and kidneys). First, he identified the wife as the gatekeeper who channeled food to the rest of the family in the 1940s. Then he analyzed the barriers to their buying organ meats.

> If one considers the psychological forces that kept housewives from using these intestinals, one is tempted to think of rather deep-seated aversions

requiring something like psychoanalytical treatment. Doubtless a change in this respect is much more difficult than, for instance, the introduction of a new vegetable, such as escarole. There were, however, only 45 minutes available. (Lewin, 1952, pp. 463–464)[1]

The most obvious way to change people's minds is to lecture them, and the researchers arranged an attractive lecture, linking the organ meets to the war effort, good nutrition, and household budgets. Speaking before groups of 13 to 17 women, the lecturer provided recipes and vivid personal stories. A follow-up showed that only 3% of the lecture attendees served the new foods to their families.

Lewin then harnessed the power of the social situation to persuade women to buy the unfamiliar food. Instead of hearing a lecture, other women participated in a small group discussion about "housewives like themselves," receiving the same information but without high-pressure tactics. At the end of the meeting, the women were asked to raise their hands if they would try one of the new meats that week. Lewin describes this as the crucial group decision (not unlike the moment when my students see other people start to fold their syllabus). At the follow-up, 32% had served one of the new meats, fully ten times the number doing so after hearing the lecture. A later study showed the same effects for feeding babies cod liver oil (see Figure 1.2).

Lewin credited the face-to-face group setting with creating a psychological group, securing involvement, and motivating a decision. As he points out, although a lecture audience puts people in a physical group, people find themselves "psychologically speaking, in an 'individual situation'" (p. 465). In the situation that feels more like a group (i.e., the discussion), the individual is reluctant to depart too far from the rest of the group. This shows the power of the social situation.

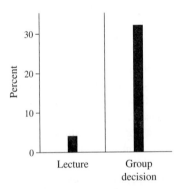

(A) Percentage of individuals serving a type of food never served before, after lecture and after group decision

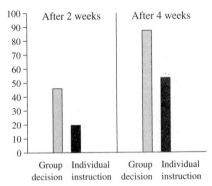

(B) Percentage of mothers completely following group decision or individual instruction in giving cod liver oil

**Figure 1.2**  The Power of Group Decisions

*Source:* From Lewin, 1952. Copyright © Lewin Estate. Adapted with permission.

---

In one sense, the impact of the situation is democratic; it brings everyone to the same level. My classes, across public and private universities, consist of incredibly varied people, but they all make the paper airplane. And you, too, have a unique personality, but you are almost certainly reading this chapter in response to a course assignment. The social situation (the class) dramatically influences all its members, regardless of individual personality. For traditional social psychologists, people's personalities are often simply "noise in the system"; they distract from the goal of recognizing powerful but subtle influences of the situation. The social situation by itself can predict people's behavior. Of course, individuals are unique, and people's personalities interplay with situations. Indeed, Lewin argued that behavior is a function of the person and the environment, but his empirical work and his legacy primarily concern the social psychology of the situation, not the individual's disposition. Social situations are the crucible of social psychological inquiry.

## Situations versus Personalities

Why do social psychologists emphasize situations as opposed to personalities? At least four reasons matter (see Table 1.2). First, ordinary people rely too much on personality in explaining behavior; a later chapter will explain why. But for the moment, think of presidential elections. How do reporters and voters discuss the candidates? Usually, the discussion centers on personality traits (Abelson, Kinder, Peters, & Fiske, 1982). Is this candidate honest? Is that candidate competent? Is this candidate caring? Is that candidate a little crazy? Is this candidate amiable? Notice that voters judge a candidate's personality instead of considering the situations that might make the candidate appear dishonest (being framed by political opponents) or incompetent (a tough economic situation that no one truly understands or could have anticipated).

Second, ordinary people underestimate—or never even consider—the power of situations. That is what makes social psychology fun. Researchers can set up studies that manipulate the social situation in tiny ways that have a huge impact on people's behavior. For example, an event as trivial as finding a coin in a phone booth can make people more helpful to the next stranger they meet. Many years ago, researchers planted dimes in the coin-return slot of public phones in San Francisco and Philadelphia shopping malls. The next caller almost invariably checked the coin-return slot, retrieved the coin, and emerged to find a woman walking in the same direction; the woman dropped a manila folder full of papers in the caller's path. In the control condition, others did not find a planted dime but did encounter the same woman.

The critical measure was the number of people helping, depending on whether or not they had just found a dime. Of those who did not find a dime, only 4%

**Table 1.2**   Why Social Psychology Emphasizes Situations over Personalities

Ordinary people overemphasize personalities
Ordinary people underemphasize situations
Complexity of personality judgments requires separate subfield
Personality explanations are incomplete

(1 of 25) helped the woman pick up her spilled belongings. Of those who had just found the dime, fully 88% helped (Isen & Levin, 1972). The implied presence of another person (the one leaving the coin) and the utility of a coin as part of an imagined social exchange (buying something) created a social situation that influenced individual behavior.

Why should an event as tiny as finding a bit of change make people's behavior so decidedly different? An observer of the behavior would doubtless say that the person is helpful or generous (a trait description). If a social psychologist said, "This person is helping because she just found a coin in the phone booth," the observer would not believe it. The impact of this tiny feature of the social situation is counterintuitive; the power of situational happenstance flies against what people think would occur. Try asking a friend what percentage of people would normally help, and then ask the friend how much the percentage would increase if the person had just picked up a coin. I'll wager your friend will not give odds of 5% versus 90%, as the data indicate. In short, people are biased to underestimate the power of situations.

A third reason why social psychologists emphasize situations rather than personality in explaining behavior is that, as scientists, they know that personality is complex enough to require its own separate subfield, with its own methods. Personality theorists sometimes disagree about how to measure personality. Nonscientists think personality is easy to assess, so they routinely use it to predict and explain behavior. But from a scientific perspective, personality defies easy measurement, which explains why it requires a separate field. Personality psychologists focus on accurately measuring individual differences and their implications for behavior. Measuring helpfulness—or any other aspect of personality—is not easy; even personality psychologists cannot always agree. Despite considerable progress, personality assessment still generates intense debates (Cervone, 2005; Funder, 2001; Mischel, 2004; Ozer & Benet-Martinez, 2006). Social psychologists choose to bite off a different piece of the problem, because one cannot study everything at once.

The fourth point is that laypeople's relying on personality instead of situations is not exactly a mistake; explanations based solely on personality are simply incomplete. Personality cannot be the whole explanation for behavior because it does not usually predict specific behavior in one random situation. Some social-personality psychologists (e.g., Mendoza-Denton, Ayduk, Mischel, Shoda, & Testa, 2001; Snyder, 2006) have demonstrated that the *combination* of situation and personality can predict behavior. Others (Ajzen & Fishbein, 2005; Epstein, 1980) have proposed looking at personality as predicting *average* behavior, aggregated across situations (and therefore ignoring any particular situation). In both cases, the point is that ordinary people's strategy of predicting one particular, specific behavior just from someone's personality is misguided. Either one must think of the person in a specific situation to predict a specific behavior, or one must think of a person's personality as predicting an average pattern of behavior across situations. Both solutions acknowledge the joint power of personality *and* situations.

As scientists, social psychologists have opted to explain behavior more in terms of the social situation precisely because the role of the social situation is so often underestimated. This book aims to convince you of the adaptive significance of the social situation, that is, other people.

## The Power of Situations as an Evolutionary Adaptation

Why does the social situation matter so much? Because social situations are so powerful, we need to understand why people so readily respond to them. Situations matter because people need other people in order to survive and thrive. Evolution has an important role to play in explaining the impact of social situations on people. People attune to social situations for functional, adaptive reasons. This book argues that people respond to other people and seek social acceptance through social motives that have evolved to help them survive and thrive in groups—and more generally. The power of social situations may be one of people's most important evolutionary adaptations.

But before we examine this approach more closely, a note of caution: Evolutionary explanations can easily be misused. For example, some writers (e.g., Rushton, 1992) have implied the existence of "inferior" and "superior" races and claimed that environmental challenge creates evolutionary pressures that result in genetically based racial differences in intelligence. Rushton also alleges that sex differences in brain size determine intelligence. Similarly, men have historically held more power than women, so some writers (e.g., Goldberg, 1973; Pratto, Sidanius, & Stallworth, 1993) might argue that patriarchy has inevitably evolved because of male and female biological differences.

This kind of biological determinism weakens some evolutionary explanations because they fail to acknowledge the integral role of social factors (Maccoby, 1973, 2000; Wood & Eagly, 2002, 2010). Moreover, determinism suggests to some critics that the current evolutionary outcomes were inevitable. Evolutionary explanations can be misused to justify the status quo, as if humans were not still evolving and as if change were not part of evolution. People also think that evolutionary pressures minimize the importance of culture, but as this chapter discusses, evolution predisposes people to participate in their culture.

Despite such problems, scientists generally agree that selective pressures clearly operate on human behavior, including social behavior. Consequently, theories based on principles of selection require empirical testing. **Evolutionary psychology** focuses on the inherited design of the mind, especially functions that improved our ancestors' success in passing on their genes (Buss, 2005). Evolutionary social psychology focuses on the parallel implications for social reactions (Schaller, Simpson, & Kenrick, 2006).

Various theorists have described evolutionary pressures at various levels, and this section considers four (see Table 1.3) that help us locate the relevant level for responsiveness to the social situation. First, when people think of evolution, they

**Table 1.3**    Levels of Evolutionary Pressures

| Name of Approach | Alternative Term | Level of Reproduction |
| --- | --- | --- |
| Natural selection | Survival of the fittest | One individual's genes |
| Kin selection | Inclusive fitness | Genetic relatives |
| Group selection | Group-level adaptation | Unrelated members of social unit |
| Social survival | Core configurations | Individual in group |

usually think about Darwin's classical theory of **natural selection** or "survival of the fittest": The strongest, wiliest, best-adapted individual survives to reproduce and thus to pass on his or her strong, wily, well-adapted genes. That was Charles Darwin's original idea. It focuses on the selfish reproductive ambitions of individuals and their genes.

At a second level, and more recently, scientists suggested that evolutionary processes might operate at the level of genetically related kin. Even if a particular individual does not survive, if several of that person's siblings survive, some of the individual's genes will be passed on. This **kin selection** idea—related to **inclusive fitness**—operates at a higher level than the individual (Hamilton, 1964).

> For a gene to receive positive selection it is not necessarily enough that it should increase the fitness of its bearer above the average if this tends to be done at the heavy expense of related individuals, because relatives, on account of their common ancestry, tend to carry replicas of the same gene. (p. 17)[2]

Kin selection thus favors the genes of those who promote the survival of their closest genetic relatives. The principle of preserving shared genes, rather than only one's own genetic material, explains why individuals might sacrifice themselves for their immediate family (Caporael, 2001). Most versions of evolutionary psychology work at one of these first two levels, and these analyses focus heavily on human reproductive strategies (Buss & Kenrick, 1998), which the chapters on attraction, close relationships, and helping discuss.

At yet another level comes the idea of **group selection**, which suggests that some groups might survive better than others (e.g., Wynne-Edwards, 1965). For example, perhaps some groups can evolve into adaptive units, compared with other groups, if they function effectively. Certain kinds of group structure (e.g., having a leader and shared goals) might well prove more effective than others (e.g., having constant battles over leadership and letting each individual go his or her own way); in other words, the survival of the well-coordinated group is encouraged by its organization as a unit. While this is undoubtedly true, the selection of one whole group instead of another has not received much empirical support (Williams, 1966, but see Wilson & Sober, 1994).

Finally, consider the social psychology of the individual *within* a group. Cutting across all these levels—individual, kin, group—one can think of individuals as surviving within groups of people, some related and some not. The key is people's ability to survive *as group members* (Caporael, 1997). Humans are adapted to fit into face-to-face groups; groups are important to survival. People are not adapted to survive as isolated individuals, as we will see.

As classic work on social support has shown, people who are more socially integrated survive better (Figure 1.3). Men live longer if they report more social ties, such as marriage, contacts with extended family and friends, church membership, and other formal or informal affiliations. This relationship holds, even controlling for

---

[2] Copyright © Elsevier. Reprinted with permission.

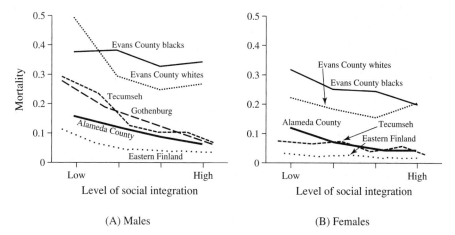

**Figure 1.3**    The Power of Social Ties: Age-adjusted Mortality Rate, Depending on Social Integration, across Several Studies

*Source:* From House et al., 1988. Copyright © American Association for the Advancement of Science. Adapted with permission

physical health, smoking, alcohol consumption, activity, obesity, social class, race, age, life satisfaction, and use of preventive health services. The benefits of social ties for women, although weaker, are still significant (House, Landis, & Umberson, 1988). According to one study (Lett et al., 2007), people who report high social support live longer after a heart attack than people who report low social support or high depression. Negative emotions—such as those resulting from social isolation—demonstrably harm the immune system and even survival (Kiecolt-Glaser, McGuire, Robles, & Glaser, 2002). Although the pathways are complex and likely to include both behavior and physiology, the point is that people's very life is affected by their social ties.

The history of human beings and related primates (as well as certain other animals) can easily justify the argument that people need social groups for survival. Social groups defend people against environment hazards, predators, and hostile outsiders. Human beings also go through long vulnerable periods as children, when they need to be protected; not all those adults protecting the young ones can be out hunting or foraging for food. People share tasks, and they share information—exploring the environment and returning to convey information and coordinate actions. Even a simple action such as grinding grain into flour works better when people do it together in a coordinated way, and so does gathering berries or hunting large animals, planning a party, or reviewing for an exam. Compelling evidence supports the idea that people are, in effect, adapted for living in social groups.

Although of course adults can survive alone and sometimes choose to do so, even hermits and monks usually depend on others for financial support and physical sustenance. Most people do not choose to live alone: Survival is easier in groups, and physical health is better in relationships (see Chapter 8). And in some environments at some times, surviving alone is nearly impossible. Hence, it makes sense that people have a built-in responsiveness to others and orient toward groups. As Aristotle said, humans are social animals, or as I would say, humans are social beings, social to the core.

## Summary of Situationism

Responsiveness to other people runs through all of social psychology: Situationism describes our orientation to social contexts, which consist of other people. Our responsiveness to social situations—and therefore their considerable impact—results from evolutionary pressures for individuals to survive in groups. An emphatically social theory of evolution holds that people are adapted at various levels. While adaptation certainly operates at the level of the individual, one's genetic relatives, or maybe the entire group, none of these quite fits the shape of a social psychological analysis. Just as the social psychologist analyzes the person as influenced by others (i.e., the social situation), so the *social* evolutionary perspective analyzes the person as adapted to living with others in that social situation. According to this theory, other people constitute our evolutionary niche.

## A NOTE ON THE SOCIAL BRAIN

Because social beings have long solved similar problems over our collective history, the social brain presumably has developed to facilitate this. Indeed, the social brain hypothesis specifically links the historically ever-increasing complexity of social life to increases in brain volume—especially in the human neocortex (Adolphs, 2009; Barrett & Henzi 2005; Dunbar & Schultz 2007). Adaptively attuned to the social situation, people have needed more grey matter to deal with it.

Over evolutionary history, humans have needed to track geometrically increasing numbers of social relationships as our social groups expanded (Massey, 2005). Human pair-bonding specifically demands extraordinary social sensitivity, as do all complex forms of human interaction described in this book. The importance of the social situation suggests that a search for relevant brain systems will be useful. Indeed, related to the importance of our social niche, early social neuroscience already shows that social exclusion activates similar systems to physical pain (Eisenberger, Lieberman, & Williams, 2003). In this book, we will note relevant social neuroscience data, mostly as promissory notes (stay tuned).

## CORE SOCIAL MOTIVES

From the idea that we need other people for our basic survival, it follows that over time we would have developed some core motives that interact with the social situation, to help us survive in groups. We are motivated to get along with other people because it is adaptive to do so. **Motives** in general are the motor for behavior. **Core social motives** describe fundamental, underlying psychological processes that impel people's thinking, feeling, and behaving in situations involving other people. This section later describes those motives as belonging, understanding, controlling, self-enhancing, and trusting.

## Five Unifying Themes in Social Psychology

Motives result from the interplay of person and situation; they are not general personality dispositions that consistently predict behavior regardless of the situation. These core social motives characterize a social psychological analysis precisely because they result from the interaction (unique combination) of the person and the situation. Lewin argued that a motive creates a psychological force for a person, who is located in a particular situation or **life space**. From the person's perspective, certain features of the environment facilitate or inhibit important goals, so they are motivating. Thus, the features acquire what Lewin (1951/1997) calls a **valence**, that is, a positive or negative value. If you want to mail a letter, a mailbox acquires a positive valence. If the mailbox potentially contains a bomb, it acquires a negative valence. If you want to acquire a mate, an attractive, available person of the appropriate gender acquires a positive valence. Because current goals shape your experience of the situation, what is meaningful is not necessarily the literal physical environment but this psychological environment, the situation as you experience it. Thus, social motives operate as person-in-situation principles.

The core social motives thus connect to situationism, the central intellectual contribution of psychology. The person's motives determine the psychological situation for that person; the person-in-situation combines what is out there with the person's own motives. Thus, the core social motives determine the nature of the situation, filtered through the person's interpretations. Social psychologists broadly agree on situationism and acknowledge that what matters is people's own interpretations of the situation. In this way, the social motives fit into situationism, social psychology's focus.

Accordingly, core social motives describe, unify, and explain seemingly unconnected lines of research. The core social motives about to be discussed in this section will help track the more specific theories and research across later chapters. These linking motives have been repeatedly identified by personality and social psychologists over the decades, so they are not my idiosyncratic invention. Describing them this way, however, is my own perspective on how to unify the varied contributions of social psychology. While the field has not explicitly adopted them as a framework, the job of textbook authors and other reviewers of scientific literature is to detect themes that provide coherence and order to the field. Hence, in this text, the core social motives serve as a set of unifying principles.

As a person new to the field, you should know some of the intellectual forebears of this enterprise. Listing motives is a risky enterprise. Social and personality psychologists listed and relisted basic motives early in the 20th century, arguing about how many, how necessary, and how they ranked. McDougall (1908), in one of the first textbooks on social psychology, undertook such a project, using the term *instincts* (see Boring, 1950, for one review of this era). Unfortunately, an instinct developed to explain every behavior, and "instincts" proliferated beyond what was scientifically useful.

So, as a newcomer, bear in mind that these five are not the only possible interpretations of core motives that could organize this field. Indeed, I am tempted to call these "five plus or minus five" core motives. Nevertheless, in the experience of my students, this framework offers a manageable number of organizing themes that recur across areas. Each chapter highlights certain motives, depending on the emphasis of the theories and research in a given area. All five motives reappear throughout the book, helping to make sense of what might otherwise seem a staggering array of theories and findings. Indeed, in practice, social psychology is somewhat scattered; different researchers stake out problems they find interesting and work in subareas that do not necessarily relate to one another. However, in my experience as a teacher, writer, and consumer of social psychology, people cannot make sense of the material if reviewers do not offer a framework. Each new idea will therefore relate to familiar themes encountered before, because some fundamentals do run through the field.

Over decades of theories and research, many major personality and social psychologists have developed ideas about people's basic motives. Five come up repeatedly (Fiske, 2008): *belonging, understanding, controlling, enhancing self*, and *trusting others*. (I like to think of these as a BUC(K)ET of motives.) All five motives orient toward making people fit better into groups, thus increasing their chances for survival. This idea that *a small number of essential, core social motives enhance people's survival in social situations* offers a unifying framework for understanding the field of social psychology.

The first core motive, belonging, underlies the other four core social motives (see Table 1.4). Two of the remaining motives, understanding and controlling, are relatively cognitive in nature. That is, they concern thinking processes, as we will see, but one is more reflective (understanding) and the other is more active in the world (controlling). The other two remaining motives, self-enhancing and trusting, are relatively affective in nature, but one is more self-directed (self-enhancing) and the other is more other-directed (trusting). Let us now turn to a detailed description of each of the five core social motives.

**Table 1.4**    Relationships among Core Social Motives

| Belonging | | | |
|---|---|---|---|
| Need for strong, stable relationships | | | |
| Relatively Cognitive Motives | | Relatively Affective Motives | |
| Understanding | Controlling | Self-enhancing | Trusting |
| Need for shared meaning and prediction | Need for perceived contingency between behavior and outcomes | Need for viewing self as basically worthy or improvable | Need for viewing others as basically benign |

## Belonging

When you first entered college, if you didn't know anyone, one of your first goals doubtless was to meet people. What drove you to find friends, groups of people who seemed like you in important ways? Wasn't it so that you could feel comfortable, having people to explain things, to support you, to make you feel less alone? Across the country, student affairs offices have discovered that students are happier and more likely to complete their degrees if they form affinity groups based on living situations, majors, sports, language, cultural identity, interests, or politics. This common experience illustrates the motive to have a stable sense of belonging.

I suggested earlier that people are adapted and motivated to belong in groups, but now let us examine some initial evidence here for **belonging**, the idea that people need strong, stable relationships with other people. People seek ongoing, secure relationships (Baumeister & Leary, 1995). In fact, some classic social psychology experiments have shown that people form social bonds incredibly easily. For example, researchers in a summer camp (Sherif, Harvey, White, Hood, & Sherif, 1961) divided previously unacquainted young boys into two random groups. On the basis of these arbitrary groups, they rapidly formed intense team loyalties. In another well-known study (Festinger, Schachter, & Back, 1950), families of returning World War II veterans who were haphazardly assigned to campus housing formed friendships with whomever happened to live the closest to them.

Having some close social ties is about the only objective factor found to correlate with subjective well-being (Baumeister, 1991b, p. 213). Being ostracized threatens people's sense of belonging, of course, but also their mood (Williams, Ceung, & Choi, 2000). The hormone oxytocin may mediate the stress response that accompanies disrupted social relationships, sometimes resulting in reparative tend-and-befriend behavior (Taylor, 2006). Problems in close relationships predict poor health (Stansfeld, Bosma, Hemingway, & Marmot, 1998). And in states where fewer people join voluntary groups, more violent crimes with firearms occur (Kennedy, Kawachi, Prothrow-Stith, Lochner, & Gupta, 1998). As Durkheim (1951) suggested, people with poor social networks are more likely to kill themselves (Berkman, Glass, Brissette, & Seeman, 2000). Many of these studies are correlational (belonging and health go together), so they do not guarantee causality (i.e., that belonging causes health; more on that in the next chapter). Nevertheless, a variety of evidence suggests that belonging is good for your health.

The motive to belong benefits the group also. If people generally cooperate with one another and want to be accepted, it helps the group coordinate its actions and operate effectively (Levine & Kerr, 2007). As mentioned earlier, ancestral examples include hunting and gathering; modern ones include networking, celebrating, and studying. An organization with a strong corporate culture encourages its employees to learn "how we do things around here" in order to fit in; one large retail company schedules a daily pep talk and group cheer to motivate its sales force each morning, and the employees view themselves as one big family, bleeding the corporate colors for each other. The power of employees' need to belong explains the loyalty built up through these daily reminders, and the company expects sales associates to work more effectively if they feel they all are in it together. Similarly, in Burkina Faso, West Africa, people cultivate their fields together, sometimes to the beat of a drum, which helps them get the job done more efficiently and pleasantly than if each worked alone. Traditional American barn-raising worked in much the same way, with collective activity, music, and reciprocal effort. A wide variety of group activities thrive best when people are motivated to cooperate, to get along, and to be accepted.

People's motive to belong may help the group survive, but the main point here is that *belonging to a group helps individuals to survive* psychologically and physically, whether on a college campus, the Burkina Faso savanna, or the Kansas prairie. Belonging may be more valued in some cultures than others, as we will see, but it remains a core motive. More evidence comes up in chapters devoted to specific topics that especially emphasize belonging. As the relevant chapters indicate, this book argues that people's need to belong reflects some kinds of attitudes, prejudices, and social influence, but belonging especially motivates close relationships, helping, and groups.

As noted earlier, belonging forms the core motive that underlies the other four. Of those, two are more cognitive in nature; that is, they concern thinking. They are the motives to understand and to control. The other two motives are more affective in nature. They are the motives to self-enhance and to trust.

## Understanding

Of the cognitive motivations, the most fundamental one encourages people to **understand** their environment—whether campus, prairie, or savanna—to predict what is going to happen in case of uncertainties and to make sense of what does happen. Most important, people prefer to develop meanings that are shared with other people. For example, if in a given year more people accept offers of admission than a college expects, quite a few students end up living in dorm lounges or the campus hotel. It is easy to understand why living in the lounge is problematic (no closet, for one thing). But what is wrong with a room at the campus hotel? After all, students in a hotel get private bathrooms, their own TV, and larger rooms. In fact, living in the hotel is problematic because the student residents are not a part of a stable group with people who will be their neighbors for the year; they must wait in limbo before finding their social niche. The uncertainty itself is the problem. People lack a shared social understanding, normally developed from membership in a stable group.

People in temporary housing or any other uncertain situation immediately wonder, "why?" and "why us?" They may develop all kinds of theories to explain what is going on: "A housing clerk retired and left a thousand checks in her desk, so they didn't realize how many housing deposits they really had." Or, "The school is greedy, overbooking its rooms to get more money." Or, "Have you noticed, all the Latino [or rural or scholarship] students don't have rooms? Maybe they did it on purpose because they don't want us here."

The motive to understand is not limited to unexpected events (housing crises, school shootings, tornadoes); it applies to any significant event that affects us in important ways (inconvenient exam schedules, recurring potholes, tick-borne diseases, terrorist attacks). Whatever the phenomenon, if it seems important, people have theories about it. Harold Kelley (1967) described how a loss of information, below acceptable levels, sets in motion the process of explaining and attributing causality, a major topic in Chapter 3.

As people struggle to understand and make sense of their world, they share their theories with other people in an effort to reach agreement. Serge Moscovici (1988) called these shared understandings **social representations** (for an integrative overview, see Augoustinos, 2001). Robert Zajonc called them **group meaning** (Zajonc & Adelmann, 1987).

One aspect of socially shared meaning emerges when groups convene to make decisions. Most often, they discuss already-shared information, rather than passing along new information. In one study, interns and medical students individually viewed videotapes of a patient describing a variety of symptoms; some information appeared on every version of the videotape (shared information), while some was unique to a particular version of the videotape (unshared information), just as might occur if several doctors separately interviewed a patient. Even though all the information was relevant to making a diagnosis (in this case, Lyme disease versus mononucleosis), when the diagnostic teams convened, they discussed shared information earlier and more often. As Table 1.5 indicates, shared information came up 24% more often and 1.5 topics sooner than the equally valuable unshared information (Larson, Christensen, Franz, & Abbott, 1998). Whether or not they know which information is shared, it has a higher probability of being discussed because more people possess it. But it means that even the simple odds favor the group learning nothing new. For good or ill, this illustrates the power of shared understanding in groups, in this case dealing with important real-world problems.

Shared understanding is adaptive for survival as a group member. Being able to understand and make sense of situations, especially to share social representations, group meaning, and other knowledge, enables people to function in groups. Even if the group meaning is not fully accurate, if it will serve the group's purposes, it enables people to coordinate with other group members. For example, in a famous study of a doomsday cult (Festinger, Reicken, & Schachter, 1956), group members followed the instructions from extraterrestrial guardians, relayed by Marian Kreech with the help of Dr. Thomas Armstrong and Daisy Armstrong. Convinced of an impending flood, cult members met, proselytized, and planned for their rescue by flying saucer. Not only

**Table 1.5**    Pooling of Shared Information by Medical Decision-Making Teams

|                                                                    | Type of Information | |
| --- | --- | --- |
| Variable                                                           | Shared | Unshared |
| Previously obtained information mentioned at least once in group    | 78%    | 54%      |
| Timing of first mention (high numbers = later)                      | 5.55   | 7.09     |

*Source:* From Larson et al., 1998. Copyright © American Psychological Association. Adapted with permission.

did they remove from their bodies all metal objects (zippers, watches, jewelry, coins), which had been deemed dangerous to their flight, but Dr. Armstrong reported that group members felt: "I've had to go a long way. I've given up just about everything. I've cut every tie; I've burned every bridge. I've turned my back on the world" (p. 168). All this occurred because of personal conviction about the group's prophecy and commitment to the group's task of coordinating their rescue from the coming cataclysm.

Even under less exotic circumstances, shared understanding explains why people try to resolve random events and mysteries ("We sent in our dorm deposits the same day, so how come you have a room and I don't?") and share their understanding with other people whom they consider relevant. For example, if students feel that the college procedures are unfair, they may be envious of those who seem to be singled out for special treatment, and student morale will suffer. Wise college administrators know that they cannot afford to have students resenting each other, so they provide information promptly.

Shared understanding aims at knowing quickly and predicting well enough to function in ordinary life. People's motive to understand adapts them to group life and its shared view of reality (Hardin & Higgins, 1996). As later chapters indicate, in social psychology, the motive to understand describes why people bother to make sense of each other, themselves, and various attitudes. Easy understanding and prediction also drive both attraction to similar others and prejudice against dissimilar others, as well as certain kinds of social influence.

## Controlling

What caused the fights you had with your parents in high school? Curfews? Car? Clothing? Hair? Friends? Whatever the specifics, control was likely the main issue: Who was going to decide, who was going to get their way? A motive related to understanding, and like it, having a cognitive flavor, the motive to control encourages people to feel effective in dealing with their social environment and themselves. **Control** entails a relationship between what people do and what they get, or in more technical terms, a contingency between behavior and outcomes. People want to be effective, to have some sense of control and competence, and a lack of control provokes information-seeking, in an effort to restore control (Gleicher & Weary, 1995; Pittman, 1998).

For example, in one study, researchers (Pittman & Pittman, 1980) decreased participants' sense of control and observed their tendency to seek control by becoming more sensitive to social information. Participants experienced a loss of control during a learning task with no right answer, about which they received only random feedback. Participants struggled to find the "correct" pattern in pairs of letters that appeared in varying combinations of black or red, upper or lower case, with circle or square borders and solid or dotted underlining. Over six problems, the experimenter gave them predetermined feedback, not contingent on their actual response; this random feedback occurred with all six problems (high helplessness) or two problems (low helplessness), or no feedback occurred (control condition).

Then, in a second apparently unrelated experiment immediately afterward, participants read about an expert on nuclear power plants who wrote an essay opposing their placement near populated areas; the expert wrote the essay either for payment (external motivation) or in his personal journal (internal motivation). When asked about the expert's motivation for writing the essay, people in both helpless conditions were more sensitive to the writer's circumstances than were the people in the control condition (see Table 1.6). That is, control-deprived participants thought harder about another person. Thus, lack of control motivates people to use socially available information, in an effort to regain a sense of control.

To the extent that people consistently feel that they are in control, they may be healthier, feel happier, and live longer (Taylor & Brown, 1988). Recent research suggests that health and longevity follow from social environments (Taylor et al., 2004) that afford more control to some races and social classes than others. And control over one's experiences improves health status. Specifically, a study of 10,308 British civil servants identified the ratio between effort and reward at work (i.e., the perceived contingency between what one does and what one gets, or perceived control). An imbalance between effort and reward (i.e., lack of control) predicted poor mental and physical health (Stansfeld, Bosma, Hemingway, & Marmot, 1998). Other measures of control, such as decision latitude at work, job demands, and work support, also correlated with health.

Needing control, wanting to be effective, is an early, basic motive even in young infants—for example, when they discover they can have an impact on their families by crying, smiling, or babbling. This is the beginning of social control and effectiveness: When the infants make faces or noises, the family reacts accordingly. Robert White (1959) identified **effectance**, a need for competence—essentially identical to the control motive being discussed here—which can be readily observed when children learn to grab, walk, or talk.

Competence and control enter adult social interactions as well, as when students try to persuade friends to room with them, have dinner at their preferred spot, or take social psychology during the same semester. If friends negotiate such matters successfully, they are controlling each other's behavior. But this is natural. Mutual control helps people fit into social groups, in several ways. It encourages cooperative behavior within the group; it also deals effectively with the social environment. If people experience a contingency between what they do in a group and what happens to them, that sense of control contributes to their psychological, social, and physical survival. If they know how to ask for certain kinds of help and then receive it (i.e.,

**Table 1.6**   Sensitivity to Social Information, as a Function of Control Deprivation

|  | Level of Control Deprivation | | |
|---|---|---|---|
|  | High helplessness | Low helplessness | No helplessness |
| Sensitivity to other's circumstances | 3.55 | 4.88 | 1.41 |

*Source:* From Pittman & Pittman, 1980. Copyright © American Psychological Association. Adapted with permission.

the group will help them meet their own goals), that constitutes social control and effectiveness.

As an alternative to personal control, people may entrust control to their group. If they know that their group can have some control over their individual outcomes, they may accept such indirect control and thus feel more secure (Morling & Fiske, 1999). Thus, control may operate at the level of the individual (as in some Western societies) or at the level of the group (as in many other societies). For example, in many Asian, African, and Latino societies, one's family might have much more impact on one's choice of college major than is typical in many Euro-American societies. Interdependent selves accept other people deciding for them, more than independent selves do (Pöhlmann, Carranza, Hannover, & Iyengar, 2007). In a group-oriented setting, the family takes care of its own, but as part of the bargain, it also expects family members to cede some individual control. Similar bargains occur in traditional small businesses in the United States and in traditional corporations in Japan. Either way, when people feel that someone (including themselves or a trusted group) is in control, they feel more secure.

The control motive encourages people to feel competent and effective at dealing with their social environment and themselves. Later chapters apply it to describe how people make sense of one another, how relationships cause emotions, why aggression sometimes occurs, and how prejudice operates.

Control is the third motive discussed so far. Recall that belonging, the first one, is the fundamental motive that runs through all five core social motives (see Table 1.4). Indeed, it overlaps with the motive to control. In describing the role of social relations in health promotion, Berkman (1995) notes, "For social support to be health promoting, it must provide both a sense of belonging and intimacy and must help people to be more competent and self-efficacious" (p. 245), that is, in control.

As described so far, understanding and control, the second and third motives, focus on getting information, thinking, believing, and problem-solving; thus, they are relatively cognitive in nature. The last two motives—self-enhancing and trusting—are relatively affective in nature; that is, they emphasize feelings and emotions. Of course, the distinction between the cognitive and affective social motives is not absolute but a matter of degree.

## Enhancing Self

The fourth basic motive, **self-enhancement**, involves either maintaining self-esteem or being motivated by the possibility of self-improvement. All else being equal, people basically like to feel good about themselves (Taylor & Brown, 1988); they like to feel that they are good and lovable. People feel instantly good when they receive positive feedback about themselves (Swann, Hixon, Stein-Seroussi, & Gilbert, 1990). For example, two experiments placed college students under mental overload, either by asking them to remember a telephone number and extension or by putting them under time pressure. Compared with other students who had more time to think, these mentally overloaded students presumably were more likely to use their spontaneous reactions. Their spontaneous reaction was to prefer interacting with someone who had

**Table 1.7**   Impact of Cognitive Load and Self-concept on Desire to Interact with Favorable Instead of Unfavorable Evaluators

|  | Cognitive Load | |
| --- | --- | --- |
| Self-Concept | Load (Spontaneous Response) | No Load (Thoughtful Response) |
| Negative | 5.00 | .50 |
| Positive | 4.56 | 4.00 |

Higher numbers indicate a greater desire to interact with a positive (versus negative) evaluator.
*Source:* From Swann et al., 1990. Copyright © American Psychological Association. Adapted with permission.

evaluated them favorably (see left column in Table 1.7). In contrast, people with more mental space chose to interact with someone who evaluated them more in line with their own self-concept, whether favorable or not. A later chapter discusses this and related studies. For now, the point is that the first, spontaneous reaction of American college students is to prefer interacting with someone who views them favorably.

Apart from the fact that self-enhancement makes a person feel good, why would individual self-esteem be useful for a group? Because people who feel truly terrible about themselves are not motivated to do even the most basic things, such as get out of bed in the morning, undertake challenges, or meet social obligations. But if people feel good about themselves, they feel optimistic enough to make the effort to be a useful and pleasant group member.

Low self-esteem can emerge through the lens of anticipated rejection by important social others (Leary, 2005). People who feel socially excluded also feel bad and engage in a number of socially destructive and self-destructive behaviors: substance abuse, irresponsible sexuality, aggression, and eating disorders. All of these behaviors further undermine the person's adaptive functioning in a socially constructive group. If instead the people in a group feel good about themselves and one another, then they want to cooperate and to relate, which can cement the group together. In short, as long as it is not overdone, self-enhancement helps maintain the group.

Note that people may gain self-esteem or enhance themselves in different ways. For example, one could feel pride in oneself as a special individual, which is the usual meaning of self-esteem in the United States. But one could also feel pride in oneself as a good member of a group (team, family, neighborhood) or for wholeheartedly performing a certain role in a group. Self-esteem lets people monitor how well they are doing socially, as group members (Baumeister & Leary, 1995; also see Leary et al., 1995); in that sense, it might result directly from the belonging motive. A later chapter will come back to the different senses of self-esteem. Note that my use of the term **self-enhancement** deliberately includes the possibility of self-improvement, whereas **self-esteem** includes the undesirable perception of self as better than others. The more balanced form of this motive (self-enhancement) will prove more adaptive than the more self-centered form (self-esteem).

In short, people need to feel good about themselves; self-enhancement comprises both self-esteem and self-improvement. Some people emphasize putting oneself first and viewing oneself in a positive light, but others emphasize the humble self, always striving to improve and putting others first. As a later section explains, cultures vary in the same way. The term **self-enhancing** captures both senses, which of course will explain many aspects of the social self. Self-enhancing also explains some aspects of attribution, attraction, helping, aggression, and prejudice, all topics appearing in later chapters.

## Trusting

**Trusting** means seeing the social world as a benevolent place. Just as people enhance the self, to some (lesser) extent they enhance others. Trust involves "confidence or faith that some other, upon whom we must depend, will not act in ways that occasion us painful consequences" (Boon, 1995, p. 656). A predisposition to trust others, given appropriate circumstances, facilitates important human behavior, ranging from bargaining to loving. Certainly trust makes us vulnerable, and under certain circumstances people do not trust other people, but those occasions are exceptions. All else being equal, people do expect fairly good outcomes (Parducci, 1964), especially from other people. When people are making sense of other people, they are biased to see the best in them (Matlin & Stang, 1978; Sears, 1983). Although people differ, on average they trust other people, expecting them to be basically benign.

Trust facilitates daily life. It makes people both liked and likable, and with good reason. Trusting people deserve trust; they are unlikely to cheat or steal. They are more successful socially, being less suspicious, vindictive, resentful, and lonely than distrusting people (Gurtman, 1992; Murray & Holmes, 1993; Rotenberg, 1994; Rotter, 1980). Trusting people go with the flow (Morling & Fiske, 1999). A trusting orientation, compared with a paranoid or depressive orientation, facilitates people's interactions with others. Think how socially ineffective people are when they always expect the worst from other people.

Indeed, researchers have studied participants in two-person games that simulate real-world choices between cooperative trust and exploitative self-interest (Orbell & Dawes, 1993). In some games, people had the choice to play or not to play, in each trial, depending on their own judgment of how they would fare if they did play; in other games, people had to play every time. In the games allowing a choice, people intending to cooperate, that is, people high in trust, usually (81% of the time) offered to play; this was more often than people intending to exploit the other person (54%). Trustful people cooperate and expect others to cooperate, more so than would-be exploiters. When they have a choice about whether to participate, as is often true in real-world relationships, the pairs gain more often than they lose (16 of 18 groups gained points in the game). Trust and cooperation reinforce each other (Ferrin, Bligh, & Kohles, 2007), but they differ. For example, Americans may tend to trust more widely (take optimistic risks), whereas Japanese are better at building durable cooperation (Cook, Yamagishi, Cheshire, Cooper, Matsuda, & Mashima, 2005).

Trust is a form of social intelligence (Yamagishi, 2002). Trust facilitates group cohesion because it is rewarding, but it is also efficient. Think of all the energy wasted in a group whose members constantly guard themselves against each other because they think everyone else is out to get them. If people can basically trust others who, for example, tell them to expect rain or to avoid a poisonous mushroom, then group life works better. People can rely on other people to share information and resources and to avoid harm. In contrast, places where many people lack trust (believing, e.g., that "most people would take advantage of you if they got the chance") are also places with more violent crime (Kennedy, Kawachi, Prothrow-Stith, Lochner, & Gupta, 1998).

Trust operates through emotional channels that automatically detect trustworthiness in other people's faces through both fixed features (Engell, Haxby, & Todorov, 2007) and dynamic expressions (Krumhuber et al., 2007). Social talk that shares emotions (e.g., funny or endearing anecdotes) also establishes trust (Peters & Kashimia, 2007). Cooperative exchanges have instrumental value, of course, but also create sentiments of trust (Molm, Schaefer, & Collett, 2007).

People's view of the (social) world as a benevolent place is most obvious when that core motive has been shattered, as when their lives are devastated by trauma, especially trauma caused by other people. Although surrounded by news reports of murder, rape, and other crime, most people "assume other people are benevolent ... basically good, kind, helpful, and caring" (Janoff-Bulman, 1992, p. 6). People essentially believe that their world is safe and decent. For example, when that world is disrupted by parental divorce, children rebuild their general view of the world as benevolent. Moreover, their assumptions about people's benevolence make them optimistic about their own marriages (Franklin, Janoff-Bulman, & Roberts, 1990). People are motivated to restore their sense that the world is trustworthy.

The potential damage caused by betrayal, exploitation, or hostility certainly makes people sensitive to signs of negative behavior by others, as a later chapter indicates. Indeed, evolutionary psychologists posit special cheater-detection modules designed to watch for untrustworthy behavior (Cosmides & Tooby, 1992). This focus on detection and monitoring is inversely related to trust (Ferrin et al., 2007), so it might be more important at earlier than later stages of a social bond. In conditional trust, when they are initially still monitoring the other person, people use demonstrably different neural systems to evaluate rewards from others, compared with unconditional trust, when they are maintaining an established social attachment (Krueger et al., 2007). Thus, different processes underlie vigilant monitoring and an established trusting baseline. Although sensitive to antisocial behavior, people typically trust others to behave prosocially.

As with the other motives, the motive to trust returns in later chapters to help describe various social phenomena. As later chapters elaborate, trusting appears in people's general positivity bias in perceiving others, but it also makes people hypersensitive to negative information about others. Trusting facilitates the attachment and interdependence found in close relationships. The general predisposition to expect good things from most people (until or unless proven otherwise) enables people to adapt to their groups, encouraging mutual helping, social influence, and group loyalty.

## Summary of Core Social Motives

The five core social motives—belonging, understanding, controlling, self-enhancing, and trusting—serve as key themes in this book. Belonging, as the motive that makes us emphatically social beings, underlies the other four and aids our social survival.

Understanding propels us to make sense of our social situation, and controlling compels us to be effective in acting on that situation; both also make us more adaptive group members. Trusting others and enhancing the self make us better group members as well. The five motives provide unity and continuity throughout the book. A subset of these core motives particularly relate to each chapter.

To be sure, other authors can and do generate other lists of motives, add a motive (justice-seeking has been suggested), subtract a motive (some people argue against trusting), or reject the whole concept of core motives. Evolutionary social psychologists might argue that survival or reproduction should be listed as the sole original motive. Nevertheless, the emphatically *social* survival perspective taken here argues that surviving in the social situation determines one's ability to survive at all and to reproduce. In any case, social psychologists constantly seek to improve our collective thinking by advocating different frameworks. Thus, while I do not claim that these five motives are the only way to organize the field, they do provide one workable framework and a starting point for discussion. The motives constitute not a theoretical model that predicts outcomes but a description of what social psychologists do, in practice.

## CULTURE AND THE CORE SOCIAL MOTIVES

Most of the research supporting the five core social motives was conducted in Western cultures. However, the motives take different forms in different cultures. For example (Triandis, 1990), North American and European cultures are more **individualist** on the whole—they emphasize the autonomous person—but Asian, African, and South American cultures on average are more **collectivist**, which means that they emphasize groups such as the family, the community, the organization, and the country. Cultures differ overall on these dimensions (Osyerman, Coon, & Kemmelmeier, 2002; see Table 1.8). On average, Asians and Asian-Americans are less individualist and more collectivist than Europeans and European-Americans. Also, Latinos and Latino-Americans are more collectivist than Europeans and European-Americans. Africans are less individualist and more collectivist. However, African-Americans

**Table 1.8**    Meta-Analysis of Individualism and Collectivism across Cultures and American Subcultures

| Compared to European-Americans | Individualism | Collectivism |
|---|---|---|
| Asians | Lower | Higher |
| Asian-Americans | Lower | Higher |
| Latinos | Same | Higher |
| Latino-Americans | Same | Higher |
| Africans | Lower | Higher |
| African-Americans | Higher | Same |

Table entries indicate cultures' standing, relative to European-American culture.
*Source:* Summary of Oyserman et al., 2002.

are *more* individualist than European-Americans (Social psychologists need to collect more data here.)

Similarly, even within the United States, although the predominant orientation is individualist, various regions differ in degrees of individualism and collectivism (Vandello & Cohen, 1999). For example (see Figure 1.4), collectivism is extremely high in Hawaii (which borders on collectivist Asia) but also in California (with many ethnically Asian immigrants), Utah (strong religious identity), the deep South (strong regional and church identity), and New York City and New Jersey (many immigrants from Asian and Latino cultures). The most individualist regions by far are the Rocky Mountain and Great Plains areas, encompassing recent frontier and livestock-herding societies. In more individualist cultures, people put each person's own needs over the group's needs, whereas in more collectivist cultures, people put group needs over individual needs.

We can reconsider the five social motives in terms of cultural variation. The core motive of belonging, for example, is even more important and basic in a collectivist culture than in an individualist one. In Latin cultures, the expression *mi casa es su casa* (my house is your house) illustrates this idea. European-Americans traveling in

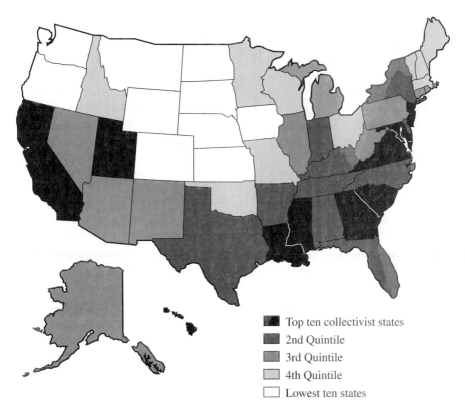

**Figure 1.4**    The Distribution of Individualism and Collectivism across the United States

*Source:* From Vandello & Cohen, 1999. Copyright © American Psychological Association. Adapted with permission.

Asia, Africa, and Latin America often remark on other cultures' hospitality. Respect for people's ties to one another permeates collectivist cultures more than individualist cultures.

The other four motives may also differ across cultures. Although people everywhere seek to understand their surroundings and function competently, their ways of doing so may vary (Triandis & Suh, 2002). For example, in some parts of rural Africa, the ways people gather information differ from those in mainstream society in the United States. Because it is impolite to ask questions directly, one cannot necessarily obtain local information that way. If a traveler asks whether a bus leaves town today, the answer may well be "yes," regardless of whether the bus actually leaves today or tomorrow. People prefer not to disappoint the stranger, and they assume that the person will eventually discover when the bus in fact leaves. One maintains the relationship at the cost of precision. In the same way, both in the United States and elsewhere, refusing a party invitation directly would be impolite. Thus, one may accept the invitation, regardless of one's plans, and then simply not show up. Information is gained and conveyed differently, depending on the social context. In certain cases (e.g., "Do you like my new haircut, sweetie?"), the consequences of brutal honesty are not always socially desirable.

People's need for control also is expressed differently across cultures. For example, in North American culture, people value control over the environment, believing that an individual can have a major impact on the surrounding social and nonsocial world (Strickland, 1989). Many North Americans show greater mental health if they score high on tests of need to control the environment. But some minority cultures in the United States—such as Asian-Americans and Latino-Americans, as well as some traditional cultures in Asia, Africa, and Latin America—may operate from a quite different sense of control, almost the opposite, in fact; they adjust themselves to their social environment and adapt their individual needs to those of the group. A person who instead places individual control over group control would be seen as immature.

Reflecting these cultural distinctions, a form of **harmony control** operates even in the United States (Morling & Fiske, 1997); harmony control contrasts with the environmental control so familiar to people in North American society. In this alternative form of control, people choose to give control over their own outcomes to other people, a higher power, or luck. Here are some expressions of harmony control:

■ "I feel secure knowing that my friends will take care of me, should I need it."

■ "Most of my own needs are met when I meet other people's needs."

■ "Sometimes when I am with others, I seem to lose track of what I personally want."

■ "Periods of good and bad luck even out in the end."

■ "I know that a higher power ultimately decides the good and bad times in our lives."

Rather than controlling the environment, they harmonize with other people and intangible forces. This form of control is somewhat higher in women and Latinos than in men and Anglos. Thus, different subcultures and groups, even within the United States, express their control needs differently, in ways that may be just as adaptive as individually trying to control other people or the environment. Control matters in both cases, but the expression differs.

As indicated earlier, cultures vary in self-enhancement, too: A person can feel good as a unique individual—which would be more appropriate in individualist and independent cultures—or a person can feel good as a group member in certain roles—which would be more appropriate in more collectivist and interdependent cultures. The chapter on the self considers this issue in detail.

Trust—expecting the world to be benevolent—probably depends on culture as well. In more interdependent cultures, such as Japan, people expect to take care of each other and to trust their immediate family, friends, colleagues, and associates, although they may not trust outsiders (Markus & Kitayama, 1991). In the more independent culture of the United States, trust and benevolence are more individually based; people believe, "Good things will happen to me personally; other people will probably treat me well." Americans trust people in general, believe reputation important, and consider themselves honest and fair (Yamagishi & Yamagishi, 1994). In a society in which people move in and out of different groups all the time, this kind of generalized trust in others and in the self is adaptive. In Japan, people are less generically trusting of others but see dealing with others through personal relations as useful; people form committed, safe, but confined relationships with few others (Yamagishi, Cook, & Watanabe, 1998). In the Japanese case, trust is confined to a small group; in the American one, trust is directed toward many more people in a more diffuse manner.

Cultures differ on more dimensions than individualism-collectivism or interdependence-independence (Bond & Smith, 1996; Triandis & Suh, 2002). For example, some cultures have high **power distance**, emphasizing the distinctions between those at the top and bottom of a hierarchy, whereas others minimize the difference between them. Some cultures are more **tight** (i.e., strictly organized), whereas some are looser and more flexible. Individualism and collectivism (or their cousins, independence and interdependence) simply reflect the most commonly studied dimensions to date.

## Summary of Culture and the Core Social Motives

Later chapters come back to all these issues; for now, just note these cultural variations. Although varying across cultures, the core social motives fit social evolutionary pressures that locate people in relationships, groups, and communities. People survive and thrive if they want to belong, to develop socially shared understandings, to be effective and have some sense of personal or social control, and to enhance themselves, as well as trust others. All these motives, despite cultural variations in their expression, facilitate living as a social being. Cultures solve similar problems in different ways (Cohen, 2001).

## KEY FEATURES OF SOCIAL PSYCHOLOGY'S APPROACH

As noted earlier, social influence forms the main scientific business of social psychology. Social influence works because people are motivated to belong and to comply with the influence of others. This holds true for most people, although we tend to ignore or deny it. Social influence includes such trivia as fashion and hairstyles (for guys, crew cuts, Afros, ponytails, shags, preppie cuts, Mohawks, mullets, and shaved heads have each had their day; for women, curly, straight, bangs over the eyes, no bangs, pulled back, big hair, and close-cropped styles have each in turn been popular). Social influence more importantly includes whether you feel comfortable telling people you want to be a nursery school teacher, a construction worker, a lawyer, a veterinarian, an investment banker, or a professor. Social influence affects choice of major, career, sports, politics, friends, mate, and haircut.

To give a scientific example, look at social influence in what is called the **autokinetic effect** ("auto" meaning self and "kinetic" meaning movement). This optical illusion creates the impression that a point of light in a dark space is moving. After the sun goes down, if you stare at the first star that comes out, without anything else nearby, you cannot tell whether it is a star or a satellite, moving or stationary. A single point of light in an otherwise dark space appears to move; this is called the autokinetic effect.

Muzafer Sherif (1935) capitalized on the autokinetic effect by bringing groups of people into a darkened room where he generated a point of light. Sherif then asked them to estimate how far it had moved on four separate trials; all participants were willing to assume that the light had moved. Some people gave one judgment alone and then voiced the three other judgments in the presence of one or two other people; others first made three judgments in a group and then made one judgment alone. Whenever people gave their judgments in the group or merely after hearing the group's judgments, they influenced each other's estimates. Some groups converged on the judgment that the light had moved several inches, while other groups converged on an inch or so. People's individual judgments, which started out quite different, were "funneled" (Sherif's term) to converge with the group (see Figure 1.5, first and third columns). Also, people who first made judgments in the group (Figure 1.5, second and fourth columns) continued to follow the group decisions even when judging alone. Both patterns reflect social influence. The groups developed **norms** (implicit social rules) about how far the point of light was moving.

In a later version of the study, researchers (Jacobs & Campbell, 1961) replaced members of the group one by one over time, such that after a "generation" no one from the original group was still there; the norms nevertheless perpetuated themselves. In the groups that had converged on a couple of inches, the next generations still claimed that the light had moved a couple of inches, and in the groups that had converged on almost a foot, the next generation still claimed almost a foot, even though no original group member was still there. This perpetuation of an arbitrary tradition through several generations illustrates the scientific study of social influence over time. Such results have successfully applied to real-world problems, as in Lewin's wartime study that persuaded people to eat organ meats. The phenomenon of influence through social norms comes up again in the chapters on attitudes and on conformity and obedience.

Research on social influence and the autokinetic effect also exemplifies the unexpectedness and importance of some social psychological findings: People influence each other on a judgment that seemingly should be objective. As you might imagine, such social factors in judgment have implications for obviously subjective norms as

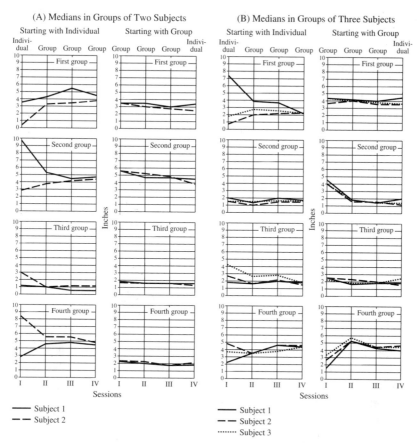

**Figure 1.5**    Median Judgments of Illusory Movement of a Point of Light, Starting with Individual or Group Judgment, for (A) Two-Person and (B) Three-Person Groups

*Source:* From Sherif, 1935. Copyright © Columbia University Board of Trustees. Adapted with permission.

trivial as what label people wear on a baseball cap, or whether they wear one at all, as well as for more important issues such as deciding whether and where to go to college. Which opportunities seem possible when one is coming out of high school and entering adult life depends on one's social setting, and social psychology has a lot to say about these life-changing effects of social influence.

The Sherif experiments on social influence illustrate some key characteristics of social psychology as a field of knowledge. The rest of this final section characterizes the intellectual territory covered by social psychology, as described by Phillip Brickman (1980). This chapter has claimed, not modestly, that social psychology relates to just about everything important in life. Many social psychologists love their field, as I do, and Brickman's perspective captures for me exactly why this is so. As the Sherif experiments show, social psychology is broad in scope, constitutes a culturally mandated source of knowledge, follows scientific methods, and reflects an ongoing search for wisdom.

## Broad Scope

The domain of social psychology is indeed broad; it provides a vantage point on major human concerns, such as conformity and deviance, altruism and aggression, loving and hating, self and groups, attitudes and action. It addresses, in some sense, all of human behavior. It discusses everything from private emotions to public trials. Social psychological principles are eagerly borrowed by economists, political scientists, management researchers, health scientists, legal scholars, education researchers, and colleagues in all the other branches of psychology (e.g., personality, clinical, developmental, cognitive, and neuro). The breadth of social psychology goes back to the crucial role of other people in our lives, which we have traced back to the human social group as the foundation of people's biological survival.

One example of an area that spans issues from close relationships to political clout is **nonverbal behavior**—all the action in a communication that is not words. Chapter 3 notes that people imitate other people's nonverbal behavior. Notice, for example, that when two people talk to each other, they often end up mirroring each other's gestures: crossing their arms at the same time, leaning their chins on their hands at the same time. Similarly, each person often reflects the other's facial expressions (Hatfield, Cacioppo, & Rapson, 1993).

Over time this can have a permanent effect on one's appearance. People do look more like their spouses after many years of marriage (see Table 1.9; Zajonc, Adelmann, Murphy, & Niedenthal, 1987). One explanation suggests that as they talk to each other and mimic each other's facial expressions, certain facial habits and muscle groups develop, with the result that the spouses eventually look more alike. Facial mimicry works even when people watch political leaders on television. Researchers (McHugo, Lanzetta, Sullivan, Masters, & Englis, 1985) attached electrodes to people's faces and found that they made tiny facial imitations of the person they were watching. So one explanation for the success of someone like President Reagan, who had a warm personality and was pleasant to watch, was that viewers subtly mimicked his facial expressions—for example, forming the ghost of a smile when he smiled. Smiling along with Reagan made people feel good. That too is a form of social influence, illustrating the broad scope of social psychology.

**Table 1.9**   Resemblance Values for Photographs of Young and Old, Married and Random Pairs

| | Years Married | |
|---|---|---|
| Status of Pairs | 1 | 25 |
| Married | 3.57 | 3.89 |
| Random | 3.77 | 3.40 |

Higher numbers indicate greater resemblance

*Source:* From Zajonc et al., 1987. Copyright © Klumer. Adapted with permission.

## Cultural Mandate

Second, and perhaps most important, social psychology is:

> a culturally mandated translation of our understanding of human behavior
> from an older language into a newer one. The older language was a
> language of religion and custom and law and etiquette. In the not too
> distant past, if we wanted to predict what someone would do or explain
> why they would do it, we would speak in religious terms or in terms of
> tradition. This would tell us quite well what kind of occupation a person
> would follow or what kind of person they would marry.... We demand an
> explanation of human behavior in language we find compelling, and this is
> now the language of science. (Brickman, 1980, p. 8)[3]

Social science in general (and social psychology in particular) supplies an explanation that modern culture respects and uses. Just as some times and some cultures
rely on tradition to explain people's lives, social psychology supplies a scientific
expertise sought by modern courts, lawmakers, educators, policy analysts, health-care
providers, managers, businesspeople, and journalists. Social psychology is culturally
accepted as a source of significant understanding, in the same way that tradition,
religion, or fortune-telling has in other times and places. In a traditional society, if
your small business is failing, you might consult an oracle to tell you whether your
competitor has put a spell on it (Evans-Pritchard, 1972). In an American city, if your
small business is failing, you might consult a social psychologist to design alternative
marketing strategies. In the United States, people who think they have been the target
of discrimination might go to court, calling a social psychological expert on stereotyping and prejudice to testify; in another society, people might simply accept their place
as a matter of tradition. Cultures mandate various forms of expertise. In the modern
world, social psychology is culturally mandated as an accepted form of knowledge.

## Scientific Methods

Scientific methods are integral to social psychology in three major ways, which the
next chapter will explain in detail. First, social psychologists develop systematic
theories and then investigate their validity to advance scientific understanding. As the
next chapter indicates, scientific theories attempt to predict causality, create coherence,
avoid excess, and facilitate investigation.

Second, social psychology relies on the scientific method—its techniques, procedures, analyses, and standards—to create scientifically reliable knowledge. Knowing
about research methods will clarify how the data help fit together pieces of the human
social puzzle. The methods aim to be precise, public, and accurate.

Third, social psychologists choose appropriate research strategies. They conduct experimental, observational, and survey research, adhering to rigorous standards

---

[3] Copyright © Elsevier. Reprinted with permission.

before making assertions about how people influence each other. Whatever the strategy, research outcomes attempt to predict the social world and to analyze people's responses.

The alternative to scientific explanation, namely, common sense, can seduce you into believing that you understand the material in this book. Beware common sense. (It will fail you on the exam!) You will frequently think that a given point is obvious or easily understood. Be careful. It may *seem* obvious because social psychology deals with face-to-face interactions, and we all are experts at face-to-face interactions, because we have them all the time. Common sense will provide a comfortable familiarity with the material.

Nevertheless, common sense cannot be trusted in learning social psychology. Often, common sense is neither common nor sensible. Common sense is contradictory and unreliable. Don't simply read a theory and say, "Yes, I get this." Study social psychology as you would any other subject, even though many social psychological concepts may make quick intuitive sense. For example, if you encounter the theory that people are attracted to people similar to themselves, you may think, "Of course, birds of a feather flock together." No doubt you can think of some examples. But what about "opposites attract" or "exotic is erotic"? Common sense might also tell you that people are attracted to others whose personalities complement theirs. Both alternatives cannot be right. Common sense thus contains a lot of truths, but also their opposites. Whereas common sense is not required to be consistent, science is. Social psychology goes beyond common sense to build a scientific understanding of human social behavior.

## Search for Wisdom

Social psychologists study practical social issues, in an effort to make the world a better place. Application to real-world problems is a key goal. Many people go into social psychology to help others. Social psychologists believe that if we understand how people influence one another, then perhaps we can understand and ameliorate some of the negative influences. Social psychology is in some ways a field for idealists.

In the end, social psychology searches for wisdom, not just knowledge. "Knowledge is an essential component of wisdom, but it is not by itself enough. Wisdom requires a fusion of moral and intellectual concerns, and also a fusion of direct and indirect experience" (Brickman, 1980, p. 12). Wisdom comprises knowledge about people and the world, combined with enduring moral, intellectual, and societal concerns, that together make sense in the social context of people's lived experience. I hope you get from this book little pieces of wisdom that you can carry with you for life.

## CHAPTER SUMMARY

This chapter began by defining social psychology as the science explaining how people influence other people. The actual, imagined, or implied presence of others influences the thoughts, feelings, and behaviors of individuals. Social psychology's level of analysis relative to other psychological and social sciences emphasizes individuals affected by other individuals or groups. As such, it highlights the often-underestimated power of the social situation, as compared with individual personalities. Moreover, people are so acutely attuned to others because we survive better in groups than as isolated individuals; evolutionary adaptation apparently favors the group-oriented person.

Our core social motives suit us to be good group members. People are motivated to belong to groups, to develop socially shared understanding, to control their interpersonal outcomes effectively, to enhance (esteem or at least improve) themselves, and to trust others by default. Not all people exhibit these motives under all circumstances, and they vary across cultures, but these five motives crop up repeatedly as organizing themes throughout social psychology, and they suit people to group life.

Social psychologists tackle the motives of the person in the situation by examining thoughts, feelings, and behavior across a broad scope, within the person, between people, within groups, and between groups. As a form of culturally mandated understanding, it is scientific, as opposed to tradition or common sense. At its best, social psychology is a search for wisdom about the human condition.

## SUGGESTIONS FOR FURTHER READING

CAPORAEL, L. R. (2001). Evolutionary psychology: Toward a unifying theory and a hybrid science. *Annual Review of Psychology*, 52, 607–628.

FUNDER, D. C., & FAST, L. A. (2010). Personality in social psychology. In S. T. FISKE, D. T. GILBERT, & G. LINDZEY (Eds.), *The handbook of social psychology*. New York: Wiley.

HEINE, S. J. (2010). Cultural psychology. In S. T. FISKE, D. T. GILBERT, & G, LINDZEY (Eds.), *The handbook of social psychology*. New York: Wiley.

JONES, E. E. (1985). Major developments in social psychology during the past five decades. In G. LINDZEY & E. ARONSON (Eds.), *The handbook of social psychology* (3rd ed., Vol. 1, pp. 47–108). New York: Random House.

LEARY, M. R. (2010). Affiliation, acceptance, and belonging: The pursuit of interpersonal connection. In S. T. FISKE, D. T. GILBERT, & G. LINDZEY (Eds.), *The handbook of social psychology*. New York: Wiley.

McGARTY C., & HASLAM, S. A. (Eds.). (1997). *The message of social psychology*. Cambridge, MA: Blackwell.

NEUBERG, S. L., KENRICK, D. T., & SCHALLER, M. (2010). Evolutionary social psychology. In S. T. FISKE, D. T. GILBERT, & G. LINDZEY (Eds.), *The handbook of social psychology*. New York: Wiley.

ROSS, L. R., & NISBETT, R. E. (1991). *The person and the situation: Perspectives of social psychology*. New York: McGraw-Hill.

ROSS, L. R., WARD, A., & LEPPER, M. (2010). A history of social psychology: Insights, challenges, and contributions to theory and application. In S. T. FISKE, D. T. GILBERT, & G. LINDZEY (Eds.), *The handbook of social psychology*. New York: Wiley.

TAYLOR, S. E. (1998). The social being in social psychology. In D. T. GILBERT, S. T. FISKE, & G. LINDZEY (Eds.), *The handbook of social psychology* (4th ed., Vol. 1, pp. 58–95). New York: McGraw-Hill.

VAN LANGE, P. A. M. (Ed.), (2006). *Bridging social psychology: Benefits of transdisciplinary approaches*. Mahwah, NJ: Erlbaum.

# Chapter **2**

# Scientific Methods for Studying People in Interaction

Could simply thinking about smart people improve your performance? Dutch researchers hypothesized that merely contemplating professors could make people more knowledgeable. Fifty-eight Dutch college students volunteered for a pair of pilot studies to develop materials for future psychology experiments. Seated in individual computer cubicles for the first pilot study, two-thirds of the participants started out by imagining and listing a typical professor's behaviors, lifestyle, and appearance; some did so for two minutes and some for nine minutes. The remaining third of the participants skipped this task. Then, in the second pilot study, all participants completed a 60-item general knowledge test, composed of items from the Trivial Pursuits game. Examples included "Who painted *La Guernica*?" (a. *Dali*, b. *Miro*, c. *Picasso*, d. *Velasquez*) and "What is the capital of Bangladesh?" (a. *Dhaka*, b. *Hanoi*, c. *Yangon*, d. *Bangkok*). Participants typically answered about 50% correctly (where 25% would be chance). None of the participants saw any link between the first pilot study and the second. In fact, however, subjects who had spent time thinking about typical professors actually performed far better on the knowledge test than those who did not (see Table 2.1): Professorial thoughts gained them an advantage of 6% to 14% on this multiple choice test of factual knowledge. What happened? Did participants become more knowledgeable merely as a result of thinking about professors? (We wish.) The experiment's authors (Dijksterhuis & van Knippenberg, 1998) speculated that having "professor" on the mind may have caused them to work harder, use better strategies, or trust their hunches. Other studies will unravel this mystery (see Chapter 4). For the present, however, this study illustrates the simultaneously elegant and provocative nature of a well-designed experiment.

This chapter aims to help you understand the unsurpassed power of the scientific experiment but also its limitations. Whether studying the influence of thinking about social roles, as in the professor study, or the impact of group decision making, as in Lewin's organ-meats study from Chapter 1, all social psychologists grapple with determining the scientific methods best suited to test their hypotheses. Methods form

**Table 2.1**   Trivial Pursuit Score, after Thinking about Professors

|  | Time Spent Thinking about the Typical Professor | | |
|---|---|---|---|
|  | 0 Minutes | 2 Minutes | 9 Minutes |
| Percent Correct | 45.2 | 51.8 | 58.9 |

*Source:* From Dijksterhuis & van Knippenberg, 1998, Experiment 2. Copyright © American Psychological Association. Adapted with permission.

the bedrock on which our field rests, and experiments are the most solid scientific rocks of all. Careful scientific methods and outcomes provide the best information about the plausibility of our ideas, whether the hypotheses concern the power of roles, the influence of group decision making, or the causes of aggression.

To explain social psychology's methods, this chapter first describes forming scientific hypotheses, which involves the process of conceptualization. Second, the chapter describes testing hypotheses, that is, the process of operationalization, whereby researchers create empirical, working definitions of their concepts. Third, the chapter describes three research strategies that utilize social psychology's operational methods: descriptive, correlational, and experimental. Fourth, we will see that some methodological challenges are peculiar to social settings and the core social motives that people bring to them. Finally, the chapter includes a brief discussion of research ethics. By the end of the chapter, I hope you will see how the research enterprise operates and what dilemmas it confronts, that is, how social psychologists conduct their science.

## FORMING HYPOTHESES: CONCEPTUALIZATION

The first chapter noted that social psychology is scientific. As a science, it involves the dynamic interplay among theory, method, and application—all three of which influence each other. This first section will tackle **conceptualization:** how social psychologists develop hypotheses, based on both theory and application to social problems (see Fiske, 2003, for other sources of ideas). The second section addresses **operationalization:** how social psychologists test scientific hypotheses, whether theory-based or application-oriented.

### Application as a Source of Hypotheses

Most textbooks and lectures assume theory as the basis of research, but most introductory students assume real-world issues as the basis of research ideas, so the chapter starts there for the moment. Many social psychologists in fact go into the field because of an interest in improving the world, and many government agencies that fund research also emphasize the importance of applications.

Indeed, some of the most famous social psychological research focuses on an important social issue, rather than a specific theory. For example, Craig Haney, Curtis Banks, and Phillip Zimbardo (1973) started from the premise that prisons fail on humanitarian, pragmatic, and economic grounds. Their approach stemmed from their social psychological analysis of why this apparent failure occurs. The most frequent explanation for the failure of prisons, they argued, is the **dispositional hypothesis:** That is, the supposed nature of the people who populate prisons (both correction officers and inmates) creates the awful conditions in prisons. By contrast, a social psychological account attends to the prison as a social situation, which itself creates the awful conditions and failures to rehabilitate. Thus, the researchers' goal was to evaluate the dispositional hypothesis (and by extension, the situational one as an alternative account) as a way to understand prisons. From an applied problem and a social psychological analysis of the setting came their situational hypothesis.

They arranged to have Stanford student volunteers "arrested" by real police in the students' own residences and taken to a temporary basement prison, where they were stripped of their normal clothes; made to wear only muslin smocks, ankle chains, and rubber sandals; forced to cover their hair with nylon stocking caps; and constantly bossed and degraded by guards. For example, guards insulted prisoners ten times as often as vice versa and threatened them five times as often; the guards acted aggressively and spoke primarily in commands, without using names or other individuating references, while the prisoners resisted and spoke primarily to ask questions (see Table 2.2). "Despite the fact that guards and prisoners were free to engage in any form of interaction (positive or negative, supportive or affrontive, etc.), the characteristic nature of their encounters tended to be negative, hostile, affrontive, and dehumanizing" (p. 80). The researchers felt compelled to halt the study when the cruelty of the guards (randomly assigned students) made the prisoners (other randomly assigned students) unbearably miserable. Five of the ten prisoners had already been released early because of extreme emotional reactions (depression, crying, rage, acute anxiety).

Before the study terminated, the guards had learned to dislike and victimize the prisoners; the prisoners adopted the guards' negative views and became passive. The study is a controversial classic in American social psychology courses, for methodological and ethical reasons, as we will see. Nevertheless, it illustrates the power of the situation—randomly assigned roles—to create extreme behavior.

As another example of application driving hypotheses, consider the Lewin organmeat study described in the last chapter. In that instance, an applied problem, namely, getting families to consume unusual and economical foods in a time of scarcity,

**Table 2.2**  Behavior as a Function of Randomly Assigned Roles: Prison Study

| | Role | |
|---|---|---|
| Behavior | Guard | Prisoner |
| Verbal threats | 27 | 5 |
| Deprecation/insults | 61 | 6 |
| Physical resistance | 2 | 32 |
| Weapon or tool use | 23 | 6 |

Entries are numbers of instances of each behavior.
*Source:* Data from Haney et al., 1973.

motivated the research. But Lewin's brilliance lay in his conceptual analyses of the social psychological processes, namely, group decisions, that are most likely to prove effective.

When novice scientists become interested in a problem, they often leap directly from the application (e.g., gender stereotyping, sexual attraction, casual lies) to the method. Nevertheless, great social psychologists analyze the problem more carefully, to identify the social forces at work, in order to conceptualize the process more scientifically and ultimately more usefully. Lewin is widely quoted as having said, "Nothing is so practical as a good theory" (although in fact he attributed this bit of wisdom to an anonymous businessman). Whatever the source, the point is that application is improved by good theory, and theory is improved by relevant application.

## Theory as a Source of Hypotheses

Hypotheses most often derive from theory, in what is called basic research. A **theory**, as a system of logical principles, attempts to explain or account for relationships among natural, observable phenomena. The theory is stated in abstract, general terms and generates more specific hypotheses (testable propositions), discussed later. What makes a good theory that can generate hypotheses for research? A good theory, first, posits causal relationships and also attempts to be coherent, parsimonious, and falsifiable. Let's address each feature in turn.

**CAUSAL RELATIONSHIPS**    Social psychologists create theories that attempt to explain people's interactions with each other. As such, social psychological theories attempt to explain why people behave as they do in social situations. In explaining why, the theories posit **causal relationships:** Some behavior occurs because of some prior situation. Thus, social psychologists aim to make valid **causal inferences** (what causes what), a topic that will focus most of this chapter. Scientists are interested not only in describing and predicting people's social reactions but also in being able to say what causes them. Knowing how and why a phenomenon occurs creates a deeper understanding of it, not to mention the possibility of influencing it.

For example, if we knew that merely assigning people to low- and high-power roles in a highly regulated environment (such as a prison) can cause people to abuse other people, then we would understand much more about social power and abuse, as well as prisons, than if we merely knew that people differ in need for social power and in abusiveness, even if we know power and abuse are sometimes correlated. If we knew that merely making people think about professors, intelligence, and great books can cause people to retrieve their knowledge more effectively, then we would understand much more about mind-set and intellectual performance than if we merely knew that people differ in mind-sets and differ in performance, even if the two tend to be correlated. Positing causal relationships—not just correlations—is an important feature of any scientific theory.

**COHERENCE**    Another characteristic of good scientific theories is that they are **coherent**, that is, (a) all the parts of the theory agree with each other, so it is not self-contradictory, and (b) the theory makes internal sense. The last chapter gave an example of how common sense could be self-contradictory (opposites attract, but birds of a feather flock). As another example, the expression "out of sight, out of mind" is a direct contradiction of the expression "absence makes the heart grow fonder." Taken together, those would not be good scientific theory, in part because they contradict each other.

Coherence goes beyond simply not contradicting each other, for it is also important that science tell a good story that hangs together and makes internal sense. Some theories in social psychology may be perfectly correct, but they do not tell a good story, so they do not generate much research. In the broad sense, coherence is an element in the aesthetics of scientific explanation; a coherent explanation is more pleasing to consider, is more feasible to test, and generates more research.

**PARSIMONY**    In addition to causality and coherence, scientific theories ideally are **parsimonious;** they are compact, explaining things simply, using as few concepts as absolutely necessary. Why garbage up the explanatory system with extra components? To predict one person's violence, surely a thousand predictors could combine to do a good job, but what use is that? If we can predict violence using three or four major factors, that is neater, more compact, and ultimately more useful, because those three or four factors will be the important ones and we can feasibly measure them. Scientists seek compact explanations, for both practical and aesthetic reasons, to the extent that reality allows simplicity and elegance.

**FALSIFIABILITY**    Finally, for theory to guide research, the ideas have to be **falsifiable**. That is, the theory has to be stated in such a way that it is possible to produce data that would make researchers conclude that the theory is wrong or that it is wrong in part, that is, not supported in the particular set of observations. If every conceivable observation that one can imagine can be explained by the theory, then something is wrong with the theory. Many a theory has lost its credibility within psychology precisely because it could explain everything. The theory was not so interesting or useful anymore because it could explain any result and its opposite.

For example, the useless prediction that the weather tomorrow will be between $-80$ and $+120$ degrees F will be correct but too vague to be falsifiable. (It is also uninteresting.) As another example, the statement that "all behavior is caused by some kind of instinct" proved to be unfalsifiable because every time a behavior seemed not be predicted by a known instinct, a new instinct was invented. As instincts proliferated, they became useless as explanatory mechanisms (Boring, 1950). Some people have accused Freudian theory of explaining virtually every kind of observation. This probably is not totally fair, for it depends on whose version of Freudian theory is meant and whether one treats it as a scientific theory or as a more humanist project. From a basic science perspective, however, if a theory digests every conceivable thing in its path, it is not falsifiable. Theories have to predict concrete observations that would support or contradict the theory.

Theories are not typically destroyed by a single critical experiment that by itself falsifies the theory. Rather, the accumulating data build up contradictions that do not fit the theory, and confidence in the theory diminishes over time. Eventually, a new theory comes along to do a better job of accounting for the overall pattern of research results. Although a theory can be undermined and discarded, established scientists rarely use the term "disproved." The process is more cumulative than that, and often the theory may hold under certain limited circumstances.

Conversely, novices often consider that a theory can be "proved"; it cannot. A theory can be supported by quantities of data that are consistent with it, or the theory can fail to gain support from data and be undermined by data that are inconsistent with it. But even if a theory is well supported, some researcher, somewhere, sometime, potentially could come up with some data that contradict the accumulated evidence, or some theorist, somewhere, sometime, could create a theory that accounts for the available data better than previous theories do. Thus, a theory can never be considered conclusively proved for all time.

With this caution, some theories may be extremely well supported, and the current consensus of scientists may agree that a given theory explains the available data better than any other available theory. Reviews of the research can even quantify the direction of results and what factors modify the results. This technique—called a **meta-analysis**—isolates the same research question across many studies, extracting a quantitative estimate of the size of the effect, and combines those effects over studies. This text uses meta-analyses whenever possible (for 322 examples, see Richard, Bond, & Stokes-Zoota, 2003) because they most reliably indicate the direction taken by a particular line of research. Meta-analysis is one method for scientists to focus on the weight of the data pro and con. Precisely because theories cannot be proved, but rather depend on the weight of the evidence, the theory must provide the possibility of enough supportive data, as well as the chance for contrary data that could falsify it.

**SUMMARY OF THEORIES AS A SOURCE OF HYPOTHESES**    Scientific theories specify causal relationships and aim for coherence, parsimony, and falsifiability. Given a coherent, parsimonious, falsifiable theory of causality, scientists generate more specific hypotheses that apply to particular situations. Whereas a theory is a broad system of ideas—for example, evolutionary theory, or the social psychological theories in the rest of this book—a single hypothesis is a more specific, testable statement.

## Hypotheses

A **hypothesis** is a statement of the relationship that is expected to exist between two or more conceptual variables. Ideally, a hypothesis takes the form of a declarative sentence consisting of "something-verb-something else." The verb in the middle usually takes the form: affects, changes, increases, decreases, is related to. The hypothesis usually has an explicitly causal structure to it—one factor influences another factor: Group decisions influence individual behavior; thinking about intelligence improves performance; being powerless reduces confrontation; violent television increases aggression.

Although nothing should be simpler, finding the hypothesis explicitly stated in some social scientific articles can be hard, as my students often discover, to their surprise. When you participate in an experiment, if you have that option, or when you read and think critically about a scientific study, the first step is to know what the hypothesis is. (It is not enough simply to copy down what the experimenter tells you or what it says somewhere in the abstract.) Put the hypothesis into this form: "*a* does something to *b*." Sometimes the hypothesis is "*a* and *b* do something to *c* and *d*." More than one factor can appear on either side of this verb-arrow. Stating the hypothesis as "something(s) affect something(s)" reveals the structure of the researcher's argument.

## Variables

Besides the verb (such as "affect") that connects them, hypotheses are made up of variables: Variable *a* influences variable *b*. A **variable** may be defined as a characteristic that varies or changes either across people or in the same person across time and place. As an active learning exercise, you might pause and generate some social psychological variables.

Actually, many of the chapter headings from here on constitute social psychological variables, or pointers to some: self (self-concept, self-esteem), attitudes and persuasion, attraction, helping, aggression, stereotyping and prejudice, conformity and obedience. For example, helping, as a variable, can influence other variables, such as liking, and helping can result from other variables, such as attraction.

In addition, the most common applications of social psychology create variables. As some of the Chapter 1 examples noted, health affects people's social situation, and the social situation affects health, even survival. Social psychologists Ellen Langer and Judith Rodin (Rodin & Langer, 1977) concluded that elderly patients actually lived longer when given control over apparently trivial aspects of their lives (Table 2.3). One group of residents heard a lecture on the importance of taking responsibility for themselves and were offered a houseplant to water, as well as being able to choose movie times; the comparison group received a lecture about staff responsibility for their care, a houseplant that the staff would water, and staff-scheduled movie times. Over a year after the intervention, nurses evaluated the residents on measures that included whether they seemed happy, actively interested, sociable, self-initiating, and vigorous. The experimental group scored higher and also lived longer. The study is not flawless, and we will come back to it. However, the point here is its striking result on a variety of social psychological variables, including survival. Although social psychologists rarely deal with death as an outcome variable, it could be one, as in this study. In other applied areas, other real-world variables enter in: arrest rates, voting participation, consumer choice.

**Table 2.3**   Effects of Perceived Control on Mortality in a Nursing Home

| Measure, 18 Months Later | Condition | |
| --- | --- | --- |
| | Responsibility Induced | Comparison |
| Mortality rate | 15% | 30% |
| Nurses' evaluation of health (scale from 45 to 630) | 352.33 | 262.00 |

*Source:* From Rodin & Langer, 1977. Copyright © American Psychological Association. Adapted with permission.

Here is another variable: "What about gender?" you ask. Isn't gender a social psychological variable? Some variables, such as gender, education, socioeconomic class, ethnicity, and age, are demographic variables; such population characteristics are one kind of person variable. Although often used in social psychology, these person variables are less often the focus of research. Social psychologists tend to look less at **person variables**—features of a research participant that the person carries all the time—and look more at **situation variables** that can change according to the social context. Later, we discuss more examples of social situation variables: how many other people were present, what role a person has in a group, whether two people depend on each other. Those are not intrinsic features of the participant; those are variables that depend on the situation. Social psychology focuses on such situational variables, although the less typical kind, person variables, also come up as well. Sometimes social psychologists will examine person variables in combination with situation variables, as we will see. Recall from Chapter 1 that field founder Kurt Lewin originally described behavior as a function of both person and situation.

## Conceptual Variables

A hypothesis focuses on the general version of any given variable. The **conceptual variable** is the abstract version of the variable used in the hypothesis; it occurs in the dictionary. In studying aggression, one could look it up in the dictionary to get a conceptual point of view and an abstract definition. Or one could examine theoretical discussions by social psychologists, for example, about the nature and causes of aggression, to consider the conceptual version of the variable. In the same way, a researcher could conceptualize attractiveness, love, helping, or prejudice; all of these are social psychological conceptual variables. All of them have definitions within social psychology that usually resemble the dictionary definition. This, then, is the abstract, conceptual version of the variable, used in stating the hypothesis.

Many conceptual variables are also **hypothetical constructs**, that is, ideas that link together various other ideas or observations as sharing some common property. For example, an attitude is a (well-established) hypothetical construct. We cannot directly observe an attitude, but we can observe many manifestations that are consistent with the concept. And the attitude concept links to other concepts (prejudice, attraction, self-esteem) in useful ways. Hypothetical constructs often are nonobservable entities inside people's heads, but they are posited because they bring together many phenomena that seem to be related. Goals, instincts, and schemas are other hypothetical constructs. People can debate their utility for clarifying scientific theory and generating research.

In contrast, other conceptual variables are less often considered hypothetical constructs because they were not invented to serve psychological theories, as the attitude concept was, but instead are considered to have some intrinsic reality. Helping, for example, while an abstract concept that may be expressed in multiple ways, occurs mainly as an observable behavior, and few would label it a hypothetical construct. Thus, all hypothetical constructs are conceptual variables, but not all conceptual variables are hypothetical constructs.

## Summary of Hypotheses

More specific than theories are hypotheses, which state an expected relationship between two or more variables. Variables are factors that can vary across people, contexts, and time. Situation variables are most common in social psychology, but person variables enter as well. Hypotheses use the abstract or conceptual versions of variables.

## TESTING HYPOTHESES: OPERATIONALIZATION

Having formulated a hypothesis, the researcher turns from conceptualizing to operationalizing, the focus of this section.

### Operational Variables

As noted, hypotheses use conceptual versions of variables. Then there is the **operational variable**—the working definition or operationalization, which refers to the concrete, specific, precise empirical definition of the variable, used in testing the hypothesis. The translation from the conceptual version to the operational version constitutes the critical step in research. How concepts are operationalized matters because social psychologists generate evidence from concrete versions of the variable: measuring it or, in the case of an experiment, manipulating it. The evidence is only as good as the operationalization.

The operational version of the variable has to be so specific and concrete that one can literally point to it. This degree of concreteness goes to what is called public reproducibility, discussed in the next section. The operationalized version of the variable has to be so specific that researchers can show other researchers exactly how they could study it too in precisely the same way. Whether the operational variable is a survey questionnaire measuring attitudes, a computer key-press measuring speed of response, or a scenario whereby two strangers meet in a waiting room, researchers have to be able to describe their operationalized variables so precisely that someone else can replicate exactly what they did, down to the last detail.

Sometimes, the potential gap between the researchers' idea (e.g., the concept of aggression) and what they actually do in their research (the operational or working definition) is problematic. Professional reviewers but also novices often judge whether the researcher's idea has been operationalized properly—whether the research effectively and realistically captures the phenomenon. This is a valid criticism, and a practical alternative can emerge from the criticism.

For example, students might feel that the operational definition trivializes a concept that matters to them: "I can't believe that they are studying love by having people meet each other for five minutes and report how attracted they are." (The answer is that it depends on what aspect of love is being studied; as an operationalization of initial attraction, that method might be acceptable, but as the close relationships chapter shows, it will not do to operationalize love that way.) For any topic, say, aggression or love, contradictions between what some people think it is (i.e., their concept) and how others study it (i.e., the particular operationalizations) can lead to creative new research directions.

## Levels of a Variable

One of the key decisions in operationalizing a variable is picking appropriate levels of the variable to use. If a variable is defined as a characteristic that varies, then it must vary through different **levels**, values, qualities, or quantities. For example, how many different levels or values does gender have? (In other words, how many different genders are there?) Two. A reasonable answer, although for some purposes, degrees of masculinity and femininity might matter, or transgender individuals might be relevant.

How many different levels or values does income have? The answer depends on how specific the researcher wants to be. Usually scientists break down income, as in a survey; the researchers provide ranges, and participants select the range that includes their own income. That way, instead of having practically infinite numbers of options (*$12,001, $12,002, . . .*), the researchers get answers that are accurate enough for their purposes (*$15,000 or less; $15,001 to $25,000*; etc.). But that is a decision on the part of the researcher, depending on the purpose of the research. For instance, in studying students, one would use income categories different from those in studying established doctors.

Take aggression as another example. When researchers consider aggression as a variable, the levels they use depend on whom they are studying and for what purpose. If they are investigating kindergarten children and focusing on interpersonal violence, homicide is not a likely level of aggression. However, if they are examining urban violence, homicide is a relevant level of the variable, whereas shoving somebody is probably not too relevant (although it can lead to homicide). In the Stanford prison study, insults and verbal put-downs constituted levels of interpersonal aggression. When social psychologists choose a variable, then, they make a choice about what levels or values of that variable they are interested in studying, depending on how detailed and inclusive they want to be.

Take, as another variable, comfort with the drinking habits of one's fellow students; such norms about alcohol consumption do influence people's own drinking. Comfort with the local customs has been measured on an 11-point scale, from 0 = *not at all comfortable* to 10 = *very comfortable* (Prentice & Miller, 1993). Participants' own comfort contrasted with what they perceived to be the comfort of all the other students, a phenomenon called **pluralistic ignorance**. For example, in September, first-year male students on average believed other students were 1.64 scale-points more comfortable with local drinking habits than they themselves were; by December, their own comfort had increased, nearly to match the (falsely) perceived norm (see Table 2.4). Women showed the opposite pattern; their discomfort did not change over the semester, as they perceived other students' comfort to increase. For men, this fit a pattern of drinking more over the course of the year, to fit in with the (at first falsely) perceived social norms.

**Table 2.4**   Ratings of Own and Others' Comfort with Norms about Drinking

| Measure | Self | Average Student |
| --- | --- | --- |
| Men: comfort in September | 5.84 | 7.48 |
| Men: comfort in December | 7.08 | 7.58 |
| Women: comfort in September | 6.08 | 7.16 |
| Women: comfort in December | 5.94 | 7.74 |

*Source:* From Prentice & Miller, 1993. Copyright © American Psychological Association. Adapted with permission.

Consider the issue of levels in the comfort variable. If the researchers had, alternatively, simply looked at a dichotomy (*comfortable/uncomfortable*), they would not have uncovered people's illusions so easily as they did with an 11-point scale. Conversely, they did not need to ask respondents to distinguish along a more detailed continuous range (on a scale from 1 = *extremely uncomfortable* to 100 = *extremely comfortable*) in order to find their effect. Even when researchers choose to use an intermediate range (typically 5–15-point scales), they must decide how to break up that range, how to label it (e.g., *strongly disagree, moderately disagree, neutral, moderately agree, strongly agree*), and whether to omit or include a neutral point.

Sometimes, consumers of research, both students and scientists, identify variables that they think are mistakenly broken up into inappropriate levels, variables that for one reason or another tend to group together people or responses that do not belong together. For example, the 2000 census faced a major dilemma in measuring ethnicity. Traditionally, the government and many survey researchers often collapse together all different kinds of Latinos into one category and all different kinds of Asians into another. Depending on the purpose of the research, that might be appropriate or not. Each of those categories lumps together people from many different backgrounds who might, in terms of their own social identity, know it as a mistaken lumping. "Asian" and "Latino" are social creations on the part of the culture, as is calling somebody "black." Whether the researchers are studying people's own identities or some people's categories for other people, different levels of the variable ethnicity might apply. Studying identity is likely to require many levels (for Asian, at least South Asian, Southeast Asian, East Asian, but more probably the specific country of ancestors and identity as well as current nationality). It might also include, as the 2000 census did for the first time, the possibility of checking multiple categories, indicating increasingly common multiracial identities. Depending on context, global identity (e.g., European) or subgroup identity (e.g., British) might matter (Crisp, Hall, & Stone, 2006). On the other hand, studying stereotypes might require only the global category "Asian" or even the mistaken belief that "they" are all "Chinese."

Conceptual and operational versions of variables both include the assumption that variables have levels, but specifying levels of variables often arises in the process of operationalization. The purpose of the research, the hypothesis in particular, helps determine the appropriate levels of the variables.

## Scientific Standards in Operationalizing Variables

In operationalizing variables for testing a scientific hypothesis, scientific standards require operational precision, public reproducibility, and accuracy.

**OPERATIONAL PRECISION**    In scientific methods, as noted earlier, an operationalization is the working definition of a concept for the purposes of studying it. **Operational precision** then forms the cornerstone of standards for scientific methods; it entails first executing one's research consistently and exactly, then describing one's sampling, procedures, manipulations, and measures in specific detail. All this entails specifying what a concept means. If social psychologists want to study aggression, for example, operationalizing the concept of aggression forces them to be scientifically precise, in order to be clear about what exactly they mean by aggression. Operational precision requires picking the exact observable variable. In studying aggression, shall they study insults, punches, homicide, or spouse abuse? As noted earlier, scientists could operationalize aggression many different ways, and choosing is the first step in operational precision.

Then, the method must be conducted in the same way every time. The exacting nature of asking the survey question consistently and of conducting the experiment the same way every time conveys operational precision. In choosing methods and conducting studies, researchers have to compromise between everyday reality and precise, feasible, scientific standards. In this compromise, operational precision helps to meet important scientific standards.

Finally, the detail of the methods sections of empirical articles also expresses the importance of operational precision. As a researcher, one must document one's method in complete detail and down to the last nuance. If one cannot do that, then it is not truly scientific. Operational precision forces social researchers to be specific and unambiguous. It requires the kind of scientific rigor necessary to progress.

**PUBLIC REPRODUCIBILITY**    Scientific methods also must be **publicly reproducible**, which means that others can examine and replicate the methods and the data they produce. Science depends on replication from one laboratory to another.

Private evidence is not evidence. One example of not being publicly reproducible comes from the early days of psychology. Around the end of the 19th century, the first laboratory psychologists, Wilhelm Wundt (1897) and Hermann Ebbinghaus (1885), relied a great deal on themselves as research subjects and sometimes just on introspection. They and their graduate students trained themselves to observe their own thought processes, specifically, their own memory systems. They would observe and reflect on how they memorized a list of numbers, for example. The problem is that if they developed a theory based on how they memorize numbers, and other scientists developed theories based on how they memorize numbers, how does one decide which is right?

Social psychologists have the same challenge because most people have strong intuitions about how they interact with other people, and they may or may not be right. People cannot tell more than they can know (Nisbett & Wilson, 1977a). In one study, students watched a teacher on one of two videotapes, one in which he behaved warmly, encouraged discussion, and described appealing assignments and another in which he behaved coldly, discouraged discussion, and gave unappealing assignments (Nisbett & Wilson, 1977b). Roughly 70% of students rated his physical appearance in his warm guise as appealing, and in his cold guise roughly the same percentage rated it as irritating. Despite these clear effects, 90% to 95% of the students claimed that his likeability had no effect or the opposite effect on their ratings of his appearance (see Figure 2.1). Participants could not accurately report what had influenced their responses.

People may be unaware of a stimulus that affects their response, unaware of the response, or unaware of the connection between the stimulus and the response. Accordingly, psychologists cannot rely on research participants' verbal reports about why they responded as they did, because those reports are unreliable. In the same way, researchers cannot report on their own internal processes, using them as a form of evidence.

Psychologists cannot get inside the head and directly observe affective and cognitive processes, so we must use outward manifestations of the interior thinking and feeling processes. Those outward manifestations then encompass scientific methods that any researcher can use. Public reproducibility (being able to replicate someone else's methods exactly) is impossible for introspection. Introspective "methods" are not appropriate in modern science, except when—along with theory and application—researchers use them in first generating hypotheses. But introspection, intuition, hunches, and common sense do not belong in the main stages, when researchers go beyond generating a hypothesis. The key to being publicly reproducible is that one laboratory has to be able to replicate what another laboratory has already done. Conducting research carefully and writing methods down in detail (operational precision) constitute the first steps, but what is done and written needs to be observable and repeatable by others (public reproducibility).

**OBSERVATIONAL ACCURACY**    Social psychologists try to generate accurate observations that conform to scientific standards. **Observational accuracy** involves both precision and lack of bias (Rosenthal, 1995).

**Observational precision** minimizes the random error—or the noise—in measurements. An example is an antique clock that runs, unpredictably, sometimes fast and sometimes slow. This form of inaccuracy is imprecision; the clock would be approximately right, but not reliably off by exactly the same amount or even the same direction each time. A sloppy human observer, coder, or data-entry typist also would lack precision. Being careful, social psychologists (and other social and behavioral scientists) acknowledge that our data are likely to contain some random error, so we average over many observations, for the errors to cancel out.

The other form of accuracy entails lack of **observational bias**, which describes a constant error. That is, suppose a watch is always fast or slow by a constant amount. For example, some people set their watches ahead by five minutes, a constant bias that improves their on-time record. Which would be preferable, a watch that has a constant bias or a watch that has random error? Having a watch with a lot of random

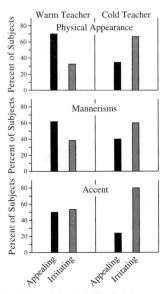

(A)    Ratings of Teacher's Physical Appearance,
        Mannerisms, and Accent as a Function of
        Manipulated Warmth versus Coldness

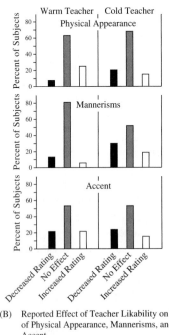

(B)    Reported Effect of Teacher Likability on Ratings
        of Physical Appearance, Mannerisms, and
        Accent

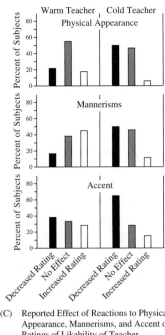

(C)    Reported Effect of Reactions to Physical
        Appearance, Mannerisms, and Accent on
        Ratings of Likability of Teacher

**Figure 2.1**    Inaccuracy of Verbal Reports

*Source:* From Nisbett and Wilson, 1977b. Copyright © American Psychological Association. Adapted with permission

error and noise would prevent effectively adjusting for its inaccuracy, for one would never know whether it was five minutes fast or five minutes slow. With constant bias, as in setting one's watch ahead, one can always adjust to get the accurate answer, although one may not always remember in a pinch (hence, this trick's usefulness for the consistently tardy). With scientific observations, of course, the trick is knowing when observations are biased and by how much. More frequently, social psychologists simply attempt to prevent bias, as described later.

## From Concept to Operation: Some Examples

As we have seen so far, both application and theory generate hypotheses, which state relationships between conceptual variables. Operational variables then test a hypothesis, adhering to scientific standards.

Consider a specific hypothesis as an example: Attractiveness increases persuasion (see Table 2.5). Without going into theoretical detail (see attraction chapter), this hypothesis seems plausible. "What is beautiful is good" applies to people, at least in some respects, according to a meta-analysis. In a quantitative review of 76 studies (Eagly, Ashmore, Makhijani, & Longo, 1991), attractive people are consistently credited with being sociable, well-adjusted, powerful, and intellectually competent, although not necessarily trustworthy or concerned about others. On some counts, but not all, attractive people might well be persuasive. Certainly, advertisers think so. And so do political parties; think of all the attention paid to managing candidates' appearance.

Suppose, then, that our hypothesis is that attractiveness increases persuasiveness. Notice that "attractiveness" and "persuasiveness" are the abstract, conceptual versions of the variables used in the hypothesis. How might one operationalize this hypothesis? One could operationalize attractiveness in many ways. The meta-analysis by Eagly et al. (1991) documents several methods in use, but the most common one is preselecting people as attractive and unattractive, according to judges' ratings, and showing them in head-and-shoulders photographs or videotapes. A minority of studies

**Table 2.5**   From Concept to Operation: Attractiveness Increases Persuasion

|  | Hypothesized Cause | → | Effect |
|---|---|---|---|
| Conceptual Variables | Attractiveness | → | Persuasion |
| Operational variables | Pretested photographs<br><br>*or*<br><br>Same person, with better or worse grooming<br><br>*or*<br><br>Same person, smiling or not |  | *Topic:* college issues, health, consumer goods, *or* social policy<br><br>*Measure:* scale of agreement (choose levels, wording)<br><br>*or*<br><br>behavior (e.g., signing petition, buying product) |

change the appearance of the same target, for example, with makeup, hairstyle, and expression.

Suppose we pick simply the amount of smiling the person does, because that is something that we could set up in an experiment with the same average-looking person smiling either a lot or very little. The meta-analysis indicates that using the same person twice produces stronger results than preselected attractive and unattractive photographs of different people. Then, to get down to the most specific form of the operationalization, we could present half the people with photographs of a communicator who is smiling and the other half with the same person not smiling. If we use a color photograph instead of black and white, the meta-analysis indicates the effects are likely to be stronger, so that would be wise. What's more, the effect is likely to be stronger if we do not present a lot of additional information about the person.

What about the operational version of persuasiveness? One could measure persuasion in lots of different ways also. First, we have to pick a topic. Another meta-analysis (Johnson & Eagly, 1989) lists topics that range from the merits of disposable razors to senior comprehensive exams to media coverage of hijacking. College issues, health, consumer products, and social policy are the most common topics in persuasion studies.

Then we have to measure persuasion. Examining the meta-analysis indicates, reasonably, that several questionnaire items tend to produce larger effects than one item, presumably because more items create more **reliable** measures (random error cancels out). Most often, researchers use an agreement scale (e.g., from 1 to 7), but we would have to decide the number of levels that make sense and how to label them. Or we could use a behavioral measure, such as signing a petition or buying a product. Each of these operational decisions would come up in measuring persuasion, to test the hypothesis that attractiveness increases persuasion.

Any decision about operationalizing a variable in a particular form is a kind of hypothesis itself. For example, a hypothesis lurks behind the idea to use smiling and unsmiling pictures to operationalize attractiveness, namely, the hypothesis that smiling is attractive. This too is an empirical question. In one study, Reis and nine students (1990) tested the hypothesis that smiling increases perceived attractiveness. Thirty undergraduates served as stimulus people. Each one was photographed with either a neutral or smiling facial expression. Attractiveness thus had two levels: The undergraduates either smiled or not. Then the researchers asked 100 other college students to rate the photographs on 20 trait adjectives, which thus measured attractiveness (see Table 2.6). They found, for example, that smiling faces seemed more sincere and likeable, sociable and exciting, as well as competent and intelligent. But a smile also indicates submission, so smiling faces seemed less independent and self-assured, and less masculine, more feminine. Thus, smiling does reliably increase certain kinds of attractiveness, so our operationalization of attractiveness as smiling makes some sense, and increases in perceived sincerity and competence might well predict increased persuasion. However, our operationalization is weak in the persuasion context because smiling people seemed less independent and self-assured. All operationalizations present trade-offs, and researchers' skill partly involves balancing among them to pick the most reasonable and convincing operationalization, which after all is simply a working definition.

**Table 2.6**    Trait Perception Scores as a Function of Smiling

| Dimension | Not Smiling | Smiling |
|---|---|---|
| Sincere, likable, modest, sensitive, kind, trustworthy, nurturing, cooperative | 3.99 | 4.58 |
| Sociable, interesting, exciting, sexually warm | 3.89 | 4.61 |
| Competent, intelligent | 4.31 | 4.53 |
| Independent, self-assured, strong | 4.36 | 4.22 |
| Masculine, not feminine | 4.11 | 3.92 |

*Source:* From Reis et al., 1990. Copyright © Wiley. Adapted with permission.

## Summary of Testing Hypotheses via Operationalization

Operationalization involves concrete versions of variables, the working definitions in the specific prediction for a particular study. Scientific standards for operationalization include operational precision, public reproducibility, and observational accuracy (precision and lack of bias), as indicated in several examples.

## CHOOSING A RESEARCH STRATEGY

All research involves variables and hypotheses. Having formulated a hypothesis with conceptual variables, and now in the process of operationalizing the variables, the researcher must choose an overall research strategy. One way to understand this choice is to consider three commonly identified basic strategies (e.g., Rosenthal, 1995; Stangor, 2006): *descriptive, correlational*, and *experimental*. Each research strategy differs in the type of hypothesis it investigates, as well as particular issues it raises.

### Descriptive Research

**Descriptive research** aims to depict accurately some characteristic in a population of interest. Descriptive research focuses on only one variable at a time, assessing the amount or average level of a given variable in a population. It concerns an atypical kind of hypothesis, raises specific issues about sampling, and addresses a unique kind of question.

**NOT A TRUE HYPOTHESIS**    In descriptive research, the "hypothesis" is an exception to our earlier definition; descriptive research does not have an explicit hypothesis in the same sense as other kinds of research. Remember that a hypothesis was defined as a statement of the expected relationship between two or more variables. Because descriptive research addresses the amounts of a single given characteristic, it cannot very well look at the relationship between two or more variables. Typical questions might include: What is the percentage of athletes on campus? How productive is the average professor? What is the violent-crime rate in New York City?

A common kind of descriptive research is a public opinion survey. What proportion of the people in the United States think we should get rid of welfare, vote Republican in a given election, or believe the president is doing a good job? The media report such poll results all the time, especially during presidential election years. Public opinion surveys address other pressing issues: In November 2007, the Harris Poll reported that 41% of adults believe in ghosts and 31% believe in witches.

The census also provides descriptive research results. Its most important figures describe population numbers by area. These numbers determine a region's share of representatives in Congress, federal allocations of money, and other critical resources. The census also paints a portrait of our lifestyle, based on a subset of questionnaires that are longer than usual. For example, which type of pet is more common: cats or dogs? Answer: Dog-owning households outnumber cat-owning households (31.2 versus 27.0 million), but more pets are cats, because cat households average 2.2 each, while dog households average 1.7 each (U.S. Bureau of the Census, 1997). Almost all (88%) claim their pet as a member of the family, according to a December 2007 Harris Poll.

**RANDOM SAMPLING**    The crucial issue in descriptive research is whether the researchers have selected a good, unbiased sample. Is it a random sample of the population to be described? For example, suppose a researcher wants to know what proportion of undergraduates on campus want to go to graduate school. A researcher could ask people in the introductory social psychology class if they are planning to go to graduate school, but these students might be a biased sample, not representative of the larger campus population. Even psychology students in general are not a good random sample of the campus population. If a researcher wanted a good, accurate description of the campus population, the person could ask literally everyone on campus, but random sampling provides a still better way. Researchers do not actually have to poll the entire student body to get an accurate estimate of the proportion of people planning to go to graduate school. They can use a sample more efficiently, but the sample does have to be random for the estimate to be accurate. In a good random sample, everyone on the campus is equally likely to be included.

A true **random sample** requires that every member of the population of interest has an equal chance of being in the sample. A random sample provides a reliable, cost-effective estimate of the population as a whole. (That is why presidential election polls can sample as few as 1,000 respondents nationwide to estimate the whole adult population within a few percentage points.) In the year 2000 national census, some politicians were suspicious of sampling and insisted on a person-by-person count, even though (a) such supposedly exhaustive counts miss a lot of people (primarily poor and homeless people), (b) intensive sampling could save the country a great deal of money, and (c) modern techniques make sampling potentially even more accurate than attempting a person-by-person count. Again, in the year 2000 presidential election, the crucial Florida votes might have been better assessed by the exit poll samples than by the unreliable machine counts and the confusing paper ballots with their incomplete punch marks. Ironically, the television networks were criticized for relying on exit polls that may have been the more accurate measure of people's intended votes.

Consider another sampling problem. Suppose researchers want to study the proportion of people on campus who have been victims of violence. They could examine campus police records, but what kinds of violence might be omitted from those reports? In particular, fights, rape, and abuse are not always reported to the police. What if researchers advertised in the campus newspaper for people to volunteer to report instances of aggression anonymously? Volunteers who would come forward for a study would be an incomplete, biased sample as well. The best approach is to draw a truly random sample (picking people by using a random number table) and then work hard to get as many of the sample as possible to respond. Indeed, victimization reports to survey researchers may best estimate crime rates (Anderson, Bartholow, & Huesmann, in press). Researchers often aim to get at least a 60–70% response rate from their intended sample, to minimize bias from non-responders. This is not easy, but researchers have found that incentives, such as unconditional gifts, do help (Tourangeau, 2004).

Why can't researchers just use volunteers, instead of contacting unsuspecting random recruits and then hounding them to respond? Unfortunately, the kinds of people who spontaneously volunteer for studies differ systematically from the kinds of people who do not (Rosenthal & Rosnow, 1975). Volunteers are better educated, higher social status, more intelligent, more sociable, and higher in need for social approval. They may also be more arousal-seeking (if the study concerns stress, sensory isolation, or hypnosis), more unconventional (especially for a study of sex), more likely to be female (unless the study is physically or emotionally stressful), less authoritarian (i.e., more comfortable with loose hierarchies), and more likely to be Jewish or perhaps Protestant than Catholic. Moreover, paying people the modest amounts researchers can usually afford does not dramatically change the volunteer biases. Going back to the most recent example, do you think the typical volunteer may be more likely, less likely, or about average on exposure to violence on campus? For such reasons, then, a random sample would be better than relying on volunteers, even paid volunteers.

The time of the semester at which people volunteer also turns out to matter. Reliable personality differences correlate with the time of the semester at which people volunteer for a study. People who participate earlier are more organized, more likely to plan ahead, and more conforming, whereas people who participate at the end of the semester tend to be more hostile to authority (Neuberg & Newson, 1993). If researchers were trying to study people exposed to violence, even the time of the semester at which they solicited their volunteers might bias their sample.

If we consider moving outside a student population for a random sample, what about going to shopping malls? Consider some of the biases in who shows up at a mall. Would they be a good random sample for assessing the incidence of violence? Consider who shows up at different times of the day or week. Would Friday night shoppers be more or less likely than Monday morning shoppers to be victims of violence? A mall does not provide a truly random, representative sample of the country.

Descriptive research asks what proportion of the population has experienced violence, believes in space aliens, gets divorced, or possesses a home computer. Or it may ask, What is the average level of trust in government? Time spent holiday shopping? To get accurate answers to these questions requires a truly random sample, in which every single member of the population has an equal chance of participating.

**COMPARED WITH WHAT?**    The utility of descriptive research comes in the comparison of the results (e.g., an average or percentage) with some baseline expectation. When pollsters say 40% of the U.S. population thinks our president is doing a good job, why is that a meaningful statistic? The statistic matters only in comparison with that president's own prior ratings, other presidents' ratings, or one's current impressions of the president's popularity. If people thought that everyone approved, then the 40% figure would surprise people as low. Or if people thought that nobody approved, then 40% percent is not so bad. Alternatively, perhaps 40% compares favorably with other presidents at the same point in their term. As another example, crime statistics interest people mainly when they have gone up or down (compared with the last report), that is, when they differ from people's expectations.

What always makes descriptive research interesting is the "compared-with-what" question, which implies an implicit or explicit baseline. A **baseline** sets a standard for comparison with new data. When somebody quotes a survey result, or when the newspaper reports one, think about precisely why the statistic matters. The implicit "compared-with-what" question always lurks behind the descriptive result: compared with what one personally might expect, what pollsters reported last time, or what people generally think? A 41% belief in ghosts is surprising because many of us would not expect the number to be so high; also, it is surprising compared with 30 years earlier, when only 11% reported believing in ghosts. If pollsters say only 25% of U.S. teens can identify Winston Churchill's country or the year of the United States' independence, why is that interesting? If would be interesting because the compared-with-what baseline is the standard that everyone ought to know history.

No single comparison is right or wrong: Different comparisons answer different questions. Knowing that, for black Americans, the last 50 years have seen steady improvements in infant survival, life expectancy, years of schooling, home ownership, and numbers of elected officials (Pettigrew, 1996; see Figure 2.2), what comparison does this make? It compares black Americans with themselves previously, and the results look encouraging. But when one compares black Americans with whites, on each of these measures, blacks are disadvantaged. The useful comparison depends on the question to be answered.

**SUMMARY OF DESCRIPTIVE RESEARCH**    Descriptive research reports the estimated amount or value of a particular variable in the population. For accuracy, the sample needs to be carefully selected at random. Behind every descriptive statistic is the baseline or compared-with-what question that answers whether and why the result matters. In that sense, then, the hypothesis in a descriptive study would indeed concern the relationship between two variables, the estimated amount of the variable in a population, compared with an implicit baseline.

## Correlational Research

Correlational research exposes the implicit comparison lurking behind descriptive research; it specifies the variable being compared with another variable. **Correlational research** investigates whether changes in one variable are related to changes in another

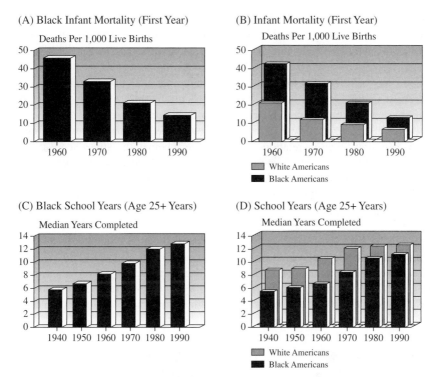

**Figure 2.2**   Blacks' Progress and Disparities Compared with Themselves and with Whites

*Source:* From Pettigrew, 1996. Copyright © Allyn & Bacon. U.S. Bureau of the Census, 1979, 1992a. Adapted with permission.

variable. Thus, it always considers at least two variables, whereas descriptive research considers only one variable at a time. If descriptive research addresses questions such as "What is the level of violence on campus?" correlational research addresses the relationship between being a perpetrator of violence and being (for example) an athlete.

**HYPOTHESIS**   Because a hypothesis in correlational research takes the form that changes in one variable are related to changes in another variable, correlational research always considers at least two variables, asking whether they reliably go together. At the conceptual level, a correlational hypothesis could propose, for example, that changes in stress relate to changes in aggression: As stress increases, aggression increases. Alternatively, to go back to an earlier hypothesis: Attractiveness increases with persuasiveness, so as somebody is more attractive, the person is also more persuasive.

Moving from the conceptual to the operational, researchers could examine for instance the stress-aggression correlation among college students, prison guards, or nursing home patients. Researchers could look at the attractiveness-persuasion hypothesis among politicians, rocket scientists, or salespeople. Focusing on the latter for a moment, one can ask, are the more attractive salespeople also the more persuasive ones? One operationalization suggested earlier was the number of smiles and the listeners' agreement to buy a product (for example, shampoo). The specific prediction in the study would be that number of salesperson smiles correlates with listeners' agreeing to buy the shampoo.

Let's go back to the stress-aggression hypothesis. What specific ways could researchers operationalize that hypothesis into observable variables for a correlational study? Researchers could measure, for instance, college students' reports of stress on a standardized scale of stressful life events (e.g., unusual pressure from academics, activities, family, relationships) and see whether the stress score correlates with self-reported or acquaintance-reported aggression. Indeed, meta-analysis suggests a clear relationship (Carlson & Miller, 1988). Whether considering the operational prediction or the conceptual hypothesis, correlational research always addresses the relationship between at least two variables.

**TYPE OF RELATIONSHIP**    As long as I teach social psychology, I will continue to borrow Robert Rosenthal's class demonstration of types of correlational relationships: One way to think about correlational studies is that each person in a sample has two variables (imagine the person in Figure 2.3 "holding" one in each hand). In the case of a **positive correlation**, the person is high on one variable and high on the other

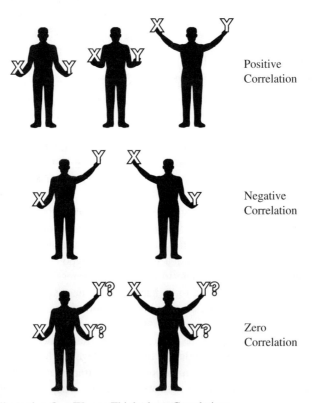

Positive Correlation

Negative Correlation

Zero Correlation

**Figure 2.3**    Illustrating One Way to Think about Correlations

(both hands raised). This would include high attractiveness and high persuasiveness, or high stress and high aggression. A positive correlation also predicts (both hands lowered) low attractiveness and low persuasiveness, or low stress and low aggression. Medium levels of each variable go together as well (both hands waist-level). You can think of it as two variables moving together: high-high, low-low, or medium-medium (in class, I am now flapping my arms). Lots of variables have positive correlations, such as the amount of sleep that you get and how well you do on your exam the next day, the number of people you know in a group and how comfortable you feel, threat to your ethnic group and prejudice against outsiders.

In contrast, **negative correlations** mean that participants are high on one variable and low on the other (one hand up, the other down, looking roughly like a semaphore). For example, people who are rude are probably not too persuasive. High on rudeness, low on persuasion. Low on rudeness, high on persuasion. Another negative correlation would be distance and attraction; people are often attracted to people who live nearby, not far away: low distance, high attraction. If the variables go opposite to each other, that is a negative correlation.

Finally, in **zero correlations**, one may know the person's value on one variable (x), but it does not predict anything about the value on the other variable (y). What is the correlation between the amount of blue you wear in your wardrobe and how much you exercise? Zero. What is the correlation between a professor's research productivity and teaching ratings? Close to zero. (On some dimensions, such as being up-to-date, organized, committed, and enthusiastic, the correlation is somewhat positive, whereas on others, such as facilitating interaction or managing the course, it is zero; Feldman, 1987; Hattie & Marsh, 1996).

Correlations range from −1.00 to +1.00. The ones in social psychology all tend to be much less than plus one and much greater than minus one. In social psychology, we never get perfect 1.00 correlations between anything; if someone does, then chances are that somebody made up the data. A strong correlation in social science is about .50 or above, a medium one about is .30, and a small one is about .10, according to psychological statisticians (Cohen, 1992). Similarly, −.50 would be a strong correlation, −.30 would be moderate, and −.10 would be weak. (Statistical significance, a separate matter, would depend on both the size of the correlation and the size of the sample, a topic beyond the scope of this text.) Correlations between social science variables rarely approach +1.00 or −1.00, in part because all our variables are measured imperfectly, so the data carry a lot of noise (random error), which attenuates the correlations. A 1.00 correlation is not plausible unless the researcher (mistakenly) measured the exact same thing twice, and even then some error would be expected.

More important, though, in social psychology, the most interesting results are the ones that are not obvious. If the correlation between two variables is perfect, they may be redundant (measuring the same thing), so it may not be interesting. The most interesting correlations show that two quite different variables are, in fact, related: for example, a correlation between warm weather and student protests.

Some people like to get a visual sense of how patterns of data generate correlations. Consider a study of stereotypes about various groups (Fiske, Cuddy, Glick, & Xu, 2002, Study 2). A group's perceived status could correlate with its perceived competence, in various ways. People could take (a) the just-world view that groups get what they deserve (a positive status-competence correlation) or (b) the sour-grapes view that high-status groups get arbitrary and unfair breaks, whereas struggling low-status groups are held back (a zero or even negative correlation). Figure 2.4 shows people's average views of various groups, where each dot is one group. Because the cloud of points runs from "southwest to northeast," it shows

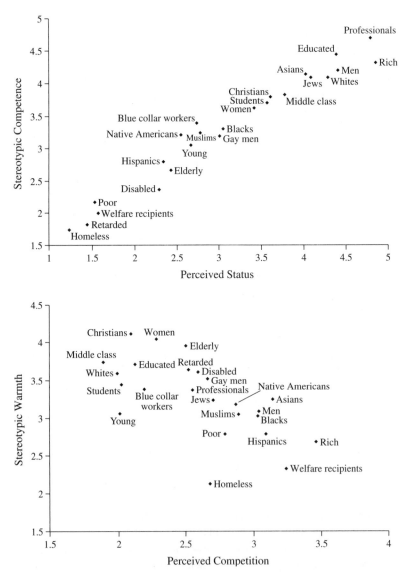

**Figure 2.4** Positive and Negative Correlations in Out-Group Stereotypes

*Source:* Data from Fiske et al., 2002, Study 2, unpublished figure.

that the perceived status-competence correlation is positive and high (.88), supporting the just-world view that as perceived status increases, perceived competence does too.

The study also examined the groups' perceived competitiveness and perceived warmth. If people think that groups who compete with the mainstream are not sincere, trustworthy, and kind, then the correlation between perceived competition and perceived warmth should be negative, which it is: −.31. The cloud of points would run from "northwest to southeast." As perceived competition increases (special breaks, power struggles), then perceived warmth decreases.

Regardless of whether one examines the numbers or figures, the overall point is that correlations express a type of relationship that can be positive, negative, or zero, and stronger or weaker.

**CAUSAL AGENDAS**    The main issue for correlation: Researchers or reporters usually are hiding a causal agenda. Usually they are not really just saying A goes with B, but they have a hidden agenda claiming that A causes B. Let's take our example of attractiveness and persuasion as correlated. Consistent with Table 2.5, you probably thought that attractiveness causes people to be more persuasive. In a typical correlational test of that hypothesis, however, the data might show only that across a series of local elections, the attractiveness of the candidate is correlated with the proportion of the vote garnered; the more attractive candidate tends to win. Given these correlational data, however, we do not really know that the attractiveness was causing the persuasion (i.e., gaining the votes), but that was our implicit idea.

In correlational research, causality is usually an implicit hidden agenda. But, in fact, researchers do not have a right to say, in a correlational study, what causes what because they do not actually know. Take this obvious example: Attractiveness causes persuasion. What about the opposite? What if winning elections makes people more attractive? It could; success and self-confidence can make people smile, or at least get them to the tailor and the hairstylist, any of which could make them more attractive. So the causality could indeed go the other way.

A correlation potentially represents any of three possible relationships: A causes B, B causes A, or some third variable causes both of them (see Table 2.7). As an example of a third variable, money could cause both winning elections and being attractive. The more money politicians have, the better their health, the better they eat, the better they dress, and the more handlers they can pay to tell them what to say, how to smile, and which awkward mannerisms to ditch. This way, a third variable, money, could cause both attractiveness and electoral success. Every time

**Table 2.7**  Three Patterns of Causality for a Correlation

| Observed Positive Correlation | Attractiveness and Persuasion | | |
|---|---|---|---|
| Possible causality | Attractiveness | → | Persuasion |
| | Persuasion | → | Attractiveness |
| | Money | → | Attractiveness |
| | Money | → | Persuasion |

you hear about a correlation between two variables, think hard about which of these causal patterns could be operating, because the person reporting the correlation almost always has a hidden causal agenda in mind. But the opposite pattern could hold, or a third variable could cause both.

Take some other examples: The weekly consumption of ice cream and the crime rate go up and down together, so sugar causes crime, right? What is an obvious third variable? Heat. Another interesting one: storks and babies. There is a positive correlation between storks nesting and babies arriving. Do storks cause babies to arrive? No, there is a third variable: heat again. Certain storks like to nest in warm chimneys, people stay inside more in cold weather, and babies result. Take measured IQ and school performance. Does IQ cause better school performance? Maybe. But doing well in school can also increase performance on an intelligence test. And third variables, such as social class and cultural experience, strongly affect both. IQ and school performance seem like obvious correlates, but people do not take account of third variables that strongly affect both those variables. In short, the problem with inferring causality from correlations is that correlations indicate only association: All one knows is that two variables go together. Storks and babies, ice cream and crime, IQ and school performance. But the correlation does not tell why or how.

**INFERRING CAUSALITY**    Inferring causality requires three factors identified originally by philosopher John Stuart Mill, plus a fourth that will help us to think about some of social scientists' assumptions. The first necessary factor is **association**, which we have just been discussing as correlation. For one variable plausibly to cause another variable, they must be associated or correlated in some fashion, positive or negative. For example, if researchers hypothesize that violent television causes aggression, then they have to show that the two are associated; people who watch more televised violence also commit more violence. Association allows survey researchers to predict one variable from another. For example, an actuary or demographer can predict someone's mortality with a reasonable degree of probability, given the person's age, gender, income, and family history. But the prediction-by-association is mute about causality.

Inferring causality in addition requires **temporal priority**, meaning the alleged cause has to come before the alleged effect. This seems obvious; causality does not run backward in time. However, in specific cases, temporal priority may not be so easy to establish. For example, to make the argument that attractiveness causes electoral success is easy because one normally considers attractiveness to be a fairly stable aspect of a person that predates running for office. But researchers would have to be careful to measure attractiveness before the election season began, in case winning (or the anticipation of it) actually made people more attractive (they cheer up and look better). Similar temporal issues arise with the example of television violence. Does a habit of watching violent television develop before or after a person becomes aggressive? In each case, temporal priority is a critical ingredient to inferring causality.

The third condition for inferring causality is ruling out alternative explanations or establishing a nonspurious relationship. A **spurious relationship** just means that a third variable explains the relationship between the two variables of interest. If cold weather causes the storks to nest in warm chimneys and people to be inside making babies, then the relationship between storks and babies is spurious. If ice cream consumption and crime are both related to hot summers, then the direct relationship between the two is spurious. In contrast, if no plausible third variable causes the two variables that are correlated, then the relationship is not spurious and one is closer to inferring causality. Establishing temporal priority and nonspurious relationships (ruling out third variables) can be tough with correlational data. However, some statistical techniques (beyond the scope of this text) can help researchers examine potential causality. Even so, correlation does not establish causation.

The other factor some social scientists would require for inferring causality is a **theoretical rationale** or reasoning. A researcher cannot convincingly argue for causality without making a plausible case for psychological **mechanisms**, exactly why and how one variable affects the other. For example, most scientific psychologists do not accept ESP (extrasensory perception or mind-reading) as a reliable phenomenon, in part because most available studies either have failed to produce evidence or have been plagued with methodological flaws. That is, nonspurious association has not been established. But even if the studies did show convincing support, the other trouble with ESP is that no one has posited plausible mechanisms by which it could operate (not to mention reliable association, temporal priority, and nonspurious relations). Lacking a theoretical rationale, researchers are reluctant to pursue causality.

**SUMMARY OF CORRELATIONAL RESEARCH**    Correlational hypotheses hold that one variable relates to another variable; the relationship can be positive (the variables tend to go together) or negative (the variables tend to go in opposite directions). Reports of correlation often have a hidden causal agenda, but three patterns are possible: causation, reverse causation, or a third variable. Correlation does not imply causation, because at best correlation can show only association, with temporal priority and theoretical rationale potentially provided as well. But the difficulty comes in showing that the correlational relationship is not spurious, that no third variable accounts for it. As a partial solution, researchers can measure plausible third variables and make convincing arguments that the patterns of correlations are consistent with their hypothesized view of causality. But only one formal method demonstrates a nonspurious relationship and therefore establishes causality, namely, the experimental method.

## Experimental Research

Let's begin the discussion of experiments by comparing them to the two previous kinds of research and then work through an example regarding media violence, using it to see how experiments allow causal inferences. With that background, we will formally define experiments and walk through various examples of experimental designs. All of this should make you a more informed consumer of experimental research presented in public forums, not to mention in this book.

**ADVANTAGE OVER DESCRIPTIVE RESEARCH**    Consider the following poll results: 61% of Americans report being bothered some or a lot by television violence, according to a 2005 Pew poll, and 83% believe that television violence causes violence in real life, according to a 2000 First Amendment Center Poll. Most people apparently think that media violence numbs people, making them insensitive to violence (76%) and telling them that violence is fun and acceptable (71%) ("Are music and movies killing America's soul?" 1995).

Suppose you are advising parents and media moguls about television and movie programming. What do these poll results tell you? Many people say they are against media violence and think it has a bad influence. These are excellent and useful descriptive statistics. Do these results tell whether media violence actually does make people more likely to aggress against other people? No.

**ADVANTAGE OVER CORRELATIONAL RESEARCH**    Suppose researchers want to pursue the hypothesis that television violence really does increase aggression; the hypothesis is stated in terms of a positive association between the two conceptual variables (television violence and aggression), with an explicit causal agenda concerning which causes which. The operational version of these variables might be, for television violence, the reported number of violent television shows regularly watched, and for aggression in children, their aggressiveness as rated by the teacher. Suppose further that, as the aggression chapter describes, researchers discover a positive association. As a statement about children's natural television-viewing habits and spontaneous aggression, this is an informative result, but it does not provide the fullest support for the hypothesis.

As just noted, three possible patterns of causality could underlie that finding:

- Television violence may indeed cause aggressive behavior.
- Aggressive behavior might cause a preference for violent television shows.
- Poor social skills (or some other third variables) cause a preference for violent television and aggressive behavior toward peers.

Clearly, a theory could account for each of these patterns of causality (and some theories will, in the chapter on aggression), so plausibility of rationale does not help differentiate among these alternatives. One could also attempt to establish temporal priority, by measuring each variable at two points in time and seeing whether television at Time 1 predicts aggression at Time 2, or aggression at Time 1 predicts television at Time 2, or both. (This would support temporal priority.) Thus, researchers could work on association, rationale, and temporal priority, given these correlations.

But what can we do about those pesky third variables, such as social skills, rotten environment, or aggressive personality? Under some circumstances, researchers can make an excellent argument for causality in correlational data, and one of the major advantages of the correlational method is that one can measure important variables in the real world. Nevertheless, despite what researchers can do statistically to control for third variables (as stated earlier, a topic beyond this book), with correlational data, researchers can never completely rest easy that they have ruled out all the alternatives, that is, that the correlation is not spurious.

**EXAMPLE AND DEFINITION OF AN EXPERIMENT**    Now consider an experiment on the same hypothesis that media violence increases aggression (Bushman, 1995): 148 college students watch *Karate Kid III*, a movie rated 7.2 on an 11-point scale for violence, and another 148 watch *Gorillas in the Mist*, a movie rated 2.2 on the same scale for violence; both are rated equally exciting, action-packed, and entertaining. Immediately afterward, each participant competes with an ostensible opponent in a reaction time game, in which the person slower to respond receives an unpleasant blast of noise. Just before each trial, each player sets the intensity of the noise blast to be administered if the opponent loses. Then researchers measure whether the first group plays more aggressively than the second group, that is, sets higher levels of noise for the opponent. Indeed, the simple effect of the violent video is to make participants select noise at 4.6 on a scale of 10, whereas nonviolent-video watchers selected 3.9, so some initial evidence fits the hypothesis. (We discuss more results later.) How do this design and set of results improve on a correlational study?

First, let's get some terms straight. In experiments, the potentially causal variable is called the independent variable, and that causal variable can affect the dependent variable, the measure. The **independent variable** is manipulated by the experimenter, such that some participants receive one level and others receive a different level (for example, viewing the violent or nonviolent movie). The independent variable is independent of other features of the individual participant, because the experimenter controls and assigns its levels. The **dependent variable** is measured by the experimenter, such that participants provide responses that the experimenter records. The dependent variable depends on the independent variable. That is, the manipulated independent variable causes changes in the measured dependent variable. Learn this distinction. When you read about experiments in this book, or if you participate in an experiment, you should be able to identify the hypothesis and the independent and dependent variables. What's the manipulation? What's the measure? The experiment will be more understandable if you know the independent variable and the dependent variable, because then you know what the researcher was trying to do.

A true **experiment** contains three components: manipulation, randomization, and control. First, the independent variable must be a **manipulation** set by the researcher. The experimenter can change the levels of the independent variable for different people, by assigning them to different experimental conditions. That is, the experimenter must be able at will to put some people in the experimental condition and others in the control condition, for example, give some people the violent movie and others the nonviolent movie. It is easy to assign different people to watch different videos in the laboratory, but it would be difficult to assign them different patterns of television or movies over a longer period.

The necessity to be able to manipulate the independent variable in an experiment determines the kinds of variables that can be operationalized experimentally. For example, an experimenter could manipulate the apparent characteristics of a partner in a two-person task (e.g., attractiveness or membership in a stereotyped group), by providing a photograph of an expected interaction partner or by employing a confederate. Equally, an experimenter could manipulate characteristics of a persuasive communication (e.g., argument quality or personal relevance). But an experimenter could not manipulate a research participant's own long-term attractiveness or membership in a stereotyped group per se, nor could an experimenter manipulate all the persuasive communications in a participant's environment. Likewise, an experimenter cannot manipulate a participant's personality, gender, age, or other person variables (called **demographic variables** when related to population variables such as ethnicity and age; called **individual difference variables** when related to personality). The first feature of an experiment, the ability to manipulate the independent variable at will, determines the kinds of independent variables experimenters can investigate. Nevertheless, you may be entertained and impressed by the ingenuity of some of the experiments in social psychology.

The second feature of a true experiment is **randomization**, that is, random assignment of participants to the different levels of the independent variable. In randomization, every participant has an equal chance of receiving each level of the independent variable. Note the similarities and differences between random assignment and random sampling to participate in the study in the first place, discussed under correlational research. In random sampling, every member of the population of interest has an equal chance of participating in the study; in random assignment (randomization), every member of the sample has an equal chance of receiving each level of the independent variable. A study can have both randomization and random assignment or either one alone, but true experiments require only random assignment to conditions.

What techniques constitute truly random assignment? Flipping a coin, if the independent variable has two levels, would randomly assign participants to conditions. A random number table could serve the same purpose. But alternating participants, one to each condition, in order of running the study, is not truly random. (What if people sign up with their heterosexual dating partners, and the women tend to sign up first? All the men could end up in one condition and all the women in the other.) What about running one condition on one day of the week and another condition on another day of the week? (Not good. Maybe some majors have labs or studios on Wednesdays and Fridays, and others on Tuesdays and Thursdays.) Morning and afternoon would not work either, because maybe morning people differ from night people.

One flaw of the nursing home study, making it less than a true experiment, is that the residents were assigned by floor, with one entire floor assigned to receive the experimental condition (control over their environment), and the other floor to serve as the baseline comparison group. Residents may not be assigned to a floor totally at random, and indeed, the experimental floor residents were healthier before the study began, which may partially or entirely account for the results. The researchers may not have been able, for practical reasons, to assign residents randomly to experimental and control groups within floors; real-world considerations often compromise the design of a true experiment.

What about self-selection into conditions? What would be the obvious problem with allowing participants to pick whether they watched the violent or nonviolent movie? Clearly, the more aggressive ones would pick the violent movie, so the experimenter would not know whether aggressive personality or the movie itself made them

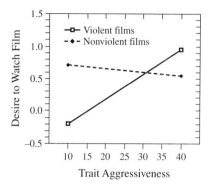

**Figure 2.5**   Trait Aggression's Influence on Choice of Violent Videos

*Source:* From Bushman, 1995. Copyright © 1995 by the American Psychological Association. Adapted with permission.

play more aggressively afterward. Indeed, in one study (Bushman, 1995, Study 1), participants who scored higher on the personality trait of aggression were more interested in violent videos than were participants low in trait aggressiveness (Figure 2.5). Because of biases inherent in self-selection, then, truly random assignment matters.

The third feature of a true experiment is **experimental control** over potential third variables to prevent confounding the independent variable with an extraneous variable. This is equivalent to compensating for potential contamination by third variables in correlational research, to prevent a spurious relationship. The unique feature of experiments is experimental control: Researchers can isolate the independent variable, making sure that nothing else correlates with it, or in other words, prevent confounding the manipulation with unwanted other factors. In **confounding**, an extraneous variable is manipulated simultaneously with the independent variable of interest. If participants watch a violent movie or a nonviolent movie, for example, it would never do to give the violent movie watchers ice cream and the nonviolent movie watchers popcorn. Snacks would be confounded with the independent variable.

One of the problems with the prison study is that it did not precisely isolate its independent variable, prison role (guard vs. prisoner). Although student volunteers were randomly assigned one role or the other, the role was confounded with a variety of theatrical effects (costumes, public "arrest") that make it hard to isolate or precisely identify the manipulation. To be fair, the researchers' aim was to recreate a variety of features of the prisoner/guard role, but the effect of that choice was to create confounds that undermine its judged validity as a true experiment.

As another example, in last chapter's organ meats study, Lewin himself identified confounds in his experiment. Recall that some participants heard a lecture, and some made a group decision about the wisdom of consuming organ meats. The finding that the group decision was more persuasive could be caused also by (a) the differing personalities of the leaders of the two groups or (b) the expectation, created only for the group-decision participants, that they would be queried later about their introduction of the new food. Lewin (1952) addresses these confounds, as social psychologists have ever since, by replicating his results on another sample but without the confounds.

To summarize, then, the three crucial features of experiments are manipulation of the independent variable, random assignment to levels of the independent variable, and control over potentially contaminating third variables to prevent confounding.

**MAIN PURPOSE OF EXPERIMENTS**   A true experiment's crucial features create its unique power as a research method to infer causality. Experiments demonstrate causality by fulfilling the four requirements outlined earlier, establishing association, temporal priority, rationale, and nonspurious relationships (see Table 2.8).

Association is established by comparing results in different experimental conditions. For example, if the participants in the violent video condition behave more aggressively than those in the nonviolent video condition, then video violence is associated with violent behavior.

Temporal priority is established in two ways. First, because experimental participants are randomly assigned, they should show no preexisting differences on the dependent variable; for example, they should average equivalent on aggressive behavior before the experiment. Second, the independent variable is manipulated before the dependent variable is measured. Participants first watched the video and then played the game that assessed their levels of aggression.

Rationale is provided by specifying the theory that underlies the hypothesis and making specific predictions about the particular operationalizations. Often, the theory will suggest measurable mechanisms for the effect; that is, exactly how does television influence aggression? For example, if a theory proposed that television violence desensitizes people, an experimenter could measure desensitization, along with aggression. Or if a theory proposed that television violence excites people, one could measure arousal and so forth.

Finally, the strength of well-designed experiments lies in their ability to rule out **alternative explanations**, that is, spurious relationships. Isolating the independent variable, the manipulation, entails being certain that it is not confounded or contaminated with another variable. In our ongoing example, the people watching the two kinds of videos are randomly assigned, so that rules out personality differences, age, gender, ethnicity, and other person variables. Moreover, they all sit in the same chairs, are instructed by the same experimenter, and so on. And the videos themselves are

**Table 2.8**   How Experiments Demonstrate Causality

| Factor Necessary to Causality | Feature of True Experiments |
| --- | --- |
| Association | Measure DV at different levels of IV |
| Temporal priority | Manipulate IV, then measure DV |
| | Random assignment to levels of IV prevents preexisting differences on DV |
| Rationale | Theory explains mechanisms |
| | Theory makes specific predictions |
| Nonspurious relationships | Isolate the IV from contaminating confounds |

IV = independent variable; DV = dependent variable.

equivalent on possibly confounding dimensions, such as interest and excitement, so that violence is the only measurable difference between them. If the only thing that differs between the experimental and control conditions in the experiment is the violence of the video, then it is the only possible cause of their subsequent differences in aggressive play.

**PROS AND CONS OF EXPERIMENTS**    As mentioned earlier, experiments limit the type, timing, and duration of variables they can manipulate and measure. Because of the types of operationalizations necessary in a laboratory setting, psychology experiments can be limited in how much they generalize beyond the laboratory. Of course, parallel limitations occur in descriptive opinion polls and in correlational studies in the field. For example, one cannot necessarily generalize from a survey response to behavior in the mall or the voting booth.

Another limitation always present in laboratory experiments (but not unique to them) is the unrepresentative samples of participants. Psychology student participants are not randomly sampled at all. So the question that any experiment raises is, how much does its sample represent the larger population? The habitual research sample in social psychology, college sophomores, do have less rigid attitudes, a less fixed sense of self, stronger cognitive skills, greater respect for authority, and more fluid relationships than older adults (Sears, 1986). These differences lead some to argue that results might well be biased by relying exclusively on college student participants (Henry, 2008; see commentaries, same issue).

Every type of research has trade-offs, strengths, and weaknesses. Researchers raise several points regarding the role of experiments in regard to the "real world." First, laboratory results on important social issues routinely replicate in field studies with more representative samples, although without the precise controls and possibility of causal inferences. Sometimes the results are stronger in the field than in the laboratory. Together, laboratory experiments and field studies converge to make strong arguments, especially in research on aggression, helping, close relationships, and discrimination.

Second, experiments are often designed as demonstrations of plausible scenarios. The experiment shows that results consistent with the hypothesis can and do occur. Experiments demonstrate that an effect *can* occur this way (these are sufficient conditions for it to occur) at least among some populations. Thus, one way to think about experiments, and what they do best, is that they show how a process could happen. An experiment demonstrates the sufficient conditions for A to produce B. The scientific hypothesis being tested is then supported under at least some circumstances.

Third, experimenters distinguish between mundane and psychological realism (Wilson, Aronson, & Carlsmith, 2010). **Mundane realism** describes how much the experimental setting resembles the comparable real world setting. For example, people often aggress by physical assault, but for obvious reasons, this dependent measure is infeasible in the laboratory. If the experimenter allows the participants to deliver noise blasts as punishment to an insulting competitor, that would have low mundane realism. But if participants get caught up in the situation—as they do—then it has high **experimental realism** (involving, impactful, taken seriously). If it also re-creates in the lab the same psychological processes that occur in daily life, then it ranks high on **psychological realism**. Experimenters must create psychological realism (avoiding artificial processes), often desire experimental realism (involvement), and worry less about mundane realism. Novices often reverse these priorities, but thereby test theory less effectively.

Fourth, generalizability is an empirical question. If researchers can establish an effect in one population and one setting, the effect plausibly might work elsewhere too. Thus, generalizability from the laboratory to other populations and settings is a testable hypothesis: An effect found with college students may also hold for other people. One summer, Amherst, Massachusetts, hosted about 3,000 Airstream trailers and their occupants on a campus athletic field. One enterprising graduate student conducted research with those people, who differ a lot from students, just to get a novel sample. Suppose the same effect occurs for college students and for members of the Wally Byam Caravan Club International, who are mostly retired and have enough money to buy an Airstream caravan. Then this effect may well hold true for "people in general," although it might still be limited, because people who go to college or own Airstream trailers are among the more privileged in society. So these questions of generalizability are always open, but it is an empirical question to see whether an effect generalizes. The question of **external validity** (or generalizability) asks whether researchers can generalize from their own sample to the population of interest. That is why social psychologists do research in the "real world" too. A random sample survey or field experiment can help to generalize effects beyond the laboratory participants and setting.

Fifth, with regard to generalizing to contexts outside the laboratory, the main purpose of experiments is to infer causality, and experiments have unparalleled elegance for doing exactly that, as reviewed here and as shown throughout social psychology. Experiments are high on **internal validity**, which means that researchers can make a causal inference if the experiment meets the standards of a true experiment, outlined before. That is, the experiment, in and of itself, can be scientifically sound, internally valid.

**EXPERIMENTAL DESIGNS AND RESULTS**    Reading the rest of this book will be easier, given some basic acquaintance with types of experimental designs. The most basic type of experiment would include one independent variable with two groups, as in the violent video example used so far: The independent variable is the violence of the video, and it has two levels, an experimental group (violent) and a control group (nonviolent). Similarly, the Stanford prison study's independent variable, social role, had two levels, to which participants were randomly assigned: prisoners and guards. And the nursing home study's independent variable had two levels, experimental (increased responsibility) and control (baseline). Our attraction-persuasion study had two levels (attractive, unattractive).

An independent variable also can have more than two levels, for example, if video violence included movies rated X, R, PG-13, and G for violence. Similarly, the independent variable attractiveness could have multiple levels, that is, the experimental conditions might include a highly attractive communicator, an average communicator, and a completely unattractive communicator. Researchers might operationalize this independent variable by selecting photographs at each level of attractiveness, as rated by independent judges. The specific prediction might be that persuasion would be highest for the attractive communicator, moderate for the average one, and lowest for the unattractive one. On the other hand, perhaps people would be most persuaded by the average communicator, who most resembles their own level of attractiveness, but they might distrust the attractive communicator and reject the unattractive one. Without three levels of the independent variable, one could not detect this inverted U–shaped effect. Using simply attractive and unattractive communicators would produce no effect. Sometimes, then, a hypothesis will specify the levels of the independent variable.

Moving up a level of complexity, let's return to the violent video example. Suppose researchers hypothesize that watching violent videos, *and* having peers who approve, jointly increase aggression, but not otherwise. This hypothesis involves two independent variables (degree of video violence and peer approval). One study (Leyens, Herman, & Dunand, 1982) paired ordinarily submissive children with peers in an independent variable with three levels: Some children watched the video alone, some with a dominant peer, and some with a submissive peer. Presumably a dominant peer represented aggressive values and encouraged subsequent aggression. The second independent variable, violence of the video they watched, had two levels, neutral and violent. Children were randomly assigned to one of six conditions formed by this 2 × 3 combination.

This type of design, with two independent variables, allows researchers to examine the **main effect** of each independent variable in isolation from the other, that is, the effect of each variable alone, averaging over levels of the other. So the researchers could examine either the effects of the violent video, averaged over the three levels (types) of peers, or the effect of peers, averaged over levels of video violence (see Table 2.9).

**Table 2.9**    Peers and Video Violence Influence Aggression

Hypothesis:

IV$_1$: Watching violent video with IV$_2$: Peers who approve → DV: Aggressive behavior

| IV$_2$: Type of Peer | IV$_1$: Video | | **Peer Main Effect** (average over videos) |
|---|---|---|---|
| | Neutral | Violent | |
| None (watch alone) | 1.86 | 3.67 | **2.76** |
| Dominant peer (approving violence) | 3.30 | 3.93 | **3.62** |
| Submissive peer (not approving violence) | 3.33 | 2.25 | **2.79** |
| **Video main effect** (average over peers) | **2.83** | **3.28** | |

Main effects: Effect of video violence (2.83 vs. 3.28) (not statistically different); effect of peer (2.76 vs. 3.62 vs. 2.79) (statistically significant difference)

Interaction:    Unique effect of combination (e.g., 1.86 vs. 3.93) (statistically significant)

IV = independent variable; DV = dependent variable.

*Source:* Data from Leyens et al., 1982.

In addition, this design allows one to examine the **interaction** or interplay of the two independent variables. Recall that the hypothesis stated that video violence had no effect, unless peers approved. The effects of one variable (video violence) depend on the level of the other variable (peer approval). In that case, only some of the six possible combinations will increase aggression (see Table 2.9). The three effects (two main effects and an interaction) can occur separately or together, as the table indicates.

The result of the video violence by peer approval study shows a statistically significant main effect for type of peer approval: Regardless of what they watch, peer attitudes matter. A dominant, violence-approving peer causes even submissive children to behave more aggressively (3.62) than they would alone (2.76) or with another submissive child (2.79). (Aggression scores ranged from 1 to 5, resulting from the degree to which the child later took an opportunity to interfere with the video quality of another child's cartoon show.) The other independent variable, video violence, does not show a statistically significant main effect by itself, although the averages indicate a slight difference between violent and nonviolent videos.

Further, the interaction of the two independent variables indicates that children are especially aggressive when a video is violent and their peers approve. The combination of a violent video and a dominant peer creates a peak of aggression (3.93), whereas that of a neutral video and no peer creates the least aggression (1.86). The other four combinations fall in between these two extremes.

A similar interaction occurred in the video violence study conducted with college students. As described earlier, they watched the *Karate Kid III* or *Gorillas in the Mist* and played a reaction-time game in which the loser receives noise blasts previously set by the opponent. In addition to the results reported earlier, the violent video (independent variable) interacted with the personality trait of aggression, to produce uniquely high levels of aggression. Aggressive participants who had watched the violent video administered far higher noise than any of the remaining three combinations (see Figure 2.6; Bushman, 1995).

The concept of an interaction effect is complex and not intuitive, so let's examine another example. Going back to the attractiveness-persuasion experiment, suppose

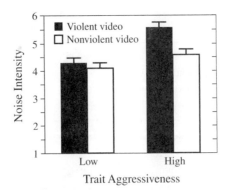

**Figure 2.6**    Interaction of Trait Aggression and Video Violence on Aggression

*Source:* From Bushman, 1995. Copyright © 1995 by the American Psychological Association. Adapted with permission.

researchers hypothesize that people are persuaded by people who match their level of attractiveness. In other words, highly attractive people like highly attractive communicators and more average people like more average communicators. Researchers could measure people's attractiveness, which would be a person variable, so it would not be an experimental manipulation. Or, alternatively, researchers could try to manipulate people's temporary feelings of attractiveness by showing them flattering or unflattering pictures of themselves. In any event, the other independent variable, the communicator's attractiveness, could be manipulated simply by presenting a photograph of a highly attractive or more average communicator and assessing persuasion. People who felt attractive might prefer communicators who were attractive, and people who felt more average might prefer communicators who were more average. Notice that the hypothesis predicts an interaction only, with no main effects (participants' own attractiveness does not make them more easily persuaded, nor does the other person's attractiveness make the person inherently more or less persuasive; it is the combination that matters). Like the previous example of video violence and peer approval, the effect of each independent variable depends on the level of the other independent variable.

**SUMMARY OF EXPERIMENTAL RESEARCH**    Experimental research has advantages over descriptive and correlational research, as well as its own pros and cons. Experiments have independent and dependent variables, along with three crucial components: manipulation of the independent variable, random assignment to experimental condition, and control over potential third variables to prevent confounding. Experiments are designed to infer causality by establishing association between independent and dependent variables, temporal priority, theoretical rationale, and nonspurious relationships. Generalizability of experiments is an empirical question, but they must create realistic psychological processes. Experiments allow researchers to assess the main effects of each independent variable separately, as well as their interaction.

## METHODOLOGICAL CHALLENGES IN SOCIAL SETTINGS

Whatever the hypotheses and whatever the research strategy (descriptive, correlational, or experimental), social psychologists face unique challenges in research methods. As in other sciences, the act of observing and measuring affects the phenomenon. The distinctive feature of most psychology is that the observer and the observed are the same species, plus the act of observation is a social phenomenon in itself. The contact between the researcher and the participant constitutes a two-way communication. For example, people adjust themselves when they know other people are watching, and observers compensate for people's efforts to manage the impressions they create.

As a social interaction between two humans, the research enterprise invokes the core social motives introduced in Chapter 1: belonging, understanding, controlling, self-enhancing, and trusting. Each motive introduces possible confounds and biases that threaten the validity of research. Social psychologists have learned to guard against these experimental **artifacts**, social threats to scientific accuracy.

## Expectancy Effects and Motives to Belong

Research participants generally want to get along with researchers. Even if the social contact is brief, participants, especially volunteers, are motivated to be part of the temporary team formed by researcher(s) and participant(s). Wanting to belong elicits compliance, so participants are typically agreeable. Wanting to belong also invites mimicry. (Recall people imitating the nonverbal behavior and facial expressions of conversation partners.) However, too much agreeableness and too much mimicry create problems for researchers.

Participants may agreeably mimic the researcher's attitude, which can be conveyed unintentionally and nonverbally. This is a problem if the researcher's attitude reveals the hypothesis. Think back to the video violence studies. If the researchers think watching violence makes people aggressive, they themselves may become subtly aggressive (abrupt behavior, irritated expression), causing the participants to imitate and reciprocate. Think back to the attractiveness and persuasion studies. If researchers believe their hypothesis, they may smile slightly as they observe the attractive communicators.

**Expectancy effects** in research consist of the researcher bringing about the expected results by inadvertently influencing participants to behave in the predicted direction. In the original instance of this phenomenon, teachers told that some of their pupils would experience an intellectual growth spurt that year and did in fact observe those students performing better by year's end. The problem is that the intellectual bloomers had been randomly selected, and the teachers' expectancies had created the effect. The interpersonal expectancy effect (Rosenthal, 1994) has been demonstrated in a variety of domains (listed from smallest to largest effects): laboratory interviews, reaction time, learning and ability, person perception, inkblot tests, everyday situations, psychophysical judgments, and especially animal learning. The mechanisms, at least for teachers advantaging certain students (and maybe even laboratory rats), are a warm attitude (climate), communicated nonverbally, and greater effort to interact with the favored few.

The discovery of expectancy effects caused a revolution in research. To this day, researchers avoid expectancy effects by remaining blind to the experimental condition of the participant until afterward (so they cannot unconsciously affect the person's behavior). Also, they verbally communicate neither the hypotheses nor the comparison conditions to the participants ahead of time, so the participants also cannot consciously or unconsciously behave as "good subjects" and produce the expected results. In short, expectancy effects can be prevented, but they are a particular concern in social psychological research, because the participants typically want to get along socially.

## Participant Construal and Motives to Understand

Another core motive, understanding, also enters the social psychology laboratory. As soon as participants arrive at this admittedly novel context, they want to make sense of it. If each participant makes sense of the situation in a unique way, then the study data will contain a lot of random error (noise) that will obscure the effects of interest (signal). For this reason, researchers provide all participants with a single understandable framework for the study.

But not just any plausible framework will do. Recall that people respond to the social situation; this is the basis of situationism, introduced in the previous chapter. Recall also that they respond to the situation as they understand it. Hence, researchers must be sensitive to the participants' perspective on the research setting. It does not matter what is objectively true, or true from the experimenter's perspective; what matters is the participants' perspective. Thus, for example, two facts might be inconsistent from the experimenter's perspective, but if they are psychologically consistent from the participants' perspective, they are consistent for the purposes of the experiment.

Understanding the participant's psychological construal of the research situation is important so that the researcher and participant have the same shared meaning. In experiments, for example, this allows experimenters to be sure that the manipulated social influences come across as intended. Getting inside the participant's head to create the intended understanding is one of the great challenges of social psychological methods.

## Demand Characteristics and Motives to Control

Participants do not wish only to understand the novel social context presented by a research setting; they also wish to have some sense of efficacy and control. From a motivational perspective, they must feel they have a choice about the role they play in research. They may follow instructions or not, figure out the hypothesis or not, confirm the hypothesis or not. Factors in the research setting (other than the independent variable) may affect their behavior, as **demand characteristics** (Orne, 1962): prior experience in psychological research, rumors about that study, the researchers' behavior, instructions, equipment, setting, and response alternatives. Participants may respond to perceived attempts to control their behavior by cooperating or resisting, so it is important that they do not react to independent variables as the researcher's attempts to influence them. The research must be set up to minimize overly overt cues to expected behavior, a requirement that also meets participant motives for control. Participants must feel able to respond freely to the research stimuli.

## Social Desirability and Motives to Self-Enhance

Participants enter the research setting with motives not only to belong, understand, and control. They also have fundamental motives to protect the self and the images of the self that they present. In the social setting of the research context, participants want to come across well. They worry about **social desirability**, that is, complying with the norms for responses that reflect positively on self.

Consequently, participants resist responding in ways that make them vulnerable to looking incompetent, unkind, dishonest, unfair, biased, and so on. Unfortunately, some of the most interesting human behavior is incompetent, unkind, dishonest, unfair, and biased. Much of what social psychologists study are flaws in human nature, with an eye to diminishing their effects, so sometimes we need to see participants at less than their best. How else can we study topics such as aggression and racism?

Researchers guard against social desirability biases in several ways. Most frequently, researchers honestly assure participants of the anonymity of their responses and the confidentiality of their data. In addition, researchers may bury sensitive questions in a series of less provocative questions, to minimize the impact of self-presentational concerns. Researchers may frame questions as neutrally as possible. They can also separately measure people's tendency to respond in a socially desirable way and statistically control for it in analyzing their data. Finally, researchers may measure subtle responses that escape the participants' notice or control, such as speed of response or distance of seating.

## Positivity Biases and Motives to Trust

Finally, according to the **positivity bias**, people are predisposed to think well of other people, at least in-group others, all else being equal. This means that they will tend to rate others positively and resist negative responses—inconvenient if one develops a 3-point scale consisting of *dislike, neutral, like*, because virtually every participant will respond *like*. Even a five-point scale will elicit a consensus around *like moderately*. We return to this point in the chapter on interpersonal attraction, but here the point is that researchers need to compensate for participants' tendencies to like and trust others.

Then there's liking and trusting the researcher. Participants expect the researcher to be competent, kind, honest, fair, and unbiased, and they will give the researcher the benefit of the doubt. Researchers need to justify that positivity bias in their demeanor toward participants. Part of that responsibility involves ethical behavior, covered next.

## Summary of Methodological Challenges in Social Settings

Researchers beware: Participants, motivated by core social motives, may create artifacts in social psychological research: (a) motivated by the belonging motive, they may conform to experimenter expectancy; (b) motivated to understand, they may construe the experiment in unintended ways; (c) motivated to control, they may react to perceived demands to respond as expected; (d) motivated to self-enhance, they may respond in socially desirable ways; and (e) motivated to trust, they may show strong positivity biases.

## ETHICS IN RESEARCH

Social psychologists rarely deal with death as a variable, but recall the nursing home study (Rodin & Langer, 1977), in which elderly patients may have lived longer when given trivial levels of control over their lives. When the researchers first hypothesized this, should they have tried to persuade the nursing home to give houseplants and movie choices to *all* the patients at the outset? Should they have halted their study when the data first started coming in? At what point should they have applied their findings?

In the nursing home study, researchers could not know with any certainty that the personal control would prolong people's lives, unless they completed the study as designed. And even then, replications and improvements are needed. This points out the importance of causal inferences in making ethical decisions about people. For example, if we know that merely perceiving control over one's environment can cause better health and well-being, as in the nursing home experiment, then we understand much more about perceived control and the causes of health than if we merely know that people differ in perceived control and in health, even if we know they are correlated. If researchers terminate the experiment before it is completed, then they may not be certain that the initial results were not just a statistical fluke. This is a major issue in medical research, where desperate patients may pressure scientists to give them unproven experimental treatments, rather than allowing themselves to be randomly assigned, perhaps to the control group, which may receive the currently standard treatment.

Similar issues arise in particularly impactful social psychology studies, such as the prison study, that dramatically affect participants' well-being. Should the Stanford prison researchers instead have studied real prisoners and guards? Or should they have tried to observe or interview people in parallel situations, such as Jennifer in her prison-like National Labor Federation, the Brooklyn cult described in the opening chapter? What are some advantages and disadvantages of each of these methods? Given their extreme results, should they have stopped the study when they did? Stopping the study deprived the researchers of complete measures and full knowledge, but how does that weigh against the miserable experience of the participants? Should they never have begun the experiment in the first place?

Even in more ordinary social psychology experiments, participants may experience temporary discomfort, and researchers must obtain their consent ahead of time and allow them to withdraw from the experiment if necessary. In every case, participants incur costs, ranging from inconvenience, to boredom, to embarrassment, to temporary anxiety. These costs must be weighed against the benefits of the research to the participants (learning about themselves), to the researcher (advancing science), to the field (greater theoretical understanding), and to society (solutions to social problems). Ethical decisions about research depend on weighing the potential costs and benefits perceived by researchers and independent review boards (present in every institution that conducts research with human participants).

## Ethical Dilemmas

Important variables (pain, failure, stress, fear, aggression) are often unpleasant. Most people are motivated to diminish human suffering and want research to inform those efforts, but researchers must confront these experiences directly, in order to study them. Researchers try to minimize the extent to which they study these experiences by inflicting them on people, but as chapters on aggression and discrimination will show, for instance, the choice of research method is not always simple.

What's more, in social psychology, unambiguous inferences may require that participants are temporarily unaware or deceived about the intent of the study. If participants know that the research is studying selfishness, prejudice, or conformity, they might shape their behavior to fit the socially desirable response, instead of acting spontaneously. Thus, researchers sometimes withhold information about the experiment until the end. Sometimes, they even have to mislead participants, to prevent their guessing the true nature of the study. Deception research was particularly popular during the 1950s to 1960s heyday of high-impact experimental social psychology, when some of the classic studies were conducted, but it decreased in the next two decades (Nicks, Korn, & Mainieri, 1997). Whenever deception appears as an option, researchers must consider more straightforward methods, before resorting to omitting or distorting information, and all researchers must inform participants afterwards about the true nature of the study and obtain permission to use their data before they leave.

Another ethical issue that arises in social psychology is the fear that the data may disadvantage the participants. Suppose a research project shows that one demographic or personality group on average scores lower than another on some socially valued dimension, whether competence, warmth, coordination, aggression, or spatial skills. The disadvantaged group might not have wanted to contribute to these research findings, if they are then used to justify discrimination. On the other hand, no one can censor scientific findings. And the interpretation of those findings is always open to debate. For instance, maybe group averages differ, but only a little, and the variation is so great *within* the groups that their distributions overlap almost completely. And average differences between, for example, the genders on aggression do not explain why they occur, as in the interactions of biology and society in producing those outcomes.

Finally, social psychologists who work with special populations—including students in psychology classes—have to consider carefully their recruitment of participants. Unintentional coercion always lurks, in both obvious and subtle forms. Recruiting students to work on the professor's own research, for extra credit, may or may not be appropriate, depending on the circumstances. Such ethical dilemmas apply even more clearly to recruiting people who are institutionalized, very young or very old, encountered in a psychological services context, or from a different culture.

## Ethical Decisions

Ethical treatment of human participants in research requires that they be respected, not be harmed, and consent to participate. As noted, ethical choices depend on weighing costs and benefits. Resolving ethical conflict includes acknowledging that no absolute answers exist; reasonable people disagree. Researchers are obligated to (a) do the best research possible and (b) protect human participants. When these goals conflict, they must consult their consciences, but they can also be biased by their investment in their own projects. To counteract their bias and ensure fair consideration of the advantages and disadvantages of their research, investigators must undergo collegial review.

Participants always need to know that they have a choice about participating in the experiment, they can stop at any time, they will receive any promised compensation, their responses will be available only to appropriate audiences, and they can get any appropriate additional information. In short, they need to be treated with respect, as humans with control over how they participate in the research experience. **Informed consent** means that the participant's agreement to engage in the research process is contingent on having a reasonable amount of information about what that will entail.

## Summary of Ethics in Research

Social psychological research raises ethical dilemmas because it involves human participants and important social problems. Sometimes it also involves deception, uncomfortable experiences, participant disadvantages, or special populations. Researchers, with the advice of colleagues and review panels, must weigh the costs and benefits of their research methods, as part of the scientific enterprise.

## CHAPTER SUMMARY

Conceptualization, the first step in research, entails forming scientific hypotheses, which come from both application and theory. Theories, broad systems of logical principles that explain or account for observed natural phenomena, adhere to certain principles: positing causal relationships and being coherent, parsimonious, and falsifiable. Derived from theory, hypotheses state relationships expected between two or more variables. Hypotheses specify variables in a conceptual version, and researchers then operationalize the hypotheses, providing working definitions of the variables in a particular research context. In operational form, studies aim to meet scientific standards of operational precision, public reproducibility, and observational accuracy (lack of bias).

Besides making tactical operational decisions about variables, social psychologists must choose an overall research strategy, which also guides how they operationalize their variables. The overall strategies involve using descriptive, correlational, or experimental research methods. Descriptive research, characteristic of polls and surveys, raises issues of random sampling for accuracy and comparison to baseline. Correlational research specifies relationships among variables, often with an implicit causal agenda, but rarely with the ability to make causal inferences. Experiments are designed precisely to infer causality, although their generalizability often remains to be tested, depending on the sample. Artifacts can affect any social research.

With this knowledge, scientists have to make ethical decisions about whether and how to run their research enterprise. Experiments, with their unique power to infer causality, can improve people's lives. Correlational data, without randomized trials, can never truly establish the certainty that a particular intervention improves a particular outcome. Public policy is best based on large-scale randomized experiments, to the extent possible, so that people may get the best we know how to provide. Donald Campbell, many years ago (1969), argued for the experimenting society that would create only those social programs that had been well-supported as accomplishing what they were designed to accomplish. Even on a more individual scale, before social psychologists generally assert that something in the social situation (an attractive person, a shampoo ad, a television show, a relationship, a prison) influences people in a particular way, an experiment generally provides the best evidence.

The chapter included accounts of research on test performance, prison roles, health, drinking habits, attractiveness, racial disparities, stereotyping, and aggression, all illustrating social influences on people as individuals and as group members, social processes that the rest of the book will now take up in earnest.

## SUGGESTIONS FOR FURTHER READING

ABELSON, R. P. (1995). *Statistics as principled argument*. Hillsdale, NJ: Erlbaum.

PELHAM, B. W., & BLANTON, H. (2006). *Conducting research in psychology: Measuring the weight of smoke*. Belmont, CA: Wadsworth.

PETTIGREW, T. F. (1996). *How to think like a social scientist*. New York: Harper Collins.

REIS, H. T., & GOSLING, S. D. (2010). Social psychological methods outside the laboratory. In S. T. FISKE, D. T. GILBERT, & G. LINDZEY (Eds.), *The handbook of social psychology* (5th ed.). New York: Wiley.

ROSENTHAL, R. (1995). Methodology. In A. TESSER (Ed.), *Advanced social psychology* (pp. 17–49). New York: McGraw-Hill.

SANSONE, C., MORF, C. C., & PANTER, A. T. (2003). *Sage handbook of methods in social psychology*. Thousand Oaks, CA: Sage.

SHAUGHNESSY, J. J., ZECHMEISTER, E. B., & ZECHMEISTER, J. S. (2006). *Research Methods in Psychology*. New York: McGraw-Hill.

STANGOR, C. (2006). *Research methods for the behavioral sciences*. New York: Houghton Mifflin.

WILSON, T. D., ARONSON, E., & CARLSMITH, K. (2010). The art of laboratory experimentation. In S. T. FISKE, D. T. GILBERT, & G. LINDZEY (Eds.), *The handbook of social psychology* (5th ed.). New York: Wiley.

# Chapter 3

# Ordinary Personology: Figuring Out Why People Do What They Do

At the American Academy of Forensic Sciences' annual awards dinner, AAFS President Don Harper Mills intrigued his San Diego audience with the legal ramifications of a death under bizarre circumstances. Here is the story he told:

> On 23 March 1994, the medical examiner viewed the body of Ronald Opus and concluded that he died from a shotgun wound of the head. The decedent had jumped from the top of a ten-story building intending to commit suicide (he left a note indicating his despondency). As he fell past the ninth floor, his life was interrupted by a shotgun blast through a window, which killed him instantly. Neither the shooter nor the decedent was aware that a safety net had been erected at the eighth floor level to protect some window washers and that Opus would not have been able to complete his suicide anyway because of this.
>
> "Ordinarily," Dr. Mills continued, "a person who sets out to commit suicide ultimately succeeds, even though the mechanism might not be what he intended. That Opus was shot on the way to certain death nine stories below probably would not have changed his mode of death from suicide to homicide. But the fact that his suicidal intent would not have been successful caused the medical examiner to feel that he had homicide on his hands."
>
> The room on the ninth floor whence the shotgun blast emanated was occupied by an elderly man and his wife. They were arguing and he was threatening her with the shotgun. He was so upset that, when he pulled the trigger, he completely missed his wife and the pellets went through a window, striking Opus.
>
> When one intends to kill subject A but kills subject B in the attempt, one is guilty of the murder of subject B. When confronted with this charge, the old man and his wife were both adamant that neither knew that the shotgun was loaded. The old man said it was his long-standing habit to threaten his wife with the

unloaded shotgun. He had no intention to murder her—therefore, the killing of Opus appeared to be an accident. That is, the gun had been accidentally loaded.

The continuing investigation turned up a witness who saw the old couple's son loading the shotgun approximately six weeks prior to the fatal incident. It transpired that the old lady had cut off her son's financial support, and the son, knowing the propensity of his father to use the shotgun threateningly, loaded the gun with the expectation that his father would shoot his mother. The case now becomes one of murder on the part of the son for the death of Ronald Opus.

There was an exquisite twist. "Further investigation revealed that the son [Ronald Opus] had become increasingly despondent over the failure of his attempt to engineer his mother's murder. This led him to jump off the ten-story building on March 23, only to be killed by a shotgun blast through a ninth story window.

The medical examiner closed the case as a suicide. (From www.cybertown.com/suicide.html)[1]

We will return to this fictional example a few times, but apart from how bizarre it is, consider how you would decide whether the death is homicide or suicide. That is, how would you explain the cause of death, the intent of the person who caused the death, and whether the person was depressed (in the case of the son) or violent (in the case of the father)?

This chapter addresses how people infer other people's shorter-term feelings (e.g., depressed) and enduring traits (e.g., violent) from their actions. We examine both kinds of inferences, as well as how people imagine each other's mind in general. In ordinary personology, people are less often concerned with homicide and suicide (although these provoke the most deeply disturbing exercises in understanding others) but more often concerned with why friends did what they did. Ordinary personology provides the foundation that underlies all social processes. People must make sense of the actual, imagined, and implied others who constitute the social situation that so influences us. As pioneers Edward Jones and John Thibaut (1958) put it, "Interpersonal perception can most fruitfully be treated as both instrumental to social interaction and conditioned by it" (p. 152).

Ordinary personology logically opens the study of social psychology. This book progresses from the micro to the macro within social psychology. Processes *within* an individual—an individual thinking about other people (ordinary personology and social cognition), the self, or attitude objects—logically underlie processes *between* individuals (attraction, relationships, helping, aggression). Processes between individuals underlie processes *within and between groups*. This *individual* to *dyads* to *groups* level of analysis mirrors the book's organization. Here, let's focus on how people think about another person, especially how we perceive each other's temporary states (e.g., feelings), long-term dispositions (e.g., personality traits), and mental life in general (e.g., consciousness and will). First, this chapter examines the field of interpersonal

---

[1] Copyright © Don Harper Mills. Reproduced with permission.

perception (personology) from a conceptual perspective. As Chapter 2 noted, before researchers can study a phenomenon, they must clarify the nature of the concept itself. In my experience, students want to know what social psychologists mean by a technical term such as personology but also by terms that overlap ordinary language (e.g., personality). With that conceptual background, the chapter overviews interpersonal perception from an operational perspective, sampling some of the ways that researchers typically manipulate and measure person perception. Again, as Chapter 2 noted, to understand how social psychology actually functions, one must know the typical working definitions.

Then, the chapter discusses the core social motives that most often surface in this line of work: understanding, controlling, and self-enhancing. Building on that background, the chapter turns to provocative findings about perceiving nonverbal behavior (how people understand other people's feelings), dispositions (how people understand other people's traits, from behavior), and mind (how people understand others' consciousness). The chapter closes with a discussion of our persistent errors and biases in interpersonal perception. Some findings will frame research in later chapters, as social psychology starts with people perceiving other people.

## WHAT IS ORDINARY PERSONOLOGY?

Ordinary personology, the daily inference of feelings, personalities, and minds, both determines our social interactions and results from them. Chapter 4 returns to this theme, focusing on how people think about other people in order to interact with them (topics include accuracy, expectancies, and goals). Chapter 4 focuses on **deductive inferences**, reasoning from abstractions to observations. Meanwhile, the current chapter focuses on **inductive inferences**, that is, how people transform concrete observations of behavior into abstract understandings, whether perceived feelings, traits, or mind.

### Conceptual Definition

Personology is the scientific study of the characteristics of individual people. **Ordinary personology** is the everyday study of persons, that is, the process by which ordinary people seek to understand the individual people around them. The term, coined by Daniel Gilbert (1998), reminds us that this is the process by which "ordinary people come to know about each other's temporary states (such as emotions, intentions, and desires) and enduring dispositions (such as beliefs, traits, and abilities)" (p. 89), as well as having a mind at all. The process is surprisingly active and oddly parallel to perceiving objects, but it also involves unique complexities that are emphatically social.

**ACTIVE CONSTRUCTION OF EXPERIENCE**    What impression did you form of Ronald Opus, the deceased son in the opening example? Was he a teenager in adolescent angst or a middle-aged man in mid-life despair, in your mind's eye? How did you form your impression of him? The story does not say, yet many readers have a spontaneous image of him, including his rough age, his appearance, his motives for financial support, his mother's motive for terminating it, and his planned revenge. Your spontaneous image probably sprang to mind without much thought.

In everyday interaction, in ordinary personology on the fly, people's inferences also are spontaneous and rarely self-conscious. Indeed, we often seem to experience directly another person's feelings, intents, or traits. The late Fritz Heider, one of the founders of what he termed the study of common-sense psychology (1958), identified **phenomenal description** as people's direct experience of their interpersonal environment. A person "not only perceives people as having certain spatial and physical properties, but also can grasp even such intangibles as their wishes, needs, and emotions by some form of immediate apprehension" (p. 22). He cites a telling quotation by Solomon Asch (1952, p. 142):

> To naïve experience, the fact of being "in touch with" other persons is most direct and unmediated by intervening events. We experience direct communication with others: emotion clashing with emotion, desire meeting desire, thought speaking to thought. Often there is virtually no lag between the psychological event in one person and its grasp in the other.[2]

Although people's experience is immediate, they in fact search the social horizon unaware that they are using mental binoculars and that things are much farther away than they appear. All our experience, as Egon Brunswik (1952) noted (building on Kant and Plato), is actually **mediated** or filtered through a psychological lens, our perceiving apparatus. Although we experience the world as if we take in a literal, unfiltered copy, each person passes reality through a different lens. Schematically,

the situation → our interpretive lens → our experience

Whether observing other people or objects, people are aware only of the end product, their experience. Chances are, when people pick up the feelings, personalities, and minds of those around them, they are not fully aware of how they filter them. People experience **naïve realism** (Pronin, Gilovich & Ross, 2004), that is, the notion that one sees the world objectively (even though others may not).

Heider points out that people's direct experience of the world contrasts with a **causal description** or scientific analysis of how people perceive it. The scientific analysis shows that people constantly interpret, construct, and frame their perceptions. People are not video cameras, passively recording all that comes along. People are more like artists, sometimes slapdash cartoonists and sometimes Grand Masters, but active interpreters of reality nonetheless. Henry James, the novelist, described people perceiving other people as if looking out their windows:

> Neighbors are watching the same show, but one seeing more where the other sees less, one seeing black where the other sees white, one seeing big where the other sees small, one seeing coarse where the other sees fine.... [The impressions are] nothing without the posted presence of the watcher. (James, 1881, pp. ix–x)

---

[2] Copyright © by Asch Estate. Reproduced with permission.

**Table 3.1**  Perceived Number of Infractions, by Own
School and Team Judged

|  | Team Judged | |
| --- | --- | --- |
| Own School | Dartmouth | Princeton |
| Dartmouth | 4.3 | 4.4 |
| Princeton | 9.8 | 5.7 |

Higher numbers indicate more perceived infractions.
*Source:* Hastorf & Cantril, 1954.

Several pieces of evidence demonstrate people's active role in making sense of social reality. One is **selective interpretation**, the tendency to shape understandings to fit one's own perspective. Consider the family situation of poor Ronald Opus. Presumably, he felt he deserved continued financial support from his family, and his mother felt he did not. Was she a heartless tyrant or a realistic judge? Was he a hapless victim or an irresponsible jerk? Or consider the fight between the father and mother. Who started it and how? Arguments are minefields of selective, interpretive processes.

Competition is also rife with interpretive processes. Early social psychologists noted the role of people's selective interpretation of the same reality in competitive settings. Albert Hastorf and Hadley Cantril's (1954) study, "They saw a game," presented participants with a film of a Dartmouth-Princeton football game. Students from the two colleges were asked to judge the number of infractions that had occurred. The students from one college perceived many more infractions by the opposing team than its own supporters did. As illustrated in Table 3.1, Dartmouth students thought the numbers of infractions were about equal, whereas Princeton students saw twice as many infractions by Dartmouth players as by Princeton players. These data indicate an interaction effect (a data pattern explained in Chapter 2): Together, the student's college and the particular team combine to affect the number of infractions perceived. Moreover, when asked, "Which team do you feel started the rough play?" 86% of Princeton students but only 36% of Dartmouth students said "Dartmouth." Both sides actively interpret the game.

Selective interpretations often occur when people take sides. In another study (Thompson, 1995), students role-played an employer-employee negotiation over a job contract (salary, raise, vacation, medical coverage, start date, and region). The negotiators themselves and partisan observers (assigned to empathize with one side or the other) both made inaccurate judgments, compared with nonpartisan observers, about the other side's true interests (see Figure 3.1). Partisans also rated their own side as more friendly and honest. Does this sound like perceptions of one's own team?

But it is not only competition and argument that trigger people's interpretive, constructive processes. Perceptual **construction** always imputes structure, stability, and meaning to the raw data of the world, whether people or objects (Schneider, Hastorf, & Ellsworth, 1979). When we see small dark things on the road, we (a) structure them as a unit, perhaps all spilled off the same truck; (b) view them as stable, the identical objects even though the image on our retina changes as we approach; and (c) create the meaning of trash that we must avoid hitting. Similar active processes

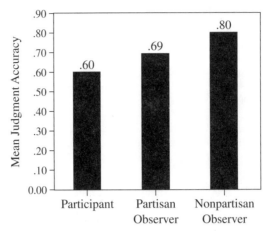

**Figure 3.1**   Judgmental Accuracy for Participants, Partisan Observers, and Nonpartisan Observers

*Source:* From Thompson, 1995. Copyright © American Psychological Association. Adapted with permission.

operate when we structure an old sweatshirt and dirty jeans as going together, view them as a habitual choice, and interpret the wearer as a homeless person or very relaxed professor.

Heider agreed with Brunswik that perceiving people is importantly similar to perceiving things. In particular, people selectively interpret, imputing structure, stability, and meaning to people as well as objects. If people observe a person brandishing a shot gun and yelling at another person, the observers structure those two actions together as part of an anger episode, as in our opening example. If people observe the same person on another occasion threatening his wife with a knife, then the observers may see stability in his behavior over time and perceive his tendency to become violent when angry. Observers may give meaning to the information as a case of domestic violence. In person perception as well as object perception, people "go beyond the information given" (Jerome Bruner's felicitous phrase in 1957a). The marked parallels in how people perceive objects and how people perceive people reflect these principles of active perception: imputing structure, stability, and meaning.

**OBJECT PERCEPTION VERSUS PERSON PERCEPTION**   People and objects differ, of course, as targets of perception. Shelley Taylor and I compiled some of the most frequently noted differences between perceiving things and people (Fiske & Taylor, 2008). First, people are *causal agents*, that is, they intend to act on their environment; when people cause an event, they can be intentional origins of action. An object can cause an event, as when a loaded gun falls off a table and fires, but the gun has no intention. A person who fires the gun more likely does it on purpose. This unique feature of people stimulated social psychologists' interest in studying how people attribute intention, as well as recent work on perceiving minds, both covered in this chapter.

Just as people are active in their intentions, so they are active in their perceptions. People, as objects of perception, perceive the perceiver back. Social perception is *mutual perception*, whereas object perception is a one-way street. This means, for example, that it is impolite to stare at a person but not at an object. Obvious gazes suggest the other person is the focus of your thoughts and perhaps intentions. The other person may well have some reactions to being a target of attention. Mutual perception means that we have to be careful about how we gather data about other people, who are simultaneously busy gathering data about us.

Related to this point, people's observations of other people *implicate the self*. When people notice another person's shocked expression, they may wonder if they should be wearing the same expression. The shocked expression may indicate a body falling past the ninth floor window behind our back, in which case the other person's expression implies a shared experience. Or the other person may simply be wearing blue jeans when we are in a business suit (or vice versa), which has more implications for us than observing whether a tree has leaves or not.

An object does not anticipate being observed, but a person does. Another person's facial expression may of course be faked to communicate an emotion not felt, whereas the tree cannot put on and take off its leaves to fool us about the season. *Self-presentation* occurs in observed persons, unlike objects. If Ronald Opus while still alive had been accused of loading his father's shotgun, he might have assumed a facial expression that belied his purpose. The next section of this chapter takes up nonverbal behavior and deception.

Because people manipulate their self-presentation, it interferes with observers' ability to know their intentions, feelings, and traits. But, because they are causal agents, their inner states are important. If they can cause events, their behavior may be predicted by knowing their intentions, feelings, and traits. For all these reasons, people's *nonobservable states and traits* are more important than the nonobservable states and traits of objects. If an object is breakable, one may infer that from its appearance. A person's psychological fragility is harder to infer from appearances, yet it may predict the person's behavior.

People are generally more *changeable* than objects, partly because they are causal agents and can change some aspects at will. This makes observations of people more tenuous than observations of objects.

It is harder to verify the *accuracy* of observations about people than observations about objects. If people judge that an object is fragile, we could theoretically verify the accuracy of that judgment by throwing it out a nine-story window. But we would not even imagine trying that experiment with a person, nor (ethically, at least) even the experiment of trying to inflict psychological damage. Observers also agree less about the properties of people than those of objects, an issue that has plagued personality psychologists trying to measure people's traits. Chapter 4 returns to this point.

**SUMMARY**   Ordinary personology describes how people infer other people's feelings, dispositions, and mind in general. People's phenomenal description (i.e., experience) is that these perceptions are spontaneous and passive. But a scientific causal description indicates that people filter reality through a psychological lens. People actively select and interpret, imputing structure, stability, and meaning to their understanding of both objects and people. Nevertheless, inherent complexities enter into perceiving people: people's status as causal agents who perceive back, implicate the self, and self-present, possessing important but nonobservable traits that are changeable and difficult to verify. The simple fact that people are unavoidably complex makes ordinary personology a miracle: Sometimes it seems amazing that we ever manage to make sense of each other at all.

## Operational Definitions

In the early 1970s (Nisbett, Caputo, Legant, & Marecek, 1973), Yale College women volunteered for a group experiment on decision making. To decrease suspicion and increase spontaneous responses, the actual experiment occurred before the alleged experiment (which never happened.). Before the alleged experiment, they were asked to help university fund-raising efforts toward a center for disadvantaged children, by volunteering to host the families of potential donors. Two confederates of the experimenter agreed first, so many participants also did, particularly if pay was high (64%) instead of low (24%). (Pay was an independent variable.) Observer participants then rated various stated reasons for the volunteer's decision (e.g., helping, interesting activities, earning money, social pressure), and predicted whether in the future she would also volunteer to canvass for the United Fund; these constituted the dependent variables. Observers ignored the social pressure (confederates) and the monetary incentive, instead predicting that she would volunteer again if she volunteered this time. The participants themselves did not make the same prediction (see Table 3.2). This illustrates some typical methods involved in personology research, namely, people observing other people's behavior, explaining why they did what they did, and rating it as predictive of their future behavior. This study also illustrates a central principle—ordinary people underestimate the very situational factors that social psychology emphasizes (mentioned in Chapter 1, this pattern featured in this chapter).

Social psychologists have empirically studied interpersonal perception ever since the beginning of the field. Earlier, we noted that ordinary personology focuses on inductive inferences, people actively constructing observed behavior (volunteering) into abstract understandings (helpful personality). Consequently, one might expect that

**Table 3.2**    Judged Probability that Participant Would Volunteer Again

| Role | Participant's Previous Behavior | |
|------|------------|------------------|
| | Volunteered | Did Not Volunteer |
| Observers | 4.25 | 2.71 |
| Participant | 3.73 | 3.38 |

Higher numbers indicate a higher perceived probability of volunteering again.

*Source:* From Nisbett et al., 1973. Copyright © American Psychological Association. Adapted with permission.

the independent variables would manipulate observed raw behavior, and dependent variables would measure inferred feelings and traits. This is only half right.

Person perception researchers typically do measure dependent variables as ratings of short-term internal states (de la Haye, 1991), such as perceived feelings, intentions, and attitudes (24% of studies), and long-term internal characteristics, such as abilities and traits (42% of studies). Some studies (17%) measure perceived causes (as in the Nisbett et al. example). These judgments often use a numbered scale (e.g., 1 to 5). Less often, personology researchers will study efficiency of responses (recognition, recall; 22%) or speed of responses (6%). Dependent variables, then, are operationalized essentially as one might expect, given the concept involved. One might wish for more open-ended responses from participants (3%), although these are not always practical to collect and to code for analysis.

But on the independent variable side, ordinary personology researchers do not present raw behavior very often. The **target**, or person to be judged, only rarely appears physically (17%) or even in video (18%) or audio (7%). Most often (45%), researchers use verbal presentations, such as narratives, behavior lists, questionnaire responses, or trait lists. To be fair, this review of methods applies to both inductive personology studies (this chapter) and deductive social cognition studies (next chapter). But one reason the illustrative study is considered a classic may be precisely that the live setting is so compelling as an operational definition.

## Core Social Motives

However social psychologists conceptualize and operationalize the process, people infer each other's feelings, personalities, and minds for good reason. Recall that Chapter 1 described how people are adapted to live in groups; people need social groups for survival. Social psychology especially concerns how people get along with each other, how people interact with each other, face to face. Thus, the basic social motives that unify this text all address people's ability to survive in groups. As noted, people not only perpetuate their own genes and even their relatives' genes but also try to make their group survive and themselves survive in the group. The adaptive pressure, then, includes making the group an adaptive group and the self an adaptive person within the group. This allows a big-picture understanding of social psychology by thinking about the ways people fit into social environments.

As Chapter 1 noted, each of the chapters highlights some of the five core social motivations. These core social motives should provide some sense that a few central, recurring themes do run through social psychology, throughout its generous array of theories. The themes fit the theories together. In this chapter on ordinary personology, the main motive that underlies most theories is understanding, but two subsidiary motives are controlling and self-enhancing.

**UNDERSTANDING**    People patently have a basic need to understand other people, to make sense of other people, in order to survive in a group. People need to form some coherent understanding of the people in their social world, unless they intend to be total isolates. People have to be able to predict what other people are going to do, to share a meaning system with them, so they can interact in the most basic ways. Sharing the same frames of reference facilitates interaction with other people, from something as simple as whether to say grinder, hoagie, or sub when ordering a foot-long sandwich, to whether one acknowledges a fleeting smile from a stranger.

Understanding creates shared meaning about the personalities and feelings that predict other people's behavior. In the bizarre suicide example, the medical examiner's job was partly to predict the future behavior of the father in the story, whether he should be charged with homicide because he intended to do harm and so might be dangerous again or should be released because he could not have foreseen the consequences of his action and so would be blameless in the future as well. Understanding the father's intentions and feelings, forming a theory concerning the father, predicts his future behavior. In the Yale study, observers tried to predict the volunteer's future behavior from her current behavior, regardless of situational constraints.

People and cultures vary in how much they are motivated to understand other individual people, as we will see. For example, individuals vary in their need for unambiguous answers, a phenomenon called **need for closure** (Webster & Kruglanski, 1994). The type of unambiguous understanding they seek may vary by culture, but in the United States, the inference of individual consistency is a socially convenient understanding. The more a given American personally needs closure (definitive understanding), the more that person makes dispositional, stable interpretations. In other cultures, a need for understanding creates a reliance on stable situational factors, such as the group (Chiu, Morris, Hong, & Menon, 2000). A later section comes back to this point, but here the implication is that increasing people's need for unambiguous understanding increases their tendency to make inferences from behavior to more stable explanations. Across cultures, understanding constitutes the core social motive that guides ordinary personology.

**CONTROLLING**    Ordinary personology also has a lot to do with the core motive of controlling, being effective. Learning about a specific other person's feelings, intentions, and personality not only allows one to predict that person, a function that overlaps with understanding, but also allows some potential control over what happens. For the legal system, of course, a decision that a person intended murder, that is, a charge of homicide, activates an entire apparatus designed to be effective in controlling that person. In a more mundane way, if a student learns about a new professor's mood, intentions, and personality, the student knows far better how to approach the professor about an extension on the term paper due on the Jewish high holiday Yom Kippur, which might necessitate an attempt to influence the professor. That student's analysis of the professor is a way of exerting some control in the environment.

Control, then, does not mean that the student can manipulate the professor to comply, but the student could interact with the professor, expecting that certain actions encourage certain responses from the professor. Some mutual influence occurs in virtually any relationship, which motivates people to be effective and have some sense of control. People high in **need for internal control** are especially likely to make inferences based on other people's behavior (Miller, Norman, & Wright, 1978), and perhaps thinking of such highly controlling people makes us all feel that it is rude, crude, or socially inept to discuss control so explicitly. But everyone does it, and control is crucial to human relationships. In a social world with no personal control, one would feel totally lost. Suppose a newcomer does not know whether smiling and greeting a stranger on the street will elicit ignoring, attacking, smiling, or conversing: an unsettling world, at least. People need to expect some contingency between what they do and what they get. Much ordinary personology, social perception, concerns people trying to understand those contingencies, to be able to influence what happens to them in social settings.

**SELF-ENHANCING** Sometimes, a third social motive will come up, namely, self-enhancing. Some of the ways people think about people's feelings and traits are shaped by the motives of self-enhancement, although this motive appears to a lesser extent than the other two. Self-enhancement surfaces in face-saving fibs and nonverbal behavior. Moreover, the end of the chapter shows that several errors and biases in people's thinking processes occur because of the motive to make themselves feel or at least look good.

## Summary of Definitions and Core Social Motives in Personology

The first motive, understanding, provides the big picture for this and the next chapter. Most theories in this chapter directly concern understanding other people and indirectly address the motives to control and self-enhance. People's understanding of other people, as conceptualized in ordinary personology, reveals active construction of experience, in contrast to people's phenomenal experience of direct, unfiltered perceptions. People selectively interpret, imputing structure, stability, and meaning to perceiving both objects and people. But people are inherently complex because they are active causal agents who perceive back, adjust their appearance, and implicate the self; they possess important characteristics that must be inferred from changeable behavior, with problematic accuracy. Operationally, social psychologists study ordinary personology by examining how people use behavior to infer feelings and traits, often presenting verbal reports of behavior but sometimes using video or audio recording and measuring judgments of feelings, intentions, or traits.

As we will see, people make inferences about other people's internal states and traits, with some accuracy but also some little-known pitfalls. The next section starts with how people infer other people's feelings, because feelings can be fleeting, then moves to inferences about more stable traits and intentions, and finally discusses the wonder of mind perception overall.

## NONVERBAL BEHAVIOR: UNDERSTANDING FEELINGS

Popular media tout "body language" as a way to read people's minds. Is it? We cannot answer that question without first knowing what it is and then what it reveals about everyday interaction, deception, and attraction.

## Conceptual and Operational Definitions

**Nonverbal behavior** consists of all features of an interaction that are not words. Non-verbal literally means "not words" (DePaulo & Friedman, 1998, p. 3): "the dynamic, mostly face-to-face exchange of information through cues other than words" (p. 4). In a play, nonverbal behaviors are everything supplied by actors when they are given a script, which contains basically only the words. Nonverbal behavior serves both as an independent variable (presented in photographs, audio records, visual records, and actual interactions) and as a dependent variable (measures of facial expressions, vocal cues, and body movement) (Gray & Ambady, 2006).

Special features characterize perceiving nonverbal behaviors. In comparison with other kinds of cues in ordinary personology, nonverbal cues stand out in a number of ways (Schneider, Hastorf, & Ellsworth, 1979, pp. 122–136). Nonverbal behavior deals in affect more than verbal cues do. Because nonverbal behavior is fleeting and changeable, it is especially suited to communicating emotions and approach-avoidance responses to others. For example, according to meta-analyses, people like other people who make eye contact, smile, and lean forward (Tickle-Degnen & Rosenthal, 1990), all positive approach behaviors.

Moreover, most people believe nonverbal behavior to be unintentional and uncontrollable, so they trust it as a genuine representation of other people's feelings, more than, say, the words spoken. In contrast, social psychologists show that people constantly regulate their nonverbal behavior, that "people's nonverbal behaviors are exquisitely responsive to self-presentational contingencies" (DePaulo & Friedman, 1998, p. 15).

Nonverbal behavior is also special in that it precedes verbal behavior in human development. Babies cry, frown, and smile long before they can express their feelings in words. Because nonverbal expressions start early, involve feelings, and are relatively unconscious (if not uncontrollable), they undergird perceptions of other people.

Finally, nonverbal behavior is special in being relatively ambiguous, more so than verbal behavior. Its meaning depends on context. For example, staring can be interpreted as a sign of attraction or aggression, but who is staring at whom and in what context can make the meaning utterly clear. Both the facial expression and the circumstances combine to signal emotions (Carroll & Russell, 1996). Being heavily influenced by context makes nonverbal behavior a good topic for social psychologists, who focus on the effects of the social situation.

People do vary in their nonverbal expressiveness and sensitivity, as a function of gender, culture, and personality. According to meta-analyses, women on average are somewhat more nonverbally expressive and sensitive than men (Hall, 1978, 1984). And cultures differ on a North-South axis (Pennebaker, Rimé, & Blankenship, 1996): In 21 northern hemisphere countries, the southerners viewed themselves and were viewed as more nonverbally expressive than the northerners in the very same countries (see Figure 3.2). Warmer temperatures perhaps encourage social interaction, spontaneity, and fewer clothes, whereas colder climes require more self-protection, more planning, and bulkier clothes that dampen nonverbal expression. Cultures also differ along an East-West axis in norms about expressiveness, for example, whether you respond to a stranger's glance with a smile, nod, or nothing (Patterson et al., 2007).

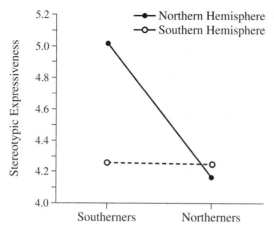

**Figure 3.2**   Stereotypic Emotional Expressiveness of Northerners and Southerners

*Source:* From Pennebaker et al., 1996. Copyright © American Psychological Association. Adapted with permission.

We must not overstate these differences, of course. Basic emotions (e.g., anger, fear, sadness, happiness, surprise, disgust) have a fair degree of cross-cultural recognition (Ekman, 1993; Russell, 1994). Cultures differ in their nonverbal "accents" (Marsh, Elfenbein, & Ambady, 2003), but people everywhere read each other's faces. In any given interaction, people tune in to each other's thoughts and feelings when they are motivated (Ickes, 1993; Ickes, Stinson, Bissonnette, & Garcia, 1990). Nonverbal behavior, a fundamental aspect of ordinary personology, aids people's basic social motive to understand others.

In summary, nonverbal behavior involves communication beyond words. Crucial to people's understanding of other people, it is trusted to communicate affect, from an early age, and some expressions are universal. Nevertheless, people and cultures do differ in their expressivity and sensitivity in nonverbal behavior, which is relatively ambiguous and context-dependent. Examples from the study of nonverbal behavior convey some surprising nonverbal aspects of deception, attraction, and intention that characterize social beings.

## Doing and Detecting Deception

Deliberatively deceptive nonverbal communication can pit the individual against the group. When people are lying, however, their nonverbal behavior may give them away: According to one meta-analysis (Sporer & Schwandt, 2007), liars inhibit their head, foot, and leg movements. Contrary to worldwide assumptions, they do easily look the listener in the eye. Unfortunately, most nonverbal cues to lying vary by the communicator's motivation, preparation, content, and sanctions, as well as the research context. People masking their emotions do leak the truth in measurable "microexpressions" (1/25–1/5 of a second), but untrained observers do not detect them (Porter & ten Brinke, 2008). Altogether, it turns out to be difficult to train people—such as customs inspectors—to detect lying. In one study, polygraph experts, judges, police officers, psychiatrists, business people, lawyers, and students all were equally poor at detecting lies; only Secret Service agents did better (Ekman & O'Sullivan, 1991).

People wrongly believe that the face is the least controlled, most revealing nonverbal channel (Zuckerman, DePaulo, & Rosenthal, 1981). Another meta-analysis compared all the occasions on which observers had any access to the potential deceivers' faces versus all those in which they did not. Having access to facial cues did not improve observers' chances of accurately detecting lies. Tone of voice appears to better indicate lying, in that people's pitch rises when they are lying. Overall, this does not leave much room for optimism about the possibility of training people to detect lying. People sometimes can detect lying, but not as much as they think they can (according to a meta-analysis by DePaulo, Charlton, Cooper, Lindsay, & Muhlenbruck, 1997).

Not all lies are equal. Some lies ("fibs") may help people interact with each other. People's inability to detect lying may fit the idea that people frequently go along to get along. Consistent with its social function, people seem to lie a lot, particularly when they are trying to impress someone. One study (Feldman, Forrest, & Happ, 2002) hypothesized that self-presentation goals would influence the amounts and kinds of lies that people told. Undergraduates participated in a getting acquainted conversation with another student and were randomly assigned to appear likable, to appear competent, or to have no goal. They later watched their own videotaped conversation and identified all lies, small and large. The average number of lies per ten-minute conversation was 1.75, with 60% of participants reporting at least one lie. Given an explicit goal to appear likable or competent, participants' most common kinds of lies (about one per session) misrepresented their feelings, for example, expressing a false opinion or evaluation, in order to get along or impress. One might argue that the goals had encouraged participants to lie, but even in the control condition, roughly one in four students lied about a feeling, an achievement, or a fact, even without explicit incentive. Besides, life outside the lab is full of situations (e.g., job interviews) where people have major incentives to present themselves as favorably as possible, and they do sometime lie, both verbally and nonverbally (Weiss & Feldman, 2006). Self-enhancement functions this way.

Sometimes lying about one's feelings ("yeah, great haircut") merely greases the social wheels. Indeed, socially skilled adolescents are better liars than unskilled adolescents (Feldman, Tomasian, & Coats, 1999). And people tell more altruistic lies to friends than strangers (DePaulo & Kashy, 1998), presumably to spare their feelings. So maybe some lying and some failure to detect lies merely reflects a face-saving norm: I will occasionally misrepresent my feelings, to smooth our interaction, and you will politely fail to notice.

## Attraction and Coordination

Nonverbal behavior serves more explicitly benign social purposes than ordinary face-saving, self-enhancing fibs. Earlier, we noted that nonverbal behavior communicates emotions and impulses to approach or avoid others in social interactions. Nonverbal behavior facilitates mutual attraction in the most ordinary interactions.

**Table 3.3**  Ratings of Nonverbal Synchrony between Mothers and
Infants

|  | Minute of Interaction | |
| Mother-Child Pair | 1st | 3rd |
| --- | --- | --- |
| Actual Pair | 5.48 | 5.97 |
| Switched Pair | 5.57 | 4.70 |

Higher numbers indicate greater nonverbal coordination.
*Source:* From Bernieri et al., 1988. Copyright © American Psychological Association. Adapted with permission.

Conversation encourages complementary nonverbal behavior: The listener gazes at the speaker, while the speaker glances only intermittently at the listener (Duncan & Fiske, 1977). Other conversational nonverbal behaviors, such as turn-taking cues, signal the end of the speaker's turn (e.g., dropped voice). What's more, interacting people generally coordinate their nonverbal behavior, smiling when the other smiles, grimacing when the other grimaces, leaning forward when the other leans, and so on. Remember from Chapter 1 that people imitate each other's gestures and expressions (Hatfield, Cacioppo, & Rapson, 1993).

Whether coordination entails complementary or simultaneous behavior, people coordinate more, the more they like each other and are satisfied in their relationship (Bernieri & Rosenthal, 1991; Chartrand & Bargh, 1999). People motivated to affiliate will nonverbally mimic their partners (Cheng & Chartrand, 2003). Affectionate nonverbal attunement starts early; watch an infant and a familiar caregiver mimicking each other's expressions. After a few moments of interaction, for example, mothers and their own infants synchronize movement, tempo, and coordination more than the same mothers and infants do with someone else (see Table 3.3; Bernieri, Reznick, & Rosenthal, 1988). Nonverbal coordination indicates attachment at all ages. Indeed, people often learn by imitation, and perhaps our brains are wired to do this. Consider the social implications of the mirror neuron system (MNS), which activates when people observe an action just as when they themselves perform the same action (Rizzolatti & Craighero, 2004). An **ideo-motor representation** of actions suggests that empathy results from a shared mental format for one's own actions and perceiving the same action by others (Iacoboni, 2009). Children's MNS activity correlates with measures of interpersonal competence and empathic concern (Pfeifer, Iacoboni, Mazziotta, & Dapretto, 2008). The MNS specifically activates to nonverbal hand communications (Montgomery, Isenberg, & Haxby, 2007), suggesting one route for social learning of gestures. Nonverbal behavior does not always invite imitation, in facilitating social interaction. Sometimes nonverbal complementarity signals opposite but interlocking roles, as in high and low status (Ambady & Weisbuch, 2010; Fiske, 2010).

Despite its importance, people rarely comment on other people's nonverbal behavior; rarely do they ask, "Why are you standing so far away from me?" or say, "Thank you for squeezing my hand." Instead, they respond nonverbally, for example by moving closer or squeezing back. Meeting nonverbal communication with nonverbal communication is the rule of **nonverbal reciprocity** (DePaulo & Friedman, 1998).

This rule holds that feelings are best reciprocated with feelings, because much non-verbal behavior appears automatic, and nonverbal communication is less direct than verbal communication. Thus, when people are feeling vulnerable, it provides a safer way to communicate attraction or rejection, with less risk of being called to account. In various ways, then, the nonverbal channels facilitate social attachment and belonging as people understand each other.

## Gaze, Attention, and Intention

Nonverbal coordination is not the only way to communicate attraction. A direct gaze, at a minimum, communicates attention (Frischen, Bayliss, & Tipper, 2007) and perhaps intention toward its target. Under some circumstances, gaze communicates a benign intent but under others a malign intent. For example, an approaching, direct-gaze, angry face signals danger, so people readily detect it (Adams, Ambady, Macrae, & Kleck, 2006). In smiling or more neutral faces, direct gaze is attractive and likeable (Jones, DeBruine, Little, Conway, & Feinberg, 2006; Mason, Tatkov, & Macrae, 2005); this fits findings on the typical positivity of eye contact (Tickle-Degnen & Rosenthal, 1990). Direct gaze tends to fit approach emotions, whereas averted gaze tends to reflect avoidance emotions such as fear (Adams & Kleck, 2005). In any case, a direct-gaze face is memorable (Mason, Hood, & Macrae, 2004), even for children (Hood, Macrae, Cole-Davies, & Dias, 2003).

Indirect gaze is also informative. When gaze is averted, people efficiently orient in that direction (Quadflieg, Mason, & Macrae, 2004). Gaze-detecting behavior occurs as early as newborns (Frischen et al., 2007). People rapidly infer that a face consistently looking away from a task-target is untrustworthy (Bayliss & Tipper, 2006). The importance of detecting gaze—and by extension, the target's intention—appears in the gaze-related activity of the superior temporal sulcus (STS) area of the brain (Haxby, Hoffman, & Gobbini, 2002), a region that matters to inferences of intent more generally, as we will soon see.

## Summary of Nonverbal Behavior

Even in situations less dramatic than observing one person threaten another with a shotgun, as in the Ronald Opus story that opened this chapter, nonverbal behavior serves perceivers' core social motives to understand other people, to control or at least influence their responses, and to present self effectively. Nonverbal behavior supplies an emotional understanding of other people, in a medium that people believe to be genuine, even if research indicates that people do lie but are not especially good at nonverbally detecting deception. Sometimes people avoid detecting face-saving fibs that grease the social wheels. Following predictable but unwritten rules, people communicate effectively in nonverbal exchanges by coordinating interaction to indicate attraction and by following another's gaze to infer attentional focus. Nonverbal behavior facilitates the motive to understand others' feelings in ordinary personology.

## ATTRIBUTION OF DISPOSITIONS: UNDERSTANDING TRAITS

In studying nonverbal behavior, researchers examine attribution of emotions, which tend to be short term. Psychologists use the term **disposition** to mean an individual quality that is relatively stable, for example, a personality trait. Various theories explain how people infer dispositions from others' and their own behavior, but errors and biases surface in the attribution process. In terms of core motives, people try to understand other people, with an eye to having some sense of control over their social environment. In their errors and biases, though, self-enhancement arises.

### Heider's Attribution Theory: The Naïve Psychology of Traits

Recall that Fritz Heider founded the study of how ordinary people (nonpsychologists) think about each other. Heider (1958) contributed two central ideas about the benefit of studying how regular folks make sense of each other. First, studying how people think about other people provides meaningful data for scientific analysis.

> We shall make use of the unformulated or half-formulated knowledge of interpersonal relations as it is expressed in our everyday language and experience—this source shall be referred to as common-sense or naïve psychology. (p. 4, emphasis added)[3]

This is the same idea as ordinary personology.

Thus, Heider suggested listening to what people say about how they think about people and how they think they think about other people, gathering people's everyday theories. Talking to laypeople can be a source of perfectly good ideas. Heider had a great deal of respect for the ordinary person, despite the fact that he invented the term naïve psychology.

Heider's second major proposal argued that psychologists have to systematize the data from people's everyday experience, making them more precise, coherent, and scientific. Heider's point was that scientific theory and research provide a conceptual framework that reveals common patterns among diverse events. Heider's work painstakingly analyzes ordinary personology, drawing on an impressive range of the then-available science.

> The study of common-sense psychology may be of value because of the truths it contains, notwithstanding the fact that many psychologists have mistrusted and even looked down on such unschooled understanding of human behavior. (p. 5)[4]

People know a lot about other people and how to think about other people. They are not always right, but they do it a lot, and they have ideas about how they do it, so psychologists should listen to them.

---

[3] Copyright © Heider Estate. Reproduced with permission.
[4] Copyright © Heider Estate. Reproduced with permission.

The idea of listening to regular folks was a radical contrast to then-current wisdom in the rest of psychology. Behaviorism dominated psychology, and people's thoughts ranked as intellectually useless garbage: **epiphenomena**, events that were irrelevant to the real causal system. Heider, a recent European refugee of World War II, first in Northampton, Massachusetts, and then in Lawrence, Kansas, created a fresh approach, compared with what most psychologists were doing. He took people's own thoughts seriously, this being a time when the rest of psychology was not really interested in people's thoughts either as data or as inspiration.

**TRAITS: QUICK AND DIRTY TOOLS FOR UNDERSTANDING**    People try to understand other people because it is adaptive for prediction and control. How can a person be effective without knowing what causes people to act the way they do? How can one have some sense of prediction and control without understanding causality, at least using some naïve theory or hunch about causality? Poor Ronald Opus apparently did not have a good theory of what would cause his mother to maintain his financial support. He thought he had a theory of his father's behavior when angry at his mother, which entailed pointing the shotgun at her, although Ronald's timing was off. Knowing how to get somebody else to do something can be a life and death matter in less peculiar but still dangerous circumstances, such as trying to involve bystanders in one's threatened mugging. Note that understanding logically predates control: One can understand and predict events without being able to control them, another person's suicide being a tragic example. Sometimes, people attempt to understand other people out of simple curiosity or entertainment value, without attempting control. Most often, though, people analyze another person in order to create a sense of contingency between what they do with the person and what they get from the interaction. People have lots of theories about what makes people tick (understanding) and what use it serves (controlling). The ordinary personology of traits describes those everyday theories.

Attribution is specifically a subtopic within naïve psychology and ordinary personology, although a major one. The term **attribution** refers to the process by which people explain why somebody did something. In particular, attribution theories focus on how people infer causality for behavior: Given a behavior, why did the person do what he or she did?

Some professors make use of attribution processes when they teach a class that is initially overenrolled. If they do not have enough seats or teaching assistants to manage the overflow, they might make a lot of discouraging comments (that the course is too hard for nonmajors or first-year students, for instance), trying to be grumpy about it, not because they want to throw specific people out but because they are constrained by the situation to limit the number of people in the class. So given that behavior, students could infer either that the professor is a rigid, grumpy person or that the behavior had something to do with the situation, the role that the person is playing, in trying to cut people out of class. What use is the inference about the professor, to a student? The inference that the professor is a grumpy, irritable, rigid person might make one want to drop the class, because who wants to spend the semester with a grumpy, irritable, rigid person? The inference, on the other hand, that the professor is rude because of his or her role and because of the situation at the beginning of the semester might lead one to give this person the benefit of the doubt: Maybe the professor will improve once the class gets down to a better size. (Indeed, the fact that the class is overenrolled might make one want to take it even more.) Those two different causal inferences—dispositional or situational—lead to two different kinds of conclusions about what one should do. Again, an understanding of the professor's motivations determines one's own actions.

**DISPOSITIONS AND SITUATIONS**    This example illustrates the two main kinds of causality that social psychologists have studied: One kind reflects **dispositional** causes, such as mood, personality traits, values, intentions. All these factors indicate internal causes of behavior. The behavior occurs because the person apparently wants to do it, so it reflects will or intent. As the next sections will show, Heider viewed people as searching for **invariance** in behavior, that is, looking for stability. A dispositional property of a person (or an object) "disposes" it to act in a certain way because of its relatively unchanging underlying properties.

Dispositional causality contrasts with **situational** or external causality. In the previous example, their respective social roles create certain demands on a professor or a student, entailing certain obligations. Whether one likes some of them or not, one buys into them when one occupies the role. A role constrains behavior, along with other situational or external causes such as rules, norms, or laws. Situational causes go beyond physical constraints.

How controllable are psychological constraints? For example, the pressure on my students to make the paper airplane the first day of class does not indicate that they have no personal control. Some are reluctant to do it, but everyone does it, so the evidence for situational causality is strong. When someone puts a gun to a person's head and demands money, handing it over counts as responding to a strong situational cause because virtually everyone would respond in the same way. When it's human nature to respond to an incredibly strong situational pressure, then we consider the cause to be the external situation, even though the person actually could resist. Our convention as ordinary people is to say that the situation caused the behavior, even though the person willingly cooperated with the situation. If everyone would do the same thing under the circumstances, we blame the situation. As Daniel Gilbert (1998) puts it:

> Speakers of English have an odd habit and a not so odd habit. The not so odd habit is that they describe behavior that is driven by extraordinary dispositions as having been driven by extraordinary dispositions. The odd habit is that they describe behavior that is driven by ordinary dispositions as having been caused by external agencies.... When situations appeal to or invoke ordinary dispositions, speakers naturally talk about the resulting actions as having been "caused by the situation." (p. 101)[5]

**TRAITS AS INVARIANCES**    Heider's core contributions set the stage for subsequent attribution theories' analysis of how people arrive at trait attributions. As noted, Heider suggested that people look for **invariance**—stable, enduring qualities—in other

---

[5] Copyright © by McGraw-Hill. Reprinted with permission.

people. He described how people observe a variety of behavior and extract the invariance from it. Putting a coin in a bucket, shoveling snow off a sidewalk, reading aloud from a book, and killing a mosquito all may illustrate the single trait of generosity to another person, although they certainly look different.

Heider focused on how people perceive other people's capacity and motivation to produce their actions. He described perceived **capacity** as what a person *can* do and perceived **motivation** as what a person will *try* to do. For example, one will not donate money to charity unless one can do so and tries to do so. Capacity reflects the person's ability, compared with environmental forces. One must have the ability (i.e., the cash), and the environment (one's bank, one's parents, one's partner) must not prevent it. Similarly, motivation reflects the combination of *intention*, that is, one's goal (helping a particular organization), and *exertion*, that is, effort (getting around to doing it). Heider described how observers infer capacity and motivation from observing invariances in people's action.

In summary, Heider noted that commonsense psychology held insights for scientists to analyze, in considering how people think about the causes of other people's behavior. Dispositions and situations provide two explanations with significant real-world implications. Traits and other dispositions reflect invariance—stable, enduring qualities of the individual—reflected in capacity and motivation. Heider set the stage for three important analyses of dispositional inference, by three theorists: Jones, Kelley, and Weiner.

## Inferring Traits from Other People's Behaviors

Attribution theory and person perception emphasize people's core social motive to understand each other and to have some control. That is, people need to have some sense of prediction about other people's actions (understanding) and about their own impact on those actions (control). Prediction and control explain why attribution theory and ordinary personology address people's basic human concerns. And, although parts may seem a little dry or complex, the basic idea is that people try to understand each other. Using an intuitive and relatively automatic process, people do not think about making attributions; they just do it. People are experts at understanding other people—at least we all think we are—but we do not actually understand how we do it until we reflect on it. And attribution theory is one way of systematically reflecting on it.

**JONES'S CORRESPONDENT INFERENCE THEORY**    Edward Jones focused on the motivation (*try*) part (rather then the capacity, *can* part) in Heider's attribution theory, specifically: how people infer other people's intentions from their actions. Having carved out a manageable portion of the entire attribution framework, **correspondent inference theory** (Jones 1979; Jones & Davis, 1965) examined how people decide that an action reflects an intention, that is, how people infer that the action corresponds to an underlying intent.

Jones's theory worked out the information that people use to determine another person's intent. The core of the theory addresses how people make sense of another person's decision to behave in a certain way, given "the number and desirability of the decision's unique consequences" (Gilbert, 1998, p. 96).

Actions have consequences, and some consequences are **unique** (or "**noncommon**," in Jones's original term). Go back to the Ronald Opus bizarre homicide/suicide: Suppose the medical examiner needs to infer Opus's intent in deciding to jump off his parents' ten-story building, as opposed to other tall buildings. A jump off any tall building could have the common consequence of causing his death. One unique consequence of jumping off his parents' building could have been to inflict his death on them, hoping they would discover his body. From this, then, one might infer his intent.

Given unique consequences, first the examiner has to consider the sheer number of them. If an action has only one unique consequence, compared with alternative choices, that unique consequence is informative as to intent. The single consequence seems to fit the choice of venue for his suicide. Similarly, consider his father's choice to brandish the shotgun at his mother, as compared with other ways of having an argument; this action could have one unique consequence, namely, terrifying her. Alternatively, if the action has multiple unique consequences (protecting himself and dominating her), then the person's intent is ambiguous, because any of the consequences might have been intended. For example, writing a suicide note, by itself, is ambiguous, for it could reveal a plan to communicate from beyond the grave, a cry for help, or the writer's need to mull over his problems. The intent behind a choice with multiple unique effects is less clear than the intent behind a choice with only one major unique effect.

The second element is the **social desirability** of the consequences. If an action, such as going up to the roof, has socially desirable effects (being outside on a nice day), then it reveals little about the person's particular dispositions because most people like nice weather. But if the action has socially undesirable effects (e.g., dying), then the action reveals much about the person's particular dispositions. Jones concentrated on intentions that set the person apart from other people, on average. Thus, the attribution process focuses on extraordinary dispositions, rather than ordinary ones.

The number and desirability of unique effects are illustrated in a classic study (Jones & Harris, 1967). Participants were observers of another person's behavior and its situational constraints. They learned that another student had written an essay for a political science exam (the behavior). As independent variables, (a) the essay either favored or opposed Cuban dictator Fidel Castro, and (b) the direction of the argument was either by choice or by assignment.

The first manipulation, perceived choice, can be seen as one way to operationalize the number of unique consequences (although this is not Jones's original interpretation). If the essay's argument results from free choice, then it has only one unique effect, namely, to express one's views. If the essay's argument is written by assignment, then it meets the assignment, and it may or may not express one's views. Writing the assigned argument is less informative because it has multiple possible effects.

The second manipulation, the essay's actual argument (pro or con Castro), operationalizes social desirability, where a pro-Castro essay would be seen as the socially undesirable direction. Thus, the study had two independent variables, perceived choice

**Table 3.4**    Attitudes Attributed to Essay Writers

| Type of Essay Written | Essay Writer's Situation | |
| --- | --- | --- |
| | Choice | No Choice |
| Pro-Castro (Socially undesirable) | 59.62 | 44.10 |
| Anti-Castro (Socially desirable) | 17.38 | 22.87 |

Higher numbers indicate attributed attitudes that are more Pro-Castro.
*Source:* From Jones & Harris, 1967, Study 1. Copyright © Elsevier. Adapted with permission.

and social desirability of essay. According to Jones, writing a freely chosen, socially undesirable essay should be most informative about the writer's attitudes. Writing the socially desirable essay, with or without choice, is not especially informative about the writer's attitudes.

The dependent variables were ten items, each implying the writer's true attitude (e.g., whether the writer would agree with statements such as "Cuba has as much right as any other country to choose her own form of government, free from outside interference by the United States"). Because the ten items appeared on 7-point scales, the total score could range from 10 (attributed attitude anti-Castro) to 70 (attributed attitude pro-Castro).

Looking at Table 3.4, notice first the main effect of the essay variable: Writing a pro-Castro essay elicits an attributed attitude that is more pro-Castro (about 52, averaged over the levels of choice), whereas an anti-Castro essay elicits an attributed attitude that is more anti-Castro (about 20, averaged over choice). There is no main effect of the choice variable averaged over essay; the averages are about 38 and 34, not statistically different.

Jones and Harris hypothesized an interaction between the two independent variables, such that participants would make stronger inferences about the essay writers when their essays were written by choice (had one primary, unique consequence) and when they were in the socially undesirable direction. Indeed, participants made more extreme inferences in this combination of circumstances.

Notice that choice interacted with essay also as follows: Remember that choice allows the inference that the person's behavior was internally caused, whereas the no-choice condition locks in an external cause. Choice indeed makes for stronger correspondent inference, in that the direction of the essay makes a bigger difference in the choice condition (59.62 versus 17.38, about 38 points difference) than in the no-choice condition (44.10 versus 22.87, about 21 points difference). That fits the theory, as Jones originally described it, namely, that choice is a prerequisite for inferring intent. It also fits the theory as described here, in that the unique consequence in the no-choice condition is fulfilling the exam requirement, whereas the consequences in the choice condition are both fulfilling the exam requirement and expressing one's opinion, so the attribution is less clear.

A third aspect of the interaction is that the socially undesirable pro-Castro essay makes a stronger correspondent inference: Comparing the 59.62 versus 44.10 in the socially undesirable pro-Castro condition shows a bigger difference than the 17.38

versus 22.87 in the socially desirable anti-Castro condition. A bigger effect of choice for the pro-Castro essay than for the anti-Castro essay occurs because the anti-Castro essay is what everybody would do. Another way to put it is that choice exaggerates the attribution about a socially undesirable response. This shows the interaction of the two independent variables.

The last point concerns what observers actually do overall. Return to the main effect for social desirability, the direction of the essay that is actually written. That's the approximately 52 versus the 20 that constitutes a main effect. Writing a pro essay (regardless of choice) resulted in attributions of a pro-Castro attitude, compared with writing an anti-Castro essay. Notice that it reflects a tendency to assume that people's behavior reflects (corresponds to) an underlying intent. Even when the essay writer had no choice, people assume the essay reflects the person's attitude to some extent. Even in the case where people should not be making an inference, the no-choice condition, they still are. Even when the writer had no choice about the direction of the essay—that is, the instructor required an exam answer in this direction—observers still assume that the essay reflects the person's attitude. Logically, the assigned essay tells nothing about the person's attitude; a later section will come back to this biased judgment.

Whether concerned with inferences about attitudes or personality, Jones termed these dispositional attributions correspondent inferences. A **correspondent inference** reflects people's attribution that somebody's behavior reveals (corresponds to) an underlying disposition, such as a trait, attitude, or intention. As noted, most of the theory concerns principles of correspondence: the number and social desirability of the action's unique (noncommon) effects.

**KELLEY'S COVARIATION THEORY**    Harold Kelley's theory (Kelley, 1967, 1972) and Jones's theory have two important differences and two important similarities (see Table 3.5). First, whereas Jones focused on the covariation (correlation) of actions and their *consequences* as a key to attribution, Kelley's **covariation theory** argued the complementary view, focusing on the covariation (correlation) of actions and their potential *causes* as the key to attribution. Second, Kelley's theory tackles a different domain from the Jones correspondent inference theory, largely because the Jones model accounts for the degree to which *one behavior*, or one choice, reflects somebody's disposition. Kelley's theory accounts for *repeated observations*, multiple encounters with the behavior. Multiple observations enable Kelley's theory to ask about consistency over time: How often has this person behaved this way? For example, in the case of Mr. Opus, Senior, the report that he habitually (consistently) threatened his wife with a shotgun is more informative than knowing that he did so on one occasion.

The two theories' similarities are often unappreciated (Gilbert, 1998). Kelley proposed that people infer the causes of action by looking at the covariation of behavior and its potential causes, using three principles, two similar to those of Jones. Suppose that we want to know why Harold chooses to live in Los Angeles. Observers first ask about **consensus**, what other people have done. Does everyone else want to live in Los Angeles, or is Harold the only one? Kelley identified consensus, similarly to

**Table 3.5**  Comparing the Jones and Kelley Attribution Theories: Why Harold Chooses to Live in Los Angeles

|  | Jones's Theory of Correspondent Inference | Kelley's Theory of Covariation |
|---|---|---|
| **Differences in scope** | | |
| Focus on | Consequences of behavior (effects of Harold's choice) | Causes of behavior (determinant of Harold's choice) |
| Explain | Single behavior (a one-time choice) | Pattern of behavior (repeated choices over time): Consistency (Does Harold always choose L.A.?) |
| **Similarities in kinds of information** | | |
| What other people do | Social desirability (Is L.A. generally preferred?) | Consensus (Do most people choose L.A.?) |
| What other entities evoke | Unique (noncommon) effects (What's special about L.A.?) | Distinctiveness (Does only L.A. get chosen?) |

Jones identifying social desirability. If consensus is high, then the action is socially desirable. If everyone wants to live in Los Angeles, then Harold's behavior reflects something about Los Angeles, whereas if hardly anyone does, then Harold's choice reflects something about Harold's unique preferences.

Observers, second, ask whether the behavior, in this case establishing a home, is distinctively addressed to a particular entity or indiscriminately addressed to various entities. Does Harold choose to live in multiple cities (suppose he is rich), or does he call only Los Angeles his home? The concern with **distinctiveness** is similar to Jones's concern with unique effects; has Harold chosen Los Angeles in particular, or is his choice more indiscriminant? The more distinctive his choice, the more it has something to do with the unique effects of living in Los Angeles; the less discriminating his choice, the more the behavior reflects Harold's disposition to adore all cities in general. The distinctiveness factor resembles Jones's unique effects criterion.

Finally, Kelley identified **consistency** over time as important to attribution. Does Harold choose to live in Los Angeles over a long period of time, or does he move around a lot? If his choice is consistent over time, then it is more likely to reflect something long-term about Harold (an enduring disposition), rather than some temporary circumstances.

One useful way to make sense of these attributional questions—consensus, distinctiveness, and consistency—is to consider the behavior in question ("chooses to live in") as part of a simple sentence the observer tries to explain. In our previous example, we have been trying to explain why "Harold chooses to live in Los Angeles." Consensus varies the subject of the verb, Harold: Is it "only Harold" or "many people" who would choose to live in Los Angeles? Distinctiveness information varies the object of the verb, Los Angeles: Does Harold live in "only Los Angeles," or "many cities"? Consistency varies the implicit adverb "all the time" or "only once." Combining all three factors, if "*only* Harold chooses *many* cities *all the time*," then we know that, respectively, consensus is low ("only Harold"), distinctiveness is low ("many cities"), and consistency is high ("all the time"), so Harold is an obsessive urban dweller, which explains his living in any city, and it has less to do with Los Angeles. On the other hand, if "everyone wants to live in Los Angeles" (consensus and therefore social desirability is high), and, moreover, this is true of "only Los Angeles" (distinctiveness to the entity is high, or there is only one, unique choice), and it is true consistently, the combination tells us that Harold lives in Los Angeles because Los Angeles is special.

This kind of attributional analysis can be applied to any behavior that occurs by choice. If only Julia arrives in class late, but she does it in all her classes and does it consistently, then she is a tardy person. If, however, everyone in the class arrives late and Julia does so in only this class, and she does it consistently, then there is something about that class that causes her lackadaisical behavior. These two patterns allow unambiguous inferences. Mixtures of these two patterns do not allow clear causal analysis, as when everyone arrives late at this class, but Julia also arrives at all her classes late, so it could be something either about Julia or about this particular class. Her arriving late to this class has two possible causes, so the role of either cause is discounted (diminished) because the other is present; Kelley called this the **discounting principle**, and Jones would have called it a lack of unique effects. If Julia is late to class *despite* the threat of detention, then the **augmenting principle** says her predisposition to be late is especially potent.

Just like Jones, Kelley realized that if a behavior covaries with more than one factor (causes, in Kelley's case; effects, in Jones's case), then the attribution is ambiguous. Think back to the methods chapter; the same principle operates in scientific causality. If a researcher does not isolate an independent variable, a potentially causal variable, but confounds it with another (unintended) variable, then the researcher cannot draw any reliable causal inferences from the variable's effects. Is it any wonder that Kelley's model evokes the image of people as scientists, albeit naïve (amateur) ones? Overall, Kelley's contribution, in true Heider fashion, systematizes the principles that people all use intuitively. People can think about the three logical types of information—consistency, distinctiveness, consensus—in order to attribute causality.

An experiment tested Kelley's theory of the information people use to attribute causes of behavior (McArthur, 1972). Participants read sentences describing people's responses: John laughs at the comedian, Sue is afraid of the dog, George translates the sentence incorrectly, Bill thinks his teacher is unfair, Ralph trips over Joan's feet while dancing. Three additional pieces of information followed each sentence: consensus ("Almost everyone ... " or "Hardly anyone ... "), distinctiveness (this person does or does not respond the same way to "almost every other ... " comedian, dog, sentence, teacher, partner's feet), and consistency ("In the past, ... has almost always ... " or "almost never"). Participants chose among four alternative causes for the initial response: something about the person, stimulus, particular circumstances, or a combination of these factors. Table 3.6 summarizes the basic results, and two of

**Table 3.6**   Which Covariation Information Influences Which Causal Attributions

| | Type of Causal Attribution | | |
| Type of Covariation | Person | Entity | Circumstances |
| --- | --- | --- | --- |
| Consensus information | **6.25%** | 5.17% | .30% |
| Distinctiveness information | 21.72% | **12.12%** | 7.58% |
| Consistency information | 15.76% | 5.88% | **41.36%** |

Higher numbers indicate that the type of attribution (column headings) was most influenced by that type of covariation information (row headings). Numbers do not add to 100% because these sources of influence are not exhaustive. Numbers in bold were hypothesized to be largest in their respective columns.
*Source:* From McArthur, 1972. Copyright © American Psychological Association. Adapted with permission.

the three types of information operate as hypothesized. Of the three types of information, distinctiveness influenced entity attributions the most, and consistency by far influenced circumstances the most. Contrary to predictions, consensus did not influence person attributions the most. Later studies confirmed this underuse of consensus information, as we will see, but all three typically have some influence on attributions, supporting the broad outlines of Kelley's theory.

**NORMATIVE MODELS: DO PEOPLE BOTHER THIS MUCH OVER CAUSAL ATTRIBUTION?**   Perhaps causal attribution seems a complex analysis for everyday use. Do people really bother this much? At least three answers tackle this question. First, research suggests that people can use these three types of information when provided, but they probably use consistency the most, distinctiveness moderately, and consensus the least (Major, 1980; McArthur, 1972). People may not always be as thorough as the Kelley theory implies.

Second, people may in fact do the full Kelley analysis mainly when the outcome truly matters, for example, in explaining their closest relationships. Suppose that Harriet rejects Tom, after a long-term relationship. What is Tom's first response, apart from feeling hurt? First, Tom checks to be absolutely certain Harriet means it; if Harriet is sure over time, then she is consistent. People always have to have high consistency to make any kind of inference. If the person flip-flops, then one cannot make an inference. (Both the earlier examples have high consistency: Harold chooses to live in Los Angeles for a while, and Julia is late to class every time.) Without consistency, one cannot attribute any causality because the rejection is just a fluke, a random blip.

If Harriet is consistently sure that the relationship is over, Tom then wonders whether this has happened only to him, as an object of Harriet's rejection. In other words, is this distinctive to him as the rejected entity, or does this person leave everyone? If Harriet has a pattern of rejection, then it is not unique to poor old Tom. Then, the last questions that Tom might ask concern consensus: Has this happened to him before? Have other people treated him this way? Does he have a history of being rejected after a certain amount of time? What is it about him? When something hurtful happens, people do consider whether other people have treated them the same way, that is, whether there is consensus about them, that is, consensus across other actors.

Third, in answer to the question about whether people actually take this much trouble in making attributions, the Jones theory and the Kelley theory are **normative models**: that is, they describe people's ideal attribution processes, when they are thinking according to an ideal or standard. Note that calling these models *normative* does not reflect how social psychologists usually use the term *norm*. Here, *normative* means a model of people thinking according to the highest standards, according to idealized models of how people would think given all the available information, unlimited time, and no biases.

## WHY DO ATTRIBUTIONS MATTER? WEINER'S APPLICATIONS

Normative or not, attributions are important in a broad range of cases. Consider perceptions of people who are poor. Two broad sets of explanations are available (Kluegel & Smith, 1986). Individual (dispositional) explanations cite a supposed lack of thrift, ability, effort, and morals, whereas structural (situational) explanations cite poor schools, chaotic environments, low wages, exploitation, and lack of jobs.

Certain political beliefs correlate with dispositional attributions. That is, individualistic, controllable, blameworthy perceived causes predict anger (Zucker & Weiner, 1993). In this view, people are poor because they refuse to work hard, do not improve themselves, cannot manage money, and abuse drugs or alcohol. These beliefs about poor people correlate with conservative political opinions. Less conservative beliefs correlate with situational attributions: perceiving societal causes, feeling pity, and intending to help. In this view, people are poor because of prejudice and discrimination, inadequate education, exploitation by the rich, and low wages (see Table 3.7). The conservative dispositional attributions imply that poor people have a controllable predisposition to stay poor.

But consider this: While many Americans believe that those who are poor will remain dependent for years on public assistance, research has found that one of three people living below poverty will lift himself or herself out of poverty within twelve months ("Welfare stereotype ... ," 1996). That does not fit a stable dispositional

**Table 3.7**   Correlations of Conservatism with Beliefs about the Causes of Poverty

| Belief | Correlation |
|---|---|
| Individual causes | .19 |
| Societal causes | −.39 |
| Controllability | .21 |
| Blame | .24 |
| Pity | −.36 |
| Anger | .20 |
| Desire to help | −.30 |
| Approval of welfare | −.37 |

All correlations are statistically significant.

*Source:* From Zucker & Weiner, 1993. Copyright © Winston. Adapted with permission.

attribution. Other people often assume that poor people live primarily off of welfare benefits, but studies have found that less than half of poor people actually receive cash benefits from the government. While the poor are assumed to be anti-work, the study found that 50% of the nation's poor are either children ineligible to work or people over 65 years of age, which also does not fit a personality predisposition to be lazy or irresponsible. Moreover, many situational events can force people onto welfare, but these are rarely discussed. A single mother might live in an area without jobs, child care, or affordable transportation, especially in remote rural areas where (contrary to myth) a great many people on welfare actually live.

The point is that if an observer thinks that poor people are lazy, immoral, and unskilled, then that causal explanation suggests certain kinds of solutions, namely, motivate them to work. If the observer thinks people are poor for situational reasons, then that causal explanation suggests other kinds of solutions, namely, improve the situation. Public policy results from people's theories about the dispositional or situational causes for other people's behavior. Much argument about who is on welfare and why is a causal argument, an argument about attribution.

Similar debates occur in attributions for educational outcomes and emotional reactions to people with social stigmas, points to which the stereotyping chapter will return. For now, consider Weiner's analysis of achievement attributions. Suppose a classmate asks to borrow your notes for a missed class. In one case, the classmate was ill and missed class. In another case, the classmate did not feel like attending class and went instead to the beach. In which case are you more likely to lend your notes? In which case do you feel pity and in which case annoyance or even anger? Weiner (1980) conducted precisely these experiments, finding what the theory predicted. Weiner (1985) has identified three attributional dimensions that describe possible causes: locus (internal/external), stability, and controllability. Generally, Weiner has found that when people fail for internal, controllable reasons, such as lack of effort, others feel anger and do not help. When a person fails for uncontrollable reasons (such as task difficulty, lack of ability, luck), others feel pity and help.

**SUMMARY**    As the methods chapter noted, psychologists (and other scientists) look for two events (or variables) to be correlated (or covary) in order to infer causality. When two events covary, one may be causing the other. According to Kelley, observers essentially analyze the effects associated with three different independent variables. That is, they look for the possible effects of: time (consistency), entity (distinctiveness), and actor (consensus). Jones essentially addressed the latter two. Not surprisingly, people talk about the Jones and Kelley attribution theories as being models of the naïve scientist. The idea of a naïve scientist fits with the core social motive to understand the social world around us. As this chapter described earlier, ordinary personology describes lay psychology, ordinary people thinking about other people. The Kelley and Jones normative models allowed researchers to compare people with idealized standards of what people would do if they were thinking carefully. Weiner's applications show how much attributions matter to social policy, so people's adherence to normative models matters to real-world issues. In fact, as we will see, people are not quite that careful, much of the time. Before getting to people's carelessness, though, let's consider two more theories about attribution of dispositions. The models discussed so far concern people making inferences about other people. Attribution principles also apply to people making inferences about themselves.

## Inferring Dispositions from Our Own Behavior

The first theory of inference about oneself concerns attributing attitudes to oneself; the second concerns attributing emotions. Both focus on the core social motive of understanding.

**BEM'S SELF-PERCEPTION THEORY OF ATTITUDES**    People do not always know their own attitudes, emotions, and traits. When people do have to infer their own dispositions, how do they do it? Daryl Bem (1972) proposed that people infer their own internal states, just as outsiders do: They observe their own behavior and, to the extent the situation is not a plausible cause, they infer that their dispositions must be the cause.

> Individuals come to "know" their own attitudes, emotions, and other
> internal states partially by inferring them from observations of their own
> overt behavior and the circumstances under which this behavior occurs.
> Thus, to the extent that internal cues are weak, ambiguous, or
> uninterpretable, the individual is functionally in the same position as an
> outside observer, an observer who must necessarily rely on those same
> external cues to infer the individual's internal states. (p. 2)[6]

Bem's peculiar and radical position claims that people have no privileged access to their own internal states, at least when the internal cues are "weak, ambiguous, or uninterpretable."

Most of the time, as an adult, one knows one's attitudes: If a friend asks, "Do you like anchovies on your pizza?" you know the answer right away. You do not even have to think about it because anchovies do not create an internal state that is "weak, ambiguous, or uninterpretable," and the attitude is already stored anyway, as it has probably come up before. Instead, suppose the friend asks about portabella mushrooms on pizza. What do you do first? Unless you automatically hate all mushrooms or all new food experiences, you consider your previous behavior with regard to these giants among mushrooms and how you reacted, assuming free choice. Similarly, people sometimes wonder if they love someone's company, like their work, or enjoy exercising by asking similar questions (e.g., do I seem to choose this activity when I have free time?). Thus, a novel question, an attitude not considered before, along with ambiguous internal reactions, fits contexts in which Bem's **self-perception theory** proposes that people think about past behavior and then infer internal states such as attitudes from the past behavior.

The challenging part of Bem's theory is that other people can make the same conclusion about one's attitude just by observing one's behavior and by looking at

---

[6] Copyright © Daryl Bem. Reprinted with permission.

the environmental constraints on it. People do not necessarily know their own attitudes better than some observer would. We are used to thinking that we know ourselves best and that we know our own preferences better than other people do. But maybe not. Have you ever had a close friend say, "You really like that person, don't you?" before you admitted it to yourself? Bem's theory best accounts for those circumstances where one does not know one's own mind or attitude ahead of time.

One of the most provocative lines of research to emerge from self-perception theory concerns the **overjustification effect**, which operates like this: If one has situational justifications for one's behavior, such as external rewards, then one does not need to make a dispositional attribution for it. If the unfortunate Ronald Opus from the chapter's outset had behaved affectionately toward his mother while she was financially supporting him, would either he himself or an outside observer assume that he truly respected or loved her? Fear, maybe, but genuine filial devotion, no, not necessarily. If he was nice to her when she was paying him, he could attribute his behavior to her financial rewards, but not necessarily to love. Consider, then, what could have happened from Ronald Opus's point-of-view, when she ceased supporting him. The external reason for his previous devotion vanishes; because of the money as a sufficient explanation for his behavior, he might not really experience himself as loving her. Does that make it easier to be angry and plot her death? Probably.

To take a more mundane example, consider the not-uncommon practice of parents rewarding their children for studying. Indeed, some New York City schools have undertaken an experiment of paying children for exam results, testing Roland Fryer's economic theory of incentives for performance (Medine, 2008). Consider the possible unintended consequences: If a child likes to read, for example, and receives a gold star for each book completed, the child may infer that the reading is motivated by the rewards. If the rewards discontinue, then the reading may too, creating in the long-term an effect opposite to that intended. A classic study demonstrated this phenomenon (Lepper, Greene, & Nisbett, 1973).

Some nursery school children, more than their classmates, loved to draw with felt-tip pens (then rare in classrooms); they were assigned to one of three conditions: expected award, unexpected award, or no award for drawing with the pens. Which children might infer that they were using the pens only because of the award? Only those children who expected the award while they were drawing. Which children might infer that they actually loved to draw with the markers? Only the children who drew without thought of a reward. Indeed, a couple of weeks later, the children were given access to the pens during a free-choice play period, now without any expectation of award, and the previously rewarded children—now that the reward had been withdrawn—played with the markers half as much as the previously unrewarded or unexpected-reward children, who had only themselves to credit for their previous interest in the markers (see Table 3.8).

Meta-analysis of later work (Deci, Koestner, & Ryan, 1999) shows that intrinsic (internal) rewards are the best motivators, with extrinsic (external) rewards undermining enduring interest. Whether rewards are contingent on merely task engagement, task completion, or performance quality, they undermine subsequent free choice of the previously rewarded behavior. Freely chosen activities are most likely to endure.

**Table 3.8**   Overjustification: Free-Choice Play with Previously Rewarded Activity

| Result of Original Choice to Play | Playing with Felt-Tip Markers |
| --- | --- |
| Expected award | 8.59 |
| No award | 16.73 |
| Unexpected award | 18.09 |

Numbers represent percent of total free-play time.

*Source:* From Lepper et al., 1973. Copyright © American Psychological Association. Adapted with permission.

People's appetite for choice is finite, however; people are more motivated by a limited array of choices (e.g., six) than by a huge array (24) (Iyengar & Lepper, 2000).

Whereas the evidence for overjustification is strong in the United States, it rests on this culture's bias toward individual autonomy and perceived choice. In more interdependent cultures, children's intrinsic motivation increases when choices are made for them by trusted authorities or peers (Iyengar & Lepper, 1999). Thus, the universality of these effects is open to investigation. In any case, the overjustification effect is but one application of self-perception theory. A later chapter revisits self-perception theory in the context of attitude change.

## SCHACHTER'S TWO-FACTOR THEORY OF ATTRIBUTING EMOTION

Another self-attributional theory, Stanley Schachter's (1964) **cognition-arousal theory**, concerns inferences about how people attribute emotions to themselves. Emotions might seem borderline as dispositions, because emotions are more transitory than personality traits or attitudes, but emotions are still internal states. This theory comes back at least twice later on in the text because early on, it captured the imagination of social psychologists. (Other theories of emotion surface in other chapters.) Schachter had an idea equally radical to Bem's, namely, that people do not always know their own feelings. He proposed that emotions result from undifferentiated physiological arousal, combined with an explanation that seems reasonable in context: "an emotional state may be considered a function of a state of physiological arousal and of a cognition appropriate to this state of arousal." He elaborated that the relevant cognitions were those "arising from the immediate situation as interpreted by past experience" (Schachter, 1964, p. 51).

To test the idea that emotions boil down to arousal plus cognition that labels the arousal, a classic experiment (Schachter & Singer, 1962) manipulated (a) physiological arousal and information about it, as well as (b) a social situation that would suggest an emotional label. To manipulate arousal, under the guise of studying a vitamin compound called Suproxin, the researchers injected participants with a placebo (inert substance) or epinephrine (adrenaline). Adrenaline initiates sympathetic arousal, and the injection's effects lasted about 15 to 20 minutes on average. Some of the adrenaline participants were informed that the injection might make them feel jittery, and others received no information. (Others were provided misleading side effects, but this complicates the design beyond our scope here.) Thus, participants were given either

(a) the placebo, so not aroused, or (b) the adrenaline, so aroused, and informed, or (c) adrenaline, so aroused, but not informed (three levels, first independent variable).

Then participants encountered an alleged fellow participant (actually a confederate of the experimenter). In a room littered with scrap paper, rubber bands, pencils, and file folders, the confederate behaved in either a goofy, euphoric manner (shooting baskets with wadded-up paper, flying paper airplanes, shooting wads of paper with rubber bands) or in an angry, outraged manner (complaining about an increasingly personal and insulting questionnaire they took, refusing to answer some items, and finally tearing and crumpling it before leaving abruptly); this emotional context, then, constituted the second independent variable. At this point, the experimenter returned and asked participants to complete a questionnaire assessing their hunger, fatigue, and mood, any of which supposedly might influence their performance on a subsequent vision test, the alleged focus of the study. The main dependent variables were their ratings of current mood, including *irritated, angry, or annoyed* and *good or happy*.

Table 3.9 summarizes the results. In the euphoria condition, as predicted, people uninformed about the epinephrine (i.e., those experiencing unexplained physiological arousal) reported feeling happier, and they acted happier than people informed about its effects (i.e., those experiencing fully explained arousal); the placebo condition fell in between, although it should have been equivalent to the unexplained group. In the anger condition, as predicted, those uninformed about the epinephrine expressed more anger than those informed; the placebo condition again fell between the two. Although the results are less clear than one might hope, and the design is complex, this classic study supports the idea that participants injected with the epinephrine, if they lacked adequate explanation for their resulting arousal, used cues from the environment to label their feelings.

In his theory, Schachter gives varied examples of arousal—in response to a figure with a gun in a dark alley, labeling the arousal as fear; suddenly learning one has made Phi Beta Kappa, labeling the arousal as joy; fighting with a spouse, labeling the arousal as anger; being in the presence of a sexy person, labeling the arousal as love or lust. This deceptively simple attributional theory thus holds that emotion results from unexplained arousal and cognitive labels from the situation. But one implication is that people can be manipulated into states of fear, euphoria, anger, or amusement, given otherwise unexplained arousal.

**Table 3.9**    Self-Reported Emotions, as a Function of Arousal and Social Context

| | Self-Reported Emotion, per Social Context | |
| --- | --- | --- |
| Arousal Condition | Euphoria | Anger |
| Informed | 0.98 | 1.91 |
| Ignorant | 1.78 | 1.39 |
| Placebo | 1.61 | 1.63 |

Higher numbers indicate more happiness and less anger. This table omits the euphoria-misinformed condition in the original study, for ease of explanation.

*Source:* From Schachter & Singer, 1962.

A series of studies explored this idea that people might misattribute their arousal and therefore their emotional reaction. A Cornell study (Dutton & Aron, 1974) arranged for men to be interviewed by an attractive young woman, either immediately or ten minutes after they had crossed a narrow, 450-foot suspension footbridge over rocks and rapids in a deep canyon, the bridge having a tendency to "tilt, sway, and wobble," thereby provoking physiological arousal. Men interviewed immediately were more likely to display sexual imagery in stories they wrote in response to ambiguous pictures. They also were twice as likely to call the attractive interviewer later, compared with men interviewed by the same woman but after their arousal had faded. In another study, men awaiting strong electric shock (and therefore aroused) were more likely to find a female confederate attractive, compared with men anticipating only weak shock. The strategy of taking one's date to a roller coaster or a thriller movie becomes apparent.

## Summary of Dispositional Attribution Theories

The attribution theories of Jones and Kelley both describe how people explain other people's behavior. Both theories are, to a great extent, normative models that describe how careful or motivated people would make attributions, considering a lot of evidence. Both theories (see Table 3.5) focus on covariation of behavior, with either potential causes (Kelley) or effects (Jones). Attribution depends on the number of unique covariates (Jones's noncommon effects; Kelley's distinctiveness over entities) and their social desirability (Jones's social desirability; Kelley's consensus over actors). Kelley added that consistency over time allows firmer attributions. Weiner applies attributional concepts of stability, locus, and controllability to achievement, poverty, and more.

Bem and Schachter both focus on how people attribute internal (quasi-dispositional) states to themselves (see Table 3.10), arguing that people observe their behavior (Bem) or their arousal (Schachter) and examine the relevant situational constraints (Bem) or labels (Schachter) to assign a feeling to themselves, whether attitude (Bem) or emotion (Schachter).

Notice that all of these theories examine situational constraints. Jones assumes that actors have to have a choice because otherwise the situation totally constrains behavior and then observers cannot make a correspondent inference. Kelley asks whether the behavior happens to everyone in that situation, in which case the situation constrains the behavior. Bem explicitly implicates environmental constraints. And Schachter also

**Table 3.10**  Comparing the Bem and Schachter Self-Attribution Theories

| People's Processes | Bem's Theory of Self-Perception | Schachter's Cognition-Arousal Theory of Emotion |
|---|---|---|
| Notice: | Own behavior | Own arousal |
| Examine situation for: | Constraints | Labels |
| Attribute: | Own attitude | Own emotion |

emphasizes environmental cues (though not exactly constraints). In their emphasis on taking account of the social situation, attribution theories are fundamentally social psychological theories, taking account of situational influences on people's behavior. Regardless, these theories describe people following the core social motive to understand their social world and (at least potentially) control what happens to them, reflecting another core social motive.

## ERRORS AND BIASES IN ATTRIBUTION: CONTROLLING AND SELF-ENHANCING

Although attribution theories specify that ordinary personologists should take some account of the social situation, by attending to social constraints, the evidence is weak that they actually do so, to any major degree. Ordinary personologists resemble everyday *personality* psychologists, emphasizing dispositions more than situations. The normative models of Jones and Kelley paint a stark contrast to **descriptive models** that specify how people actually function, complete with all their errors and biases. Whereas the normative models reflect the core social motive of understanding and to some extent control, the descriptive models especially reflect core social motives of control and self-enhancement. Descriptive models come in two kinds: ones showing that people err by believing someone is in control, when no one is, and ones showing that people err by enhancing themselves. These descriptive models also vary as a function of cultures and individuals.

### Believing Someone Is in Control: Ignoring the Hidden Power of Situations

What happens when normative models meet reality? People turn out not to be so rational. They are not quite such good scientists as expected and instead are prone to a whole litany of mistakes. These biases all overemphasize the role of individual dispositions in guiding people's behavior, implying that other people control their own behavior more than they feel they do. Several of these biases share the property of believing that *someone* controls the behavior and, by extension, that the situation or random events do not. Believing someone is in control ignores the hidden power of situations. The biases promote the idea that some person—rather than impersonal forces—controls behavior.

**UNDERUSE OF CONSENSUS INFORMATION**    The first bias that social psychologists discovered is that people do not use Kelley's consensus information as much as theoretically supposed (Kassin, 1979). Recall McArthur's (1972) data (Table 3.6) showing that people use distinctiveness information to make entity attributions and consistency information to make circumstance attributions, but unexpectedly, people do not use consensus information to make person attributions. People underuse information about what everyone else does. If observers fail to take everyone else into account, then observers will tend to view the actor's behavior as unique to that actor, increasing the odds of dispositional attributions.

**CORRESPONDENCE BIAS**  Jones (1990) identified this phenomenon as the **correspondence bias**, namely that observers have a broad tendency to see behavior as corresponding to dispositions even when it may not. This is illustrated by the study (Jones & Harris, 1967; see Table 3.5), in which essay writers praised or criticized Fidel Castro. Even those writers who had no choice of essay topics were seen as endorsing the position they represented on paper; if observers had taken full account of the situational constraints, the direction of the essay should not have mattered and the 21-point difference on a scale of 10 to 70 should not have occurred. This, of course, is an unreasonable but all-too-human inference, as any debate-team member knows. Advocates worry that the audience will think that they must believe the side they are arguing. However, people overestimate observers' correspondence bias (Van Boven, Kamada, & Gilovich, 1999), so maybe opinion advocates worry too much.

**FUNDAMENTAL ATTRIBUTION ERROR**  In a similar vein, Lee Ross (1977) identified the **fundamental attribution error** as being the "general tendency to overestimate the importance of personal or dispositional factors relative to environmental influences" (p. 184). This error plagues students and professionals in social psychology as well:

> Many of the best known and most provocative studies in our field depend, for their impact, on the reader's erroneous expectation that individual differences and personal dispositions will overcome relative mundane situational variables. (p. 186)[7]

Recall, from this book's opening chapter, that people are likely to explain other people's behavior in terms of their personalities and not so much in terms of the situation, yet the situation often matters more. Alerting people to the often-ignored impact of the situation defines social psychology's mission, of course, but it can be a mission only if no one else (i.e., the average person) has chosen to accept it. The widespread assumption that mainly dispositions cause behavior gives the field its impact.

**ACTOR-OBSERVER EFFECT**  For a change of pace and an illustration, consider the following: Take a break from reading, and rate on a scale from 1 (*low*) to 5 (*high*) to what extent each of the following are the reasons you chose your college:

- Parental wishes
- Desire to get away from home
- Friends' choices
- Good location
- Prestige
- Desire to find a marriage partner
- A good social life
- Ease of getting admitted.

---

[7] Copyright © Lee Ross. Reprinted with permission.

(This illustration works best if you record the numbers.) Now rate all the reasons the typical student at your college picked it, again recording the answers.

When you are done, see how often you rated the typical student higher than yourself, yourself higher than the typical student, or the two about equally. Usually, when my students do this, all the motivations on average are more easily attributed to the typical student than to one's self. Rating these motives as important is akin to making a dispositional attribution. Any given dispositional motivation is easier to attribute to other people than to attribute to yourself. Other people pick college for dispositional reasons, whereas our own reasons for picking college are never quite so predictable. This illustrates one way of looking at the actor-observer effect.

The **actor-observer effect** goes one step farther than the previous three—the underuse of consensus information, the correspondence bias, and the fundamental attribution error—all of which concern judgments about someone else's behavior being caused by dispositions more than it actually is. Observers do overattribute actors' behavior to dispositions, as noted, but to what do actors attribute their own behavior? Actors tend to see their own behavior in terms of the situation, according to Jones and Nisbett (1972).

The actor-observer effect holds that attributing dispositions to other people comes easily (that part comprises the underuse of consensus, the correspondence bias, the fundamental attribution error). What's more, however, the actor-observer effect adds that people do not like to attribute dispositions to themselves. Instead, people tend to explain their own behavior much more by pointing to the particular situation (and not a particular disposition). So, for example, suppose an applicant is late to a job interview; for the interviewer, an internal reason is the cause (the applicant is careless), but for the applicant, an external situation is the cause (the dog ate my car). The actor-observer asymmetry is clearest for negative behavior, idiosyncratic actors, hypothetical events, free-response explanations, and intimate relationships (Malle, 2006). Some of these factors hint at a defense explanation for the asymmetry; we will come back to this.

Perversely, people reinforce the actor-observer phenomenon by claiming a whole gamut of *potential* dispositions (and again not one particular disposition) for themselves. Thus, people view themselves as multifaceted and less predictable than other people because which particular disposition they express depends on the situation. A handful of personality traits may describe you, but it does not suffice to describe complicated me. People see themselves as having rich, deep, and adaptive personalities, able to express almost any given trait and its opposite, depending on the circumstances (Sande, Goethals, & Radloff, 1988). Other people, of course, are ruled by their personalities, which have fewer traits than our own personalities, which have many.

## Explaining the Dispositional Bias in Attributions

Recall that ordinary people's dispositional bias fundamentally distinguishes ordinary personology (Heider's phenomenal description) from social psychological analyses emphasizing the situation (Heider's causal description). Hence, understanding the origins (why?) and boundaries (where? who? what?) of dispositional bias is important.

**WHY?**   Various dispositional biases—the underuse of consensus information, the correspondence bias, the fundamental attribution error, and the actor-observer effect—all would suggest that observers are eager to attribute other people's behavior to their (supposedly not terribly complex) personalities. Observers' dispositional bias may come from various mechanisms (Gawronski, 2004; Gilbert & Malone, 1995):

- Dim awareness of another person's situational constraints, which are invisible and difficult to construe properly;
- Categorizing situation-appropriate behavior as nevertheless diagnostic about the actor; and
- People's propensity to start with the dispositional implications of behavior, but not to correct adequately for the impact of the situation.

All these factors implicate observers' underusing the situation as an explanation for their dispositional bias. Some related theories capitalize on the last type of process (Gilbert, Pelham, & Krull, 1988; Quattrone, 1982; Trope, 1986); all contrast a relatively automatic initial stage and a more controlled second stage: People first automatically **categorize** and **characterize** or **identify** (label) the behavior, then they make more deliberate attributional **inferences**, which are **anchored** in that initial labeling of the behavior. This latter stage includes a relatively controlled process of **adjusting** or **correcting** for the situation as a mitigating circumstance. The net result is an attribution that sticks closer to the trait implications of the behavior, having automatically started there, with more controlled and optional adjustments for the situation.

This contrast between relatively automatic and dispositional first steps and relatively controlled and corrective second steps may even be related to reflexive versus more reflective types of brain activity (Lieberman, Gaunt, Gilbert, & Trope, 2002). Relatively automatic dispositional inferences in the Kelley model result from just one combination out of eight (low consensus, high consistency, low distinctiveness), and that particular combination uniquely activates the superior temporal sulcus, a brain region often implicated in inferring people's intent (Harris, Todorov, & Fiske, 2005). Collapsing over consensus information (given its often-weak role), the medial prefrontal cortex also activates (to high consistency, low distinctiveness combinations); this area plays a common role in thinking about individual people. Thus, our brains identifiably respond to dispositional inferences. Work with children identifies these two regions and another (temporo-parietal junction) as critical in making inferences about others' minds (Saxe, Carey, & Kanwisher, 2004).

Why might people have this relatively automatic tendency to emphasize the intrinsic, personal, dispositional causes of behavior? How might it be adaptive? People spontaneously understand behavior in relation to the traits it represents (Uleman, Saribay, & Gonzalez, 2008), and they do so without any instructions. These **spontaneous trait inferences** allow people to form abstract representations instead of merely concrete mental representations. In other words, people make rapid dispositional inferences in order to characterize the behavior. Furthermore, people efficiently form a lasting link from the spontaneously inferred trait to the face of the person doing the behavior (Todorov & Uleman, 2004). Seeing the face, even later, activates brain areas associated with the emotional implications of the spontaneous trait inference (Todorov, Gobbini, Evans, & Haxby, 2007).

This spontaneous tendency to believe the implication of behavior may go far beyond spontaneous dispositional attributions from behavior. Perhaps people can't not believe everything they see (at first) (Gilbert, 1991): People have an automatic tendency to believe that things are what they seem, that facts they read are true, that behavior corresponds to dispositions—until and unless time allows correction for mitigating circumstances. This is cognitive inertia:

> Although the perceiver is misled occasionally, that expense if worth bearing for the advantage of usable cognitive energy that is released. If, indeed, it requires cognitive effort to assess or reassess the truth value of everything we hear or see, one can easily imagine a poor, ineffective, overtaxed organism, too busy wallowing in doubt to get through the day. Furthermore, it is probably fair to say that most of the things we see and hear need little correction. (Jones, 1990, p. 153)[8]

The dispositional bias serves two core social motives: understanding and control. As long as people can believe that behavior represents people's intentions, goals, attitudes, and personalities, then we can believe that people are predictable, which makes them more understandable, as well as more open to our influence.

**WHERE?**    Not every culture shows dispositional biases to the same degree, directed to the same social objects, or even perhaps at all. Recall the idea described in the introductory chapter that traditional European and North American cultures are relatively individualistic, whereas traditional Asian cultures are relatively more collectivistic. An individual emphasis suggests individual, dispositional causality, whereas a collective emphasis suggests social situational causality (Heine & Buchtel, 2009). In accord with this distinction, people in India and the United States show a relative bias in descriptions and explanations of other people, with Indians emphasizing (collective) situations relatively more, and Americans emphasizing (individual) dispositions relatively more (Miller, 1984, 1987).

The relative cultural emphases on person and situation occur in the laboratory as well as the field. American high school students emphasized internal causes relative to Chinese students' emphasis on external causes, in their accounts ranging from the causes of murder to the social behavior of fish (Morris & Peng, 1994). American English–language newspapers writing about murders emphasized dispositional causes (e.g., a deeply disturbed, driven personality or a very bad temper, short fuse), whereas Chinese-language newspapers describing the same crime emphasized situational causes such as relationships (rivalry, isolation), society (availability of guns, achievement pressure), and immediate context (recently being fired, a recent mass slaying).

For example, Figure 3.3 shows that American graduate students explaining murders emphasize personal causes overall (but especially for murderers outside their own

---

[8] Copyright © Freeman. Reprinted with permission.

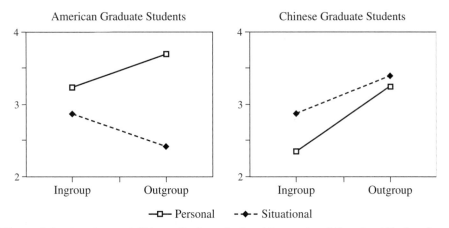

**Figure 3.3**   American and Chinese Graduate Students' Personal and Situational Explanations, Separately for Ingroup and Outgroup Murders

*Source:* From Morris & Peng, 1994. Copyright © American Psychological Association. Adapted with permission.

group); Chinese graduate students emphasize situational causes overall (although they provide more of every cause for outgroups than ingroups). Similarly, East Asians tend to view collective groups as powerful causes of individual behavior, whereas North Americans place individuals in that role (Menon, Morris, Chiu, & Hong, 1999). Relative to each other, some cultures construe agency as an individual property, whereas others construe it as a collective property of social situations or of groups (Morris, Menon, & Ames, 2001). In this view, all cultures encourage a search for invariant dispositions, but some locate them more in individual actors and some more in collective actors. What's more, Asians do not so much deemphasize dispositions as recognize the at least equal importance of situations (Choi, Nisbett, & Norenzayan, 1999).

**WHO?**   Individuals vary as much as cultures do. Just as some cultural contexts encourage or discourage attributions to dispositions, some individuals have private theories that people's behavior is caused by relatively fixed dispositions—**entity theorists**—or by relatively malleable personal qualities—**incremental theorists**. (Note that this usage of entity differs from Kelley's; the entity or "thing" in Kelley's case is the stimulus, whereas the entity or "thing" is this case is the disposition as a fixed thing.) Both Chinese and American students can hold either kind of private theory, with entity theorists in both cultures making more dispositional attributions than incremental theorists in both cultures (Chiu, Hong, & Dweck, 1997).

**WHAT?**   Not all behavior is equally easy to attribute to dispositional factors. Recall that Jones directly (social desirability) and Kelley indirectly (consensus information) observed that socially desirable behavior has two potential explanations: The person is doing it because of some inner dispositional impetus or because social context calls for it. Socially undesirable behavior, in contrast, does not lend itself to a situational explanation, because it flies in the face of the situation. Hence, negative behavior shows more dispositional bias than positive behavior (Malle; 2006; Ybarra & Stephan, 1999).

Besides negative behavior, distant behavior shows more dispositional bias. **Construal level theory** (Trope & Liberman, 2003) posits that the farther-off the behavior, in time or space, the more people use abstract (e.g., dispositional) construals to predict it. This means, in a variant on the Jones-Harris essay study, that students see a fellow student who advocates for an unpopular cause (senior comprehensive exams) as having a stronger attitude when writing the essay in a study-abroad tour than when writing it on their home campus (Henderson, Fujita, Trope, & Liberman, 2006). It also explains why we overcommit ourselves to far-distant obligations: In the abstract, the commitment fits general dispositions (goals, attitudes, values), but when the event comes upon us, we notice the concrete hassles of fulfilling the obligation, which suddenly does not seem like such a great idea any more. In the distant future or past, we seem to ourselves more the way we see another person, for whom dispositional explanations work well (Pronin & Ross, 2006). Not so in the immediate situation.

**SUMMARY OF DISPOSITIONAL BIASES**    With all this, at least Western, dispositional bias in mind, why did Ronald Opus attempt to kill his mother and then to kill himself? His own explanation as the actor and that of many traditional Asians and incremental theorists would likely hinge on his desperate circumstances, but many traditional Western observers' explanations, as well as entity theorists in any culture, would likely hinge on his unusual personality. On average, overall, Westerners do have a clear dispositional bias, but it is not necessarily a universal human tendency. Nevertheless, either dispositional or situational attributions can serve the core social motive to attain understanding. In addition, the average Western emphasis on dispositions may be traced to culturally based social motives for control and the need to believe that people are in dispositional control of their behavior.

## Self-Enhancing Attributions: Feeling Good by Credit and Blame

In addition to understanding and control, ordinary personology serves self-enhancement motives, people's need to feel good, and this describes the second batch of attribution biases. Indeed, people have a **bias blind spot**, perceiving themselves to be free of the biases that plague others (Pronin, Gilovich, & Ross, 2004).

**DEFENSIVE ATTRIBUTIONS**    The need to believe someone is in control links to the belief that when something terrible happens, some blameworthy person caused it. The more serious an offense, whether domestic violence, plagiarism, shoplifting, or political protest, the more people perceive the individual actor to be responsible (Feather, 1996). The idea of pure chance accident is not comforting. When something goes wrong, when a major accident occurs, for example, the worse it is, the more people want to blame somebody for it (Shaver, 1970). They want to be able to attribute responsibility for bad things that happen in the world. People do not like to attribute significant events to chance; flukes make them uncomfortable. In **defensive attributions**, people would rather blame a person for adversity, especially the worse it is, because then it gives them the feeling that they personally can avoid it: "Oh, that won't happen to me because I don't ride a motorcycle in the rain at night." By definition, a defensive attribution makes it self-protective to believe that a bad event will not happen to you, a common human belief. Is it rational? Is it logical? No. But it's part of people's need to feel in control of their lives.

Some 22 studies tested the prediction that if the accident perpetrator is dissimilar to the self, then people will blame the person more, the more severe the accident (Burger, 1981). In contrast, if the perpetrator is similar to themselves, then people blame the person less, the more severe the accident. The net effect is to distance oneself from causing anything really bad to happen.

**SELF-SERVING ATTRIBUTION** In a related way, if something bad does happen to people personally, they are especially likely to avail themselves of the actor part of the actor-observer effect and blame it on the situation. But people are willing to take credit for successes. This is a **self-serving attribution**, of course, to take credit for success and to blame other people or situations for failure. According to meta-analyses, both children and adults make internal attributions for success (Whitley & Frieze, 1985, 1986; Mullen & Riordan, 1988). The evidence is clearest that people take credit for success rather than assigning blame for failure (Miller & Ross, 1975).

People are especially likely to blame the situation for their failure when the task is important (Miller, 1976). Table 3.11 shows participants' attributions for their performance on a social-perceptiveness test, depending on whether they succeeded or failed, and how important it allegedly was to life success. Notice, first, that people generally attribute failure more than success to external factors (task difficulty, luck); this compares the four means on the top left with the four means on the top right. This pattern is exaggerated when importance is high (of those means, just those in the high-importance columns). Conversely, when people succeed, they attribute their performance to themselves (their own social perceptiveness, effort); this compares the four means on the lower left with the four on the lower right. Again, this pattern is exaggerated when importance is high.

Moreover, people do the same with their favorite sports teams. In 91 tests of self-serving (team-serving) attribution bias (Mullen & Riordan, 1988), stronger evidence supports attributing the team's wins to ability (an internal, dispositional factor), rather

**Table 3.11** Defensive Attributions for Success and Failure, Depending on Importance

| | Outcome and Its Importance | | | |
| | Success | | Failure | |
| Measure | High | Low | High | Low |
| --- | --- | --- | --- | --- |
| Difficulty | 1.54 | 2.50 | 3.70 | 2.85 |
| Luck | 1.47 | 1.47 | 4.24 | 2.62 |
| Perceptiveness | 4.77 | 3.85 | 1.16 | 2.77 |
| Effort | 4.85 | 4.93 | 3.24 | 4.31 |

Higher numbers indicate greater attribution to factor indicated in left column.

*Source:* From Miller, 1976. Copyright © American Psychological Association. Adapted with permission.

than, say, luck or the game being easy (shades of the Princeton-Dartmouth game in the chapter's opening pages).

In real-life settings, blaming others can be hazardous to your health and your marriage. In 25 studies, blaming others for one's misfortunes is correlated with impaired health and well-being (Tennen & Affleck, 1990). Similarly, blaming one's spouse is correlated with marital dissatisfaction, and various data suggest the causality runs from blame to unhappiness, rather than the other way around (Bradbury & Fincham, 1990). Though self-serving in the short-run, this bias is not adaptive in the long-run.

**SELF-CENTERED ATTRIBUTION BIAS**   The final bias in this self-enhancing set is best illustrated by example. Think about your roommate, if you have one, or else someone with whom you've shared chores. Do this experiment: Ask yourself how much of the household maintenance you do. Now, if your roommate is handy, ask how much of the household maintenance that person thinks he or she does. (If you have more than one roommate, ask each to estimate his or her own contribution.) Add up each person's percentage, including your own, and you should find that it adds up to more than 100%. This means that each of you overestimates how much you do, relative to what the other person says you do, which is why it adds up to more than 100%.

This **self-centered bias**—both people thinking they contributed more to a joint project than the other person thinks they did—occurs for married couples estimating their individual contributions to household responsibilities, students taking responsibility for ideas generated in a team's psychological assessment, basketball players owning responsibility for an important turning point in a game, psychology majors rating who controlled a brainstorming session for an antismoking campaign, and psychology graduate students indicating their own and their advisor's relative contributions to their senior thesis (Ross & Sicoly, 1979). The self-serving bias is often a problem for researchers trying to decide who should be first author on joint papers (the order of authorship reflects relative contribution and therefore credit). Supposing that both authors actually did about 50%, but each estimates 60%, and therefore each author claims to be first. This bias underlies all too many professional resentments. In these settings, the bias seems to depend on people's ability to remember their own contributions more than others', not so much on their failure to pay attention at the time or on a motivation to distort their own responsibility.

According to subsequent evidence, people inadvertently even plagiarize their partners' work (the ultimate form of taking credit), when they simultaneously engage in irrelevant effort, as if they are actively working on the task themselves (Preston & Wegner, 2007). Priming agentic thoughts (e.g., "I" versus "computer") also increases people's own feelings of authorship (that is, sense of having originated an action) (Dijksterhuis, Preston, Wegner, & Aarts, 2008). This kind of self-attribution occurs even for other people's actions, for example, when we root for our team's televised victory, as if our wishes made a difference (Pronin, Wegner, McCarthy, & Rodriguez, 2006). If our thoughts precede, fit, and explain an action—whether our own or someone else's—we take credit for it (Wegner, 2003), in a self-serving way.

## Normative and Descriptive Models

Whether emphasizing self-enhancement or control, all of these errors and biases fall under the rubric of descriptive models in psychology. As noted earlier, the normative models, such as Kelley's covariation theory, state more or less ideally what people should do. In contrast, as we see here, descriptive models emphasize what people actually do when observed directly. In the social sciences, and in psychological science particularly, researchers compare normative models (what people ought to be doing) with descriptive models (what they actually do). In economics, for example, the rational actor represents an ideal model of a person gathering all the relevant information, weighing it carefully, and coming to an unbiased decision. However, what people ought to do if they are being totally rational is often not what they actually do. The descriptive models, by documenting biases, capture that discrepancy. In the case of ordinary personology, Westerners ignore the hidden power of situations and focus on other people's dispositions more than they should, especially for negative behavior, and people generally attribute more personal responsibility to themselves for good events than they should.

## MIND PERCEPTION

As we have seen, people make sense of each other's feelings, mostly via nonverbal behavior, and each other's dispositions, from a variety of information—with more or less bias—all operating on the obvious assumption that other people have minds like their own. Philosophers call this the "problem of other minds," only problematic if you consider that we don't really know other people's minds directly, only indirectly (Epley, 2008). Nonetheless, people eagerly attribute minds to other beings, from frogs to fetuses, from robots to God, not to mention other people, along two primary dimensions (Gray, Gray, & Wegner, 2007), namely, agency and experience. **Experience** means that the other being feels things (hunger, pain, embarrassment, joy), has consciousness, and possesses a personality. **Agency** means that the other has self-control, memory, planning, and communication. Some of our biases (e.g., making overly dispositional attributions, taking credit where we should not) make sense as imputing agency where none exists.

People routinely do this. We assign agency and experience to computers and cars all the time. **Anthropomorphism** imputes human experience and agency to nonhuman objects (Kwan & Fiske, 2008). People anthropomorphize their pets, projecting their own personalities onto their dogs as much as onto other people (Kwan, Gosling, & John, 2008). And pets' perceived personalities affect even people's own behavior (Chartrand, Fitzsimons, & Fitzsimons, 2008). People claim personal relationships with favorite television characters (Gardner & Knowles, 2008), and they reveal their private symptoms to sympathetic robot nurses (Kiesler, Powers, Fussell, & Torrey, 2008). People anthropomorphize nature (Norenzayan, Hansen, & Cady, 2008), and when they attribute human characteristics to God, they make more severe moral judgments, viewing transgression as personally offending God (Morewedge & Clear,

2008). Anthropomorphism is a common phenomenon, but the relevant research does not necessarily claim it as an error. Indeed, it serves useful functions.

People attribute dispositions to nonhuman others more often when they have easily accessible knowledge, along with motives to understand and explain, as well as motives to connect with others (Epley, Waytz, & Cacioppo, 2007); these motives respectively resemble this text's core understanding, controlling, and belonging motives, so they fit broader human tendencies. One impact of the belonging motive in particular is that people especially anthropomorphize when they are lonely (Epley, Akalis, Waytz, & Cacioppo, 2009).

## CHAPTER SUMMARY

Our running example of the Opus homicide/suicide was originally fabricated to show how difficult it is to infer motives. Although that venue was forensic, and ours is social interaction, many of the principles are the same in the legal system and in everyday life. People seek an understanding of their world and of each other, especially in detecting short-term feelings, attributing traits or other stable dispositions, and perceiving other people's minds in general. The most relevant core social motive is understanding, but controlling and self-enhancing come in as well, and belonging apparently encourages the mind perception of anthropomorphism. People actively construct their perceptions, balanced of course by reality. People as targets of social perception are causal agents who perceive the perceiver back, implicate the self, and self-present. People possess important traits, feelings, and minds that are not directly observable but are changeable and difficult to verify, making people incredibly complex as perceptual stimuli.

People perceive other people's feelings in large part through nonverbal cues, which ordinary people view as reliable. Some nonverbal cues communicate across cultures and across the life span. Although nonverbal behaviors can be ambiguous, they constitute a crucial aspect of social life. Examples include people's use of nonverbals in enacting and detecting deception, attraction, and intention

People perceive each other's more enduring personality traits as invariances that predict behavior across situations. Jones's correspondent inference theory and Kelley's covariation theory both examine how people perceive behavior to correlate with certain causes (Kelley) or certain effects (Jones), then make their attributions accordingly. Jones's theory focuses on single events, whereas Kelley's theory focuses on a series of events. Weiner applies attributional principles to social issues such as poverty and achievement.

People also infer their own dispositional qualities. Bem's self-perception theory describes people inferring their attitudes from their own behavior and situational demands. Schachter's theory describes people inferring their feelings from their arousal and situational explanations.

In contrast to the normative or ideal models, descriptive theories focus on actual behavior that may fall short of ideals. Many attributional errors and biases stem from ordinary personologists ignoring the subtle but strong power of situations, believing someone must be in control. Others stem from people protecting their self-image. Mind perception causes people to anthropomorphize nonhuman targets. All these theories examine how individuals make sense of the underlying causes of behavior, whether traits or feelings, in an effort to understand, perhaps control, perhaps self-enhance, and sometimes even belong.

## SUGGESTIONS FOR FURTHER READING

AMBADY, N., & WEISBUCH, M. (2010). Nonverbal behavior. In S. T. FISKE, D. T. GILBERT, & G. LINDZEY (Eds.), *Handbook of social psychology* (5th ed.). New York: Wiley.

EPLEY, N., & WAYTZ, A. (2010). Mind perception. In S. T. FISKE, D. T. GILBERT, & G. LINDZEY (Eds.), *Handbook of social psychology* (5th ed.). New York: Wiley.

GILBERT, D. T. (1998). Ordinary personology. In D. T. GILBERT, S. T. FISKE, & G. LINDZEY (Eds.), *Handbook of social psychology* (4th ed., Vol. 2, 89–150). New York: Wiley.

HILTON, D. (2007). Causal explanation: From social perception to knowledge-based causal attribution. In A. W. KRUGLANSKI & E. T. HIGGINS (Eds.), *Social psychology: Handbook of basic principles* (2nd ed., pp. 232–253). New York: Guilford.

JONES, E. E. (1990). *Interpersonal perception*. New York: W. H. Freeman.

MACRAE, C. N., & QUADFLEIG, S. (2010). Perceiving people. In S. T. FISKE, D. T. GILBERT, & G. LINDZEY (Eds.), *Handbook of social psychology* (5th ed.). New York: Wiley.

# Chapter 4

# Social Cognition: Making Sense of Others

Federico Peña, secretary of energy under Bill Clinton, told a story about hosting his first formal dinner as newly elected mayor of Denver. The guest list included rich and influential Southern Californians. As he stood near the door in his new tuxedo, he was greeted by a guest thus: "Waiter, get me a drink." The next moment, a city official arrived on the scene, recognizing him as "Mr. Mayor." The guest turned beet red, and Mayor Peña duly led the way to a much-needed drink all around.

In contrast to this interpersonal fumble, consider Sherlock Holmes explaining to Dr. Watson how, at their first meeting, he knew that Watson had just come from Afghanistan:

> I *knew* you came from Afghanistan.... The train of reasoning ran, "Here is a gentleman of a medical type, but with the air of a military man. Clearly an army doctor, then. He has just come from the tropics, for his face is dark, and that is not the natural tint of his skin, for his wrists are fair. He has undergone hardship and sickness, as his haggard face says clearly. His left arm has been injured. He holds it in a stiff and unnatural manner. Where in the tropics could an English army doctor have seen much hardship and got his arm wounded? Clearly in Afghanistan." The whole train of thought did not occupy a second. (Doyle, 1892–1927, p. 24)[1]

Between our all-too-human foibles and the superhuman deductive powers of a fictional detective lie most people's efforts to make sense of other people. Social cognition is both a miracle and a debacle: It is amazing that people manage to make sense of each other, in milliseconds, but it is terrible the errors that people sometimes commit, using some of the same processes. Sometimes the errors are deadly, as in police shooting an innocent but stereotyped bystander.

---

[1] Copyright © Doyle Estate. Reprinted with permission.

Three central issues dominate people's understandings of others: accuracy and inaccuracy, reliance on familiar expectations, and degrees of control and automaticity in these processes. In discussing accuracy, we will see that people seek good-enough understanding, depending on degree of acquaintance, the relevant dimensions, and specific contexts. People often make biased inferences and use shortcuts that only sometimes work well. In relying on familiar expectations, people tend to be conservative perceivers, although with adequate information and motivation, they will assimilate more data. In discussing people's degree of control over these processes, we will see that people can't always think what they want. But if they try sometimes, they just might find, they think what they need (to paraphrase another great British thinker, Mick Jagger). Even our neural systems reflect these dual processes of automaticity and control. Overall, social psychologists find that people are often efficient but approximate in their social cognitions. As they follow the core social motives of understanding and trusting, people think quickly, but not always well.

## WHAT IS SOCIAL COGNITION?

### Conceptual Definition

The study of social cognition builds on attribution theory and, in particular, naïve psychology (Chapter 3). Think back to Heider's interest in examining naïve psychology: how people think about other people. **Social cognition**, more generally, constitutes the process by which people think about and make sense of other people, themselves, and social situations (Augoustinos, Walker, & Donaghue, 2006; Fiske & Taylor, 2008; Kunda, 1999; Moskowitz, 2004). It especially focuses on how people initially form impressions of each other's personalities, emotions, roles, and identities—a process so natural that people are not often aware of it. Recall Heider's contrast between people's own phenomenal description and scientists' causal description. As Holmes put it, "From long habit the train of thoughts ran so swiftly through my mind that I arrived at the conclusion without being conscious of intermediate steps. There were such steps, however" (Doyle, 1892, p. 24). Social cognition analyzes the steps in people's train of thoughts about other people. Consider this: What makes a person seem warm, responsible, intelligent, neurotic, or open? Depressed or angry? Mayor or waiter? Recently from Afghanistan or Brighton Beach?

As noted, Chapter 3 focused on inductive processes by which people move from behavior to abstractions such as feelings and traits. This chapter will focus on more deductive processes, by which people's already-abstracted expectancies, heuristics, and goals influence how they interpret the data presented by the social world.

### Operational Definition

From an operational perspective, social cognition experiments apply cognitive psychology's methods and theories to social psychology. Social cognition research examines **cognitive structure** and **process**—attention, memory, inference, and concept formation—but applied to perceptions of people. For example, in one study (Bargh,

Chen, & Burrows, 1996) college students briefly saw words related to stereotypes of elderly people (*worried, Florida, old, lonely, gray*). Afterward, the students then walked to the elevator more slowly, as if they were enacting the stereotype. In another study by the same researchers, white students briefly saw either black faces or white faces (first independent variable) and then were either provoked by the experimenter or not (second independent variable). The students who had been both provoked and exposed to black faces then responded in a more hostile manner, thereby enacting their stereotype of a hostile black man. Similarly, recall the study that opened Chapter 2, in which students who thought about professors then performed better on a trivia quiz (Dijksterhuis & van Knippenberg, 1998). We discuss these ideas in more detail later, but for now, the point is that all these researchers used the cognitive finding that people, if recently exposed to a concept, then readily apply it to new contexts, some more relevant than others. As we will see, the use of this cognitive finding has made some provocative points about how people use social categories in thinking about others.

Social neuroscience has increasingly informed social cognition research (e.g., Adolphs, 2009; Fiske & Taylor, 2008; Lieberman, 2007, 2010; Mitchell, 2008). Indeed, the brain region that typically responds to other people, the medial prefrontal cortex, is implicated in scores of social cognition studies (Amodio & Frith, 2006). What's more, people's default, resting-state preoccupation may well be thoughts of themselves and other people, according to some neural evidence (Iacoboni et al., 2004; Mason, et al., 2007). Given the centrality of social cognition, our brains are acutely attuned to others.

## Core Social Motives

As people make sense of other people, the core social motive of understanding is prominent. But because they are thinking about people instead of objects, trust and control become important as well.

**UNDERSTANDING**   People think about other people in order to interact with them. Social cognition is a practical business (S. T. Fiske, 1992, 1993b). William James was one of the founders of American psychology and of the American school of **pragmatism**, which determined the validity of concepts by their practical results. As James put it, "My thinking is first and last and always for my doing, and I can only do one thing at a time" (1890, p. 960). As noted in Chapter 3, thinking about other people determines social interaction (e.g., deciding how to approach a boss for a favor), but it also results from social interaction (with each conversation, the employee gains a better understanding of the boss) (Jones & Thibaut, 1958). The banquet guest gave little thought to the alleged waiter, but the new mayor's staff probably gave a lot of thought to Mayor Peña (and rarely mistook him for a waiter). Since the dawn of the discipline, social psychologists have investigated people's everyday social cognition, both as a fundamental result of social interaction and as a fundamental determinant of social interaction.

When social cognition results from social interaction, people gather data about other people, but the data reflect the active role of the observer (noted in the last chapter with regard to the Dartmouth-Princeton game). As another early example, researchers (Dornbusch, Hastorf, Richardson, Muzzy, & Vreeland, 1965) hypothesized that an overall impression results from the perspective of the particular perceiver *at least as much as* from the characteristics of the person being perceived. That is, one person's judgments of two different people may have more in common than two people's judgments of one person because each perceiver may have favorite and habitual ways of describing other people.

Interviewers asked 10- to 11-year-old children at a summer camp about their tent-mates after they had been living together for two to three weeks. The questions were open-ended ("Tell me about _____"). The researchers scored the descriptions according to various categories, such as the traits *neatness/sloppiness*. As Table 4.1 indicates, the overlap due to a single perceiver (one child describing two different others) was actually larger (57%) than the overlap due to a single target (45%; two children describing the same other child). As a baseline, the average overlap between any two children describing any two other targets was (38%), which might be viewed as overlap due to the common camp culture. In at least some circumstances, then, perceivers contribute greatly to their own perceptions. As noted in the previous chapter, ordinary personologists actively contribute to their impressions by imputing structure, stability, and meaning to other people and their interactions, and people may have habitual dimensions or categories that they use all the time. We come back to this point at the end of the chapter.

As noted in the previous chapter, human beings are inherently complex, and thinking about one another as we interact makes the job of perception even more complicated. To cope with this complexity, people have to simplify. The term **cognitive miser** (Fiske & Taylor, 1984) describes how people conserve their scarce mental resources and cut corners when trying to make sense of other people. That is, rather than always thinking hard about other people, people often use habitual dimensions or categories. Their first, automatic impressions or well-learned expectations are shortcuts to understanding. The world is too complicated and people are too easily overloaded to be completely careful all the time, especially when forming impressions from interactions.

**Table 4.1**    Contributions to Impressions by the Person Perceiving and the Person Perceived

| Person perceiving | Same | Different | Different |
|---|---|---|---|
| Person perceived | Different | Same | Different |
| Who describes whom | One describes two | Two describe one | Two describe two |
| Overlap between descriptions | 57% | 45% | 38% |

Higher numbers indicate higher percentages of categories that overlap between the two descriptions specified.

*Source:* From Dornbusch et al., 1965. Copyright © American Psychological Association. Adapted with permission.

Social cognition also guides social interaction (S. T. Fiske, 1992, 1993b). "The relative smoothness of operation of day-to-day living reflects the fact that one person is in some degree aware of what another person does, feels, wants, and is about to do." This classic observation (Tagiuri & Petrullo, 1958, p. ix) underlines James's point that thinking is for doing. In social cognition, people balance cognitive necessity (cognitive miserliness) against smooth social interaction (everyday coordination between people). This balance shows social thinkers to be **motivated tacticians** (Fiske & Taylor, 1991). That is, depending on motivation, people shift from quick-and-dirty cognitively economical tactics to more thoughtful, thorough strategies for forming impressions. People think as hard as the social situation requires. If you are forming an impression of a professor, you think harder if you intend to take that professor's seminar than if you never expect to attend his or her classes. You couldn't possibly think hard about all the professors you ever encounter! The concept of the motivated tactician reflects such balance in social cognition used for social interaction.

Social cognition is important primarily because understanding what another person does, feels, wants, and intends can determine one's own reactions. Going back to the theme of social adaptation, people have evolved in the context of living with other people. Being part of a social group demands the ability to make sense of other people and thus to interact adequately. Understanding does not have to be perfect or completely accurate, but it does have to be good enough, specifically, coherent and simple. Figuring out another person's feelings guides one in dealing with that person. For example, if Professor Funk is in a foul temper, being punitive, abrupt, and giving pop quizzes, a student needs to be aware of the professor's mood. Another example would be a project partner. What if one person suddenly decides not to work on it any more? Knowing that person's mind matters a lot.

Understanding matters in groups as well as in one-on-one interactions. Consider a group's initial meeting. When members first arrive, they may wonder, "Who are all these people in this group that I've joined? Who is friendly, and who is stand-offish? Who is going to run things? Who is unpredictable, and who is reliable? Who is going to be the note taker? Who is funny? Who is going to be someone I can count on to get the inside story? Who is going to be a little slick and maybe not too trustworthy?" Social cognition both determines and results from social interaction. In this light, social cognition lies at the center of human social life. How people understand other people helps determine their happiness or unhappiness.

**CONTROLLING**    People struggle for understanding in order to predict their outcomes and perhaps to control them. Many of the studies based on understanding in the service of interacting also reflect people's desire for control. However, the control motive will emerge most clearly at the end of the chapter, in people's efforts to control their own thoughts (harder than you think) and in the effects of control motives on how people think about others.

**TRUSTING**    Although understanding (and to a lesser extent, control) is the core social motive most studied with regard to social cognition, the motivation to trust, a rarely acknowledged undercurrent, also runs through social cognition. Because people are thinking about other people, trust is central. This motivation reflects two premises: Other people are usually good, and unexpected bad behavior requires immediate attention. Perhaps the best summary is that people "trust but keep their eyes open."

First, consider the premise that other people are usually good, the **positivity bias**. People expect other people to be fairly competent, fairly nice, and fairly honest, in other words, trustworthy. As remarked in Chapter 1, a range of evidence supports the idea that most people expect other people to be benevolent, all else being equal. People have a positivity bias even toward their pets (Rajecki, Rasmussen, & Conner, 2007). An entire book (Matlin & Stang, 1978) documents the "Pollyanna principle": People seek the pleasant and avoid the unpleasant, communicate good news more frequently than bad, judge pleasant events as more likely than unpleasant ones, recall pleasant life experiences more accurately than unpleasant ones, rate themselves as better than average and more happy than not, and evaluate each other positively. Moreover, desirable traits are perceived to be more common than undesirable ones (Rothbart & Park, 1986).

In a phenomenon dubbed the **person positivity bias** (Sears, 1983), people evaluate other people positively, even compared with comparable nonhuman entities. That is, students evaluate individual professors more favorably than their courses and individual politicians more favorably than politicians in general. In both cases, the individual person fares better than the impersonal course or the stereotyped group. In the case of the course, it is odd that students like the professor better than the course, given that they are rating the same experience in two different ways. In the case of the politicians, the combined average of the individual politicians should equal the rating of the politicians as a group, but it does not, because people like each individual politician more than they like the group as a whole.

From an operational standpoint, the psychological midpoint of people's expectations of other people is not the arithmetic midpoint. This is reflected in their ratings. For example, if a scale runs from 1 to 9, most ratings of a specific other person will be 5 or above, so a psychologically neutral score is not 5 (the numerical midpoint), but 6 or 7. This positivity bias matters in real-world settings, such as when students grade one another. Almost no one is merely middling; to paraphrase public radio storyteller Garrison Keillor, "everyone is above average."

The positivity bias goes beyond expectations of other people to general expectations of positive life outcomes. When people imagine life outcomes, they expect more good than bad events (Parducci, 1968). As Figure 4.1 indicates, the preponderance of expected events appears on the positive side of neutral. People (North Americans, at least) view their futures as unequivocally positive (Ross & Newby-Clark, 1998), and this bias appears automatic (Lench & Ditto, 2008). Positive words even outnumber negative words in most languages (Zajonc, 1998).

The positivity assumption, then, is widespread in people's expectations about life experiences, but people expect positive outcomes from other people even more than from events in general. A positive outlook promotes exploration and curiosity. That is, positivity implies approach rather than avoidance, so it encourages interaction with other people and the environment. Openness and trust encourage discovery and connection to others.

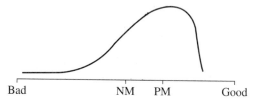

**Figure 4.1** Hypothetical Distribution of Life Outcomes, Showing a Positive Psychological (versus Numerical) Midpoint

*Source:* Parducci, 1968. Copyright © General Learning Press. Adapted with permission.

In addition to the positivity bias, trusting carries a corollary, **vigilance**, an acute sensitivity to negativity. Other people's negative attributes and behavior require immediate attention. Exploration is all very well, but one poisonous mushroom can ruin your day (Kanouse & Hanson, 1972; Peeters & Czapinski, 1990). So can one poisonous friend. Acute sensitivity to negative features and behavior, when they do crop up, protects people from death and destruction, whether physical or psychic. Thus, the positivity (which enables exploration, information-seeking, getting to know others) is offset by vigilance.

Negative behavior indeed does grab people's attention. For example, in one experiment (Fiske, 1980), people formed impressions of other people from slides, which depicted them as more or less sociable with friends, as well as more or less active in a good cause (against child pornography). Hence, one independent variable was degree of sociability; the other was degree of community responsibility. Participants controlled the slide projector switch, which recorded how long they looked at the slides showing positive and negative behavior (the dependent variable). Not only did people look longer at negative behavior (unsociable or unhelpful actions), but they looked longer at the behavior the more negative it was (really rude or completely selfish actions). The behavior that attracted the most attention also carried the most weight in people's subsequent impressions.

Vigilance for negative personality trait words appears to be automatic (Pratto & John, 1991); people take longer to process words such as *sadistic, mean*, and *hostile*, compared with words such as *kind, sincere*, and *talented*. In people's open-ended descriptions of others (Vonk, 1993), unexpected negative behavior (e.g., in a likeable person, ordering the most expensive drink after someone else has offered to pay) had more impact than unexpected positive behavior (e.g., in an unlikeable person, jumping up to embrace a friend who has passed an exam). Negativity more consistently activates the brain's amygdala, a region implicated in vigilance for motivationally relevant inputs (Cunningham, Van Bavel, & Johnsen, 2008); positive events also activate the amygdala, but more flexibly, depending on stimulus relevance to current goals.

Two highly related explanations account for people's acute sensitivity to bad behavior and terrible traits. If negative events are perceived to be rare, they should provide more information about the individual; that is, if they are rare, they set the person apart from the norm (Fiske, 1980). Relatedly, negative events might also be more diagnostic, that is, allow more confident categorization of a person as one particular kind or another, regardless of the norm (Skowronski & Carlston, 1989). Honest behavior, for example, is not so diagnostic in the short run; it can be exhibited by both honest and dishonest people. But dishonest behavior immediately places the actor squarely in the dishonest category. This negative-positive asymmetry flips for competence traits; the diagnostic value of negative behavior indeed is greater for interpersonal traits, such as sociability or morality, but tends in the opposite direction for ability. To put it bluntly, a smart person does something dumb more often than a dumb person does something smart (Reeder & Brewer, 1979).

How can people continually expect good events, despite constant vigilance for bad ones? People do mobilize in response to negative events, using physiological, cognitive, emotional, and social resources to assess and cope, but they cannot maintain high alert at all times. Therefore, they soon minimize the negative, allowing a return to a more positive baseline state (Taylor, 1991). Among the mechanisms that allow people to minimize the long-term impact of adversity are people's positive biases, simultaneous moderating life events, ability to make the best of a bad situation, and facility at explaining away some negative outcomes. Indeed, people's positive outlook recovers surprisingly soon after major adversity. People tend to overestimate how long they will be upset by negative life events, compared with how quickly their life satisfaction actually returns (Gilbert, Pinel, Wilson, Blumberg, & Wheatley, 1998; Wilson, Wheatley, Meyers, Gilbert, & Axsom, 2000; the self chapter revisits this issue). Specifically, rebuilding their trust in other people is a major task for trauma victims, and their success testifies to human resilience (Janoff-Bulman, 1992).

## Summary of Definitions and Core Motives

Social cognition comprises the processes by which people seek to understand and make sense of one another. Operationally, this means social psychologists adapting cognitive theories and methods for their own research. Understanding other people is pragmatic; it both results from and determines social interactions. Controlling follows from understanding. The motive to trust also enters in: Other people are expected to be interpersonally good, but bad behavior captures immediate attention and analysis.

If thinking indeed is for doing, as James claimed, and social thinking is for social doing, as social cognition researchers claim, then three themes follow. People's social cognition must be *accurate* enough to guide their everyday interactions. People must have workable *structures* to organize and anticipate their interactions. And people's social cognition must be *flexible* enough to change with changing goals and circumstances. Social cognition research takes up each of these themes, as we will see.

## ACCURACY AND INACCURACY: PEOPLE SEEK GOOD-ENOUGH UNDERSTANDING

Social cognition is sometimes mistaken, as in the chapter's opening, chagrin-filled story of the guest who mistook the mayor for a waiter. Such a mistake seems especially appalling in comparison with the perfect logic of Sherlock Holmes.

On the other hand, most of the time the presumed "waiter" is indeed a waiter. Although we are not totally rational and accurate, most of us do not construct our own delusional realities totally without reference to the outside world. People could not function effectively if they constantly misunderstood one another's social roles. Similarly, people sometimes do misjudge other people's personalities, as when the nice stranger turns out to be a con artist or the gruff boss has a kind heart. Nevertheless, most of the time people must be accurate enough for everyday purposes. Social psychologists have demonstrated people's good-enough accuracy of impressions and judgments.

## Accuracy of Impressions

Most people think they are good judges of other people's personalities. What do they mean by that? Usually they mean that their impressions are accurate. However, what psychologists mean by accuracy is more precise and nuanced than what laypeople mean. Social psychologists have distinguished who is accurate about whom and examined accuracy as a function of acquaintanceship, relevant dimensions, and specific context.

**WHO IS ACCURATE ABOUT WHOM?**    Researchers have broken accuracy down into its interpersonal components. For example (Kenny, 1991; Kenny & Albright, 1987), certainly some people can be more accurate judges of personality, across a variety of people, which is what most laypeople mean by accuracy. But certain people as targets can actually elicit more accuracy, across a variety of judges. That is, some people are easier to "read" than others. What's more, sometimes a particular judge can read a particular person especially well, but this ability may not extend to people in general. An example would be a couple in which one partner is highly attuned to the other partner, but not to people in general. Putting it into the statistical terms introduced in Chapter 2, accuracy can reflect a main effect for judge, a main effect for target, or the interaction of the two. For example, nine-year-old boys all judge some classmates' aggression more accurately than others (target effects), but individual perceivers and unique dyads do not systematically vary in accuracy (Kenny et al., 2007).

In all three kinds of accuracy, one might well ask, accurate compared with what? Accuracy mostly means agreement with some standard or **criterion**, but the appropriate standard is not always obvious (Biernat & Eidelman, 2007; Kruglanski, 1989). An external standard is not always preferable to a personal one. For example, all your friends and relatives might recommend a particular marriage partner, but you might have no feelings for the person they recommend. Which would be the proper standard? In less intimate cases, consensus (agreement) among a group of people does often operate as a proxy for accuracy (Funder, 1987), particularly in judging a person's personality traits; two people may agree that a particular person is extroverted. But what matters more: consensus between two outside observers or consensus between an observer and the target of the judgment? If observers and target disagree, who is accurate? What if experts disagree with a consensus of laypeople; who is accurate then?

The answers to this issue depend on who judges whom. Targets might be the most accurate regarding their own current thoughts and feelings (Andersen, 1984); observers might be most accurate regarding observable traits, such as extroversion (Park & Judd, 1989); and experts might be the most accurate clinical judges on traits such as emotional stability. However, undergraduates even without clinical training can detect pathological traits from brief clips of verbal and nonverbal behavior (Friedman, Oltmanns, Gleason, & Turkheimer, 2006). The problem is that people are not generally as accurate as they think they are. What's more, people see other people as more biased than they themselves are (Pronin, Gilovich, & Ross, 2004; Pronin, Lin, & Ross, 2002), partly because they rely on introspection to judge themselves but discount the other person's thoughts and feelings as a basis for judgment (Pronin & Kugler, 2007).

**ACCURACY AND ACQUAINTANCE**   Accuracy of impressions surely increases with time and acquaintance; that much seems obvious. But it's mostly wrong. In 32 studies of agreement among judges about another person's personality, consensus did not increase with acquaintance (Kenny, Albright, Malloy, & Kashy, 1994). For acquaintance to improve consensus, judges would have to see increasing amounts of overlapping, consistent, unambiguous behavior, but this is not necessarily what people see. Under variable circumstances (different observations, inconsistent behavior, ambiguous behavior), acquaintance would not increase consensus. So maybe acquaintance does not dramatically increase accuracy.

When acquaintance seems to improve accuracy (defined as observer consensus with the target and peers), it may be for extraneous reasons. For example (Stinson & Ickes, 1992), male friends were more accurate than male strangers at inferring each other's thoughts and feelings. Of course, that might be because they had more detailed knowledge of each other, but it might also be because, being friends, they had more similar personalities than two strangers would. In another study (Paunonen, 1989), participants signed up with a close friend and then were mixed with 6–12 other participants seated around a large table; participants rated their own personality and that of another person, randomly assigned by the researcher. Degree of acquaintance thus varied from the close friend to complete strangers. Acquaintance predicted degree of agreement between the self-rating and peer rating, but again similarity is a possible alternative explanation.

How can acquaintance *not* improve accuracy? Maybe accuracy is high from the beginning. People indeed are remarkably accurate at observing **thin slices of behavior**, brief excerpts of expressive behavior drawn from ongoing interaction. Even the briefest exposure to a stranger at zero acquaintance allows surprisingly accurate ratings. One review examined studies in which the criterion for accuracy was objectively observable behavior or ratings by experts. Some of the judgments were clinical (patient commitment, anxiety, depression), some were social (teacher effectiveness, status, bias), and some focused on deception (covered in Chapter 2). Across 38 independent findings (Ambady & Rosenthal, 1992), judges' accuracy approximated a correlation of .39 (medium to large, by social science standards), and this substantial accuracy showed up in ratings all based on less than five minutes of behavior. What's more, accuracy did not differ between observations lasting merely 30 seconds or the full five minutes. And this zero-acquaintance accuracy held true, regardless of whether the behavior was

**Table 4.2**   Accuracy of Judgments for Different Channels

| Channel | Correlation with Objective Standard |
| --- | --- |
| Face + body | .54 |
| Face + speech | .41 |
| Face | .40 |
| Speech | .36 |
| Body + speech | .33 |
| Transcripts | .29 |
| Body | .28 |
| Face + body + speech | .28 |
| Tone of voice | .26 |

Higher correlations indicate greater accuracy.

*Source:* From Ambady & Rosenthal, 1992. Copyright © American Psychological Association. Adapted with permission.

observed in a laboratory or in a natural setting. Table 4.2 shows degrees of accuracy across different channels of communication; the face is the most useful, but even transcripts prove adequate. A variety of predictions can result from thin slices: teaching ratings, work performance, interview outcome, relationship quality, sexual orientation, and personality (Ambady, Bernieri, & Richeson, 2000). People can judge even the more observable aspects of a salesperson's effectiveness, based on 30 seconds' exposure (Ambady, Krabbenhoft, & Hogan, 2006). Finally, zero-acquaintance accuracy extends to cross cultural judgments between American and Chinese participants, who again show high levels of mutual accuracy (Albright et al., 1997). Cultural experience increases accuracy (Elfenbein & Ambady, 2003).

Accurate social perception at zero acquaintance may reflect some physical realities (Engell et al., 2007; Zebrowitz & Collins, 1997). For example, both physical appearance (rapid movements) and a personality trait (extroversion) could have the same underlying biological cause (level of activity). Or appearance and a trait could have the same environmental cause, as when socioeconomic status (occupation) underlies both physical (weight) and behavioral (nutrition, exercise) characteristics. Moreover, physical appearance can cause psychological qualities and vice versa, making inferences accurate. Having a hostile temperament, for example, could cause facial scars or a battle-flattened nose. Conversely, being physically attractive could cause people to feel more self-confident. By all these routes, then, appearance and psychological reality can sometimes correspond, making it possible, after all, to judge a book by its cover.

Another social reality may inform the accuracy of instantaneous impressions. Defining accuracy as consensus, people tend to agree about which faces appear instantly competent or trustworthy. Consensus on candidates' perceived facial competence predicts more than two-thirds of 2004 Senate election outcomes (Todorov, Mandisodza, Goren, & Hall, 2005). Facial competence appears related to facial dominance, which in men relates to facial maturity (Oosterhof & Todorov, 2008). On the other important dimensions, consensus on a face's trustworthiness predicts neural responses in the amygdala, a region that activates to emotional significance (Todorov, Baron, & Oosterhof, 2008; Todorov & Engell, 2008). At the extremes, trustworthy faces mimic happy faces, and untrustworthy faces mimic angry faces, so the trait inferences may follow from adaptive (and perhaps accurate) responses to facial emotion (Todorov, 2008).

**ACCURACY ON DIFFERENT DIMENSIONS**    Another issue concerns accuracy along different personality dimensions. Simple descriptions of personality generally focus on social likeability and task competence (Fiske, Cuddy, & Glick, 2007; Rosenberg & Sedlak, 1972), similar to the dimensions of trustworthiness and competence, just described. More complex descriptions (e.g., John, 1990) reflect five dimensions from most to least relative importance:

- Extroversion
- Agreeableness
- Conscientiousness
- Emotional stability or neuroticism
- Intellect or openness to experience.

These dimensions appear widespread, showing up with slight variations in languages other than English (Heine & Buchtel, 2009).

Whether the number of relevant dimensions is 2, 5, or 107, accuracy is higher for the more quickly observable, social dimensions (extroversion, agreeableness) than for the less immediately observable, competence-oriented ones (conscientiousness, intellect, and openness to experience). Some traits, such as extroversion, are more easily judged than others, as noted earlier. In one study (Ambady, Hallahan, & Rosenthal, 1995), unacquainted summer school students sat around a large table in groups of three to seven; they completed questionnaires and two audiovisual tests of nonverbal and verbal sensitivity. Participants also rated themselves and the other participants on clusters of traits reflecting extroversion, agreeableness, emotional stability, and conscientiousness. In this study, the accuracy criterion was target-other agreement: If a rater tended to agree with targets' self-ratings, that person was judged to be relatively accurate. The researchers found that more sociable and extroverted people are easier to read, that is, to judge more accurately.

**ACCURACY IN DIFFERENT CONTEXTS**    Context influences accuracy. People may be accurate in some settings but not others, consistent with a pragmatic perspective (Swann, 1984). For example, people may have **circumscribed accuracy:** They may be accurate about a particular person in the limited context in which the two interact (e.g., work) but perhaps not in other contexts (e.g., home). People also choose to interact with others who are similar to themselves, thereby increasing their accuracy in the context of that relationship. Moreover, people deliberately give off cues to their identity in a particular context (a lawyer's briefcase, a carpenter's toolbox, a college T-shirt, a political button); such cues again would increase accuracy. What's more, people often meet each other in contexts that one of them has created (e.g., dorm-room or office), and observers can learn a lot about other people from their rooms' cues

(Gosling, Ko, Mannarelli, & Morris, 2002). Finally, in a single interaction, a person may influence the other person to fit predictions; as we will see, expectancies can bring about the very results predicted.

Some degree of accuracy does facilitate particular interactions in particular contexts. Knowing one's specific audience is a crucial feature of any interaction, allowing both verbal and nonverbal coordination. For example (Fussell & Krauss, 1989; Krauss & Fussell, 1991), speakers elaborate their explanations to suit the listener's knowledge, which in turn facilitates comprehension in that context. Accuracy may facilitate closeness, as when one spouse understands another's positive feelings, but accuracy can undermine closeness, if a spouse's feelings are instead negative, and the empathic partner would rather avoid dealing with them (Simpson, Oriña, & Ickes, 2003). In general, though, the more people are motivated to belong, the more accurate they are (Pickett, Gardner, & Knowles, 2004), suggesting that some accuracy is adaptive.

**SUMMARY**    Accuracy varies by judge, target, and their unique combination. The criterion is often self-ratings or consensus among peers, but objective or expert measures are sometimes available. People do not necessarily become more accurate with acquaintance, but they can be surprisingly accurate within minutes of meeting. Social dimensions are easier to judge than competence-related ones. And the context matters, considering both circumscribed accuracy and people's ability to choose or create contexts in which they can be accurate.

In sum, good-enough accuracy in forming impressions allows us to navigate our social seas and not collide or run aground too often. Understanding others is thus socially adaptive. This assertion—apparently reasonable in studies of accuracy—confronts a tougher challenge in studies of people's shortcuts in the inference process.

## Inferences and Heuristics

Consider these two examples of human inference.

- A man planning to meet a friend for a predawn run goes to bed early and sets the alarm extra early. When the alarm goes off, it is still dark outside, as expected. He pulls on his running togs, wondering why last night's dinner still sits so heavy in his belly. He waits in vain for his friend and finally in frustration takes off without him, but also without his usual energy. Upon returning home, he is quizzed by his frantic wife, who wants to know where he has been at 1 a.m. They are both confused until they realize that a power outage had reset the alarm clock by several hours, and with it, the runner's predawn schedule.

- Sherlock Holmes uses a pocket-watch to judge Watson's brother:

    > He was a man of untidy habits—very untidy and careless. He was left with good prospects, but he threw away his chances, lived for some time in poverty with occasional short intervals of prosperity, and finally, taking to drink, he died.

Holmes's explanation:

> I began by stating that your brother was careless. When you observe the lower part of the watch-case you notice that it is not only dented in two places but it is cut and marked all over from the habit of keeping other hard objects, such as coins or keys, in the same pocket. Surely it is no great feat to assume that a man who treats a fifty-guinea watch so cavalierly must be a careless man. Neither is it a very far-fetched inference that a man who inherits one article of such value is pretty well provided for in other respects.
>
> [Furthermore], it is very customary for pawnbrokers in England, when they take a watch, to scratch the numbers of the ticket with a pinpoint upon the inside of the case. It is handier than a label as there is no risk of the number being lost or transposed. There are no less than four such numbers visible to my lens on the inside of this case. Inference—that your brother was often at low water.
>
> Secondary inference—that he had occasional bursts of prosperity, or he could not have redeemed the pledge. Finally, I ask you to look at the inner plate, which contains the holes—marks where the key has slipped. What sober man's key could have scored those grooves? But you will never see a drunkard's watch without them. He winds it at night, and he leaves these traces of his unsteady hand. Where is the mystery in all this? (Doyle, 1892–1927, pp. 92–93)[2]

Just as most people consider themselves really good judges of other people's behavior, although in fact they are just good enough, so too people consider themselves good at making inferences in general, as if they were all as good as Holmes. But in truth people make a lot of systematic errors, more like Watson or the misled runner. The major research strategy in inference, judgment, and decision making contrasts how good we think we are (Holmes) versus how we actually make decisions (the runner): Researchers contrast **normative models** (discussed in Chapter 3), which specify how people ideally, rationally ought to make decisions—Sherlock Holmes being a prime example—with **descriptive models** of how people actually make decisions, the case of the predawn runner illustrating normal human foibles. The gap between the normative and descriptive models reveals errors and biases in social cognition as it did in attribution. Overall, people are prone to seek or interpret evidence that will confirm their existing beliefs, expectations, and hypotheses (Nickerson, 1998). As this section shows, one set of errors occurs as people are making inferences or judgments, and another set reflects the heuristics that shortcut the rational process.

**MAKING INFERENCES**   People constantly have to make **inferences**, judgments from limited information to uncertain outcomes. Suppose a person about to be married wants to consider the odds that the marriage will end in divorce. Confronting the overall U.S. divorce rate of about 50%, the person nevertheless will most likely

---

[2] Copyright © Doyle Estate. Reprinted with permission.

**Table 4.3**    Rated Contributions of Some Personal Attributes to a Stable Marriage

| Target's Attribute | Participant Matches | Participant Does Not Match |
|---|---|---|
| Employed mother | 5.53 | 4.40 |
| Nonemployed mother | 4.96 | 4.48 |
| Early relationship | 6.47 | 5.75 |
| No early relationship | 4.43 | 3.57 |
| Nonreligious | 4.80 | 4.12 |
| Religious | 6.81 | 6.33 |

Higher numbers indicate that the attribute is judged to make a stable marriage more likely. Only statistically significant differences are shown.

*Source:* From Kunda, 1987. Copyright © American Psychological Association. Adapted with permission.

reason that "it can't happen to us." In one study (Kunda, 1987), participants read about a person's background under one of three conditions of the independent variable, marital outcome: now happily married, now divorced, or marriage outcomes not given. They all read that this person had various attributes that might contribute to continued marriage or to divorce: One person was religious, conservative, dependent, and extraverted; the person had a nonemployed mother and in high school had not had a serious relationship. The other person was the opposite (nonreligious, liberal, independent, introverted, employed mother, previous relationship). Regardless of which target person they judged, people who matched that person on a particular attribute conveniently viewed it as better for that person's marriage, probably because they viewed their own attributes as predictive of a good marriage. That is, people who matched the target on being religious saw that attribute as predicting a stable marriage, but people who matched the other target on being nonreligious likewise saw that attribute as predicting a stable marriage (see Table 4.3). People apparently construct private theories that explain divorce, but they do so in a way that gives them reason for personal optimism, despite the odds. Such causal theories contribute to people's adaptively unrealistic estimates of their marital odds and other life experiences (see the self and the relationships chapters). For example, people may underestimate their genetic susceptibility to lung cancer, mis-recalling or misinterpreting test results (Lipkus, McBride, Pollak, Lyna, & Bepler, 2004).

Such inference processes have distinct stages (Holmes's "intermediate steps in the train of thought"): attending, encoding, and combining information (Crocker, 1981; Weber & Johnson, 2009). Let's begin with **attending** (see Table 4.4). People tend to be distracted by irrelevant factors, such as information **salience** (what attracts attention). For example, people tend to notice hypothesis-confirming cases, but not all the relevant evidence. A full consideration requires four kinds of data (Nisbett & Ross, 1980): all combinations of whether people are married or divorced and whether people have had previous relationships or not. Noticing just the number of cases that would confirm the hypothesis (married people with previous relationships) does not help as much as knowing the relative proportions of married and divorced people who have and have not had previous relationships. Thus, people often limit their attention to the easiest, first, most convenient information. As another example, people will often select the

**Table 4.4**   Stages of Making Inferences

| Stage | Process | Common Bias |
|---|---|---|
| Attending | Which data are relevant | Focus on confirming cases<br>Ignore population base rates |
| Encoding | How to interpret the data | Over-use outliers<br>Over-rely on information fluency |
| Combining | How to put data together | Dilute with nondiagnostic information<br>Over-estimate plausible conjunctions<br>Perceive illusory correlations<br>Use subjective, inconsistent weights |

first candidate on a ballot, not bothering to look farther down the list (Krosnick, Miller, & Tichy, 2004).

Besides being distracted by the most obvious information, people also have a marked propensity to ignore background information such as **base rates**, that is, population statistics. If the divorce rate for the entire population averages 50%, then that base rate is the best estimate for oneself, without a scientific sample more directly relevant to oneself. But people routinely underuse base-rate information in favor of vivid examples (Hamill, Wilson, & Nisbett, 1980), such as celebrities, even when they know the examples are atypical. What's more, people fail to consider that the available sample does not represent the starting base rate: the current sample includes only survivors, so when people consider risky behavior, they under-estimate the failure rate because they are no longer in the sample; this occurs for individuals and even for entire organizations (Denrell, 2003).

After attending, a person's next step is **encoding** (interpreting and classifying). For example, people are likely to be misled by extreme data values (six divorces), which are more than likely to be flukes, that is, chance events unlikely to repeat. People do not appreciate the role of chance in creating **outliers**, extremes that should be ignored. To use another example, an extraordinarily good or bad performance is most likely to be followed by a more moderate performance, rather than by an equally outstanding performance the next time (Jennings, Amabile, & Ross, 1982), a phenomenon termed **regression to the mean**. Thus, it is a mistake to rely too heavily on one peak performance or one disaster to predict future patterns.

Encoding also depends on **fluency**, that is, the sheer ease of processing. People over-rely on information that goes down easy. For example, easy-to-say names give short-term advantages to some stocks over those with hard-to-say names (Alter & Oppenheimer, 2006). Fluency affects judged importance, familiarity, frequency, typicality, and confidence (Oppenheimer & Frank, 2008).

**Combining data** presents the last set of potential pitfalls. With encoded information in hand, information on more than one dimension has to be combined to make a judgment. Three major errors can occur in this process. First, some information is more **diagnostic** (relevant and informative) than other information. Logically, the diagnostic information should be used and the nondiagnostic information ignored. However, people have a weakness for allowing the nondiagnostic information to dilute the diagnostic information (Nisbett, Zukier, & Lemley, 1981). One reason people fall prey to the **dilution effect** is that they use information that is diagnostic elsewhere as if it were relevant everywhere (Hilton & Fein, 1989). Similarly, people may use unjustifiable factors when they can stretch them to fit, given elastic guidelines (Hsee, 1996; Norton, Sommers, & Brauner, 2007).

A second error in combining information is the **conjunction error**, whereby people think the simultaneous occurrence of several specific bits of information is more likely than the occurrence of any one of them alone, a logical impossibility. For example (Tversky & Kahneman, 1983, p. 297), suppose Linda is

> 31 years old, single, outspoken, and very bright. She majored in philosophy. As a student, she was deeply concerned with issues of discrimination and social justice, and also participated in antinuclear demonstrations.

In one study, participants ranked the possibilities for what Linda is doing now. They ranked "bank teller and active in the feminist movement" higher than just plain "bank teller." Logically, the odds that Linda is a feminist bank teller should be lower than the odds of her being simply a bank teller, but people often do not operate this way (see also Leddo, Abelson, & Gross, 1984).

A third error of combining information comes in **illusory correlation**, which happens when people overestimate how often two events occur together. For example, people over-estimate the frequency of criminal behavior by members of minority groups, partly because both are rare and therefore distinctive, and their paired distinctiveness stands out when it does occur. The same perceptual phenomenon would occur with a sample of 80% squares and 20% circles, each being 90% green and 10% red. The circles stand out, the red shapes stand out, and the red circles especially stand out. Of course, applied to crime and ethnic minorities, the stereotypic expectations merely exacerbate the perceptual effect (Hamilton & Rose, 1980). In an odd twist, the illusory correlation bias may befall Westerners more often than East Asians, on average. To the extent that individualist Westerners emphasize individual objects, they may not see the holistic big picture. In one study (Ji, Peng, & Nisbett, 2000), Chinese participants were more sensitive to and confident about differences in actual patterns of covariation than Americans were. These differences disappeared when perceived control was increased, to create a more Western context.

A fourth error in combining information is improper **weighting** of information. When people must arrive at an overall judgment, they do not consistently and appropriately weight the information they have elected to use. Arguably (Dawes, Faust, & Meehl, 1989), decisions about people—whether clinical diagnoses, admission choices, or hiring decisions—operate best through a computer programmed to weight certain scores consistently (e.g., so much to Graduate Record Examination score, so much to grade-point average, so much to letters of reference). Yet decision makers (and candidates) are attached to the idea of making individual decisions on the basis of each person's unique story or configuration of characteristics. Fierce battles over this issue arise in the research literature, and the issue is not yet resolved. But it lies at the heart of the proper role for normative (computerized) versus descriptive (intuitive) models.

To summarize, people attend to insufficient data, encode erroneously, and combine information poorly (see Table 4.4). The litany of possible errors and biases may seem endless (Ajzen, 1996; Dawes, 1998; Fiske & Taylor, 2008; Kunda, 2000). Apparently, we cannot even get out of the docks, let alone successfully navigate the social sea. Nevertheless, some remedies do counteract these errors and biases, as we will see later.

**USING HEURISTICS**   Some patterns of inference shortcut the stages just described, in favor of **heuristics** that allow quick-and-dirty estimates, relying on relatively automatic processes. Research on heuristics, perhaps the most famous area of social decision making, won the 2002 Nobel Award in economics for its implications. In the core series of experiments, Amos Tversky and Daniel Kahneman (e.g., 1974) demonstrated some significant shortcuts that depart from the idea that people are rational decision makers, thus violating a basic tenet of classical economic theory. Social psychologists imported these insights, thereby developing principles of social decision making (Nisbett & Ross, 1980); four key heuristics appear next (see Table 4.5).

Suppose that one must judge whether a random sequence is truly random—for example, which series of coin tosses (HHTHTTHT or HHHHTTTT) is more likely? Most people answer that the former is more likely. Each specific sequence is equally likely, yet the first one looks more like a random sequence. The **representativeness heuristic**, as it is called, prompts decision making on the basis of appearances, that is, instances that resemble stereotyped expectations (e.g., how a random sequence is supposed to appear). In a similar vein, the representativeness heuristic may explain the conjunction error described earlier. Linda, who was deeply concerned with discrimination and social justice, just seems like the kind of person who should be a feminist now; she is representative of that category, so "feminist bank teller" resembles the idea of Linda more than "bank teller" does. The representativeness heuristic describes people's tendency to rely on resemblance rather than logical odds.

The **availability heuristic** describes people's tendency to make decisions based on the ease with which examples come to mind. (It overlaps with representativeness in that representative examples come to mind more easily, but availability is broader.) As an example, how many words can you generate quickly that have this pattern: _____ N_? (Try it.) Most people struggle to generate such words, and if asked, report that they are likely to be relatively rare. But if people are asked to generate four-letter

**Table 4.5**   Heuristics, Definitions, and Examples

| Heuristic | Overrelies On | Examples |
| --- | --- | --- |
| Representativeness | Instances that resemble expectations | Stereotyped coin-flip sequences Feminist bank teller |
| Availability | Ease with which instances come to mind | Words with "n" next to last Dramatic causes of death |
| Simulation | Ease of imagining alternatives | Missed plane Olympic bronze |
| Anchoring and adjustment | Initial starting point and insufficient shift | Estimated homicides Murder trial verdicts |

verbs ending in "ing," many more examples come to mind, and they infer that such words are more common. Turn to a social example (Fischhoff, Lichtenstein, Slovic, Derby, & Kenney, 1981): People over-estimate the frequency of dramatic causes of death (botulism, tornadoes, floods) and under-estimate the frequency of less dramatic ones (diabetes, stomach cancer, heart disease). Moreover, estimates of the causes of death highly correlate with the number of column-inches devoted to each type of death in recent newspapers, that is, **salience** in the news. Events that come readily to mind are estimated to be more frequent. Similar phenomena occur in using one's acquaintances as a basis for informal estimates of divorce likelihood, unemployment rate, average education, and the like.

To understand the **simulation heuristic**, consider another puzzler (Kahneman & Tversky, 1982, p. 203):

> Mr. Crane and Mr. Tees were scheduled to leave the airport on different flights, at the same time. They traveled from town in the same limousine, were caught in a traffic jam, and arrived at the airport thirty minutes after the scheduled departure time of their flights. Mr. Crane is told that his flight left on time. Mr. Tees is told that his flight was delayed and just left five minutes ago. Who is more upset, Mr. Crane or Mr. Tees?[3]

Most people say that Mr. Tees is more upset. Why? It is easier to imagine, or mentally simulate, how it might have been otherwise for him than for Mr. Crane. If only the traffic lights had not all been against them, if only the departure gate had been closer, if only the plane had been delayed just a tiny bit longer.... The simulation heuristic addresses these "if only" **counterfactual** imaginings. The easier it is to imagine how things might have been otherwise—to mentally undo the misfortune—the more tragic it seems. People mentally undo action more easily than inaction, so their emotional responses are stronger when a mishap results from an error of commission rather than omission (Kahneman & Miller, 1986). For example, people feel worse about inappropriate things they said than about appropriate things they failed to say. Similarly, Olympic bronze medalists are actually happier than Olympic silver medalists, presumably because the silver winners are simulating the gold they could have won and the bronze are simulating not winning at all (Medvec, Madey, & Gilovich, 1995).

To understand the **anchoring-and-adjustment heuristic**, try to estimate how many people died in 1999 from homicides in the United States. With no prior idea, perhaps it would be helpful to know how many people were killed the previous year (16,974, according to the FBI) and that the crime rate went down. In estimating probabilities and frequencies, people often start with an **anchor**, or starting point, and adjust it up or down. This useful strategy works if the anchor is accurate and if the adjustment is adequate. Unfortunately, people may use the wrong anchor—for example, starting with the number of homicides in their neighborhood—and then adjust inadequately. Even if they have a good anchor, such as 17,000 homicides during the previous year, they tend to adjust insufficiently, not coming close to 15,533, the correct answer.

---

[3] Copyright © Cambridge University Press. Reprinted with permission.

Decisions are strongly affected by insufficient adjustment from arbitrary anchors (Epley & Gilovich, 2006). For example, in a murder trial, the judge instructs the jurors to consider first the most severe crime charged (e.g., premeditated murder) and then, if the evidence is inadequate, to proceed down to the next most severe charge (e.g., manslaughter). Starting with the most severe potential verdict results in harsher judgments than the reverse order (Greenberg, Williams, & O'Brien, 1986).

The four decision heuristics—representativeness, availability, simulation, and anchoring and adjustment—all address how people ordinarily estimate probabilities in order to judge and make decisions (see Table 4.5). In each case, the heuristic provides a shortcut for estimating probabilities—a shortcut that works well enough most of the time. Also, in each case, the heuristic estimates probabilities on the basis of what is salient or comes to mind most easily. In a sense, therefore, all four boil down to variants of the availability heuristic, which explicitly concerns ease of bringing information to mind (for a review of others, see Weber & Johnson, 2009).

**DEFENDING ORDINARY DECISION MAKING**    Judgmental errors, whether due to biases at various stages of inference or to the use of heuristics, seem to threaten people's ability to function at all. But maybe the errors are not so bad, and maybe other factors counteract them anyway (Fiske & Taylor, 2008; Wilson & Brekke, 1994). Besides, how could we have evolved to be such idiots?

One possibility is that the errors are more apparent than real, being identified mainly in laboratory studies, with use of unnatural tasks. Some of the studies seem designed expressly to make people look stupid. Granted, if a study unfairly sets them up, people can make these mistakes, but how often do they do so in life outside the laboratory?

Relatedly, the cards may be stacked against research participants, by presenting the information in a way that would make it difficult to use a normative statistical model. For example, different information formats make it harder (admissions folders) or easier (systematic tables) to extract and combine information consistently. Some forms of narrative (a coherent essay) facilitate understanding and combining information appropriately (Mulligan & Hastie, 2005; Sanfey & Hastie, 1998).

Alternatively, maybe the normative models are inappropriate standards. People rarely operate in the ideal conditions of complete information and unlimited time. Sometimes making a quick decision, any decision, matters most. Sometimes admittedly biased, positive judgments may help. For example, close relationships in which partners have positive illusions about each other tend to do better (see relationships chapter).

Another important factor is domain-specific knowledge. For example, some domains of knowledge remain more stable (the old diner's breakfast menu) than others (available cancer treatments). Errors may be more problematic in some domains than in others (again, consider the breakfast menu versus the cancer treatment). Different types of judgments entail different kinds of domain-specific knowledge and significance.

Ordinary decision making can also be defended by its function, that is, adaptability. Some decision-making strategies may have developed because they work well enough most of the time. For example, in a circumscribed social setting with a limited number of similar people (your friends), estimating divorce frequency by availability (the ease with which instances of divorce come to mind) may be quite reasonable.

Moreover, evolutionary psychologists have combined the ideas of domain-specific knowledge and function to argue for specific **modules**, specific inference systems that preempt more general systems, to govern decisions of importance to survival and reproduction (Klein, Cosmides, Tooby, & Chance, 2002; Pinker, 1997). For example, as noted earlier, when people have to make a decision about what combinations of information to seek, they often fail to search for appropriate information. Many of those problems are presented out of a social context. However, people search for more appropriate information if the problem is cast in terms of who is cheating and who is not, than when the same logical problem is not framed in terms of social contracts (see Table 4.6); different brain regions activate to social versus formally equivalent but nonsocial tasks (Ermer, Guerin, Cosmides, Tooby, & Miller, 2006). Moreover, people are better at estimating frequencies than probabilities, the former having a more ecologically realistic function (Cosmides & Tooby, 1996). Although these claims are controversial, they emphasize the point that decision-making strategies may be domain-specific and adaptive, unless taken out of their original context for the purposes of research.

Finally, many errors are self-correcting anyway. For example, as noted earlier, people overestimate the diagnosticity of initial extreme performance (ignoring

**Table 4.6**   Reasoning with and without Social Content

Instruction: Turn over the card(s) needed to tell whether the sentence is true or false.

| Version | Rule to Test | On Front Side of Cards | | | | % Correct |
|---|---|---|---|---|---|---|
| Original (Wason, 1968) | If there is a D on one side of any card, then there is a 3 on its other side. | D | 3 | B | 7 | 6% |
| Social Contract: Social Law (Cosmides, 1989) | If a man eats cassava root, then he must have a tattoo on his face. | Eats cassava root | Tattoo | Eats molo nuts | No tattoo | 75% |
| Social Contract: Private Exchange (Cosmides, 1989) | If he gives Bo his ostrich eggshell, Bo will give him duiker meat. | He gave his ostrich eggshell to Bo | Bo gave him duiker meat | He gave Bo nothing | Bo gave him nothing | 71% |

In each case, the first and fourth cards must be flipped to determine whether the sentence is true or false.

probable regression to the mean in subsequent performance). A brilliant opening lecture may be followed by a more modest second one, so the students' enthusiasm may give way to disappointment. But during the initial lecture, other (irrelevant) information about the professor is gleaned, so it may dilute the diagnostic information the lecture seems to provide, tending to moderate the overly extreme judgments anyway. Other errors cancel each other out, if they occur in random combinations.

Perhaps errors will be corrected socially, as when collective decisions correct individual errors and biases. Some goofs are fixed by feedback from the social environment ("Mr. Mayor!"); others reflect social rules of conversation (Hilton, 1990). (A later chapter compares group and individual performance.) And some errors do not matter much, as when one buys the "wrong" brand of toothpaste.

**IMPROVING ORDINARY DECISION MAKING**    Although ordinary decision making can be defended, decision makers still do commit errors. Accordingly, researchers have taken up the challenge to reduce them. For example, whereas higher education does not automatically improve people's decision-making strategies, education about inference processes in specific disciplines—such as graduate school in psychology or medicine, but not chemistry or law—improves decision-making strategies (Lehman, Lempert, & Nisbett, 1988).

Making information easier to process can improve the quality of decision-making. For example, on food labels, nutritional information about negative ingredients (e.g., sodium, fat, sugar content) helps consumers make better choices (Russo et al., 1986). As noted earlier, information can be arranged in ways that are easier to process in a normatively correct way, as when the critical information is extracted and presented systematically or, even better, integrated into a coherent story.

Compensating for errors and biases or **mental contamination** (Wilson & Brekke, 1994) depends on several factors all being present at once: being motivated to correct the problem, being aware of the direction and magnitude of the bias, and having control over one's responses. For example, forewarning people of the possibility of one of the specific biases covered here can indeed avert it, if all three of the listed factors are present. Similarly, **debiasing** (identifying the possibility of bias after receiving information or making an initial decision) works if and only if the process addresses each of these factors. With the various caveats in mind, being conscious of one's judgment processes may make one's inferences more satisfactory, within a given context. People differ in their ability to regulate their biases, perhaps based on neural mechanisms for monitoring conflict (Amodio, Devine, & Harmon-Jones, 2008).

Finally, people can analyze the decision-making process relative to their own values and criteria. For example, different cultures endorse different types of decision-making processes. Western, individualist cultures focus more on rules, clear-cut categories, and individual entities—a style termed **analytic**—whereas Eastern, collectivist cultures focus more on context, similarities, and relationships—a style termed **holistic** (Nisbett, Peng, Choi, & Norenzayan, 2001). Thus, decision making that might seem illogical and biased in one culture, such as holding two contradictory beliefs, might seem mature and wise in another culture.

## Summary of Accuracy and Inaccuracy

People are good-enough social thinkers in many respects, their judgments serviceable for everyday transactions, but not up to the normative standards of Sherlock Holmes. People are remarkably accurate in judging thin slices of behavior at zero acquaintance. And their choice of similar friends, prescribed roles, and circumscribed contexts all probably increase accuracy in forming impressions of others, especially on the most observable social dimensions.

People's inferences and judgments do not seem to fare as well as their daily social impressions. What's the difference? Impression formation in general does not allow as clear a criterion of accuracy, so people's "errors" are less evident. Judgments and inferences about many nonhuman targets do permit a normative ideal as a standard of comparison. People make mistakes at all stages of inference, and heuristics provide short-cuts that work only sometimes. Looked at logically, people's judgments come up short, especially if the format of the judgments is unfamiliar.

Nevertheless, people are rescued by the social checks and balances in much decision making. Many decision-making strategies may be adaptive and functional in social contexts. An optimistic viewpoint would argue that people's motive to understand gives them at least a sense of accuracy and often good-enough accuracy in forming impressions and making decisions about others. Next, we turn to research on one particular strategy that both helps and hinders people's accuracy, the use of prior knowledge to make sense of new information.

## EXPECTATIONS: PEOPLE UNDERSTAND AND TRUST THE FAMILIAR

According to Bill James (1986), Chicago Cubs baseball player Ernie Banks

> was a good-to-excellent shortstop.... Certainly it is true that his batting statistics were helped by playing in Wrigley Field.... But I think it is generally true that all power-hitting shortstops get a bad rap as defensive players.... they always seem to have better defensive statistics than reputations.... People think in terms of images; I do, you do, everybody does. That's how we make sense of an overpowering world; we reduce impossibly complex and detailed realities to simple images that can be stored and recalled. People have trouble reconciling the image of the powerful hitter—the slow, strong muscleman with the uppercut—with the image of the shortstop, who is lithe, quick, agile. When confronted with incontrovertible evidence that a man is a slugger—no one really doubts the validity of batting statistics—there is a [discrepancy] with the idea that he was also a good shortstop. The image of him as a shortstop, being not locked in place by a battery of statistics, gets pushed aside so it can accommodate the image of him as a slugger. Education is not eliminating images, but building more complex, detailed images that better represent the realities. (p. 377)[4]

---

[4] Copyright © Darhansoff, Verrill, Feldman. Reprinted with permission.

Not myself having an image of a shortstop or a power hitter, I nonetheless find this a compelling description of the functioning of expectations. People make sense of the world by relating it to familiar images or coherent prior knowledge. People's core motive for understanding their world is served by expectations or mental representations of prior knowledge (traits, stereotypes, stories, and the like), which act as coherent concepts or naïve theories that render the world manageable. These **mental representations** go by several related names—schema, category, concept, expectation—but they share the idea of being a cognitive structure organizing the attributes of a concept or type of stimulus and the relationships among the attributes.

If thinking is for the pragmatic purpose of doing, people must have such workable structures to organize and anticipate the data they experience. Various expectations provide the scaffolding on which we build our impressions of others from the information available. People use workable, habitual structures for social cognition: We understand new information by reference to old, familiar expectations.

## Impression Formation before the Cognitive Revolution: A Tale of Two Processes

Before cognitive psychology attained prominence in the 1970s and long before neuroscience examined social cognition, social psychologists had developed two contrasting approaches to explain how people form impressions of other people. One focused on coherence, which anticipated the work on expectations and other mental representations; the other focused on simple evaluation, which rejected the notion of coherence, providing a counterpoint to the idea of mental representations.

**COHERENT IMPRESSIONS**    Suppose that Professor Busy comes to class and describes two new teaching assistants, based on previous students' reactions. One assistant, Ms. Popular, is generally viewed as "intelligent, industrious, and impulsive." The other, Ms. Awful, is generally viewed as "critical, stubborn, and envious." The professor asks students to indicate which teaching assistant they prefer. The choice is not difficult. The students' impressions of Ms. Popular differ a lot from their impressions of Ms. Awful. Now suppose Professor Busy checks his notes and realizes belatedly that Ms. Popular and Ms. Awful are the same person, Ms. Terry who is simultaneously "intelligent, industrious, and impulsive," *as well as* "critical, stubborn, and envious." How can one reconcile these opposing impressions?

Participants in an experiment conducted by Solomon Asch over 50 years ago (1946) considered someone equivalent to our Ms. Terry to be a "mass of contradictions," "Jekyll and Hyde," or more benignly, split into a business half and a social half. Some participants refused to believe that all of the traits could fit the same person. Nevertheless, when other participants in Asch's experiment encountered Ms. Terry from the outset as one individual, not two, they easily combined the various traits into a coherent portrait of a single person. The first set of participants, who initially encountered the two separate people, found that the two separate coherent impressions made it hard to synthesize the two into one person. The second set of participants, who started out with a coherent impression of a single person, easily synthesized all six traits into one coherent portrait.

Now suppose that Professor New comes to give a guest lecture. The regular professor has described him as "intelligent, skillful, industrious, warm, determined, practical, and cautious." Think about this person a moment. Participants in another experiment expected this person to be generous, wise, happy, good-natured, humorous, sociable, popular, humane, altruistic, and imaginative: "A person who believes certain things to be right, wants others to see his point, would be sincere in an argument, and would like to see his point won." Suppose that a second guest lecture is given by Professor Next, who is described in advance as "intelligent, skillful, industrious, cold, determined, practical, and cautious." The students now expect "a rather snobbish person who feels his success and intelligence set him apart from the run-of-the-mill individual. Calculating and unsympathetic." He tends to be more ungenerous, shrewd, unhappy, irritable, humorless, unsociable, hard-headed, and so on. Why is the second lecturer so different from the first? Six of seven adjectives remained the same in the two descriptions.

Switching one trait term, *warm* versus *cold*, changes sociable to unsociable; that much follows directly from the meanings of warm and cold. But how does this change wise to shrewd, imaginative to hard-headed? These terms do not come directly from *warm* and *cold*, but from the impact of *warm* or *cold* on other terms in the impression. The meaning of *intelligent*, which is common to both Professor New and Professor Next, changes depending on the context. A warm intelligence differs from a cold intelligence. Again, the principle of coherence makes all the traits fit together into a well-integrated portrait, known as a **Gestalt** or good, coherent configuration.

Solomon Asch demonstrated that people's understanding of other people is coherent. His Gestalt configural model held that impressions have at least six features that lend coherence:

- Impressions view the entire person as a unit, as the Ms. Terry experiment indicates.
- Impressions unify and integrate traits, as when "critical, stubborn, and envious" fit together to portray the teaching assistant from hell.
- Impressions organize around central traits, a point made by the disproportionate and unifying impact of *warm* versus *cold*, which is substantially stronger than, for example, *polite* versus *blunt* would be.
- Impressions include traits as parts of a whole, each one contributing to a unified impression. Hence, *industrious* adds to the impression of a hard-working academic in both cases.
- Impressions can change the meaning of traits, as when a warm, intelligent person is wise, but a cold, intelligent person is shrewd.
- Impressions emerge within an overall context that the traits create for each other.

Subsequent research replicated these results with actual people instead of trait lists (Kelley, 1950), showed that the processes can be unconscious (Nisbett & Wilson,

**Table 4.7** Frequent Resolutions for Trait Pairs

| Mode of Resolution | Pair | Example |
| --- | --- | --- |
| Enabling | Intelligent—witty | *Witty* presupposes *intelligent*. |
| Segregation | Brilliant—foolish | Each occurs in a different sphere of person's life. |
| Cause—effect | Hostile—dependent | *Dependence* breeds *hostility*. |
| Common source | Cheerful—gloomy | A *moody* person appears alternately *cheerful* and *gloomy*. |
| Inner—outer | Sociable—lonely | The person is outwardly *sociable* but inwardly *lonely*. |
| Means—end | Strict—kind | Being *strict* can serve being ultimately *kind*. |
| Interpolation | Intelligent—unambitious | An *intelligent* person's failure made him *unambitious*. |

*Source:* From Asch & Zukier, 1984. Copyright © American Psychological Association. Adapted with permission.

1977), and identified some of those key processes that create coherence in impressions, especially when traits do not obviously fit together (Asch & Zukier, 1984; see Table 4.7). For example, *cheerful* and *gloomy* can be reconciled under *moody*. Recalling Jerome Bruner's (1957a) felicitous phrase also cited in Chapter 3, the impression "goes beyond the information given"; people feel comfortable inferring, for example, that the intelligent, determined, warm person would be "sincere in an argument." All these processes create coherence in impressions, a process that creates a holistic Gestalt, akin to an expectation or mental representation, but in contrast to the elemental process discussed next.

**EVALUATIVE IMPRESSIONS**     In marked contrast to the Gestalt coherence model, another approach focuses on the simple evaluation that can result from forming an impression of another person. Norman Anderson (1974) proposed that people understand other people by distilling out the evaluative element of each component of the impression (i.e., each trait's inherent likeability) and then averaging the separate evaluations into an overall evaluation. In contrast to the coherence model, Anderson's **averaging** or **algebraic model** is explicitly oriented toward piecemeal, separate elements.

In this view, impressions are weighted averages. The impression equals $\Sigma w_i s_i$, where $w_i$ equals the weight or importance of a trait and $s_i$ equals the isolated evaluation of the trait. For example, the likeability of being practical, on a 10-point scale, might be 8; *practical* is a positive attribute. In contrast, the likeability of being *mean* might be 1; *mean* is a negative attribute. The scale value of *practical* would be 8, and the scale value of *mean* would be 1.

How important is each attribute to an overall impression of a person? Being practical, while nice, might not be very important—accounting for only 25% of the overall impression. Being mean, on the other hand, might be extremely important—accounting for at least 75% of the overall impression. The relative weight of being mean far exceeds the relative weight of being practical, so overall likeability is determined mostly by *mean*.

In algebraic terms, $\Sigma w_i s_i$ equals the weight (0.25) times the scale value (8) of *practical* plus the weight (0.75) times the scale value (1) of *mean:* $(.25)(8) + (.75)(1) = 2.75$. The impression of the other person is thus expressed in a simple numerical evaluation.

While this model might be viewed as a simple, focused approach to the understanding motive, it also provides a quantitative approach to the other motive most relevant in social cognition, the trusting motive. Anderson (1974) had to add a positivity constant to his equation to predict people's overall ratings of another person. That is, a likeability impression equals a positive starting value plus the $\Sigma w_i s_i$ just described; he added this positivity constant after finding that people's baseline expectancy about another person is slightly positive, not neutral.

Anderson's model has been termed **elemental**, because it predicts that the traits are completely independent of each other and do not affect each other, except that their relative weights may vary. The idea that a practical (+), mean (−) person might be worse than an impractical (−), mean (−) person does not enter into this piecemeal, elemental model, in contrast to the holistic, Gestalt model.

**SUMMARY**    Two theories of impressions predated the subsequent theories: coherence of the impression's various aspects versus simple distillation of isolated traits into overall likeability. The emphasis on coherence reflects a more configural, holistic, Gestalt process, whereas the emphasis on isolated traits, which are then combined piecemeal, reflects a more elemental process. Both processes serve the core motive of understanding one's social world. Gestalt-type processes underlie expectations, covered next. Elemental evaluation appears in some attitude theories discussed in that chapter. The elemental/analytic process contrasts with the holistic/configural processing style, both identified in cultural psychology, as we have seen, respectively for Westerners and Easterners. Individual differences in processing style, even within Westerners, affect people's sensitivity to the framing of a decision (McElroy & Seta, 2003). For now, these two approaches provide a historical context for research examining mental representation in impression formation.

## Mental Representations in Other Domains of Psychology

The mental representation idea is not new, having surfaced previously in cognitive, social, and developmental psychology. In each case, it has provided a configural contrast, as in Solomon Asch's Gestalt model, to views of mental representation that focus on separate elements, as in Norman Anderson's algebraic model. Throughout psychology, mental structure emphasizes a Gestalt whole, greater than the sum of its parts, that is, with emergent properties beyond simple combinations of the isolated components. Perhaps the earliest schema theory emerged in Frederick Bartlett's book *Remembering* (1932), which described memory for figures, pictures, and stories. The theory was offered in explicit opposition to the then-dominant views that memory collected isolated elements; Bartlett described how people organize stories and experiences into patterns that facilitate understanding and behavior.

In a similar way, Jerome Bruner (1957b) described how perceivers use organized prior knowledge to make meaning. And Fritz Heider (1958), the grandfather of attribution theory, described social relationships that form good psychological units (e.g., agreeing friends versus disagreeing friends; later chapters come back to this "balance theory."). In developmental psychology, Jean Piaget (e.g., 1952), described how children engage "the coordination of the new with the old, which foretells the process of judgment" (p. 43). All these historical precedents emphasized how people assimilate new information to an existing configuration that they have generalized from experience; as we will see, the mental representation idea contrasts with the idea that people accumulate isolated elements or react completely afresh to each new encounter with a stimulus in their environment.

In the 1960s and 1970s, **schema** theories appeared, mostly in experimental psychology, which was being transformed by its cognitive revolution. Cognitive researchers noted how expectations, generalizations, and inferences operate in memory for text: Memory relies on coherent frameworks to determine relevance; people's memory improves when they have an appropriate organizing theme for a text; and people recognize material faster when they apply organized prior knowledge. To illustrate, consider the following passage without an appropriate expectation:

> The procedure is actually quite simple. First, you arrange things into different groups. Of course, one pile may be sufficient depending on how much there is to do. If you have to go somewhere else due to lack of facilities, that is the next step; otherwise you are pretty well set. It is important not to overdo things. That is, it is better to do too few things at once than too many. In the short run this may not seem important, but complications can easily arise. A mistake can be expensive as well. At first, the whole procedure will seem complicated. Soon, however, it will become just another facet of life.... After the procedure is completed one arranges the materials into different groups again. They can then be put into their appropriate places. Eventually they will be used once more and the whole cycle will have to be repeated. However, that is part of life. (Bransford & Johnson, 1972, p. 722)[5]

People have schemas for everyday objects, to the extent that they have experience with them. Thus, just as I might be clueless about baseball shortstops, a Saudi princess might be clueless about how to operate a washing machine, the mystery object in the example just given.

## Kinds of Expectations

Consider the following examples of expectations:

- Late one summer, a new female assistant professor tried to communicate with the university bookstore, so it could order the required textbooks in time

---

for sale to her students at the start of the upcoming semester. Apparently mistaking her identity, the clerk explained that the books were not in yet for the fall semester. The young professor replied, "I know; I want to *order* the books for the fall semester." Now the clerk replied: "Well, what books does the professor want?" The frustrated answer: "I *am* the professor."

■ Watson and Holmes were seated at the breakfast table; Watson recounts their conversation: "But here"—I picked up the morning paper from the ground—"let us put it to a practical test. Here is the first heading upon which I come. 'A husband's cruelty to his wife.' There is half a column of print, but I know without reading it that it is all perfectly familiar to me. There is, of course, the other woman, the drink, the push, the blow, the bruise, the sympathetic sister or landlady. The crudest of writers could invent nothing more crude."

"Indeed, your example is an unfortunate one for your argument," said Holmes, taking the paper and glancing his eye down it. "This is the Dundas separation case, and, as it happens, I was engaged in clearing up some small points in connection with it. The husband was a teetotaler, there was no other woman, and the conduct complained of was that he had drifted into the habit of winding up every meal by taking out his false teeth and hurling them at his wife, which, you will allow, is not an action likely to occur to the imagination of the average story-teller. Take a pinch of snuff, Doctor, and acknowledge that I have scored over you in your example." (Doyle, 1892–1927, p. 191)[6]

People have a host of expectations for social objects and events, including those for the average professor and the typical domestic abuse case. In the late 1970s, social and personality psychologists also began to demonstrate the cognitive convenience (information processing speed and confidence) of schemas, particularly as applied to personality traits, self-schemas, social roles, social groups, and social events—which this section examines in turn (Fiske & Taylor, 1991; Olson, Roese, & Zanna, 1996).

**PERSONALITY TRAITS**    People's mental representations for personality have at least two dimensions. As noted earlier, two central dimensions of people's trait impressions are competence and likeability, which are somewhat independent of each other (Abele & Wojciszke, 2007; Fiske, Cuddy, & Glick, 2007; Judd, James-Hawkins, Yzerbyt, & Kashima, 2005; Rosenberg & Sedlak, 1972). Likeable traits range from socially good (sociable, popular, happy, good-natured, tolerant, honest, helpful) to socially bad (unsociable, humorless, cold, pessimistic, irritable, moody, unhappy, unpopular). The competence dimension also ranges from good (industrious, intelligent, imaginative, scientific, persistent) to bad (foolish, irresponsible, wasteful, unintelligent, wavering, unreliable). Not only do people have **implicit personality theories** that tend to cluster these groups of traits together, but also they know the implications of each trait dimension; they know that outgoing people are likeable, talkative, friendly, and fun at a party, but a pain when one is working against a deadline. Similar analyses would be

---

[6] Copyright © Doyle Estate. Reprinted with permission.

possible for the Big Five traits noted earlier (extroversion, agreeableness, conscientiousness, emotional stability or neuroticism, and intellect or openness to experience). In short, people have organized knowledge about personality traits.

People locate this trait knowledge in social contexts (Cantor, Mischel, & Schwartz, 1982): They think about traits as representing the **person in the situation**, for example, an extrovert at a party versus at the library. They use traits to predict other people's goals, which then predict people's behavior. The extrovert has a goal of being friendly and talking with people, whereas an introvert has a goal of looking inward. People use others' goals to predict their behavior in particular situations, such as being seated next to them on the airplane. Trait expectations are also useful for communicating with other people; being compact, they carry much information in shorthand.

**SELF-SCHEMAS**    People have **self-schemas**, that is, expectations for themselves; these comprise their most salient and central understandings of themselves (Markus, 1977). Toni Morrison described a developing self-schema in *The Bluest Eye* (1970, p. 126):

> When Sammy and Pecola were still young, Pauline had to go back to work.
> She was older now, with no time for dreams and movies. It was time to put
> all of the pieces together, make coherence where before there was none.
> The children gave her this need; she herself was no longer a child. So she
> became, and her process of becoming was like most of ours: she developed
> a hatred for things that mystified or obstructed her; acquired virtues that
> were easy to maintain; assigned herself a role in the scheme of things; and
> harked back to simpler times for gratification.[7]

Self-schemas, as do other expectations, "make coherence where before there was none," as we see in the self chapter.

**SOCIAL ROLES**    People have expectations for social roles, such as librarian (orderly, quiet, wears glasses, drinks wine and not beer). Social roles guide people's daily interactions (Goffman, 1967). Understanding roles is especially pragmatic; they tell us what to do and with whom. We interact differently with a bank president than with a gas station attendant. People's representations of social roles (see Figure 4.2) operate at a **middle level** (comic joker), rather than **superordinate level** (extraverted person) or **subordinate level** (TV comedian). The middle level carries the greatest richness, differentiation, and vividness in person knowledge (Cantor & Mischel, 1979), as in other kinds of categories (Rosch, Mervis, Gray, Johnson, & Boyes-Braem, 1976). Even three-year-old children and baboons can think at appropriate levels for different contexts (Bovet, Vauclair, & Blaye, 2005). Roles focus on context more than traits do.

Compared with people in other cultures, Europeans and Euro-Americans underestimate the importance of social roles. Instead of revolving around fixed personality

---

[7] Copyright © Toni Morrison. Reprinted with permission.

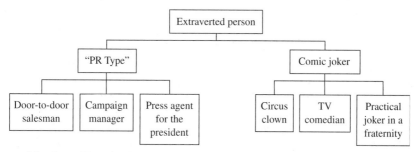

**Figure 4.2**   Some Tentative Taxonomies of Persons
*Source:* From Cantor & Mischel, 1979. Copyright © Nancy Cantor. Adapted with permission.

traits, one's concept of a person might just as easily center on transferable roles (Shweder & Bourne, 1982). Consider the following:

> Balinese culture [includes the] ... persistent and systematic attempt to stylize all aspects of personal expression to the point where anything idiosyncratic, anything characteristic of the individual merely because he is who he is physically, psychologically or biographically, is muted in favor of his assigned place in the continuing, and, so it is thought, never-changing pageant that is Balinese life. It is dramatis personae, not actors, that endure; indeed it is dramatis personae, not actors, that in the proper sense really exist. Physically men come and go—mere incidents in a happen-stance history of no genuine importance, even to themselves. But the masks they wear, the stage they occupy, the parts they play, and most important, the spectacle they mount remain and constitute not the facade but the substance of things, not least the self. (Geertz, 1975, p. 50)[8]

Similarly, Camara Laye of Guinea (1954) writes about his father's self-effacement in light of his endowed role as a prominent blacksmith, itself a prestigious occupation in rural West Africa:

> Was not my father the head man in our concession [extended family courtyard]? Was it not my father who had authority over all the blacksmiths in our district? Was he not the most skilled? ... My father again was silent for a moment, then he said:
>
> "You can see for yourself that I am not more gifted than other men, that I have nothing which other men have not also, and even that I have less than others, since I give everything away, and would give away even the last thing I had, the shirt on my back. Nevertheless, I am better known. My name is on everyone's tongue, and it is I who have authority over all the blacksmiths in the five cantons. If these things are so, it is by virtue of ... the guiding spirit of our race. It is to this ... that I owe everything." (Laye, p. 25)[9]

---

[8] Copyright © Clifford Geertz. Reprinted with permission.
[9] Copyright © Farrar, Straus, and Giroux. Reprinted with permission.

**SOCIAL GROUPS**    People have expectations for social groups, especially **outgroups**, those groups to which they do not belong. These outgroup **stereotypes** will feature in a later chapter, in much more detail than is possible here. For now, the point is that people's concepts about outgroups can guide their action, sometimes in tragic ways. For example, in one large New York bank building, a long-time computer operator arrived for his midnight shift a little early, after working out at a nearby gym. He signed in at the security desk and went to the upper floor with his gym bag. An hour later, he was surrounded and seized by security guards who had been alerted to the presence of a "suspicious black male." Despite his company badge, he was hustled downstairs and interrogated in the lobby, in full view of his arriving colleagues and passersby, until his supervisor intervened. Similar experiences are repeated countless times by innocent motorists who are pulled over for the "crime" of DWB (driving while black). In short, expectations about social groups motivate many assumptions, mostly not benign.

**SOCIAL EVENTS**    Finally, people organize common events into **scripts**, that is, expectations for events, sequences of typical actions such as eating in a restaurant (Schank & Abelson, 1977). If John goes to a restaurant, orders fettuccine Alfredo, drinks some wine, pays the bill, and leaves a tip, everything seems fairly normal. If asked what John ate for dinner, most people would respond, "fettuccine Alfredo." But that answer actually fills in a gap in the account, which said only that he ordered it and paid his bill. These actions imply, but do not state, that he accepted his dinner and ate what he ordered. One rule of scripts is that if something abnormal occurs, the communicator is obligated to report it. So, lacking a report that John sent his plate back, one assumes that he followed the normal sequence of actions constituting a meal in a restaurant, which includes eating the food one orders. Scripts concern such common, predictable events, a crucial part of social interaction (Goffman, 1967).

Even unique events, whether told or remembered, may include a coherent configuration—a story or **narrative**. Narratives have a set of rules that are schematic in nature: They must be consistent, plausible, and complete; they have causal sequences in which one event **enables** (makes possible) subsequent events, and some events precede others in time. These causal and temporal links create the narrative flow. Jurors, for example, use narratives to understand the events of a trial and to render a verdict, according to the **story model** (Pennington & Hastie, 1991). Narratives create coherence among isolated events and bits of evidence, allowing the jurors to test their conclusions. Stories can also explain contradictions, predict plausible futures, and interpret the past.

## Uses of Social Expectations

Expectations are everyday subjective theories about how the world operates. Whatever content they address—whether personality traits, self-concept, social roles, social groups, or social events—expectations represent the general case. They abstract broad knowledge across many particular instances; for instance, multiple dining experiences create the abstract restaurant script. Expectations (or knowledge structures, in general) generalize over numerous instances, resulting in a mental abstraction stored in memory. They guide how people **encode** (attend and interpret), remember, and respond (judge and interact) in their social worlds.

**ENCODING**    When people are first considering information, relevant expectations apparently come to mind in an all-or-none fashion, creating a unitary representation. That is, activating a portion of the concept tends to activate the whole unit at once. As a tight unit, such expectations are at once efficient to use and difficult to dismantle. If a person activates one part of a concept, that tends to activate the whole concept (Sentis & Burnstein, 1979). Activating the restaurant script brings to mind all its key parts, as we saw earlier.

How do mental representations come to mind in the first place? Concepts are cued by labels ("This is my friend Fred, a firefighter.") or by categorization based on salient features (a yellow slicker, black boots, and a distinctive hat). As a later chapter indicates, people categorize other people according to gender, race, and age (and sometimes uniform) within milliseconds. Expectations, especially well-learned ones, then allow people to eliminate redundant information, fill in missing details, rearrange minor disorder, and resolve confusions, all within the first moments of perception. People interpret ambiguous or missing information to fit familiar frameworks, as when one assumes the firefighter's hat to be the standard-issue firefighter hat, not a child's costume hat.

People typically attend to dramatically inconsistent information and process it longer than consistent information, especially when they have to choose because their attentional capacity is overloaded. In one study (Sherman, Lee, Bessenoff, & Frost, 1998), participants read about Bob Hamilton, who was labeled either a skinhead or a priest. The description then included 30 behaviors, 10 kind ("gave a stranger a quarter to make a phone call"), 10 unkind ("shoved his way to the center seat in the movie theater"), and 10 irrelevant ("bought a new shirt"). The kind behaviors were consistent with participants' priest concept but inconsistent with their skinhead concept, and vice versa for the unkind behaviors. Participants read the behaviors, which appeared one at a time on a computer screen, and they pressed the space bar to cue the next behavior after they finished reading each one, which allowed the experimenters to measure attention, operationalized as reading time. Half the participants had reduced attentional capacity because they had to hold in memory an eight-digit number at the same time as reading the descriptions; the other half of the participants had no additional task, so their attentional capacity was high.

As Figure 4.3 indicates, when people's processing capacity was high, they could attend to both kinds of information equally, but when their capacity was low, they took longer at both kinds, but especially focused on the inconsistent information because they more easily comprehended the consistent information. That is, under low capacity, they had to make attentional trade-offs. In general, as people attend to inconsistencies, they may follow one of several routes: resolve the discrepancy in favor of confirming a well-developed expectation, abandon the expectation as inappropriate, or combine the inconsistency with the expectation as a tagged exception. (On the other hand, people virtually ignore expectation-irrelevant information.) Evidence

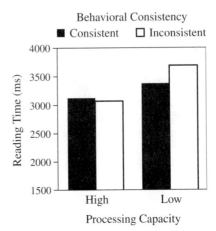

**Figure 4.3** Reading Times as a Function of Stereotype Consistency and Processing Capacity

*Source:* From Sherman et al., 1998. Copyright © American Psychological Association. Adapted with permission.

from neuroscience implicates a particular neural region, the anterior cingulate cortex, in detecting such discrepancies and triggering attention (Botvinick, Cohen, & Carter, 2004).

**REMEMBERING**    Mental representations may be structured in memory in a variety of ways (Fiske & Taylor, 2008; Smith, 1998). They may be lists of features connected by links; this view has been termed an **associative memory model**. Such a model has nodes for concepts (firefighter) and links to conceptually related nodes (attributes such as the distinctive hat and related concepts such as police officer). Mental representations may appear as **prototypes** (the average firefighter) or ideal instances (the best firefighter), with more typical or central examples clustered around the prototype and more peripheral examples (dispatcher) farther away in mental space. Mental representations may include only concrete **exemplars**, as we will see in views that contrast to the generalized expectations covered in this section.

However the expectation is represented in memory, people's **recognition** memory generally favors the expectation, if they are guessing among multiple choices (Cantor & Mischel, 1977). People recognize schema-consistent features as familiar (e.g., eating is a usual part of the restaurant script); this can lead them to assume that they had seen the schema-consistent features in a particular instance (as when you probably assumed that John ate his fettuccine Alfredo).

In **free-recall** memory—that is, when the memory question is open-ended—strong, well-established expectations encourage memory for consistent details (your retelling of the restaurant story would emphasize the most typical details). However, weaker or novel expectations, such as those an experimenter might create in the laboratory or (for an American) the script for a Japanese tea ceremony, actually encourage the opposite. When learning a new concept, people preferentially recall the discrepancies, as if they are trying to understand and resolve them. Thus, recall depends on the strength of the expectancy (as Stangor & McMillan, 1992, showed in a meta-analysis of 54 experiments). The advantage to expectancy-consistent information appears most often in demanding, complex, realistic settings, for people who are not otherwise motivated (S. T. Fiske, 1993b). A variety of sophisticated models of social memory draw on classic and recent advances in memory research (Wyer, 2007). However, social memory differs from nonsocial memory in important respects; for example, the self inevitably appears in truly social cognition (Doosje, Spears, de Redelijkheid, & van Onna, 2007). Across types of social memory, some principles emerge (e.g., Heider et al., 2007); for example, people best recall expectancy-inconsistent information when the expectancy is overt, but better recall expectancy-consistent information when it is covert.

**RESPONDING**    How are people's overall impressions affected by expectations? Does memory for the specific details that compose an expectation determine the overall impression? Surprisingly, it does not; recall and judgment often are uncorrelated ("I know what I feel about that person, but I can't remember anything about her"). In effect, an expectation can become independent of its origins in the original data that gave rise to it (Hastie & Park, 1986). That is, once the expectation forms, it has a life of its own, separate from its components. The correlation between a judgment and memory for the data on which it was based can be surprisingly low. The key seems to be this: People often make a judgment **online**, as they receive information, which is irrelevant to whether or not they remember that information later. Automatic evaluation is the rule (Bargh & Chartrand, 1999), and too much marshalling of evidence can actually undermine a decision (Wilson & Schooler, 1991).

People often use expectations to make a judgment ("I know how I feel about those kinds of people"). But sometimes they do not use any expectation, as when admissions officers screen hundreds of candidates on the basis of a few criteria (grades, tests, activities). This would be a more piecemeal, elemental kind of decision. And sometimes people do not use expectations because they want to form a more detailed, individual impression—for example, of a new boss or office mate. When do people use expectations for judgments and when do they use individual attributes?

The **continuum model** (Fiske & Neuberg, 1990; Fiske, Lin, & Neuberg, 1999) describes responses that are more category-based and schematic versus those that are more piecemeal, elemental, and individuated. People's use of general expectations versus individual information depends on (a) adequate fit to the available information and (b) motivation. Given good fit and a motivation to be decisive, judgments often are schematic (e.g., choosing a person in work-out clothes as a seat-mate on the bus). Given questionable fit to the available information (e.g., a stereotypic athlete reading astrophysics), judgments tend to compromise between expectation and conflicting data, especially if people have time and are motivated mainly by accuracy (the athlete is one's lab partner). Given really bad fit (the alleged athlete is out of shape and uncoordinated), judgments may use no expectations at all, regardless of motivation; such judgments become aschematic or what the model calls piecemeal. Manipulations of the information's fit or lack of fit produce the predicted result (Fiske, Neuberg, Beattie, & Milberg, 1987). And manipulations of motivation do also. For example, instructing people to categorize or individuate leads respectively to more expectation-based or piecemeal processing (Pavelchak, 1989). Other motivations appear at the end of this chapter, and they also support this dual-process model of schematic versus individuating processes.

Once invoked, expectations guide social interaction. For example, 40 years of research on interpersonal expectancies (e.g., Rosenthal, 1994) indicates that when people expect excellence from other people, they can induce that excellence through their own behavior; the result is a **self-fulfilling prophecy**. Various expectations can invoke positive and negative expectancies, as when teacher expectancies cause some children to perform better in school than others. As noted earlier, the message of this research is that teachers create a warmer climate for students they consider special, and they teach more material to those students, thereby confirming their expectations that those students indeed will perform better. A later chapter returns to expectancy confirmation in the context of stereotypes, but for now the point is that expectancies guide a variety of important responses, even automatically (Dijksterhuis, Spears, & Lépinasse, 2001).

## Expectations Develop and Change

People learn expectations and other naïve theories from their own experiences or from other people telling them about the world (Anderson & Lindsay, 1998). However, secondhand expectations tend to incorporate less variability than the self-generated kind, so they create more extreme impressions. In one study (Gilovich, 1987), pairs of friends rated a third party whom one knew well and the other knew only from the first person's reports. As Table 4.8 indicates, ratings became more extreme for secondhand as compared to firsthand acquaintance; similar results occurred in laboratory manipulations of knowing a new acquaintance firsthand or secondhand.

In forming their own expectations, people rapidly generalize, sometimes even from just two instances (ask any young child, after the first two birthday parties, whether cake and presents are standard). Expectations then become more abstract, complex, organized, compact, and resilient, with increased experience (consider an adult's birthday party script).

Several psychological pressures tend to maintain expectations, making them resist change. For one, people reinterpret ambiguous or mixed information that might challenge their expectation; they make the information fit the expectation. For another,

**Table 4.8**    Extremity of Trait Ratings for Firsthand or Secondhand Acquaintances

| Consensual Evaluation of Acquaintance | Acquaintance | | |
| --- | --- | --- | --- |
| | Firsthand | Secondhand | Difference |
| Likeable | 29.43 | 32.14 | 2.71 |
| Unlikeable | −29.28 | −33.21 | −3.93 |

Ratings potentially range from −36 to +36.

*Source:* From Gilovich, 1987. Copyright © American Psychological Association. Adapted with permission.

people's thinking makes their expectations more extreme (Tesser, 1978; the more you think about your favorite hobby, the more you like it). Finally, the cost of constructing a new expectation seems psychologically prohibitive. Even so, people are no fools. Expectations do change in response to clear disconfirmation, encounters with alternative expectations, and scrutiny of the unique individual instance.

## Mental Representation of Specific Experience

Schemas and expectations form only one hypothesized kind of mental representation. With all this emphasis on them, one might wonder whether people ever scrutinize individual instances at all. Do people even use the raw data? Yes, people do have multiple mental representations of specific stimuli or experiences, derived from first-hand or secondhand experience. Not only do people generalize and store expectations, but also the specific experiences themselves aid understanding. People can understand other people on the basis of concrete experiences, stored as a collection of **exemplars** (Smith, 1998; Wyer, 2007). Unlike an abstract summary of someone in an overall Gestalt impression, understanding by exemplars collects direct and indirect experiences, storing them for future reference. Later the person can aggregate those experiences or exemplars to answer a general question. For example, if one needed to know whether professors are witty, one would think of various specific interactions with professors and generalize on the basis of experiences.

An advantage of this kind of process is the ability to calculate unexpected answers. People realize in birds, for example, the connections between small size and singing or large size and squawking (Malt & Smith, 1984). Exemplars can also be sensitive to the immediate context (Barsalou, 1987): Do birds have beaks and feathers? Yes. Do birds sing? Yes, in the context of "typical" birds such as robins and sparrows. But now consider barnyard birds. Think of all that squawking, clucking, crowing, gobbling, honking, and quacking; one might hesitate to call it singing. In that context, maybe singing is not a core feature of birds. One could extrapolate this example to professors singing ("no, not well"), unless one specifically considers humanities and fine arts faculty, in which case many fine professional singers come to mind. The power of the exemplar to calculate answers to unusual questions is clear, but it depends on context.

The **grounded cognition** approach (Barsalou, 2008) suggests that concrete experiences create **embodied cognition**, such that the original perceptual experience and bodily state reemerges in recollecting cognitions, a process that simulates the original experiences. This highly specific type of process rejects abstracted symbolic and computational processes, and it is gaining currency within social cognition research, especially to describe the role of emotion (e.g., Niedenthal, Barsalou, Winkielman, Krauth-Gruber, & Ric, 2005).

## Summary of Expectations

Schemas and expectations have a long history in psychology, cutting across developmental, cognitive, social, and clinical psychology. This broad application continues: Psychological researchers have applied schema theories to, for example, text processing, self-concept, personality disorders, visual perception, body image, managerial decision-making, math instruction, clinical diagnosis, sexuality, marketing, verbal causality, criminal justice, leadership, health behavior, intended actions, story construction, stereotypes, causal explanations, geometry tests, pragmatic reasoning, gender roles, reading comprehension, close relationships, political decision-making, and propensity to sue (Fiske, 2000b).

In social psychology, the most common kinds of expectations are personality traits, self-concepts, social roles, social groups, and social events. Social expectations guide encoding, remembering, and responding, mostly to make social thinking more efficient and generally to maintain expectations. Expectations do develop and change in response to new information, but they tend to be conservative. Memory for specific experiences, that is, exemplars and embodied cognitions, also guides social understanding.

## GOALS, AUTOMATICITY, AND CONTROL: PEOPLE CAN'T ALWAYS CONTROL WHAT THEY THINK

A harried parent trying to get the family out the door to work and school places the child's cereal on the floor for the dog and the kibbles on the table for the child. This merely supplements occasions on which the parent calls the child by the dog's name and vice versa (Fiske, Haslam, & Fiske, 1991).

Clearly, this is an instance of careless use of expectations, under time pressure. Contrast it with Dr. Watson's efforts to use scientific deduction in analyzing a walking stick engraved to a Dr. Mortimer "from his friends at C.C.H. 1884." Watson deduces that the walking stick implies a "successful, elderly medical man, well-esteemed," who must be a country doctor because the stick "has been so knocked about" and "the thick iron ferrule [tip] is worn down." Holmes sets him straight.

> On what occasion would it be most probable that such a presentation would be made? When would his friends unite to give him a pledge of their good will? Obviously at the moment when Dr. Mortimer withdrew from the service of the [Charing Cross] hospital in order to start in practice for himself. We know there has been a change from a town hospital to a country practice. . . .
>
> He could not have been on the staff of the hospital, since only a man well-established in a London practice could hold such a position, and such a one would not drift into the country. What was he, then? If he was in the hospital and yet not on the staff he could only have been a house-surgeon or a house-physician—little more than a senior student. And he left five years ago—the date is on the stick. So your grave, middle-aged family practitioner vanishes into thin air, my dear Watson, and there emerges a young fellow under thirty, amiable, unambitious, absent-minded, and the possessor of a favorite dog, which I should describe roughly as being larger than a terrier and smaller than a mastiff.

... It is my experience that it is only an amiable man in this world who receives testimonials, only an unambitious one who abandons a London career for the country, and only an absent-minded one who leaves his stick and not his visiting-card after waiting an hour in your room.

And the dog?

Has been in the habit of carrying this stick behind his master. Being a heavy stick, the dog has held it tightly by the middle, and the marks of his teeth are very plainly visible. (Doyle, 1892–1927, pp. 670–671)[10]

As these examples illustrate, the process of applying expectations depends on people's goals. In the kibbles/cereal mix-up, the harried parent focused on a goal of responding rapidly and seems to have applied the feed-smaller-creatures script to pet and child indiscriminately. In the Watson-Holmes example, both men focused on a goal of thinking slowly and deliberately about Dr. Mortimer, though apparently with different degrees of accuracy.

People's processes, whether accurate or not, must be sensitive to changing goals and circumstances (Fishbach & Ferguson, 2007; S. T. Fiske, 1992, 1993b; Jones & Thibaut, 1958; Shah & Gardner, 2008). People's goals guide them between the poles of **dual processes**, automatic and controlled. Sometimes we can fly on automatic pilot, and sometimes we need to control the plane ourselves. Degrees of automaticity and control are evoked by various social interaction goals, showing that indeed thinking is for doing. People's understanding processes are catalyzed by their motive to understand their social words, in the service of social interaction. Whether aiming for accuracy in social impressions or using schemas and expectations to understand what seems familiar, people are motivated to reach good-enough, not obviously wrong, understandings of their social surroundings. People also are motivated to trust others, all else being equal, seeing the positive whenever plausible. Both understanding and trusting operate in the context of acting effectively in one's social environment. The goal of coordinating with other people requires understanding and trusting them well enough.

People are concerned not only with coordination, cooperation, and control regarding others, but also coordinating and controlling themselves. In this chapter, a final feature of social cognition concerns how controllable it is—or is not. Some researchers (e.g., Bargh, 1997) argue that 99.44% of people's thoughts and actions are automatic, whereas others believe that people have more choice than that. Some of the most exciting new work in social psychology revolves around these issues. After reading about varieties of automaticity and control, see where you think the balance lies between these dual processes.

## Automaticity, the New Unconscious

"The whole train of thought did not occupy a second." A fully **automatic** mental action occurs unintentionally, involuntarily, effortlessly, and outside awareness. Automaticity can be defined in if-then terms: "Given the presence or occurrence of a

---

[10] Copyright © Doyle Estate. Reprinted with permission.

particular set of situational features (e.g., a person or event), a certain psychological, emotional, or behavioral effect will follow" (Bargh, 1997, p. 2). Knowing the sum of 2 + 2 would qualify as a simple sort of automaticity, as would backing away from a creepy-looking person. Typing and driving are more complex kinds of automatic nonsocial actions. More social forms of complex automaticity are far-reaching, as the next section indicates, but here is an illustration:

> A number of years ago, in Cambridge, Massachusetts, I was sitting on a bench in a shopping complex with a friend of mine. The two of us were talking casually, classical music drifting through the air, when all of a sudden we heard behind us the sound of running feet. Just as we turned around, we saw tearing past us two black men followed by a white man in a security guard's uniform. My friend, who has an active civic conscience, jumped up, too late to catch the first guy, but tackled the second guy. They both went sprawling to the floor, my friend broke his glasses, and the security guard nearly landed on the two of them, my friend and the second black guy. The first guy got away. It turned out that the guy my friend had tackled was the owner of the store that had just been robbed. So the real thief, who was the first African American fellow, escaped, thanks to my friend. For everyone involved, it was truly maddening and humiliating. (Fiske, 1995, p. 150)[11]

How do such reactions become automatic? Such processes do not happen overnight. It takes practice to assume that two black men are necessarily together and that if one is a thief, then the other is too. Automatic processes are not either on or off, like a light switch. Instead, like a dimmer, they move from the bright light of full consciousness to the darkness of the fully unconscious. They move into automaticity by repetition. People learning any new physical skill know this, as they practice the skill until it becomes habitual. Social psychological processes also become automatic through practice (Smith, 1998). For example, a probation officer might make repeated judgments of another person's stability, reliability, and honesty, becoming more automatic than deliberate, whereas a professor giving 100 oral exams learns to judge students' performance relatively quickly, and a panhandler judges potential givers' generosity almost instantly. Social cognitive processes range from most practiced and automatic to most controlled (Bargh, 1984, 1996), as follows.

**PRECONSCIOUS AUTOMATICITY**    Suppose that an experimenter seats you in front of a computer screen and you see a series of small flashes, each followed by a Chinese ideograph. Afterward you must rate the novel ideographs, and although it seems arbitrary, you find that you like some better than others. Reliably, participants like best those ideographs that had been preceded by a suboptimal or **subliminal** positive prime. That is, each initial flash of light was actually the independent variable; it was a picture of a smiling or angry face displayed for 4 milliseconds (4/1000 of a second). These flashed faces affected ratings of the ideographs that followed them

---

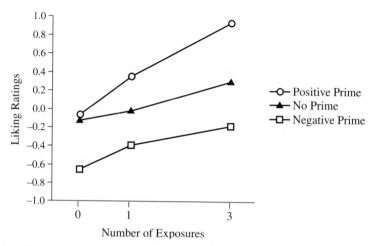

**Figure 4.4**   Liking as a Function of Suboptimal Affective Primes and Number of Exposures

*Source:* From Murphy et al., 1995. Copyright © American Psychological Association. Adapted with permission.

(Murphy, Monahan, & Zajonc, 1995). In other words, the flashed faces each acted as a **prime** (a prior stimulus activating concepts that affect interpretation of what follows). Positive primes created more liking for the ideographs, and negative ones created more disliking, in comparison with a no-prime control group. These effects increased with numbers of exposures to the prime-ideograph pair (see Figure 4.4).

This result illustrates **preconscious automaticity**, for the priming stimulus (the happy or angry face) appears below awareness, yet it affects ratings nonetheless. Preconscious automaticity is the gold standard of automatic processes, the most purely automatic kind of response, with surprising results. In line with the public's worst fears, movie theaters could use this technique to get customers to rush out for soda during a film (Cooper & Cooper, 2002). Clearly this kind of subliminal priming can occur in real life—for example, when one sees the flash of a frown, or someone else's hand at cards; willy nilly, these brief exposures have an unconscious impact. Nonetheless, even this kind of subliminal processing depends on one's goals (Stapel & Koomen, 2006).

Another kind of preconscious automaticity occurs even more often in daily life. Unconsciously, people are primed permanently or chronically, as it were, for certain dimensions of social cognition. For example, one of my elderly relatives appraises all women on their appearance and all men on their importance. Some undergraduates consistently describe other people in particular terms—for example, as humorous, intelligent, friendly, loud, or concerned. People focus on these chronically accessible dimensions and ignore other dimensions that are not chronic for them. These **chronically accessible** traits thus preconsciously influence their impressions and memory of other people (Higgins, King, & Mavin, 1982). The individual difference interacts with contextual primes. For example, unconsciously priming chronic competitors with competence promotes competing, whereas the opposite holds for chronic cooperators (Utz, Ouwerkerk, & Van Lange, 2004). Like subliminal primes, chronic accessibility operates at a preconscious level to filter and shape our experience of other people, depending on context.

**POSTCONSCIOUS AUTOMATICITY**    As an exercise, memorize the following words: *adventurous, independent, self-confident, persistent*. What technique are you using? Some students simply rehearse the words by repeating them. Some try to make the first letters into an acronym, such as P(ersistent), I(ndependent), S(elf-confident), A(dventurous). Others try to imagine a person with all these characteristics; can you form an impression of that person easily?

Now consider which technique is most likely to be effective. It turns out that using the words to form an impression of the person works best (Hamilton, Katz, & Leirer, 1980). This illustrates **postconscious automaticity**, insofar as one is aware of the words and of engaging in the process (forming an impression) but not necessarily aware of the effects of impression formation on the memorizing process.

Now try another experiment. First, familiarize yourself with the following paragraph:

> Donald spent a great deal of time in search of what he liked to call
> excitement. He had already climbed Mt. McKinley, shot the Colorado
> Rapids in a kayak, driven in a demolition derby, and piloted a jet-powered
> boat without knowing very much about boats. He had risked injury and
> even death a number of times. Now he was in search of new excitement.
> He was thinking, perhaps, that maybe he would do some skydiving, or
> maybe cross the Atlantic in a sailboat. By the way he acted, one could
> really guess that Donald was well aware of his ability to do many things
> well. Other than business engagements, Donald's contacts with other people
> were rather limited. He felt that he did not need to rely on anyone. Once
> Donald made up his mind to do something, it was as good as done, no
> matter how long it might take or how difficult the going might be. Only
> rarely did he change his mind, even when it might have been better if he
> had. (Higgins, Rholes, & Jones, 1977)[12]

How generally likeable do you find Donald: more positive than negative or more negative than positive? If you react as did participants in one study (Higgins, Rholes, & Jones, 1977), you should find him more positive than negative. Part of the reason is the list of trait words you memorized (or at least read several times) in the previous paragraph. Not only was I using those words to illustrate a point, but I was also using them to prime you postconsciously with a positive impression of Donald. Try the alternative experimental condition at home, on a roommate or relative. Ask the person to memorize *reckless, conceited, aloof, stubborn*. Then as part of a "separate experiment," ask the person to read and rate the Donald paragraph; the person's reaction should be more negative than yours, on average. Again, this constitutes a type of postconscious priming effect, in which the primes and the stimulus are conscious, but the link between the two is not.

---

[12] Copyright © Elsevier. Reprinted with permission.

For example, consciously priming the concept of distance makes people report weaker attachments to family and home town (Williams & Bargh, 2008). One study (Bargh, Chen, & Burrows, 1996) discussed earlier in this chapter also exemplifies postconscious priming, in that participants consciously saw words related to their elderly stereotypes, which then caused them to walk more slowly. (These researchers' priming of the black male stereotype, in contrast, was subliminal and therefore preconscious.) The behavior primed may prepare perceivers to interact with that social group (Cesario, Plaks, & Higgins, 2006), most often by behavior matching.

One puzzle, related to stereotypes in particular, concerns whether automaticity results in people imitating the stereotype versus responding in the opposite direction. For example, they may behave in the complementary way (subordinate reaction to dominance) or they react against it (reject the stereotype). Whether the person appears cognitively as a prototypical group member versus a specific individual, automatic behavior shows opposite patterns (Dijksterhuis, Spears, & Lépinasse, 2001). Consider first **assimilation** (fitting a stimulus to a prior conception). Abstract concepts, such as stereotypes, function as relatively automatic frameworks to interpret specific encounters, as in this chapter's earlier account of expectations. Similarly, when primed by a group stereotype or prototype, people assimilate related individuals to the group and behave stereotypically. They also assimilate when they are operating under cognitive load or no particular accuracy motivation, presumably because the automatic reactions predominate.

On the other hand, consider **contrast** (opposing the stimulus to the existing standard). When primed by a specific individual exemplar of a category, people compare themselves to the individual, using the person as a standard. When the person is an outgroup member, people emphasize the difference between themselves and the other individual. As a result, people contrast when exposed to an individual exemplar. People also contrast when motivated to be accurate (going beyond general group stereotypes) or when self-focused, because they can override the automatic effects of stereotype activation (Dijksterhuis & van Knippenberg, 2000).

Thus, priming the overall stereotype of brainy professors or airhead supermodels leads to respectively better or worse performance on a knowledge test—assimilation—but priming specific exemplars leads to the opposite pattern—contrast (Dijksterhuis et al., 1998). Presumably, also, stereotypic associations to the general category would be stronger than stereotypic associations to any given unique individual. Thus, a related principle also fits these assimilation-contrast effects: The sheer degree of association in memory between the relevant outgroup category (e.g., elderly) and the relevant trait (forgetful) determines these automatic behavior effects (Dijksterhuis, Aarts, Bargh, & van Knippenberg, 2000). Contact with the outgroup can strengthen stereotypic associations if the experience reinforces the stereotype. Associations are stronger when perceivers have encountered group members whose stereotype-relevant traits fit expected averages with low variability (Dijksterhuis & van Knippenberg, 1999). Work to date has emphasized cognitive routes to automatic activation of stereotypic behavior, fitting our core social motive of understanding (Wheeler & Petty, 2001).

Another example of postconscious automaticity—besides priming abstract concepts and concrete exemplars—is mood's effect on everyday behavior. For example, students arriving to study in a library once discovered at a vacant desk a large envelope containing pictures designed to induce either a positive mood (humorous cartoons) or a negative mood (car accidents). Moments later, a stranger approached them and requested some paper. When the students were in a negative mood, especially if the request sounded impolite ("Give me some paper"), they were more likely to resist the request and to criticize it later, compared to those primed to be in a good mood (Forgas, 1998). This effect is postconscious because, again, the participants were entirely aware of the pictures but not of their effects on subsequent responses. Mood also affects memory and judgment (Schwarz & Clore, 2007): People tend to judge events as congruent with their current mood (Mayer, Gaschke, Braverman, & Evans, 1992). People judge even their lives as better when they are in a good mood due to the weather (Schwarz & Clore, 1983). The automatic effects of chronic negative mood can create a downward spiral in conditions such as ongoing depression.

As still another type of postconscious automaticity, **salience** describes effects of capturing people's conscious attention. For example, mere physical point of view alters significant social judgments (Taylor & Fiske, 1975). Students sat in a circle observing two conversationalists and later judged which one influenced the conversation most. Although their seating positions were entirely arbitrary, the participants rated whichever person they faced as more important than the other in setting the tone and content of the conversation. (A word to the wise: Seating position in a seminar—opposite the instructor—can determine which students are viewed as contributing more to the discussion.) Subsequently, we (Taylor & Fiske, 1978) also found greater extremity in ratings of people who stand out in a group (e.g., the only man or woman in a group of the other sex, the only black person in a group of whites). The common theme here is that people who are salient, who stand out and attract visual attention, receive more credit and blame than people who attract less notice.

A final example comes from the mere effects of **gaze direction** (Macrae, Hood, Milne, Rowe, & Mason, 2002), noted in the last chapter. When a person gazes directly at you, you can more quickly categorize the person and access stereotypic information. Presumably, the person's direct gaze indicates that you are the focus of attention, suggesting that the person may have intention as well as attention directed toward you. In that case, quick decisions about the person may be adaptive. As with impression priming, mood, and salience effects, gaze effects are postconscious because the stimulus eliciting the effect is fully conscious, although its impact is not. Thus, the process may be unintentional, involuntary, effortless, and itself outside awareness, but the eliciting stimulus is not outside awareness.

**GOAL-DEPENDENT AUTOMATICITY**   Moving up the ladder from fully automatic toward more controlled responses, **goal-dependent** forms of automaticity are involuntary, effortless, and outside awareness, but they depend on conscious intents. That is, when people have goals in mind, the goals recruit automatic processes to help out. Indeed, people may make superior decisions when they let their unconscious do the deciding, once they deliberately set the choice process in motion and then ignore it for a while (Dijksterhuis, Bos, Nordgren, & van Baaren, 2006). People's thoughts demonstrate goal-dependent automaticity in at least three other ways: making it difficult to suppress unwanted thoughts, ruminations, and habits.

To appreciate this point, do a **thought-suppression** experiment. Stop reading, and try *not* to think of a white bear for one full minute. If you happen to think of one, mark a piece of paper each time. But try your best not to think of one. When people try to suppress a thought, they tend to be unsuccessful because, ironically, the effort to suppress causes the opposite result (Wegner, 1994). If you did the white-bear experiment, chances are you failed to suppress the thought completely. The very act of monitoring to see if you have thought the thought causes it to be activated automatically. As well, any distractors you may dream up (red Volkswagens) become associated with the forbidden thoughts (bears climbing out of VWs), bringing the thought to mind yet again. The processes that bring the thought to mind are automatic, but the goal that sets them in motion is not.

In a similar vein, people's **ruminations**—conscious thoughts directed toward a given object over an extended period—result from goals (Martin & Tesser, 1989). When people's goals are frustrated (e.g., getting together with their inaccessible dream date), the frustration motivates them to try again (asking again and getting rebuffed). Then they tend to think about other ways of getting to their goal, daydream about the unattained outcome, and eventually try to give up on the goal (a difficulty enshrined in several popular songs about romantic obsessions).

Whenever activated, goals rapidly cue related **habits**, goal-directed automatic behavior (Aarts & Dijksterhuis, 2000). For example, habitual bicycle-riders rapidly respond to the word *bicycle* when primed with the goal of traveling to nearby locations (e.g., the university). Nonhabitual bicycle riders do not (see Table 4.9). Thus, for better or worse, goals cue habitual thoughts and behaviors.

All is not lost, however. Although people may not be good at suppressing unwanted thoughts and derailing unbidden ruminations, practice makes progress. When people develop a goal that entails repeated social cognitive processes, the process can become automatic, as noted earlier. Repetition facilitates subsequent responses to the same task (Smith, 1998). Practice also can be harnessed to achieve alternative goals, alternative thought processes, and other freely chosen goals. With regard to the experiment's travel goal that primed *bicycle*, one can deliberately think about alternative goals (working from home), alternative thought processes

**Table 4.9**   Speed of Response to the Word *Bicycle*

| Habit Strength | Travel Goal Primed | |
| --- | --- | --- |
| | No | Yes |
| Nonhabitual bicycle riders | 863 | 958 |
| Habitual bicycle riders | 883 | 759 |

Numbers indicate milliseconds to respond, so lower numbers indicate faster responses.

*Source:* From Aarts & Dijksterhuis, 2000. Copyright © American Psychological Association. Adapted with permission.

(focusing on the pleasures of biking or walking), or creating an altogether new goal (exercising). What starts as deliberate can become automatic with repetition.

Before leaving goal-dependent automaticity, recall two forms of dispositional inference, discussed in Chapter 3; these also illustrate automaticity that depends on goals. People can observe behavior and categorize it instantly according to relevant personality traits (Todorov & Uleman, 2002; Winter & Uleman, 1984), and they can make dispositional attributions relatively automatically (Gilbert, 1998). Spontaneous trait inferences fit goal-dependent automaticity, in that they seem more likely when the perceiver has a goal of forming an impression of the other person.

**FULLY INTENTIONAL CONTROL**    To exercise **intent**, a person must (a) have options, (b) make the hard choice, and (c) pay attention (Fiske, 1989). To demonstrate intent, a person must first have a choice, as in the following timeless dilemmas: getting out of bed on a cold morning or staying put; squandering one's money or saving it; assenting to a seduction or declining it. In these cases, one has options and therefore intent. In contrast, flinching from a hot flame is not intentional. Generally, when one has a choice, one option is the easy, dominant alternative, in which case intent is less obvious ("I couldn't help it"); the other alternative, if chosen, demonstrates intent in a more obvious way (making the hard choice). To implement the chosen alternative, the intentional actor must concentrate on it (imagine what has to be done after getting up; plan how to save money; visualize a healthier relationship). Paying attention, forming mental images of the action, or simulating the entire process all facilitate enacting the intention.

Enacting an intent entails an **implemental mind-set**, which differs from the **deliberative mind-set** of decision making prior to action (Gollwitzer, Heckhausen, & Steller, 1990). When people are deciding, they consider their options and weigh all kinds of information. Having decided, they shift to implementing their decision and focus on information that will help them enact their choice. People are more likely to enact their intentions (e.g., getting a project done over winter break) when they form specific implementation plans (in situation $y$, I will perform behavior $z$) (Gollwitzer & Brandsdätter, 1997). For example, one might think, "I will start the term paper the morning after Christmas, when my family always goes out to exchange unwanted gifts." This specific implementation plan works better than "I'll do the term paper over winter break." These if-then intentions reliably facilitate goal attainment (Gollwitzer & Sheeran, 2006).

## Goals That Prompt Automaticity and Control

Knowing that social cognition ranges from preconscious automaticity, through postconscious automaticity and goal-dependent automaticity, to fully intentional control, one might well wonder how people arrive at these relatively automatic or controlled processes in the first place. In keeping with the view of people as motivated tacticians (mentioned earlier in this chapter), social cognizers may take the automatic, easy way if they are motivated to be decisive, but the more controlled, effortful process if motivated to avoid being wrong. This dual-process tactic (one more automatic, one more controlled) characterizes a range of social behavior (Chaiken & Trope, 1999) and judgment (Evans, 2008; Kruglanski & Orehek, 2007), even distinguishing different neural systems that underlie social cognition (Adolphs, 2009; Lieberman, 2007). Both processes, although contrasting, serve the core social motive of understanding.

**AVOIDING INDECISION**  The motive to control—that is, to be effective in the environment—increases the cost of being indecisive. Making a decision, any good-enough decision, can dominate all other goals (Kruglanski & Webster, 1991, 1996). Various situational variables create subgoals aiming for **urgency** (decide fast) and **permanence** (never reconsider). Time pressure, ambient noise, mental fatigue, a demanded judgment, and the threat of boredom all motivate people to reach closure on a decision, immediately seizing on accessible information and quickly freezing on an initial judgment.

Besides these situational motivators toward decisiveness, individual differences in **need for closure** work in a similar way, creating preference for order and predictability, decisiveness, discomfort with ambiguity, and closed-mindedness. Chapter 3 introduced need for closure in the context of high-scoring people who seek stable explanations that differ by culture (individual or group dispositions). People differ not only as individuals but also by self-sorting into vocations: Accounting students score higher on need for closure than studio arts students do (Webster & Kruglanski, 1994). A related construct, **personal need for structure** (Neuberg & Newsom, 1993), disposes people to favor relatively simple organization and understanding. Overall, the motive to be decisive encourages relatively automatic processes and inhibits more controlled processes for making sense of the social world.

**AVOIDING ERROR**  People are not always motivated to be decisive, in order to satisfy the understanding motive. The desire for accuracy also reflects people's need for understanding. Because that understanding preferably is socially shared, the core social motives of understanding and belonging both are relevant here.

Various processes alert people to the possibility of error: Increasing the costs of a bad decision, requesting caution, and subjecting decisions to scrutiny all cause people to use more information in an effort to feel accurate, although they may or may not increase their actual accuracy. For example, making people **accountable** for their decisions by telling them that they will have to justify their decisions to a third party causes them to use available information even when it is inappropriate (Tetlock, 1992).

Making people dependent on other people has parallel effects (Erber & Fiske, 1984). When people need each other to achieve a goal, when they are **outcome dependent**, they learn about each other in more detail, focusing especially on the information that challenges their expectations for the other person. They make more dispositional inferences about this unexpected information and form more idiosyncratic responses. For these processes to operate, people do not have to be on a team together, although that is one obvious instance of interdependence. People's outcomes merely have to be correlated, even if negatively, as in a singles tennis competition, for them to be motivated to be accurate in judging another person (Ruscher & Fiske, 1990). Depending on other people, whether cooperatively or competitively, creates a need to understand them accurately in order to increase one's own sense of prediction and control (Neuberg, 1989; Neuberg & Fiske, 1987). The control motive is thus also important here. As noted in Chapter 1 (Pittman & Pittman, 1980), people temporarily deprived of control think harder about other people. Moreover, accountability and interdependence also reflect the core social motives to belong and to understand other people in ways that make social sense.

Individual differences in experienced lack of control influence social cognition. People who are chronically uncertain about the causes of their own and other's outcomes think more sensitively and carefully about social information (Weary & Edwards, 1994). People who are depressed and chronically low on sense of control also focus on piecemeal understanding (Edwards & Weary, 1993). **Causal uncertainty** makes people think harder in an effort to find predictability and control.

## CHAPTER SUMMARY

A last bit of social cognition from Sherlock Holmes, explaining how he knew that Watson had just recovered from a summer cold:

> "Your slippers are new," he said. "You could not have had them more than
> a few weeks. The soles which you are at this moment presenting to me are
> slightly scorched. For a moment I thought they might have got wet and
> been burned in the drying. But near the instep there is a small circular
> wafer of paper with the shopman's hieroglyphics upon it. Damp would of
> course have removed this. You had, then, been sitting with your feet
> outstretched to the fire, which a man would hardly do even in so wet a June
> as this if he were in his full health." (Doyle, 1892–1927, p. 363)[13]

Ordinary mortals do not match Sherlock Holmes's knowledge of behavior, motivations, and occupations, as revealed by traces on body, clothing, and possessions, nor his ability to construct the most likely and coherent explanations. Yet ordinary social cognition—the process by which people think about and make sense of other people, themselves, and social situations—serves everyday purposes. Pragmatically, it works much of the time, people's foibles not withstanding. People's core motive to understand is influenced by being motivated tacticians who balance the use of mental resources against a need for pragmatic accuracy. People's motive to trust others and think well of them is tempered by their vigilance for negative information. Social psychologists examining cognitive structure and process in view of these core social motives have discovered a variety of pragmatic phenomena related to impression and inferential accuracy, expectations, and goals.

Impressions are remarkably accurate, as indicated by consensus from the first moments of interaction, especially on interpersonal traits such as extroversion and agreeableness and especially in familiar contexts. People's inferences fall far short of normative models at every stage because people use heuristic shortcuts. However, social settings provide some checks and balances, and certain kinds of training can improve decision making.

---

[13] Copyright © Doyle Estate. Reprinted with permission.

The expectation concept arose in psychology generally as a way to describe people's reliance on organized, familiar cognitive structures. In social psychology, it built on Gestalt models of impression formation, in contrast to more elemental models. People understand their social worlds via expectations for personalities, self, roles, groups, and events, which guide encoding, remembering, and responding. Expectations generally favor expectation-consistent information and develop from firsthand or secondhand experiences.

Social cognitive processes can range from preconscious automaticity (through postconscious automaticity and goal-dependent automaticity) to fully intentional control. People's goals guide them to be more decisive or more careful, depending on circumstances and individual differences.

All these processes—related to decision making, expectations, and goals—serve the core social motive of understanding other people. Understanding primarily drives social cognition in the service of control, although people do seem generally motivated to trust other people, within limits. As social thinkers, we muddle through, no Sherlock Holmeses, but no fools, either.

## SUGGESTIONS FOR FURTHER READING

ANDERSEN, S. M., MOSKOWITZ, G. B., BLAIR, I. V., & NOSEK, B. A. (2007). Automatic thought. In A. W. KRUGLANSKI & E. T. HIGGINS (Eds.), *Social psychology: Handbook of basic principles* (2nd ed., pp. 138–175). New York: Guilford.

AUGOUSTINOS, M., WALKER, I., & DONAGHUE, N. (2006). *Social cognition: An integrated introduction* (2nd ed.). Thousand Oaks, CA: Sage.

BARGH, J. A., GOLLWITZER, P. M., & OETTINGEN, G. (2010). Motivation. In S. T. FISKE, D. T. GILBERT, & G. LINDZEY (Eds.), *Handbook of social psychology* (5th ed.). New York: Wiley.

CHAIKEN, S., & TROPE, Y. (Eds.). (1999). *Dual process theories in social psychology*. New York: Guilford.

DIJKSTERHUIS, A. (2010). Automaticity and the unconscious. In S. T. FISKE, D. T. GILBERT, & G. LINDZEY (Eds.), *Handbook of social psychology* (5th ed.). New York: Wiley.

FISKE, S. T., & TAYLOR, S. E. (2008). *Social cognition: From brains to culture*. New York: McGraw-Hill.

GILOVICH, T. D., & GRIFFIN, D. W. (2009). Judgment and decision making in social psychology. In S. T. FISKE, D. T. GILBERT, & G. LINDZEY, (Eds.), *Handbook of social psychology* (5th ed.). New York: Wiley.

KUNDA, Z. (1999). *Social cognition: Making sense of people*. Cambridge, MA: MIT Press.

LIEBERMAN, M. D. (2010). Social cognitive neuroscience. In S. T. FISKE, D. T. GILBERT, & G. LINDZEY, (Eds.), *Handbook of social psychology* (5th ed.). New York: Wiley.

MOSKOWITZ, G. B. (2004). *Social cognition: Understanding self and others*. New York: Guilford.

SHAFIR, E. (2007). Decisions constructed locally: Some fundamental principles of the psychology of decision-making. In A. W. KRUGLANSKI & E. T. HIGGINS (Eds.), *Social psychology: Handbook of basic principles* (2nd ed., pp. 334–352). New York: Guilford.

ROESE, N. J., & SHERMAN, J. W. (2007). Expectancy. In A. W. KRUGLANSKI & E. T. HIGGINS (Eds.), *Social psychology: Handbook of basic principles* (2nd ed., pp. 91–115). New York: Guilford.

SMITH, E. (1998). Mental representation and memory. In D. T. GILBERT, S. T. FISKE, & G. LINDZEY (Eds.), *Handbook of social psychology* (4th ed., Vol. 1, pp. 391–445). Boston: McGraw-Hill.

WEGNER, D. M., & BARGH, J. A. (1998). Control and automaticity in social life. In D. T. GILBERT, S. T. FISKE, & G. LINDZEY (Eds.), *Handbook of social psychology* (4th ed., Vol. 1, pp. 446–496). Boston: McGraw-Hill.

WYER, R. S., Jr. (2007). Mental representation. In A. W. KRUGLANSKI & E. T. HIGGINS (Eds.), *Social psychology: Handbook of basic principles* (2nd ed., pp. 285–307). New York: Guilford.

# Chapter 5

# The Self: Social to the Core

What is the self? Why have humans evolved a self? How do different cultures construct the self? Social psychology has addressed these questions and more. As we will see, three core social motives best explain the self in its cognitive, affective, and behavioral manifestations: The motive to understand underlies the cognitive self-concept; the motive to self-enhance explains feelings about the self; and the motive to belong accounts for the interplay between self and behavior. The cognitive self-concept shows the simultaneous coherence but complexity of the self and how people come to know themselves. The affective self shows self-enhancing biases that predict emotional reactions to adverse feedback. And the behaving self shows various forms of strategic self-presentation, self-monitoring, and self-regulating, all designed to gain acceptance by others. But first, we will conceptually and operationally define the self and illustrate the role of the core social motives, in order to frame what research has uncovered about the self, which turns out to be social to the core.

Now that we are a few chapters in, keep in mind that the book flows from within the person, to between people, to between groups. The book's overall level of analysis continues from micro to macro within social settings. Because of this flow, your perspective on the psychology of the self will be better if you have already read about social cognition (Chapter 4), which involves self-schemas, and person perception (Chapter 3), which involves dispositional inferences about self and others.

## WHAT IS THE SELF?

Before you read on, take a minute and write 20 responses to "I am ... " Even if you have already done it for class, take a minute now.

On the first day of my social psychology class, students also answer, "Who am I?" Here are some of their responses (printed here with permission!):

- "Thoughtful. Understanding. Flexible. Reasonable. Often timid. Cautious. Focused but confused. Mellow."

- "Female. Student. Active. Musical/creative. Dedicated. Ethical. Sarcastic. Caring. Loving. Independent. Faster than _____. Enthusiastic. Over analyzer. Deep thinker. Casual drinker. Loyal. Selfish. Opinionated. Accepting. Almost graduate."
- "Male. Brown hair. Blue eyes. Like sports. Like guitar. Friendly. Sociable. Organized. Goal oriented. Neat."

What stands out about these responses? Most are trait adjectives, apparently fixed dispositions. Many students consider themselves to have a particular personality that constitutes the self.

What is missing from these descriptions? To answer this question, compare these answers with some from my psychology of racism class:

- "Female. Student/psych major. From New York. Of Irish descent. Passive/shy (at first). Open-minded. Terrible decision-maker."
- "A woman. A Hispanic. A student. A secretary. A daughter. A sister. A fiancée. Someone who cares for others. A faithful Catholic. A friend. A human. An independent person. A lover of classical music. A great cook."
- "A woman. Young, 21. Black. College student. Studying psychology. Happy, caring. Sympathetic. Fun, with a sense of humor. Outgoing. Studious. Adventurous. Person who likes to do things. Intelligent. Me."

In the psychology of racism class, twice or three times as many people answer "Who am I?" by mentioning their ethnic background, compared with those who do so in the social psychology class. Why? It might be that different people take the two different courses, but even when the same people overlap, they do not answer identically in the two different classes. Why? Probably because of the situation. Consider how differently people describe themselves on Facebook or other internet sites when they think their family (or employers) will have access—or not (Bargh & McKenna, 2004; Hart, 2008). When students answer the question "Who am I?" or construct a profile online, the self they describe is not a fixed entity. Who they are—or who they communicate themselves to be—depends on the social situation. The **dynamic self** is not a simple fixed entity (Markus & Wurf, 1987): "What began [for researchers] as an apparently singular, static, lumplike entity has become a multidimensional, multifaceted dynamic structure" (p. 301). Evidence of the dynamic self comes from people's **self-reports** (what they say about themselves). As my two classes' "who-am-I" examples illustrate, people report different selves, depending on the social context. Researchers studying the self, as we will see, provide several accounts for the differences. Of course, the self-reported self provides only one window on the self, but other research more systematically illuminates the variety of selves.

In response to the in-class exercise, one student replied, "Who am I? That's a lot to ask the first time we meet." Nevertheless, social psychologists persist in asking. Let's define some terms and differentiate, as always, between what social psychologists mean conceptually (that is, the abstract definition), and what we mean operationally (namely, how the concept is concretely studied), the working definition that includes how to measure or experimentally manipulate it. Although other examples from my students will pepper the rest of the chapter, these informal examples are not to be confused with formal evidence, being merely spice.

## Conceptual Definitions

Several authors discussing the self have pointed to the distinctions we have just illustrated. More formally now, examine conceptual levels of the self from the most direct experience to the more indirect. At the most direct level (Baumeister, 1995; Brown, 1998) is the **body self**, an idea that William James (1890) also endorsed as the **material self**. The simplest level, then, would be that the self includes and extends the boundaries of the body.

According to these two physical definitions, one's possessions, clothes, room, car, pet, all are parts of the self. Most clearly, one's head, body, fingers and toes, and one's hair while it still attached to the head all are part of one's self in Western culture. The voice is a bit ambiguous, but e-mail messages once sent are no longer one's self, just as hair, when it falls on the floor after a haircut, is no longer really self (at least in Western culture). And one's perfume or the smell left behind after a particularly sticky workout do not really constitute the self, although they are certainly traces of self, for better or worse. It seems to me that one clue to the self versus not-self distinction would be one's emotional reaction to its loss, damage, or derogation. If you get defensive, it's part of you.

Move up a level, to people's own experience of an **inner self**, what James (1890) called the **spiritual self:** individual, private, intrapersonal, self-reflective identity (e.g., Baumeister, 1998; Brewer & Gardner, 1996; Brown, 1998; Markus & Wurf, 1987; Snyder & Cantor, 1998). People feel that their inner thoughts and feelings best represent their experiences of themselves (Andersen, 1984; Andersen & Ross, 1984), as a later section addresses. One European-American college student answered the "Who am I?" question with internal feelings, thoughts, interests, and abilities: "Stressed and confused. One of many scared & desperate graduate school applicants. . . . Quiet, until you get to know me. Funny. Dramaqueen. A basket of stress. Empathetic. In love." People's attitudes, abilities, interests, and emotions all constitute the inner self. Again, a diagnostic clue to what is self or not comes from self-defense: What aspects of inner experience does the person defend when attacked? Consider an attitude as a possession of the self (Abelson, 1986; Prentice, 1987): One acquires, possesses, and defends an attitude, just like the material aspects of the self—say, a hat or a car. In various ways, then, people experience an inner self, which is typically within but separate from the body and from more obviously social selves.

The **interpersonal, social,** or **relational self** depends on connections between people (Andersen & Chen, 2002; Baumeister, 1998; Brewer & Gardner, 1996; Brown, 1998; James, 1890). The relational self can operate automatically to orient people in the particular social context (Chen, Boucher, & Tapias, 2006). This interpersonal self includes a person's collection of roles: "Student. Swimmer (athlete). Daughter. Sister. Friend. Psychology major." When they answer the question "Who am I?" many students focus on various social selves. People list their ages, their roles in their family, their career plans, their current majors, their interests, their values, and their attitudes; these fit into interpersonal identities, the face-to-face selves that people have and might take on. The roles that constitute the interpersonal self all have in common prescriptions for behavior. A **role** comprises the behavior expected of a person who fills a certain socially defined position.

Moving beyond the interpersonal self to the broader level of the entire culture, the final useful level is the **societal self**. The societal self represents **social identities** defined at the level of the collective or the culture (Brewer & Gardner, 1996). One's ethnicity, gender, age, and religion all contribute to identity. Identity is not defined by face-to-face interaction, the way roles are, but by one's concept of oneself as a member of society and by other people in general having a concept of one's group membership as meaningful. A later section takes up identity in more detail, because it does have important ramifications for individual psychology.

Besides these four levels—body self, inner self, interpersonal self, societal self—one can carve up the self in other ways. For example, William James (1890) distinguished between the "I" and the "me," emphasizing the self in two different forms. One is *I*, which is the agent, the actor: "I choose to do this." The active part of the self, the *I*, is the intentional part of the self. The *I* holds the will and resembles an **agent self** (Baumeister, 1998). People normally do not necessarily consider the self as an agent because we are not so conscious of our own causality (remember Chapter 3's actor-observer effect in attribution: My actions are caused by the situation; yours are caused by your disposition). Then there is the *me*, which is how I am seen—or at least how I think I am seen—the self as an **object** of other people's observation (Duval & Wicklund, 1972): "What do you think of me?" The part of the self that is *me* constitutes the self being observed by others. Distinguishing between the *I* and the *me* illustrates another way to analyze the self besides the four levels that many social psychologists have used.

## Operational Definitions

What are the working definitions of the self? That is, how do social psychologists operationalize the self and make it concrete enough to study? The conceptual definitions of self tell the potential domain of study, but the operational definitions tell how social psychologists actually measure the self. The research divides into (a) self and cognition (self-concept), (b) self and emotion (e.g., self-esteem), and then (c) self and behavior (e.g., self-presentation), to mirror the cognition-affect-behavior tripod discussed in the opening chapter. Note that laypeople often use the terms *self-concept, self-esteem*, and *self-presentation* interchangeably, but social psychologists do not.

**SELF-CONCEPT**   Social psychologists have been particularly interested in the **self-concept**, or cognitive representation of the self. With the use of a cognitive approach, studying the self has overwhelmingly focused, lately, on the content of people's knowledge of themselves or beliefs about themselves. Having just read about social cognition, many students raise the question of overlap between the self-concept and **self-schema**, which the social cognition chapter examined. The overlap is considerable. Self-schemas make up one particular operational way of looking at the self-concept, namely, a dimension on which one rates oneself as high (e.g., *very independent*), as definitely not the opposite (*not at all dependent*), and as important (*most central*) (Markus, 1977). Not all aspects of the self are self-schematic. And not everybody who studies the self-concept endorses the idea of a schema; social psychologists hypothesize different approaches to how the mind might structure self knowledge. In general, though, self-schema and self-concept are close cousins, and a schema is one way to operationalize the most important aspects of the self-concept. Another operational definition of the self-concept comes from answers to the question "Who am I?", as illustrated in the self-descriptions from my classes. For example, the "Twenty Statements Test (TST)" (the who-am-I exercise constrained to 20 answers) contrasts Japanese and American self-concepts (Cousins, 1989), as described later.

**SELF-ESTEEM**    Another area of self research—namely, work on **self-esteem**—illustrates different working definitions that focus on self and emotion: Social psychologists often measure whether people feel good about themselves and feel that they are lovable and worthwhile people. Researchers differentiate **trait self-esteem** (a stable personality disposition) and **state self-esteem** (short-lived self-regard). Social psychologists are primarily interested in state self-esteem. Ever since the beginning of social psychology, about 100 years ago, researchers have pondered state self-esteem and measured it in a variety of ways. Momentary, context-dependent changes in self-evaluation respond like a barometer of one's success, ideally calculated as "outcomes over pretensions [aspirations]" (James, 1890).

The most common measure of self-esteem (Rosenberg, 1965) appears in Table 5.1. Although it is designed to measure trait self-esteem, researchers sometimes use it to measure state self-esteem. More appropriate operationalizations exemplify short-lived, personal, global self-regard. For example, one field researcher (Wells, 1988) measured state self-esteem by lending beepers to mothers and paging them at random moments to have them report how good they were feeling about themselves and how satisfied they were with what they were doing. Researchers sometimes measure three dimensions of state self-esteem (Heatherton & Polivy, 1991): performance ("I feel confident about my abilities"), social regard ("I am worried about what other people think of me"), and appearance ("I feel satisfied with the way my body looks right now"). Still more measures of self-esteem (collective, domain-specific) lie beyond our scope in this chapter.

**SELF-PRESENTATION**    The final area of work operationalizing the self has considered **self-presentation**, which concerns behavior in everyday social psychology—how people try to convey certain identities or images to other people. Toward the end, the chapter discusses self-presentation, the goals people have when they try to convey certain impressions and how they do it. But for now, let us consider some operational definitions of self-presentation. One strategy has simply contrasted public versus anonymous behavior (Baumeister, 1982); any differences presumably result from self-presentation concerns. Other operationalizations (Leary & Kowalski, 1990) observe how public failure or an embarrassing incident makes people hurry to repair the damage, for example, by stressing their positive attributes, doing favors, associating themselves with successful people, or explaining away their failure.

**Table 5.1** Rosenberg Self-Esteem Scale

Instruction: Circle the number that best represents your response.

*1. I feel that I am a person of worth, at least on an equal basis with others.
    1. Strongly agree        2. Agree        3. Disagree        4. Strongly disagree

*2. I feel that I have a number of good qualities.
    1. Strongly agree        2. Agree        3. Disagree        4. Strongly disagree

3. All in all, I am inclined to think that I am a failure.
    1. Strongly agree        2. Agree        3. Disagree        4. Strongly disagree

*4. I am able to do things as well as most other people.
    1. Strongly agree        2. Agree        3. Disagree        4. Strongly disagree

5. I feel I do not have much to be proud of.
    1. Strongly agree        2. Agree        3. Disagree        4. Strongly disagree

*6. I take a positive attitude toward myself.
    1. Strongly agree        2. Agree        3. Disagree        4. Strongly disagree

*7. On the whole, I am satisfied with myself.
    1. Strongly agree        2. Agree        3. Disagree        4. Strongly disagree

8. I wish I could have more respect for myself.
    1. Strongly agree        2. Agree        3. Disagree        4. Strongly disagree

9. I certainly feel useless at times.
    1. Strongly agree        2. Agree        3. Disagree        4. Strongly disagree

10. At times I think I am no good at all.
    1. Strongly agree        2. Agree        3. Disagree        4. Strongly disagree

To get your total score, reverse-score *'d items 1, 2, 4, 6, and 7 (make 1 = 4, 2 = 3, 3 = 2, and 4 = 1). Then add the new scores to your original scores on items 3, 5, 8, 9, and 10. Scored this way, higher numbers indicate more positive feelings about oneself.
*Source:* From Rosenberg, 1965.

These sample operationalizations of self-concept, self-esteem, and self-presentation illustrate how social psychologists study people's selves, in cognitive, affective, and behavioral terms.

## Core Social Motives

Now return to the larger context, that is, some core human motives that have evolved to help people live in groups. The three that best characterize the social role of the self are understanding, enhancing, and belonging. As just illustrated, much of the work on the self within social psychology examines the self from either the context of understanding—trying to develop a clear self-concept, which is cognitive—or the context of self-enhancing—trying to maintain self-esteem as worthwhile, which is primarily affective. The tension between understanding and enhancing creates a dilemma when one tries simultaneously to acknowledge and deny one's negative features. Understanding and enhancing make up two of the themes in research on the self, and they build on the third, namely, belonging: Understanding and enhancing the self help people fit into their social groups.

In the world of ideas, parallel invention helps to validate the utility of similar frameworks created by different people thinking about the same issues. Other writers have parsed the self-motives in a related, though slightly different, way (e.g., Banaji & Prentice, 1994). Their motive for **self-knowledge** resembles this text's "understanding" motive. Their self-enhancement motive (defined solely as seeking positive feedback about the self) is separated from their **self-improvement** motive (the desire to bring oneself closer to one's ideal). As this chapter's section on cultural differences suggests, self-improvement may be one form of self-enhancement (here defined as striving to make oneself worthy). For consistency with the rest of the text, then, this chapter will view **self-enhancement** (increasing the value of the self) as including both attempts to make oneself *be* better and attempts to make oneself *feel* better. (Banaji and Prentice do not discuss the belonging motive, but it is implicit in their discussion of the self in social contexts.)

Another parallel framework for understanding self motives is titled "to thine own self be good, … sure, … true, and … better" (Sedikides & Strube, 1997); these reviewers capture research on the self as, respectively, self-enhancement, self-verification, self-assessment, and self-improvement. Again, they find it useful to separate self-enhancement (positivity) from self-improvement (betterment), and they separate self-assessment (understanding) from self-verification (controlling by confirming one's self-view). We will come back to all these motives throughout the chapter, but framed in terms of three core motives that subsume these more detailed breakdowns. With these clarifications, and reassurance that parallel ideas have already proved useful in discussions of the self, let's consider next how understanding, enhancing, and belonging motives underlie some broad functions of the self.

**UNDERSTANDING**    One student wrote, with the emphasis hers: "I am a *seeker* of *wisdom, knowledge*. A student. A spirit, soul, and physical body combined into one being. 20, female, happy." Clearly, this person's motive for understanding sits squarely in the middle of her sense of self. More generally, people function more effectively with accurate-enough self-knowledge.

People's motive for self-knowledge adapts them to group life, in several ways. First, seeking self-understanding can propel them into groups, to see the self in group context. People may join a club, for example, to see if they fit in with the kind of people who enjoy its goals, whether bird-watching, fraternity parties, or cannabis reform. Second, as a group member, self-understanding allows one to function in a group, because one can fulfill the roles for which one is best suited (organizer, archivist, clown). Third, having a clear sense of self (as a group member) permits action on behalf of the group, a sense of agency that can serve the group. Finally, the more one is committed to the group, the more the group becomes a part of the self-understanding, which then perpetuates the commitment. In all these ways, a motive to understand oneself can be adaptive for social survival (see also Leary, 2007).

More specific evolutionary arguments for an abstract sense of self (Sedikides & Skowronski, 1997) suggest that increased cognitive capacity in human ancestors who hunted and foraged would have facilitated planning, which entails a self. And the group context specifically would have required a self that could speak, take the perspectives of others, and manage impressions. In this way, one social evolutionary perspective makes an argument that self-understanding would plausibly be adaptive for people in groups.

**ENHANCING SELF**    "19 year-old male. European-American. College student. A pretty neat and interesting person. A native of the cornfields of Illinois who was transplanted to the big city." Feeling like a worthy or at least "a pretty neat and interesting person" also is adaptive within group life. Having adequate self-esteem motivates people to pursue group goals optimistically and to function in a healthy way (Taylor & Brown, 1988). People tend to be optimistic about the future, whereas they see the past in more balanced fashion (Ross & Newby-Clark, 1998). However, depressed people have more negative views of their interactions (Rook, Pietromonaco, & Lewis, 1994). People who feel "pretty neat and interesting" make better group members than people who feel "pretty terrible and boring." For example, women who display positive affect in college yearbook photographs foster others' expectations that interaction with them will be rewarding. And indeed, their marriages and personal well-being are more favorable 30 years later (Harker & Keltner, 2001).

Also, even if we consider self-enhancement to include the desire to self-improve, a person motivated to do better adapts well to group life, compared with someone unresponsive to feedback. Indeed, self-esteem serves as a **sociometer** for one's standing in the group (Leary 2007). Thus, if one is in danger of group rejection, one's self-esteem falls, presumably motivating one to try harder to get along with the group.

**BELONGING**    For many students, their relationships, roles, and memberships figure prominently in their sense of self: "Female. Student at ____. Friend. Daughter. Sister. Psychology major." "Son of M. and E. Brother of J. and M. ____ marketing major. Occupant of 49 ____. Photographer. Struggling tennis player. Friend. Lifeguard at ____ Beach."

People's sense of self depends on their standing within various groups, which spotlights belonging (Baumeister & Leary, 1995; Leary & Baumeister, 2000). In the same way, ostracism (involuntary solitude, exclusion by other people, or exile from a group) is an ancient form of group sanction (Williams, 2007). According to one account of life in a West African village, people are punished by being ignored and nurtured by being accompanied (Bowen, 1954); threats of ostracism contrast with the comforts of social submersion in groups as varied as Mormons, Amish, Japanese, and American fraternities. Involuntary solitude disheartens, and social support heals. A positive image of the self as attached to others starts early and persists, as attachment theorists have argued (see the relationships chapter).

People's motivation to keep the self belonging to a group obviously makes people more adaptable and compliant to the needs of the group. People's selves, as later sections will indicate, allow them to regulate their own behavior, an advantage for both self and group.

The motives of self-understanding, self-enhancing, and self-belonging run through a variety of work on the self, and all contribute to people's social survival. The self can serve various social psychological functions; having a self is not only knowing where your skin ends, but also how to get along in a group.

## Summary of Definitions and Motives

The self is not a fixed entity but depends on the situation. A conceptual definition of the self includes the body, the inner self, the interpersonal self, and the collective self. Operationally, social psychologists have examined the self-concept (e.g., the who-am-I statements), self-esteem (e.g., the Rosenberg scale), and self-presentation (e.g., how behavior differs in public and private). Self-understanding, self-enhancing, and self-belonging all facilitate survival within the group.

## SELF-CONCEPTS: UNDERSTANDING THE SELF

Before going further, do a little experiment. (a) Read the following words, thinking about how much each one, in turn, describes you. (To play fair, you should take about three seconds per word.) Ready? OK, to what extent are you: *Friendly. Smart. Silly. Creative. Athletic. Gloomy. Dedicated*. (b) Now, without looking back at the words, think of the whole first verse of the "Star Spangled Banner." Look away from the book until you are finished. (c) Now, without looking back at the personality trait words, write down as many of them as possible. Give yourself enough time. How many did you get?

When I teach social psychology, half the class is assigned to do what you did, apply the words to themselves in part (a), and the other half of the class is assigned to consider the words just by counting the vowels in them. The vowel-counters remember only two or three words, if that; they can rapidly identify vowels without reading the words. The self-description people typically get five or more. When they read each word, considering how it relates to themselves, they are accessing a whole storehouse of knowledge about self. Consequently, you remember the list better than if you are doing something trivial with it, just as in Chapter 4, you recalled the list of trait words better if you formed an impression of such a person than if you merely memorized the list by rote. The difference here is that the person in question is yourself.

This exercise illustrates the role of the self in memory. In one study (Kuiper & Rogers, 1979), participants read 40 personality trait adjectives, one at a time, on a computer screen. Preceding each adjective, one of four questions flashes on the screen: *Describes you?* [the self-referent task you just did]; *Describes him?* [i.e., an other-referent task concerning the experimenter]; *Specific?* [a semantic judgment about the word's concreteness]; or *Long?* [a structural task concerning word length]. Participants recall the words seen under the self-referent task about three or four times more accurately, easily, and confidently and generally faster than under the other tasks (see Table 5.2). According to one meta-analysis (Symons & Johnson, 1997), the **self-reference effect** (superior memory for information encountered and related to the self) is robust. Referring material to self makes it memorable because it is easy to **elaborate** (flesh out some related thoughts) and **organize** (put into categories). Both processes make self-referred material more memorable. Self-reference invokes overlapping but distinct neural systems from other-reference, if the other person is not

**Table 5.2**    Self-Reference Effects

| Rating task | Question | Recall | | | |
| --- | --- | --- | --- | --- | --- |
| | | Accuracy | Difficulty | Confidence | Speed |
| Structural | Long? | 16% | 3.08 | 3.83 | 1.28 |
| Semantic | Specific? | 16% | 4.25 | 3.83 | 2.64 |
| Other-referent | Describes him? | 9% | 5.00 | 2.75 | 2.86 |
| Self-referent | Describes you? | 42% | 2.00 | 6.00 | 2.54 |

Text describes rating task in more detail. Accuracy measures recall for items to which the task question's answer was "yes." Difficulty and confidence were measured on scales from 1 to 7, with higher numbers indicating more difficulty and more confidence. Speed is time to respond to the question, in seconds, so lower numbers indicate greater speed; the speed data come from a separate study.

*Source:* From Kuiper & Rogers, 1979. Copyright © American Psychological Association. Adapted with permission.

close; the closer the other, the more the neural systems for encoding tend to overlap (Heatherton et al., 2006; Ochsner et al., 2004).

The self-reference effect points out a peculiar puzzle. On the one hand, the self is rich, messy, and complex. People can relate to just about any personality trait word as true of themselves, under at least some circumstances. (That's why the self-reference effect works, also why horoscopes do.) Because the self is so detailed and elaborate, it is not a simple, single, compact unit. On the other hand, the self is structured, consistent, and coherent; it does fit together. People view themselves as having "a self." How social psychologists reconcile the messy complexity of the multifaceted self with the apparent coherence of the consistent self tells the story of self-concept research. Both the complex, rich, messy self and the seemly stable, consistent, coherent self facilitate self-understanding and ultimately adaptation to group life.

## The Rich, Elaborate, Complex Self: The Self Is Not a Bowling Ball

"Who am I? A second-year Senior. Psych major. A person into physical fitness, go to the gym. I work with a mentally challenged person. A cook. I live at 58 _____ Street. A person who enjoys the outdoors. Who is doing a project with the Community Center. 5'7"."

As this example illustrates, the self is, among other things, a loose-knit knowledge structure, a concept. Talking about *the* self-concept often makes people reify ("thingify") it, make it into a discrete unitary **entity**. The self is not a single thing. In the words of Edward E. Jones, "the self is not a bowling ball." Or to paraphrase Hazel Markus and Elissa Wurf (1987), quoted earlier, the self is not a lump. Instead, the self is a set of semi-attached ideas. Maybe the self is a coral reef: a complex, well-adapted system with many parts and many interrelated functions, no clear boundaries, but lots of psychic flora and fauna coexisting in a complex ecosystem. A coral reef is more interesting to contemplate, anyway, than a bowling ball or a lump. If the self is a complex system, what are the features of its complexity?

**SELF-SCHEMAS**   The complex system of self can be described as collected **self-schemas**, noted earlier and introduced in a previous chapter (Markus & Wurf, 1987). The self-schema idea explains the self as a rich, multifaceted cognitive structure. People's self-schemas include, in particular, a sense of their traits, which make up a big piece of Americans' answer to "Who am I?" ("Athletic. Kind. Caring. Stubborn. Strong. Intelligent. Intuitive. Generous. Trusting. Trustworthy. A little crazy. Confident.") Self-schemas can include other thoughts, but primarily, they have been operationalized in terms of personality traits. In particular, as noted, self-schemas contain those traits on which people rate themselves highly, without contradiction, and as important to their self-concept. Those self-schematic traits constitute people's core self-concept, and neural systems process such self-schematic information somewhat differently than non-schematic information (Lieberman, Jarcho, & Satpute, 2004).

Self-schemas affect important behavior. For example, people's chronic self-views (e.g., *bad at science*) led them to inaccurate views of their own performance and consequently to avoid entering a science contest, despite evidence to the contrary that they had performed well (Ehrlinger & Dunning, 2003). Sometimes such self-views of chronic traits resist feedback. People's overall self-knowledge is limited but improvable (Wilson & Dunn, 2004).

How does all this emphasis on personality traits in the self-concept or self-schema fit with the actor-observer effect, covered in the personology chapter? (Remember: People report that *other* people's behavior is caused by their traits, but their *own* behavior is caused by the situation.) As noted, people basically view themselves as more complex than other people; they believe they have more personality traits than other people, their own varied traits emerging in different situations (Sande, Goethals & Radloff, 1988). People are more likely to rate themselves as having both a trait and its opposite (e.g., both serious and carefree), so they rate themselves as having more traits and being less predictable than other people. "Can I be stubborn? Yeah, I can be stubborn. Flexible, I can be flexible, too. Generous? Yeah, generous. Stingy? Under some circumstances, with some things, yes, I suppose." Basically, it is not that people do not believe that they personally do not have traits; it is more that people do not limit themselves to just a few. People believe they have a rich and varied set of traits, at different times and in different circumstances, so the self defies simple description. One trait could reflect self in one setting, and another trait could reflect self in another setting. It's all still self, though it is a self-in-situation (Mendoza-Denton et al., 2001). This variety of self-schemas, depending on the situation, generates the complex self-concept.

**SELF-COMPLEXITY**   Although most people may believe themselves more complex than other people, people do vary in **self-complexity** (Linville, 1985, 1987). For example, one student wrote 31 separate, nonredundant responses to the who-am-I question, starting with "young" and ending with "talkative"—with stops along the way for shoe size, "mall woman," and "master mindful"—whereas another wrote only gender, age, and major. Period.

Self-complexity researchers' method involves giving participants a stack of cards, each listing a different personality trait. Participants sort the traits into piles, each of which represents a distinct aspect of self (they can use the same trait twice or add a new one by writing on a blank card). The researcher then calculates the number of nonredundant clusters each person creates. For some people, more dimensions matter, and for other people, fewer dimensions matter. People with complex self-concepts are demonstrably less moody. Life events have less global impact on them because the events can be compartmentalized to one limited aspect of the self, leaving many others unaffected. People with more complex selves (more self-aspects) have more moderate reactions to stress, reflected in less depression and illness. A complex self-concept buffers against the slings and arrows of daily experience, generally, although self-complexity protects only those who feel in control of their varied self aspects (McConnell et al., 2005).

In a related way, people have multiple **possible selves** that can help them adapt—or not: "Possible selves provide for a complex and variable self-concept but are authentic in the sense that they represent the individual's persistent hopes and fears and indicate what could be realized given appropriate social conditions" (Markus & Nurius, 1986, p. 965). For example, one student included "Peace Corps after graduation. Professor, restaurant business some day." More commonly, American college students consider these types of possible selves: happy, confident, depressed, lazy, traveling widely, having lots of friends, sexy, in good shape, paralyzed, speaking well publicly, making own decisions, manipulating people, powerful, trusted, a media personality, or a business owner. Few consider possible selves as a janitor, prison guard, or tax cheat. The more students imagine an academically successful possible self, the more they indeed achieve and the better they feel (Oyserman, Bybee, & Terry, 2006). In the opposite time horizon, when older people replay a foregone possible self, the worse they feel in the short term, but the more complex and happy (mature) they feel in the long term (King & Hicks, 2007). Overall, people have complex views of their hypothetical futures and lost past possibilities, just as they do of their present, rich self-schemas.

**IDENTITIES**    A particular version of people's multiple selves, their multiple **identities** (Deaux, 1993; Frable, 1997), explicitly emphasizes roles and group memberships, taking a more societal than purely psychological view of the self. Identity is social; self-concept can be personal or social. One student's self statements emphasized identities: "Student at ____. Woman. Nigerian-American. Catholic. Sister to 3. Oldest daughter. Member of [singing group]. [Student government committee] chair." More formally, identities break down into several components. Various central relationships might include daughter and sister, in this example, or fiancée and friend, in an earlier example. People's vocations and avocations are important to their identities, such as student, Catholic, singer, and chair, in this example, or lover of classical music and great cook in the earlier one. Political affiliations, too, and stigmatized identities, if any, matter too. Finally, ethnic identities, such as Nigerian-American or Hispanic, appear. Identities are all different roles that people have. The emphasis in identity is more on roles, relatively speaking, and the emphasis in the self-schema is usually much more on personality traits, but both are critical parts of people's multifaceted self-concept.

Identities are socially created. For example, some students currently describe themselves as "multiracial," whereas an earlier generation might have used "mulatto" or other terms. At different times and places, different definitions of racial identity apply, and ethnic identity follows. For example, the social construction of a "black" racial identity has changed over time. In 1938, for example, a court had to decide whether a woman whose great-great-grandmother allegedly was a "Negro" was herself black, although all her other ancestors were white. If she were 1/16 black, her white ex-husband could annul their marriage (black-white intermarriage then being illegal) and not pay alimony (Banks & Eberhardt, 1998). Her own contention was that her great-great-grandmother had been American Indian, but a contemporaneous document had described her as a "free woman of color," leaving open either possibility. The court then relied on reported physical evidence of the great-great-grandmother's hair texture, straight or kinky. All this aimed to decide if the ex-wife was 6.25% black, which would then qualify her as a black person, according to the then-current "one-drop" rule of racial identity. Her identity became a matter determined by the court (her long straight black hair and possibly blue eyes and copper-colored skin all decided the court).

As another example of society's impact on our ethnic identities, the term "Asian-American" is relatively new. Previously, people whose ancestors immigrated from that significant part of the world might have viewed themselves as, for example, Chinese, Japanese, or Indian. But in the American cultural context, people whose ancestors emigrated from Europe tended to lump them together as Asian. Over time, it has become socially, politically, and psychologically useful for some Americans of those various Asian origins to have an identity that includes Asian-American (along with all their other identities). Being multiracial, an increasingly common identity, allows people to choose one identity over the other, often depending on other people's feedback about their appearance and apparent cultural knowledge (Khanna, 2004). Or people may insist on retaining all applicable racial identities.

Just as people vary in self-complexity, as noted, people also vary in identity complexity (Roccas & Brewer, 2002). Some people have several social identities (e.g., white, American, student, Protestant) that they view as complex (nonoverlapping and dissimilar). Identity complexity buffers them from stress (worry, agitation) and correlates with tolerance for ambiguity (openness to change, versus conservatism). Some people are put off by the possibility of having multiple identities. Some situations, such as group threat, also discourage identity complexity.

The array of potential identities—relationships, avocations, politics, stigma, ethnicity—does not dazzle social psychologists, however, into viewing the self as a hodge-podge collection. Although the self may not be a bowling ball, it is also not just the bowling pins scattered after a strike.

## The Coherent Self: The Self Is Not Just Scattered Bowling Pins

As the last section showed, the self is not a single unitary thing; it is rich, elaborate, and complex. Nevertheless, the self hangs together, in all its facets. It attains coherence in three primary ways: Only some aspects are accessible at any given time; consistency pressures create harmony; and situational attributions explain away disruptions.

**ACCESSIBILITY**    So far, we have emphasized the multiple aspects of the self. If people kept all these aspects in mind every minute, they would be paralyzed. If only one self can respond at a time, which self responds when? On a date, one's scientist self is not the best entertainment to trot out to one's partner. Conversely, an exam is probably not the best place to trot out one's clown self. How do people manage the tension between the complex self and the need for action?

Only part of one's complex self-concept is at the top of the mental heap at any given time. The aspect of self that is most **accessible**, most easily comes to mind, depends on the context. This is why researchers sometimes discuss the working self-concept (Markus & Wurf, 1987). With all the rich and elaborate self-concepts, present and possible, traits and identities, the **working self-concept** identifies the currently active aspects of the self (Markus & Nurius, 1986). As the self-concept of the moment, the working self-concept is not fixed but depends on the social circumstances, in large part, on one's different roles. One's working self-concept supports the experience of oneself as a unitary, coherent person.

A related way of thinking about the self-concept assesses people's **chronically accessible constructs** (Higgins, King, & Mavin, 1982). In this research, people list adjectives to describe, in turn: themselves, a liked person, a disliked person, someone they avoid, and someone they seek. Certain themes tend to come up consistently across all these people. For example, whether or not someone is kind might come up in three of four descriptions of other people, or in describing self and someone else, indicating that *kind* is a personality trait at the top of the head, chronically accessible. Some of the top chronically accessible traits for a lot of undergraduates include *humorous, intelligent, friendly*, and *outgoing*. Chronically accessible constructs—often part of the self-concept—shape what people view as important in other people as well. One experiment described a person as possessing a mixture of traits. Some traits were chronically accessible and some chronically inaccessible, individually tailored, separately for each participant in the study. Participants then tried to recall the essay and to describe the person themselves, both immediately and after a delay. As Table 5.3 indicates, they consistently used more of their own personally accessible attributes and deleted more of their own personally inaccessible attributes in subsequent depictions of the other person.

The working or accessible self is the *now* self-concept that guides reactions in any given context. One way the self maintains coherence is thus by activating only a subset of the self-concept at any particular moment. Knowledge activation makes accessible a subset of self-knowledge, much as for any of our other vast stores of knowledge (Förster & Liberman, 2007).

**Table 5.3**  Use of Chronically Accessible Aspects of Self to Describe Others

| Deletion Measure | Traits Given in Original Description | |
| --- | --- | --- |
| | Accessible | Inaccessible |
| Immediate recall | 17.7% | 35.3% |
| Delayed recall | 26.7% | 52.7% |
| Immediate impression | 45.1% | 69.4% |
| Delayed impression | 53.9% | 75.2% |

Numbers indicate percentages *deleted* from traits originally provided in describing a target person; thus, accessible traits are deleted less often and therefore used more often than inaccessible ones.
*Source:* Data from Higgins et al., 1982.

**CONSISTENCY PRESSURES**    Another way to maintain coherence is by fitting together disparate pieces. Americans and Europeans do not like to see themselves as inconsistent. One of the ways that people maintain a coherent sense of self is to have biased views of themselves that maintain consistency within the self, including consistency with own past behavior. Consistency pressures rein in the multiple self-concepts, in one of two ways. People seek consistency in feedback from other people, in a process called **self-verification**, which is covered soon. And people reinterpret inconsistencies to make them fit, in processes related to **cognitive dissonance**, which is covered in the attitudes chapter. Earlier, we noted that people think of themselves as having almost every trait, depending on the circumstances, so it is easy for them to make many possible inconsistencies fit at least one view of themselves.

**SITUATIONAL ATTRIBUTIONS**    Finally, people maintain a coherent sense of self in another way, namely, explaining apparently inconsistent behavior by blaming it on the situation—making **situational attributions**. As noted, according to the actor-observer effect (discussed in the personology chapter) attributions to the situation are prominent in people's explanations of themselves. They also help maintain a coherent sense of self. If one behaves in a way that is really unusual for oneself and does not fit one's self-concept, one can explain it away by blaming the situation: "I was just following orders." "My friends made me do it." "It was late at night."

**SUMMARY OF THE COMPLEX YET COHERENT SELF**    People have self-schemas, possible selves, self-complexity, and multiple identities, which create a rich, elaborate self-system. That rich, elaborate, complex self is kept in check by accessibility (the working self-concept, chronic accessibility), consistency pressures, and situational attributions. The self is a dynamic system of related but changing parts.

## How People Get to Know Themselves

If the self resembles the complex ecosystem of a coral reef, complete with a colorful variety of inhabitants, and like a coral reef, partly above water, partly submerged but still visible, and partly visible only upon diving deeper, the self certainly challenges superficial investigation. How do people get to know themselves? The self stores and coordinates a lot of knowledge. Given time, people could easily write 100 answers to the question "Who am I?" instead of the usual 20. We next examine four sources of the self-knowledge that helps people develop a self-concept in the first place. The first two sources (self-perception and introspection) come from the **isolated self-concept**, the identity that develops as an individual separate from family and friends. The second two (social comparison and social feedback) come from self in relationship to others, the **interrelated self-concept**. This distinction between the isolated and interrelated views of self parallels differences between independent and interdependent cultural selves (Brewer & Chen, 2007; Niedenthal & Beike, 1997).

**LOOK AT YOURSELF: SELF-PERCEPTION OF BEHAVIOR**    "Loves: hot chocolate, flannel, the smell when I open the dishwasher, pizza, yellow, lace-making, summer, babies, camping, shag rugs, backpacking aimlessly around cities, my mom, hamsters." How does this person know she likes flannel? Perhaps, in part, because when she opens her closet, that's what she seems to have bought. One major source of knowledge about self is observing one's own behavior. In the personology chapter, **self-perception theory** (Bem, 1972) noted that people learn about themselves from their own behavior. One isolated way that people acquire a self-concept is by watching what they do, just as an outside observer might; remember the portabella mushrooms example (I must like portabella mushrooms a lot because I always order them). One of the ways that people know their own taste in food is by observing what they typically eat. One of the ways that people know what they value is how they spend their time. Over the years, if George discovers that he always contributes money to education, ecology, and elephants, he might well infer that he has a special fondness for these causes. He observes his own behavior and infers his own preferences. Observing our own behavior certainly is one isolated way that people learn about themselves. A closet full of flannel sends a message to one's self-concept.

More formally, self-observation can indeed make people relatively accurate about how other people perceive them. For example, when the behavior is relatively public—as in children's academic performance—both self-perception and others' perception of a child's ability tend to agree (Malloy, Albright, & Scarpati, 2007). Normally, we do not see ourselves as others see us; that is, we do not typically observe our own behavior from the outside, as others do. In one study (Albright & Malloy, 1999), when group members saw themselves on videotape, they were better able to determine how others would judge them. Nevertheless, people rarely see themselves from the outside, except in acting classes, education seminars, and psychology experiments.

**LISTEN TO YOURSELF: INTROSPECTION ABOUT INNER THOUGHTS AND FEELINGS**    Behavior is not people's favorite way to learn about themselves. The same person who liked flannel and the smell of clean dishes also noted elsewhere her tendency for nightmares. People writing about themselves noted, for example, being stressed and confused, "hot in this sweater," and liking summer classes. American students report drawing their sense of themselves, their self-concept, mostly from their inner thoughts and feelings. When asked about "the most crucial part of yourself, your true self," they report their own inner experience, not their behavior (Andersen, 1984; Andersen & Ross, 1984). In one study, college students were interviewed about their careers, relationships, conflicts, and formative experiences, under instructions to focus either on their thoughts and feelings or on their overt actions. Interviewees overwhelmingly rated the cognitive/affective (thoughts and feelings) interviews as more informative about themselves, in terms of accuracy, completeness, observers' knowledge, and observers' ability to predict their future thoughts, feelings, and behavior.

This is hypocritical, however. In fact, people believe their own thoughts and feelings to be most revealing about themselves, but their peers' overt behavior to be most revealing about them. Thus, people have the sense that they know their peers well (as revealed by the peers' behavior), but they simultaneously claim their peers do not know them (lacking access to their inner thoughts and feelings). The illusion of asymmetric insight claims that "you don't know me, but I know you" (Pronin, Kruger, Savitsky, & Ross, 2001). What's more, people think they are less biased than other people because their own introspections seem to provide evidence of their own objectivity, but they do not grant the same credit to others' introspections (Pronin & Kugler, 2007).

So far, we have seen people's independent judgments of themselves. People observing their own behavior and people examining their own thoughts and feelings together constitute socially isolated sources of self-knowledge, in comparison to the interpersonal self-knowledge sources we consider next.

**LOOK AT OTHER PEOPLE: SOCIAL COMPARISON**    "I'm someone who likes to travel. I love meeting new people. I feel that every person I've met has taught me a thing or two. From traveling, new ideas and new life strategies are found." People get information about themselves by considering other people, comparing themselves to other people with regard to long-term (life strategies) and temporary aspects. Are you taking the right amount of notes on this book? It's hard to know, unless you sneak a peek at someone else's notes. It's easier to know whether you are writing the right amount of notes in a lecture: You look at other people and see how much they are writing. As a lecturer, I often observe a phenomenon in which people may be listening to an example, and nobody's writing any notes, and then one person in the front row starts to scribble madly, and everybody else startles and begins to write. Social comparison entails learning about the self's capabilities by measuring against other people. Social comparison is rampant right after test grades come back: "How did you do? What did you get?"

**Social comparison theory** captures the idea that people tend to compare themselves with other people, to assess how they are doing. Leon Festinger, one of the most prominent social psychologists of the 1950s and 1960s, contributed this and other central theories to social psychology (Guimond, 2006). Social comparison serves at least two functions. First, social comparison serves an understanding function, which Festinger (1954) emphasized, especially in achievement situations. That is, people want to know "How good am I?" and they seek accurate comparisons with similar others. This kind of social comparison helps to predict one's own future performance (Wheeler, Martin, & Suls, 1997). For example, to predict how one might do in a difficult class, one might ask similar others who have already taken the class.

Second, social comparison also serves a self-enhancement function, in the sense that people compare themselves especially with people who are doing less well than they are. It answers the question, "How can I make myself feel good about how I've done?" People often engage in **downward comparison** (Wills, 1981), when they seek self-enhancing comparisons with others who are less well off. This kind of social comparison helps to make their actual performance feel adequate. To assess how they are doing in classes, for example, people often compare downward because it feels better.

People also compare downward in health domains. In one interview study (Rickabaugh & Tomlinson-Keasey, 1997), the majority of elderly people (aged 65–93 years) reported downward comparisons, seeing themselves as relatively better off than their peers or at least as well off as their younger selves (see Table 5.4). Even breast cancer patients, people in bad shape in comparison with the population as a whole, will compare themselves with other patients who are even worse off (Taylor, 1983). Similarly, when people have had accidents, they almost invariably say, "It could have been worse." After a fender bender: "My car could have been totaled." After the car is totaled: "I could have been in a coma." After a coma: "I could have died." Victims of stressful life events will often describe themselves as a better person for having lived through the event (McFarland & Alvaro, 2000). They come to this conclusion by comparing their present selves with a preevent self whom they derogate. Perhaps it is adaptive to compare oneself with a worse scenario. Maybe downward comparison explains the popularity of soap operas. (No one's life is really *that* bad.)

**Table 5.4**    Social Comparisons by Older Adults

|  | More Frequent Type of Comparison | |
| --- | --- | --- |
| Measure | Upward | Downward |
| Social comparisons | 19.3% | 68.4% |
| Temporal comparisons | 24.1% | 75.9%* |

*Includes both downward and stable temporal comparisons.
Social comparisons involve comparing self with others, who are better off (upward) or worse off (downward). Temporal comparisons involve comparing self at present with self in the past, as better off (upward) or worse off (downward).
*Source:* Data from Rickabaugh & Tomlinson-Keasey, 1997.

The exception is clear attempts at self-improvement, when people compare slightly upward to people they want to emulate. For example, if a college student works with a graduate student or a professor, comparing himself or herself to one of them as a role model would be an aspiration, comparing upward. That kind of upward comparison does not feel bad, precisely because it represents a goal. Upward social comparison provides information useful for self-improvement, and it can be self-enhancing (Collins, 1996).

People have reported other motives for social comparison, which include bonding, altruism, and self-destruction (Helgeson & Mickelson, 1995). With regard to self-destruction, for example, either upward or downward comparison can be a negative experience. One may envy the upward comparison; one may dread the downward comparison as a possible self. People with low self-esteem, especially those who feel uncertain or not in control, experience negative comparisons in domains ranging from cancer symptoms to marital relationships (Buunk, Collins, Taylor, Van Yperen, & Dakof, 1990). For most people, however, social comparison is useful. For example, both directions—to compare upward and to compare downward—independently predict future performance of secondary school students (Blanton, Buunk, Gibbons, & Kuyper, 1999).

In sum, everybody uses social comparison, throughout their lives, to understand how they are doing (through comparison with similar others), to feel better (through downward comparison), and to improve (through upward comparison). Social comparison reflects a variety of goals, of which accuracy is only one. Some social comparison operates unconsciously, outside of explicit goals (e.g., Blanton & Stapel, 2008); moreover, the environment may impose unwanted comparisons (Wood, 1989).

**LISTEN TO OTHER PEOPLE: SOCIAL FEEDBACK**   In partial response to "Who am I?" one student wrote, "I love and am loved." Other people are potential sources of feedback to know oneself: "I am who other people see me to be." **Symbolic interaction** theorists (e.g., Shrauger & Schoeneman, 1979) would argue that the self consists totally of how one thinks other people react. In this approach, the sense of self is entirely social, derived from how other people interact with and apparently perceive one. In this view, even the private self is a social phenomenon, based on one's history of social interactions. This observation led early theorists to identify the **looking-glass self** (Cooley, 1902; Mead, 1934; Scheibe, 1985; see Brown, 1998, for a review).

Recent researchers have measured the **reflected appraisals** that make up the looking-glass self. Specifically, self-concept correlates *with perceived* appraisals (Kenny & DePaulo, 1993). That is, people's sense of self (self-appraisal) does not relate to how other people actually see them (actual appraisal) but instead relates to how they *think* other people see them (perceived appraisal). People are reasonably accurate at understanding how people in general view their personalities and even reasonably accurate at knowing whether they are generally liked. Self-evaluation may guide perceived social standing, so people's view of themselves may guide their beliefs about how they are viewed by others, not the other way around: "As I am, so other people see me." Of course, this begs the question of how those self-views develop in the first place. Quite possibly (Demo, 1992), self-views develop early, among family and friends, but then become more fixed.

People tend to think other people notice and evaluate them more than they actually do, a phenomenon termed the **spotlight effect** (Gilovich & Savitsky, 1999). And people tend to think that their inner selves leak out and are detected by others, the **transparency effect** (Gilovich, Savitsky, & Medvec, 1998). What's more, as noted in Chapter 3, people think others are drawing stronger dispositional inferences about their behavior than they really are (Van Boven, Kamada, & Gilovich, 1999), whereas the observers actually do manage to moderate their correspondence bias by taking some account of the actor's circumstances (Epley, Savitsky, & Gilovich, 2002). So people have some accuracy in their general idea about how others perceive them, except that they think others are attending more closely and more accurately than they really are and that they are drawing stronger dispositional inferences than they really are. People's self-concepts correlate more closely with how they think others perceive them than with how others actually see them.

**SUMMARY**    People acquire their self-concept from self-perception, introspection, social comparison, and reflected appraisals. Thus, they look at their own behavior, feelings, and thoughts; compare themselves with other people; and perceive how other people view them. The motives that run through all these self-concept processes especially feature self-enhancement and self-understanding. Are these two motives always compatible?

## Self-Enhancement versus Self-Verification

People can be threatened by a potential tension between self-enhancement and self-understanding. Certain versions of these motives can be incompatible. For example, self-enhancement in the narrow sense of feeling good about oneself can conflict with self-understanding in the narrow sense of **self-verification** (socially confirming what one believes about oneself). As a final example of work on the self-concept, and building on the discussion of other people's actual appraisals, consider this tension between self-verification versus self-enhancement (Swann, 1990).

**SELF-VERIFICATION**    Self-verification entails getting other people to see you as you see yourself, getting them to be "accurate" by agreeing with you. Self-verification greases the social wheels and reduces conflicts in interaction, so it serves social survival needs. People do seem to strive for self-verification, which indeed is accuracy, in the sense of consensus about the person's self-views. This serves the core social motive for understanding, in that the socially shared view affirms the self-concept. In general, the social world works better if people's self-views essentially agree with other people's views of them.

In one test of the social benefits of self-verification, researchers contacted first-semester business school students, who were meeting in small study groups for all their group projects (Swann, Milton, & Polzer, 2000). Self-concepts were measured before the groups met and then again nine and 15 weeks later. Appraisals

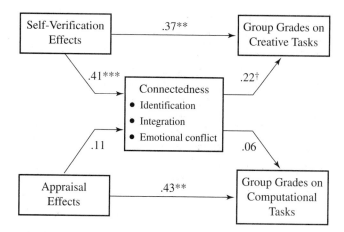

Values represent predictors from one step to the next; *s indicate
statistical significance.

**Figure 5.1**   Self-Verification and Group Functioning

*Source:* From Swann et al., 2000. Copyright © American Psychological Association. Reprinted with permission

by others were measured just after the first group meeting, then again nine and 15
weeks later. Thus, the researchers could compare self-verification effects (whether
peer appraisals moved closer to self-concepts over time) and appraisal effects
(whether self-concepts moved closer to peer appraisals over time). Participants also
rated the group atmosphere, and instructors provided group grades. This way, the
researchers could see whether self-verification or appraisal effects (if they occurred)
benefited group functioning. Figure 5.1 shows that they both did. As predicted by
the idea that groups benefit when members feel that others see them as they see
themselves, self-verification improved connections to the group, which in turn tended
to affect group creativity grades. On the other hand, appraisal effects (i.e., the group's
influence on the individual self-concept) improved computational task accuracy but
had no effect on connections to the group. In a related analysis, self-verification
fostered harmony and productivity in diverse work groups (Swann, Kwan, Polzer, &
Milton, 2003). Thus, self-understanding, especially self-verification, but also reflected
appraisals, benefits group functioning, in different respects (Leary, 2007).

Not only individual, but also collective self-verification can benefit the individual
as a group member. To the extent a collective identity (e.g., one's self-view regarding
one's gender) is certain, salient, and important, and when the source of self-verification
matters, then the collective self also benefits form self-verification (Chen, Chen, &
Shaw, 2004).

**SELF-ENHANCEMENT**   At the same time, people (many Americans, at least)
seem to strive for self-enhancement in the sense of wanting to see themselves and be
seen in a positive light. For example, people have particular difficulties recognizing
their own incompetence and tend to overestimate their performance if it is low (Kruger

& Dunning, 1999). But this may motivate them to keep trying, which would benefit the group. Recall the women whose college pictures conveyed positive emotions—who arguably felt good about themselves—reported more affiliation and better marriages up to 30 years later. Observers expected interactions with them to be more rewarding, and their personal well-being reflected all these benefits (Harker & Keltner, 2001). Communicating positive personal events improves one's own well-being (assuming the other responds positively) and also enhances relationship quality (Gable, Reis, Impett, & Asher, 2004). Reasonable self-enhancement thus encourages social belonging, to the extent that positive self-feelings encourage relationships (Leary, 2007).

**TENSION BETWEEN SELF-VERIFICATION AND SELF-ENHANCEMENT**
Although both motives serve social survival, a problem arises when they conflict. A negative self-verifying view would conflict with self-enhancement. People with low opinions of themselves may actually opt to maintain self-consistency at the cost of self-enhancement. In one study, people were more committed to their marriages if they had picked long-term partners who verified their views of themselves, even if those shared views were in fact negative (Swann, Hixon & De La Ronde, 1992). This way, in the long term, relationships can reinforce (negative) self-views and people's self-verifying, as opposed to self-enhancing, view of themselves. This insight explains certain kinds of abusive relationships: Negative self-verification wins over self-enhancement. Self-enhancement (in the sense of self-esteem) clearly matters but qualified by self-verification (self-understanding) in the long-run.

Another way to understand how these two motives co-occur is to see that self-enhancement and self-verification operate at different speeds. Self-enhancement (positive feedback) feels good instantly. Then moments later, milliseconds later, if the positive feedback disagrees with what makes sense, what is plausible, or how they view themselves, people reject it. After the immediate feel-good glow, a slower process evaluates whether the feedback fits or not. In a study noted in Chapter 1, researchers (Swann, Hixon, Stein-Seroussi, & Gilbert, 1990) made some people cognitively busy (in one study, participants were made to hurry, and in another, they had to keep a phone number in their heads), so their cognitive capacity was taxed. These busy people could only do whatever came automatically, which turned out to be self-enhancement. In support of the idea that self-enhancement is relatively automatic, busy people preferred positive feedback: the instant feel-good reaction when someone says something nice. In contrast, people who were not cognitively overloaded—people who had time to think about the feedback—preferred feedback that fit their own view of themselves, even if it was negative. Thus, the paradox between narrow self-enhancement and self-verification resolves by regarding self-enhancement as an instantaneous, automatic preference (i.e., when one is busy) but self-verification as prevailing in the long run.

## Cultural Differences: Interdependent and Independent Self-Concepts

Do people everywhere automatically prefer self-enhancing feedback? Do people everywhere privilege their inner thoughts and feelings over social behavior? Do people everywhere have self-concepts that consist largely of personality traits? Ideas about the self are culturally bounded (M. H. Bond & Smith, 1996; Heine & Buchtel, 2009): The self-concept differs dramatically in European-American cultures and certain East Asian cultures (and perhaps South Asian, African, and South American ones, but empirical social psychologists have not written enough about these cultures yet).

An initial way to think about these differences is the distinction between being more individually oriented and more collectively oriented. Recall from Chapter 1 the distinction between individualist and collectivist cultures, which also applies to selves (Triandis, 1990). Analysis of more collectivist cultures reveals that the individualist American mainstream idea of self as autonomous and primary is not universal. Triandis describes cultural **collectivism**, as noted, which emphasizes the group's needs over the individual's needs, whereas cultural **individualism** prioritizes the individual over the group. People's self-concepts respond to individualist and collectivist primes, according to meta-analysis (Oyserman & Lee, 2008). Chronic priming of one type or the other could be a model of how cultures influence selves.

A related idea distinguishes the independent self and the interdependent self (Kitayama & Markus, 1999; Markus & Kitayama, 1991). **Interdependence** characterizes people's sense of self in collectivist cultures, as deeply embedded in one's groups, and **independence** characterizes people's sense of self in individualist cultures, as autonomous from one's groups. Layers of interdependence clarify all these cultural contrasts: **individual, relational,** and **collective selves** all reflect cultural differences (Brewer & Chen, 2007). The self differs in definition, structure, importance, life tasks, role of others, and self-esteem, in the following ways.

**SELF-DEFINITION**    The core independence-interdependence distinction appears in initial work on cultural definitions of the individual and relational self. The self in more independent, European-American settings is unique and separate. Not coincidentally, American social psychologists often emphasize this view of self, as this chapter indicates. And American students also emphasize this view of self (Cousins, 1989): They provide many more abstract psychological attributes (predominantly personality traits) when asked the question, "Who am I?" In American culture (but it holds for most of Europe as well), the self makes choices, is autonomous, and is unique. A typical American answer to the bald "Who am I?" question might be one student's response: "Logical. Aware. Optimistic. Creative. Not always on time. Motivated. Healthy. Sexual." Notice the string of abstract trait adjectives.

In contrast, Japanese students provide more concrete behavioral responses ("I play tennis") to this out-of-context question. The Japanese students do provide many more abstract psychological attributes when given a specific context, such as "Who am I at home [with friends; at school]?" The interdependent view of the self embeds, connects, and enmeshes in the social context; the person is the intersection of a lot of different roles and groups: "My father's son. My mother's son. Brother. Residence assistant. AIPAC liaison.... Friend. Boyfriend."

Not that roles and contexts are absent from all American students' who-am-I statements; in fact, this last example is American, and other American students do mention family, teams, clubs, majors, college or university, jobs, and relationships.

**Table 5.5**    Relational-Interdependent Self-Construal Scale Items

---

1. My close relationships are an important reflection of who I am.
2. When I feel very close to someone, it often feels to me like that person is an important part of who I am.
3. I usually feel a strong sense of pride when someone close to me has an important accomplishment.
4. I think one of the most important parts of who I am can be captured by looking at my close friends and understanding who they are.
5. When I think of myself, I often think of my close friends or family also.
6. If a person hurts someone close to me, I feel personally hurt as well.
7. In general, my close relationships are an important part of my self-image.
8. Overall, my close relationships have very little to do with how I feel about myself.*
9. My close relationships are unimportant to my sense of what kind of person I am.*
10. My sense of pride comes from knowing who I have as close friends.
11. When I establish a close friendship with someone, I usually develop a strong sense of identification with that person.

---

Response scale ranges from 1 *(strongly disagree)* to 7 *(strongly agree)*.
*Reverse-scored items.
*Source:* From Cross et al., 2000. Copyright © American Psychological Association. Adapted with permission.

Table 5.5 shows items that measure individual differences in interdependent (relational) self-construals, which predict responsiveness to the needs of others (Cross, Bacon, & Morris, 2000). Americans differ among themselves on this measure as, for example, Japanese doubtless do also. The point is that on average, American students display interdependent selves less often than students from many Asian countries, such as Japan.

People's sense of themselves as independent or interdependent selves goes back to their earliest reported memories. In one study, American students reported self-focused, individual, trait-oriented memories that dated six months younger than those reported by Chinese students, whose earliest memories were more collective (family and neighborhood), included more other people, and were more general (e.g., routines and roles; Wang, 2001). The Americans' memories were also more emotionally elaborate, whereas the Chinese memories were more neutral, in keeping with an emphasis on interdependent social harmony.

The same behavior can have very different meanings for a self defined as independent or interdependent. A high-achieving person in the United States usually views the self as achieving mostly for self, as in the old Army recruiting slogan: "Be all that you can be" or the later "An Army of One." Being in the honors program, working hard in college, playing trumpet, or weight-lifting means wanting to do one's personal best, as a unique individual, in this cultural context.

Of course, achievement orientation can also be shared by someone from a collectivist, interdependent culture, but the motivation differs (Yu & Yang, 1994). North American and European cultures emphasize individually oriented achievement motivation, whereas Asian cultures often emphasize socially oriented achievement motivation. In the latter case, one achieves to obey and honor the family, the teachers, the school, the hometown, and so on. The idea here is that if one achieves, it is not for oneself; it is for the groups one holds dear. In fact, a mature person might suppress "self" in order to achieve on behalf of cherished groups. One might deny personal desires, and one might even do what one does not want to do; one might achieve at being a doctor, not because of personal preferences but because of group needs. The sense of achievement differs; the same self-definitions, "I'm an honors student" or "I'm a psychology student," can carry a different meaning, depending on whether one is more independent or interdependent. These dichotomies are not absolute, of course. For example, a relatively individualist American guy can achieve both for his football team and for himself, but the relative cultural emphasis on the unique, independent, individual self over the connected, interdependent self still holds.

**SELF-STRUCTURE**    A second dimension (Markus & Kitayama, 1991) contrasts the structure of the self in the independent and interdependent orientations. The structure of the independent, autonomous self is more unitary and more stable. The structure of the interdependent, relational self is more fluid and variable: One adjusts oneself to different settings and relationships depending on what is needed. One may become a different person, and that person is equally true to one's self because one's self *is* the role and the relationships. A dutiful daughter or son in a collectivist culture does whatever is demanded by that role, and personal preferences are totally irrelevant. It would be immature to insist on having one's own way. Or a responsible employee in a collectivist culture, again, does what the role requires, and personal preferences do not matter. The private self is not even in the equation. One might be a different person in different roles because the roles call for it.

Henry James (the novelist, brother of psychologist William) gives an example from a more collectivist era in one European culture:

> In France, you must never say Nay to your mother, whatever she requires of you. She may be the most abominable old woman in the world, and make your life a purgatory; but after all she is *ma mère*, and you have no right to judge her. You simply have to obey.... With these people the family is everything; you must act, not for your own pleasure, but for the advantage of the family. (H. James, 1876, p. 120)[1]

Because one's roles differ, the self is stable *within* relational contexts, in a collectivist culture, but *across* relational contexts in an individualist culture (English & Chen, 2007). Similarly, people view themselves as fixed entities in individualistic cultures, but as more malleable and improvable in collectivist cultures (Heine & Buchtel, 2009).

---

[1] Copyright © James Estate. Reprinted with permission.

**IMPORTANCE**    In an independent culture, the internal, private self predominates, considered most real and important. The authentic self, according to European-Americans, is the internal and private experience. One European-American second-grader, asked whether the presence of old friends eased a new summer-camp experience, replied, "It's not who I'm with; it's how *I feel*." One's self-view retains consistent importance across contexts, in an individualist culture (English & Chen, 2007).

In a more interdependent culture, however, one's self-view carries importance depending on the context. Relationships matter more—external, public, social ties loom large. In a sense, appearance matters more for social behaviors than interior states do. It is not that interdependent people are fake: The harmony with others *is* a critical part of them; the relationship with others *is* a major aspect of their true self. Although they may suffer internally, their true selves are serving what the social scene needs them to be, and the better one can do that, the better person one is. (Much traditional and modern Japanese literature addresses the conflict between inner wishes and outer duty.) For an interdependent self, harmony is the best policy. For an independent self, honesty is the best policy.

**LIFE TASKS**    The fourth implication of the independent-interdependent distinction concerns the life tasks that people have. One major life task, relevant to the college years, is finding one's own identity. The whole idea of an identity crisis is very European-American: to be unique, express self, follow one's own goals, and be direct; all of that is very Western and independent.

On the other hand, belonging, fitting in, acting appropriately, following group goals, being diplomatic and subtle, those norms are prized in places that value saving face, creating harmony in the group, getting along well with each other, and not being angry. Expressing anger, for example, can be considered crude and immature. In Japan, children are socialized not to express anger, and arguably, adults may not even experience anger as often as people in the United States do (Kitayama & Markus, 1999). Anger happens when one feels that somebody is illegitimately harming one personally. If the personal self takes a backseat, if harmony and fitting in come first, then anger diminishes. Getting angry and defending one's rights recede as an issue. Possibly, some of the anger most commonly expressed in Japan focuses on somebody who violates a norm (recall: an unwritten social rule). Personal anger (somebody has harmed me, so I have a right to be angry) might be experienced less often due to a group self-definition. Thus, relationship harmony predicts life satisfaction (Kwan, Bond, & Singelis, 1997).

**ROLE OF OTHERS**    A fifth dimension identified by Markus and Kitayama is the role of others: For an independent self, others serve as social comparison, to self-evaluate. It is as if independent selves are always being graded on a curve, relative to others. One meets someone relevant to oneself and checks the person out—looks, clothes, grades, social success—and feels good or bad accordingly. Independent selves automatically orient toward the evaluative meaning of words (essentially, good for me or bad for me). In contrast, more interdependent selves automatically attune to the emotional tone of the other's communication (Kitayama & Ishii, 2002). For an inter-dependent self, others serve as social definition. One defines oneself in that context according to the relationship: What are the relative roles, as student to teacher, older student to younger student, guest to host, and so on? The interdependent frame of reference is external others' standards, compared with an independent frame of reference being one's own internal standards (Heine & Buchtel, 2009).

**SELF-ENHANCEMENT AS SELF-SYMPATHY**    Finally, the interdependent emphasis in some cultures suggests that we will need to expand our idea of self-enhancement as a motive. People can enhance themselves in two ways: The independent, individualistic culture's way is pure self-esteem ("I'm the greatest!" or at least "a pretty neat and interesting person"), to have optimistic illusions about oneself. Westerners self-enhance reliably more than do East Asians (Heine & Bechtel, 2009). But interdependent, relational cultures' way is self-improvement, self-adjustment, and **self-sympathy** (Heine, Lehman, Markus, & Kitayama, 1999). One can improve oneself by seeing all one's faults and striving to do better, and one can adjust oneself to create harmony in one's social relationships, but one can still sympathize with one's own weakness. Westerners vary in their degree of self-compassion, but when they are kind to themselves, they benefit in ways that are distinct from self-esteem; for example, self-compassion acts as an emotional buffer against over-reacting to negative events (Leary et al., 2007).

On the whole, however, independent and interdependent cultural contexts respec-tively encourage self-enhancement or self-criticism (Kitayama, Markus, Matsumoto, & Norasakkunkit, 1997). When Japanese people describe themselves and a typical student in a Japanese cultural context, they show low self-esteem; Americans describ-ing themselves in an American cultural context show the most self-esteem. Japanese in American context (or vice versa) show intermediate self-esteem (see Figure 5.2).

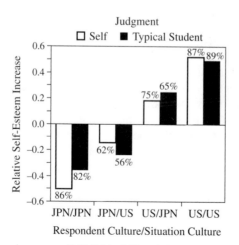

**Figure 5.2**   Self-Enhancing versus Self-Critical Situations

As further evidence of the importance of cultural context, Americans and Hong Kong Chinese reported different kinds of daily interactions in a diary study (Wheeler, Reis, & Bond, 1989). The Hong Kong students reported a more collectivist and relational interaction context: more group interactions and longer interactions with fewer but closer people. Americans move like free agents in and out of superficial interactions with more people. Generally, Americans rate their emotional lives as pleasant (as in the positivity bias from Chapter 4). However, for relatively relational Japanese, their experience of pleasant emotions depends on interdependent concerns (Mesquita & Karasawa, 2002),

Independent self-esteem differs from interdependent self-improvement, self-sympathy, or self-adjustment, but both are valid ways of enhancing self: One way changes perceptions (perhaps false, perhaps accurate), and the other motivates efforts (perhaps realistic, perhaps futile). What's more, both independent and interdependent selves may carve out domains in which they can feel they are better than others: individualist attributes for independent selves (free, independent, unique) and relational attributes for interdependent selves (cooperative, loyal, compromising). In that sense, some form of positive self-regard occurs everywhere (Sedikides, Gaertner, & Toguchi, 2003). To make our discussion more sensitive to cultural variation, we need to amend our understanding of self-enhancement to include maintaining individualist self-esteem, which is the traditional European-American social psychology, as well as self-sympathy, self-improvement, self-adjustment, and pride in being a group member, which are part of Asian and perhaps other interdependent cultures (Fiske, Kitayama, Markus, & Nisbett, 1998).

All these contrasts between independent, individualistic cultures and interdependent, collectivist cultures risk creating major cultural stereotypes. One must not draw this contrast too sharply. People in Japan vary a lot; some are more Western, independent, and individualist, and some are more collectivist, relational, interdependent, and traditional.

In the United States, people also vary a lot along these dimensions. Ethnicity, culture, perhaps gender, and other individual differences create differences in levels of individualism among North Americans. Moreover, not all Japanese agree with this characterization of contrasting selves (Kashima & Yamaguchi, 1999). Nevertheless, with the proviso that this is a broad-brush understanding—research in progress—the sense of the self potentially differs in various cultural settings that tend to emphasize either social harmony or the individual.

A final warning: One might think that people with interdependent selves would belong to more groups, because they depend on them so much, than people with independent selves, because they are more autonomous. People in independent cultures like the United States actually belong to more groups, but their identity—the relationship with the group—is not as strong, in each case. Basically, Americans move in and out of more groups than people do in more traditional, collectivist cultures because the groups do not mean as much. In fact, on average, European-Americans have a certain kind of social skill that facilitates transporting self into and out of a variety of groups (Heine & Buchtel, 2009). But different kinds of social skills result from being successful and harmonious in a long-term group, where one has to live with people for the rest of one's life. The whole collectivist notion is, for example, that once you take a job, traditionally, the organization will take care of you for life, but also you have to be loyal for life to this corporation. This kind of relationship in traditional Japan differs from some other places. North Americans are more likely to consider themselves free agents: One can quit, or one can be fired, or one could get a better job with a better salary; one may be moving into lots of different jobs in a lifetime, thereby requiring less sense of mutual loyalty and need for harmony. Ironically, collectivist, interdependent societies may foster fewer group memberships than individualist, independent societies do.

## Summary of Self-Concepts

Social psychology has studied self-understanding in several ways. The loose-knit knowledge structure, the self-concept, appears as a self-schema, with varying degrees of complexity, possible selves, and multiple identities. These varied selves are often dormant, activated in the working or accessible self-concept in any given context, with consistency pressures maintaining coherence and situational attributions discounting any remaining inconsistencies. People develop their self-concepts from self-perception of their own behavior, from introspection about their own thoughts and feelings, from comparison to other people, and from appraisals provided by others. Self-concept promotes both self-enhancement in the short run and consistent self-understanding (self-verification) in the long run. Finally, cultural differences underlie the independent expression of the self in individualist societies and the interdependent, relartional expression of the self in collectivist societies; these cultural patterns have implications for both self-understanding (self-concept) and self-enhancement (self-esteem and related emotions).

## SELF AND EMOTION: ENHANCING THE SELF

For a change of pace, do another little experiment. Make two lists: one of your strengths and one of your weaknesses. (The example will not work well after you read on. Active learning works better than passive learning. . . .)

Now, count the number of strengths and weaknesses separately. In sheer numbers, did your strengths outweigh your weaknesses? Most of my students report more strengths than weaknesses. (Typically, for 10% of the people, the strengths and weaknesses are the same number. For maybe another 10%, it is the opposite. As just noted, this may reflect cultural or individual variation.) This exercise typically shows more positive than negative self-aspects.

The tension between self-verification and self-enhancement, just covered (toward the end of the self-concept section), began our transition from self-knowledge to emotion. Social psychologists have studied a variety of self-related feelings (e.g., Brown, 1998), differentiating **global self-esteem** (general fondness or affection for self), **self-evaluations** (appraisal of one's specific characteristics), and **self-worth** (momentary self feelings). As noted, sometimes researchers refer to **trait self-esteem** (enduring, global) and **state self-esteem** (temporary, specific). The Rosenberg self-esteem scale, reproduced as Table 5.1, was designed to measure trait self-esteem, which tends to be in fact fairly stable, especially in young adults (Trzesniewski, Donnellan, & Robins, 2003).

## Biases in Self-Esteem

Though we've seen this self-description earlier, consider it now, focusing on its global self-esteem: "I'm a woman. Young, 21. Black. College student. Studying psychology. Happy. Caring. Sympathetic. Fun, with a sense of humor. Outgoing. Studious. Adventurous. A person who likes to do things. Intelligent. Me." This upbeat attitude reflects not only the class averages on positive versus negative aspects of self but also the positive tone of people's responses to the who-am-I test. Why does the positive outweigh the negative in both instances? In fact, most Americans do have a positive bias, as noted in Chapters 1 and 4 (Matlin & Stang, 1978). That is, they expect good events and a rosy future. Recall the study (Kunda, 1990) in which participants supported elaborate theories about why *their* marriage was going to be fine, despite the 50% divorce rate.

If people enhance themselves relative to others, are they inflating themselves or deflating those others? In four studies, students held overly charitable views of themselves but relatively accurate views of others (Epley & Dunning, 2000). A related question is whether self-enhancement means we see ourselves as better than other people or as better than other people see us (Kwan, John, Kenny, Bond, & Robins, 2004, Kwan, John, Robins, & Kuang, 2008). Certainly European-Americans retain a positive outlook in general; as just noted, the positive self-esteem bias may be less true in more collectivist cultures or for more interdependent selves.

Of course, even if individualist people on average accentuate the positive, situations still vary. For example, if you personally did not accentuate the positive in the exercise that opened this section, one possibility could be that it is simply a mental habit that could change, upon serious reflection (Verplanken, Friborg, Wang, Trafimow, & Woolf, 2007). Another possibility is your present state of mind. When people have just received some bad news and feel depressed, they think more about negative aspects of self. The context in which people think about self would be a short-term factor, affecting momentary self-worth. Research on mood shows precisely that. When people read a positive newspaper story, they judged twenty-one personal risks as less probable for themselves, and the opposite occurred for people who read a negative newspaper story, even though both stories were irrelevant to the personal risks they rated. As Figure 5.3 shows, their self-relevant judgments were affected by the temporary context (Johnson & Tversky, 1983). Both short-term and long-term state of mind powerfully affect people's transitory positive and negative self-judgments.

These short-term effects aside, positive self-views are valued in the U.S. individualistic mainstream culture—and for some good reasons. People with high self-esteem persist at tasks, despite setbacks; have more and better friends; deal constructively with health threats; and resist illness. Self-esteem generally associates with psychological, social, and physical well-being (Armor & Taylor, 1998; Brown, 1998; Taylor & Brown, 1988). People with high self-esteem may sometimes be right, in the sense that

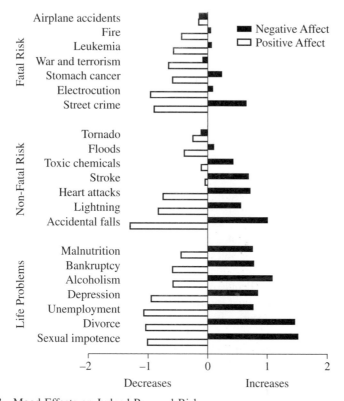

**Figure 5.3**   Mood Effects on Judged Personal Risks

*Source:* From Tversky & Johnson, 1983. Copyright © American Psychological Association. Adapted with permission

other people also think they are better than average (Kwan, John, Robins, & Kuang, 2008). In contrast, low-self-esteem undermines social bonds and thereby endangers people's health (Stinson et al., 2008). People with low self-esteem have vulnerable self-worth because it is conditional on recent success and failure, whereas people with high self-esteem have more resilient feelings of self-worth. Contingent self-esteem is unhealthy: It undermines autonomy, self-regulation, learning, health, and relationships when people constantly seek to validate their self-worth (Crocker & Knight, 2005). The benefits of high, stable self-esteem are real, but they can be taken too far. Nowadays, self-esteem is all the rage, as attested by the self-help section of the nearest bookstore. Self-esteem is the great cure-all, the great panacea for the problems that ail us. If somebody is in lousy relationships, it is because the person does not have enough self-esteem, or if somebody is not physically healthy, it is because the person does not have enough self-esteem to fight the illness. Self-esteem features as the 21st century cure for all ills.

Maybe this is not so. Baumeister (1998), for example, has debunked this myth; he argues that self-esteem is not a cure for everything, at all—quite the opposite. For example (Baumeister, Smart, & Boden, 1996), some of the most aggressive people have incredibly high self-esteem; the danger lies in having high but fragile self-esteem. Fragile self-esteem (e.g., because inflated) could more easily be damaged and threatened, leading to aggression. That is, high but unstable, tentative, or inflated self-esteem is readily defensive and may protect itself through aggression. For example, high self-esteem participants whose egos had been threatened by poor test scores became antagonistic and were rated as less likeable. Low self-esteem participants who received the ego threat became more restrained and were more likeable afterward (Heatherton & Vohs, 2000). What's more, nobody likes a narcissist because they fail to self-regulate, given a reactive, vulnerable, and insensitive grandiosity (Morf & Rhodewalt, 2001).

Stable, moderate self-esteem does not overreact. As an everyday example (Robins & Beer, 2001), inflated self-esteem, in the form of biased judgments of one's own performance, correlates with initial positive affect but also with narcissism, ego involvement, self-serving attributions, decreased self-esteem over time, and disengagement from later performance. Thus, biases in self-esteem may work in the short run but not in the long run or if too extreme.

Similarly, optimism and self-esteem can be so unrealistic as to encounter disconfirming evidence, promote inappropriate persistence, or endanger one's safety (Armor & Taylor, 1998). People will see what they want to see (Balcetis & Dunning, 2006) and use discredited information if the invalidated information supports a positive self-concept; inaccurate perseverance hardly seems ideal (Guenther & Alicke, 2008). The point here is that self-esteem is not a psychic aspirin for all ills. Instead, self-esteem reflects many angles of the emotional self.

## Self-Discrepancy Theory

Self-esteem concerns simple positive and negative self-evaluation. Self-discrepancy theory links the self-concept with rich, specific emotions, such as sadness, fear, anger, or happiness. It also goes beyond merely positive and negative feelings (pleasure and pain) by analyzing what exactly people approach and avoid (Higgins, 1997, 1998).

**SELF-GUIDES**    One of the major theories in the social psychology of the self and emotion, **self-discrepancy theory** (Higgins, 1987), concerns the impact of self-knowledge on how people feel and behave. The theory addresses how people use self-knowledge to fit social standards and adapt to group life. Various **self-guides**—standards—regulate behavior; different self-guides include the actual self, the ought self, and the ideal self.

The **actual self** is people's own image of who they really are right now. The "Who am I?" statements throughout this chapter are one operationalization of people's actual selves. (Of course, they might be accurate or not; perceived self is the point here.)

Then, the **ought self** represents who people feel they morally should be or who significant people in their lives—for example, parents—feel they should be. The ought self emphasizes responsibilities. These "shoulds" reflect conscience in the sense that people would feel guilty if they did not perform. *Ought* has a punitive overtone: If one does not measure up to the ought self, some bad consequences (punishment) will follow. If one does meet the ought responsibilities, one can be safe and secure.

Last, the **ideal self** represents who a person wants to be or who somebody else wants the person to be. The ideal self concerns desires, wishes, and aspirations. If a person fails to reach an ideal, the consequence is disappointment over losing the reward, not fear of punishment. If one does not attain one's ideals, one feels sad but not guilty. If one does meet the ideal aspirations, one can feel accomplished and rewarded.

The ought versus ideal is a distinction worth pondering. Because the ought self concerns *should*, if one fails to reach the "oughts," then one feels that someone might punish oneself. The ought self emphasizes a **prevention focus**, avoiding negative consequences: "Do this, or else." People who reach their *oughts* feel relief. On the other hand, the ideal self emphasizes a **promotion focus**, obtaining positive consequences: "Do this, and win that." People who achieve their ideals feel happy. The *ought* avoids the negative; the *ideal* seeks the positive.

Sometimes the differences between oughts and ideals can be subtle. One student described herself: "A senior. An Italian minor. A young lady (woman). A friend/roommate. A singer. A problem-solver. A slacker. A camp counselor. A procrastinator. A thinker. Sister/daughter. An Italian wannabe. Catholic. Aspiring politician." Chances are, "Italian wannabe," "singer," and "aspiring politician" represent ideals, whereas "a young lady" might be an ought, but "slacker" and "procrastinator" might represent failed oughts.

**SELF-DISCREPANCIES**  When the actual self diverges from the ideal or ought self, then the person has a self-discrepancy. People hardly ever live up totally to all their obligations or aspirations, so discrepancies will always come along.

People differ in which of the two discrepancies dominates. Some people experience a large **actual-ideal** discrepancy; they feel a chasm between who they are and who they hope to be, and they experience disappointment. For some people (sometimes the same people, but sometimes different people), the discrepancy between who they are and who they feel they should be—the **actual-ought** discrepancy—constitutes the chasm. They feel that they constantly fail at their obligations, and their conscience bothers them.

**EMOTIONAL VULNERABILITIES**  Emotional implications come out of self-knowledge and its discrepancies. "Knowledge," of course, is not necessarily accurate, but rather one's own perceptions, including internalization of perceptions from important other people (parents, major advisor, grandparents), all create ought and ideal self-guides. Whatever their source, the self-guides can be discrepant, and different discrepancies elicit different emotions. Depending on whether a person has a greater actual-ideal discrepancy or actual-ought discrepancy, the theory predicts different emotions. An actual-ideal discrepancy, not reaching ideals, reflects a failure to obtain a gain. As a failure of promotion focus, it predicts feeling disappointed, sad, lethargic, and in the long term, depressed. An actual-ought discrepancy, not fulfilling obligations, reflects a failure to avoid a loss. As a failure of prevention focus, it predicts feeling worried, nervous, and agitated, and in the long run, anxious.

Research on self-discrepancy theory directly demonstrates emotional vulnerabilities as a function of self-knowledge (Higgins, Bond, Klein, & Strauman, 1986). People tested on their self-discrepancies—actual-ought and actual-ideal—in a mass testing

**Table 5.6**    Self-Discrepancy and Positive-Negative Focus Effects on Writing Speed and Mood

| | Self-Concept Discrepancy | | | |
| | Actual-Ideal | | Actual-Ought | |
| Measure | Negative Focus | Positive Focus | Negative Focus | Positive Focus |
|---|---|---|---|---|
| Writing speed | **−5.1%** | 4.3% | **3.9%** | .50% |
| Dejection | **.24** | .03 | .04 | .06 |
| Agitation | .00 | .03 | **.11** | .09 |

Writing speed represents percent change from baseline. Mood scores could range from 0 to 1. Numbers in bold represent results cited in text.
*Source:* From Higgins et al., 1986. Copyright © American Psychological Association. Adapted with permission.

session at the beginning of the semester listed up to 10 attributes associated with their actual, ideal, and ought selves (which the investigators defined). Some people had bigger actual-ought or actual-ideal discrepancies, and they were invited into the laboratory. Researchers then had participants focus on a negative or positive event, to see whether a negative event would produce different types of discomfort depending on self-discrepancy. Under negative focus, participants were dejected or agitated, depending on whether they had a high actual-ideal or actual-ought discrepancy (see Table 5.6). Those with a high actual-ideal discrepancy even wrote more slowly when they had focused on a negative event (i.e., they started to get depressed), and those with a high actual-ought discrepancy wrote faster when they had focused on a negative event (i.e., they became anxious).

Prevention and promotion focuses create different patterns of achieving one's goals (Higgins, 2007). People with a promotion focus work on attaining their ideals (minimizing the actual-ideal discrepancy). They approach achievement from this perspective, as they

- Generate many hypotheses and keep them all open
- Are open to change
- May wait to pursue their goals
- May be distracted by competing temptations
- Quickly appraise how cheerful or dejected objects in the world would make them feel
- React with more cheerfulness when they do attain their goals or more dejection when they do not
- Feel more pleasure over gains and less pain over losses

In contrast, people with a prevention focus work to maintain safety and security (minimizing the actual-ought discrepancy). Their approach to achievement makes them

- Generate fewer hypotheses and commit to one
- Prefer stability
- Pursue goals immediately

- Resist distraction
- Quickly appraise how calm or agitated objects in the world would make them feel
- React with more calm when they do attain their goals or more agitation when they do not
- Feel more pain over losses and less pleasure over gains

Neither prevention nor promotion focus is inherently superior in all contexts. Regulatory focus that matches the task means and incentives works the best (Shah, Higgins, & Friedman, 1998). Regulatory fit between the self-system and the experience helps motivate people (Higgins, 2006). Besides sheer valence (pleasure-pain), the intensity of engagement matters to persuasion, judgment, and emotion.

Relative emphasis on promoting ideals and preventing the failure of oughts will vary, beyond the specific individual difference in regulatory focus (i.e., discrepancy type). Independent people, cultures, and situations all seem to encourage a promotion-focused orientation, whereby ideal self-guides predominate. In contrast, interdependent people, cultures, and situations all seem to encourage a prevention-focused orientation, whereby ought self-guides predominate (Lee, Aaker, & Gardner, 2000). More generally, independent cultures encourage approach motivations, whereas interdependent cultures encourage avoidance motivations (Heine & Buchtel, 2009).

This theory relates to this book's overall themes of self-understanding and self-enhancement in the service of group life. Although one's parents may be the most obvious sources of self-guides, self-guides are internalized also from the larger group. As noted earlier, norms are unwritten rules of the group; norms in effect are obligations. The group benefits if people feel guilty and anxious when they fail to follow its norms. In a similar way, the group benefits if people are motivated to set goals (ideals) and strive for them—so long as the goals are consistent with the group's values. The norms and values of the group become self-guides as ought and ideal selves. What's more, both obligations and aspirations reflect motives for self-understanding (seeing oneself in terms of these internalized standards) and self-enhancement (in the sense of self-improvement), both of which can benefit the group and hence one's survival in it.

## Self-Evaluation Maintenance Theory

One student wrote, "An athlete. A friend. Listener. African. Advisor. Helper. Student. Dancer. Dreamer. Perfectionist. An older sister. Intelligent. A fighter. Feminist." For this student, if "athlete" is central to her self-concept, coming first in her list, then she may not be pleased if her younger sister overtakes her athletic ability. If self-discrepancy theory addresses discrepancies *within* one's own understanding of self, with certain emotional fallout, **self-evaluation maintenance theory** addresses discrepancies *between* two people in a relationship, again with certain emotional fallout. Two people in a relationship each aim to keep themselves feeling good, given social comparison with their partner (Tesser, 1988). The basic idea is this: Each person has certain areas of self that are central and self-defining. They might include piano-playing, generosity, sense of humor, or athletic ability. Someone else taking over certain self-defining areas of one's self-concept can lead to discomfort. For example, if a brother or sister starts excelling at the piano, and you are the family piano player, you may not be exactly pleased.

Self-evaluation maintenance theory considers two factors to see whether people will be threatened or pleased by the accomplishments of people who are close to them: First, the more relevant the area is to one's own self-concept, the more threat increases. For example, although a sibling's piano virtuosity would be threatening, that sibling's violin playing instead could cause pride, because that is further away (and maybe the siblings could do sonatas together). Moving still farther from one's own bailiwick, one could be even more proud if the sibling were accepted to graduate school in physics, that being not at all part of one's self-concept as a musician.

Second, the theory singles out how close the two people are. The closer the person is, the more emotion results, either positive or negative. If one feels threatened, in the case of the competing piano player, one would feel less threat if the person were a cousin instead of a sibling, and even less if the person were a distant acquaintance. To feel proud, as in the case of the physics graduate student, one would feel most proud of a sibling, less proud of a cousin, and not much about the distant acquaintance.

These threat and pride emotions affect people's self-evaluation (as in the name of the theory). The more one feels proud, the more the other person's accomplishments raise one's self-esteem; the more one feels threatened, the more the other person's accomplishments lower self-esteem. Other emotions also follow the self-evaluation maintenance model. In one study (Tesser, Millar, & Moore, 1988), pairs of women friends came into the laboratory and indicated individually whether aesthetic judgment or logical thinking ability was more self-relevant. The women then separately performed a series of short aesthetic and logical games on a computer, receiving feedback about their performance each time. Their feedback compared them either with their friend or a stranger who had played the games earlier. The researchers surreptitiously videotaped expressions on the women's faces, as they received the feedback from the computer. The tapes showed them looking more pleased about outperforming a friend than a stranger, when the game was self-relevant, presumably the most threatening situation. When the game was less self-relevant, they cared less. If the other person beat them in the low-relevance game, it was better to have the reflected glory of a friend than to be beaten by a stranger. The results show the operation of closeness, relevance, and relative performance, in accord with the theory's predictions.

Self-evaluation maintenance echoes themes of social comparison theory, covered earlier, but it explains how one can maintain self-evaluations in the face of demoralizing upward comparisons. For example, if the target outperforms you in one domain (e.g., analytic), your own performance can improve in a separate domain (e.g., verbal), rescuing your self-esteem (Johnson & Stapel, 2007). This theory clearly addresses motives for self-enhancement (maintaining positive self-evaluation). The theory also relates somewhat to self-understanding (social comparison). It links to compatibility in group life, too, in that people prefer to carve out different, complementary areas of expertise, so as not to feel threatened by close others, and that helps the group to get more different bases covered.

## Affective Forecasting

For all their attempts to protect themselves from feeling bad, people turn out to be not very accurate at knowing what will indeed make them feel lousy. People also are not very accurate about how very effective they will be at self-enhancing to remedy negative events. **Affective forecasting** describes people's attempts to predict how future events will make them feel (Gilbert & Wilson, 2007; Wilson & Gilbert, 2005). People fall prey to **durability bias**—overestimating the duration of their reactions to negative events—because they are unaware of the various self-enhancement processes that social psychologists have uncovered. People's self-understandings fall short of their self-enhancement skills.

For example, people know that positive events will make them feel good (match the first two columns of Table 5.7), but they apparently do not realize that they will recover quickly from negative events, such as romantic breakups, not getting tenure, not getting hired, and negative personal feedback (compare the last two columns of Table 5.7; Gilbert, Pinel, Wilson, Blumberg, & Wheatley, 1998). People's **psychological immune systems** help them to cope with horrible life events, but people neglect to credit these spontaneous self-protective processes. Similarly, people engage in **focalism**, assuming that the negative event will be the center of their lives and no other events will moderate its impact (Wilson, Wheatley, Meyers, Gilbert, & Axsom, 2000). People so fail to notice their own capacities for generating self-enhancement that they tend to attribute their self-satisfying choices to benevolent **external agency** (Gilbert, Brown, Pinel, & Wilson, 2000).

## Summary of Self and Emotion

Work on self and emotion has focused on one phenomenon—self-enhancing biases in self-feelings—and three major theories. Self-discrepancy theory proposes that gaps between the actual and ideal self emphasize a failure to obtain positive outcomes and

**Table 5.7**  Inaccuracy of Affective Forecasting for Negative Events

| Variable | Positive Events | | Negative Events | |
|---|---|---|---|---|
| | Forecast | Actual | Forecast | Actual |
| Romantic experience | 5.79 | 5.81 | 3.89 | 5.44 |
| Tenure decision | 5.78 | 5.53 | 4.10 | 5.05 |
| Election outcome | 4.90 | 4.40 | 4.07 | 5.33 |
| Personal feedback | — | — | 3.40 | 5.31 |
| Hiring decision | — | — | −2.00* | −.24* |

*Change from predecision baseline.
Higher numbers indicated greater anticipated or actual happiness. Blanks indicate data not gathered in that study. Means include experimental conditions most relevant to current discussion, some collapsed over immediate and delayed conditions.
*Source:* Data from Gilbert et al., 1998.

thereby predict depression, whereas gaps between the actual and ought self emphasize avoiding negative outcomes and thereby predict anxiety. Self-evaluation maintenance theory examines gaps between people and proposes that people feel proud when close others perform well in areas of low self-relevance but feel threatened when those same close others perform well in areas of high self-relevance. Affective forecasting theory proposes that people overestimate the impact of negative events and underestimate their own capacities for coping. All three theories focus primarily on self-enhancement motives, but they have implications for self-understanding and belonging as well.

## SELF AND BEHAVIOR: WANTING TO BELONG

So far we have examined what the self is and how it functions, and then how people understand the self, and most recently how the self relates to certain emotions. Now let's turn to the behaving self, focusing on how people present themselves to others and why. Self-presentation aims to maintain and save one's social face—the positive front one puts on in public (Goffman, 1967). Throughout this chapter, students' self-descriptions have illustrated aspects of the self-concept and self-related emotions. The self-descriptions represent **self-presentation**, the desired view of self as expressed in social behavior. Writing a self-description to hand in to a psychology professor is a social act, presenting oneself and monitoring the situation for appropriate cues.

### Self-Presentation Contexts

Recall that students in my social psychology classes are less likely to mention ethnicity than students in my psychology of racism class. Their self-presentations depend on context, for at least four reasons reflected by my students: personal goals, audience, situation, and societal context.

**PERSONAL GOALS**    First, students who take psychology of racism may on average have different personal goals than students in the broader course. Hence, they would be more likely to mention ethnicity because it fits their goals, for example, exploring ethnicity in their current self-concept and possible selves. Self-concept defines one's view of what is accurate, plausible, and ethical, which fits people's motives of self-understanding and self-enhancement. For example, a student who portrays herself as "A good friend. An avid reader. A person who usually smiles. A person who supports other people" may note positive aspects about herself but none exaggerated or implausible. Similarly, one's possible selves (desired and undesired identities) determine how one tries to portray oneself; the motives of self-understanding and self-enhancement both constrain possible selves. For example, the same student noted that she is "committed to improving" and "committed to working toward a more just society," both desired identities, goals that determine self-presentation in a particular context.

**AUDIENCE**    Students have expectations, based on the audience, namely the professor and what they think she wants. In the racism class, they may assume I want to know their ethnic background. Also, they presumably shift their answers for a professor as opposed to a peer. Audience factors include both sides' relative roles and the audience's values (Leary & Kowalski, 1990). Social roles constrain self-presentation because maintaining one's role in the group depends on presenting oneself as appropriate to fill that role. For example, the same student portrayed herself as a "good neighbor" and immediately added the context of "a giving person," which fits the good-neighbor role. Similarly, the audience's values shape self-presentation, which again fits the motivation to belong. People select aspects of themselves likely to please the audience. The student perhaps was conscious of her audience (her professor in psychology of racism) when she emphasized her "concerns with discrimination and oppression," undoubtedly also a core aspect of her self-concept, but one she may have mentioned because of the audience for her self-presentation.

**IMMEDIATE SITUATION**   The situation shapes self-presentation in several ways. People describe themselves partly on the basis of what identifies them in a particular setting. For example, some dimensions make one distinct (McGuire & McGuire, 1988). Even in a racism class, people of color may be distinct by virtue of being a minority, so they would mention it to identify themselves. In addition, students may feel similar to others of their ethnicity, so they would mention it to establish their social group identity (Oakes, Haslam, & Turner, 1994). And, of course, if the class topic is racism, people's own ethnicity would be primed in their own minds (remember priming from the social cognition chapter). In any given situation, self-presenters are limited by their current or potential social image (Leary & Kowalski, 1990); to maintain credibility and belonging within the group, self-presenters may be constrained, compelled, or entitled by what people already know about them or are likely to learn in the future. For example, a student new to a course would be unlikely to claim a perfect academic record, in case that image could not be maintained in the new class.

**SOCIETY**   Dimensions of the broader society matter too. In my social psychology class, few students mention their ethnicity, but almost all the exceptions come from people of minority ethnicities. Most people of color and Jewish people in my class mention their ethnicity, whereas less than a fifth of the white, non-Jewish people do. The reasons are complex, as the chapter on stereotyping and stigma discusses, but the point here is that people describing themselves are affected by the composition of their society.

**SUMMARY**   Self-presentation adapts to context (goals, audience, situation, and society). People's self-presentations increase their subjective well-being by meeting three primary motivations (Leary & Kowalski, 1990): maximizing the rewards of social relations (belonging), enhancing self-esteem (self-enhancement), and establishing desired identities (self-understanding) (see also Schlenker & Weigold, 1992). Self-presentation mainly facilitates belonging but also serves self-enhancement and self-understanding. The central role of belonging motives appears when ostracism makes people more attentive to their impact on others (Williams, 2007). People high on need to belong are more socially sensitive (Pickett, Gardner, & Knowles, 2004). Similarly, loneliness increases social monitoring (Gardner, Pickett, Jefferis, &

Knowles, 2005). Belonging motives mainly drive attunement to others and strategic self-presentation.

## Strategic Self-Presentation

How does the self express itself through behavior? One of the first chapters discussed how social perception differs from object perception, in that, when one is perceiving somebody else, that person is perceiving back, so one may become self-conscious and adjust accordingly. Self-presentation goes beyond wanting to look good physically; people care even more about what other people think of them as human beings. As noted, people have a complex and multiple self-concept. People use many **self-presentation strategies** to convey their preferred self-concept, with the motives to understand, enhance, and belong influencing choice of strategy.

Self-presenters aim to elicit a particular perception that they want other people to hold, using several everyday strategies (Jones & Pittman, 1982). Each strategy has four aspects: the trait attribution (or image) the self-presenter seeks, the downside risk (the attribution if the strategy fails), the affect (emotion) sought, and the strategic behaviors themselves (see Table 5.8).

**INGRATIATION**    The most obvious strategy is **ingratiation**, which means behavior to promote being liked. The hoped-for attribution is that one is *nice*. As just noted, each of these strategies revolves around a desired trait attribution, wanting the other person to perceive a certain personality trait, so self-presenters pick their strategies accordingly.

Probability of success also determines the strategy self-presenters pick. What if one fails to come across as nice? What if the other person realizes the self-presenter is ingratiating? For example, suppose a student says, "Oh, Professor Fiske, I just love your lectures; they're so great." The risk there, the downside, explains why students typically wait to gush (if they do) until after grades are due. Students do not want to be seen as *hypocrites* or *sycophants* (we'll skip the cruder ways to put this). One social psychologist (Vonk, 1998) coined the verb to **slime** someone, an evocative description. The behavior of salespeople toward customers (DeCarlo, 2005) and of subordinates toward superiors (Struthers, Eaton, Czyznielewski, & Dupuis, 2005) each carries this downside risk of ingratiation.

Next, consider the desired affect (remember this is not "effect"; this is the emotional reaction sought). Ingratiation seeks *affection:* wanting to be liked. Each strategy has a desired affect, the emotion the self-presenter seeks to elicit from the other person.

Finally, consider some typical behaviors that one could perform in order to be seen as nice and likeable. Do people have other ways to ingratiate, besides indiscriminate agreement and flattery? Students often mention smiling, complimenting, nodding, recognizing, attending, and appreciating. I know of at least one marriage and one substantial charitable donation each attributed to someone laughing at someone else's jokes. Various strategic behaviors, from agreeing to laughing, illustrate how people try to get the attribution they want (being likeable) and to receive the feelings they want (affection). Sometimes they even get the mate or the money they want.

**Table 5.8**  Taxonomy of Self-Presentational Strategies, Classified Primarily by Attribution Sought

| *Strategy* and Attribution Sought | Negative Attributions Risked | Emotion to Be Aroused | Prototypical Actions |
|---|---|---|---|
| *Ingratiation* | | | |
| Likeable | Sycophant, conformist, obsequious | Affection | Self-characterization, opinion conformity, other enhancement, favors |
| *Self-promotion* | | | |
| Competent (effective, "a winner") | Fraudulent, conceited, defensive | Respect (awe, deference) | Performances, performance claims, performance accounts |
| *Intimidation* | | | |
| Dangerous (ruthless, volatile) | Blusterer, wishy-washy, ineffectual | Fear | Threats, anger (incipient), breakdown (incipient) |
| *Exemplification* | | | |
| Worthy (suffering, dedicated) | Hypocrite, sanctimonious, exploitative | Guilt (shame, emulation) | Self-denial, helping, militancy for a cause |
| *Supplication* | | | |
| Helpless (handicapped, unfortunate) | Stigmatized, lazy, demeaning | Nurturance (obligation) | Self-deprecation, entreaties for help |

*Source:* From Jones & Pittman, 1982. Copyright © Erlbaum. Adapted with permission.

**SELF-PROMOTION**    Another form of self-presentation, **self-promotion**, carries the goal to be seen as *competent*, which can conflict with being seen as likeable. Self-promotion is not ingratiating (Godfrey, Jones, & Lord, 1986). After pairs of participants held an unstructured conversation, one of them was given a self-presentational goal: to try to be either as likeable as possible or as competent as possible, in a second conversation. The would-be ingratiators gained in likeability, while their perceived competence remained the same, whereas the would-be self-promoters sacrificed likeability but did not manage to impress their partners. Self-promotion may be a skill that requires more than a brief conversation; in a 20-minute conversation, self-promoters could present their credentials only by taking charge of the conversation, not a likeable tactic.

The distinction between ingratiation and self-promotion comes across in a job interview. An interviewee does not want to be seen as just likeable; it is far more important to be seen as competent. Employers want to feel that they could work with someone who has good interpersonal skills, but at a minimum, they want someone competent. Two studies (Operario & Fiske, 2001a) show how useless it is to be seen as only likeable in a job interview. Pairs of participants enacted a job interview to be a research assistant. Half the interviewees had the goal of making the interviewer like them (ingratiation), and half had the goal of making the interviewer respect them (self-promotion). If the interviewer was a high-dominance personality, the interviewer liked the ingratiator and wanted to go afterward for coffee with this likeable person, but the high-dominance interviewer did not want to hire that person. The low-dominance interviewers simply wanted to hire the person who was competent. So, interviewees need to be careful about not just ingratiating in situations that call for self-promotion. One may go out of the interview feeling good about being appreciated as nice, but one will not necessarily get hired. On the other hand, behaving in a competent yet cold way could backfire, too. But competence comes first.

What is the downside risk of self-promotion? One risks being seen as *a fraud* at worst or as simply *conceited*. In the Godfrey et al. study, the unsuccessful self-promoters were seen as mechanically reciting their successes and being dull. Moreover, even moderate and honest self-promotion is appropriate only in certain settings. A new roommate who immediately reels off accomplishments—stellar GPA, prestigious summer jobs, and meeting the President—has hardly ingratiated.

The affect or emotions that self-promoters are trying to elicit are *respect* and *awe*. In the study by Godfrey et al., self-promoters reported that they mentioned their accomplishments, attempted to lead the conversation, showed nonverbal confidence, expressed verbal confidence, and avoided their partner's areas of expertise. Self-promotion is a common form of office politics (Buchanan, 2008).

**INTIMIDATION**    Now here's a different line to take. The first two, self-promotion and ingratiation, are perhaps obvious, but the next three are less obvious. In **intimidation**, people want to come across as *dangerous*. For example, faculty in the first few meetings of a large class may act a bit tough and intimidating, to avoid crowd control issues. The desired attribution is "Don't mess with that professor." In general, people and other animals might have developed intimidation to exploit others, acquiring their resources (Buss & Duntley, 2008).

What is the downside risk of intimidation? The professor who threatens to throw out people who chat in the back row, but does not actually do it, is *absurd, a paper tiger, insincere*. Parents sometimes fall into this trap of making empty threats that rapidly lose credibility.

The emotion that the intimidator wants to inspire in people *is fear*, just enough fear to control them. The typical behaviors to intimidate somebody include nonverbal behaviors, such as standing too close ("in their face"), staring, or frowning. People can also intimidate by setting high standards, being volatile and unpredictable, or being unavailable and hard to reach. Expressing anger intimidates others and reinforces power hierarchies (Tiedens, 2001).

Although the examples so far involve people in official power being intimidating and dangerous, the traditionally powerless can also intimidate. The four-year-old who communicates, in the middle of the grocery store, "If you don't buy those special cookies, I'm going to have a temper tantrum!" in effect threatens the parent. Some-times, even adults do that, if their relationship deteriorates enough. For example, if the other person is threatening to make a scene in public, that could be intimidating and dangerous. People do not have to wield just traditionally recognized forms of power in order to intimidate and control. Jones (1990) suggested that because it produces aversion, intimidation is most likely in committed long-term relationships. Intimidated people in nonbinding relationships may just leave.

**EXEMPLIFICATION**   This one intrigues people because they do not think of it as a self-presentation strategy. In **exemplification**, the person wants to be seen as *worthy, moral*, and *saintly*, to set an example. Parents and professors try to exemplify, as do religious and political leaders.

The downside to exemplification is being seen as *sanctimonious, holier than thou*, or *a pain*. An exemplifier could even be *exploitative* by guilt-tripping or manipulating people into compliance as compensation for one's sacrifices. Jones (1990) suggested that *self-deceptive* is also an attribution risked by failed exemplification. As with all these strategies, political skill enables success; without skill, one is better off not attempting exemplification (or any of the other strategies) (Harris, Kacmar, Zivnuska, & Shaw, 2007).

The affect desired from the other person is *guilt*. (Maybe the exemplifier is try-ing to maximize the other person's actual-ought discrepancies, by being the ought.) People are supposed to feel guilty because they feel that they are not living up to the exemplifier's example (Jones, 1990). Guilt may not be the only desired emotion. An exemplifier wanting to be seen as a worthy, moral example may want to *inspire* people to follow. Moral leaders often try to instill a little guilt and a little inspiration.

Some typical behaviors include just talking about one's virtues or doing good deeds in a noisy way. Sometimes it is the self-other discrepancy that is the killer: "When I was your age, I never drank; how can you drink so much?"

**SUPPLICATION**   The final self-presentational strategy (Jones & Pittman, 1982) may seem odd at first, and it is the strategy of last resort (Jones, 1990). The goal of **supplication** is to be seen as *helpless*. Why might it be useful? To get other people to help out, whether it is changing a tire or cooking dinner, people may self-present as helpless. Think of it as strategic incompetence.

All of these strategies can backfire, and certainly supplication can cause a reaction; the downside risk is being seen as *lazy, calculating*, or *repulsive*. The risk is the perception that the person is just trying to get out of doing a job. The desired emotion is *nurturance*, either maternalistic or paternalistic: "Let me take care of that; let me take care of you." Mutual trust is key here (Van Kleef, De Dreu, & Manstead, 2006). The typical behaviors emphasize the supplicator's helplessness and incompetence but in ways that maintain self-esteem and do not make the other person disgusted; it's a trick to pull it off.

**ARE THESE THE ONLY SELF-PRESENTATION STRATEGIES USED?**
Virtually everybody wants to be seen, sometimes, as likeable, competent, intimidating, saintly, or helpless. For example, everybody ingratiates sometimes; almost all people

want other people to like them; the core social motive to belong reflects this desire. Ingratiation in small doses just greases the social wheels among people; part of social interaction involves being nice to people. Similarly, trying to appear competent (self-promoting) fits the core social motive of self-enhancing. Trying to appear potentially dangerous (intimidation) fits the core social motive of control. Trying to appear helpless (supplication) fits core motives to trust and depend on other people. Trying to appear saintly (exemplification) does not uniquely fit any of the core social motives; it could entail self-enhancement (holier than thou), understanding (setting a good example), or control (do as I do).

The five strategies and the five motives do not map one-to-one on each other, but the misfits allow us to consider whether people might have still other self-presentation goals. Perhaps people try to elicit from other people a whole other class of trait attributions reflected by, for example, the core social motive of shared social understanding. One might try to appear wise, in the know, and socially central, in a strategy of establishing one's indispensability.

Similarly, of course, ideas such as this self-presentation theory can suggest core motives potentially omitted here (perhaps the motive for justice, reflected by exemplification?). In any conceptual framework, social psychologists identify an essential set of factors critical to their approach. In these two cases, the five particular strategies seem to cover a lot of common situations, but they need not be five versus four or seven. Theoretically, no reason limits us to these five and only these five.

Even these five self-presentation strategies, however, make one think differently about some of one's daily interactions. They all make people more firmly part of their group; even as they may be trying to influence the group, they want to maintain their place in the group. More generally, our social adaptation viewpoint would argue that people survive better in the group, by knowing how to present themselves effectively, without provoking undue costs.

## Self-Monitoring

Take a minute to complete the scale in Table 5.9. Like self-presentation, **self-monitoring** (Snyder, 1974, 1987) also concerns the self and behavior because it describes how much people monitor themselves to fit the social situation. Guiding one's behavior to fit the situation often facilitates fitting into the group. The self-monitoring concept nicely illustrates a very social psychological individual difference. By definition, social psychology does not much address individual differences; as the introductory chapter noted, mostly social psychology does not study personality. Nevertheless, self-monitoring constitutes one individual difference that has everything to do with how much people attend to the social situation, so it is profoundly social psychological.

High self-monitors attend to the social situation a lot; the situation matters to them, and they are sensitively attuned to it. Low self-monitors attend to their own interior cues a lot; the self matters to them, and they are sensitively attuned to it. Neither a high nor low score is better than the other; both are healthy. Self-monitoring supplies one of the few personality scales where the author worked hard to make both ends of the scale acceptable. (So don't start feeling bad about being on either end or in the middle.)

**Table 5.9**  Self-Monitoring Scale

Indicate True or False for each of these statements:

1.  I find it hard to imitate the behavior of other people.
2.  I guess I put on a show to impress or entertain people.
3.  I would probably make a good actor.
4.  I sometimes appear to others to be experiencing deeper emotions than I actually am.
5.  In a group of people, I am rarely the center of attention.
6.  In different situations and with different people, I often act like very different persons.
7.  I can only argue for ideas I already believe.
8.  In order to get along and be liked, I tend to be what people expect me to be rather than anything else.
9.  I may deceive people by being friendly when I really dislike them.
10.  I am not always the person I appear to be.

Look at your answers to questions 1, 5, and 7. Give yourself a point for each of those questions that you answered False. Now give yourself a point for each of the remaining questions that you answered T. Add up your points. If you scored 7 or above, you probably are a high self-monitor; if you scored 3 or below, you probably are a low self-monitor.
*Source:* From Snyder, 1974. Copyright © American Psychological Association. Adapted with permission.

Low self-monitors see themselves as principled, and their view of themselves cues their behavior. We will see when we get to attitudes, the next chapter's topic, that for the low self-monitors, their attitudes guide their behavior more than for other people because they do what they believe in, what they want to do, and what they like. They do not do what they do not like or what they do not believe in, even if it has substantial social costs. They might or might not be good group members, being more motivated by individual understanding, controlling, or self-enhancing.

High self-monitors, on the other hand, view themselves as pragmatic and flexible. The social situation guides their behavior. They are much more tuned into what the social situation requires, very sensitive to it. They are much more likely to do, not what they personally prefer, but what is necessary in the situation: what other people need for them to do or what is appropriate. High self-monitors are particularly adapted to survive well in social groups, so they especially fit the core social motive to belong and perhaps the core social motive to trust (at least to trust others to behave appropriately).

Both these dimensions have an undesirable side: Low self-monitors could behave in ways that are situationally insensitive or inappropriate, and high self-monitors could behave in ways that contradict what they honestly believe. Neither low nor high self-monitoring is perfect.

Consider some of the important implications of high and low self-monitoring (Gangestad & Snyder, 2000). Who acts on their attitudes? (Low self-monitors.) Who is sensitive to situational norms? (High self-monitors.) Who picks their friends on the basis of activities that they both like to do? (Lows.) Who picks their friends on the basis of how they look? (Highs.) Who picks their friends based on their personality and how they feel about them? (Lows.) Who is more oriented to other people? (Highs.) Who most expresses their own personal feelings? (Lows.)

Now: Who believes feedback from personality tests? One might think, "highs." After all, they respond to external cues. Actually, the result is counter-intuitive: It turns out that the lows use the personality test feedback the most (Fiske & Von Hendy, 1992). If low self-monitors believe the feedback—even when it is random—they presumably assimilate it to their self-concept, and they behave accordingly. People often have the idea that low self-monitors are accurate about themselves, but they may have a mistaken view of who they are and act on it. The experimenter told some people that a personality test rated them a certain way, and the low self-monitors acted on that. In the same way, the experimenter told high self-monitors that the social norms were a certain way, and the high self-monitors acted on that. Nobody has a monopoly on truth.

Both levels of self-monitoring can be useful in the social world. High self-monitors and people high on need-to-belong respond to significant-other primes (i.e., roommate, mother) by assimilating their goals to those close others (Morrison, Wheeler, & Smeesters, 2007). Groups need people who are sensitive to norms and flexible about adjusting to them. But groups also need people who stand up for enduring principles, so a mix of high and low self-monitors is arguably good for group survival.

## Self-Regulation

In both self-monitoring and self-presentation, people aim to regulate their behavior. Both describe people's motives and strategies, but they do not describe their success. Work on **self-regulation** suggests when people can and cannot control their behavior. Social psychologists would like to understand why people drive drunk, abuse drugs, and risk unprotected sex, but researchers cannot ethically encourage people to engage in these behaviors. Much laboratory research has focused instead on dieting, a common attempt at self-control that actually fails most of the time.

One model of self-regulation, the **ego depletion model** (Baumeister, Bratslavsky, Muraven & Tice, 1998), argues that all kinds of volition (e.g., choice, self-regulation) draw on the same limited inner resources. If one resists one temptation, one may more easily fall prey to the next immediate risk. For example, a study ostensibly about taste perception asked participants to eat two or three radishes in five minutes but resist some nearby chocolate candy and fresh-baked chocolate chip cookies, or asked them to eat two or three cookies and candies but resist some nearby radishes. Participants in the control group skipped this stage of the study. All participants then tried to solve a geometric drawing puzzle which was (unbeknownst to them) unsolvable. The measure of persistence (self-regulation) was number of attempts and time trying to solve the problems. Presumably, participants who had to resist chocolate used up more self-regulatory resources than those who had to resist radishes or those who had no self-regulation. As Table 5.10 indicates, radish eaters tried less often and gave up sooner than chocolate eaters or the no-food control group. These results fit the idea that resisting chocolate used up inner resources that could have been spent on task persistence.

**Table 5.10**    Persistence on Unsolvable Puzzles

| Condition | Time (minutes) | Attempts |
|---|---|---|
| Chocolate resisters | 8.35 | 19.40 |
| Radish resisters | 18.90 | 34.29 |
| No food control | 20.86 | 32.81 |

*Source:* From Baumeister et al., 1998. Copyright © American Psychological Association. Adapted with permission.

Similarly, chronic dieters seated next to tasty snacks (Doritos and M&Ms), who presumably had to exert self-control, then failed to self-regulate effectively on a second chance to resist overeating (ice cream the second time) (Vohs & Heatherton, 2000). Self-control attempts of all kinds seem to deplete one's self-regulatory resources. All kinds of self-regulation depress blood glucose levels, depleting resources for the next attempt at self-regulation, but consuming a high-glucose drink enables subsequent self-regulation (Gailliot et al., 2007). This helps explain eating as a release. Controlling one's emotions or coping with emotional distress leads to uncontrolled eating (Heatherton, Striepe, & Wittenberg, 1998). However, uncontrolled eating occurs when people are upset but not wanting to think about themselves being upset. Binge eating fits this escape from aversive self-awareness (Heatherton & Baumeister, 1991).

Not just controlling distress, but maintaining optimistic illusions also requires regulatory resources (Fischer, Greitemeyer, & Frey, 2007). When not overtaxed, optimism and appropriate goals aid self-regulation in the service of good health (Rasmussen, Wrosch, Scheier, & Carver, 2006). People differ a lot in their self-regulatory patterns, however, and these systems construct our unique selves (Morf, 2006), determining our health and well-being (Leventhal, Weinman, Leventhal, & Phillips, 2008).

## CHAPTER SUMMARY

"I am a TA for Psych 100. Resident assistant in [dorm]. Student Admissions Assistant. Rollerblader (not a good one). Tennis player (average). Runner (used to run for the university). Extremely hard worker. Sometimes too hard. Undergrad psych advisor. Fun/enjoy humor and try to be funny. Active. Member of Psi Chi." This last self-description reflects many aspects of the self studied by social psychologists.

The self includes various levels, including the body, inner, interpersonal, and societal selves, as well as the active "I" and the object "me." Operationally, social psychologists most often use working definitions that measure self-concept (e.g., the who-am-I test), self-esteem (e.g., the Rosenberg scale), and self-presentation (public-private differences in behavior). In various socially adaptive ways, the self-concept fulfills motives to understand, while self-esteem and self-improvement fulfill motives to self-enhance, and self-regulation fulfills motives to belong.

The self is not a unit, but it glues together a range of knowledge about ourselves. Although complex, the self achieves some coherence via selective accessibility, consistency pressures, and situational attributions. People get to know their complex selves by observing their own behavior, introspecting about thoughts and feelings, comparing themselves to others, and attending to social feedback. Sometimes they prefer self-verifying feedback from others, even if it fits a negative self-concept. Independent and interdependent self-concepts occur respectively in individualist and collectivist cultures, with characteristic differences in the role of the self.

People strive to enhance themselves, but cultures vary as to whether that is merely believing the best about oneself (self-esteem biases) or focusing more on self-sympathy and self-improvement. More specific emotions such as anxiety and depression respectively result from discrepancies between one's actual and ought selves or one's actual and ideal selves. At a more interpersonal level, pride and threat emotions result from discrepancies between self and close others, depending on closeness and self-relevance. At a temporal level, people show major discrepancies between how badly they think they will feel after a negative experience (affective forecasts) and how well they actually manage to feel.

The behaving self, striving to belong, affects people's self-presentation, self-monitoring, and self-regulation. People's self-presentations depend on context (goals, audience, situation, society) but generally help subjective well-being. Among people's self-presentational strategies, striving to get others to make particular attributions about self, are ingratiation, self-promotion, intimidation, exemplification, and supplication. High self-monitors are more concerned with and skilled at self-presentation, whereas low self-monitors are more skilled at acting on their own beliefs. Whatever people's behavioral goals, self-regulation depends on inner resources, which self-control depletes. The self functions in our core motives not only of understanding and self-enhancing but of belonging as well.

## SUGGESTIONS FOR FURTHER READING

BAUMEISTER, R. F., SCHMEICHEL, B. J., & VOHS, K. D. (2007). Self-regulation and the executive function: The self as controlling agent. In A. W. KRUGLANSKI & E. T. HIGGINS (Eds.), *Social psychology: Handbook of basic principles* (2nd ed., pp. 516–539). New York: Guilford.

BREWER, M. B., & CHEN, Y. (2007). Where (who) are collectives in collectivism? Toward conceptual clarification of individualism and collectivism. *Psychological Review*, 114, 133–151.

BROWN, J. D. (1998). *The self*. New York: McGraw-Hill.

ELLEMERS, N., SPEARS, R., & DOOSJE, B. (2002). Self and social identity. *Annual Review of Psychology*, 53, 161–186.

SNYDER, M., & CANTOR, N. (1998). Personality and social behavior. In D. T. GILBERT, S. T. FISKE, & G. LINDZEY (Eds.), *Handbook of social psychology* (4th ed., Vol. 1, pp. 635–679). New York: McGraw-Hill.

SWANN, W., Jr., & BOSSON, J. (2010). Self and identity. In S. T. FISKE, D. T GILBERT, & G. LINDZEY (Eds.), *Handbook of social psychology* (5th ed.). New York: Wiley.

# Chapter 6

# Attitudes and Persuasion: Changing Hearts and Minds

The world's largest completed industrial merger to that date, between Daimler-Benz, Germany's largest company, and Chrysler Corporation, was announced May 7, 1998. The companies spent $25 million on public relations targeted to the merger alone. On the day of the announcement, across four continents, they telephoned 147 world leaders; held news conferences for 502 journalists; briefed 950 industry analysts; beamed 5,000 videos to television; phoned 10,000 union, political, and civic leaders; sent 140,000 e-mails; delivered letters and gifts to each of their 428,000 employees; and popped countless champagne corks. Nearly a year later, the head of Daimler-Chrysler reported that he was spending 40% to 50% of his time networking, still trying to convince his many audiences that the merger was a good idea. What were the issues, and why was it so urgent to persuade all these constituencies?

"Controlling and shaping a corporate image creeps into nearly every corner of a chief executive's day" (Ibrahim, 1999, p. C7). CEO Jürgen Schrempp's speaking engagements were booked more than a year in advance, including such venues as the World Economic Forum, industry executive clubs, and universities. In this merger, three top PR firms identified the major issues: American Jews' reactions to Daimler's use of World War II slave labor; Chrysler's diversity commitment, allegedly less a concern to Germans; and employee fears that the company would become all German or all American. These issues could have broken the deal, sparked strikes, lowered morale, tainted the product, killed the managers' careers, or ruined the merged company's stock. Ten years later, Daimler sold its plummeting Chrysler division. Daimler turned a tidy profit within a year, while Chrysler tapped a $2 billion credit-line, scrambling to redefine its image, tuning in to changing American economic conditions. Globalization has intensified the need for finely honed persuasive skills suited to multiple audiences, across multiple media.

At the turn of the 21st century, each of students' currently most popular career choices—business, health, law, communications, politics, education, art, and science—requires the science of persuasion. Business people have to pitch their product; health practitioners have to induce patient compliance; lawyers have to argue their case; communications media have to win audiences; politicians have to impress their constituencies; educators have to sway their students; artists have to intrigue their viewers; and scientists have to convince their colleagues. Understanding attitudes and persuasion propels almost any professional career, even absent an unprecedented global industrial merger. Social psychologists have much to offer on this score, having studied attitudes from the outset of the field a century ago.

Attitudes have both conceptual and operational definitions, of course, and attitudes' functions fit some of the familiar core social motives, which appeared in the earliest social science of attitudes. As this chapter shows, the life course of an attitude includes how it forms, primarily as a rapid, affect-based, perhaps unconscious understanding of what to approach or avoid; how it may or may not change via cognitively consistent understanding or via understanding a newly encountered persuasive communication; and how an attitude may or may not affect behavior, as a result of varied understandings and belongings.

## WHAT ARE ATTITUDES? THE IMPORTANCE OF BEING PERSUASIVE

### Conceptual Definitions

At a minimum, attitudes entail evaluation. Experts agree that the *sine qua non* (without which, nothing) of an **attitude** is the positive or negative judgment of an **attitude object** (i.e., the entity about which one bears an attitude). Attitudes link an object to an evaluation (Albarracín & Vargas, 2009; Crano & Prislin, 2006). "Evaluating a particular entity with some degree of favor or disfavor" captures the flavor for Alice Eagly and Shelly Chaiken (1998, p. 269; Eagly & Chaiken, 2007), while Richard Petty and Duane Wegener (1998, p. 323) describe an "overall evaluation of persons (including oneself), objects, and issues."

The focus on evaluation notwithstanding, attitudes can elicit three types of responses that reflect the more general psychological tripod within social psychology (Chapter 1): affect, behavior, and cognition. The **affective correlates** of response comprise the emotions and feelings the attitude object elicits (whether "Never!", "Yuck!", "Hmmm...", "Wow!", or "Yes! Yes!"). The **cognitive correlates** correspond to the beliefs the object elicits ("Is it safe, kind, fair, or fun?"). And the **behavioral correlates** reflect fundamental tendencies toward approach and avoidance (historically, the first meaning of attitude: a **set** or predisposition to respond).

Attitudes not only result in different types of responses—affective, cognitive, and behavioral—but they also result *from* the same three different types of processes. The major attitude processes that this chapter considers (affective learning, cognitive dissonance, cognitive persuasion, and behavioral response) roughly reflect different relative emphases among these three different types of responses. Readers who relish tidy categories should not push this tripartite distinction too hard; the distinctions often blur and overlap. Nonetheless, it provides a convenient way of talking about various aspects of attitudes.

Attitudes are conceptualized as **structures** stored in memory (Judd, Drake, Downing, & Krosnick, 1991). Attitudes differ in their structure, some reflecting the cognitive, affective, and behavioral correlates more than others; the correlates of an attitude show how it **covaries** (goes along) with the various types of origins and responses (Olson & Zanna, 1993).

Attitude structures can be **bipolar**, as is typical of controversial issues (Pratkanis, 1989). A bipolar attitude scale would range from *pro*, through *neutral*, to *anti*. For example, most Americans are familiar with arguments on both sides of current debates—immigration, abortion, gun control, death penalty—and could place themselves on that continuum. Other attitudes may be **unipolar**, representing mainly one's own perspective: matters of taste in music, sports, food, or movies may more often be of the unipolar variety, reflecting less information on the opposing viewpoint. A unipolar attitude scale would range from *pro* to *neutral* (liking to indifference). In matters of taste, the negative side of the attitude is less well-developed in people's minds (Pratkanis, 1989).

A separate feature of attitude structure is **complexity:** Attitudes may be complex in that the cognitive component, one's belief system, has multiple dimensions. A simple attitude toward the death penalty, for example, would be "an eye for an eye; murderers must die," whereas a more complex set of beliefs would consider retribution, incapacitation, deterrence, and just deserts (Carlsmith, Darley, & Robinson, 2001; Darley, Carlsmith, & Robinson, 2000). Complex attitudes often are more moderate ones (Linville, 1982). As the number of purely independent dimensions increases, the more likely it is that one has to consider both pros and cons, becoming more moderate. If the world contains both supporting and contrary information, the more information one obtains—as long as the separate pieces of information are independent of each other—the more moderate one becomes.

Just as attitudes may be cognitively complex, they may be evaluatively complex, in being more or less **ambivalent**, that is, relatively mixed or unmixed. Ambivalent attitudes tend to be weak (Crano & Prislin, 2006). Such ambivalence can lead to highly variable responses, sometimes on one pole and sometimes on the other. For example, racism can prove ambivalent and volatile (Hass, Katz, Rizzo, Bailey, & Eisenstadt, 1991). Ambivalent white racists see black people as both deviant, eliciting aversive disdain, and disadvantaged, eliciting friendly concern. Ambivalence results in more changeable white reactions to blacks who either help or hinder them than to comparable other whites. Similar ambivalence occurs for sexism, in that sexists view some women in benevolent terms (as pure, necessary partners, to be protected) but some in hostile terms (as sexually threatening competitors) (Glick & Fiske, 1996). A later chapter will return to these specific kinds of intergroup ambivalence.

Not only social groups, but also politicians elicit ambivalence; the positive and negative feelings aroused by any given presidential candidate are nearly independent. That is, the correlation between feeling good (*hopeful, proud, sympathetic*) and feeling bad (*afraid, angry, disgusted, uneasy*) about a particular political candidate averaged only $-.26$ (Abelson, Kinder, Peters, & Fiske, 1982). For example, many years ago, pride in Edward Kennedy's mystique and care for the common people was offset by disgust at his perceived betrayal of moral standards. In 1998 opinion polls, the American public distinguished sharply between their affective reactions to Bill Clinton's governing (good) and his personal life (bad).

Indeed, attitude objects usually entail separate positive and negative evaluations (Cacioppo & Berntson, 1999). Although people are constrained either to approach or to avoid an attitude object on any given occasion, their reactions probably result from two separate underlying positive and negative affect systems, which combine to produce any given response. Being high on both positive and negative evaluation results in ambivalence.

Attitudes differ too in the **consistency** between overall evaluation and any of the three cognitive, affective, and behavioral responses; sometimes the heart and mind disagree, as when an affable politician can make people feel warm and fuzzy, even when they disagree completely with his policies. Attitudes that are more internally consistent (e.g., one's feelings match beliefs about censorship) are more likely to polarize, becoming more extreme, the more one thinks about them (Chaiken & Yates, 1985). That is, if all the aspects of the attitude point in the same direction (censorship feels abhorrent, plus one believes that it endangers democracy), then additional thought makes the attitude firmer and more extreme. Conversely, if the heart and mind disagree, additional thought may simply confuse one's attitude (Wilson, Dunn, Kraft, & Lisle, 1989).

Finally, attitudes differ along some other dimensions that will come up later, notably, their **importance, strength**, and **accessibility**. Overall, though, the concept of an attitude hinges most centrally on evaluation, with additional consideration of its affective, cognitive, and behavioral correlates, as well as its complexity and internal consistency.

## Operational Definitions

Suppose you had to survey employees to find out how sympathetic to corporate merger they are likely to be, a strategy that Daimler-Chrysler's PR firms might well have used to discover and circumvent the potential liabilities of the merger. How might you assess attitudes toward the merger? The most common techniques employ **self-reports** as operational definitions of attitudes. These comprise the familiar telephone surveys, course evaluations, and customer satisfaction questionnaires. Other, more innovative techniques have developed recently, as a later section will show.

Many self-report techniques start by considering various aspects of the attitude object (corporate merger) and writing items to reflect their salient dimensions. For example: "Corporate mergers fuel the American economy"; "Most corporate mergers have consumers' best interests at heart"; "Most corporate mergers try to protect the rich"; "Corporate mergers generally do not protect their workers" (the last two items, being anti, would be scored in reverse of the first two, being pro). Having written the items, the simplest technique is to use a **Likert Scale**, for example, asking respondents the extent to which they agree or disagree with each item, on a scale from 1 (*disagree completely*) to 5 (*agree completely*). People's summed or averaged response to a series of Likert Scale items gives the researcher a way to locate each respondent relative to others (Himmelfarb, 1993), for example, as more or less favorable toward corporate mergers. "On a scale from 1 to 10, how much do you like [the merger, the dinner, the President, high school]" is probably the best-known technique for measuring attitudes.

Another common operational self-report definition of attitudes uses **semantic differential scales** (Osgood, Suci, & Tannenbaum, 1957), again to locate each respondent on a continuum of favorability toward the attitude object. As an example, check one space on each of the following lines to describe your attitude toward corporate mergers: Scores are usually summed from −3 to +3, to provide the respondent's overall attitude, thus locating each person's attitude relative to other respondents' attitudes.

Beautiful ___ : ___ : ___ : ___ : ___ : ___ : ___ Ugly

Bad ___ : ___ : ___ : ___ : ___ : ___ : ___ Good

Pleasant ___ : ___ : ___ : ___ : ___ : ___ : ___ Unpleasant

Dirty ___ : ___ : ___ : ___ : ___ : ___ : ___ Clean

Wise ___ : ___ : ___ : ___ : ___ : ___ : ___ Foolish

Other types of self-report measures, perhaps less familiar, locate the items first, and then the people. In **Thurstone scales**, judges sort items into, say, nine categories of favorableness. The average rating of each item then determines its scale value. So, for example, an Attitudes toward Blood Donation scale (Breckler & Wiggins, 1989) includes items scaled as low (1 = *Blood donation makes me feel ill.*), moderate (3 = *Blood donation makes me feel bored.*), and high (7 = *Blood donation makes me feel overjoyed.*). Having scaled the items, researchers next administer them to respondents who then agree or disagree with each item (without knowing the scale values, of course). A respondent's score consists of the average scale value of the item or items endorsed. Louis Thurstone pioneered this technique now named after him. It has the advantage of locating both items and persons along the same continuum from unfavorable to favorable.

The Likert, semantic-differential, and Thurstone scales, supplemented by other self-report measures, all suffer from the same threat that plagues most verbal measures in social psychology: People may distort their responses to accord with **socially desirable** reactions. Several solutions to the self-report problem have arisen. An antidote called the **bogus pipeline** (Jones & Sigall, 1971) hooks up laboratory participants to an elaborate but fake psycho-physiological apparatus and leads them to believe it can read their true feelings.

For example, researchers were concerned about whether people answer truthfully when asked about sensitive issues such as their amounts of drinking, smoking, sexual behavior, illicit drug use, and exercise (Tourangeau, Smith, & Rasinski, 1997). Adult volunteers from an urban university community came in for interviews concerning "health questions of a personal nature, such as sexual activity, drug use, and birth control," to help researchers studying the spread of the AIDS virus. Half the respondents were randomly assigned to a bogus pipeline condition, in which they were told that a physiological recording device could detect inaccurate answers. The bogus pipeline condition made them more honest: It increased their reported frequencies for many of the socially sensitive (perhaps undesirable) behaviors, except for the one socially desirable behavior, exercise, for which reports decreased (see Table 6.1). Thus, people were not simply motivated by the apparatus to report higher frequencies of everything (as they might if it made them anxious), but in fact were motivated to be

**Table 6.1**    Self-Reported Socially Sensitive Behaviors, under Bogus
Pipeline and Control Conditions

|  | % Answering Yes | |
| --- | --- | --- |
| Topic and Item | Control | Bogus Pipeline |
| Drinking | | |
| Drink more than average? | 3.4 | 21.0 |
| Ever drink more than you should? | 15.5 | 33.9 |
| Ever drink and drive? | 17.2 | 30.6 |
| Sexual behavior | | |
| Often have oral sex? | 32.1 | 51.7 |
| Illicit drug use | | |
| Ever smoke pot? | 56.9 | 71.0 |
| Ever use cocaine? | 25.9 | 43.5 |
| Ever use amphetamines? | 19.0 | 38.7 |
| Ever use other drugs? | 19.0 | 38.7 |
| Other | | |
| Do you smoke? | 20.7 | 33.9 |
| Exercise 4 or more times a week? | 44.8 | 22.6 |

Note. Results appear here only if they were statistically significant or nearly so.
*Source:* From Tourangeau et al., 1997. Copyright © Winston. Adapted with permission.

more accurate about socially sensitive behavior that they might otherwise distort. The
sheer frequencies should be interpreted with caution, for this is not a representative
sample. (Consider the biases in who might volunteer for such a study of personal
health.) However, the differences between the two experimental conditions confirm
the socially desirable direction of responses under the control condition. Twenty years
of research indicate that the bogus pipeline does indeed lead people to respond more
truthfully (Roese & Jamieson, 1993). Ironically, because the bogus pipeline depends
on this belief, **physiological measures** of attitudes at first fared much worse than
people thought (Himmelfarb, 1993).

Nevertheless, given recent advances in knowledge, sociophysiological measures
can be useful (Blascovich & Mendes, 2010): One aspect of EEG (electroen-
cephalogram) brain waves (namely, late positive potentials) represents an evaluative
categorization (essentially, a primitive attitude measure) in response to specific
positive and negative stimuli (in this case, personality traits) (Cacioppo, Crites,
Gardner, & Berntson, 1994). Similarly, functional brain imaging methods are
beginning to allow social psychologists to locate approach and avoidance reactions
in particular areas of the brain (e.g., Ochsner & Lieberman, 2001). For example,
distinct brain areas respond to the positive-negative valence (right insula) and
emotional intensity (amygdala) of an attitude (Cunningham, Raye, & Johnson, 2004).
While an intriguing solution to the self-report problem, neuroscientific measures
are still cumbersome, expensive, and beyond the current expertise of many social
psychologists, not to mention persuasion practitioners in the larger world. What's
more, they are controversial because they tend to be disproportionately believable.

For example, legal scholars worry that expert witnesses who present brain-imaging data will come across as unassailable, when in fact these measures are still evolving (Tancredi & Brodie, 2007). But neuroscience increasingly contributes to measuring the affective underpinnings of attitudes, as this chapter will show.

Another antidote to the self-report problem comes from an **unobtrusive measure**, namely, any measure that does not impinge on respondents, in that they do not know it is being taken. For example, nonverbal behavior is sometimes an unobtrusive measure of attitudes. Interracial attitudes can be operationalized via nonverbal indicators of **immediacy** that have included physical distance, forward lean, eye contact, and shoulder orientation (i.e., how directly one person faces the other), as well as length of interview (Word, Zanna, & Cooper, 1974).

Other kinds of unobtrusive measures are more cognitive. For example, cognitive activation can unobtrusively measure racial attitudes (Fazio & Olson, 2003; see a later section and also the prejudice chapter). To the extent that a negative category is **primed** or **activated** (mentally available; recall from Chapter 4), another, immediately-following negative category is recognized more quickly. That is, a person first primed with *cancer* responds more quickly to the next word when it is *crime* (negative) than *candy* (positive). In one study (Fazio, Jackson, Dunton, & Williams, 1995), color photographs of students from various racial groups served as positive and negative primes, to the extent a respondent was prejudiced. Students first viewed a photograph and then a positive or negative adjective. They more quickly responded *good* or *bad* when the adjective's evaluation matched their race-based evaluation of the photograph. This **facilitation** or speed-up of evaluatively matching responses (own racial group—good, other racial group—bad) indicated their negative judgments of other-group races and correlated with various racial attitude scales. This measure clearly circumvents the self-report problem. The Implicit Associations Test relies on a similar method (Greenwald, McGhee, & Schwartz, 1998; see later sections of this chapter and the prejudice chapter).

Finally, some novel and entertaining unobtrusive measures focus on group-level data. At the Museum of Science and Industry in Chicago, researchers once measured interest in various exhibits by how often the museum had to replace the floor tiles in those locations (the chick-hatching exhibit was tops). They could estimate even the relative ages of people interested in various exhibits by the height of the nose-prints on the glass cases. These and other oddball examples of unobtrusive measures (collected by Webb, Campbell, Schwartz, Sechrest, & Grove, 1981) typically do not focus on individual respondents, but rather on group-level data (e.g., all the museum visitors over a certain time period), so social psychologists, who are typically interested in individual behavior, rarely use them. But they remind us that the measurement of attitudes is limited only by the creativity of the researcher.

## Core Social Motives as Functions of Attitudes

Early attitude theorists (e.g., Katz, 1960; Smith, 1947) pointed out that attitudes can serve various functions for people; these functions correspond to the core social motives that run through all of social psychology in one form or another. Attitude research focuses on two, which here are called understanding and belonging (see Table 6.2).

**Table 6.2**   Attitude Functions and Core Social Motives

| Attitude Function | Core Social Motive |
| --- | --- |
| Object appraisal (+/−) | Understanding (approach/avoid) |
|   Utilitarian (specific goal helped or hindered) | |
| Value Expressive | Belonging |
|   Public: Social adjustive | |
|   Private: Pure value-expression | |

**OBJECT APPRAISAL: UNDERSTANDING**   The clearest function of attitudes is **object appraisal**, which fits our core social motive of understanding: Attitudes categorize entities, so the person can decide which to approach or avoid. The object appraisal function may hold universally, for all attitudes and all people (Eagly & Chaiken, 1998). Object appraisal generally facilitates people's goals in the world because people first form categories and then instrumentally assess whether the category helps or hinders the goal. Object appraisal is a primitive form of categorization and as such overlaps with a basic **knowledge function**, which furthers rapid understanding of one's world.

The **automatic accessibility** of one's attitude, that is, having an evaluation immediately upon encountering an object, fits the broad view of object appraisal functions (Fazio, 1989). In keeping with a social adaptation view, the general object appraisal function is good for your health. In other words, knowing what one feels, and therefore not having to struggle with one's judgments and decisions, relieves stress. Being in limbo, wallowing in indecision, worsens stress. The distraction, vigilance, worry, and preoccupation evidently all take a toll.

In one study (Fazio & Powell, 1997), researchers found that first-year college students varied in the extent to which they had accessible (rapid) attitudes toward academics—that is, some instantly knew their attitudes toward various classes, majors, schedules, and study strategies; others did not. The decisive students, who had their minds made up with more accessible attitudes, were buffered in their dealings with life stress. For example, consider initially healthy first-year students (depicted by the two solid lines in Figure 6.1). If major adversity (e.g., family problems) came into their lives, as reflected by their reported stress scores (horizontal axis of the figure), everyone was more likely to become physically ill (vertical axis). However, the students with accessible attitudes (circle endpoints in the figure) showed less impact of life stresses on illness, compared with those with inaccessible attitudes (triangle endpoints). That is, the illnesses of students with accessible attitudes did not increase as steeply with their life stress. In short, accessible attitudes diminished the stressors' negative impact, resulting in fewer doctor visits, days lost to illness, and physical symptoms, compared with students with less accessible attitudes, who presumably had to agonize over academics as well as cope with other life stresses. In effect, knowing what you want saves the added burden of indecision, if you are stressed but otherwise healthy.

In contrast, initially unhealthy students with accessible attitudes (in the figure, dotted lines with circle endpoints) benefited only at low levels of life stress; presumably,

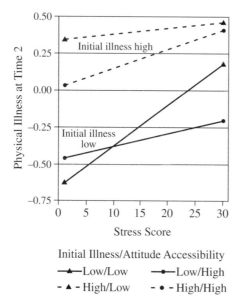

Initial Illness/Attitude Accessibility

&#9652;Low/Low          &#9679;Low/High

-&#9652;-High/Low        -&#9679;-High/High

High attitude accessibility moderates the effects of
stress on illness.

**Figure 6.1**   First-Year Students' Physical Illness, as a Function of Initial Illness, Life Stress,
and Attitude Accessibility

*Source:* From Fazio & Powell, 1997. Copyright © Blackwell. Adapted with permission.

high levels of stress, coupled with ill health, either put them over the top or reflected
their inability to cope effectively in the first place. Thus, apart from overwhelming
health problems and life stress, the main point is that rapid object appraisal can serve
a real function in people's lives.

A more delimited kind of appraisal function is the more narrowly **utilitarian
function**, using attitudes to further one's specific self-interests. Attitudes can facilitate
one's access to money or other resources, as one example (Eagly & Chaiken, 1998).
Consider politicians who change political parties to get elected more easily in the other
party; consider lawyers who adopt a positive attitude toward their clients—whether
justified or not—in order to plead more effectively for them; consider the employee
who adopts a positive attitude toward a corporate merger, hoping to advance in the
company faster than a recalcitrant employee. Actually, people overestimate the effects
of utilitarian self-interest on other people's attitudes (Miller & Ratner, 1998), so maybe
it is a less important function than one might think. In any case, the utilitarian function has a narrower purview than the pure object appraisal function, which entails
understanding in a broader context (see Table 6.2). Although object appraisal may
be universal, people differ in their **need to evaluate**, that is, the degree to which
they report having attitudes and thinking evaluative thoughts (Jarvis & Petty, 1996).
People high on need to evaluate respond in both more positive and more negative
terms to paintings, politics, and life events. One might say they have an opinion about

everything. (This need to express one's evaluations differs from a need to think, so the omnipresent opinions may or may not be thoughtful!) As with all the core social motives, object appraisal drives social responses for everyone, but perhaps for some even more than for others.

**VALUE EXPRESSION: BELONGING**    In contrast to understanding for self-relevance—the main message of object appraisal—**value-expressive functions** align with important standards or social approval (Olson & Zanna, 1993); value-expressive attitudes represent one's identity, either publicly or privately (Shavitt, 1990). Thus, value expression creates a sense of belonging to desirable social groups, by seeming to share their attitudes and underlying values. The public side of this has been termed a **social adjustive function** ("I want to be part of that group who defends civil liberties"), and the private side has been termed **pure value expression** ("I'm the kind of person who believes in civil liberties").

The contrast between object appraisal and value expression as a functional basis of attitudes matters in a practical way. For example, attitudes toward people with AIDS can serve an object-appraisal function (e.g., fear of contamination), but they can also serve a value-expressive function (e.g., antipathy toward homosexuals). Educating employees about the improbability of AIDS transmission in the workplace—addressing the knowledge or object appraisal function—had no impact on people with negative attitudes toward homosexuals, for whom AIDS symbolizes alleged homosexual promiscuity and moral decadence, serving a value-expressive function (Pryor, Reeder, & McManus, 1991). Presumably, attitude change would require addressing the values underlying attitudes toward people with AIDS, emphasizing not only knowledge and object-appraisal but also the value-expressive function of the attitudes.

**WHICH FUNCTION WHEN?**    Some people, some situations, and some attitude objects elicit the more practical function of object appraisal, and some elicit the more social value-expressive function (Tesser & Shaffer, 1990).

Start with people: Some people emphasize the public and others the private aspects, even within the value-expressive function (e.g., social adjustive vs. pure value-expression). As noted in the self chapter, and as a later section elaborates, high self-monitors (who are more sensitive to the public, social environment) respond differently than low self-monitors (who are more sensitive to their private, internal values). Consequently, high self-monitors should focus more on public images in advertising, responding to the soft sell, while low self-monitors should focus more on alleged quality, responding to the hard sell. Researchers (Snyder & DeBono, 1989) tested these hypotheses by creating ads for products as varied as coffee, cars, whiskey, shampoo, and cigarettes, and they varied only the ad copy to create a soft sell (image) or hard sell (information). One ad showed a bottle of Canadian Club whiskey sitting on a set of house blueprints, with copy featuring either image ("You're not just moving in, you're moving up.") or information ("When it comes to great taste, everyone draws the same conclusion."). Indeed, high (compared with low) self-monitors found the image-oriented ads better, more appealing, and more effective, plus they were willing to pay more money for the product and were more likely to try it. Apparently, the attitudes of high self-monitors serve a social-adjustive (public belonging) function; they care about how their attitudes help them to function with group members they value. In contrast, the attitudes of low self-monitors serve an internal value-expressive (private belonging) function, although low-self monitors may also be likely to emphasize utilitarian and knowledge (pure object-appraisal) functions.

Situations also emphasize different attitude functions. In one study, some ads urged donations to cancer research by emphasizing value-expressive ("help people to live") or utilitarian object-appraisal ("protect your future") functions. Values about altruism and helpfulness predicted attitudes toward donation in the value-expressive condition only (Maio & Olson, 1995). In contrast, pressures toward snap judgments would engage the object-appraisal function (Jamieson & Zanna, 1989).

Finally, some attitude objects tend to elicit certain functions more than others. For example (Prentice, 1987; Shavitt, 1990), attitudes toward family heirlooms and bibles serve symbolic (belonging, value-expressive) functions, whereas attitudes toward televisions and bicycles primarily serve utilitarian functions.

### Summary of Definitions and Motives

Attitudes are primarily evaluative responses to entities, with affective, cognitive, and behavioral correlates. Social psychologists usually measure attitudes by verbal self-reports on numerical scales. All attitudes serve the object-appraisal function of understanding: categorizing entities with favor or disfavor, tendencies to approach or avoid. Some attitudes fill this object appraisal function more narrowly as utilitarian attitudes serving particular self-interested goals. Besides object appraisal, the other major function is value expression. In the public sense, this is also social adjustive, and in the private sense, this is also pure value expression, but both promote identity with groups and standards and therefore a sense of belonging.

## HOW ATTITUDES FORM VIA AFFECT FIRST: UNDERSTANDING WHAT TO APPROACH OR AVOID

The average citizen has shockingly few real political attitudes, defined as those that display much knowledge and stability. Ideology is beyond the reach of what most Americans can or care to manage (Kinder, 1998). The prevalence of **nonattitudes**— insubstantial political fads and whims, here today and gone tomorrow—would seem to threaten the basic principles of democracy, which presumes a thinking public (Krosnick & Visser, 2010). Yet, as Kinder puts it felicitously, if unkindly, American citizens are awash in ignorance, show intolerance galore, and are unsophisticated in the extreme. For example, "in late 1995, more than twice as many Americans believed, stupendously incorrectly, that the federal government spends more money on foreign aid than on Medicare" (Kinder, 1998, p. 785). Nevertheless, when the pollster calls, people willingly express opinions that we spend too much public money bailing out foreign countries and too little taking care of our own elderly. Whatever their proclivities, having the underlying facts would make their opinions more compelling than when they are innocent of the facts. People respond out of "wretched ignorance," with bias against opinions and groups that differ from their own, and with a preference for easy answers. This shocking accusation becomes commonplace, however, when one examines how attitudes form. The opinion (knowledge) component does not figure greatly in most attitude acquisition, as it happens.

Instead, affective processes predominate. People want to understand what to approach and what to avoid (Cacioppo & Berntson, 1999). Arguably, knowing a bunch of obscure facts matters less to democratic politics than does having a consistent attitudinal evaluation (Krosnick & Visser, 2010). If attitudes are nothing if not evaluative, according to the usual definition, then it makes sense that the most basic forms of attitude acquisition emphasize affective processes, not cognitive content. This section addresses some affectively-oriented forms: learning theories, primary emotional appraisals, and mere exposure, all unreasoned attitudes. Then it addresses relatively unconscious evaluative associations, implicit attitudes. It closes with a more focused discussion of emotions and attitudes.

## Learning Theories

One of the most basic and affective attitude formation processes, conditioning, does not surprise laypeople (Snell, Gibbs, & Varey, 1995); people's everyday theories of attitude formation fit conditioning, perhaps because the principles of learning have filtered into society. And no wonder. Starting with rats, pigeons, dogs, and the occasional cat, researchers mapped the outlines of fundamental learning processes during half a century. Although the origins of this research lay in animal models, the generalization to humans proved fruitful. The next two brief sections summarize some basic principles of animal learning theories, in order to apply them to people. The power of the situation (learning) shapes affective and behavioral preferences.

**CLASSICAL CONDITIONING**   Introductory psychology classes teach the principles of **classical conditioning**, as famously uncovered by Ivan Petrovich Pavlov and his nameless dog. **Repetition** and **association** were the combination that unlocked classical conditioning. The dog initially, spontaneously, reflexively salivates upon encountering food powder. Salivation is an **unconditioned response** (UCR) to food, which is the **unconditioned stimulus** (UCS). To this preexisting UCS-UCR pairing (food-salivation) is added the to-be **conditioned stimulus** (CS), in this case a metronome beat. As the metronome beat is repeatedly paired with food, it too comes to elicit the **conditioned response** (CR, here salivation), until it can do so independently. The UCS-UCR pairing becomes a CS-CR pairing.

An analogous process operates in the classical conditioning of attitudes (Staats & Staats, 1958). People naturally dislike (UCR) electric shock (UCS), and when shock is repeatedly paired with certain words (CS), the words take on a negative association (CR). One could imagine a child responding, reflexively, negatively, to the unconditioned stimulus of a parent's nonverbal cues of fear or anger. When those are paired repeatedly with a particular political party or various ethnic groups, the child may develop the same negative associations to those groups. Classical conditioning accounts for a range of attitudes (Walther, Nagengast, & Trasselli, 2005).

Classical conditioning works best when prior knowledge is low (Cacioppo, Marshall-Goodell, Tassinary, & Petty, 1992). Neutral words (e.g., *player*) condition less effectively than equally neutral nonwords (e.g., *trames*). When researchers paired words with shocks, they were disliked, but not as much as nonwords that had been paired with shocks (see Figure 6.2). This result indicates that classical conditioning works best with unfamiliar stimuli, which is consistent with viewing conditioning as a form of initial, affect-based attitude acquisition. Classical conditioning results in an attitude represented by feelings, predicting impulsive and nonrational (e.g., affectively based) behaviors.

Other research (Kim, Lim, & Bhargava, 1998) supports this interpretation. The direct transfer of affect in classical conditioning (i.e., the positive affect associated with a close-up of a kitten), over repeated associations, can create attitudes toward irrelevant consumer products such as "Brand L Pizza House," in the absence of any beliefs about the product. Thought-listing in response to the kitten photos included "cute, soft, playful, and curious," not attributes related to pizza. Nonetheless, the kitten-related positive feelings transferred to the pizza. Moreover, affect outweighed beliefs in attitude formation, when the photo and the pizza house were paired as many as ten times.

Classical conditioning works even for people as stimuli: Pairing a neutral person with someone liked or disliked spread affect not only to that person but also to another person associated with that second person (Walther, 2002); be careful who your friends are! Classical conditioning elicits pure affect, and it fits the object appraisal function of

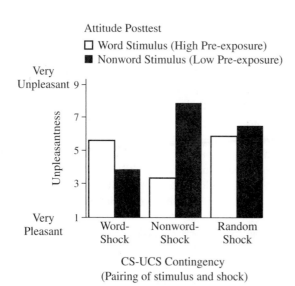

**Figure 6.2**   Classical Conditioning of Attitudes toward Words and Nonwords

*Source:* From Cacioppo et al., 1992. Copyright © Elsevier. Adapted with permission.

attitudes, namely the motive to understand which objects are "good for me" and which "bad for me." It may especially underlie attitudes that are less than fully conscious (Olson & Fazio, 2001).

**INSTRUMENTAL CONDITIONING** **Instrumental** (also known as **operant**) **conditioning** works on this simple principle: Animals emit various random behaviors, some reinforced (rewarded or punished) by the environment, which in turn changes the frequency of the behavior. In B. F. Skinner's laboratory, pigeons pecked around their cages, until randomly pecking a key that released a food pellet; that reward encouraged the pigeon to repeat the behavior. Instrumental conditioning is aptly named because the consequence of the behavior becomes its (instrumental) cause. The behavior is repeated in order to obtain rewards or avoid punishments, collectively known as **reinforcements**.

Instrumental conditioning of attitudes is illustrated by studies in which telephone interviewers say "good" every time the respondent happens to emit a response in the desired direction. For example (Insko, 1965), students at the University of Hawaii, subtly conditioned in this way, developed positive or negative attitudes toward creating a springtime Aloha Week, attitudes that held up as much as a week later.

Among researchers, an intense debate raged for years over whether or not attitudes are conditioned only when people become aware of the contingency between the attitudes they express and the verbal reinforcement. If awareness is necessary, perhaps people's attitudes change only because they are trying to please the experimenter or conform to social norms. If so, conditioning might be a trivial methodological artifact, not the affective learning process it was presumed to be. In the end, although beyond the scope of this text, awareness probably is not required for the instrumental conditioning of attitudes (Eagly & Chaiken, 1993).

**SOCIAL LEARNING** Social learning theories introduce uniquely interpersonal processes into the conditioning equations. Two kinds of social learning theories provide respective conceptual parallels to the classical and instrumental conditioning of attitudes. A subsequent chapter elaborates, but the initial comparison is useful now. Classical conditioning and instrumental conditioning each have interpersonal analogues in social learning.

A process termed **modeling** essentially describes learning by imitation of another person, a process that roughly parallels classical conditioning, thus: An admired other (older sibling, parent, popular peer) repeatedly endorses a presidential candidate (or any other opinion), and the positive feelings (UCR) associated with the admired other (UCS) become associated as a conditioned positive response (CR) to the opinion (favoring the presidential candidate) (CS). Although other interpretations are possible (Lott & Lott, 1985), modeling or imitation constitutes a relatively simple form of social learning.

Another process, termed **vicarious conditioning** or **observational learning**, roughly parallels instrumental conditioning. Watching another person receive rewards and punishments allows observers to shape their own behavior according to those reinforcements without having to experience them directly (Berger & Lambert, 1968).

How many teenagers have learned the cool attitudes by watching peers reward or punish other teens for endorsing certain music, styles, or convictions? How many children have watched another child in trouble with the teacher and learned to avoid the same provocative behavior and its inevitable consequences? Later chapters on helping and on aggression take up social learning in more detail, but for now, social learning illustrates some processes of attitude formation, emphasizing affect. Again, it relates most closely to the object-appraisal function of attitudes, understanding what features of the environment to approach and avoid.

## Emotional Appraisal

A broader view of object appraisal has long appeared in emotion theories, and it fits with newer attitude approaches that incorporate complex emotions into the basic approach-avoidance view of attitudes. Emotion theories of attitudes distinguish immediate **primary appraisals** (good for me, bad for me) from subsequent **secondary appraisals**, a more complex reaction implicating causality, responsibility, certainty, and timing (Ellsworth & Scherer, 2003). Primary appraisals resemble the approach-avoid, positive-negative object appraisals we have seen so far, but emphasizing their speed. More specific emotional appraisals result from specific events (Schwarz & Clore, 2007). For example, anger implies an illegitimate negative outcome controlled by another person, whereas guilt implies a negative outcome controlled by the self. By going beyond simple evaluative valence, specific emotions thus distinctively influence judgment and behavior, in predictable ways, based on the underlying appraisals (Lerner & Keltner, 2000).

Specific emotional appraisals shape attitudes in ways that go beyond valence. For example, inducing anger causes automatic negative evaluations of an outgroup, whereas inducing sadness or neutrality does not, presumably because they are normally less relevant to intergroup relations (DeSteno, Dasgupta, Bartlett, & Cajdric, 2004). Similarly, anger and sadness each elicit distinct attitudes regarding policy preferences ranging from social welfare to terrorism (Small & Lerner, 2008; Small, Lerner, & Fischhoff, 2006). Political candidates who exploit fear, anger, or hope know their distinct implications for voting behavior.

## Mere Exposure

Most political campaign tactics do not afford much thought, and the minimalist campaign outlet consists of a billboard simply stating the candidate's name and the office sought. The more the billboards, the more voters like the candidate, and conditioning is not required; no positive associations or rewards matter. **Mere exposure**, the sheer frequency of encountering an initially neutral or positive stimulus, enhances evaluations of it, a now-classic phenomenon discovered by Robert Zajonc (1968). Indeed, frequency of exposure predicts attitudes toward Chinese ideographs and yearbook photographs, as well as names; it is a small leap from here to bumper stickers as a means of establishing favorable attitudes toward a candidate. In a 20-year review (Bornstein, 1989), mere exposure studies show a moderate correlation of about .26

between frequency of exposure and liking, but the effect is variable. Stronger exposure effects hold for adults viewing photographs, meaningful words, and polygons, when they are presented 10–20 times, under brief exposure (less than a second), and later rated for liking, after a considerable delay. Fortunately for advertisers, the effects are even stronger in natural settings than in the laboratory.

Most impressive is evidence that the mere exposure effect does not depend on the exposure itself being conscious (Murphy, Monahan, & Zajonc, 1995), nor does it even depend on later recognizing the frequent stimulus as familiar (Moreland & Zajonc, 1977). In the world, more common than unconscious (**subliminal**) advertising is the technique of frequent and broad exposure of a product. Similarly, the political publicist maximizes airtime, in keeping with the adage, "no such thing as bad publicity"; whatever gets the name out, it helps (although the mere exposure effect suggests the context has to be neutral or positive).

One mechanism appears to be perceptual **fluency** (ease of processing), which produces positive affect, as indexed by micro-muscular movements in the smile muscles (zygotmaticus major; Winkielman & Cacioppo, 2001). More generally, processing fluency—whether based on aesthetic principles (e.g., figural goodness, figure-ground contrast, stimulus repetition, symmetry, prototypicality) or priming—increases pleasure (Reber, Schwarz, & Winkielman, 2004). Consumers often base choices on products that "feel right," because they are encoded or remembered easily (Ariely & Norton, 2009). For example, on the New York Stock Exchange, stocks with fluent (pronounceable) ticker codes outperform those with unpronounceable ticker codes (Alter & Oppenheimer, 2006). Again, though, attitudes formed this way have no cognitive content, only affect.

## Automatic and Implicit Attitudes

The rapidity of forming good-bad, approach-avoid appraisals means that these processes often operate with minimal or no conscious awareness. Prejudice researchers particularly need to understand people's hidden biases (see that chapter), but implicit and automatic attitudes apply to all kinds of object appraisals (Fazio & Olson, 2003). We have already discussed attitude accessibility and facilitation of responding to attitude objects, following matched, evaluative-consistent primes.

Another well-known theory concerns **implicit attitudes**, people's simultaneous associations between the attitude object and positive or negative words (Fazio & Olson, 2003). This phenomenon concerns implicit attitudes because it displays traces of past experiences (i.e., associations) that are not accurately represented in conscious awareness. One of the most convincing demonstrations of relatively automatic implicit attitudes is the Implicit Associations Test (IAT; Dasgupta, McGhee, Greenwald, & Banaji, 2000; Greenwald, McGhee, & Schwartz, 1998). At this writing, the IAT is available on the Internet (put the name of the test into any standard search engine), so one can take the IAT online; for example, one may associate presidential candidates with good and bad concepts, showing one's subtle evaluations of them. The IAT shows how rapidly and easily—implicitly—people do this.

The IAT has invited more controversy than usual for an attitude theory, perhaps because of its use in measuring racial attitudes (see this and the prejudice chapter)—or perhaps more generally, associations that people prefer not to report on a more deliberate, explicit basis. Many observers ask whether the "real" attitude is the implicit attitude (e.g., the faster association between career and male, versus family and female) or the explicit endorsement (e.g., of egalitarian attitudes). Consequently, the IAT has sparked considerable efforts to validate the meaning of the measure (Greenwald, Nosek, & Banaji, 2003; Greenwald, Poehlman, Uhlmann, & Banaji, 2009; Nosek, Greenwald, & Banaji, 2005; Olson & Fazio, 2003). At this point, meta-analyses (more than 100 studies on more than 10,000 participants) indicate its predictive validity for a range of behavior, physiology, and judgment (Greenwald et al., 2009). The IAT is especially effective in socially sensitive domains, adding incremental validity to explicit self-reports in delicate areas such as prejudice. Overall, implicit attitudes express affect-laden associations that people may or may not endorse, that come from either cultural or personal experience; in contrast, explicit attitudes express propositions that people regard as true, involving more overt, logic-oriented (but not necessarily objective or accurate) reasoning (Gawronski & Bodenhausen, 2006).

## The Importance of Affect and Emotion

Why do theories of attitude formation tend to emphasize affect and to neglect cognition? Affect is the foundation of attitudes. As we will see, most theories of attitude *change*, as opposed to attitude formation, focus at least equally, if not more heavily, on cognition. Those theories of attitude change (persuasion) assume an existing attitude and mostly cognitive processes to change it. In contrast, the theories of attitude formation assume no prior attitude. The relative emphasis on affect in theories of attitude formation reflects the **primacy of affect** (Zajonc, 1980); that is, affective reactions, relative to cognitive ones, are more immediate, involving, inescapable, irrevocable, and compelling. Thus, affect enters in at the first stages that make an attitude an attitude (a reaction with a strong affective-evaluative component). Recall that the chapter opening defined an attitude as, at a minimum, an evaluative (affective) reaction. Moreover, people react faster in reporting how they feel than how they think about various attitude objects, such as brand names and countries (Verplanken, Hofstee, & Janssen, 1998). Affect is primary in many respects, although people differ in their reliance on heart and mind as bases for their attitudes (Haddock & Zanna, 1998). Subsequent work confirms that the affect is primary mainly for attitudes with a heavy evaluative basis (Giner-Sorolla, 2004).

The Zajonc position on the primacy of affect caused quite a controversy in the field (Fiske & Taylor, 2008, Chapter 14). For example, some (e.g., Epstein, 1984; Lazarus, 1982) argued that primitive forms of nonconscious cognition, object appraisals, have to precede emotion. Some forms of cognition can be just as rapid as affective responses and not necessarily more rational (Holyoak & Gordon, 1984). Zajonc (1984) countered that cognition must be distinguished from initial perception; his point was to contrast more intellectual from more affective forms of understanding. The current consensus is that affect and cognition are deeply interdependent (Storbeck & Clore, 2007), in attitudes as elsewhere, although cognitive approaches tended to dominate the field in certain eras, notably during the 1950s communication and persuasion emphasis and during the 1980s dual-process persuasion models, both covered in later sections.

The importance of emotion in attitudes has become even more evident with new theories and methods for understanding social emotions (Keltner & Lerner, 2010). For example, attitudes are **embodied** or represented by consistent physical enactments (recall embodied cognition from Chapter 3). People express approach (usually positive) evaluations more rapidly by pulling a lever toward themselves and avoidance (negative) evaluations more rapidly by pushing it away (Centerbar & Clore, 2006). Nodding while listening to a strong persuasive communication facilitates agreement, whereas shaking one's head facilitates disagreement (Briñol & Petty, 2003). Beyond physical representations of attitudes, affective neuroscience implicates the amygdala and right insula, as noted earlier, plus reward areas such as orbital frontal cortex (O'Doherty, Kringelbach, Rolls, Hornak, & Andrews, 2001). Earlier, we noted the involvement of the amygdala in affect intensity; in this vein, people viewing politicians showed amygdala activation that correlated with strength of emotion (Knutson, Wood, Spampinato, & Grafman, 2006). Whatever way affect emerges, the core of attitudes emerges in such evaluations and more complex emotions.

Logically, attitude formation could employ either cognitive or affective processes to form an initial attitude. For example, one study (Edwards, 1990) compared affect-based and cognition-based attitudes, to see whether they most easily change by persuasion methods that match, respectively, being affective or cognitive. Participants formed attitudes toward Chinese ideographs, either affectively first or cognitively first. In the affective formation, a smiling or frowning face preceded the slide for the ideograph; the face appeared so rapidly (10 milliseconds) that it was outside awareness but could still influence affective reactions to the ideograph that followed. In the cognitive formation, an informative paragraph described the calligraphy favorably or unfavorably. Participants then rated the ideographs, indicating that positive and negative attitudes had formed. Then the sequence repeated, in order to try to change the attitude. Change was most effective when it matched the basis of persuasion: Subliminal faces changed attitudes that had formed using subliminal faces, and information-based paragraphs changed attitudes that had formed by information-based paragraphs (see Figure 6.3). Thus, although evaluation is essential and emotions are deeply involved, some attitudes are even more affective and some relatively more cognitive than others.

## Can People Control Affectively Formed Attitudes? Prejudice as a Critical Case

Classical, instrumental, and social learning, emotional appraisals, mere exposure, and implicit associations—as well as the more emphatically emotion-oriented approaches—together raise the question of how much we control our attitudes. As noted in the social cognition chapter, more of our reactions are automatic than we like to think (Bargh & Chartrand, 1999), and where affect is concerned, the question of control becomes even more dicey. The limits of our control are moderated, however,

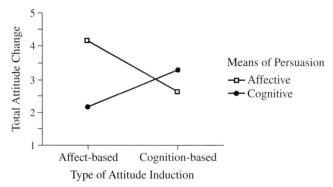

**Figure 6.3**    Match between Cognitive or Affective Basis for Attitude and Most Effective Form of Persuasion

*Source:* From Edwards, 1990. Copyright © American Psychological Association. Adapted with permission.

by individual differences, situational motivators, and context. The attitude domain where this has been most aptly demonstrated is prejudice, precisely because most people would prefer to control their prejudices. A later chapter addresses these biases in detail, but for now they illustrate the automaticity and control of affect-laden attitudes.

**INDIVIDUAL DIFFERENCES IN CONTROL**    People differ in their motivation to control their own expressed attitudes, and two types of cognitive processes reflect this motivation. Researchers typically compare relatively automatic, subtle, implicit, spontaneous reactions with relatively controlled, blatant, explicit, deliberate reactions. The more automatic reactions allow less capacity for control, and the relatively deliberate responses allow more capacity for control. We would expect people to be able to control the more deliberate responses, if they are motivated, because the capacity is present. But to what extent do they control the more spontaneous responses, where capacity is limited, even if they are motivated?

People experience a need to control their responses when they violate their own **standards** for acceptable behavior. Everyone sometimes experiences discrepancies between the way they feel they should behave and the way they do behave, as the self chapter indicates. Control over one's prejudice exemplifies this rule (Devine, Plant, & Buswell, 2000; Monteith & Mark, 2005). For example, people with large should-would discrepancies might laugh at a racist or sexist joke, failing to monitor their own behavior, especially if they are distracted (Monteith & Voils, 1998). Besides should-would discrepancies, researchers more often measure individual differences in prejudice and split people into low- and high-prejudice groups on that basis. Both high- and low-prejudice people can have should-would discrepancies, which potentially motivate them to behave better, but the dynamics differ for high- and low-prejudice people.

Low-prejudice people experience a discrepancy when cultural stereotypes surface automatically in their own responses, which then conflict with their own unbiased beliefs (Devine, 1989). When they do transgress their own internalized standards, low-prejudice participants slow down and think about the discrepancy, and they feel compunction, guilt, and self-criticism. As a result of discrepancy, they can effectively inhibit their spontaneous affective reactions, such as laughing at biased jokes (Devine, Monteith, Zuwerink, & Elliot, 1991; Monteith, 1993; Monteith, Devine, & Zuwerink, 1993). Low-prejudice participants can inhibit stereotype activation under both automatic and controlled conditions (Kawakami, Dion, & Dovidio, 1998; Lepore & Brown, 1997). Thus, they make the motivated effort and indeed have some success at controlling their prejudices, even automatic ones. **Compunction** plays an important role in overriding spontaneous affect-laden attitudinal responses.

In contrast, more prejudiced people readily endorse and activate cultural stereotypes (Kawakami et al., 1998). Highly prejudiced people do have standards for what constitutes unacceptably biased behavior; they have their own moral obligations about being tolerant, particularly when they focus on equality of opportunity (Monteith & Walters, 1998). People who are relatively prejudiced sometimes feel guilty about their transgressions, even though their standards are lower, relative to less prejudiced people's high internal standards (Monteith, 1996). More prejudiced people sometimes feel uncomfortable and angry about being constrained by other people's higher standards (Devine et al., 1991; Monteith et al. 1993). (A better description of resentment around political correctness I cannot imagine.) The bottom line is that highly prejudiced people make less effort to inhibit their automatic attitudes and may be more likely to blame others when they themselves go astray.

Besides measuring people's prejudice directly, researchers sometimes use **known groups**, that is, categories of people expected a priori to differ on a given attitude (e.g., prejudice). For example, black students differ on average from nonblack students in antiblack prejudice, both the implicit and explicit kinds (Rudman, Ashmore, & Gary, 2001). In another known-groups variant, students who had just taken a seminar on prejudice and conflict might well be expected to differ on average from those enrolled in a large lecture course or a research methods course. Although they did not differ at the beginning of the course, by the end of the course, their scores on both implicit and explicit measures of both stereotyping and prejudice improved (Rudman et al., 2001). Over the longer term, groups of whites who report having had both unprejudiced parents and some childhood experiences with blacks show greater explicit concern with avoiding discriminatory actions, although their automatic reactions differ only if their positive interracial experiences have been recent (Towles-Schwen & Fazio, 2001).

Known groups also differ in their attitudinal dynamics. Dominant group members (i.e., whites) worry about how they themselves are evaluated in intergroup interactions (Vorauer, Main, & O'Connell, 1998). Some whites are more interracially anxious than others (Britt, Boniecki, Vescio, Biernat, & Brown, 1996). Low-prejudice white people have a more negative **meta-stereotype** (belief about what other groups think of their group), but high-prejudice people feel more personally stereotyped by the outgroup ("Why do those black people always assume I am prejudiced just because I am white?"). Meta-stereotypes activate when people are concerned about being socially evaluated by the outgroup member, and it matters to them (Vorauer, Hunter, Main, & Roy, 2000). Whites who are concerned about appearing prejudiced are more anxious and enjoy an interracial interaction less, but ironically their black partners enjoy it more, suggesting that the white person's efforts to inhibit prejudice are costly but effective (Shelton, 2003). Indeed, managing interracial contact can be distracting for prejudiced whites (Richeson & Shelton, 2003).

Criteria less obvious than race also can guide the selection of known groups to assess attitudes. For example, one set of basketball fans with a reputation for expressing enthusiastic and overt outgroup hostility differed from another group of fans known for its more restrained style (Franco & Maass, 1996). The more aggressive fans showed more prejudice and discrimination on explicit measures (reward allocation and trait attributions) but no difference on more subtle measures (biased language), suggesting that the relatively automatic attitude is indeed more implicit, harder for people to control. As another example, older people might be less able to inhibit their reactions than younger people (von Hippel, Silver, & Lynch, 2000). Although they report feeling more motivated to control their prejudice, the older people's weakened inhibitory capacity made them respond in more prejudiced and stereotyped ways than they wanted, even on subtle (but not automatic) indicators of stereotyping. Both capacity and motivation are necessary, and the older people lacked the capacity, although not the motivation.

Besides the work splitting people on high and low prejudiced attitudes, using known groups, other work examines correlations between people's implicit and explicit (roughly, automatic and controlled) attitudes. Here's the logic: If the more spontaneous, implicit, automatic attitudes are indeed not controllable, then they should diverge from the controlled ones for people motivated and able to exercise that control. Presumably, the automatic attitudes would be more prejudiced and the controlled ones more or less prejudiced, so their correlation would be low. If the relatively automatic ones instead are controllable, then the two should correlate. Both would depend on the person's motivation and ability to control prejudice. Sometimes the two kinds of attitudes correlate nicely, suggesting the possibility of control (e.g., Rudman et al., 2001; Wittenbrink, Judd, & Park, 1997), and sometimes they do not, suggesting the difficulty of control (e.g., Brauer, Wasel, & Niedenthal, 2000; Karpinski & Hilton, 2001; von Hippel, Sekaquaptewa, & Vargas, 1995, 1997).

Suppose, given the mixed evidence, that the automatic attitudes are in fact fully automatic and typically not controllable. The relationship between automatic and controlled attitudes may depend on the target group being normatively protected (no correlation, because controlled attitudes respond to motivation, but more automatic ones do not). In contrast, if the group is not protected, automatic and controlled attitudes should correlate, precisely because there is no effort at control. Indeed, one study showed that only if the group is *not* protected do people's controlled and spontaneous attitudes correlate (Franco & Maass, 1999). More remains to be discovered about degrees of automaticity and control in affect-laden attitudes.

Motivation to control prejudice also does moderate people's ability to control their automatic responses (Payne, 2001). In a direct parallel to the circumstances that can cause police mistakenly to shoot unarmed black men, white people misidentify a hand tool as a gun more often when it is associated with a black male face than when it is associated with a white male face. They are most likely to make this (potentially tragic) mistake when they are operating on automatic, with little time to consider their response. For those not at all motivated to control bias, their automatic bias is directly related to their explicit racism, again because the failure to control leaves the two types of response free to be the same. For those highly motivated to control bias, their racism scores are inversely related to their explicit racism (i.e., the higher their racism, the more they have to control the automatic bias). These studies again show that capacity (automatic versus controlled levels of time to respond) and motivation (effort to control bias; lower racism scores) both influence responses, in particular the extent to which automatic and controlled responses correlate. Notably, however, even seemingly automatic responses are sometimes controllable.

People do differ in their orientation to being egalitarian, and chronically active **egalitarian goals** sometimes can prevent preconscious, automatic activation of stereotypes (Moskowitz, Gollwitzer, Wasel, & Schaal, 1999); this occurs even when the goal is activated preconsciously, as well as when the stereotype control operates below consciousness (Moskowitz, Salomon, & Taylor, 2000). A parallel set of findings emerges for people who typically feel uncertain about why things happen as they do; **chronic causal uncertainty** can lead people to have an accuracy goal in understanding other people, and they consequently use stereotypes less (Weary, Jacobson, Edwards, & Tobin, 2001).

A final type of individual control entails people's assessment that they may not be entitled to judge the other person. **Social judgeability theory** supposes that people do not always judge other people; instead, they must feel entitled to judge (Leyens, Yzerbyt, & Schadron, 1992), based on available data, appropriate roles, relevant values, and so on.

To summarize, motivation and capacity operate in these studies of control over automatic affect-laden attitudes, most of which examine individual differences in motivation through should-would discrepancies, prejudice scales, known groups, or motivations to control prejudice. These studies mostly operationalize capacity by creating stimulus exposures at automatic or controlled levels. Across the board, both capacity and motivation interact with individual differences in motivation to control attitudes.

**SITUATIONAL GOALS CONTROL AUTOMATIC ATTITUDES**    Just as individual differences allow capacity and motivation to combine in controlling biased responses, so too can situational goals combine capacity and motivation. For example, one set of studies (Blair & Banaji, 1996) compared motivation (intentions to respond in stereotypic or counterstereotypic ways) and capacity (rapid exposures requiring automatic responses versus slower exposures allowing controlled responses). People saw a series of common first names on a computer screen, judging gender as quickly and accurately as possible, by pressing an M or F key on the keyboard. Some received instructions that the name would always follow a stereotypic word (e.g., for males, *decisive, crude, jeep, wrestling;* and for females, *caring, dependent, perfume, laundry*), and others learned that the name would always follow a counterstereotypic word. In either case, they could respond more effectively by using the first word as a strategy for responding to the names.

When people intended to respond in a nonstereotypic way and had few capacity constraints, they were able to control their nonautomatic stereotypic associations. Start with Figure 6.4(A). In a baseline condition of automatic responding without

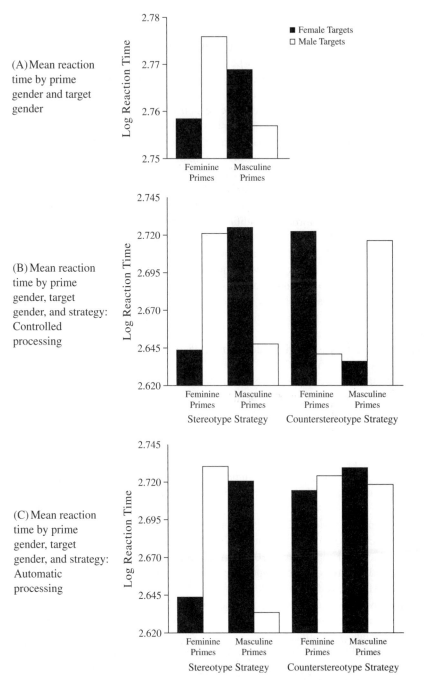

(A) Mean reaction time by prime gender and target gender

(B) Mean reaction time by prime gender, target gender, and strategy: Controlled processing

(C) Mean reaction time by prime gender, target gender, and strategy: Automatic processing

**Figure 6.4**   Automatic and Controlled Attitude Processes, as a Function of Intent (Strategy)

*Note:* Shorter bars indicate faster responses, for example when prime and target gender match.

*Source:* From Blair & Banaji, 1996. Copyright © American Psychological Association. Adapted with permission.

any strategic intention, people responded faster to male-male matches and female-female matches, as is typical in stereotyping research. They also responded faster to stereotype matches in either automatic (left side of Figure 6.4(B)) or controlled (left side of Figure 6.4(C)) conditions when using a stereotype strategy.

However, when they intended to respond counter-stereotypically, they were completely able to do so under controlled conditions (right side of Figure 6.4(B)) and were even able to moderate their stereotypic responses under automatic conditions (right side of Figure 6.4(C)). This last point is key: Their intention to respond nonstereotypically allowed them to moderate their associations even when cognitive constraints were high, operating automatically. What's more, in other research, people's motivation and capacity combined to enable them to block not only automatic stereotypic associations but also stereotypic memories (Macrae, Bodenhausen, Milne, & Ford, 1997).

Situational goals can also motivate people to learn new ways of responding. Just as attitudes can form through conditioning, so too can they change through implicit evaluative conditioning (Olson & Fazio, 2006). People can even train themselves, through practice, to "just say no to stereotyping" (paraphrasing an old antidrug campaign slogan). In one study (Kawakami, Dovidio, Moll, Hermsen, & Russin, 2000), people's automatic associations were stereotypic and remained so when they were trained to say no to an irrelevant category. But if they practiced negating a particular stereotypic category, they could control the otherwise automatic activation of skinhead and racial stereotypes. Further, this kind of training against stereotypic associations can carry over to less discriminatory hiring decisions, at least sometimes (Kawakami, Dovidio, & van Kamp, 2005).

Similarly, the goal of perspective-taking can decrease even automatic stereotyping and increase perceived overlap between self and outgroup, as well as evaluations of the outgroup (Galinsky & Moskowitz, 2000). Empathy apparently mediates the relationship between perspective-taking and reduced prejudice (Dovidio et al., 2004; Vescio, Sechrist, & Paolucci, 2003).

Alerting people to their own moral hypocrisy (their general egalitarian values versus specific failures around prejudice) makes implicitly prejudiced people feel uncomfortable and guilty, as well as behave better (Son Hing, Li, & Zanna, 2002). Guilt motivates people to control their prejudice (Amodio, Devine, & Harmon-Jones, 2007). As noted earlier, self-focus also reminds people of their better selves, and they override activated stereotypes, instead of behaving automatically in tune with them (Dijksterhuis & Knippenberg, 2000). And people instructed that "your job is to be as unprejudiced as possible" respond less stereotypically even on automatic reactions (Lowery, Hardin, & Sinclair, 2001).

We have known for a while that goals control less automatic forms of prejudice, as when people are instructed to be accurate (Biesanz, Neuberg, Judice, & Smith, 1999; Biesanz, Neuberg, Smith, Asher, & Judice, 2001; Neuberg, 1989; Neuberg & Fiske, 1987) or colorblind (Wolsko, Park, Judd, & Wittenbrink, 2000). The important insight here is that situational goals, especially given adequate capacity, can reduce even automatic forms of prejudice, an attitude that especially provokes control attempts.

People sometimes attempt to suppress stereotypes altogether, to keep them out of mind. Naturally, stereotype suppression fails when capacity is limited (e.g., by time pressure: Wegner et al., 1993; or by alcohol: Bartholow, Dickter, & Sestir, 2006). And the other necessary ingredient, motivation, appears in several guises—spontaneous and instructed suppression, which seem to operate in similar ways (Macrae, Bodenhausen, & Milne, 1998; Wyer, Sherman, & Stroessner, 1998), and self-focus, but only for people whose personal standards require it (Macrae et al., 1994).

People can be effective when their motivation is internal, rather than given external motivations for control; they monitor better their conflicting responses, as indexed by neural signals for control (Amodio, Devine, & Harmon-Jones, 2008). The mechanisms differ for internal versus external cues to control (Amodio, Kubota, Harmon-Jones, & Devine, 2006). Specifically, although regulating racial responses activates the anterior cingulate cortex, internal cues implicate a more dorsal region, whereas external cues implicate a more rostral region. Nevertheless, activating this region does not guarantee success in regulating racial bias, only the intent to try (Amodio et al., 2004).

Worse yet, these efforts can backfire. People who actively try to suppress a stereotype may experience afterward a **rebound:** increased stereotypic responding, relative to baseline participants who never attempted suppression (Macrae, Bodenhausen, Milne, & Jetten, 1994; Wegner, 1994). Again, both motivation (goal) and capacity (cognitive load) determine whether rebound follows stereotype suppression (Monteith, Sherman, & Devine, 1998; Wyer, Sherman, & Stroessner, 2000). Lacking motivation, highly prejudiced people may be most vulnerable to rebounds after suppression (Monteith, Spicer, & Tooman, 1998). Indeed, prejudice and goals together determine the degree of rebound after suppression (Monteith et al., 1998).

Just as the best intentions can backfire, so too are people's intentions not always good. Other, less benign situational goals also determine biases. Leaving aside overtly prejudiced people, stereotyping and prejudice can result from motivations to support one's desired point of view (Kunda & Sinclair, 1999). For example, students negatively evaluated by a female professor rate her as less competent than a male professor who negatively evaluates them and as less competent than either a male or female who evaluates them positively (Sinclair & Kunda, 2000). Praise or blame by a black doctor had the same effect on white students, especially those high in prejudice (Sinclair & Kunda, 1999).

More generally, a situationally driven threat to one's self-image encourages stereotyping even of those not responsible for the threat (Fein & Spencer, 1997), and this is especially true when people are overloaded (Spencer, Fein, Wolfe, Fong, & Dunn, 1998). Downward comparison and stereotyping (which derogates the outgroup) both can raise self-esteem (Fein & Spencer, 1997). As noted earlier, people with high self-esteem may be more likely to use downward comparisons and outgroup derogation to restore or maintain their self-esteem under threat (Brockner & Chen, 1996; Crocker, Thompson, McGraw, & Ingerman, 1987), a point to which we will return.

Being in a bad mood for whatever reason also can accentuate prejudices and discrimination, especially when the group is personally relevant (Forgas & Fiedler, 1996). When the context puts them in a bad mood, people change the meaning of the outgroup's stereotypic characteristics (e.g., *assertive* becomes *aggressive;* Esses & Zanna, 1995). However, the type of bad mood matters. Being in a sad mood can make people more careful to avoid stereotyping (Bodenhausen, Gabriel, & Lineberger, 2000; Lambert, Khan, Lickel, & Fricke, 1997; Park & Banaji, 2000), whereas an angry mood makes people more likely to stereotype (Bodenhausen, Sheppard, & Kramer, 1994). Conversely, being cheerful can make people careless about using stereotypes (Bodenhausen, Kramer, & Suesser, 1994; Park & Banaji, 2000).

Most often, given current norms, situation-driven motivation takes the form of attempting to avoid biases, and, if so, sufficient cognitive capacity is required. Sometimes, motivations may encourage bias, and then capacity appears irrelevant because the automatic default response and the motivated response both facilitate prejudiced attitudes.

But capacity matters at the earliest processing stages. All the manipulations of situational goals and motivations take as a default the automatic activation of attitudes as soon as people encounter another person. However, the activation and application of stereotypes does differ, depending on capacity (Gilbert & Hixon, 1991). Capacity constraints can undermine the initial **activation** (accessibility) of stereotypes but can facilitate their **application** (use) once activated. Given this distinction, goals can interact with either the activation or application stage. The studies described so far usually focus on suppression and inhibition of attitudes otherwise already activated.

However, some goals may intervene at very early stages of activation. For example, people observing faces normally categorize them quickly on the basis of age, ethnicity, and gender. But when people view the faces in a presemantic fashion—for example, search for a scratch on a photographic negative—they may not even see the face as a face. In one pair of studies (Macrae, Bodenhausen, Milne, Thorn, & Castelli, 1997), some people viewed a photograph while searching for a white dot on the surface (presemantic), others while judging whether it was an animate or inanimate object (requiring categorization), and others simply reporting that a stimulus had appeared (presemantic). Only the people who had processed the faces under a categorization task subsequently showed stereotype activation, and this occurred at both longer and shorter processing times, so it was not a function of sheer capacity.

Overall, a variety of situational goals can affect even automatic attitudes (prejudices, stereotypes, discriminatory tendencies), depending on people's available capacity. The goals provide the motivation, and capacity determines how effective it can be. The surprise is that even fairly low-capacity, relatively automatic processes are open to influence.

**STIMULUS CONTEXT AS CONTROL**    Stimulus context (i.e., the setting in which the target person appears) also determines automatic activation of attitudes. Here, motivation and capacity are less apparent factors than are initial categorization processes. Negative stereotypes and prejudices can dissipate when whites view blacks in a positive context (family barbecue, church) versus a negative one (gang incident, street corner), and these effects operate at automatic levels (Wittenbrink, Judd, & Park, 2001b). Context created by positive and negative exemplars has the same effect on subsequent implicit prejudices (Dasgupta & Greenwald, 2001). An immediately prior context that repeatedly pairs an outgroup with positive associations (Denzel Washington) and an ingroup with negative ones (Jeffrey Dahmer) can attenuate whites' implicit prejudices (Karpinski & Hilton, 2001). Focused mental imagery that is counterstereo-typic (e.g., a strong woman) can counteract typical implicit stereotypic associations. So too a black experimenter reduces implicit and automatic prejudices (Lowery, Hardin, & Sinclair, 2001). Conversely, repeated associations of a particular person and stereotypic behavior speed up trait judgments, especially for high-prejudice perceivers (Stewart, Doan, Gingrich, & Smith, 1998). Finally, a short-term context that creates arbitrary new ingroups and outgroups can elicit automatic biases (Ashburn-Nardo, Voils, & Monteith, 2001). All these immediate effects of stimulus context apparently operate at relatively early stages of categorization, facilitating some associations over others.

**SUMMARY OF CONTROL OVER AFFECT-LADEN ATTITUDES**   Capacity and motivation combine to allow individual differences and situational goals to create varieties of control over prejudices. Individual differences in prejudice, motivation to control prejudice, and should-would discrepancies, as well as known group differences, all operate under combinations of capacity and motivation to exert sometimes surprising degrees of control over subtle bias. Situational goals to respond counter-stereotypically have similar effects. Finally, immediate stimulus context determines degrees of control over relatively automatic attitudes.

## Summary of Attitude Formation via Affect

Attitudes can form or change, either affectively or cognitively, and matching seems effective. Nevertheless, the bulk of social psychology's work on attitude formation has had an affective flavor, as we have seen, and the bulk of the work on attitude change has had a cognitive flavor, as we shall see.

To review, attitudes can form through classical conditioning (repetition and association), instrumental conditioning (rewards and punishments), and their social learning counterparts: modeling (imitation) and vicarious reinforcement (observational learning). All these processes can operate with minimal cognitive activity of the opinion-formation variety; instead, they rely on affective processes, such as pleasure and pain. For example, many of people's political opinions are probably based on repetition and association (the smiling candidate appearing in pleasant or important contexts), reinforcement (friends' agreement), modeling (following opinion leaders), and vicarious reinforcement (watching other people get praised or trashed for their attitudes).

Another minimally cognitive and maximally affective process, mere exposure, increases liking via the sheer frequency of encounter with an initially neutral attitude object (the candidate's name on billboards or bumper stickers). The process can operate below awareness. Primary emotional appraisals also occur quickly, preceding more complex emotional reactions. Affective processes appear to be primary and automatic in many respects. Nevertheless, as prejudice research shows, individual differences, situational goals, and stimulus context all can moderate automatic attitudes. Further, attitudes can form either affectively or cognitively, and attitude change may work best when it matches the original basis of the attitude.

Neither conditioned learning nor mere exposure as a basis of opinion formation provides any cognitive content, only affective leanings, which do not exactly build the foundation for an informed democratic citizenry. Nonetheless, even simple, affect-based attitudes serve the object appraisal function of approach and avoidance, contributing to the core motive of understanding and perhaps even democratic expression.

## ATTITUDE CHANGE VIA DISCOMFORT WITH CONTRADICTION: UNDERSTANDING AS COGNITIVE CONSISTENCY

Having formed an attitude, however preliminary and merely affect-based, people over time develop cognitions that support that affect. One of the mechanisms for moving from affect-based attitudes to more multidimensional attitudes is probably cognitive consistency. People have a penchant for internally consistent attitudes, as several theories proposed at the end of the 1950s, a decade of convention and consistency. The penchant for consistency fuels the core social motive of coherent understanding and the corresponding attitude function of unambiguous object-appraisal.

### Theories of Cognitive Consistency

Consistency theories dominated social psychology in the 1960s. Collected in *Theories of Cognitive Consistency: A Sourcebook* (Abelson et al., 1968)—informally known by its unfortunate acronym TOCCAS—they home in on the cognitive correlates of attitudes. The **consistency theories** make the simple but profound point that inconsistency begets attitude change. When important cognitions collide, the attitude destabilizes, and some aspect usually caves. Inconsistency can occur within or among the cognitive, affective, and behavioral correlates of attitudes, but most of the theories emphasize cognition and cognitions about behavior.

The experienced inconsistency is psychological, not objective. Thus, if a dieter has salad and a diet drink for dinner, followed by a hot fudge sundae with whipped cream, that objective inconsistency may or may not constitute a felt inconsistency, depending of course on the adroitness of the dieter's ability to rationalize. The comments of outside observers, such as one's partner or parent, are psychologically irrelevant, unless adopted as one's own standard.

If the inconsistency is indeed experienced, consistency theories posit the inconsistency to be an unpleasant state of affairs, in need of quick remedy. Just as hunger or thirst or sexual deprivation causes a drive to satisfy the need, restoring comfort, so too does perceived inconsistency. According to this kind of formula, called a **drive reduction model**, inconsistency (or hunger, etc.) leads to tension and arousal, which motivates a drive to reduce that discomfort, which encourages remedial activity, in this case, to restore consistency. Examples of consistency models include **balance theory** (Heider, 1958), which is postponed until the next chapter, and cognitive dissonance theory, addressed next.

## Dissonance Theory

People do not believe in cognitive dissonance as an effective way to change attitudes (Snell et al., 1995), perhaps because it is counterintuitive. The best-known theory in social psychology, cognitive dissonance theory has worked its way into everyday language, with all kinds of people claiming to experience "cognitive dissonance" when one attitude is incongruent with another or when they behave incongruently with their attitudes. And, to that degree, people do understand the theory. However, they do not believe that the dissonance they experience could change their attitudes. The details, moreover, explain exactly how the psychology of dissonance does shift attitudes.

**THEORY**   The inventor of **cognitive dissonance theory**, Leon Festinger (1957), proposed that cognitions can be relevant or irrelevant, and—if relevant—consonant or dissonant. **Dissonance** describes both the perceived incongruity and the discomfort predicted to result; people feel tense, aroused, and uneasy from salient, self-involving incongruities. This state of dissonance comes from the ratio of dissonant to consonant cognitions. A typical example includes the cognition "I smoke," along with all the supporting and countervailing reasons (see Table 6.3; note that smokers naturally muster more consonant than dissonant cognitions).

Another, less typical example would be one's active support for a respected, famous person (the president, a Supreme Court justice, a well-known professor), coupled with the knowledge that the person regularly participates in extramarital affairs or sexual harassment. The incongruity causes psychological discomfort and aversive arousal that beg for resolution. People resolve dissonance in several ways, most easily by self-generated attitude change, that is, changing the dissonant cognitions (I can quit smoking any time; the famous sexual harasser's accomplishments outweigh his poor interpersonal judgment).

People change their attitudes and reduce their dissonance specifically by adding consonant or subtracting dissonant cognitions, as well as minimizing the importance of the dissonant ones. Consider an example of subtracting dissonant cognitions (Gibbons, Eggleston, & Benthin, 1997): Smokers who participated in a cessation program fully appreciated the health risks associated with smoking, that is, they accumulated cognitions dissonant with smoking. But if they relapsed afterward, their perceptions of the risks declined, presumably because they subtracted dissonant cognitions about the dangers of smoking. They could not change their behavior, so they changed their cognitions about smoking instead, thereby maintaining consonance and a view of themselves as sensible.

**CLASSIC STUDIES**   One of social psychology's classic experiments demonstrated attitude change as a function of dissonance between perceived actions and attitudes. The hypothesis was that incongruity between one's attitudes and actual behavior would produce dissonance, which in turn would cause attitudes to change in line with past behavior, which cannot be changed. In the study (Festinger & Carlsmith, 1959), which established the **induced compliance paradigm**, Stanford undergraduates spent half an hour using one hand to put 12 wooden spools into a tray, empty it, and then refill it again.

**Table 6.3** Cognitive Dissonance in Action: Teenagers' Reasons for Smoking

---

"We smoke because we want to try something new—not because our friends are pressuring us to."

"I tried to quit recently, but I found it's pretty hard to live in New York and not smoke."

"It's not something I'm proud of. The later high-school years and college almost provoke smoking. Life can get overbearing, and smoking is a relaxing outlet."

"Smoking in high school was definitely cool. In college, it's a social thing. But that's not why I smoke. I enjoy a cigarette with a drink."

"I think it's a nasty and expensive habit, and I'm quitting in about two weeks. I wouldn't recommend starting."

"I don't have anything good to say about it. I'm more of a social smoker. I smoke a lot when I'm drinking. I usually smoke one cigarette a day. But when I'm being social, I smoke half a pack."

"I love it. I love the taste of it, the action of smoking. It's very soothing. I don't plan on quitting in the near future."

"I was 16 when I started. I'm glad I wasn't younger—I would have regrets. I don't think it's a great thing, but it's okay as long as it's under control. There's no peer pressure. We try to support each other and make sure we're not smoking too much."

"It's really hard to quit once you start. I tried to quit, but it didn't really work out."

"I started smoking when I was 5 years old. My sisters, my mother, my brother—everyone—smoked, and I wanted to be like them. My mother found out when I was 13. I smoke in front of her. I'm trying to stop."

---

*Source:* From *New York Times Magazine*, December 26, 1999. Copyright © *New York Times*. Reprinted with permission.

The next half-hour's task required using one hand to turn 48 square wooden pegs a quarter turn each, one after another, row by row, and then starting over when reaching the end. After the experiment was apparently over, participants were offered $1 or $20 to tell the next participant that the task was interesting, supposedly to help the experimenter. A control condition received no payment and told no lie.

After telling the lie, the people paid only $1 had considerable dissonance to resolve (the $20 people had a ready explanation for their lie, so no dissonance). The people paid *less* were *more* likely to change their own attitudes and rate the experiment as more enjoyable and important (see Table 6.4). This readjustment of their attitude resolved their dissonance (not so much pay, but not really a lie). This counterintuitive finding—less incentive causes more attitude change—flies in the face of learning theory predictions, which would predict that bigger incentives cause bigger change. As noted earlier, laypeople believe in learning theory more than in dissonance as a

**Table 6.4**  Effects of Cognitive Dissonance on Interview Questions

| Question | Experimental Condition | | |
|---|---|---|---|
| | Control | $1.00 | $20.00 |
| How enjoyable tasks were (scale of −5 to +5) | −0.45 | +1.35 | −0.05 |
| Scientific importance (scale of 0 to 10) | 5.60 | 6.45 | 5.18 |
| Would participate in similar experiment (scale of −5 to +5) | −0.62 | +1.20 | −0.25 |

*Source:* From Festinger & Carlsmith, 1959. Copyright © American Psychological Association. Adapted with permission.

source of attitude change. What's more, people overestimate the power of self-interest (Miller & Ratner, 1998), so the idea that $1 changes an attitude more than $20 remains especially intriguing.

In the Festinger-Carlsmith experiment, participants' option to resolve dissonance by changing their behavior was blocked. Past behavior cannot be changed. Even continuing behavior resists change more than cognitions do, so attitude change is the easier route. In the case of smoking, one can attempt to quit, thereby resolving dissonance, but changing one's attitudes toward smoking is easier than overcoming the addiction. Consistent with the idea that cognitions are easier to change than behavior, people sometimes misremember their previous behavior as fitting their current attitudes and behavior, thereby changing their cognitions about their prior behavior (Ross, 1989).

Another classic study established the **free-choice paradigm** (Brehm, 1956). Dissonance theory predicts that when people make a choice, the positive features of the rejected alternatives and the negative features of the chosen alternative provoke dissonance. Hence, people are predicted to bolster their choices, once made, by downplaying these dissonant aspects of the chosen and rejected alternatives. In the context of a marketing study, women rated eight housewares (e.g., toasters, coffeemakers) and could choose to keep one of two then offered to them. The items in the choice pair were selected to be close in desirability (hard choice) or distant in desirability (easy choice). After choosing one, the women again rated the products. Under the hard choice condition, dissonance should be higher, and the women indeed bolstered their choice by **spreading the alternatives**, that is, liking the chosen one more than before and disliking the rejected one more than before. For the easy choice, with less dissonance, the spreading of alternatives was less, as predicted.

Another classic method of dissonance research, the **effort justification paradigm**, rests on the prediction that the more unpleasant the attempt to attain a desired goal, the more people should like the goal once it is obtained (Aronson & Mills, 1959). The unpleasant effort is dissonant with the positive features of the goal, and resolving the dissonance requires bolstering the desirability of the obtained outcome. In the classic study, women underwent a screening test to join a group that would discuss sexual topics. That initiation involved reading sex-related words to a male experimenter (supposedly to see whether the women would be able to participate in the group), and the words were either explicitly embarrassing or mildly suggestive. Then the participants listened to a tape of the group having a technical and boring discussion about animal sex. In the severe, high-effort condition, the women had more unpleasant effort to justify, so they reported liking the group more than in the mild, low-effort condition.

One of the obvious predictions from dissonance theory is **selective perception;** that is, people should be prone to heeding, interpreting, and remembering information that supports their beliefs, thereby adding to their consonant cognitive reserves. Although a principle that deserved to be true, early research found that people do not actively avoid dissonant information, but in the course of their lives, they tend *de facto* (by default) to be exposed to more information that supports their views (Freedman & Sears, 1965). Further, notions of utility, fairness, and novelty can override the tendency to avoid views that disagree with one's own. Under some conditions, some versions of dissonance do affect early perceptual processes. Participants who thought they freely chose to wear a Carmen-Miranda-type costume, while crossing campus, or to push themselves uphill, while kneeling on a skateboard, reported that the environment was less aversive than did low-choice participants performing the same embarrassing feats (Balcetis & Dunning, 2007); dissonance effects on perception explain these results.

The entirely compatible tendency toward **seeking supportive (consonant) information** (rather than actively avoiding dissonant information) was pointed out later (Eagly & Chaiken, 1998; Frey, 1986). **Selective exposure** to supportive views occurs when people have freely chosen the dissonant activity and are publicly committed, but also when people's attitudes are moderately stable, neither so tentative that they are seeking the widest range of information, nor so fixed that they are checking for dissonant information that might be useful in the long run. High authoritarians (who have rigid attitudes), when under threat (from thinking about their own death), especially show selective exposure (Lavine, Lodge, & Freitas, 2005), suggesting its utility for people with defensive, protective stances and low tolerance for the ambiguity of opposing views.

Similarly, **selective interpretation** allows people to evaluate unfavorably any information that might dispute their views. Recall from Chapter 1 the doomsday cult that reinterpreted information to fit their shared understanding, especially when doomsday failed to arrive as prophesied (Festinger, Reicken, & Schachter, 1956).

However, evidence of **selective memory** for supportive information is less clear (Eagly, Chen, Chaiken, & Shaw-Barnes, 1999); for example, strong opinions on controversial subjects allow people to remember their own side, but also the other side. Moreover, amnesiacs as well as participants with normal memory but distracted by cognitive load (Lieberman, Ochsner, Gilbert, & Schacter, 2001) still show dissonance reduction, suggesting that it does not require explicit memory at all. Thus, the evidence for selective exposure and interpretation is stronger and clearer than the evidence for selective perception and memory. As in social cognition, most of the interesting processes occur on-line (in exposure and interpretation), rather than on the basis of memory.

**CONTROVERSIES**    Dissonance theory provoked some controversy in its heyday (Aronson, 1992; Harmon-Jones & Mills, 1999; Petty & Wegener, 1998). The first challenge, **self-perception theory** (Bem, 1967; recall from Chapter 3), held that people infer their attitudes from observing their own behavior and its context. Therefore, when people observe their own effort, choices, or incentives, they infer the corresponding attitudes. No sense of dissonant discomfort or changed cognitions is necessary, in this view. Another challenge also rejected the idea of dissonance-provoked tension, arguing that the findings all result from impression management, that is, participants trying to appear rational and consistent to the experimenter (Tedeschi, Schlenker, & Bonoma, 1971), suggesting a role for self-enhancing or belonging motives.

In response, the ongoing debate centered around the hypothesized state of dissonance, the discomfort itself. If people experience psychological discomfort or physiological arousal from dissonance, then the self-perception and impression management explanations are less plausible. Indeed, dissonance does elicit tension, measurable discomfort, and unpleasant physiological arousal, thereby supporting the original theory as an explanation (for reviews, see Cooper, 1995; Harmon-Jones & Mills, 1999). Impression management seems even less likely, considering that dissonance activates left frontal brain regions that correlate with questionnaire measures of dissonance-based attitude change (Harmon-Jones, Harmon-Jones, Fearn, Sigelman, & Johnson, 2008).

Recent variants on the theory abound (Harmon-Jones & Mills, 1999). According to the **self-standards model** (Stone & Cooper, 2001), all variants concern people violating self-standards, either personal or normative. Personal standards suggest a role for self-enhancing motives, and normative standards for belonging motives. Combined, as in public advocacy and private reminders of one's failures to live up to self-standards, dissonance can change behavior toward more healthy, environmentally friendly, and interpersonally responsible behavior (Stone & Fernandez, 2008). In other more specific models, the self fails either private or public standards, as follows.

If people's behavior violates norms, that is, external self-standards, then self-esteem plays no role in dissonance reduction. Under these circumstances, described by the **new look** at dissonance theory (Cooper & Fazio, 1984), dissonance may simply require people to believe that they have freely chosen an action with foreseeable **aversive consequences**. To experience dissonance, people essentially have to feel guilty. Felt responsibility for aversive consequences can provoke dissonance, even when one's behavior is consistent with one's beliefs, because the aversive consequences are inconsistent with one's socially established preferences (Scher & Cooper, 1989). The relevant social norms (self-standards) are external to the self, so self-esteem is irrelevant.

Alternatively, any action may produce dissonance if it violates one's **self-consistency**, that is, personal expectancies about one's own competent and moral behavior. The higher one's self-esteem, the higher one's personal expectations, and the more vulnerable to dissonance one would be. In this view, people change their attitudes to maintain self-esteem (Aronson, 1968, 1992). This emphasizes one's personal self-standards.

Finally, people may violate personal standards in the context of a broader view of self. If one has abundant, accessible, positive cognitions about self, and if one has violated a personal standard, the repair work is easy. Thus, people with high self-esteem would be *less* vulnerable to dissonance. In this broader view, dissonance results from threats to self-integrity, leading people to affirm their worth in a variety of ways, which include but are not limited to attitude change (Steele, 1988). In this view, the self is a resource enabling **self-affirmation** in the face of dissonance. Dissonance persists when people attempt self-affirmation but fail (Galinsky, Stone, & Cooper, 2000).

## Summary of Attitude Change via Discomfort

Consistency theories focus on people's tendency to maintain clusters of coherent attitudes, cognition, affect, and behavior. Operationally, tests of the theories have emphasized people's cognitions about their actions and their beliefs. Cognitive dissonance theory shows that people seek to keep their cognitions consistent, including their cognitions about their attitude-relevant behavior. Thus, cognitive consistency theories partly illustrate the core social motives of self-enhancing and belonging, seeing oneself as not violating personal or normative self-standards. Nevertheless, the core social motive of understanding primarily underlies consistency processes, in that people seek the clear object appraisals afforded by cognitively consistent attitudes. Most dissonance research emphasizes self-inflicted attitude change; we now turn to attitude change engineered by others.

## ATTITUDE CHANGE VIA UNDERSTANDING PERSUASIVE COMMUNICATION

Recall the corporate merger that opened this chapter. The public relations persuasion campaign consumed millions of dollars and person-hours. Persuasion theories focus on just such deliberate attempts to change people's attitudes, as in advertising, propaganda, legal argument, and health education. People think they can resist persuasion (Wilson, Houston, & Meyers, 1998): People say they are unwilling to change their attitudes, think they can generate effective counterarguments, and later underestimate how much their attitudes indeed have changed. Social psychologists know better. Researchers analyze persuasive communications for their effectiveness, typically by breaking down the process, as this section will show in two major approaches, one old and one new. The object appraisal function, exemplifying the core social motive of understanding, especially represents how persuasive communications succeed. Note the general focus on cognitive processes of persuasion, as compared with the more emphatically affective processes of attitude formation described earlier. The persuasive communication theories take more account of people's abilities to understand issues and ideology, which indeed predict important behavior, such as voting (Jost, Federico, & Napier, 2009).

### Yale Communication and Persuasion Approach

Persuasive communication analyses proceed by dissection. Breaking processes down into their components, these theories achieve precise and rigorous enumeration of all the likely relevant variables, just as any dissection lays all the functional parts on the table.

**MCGUIRE'S INFORMATION-PROCESSING STAGES**   Consider a theory that slices persuasion according to audiences' information-processing stages. William McGuire (1969) emphasized people's initial **reception** of messages, as comprising exposure, attention, and comprehension. For example, in a political campaign, if aspirants do not get the message out, they cannot be effective. Exposure, as in distributing campaign messages under windshield wipers or making 30-second television spots, famously requires resources (money, staff). But no amount of exposure is effective if people do not attend, instead using the leaflet to scrape mud off their feet or the television spot to take a nacho break. And comprehension, of course, must follow attention: If the ad is confusing or obscure, the audience cannot take it in. Message reception matters most when it is problematic (Eagly & Chaiken, 1993): when the audience is strongly distracted, verbally unintelligent, or receiving a difficult message in an audio or video modality (as apart from written messages, which can be read at one's own pace). Early researchers measured reception only as memory for the message, but subsequent researchers have realized that a recipient could form an attitude on-line, retaining the attitude but forgetting the details of the message. In that case, memory for the message would not appropriately measure reception (Chaiken, Wood, & Eagly, 1996).

Once the message is received, successful persuasion requires **yielding**, that is, accepting and using the message. The major stages—reception and yielding—can be sensitive to different processes, so they are useful to separate. For example, self-esteem effects on persuasion are independently explained by both message reception and yielding (see Rhodes & Wood meta-analysis, 1992): People low in self-esteem have difficulty *receiving* a message, perhaps because they are too distracted and withdrawn; they indeed fail to recall messages. At the other end, people high in self-esteem do not *yield* easily because they are especially confident in their opinions. The net effect is that people of moderate self-esteem are most easily persuaded because the reception and yielding processes both cooperate.

McGuire broke the yielding process down into its components: yielding (the actual agreement), retention (keeping and remembering the changed opinion), and acting on it. Other theories of persuasion and attitude-behavior relations more fully address these latter stages, so we now turn to those.

**COMMUNICATION AND PERSUASION VARIABLES**   World War II brought many psychologists into the military, and among them were those studying enemy propaganda. These studies resulted in a postwar Yale research laboratory including Carl Hovland, Irving Janis, and Harold Kelley. Theoretically eclectic, their research systematically examined each component of persuasion, breaking the interpersonal process down according to a well-known formulation by Harold Lasswell (1948): Who says what to whom with what effect. Their research program focused on these variables, more than on theoretical analysis: **source, message, recipient**, and **context**. For example, features of the source influence the success of persuasion, for whether the source possesses credibility (e.g., expertise and trust) affects persuasion.

The feature of the message most often studied is the strength of the argument. As one classic example, the Yale laboratory's research program examined the impact of **fear appeals** (Janis & Feshbach, 1953), that is, messages that scare people. Researchers presented participants with tooth-brushing messages, embedded in varying degrees of threat. The most severe fear appeal contained 71 separate references to negative consequences of dental neglect, from tooth decay to gum disease to oral cancer, coupled with vivid photographs of same, and couched in accusatory language ("This can happen to you"). Low levels of fear were created by minimal references to mild negative consequences of neglect, primarily tooth decay, coupled with photographs of healthy teeth, and couched in impersonal language. The two fear appeal groups and a control group (who received an irrelevant message about the human eye) were asked a week later how much they had complied with various dental hygiene recommendations. Only the low-fear appeal was effective, whereas the high-fear appeal did not differ from the control message.

These results suggested that too much (or too little) fear undermines persuasion, a result again explained by McGuire's emphasis on reception versus yielding processes, just covered. McGuire suggested that (like self-esteem) fear has opposite effects on the two processes: Fear blocks reception but enhances yielding. Adding the two processes together, the lowest levels of fear should allow reception but not motivate yielding, whereas the highest levels would allow yielding but block the initial reception. Moderate fear balances the ill effects on reception with the beneficial effects on persuasion, in this view. Thus, the effect of fear on persuasion should be an inverted U, with most persuasion at moderate levels (see Figure 6.5).

The problem with an inverted-U prediction is that researchers must sample the entire range of the predictor variable, in this case fear. If a researcher samples only the low-to-moderate end of the range, the observed relationship will be positive: Moving from low to moderate fear increases persuasion. If a researcher samples only moderate-to-high levels of fear, then the observed relationship will be negative: Moving from moderate to high fear decreases persuasion. The Janis and Feshbach study, which showed a negative relationship, may not have sampled enough of the low-to-moderate end of the range. Most of the fear appeals research does show that

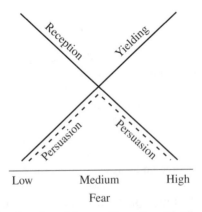

**Figure 6.5**   Effects of Fear Levels on Message Reception, Yielding, and Ultimate Persuasion

*Source:* Drawn from model described by McGuire, 1969.

threat enhances persuasion (Eagly & Chaiken, 1993; Witte & Allen, 2000), but maybe most of the recent research neglects the graphic, high-level fear appeal invoked by the original study, so it does not show the curvilinear effect. People's perceived vulnerability and outcome severity also interact with fear effects (de Hoog, Stroebe, & de Wit, 2007), so fear is not a simple variable.

We have illustrated communicator and message variables; the next two sections address recipient and context variables in discussing two later models of persuasion processes. Overall, the contributions of the Yale communication and persuasion approach are considerable, although many specific findings have been qualified in subsequent research. Essentially, this single persuasion laboratory set the scientific agenda for subsequent persuasion researchers, establishing persuasion as a topic to study, specifying the important variables, and demonstrating experimental rigor. However, the resulting research perhaps overemphasized deliberate, thoughtful persuasion processes, based on careful processing of message content. Other persuasion processes—considerably more superficial—matter as well.

## Dual-Process Persuasion Models

People search for understanding and specifically object-appraisal in different ways at different times. In the social cognition chapter, more automatic versus more controlled processes divided, respectively, the rapid, expectancy-based, heuristic processes from slower, more detailed deliberate processes. Simultaneously, attitude theorists had identified persuasion operating via two routes, one fast and superficial versus one slow and analytic. The heuristic-systematic model and the elaboration likelihood model both make this point.

**HEURISTIC-SYSTEMATIC MODEL**    Imagine that your university contemplates switching from its present two-semester system to a trimester system, but not for at least another five years. The change advocate is a cynical administrator who views students as irresponsible and immature, as unconcerned with their societal role, and as getting more public credit than they deserve. The proposed change would mean 50% more courses, exposing students to a wider variety of material, and each course would cover 70% of the standard material. The year would start later, and the first term would still end before winter holidays. Many schools use this trimester system and view it as advantageous to their graduates. To what extent do you think carefully about this issue? If the change is delayed for more than five years, it seems remote and irrelevant. And the fellow pushing it sounds like a jerk, so it is probably a bad idea.

On the other hand, suppose you hear advice that it is actually healthier to sleep less than eight hours a night, and soon you will have to be interviewed about your opinion on this topic. The less-sleep position, advocated by a well-loved campus figure, includes arguments such as the cultural and seasonal nature of sleep patterns, the efficacy of REM (dreaming) sleep over non-REM sleep, the utility of naps and meditation, correlations between excessive sleep and illness, as well as famous high achievers who sleep less than average. To what extent do you think carefully about this issue? In this case, given that it affects you, and that you soon will have to have a considered opinion, the likeability of the person who conveyed this opinion matters less than the quality of the arguments.

Using a refined version of this methodology, Shelly Chaiken (1980) proposed that (a) highly involved people use **systematic processes** to understand a persuasive message, deciding its merits by evaluating the arguments, whereas (b) uninvolved people use **heuristic processes**, simple decision rules such as the likeability of the communicator, to give a more superficial opinion. Systematic, message-based persuasion persists longer than heuristic, superficial persuasion. This work generated the **heuristic-systematic model**, which proposes that persuasion sometimes operates by simple and effortless shortcuts, while at other times it operates with more careful thought.

A subsequent research program (Chen & Chaiken, 1999) identified sample heuristic shortcuts for superficial persuasion:

- Length implies strength (a message with many arguments is probably right).
- Consensus is correct (if a lot of people agree, then it must be true).
- Go along to get along (whatever your conversation partner asserts is acceptable).
- Experts can be trusted (expert sources are accurate).

These heuristics save mental time and energy, triggering persuasion when capacity and motivation are low. People with limited time or knowledge have reduced capacity for thoughtful processing of persuasive messages, so they rely on heuristics. People motivated to be accurate and confident, in contrast, increase their effort toward systematic processing. In the short term, in the rush of events, people may be distracted by superficial heuristics, focusing on secondary characteristics, whereas when thinking into the distant future, people are more able to focus systematically on primary characteristics and abstract principles (Fujita, Eyal, Chaiken, Trope, & Liberman, 2008).

Heuristic and systematic processes do not constitute a dichotomy or even opposite extremes; they can occur simultaneously (Chen, Shechter, & Chaiken, 1996). Researchers primed either an accuracy motive (systematic) or social-impression motive (heuristic) by having participants read scenarios that all emphasized either objectivity (systematic accuracy) or social norms (heuristic impressions). As the first line of Table 6.5 indicates, impression-minded participants then simply agreed with their partners (a heuristic process; in effect, "go along to get along"), whereas accuracy-minded participants were unaffected by their partners' opinions (thereby not showing any heuristic process). Similarly, impression-minded partners' systematic *thoughts* about the message also were biased by their partners' views (see second line of Table 6.5), whereas the thoughts of accuracy-minded participants were not significantly affected by their partners' views. Thus, for the impression-minded participants, both heuristic processing (agree with partner) and systematic processing (use message content) operated simultaneously.

**Table 6.5**   Heuristic and Systematic Processing: Own Favorability under Impression and Accuracy Motives, Depending on Partner Attitudes

| | Motivation | | | |
| --- | --- | --- | --- | --- |
| | Accuracy | | Impression | |
| | Partner attitude | | Partner attitude | |
| Measure of own favorability | Favorable | Unfavorable | Favorable | Unfavorable |
| Attitudes | 7.60 | 7.22 | 9.56 | 5.38 |
| Thoughts | −0.41 | 0.32 | 1.01 | −0.28 |

*Source:* From Chen et al., 1996. Copyright © American Psychological Association. Adapted with permission.

In general, the heuristic-systematic model proposes two parallel routes to persuasion, detailing the heuristic route in particular, as well as demonstrating some of the interpersonal motivations that encourage one or the other type of processing. Note that the interpersonal motives partly illustrate the Yale approach's context variable. Note too the similarity of the accuracy motive to the core social motive of understanding and the resemblance of the impression motive to the core social motive of belonging.

**ELABORATION LIKELIHOOD MODEL**    At about the same time that the heuristic-systematic theory emerged, Richard Petty and John Cacioppo (1981) also developed a model of persuasion by two routes: peripheral and central. The **peripheral route**, like Chaiken's, includes heuristics but also other potential shortcuts, such as mood. The **central route**, like Chaiken's, involves careful (though not necessarily accurate) processing of message information. The difference from Chaiken's heuristic-systematic model is that the **elaboration likelihood model** operates at a broader level, less focused on specific heuristic and motivational processes.

The elaboration likelihood model posits the probabilities of **elaborating** (considering and extending) message content, hence the name of the model. Stated simply, various persuasion variables (source, message, context, and recipient), which are familiar from the Yale approach, act to increase or decrease the recipient's likelihood of thinking about the persuasive communication. The valence (pro or con) of these thoughts then determines persuasion.

The difference from the Yale approach is that the elaboration likelihood model (like Chaiken's heuristic-systematic model) examines *on-line* message processing, whereas the Yale model had focused on learning and *recall* of message content. That is, the Yale model had assumed that, to the extent people first learn message arguments, they are persuaded. Thus, the research typically tested people's memory for message content, as an index of message learning, to see if it predicted persuasion. In contrast, the more recent models find that people's **online responses**—their thoughts as they are receiving the message—more reliably predict their persuasion. Literal memory for message content (which is determined by extraneous factors) is not particularly associated with persuasion. The elaboration likelihood model's central point remains

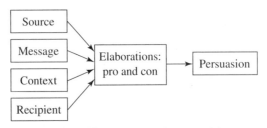

**Figure 6.6**   Elaboration Likelihood Model

*Source:* From description by Cacioppo & Petty, 1981.

that degree and type of thinking **mediate** (intervene) between the persuasion attempt and potential attitude change (see Figure 6.6).

One test of this model, then, compares people who like to think with those who do not. People differ in their **need for cognition**, that is, the extent to which they enjoy and tend to engage in cognitive effort; it is measured by a scale including items such as "I would prefer complex to simple problems"; "I find satisfaction in deliberating hard and for long hours" versus "Thinking is not my idea of fun"; "I only think as hard as I have to." Over 100 studies on need for cognition (Cacioppo, Petty, Feinstein, & Jarvis, 1996) find that individuals high in need for cognition indeed do think more than those who do not. All else being equal, then, their likelihood of elaborating on message content should be higher than people who do not like to think. For example, people high in need for cognition discern argument quality more than those low in need for cognition. In one study (Smith & Petty, 1996), people high in need for cognition markedly differentiated strong and weak arguments for taking a fictitious Vitamin K, and they were more persuaded only if the arguments were cogent.

Besides need for cognition, other **recipient variables** include gender, age, self-esteem, intelligence, self-monitoring, knowledge, attitude accessibility, and involvement. As an example of **involvement** effects, a meta-analysis (Johnson & Eagly, 1989) found that recipients highly involved in a message, either because it was relevant to their enduring values or because they cared about the impression their attitude would make on others, were less easily persuaded than uninvolved recipients. Recipients involved in an outcome relevant to the persuasive message (e.g., a policy change affecting one's own academic fate) differentiated more carefully between strong and weak arguments than uninvolved recipients, a finding consistent with the elaboration likelihood model.

The Vitamin K study illustrates not only a recipient variable (individual differences in need for cognition) but also a **message variable**. Messages framed negatively ("Not taking Vitamin K can lead to illnesses that shorten life span") versus positively ("Vitamin K helps you live a longer, healthier life") elicit more thought and persuasion when the frame is unexpected—but only for those low in need for cognition, because the high-need-for-cognition individuals are already thinking as much as they can. Other message variables, besides framing, include the message's relevance to the recipient and the agreeability of its position. Also, its format matters: whether or not it uses rhetorical questions, draws conclusions, presents both sides, scares people, or invokes other emotional appeals. The most important single factor of course is whether it argues strongly. As to which persuasion technique is most effective, the simple answer is: It depends. It depends on the recipient, the context, and the source. Persuasive messages have to be tailored to particular settings and purposes. Small wonder Daimler-Chrysler's highly effective, carefully crafted advertising blitz cost $25 million.

To understand the complexities of crafting a persuasive appeal, and the importance of **context variables**, consider the effects of mood on persuasion. When a situation makes them happy, people do not like to think, if it will interfere with their mood, but they do like to think, if it will reinforce their good mood. So, they may avoid thinking about doom-and-gloom messages, but be happy to think about a heart-warming one. And if they do think, persuasion depends not only on the quality of the arguments but also on the positive associations made available by the positive mood. Thus, mood has multiple roles in persuasion (Petty & Wegener, 1998). Other context variables have prominently included distraction and time delay between message and measure.

**Source variables** have prominently featured the communicator's credibility and attractiveness. Using communicator attractiveness reflects a more peripheral route to persuasion, whereas credibility could motivate either a peripheral route (this expert must be right) or a central route (it is worthwhile to think about an expert's arguments). These source variables, along with recipient, message, and context variables, reflect the range of topics addressed by the elaboration likelihood model. The model potentially helps explain the processes by which each variable affects persuasion. As noted, each variable (e.g., mood) can have multiple effects by different processes in different situations (Petty & Briñol, 2008), so unpacking the circumstances and processes matters a lot.

### Summary of Persuasive Communication

Persuasion research examines deliberate attempts to change another person's attitude. The earliest work, coming out of wartime propaganda research, established persuasion as an area of rigorous scientific study, laid out the relevant variables, and set the research agenda. Although it emphasized effective processing (i.e., learning) of messages, more recent models emphasize alternative routes to persuasion, based on relatively superficial or in-depth processing. While the broad generalizations are few in this area of knowledge, because persuasion variables have multiple effects, the fine-grained knowledge of persuasion techniques is well developed. Research in this area tends to emphasize the core social motive of understanding when it describes systematic information processing. Other core social motives, such as belonging, appear when research turns to heuristic processes, such as going along to get along. In either case, attitudes matter most when they guide behavior, which occupies the next section.

### WHEN AND WHY ATTITUDES MATTER: PREDICTING BEHAVIOR VIA UNDERSTANDING AND BELONGING

If a lawyer persuades a judge, an advertiser persuades a consumer, or a politician persuades a voter, but the judge does not judge, the consumer does not consume, or the voter does not vote, what use is the attitude change without the behavior?

Social psychologists at first assumed that attitudes do predict behavior; it seemed so obvious. But a classic study and a later literature review raised the tough question that maybe attitudes do not always predict behavior after all. If attitudes do not predict behavior, then maybe they are mere **epiphenomena**—byproducts of more substantial processes, mere passing trifles of no intrinsic interest. If so, why would researchers research them, pollsters poll them, and the rest of us express them?

## Attitudes Don't Always Predict Behavior

In 1930, social psychologist Richard LaPiere approached a hotel clerk, "with some trepidation," to obtain rooms for himself and a young Chinese couple. To his great relief, given the small town's reputation for bigoted attitudes toward Asians, they were accommodated without a murmur. Passing through two months later, he phoned the same hotel, out of curiosity, asking if they would lodge "an important Chinese gentleman"; they declined. Struck by this discrepancy, LaPiere began keeping track of their treatment as he and the couple together embarked on a 10,000-mile cross-country car trip. In what was to become a citation classic, LaPiere (1934) documented their treatment. As they stopped for 184 meals and 66 overnights at hotels, auto camps, and tourist homes, they were received graciously in all but one instance, when the owner of a dilapidated car camp refused to lodge them, referring to the Chinese couple as "Japs." Six months later, LaPiere sent a questionnaire to the same establishments, asking whether they would accept "members of the Chinese race" as guests. Fully 92% claimed they would not, again a marked discrepancy from their face-to-face behavior. The study is methodologically flawed; for example, the same people might not have made the face-to-face decisions as answered the letters. Nevertheless, for years, the study was used as a caveat, warning about limitations to the predictive power of survey research, but it hardly dampened researchers' enthusiasm for measuring and reporting attitudes.

Then, in the late 1960s, a review of 47 empirical studies of attitudes and behavior (Wicker, 1969) also concluded that attitudes barely predict behavior, usually correlating less than .30. The studies included job attitudes and absenteeism among aircraft plant employees, young mothers' attitudes and behavior about breast-feeding, plus students' and businessmen's attitudes and behavior toward football, movies, career, and sleep. The correlations were quite variable, but frequently low. Consequently, Wicker dismissed the significance of attitudes: "Taken as a whole, these studies suggest that it is considerably more likely that attitudes will be unrelated or only slightly related to overt behaviors than that attitudes will be closely related to actions" (p. 65). What ails attitude-behavior relations? Several diagnoses emerged, concerning theory, variables, and measurement.

**THEORY**    First, the theory can be at fault. Researchers had assumed that attitudes cause behavior, but dissonance theory teaches us that behavior can cause attitudes. (Recall that counter-attitudinal behavior can shift attitudes.) And self-perception theory (Bem's theory, noted in Chapter 3) teaches us that people's behavior can lead them to infer their attitudes, again making the behavior precede the attitude (at least in conscious form). If the behavior does predate the attitude, the attitude could be a mere epiphenomenon, insignificant in its own right.

**OTHER VARIABLES**    Another diagnosis of the attitude-behavior problem is that other variables, besides attitudes, influence behavior. As the social influence chapter demonstrates, and as the core motive of belonging reminds us, people's behavior follows **norms**—the unwritten rules, standards, and values of their social groups—sometimes minimizing the role of personal attitudes. Not only do norms influence behavior, but norms influence the attitudes that people express. Thus, people's so-called attitudes on a survey may not be their only attitudes, and again have little bearing on their behavior. The problem of other variables, beyond the direct attitude-behavior relation, complicates prediction.

**MEASUREMENT**    Finally, measurement of attitudes and behavior can be faulty. The test of the theory—that attitudes cause behavior—is only as good as the operationalizations of attitude and behavior (as Chapter 2 argued, this holds for all theories and operationalizations). Two kinds of measurement issues come to the forefront. First, different measurement methods have different *biases*. For example, self-reports (as opposed to observer ratings) tend to reflect people's efforts to look good. Thus, when self-report methods measure both the behavior and the attitude, attitude-behavior relations are stronger (Kraus, 1995), probably because people present themselves as more consistent than they are or perhaps because their own definition of the behavior corresponds more closely to their own attitude toward the behavior, compared with an outside observer's definition of the behavior.

With regard to a second measurement issue: *A general* attitude toward, say, the environment, may not predict the *specific* behavior of recycling scrap paper when writing a late-night essay for psychology class (see Table 6.6). The mismatch between general attitudes and specific behaviors suggests either making the attitude more specific ("What is your attitude toward recycling paper from school work?") or making

**Table 6.6**  Match between Attitudes and Behavior

| Attitude | Behavior |
| --- | --- |
| General: support for environment | Behavioral index, e.g., |
| | Recycle newspapers |
| | Recycle office paper |
| | Recycle bottles and cans |
| | Use public transport |
| | Bike |
| | Walk |
| | Conserve water |
| Specific: support for recycling paper from school work | Recycle paper from schoolwork |

the behavior more general (a combination of answers to the questions "To what extent do you recycle newspaper, office paper, containers? To what extent do you use public transport, walk, or bike, instead of using a car? To what extent do you conserve water?"). As the next section indicates, matched levels of analysis (specific attitude, specific behavior, or general attitude, general behavior) allow more accurate prediction (Ajzen, 1987).

In short, the sorry state of attitude-behavior correlations as of 1969—and whenever researchers fail to heed the lessons learned—probably reflects various factors: theory, omitted other variables, and measurement.

## When Attitudes Do Predict Behavior

Wicker's pronouncement provoked a response. Researchers set to work to prove him wrong, developing more precise measurements and also more careful theories, which specified that the attitude-behavior relation depends on variables related to the attitude, the situation, and the person.

**IT DEPENDS ON PRECISION MEASUREMENT**    Icek Ajzen and Martin Fishbein (1973; Fishbein & Ajzen, 1975) proposed the **theory of reasoned action** to account for careful prediction of behavior from attitudes. Their theory holds that attitudes and subjective norms predict **behavioral intentions**, which are the best predictors of behavior. Hundreds of studies have assessed the correlations between intentions and actions, finding them to be high on average (.44 to .62). And the prediction of intentions from attitudes toward the behavior and from subjective norms, combined, is also high (.63 to .71), according to a summary of various meta-analyses (Sutton, 1998). Widely applied, the theory predicts, for example, people's use of condoms, dental floss, and doctor visits, among other health behaviors.

The success of this theory depends on accurate measurement. Attitudes are assessed by asking respondents for their evaluations of every aspect of the attitude object: for example, all the perceived consequences of voting for a particular presidential candidate. Once respondents provide all their **subjective values** (perceived consequences) associated with the attitude object (excellent for the economy; good at international relations; not so good at dealing with Congress), they also provide the **subjective likelihood** (perceived probability) for each (how certain they are that the candidate will be excellent for the economy). The subjective probability and value are multiplied (to give the more certain values more weight than the uncertain ones) and summed, to create an overall measure of attitude. **Subjective norms** are assessed in the same way: what various important people are perceived to think of the respondent voting for this candidate and how certain the respondent is about their opinions.

Finally, a third variable, besides attitudes and norms, was added by Ajzen in an updated **theory of planned behavior** (Ajzen, 1991; Madden, Ellen, & Ajzen, 1992). The new predictor variable was **perceived behavioral control**, the probability that one can perform the behavior in question (the respondent's estimate of likely control over acting on the intention, once formed). Together, attitudes, subjective norms, and perceived behavioral control predict intention to perform the behavior, which in turn predicts behavior (Ajzen, 2001).

This theory makes explicit the nature of the attitude that best predicts behavior. One could best predict voting for a particular candidate by the person's attitudes toward voting for that particular candidate. A less good predictor would be the general attitude toward the candidate, without any mention of voting. And still less good would be general attitude toward the candidate's political party, absent any specific application to this candidate in this election. The theory also makes explicit the other variables that interfere between attitudes and intentions, namely, what other people are perceived to think and how much personal control one perceives over the behavior. With careful theory, careful specification of the other variables, and careful measurement, especially matching of the specific attitude to the specific behavior, attitudes successfully predict behavior.

One everyday parallel, noted in Chapter 4: When people report their specific intentions for implementing behavior, as opposed to merely having a general goal, they are more likely to carry out their intentions (Gollwitzer & Brandstätter, 1997). As noted, difficult personal projects (e.g., write a paper, find an apartment, settle a conflict) were fully three times more likely to be completed if students spontaneously provided **implementational intentions**, that is, had thought of specific actions in response to certain situational contexts ("when I am in situation $y$, I will perform behavior $z$"). Again, specificity matters not only in research but also in life, for attitudes and intentions to predict behavior.

**IT DEPENDS ON THE ATTITUDE**    Some attitudes predict behavior better than others. In 88 attitude-behavior studies, various variables **moderate** (qualify) the attitude-behavior relation (Kraus, 1995): Attitudes that are certain, stable, consistent, accessible, and based on direct experience predict behavior the best. In addition (Petty & Wegener, 1998), attitudes high on issue-relevant knowledge and personal relevance also predict behavior. In other words, if people are certain, knowledgeable, and involved in an attitude that is stable over time and place, based on mutually consistent thoughts and feelings, based on direct (rather than second-hand) experience, and mentally accessible at the time of their behavior, all these aspects of the attitude will contribute to its predicting behavior. Essentially, the overriding principles are that highly **accessible attitudes** predict behavior (Ajzen, 2001; Fazio, 1990) and **strong attitudes** predict behavior (Ajzen, 2001; Petty & Krosnick, 1995). Strong attitudes are stable and consequential (Krosnick, Boninger, Chuang, Berent, & Carnot, 1993).

As an example of accessible attitudes predicting behavior, researchers (Regan & Fazio, 1977) found that **direct experience** leads to highly accessible attitudes. A temporary housing crisis at Cornell University demonstrated the importance of direct experience on attitude-behavior correlations. One fall, as happens occasionally at every college, the number of entering first-year students outstripped the number of dormitory beds available. Some students had to sleep on cots in dorm lounges for as long as two months while the situation was being resolved (an example mentioned in Chapter 1). The researchers measured attitudes about the crisis (how tolerable it was; how much suffering it caused; perceived administration efforts, concerns, and priorities) and behavior (the number of actions students agreed to take to resolve the crisis, from signing a petition to joining a committee working on the problem). Students in temporary housing, that is, those with direct experience and presumably accessible attitudes, showed attitude-behavior correlations of about .30, whereas other students—who knew about the problem but had no personal experience with it and held less accessible attitudes—showed attitude-behavior correlations of about zero.

Attitude strength includes many factors (Krosnick et al., 1993). For example, unambivalent attitudes are stronger than ambivalent ones. That is, people's emotions can predict their behavior better than their beliefs do, at least when heart and mind conflict. Voters with unconflicted thoughts and feelings about presidential candidates, that is, unambivalent voters, had **internally consistent attitudes** that predicted behavior fairly well, and equally from both heart and mind. In contrast, ambivalent, conflicted voters were more likely to vote with their heart than with their mind (Lavine, Thomsen, Zanna, & Borgida, 1998). Internal consistency strengthens an attitude, but absent consistency, affect seems stronger, as we saw earlier.

Attitudes can be strong because of internal consistency but also because of their **extremity** (Prislin, 1996). This is what laypeople normally consider to be feeling strongly about something: having an extreme viewpoint. More generally, strong attitudes are embedded in one's self-concept, personal importance, values, and knowledge, but they also represent a commitment: extremity, resistance, and certainty (Pomerantz, Chaiken, & Tordesillas, 1995). Strong attitudes resist persuasion and predict behavior.

According to Kraus (1995), in general, correlations with behavior for strong, accessible attitudes average around .50, whereas the same correlations for weak, inaccessible attitudes are less than .20, a substantial difference between a small correlation and a large one, by social science standards. Overall, studies on features of the attitude itself summarize easily: Strong, accessible attitudes predict behavior better than weak, inaccessible ones do.

**IT DEPENDS ON THE SITUATION** Some situations emphasize going along with social demands, so they undermine attitude-behavior correlations. In those cases, norms predict behavior better than individual attitudes do. For example, attitude-behavior correlations for reported attitudes toward minority groups show low correlations with actual behavior (.24), presumably because of norms to appear unprejudiced, whatever one's personal views. In contrast, voting and contraceptive use—both behaviors that occur in private—show high attitude-behavior correlations (both .58). Kraus (1995) indicates that attitude-behavior correlations vary a lot, depending on circumstances.

Other situations emphasize the importance of acting on one's attitudes. An experimental demonstration of making one's attitude relevant comes from a classic study (Snyder & Swann, 1976). Male undergraduates rated their attitudes toward affirmative action as part of a larger set of questionnaires, and then two weeks later they came into the laboratory to participate in a mock court case, in which they had to judge liability in a sex-discrimination case. The situation made more or less salient the participants' relevant attitudes. In the basic condition, when attitudes were not salient, attitude-behavior correlations were .07, essentially zero. In the salient-attitude condition, participants were asked to "organize your thoughts and views on the affirmative action issue (e.g., Is it important to you that everyone is given equal opportunity in obtaining employment? Should women and minorities be actively recruited to help equalize employment ratios?...)." Under these circumstances, participants' prior attitudes predicted their verdict in the specific case, with a correlation of .58. Thus, the situation can emphasize or deemphasize one's attitudes and hence their predictive power.

The situation can also emphasize different aspects of one's attitudes in different contexts. Merely thinking about one's attitude can make different aspects accessible in different circumstances, changing attitudes and undermining attitude-behavior correlations (Wilson, Dunn, Kraft, & Lisle, 1989). When people lack a well-defined set of reasons for their attitudes, they generate reasons on the spot, not necessarily reflecting their core beliefs, but instead what is verbalizable, accessible, plausible, and self-enhancing.

This points out, then, that the attitude object is ambiguous and shifts with context. For example (Smith, Fazio, & Cejka, 1996), one can categorize sunbathing as a beach activity or a cancer risk, and Pete Rose as a baseball player or a gambler, with different attitudes elicited in each case. Whichever category is more accessible in a given setting will guide attitudes and presumably behavior. Similarly (Sia, Lord, Blessum, Ratcliff, & Lepper, 1997), when different **exemplars** come to mind (i.e., for a black person, Oprah Winfrey and Bill Cosby versus a drug dealer and an armed robber), attitudes change and undermine attitude-behavior consistency. In line with these studies, people introspecting about reasons focus on whichever happen to be their most accessible thoughts, viewing them as applicable to their current attitude (Wilson, Hodges, & LaFleur, 1995). If different situations prime different aspects of attitudes, then attitudes and behavior will be unstable over time.

The setting matters in a broader way as well. The assumption that attitudes should predict behavior is a peculiarly Western one. In more interdependent, collective settings, using one's own personal views to guide social behavior might be seen as selfish and immature. In contrast, sensitivity—to the other's needs, to the group's goals, and to the situation's requirements—might be the more appropriate and valued response. In Japanese culture, for example, the belief in attitude-behavior consistency is less strong than in English-speaking countries, such as Australia (Kashima, Siegel, Tanaka, & Kashima, 1992). Thus, the larger situation, culture, matters as well.

**IT DEPENDS ON THE PERSON**   Some people more than others show attitude-behavior consistency. Recall individual differences in **self-monitoring** from the self chapter: High self-monitors are sensitive to and mold themselves to the demands of the situation, whereas low self-monitors are sensitive to and follow their inner selves as guides to behavior. It follows, then, that high self-monitors (those who monitor themselves to fit the situation) would show lower attitude-behavior correlations than low self-monitors. Kraus (1995) reports that four studies' average correlation for low self-monitors was a substantial .50, whereas high self-monitors' correlation was only .25.

A completely different kind of individual difference is **need for cognition**, mentioned earlier, the extent to which people seek and enjoy thinking hard. People high on need for cognition, as predicted, not only base their attitudes on issue-relevant thinking but also show higher attitude-behavior correlations: a whopping .87 between their attitudes toward presidential candidates before the fall election and their reported voting behavior eight weeks later; people low in need for cognition showed a correlation of .46 (Cacioppo, Petty, Kao, & Rodriguez, 1986).

Another way that attitude-behavior correlations depend on the person comes from researchers' habit of using college students as participants. David Sears (1986) has suggested that student attitudes are not as fixed as those of their elders and that the resulting instability may undermine attitude-behavior correlations. However, more recent evidence indicates that young adults and elderly adults both have less rigid attitudes, whereas middle-aged adults have strong attitudes, not susceptible to change, because they perceive their attitudes to be central, important, and well supported (Visser & Krosnick, 1998). Kraus (1995) reports a small but significant effect across studies, with an attitude-behavior correlation of .49 for nonstudents and .34 for students, but his non-student samples probably included more middle-aged than elderly adults, who were not analyzed separately.

**IT DEPENDS ON THE PROCESS**    Earlier, we described dual-process models of persuasion, contrasting more rapid, unconscious, automatic processes with slower, more conscious, deliberate processes of attitude change. Attitude-behavior linkages also depend on whether the process involved is relative more **impulsive** versus **reflective** (Strack & Deutsch, 2004). A reflective system operates on knowledge and values, to produce behavior, while the impulsive system operates through simpler and more direct associations and motivations. The systems operate in parallel, though the impulsive one is faster, it may respond first, all else being equal. In Fazio's (2001) related **MODE** approach (Motivation and Opportunity Determine Behavior), highly accessible attitudes generate spontaneous behavior, as mentioned in the earlier discussion of distinct types of attitudes predicting behavior. In both approaches, behavior can come from a rapid association between an attitude object, the attitude, and the relevant behavior, or behavior can come from more conscious deliberation, given capacity and motivation.

The unconscious operation of attitudes on behavior is the more surprising type of process. For example, people do not often consider their voting choices to be driven by automatic, unconscious processes, but they often are (Burdein, Lodge, & Taber, 2006). People often act on what "feels right," as noted earlier with regard to perceptual fluency increasing pleasure (and stock purchases!). The broader principle is that people take **feelings as information** (Schwarz, 2004). Experiences that "go down easy" must be positive: fluent perception and accessible thoughts form the basis of judgments and behavior at the expense of more difficult knowledge retrieval. This may depend on the person: Prevention-focus participants prefer a vigilant nonverbal communicator, whereas promotion-focus people prefer an eager nonverbal communicator (Cesario & Higgins, 2008). Whichever style feels right has more influence.

People can be jolted out of this kind of impulsive, associative, go-with-your-gut process by experiencing difficulty in obtaining or using information (Alter, Oppenheimer, Epley, & Eyre, 2007), or presumably in applying it to behavior. Likewise, irrelevant affect has less influence not only at excessively high levels of effort, but also at excessively low levels of effort, when it barely registers (Albarracín & Kumkale, 2003).

## Summary of Attitude-Behavior Research

Not all seemingly relevant attitudes predict seemingly relevant behavior. The level of specificity between attitudes and behavior has to match. Both attitude and behavior have to be measured carefully. Attitude-behavior correspondence depends on the attitude's mental accessibility and its overall strength. It also depends on the extent to which the situation or the person focuses on inner thoughts and feelings or on social norms as a guide to behavior, reflecting the core social motives of understanding versus belonging. Some people like to think, but not all introspection increases attitude-behavior correspondence; justifying reasons for one's attitude decidedly does not improve its predictive role. The attitude-behavior relation underscores the object-appraisal function of attitudes, akin to the core social motive of understanding. However, attitude-behavior consistency depends on culture as well. In the case of more collectivist, interdependent cultures, attitudes may more often serve value-expressive functions and therefore the core motive to belong. The process of generating the attitude and its behavior also determines the degree and type of linkage.

## CHAPTER SUMMARY

Attitudes are evaluative responses to entities in the social world, and they have affective, cognitive, and behavioral correlates. Attitudes are most often measured by self-report, but other operational definitions supplement these. Attitudes all serve the object-appraisal function, equivalent to the core social motive of understanding. Some attitudes serve narrow self-interest functions, utilitarian goals. The other major attitude function, value-expression, resonates with the core social motive of belonging, either public or private identity with groups. Affective, cognitive, and behavioral processes relate to attitudes as primarily reflecting both understanding and belonging motives.

Attitudes often form through affective processes such as classical conditioning (repetition and association), instrumental conditioning (rewards and punishments), modeling (imitation), and vicarious reinforcement (observational learning). Another affect-based process of attitude formation is mere exposure, the increasing evaluation of entities frequently encountered. As noted, all these processes entail minimal cognitive activity of the systematic, thoughtful type that forms opinions, focusing instead on affect, such as pleasure and pain. Nevertheless, such primitive, affect-based attitudes serve the function of object appraisal.

Given an attitude, even if affect-based, object appraisal becomes richer and deepens understanding as people develop cognitions through a variety of processes, including consistency pressures and persuasive communication. Consistency theories are premised on people's tendency to fit together affect, cognition, and behavior relevant to a particular attitude. Accordingly, people seek and interpret information to support their attitudes. Cognitive consistency theories illustrate not only the core motive of understanding but also the core social motive of self-enhancement, seeing oneself as consistent and as not freely choosing actions with aversive consequences. The object appraisal function of understanding is served by consistent, not arbitrary, attitudes. The attitude change that results from consistency pressures represents processes primarily internal to the person, described as self-inflicted attitude change.

Persuasion represents deliberate attempts to change the attitudes of another. The object appraisal function, exemplifying the core social motive of understanding, especially represents the persuasive communication approaches. In analyzing persuasive communications for their effectiveness, researchers typically break down the process, as reflected in four major theories. The Yale communication and persuasion approach—both McGuire's stages of reception and yielding, as well as the larger communication and persuasion program of source, message, recipient, and context variables—set the scientific agenda for subsequent researchers, establishing persuasion as a topic, specifying variables, and establishing experimental approaches. However, the resulting research perhaps overemphasized deliberate, thoughtful persuasion processes, based on careful processing of message content. Other persuasion processes—considerably more superficial—matter as well. More recent models, namely the heuristic-systematic model and elaboration likelihood model, emphasize alternative routes to persuasion based on relatively superficial or in-depth processing. While the generalizations are few in this area of knowledge, the fine-grained understanding of effective persuasion techniques is well-developed.

Having focused on affective processes in attitude formation and cognitive processes in attitude change, attitude research also concerns behavior. Just how much attitudes concern behavior proved contentious, as early researchers first assumed and then denied that attitudes predict behavior. Increased theoretical precision, consideration of omitted variables, and matching levels of attitude-behavior specificity all rescued attitude-behavior research from its predicament. Extending a theory of reasoned action, the theory of planned behavior specifies three predictors of behavioral intention: subjective beliefs, subjective norms, and perceived behavioral control; specific intentions, in turn, predict behavior. Moreover, attitudes predict behavior when the attitude itself is strong and accessible, when the situation encourages acting on one's attitudes (and not going along with social norms), and when the person's personality predisposes acting on attitudes. The attitude-behavior scandal is over, and the resolution emerges as one of social psychology's success stories.

## SUGGESTIONS FOR FURTHER READING

AJZEN, I. (2001). Nature and operation of attitudes. *Annual Review of Psychology, 52*, 27–58.

ALBARRACÍN, D., & VARGAS, P. (2010). Attitude formation and change: From biology to social responses to persuasive intent. In S. T. FISKE, D. T. GILBERT, & G. LINDZEY (Eds.), *Handbook of social psychology* (5th ed.). New York: Wiley.

BANAJI, M. R., & HEIPHETZ, L. (2010). Attitudes. In S. T. FISKE, D. T. GILBERT, & G. LINDZEY (Eds.), *Handbook of social psychology* (5th ed.). New York: Wiley.

CRANO, W. D., & PRISLIN, R. (2006). Attitudes and persuasion. *Annual Review of Psychology*, *57*, 345–374.

EAGLY, A. H., & CHAIKEN, S. (1998). Attitude structure and function. In D. T. GILBERT, S. T. FISKE, & G. LINDZEY (Eds.), *Handbook of social psychology* (4th ed., Vol. 1, pp. 269–322). New York: McGraw-Hill.

KELTNER, D., & LERNER, J. S. (2010). Emotion. In S. T. FISKE, D. T. GILBERT, & G. LINDZEY (Eds.), *Handbook of social psychology* (5th ed.). New York: Wiley.

KROSNICK, J. A., & VISSER, P. S. (2010). The psychological underpinning of political behavior. In S. T. FISKE, D. T. GILBERT, & G. LINDZEY (Eds.), *Handbook of social psychology* (5th ed.). New York: Wiley.

MAIO, G. R., & HADDOCK, G. (2007). Attitude change. In A. W. KRUGLANSKI & E. T. HIGGINS (Eds.), *Social psychology: Handbook of basic principles* (2nd ed., pp. 565–586). New York: Guilford.

PETTY, R. E., & WEGENER, D. T. (1998). Attitude change: Multiple roles for persuasion variables. In D. T. GILBERT, S. T. FISKE, & G. LINDZEY (Eds.), *Handbook of social psychology* (4th ed., Vol. 1, pp. 323–390). New York: McGraw-Hill.

# Chapter 7

# Attraction: Initiating Romance, Friendship, and Other Relationships

Inman had attended church expressly for the purpose of viewing her. In the weeks following Ada's arrival in Cold Mountain, Inman had heard much about her before he saw her. She and her father had stayed too long green in the country they had taken up, and they soon became a source of great comedy to many households along the river road.... So one Sunday morning Inman dressed himself carefully—in a new black suit, white shirt, black tie, black hat—and set out for church to view Ada.... Inman had but the back of her head to find Ada by, yet that took only a moment since her dark hair was done up in a heavy and intricate plait of such recent fashion that it was not then known in the mountains. Below where her hair was twisted up, two faint cords of muscle ran up under the skin on either side of her white neck to hold her head on. Between them a scoop, a shaded hollow of skin. Curls too fine to be worked up into the plait. All through the hymn, Inman's eyes rested there, so that after awhile, even before he saw her face, all he wanted was to press two fingertips against that mystery place. (Frazier, 1997, pp. 59–60)[1]

Attraction impels one person to seek another, and attraction changes lives. Yet, according to social psychologists who study the mystery of attraction, the underlying principles turn out to be surprisingly simple. Core social motives prominent in attraction include both self-enhancing (i.e., liking those who make us feel good) and understanding (i.e., liking those we can know easily). Both self-enhancing and understanding are served by liking those who are most familiar. This is the unifying principle of attraction: sheer familiarity, despite what fiction says.

This chapter shows that those we seek for love, friendship, and other relationships tend to seem familiar directly as well as indirectly, by way of physical attractiveness,

---

similarity, and reciprocity. And sometimes even a "plait of such recent fashion" above "a shaded hollow of skin." We return also to exotic attractions.

## ATTRACTION IN DAILY LIFE AND IN SCIENCE

Poets, novelists, philosophers, and plain folks contemplate the meaning of attraction, but scientists, too, are fascinated by liking and loving. Attraction does not submit to direct dissection, as Ellen Berscheid (1985) pointed out, for it is a **hypothetical construct** (a term introduced in Chapter 2 as an idea that links together various other ideas or observations sharing some common property). The self and attitudes both are hypothetical constructs as well. As with any hypothetical construct, we can know the symptoms of attraction, but we cannot point to the thing itself. Because researchers cannot directly observe attraction, definitions differ, but they do agree on central themes.

### Conceptual Definitions

**Attraction** concerns a desire for a voluntary relationship, sustained because the participants enjoy each other (Huston & Levinger, 1978). Attraction is a prelude to intimacy, but intimacy implies an established close relationship. (As the next chapter shows, intimacy is a wonderfully complex topic in its own right.) Here, we address people's initial feelings for each other in a wide variety of potential relationships.

Western researchers tend to view affiliation as a matter of personal choice, discounting the seemingly arbitrary effects of the social situation. Yet, whom we happen to seek for interaction is not just sheer attraction. Social structure sometimes demands that we interact with coworkers, teammates, teachers, students, ex-spouses, and cousins we may or may not like. These interactions, the structural barriers around them, and other people also determine our relationships. Asian psychologists appreciate the role of social structure over personal choice in determining relationships, and the chapter will return to this point. But not all affiliation comes from attraction (Berscheid & Reis, 1998): Who interacts with whom is not equivalent to who is attracted to whom. While situation-based affiliation determines many of our relationships, attraction—liking or disliking another—is still an element in all social relationships, whether with one's lover, friend, employer, coworker, garbage collector, or clerk.

### Operational Definitions

Traditionally, the scientific approach to attraction has always built on attitudes research (Berscheid, 1985). Conceptually, therefore, attraction entails three correlates standard to attitudes:

- Primarily affect, a simple evaluation of another person, the liking-disliking component
- Cognition, one's beliefs about the other person
- Behavior, one's tendencies to approach or avoid the other person

Nevertheless, although an attitude, attraction merits special status because its consequences loom so large for people. We examine what this special importance means for our understanding of attraction, throughout.

The most frequent operationalization, attraction between two strangers in the laboratory, has assessed liking and disliking on verbal yardsticks. A **Likert scale** predominates, usually a scale from 1 *(dislike a lot)* to 7 *(like a lot)*, or some variant. Here one sees the high personal importance of attraction, as apart from other attitudes: People rating other people tend to use just the top half of the scale. The psychological midpoint is not the middle of the scale in rating people (Fiske, 1980; see Chapter 4). On a 7-point scale, the subjective midpoint might be 5 or just above; the other person would have to be actively obnoxious to receive a rating of 3, and 1 or 2 would constitute serious verbal violence or striking violation of social norms. In effect, a 7-point scale might as well be a 4-point scale, from 4 to 7; this is one reason that attraction researchers often use longer scales (e.g., 1 to 11, to get operational use of 6 to 11).

Note that people's underuse of the negative end of the scale fits the importance of attraction as an attitude. Perhaps people do not like to reveal their negative attitudes because disliking reflects badly on both parties. Or perhaps people like to like others because disliking is uncomfortable; it invites reciprocal disliking, as we will see, and potential harm. Chapter 4 discussed people's positivity bias as an example of the motive to trust, giving others the benefit of the doubt. People show more positivity bias toward people than toward things. Also, self-protection or social desirability easily enters into attraction ratings, reflections of the self-enhancing motive.

Because of these positivity biases, attraction may be more subtly indicated by **unobtrusive measures** (remember the nonverbal indicators of attraction, Chapter 3; also see the chapter on prejudice). One particular nonverbal behavior, eye contact, correlates highly with liking and loving (Rubin, 1973). And social psychologists have even used this fact to manipulate attraction between strangers. Artificially inducing opposite-sex single people to stare into each other's eyes makes them feel attracted. Researchers (Kellerman, Lewis, & Laird, 1989) assigned opposite-sex strangers either to (a) gaze into each other's eyes or (b) stare at each other's hands or (c) have one gaze into the other's eyes and the other stare at the first one's hands. Another control condition included (d) gazing into the other's eyes but counting eye-blinks. Overwhelmingly, the strangers expressed more affection and respect for each other after two minutes of mutual gaze than under any other condition (see Table 7.1). Scientists and laypeople alike infer liking, even their own liking, from eye contact.

Other favorite nonverbal measures are interpersonal distance (18″ or less is intimate distance). To infer who likes whom, try observing people at a not-too-crowded party. Talking distance serves as an excellent proxy for attraction. Posture (facing and leaning forward) also indicates attraction. Other kinds of unobtrusive measures include helping someone (as that chapter shows) and choosing someone as a partner (Moreno, 1953). Unobtrusive measures may be particularly germane for attraction because people are self-conscious about letting others know what they feel about them, again because attraction is so important, compared with many other attitudes.

**Table 7.1**    Affection and Respect Scores under Different Gaze Conditions

| | | | | | | |
|---|---|---|---|---|---|---|
| | | Gaze Condition | | | | |
| Scale | Subject:<br>Partner: | Eyes<br>Eyes | Hands<br>Hands | Eyes<br>Hands | Hands<br>Eyes | Eye-blink<br>Eye-blink or Eye gaze |
| Affection | | 62.4 | 53.0 | 52.8 | 54.6 | 55.8 |
| Respect | | 67.4 | 58.8 | 54.6 | 60.5 | 64.7 |

*Source:* From Kellerman et al., 1989. Copyright © Elsevier. Adapted with permission.

## Core Social Motives

Attraction serves the core social motive of belonging, clearly, as people want to be with other people. Chapter 1 defined the belonging motive as needing strong, stable relationships with other people. Thus, as an explanatory theme, belonging particularly explains the phenomenon of long-term close relationships, as the next chapter indicates. For more superficial encounters based on initial attraction, the social motives are simpler: We like those we feel we already know and those who make us feel good. Familiarity underlies both understanding and self-enhancing and thus explains a broad array of attraction principles.

**UNDERSTANDING: LIKING THOSE WE CAN GET TO KNOW EASILY**
People seek shared social understanding in order to belong more securely. In Chapters 3 and 4, we saw that people use conveniently packaged personality traits or other coherent expectations to understand themselves or others. And in the previous chapter, we saw that people use prior attitudes to respond efficiently to the social world. Similarly, people use familiarity as a basis for attraction in part because it relies on comfortable prior knowledge. Familiarity leads to attraction, for people are attracted to those they feel they can understand easily. Recall too that processing fluency pleases people, leading to liking the easily understood. The familiar, the similar, and the known all appeal more fundamentally than do the unfamiliar, the dissimilar, and the unknown. Some of the appeal of familiar and similar others may stem from felt understanding; if this person resembles prior experience or the self, then one has at least the illusion of knowing what makes the other person tick. People like other people whom they think they can understand and, not coincidentally, control (predict and perhaps influence). Familiar people also are safe, so trust is relevant as well. One could argue that belonging, controlling, and trusting, as well as understanding, all enter into people's attraction to familiarity, but a sense of understanding arguably precedes belonging, controlling, and trusting, in interpersonal attraction.

**SELF-ENHANCING: LIKING THOSE WHO MAKE US FEEL GOOD**    Just as people make self-serving attributions and develop self-schemas that reinforce their better attributes, so do people mostly seek out others who make them feel good about themselves. People who resemble us or agree with us also reassure us. People who validate us and like us presumably won't do us any harm.

Research suggests too that physical attractiveness may stem from familiarity, as we will see. Being with physically attractive people also rewards our self-esteem, as well as our aesthetic sensibilities. The principles of physical attractiveness, reciprocal liking, and similarity serve self-enhancing motives.

## Summary of Definitions and Motives

People like other people they feel they can understand comfortably, and they like others who make them feel good. More broadly, drawing on both understanding and self-enhancing motives, attraction research shows that basic principles of attraction—familiarity, physical attractiveness, similarity, and reciprocity—all may fall under the principle of familiarity. What is familiar is easily understood and reaffirms the self, as we will see.

## FAMILIARITY: LIKING THOSE WE KNOW (AND UNDERSTAND)

This insight is from British governess Jane Eyre, on being introduced to her young charge:

> The promise of a smooth career, which my first calm introduction to Thornfield Hall seemed to pledge, was not belied on longer acquaintance with the place and its inmates.... My pupil was a lively child, who had been spoilt and indulged, and therefore was sometimes wayward.... She had no great talents, no marked traits of character, no peculiar development of feeling or taste, which raised her one inch above the ordinary level of childhood; but neither had she any deficiency or vice which sunk her below it.... By her simplicity, gay prattle, and efforts to please, [she] inspired me, in return, with a degree of attachment sufficient to make us both content in each other's society. (Brontë, 1847, p. 140)[2]

People often grow attached to those average, everyday people around them all the time, just because they encounter them a lot. Oddly, the more we see people—assuming they do not have any "deficiency or vice which sinks them below the ordinary level"—the more we are inspired with Brontë's "sufficient degree of attachment." Social psychologists call this mere exposure (introduced in the last chapter).

As a corollary, the situations that throw us together mold our attractions. Nevertheless, when people explain their friendships and loves, they rarely mention such seemingly arbitrary factors as overlapping offices, adjacent apartments, shared schedules, or habitual haunts. Social psychologists show that proximity matters, as we will see.

---

[2] Copyright © Brontë Estate. Reprinted with permission.

## Mere Exposure

Recall the phenomenon of **mere exposure:** The sheer frequency of encountering an initially neutral or positive stimulus enhances its evaluation (Zajonc, 1968). In the attitude chapter, we reviewed the mere exposure demonstrations of liking for polygons and unfamiliar ideographs. People even like people whose photographs they have encountered frequently. For example, duration of subliminal (unconscious) exposure to facial photographs determines liking for them (Bornstein, Leone, & Galley, 1987). What's more, people agreed more often with another person whose photograph they had subliminally encountered just beforehand, again indicating attraction. Mere exposure does not have to be unconscious, and it may or may not involve conscious recognition, but the strength of its effects are evident in laboratory studies that use subliminal exposures and show that its effects can be independent of recognition.

Taking mere exposure one step further into the world, in one study, several women attended a 130-person class either 0, 5, 10, or 15 times during a semester (Moreland & Beach, 1992). The women were chosen to be similar-looking, so other students might easily confuse them with each other. At the end of the term, although mere exposure had only weak effects on students' ability to recognize the women, they liked best and felt most similar to the ones they had seen most often (see Table 7.2).

A study on friendship corroborates these findings (Brockner & Swap, 1976): People liked other people they saw most often, and they even tended to self-disclose

**Table 7.2**    Effects of Mere Exposure on Familiarity, Attraction, and Similarity

| Dependent Measure | Number of Visits | | | |
|---|---|---|---|---|
| | 0 | 5 | 10 | 15 |
| Familiarity | | | | |
|    Know her? | 0.00 | 0.00 | 0.00 | 0.00 |
|    Seen her? | 0.13 | 0.08 | 0.08 | 0.12 |
|    Familiar? | 2.87 | 2.95 | 3.39 | 3.15 |
| Attraction | | | | |
|    Index | 3.62 | 3.88 | 4.25 | 4.38 |
|    Become friends? | 0.41 | 0.43 | 0.57 | 0.60 |
|    Enjoy time? | 0.36 | 0.37 | 0.49 | 0.54 |
|    Work together? | 0.32 | 0.37 | 0.41 | 0.44 |
| Similarity | | | | |
|    Index | 1.88 | 1.93 | 2.11 | 2.23 |
|    Same background? | 0.34 | 0.37 | 0.47 | 0.45 |
|    Understand her? | 0.44 | 0.44 | 0.55 | 0.57 |
|    Similar plans? | 0.34 | 0.35 | 0.39 | 0.40 |

The first two measures were coded *0 = no* and 1 = *yes*. They show nonsignificant effects of mere exposure; all other effects are significantly different.

*Source:* From Moreland & Beach, 1992. Copyright © Elsevier. Adapted with permission.

more to those people. Mere exposure effects may actually be stronger in real-world settings than in the laboratory, according to meta-analysis (Bornstein, 1989). One reason for this is that people control whom they encounter, based on initial impressions. When people form an initially negative first impression—whether accurate or not—they tend to avoid the other person, so negativity correlates with (chosen) low exposure. An initially positive first impression increases the odds of repeating the interaction, so positivity naturally correlates with increased exposure. If the initial positive impression proves inaccurate, exposure can be reduced. This means that people's experience of others in the real-world is hardly random but instead selects for positivity (Denrell, 2005).

## Proximity

What natural conditions create mere exposure? In a pioneering study, Leon Festinger, Stanley Schachter, and Kurt Back (1950) studied World War II veterans going to the Massachusetts Institute of Technology and living in married student housing. They were a homogeneous group, slightly older than most college men, upper middle class in origin, majoring in engineering or natural science, aspiring to own their own home in the near future. The researchers were interested in friendship choice, as determined by **proximity**, defined to include both physical distance and functional distance. **Physical distance** measures distance (e.g., between front doors), whereas **functional distance** measures the contact encouraged by the design and relative positions in the environment (i.e., adjoining houses could have front walkways leading in opposite directions). Functional distance modifies physical distance because people's paths may be more likely to cross if they share mailboxes, walkways, or parking. The smaller the functional distance, the more likely people are to bump into each other and perhaps become friends.

Two types of housing provided a natural replication of the researchers' study (see Figure 7.1). In one, Westgate West, apartments on the same floor shared common entrance porches in a two-story building with external stairs between floors. In the other, Westgate Court, the duplex houses shared a common courtyard, with shared paths to the street. In both housing complexes, researchers measured the distance between people's apartments—that is, proximity—as a predictor of friendship. Residents nominated their top three social contacts. Within one floor of Westgate West, over 41% of top choices were next-door neighbors, with over 22% more being next-but-one. People's seemingly arbitrary assignment to apartments determined that nearly two-thirds of their friends would be within a door or two of their own place. Similar results predicted, though less strongly, friendship choice within a row of houses in a Westgate West courtyard. Functional distance worked much the same way as literal physical distance: People whose houses faced away from the courtyard, toward the street, were much less often chosen as friends.

People form friendships with those they encounter frequently, as mere exposure would predict. A later study went one step farther, randomly assigning people to proximity and measuring their friendships a year later (Back, Schmukle, & Egloff, 2008). Findings were reminiscent of Westgate, only with true random assignment.

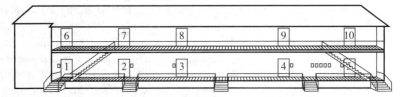

(A) Schematic Diagram of a Westgate West Building

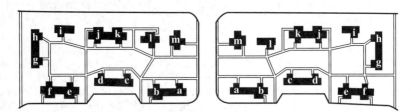

(B) Schematic Diagram of the Arrangement of the Westgate Court

**Figure 7.1**    Diagrams of Physical Distance between Household Units in (A) Westgate West and (B) Westgate Court

*Source:* Festinger et al., 1950. Copyright © Stanford University Press. Adapted with permission.

Not only sheer opportunity for interacting but also mere frequency of exposure seems to be key, in a variety of ethnic groups and life stages. Asian-Americans date Euro-Americans when they are in close proximity (Fujino, 1997). High school students form friendships within their own academic tracks, in which they take most of their classes, one version of proximity (Kubitschek & Hallinan, 1998). Older, relocated adults form new friendships based on proximity (Dugan & Kivett, 1998). For example, proximity predicts supportive behaviors such as checking on each other, shared activities, and exchanging gifts, as well as sheer frequency of contact. Although alternative ideas could explain each of these findings, mere exposure as the common thread clearly strengthens proximity effects.

Are there limits on proximity? Of course. The effects of close physical context have notable limits (Baum & Valins, 1979). In dormitories with long corridors, as compared with short-corridor and suite-based dorms, physical density may hold constant, but the experienced crowding can interfere with forming friendships. Residents of long-corridor dorms felt less control over their passive contacts with others; that is, they had less choice over their casual encounters. Too-dense proximity leads people to feel out of control and can impede liking.

## Summary of Familiarity

Familiarity, whether operationalized as laboratory-controlled mere exposure or real-world passive contacts through proximity, enhances liking. Familiarity suggests that the other person is knowable, safe, and predictable.

# PHYSICAL ATTRACTIVENESS: LIKING THOSE WHO LOOK GOOD (AND ENHANCE US)

Of all the people passively encountered via proximity, what determines attraction, apart from sheer frequency? Certain people catch our eye, please our aesthetics, and invite approach. Knowing their roles on both sides of this dynamic, people spend quantities of money and time making themselves attractive. Social psychology suggests they are not wrong to do so, if good first impressions and initial attraction are their primary goal. Whether it is fundamentally right or wrong, **physical attractiveness**—the quality of being consensually judged as good-looking—has predictable effects on attraction, even outside romantic and sexual attraction.

## Images of Attractive People

Physical attractiveness opens doors; it cues in others an immediate (if not fully conscious) positive attitude (McConnell, Rydell, Strain, & Mackie, 2008). Attractive people freely get credited with success and social competence, although not particularly integrity or concern for others, according to meta-analyses (Eagly, Ashmore, Makhijani, & Longo, 1991; Feingold, 1992a). Are attractive people really more sociable? If they are treated better, over time, maybe they indeed become better at interacting with others. Good-looking people do rate higher on independently measured social skill, popularity, and being sexual experienced; they report less loneliness and anxiety, according to meta-analyses (Feingold, 1992a). What is beautiful is socially good. In addition, meta-analyses show that attractive people are viewed as somewhat more competent, especially when they are men and little explicit information is available; however, good-looking adults are not in fact more competent (Eagly et al., 1991; Feingold, 1992a; Jackson, Hunter, & Hodge, 1995).

The power of the physical attractiveness stereotype comes across in a classic experiment (Snyder, Tanke, & Berscheid, 1977), in which male undergraduates received photographs of women before a getting-acquainted telephone conversation. The photographs, either quite attractive or quite unattractive, did not depict their actual partners, who were unaware of the experimental manipulation. Before the conversation, the men rated their supposedly attractive partner as more sociable, poised, humorous, and adept. During the conversation, as rated by independent judges, the men themselves acted more sociable, sexually warm, interesting, independent, bold, humorous, and adept. In response, the women, also by independent ratings, behaved in more sociable, outgoing, sexually warm, and poised ways. The expectation in the minds of the men had become reality in the behavior of the women, based entirely on random assignment to being thought beautiful or not.

In another study of mixed-gender dyads (Garcia, Stonson, Ickes, Bissonnette, & Briggs, 1991), as the men's attractiveness increased, the women set a more exclusive tone (referring less often to third parties). As the women's attractiveness increased, both partners became more involved and satisfied with the interaction, and the men empathized more with their partner (adopting her perspective, thoughts, and feelings).

Both exclusivity and empathy are interpersonal rewards likely to accrue to physically attractive individuals, making them perhaps more socially effective.

## Functions of Physical Attractiveness Stereotypes

Assuming the physical attractiveness stereotype is exactly that, a stereotype, why would it be functional? One possibility is that attractive people presumably have more social opportunities, so they become more socially skilled and powerful (Eagly et al., 1991); therefore, people do well to affiliate with them. Schematically, this idea would be: attractiveness → opportunity → potency.

Although plausible in the individualistic American context, the prediction breaks down cross-culturally. Chinese immigrants to Canada, those most involved in their Chinese community, did not show the stereotype (Dion, Pak, & Dion, 1990). A physical attractiveness stereotype, however, does emerge in some collectivist cultures (Korea and Taiwan), but the content differs. Unlike the United States, in Korea, attractive people are not presumed to be more powerful but instead are presumed to show more concern for others and more integrity. American and Korean views of social potency apparently differ (Wheeler & Kim, 1997). For Taiwanese participants, culture context also mattered: Taiwanese who endorsed Western values showed the stereotype most on individualist traits (Shaffer, Crepaz, & Sun, 2000), whereas those who most accepted Chinese traditions showed the stereotype on the most extreme (positive and negative) traits but not more moderate ones, presumably less important (Chen, Shaffer, & Wu, 1997).

A larger principle may explain these effects: Attractiveness is an **ascribed status**, bestowed, as is race or family lineage (e.g., royalty). It is not an **achieved status**, earned, as is education or profession. As an ascribed status given by society to people with certain inherent qualities, the beautiful receive the benefits of social status, embodying that culture's ideal values, that is, individual power in the United States and among Westernized Taiwanese, but the beautiful receive credit for a collective orientation in Korea and among traditionally collectivist Taiwanese.

Regardless of cultural variation in the stereotype content, cultures do tend to agree about what is attractive in the first place (Berry, 2000). For both men and women, having features that appear young, symmetrical, and prototypical is good. Some features obviously depend on gender; for example, in women, favorites include (Cunningham, 1986; Cunningham, Roberts, Barbee, Druen, & Wu, 1995): childlike features (large eyes, spaced far apart, small nose, small chin), some mature features that might also indicate being slender (narrow face, prominent cheekbones), expressive features (high eyebrows, large smile), and sexual cues (larger lower lip, well-groomed full hair). What is attractive in men is less often studied, but high cheekbones and rugged jaws (Berry, 2000), as well as thick brows, thin lips, square chin, and small eyes (Rhodes, 2006) appear to be favored. Although masculine appearance is desirable, moderate masculinity may be best; a masculine face tempered by slightly feminine features implies more agreeable traits, such as being warm, honest, cooperative, nurturing, and less dominant (Rhodes, 2006).

## Qualifications of Physical Attractiveness Effects

Although physical attractiveness ranks high on people's preferences, some qualifications are in order. First, although people theoretically revere attractive others, they do not always know what they actually want (Eastwick & Finkel, 2008). People often end up with people of attractiveness similar to their own. Why? Either the very most attractive people pair up with each other, leaving the rest to pair off among themselves, or people are afraid to approach someone too discrepantly better-looking, for fear of rejection. Whatever the reasons, spouses tend to be of similar attractiveness, and for men, friends are too. The average correlation between romantic partners' attractiveness is high (Feingold, 1988), and the correlation is almost as high for male friendships. But for female friends, attractiveness of one person is uncorrelated with attractiveness of the other (see Table 7.3). An early study of dating (Berscheid, Dion, Walster & Walster, 1971) indicated that both men and women chose dates whose physical attractiveness matched their own, although in general men cared more than women about appearance. Recent brain-imaging data suggest that men experience more reward value from attractive female faces than women do for attractive male faces (Cloutier, Heatherton, Whalen, & Kelley, 2008). In addition, people who conform closely to gender roles—that is, more sex-typed individuals—prioritize physical appearance (Andersen & Bem, 1981).

Second, individual differences are big, as these results suggest. Although men in the past have emphasized physical attractiveness more than women have, this may be changing to a different kind of individual difference. As women's economic power increases, they too care more about the physical appearance of potential partners (Gangestad, 1993), so perhaps the earlier gender disparity relates to resource issues and who can afford to care about appearance. Thus, gender differences may be replaced by social status differences.

Other individual differences continue to matter. For example, high self-monitors care about appearance more than low self-monitors do (Snyder, Berscheid, & Glick, 1985). Again, to the extent that people see a partner as showing their own or lower social standing, appearance will be more important. Appearance reflects social desirability, which concerns some people more than others.

Third, physical attractiveness conveys an expectation that the person will be socially skilled and desirable but not necessarily concerned with others (in a Western context). Recall that the Western meta-analyses indicate that attractive people are not credited with integrity or concern for others. Perhaps because they have so many

**Table 7.3**  Matching Physical Attractiveness in Relationships

| Relationship Type | Romantic partners | Male friends | Female friends |
|---|---|---|---|
| Correlation between partners' physical attractiveness | 0.49 | 0.38 | 0.00 |

*Source:* Data from a meta-analysis by Feingold, 1988.

social opportunities, they are therefore less in need of ingratiating themselves and less concerned about others (Eagly et al., 1991).

Finally, people's preferences in short-term sexual partners rely more on appearance than do their preferences in long-term mates. People in general, men and women alike, prefer long-term mates who are good companions, considerate, honest, affectionate, dependable, intelligent, kind, understanding, interesting, and loyal (Buss & Barnes, 1986). Much of the research on physical attractiveness examines preferences (not behavior), as measured by self-reports (maximizing social desirability), and in short-term relationships (not actual long-term choices). Recall that people do not always know (or get) what they want (Eastwick & Finkel, 2008). (For more discussion, see the later section on reciprocity and Berscheid & Reis, 1998.)

### Conclusion: Linking Physical Attractiveness to Other Principles

Despite some qualifications, physical attractiveness remains a component of attraction; moreover, it fits with principles we have already seen. The idea that attractive people presumably possess high status—that is, represent the culturally good and the socially desirable—further fits findings that link attractiveness to familiarity. That is, the face that most represents the culture is arguably most attractive. The most familiar possible face, created by averaging together many faces, turns out highly attractive (e.g., Berry, 2000; Langlois & Roggman, 1990; Rhodes, 2006). Think about what makes a face unattractive: nose or chin too big or small, cheeks too thin or fat, shape too long or short. Average features omit every "too" (big, small, short, long, thin, fat). Fluency of processing an average face makes it seem familiar and attractive.

If familiarity fundamentally underlies perceived attractiveness, then both proximity and attractiveness are explained by the same familiarity principle (Berscheid & Reis, 1998): What is familiar is good. In keeping with the core social motives, what is familiar is known (aids understanding), predictable (aids controlling), established (aids trusting), perhaps similar to self (aids self-enhancing), and probably from one's own group (aids belonging). For all these reasons, then, familiarity remains a powerful principle of attraction, in physical appearance, as in proximity.

### SIMILARITY: LIKING THOSE LIKE US (UNDERSTANDABLE AND ENHANCING)

The most familiar person in the world is our self, and those like us rank a close second. If familiarity underlies attraction, and if the most familiar people are those like us, then people like us are attractive. This is the **similarity-attraction principle**. Indeed, as a predictor of people's liking, similarity stands alone. If proximity determines whom you encounter, and physical features determine who theoretically appeals, the most solid principle apart from those is similarity—for example, shared interests, personality, and background. Going back to *Cold Mountain*:

> The girl's name, Ada soon discovered, was Ruby, and though the look of
> her was not confidence-inspiring, she convincingly depicted herself as

capable of any and all farm tasks.... And there was this: like Ada, Ruby was a motherless child from the day she was born. They had that to understand each other by. (Frazier, 1997, pp. 51–52)[3]

Discovering similarities cements acquaintances into something more.

## Balancing Friends and Attitudes

As this section shows, the similarity-attraction principle comes in part from consistency theories—which appeared in the attitudes chapter, illustrated by cognitive dissonance theory in particular. Another prominent consistency theory, **balance theory**, also subscribes to the view that people prefer and infer affective, cognitive, and behavioral consistency in themselves and others. From this general approach follows balance theory's premise that psychologically related individuals will see each other as similar if they like each other, and that they will see each other as likeable if they are similar. That is, balance theory predicts that people like to agree with their friends and to befriend those who agree with them.

What is **interpersonal balance**? Fritz Heider (1958) noted: "By a balanced state (or situation) is meant a harmonious state, one in which the entities comprising the situation and the feelings about them fit together without stress" (p. 180). Heider considered psychological entities such as people (e.g., two friends) and attitude objects (e.g., leisure activities or politics). He examined balance from the perspective of one person, P, related to another person, O, and a mutual attitude object, X. For example:

> Bob thinks Jim very stupid and a first-class bore. One day Bob reads some poetry he likes so well that he takes the trouble to track down the author in order to shake his hand. He finds that Jim wrote the poem. (Heider, 1958, p. 176)[4]

Heider then went on to ask 101 participants, "What would happen nine times out of ten when something like this occurs?" About half the people responded that Bob would grudgingly change his mind about Jim, and over a quarter of them that he would change his mind about the poems; the remaining quarter thought Bob might question Jim's authorship, distinguish between Jim the poet and Jim the stupid bore, or live with the confusing inconsistency. In most cases, people read a disharmony or imbalance into the initial social triad of Bob, dislikeable Jim, and Jim's marvelous poetry.

Heider specified two types of relationships: unit and sentiment. **Unit relationships** include people and objects that belong together, by virtue of authorship (Jim's poetry), ownership (say, Maria's car), proximity (neighbors), similarity (twins), and such. On the other hand, **sentiment relationships** involve liking and disliking. Heider's social triads, P-O-X, predict balance for both agreeing friends and disagreeing enemies, as well as imbalance for both disagreeing friends and agreeing enemies (see Figure 7.2). Later research showed that imbalance applies to disagreeing friends, whereas people are indifferent to agreeing enemies (Price, Harburg, & Newcomb, 1966).

---

[3] Copyright © Grove/Atlantic. Reprinted with permission.
[4] Copyright Heider Estate. Reprinted with permission

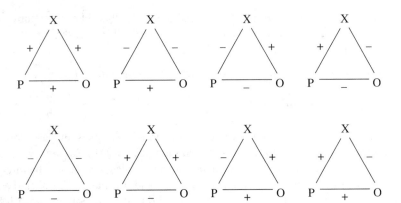

**Figure 7.2**    Balanced (top row) and Imbalanced (bottom row) Social Triads: P = Perceiver, O = Other, and X = Mutual Attitude Object

*Source:* As described by Heider, 1958.

A simple mathematical rule for determining balance multiplies the signs of the relationships: If Jim authors (+) some poetry, Bob likes (+) the poetry, and Bob likes (+) Jim, balance results (the +++ product is +). Change one sign, say, Bob dislikes (−) Jim, the ++−product is − and imbalance results, at least until Bob changes his mind about Jim or about his poetry. Imbalance presses toward balance. The similarity-liking principle follows, for if two people share attitudes toward the same object (++ or − −); that is, they are similar, the third sign in the relationship should be positive, to create balance.

Besides similarity-attraction, balance theory also makes the intriguing prediction that attraction should lead to perceived similarity. Liking someone, and knowing one's own attitudes and interests, one naturally assumes that the liked person shares those preferences. Indeed, couples who overestimate each other's similarity may get along better than couples who are more realistic (Levinger & Breedlove, 1966). Assumed agreement correlates with marital satisfaction. Actual agreement correlates with marital attraction only in areas relevant to promoting the couple's goals. Another study showed this attraction-similarity correlation: People's impressions of their partners reflected their own self-images and ideals more than their partners' self-reports. Nevertheless, these idealizations predict satisfaction, so a little illusion is a good thing (Murray, Holmes, & Griffin, 1996). In cross-sex friendships, people who are most satisfied also see their friends as most similar to themselves, and accuracy is irrelevant (Morry, 2007).

## Becoming a Unit

The similarity-attraction relation follows from balance theory in another way. A unit relationship (belonging) implies a sentiment relationship (liking), according to Heider. If two people belong together in a unit relationship (say, as partners, spouses, teammates, or roommates), they are presumed to like each other. Several studies demonstrate that positive unit relations lead to positive sentiment relations.

In general, anticipated interactions (prospective unit relations) create positive sentiments (for a review, see de la Haye, 1975). An example of anticipated interaction: Young women who anticipated joining a partner—to discuss proper standards for sexual behavior in dating relationships—reported liking their prospective partner more than a comparable nonpartner (Darley & Berscheid, 1967; see Table 7.4). It might seem that the personal nature of the discussion would determine liking (wishfully hoping the other person will be reasonable and sympatico). This feature indeed enhances the effect (Sutherland & Insko, 1973), compared with less involving topics. Generally, when people worry about being evaluated by another person, they engage in wishful thinking (Stevens & Fiske, 2000). Going beyond short-term encounters to hoped-for personal relationships, some experiments manipulated people's romantic interest in an opposite-sex partner (both signed up for a dating study). Participants who expected to go on a date viewed their partner positively, but only on relationship-irrelevant dimensions (e.g., task competence) or in the absence of relevant information. They were selectively accurate about their could-be romantic partner's attributes on potentially relevant dimensions (e.g., social skill) (Goodwin, Fiske, Rosen, & Rosenthal, 2002). So prospective unit relations do promote positive sentiments, as Heider predicted, but with limits.

Balance theory's predictions about social units and positive sentiments rely on the principle of consistency among linked entities (as in the P-O-X triads). Given a social unit, similarity and positivity create balance, one form of consistency. A consistency-oriented response to social units and attraction varies with individual differences. For example, low self-monitors, who particularly care about maintaining internal consistency, especially express liking for a prospective conversation partner (Lassiter & Briggs, 1990). But everyone finds similarity attractive; the kind just differs. Low self-monitors like people whose attitudes they share, whereas high self-monitors like people whose activities they share (Jamieson, Lydon, & Zanna, 1987). Low self-monitors care more about self-other consistency on internal dimensions (similar attitudes), and high self-monitors care more about self-other consistency on social dimensions (similar activities). Overall, not only does balance (similarity) create attraction, but so does belonging to a social unit, which also creates similarity (part of the same team, same pair).

**Table 7.4**    Sentiment Relations from Unit Relations: Liking as a Function of Anticipated Contact

| Description of partner | Person Rated Higher | | |
| --- | --- | --- | --- |
| | Partner | Nonpartner | Total |
| Personality A | 14 | 7 | 21 |
| Personality B | 12 | 5 | 17 |
| Total | 26 | 12 | 38 |

*Source:* From Darley & Berscheid, 1967. Copyright © Sage. Adapted with permission.

All told, the similarity-attraction effect deserves the status of similarity-attraction principle. Classic studies support this point. In the field, Theodore Newcomb (1961) demonstrated that housemates progressed from being strangers to friends, as a function of similarity. A group of 17 male undergraduates, strangers to each other, lived rent-free in a house provided by Newcomb, in exchange for providing weekly data. The power of shared attitudes emerged: Of those whose attitudes closely agreed during the first weeks, 58% ended up friends, whereas, among those without close agreement, only 33% ended up good friends. Donn Byrne (1971) experimentally tested the power of agreement, inviting people to evaluate strangers with whom they anticipated interaction. The strangers allegedly shared their attitudes or did not; people preferred the similar others consistently over multiple studies.

Cross-culturally, people prefer people like themselves (M. H. Bond & Smith, 1996), a global affirmation of similarity-attraction and balance principles. For example, Americans and Italians both prefer political leaders whom they view as similar to themselves (Caprara, Vecchione, Barbaranelli, & Fraley, 2007). Hindu and Muslim Indian undergraduates were most attracted to someone who shared their attitudes toward religion, society, and economy (Rai & Rathore, 1988). Similarly, Chinese adolescents rated ideal best friends as similar to themselves on extroversion, openness to experience, and emotional stability, though they said they prefer complementarity in assertiveness (Cheng, Bond, & Chan, 1995).

## Complementarity in Attraction

What about "opposites attract"? Although social psychologists have investigated this possibility, framed as a **complementarity principle**, the overwhelming evidence favors similarity (Berscheid & Reis, 1998). That is, people are most typically attracted to and satisfied with initial interactions when their attitudes, personalities, and interests are similar. The complementarity idea proposes that people might be attracted to people whose characteristics complement their own. For example, a masculine person and a feminine person might be attracted more than, say, two feminine people (of any actual gender mix). Even though opposite gender roles might seem complementary, in fact, people get along better when they are matched on levels of expressiveness ("femininity"); that is, matched femininity (social skill) facilitates attraction and interaction. Indeed, in direct rebuttal of the opposites-attract hypothesis, one study examined so-called fatal attractions to a partner with qualities that differed from the person or that differed from average. Descriptions of these terminated romantic relationships indicated that even when these dissimilar, unique, or extreme qualities might have been initially intriguing or appealing, those very qualities subsequently elicited disenchantment (Felmlee, 1998). Fatal attractions result between opposites, a popular theme in fiction (like our opening example).

Another possible exception would be the **exotic becomes erotic** hypothesis (Bem, 1996). This theory proposes that children's temperaments differ, suiting them to play with same-sex or opposite-sex peers. Whichever group they do not prefer as a child becomes strange to them and autonomically arousing. Thus, according to the theory, for boys who affiliate with other boys as children, girls are exotic and become arousing, first as a non-specific reaction to novelty and later as a specifically erotic reaction. The theory generates some consistent evidence for the role of childhood gender conformity and nonconformity in the development of heterosexual and homosexual orientations (Bem, 2000). It is also easy to imagine how it might apply to the fabled allure of the strange. However, other researchers object that the theory and evidence are flawed and that they fail to capture female experiences (Peplau, Garnets, Spaulding, Conley, & Veniegas, 1998, vs. Bem, 1998). The status of this theory remains an empirical question. Altogether, support is weak for people's intuition that opposites, exotics, or mysteries form the primary basis for attraction, whereas support is strong for the similarity-attraction principle.

## Explaining the Similarity-Attraction Principle

At least three models predict the similarity-attraction relationship. Byrne proposed that people like similar others because they create **positive reinforcement;** shared attitudes reaffirm and validate one's own attitudes (if we agree, I must be right), which boosts self-esteem (if I am right, I am a good person), which leads to attraction (I feel so good around you). In effect, shared values satisfy the drive to understand and be effective (our understanding and controlling motives), so the agreeing other person becomes rewarding, as a function of satisfying that drive. This explanation rests on the Western version of our core social motive of self-enhancement, that is, building one's self-esteem.

A less culturally narrow version might run: Shared attitudes reaffirm our **mutual group membership** (if we agree, we can't be so far apart), which boosts belonging (we are part of the same group), which leads to attraction as a natural by-product (group loyalty encourages attraction). As a later chapter shows, group cohesion results from mutual attraction among group members. Unfortunately, shared belonging to a mutual ingroup, as another chapter demonstrates, also catalyzes many a tragic and unjust intergroup conflict, when it pits "us" against "them." On a more personal level, however, shared attitudes imply shared ingroup belonging, which plants the seeds for romance and friendship.

Finally, shared attitudes suggest **mutual attraction**, by the principles of balance theory alone. If Diana adores Motown music, and she discovers that Smokey does too, then she can infer that he will like her. If she expects him to like her, then, by reciprocity, she will like him, as the next section shows. Attitude similarity, leading to inferred liking, predicts rewards: If Smokey agrees with Diana, she can infer that he will like her and do nice things for her.

To illustrate the impact of shared attitudes on inferred liking: In one study (Condon & Crano, 1988), college students reported their attitudes about (e.g.) politics, God, foreign movies, sexual relations, college education, child-rearing, and creativity. Two days later, they judged a person who had demonstrated perfect 100% agreement, 75%, 25%, or 0% agreement with their own attitudes. Moreover, half the students also read that the other person had seen their survey and judged them to be intelligent, knowledgeable, moral, and well-adjusted, expecting to like them and to enjoy working

**Table 7.5**   Attitude Similarity Implies Other's Attraction and Increases Own Attraction

| | Initial Evaluation by Other | | | |
| | None | | Positive | |
| Attitude Similarity | Inferred Attraction | Own Attraction | Inferred Attraction | Own Attraction |
| --- | --- | --- | --- | --- |
| 0% | 7.48 | 7.48 | 8.66 | 9.59 |
| 33% | 8.46 | 8.93 | 9.52 | 10.14 |
| 67% | 9.78 | 9.97 | 10.86 | 11.18 |
| 100% | 11.54 | 11.42 | 11.80 | 12.28 |

*Source:* From Condon & Crano, 1988. Copyright © American Psychological Association. Adapted with permission.

together. In a control condition, students received no evaluation from the stranger. Participants rated both their own liking for the other person and how much they inferred that the other person would like them. In keeping with the similarity-inferred liking hypothesis, attitude similarity did affect the stranger's inferred liking (see Table 7.5). And, as usual, people liked others with similar attitudes (again see Table 7.5). In addition, the correlation between attitude similarity and liking was .64. What's more, this correlation depended entirely on the stranger's inferred liking. That is, similarity apparently led to inferred liking, which led to attraction.

## Summary of Similarity

Similar others are familiar, safe, understandable, and probably will like us. Balance theory predicts that similarity and liking will correlate. Several explanations can account for the similarity-attraction principle: reinforcement, mutual group membership, and mutual inferred liking, to which we turn next.

## RECIPROCITY: LIKING THOSE WHO LIKE (AND ENHANCE) US

Let's hear again from governess Jane Eyre, on the topic of her fellow employee, the housekeeper:

> Mrs. Fairfax turned out to be what she appeared, a placid-tempered, kind-natured woman, of competent education and average intelligence.... I cherished toward Mrs. Fairfax a thankfulness for her kindness, and a pleasure in her society proportionate to the tranquil regard she had for me, and the moderation of her mind and character. (Brontë, 1847, p. 140)[5]

Charlotte Brontë reminds us that an average person with "moderation of mind and character" may produce "a pleasure in her society proportionate to the tranquil

[5] Copyright © Brontë Estate. Reprinted with permission.

regard" she holds for us. In the Condon and Crano study, students not only liked strangers purportedly similar to themselves, but also liked strangers who indicated that they liked them. Next to similarity, reciprocity is the most powerful predictor of attraction. The **reciprocity principle** can operate directly, as mutual liking, but it may also be mediated by way of mood and rewards, as we will see. What people view as indicating reciprocal liking—that is, what they want to reciprocate in mutual liking—may also differ by gender, for evolutionary or social structural reasons.

## Direct Reciprocity

People like others who like them, according to meta-analysis (Kenny, 1994). This robust effect occurs for several reasons. First, **social approval**—that is, being positively evaluated by others—is intrinsically rewarding. Moreover, how other people evaluate us influences how we evaluate ourselves; the sociometer hypothesis reviewed in Chapter 1 indicates that social approval serves as a barometer for self-esteem (Baumeister & Leary, 1995). Finally, social approval motivates people to fit in with their groups, so it is healthy for group survival and for individual survival in groups. One of the great social survivalists, Dale Carnegie (1936), suggests *How to Win Friends and Influence People* by, essentially, acting as if we like them: smile, listen, be genuinely interested, use the other person's name, talk about the other person's interests, and make the other person feel important. Most people like others who at least seem to like them.

Across 10 studies and over 1,000 people, for long-term acquaintances, correlations between two people's mutual liking are substantial: .52. This correlation comes to be high for three possible reasons. The **social relations model** (Kenny & LaVoie, 1984) isolates person (P), other (O), and relationship effects (P × O). For example, a P effect would be the general extent to which a given person is a liker, that is, likes people in general. If acquaintances tend to match each other's liking, it could be because acquaintances tend to match on their respective liking of others in general. (People vary in how much they are likers, who like everyone.) Two people who both like people in general may match on positivity or optimism, so trait similarity would explain this P part of the social relations reciprocity main effect. This is a perceiver effect, where two people's common positivity bias would explain their tendency to like each other (though each likes most other people too).

Or the reciprocity correlation could come from acquaintances tending to match in their respective inherent likeability. (People vary in how much they are likeable, so the pair, but everyone else too, likes each of these two likeables; this would be an O effect.) Two likable people might match on personality traits such as agreeableness or conscientiousness, which increases their being generally liked, including by each other, so a different kind of trait similarity might explain this O part of the reciprocity effect.

Finally, besides each of these two main effects (remember from Chapter 2), the dyad may like each other because of the unique combination, equivalent to the statistical interaction effect. The correlation could result from the source most people consider, that is, their mutual liking special to their relationship. (This P likes this

O, and vice versa, regardless of everyone else as perceivers or targets.) The social relations model typically studies groups in which everyone rates everyone, creating a round-robin of raters (perceivers) and targets (others), where everyone plays both roles. Whatever the underlying causes (P, O, or P × O), the reciprocity effect is large and general.

General as the reciprocity effect may be, groups of people nevertheless do not always agree in their inferences about each other's liking. That is, they differ in their interpretations of how much another person's behavior indicates attraction. For example, men may misperceive women's friendliness as sexual availability (Abbey, 1982; Edmonson & Conger, 1995). Men in general perceive more sexuality than women do, and female targets in general receive higher ratings of sexuality than male targets do. Adding together these two effects, women rated by men seem more sexual than any other combination of rater and target, and these combined effects do not occur for other types of ratings (see Table 7.6). So, while both parties may feel reciprocally positive, their meanings may differ (sexual vs. nice).

Similar cross-cultural misunderstandings can occur between Anglos and Latinos. Anglo reserve may be misperceived as unfriendly; Hispanics expect a higher baseline of friendly behavior than Anglos do, in keeping with a cultural script of **simpatia** (Triandis, Martin, Lisansky, & Betancourt, 1984). But in general, within and between groups, friendly, positive behavior elicits friendly, positive behavior and liking.

## Reciprocal Liking via Good Moods

When 99 German students (mostly women) were asked how they could tell they liked or loved someone, most of them mentioned feeling a good mood in the other person's presence (Lamm & Wiesmann, 1997). Good moods and reciprocal liking reinforce each other. Cheerfulness leads to helpful behavior, for example, donating money, blood, or time; mailing a lost letter or making a phone call for a stranger; or picking up somebody's spilled belongings. Cheerful people are also more likely to start conversations, express liking, self-disclose, cooperate, not aggress, and give positive advice. Good moods lead people to behave in a variety of sociable ways that make them more appealing to other people (Blaney, 1986; Fiske & Taylor, 2008, Ch. 14; Isen, 1987; Mayer & Salovey, 1988). Charismatic leaders may inspire positive moods

**Table 7.6**    Gender Differences in Perceived Sexuality

|  | Sexuality | Niceness |
|---|---|---|
| Male raters | 15.22 | 43.00 |
| Female raters | 13.56 | 43.56 |
| Male targets | 13.59 | 41.68 |
| Female targets | 15.19 | 57.45 |

The main effect for rater was significant for sexuality; the main effects for target were significant for sexuality and niceness. The interactions of the two independent variables (rater and target) were not significant. *Source:* From Edmonson & Conger, 1995. Copyright © Kluwer. Adapted with permission.

by contagion from their own upbeat expressions (Bono & Ilies, 2006), and positive affect contagion can benefit the workplace (Walter & Bruch, 2008).

Cheerful, outgoing, helpful people are intrinsically more attractive and additionally more likely to act on any feelings of attraction, eliciting reciprocity. Cheerful people also like (almost) everything and everyone better, again making them more attractive. Cheerful people remember happy events, so they are more likely to be pleasant company and to sustain good moods. Finally, cheerful people are flexible and creative in their ideas and open to persuasion, so they make easy and fun companions. In short, good moods are contagious and rewarding, eliciting reciprocity.

## Reciprocal Liking via Rewards

One narrow version of reciprocity is the expectation that the other person will be rewarding to oneself. This follows from one of the two core social motives in attraction being self-enhancement, manifested in feeling good. In a more utilitarian exchange view, consistent with people's core motive to have some sense of control, esteem is a commodity than can be traded for other commodities in the relationship.

Not surprisingly, then, the language and concepts of **social reinforcement** crop up throughout attraction phenomena. In **reward theories of attraction**, people feel rewarded by people who like them but also by people who make them feel good, agree with them, and look good. Indeed, besides the reward power of good looks, liking, and agreement, we like people who are merely present when we are rewarded in other ways. For example, children who won candy with two other children were more likely later to select those children as guests on a hypothetical family vacation (Lott & Lott, 1960, 1972). Students who receive bonus extra credit points with strangers reliably like those strangers better than do students who do not receive extra credit (Griffitt, 1968). In contrast, people who interact in unpleasant environments (crowded or hot, humid rooms) like each other less (Griffitt & Veitch, 1971).

In general, the impact of social rewards is clearer than the impact of social costs (Clark & Grote, 1998). As with reinforcement theory more broadly, where positive reinforcements outweigh negative ones, whose effects are more elusive, so too in attraction. The other person's unpleasant aspects, either intentional (rudeness, insensitivity) or unintentional (mannerisms, associates), do matter to both long-term and short-term satisfaction. However, people at the beginning of a relationship may hope for the best and overlook these costs, in the stage of initial attraction.

## Exception to Reciprocity? Evoking Dissonance and Playing Hard to Get

Are there exceptions to reciprocity and liking? Although people enthralled in the initial stages of attraction may overlook the costs of minor unpleasantries and rejections, moderate investment and effort can actually enhance initial attraction. In a classic experiment described briefly in Chapter 6, Aronson and Mills (1959) showed that an unpleasant initiation into a group could increase attraction to the group. In a hypothesis derived from cognitive dissonance—and often applied by fraternities—if a person chooses to incur some costs in order to join the group, the costs increase dissonance, which can be resolved by increased liking for the group. And indeed, recall from Chapter 6 that women who had to read sexually embarrassing material aloud to a male experimenter before being admitted to a discussion group subsequently liked the group better than those who read less embarrassing material or nothing.

From this, one might assume that individuals who provoke cognitive dissonance would be more attractive as well. That is, playing hard-to-get might work. (The effort in pursuing the person would be justified only if the pursuer's attraction—attitude—was quite positive; the harder the pursuit, the more attraction would have to be elevated, by this logic, to reduce the dissonance incurred.) But, as it turns out, this works only sometimes. Women who are selective about their partners (hard-to-get in general) are preferred by a man for whom they personally are not hard-to-get (Walster et al., 1973); the men like to feel that she is attracted to them specifically, a more flattering interpretation than either her being attracted to men in general, including them, or not so attracted to anyone, including them. So the hard-to-get principle again boils down to reciprocity.

### Reciprocity via Sex or Resources: Who Reciprocates What?

Men and women may differ in how readily and in what they reciprocate at the initial stages of attraction. As we will see, some evidence indicates that men tend to view sex as a medium of reciprocal liking, whereas women tend to view resources as a medium of reciprocal liking. The differences may be explained in either evolutionary or more social structural terms.

**EVOLUTIONARY PERSPECTIVES ON GENDER DIFFERENCES IN MATE PREFERENCES**    Some interpretations of evolutionary theory argue that perpetuating one's genes is best served for men by promiscuity but best served for women by stable, long-term relationships. At a minimum, women reproduce their genes by being pregnant for nine months and most typically by also caring for infants and children for many years. So, the argument runs, women will be more invested in selecting mates who will stay around and provide for them and their children. But, by this evolutionary logic, men can impregnate many women and move on. Then, by this argument, men are less adapted to long-term relationships and focus on women's apparent health as an indicator of reproductive fitness (e.g., Buss & Schmitt, 1993; but see Berry, 2000). Indeed, attractiveness and health do show a slight correlation (Rhodes, 2006), but it is not always reliable (Kalick, Zebrowitz, Langlois, & Johnson, 1998). In humans, regardless, both parents typically invest in their offspring and historically have done so, but the argument still runs that women will be more invested than men (Trivers, 1985).

Some specific hypotheses follow from this theory (Buss, 1989). Women should be choosier about their sexual partners than men are, because women bear the costs of pregnancy. By this logic, women should focus on men who have resources to support them and their joint offspring, with industriousness and earning potential as relevant cues. And men, in this view, should focus on women who have good reproductive capacity, with youth and appearance as relevant cues. Further, men can be less sure of paternity for any given child, compared to maternal certainty for women. Therefore, men should value sexual loyalty in women more than vice versa, by this logic.

When adults complete questionnaires assessing preferences in mates (Buss & Barnes, 1986), both men and women most value kindness, intelligence, and social skills. Kindness and intelligence hold as preferences across 37 cultures (Buss, 1989). This point is often lost in debates over the meaning of these provocative data. Kindness and intelligence are necessities to both men and women (Li, Bailey, Kenrick, & Linsenmeier, 2002). Also, these variables interact: Women like men who are prosocial—altruistic—as well as dominant, but dominance alone is not appealing (Jensen-Campbell, Graziano, & West, 1995).

Beyond this universal principle—namely, attraction to those who are kind and smart—come the hypothesized gender differences (Buss, 1989): Women do prefer men with resources more than vice versa; men do prefer women who are physically attractive more than vice versa; and men do worry about chastity in women more than vice versa. Similarly, meta-analyses of mate selection research (Feingold, 1992b) indicate that women value status and ambition in men more than vice versa. And men value attractiveness more than women do (see Table 7.7). Similarly, male dominance attracts attention, but female attractiveness does (Maner, DeWall, & Gailliot, 2008). Perhaps because of its correlation with status (Robinson & Smith-Lovin, 2001), a sense of humor is more valued in men than in women (who tend to act more as an appreciative audience; Bressler, Martin, & Balshine, 2006). Although status and attractiveness are viewed as necessities by each gender in designing an ideal mate (Li et al., 2002), the gender differences seem to be clearest for casual liaisons and less so for long-term relationships (Kenrick, Groth, Trost, & Sadalla, 1993).

Moreover, although both genders on average prefer mates approximately their own age, sometimes they deviate from age similarity. When they do diverge from age-mates, men tend to prefer younger women, and women tend to prefer older men

**Table 7.7**  Gender Differences in Mate Preferences

| Characteristic | Direction of Preference, Women Relative to Men |
|---|---|
| Attractiveness | −.88 |
| Social class | .69 |
| Ambitiousness | .67 |
| Character | .35 |
| Intelligence | .30 |
| Humor | .22 |
| Personality | .08 |

Positive numbers indicate that women weight the attribute higher than men do; negative numbers indicate that men weight the attribute higher than women do.
*Source:* From Feingold, 1992b. Copyright © American Psychological Association. Adapted with permission.

(Kenrick & Keefe, 1992). An evolutionary perspective could argue that men prefer to invest in women with a longer reproductive life in front of them, whereas women prefer men who have accumulated resources with age. These kinds of gender differences are described as **sexual selection**, as apart from natural selection. Sexual selection reflects different pressures on the two genders, based on differing sexual reproductive pressures, and results in different mating strategies.

Some warnings are in order. These gender differences may result from the forced-choice format of the questions themselves (DeSteno, Bartlett, Braverman, & Salovey, 2002). That is, when people are not forced to choose which would be worse, sexual or emotional infidelity, the gender differences predicted by evolutionary approaches disappear in questions asked in other formats. When asked to report their jealousy, men and women do not differ when they respond on automatic; both have a knee-jerk reaction that sexual infidelity is worse. But when women reflect on it, they apparently assume that emotional infidelity would probably involve sexual infidelity as well, making it upsetting on two counts and therefore worse (DeSteno & Salovey, 1996). In situations requiring little thought, evolutionary holdovers (gender differences) should be most apparent, but they are not, suggesting a role for socialization and culture.

**SOCIAL STRUCTURAL PERSPECTIVES ON GENDER DIFFERENCES IN MATE PREFERENCES**   While these mating preferences fit some evolutionary hypotheses about sexual selection, they also fit hypotheses about gender differences within the social structure, as reflected by available resources (Caporael, 1989; Eagly & Wood, 1999). That is, if women typically have fewer resources, they might well care more about whether their mates do. If men typically have more resources, they could well afford preferring an attractive mate more than women could. That is, maybe everyone prefers an attractive mate, but men have been better positioned to express that preference. Similarly, gender differences in the age of preferred mates also fit the social structure analysis. From a structural perspective, men's ability as resource provider becomes clearer with age, and women's relative youth would preserve traditional gender roles that cede more power to men.

More broadly (Eagly & Wood, 1999), the social structural theory recognizes a typical division of labor and gender hierarchy, which may well result from women's greater physical investment in child-bearing and nursing, coupled with average gender differences in size and strength. Status differences result from men's greater control and aggression, as well as women's greater orientation toward cooperation and nurturing. Typical roles result: women's stereotypical **communal roles**, emphasizing cooperation and care for others, along with men's stereotypical **agentic roles**, emphasizing competition and providing resources for others. As social structures develop, gender roles shape people's preferences along traditional gender lines.

Compelling evidence for the role of social structure comes from correlations that indicate clusters of traditional, conservative gender preferences, such as for preferred age and provider/homemaker roles. That is, some people subscribe to these views more than others, and their attitudes (preferences) tend to go together, along a more traditional or progressive direction (Eastwick et al., 2006).

As with individuals, so with societies: The United Nations publishes a gender empowerment measure, ranking societies on the degree of political and financial disparity between men and women; a similar United Nations measure of gender development reflects gender disparities in health, education, and money. These measures correlate substantially (.20 to .70) with mate preferences regarding age, resources, and homemaking skills (Eagly & Wood, 1999). Moreover, the same United Nations measures correlate, across countries, with measures of sexism (Glick et al., 2000). These correlations reinforce the argument that social structure can account for many gender differences, at least as well as evolutionary pressures can. Both evolutionary and social structural accounts are theories that can generate testable hypotheses, and research will yield more progress than merely accepting or rejecting the plausibility of these controversial theories without supporting data.

## Summary of Reciprocity

People like others who like them. The reciprocity principle can operate directly because of people matching on either a general propensity to like others or to be likeable. Or people may simply reciprocate a particular relationship. Reciprocity can operate by way of good moods; liking makes people cheerful, and cheery people are both attracted and attractive to others. Reciprocity can operate by way of rewards; mutual liking indicates that people will benefit each other. Withholding reciprocal liking (playing hard-to-get) does not work well. Men and women may differ in their priorities for the medium of reciprocal exchange. That is, men may be more likely to prioritize sexual availability and women to prioritize resources as indicators of reciprocal attraction. Both evolutionary and social structural theories can explain these differences in who prefers to reciprocate what.

## CHAPTER SUMMARY

The chapter opened with a quotation from Frazier's *Cold Mountain* about initial attraction, but that attraction had an unfortunate end. *Jane Eyre*, our other running example, did better, but not without some tragedy along the way. Let's move from tragic fiction to idealized fantasy for our chapter summary, providing a more hopeful outlook.

We can summarize the social psychology of attraction by designing the ideal first date: Using well-known principles, how would one create a social situation to maximize attraction? Attraction, defined as an attitude, consists of a positive evaluation, as well as cognitions and behaviors to match. So, dating can be a form of persuasion. Knowing that attraction serves core social motives of understanding and self-enhancing, one's overall goal would be to make the other person feel that one is known and knowable, as well as good for the other person's sense of self. Attraction principles therefore revolve around familiarity. What is familiar is reassuring: both understood and self-affirming.

So, on the perfect date, how can one make oneself familiar? Beforehand, frequency of exposure can increase liking. Running into each other (allegedly by chance, of course) results from proximity; that is, living or sitting near each other, for example. So, for starters, one can arrange chance encounters, without seeming overeager, of course. Beyond mere exposure and proximity—the foundations of familiarity—physical attractiveness does matter. Even though we all know better than to judge books by their covers, people's appearance does matter, especially to perceived social skills. Thus, on that first date, one would be well-advised to look as good as possible.

Similarity attracts, so discovering and emphasizing commonalities increases attraction. Talking about joint interests, therefore, makes strategic sense. Engaging in shared activities makes sense. Making links to friends in common makes sense. Arguing about politics makes no sense.

Finally, reciprocity. Making the other person feel liked will increase the odds that the person will like you. People like to be liked. So, letting the other person know one's positive feelings, in appropriate ways, of course, makes sense. Being cheerful and rewarding also makes one more likeable. Likewise, arranging to go to a cheery, upbeat movie might make more sense than a depressing movie. Attending a home-team winning sports event, rather than a losing event, probably bodes better for that first date. A sense of humor, however, may compensate for the pall of unavoidable losses. If you are interested in attracting a man, appearance matters; if you are interested in attracting a woman, status matters. For both genders, displaying kindness and intelligence is important. (There is no reason to suppose that same-sex romantic attraction would differ.)

Drawing on people's core motives to understand and self-affirm, then, familiarity, appearance, similarity, and reciprocity all attract. These principles return in a later chapter on prejudice and intergroup relations: People like the familiar, similar, loyal ingroup better than the unfamiliar, dissimilar, separate outgroup.

From attraction can come close relationships. The next chapter indicates the many complexities of intimacy that build on initial attraction. Without attraction, intimacy cannot begin. Nevertheless, enduring close relationships introduce new principles that differ from initial attraction.

## SUGGESTIONS FOR FURTHER READING

BERSCHEID, E., & REIS, H. T. (1998). Attraction and close relationships. In D. T. GILBERT, S. T. FISKE, & G. LINDZEY (Eds.), *Handbook of social psychology* (4th ed., Vol. 2, pp. 193–281). New York: McGraw-Hill.

FEHR, B. (1996). *Friendship processes*. Thousand Oaks, CA: Sage.

LEARY, M. R. (2010). Affiliation, acceptance, and belonging: The pursuit of interpersonal connection In S. T. FISKE, D. T. GILBERT, & G. LINDZEY (Eds.), *Handbook of social psychology* (5th ed., in press). New York: Wiley.

# Chapter 8

# Close Relationships: Passion, Interdependence, Commitment, and Intimacy

Marie loved me and I loved her, but we never called what we felt by the sweet and terrible name of "love." Perhaps it was not exactly love, though there was something of that in it. What was it? It was something big and noble, a marvelous tenderness and an immense happiness. I mean happiness unalloyed, pure and as yet untroubled by desire. Perhaps it was more happiness than love, though the one cannot exist without the other. I could not touch Marie by the hand without trembling. I could not feel the light touch of her hair without being deeply moved. Happiness and passion! (Laye, 1954, p. 162)[1]

This chapter considers close relationships, "sweet and terrible." Friendship, romance, marriage, and family all entail some common experiences. First, we will address how social psychologists conceptually and operationally define close relationships, which go beyond initial attraction by potentially including passion, interdependence, commitment, and intimacy. We consider relationships across a range of ages and cultures. The core social motives (especially controlling, trusting, belonging, and understanding) will enter in. Using various combinations of the core motives, three main research approaches capture the frameworks that social psychologists use to study close relationships: **interdependence** (relying on each other, which entails controlling and trusting), **attachment** (secure links to others through belonging and trusting), and **social norms** (unwritten societal rules for belonging and understanding).

---

[1] Copyright © Farrar, Straus, & Giroux. Reprinted with permission.

## WHAT IS A CLOSE RELATIONSHIP?

Everyone cherishes strong opinions about the nature of love, intimacy, and friendship, yet people do not necessarily agree about them. Some nonpsychologists are even offended by the idea of studying, quantifying, and predicting the course of relationships. Yet relationships entail social beings interacting with other social beings, and as such, we know a lot about how they operate and can provide some insight into healthier ones. Social psychologists have clarified key ingredients of closeness, analyzing what works both conceptually and operationally and getting at some of the dimensions so important to all of us in love, friendship, and family.

### Conceptual Definitions

**Close relationships** involve people interacting with and influencing each other, for a while, with a mutual understanding of intimacy and the potential for strong feelings (Berscheid & Reis, 1998; Brehm, 1992; Harvey & Pauwels, 1999). As just noted, the main sections of this chapter will reflect these components: interdependence (relying on each other) entails interaction and mutual influence; attachment presupposes mutually linking the self to the close other; social norms describe people's mutual understanding; and all enable potentially intense emotions. The core social motives enter variously into each research area. But, before delving into theory and research, consider the concept of close relationships in more detail.

As a relationship develops beyond mere attraction (liking another and wanting a relationship; Chapter 7), close relationships engage people far more complexly. Consider French Guinean author Camara Laye and his friend Marie's tender happiness, a major development beyond mere attraction. Recall from the last chapter that because attraction looms so large for people, it tends to be expressed only if positive, with people reluctant to report disliking, and indeed, reluctant to express attraction too directly, at least initially. As attraction develops into relationship, its qualities become delightfully or tragically more complex: The feelings range in intensity, variability, variety, and ambivalence, each worth elaborating here.

Compared with initial attraction and especially compared with attitudes toward most nonhuman objects, people's feelings about close others intensify and vary (though one's pet, computer, or car comes close). Relationships range in **intensity** and physiological arousal, even without a sexual component, which of course entails its own intensity and arousal. Whereas relationships show **variability** as people's needs change or as the other person responds differently to those needs, most ordinary attitudes in contrast normally assume stability.

What's more, feelings about other people involve more dimensions than simply good-bad, the bipolar evaluative core of attitudes and attraction. In close relationships, even positive feelings differ in quality: respect, nurturance, liking, and lust. Feelings about close others come in all **varieties** (Berscheid, 1985).

Also, feelings about close others frequently involve **affective disharmony** (heterogeneity). That is, another person feels good to us on some dimensions and bad to us on others. While **ambivalence** also can hold for common attitudes, the affective heterogeneity in close relationships is far more complex and matters far more.

Overall, intensity, variance, variety, and ambivalence add up to relationships rich in complexity, though knowable, nonetheless. Researchers have defined them in many ways, but one useful framework particularly speaks to the complex, special nature of close relationships: potentials for passion, interdependence, commitment, and intimacy (Aron & Westbay, 1996). We examine each in turn.

**PASSION: POTENTIAL FOR EMOTION IN RELATIONSHIPS**    Consider this example:

> Margaret had never seen anything like it in her life. The man slammed the door shut, turned on the ignition, then there was a cloud of dust. First one goat jumped out of the road. Then six, seven or eight more. People jumped. Both people and goats looked outraged. He kept on smiling. He was royalty, the son of a chief. He'd grown up making goats and people jump. It was nothing. By the time the van swooped up a hill towards a small building she was white around the mouth from shock. . . . The man frightened her deeply. . . . A big black scorpion, disturbed by their entry, scuttled with angry speed across the room, its tail poised alertly to strike. . . .
>
> "I am afraid of the scorpions," she said.
>
> He turned round slowly.
>
> "I knew you were going to say that," he said, as though he were talking to an old friend, whose faults and failings were quite well known to him. But there was a trick to him, some shocking, unexpected magic. A moment ago he had been a hateful, arrogant man. Now, he had another face which made him seem the most beautiful person on earth. It was only his eyes, as though a stormy sky had cleared. What was behind was a rainbow of dazzling light. Though unaware of any feeling, something inside her chest went "bang!" Her mouth silently shaped the word: "Oh," and she raised her hand towards her heart. (Head, 1971, pp. 28–30)[2]

The scary car ride, the fright associated with the scorpion, and then the sudden relief at a man who will eliminate the danger—is that "some shocking unexpected magic"? Could fear turn into love?

Surprisingly, some social psychology emotion theories make precisely this prediction. Recall from Chapter 3, Schachter's **two-factor theory of emotion:** unexplained arousal plus cognitive labels from the situation. That chapter illustrated Schachter's theory by using Dutton and Aron's (1974) study, in which young men aroused by fear—due to a wobbly suspension bridge—subsequently felt attracted to a nice-looking young woman they met immediately afterward. Initial attraction followed from fear.

Yes, but do this finding and this theory generalize to common dating scenarios? **Passion** may be defined as a strong emotion of sexual attraction, so let us confine ourselves to romantic relationships for the moment. Should romantic hopefuls

---

[2] Copyright © Bessie Head estate. Reprinted with permission.

attempt to scare the daylights out of their dates to increase passion? Researchers (Zillmann, Weaver, Mundorf, & Aust, 1986) attempted to find out, by showing a horror film to men and women in the presence of an opposite-sex companion, a confederate of the experimenters, who was physically appealing or not (first independent variable). Participants watched 14 minutes of *Friday the 13th, Part 3*, in which a homicidal maniac murders several friends, then terrorizes, pursues, and attacks a young woman in a deserted farm house. While watching the terrifying movie, the participant's opposite-sex companion affected distress, indifference, or mastery (second independent variable).

The two independent variables showed an interaction effect: Men who were initially appealing did not need the movie to maintain their appeal; they were attractive anyway. Unappealing men, however, could enhance their appeal by masterful behavior during the movie, completely compensating for their initial lack of attractiveness. Moreover, the women acquiesced most to the masterful man, perhaps because they were intimidated or perhaps because they admired him. Like the car-ride excerpt from South African Bessie Head's book, women's fear transformed into attraction when the man mastered the danger. Comparable effects did not emerge for men; they typically enjoyed the movie more than women did, especially in the presence of a distressed woman, who perhaps heightened their arousal during the movie, but her distress did not make her more attractive. This study suggests that gender roles prevail, at least during horror movies. But the broader point remains: Fear can increase attraction in a date-like situation.

Arousal from one source—a wobbly bridge, a scary movie, a reckless ride—can transfer from fear to attraction or can intensify attraction. Whether or not this result would generalize to ongoing romantic relationships, arousal can indeed intensify affect (Berscheid, 1994). The potential for emotion enters into all close relationships, not just romantic ones. As people move from superficial attraction to entwined lives, the potential for emotion will be evident in all the theories we will encounter.

## INTERDEPENDENCE: RELYING ON EACH OTHER'S BEHAVIOR
Another example:

> As a young woman I believed that passion must surely fade with age, just
> as a cup left standing in a room will gradually give up its contents to the
> air. But when [my lifelong lover] and I returned to my apartment, we drank
> each other up with so much yearning and need that afterward I felt myself
> drained of all the things [he] had taken from me, and yet filled with all that
> I had taken from him. (Golden, 1998, p. 427)[3]

In relationships, people rely on each other, giving all the things we also take from each other. **Interdependence** means that each person's goals depend on both people's behavior; what each partner does affects the other (Kelley et al., 1983; Rusbult & Van Lange, 1996). Figure 8.1 shows one chain of events between two mutually attracted people who may be building toward a close relationship. The goal (finding

---

[3] Copyright © Knopf. Reprinted with permission.

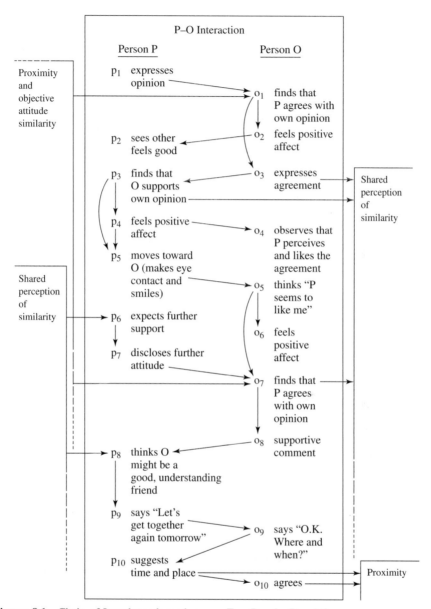

**Figure 8.1**  Chain of Interdependence between Two People, P and O

*Source:* Kelley et al., 1983. Copyright © Ellen Berscheid. Reprinted with permission.

a good friend) is facilitated by proximity and attitude similarity. Over time, people's mutual influences can facilitate (help) or interfere with (hinder) each other's outcomes—matters as trivial as what television show to watch or as important as emotional support. **Outcomes** can be tangible (groceries, money, possessions) or intangible (time, status, esteem). Although this might seem like a crass, economic view of relationships, interdependence does create the potential for intense emotions, as the literary excerpt and a later section will show.

Ordinarily, one's outcomes in life can depend on oneself (which Thibaut & Kelley, 1959, term **reflexive control**), another person (**fate control**), or both people together (**behavior control**). Interdependence refers to the third case, in which each person's behavior affects the other, as in any joint project or intertwined relationship. Interdependence varies in kind (choosing a TV show versus providing support) and pattern (mutual behavior control can occur with or without some unilateral fate control). Interdependent people can facilitate or block each other's goals, and one person may have more control than the other, over longer and shorter periods of time.

High interdependence is closeness. To define **closeness**, the most crucial variables comprise the strength, frequency, and diversity of interdependence. **Strength** refers to how much, how quickly, and how reliably one person influences the other. **Frequency** defines the sheer number of interconnections, and **diversity** describes the span of domains. A couple who collaborate on work, cooperate as parents, and share avocations will be more interdependent and close than a couple whose work does not overlap, who trade off parenting, and who relax independently.

While this definition of closeness may seem cold-blooded (as if each partner asks, "What have you done for me lately?"), the outcomes in question are not limited to raw self-interest. A valued outcome might include growth in the relationship or the other partner's happiness. This is called the **transformation** of the individual's outcome matrix to include the interests of the other person and the relationship. While interdependence increases perceived closeness, longevity, and positive feelings, of course depending on another person also creates the possibility of disappointment and negative feelings. We will come back to this point.

**COMMITMENT: INTENT TO CONTINUE**    "Commitment summarizes the nature of an individual's dependence on a partner, and represents broad, long-term orientation toward a relationship" (Rusbult & Buunk, 1993, p. 175). **Commitment** reflects wanting to maintain the relationship, wanting it to last a long time, and orienting toward the long-term future (Rusbult, Martz, & Agnew, 1998). In short, commitment reflects an intent to continue the relationship.

Commitment partly depends on whether people feel they are getting what they deserve from the relationship. A later section elaborates, but for now, the role of **comparison level** is most relevant. "This concept refers to the tendency of people to compare their obtained outcomes with the level of outcomes they believe they deserve from the relationship. This comparison is often made with the outcomes other persons are experiencing" (Kelley, 1979, p. 58). When people's outcomes exceed their comparisons, then they feel satisfied, but when their outcomes fall below, they feel dissatisfied. People may also compare their outcomes in the current relationship with those they might experience in other relationships, a concept termed **comparison level for alternatives**. Clearly, both comparison level and comparison level for alternatives contribute to people's commitment in the relationship.

Interdependence and commitment in a relationship fit with a cognitive view of self-in-relationship (Agnew, Van Lange, Rusbult, & Langston, 1998). Interdependent, committed selves merge, as the next component indicates.

**INTIMACY: SELF IN OTHER AND OTHER IN SELF**    **Intimacy** entails feeling understood and validated by the partner's responses. Intimacy is conceptually distinct from interdependence. People can be interdependent (close) without being intimate, as when one depends on someone but nevertheless feels misunderstood. Intimacy takes time:

> I have now been married ten years. I know what it is to live entirely for and with what I love best on earth. I hold myself supremely blest—blest beyond what language can express; because I am my husband's life as fully as he is mine. No woman was ever nearer to her mate than I am: ever more absolutely bone of his bone and flesh of his flesh. I know no weariness of [his] society: he knows none of mine, any more than we each do of the pulsation of the heart that beats in our separate bosoms; consequently, we are ever together. To be together is for us to be at once as free as in solitude, as gay as in company. We talk, I believe, all day long: to talk to each other is but a more animated and an audible thinking. All my confidence is bestowed on him, all his confidence is devoted to me. (Brontë, 1847, pp. 475–476)[4]

Being "ever together," intimacy is a process, not an outcome. Partners interact, respond to each other, and come to feel understood, validated, and cared for (Reis & Patrick, 1996; Reis & Shaver, 1988). The **intimacy process** begins when one person expresses personally revealing feelings or information and continues if the other person responds empathically. Being together and talking ("all day long"), self-disclosing ("all my confidence"), creates the conditions for intimacy. **Self-disclosure**, revealing oneself to another person, enhances liking, according to meta-analysis (Collins & Miller, 1994). Liking and self-disclosure make a mutually reinforcing system: People disclose more to people they like, naturally, but people also like others better as a result of disclosing to them. Plus, people like others who self-disclose. Mutual self-disclosure parallels and encourages the developing relationship (Derlega, Metts, Petronio, & Margulis, 1993; Reis & Shaver, 1988). People who appropriately lower their boundaries to reveal themselves can foster the overlap of self and other.

One of the most intimate of relationships, being in love, blurs boundaries between self and other, as the Brontë example illustrates. People's representations of themselves change in close relationships, as they **include the other in the self** (Aron, Aron, Tudor, & Nelson, 1991; Aron, Paris, & Aron, 1995). Their resources, perspectives, and characteristics overlap with the close other, so they merge lives.

Because relationships blur the mental boundary between self and other, but self and other are contained in separate skins, continuing the close relationship requires **minding** it (Harvey & Omarzu, 1997). Minding entails several aspects: getting to know the other; understanding the other's motivations and dispositions; and reciprocating thoughts, feelings, and behavior. The opposite of minding is taking for granted, not a good strategy for continuing a close relationship.

---

[4] Copyright © Brontë estate. Reprinted with permission.

## Operational Definitions

If passionate emotions, interdependent behavior, committed intent, and overlapping self-concept together constitute close relationships, how have researchers studied these complex affective, behavioral, and cognitive riches?

Most often, relationships research has surveyed dating couples, recruited from college campuses or newspaper ads, but participants also include married couples, and sometimes couples seeking therapy. The results are usually global, descriptive, and correlational. Sometimes, observational research may study married or dating couples in the laboratory or even in their homes. Occasionally, relationships researchers can also conduct experiments. Causal hypotheses require experiments using fine-grained methods. Although often experimental participants are limited to strangers, hardly the best venue for studying enduring, intimate relationships, sometimes researchers will recruit established couples and manipulate the type of interaction they have (e.g., Murray, Rose, Bellavia, Holmes, & Kusche, 2002).

Various measures operationalize specific cognitive, emotional, and behavioral aspects of relationships. Almost all use self-report measures. For example, cognition about overlapping self-concept has been measured by a scale of relationship closeness: the Inclusion of Other in the Self Scale (Aron, Aron, & Smollan, 1992). As Figure 8.2 indicates, the scale consists entirely of a series of Venn-like diagrams showing two circles (selves) that overlap to varying degrees; participants circle whichever of the seven pairs best describes their relationship. The scale predicted which relationships were intact three months later, with a good-sized correlation of .46. More cognitive representation of overlap predicts more endurance.

Similarly, for affect: Passionate emotions in relationships have been studied mostly by self-report, for example (Berscheid, Snyder, & Omoto, 1989), "How frequently have you felt elated?" (from 1 = *never* to 7 = *almost always*). That measure of emotions in close relationships includes a total of 27 emotions, both positive and negative, more and less intense.

Turning to behavior, let's see how interdependence can be represented as a matrix of people's outcomes in a particular domain of the relationship. Take, for example,

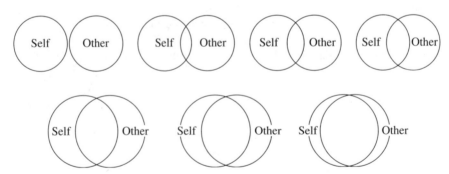

**Figure 8.2**    Including the Other in the Self, a Scale of Self-Concept Closeness

*Source:* Aron et al., 1992. Copyright © American Psychological Association. Reprinted with permission.

cleaning a shared apartment. UCLA researchers asked young heterosexual couples in relationships of at least three months' duration:

> Assume that you and your partner share an apartment. Cleaning it is a disagreeable job, but it has reached a point where it must be done. However, each of you has other time-consuming things to do (work, study, etc.). Rate each of the following possible events as to the degree of satisfaction or dissatisfaction you would feel (from −10, *very dissatisfied*, to +10, *very satisfied*).

- Both of you clean.
- You clean and your partner does other things.
- You do other things and your partner cleans.
- You both do other things.

Figure 8.3 shows the average matrix of each person's satisfaction. For example, female partners react more strongly if both partners clean (8.3) or both do not (−4.0) than male partners do (6.8 and −3.1, respectively). In effect, women report caring more about joint cleaning activity than men do. Both genders are upset if traditional gender roles are violated (i.e., the man cleans, and the woman does not), but women are surprisingly more upset (−2.6) than men (−1.1). (Maybe she feels guilty? Judges his cleaning to be inadequate?) If traditional gender roles are observed (the woman cleans, and the man does not), men are somewhat satisfied (0.9) and women are neutral (0.2) (Kelley, 1979). Before assuming that this example is outdated (as my students did), you should know that more recent research corroborates the continuing inequality in gender roles with regard to parenting and household tasks (e.g., Biernat & Wortman, 1991; Crosby, 1991; Deutsch & Saxon, 1998; Epstein, 2007; Kobrynowicz & Biernat, 1997), although things are slowly improving, at least for upper social classes (Deutsch, 1999, 2001; Massey, 2007). Gay couples, by the way, are more egalitarian (Peplau & Fingerhut, 2007).

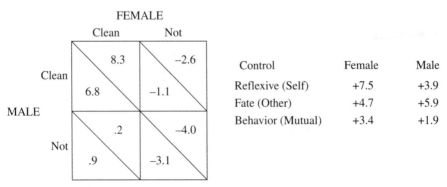

| Control | Female | Male |
|---|---|---|
| Reflexive (Self) | +7.5 | +3.9 |
| Fate (Other) | +4.7 | +5.9 |
| Behavior (Mutual) | +3.4 | +1.9 |

**Figure 8.3**  Outcome Matrix in Interdependence Theory

*Source:* Kelley, 1979. Copyright © Erlbaum. Adapted with permission.

The point of the outcome matrices is that researchers can represent different contingencies of satisfaction. Reflexive control describes how much difference on average the female partner (for example) can make in her own outcomes by unilaterally varying her own behavior; her reflexive control calculated from this example averages 7.5. (The man's is 3.9.) The matrices also allow researchers to calculate fate control, how much on average her outcomes are affected by her partner's unilateral behavior choices (4.7) and vice versa (5.9). Finally, mutual behavior control describes the extent to which each is affected by their joint, combined actions (the woman, 3.4; the man, 1.9). Mutual behavior control, the impact of mutual dependence, operationalizes interdependence.

Interdependent behavior also is measured by means of a simpler self-report questionnaire, for example, the Relationships Closeness Inventory (described later). Thus, most measures—whether affective, behavioral, or cognitive—operationalize aspects of relationships via self-report, a reasonable technique.

## Variations: Love, Family, and Friendship across Culture, Age, Gender, and Sexual Orientation

Most relationship research conducted in North America has focused on romantic relationships, but researchers also study friendships and family relations. Friendships sometimes lead to romantic relationships, and romantic relationships sometimes lead to families, but of course friendships and families also exist independently of romance.

**ROMANTIC LOVE AND MARRIAGE**   In North America, **romantic relationships** involve strong feelings, interdependent behavior, committed intent, and overlapping self-concept—dimensions shared with other close relationships. But, compared with other kinds of close relationships, romance especially involves passion and exclusive commitment. In romance, the feelings are stronger, and the interdependence is more exclusive and committed.

According to one theory (Sternberg, 1986), love has three components noted by others already named here:

- Intimacy (feeling close, connected, and bonded, as in interdependent behavior and the overlapping self-concept)
- Passion (romance, physical and sexual attraction, as in strong emotions)
- Commitment (deciding about and maintaining love)

Although other theorists separate intimacy (overlapping self-concepts) and interdependence (influencing each other's behavior), as we have seen, the unique contribution of this **triangular theory of love** is to name eight kinds of love, allowing for all combinations. For example, mere liking (that death knell of any dating relationship) consists of intimacy without passion or commitment. Purely romantic love consists of intimacy and passion without commitment. Consummate love consists of all three. Table 8.1 lists all the combinations, including some combinations describing other kinds of relationships that may be more frequent in other cultures.

**Table 8.1**  A Triangular Theory of Love

| Kind of love | Intimacy | Passion | Decision/Commitment |
| --- | --- | --- | --- |
| Nonlove | − | − | − |
| Liking | + | − | − |
| Infatuated love | − | + | − |
| Empty love | − | − | + |
| Romantic love | + | + | − |
| Companionate love | + | − | + |
| Fatuous love | − | + | + |
| Consummate love | + | + | + |

+ = component present; − = component absent
*Source:* Sternberg, 1986. Copyright American Psychological Association. Reprinted with permission.

As noted, most U.S. researchers' definitions of close relationships have focused on romantic relationships. Romantic love (i.e., intimacy and passion) as a basis for marriage has traditionally preoccupied Western researchers. This preoccupation reflects cultural differences in traditional expectations about marriage (M. H. Bond & Smith, 1996; Smith & Bond, 1994). Because Western cultures tend to be more independent and individualist, people's dispositions are presumed to drive their behavior, as Chapter 3 described. Thus, romantic love presumably motivates marriage; the free choices of two mutually attracted individuals drive the commitment. But this Western perspective is not the only possible view.

How does romance look across cultures? In more interdependent, collectivist settings, social networks motivate marriages. Families play an active, if not determining, role picking marriage partners in many traditional societies. Arranged marriages are not uncommon still, in much of the world. Before dismissing arranged marriages, consider the possibility that, in a given cultural context, they have some advantages. Families may arrange for the financial, social, and emotional well-being of their young-adult children. What results may range from Sternberg's **companionate love** (intimacy and commitment, but not much passion) to **empty love** (commitment without passion or intimacy), **fatuous love** (passion and commitment without intimacy), or possibly **consummate love** (all three). Of course, commitment before intimacy and passion flies in the face of Western proclivities. But traditionalists would argue that, with a 50% divorce rate and a seven-year average length for U.S. marriages, can modern Western methods necessarily claim superiority?

Traditional forms of matchmaking are on the wane in most cultures, as modern expectations about marriage confer more choice on the romantic couple. However, gender-role traditionalism for marriage may be higher, for example, in China (Chen, Fiske, & Lee, in press; Lee, Fiske, & Glick, in press), creating norms for less self-disclosure and intimacy in romantic relationships (Marshall, 2008). Even within the United States, different people's ideal romantic involvements vary from more intimate to more superficial and from more romantic to more practical (Rusbult, Onizuka, & Lipkus, 1993). Thus, individuals from every culture may vary in how romantic (passionate and intimate) or companionate (intimate and committed) they prefer their love relationships. So, too, for other demographic differences. Age, for example, predicts a greater focus on companionate love (Bulcroft & O'Connor, 1986). Being a gay man promotes a focus on sexuality, whereas being a lesbian focuses more on companionate issues of intimacy and commitment (Peplau & Fingerhut, 2007). Otherwise, though, the relationship dynamics of homosexual couples closely resemble those of heterosexual ones.

**FRIENDSHIP**    Many types of close relationships emphasize confiding and self-disclosure, but **friendship** especially does so (Fehr, 1996). Family relationships more likely provide concrete assistance, and romantic relationships provide passion and exclusivity, whereas friendship includes egalitarian and cooperative norms.

In the United States and Canada, the nature of friendship varies by age (Blieszner & Adams, 1992; Fehr, 1996; Newcomb & Bagwell, 1995). Childhood friends play, share, and don't hit; their friendship entails intense socializing, resolving conflicts, performing effectively, and reciprocal, intimate affiliation. In college, "play, share, and don't hit" transforms to "hang out, help, and don't betray." Mutual confiding becomes central as well. College friendship networks are likely to be large (especially for women), intimate, age-segregated, and demographically homogeneous.

Adults have fewer friends and more relationships that are not as intimate or important, but adults' friends are more varied with regard to age and circumstances. Like children and college students, adults expect friends they can enjoy (the adult version of play, hang out) and trust (adult versions of don't hit, don't betray), but direct sharing or helping matters less than intimacy. Older adults, who may be retired and less mobile, tend to have smaller, homogeneous, age-segregated friendships and fewer casual contacts; the immediate environment (institution or neighborhood) matters more, as mobility decreases.

Gender differences in friendship norms suggest that women prefer greater intimacy—self-disclosure, communication, and support—but men prefer shared activities (Reis, Senchak, & Solomon, 1985; Sapadin, 1988). Women as friends with either men or other women tend to increase relationship intimacy.

Cross-cultural perspectives on friendship are limited, but some illustrative differences show that the Western models are not the only possible, healthy styles. As with romantic relationships, choice in friendship may be subsumed under collectivist concerns. For a person who is born, raised, and expects to stay in the same village or company over a lifetime, many significant relationships are involuntary, stable, and good enough (Ho, 1998). Whether harmonious or not, the relationship created by social structures must endure. To the extent that a friendship emerges, more collectivist people have fewer, closer, more sensitive friendships, which are bound by implicit rules about intimacy (Verkuyten & Masson, 1996). Cultures differ in what people value in a friend: British respondents may desire friends who are funny and sensitive, whereas Chinese respondents may desire friends who are creative and money-minded (Goodwin & Tang, 1991). Kindness, sociability, and sensitivity are common dimensions in friendship across cultures.

**FAMILY RELATIONSHIPS**    Social psychologists tend not to study family relationships so often. However, family relationships clearly differ from romance and
friendship. Whereas friendship includes egalitarian and cooperative norms, family
does not. **Families** entail clear authority relationships, as well as communal sharing
relationships (A. P. Fiske, 1992). More often than friendships and romantic relationships, family relationships provide concrete assistance. Unlike romantic relationships,
families do not operate by passion and dyadic exclusivity.

Cross culturally, families may matter more in interdependent, relational, collectivist cultures than in independent, individualistic ones. For example, in Confucian
thought, the five cardinal relationships are (in order): ruler and minister, father and
son, husband and wife, brothers, and friends (Ho, 1998). Note that three of the five
are family, and all deemphasize women. The father-son relationship dominates the
family, with the husband-wife relationship secondary; both entail significant authority
relationships. In contrast, in U.S. families, the husband-wife relationship dominates,
and it entails relatively egalitarian standing. In East Asian cultures, most relationships
typically dominate individual preferences, and respective roles within the relationship
guide and constrain behavior to a greater degree than in Western contexts.

Warning: All these cultural variations—in love, friends, and family—provide
only an approximate flavor, not absolute differences in relationships. People's
individual endorsements of cultural values matter more than where they live.
Some individualists live in collectivist cultures and vice versa. Nevertheless, across
individuals and cultures, people apparently all believe that their own relationships
are better than other people's (Endo, Heine, & Lehman, 2000; Martz et al., 1998;
Van Lange & Rusbult, 1995).

## Core Social Motives

**BELONGING**    Some universal themes endure across cultures: People enter into
close relationships to satisfy core social motives to belong with other people, whether
one special person in a romantic relationship or best friendship or a small tight cluster
of people in a family. A sense of belonging is adaptive. People not in close relationships more often become ill with cancer and heart disease, suffer damaged immune
systems, and risk dying; "the age-adjusted mortality risk of social isolation exceeds
the comparable risk for cigarette smoking" (Berscheid & Reis, 1998, p. 245). Of
course, the causality could go either way, namely, relationships could protect one's
health (as implied), health could promote relationships, or third variables (positive
outlook, financial security, pleasant location) could encourage both physical health
and relationships. Anyway, the link between social ties and mortality is independent
of initial health and health practices, such as smoking, drinking, exercising, and getting checkups (Berkman & Syme, 1979). Perhaps people whose mortality is salient
to them are not wrong to express higher levels of commitment (Florian, Mikulincer,
& Herschberger, 2002). The advantages of belonging will come up in theories of
attachment and of social norms.

**TRUSTING** Apart from the broad general need to belong with particular other people, the predisposition to trust other people facilitates close relationships. Trusting, in close relationships, includes predictability, dependability, and faith (Rempel, Holmes, & Zanna, 1985). As Chapter 1 noted, not everyone is trustworthy, and overly gullible people can be hurt. Nevertheless, trusting people have higher self-esteem; they like other people and are themselves well-liked; they cheat or steal less often, and they are less suspicious, vindictive, resentful, and lonely (Gurtman, 1992; Murray & Holmes, 1993; Murray, Holmes, & Griffin, 2000; Rotenberg, 1994; Rotter, 1980). Trust allows others to influence one's lot in life (Murray, Holmes, Griffin, Bellavia, & Rose, 2001; Murray, Rose, Bellavia, Holmes, & Kusche, 2002). One version of trust, harmony with others, entails letting others decide and correlates with letting a higher power or luck impact one's life (Morling & Fiske, 1999). Trust balances dependency and risk of rejection (Murray, Holmes, & Collins, 2006). People regulate this risk by (a) appraising partner acceptance or rejection, (b) signaling to self through gratified or hurt feelings and changed self-esteem, and finally (c) regulating dependence as a result. Well-regulated trust is crucial to both the interdependence and attachment of close relationships.

**CONTROLLING** Controlling one's own experiences also matters deeply. Trusting and controlling balance each other in close relationships, as the section on attachment will note. People's need to control their relationship outcomes figures prominently in the emotions they experience, as the interdependence theory argues in the next section. (Understanding comes up mainly in accounts of relationships norms, at the end of the chapter.)

## Summary of Definitions, Variations, and Motives

Close relationships pick up from initial attraction, when it matures into people interacting and influencing each other, for a while, with a mutual understanding of close intimacy and the potential for strong feelings. The components—potentials for passion, interdependence, commitment, and intimacy—define important dimensions of close relationships. Passion (whether strong feelings or sexual arousal) can transfer from arousal originating in other sources, such as a scary movie. Interdependence focuses on people's behavior influencing each other, broken down into reflexive control (own), fate control (other's), and behavior control (both). Frequency, strength, and diversity of influence define the degree of closeness. Commitment entails intending the relationship to continue, and orienting toward the long-term future. Commitment depends on comparison level to calibrate satisfaction and comparison level for alternatives to calibrate the other options available. Intimacy includes the other in the self-concept. Operational definitions of these concepts address each in turn, most often through self-report scales. Whether studied in the United States or elsewhere, close relationships may include different kinds: romantic love, family relations, and friendships. In more collectivist cultures, individual choice in marriage, friends, and family takes a backseat to the group's needs. Everywhere, belonging, trusting, controlling, and, to a lesser extent, understanding are motives prominent in close relationships. Though self-enhancing is not irrelevant, it has not been a primary research focus.

# INTERDEPENDENCE: CONTROLLING AND TRUSTING

Shakespeare's (1595–1596) Romeo Montague and Juliet Capulet, "a pair of star-crossed lovers" (prologue, line 6), stand as Western icons of intense romantic passion. Yet, Romeo moans "My only love sprung from my only hate!" (Act I, Scene v, 142), and Juliet famously muses "O Romeo, Romeo! Wherefore art thou Romeo? Deny thy father, and refuse thy name; Or, if thou wilt not, be but sworn my love, And I'll no longer be a Capulet" (II, ii, 33). The lovers' feuding families condemned the forbidden passion and wished to prevent it, but they may have actually intensified it. Why should obstacles (such as feuding families) intensify passion? The answer, curiously, may lie in interdependence as a source of emotion in close relationships.

## Interdependence, Control, and Emotion

As noted, two critical components of close relationships often matter: interdependent behavior and passionate emotion. According to one theory, the one component may determine the other. That is, the very fact of interdependence may provide the well-spring for passion. As explained earlier, Harold Kelley and colleagues (1983) define closeness as a function of interdependence, that is, the extent to which two people depend on each other for important goals. Also, as noted earlier, interdependence can vary in its strength, frequency, and diversity. These features have direct implications for people's emotional life.

**THEORETICAL BACKGROUND**    To understand the effect of interdependence on emotion, consider first Mandler's **interrupt theory of emotion** (1975), which builds on Schachter's two-factor theory. Recall that his theory of emotion argues for the role of unexplained physiological arousal, plus a cognitive label from the situation, resulting in the experience of emotion. Mandler takes this theory upstream by inquiring as to the origins of the arousal (see Figure 8.4). In his view, first, arousal comes from **interruptions** that interfere with ongoing sequences of behavior. For example, if the telephone rings while you are trying to study, that event interrupts ongoing activities, increasing arousal, as if preparing you to take new action. The more important

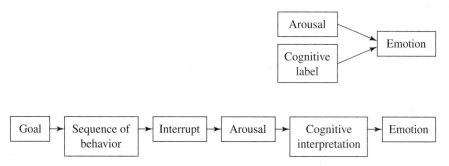

**Figure 8.4**    Schachter's (top) and Mandler's (bottom) Theories of Emotion

the goal represented by the ongoing activity, the bigger the interruption (studying for a final exam matters more than doing an optional problem set). Second, the arousal then evokes **cognitive interpretation**, asking why, which is the cognitive component of the earlier theory. Thus, Mandler links the two components of Schachter's theory, cognition and arousal, with arousal causing the search for a cognitive label. In summary, a given goal can be interrupted, which leads to arousal, which in turn leads to cognitive interpretation, which ultimately results in the experience of an emotion.

**INTERRUPTION AND EMOTION**    Ellen Berscheid (1983) applied these ideas to close relationships and an **interdependence theory of emotion**. Given interdependence, two people need each other; that is, their goals are intertwined. If your room-mate's phone calls keep interrupting your joint work together under a deadline, an important goal has been interrupted. More generally, in the course of any ongoing relationship, people depend on each other, and one person can come through for the other (**facilitation**) or one person can fail the other (**interference**), thereby disrupting the desired goal. The potential for shared completion or for interruption occurs any time two people make plans together or rely on each other.

Potential interruption creates the potential for arousal and thereby the potential for emotion. Consider some examples. If a job-seeker counts on a close friend for help completing a résumé but that help never arrives, the job-seeker becomes aroused by the inability to complete the goal, knows why, and becomes angry. Such interruptions do indeed cause emotions in relationships (Fehr & Harasymchuk, 2005). Conversely, if the friend interrupts the goal in a positive way (with unexpected facilitation, such as discovering that the résumé is unnecessary, thereby saving wasted time and trouble), the positive interruption also leads to arousal, but this time a positive interpretation, and gratitude, joy, or delight result.

In contrast to these two emotion-evoking interruptions, consider a more routinized, predictable facilitation of interdependent goals: One person always mails the couple's letters and one day, as usual, mails the completed résumé along with the electric bill. This predictable event contains no surprises, no interruptions positive or negative, so it does not elicit much emotion. Predictable, scripted help does not elicit emotions except perhaps low-level contentment.

Interdependence in a close relationship implies, as these examples indicate, only the potential for emotion, but not actual emotion. Thus, the intensity of emotion experienced in a relationship does not diagnose its commitment or closeness. Ironically, one may know the closeness of the relationship only if it ends and the array of heretofore quiet interdependences all terminate at once. This can cause either minimal or maximal disturbance, depending on the degree of interdependence.

Indeed, research supports this prediction. Researchers developed a measure of interdependence in relationships and found that it predicted emotion on break-up (Berscheid, Snyder, & Omoto, 1989). The Relationship Closeness Inventory (RCI) asked college students to "choose the *one* person with whom you have the *closest, deepest, most involved, most intimate relationship.*" This dating partner, friend, family member, or companion they then rated on characteristics of interdependence (try it; see Table 8.2): frequency (average time spent alone together per day, morning, afternoon,

**Table 8.2**   Excerpts from the Relationships Closeness Inventory

---

*Frequency*

---

DURING THE PAST WEEK, what is the average amount of time, per day, that you spent? *alone with X* in the EVENING (e.g., between 6 pm and bedtime)?

—————— hour(s) —————— minutes

---

*Diversity*

---

*In the past week*, I did the following activities *alone with X:*

—watched TV

—went to an auction/antique show

—attended a non-class lecture or presentation

—went to a restaurant

—went to a grocery store

—went to a movie

—ate a meal

—participated in a sporting activity

—outdoor recreation (e.g., sailing)

—went to a play

---

*Strength*

---

The following questions concern the amount of influence X has on your thoughts, feelings, and behavior. Using the 7-point scale below, please indicate the extent to which you agree or disagree.

I strongly disagree      1      2      3      4      5      6      7      I strongly agree

1.—X will influence my future financial security.

2.—X does *not* influence everyday things in my life.*

3.—X influences important things in my life.

4.—X does *not* influence the type of career I have.*

5.—X influences or will influence how much time I devote to my career.

6.—X does *not* influence my chances of get- ting a good job in the future.*

*Reverse-scored item.

---

Now we would like you to tell us how much X affects your future plans and goals. Using the 7-point scale below, please indicate the degree to which your future plans and goals are. affected by X.

Not at all      1      2      3      4      5      6      7      A great extent

1.  My vacation plans

2.  My marriage plans

3.  My plans to have children

4.  My plans to make major investments

---

*Source:* Berscheid et al., 1989. Copyright © American Psychological Association.
Adapted with permission.

and evening in the past week), diversity (number of 38 possible different activities done together, from doing laundry together to planning a party together), and strength (rated influence of the other on 34 domains, ranging from what television program one watches to career and family plans). For each domain, closeness scores are calculated and then averaged to form the relationship's closeness score.

By the RCI measure, romantic relationships were closer than friends and family; men and women reported equally close relationships; and the closest relationships differed from not-so-close relationships on interdependence. Relationships also last longer if they score higher on the RCI (see Table 8.3). Other factors help, such as ratings of satisfaction, closeness, length, exclusivity, and sexual involvement; factors that hinder include comparison level for alternatives, openness to casual sex, and availability of actual and imagined alternative partners (Simpson, 1987). Most relevant here, the RCI did not predict emotion within an ongoing relationship, but distress among those couples that did break up (see Table 8.3). Thus, if few interruptions occur, a close relationship predicts potential, but not necessarily experienced, emotions.

The interdependence theory explains much about the emotional experience of close relationships. For example, consider the sequence of a relationship. Patterns of interdependence tell the story of a relationship (Levinger, 1980), and with it, the experience of emotions over time (see Figure 8.5). At first, during the **attraction stage**, prospective partners size each other up, and during the **beginning stage**, the partners become aware of various benefits (and some costs) of the relationship. Over these two stages, interdependence, or relying on each other, increases. At some point, if the relationship will continue, it requires **commitment**, a decision to continue stable interdependence, after which levels of interdependence may grow or hold steady during the **continuing relationship**. Alternatively, it may reach **deterioration** and possibly an **ending**.

**Table 8.3**    Interdependence Predicting Relationship Stability and Distress at Break-up

| Predictor Variable | Relationship Stability | Distress at Break-up |
|---|---|---|
| Length of relationship | **.36** | **.36** |
| Relationship closeness inventory | .35 | **.34** |
| Ease of finding alternative partner | −.47 | **−.30** |
| Satisfaction | **.40** | .14 |
| Best alternative partner | −.35 | −.10 |
| Best imagined alternative partner | −.30 | −.06 |
| Orientation to sexual relations | −.24 | −.05 |
| Sexual nature of relationship | **.31** | −.02 |
| Exclusivity | **−.40** | .00 |

Entries are correlations, significant if .21 or larger. These correlations do not control for the effects of the other predictors with which they are correlated. Entries in bold remain significant after controlling for the other variables.
*Source:* Simpson, 1987. Copyright © American Psychological Association. Adapted with permission.

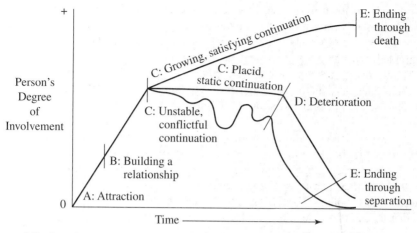

**Figure 8.5**   Development of Relationships

*Source:* Levinger, 1980. Copyright © Elsevier. Adapted with permission.

The emotional course of the relationship follows degree of involvement and interdependence. Over time, relationships often start out intense, as two people's desires, needs, wishes, and wants bump up against each other. As two people get to know each other, each revelation about the other's wonderful characteristics, shared goals, common ideals, and appealing opportunities adds arousal (read excitement) to the new relationship. Both pleasant and unpleasant surprises loom large. Over time, though, there are fewer surprises. People and relationships develop patterns. People facilitate each other's lives in predictable ways, so excitement decreases, although reliable companionship increases. As relationships mature, couples often wonder where the excitement went; one explanation is that the relationship simply becomes predictable and reliable and thus intrinsically less exciting, although far more stable.

Research supports this prediction (Aron, Norman, Aron, McKenna, & Heyman, 2000). In several survey measures of long-term relationships, quality increases as couples report participating together in novel and exciting activities. In three experiments, some couples were assigned to a seven-minute novel-arousing activity: Bound together by Velcro at wrist and ankle, they had to travel down and back across nine meters of gym mats, including a one-meter barrier (rolled up gym mat), on their hands and knees, holding a cylindrical pillow between their bodies (no hands, arms, or teeth allowed)—all in less than a minute. The mundane task involved rolling a ball and crawling to the center of the same room. Reports of relationship quality and friendly, accepting behavior both increased after the novel and arousing activity, compared with a mundane one and a no-activity control. The novel-arousing activities increase positive emotional arousal and relieve boredom, thereby improving the relationship.

Positive goals in general increase relationship quality. Having approach goals—oriented toward fun, development, and growth—creates good outcomes, including less loneliness, more satisfaction, and maintained sexual desire (Gable, 2006; Impett, Strachman, Finkel, & Gable, 2008). Successful interdependence involves facilitating each other's positive experiences, by conveying gratitude, sharing the partner's successes, and sacrificing in order to please the partner (Algoe, Haidt, & Gable, 2008; Gable, Reis, Impett, & Asher, 2004; Impett, Gable, & Peplau, 2005). Taking the other for granted, envying the partner, and sacrificing only to avoid disappointing the partner predict dissatisfaction. Similarly, facilitating the partner's movement toward an ideal self (a locomotion mindset), rather than judging the partner (an assessment mindset) likewise facilitates the relationship (Kumashiro, Rusbult, Finkenauer, & Stocker, 2007).

As two people become increasingly interdependent, conflict is all but inevitable, and that conflict is the source of affective disharmony. Conflict arises because people want some different things, and each may interfere with, rather than facilitate, the fulfillment of their partner's desires, needs, and wishes. According to the interdependence theory, conflict arises from interference (hindering interruptions) and results in negative emotions. People may develop **anger scripts**, that is, expected negative, blaming sequences of events between self and partner (Fehr, Baldwin, Collins, Patterson, & Benditt, 1999; Fehr & Harasymchuk, 2005). People's angry behavior depends on the partner's anticipated response, and so on, in a self-perpetuating sequence.

With enough repetitions in long-term relationships, the theory explains couples who have a **conflict habit**. That is, some couples fight all the time but seem not to have lasting emotional difficulties. If the fights are completely predictable, highly scripted, then they may contain no truly upsetting surprises and ironically little emotion, despite all the commotion. An example from *The Bluest Eye* illustrates:

> An escapade of drunkenness, no matter how routine, had its ceremonial close. The tiny, undistinguished days that Mrs. Breedlove lived were identified, grouped, and classed by these quarrels. They gave substance to the minutes and hours otherwise dim and unrecalled. They relieved the tiresomeness of poverty, gave grandeur to the dead rooms. In these violent breaks from routine that were themselves routine, she could display the style and imagination of what she believed to be her own true self. To deprive her of these fights was to deprive her of all the zest. (Morrison, 1993, pp. 41–42)[5]

The "violent breaks from routine that were themselves routine" could aptly describes how habitual conflict loses its emotional edge as it becomes predictable.

The interdependence theory of emotion also provides one way to think about jealousy. If one partner begins to depend on someone outside the relationship, it interrupts the interdependence within the relationship. In other words, if one partner's needs are being met elsewhere, then that person is paying less attention to the first partner's needs within the relationship, and those needs and related goals are not being met. The excluded partner feels distress because of the disruption. The more dependent partner is more vulnerable to jealousy: Dependence is greatest, and potential for emotions is greatest, when important outcomes in the relationship are not available elsewhere.

---

[5] Copyright © Toni Morrison. Reprinted with permission.

Dependence predicts wanting to stay in the relationship (Drigotas & Rusbult, 1992) and thus probably jealousy at threats to it.

In each case, Berscheid's interdependence theory of emotion goes from goal-related surprises to emotions—or from lack of surprises to lack of emotions. In any case, closeness (interdependence) provides the potential for emotion.

**PASSION AND DRAMATIC CHANGES IN INTIMACY**   Relatedly, and building on this theory, **passionate love** (strong feelings of attraction and excitement) may be viewed as any sudden, dramatic increase in intimacy (Baumeister & Bratslavsky, 1999). Recall that intimacy was defined earlier as feeling understood and validated by the other, resulting from mutual self-disclosure and resulting in overlapping self-concepts. To this definition, the intimacy-passion theory adds positive feelings that are communicated. The theory holds that intimacy generally increases slowly over time, but when it increases suddenly, excited passion arrives in intense, short episodes. If passion results from abrupt changes in intimacy, then new couples should show a lot of passion, with the dramatic change from not knowing each other (or only just a little), to knowing each other much better. Thus, new couples may feel passionate because of a sudden increase from no intimacy to some intimacy, creating passion before they know each other well enough to be highly intimate. By the same principle, long-term couples, who know everything about each other, might feel not so passionate anymore, except when reuniting after a separation or a fight, both times that might represent dramatic increases in intimacy. Long-term couples may be intimate without a lot of passion because few sudden increases occur.

Furthermore, gender nuances may fit this theory. Contrary to the myth about women demanding relationships and men eschewing them, men tend to fall in love faster than women do (Baumeister & Bratslavsky, 1999). That is, men show more emotional reactivity. In this view, men respond more rapidly to any changes in intimacy, feeling passionate more quickly with small changes in intimacy, at earlier or later stages of a relationship. In general, women may require a bigger change in intimacy in order to feel passionate. Thus, women would be slower (more cautious) about passion in early stages of a relationship and also may experience less passion when changes in intimacy taper off in the long run. Similar patterns obtain respectively for extraverts (more intimacy more easily, so more passion) and introverts (more caution about intimacy, more selective passion).

Romeo and Juliet opened this section, with their passion intensified by barriers to their love. Theories of passionate love explain precisely why obstacles, interruptions, and dramatic changes all contribute to the experience of passion.

## Commitment and Accommodation

She knew, somehow, that he was awake. After all these years, of course she knew, just from that bated quality to the air.... She whispered, "Sam?"
  "Yes," he said.
  "You know that letter you wrote me in Bay Borough."
  "Yes."

"Well, what was the line you crossed out?"

He stirred beneath the bedclothes. "Oh," he said, "I crossed out so many lines. That letter was a mess."

"I mean the very last line. The one you put so many x's through I couldn't possibly read it."

He didn't answer at first. Then he said, "I forget."

Her impulse was to stand up and leave, but she forced herself to stay.

She sat motionless, waiting and waiting.

"I think," he said finally, "that maybe it was ... Was there anything that would, you know. Would persuade you to come back."

She said, "Oh, Sam. All you had to do was ask."

Then he turned toward her, and Delia slipped under the blankets and he drew her close against him. Although, in fact, he still had not asked. Not in so many words. (Tyler, 1995, p. 324)[6]

In this novel, a woman married for decades walks away from her family on the beach and disappears. But ultimately, her commitment to her marriage, and both partners' willingness to accommodate, draws her back. Social psychologists as well as novelists have delved into the forces that maintain and repair relationships.

Earlier sections described commitment and interdependence, saying that interdependence is closeness and commitment is the intent to continue. The **investment model** describes how individuals become committed to their relationships (Rusbult, 1980). Commitment comes from high satisfaction, few alternatives, and high investment. **Satisfaction** reflects outcomes (rewards minus costs), resulting in feelings that the relationship makes one happy, is better than others, close to ideal, and satisfying. **Alternatives** reflect the desirability of other relationships perceived to be available, finding others to be appealing, attractive, and close to ideal, so the availability of alternatives undermines commitment. This builds on the concept of comparison level for alternatives, described earlier. And **investment** reflects resources put into the relationship, resources that would be lost if the relationship ended: emotional energy, time, money, and shared possessions. Investment means putting a lot into the relationship, feeling very involved, linking many life aspects to the partner. The more satisfaction, the fewer alternatives, and the more investment in a relationship, then the more committed and less likely people are to leave a relationship.

The reverse may also be true: the more committed people are, the more satisfied and invested they may be in the relationship. And people may maintain commitment also by seeing alternatives as less attractive. People already in dating relationships judge opposite-sex people as less physically and sexually attractive, compared with people not in a current relationship (Simpson, Gangestad, & Lerma, 2000).

In both China and the United States, for both men and women, commitment to cross-sex friendships and dating relationships comes from satisfaction and investment (Lin & Rusbult, 1995). Thus, these two variables from the model generalize beyond marriages, beyond the United States, and across gender. The third predictor of commitment, poor alternatives, works mainly for dating partners, for women,

---

[6] Copyright © Anne Tyler. Reprinted with permission.

and for Americans. With that caveat, though, commitment maintains and prolongs relationships with some generality.

Often, the effects of commitment are beneficial, but commitment sometimes reflects involuntary dependence, as when battered women stay in abusive relationships (Rusbult & Martz, 1995). Those women report more commitment if they report less severe abuse (i.e., are less unsatisfied), have poorer economic alternatives (e.g., are not self-sufficient), and are heavily invested (i.e., married). Commitment predicts staying even in destructive relationships.

More specifically, for good or ill, commitment predicts willingness to accommodate in close relationships. **Accommodation**—the willingness to reciprocate a destructive act with a constructive one—reflects in general a healthier couple that is more likely to stay together (Rusbult, Verette, Whitney, Slovik, & Lipkus, 1991; Van Lange et al., 1997). When people are committed, forgiving their partner reduces tension and increases well-being (Karremans, Van Lange, Ouwerkerk, & Kluwer, 2003). This requires less narcissistic concern with oneself and one's rights but more concern with the relationship (Exline, Baumeister, Bushman, Campbell, & Finkel, 2004).

People's reactions to destructive behavior may be more or less active and more or less constructive, leading to four combinations (Rusbult et al., 1991; see Table 8.4). Destructive behavior can provoke **exit** from the relationship (active and destructive), or it can elicit **voice** concerning dissatisfaction (active and constructive). Destructive behavior can also provoke **neglect** (passive and destructive) or elicit **loyalty** (passive and constructive). Accommodation may involve simple constructive, passive loyalty, which often remains unnoticed, but it can also involve giving constructive, active voice to concerns and working on them (Drigotas, Whitney, & Rusbult, 1995). Voice requires an independent self-construal, whereas loyalty comes from a more interdependent self-construal (Sinclair & Fehr, 2005).

Accommodation clearly matters, so who does it and when? People accommodate more when they take each other's perspective, when they are socially concerned, and when they depend more on each other (Arriaga & Rusbult, 1998). People are more likely to accommodate their partner also if they score high on psychological femininity (regardless of being biologically male or female). Similarly, people are more willing to sacrifice in ongoing close relationships if they are personally committed (Van Lange, Agnew, Harinck, & Steemers, 1997). One's own willingness to sacrifice is associated

**Table 8.4**  Reactions to Destructive Behavior in a Relationship

|              | Active                                        | Passive                                          |
| ------------ | --------------------------------------------- | ------------------------------------------------ |
| Constructive | Voice: discuss, seek help, suggest, change    | Loyalty: wait, hope, pray, support               |
| Destructive  | Exit: abuse, scream, threaten, separate, divorce | Neglect: ignore, avoid, be cross, criticize, let fall apart |

*Source:* From Rusbult et al., 1991. Copyright © American Psychological Association. Reprinted with permission.

with the actual and perceived willingness of one's partner to sacrifice. Perhaps such willingness creates a positive feedback loop for maintaining relationships.

## (Mis)handling Conflict

Potential conflict occurs when two people's preferences, needs, or desires differ and they do not accommodate. Potential conflict may or may not emerge in overt conflict interactions. If it does, though, some amount of overt conflict can improve a relationship, as when one partner gives voice to a difference and they work it out. In other cases, differences can lead to destructive behavior, as when people neglect or exit, utterly failing to accommodate each other.

If, instead of accommodation, destructive behavior reciprocates destructive behavior, a **conflict spiral** results (in which negative affect reciprocates negative affect). Then the marriage or other close relationship may ultimately dissolve. A **cascade of processes** (Gottman & Levenson, 1992) can create its own irresistible force: severe problems followed by dissatisfaction. These processes can create chronic arousal (at least in women, who are often the relationship minder, so their reactions signal danger). The resulting stress can damage health in both partners. Negative interactions and poor emotional regulation can also follow, with partners expressing more negative emotions and fewer positive emotions. **Unregulated couples** who do not balance their negative reactions with at least an equal number of positive reactions are headed for trouble. Interactions then display stubbornness, withdrawal, and defensiveness, sometimes leading partners to consider a dissolution and actually to separate. This view of conflicted relationships falling apart over time describes one specific pattern that can undermine relationships, namely, an unregulated imbalance of negative over positive emotions.

Other relationship dynamics can be destructive as well. For example, couples in distressed relationships make a lot of attributions about their spouse's most frequent negative behavior. They engage in **negative tracking**, focusing on the aversive events and trying to explain them (Holtzworth-Munroe & Jacobson, 1985). Unfortunately for the marriage, distressed couples attribute their partners' negative behaviors to their partners' dispositions—intentional and voluntary, stable and global. That is, the negative events are expected to endure and are the partner's fault. Distressed couples dismiss any positive behavior from their partners as due to short-term circumstances or the partners' temporary state—unintentional and involuntary, unstable and specific. Such unflattering attributions do not predict future positive behavior.

Nondistressed couples make more flattering and optimistic interpretations of their partners' behavior. Positive events are caused by their partner's personality, on purpose, and negative events are due to short-term circumstances, not their partners' fault (Holtzworth-Munroe & Jacobson, 1985). Relationships characterized by trust differ from low-trust relationships in the attributions made. High-trust couples make attributions emphasizing positive aspects of the relationship. Medium-trust couples focus more on negative events and attributions, though at least they are discussing their issues. Low-trust couples avoid escalating conflict, instead focusing on specific, affectively moderate attributions (Rempel, Ross, & Holmes, 2001). Couples do not seem to have enduring attributional styles. Instead, their changing attributions over time predict their marital satisfaction, more than satisfaction predicts attributions (Karney & Bradbury, 2000). Clearly, relationship-enhancing and distress-maintaining attributions play a role in handling (or mishandling) conflict.

Another widespread, negative dynamic in couples occurs when one (usually the man) withdraws and the other (usually the woman) makes demands. Or the cycle may start with the woman making demands and the man withdrawing. The researchers typically refer to this as **demand-withdraw interaction**, emphasizing the woman's active role (demand) and the man's passive response (withdraw). Theoretically, of course, her demands could be a response to his withdrawal. And of course, men can demand, and women can withdraw, but that pattern is half as likely as the reverse (Christensen & Heavey, 1993). Regardless, the demand-withdraw pattern correlates across several studies with marital dissatisfaction.

Most people want the same things: Both men and women seek clear expression of emotions, appreciation, and fewer arguments. Women more often than men want changes in their marriages, most often around sharing housework, child care, finances, communication, and companionship, as well as desiring attention, appreciation, and conversation. Men more often want increased sexual activity and timely meals (Margolin, Talovic, & Weinstein, 1983). In any case, the person who wants change has to make demands in order to get his or her needs met. So if women more often seek change, they will more often make demands. The demand-withdraw cycle, at its worst, correlates with violence in distressed relationships (Holtzworth-Munroe, Smutzler, & Stuart, 1998).

The worst mishandling of conflict, namely, violence, entails all these patterns. Maritally violent men attribute negative intent, selfish motivation, and blame to their wives' behavior (Holtzworth-Munroe & Hutchinson, 1993). They offer less social support for their wives' problems and are less positive; they are more belligerent or domineering, more contemptuous or disgusted, more upset, and display more anger and tension (Holtzworth-Munroe, Stuart, Sandin, Smutzler, & McLaughlin, 1997). Maritally violent men are less socially competent (Holtzworth-Munroe & Stuart, 1994), which provides one social psychological explanation for their resorting to violence in conflicts. Although relationship violence is not limited to men, its effects are more severe when men are violent than when women are. Nor is it limited to heterosexual relationships; both lesbian and gay relationships can entail violence. Of course, relationship violence varies in severity and psychopathology (Holtzworth-Munroe & Stuart, 1994, 1998). The interpersonal dynamics have been of particular interest to social psychologists, who point to interpersonal deficits and distress-maintaining attributions.

More constructive approaches to conflict reflect the inverse of patterns seen in distressed couples. Happy couples accommodate, support, and trust each other. Happy couples assume their partner has reactions similar to their own, whether or not that assumption is accurate (Kenny & Acitelli, 2001; Levinger & Breedlove, 1966; Murray, Holmes, Bellavia, Griffin, & Dolderman, 2002; Murray, Holmes, & Griffin, 1996; Thomas, Fletcher, & Lange, 1997). Pleasant illusions and false consensus, not just total empathic accuracy, can prolong relationships. As people interact in a couple, their attitudes tend to become more similar in reality, showing attitude alignment (Davis & Rusbult, 2001).

More generally, when people feel valued in the relationship, they deal with the inevitable stresses by drawing closer to their partner; when they do not feel valued, they respond by treating the partner badly (Murray, Bellavia, Rose, & Griffin, 2003). Empathy matters also. People who are naturally empathic or induced to be empathic are more likely to forgive their partner. They inhibit destructive responses and behave constructively toward someone who has behaved destructively toward them (McCullough, Worthington, & Rachal, 1997); in other words, they accommodate. More generally, older couples in long-term marriages show more positivity and less chronic arousal. They do not show the negative affect reciprocity characteristic of younger distressed couples (Levenson, Carstensen, & Gottman, 1994) but accommodate any negative affect with neutral or positive affect. Satisfied romantic partners even tease each other in more prosocial, less aggressive ways; they tease in a less threatening way and afterward engage in redress (i.e., they compensate) (Keltner, Young, Heerey, Oemig, & Monarch, 1998). A variety of processes sustain relationships, all balancing positive views of the relationship and inhibiting negative reactions by the individual.

## Summary of Interdependence

Interdependence signals commitment, when two people depend on each other in important and varied ways over time. Interruptions—both pleasant surprises and unpleasant disruptions—create intense emotions in close relationships. Commitment, which comes from satisfaction, inferior alternatives, and investment, makes people willing to accommodate in close relationships. Reciprocating destructive behavior with neutral or positive behavior sustains relationships, as reflected in forgiving and supporting. Conflicts, when they arise, escalate when partners reciprocate negative affect, blaming attributions, and destructive behavior, in the worst case, causing violence. But long-term relationships can survive and thrive, given positive interdependence, satisfying people's core motives to belong, to control, and to trust.

## ATTACHMENT: BELONGING AND TRUSTING

All people become attached to other people. As earlier chapters have emphasized, the core social motive of belonging cuts across many domains in our lives. But people do have different styles of belonging, which affect their close relationships with others (for overviews, see Berscheid & Reis, 1998; Reis & Patrick, 1996; Simpson & Rholes, 1998).

Consider which of the following best describes your experiences:

1. I find that others are reluctant to get as close as I would like. I often worry that my partner doesn't really love me or won't want to stay with me. I want to merge completely with another person, and this desire sometimes scares people away.

2. I am somewhat uncomfortable being close to others; I find it difficult to trust them completely, difficult to allow myself to depend on them. I am nervous

when anyone gets too close, and often, love partners want me to be more intimate than I feel comfortable being.

3.   I find it relatively easy to get close to others and am comfortable depending on them and having them depend on me. I don't often worry about being abandoned or about someone getting too close to me.

These styles of trusting and belonging reflect attachment.

## Theoretical Background

During World War II, many English children were sent to the countryside to protect them from the bombing of London. John Bowlby observed some of these young children separated from their parents. He noted that separated infants protested and sought proximity to their primary caregivers. If protest succeeded in reuniting them with their caregiver, they were comforted and happy. If protest failed, they sometimes despaired and, over time, became detached. These attachment reactions make evolutionary sense, given the prolonged dependence and vulnerability of human infants compared with other animals. Infants who maintain proximity to their caregivers, thereby receiving protection and nurturing, are more likely to survive into adulthood. Consistent with the adaptive function, even infant rhesus monkeys show similar distress reactions when separated from their mothers (e.g., Seay, Hansen, & Harlow, 1962; Suomi, Collins, & Harlow, 1973).

When the **attachment system** works well, young children treat the caregiver as a **secure base**. These children are smiling, playing, more sociable, more open to exploring, and less inhibited. Secure attachment allows young children to crawl or toddle away from their caregivers, occasionally glancing back or coming back to check in for reassurance. Again consistent with its evolved function, baby monkeys also play more and socialize more when attached than when separated (Seay & Harlow, 1965).

Different children respond differently to separation from and reunion with their primary caregivers. If their protests bring reunion, they repeatedly experience stable, reliable attachment. If their protests do not work, or work only sporadically, they experience unstable, unreliable attachment. From these experiences, children develop understandings of themselves and their relationships, forming **internal working models** of relationships. Mary Ainsworth (Ainsworth et al., 1978) observed that most children (56%) seemed securely attached, apparently feeling loved and confident, behaving openly and sociably even in strange situations. Other children (24%) behaved anxiously and fearfully (checking frequently for their caregivers, protesting, calling, and pleading), as if they had had unreliable experiences and expected relationships to be unstable and unpredictable. Still other children (20%) responded in an avoidant, detached manner (maintaining proximity, yet avoiding close contact); these children behaved as if they had had consistently unresponsive caregivers, with attachment bringing them mainly disappointment. Note, however, that all these children were attached to their caregivers; their styles depended on their relationship experiences. **Attachment theory** holds that these internal working models remain fairly stable into adulthood, where they affect other relationships. Similarly, baby monkeys separated early from their mothers later turn out to be terrible mothers themselves

(Harlow, 1962). Attachment theory concerns the formation of relationships over a lifetime, and the process fills a basic survival function.

## Styles of Belonging: Attachment Models and Relationships

Think back to the three-item questionnaire at the beginning of this section. Readers in the Denver area responded to these items in the *Rocky Mountain News*, assessing adult versions of the early attachment styles just described (Hazan & Shaver, 1987). The distribution of adult attachment styles came uncannily close to the Ainsworth-Bowlby 56–24–20% observations of infants, making it plausible that these styles persist from infancy into adulthood, perhaps explaining why the proportions remained constant. **Avoidant** people uncomfortable with close relationships, **anxious-ambivalent** people worried about their relationships, and **secure** people comfortable in their relationships may have been that way all their lives, as a result of early experiences.

The three styles, however, may work better as four (see Table 8.5). An elegant revision suggested that people have mental models about both themselves and others in close relationships, resulting in four combinations (Bartholomew & Horowitz, 1991). **Secure** people feel good about both themselves and others. **Preoccupied** people feel personally unacceptable and unlovable but feel that others are good; this corresponds to the anxious/ambivalent type. This new scheme separates avoidant styles into two kinds. Both kinds view other people as untrustworthy and unavailable. But one kind, **dismissing**, feels good about the self, in effect viewing others unworthy of relationship. The other kind, **fearful**, feels personally unacceptable and unlovable as well as feeling bad about others, making the fearful type socially avoidant and fearful of intimacy.

**Table 8.5**    Attachment Styles

| Feelings about Self (Range from self-confidence to anxiety) | Feelings about Others (Range from openness to avoidance) | |
| --- | --- | --- |
| | Positive, open | Negative, avoidant |
| Positive, confident | Secure | Dismissing (avoidant) |
| Negative, anxious | Preoccupied (anxious/ambivalent) | Fearful (avoidant) |

*Source:* Table after Bartholomew & Horowitz (1991); Hazan & Shaver's (1987) original categories in cell parentheses; Brennan, Clark, & Shaver's (1998) dimensions in heading parentheses.

Revised measures follow. *Secure:* It is easy for me to become emotionally close to others. I am comfortable depending on others and having others depend on me. I don't worry about being alone or having others not accept me. *Dismissing:* I am comfortable without close emotional relationships. It is very important to me to feel independent and self-sufficient, and I prefer not to depend on others or to have others depend on me. *Preoccupied:* I want to be completely emotionally intimate with others, but I often find that others are reluctant to get as close as I would like. I am uncomfortable being without close relationships, but I sometimes worry that others don't value me as much as I value them. *Fearful:* I am uncomfortable getting close to others. I want emotionally close relationships, but I find it difficult to trust others completely or to depend on them. I worry that I will be hurt if I allow myself to become too close to others.

Of course, these categories represent extreme combinations of positive-negative views of self and other, so perhaps it makes more sense to think of self-views and other-views as dimensions, with gradations, rather than as absolute categories (Brennan, Clark, & Shaver, 1998). Positive-to-negative views of self represent degrees of self-confidence or anxiety, whereas positive-to-negative views of others represent degrees of openness or avoidance. Anxiety about self shows up in endorsing items such as "I worry about being abandoned," "I worry a lot about my relationships," and "I worry that romantic partners won't care as much about me as I care about them." Avoidance of others shows up in endorsing items such as "I prefer not to show a partner how I feel deep down," "I get nervous when partners get too close to me," and "I find it difficult to allow myself to depend on romantic partners."

People internalize their relationships with significant others into general working models, a central tenet of attachment theory. These working models affect how people understand and respond in their relationships (Collins, 1996). People who are preoccupied and people who are avoidant both interpret partner behavior in negative ways, but only the preoccupied report distress as a result. Both kinds of insecurely attached people (preoccupied and avoidant) are especially undermined when partners fail to support them, and when they do receive partner support, they fail to appreciate it (Collins & Feeney, 2004). Insecure people react destructively to partner transgressions (Collins, Ford, Guichard, & Allard, 2006). Altogether, people with insecure working models of attachment undermine close-relationship dynamics.

Besides life-long working models, people also form specific scripts for interaction patterns ("If I am successful, they will love me."). These **relational schemas** describe "if . . . then" patterns in relationships with others (Baldwin, 1992). For some people, their relationships are noncontingent; they expect to love and be loved regardless of their successes and failures, reflecting security (or perhaps a secure attachment style). For other people, their relationships depend on success and failure, respectively creating love and rejection, the contingency itself resulting in low self-esteem (Baldwin & Sinclair, 1996); perhaps contingent relationships also lead to a preoccupied (anxious-to-please) or fearful (rejecting) attachment style, based on a sense of unreliable, performance-based relationships.

Whatever the scheme for classifying attachment styles, their effects are real. For example, 125 students kept structured diaries of social interactions for a week (Tidwell, Reis, & Shaver, 1996). People previously classified as avoidant (in the first, three-way scheme noted earlier) reported less intimate, enjoyable, supportive, and happy interactions, as well as more saddening, frustrating, and rejecting interactions, especially with opposite-sex others. People classified as secure reported more positive interactions; they also differentiated appropriately between romantic interactions and nonromantic opposite-sex interactions. People classified as anxious-ambivalent reported more variable experiences with happiness and support in opposite-sex interactions than did the other two types.

Although the different attachment styles allow us to classify ourselves and others, recall that attachment represents a universal form of belonging. Like the wartime babies separated from family, adults likewise separated from family by war or job react similarly to disrupted intimacy (Vormbrock, 1993). For example, commuter marriages,

POW/MIA families, and spouses who travel for their jobs all have separations built into their relationships. Adult spouses react similarly across different kinds of separation experiences and similarly to the way children do. Emotional reactions to being left include anxiety, depression, and anger; these emotions are more intense during long-term, routine separations than during repeated, short separations. Like Bowlby's war babies, home-based spouses may follow periods of distress with detachment and emotional distancing, instead seeking contact with relatives or even alternative attachment figures. Meanwhile, absent spouses tend to feel guilty. Reunions are difficult: Returning spouses seek intimacy, while home-based spouses feel ambivalent. The similarity of these reactions across different kinds of separation and across adulthood and childhood legitimizes the view that attachment is a life-long system that operates in all people.

Cultural critics of attachment theory suggest that the Western view of attachment focuses on a **generative tension** between self and other, for example, separation and reunion. In Japan, the focus is **symbiotic harmony**, dependence and caregiving (Table 8.6). Relationships are important in both cultures, but the meaning and the dynamics can differ. Attachment is measured in the West by examining caregiver sensitivity, which allows the child a secure base for exploration, leading to later social competence. In Japan, caregivers emphasize dependency instead of autonomy, group harmony instead of individuation, emotional restraint instead of self-expression, and dependence instead of exploration (Rothbaum, Weisz, Pott, Miyake, & Morelli, 2000). North Americans seek social support, that is, comfort, in relationships, whereas East Asians avoid seeking support when it might disturb relationship harmony (Kim, Sherman, Ko, & Taylor, 2006). Americans are less concerned with relationship harmony, but closer to nonbiological family (i.e., spouse) and friends, whereas Japanese are closer to biological family (Takahashi, Ohara, Antonucci, & Akiyama, 2002). People are attached to close others everywhere, but the development and expression vary with culture. As noted, people of various cultural groups view their own close relationships as better than other people's (Endo, Heine, & Lehman, 2000). Nowhere do these biases correlate with self-esteem or self-serving biases, suggesting a belonging motive rather than a self-enhancing motive. But in Japan, the positive illusions about one's relationship correlate with viewing one's relationship partner more positively than oneself, suggesting a dependency of self on other.

**Table 8.6**    Cultural Paths to Attachment in Japan and the United States

| Age | U.S.: Generative Tension | Japan: Symbiotic Harmony |
|---|---|---|
| Infancy | Separation and reunion | Union |
| Childhood | Personal preferences | Others' expectations |
| Adolescence | Transfer of closeness from parents to peers | Stability of peer and parent relationships |
| Adulthood | Trust; faith and hope in new relationships | Assurance about the mate relationship |

*Source:* As described by Rothbaum et al., 2000.

Caregiving forms the other side of the attachment system. In the West, secure adults' caretaking styles produce secure infants, according to meta-analysis (van IJzendoorn, 1995). Secure caregivers, responsive to infants, are physically warm, accepting, and sensitive to their child's needs, distress, and circumstances (Kunce & Shaver, 1994). Secure adults, responsive to their partners' needs, also maintain proximity, sensitivity, and cooperation. Adult-child and adult-adult caregiving differ importantly in power and status differences, verbal communication, and sexuality; nevertheless, the similarities are striking (Reis & Patrick, 1996).

Breakdown in the attachment system perpetuates itself across generations. Infants with unresponsive caretakers tend to develop negative mental models of self and other. In adults, these mental models lead to maladaptive interactions. Anxious (negative) views of self particularly create problems. In the worst cases, adult males' anxious attachment styles, especially fearful attachments (where both self and other are viewed negatively), correlate with relationship violence (Dutton, Saunders, Starzomski, & Bartholomew, 1994). And adult females' anxious attachment styles predict involvement in abusive relationships, whereas the preoccupied style (negative view of self, positive view of other) predicts an inability to extricate themselves from the abusive relationships (Henderson, Bartholomew, & Dutton, 1997). People with insecure attachment styles, under threat, also endorse more conservative, rigid, and violent solutions even to political problems (Weise et al., 2008).

Attachment fundamentally reflects the core social motive of belonging, and secure attachment reflects trust (Berscheid, 1994). Successful relationships depend on trust, expressed as seeking closeness, responding sensitively, and cooperating. Such behavior assumes a positive internal model of the other person, as in secure attachment. Thus, attachment returns us to the core social motives of belonging and trust, in particular.

**EVOLUTIONARY PERSPECTIVES ON ATTACHMENT**    Attachment theory takes an explicitly evolutionary view of the attachment bond. If the young of various species are relatively immature, they attach firmly to a primary caregiver, compared with species that bear young mature enough to survive on their own. The long vulnerable period for human infants and other primates (as noted), compared with some animals, necessitates attachment bonds. The original bond between infant and caregiver favors the infant's survival: The vulnerable infant's distress at separation encourages renewed contact, and the caregiver's attachment to the infant also fosters nurturing behavior. Bowlby (1969, 1973, 1980, 1982) observed prolonged distress among infants separated from their primary caregivers, even when their physical needs were met by surrogates. Infants and young children need the security of a primary caregiver in the immediate vicinity. Maintaining proximity maintains comfort. Attachment in adults also offers the promise of security through a relationship with a trusted other (Zeifman & Hazan, 1997), as the last section showed.

From an evolutionary perspective, the long vulnerable period for human children and the required presence of one caregiver suggests the evolutionary adaptiveness of sustained pair-bonds in adults. To ensure the survival of one's offspring, it helps to have two adults, one to remain proximate to young children at any given time and the other to engage in activities incompatible with simultaneous caregiving (e.g., hunting, warfare, some kinds of agriculture, some kinds of trading). The mechanisms that bond infants and caregivers could also usefully bond adults (Hazan & Shaver, 1987, 1994). The similarities between the two kinds of bonds, child-adult and adult-adult, support the evolutionary argument: Dynamics both include separation causing first anxiety, then distress, and eventually detachment. Selection criteria both include looking for a familiar, similar other, who is kind. And processes both entail preoccupation, arousal, physical closeness, viewing the attachment figure as a safe haven and a secure base from which to go out into the world and return (Zeifman & Hazan, 1997). Physical contact between attached infants and caregivers remarkably resembles the behavior of lovers: mutual gaze, cuddling, nuzzling, kissing, and skin-to-skin, especially belly-to-belly contact. People, especially women, can respond to stress with attachment-generating behaviors, termed **tend-and-befriend** (Taylor et al., 2000). Tending involves behavior that protects self, close others, and offspring, especially adaptive in a stressful environment. The attachment-caregiving system is mediated by the hormone oxytocin, and together with opiods in the brain, it relieves stress and reinforces attachment (Taylor, 2006). Oxytocin signals attachment gaps in relationships and motivates affiliative behavior, providing a biomarker of social distress and attachment seeking.

This evolutionary perspective on attachment represents a universal model, in the sense that virtually everyone forms attachments and in similar ways. This is further supported by near-unanimous preferences for a mate who is kind, intelligent, and socially skilled (Berscheid & Reis, 1998), in other words, a secure attachment object.

## Summary of Attachment

The attachment system functions to keep infants near their primary caregivers. Separation causes distress, in an effort to reunite, but prolonged separation can cause depression and detachment. Children develop more and less secure attachment styles, depending on their experiences with primary caregivers. These result in internal working models of self and other that are more or less positive. Confident views of self and open views of others predict secure attachment styles in adulthood. Maladaptive attachment styles undermine relationships. Although cultures may vary in the development and dynamics of attachment, trusting close others and belonging together are essentially universal impulses, perhaps associated with evolutionary adaptation.

## SOCIAL NORMS: BELONGING AND UNDERSTANDING

In closing, consider briefly some theories that emphasize social norms defining different kinds of relationships across dynamics of attachment and interdependence. People need shared norms—such as equity and exchange systems, communal norms, or other relational models—to understand what rules apply to different relationships. In order to belong to groups, people want to understand the shared ground rules about different kinds of relationships. Just how norms describe different kinds of close relationships, however, is not so obvious at first glance.

## Equity and Exchange

> Let us live in as small a circle as we will, we are either debtors or creditors
> before we have time to look around. (von Goethe, 1808, book II, ch. 4)

Some early views of close relationships (Walster, Walster, & Berscheid, 1978) argued that social relationships primarily revolve around debits and credits. According to **equity theory**, relationships are perceived to be fair if each person's outcomes are *proportional* to that person's contributions. So, if one partner puts little time, thought, commitment, money, or opportunities into the relationship, that person should receive fewer rewards. Equity seemed to predict satisfaction and liking in relationships (Walster, Walster, & Berscheid, 1978). However, contrary to equity theory, relationships do not become more equitable over time, and equity does not predict the stability and quality of relationships over time (Van Yperen & Buunk, 1990).

A special case of equity is **exchange**, in which people reciprocate benefit for benefit, creating an *equivalence* of outcomes (not just outcomes relative to inputs). If I invite you to dinner, you invite me back. If you pay for our lunch this time, I'll pay for it next time. Sheer equality and positivity of outcomes do matter to relationship satisfaction, and sheer instrumental value does predict behavioral preferences for a reciprocating partner. In contrast, more affective responses—trust, regard, and solidarity—result from the symbolic value conveyed by reliable reciprocity (Molm, Schaefer, & Collett, 2007). People feel solidarity with people through generalized exchange, more than with directly negotiated exchange (Molm, Collett, & Schaefer, 2007). But exchange and reciprocity miss the mark in describing close relationships. Sheer reciprocity matters less to ongoing relationships than perceived benefactor responsiveness (Algoe, Haidt, & Gable, 2008). So perhaps equity and exchange norms do not provide the most comprehensive and applicable descriptions of close relationships.

## Communal and Exchange Relationships

> The sum which two married people owe to one another defies calculation. It
> is an infinite debt; which can only be discharged through all eternity. (von
> Goethe, 1808, book I, ch. 9)

Why should people stay in a relationship whose debt cannot be calculated and discharged in this lifetime? Why do families care for their very young and very old, who cannot reciprocate? Why could it be rude to return a favor too quickly? Perhaps exchange characterizes only some kinds of relationships (Clark & Mills, 1979, 1993), such as impersonal friendships and business relationships. Another kind of relationship does not track outcomes (who did what for whom). In **communal relationships**, people keep track of each other's needs. When people respond to each other's needs, one person may end up needing more than the other, at different times or even throughout the relationship. Thinking of family relationships as communal explains why normal parents don't bill their children for their upbringing. In a communal relationship, people actually may prefer obligation because it signals a willingness to continue a relationship in which the ground rule is meeting each other's needs. Going to the neighbor for a cup of sugar signals a need but also an openness to a relationship. Returning a cup of sugar (instead of some cookies) implies an impersonal relationship and could be insulting.

Early studies differentiating communal and exchange relationships introduced students to a campus newcomer, who indicated that she was either available to form friendships (expected communal relationship) or not available after the experiment (limited exchange relationship). When participants expected an exchange relationship, they liked her better when she immediately reciprocated a benefit for a benefit, in keeping with exchange principles. When they expected a possible communal relationship, they liked her *more* when she did *not* immediately pay them back (Clark & Mills, 1979). Paying back too soon is like discussing money at an intimate social occasion; it implies insensitivity to the appropriate norms, and it distances people from each other (Vohs, Mead, & Goode, 2006). Although people in an exchange relationship do keep track of each other's inputs into a joint task, people in a communal relationship do not keep track (Clark, 1984). In contrast, people in a communal relationship keep track of each others' needs, which people in exchange relationships do not (Clark, Mills, & Powell, 1986).

Communal relationships thrive when caring partners project their own responsiveness onto their partner, leading them to expect positive responses to their needs, which perpetuates relationship-promoting behavior (Lemay & Clark, 2008). This facilitates close relationships regardless of attachment style and other individual differences (Lemay, Clark, & Feeney, 2007). To be sure, communal motivation itself is a reliable individual difference that predicts satisfying relationships (Mills, Clark, Ford, & Johnson, 2004).

Overall, a communal relationship's quality is unrelated or even positively related to costs incurred to meet the partner's needs, consistent with the idea that communal relationships operate by different norms than exchange relationships do (Clark & Grote, 1998). But relationship costs incurred because of the partner's intentionally poor behavior do damage communal relationship quality, precisely because the partner is not attending to the other person's needs. In communal relationships, partners can express even negative emotions, especially if they are personally high in communal orientation (Clark & Finkel, 2005). A strong case supports distinct norms for belonging to and understanding communal relationships, as compared with exchange ones.

## Relational Models Theory

Perhaps there are not just two kinds of relationships, but more. The **relational models theory** (A. P. Fiske, 1992) suggests four universal types (see Table 8.7). In families, for example, children start at infancy with **communal sharing**, in which each person receives according to need, and people maintain few boundaries between them. By age 3 years or so, children become aware of hierarchies and **authority ranking** (similar to the military), in which higher-ups decide what happens to subordinates. **Equality matching** follows soon after, when children around age 4 years reach the

**Table 8.7**  Relational Models Theory

| Model | First Age | Example | Scale | Dominant Rules |
|---|---|---|---|---|
| Communal sharing | Infancy | Families | Nominal | Each according to need; few boundaries |
| Authority ranking | 3 years | Military | Ordinal | Higher-ups decide for subordinates |
| Equality matching | 4 years | Peer groups | Interval | Equal portions |
| Market pricing | 8 years | Business | Ratio | Benefits proportional to cost |

*Source:* From A. P. Fiske, 1992. Copyright © American Psychological Association. Adapted with permission.

one-for-me, one-for-you, exactly-equal-portions stage (seen in peer groups throughout life). Finally, **market pricing** concepts develop around age 8 years, when children begin to understand bartering, money, trading, and other commerce; the best adult example of this is business, in which people get what they pay for. What is fair under one type of relationship is not fair under another. For example, you would not share a toothbrush with your boss or charge your own infant a child care fee.

What's more, as Table 8.7 indicates, the relationship types apparently operate according to different scales. That is, differences between communal sharing relationships are categorical (all Montagues are equivalently family members and distinct from the Capulet family). Authority ranking adds order, with some people higher and some lower; this fits an ordinal scale. Equality matching adds intervals: If I get 3, you get 3; if I get 10, you get 10. And market pricing adds ratios: If I pay twice as much as you for my room, I should get twice as much space.

Cross-culturally valid, these types of relationships fundamentally structure people's transactions with each other (A. P. Fiske, 1993). People will mix up others who fall into the same category, suggesting that these are fundamental social cognitive categories (Fiske & Haslam, 1996; Fiske, Haslam, & Fiske, 1991). People will misremember which subordinate said something but less often mix up something said by a boss with something said by a subordinate. Similarly, one might call the children by each other's names, because one has the same general type of relationship with them. Sometimes people even feed the cereal to the dog and the kibbles to the kid.

## Summary of Norms

People follow shared norms about relationships. In exchange relationships, people's outcomes are equal, and under equity, their rewards are proportionate to their costs, relative to each other. Communal relationships do not keep track of costs and benefits but instead track each partner's needs. Relational models theory subsumes these types, specifying four models: communal sharing, authority ranking, equality matching, and market pricing, with different norms applying to each. This last theory has seen less research specifically on close relationships, but has considerable potential.

## CHAPTER SUMMARY

Think about your closest personal relationship and consider how social psychology bears on it. Close relationships are defined as potentially passionate, interdependent, committed, and intimate, respectively involving varying degrees of potential emotion, mutually influenced behavior, intent to continue, and merged self-concepts. Although often using self-report measures and correlational methods, relationship science knows a lot about the working of relationships. Across age and culture, people seek friends they can trust and enjoy, to satisfy the core motive of belonging. Romantic love, emphasizing passion and intimacy, tends to be more individualistic, in its Western form, whereas commitment looms larger in more collectivist, non-Western societies. Families entail authority relations not necessarily present in romances, marriages, and friendships.

As anyone in a close relationship knows from experience, interdependence—relying on another for significant outcomes—raises issues of trust and control, as the other may facilitate or hinder one's important life goals. Emotions result from goal-related surprises: The other person may unexpectedly help or hinder, causing joy or anger. Intense emotions characterize the early stages of relationships, in which discoveries provide surprise; calm emotions characterize stable, long-term relationships that have fewer surprises; the termination of a relationship can reveal how much potential emotion was there, because of entwined interdependence, now broken. Interdependence constitutes relationship closeness. Sudden changes in closeness may predict passion.

People become committed to interdependent relationships when they are satisfied, invested, and see few alternatives. Commitment allows accommodation, reciprocating destructive behavior with constructive behavior, which prolongs the relationship. A balance of more positive than negative expressed emotions supports relationships, as do the presumption of similarity and the exercise of empathy. Destructive relationships result from reciprocated negative behavior, unsympathetic attributions for the other's behavior, and demand-withdraw (or withdraw-demand) cycles.

Attachment, a system motivated to maintain belonging with primary caregivers in childhood and with close partners in adulthood, comes in different styles. Varying views of self—confidence or anxiety—combined with varying views of other—openness or avoidance—together create distinct ways of relating to close others. People who are self-confident and open fare better than insecure people, who are more anxious or avoidant. Although sometimes it works better than others, the attachment system encourages all infants to bond with a primary caregiver and most adults to bond with a partner. Both kinds of bond have adaptive benefits. In general, people seek stable attachments; people prefer partners who are kind, intelligent, and socially skilled.

In general, norms suggest several kinds of rules for relationships, including communal and exchange relationships, as well as authority and equality relationships. People's shared understanding about the implicit rules for relationships help them to belong with other people.

Regardless of relationship type, culture, or age—or social psychological theory—people tend to believe that their own relationships are better than other people's. Relationship science suggests that this is an adaptive illusion, which fosters the core motive to belong, as well as to have a reasonable degree of trust, control, and understanding.

## SUGGESTIONS FOR FURTHER READING

BERSCHEID, E., & REIS, H. T. (1998). Attraction and close relationships. In D. T. GILBERT, S. T. FISKE, & G. LINDZEY (Eds.), *Handbook of social psychology* (4th ed., Vol. 2, pp. 193–281). New York: McGraw-Hill.

CLARK, M. S., & LEMAY, E. P. (2010). Close relationships. In S. T. FISKE, D. T. GILBERT, & G. LINDZEY (Eds.), *Handbook of social psychology* (5th ed.). New York: Wiley.

FEHR, B. (1996). *Friendship processes.* Thousand Oaks, CA: Sage.

FLETCHER, G. J. O., & CLARK, M. S. (Eds.) (2001). *Blackwell handbook of social psychology: Interpersonal processes.* Malden, MA: Blackwell.

HARTUP, W. W., & STEVENS, N. (1999). Friendship and adaptation across the life span. *Current Directions in Psychological Science,* 8, 76–79.

HARVEY, J. H., & PAUWELS, B. G. (1999). Recent developments in close-relationships theory. *Current Directions in Psychological Science,* 8, 93–95.

PEPLAU, L. A., & FINGERHUT, A. W. (2007). The close relationships of lesbians and gay men. *Annual Review of Psychology,* 58, 405–424.

RUDMAN, L., & GLICK, P. (2008). *The social psychology of gender: How power and intimacy shape gender relations.* New York: Guilford.

RUSBULT, C. E., & VAN LANGE, P. A. M. (2003). Interdependence, interaction, and relationships. *Annual Review of Psychology,* 54, 351–375.

SHAVER, P. R., & MIKULINCER, M. (2007). Attachment theory and research: Core concepts, basic principles, conceptual bridges. In A. W. KRUGLANSKI & E. T. HIGGINS (Eds.), *Social psychology: Handbook of basic principles* (2nd ed., pp. 650–677). New York: Guilford.

SIMPSON, J. A., (2007). Foundations of interpersonal trust. In A. W. KRUGLANSKI & E. T. HIGGINS (Eds.), *Social psychology: Handbook of basic principles* (2nd ed., pp. 587–607). New York: Guilford.

# Chapter 9

# Helping: Prosocial Behavior

Hattiesburg, Miss.—The washerwoman's gift of $150,000 to finance scholarships at the local college had taken much of her long and lonely life to save. Oseola McCarty made the gift as she felt her own time creeping to a close, as worsening arthritis made it hard for her to work or sometimes even stand. She had lived by herself since 1967, between rows of clothes, a shy, stooped woman of 88 years who always had a lot to say, just no one to say it to in the quiet house on Miller Street. Who else might she give her savings to, if not strangers? (Bragg, 1996, p. 1)[1]

Why did Ms. McCarty give her unselfish gift? Social psychologists study such prosocial behavior, examining its underlying causes—both dispositional and situational. Social psychologists also debate its core motives—egoistic, altruistic, collectivist, or principled. This chapter argues that these motives fit combinations of our core social motives. Debates have raged over the evolutionary significance of self-sacrificial behavior, as we will see, and the core motives shed some light on this contentious issue. We will examine how prosocial behavior can result from specific factors as varied as social learning, mood, attributed responsibility, empathy, identity, norms, and moral reasoning. But first, let's define our terms and organize these topics according to clusters of motivations.

## WHAT IS PROSOCIAL BEHAVIOR?

No one would disagree that Oseola McCarty's gift represents prosocial behavior. But what about a fictional family whose son dies, and they take in his young widow? Blamed for his death and hideously disfigured by a botched suicide attempt, she is

---

[1] Copyright © New York Times. Reprinted by permission.

barely tolerated, but she is called Precious Auntie and lives with the family nonethe-less. In keeping with ancient beliefs in traditional China, the son's ghost came to the grandmother

> in a dream and warned that if Precious Auntie died, he and his ghost bride
> would roam the house and seek revenge on those who had not pitied her.
> Everyone knew there was nothing worse than a vengeful ghost. They caused
> rooms to stink like corpses. They turned bean curd rancid in a moment's
> breath. They let wild creatures climb over walls and gates. With a ghost in
> the house, you could never get a good night's sleep. (Tan, 2001, p. 175)[2]

Given their beliefs, was caring for her a prosocial act, and if so, was it egois-tic self-interest, empathic altruism, collective family loyalty, or principled morality? As we will see when we define these terms and the research they each encompass, cultures differ in their interpretations of responsibility, with some Eastern ones empha-sizing broad responsibility (for ingroup members, at least) and some Western ones emphasizing more personal factors such as liking and direct self-interest.

## Conceptual Definitions

**Prosocial behavior** includes behavior intended to benefit others—behaviors such as helping, comforting, sharing, cooperating, reassuring, defending, and showing concern (Schroeder, Penner, Dovidio, & Piliavin, 1995, p. 15). Note several features of this definition: First, it includes the *intent* to help others, so acts that unintentionally help others do not count (for example, taking a new job may benefit another person who fills the old one, but that was probably not the intended consequence). However, acts intended to help, which may actually fail to help, would be included (for example, it would be useless, but still prosocial, to shovel snow off the front walk of some-one who uses only the back door). Second, what actually *benefits* another person is socially defined, changing with time and place. Depending on the context, proso-cial acts might include circumcision, foot-binding, piercing, scarring, tooth-pulling, or ruthless criticism. Finally, note that benefit to one or more *others*, including society, but not benefit to self, is key. The positive behavior is social and interpersonal, not self-directed in its intent.

Social psychologists often distinguish a subset of prosocial behaviors according to their motivations. Although prosocial behaviors are intended to benefit others, the underlying motivation might or might not be other-oriented. **Altruism** conceptually underlies the subset of prosocial behavior that is "motivated mainly out of a consider-ation of another's needs rather than one's own" (Piliavin & Charng, 1990, p. 30). As a motive, altruism involves self-sacrificial costs, absent "obvious, external rewards" (Batson, 1998, p. 282). Altruism thus involves concern for others' needs, independent of hoped reward or feared punishment outside the self (Grusec, 1991). By these def-initions, then, the traditional family that took in their widowed daughter-in-law, for fear of her ghost, acted prosocially but not altruistically.

---

[2] Copyright © Putnam. Reprinted by permission.

## Operational Definitions

Prosocial behavior is good. Social psychologists, like everyone else, want to promote it, but to do so, they must first explain it. They have pursued two approaches, dispositional and situational. One possible explanation is that people behave prosocially because they have prosocial personalities. In this view, the Oseola McCarties of the world differ from the rest of us, and the trick is to socialize children to become more prosocial. Researchers pursuing this track use personality questionnaires, combining various personality variables to predict helping, for example, a fellow student with severe stomach cramps (Staub, 1974; see Table 9.1).

Another personality method, besides questionnaires, uses people's initial reactions to choosing cooperative or competitive options in experimental games. You might try this method before reading further (Table 9.2). This test allows researchers to see what

**Table 9.1**   Personality Predictors of Helping Another Student

Positive predictors

Valuing helpfulness
Valuing equality
Taking responsibility for others, e.g.:
  If a good friend of mine wanted to injure an enemy of his or hers, it would be my duty
    to try to stop the friend.
  Professional obligations can never justify neglecting the welfare of others.
  I would be obligated to do a favor for a person who needed it, even though the friend
    had not shown gratitude for past favors.
Endorsing social responsibility, e.g.:
  I am the kind of person that people can count on.
  I usually volunteer for special projects at school.
  Cheating on examinations is not so bad as long as nobody ever knows.*
Moral reasoning (see Figure 9.5)

Negative predictors

Valuing comfortable life
Valuing ambition
Valuing cleanliness
Machiavelli scale
  The best way to handle people is to tell them what they want to hear.
  It is hard to get ahead without cutting corners here and there.
  Most people are basically good and kind.*

*Indicates a negatively worded item that researchers reverse-coded from others in the same set. Each questionnaire included other negatively worded items, to control for acquiescence response bias, but they are omitted here for clarity. Items listed are examples, not entire scale.

**Table 9.2**   An Instrument to Measure Social Value Orientation

In this task we ask you to imagine that you have been randomly paired with another person, whom we will refer to simply as the "Other." This other person is someone you do not know and you will not knowingly meet in the future. Both you and the "Other" person will be making choices by circling the letter A, B, or C. Your own choices will produce points for both yourself and the "Other" person. Likewise, the other's choice will produce points for him/her and for you. Every point has value: the more points you receive, the better for you, and the more points the "Other" receives, the better for him/her.

For each of the choice situations, circle A, B, or C, depending on which column you prefer most.

|   | | A | B | C |   | | A | B | C |
|---|---|---|---|---|---|---|---|---|---|
| (1) | You get | 480 | 540 | 480 | (5) | You get | 560 | 500 | 490 |
|   | Other gets | 80 | 280 | 480 |   | Other gets | 300 | 500 | 90 |
| (2) | You get | 560 | 500 | 500 | (6) | You get | 500 | 500 | 570 |
|   | Other gets | 300 | 500 | 100 |   | Other gets | 500 | 100 | 300 |
| (3) | You get | 520 | 520 | 580 | (7) | You get | 510 | 560 | 510 |
|   | Other gets | 520 | 120 | 320 |   | Other gets | 510 | 300 | 110 |
| (4) | You get | 500 | 560 | 490 | (8) | You get | 550 | 500 | 500 |
|   | Other gets | 100 | 300 | 490 |   | Other gets | 300 | 100 | 500 |

Participants are classified when they make six or more consistent choices. Prosocial choices are 1c, 2b, 3a, 4c, 5b, 6a, 7a, 8c; individualistic choices are 1b, 2a, 3c, 4b, 5a, 6c, 7b, 8a; and competitive choices are 1a, 2c, 3b, 4a, 5c, 6b, 7c, 8b.
*Source:* Excerpted from Van Lange et al., 1997. Copyright © American Psychological Association. Adapted with permission.

kind of **social value orientation** people spontaneously choose (Messick & McClintock, 1968), that is, what degree of rewards they generally prefer for themselves relative to a generalized other person. Three kinds emerge: **individualistic** (simple self-interest, also called *max own*), **cooperative** (helping self and the other simultaneously, called *max both*), or **competitive** (creating the biggest discrepancy of self over other, called *max diff*). When people choose consistently, they are classified as having one of these three orientations (Van Lange, De Bruin, Otten, & Joireman, 1997). Other individual differences involve **empathy** and **perspective-taking** (Eisenberg, 1991), described later.

In measuring the ways that personality predicts helping, researchers must consider measuring both personality and situation because they interact. In other words, different personalities are suited to different kinds of helping situations (Dovidio, Piliavin, Gaertner, Schroeder, & Clark, 1991). For example, in emergencies, the likely helpers are more impulsive, emotional, socially responsible, esteem oriented, and less oriented to safety and reality. These people and situations implicate helping based on sheer arousal. In long-term helping, the likely helpers are thoughtful about pros and cons, competent, confident, and responsible. These people and situations implicate helping based on a cost-benefit analysis. This distinction between people and situations suggests different research strategies about what variables to measure and manipulate, depending on the focus (e.g., emergency versus long-term).

Most often, rather than measuring personalities or personalities in specific situations, social psychologists focus on situational causes. Experimental games as one operationalization of prosocial behavior can assess situational variables (as well as personality differences in social value orientation). Instead of merely choosing preferred outcomes, as in the social value orientation test of personality, participants actually play experimental games with strangers. This method developed as part of **game theory** (Colman, 1982; Luce & Raiffa, 1957). Normally the researcher sets up cooperative and competitive choices, as displayed in Figure 9.1. (Notice that the payoff matrix in Chapter 8's discussion of interdependence theory derives from this kind of work.) The cooperative choice helps the partner, and the competitive one hurts the partner. Thus, a cooperative choice benefits both parties only if both parties cooperate (both people gain 2). But if one party cooperates while the other competes, then the competitor gains disproportionately (3) to the partner (0). If both compete, both lose, relative to most other outcomes (both get 1). Researchers manipulate situational variables, such as degree of communication allowed or patterns of partner choices, to track the frequency of cooperative (prosocial) and competitive choices.

In examining situational theories of prosocial behavior, social psychologists have elaborately staged some of our field's most inventive operational definitions of helping. Many studies use emergency situations, based on the original classic, Darley and Latané's 1968 study of bystander intervention in emergencies. That study, modeled after a gruesome and very public murder on the streets of New York, examined why bystanders might fail to intervene—precisely because the presence of other bystanders diffuses each individual's sense of personal responsibility. (For present purposes, we describe just the method; we examine the theory later.) In the classic study, participants listened through earphones as a series of alleged other participants took turns

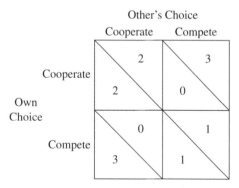

Within each cell, the lower left triangle represents own payoffs
and the upper right triangle represents the other's payoff.

**Figure 9.1**  Payoff Matrix for an Experimental Game of Cooperation (Prosocial) and Competition (Self-interest) Choices

**Table 9.3**    Effects of Group Size on Helping

| Group Size | % Responding by End of Seizure | Time (sec.) |
|---|---|---|
| 2 (Participant and victim) | 85 | 52 |
| 3 (Participant, victim, and 1 other) | 62 | 93 |
| 6 (Participant, victim, and 4 others) | 31 | 166 |

*Source:* From Darley & Latané, 1968. Copyright © American Psychological Association. Adapted with permission.

discussing personal problems associated with college life. On his first speaking turn, one person mentioned hesitantly that he was prone to seizures. On his second turn, the victim began to have an audible epileptic seizure, over three full minutes. Experimenters timed how long it took participants to leave their experimental cubicle to help, if they helped at all.

As Table 9.3 indicates, participants' helping was a direct function of the number of other people available to help (more bystanders, *less* helping). We come back to this study, but the relevant point for now is that this study introduced the now standard emergency-helping paradigm. Since that study, participants have overheard explosions and toppling bookcases, and they have encountered people needing a ride to the pharmacy, a call for the towing service, an ambulance, or help picking up spilled groceries. Some of the staged emergencies represent social psychology at its most theatrical. But the impact of the operationalized emergencies is important, for researchers need to know how people respond when they are startled, aroused, and genuinely worried.

Not all helping occurs under emergency, in the real world or in the laboratory. Some prosocial behavior is dogged and reliable over time. For example, research participants may respond to videotaped or written scenarios depicting victims of ongoing distress (e.g., family, relationship, or school troubles). Participants may report their willingness to donate hours, blood, or money for charity. In field studies, participants may report their actual time spent volunteering with AIDS patients or other community efforts.

## Core Social Motives

Why do people help in emergencies or donate resources over time? Prosocial behavior explicitly reflects four types of social motivation (Batson, 1994), which arguably reflect our core social motives. (1) Egoism (self-enhancement and controlling outcomes) contrasts with (2) altruism (which both indicates and maintains trust in the social world). (3) Collectivism represents group belonging, and (4) principlism reflects socially shared understanding of the moral world by those belonging to particular groups, as well as a sense of control over how people should behave. A partly overlapping set of motives surfaces in the self-reports of people who volunteer to work with people with AIDS (Snyder & Omoto, 1992). Social psychologists debate all these motives as if they were competing, even mutually exclusive explanations for prosocial behavior, but arguably each sometimes contributes to actual prosocial behavior—often in combination—so it is helpful to unpack them.

**SELF-ENHANCING AND CONTROLLING**   **Egoism** focuses on self-interest as a motive for prosocial behavior. Self-benefit is the ultimate goal. For social psychologists who endorse this view, people help only because it fosters their own survival or that of their genetic kin or is an accidental spillover from mechanisms evolved to help genetic kin. Similarly, people might help only in order to obtain personal rewards or avoid personal punishments, including self or public esteem. Or people might help merely in order to alleviate their own distress at watching someone else suffer. Thus, egoism combines our motives for controlling one's outcomes (contingency between what you do and what you get) and self-enhancing (protecting self-esteem). The controlling motive reflects the self-interest benefits just mentioned. As a self-reported example of self-enhancement, people who volunteer to help people with AIDS sometimes cite what the researchers label **esteem enhancement** ("to feel better about myself") as a motivation (Snyder & Omoto, 1992).

**TRUSTING**   In direct contrast to egoism, **altruism** describes a motive that makes people help because of genuine concern for others, to increase the welfare of others. They expect people to be responsible for each other. Recall that we defined the trusting motive to reflect a need to believe that the social world is a benevolent place. With altruism, people interpret the situation to be one that deserves help, and they experience empathy for the victim. Feeling the other person's pain motivates prosocial acts. The experience of individual sympathy and empathy distinguishes this motive from all the others. Apparently none of the AIDS volunteers explicitly cited simple altruism as their self-reported motive, perhaps because it would sound immodest. Regardless, altruism reflects the core social motive to trust, because it reflects the need to see the world and people in it as fundamentally benevolent.

**BELONGING**   **Collectivism** places the group's welfare as a central motive. Here, maintaining the group and one's belonging to it motivates prosocial behavior. Helping ingroup others, following the group's rules about reciprocity, playing one's role, and adhering to norms all facilitate collective life. One helps one's ingroup in order to maintain one's ingroup identity. AIDS volunteers who cite **community concern** ("because of my concern and worry about the gay community") illustrate collectivism. Note that the concern is for the group, not a specific individual, so this motive relates to the need to maintain belonging to a group. One's own inconvenience and comfort are sacrificed for a group one cherishes.

**UNDERSTANDING (AND CONTROLLING)**   **Principlism** is motivated to uphold moral standards. Impartial and universal, moral standards result from people's understanding of what is right and what is wrong. Principlism also relates to controlling outcomes, what people do and what they (deserve to) get. Thus, it implicates both understanding and controlling motives. People can reason at different moral levels, but principles or abstract standards guide prosocial behavior beyond self and group interest. Debatably, principlism reflects the core social motive of maintaining a coherent understanding of how the world ought to operate, perhaps mixed with a need for control, believing that certain ideas should guide one's own and others' behavior. As one example, AIDS volunteers who cite **values** ("because of my humanitarian obligation to help others") illustrate principlism.

Not all the motives listed by the AIDS volunteers are covered here, because they do not typically appear in other research on prosocial behavior. For example, a direct application of our understanding motive might seem to be illustrated by AIDS volunteers who cite what the researchers label **understanding** ("to learn about how people cope with AIDS"), but a pure curiosity motive, which is not here elaborated to indicate altruism (e.g., if they had added, "so I can relieve the suffering of others"), seems simply self-serving. In any case, this curiosity motive does not figure prominently in research on motives for helping. AIDS volunteers who cite **personal development** ("to challenge myself and test my skills") might be self-enhancing or might illustrate a possible role for the core social motive of controlling—efficacy and competence. The relevance of control and efficacy fits with dispositional findings that helpers often are high on general or task-specific competence, but the prosocial research has not explored this motive specifically, so we will not pursue it here. The four main motives in research on prosocial behavior thus are egotism, altruism, collectivism, and principlism, variously reflecting our core social motives.

## Summary of Definitions and Motives

Prosocial behavior intends to benefit others. Social and personality psychologists have operationalized individual differences in prosocial behavior via questionnaire studies, finding that emergency helping relates to dispositional impulsivity, whereas long-term helping relates to dispositional social responsibility. Situational factors related to prosocial behavior have prompted compelling and creative experimental methods to simulate impactful situations comparable to real cases of need. Dependent measures include participants' rate and speed of helping. Other methods include laboratory scenario studies and real-world volunteering. When people act prosocially, they do so for a variety of motivational reasons (egotism, altruism, collectivism, and principlism, at least), which variously address our core social motives, egoism reflecting both controlling and self-enhancing, altruism creating and maintaining the motive to trust the social world, collectivism helping to maintain group belonging, and principlism reflecting moral understanding and controlling.

## EGOISM HYPOTHESES: PURELY SELF-ENHANCING AND CONTROLLING

In the novel by Amy Tan, an American couple—who have been living together for years but temporarily separate when the woman goes to care for her ill elderly mother—discuss putting her into a nursing home:

> She was both shocked at the expense and amazed that Art would be willing to pay that for three months, nearly twelve thousand dollars. She stared at him, openmouthed.
> "It's worth it," he whispered. . . .
> Ruth exhaled heavily. "Listen, I'll pay half, and if it works out, I'll pay you back."

"We already went through this. No halves and there is nothing to pay back. I have some money saved, and I want to do this. And I don't mean it as a condition for us getting back together or getting rid of your mother or any of that. It's not a condition for anything. It's not pressure for you to make a decision one way or the other. There are no expectations, no strings attached." (Tan, 2001, p. 322)[3]

In this instance, it would be easy to interpret Art's apparent gift as a manipulative, self-serving ploy, no matter what he says. Although subsequent events suggest this to be a truly selfless act, it conceivably could also be motivated by selfish ends. And even more so, the traditional, rural Chinese family who takes in their daughter-in-law, ostensibly to avoid the ghosts' revenge, would be most obviously interpreted as self-serving. But go back to Oseola McCarty. How can we possibly view her gift as self-interest? Maybe, being childless, she did it because the local branch of the state university held the closest thing to genetic relatives? Maybe she did it to get social rewards in a lonely life? Maybe she did it to feel good despite her arthritic pain?

Social psychologists hotly debate whether prosocial behavior is ever truly altruistic or all ultimately reduces to egoism (e.g., Batson, 1998; Hoffman, 1981; Piliavin & Charng, 1990; Schroeder, Penner, Dovidio, & Piliavin, 1995). **Egoism** seeks the ultimate goal of increasing one's own welfare. This of course fits a simple interpretation of one evolutionary perspective. According to this approach, purely altruistic self-sacrifice would pose a nonadaptive puzzle. Why should an organism diminish or eliminate its chances of passing on its genes by sacrificing itself for another organism? Surely, this argument runs, such genetic self-sacrifice would not be selected over time, because the altruistic genes would never be passed along.

The simple analysis, it turns out, is deceptive, and the debate is more genuine, complex, and interesting. The proposed forms of egoistic motives include (1) kin selection (stemming from inclusive fitness), (2) social learning (including reciprocity and esteem seeking), and (3) mood protection, all forms of self-enhancement. And each could explain taking in your son's widow, subsidizing your partner's mother, and maybe even donating scholarships to strangers. Egoism is one of many convincing motives for prosocial behavior, but later we will see that it is not the only one.

## Kin Selection

As noted in Chapter 1, the unit of natural selection, evolutionary scientists point out, is the gene, not the individual, and this basic principle is called **inclusive fitness** (Hamilton, 1964; Wilson & Sober, 1994). Thus, **kin selection** might involve adaptive pressures promoting the survival of one's genetically related relatives. This suggests one plausible account for the evolution of prosocial behavior. If people predisposed to help their genetic relatives encourage the reproduction of such genes better than those who do not, people might be genetically predisposed to prosocial behavior. This does not mean that there is an "altruism gene," merely that people (and other social animals)

---

might have developed a propensity to respond to the needs of genetically related others, particularly those with reproductive potential. Kin selection could operate through a variety of motives, including pure egoism or even altruism. Evolutionary psychologists talk about people acting as if they are altruistically motivated, but with the underlying reality being genetic reproduction, in their view.

Evidence favoring the kin selection idea does suggest that people are more motivated to help genetically related others (Burnstein, Crandall, & Kitayama, 1994). As Figure 9.2 indicates, people are especially more likely to report that they would help kin, the more genetically related they are, especially under life-and-death circumstances. Women report receiving help from closer kin more than from distant kin (Essock-Vitale & McGuire, 1985). Genetic kin helping occurs for both Hong Kong Chinese and English participants (Ma, 1985).

People report being more likely to try to save another person than an animal and close relatives over strangers, and this focus on people and on relatives is consistent with the genetic relatedness hypothesis. But their propensity to help an innocent person over a uniformed Nazi suggests that similarity or empathy is important as well (Petrinovich, O'Neill, & Jorgensen, 1993). The dimensions shown in the United States are important in Taiwan also (O'Neill & Petrinovich, 1998), again suggesting cross-cultural generality. Although kinship matters and, by extension, egoism (self-enhancing and controlling), other motives (similarity and empathy) evidently matter as well. For example, meta-analysis indicates that dependency is a cue for helping (Bornstein, 1994). Many social factors are confounded with genetic relatedness and could equally account for the results.

If the evolution of pro-kin behavior makes sense, then some social psychological mechanisms would have to include recognizing kin and detecting their distress (Hoffman, 1981; Piliavin & Charng, 1990), as well as being motivated to act. With regard to recognizing kin, mothers recognize even their newborn infants by sight and odor (Porter, 1987). Adults report feeling closer to kin the more biologically related

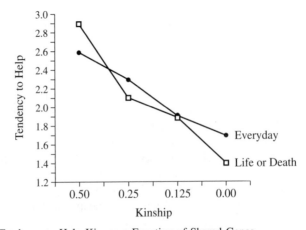

**Figure 9.2**    Tendency to Help Kin, as a Function of Shared Genes

*Source:* Burnstein et al., 1994. Copyright © American Psychological Association. Adapted with permission.

they are (Burnstein, Crandall, & Kitayama, 1994). People help people who are similar (Schroeder, Penner, Dovidio, & Piliavin, 1995), which may be a cue for recognizing genetic relatedness.

As for detecting distress, even newborns cry when they hear other infants cry. And very young children are distressed when another is distressed. Some researchers (Buck & Ginsburg, 1991) argue that human spontaneous communication of emotions (e.g., facial expressions) could mediate helping. But the underlying motives for responding to another's distress could still include altruistic empathy, collectivism, or principlism, as well as egoism.

Even if people have evolved to behave more prosocially toward kin, they would have to be motivated to act. The immediate psychological mediators for behavior remain unclear. For example, people could help those to whom they feel emotionally close. This could represent either altruistic empathy or collectivism or an evolutionary spillover from a tendency to help genetic relatives. Self-reported probable helping in a series of hypothetical life-or-death dilemmas showed that emotional closeness partially accounted for the effects of genetic relatedness (Korchmaros & Kenny, 2001). That is, emotional closeness, not merely genetic relatedness, explains the kin-helping phenomenon. Besides emotional closeness, other possible mechanisms for kin favoritism include mere exposure (introduced in Chapters 6 and 7) and other mechanisms discussed in the rest of this chapter: positive mood, guilt, empathic distress, and attributions of responsibility (Cunningham, 1985–1986). Helping genetic relatives fits the kin selection idea, but it is silent on some of the psychological processes by which it would occur. And the data also fit other possible motives, for example, the ingroup we-ness of collectivism (Dovidio, Piliavin, Gaertner, Schroeder, & Clark, 1991), discussed later in this chapter.

## Social Learning

People might help other people for egoistic reasons other than genetic survival. For example, people might learn that prosocial behavior ultimately pays off for the self. **Social learning** (introduced in Chapter 6 with regard to attitudes) highlights the uniquely interpersonal processes in conditioning such social phenomena as attitudes, helping, and aggression. Processes that illustrate the prosocial kind of social learning primarily include reciprocity and social rewards. Both support egoism (self-enhancing and controlling) in that what's-in-it-for-me constitutes the primary motive.

**RECIPROCITY**   People might learn that if they supply help, they will receive help in return, the principle of **reciprocity** (introduced in Chapter 7). Reciprocity could benefit genetic survival, as a form of symbiosis (literally, living together). In so-called **reciprocal altruism** (Trivers, 1971), if people help others who help them, then the survival of both is more likely. Regardless of an evolutionary explanation, reciprocity could simply result from short-term social learning: Helping is rewarded by the reciprocal return of the favor in some form. Recall from Chapter 7 that people like others who like them. Similarly, people help others who help them.

In relatively impersonal relationships, **equity** (introduced in Chapter 8) prevails, whereby people hold equivalent their respective outcomes relative to inputs. Thus, for example, if one person is overhelped, that person may be able to reciprocate other benefits, such as deference and esteem instead of reciprocal helping. In **exchange**, people reciprocate benefit for benefit, creating an equivalence of outcomes. If you photocopy articles for the seminar one week, other students should photocopy them other weeks. Norms favoring pure exchange-based reciprocity are strong (Gouldner, 1960). Business school alumni, for instance, cite reciprocity as one of the main reasons for donating to their alma mater, even years later (Diamond & Kashyap, 1997). The community-oriented notion of "giving-back" as an adult for what you received growing up also fits the idea of social exchange and reciprocity.

Reciprocity clearly occurs in short-term interactions. When people play experimental games with strangers, normally the researcher sets up cooperative and competitive choices, introduced earlier (Figure 9.1). Recall that the cooperative (prosocial) choice helps the partner and the competitive one hurts the partner. When people make their choices simultaneously on each trial, they eventually figure out that they both are better off if they both cooperate (Kelley, Thibaut, Radloff, & Mundy, 1962). Most relevant to considerations of reciprocal helping, research participants typically discover the most effective strategy, namely tit-for-tat (Pruitt, 1998). A **tit-for-tat** player cooperates only so long as the partner cooperates, but as soon as the partner defects to compete, the player also competes, until the partner cooperates again (Axelrod & Hamilton, 1981). This suggests reciprocity of both helping and hindering, a form of self-interested prosocial behavior.

Tit-for-tat is effective partly because it punishes cheaters. **Cheater detection** (introduced in Chapter 4; the idea that we have evolved sensitivities to notice the violation of social contracts) is important to evolutionary accounts of self-interested helping behavior. If the model holds true, the basic evolutionary principles are that (1) needs arise, (2) nearby others can help, and (3) cheating does not pay (Trivers, 1971). If cheating indeed does not pay, then evolutionary psychologists need to look for a detection and enforcement mechanism. This analysis led to the idea that people might be adapted to detect people who cheat on a social contract (Cosmides, 1989; Cosmides & Tooby, 1992, 1996; see Chapter 4). People who are chronically **free-riders** (letting others pay the cost of **public goods**, i.e., shared benefits, such as public television) are less helpful in general (Piliavin & Charng, 1990). If individuals detect cheaters and free-riders, they can minimize personal costs.

Yet another form of reciprocity is **indirect reciprocity**, whereby people help others mainly to develop an altruistic reputation, which then leads to third-parties benefiting them in the future (Nowak, 2006). Indirect reciprocity is still egoistic, being incentive-driven. Individual differences in egoism-altruism drive people's motivation toward indirect reciprocity: Egoists help when future rewards from others are possible, while altruists are less affected by such incentives (Simpson & Willer, 2008). Thus, some people may help strategically, when they know their reputation will profit them in future encounters (Semmann, Krambeck, & Milinski, 2004). Indirect reciprocity is cognitively demanding because people need to track own interactions but also the whole network of interactions, suggesting the evolution of norms in groups and abstract principles of morality (see those later sections). Indirect reciprocity depends on the probability of knowing someone else's reputation before helping (Nowak, 2006), so social controls are crucial shortcuts.

A more advanced form of indirect reciprocity, **network reciprocity**, also can encourage cooperation among a limited number of immediate neighbors. These ideas also suggest a revived form of **group selection**, whereby a group of cooperators (mutually helpful people) survives better than a group of entirely selfish, so-called defectors. All these forms of social learning related to reciprocity and exchange fit the idea that people acquire **enlightened self-interest**, learning that selfish behavior pays off in the short term but not the long term. People believe this even in large-scale social dilemmas, such as pollution, overfishing, and other ecological issues (Baron, 1997). One could argue that these kinds of social learning fit ultimately egoistic motives, but one could perfectly well also argue that social norms establish the collective rules and that belonging instead motivates reciprocity.

**SOCIAL REWARDS AND COSTS**    People often have too narrow a view of rewards and costs. Helping can entail a range of costs, such as time, money, effort, pain, danger, embarrassment, disgust, disapproval, and uncertainty (Dovidio, Piliavin, Gaertner, Schroeder, & Clark, 1991). But it can also entail a range of rewards, such as money, praise, recognition, gratitude, and relief. Tangible rewards clearly would undermine labeling a particular behavior as motivated by altruism, according to our earlier definition, whereas intangible rewards are more ambiguous. For example, cooperative behavior appears to be intrinsically rewarding; the same areas of the brain activate under cooperation as under rewards (Rilling et al., 2002). People benefit even more from giving social support than they do from receiving it (Brown, Nesse, Vinokur, & Smith, 2003). Even without self-reward, one might receive praise, approval, or social connection for helping; might that be an egoistic motive for otherwise apparently altruistic prosocial behavior?

People do weigh costs against rewards in deciding whether to help, except under the most impulsive helping. For example, in a review of 12 experiments, Dovidio (1984) found that helping decreased, as the cost of helping increased. Furthermore, in a meta-analysis of 13 studies, helping *increased*, as the personal costs of *not* helping increased (Dovidio et al., 1991). If a cost-benefit analysis operates, perhaps helping is fundamentally self-interested because people do not help unless they are on balance rewarded.

People might learn that if they help, they will receive **social rewards**, such as public esteem. This constitutes a form of social learning because the rewards come from other people, mandated by their shared social groups. In one such egoistic view of social learning (Cialdini, Baumann, & Kenrick, 1981), children only rarely help, in part because it constitutes a material cost, but later they help more when they learn that social rewards accompany prosocial acts. Adults' helping results from internalized self-reward, in this model. And indeed, both adults and children do help more after prior helping has just been rewarded, especially if the rewards are social and not material (Grusec, 1991). Any reward seen as a bribe undermines **intrinsic motivation** to help (Fabes, Fultz, Eisenberg, May-Plumlee, & Christopher, 1989), as self-perception

**Table 9.4** Naturalistic Studies of Models and Prosocial Behavior

| | No. of helpers or donors | |
| --- | --- | --- |
| Setting | Model | No Model |
| Flat tire on highway, Los Angeles | 58 | 35 |
| Salvation Army kettle, Princeton | 69 | 43 |
| Salvation Army kettle, Trenton | 84 | 56 |

*Source:* Data from Bryan & Test, 1967.

theory, noted in Chapter 3, predicts. Thus, to increase intrinsic motivation to help, social rewards are likely to be more effective than material rewards. In addition to their own reward experiences, people also probably help more when they see someone else rewarded for helping, a process called **vicarious conditioning** or **observational learning** (introduced in Chapter 6), although not a lot of research has addressed this idea.

In another form of social learning, **modeling**, people imitate someone else who helps. In one classic study (Bryan & Test, 1967), drivers saw a female undergraduate standing near a Ford Mustang with a flat tire, along the side of the road. A spare tire leaned up against the car. Half the time, her car was preceded, one-quarter mile away, by an Oldsmobile with a flat tire, where another young woman watched a man changing the tire; half the time no model was present. The conditions with a model present or absent were compared for 2000 passing motorists apiece, to see how many would stop to help. As the first line of Table 9.4 shows, many more people stopped to help when they had just seen someone else helping. Two other studies varied the presence or absence of a model on the number of donations to a Salvation Army kettle during the December holiday season. Again, seeing someone else donate made passersby more likely to donate as well.

This effect of modeling has been demonstrated among adults reporting that they imitated their parents' prosocial behavior in settings as mundane as blood donation (Piliavin & Callero, 1991) and as historic as gentiles who rescued Jews from Nazi extermination (London, 1970) or the most fully committed whites who worked for civil rights in the Southern United States (Rosenhan, 1970). Also consistent with a modeling account, prosocial behavior by family members clearly influences children's prosocial behavior (Radke-Yarrow & Zahn-Waxler, 1986). In contrast, people also imitate a model's selfish, exploiting behavior, even if it makes them indignant (Masor, Hornstein, & Tobin, 1973).

## Mood Protection

People's moods reliably affect their likelihood of helping, with most good moods facilitating help and some bad moods also facilitating help, but for very different reasons (Cunningham et al., 1980; Cunningham et al., 1990; Eisenberg, 1991). Both can be viewed as egoistic motives, if the primary cause of helping is maintaining or improving one's mood.

**MAINTAINING GOOD MOODS**    Good moods reliably help helping. Recall the example from Chapter 1, in which finding a dime in a phone booth encouraged people to help a stranger pick up spilled papers (Isen & Levin, 1972). In 61 tests of the feeling good → helping hypothesis, a meta-analysis showed that the average study obtains a large effect (Carlson, Charlin, & Miller, 1988). Experimental manipulations of positive moods have given participants success experiences, money, gifts, pleasant music, or an instruction to think happy thoughts (Salovey, Mayer, & Rosenhan, 1991). The resulting prosocial behaviors have included picking up someone's dropped books and papers, searching for lost contact lenses, donating money or time, tutoring a needy student, donating blood, and participating in another experiment.

The effect of cheerfulness on helping, though large, is variable, which suggests some **moderating variables**, that is, variables that increase or decrease the size of the effect. For example, the more positive the appeal for help, the more likely cheerful people are to help (Cunningham, Steinberg, & Grev, 1980). Conversely, helping that requires attending to *unpleasantness* undermines the effects of feeling good on helping (Isen & Simmonds, 1978). A whole series of moderating variables suggests that people in a good mood will help mainly when it maintains their cheerful mood (see Table 9.5; Carlson et al., 1988). For example, the more the good mood improves people's **social outlook** (focus on the social community), the more likely the mood is to motivate helping (Holloway, Tucker, & Hornstein, 1977; Hornstein, LaKind, Frankel, & Manne, 1975). The more *pleasant the task*, the more people in good moods are helpful (Forest, Clark, Mills, & Isen, 1979). The more people's mood reflects *self-satisfaction* (i.e., their relative advantage in resources and good fortune), the more happy people help (Rosenhan, Salovey, & Hargis, 1981; Salovey, Mayer, & Rosenhan, 1991).

**Table 9.5**    Variables that Increase the Impact of Good Moods on Helping

| Variable | Correlation with the Mood-Helping Effect |
|---|---|
| Self as target of positive event (i.e., own relative advantage) | .49 |
| Pleasantness of the helping task | .34 |
| Social outlook (i.e., positive attitude toward community) | .31 |
| Sustained helpfulness (i.e., burden over time) | −.37 |
| Extreme high or low positive affect (i.e., deviation from moderate) | −.38 |
| Guilt | −.44 |

Entries are partial correlations, which isolate the effect of the variable, controlling for other variables. The higher a positive correlation, the more the variable facilitates the effect of good moods on helping; negative numbers indicate interference with the effect. All listed variables are statistically significant, in the hypothesized direction.

*Source:* From Carlson et al., 1988. Copyright © American Psychological Association. Adapted with permission.

In contrast, when people are happy because of someone else's good fortune, *envy* apparently sets in, and they are less helpful (Rosenhan et al., 1981; Salovey et al., 1991). Other kinds of helping that would damage a good mood also discourage helping: Feeling *guilty* decreases helping when people are cheerful (Cunningham et al., 1980). *Burdensome* helping that would entail an obligation sustained over time also dissuades cheerful people from helping (Carlson et al., 1988). Being in *only a little bit of a good mood* decreases helping because dealing with any negative experience (someone else's distress, one's own effort) would easily eliminate one's mood. And being in *too good a mood* decreases helping because when elated, one would not bother with someone else's problem (Carlson et al., 1988). Another way to think about these moderating variables is as **boundary conditions**, that is, situations in which the positive mood effect on helping does not occur, primarily cases that endanger one's mood.

Given these moderators, what might be the **mediating variables**—processes by which positive mood enhances helping? **Mood maintenance** (prolonging a good mood) fits most of the moderating variables. For example, when a model reports feeling good about helping, people are more likely to help. In one study (Hornstein, Fisch, & Holmes, 1968), Manhattan pedestrians encountered a man's wallet protruding out of an open envelope. The wallet obviously contained money, and wrapped around it was a letter from a previous finder reporting his feelings about being able to return the wallet. Participants were more likely to return the wallet intact, when the letter said:

> Dear Mr. Erwin: I found your wallet which I am returning. Everything is here just as I found it. I must say that it has been a pleasure to be able to help somebody in the small things that make life nicer. It's really been no problem at all and I'm glad to be able to help.

They were also likely to help when the letter said nothing about feelings (both neutral and positive conditions would not interfere with a good mood). But they helped less when the letter said:

> Dear Mr. Erwin: I found your wallet which I am returning. Everything is here just as I found it. I must say that taking responsibility for the wallet and having to return it has been a great inconvenience. I was quite annoyed at having to bother with the whole problem of returning it. I hope you appreciate the efforts I have gone through.[4]

The results (see Table 9.6) fit the idea that people learn vicariously from the model's reported experience what their own likely experience will be. This fits an egoistic effort to maintain one's mood and to avoid bad feelings.

But the egoistic desire to hold onto one's good mood is not the only possible motive. For example, the research goes beyond egoistic mood maintenance in that a positive outlook must be specifically social (e.g., lives saved because of people's intervention) to enhance helping, whereas a nonsocial positive outlook (e.g., lives saved because of natural events) does not (Holloway et al., 1977). Perhaps, then,

---

[4] Copyright © American Psychological Association. Reprinted with permission.

**Table 9.6**    Returned Wallets as a Function of Previous Finder's Experience

| Finder's Reported Experience | Returned | Not Returned |
| --- | --- | --- |
| Positive | 14 | 6 |
| Neutral | 12 | 8 |
| Negative | 2 | 18 |

*Source:* From Hornstein et al., 1968, first study and replication. Copyright ©1968 American Psychological Association. Adapted with permission.

some of the mood maintenance data also fit a collectivist (group-oriented) motive, given the specifically social nature of good moods that enhance helping.

In line with this view of mood priming positive views of others, positive moods increase attraction to others, their perceived positive features, and overall positive evaluations (e.g., Isen, Shalker, Clark, & Karp, 1978). Positive moods specifically increase positive associations with helping situations and with people one expects to meet (Clark & Waddell, 1983). All this fits the idea that good moods improve people's social outlook, which in turn leads to helping. However, as noted, a social outlook could prime collectivism and belonging motives (or perhaps altruism and trusting motives), so this questions the assumption that the relationship between positive mood and helping must be egoistic.

Nonetheless, as an alternative to the egoism, collectivism, and altruism motives, the **concomitance hypothesis** (Manucia, Baumann, & Cialdini, 1984) holds that although a good mood makes people help, it is a side effect (mere concomitant), not intended to maintain one's mood. That is, feeling good makes people more optimistic, the positive features of situations more salient, and other people more attractive. In this view, any of the effects can facilitate helping, but the effect is indirect and not instrumentally directed toward mood maintenance. Some psychologists might view this hypothesis as simply explaining the mechanisms or mediating variables.

Whatever the mediators and moderators, good moods do reliably lead to helping in many circumstances. In organizations, for example, various factors promote good moods, which in turn promote spontaneous acts of good will. Specific causes of good moods might include one's immediate work group and one's context, as well as dispositions and life history. Good moods in turn predict **organizational spontaneity**, which includes "helping co-workers, protecting the organization, making constructive suggestions, developing oneself, and spreading goodwill" (George & Brief, 1992, p. 310).

**RELIEVING BAD MOODS**    People sometimes help when they feel bad, but it depends on exactly *how* they feel bad. If they feel bad because of **guilt** (i.e., they feel personally responsible for an aversive outcome), that consistently encourages prosocial behavior (Carlson & Miller, 1987; Salovey, Mayer, & Rosenhan, 1991). Notice that this differs from the way guilt decreases helping when people are originally in a good mood. Here, the point is that being in a bad mood, specifically because of guilt, increases help. When people believe they have transgressed (lied, cheated, broken equipment, harmed someone, touched museum displays, fed zoo animals), they presumably feel guilty and in a bad mood (guilt and mood are not always measured). Then, they are more likely to donate to charity, help an accident victim, pick up someone's dropped items, and volunteer for an experiment (Katzev, Edelsack, Steinmetz, Walker, & Wright, 1978; Kidd & Berkowitz, 1976; Riordan, Dunaway, Hass, James, & Kruger, 1984). If they are excused, pardoned, or cheered up after transgressing (and presumably not in a guilty, bad mood), they do not help as often.

Guilt as a cause of prosocial behavior fits a model whereby people assume personal responsibility, but only when they are **objectively self-aware** (Duval & Wicklund, 1972; Wicklund, 1975). This concept refers to the idea that when people are self-focused, they compare themselves to salient ideals (and usually find themselves wanting), so they try to escape from self-awareness or correct their behavior to bring it closer to salient standards (Scheier & Carver, 1983). Participants become objectively self-aware when, for example, they see their images on television or fill out an autobiographical questionnaire (Duval, Duval, & Neely, 1979). If they are exposed immediately to a victim of disease or poverty, self-aware people are more likely to feel personally responsible and to volunteer help than they would otherwise (Table 9.7). These data are consistent with the idea that guilt increases helping through self-awareness. A meta-analysis indicates that, indeed, high self-awareness, combined with salient values or requests for helping, increases the effect of bad moods (presumably guilt) on helping (Carlson & Miller, 1987).

Guilt as a cause of prosocial behavior also fits an **attentional model**, whereby attending to another person's misfortune increases empathy or increases awareness of the other person's needs (Thompson, Cowan, & Rosenhan, 1980). And indeed, a focus on the other person's misfortune, as opposed to one's own misfortune, increases the effect of negative moods on helping (Carlson & Miller, 1987). This fits an empathy-altruism motive. In much of the work on guilt, the mediating processes are not always specified but must be inferred from manipulations and outcomes.

**Table 9.7** Mean Willingness to Help Victims of Sexually Transmitted Disease

| Item | Immediate (Self-Aware) | | Delayed (Not Self-Aware) | | Control |
|---|---|---|---|---|---|
| | Before | After | Before | After | |
| Attribution of responsibility to self | 9.0 | 10.3 | 6.9 | 7.9 | 6.5 |
| Teach class | 11.2 | 11.2 | 8.5 | 7.9 | 7.0 |
| Volunteer work at clinic | 7.6 | 8.9 | 7.6 | 6.0 | 8.2 |
| Personal contribution | 6.9 | 7.7 | 3.3 | 6.6 | 5.2 |
| Combined helping | 25.7 | 27.8 | 19.4 | 20.5 | 20.4 |

Numbers represent means for each condition. The higher the number, the greater the willingness to help. *Source:* From Duval et al., 1979. Copyright © American Psychological Association. Adapted with permission.

**Sadness** (depressed feelings resulting from awareness of negative events) might seem to operate in the same way as guilt, but its effects on helping are more mixed. In one view, people rarely enjoy sadness and by adulthood have learned ways to avoid it. Building on this idea, people might use helping as a form of **negative state relief** because helping has acquired its own reward value. If one is brought up being praised for helping, then helping becomes an internalized reward, and it could relieve sadness. This fits the social learning framework of the previous section as well as the mood maintenance framework of this section.

The earliest proposal of negative-state-relief idea (Cialdini, Darby, & Vincent, 1973) involved participants induced to harm or witness harm against another person. A chair was rigged so that when it was pulled out from the desk, either the undergraduate experimenter or participant spilled three boxes of a graduate student's data, thereby putting the records completely out of order. This event—amplified by the experimenter's apparent distress—presumably put participants into a negative state (though this was not measured directly). Some of them then received an independent positive event (money or approval). Finally, all had a chance to help a fellow student by volunteering for an experiment. The witnesses and doers of harm helped *only* if they had received no positive event, so this fits the idea that they helped the other person in order to make themselves feel better. Those who had already been rewarded (and presumably felt better already) helped about as much as control subjects, who had never been exposed to the harm doing (see Table 9.8). Note that guilt alone is not a parsimonious explanation because (1) it was not measured and (2) people who had merely witnessed the misfortune (so probably did not feel guilty) behaved just as did those who had caused it.

The negative-state-relief model takes an explicitly self-serving and instrumental view of helping, and various findings are consistent with this view. People help the most when they believe their sad mood is **labile** (i.e., not fixed) and thus can be changed (Manucia, Baumann, & Cialdini, 1984). Negative moods cause helping only when the costs are low (and would not undermine mood enhancement; Weyant, 1978). And helping indeed is intrinsically rewarding (Weiss, Boyer, Lombardo, & Stich, 1973).

**Table 9.8**  Negative State Relief Reduces Helping

| | No Relief from Negative State | | Relief from Negative State | | No Harm |
|---|---|---|---|---|---|
| | No Task | Additional Task | Money | Approval | |
| Harm doer | 5.43 | 3.50 | 1.86 | 1.44 | |
| Witness | 3.38 | 6.29 | 2.86 | 2.43 | |
| Neither | | | | | 2.75 |

The means in the No-Relief and Relief conditions reflect nonoverlapping distributions and thus show a large effect.
*Source:* From Cialdini et al., 1973. Copyright © Elsevier. Adapted with permission.

The negative-state-relief model is controversial. A meta-analysis (Carlson & Miller, 1987) found no support for some of the conditions that should encourage helping according to the model. According to the model, negative mood effects on helping should increase with age, as children learn to relieve their negative moods (Cialdini, Baumann, & Kenrick, 1981); they do not. Negative mood effects on helping should increase with the degree of bad mood; they do not. Negative mood effects on helping should decrease if the helping task itself is aversive (because it would undermine its role in mood enhancement); they do not. The failures to find results are disappointing for the model. Moreover, empathy causes people to help even when they know their mood will improve for other reasons, so that helping per se will not improve their mood (Batson et al., 1989). And some people continue to feel bad when their help fails, even though their failure may be fully justified and they could still self-reward their efforts, if mood enhancement were their main reason for helping (Batson & Weeks, 1996).

All this has led some researchers to question the generality of the negative-state-relief model (Batson, 1998; Eisenberg, 1991; Salovey, Mayer, & Rosenhan, 1991), although others still defend it (Cialdini & Fultz, 1990; Schaller & Cialdini, 1988). Nevertheless, the results of the original studies remain, and researchers have found results consistent with the model.

In short, good moods and bad moods (when they do facilitate helping) might do so for entirely different reasons. In the case of good moods, people help because they see the good side of everything, including helping. In the case of a bad mood from guilt, they help out of personal responsibility and obligation (Cunningham, Steinberg, & Grev, 1980). In the case of a bad mood from sadness, they might help to relieve sadness, at least some of the people, some of the time. Some evidence suggests that people in good moods, compared with neutral or bad ones, think the hardest about the affective consequences of their helping (Wegener & Petty, 1994).

## Summary of Egoism Hypotheses

Egoistic motives for helping could include genetic kin selection, whereby people help others in direct proportion to their genetic relatedness, a phenomenon that occurs cross-culturally. Possible mechanisms might have evolved for helping as a way to perpetuate one's genes: recognizing kin and detecting distress, both of which people do well and early in life. However, some of the variables that mediate between detecting the distress of kin and coming to their aid are compatible with other theories. Emotional closeness and empathy could fit kin selection, but they could also fit more altruistic motives, throwing into doubt kin selection (sometimes interpreted to be pure egoism) as a sole motive.

Social learning is another mechanism proposed to reflect egoistic motives. People learn that helping other people pays off. So they might help others only because they expect to be helped in return. But the reciprocity principle also fits equity and exchange theories of social norms. In short-term, artificial experimental games, people quickly evolve tit-for-tat rules of reciprocity. People are alert to detect cheaters who fail to abide by these social rules. And people do believe in enlightened self-interest, namely that prosocial behavior pays off in the long run.

Besides reciprocity, people help when the social rewards outweigh the social costs. They learn these contingencies through vicarious conditioning or observational learning, but especially by imitating the behavior of others, in the process called modeling (all introduced in Chapter 6).

Finally, people might help others mainly in order to protect their own moods. Cheerful people do help more, perhaps to maintain their good moods (egoism) or perhaps because they see the good side of everything. When people feel good, they do see good in others and in the social outlook more generally. When people feel personally advantaged, they are more likely to help than when they are happy because of someone else's good fortune. And unpleasant helping does not increase under good moods. Although these findings fit an egoistic self-enhancement motive, they also fit altruistic, collectivist, and perhaps even principled helping.

People in bad moods clearly help when the mood is guilt. Feeling responsible for another's misfortune reliably increases helping, which may relieve guilt, a negative mood. When the bad mood is sadness, the results are more mixed, and researchers disagree. Sad people do help under some circumstances that seem designed to make themselves feel better, but sad people also help sometimes when it will not improve their mood. The negative-state-relief hypothesis continues to provoke controversy.

## ALTRUISM HYPOTHESES: MAINTAINING TRUST IN THE WORLD AS BENEVOLENT

Why would Art offer to pay for a nursing home for his live-in partner Ruth's mother? Kin selection is unlikely, because he does not expect to have children with Ruth. Nevertheless, evolutionary psychologists would argue that the evolved mechanism for kin selection might spill over to surrogate relationships that mimic the conditions of kin selection. Social learning is also plausible, specifically, belief in reciprocity, although Art denies expecting anything in return. Mood might be an explanation, although he makes the decision over a period of time when he doesn't seem particularly happy, guilty, or sad. One could make parallel arguments about Ms. McCarty. Maybe, instead of all these motives that social psychologists have interpreted as egoistic, just maybe their motives are pure altruism.

**Altruism**, as introduced earlier, constitutes the motivation to help out of a concern for others and their welfare. Rather than self-interest, in this view, people are motivated by other-interest. Altruism goes with a belief that people are responsible for each other and that they deserve help. As such, it fits with motives to believe the best of other people, the core social motive here termed trusting. Trust in others goes with a concern for others. Individual differences in empathy correlate with the tendency to trust others (Piliavin & Charng, 1990). People have a strong need to believe that the world is benevolent and will go to great lengths to restore that belief (Janoff-Bulman, 1992).

Evidence for altruism consists partly in showing that prosocial behavior is (1) based on processes demonstrating concern, such as attributions of responsibility to self, and (2) partly based on showing that people and situations high on empathy tend to facilitate helping. The best situational predictors of helping are the victim's unambiguous and severe need, attractive appearance, and similarity to the potential helper. Also, more bystanders present (as noted earlier) and being in a big city (with stimulus overload) are factors that reliably decrease helping (Batson, 1998). All these situational factors impact people's felt responsibility and empathy, consistent with altruistic motivations.

## Attributions of Responsibility

In New York City's Queens borough, Kitty Genovese was repeatedly stabbed, over a period of 30 minutes, and died, screaming for help, as 38 of her neighbors watched from their homes, without intervening or even calling the police. Why?

People confronting other people's misfortunes are more likely to help if they attribute responsibility to themselves for alleviating the victims' distress, if they do not see others as responsible, and if they do not see the victims as responsible for their own distress. Research suggests that the neighbors did not attribute personal responsibility for helping, thought other neighbors might help, and may have thought the assault was a lovers' quarrel, thereby apparently implicating the victim as partly responsible. We address each factor in turn.

**HELPERS' FELT RESPONSIBILITY**   The classic studies in prosocial behavior are the series on bystander intervention, introduced earlier (Table 9.3). The basic counterintuitive finding shows that the *more* bystanders present, the *less* likely a given person is to help (Darley & Latané, 1968; Latané & Darley, 1968). The explanation is that, the more people present, the more the witnesses experience a **diffusion of responsibility**. That is, people believe that others may take action, so they are not personally responsible. In the Genovese case, the neighbors apparently assumed that someone else would intervene if appropriate. The crucial process here is **felt responsibility**. What does it take for people to feel that they personally must take action on someone else's behalf? Several steps pave the way for bystander intervention. People must

- Notice the events
- Interpret the events as an emergency
- Feel personal responsibility for acting
- Consider what form of assistance is needed
- Implement action (Latané & Darley, 1970)

The first three steps are less likely the more other people are around and not reacting. In one study, male undergraduates sat in a room that gradually began to fill with smoke as they completed questionnaires. When alone, 75% reported the smoke, but when in groups of three participants, only 38% of participants responded, showing that people respond less to an emergency, the more of them there are. Consistent with the idea that it is the passivity of the other bystanders that inhibits people, when the participant was in a group of three with two confederates trained to be passive, only 10% reported the smoke. "A crowd can . . . force inaction on its members" (Latané

& Darley, 1968, p. 217). If everyone else seems to interpret the event as not seᴀ then the apparent consensus favoring nonintervention will guide the onlooker. 'ᴀ irony, of course, is that as each person tries to appear calm, while covertly watchinᵍ other people's reactions, everyone is fooled into thinking no one is worried. This exemplifies **pluralistic ignorance** (previously introduced in Chapter 2).

Bystanders have inhibited intervention for victims of seizures (Darley & Latané, 1968; Schwartz & Clausen, 1970), theft of belongings in a library (Shaffer, Rogel, & Hendrick, 1975), shoplifting in a supermarket (Bickman & Rosenbaum, 1977), and preventing a peer's driving while drunk (Rabow, Newcomb, Monto, & Hernandez, 1990). The interventions seem to turn on people's felt responsibility, which emerges from the decision-making stages just described (Bickman & Rosenbaum, 1977).

**VICTIMS' ASSIGNED RESPONSIBILITY**   Attributions of responsibility depend not only on potential helpers but also on the victims' apparent responsibility for their own plight. People are less likely to help others they perceive as responsible for their own misfortune. In an **attributional theory of motivation** (Weiner, 1980, 1985), causes can be **internal** or **external**, as in other attribution theories that contrast, respectively, dispositional and situational causes (Chapter 3). In addition, causes can be **controllable** or **uncontrollable**, that is, subject to human volition. People are least likely to help someone whose misfortune is attributed to internal, controllable factors (see Table 9.9), that is, when it's their own fault. A student who has no notes to study because he didn't bother to attend class (internal, controllable) will receive less help than a noteless student who could not attend class for internal, uncontrollable reasons (broken leg) or for external reasons, either controllable (the TA did not bother to communicate a room change) or uncontrollable (the TA was unable to communicate a room change).

As the table indicates, different attributions elicit different emotions. Internal, controllable problems (the person's own fault) generate anger, disgust, and distaste, as well as neglect. External and uncontrollable misfortunes generate sympathy, pity, and concern, as well as helping. Recall from Chapter 3 that such attributions for poverty generate differing policy implications for degree of government aid (Zucker & Weiner, 1993). Similarly, physical stigmas (e.g., disabilities, either congenital or acquired) elicit pity and helping, because they are usually considered uncontrollable and external. In contrast, mental-behavioral stigmas (e.g., mental illness, alcoholism) elicit less pity, more anger, and neglect because they are considered internal and controllable (Weiner,

**Table 9.9**   Attributions of Responsibility to Victims

| Locus | Controllable | Uncontrollable |
|---|---|---|
| Internal | Disgust, anger | Pity, sympathy |
| | No help | Help |
| External | Pity, sympathy | Pity, sympathy |
| | Help | Help |

*Source:* From Weiner, 1980. Copyright © American Psychological Association. Adapted with permission.

Perry, & Magnusson, 1988). As another example, when researchers staged a person's collapse on a subway car, an apparently ill person (uncontrollable) received more help than an apparently drunk person (controllable) (Piliavin, Rodin, & Piliavin, 1969).

Political conservatives put more weight on perceived personal responsibility than liberals do, as noted. In one study, conservatives withheld assistance from people personally responsible for their fate, across policy domains (e.g., drug subsidies for people with AIDS, low-income housing, help to victims of natural disasters). Their reported motivations emphasize punishing people who violate social norms and deterring free-riders (Skitka, 1999; Skitka & Tetlock, 1993). Liberals tend to help everyone equally, their reported motivations aiming to avoid awkward social value trade-offs that place monetary value on people's lives. That is, compared with conservatives, they do not penalize people responsible for their own fate more than people not responsible. In a related vein, religious fundamentalists hold different attributions about outgroup members who do and do not contradict their values. They view single mothers and homosexuals as responsible for their predicament (e.g., unemployment) but do not hold students and Native Canadians responsible for the same predicament (Jackson & Esses, 1997). Regardless of where they stand, most people are morally outraged at putting a price tag on their sacred values, as we will see (Tetlock, Kristel, Elson, Green, & Lerner, 2000).

**COMBINED RESPONSIBILITY FOR CAUSE AND CURE**    People are concerned not just with causes but also with cures. Combining responsibility assigned to victims for causes and cures, along with responsibility felt by witnesses for causes and cures, creates four **models of helping and coping** (Brickman et al., 1982). The distinction between responsibility for a problem and its solution has several implications: who should act, how to perceive the victim, how to view human nature, and what the potential pathologies are (see Table 9.10). Helping-coping models tend to vary across helping professions. For example, a **medical model** absolves the victim of responsibility for either cause or cure: The victim is ill because humans are weak and must accept treatment by experts. In a **moral model**, espoused by some religions, the victim is responsible for both the problem and its solution: The victim is lazy and must strive with peers, who exhort each other because humans can be strong. In an **enlightenment model**, espoused by some religions and some cults, victims are responsible for the cause because humans are basically bad or sinful, so they are guilty and must submit to the discipline of authorities. Alcoholics Anonymous, for example, requires people to admit their responsibility for their drinking problem but also to admit they are powerless to restore themselves and must turn themselves over to a higher power, who will remove their shortcomings; the label *enlightenment* reflects the need to have a spiritual awakening, according to the Alcoholics Anonymous 12-step program. Finally, the **compensatory model** reflects Jesse Jackson's reputed motto: "You are not responsible for being down, but you are responsible for getting up." Victims are deprived, but they must assert themselves, along with other subordinates who must mobilize because humans are basically good and can bring about change for the better. Although largely untested by social psychologists, other psychologists have applied these four models to understand people's attributions for

**Table 9.10**    Consequences of Attribution of Responsibility in Four Models
of Helping and Coping

| Attribution to Self of Responsibility for Problem | Attribution to Self of Responsibility for Solution | |
|---|---|---|
| | High | Low |
| **High** | **Moral model** | **Enlightenment model** |
| Perception of self | Lazy | Guilty |
| Actions expected of self | Striving | Submission |
| Others besides self who must act | Peers | Authorities |
| Actions expected of others | Exhortation | Discipline |
| Implicit view of human nature | Strong | Bad |
| Potential pathology | Loneliness | Fanaticism |
| **Low** | **Compensatory model** | **Medical model** |
| Perception of self | Deprived | Ill |
| Actions expected of self | Assertion | Acceptance |
| Others besides self who must act | Subordinates | Experts |
| Actions expected of others | Mobilization | Treatment |
| Implicit view of human nature | Good | Weak |
| Potential pathology | Alienation | Dependency |

*Source:* From Brickman et al., 1982. Copyright © American Psychological Association. Adapted with permission.

individual unemployment, depression, alcoholism, self-poisoning, counseling, cancer care, elder care, and dissertation completion (author's PsycInfo search, 2003).

The more severe the problem, the more people want to believe someone is responsible for it; this is termed the **defensive attribution** bias, introduced in Chapter 3. People will go to considerable effort to figure out why a personal tragedy allegedly occurred. This aspect of the attribution process fits our core social motive of understanding. But more broadly, as noted, explaining negative events helps people's core motive to maintain trust in the benevolence of the world and especially other people (Janoff-Bulman, 1992). When people's assumptions about trust are shattered by tragedy, one of their main tasks is to rebuild that basic trust, by attributions of responsibility and by trying to relieve distress.

## Empathy, Sympathy, and Altruism

As we have just seen, attributions of responsibility can result in prosocial feelings and actions. Other kinds of feelings also guide prosocial behavior. **Empathy** is an affective response that mimics another person's emotional state (Eisenberg, 2000). When people observe another person experiencing an aversive event, at least one of the same neural areas (i.e., the amygdala) activates as when they personally fear experiencing the event (Olsson, Nearing, & Phelps, 2007). But people also have to differentiate self and other, so other neural areas implicated in empathy also include the insula, the anterior cingulate cortex, and the right temporo-parietal region (Decety & Jackson, 2006). Among other evidence, all this implies a neural basis for empathy and social learning. Further, altruism in response to another can operate through empathy even in mammals and birds via matching emotional states (de Waal, 2008).

Usually, empathy turns into either sympathy or personal distress (Eisenberg, 2000). **Sympathy** entails feeling compassion or tenderness for another person's distress. Sometimes sympathy is interchangeably called empathy (Batson, 1987, 1998), and both are sources of altruistic motivations. However, the difference between truly *feeling* what the other person feels (empathy) and compassionately *apprehending* what another person feels (sympathy) seems useful. Knowing what someone feels is not the same as experiencing similar feelings. Indeed, people trying to take someone else's perspective often erroneously start with their own experience and adjust inadequately, to imagine the other's experience (Epley, Keysar, Van Boven, & Gilovich, 2004); most likely their well-intentioned feelings are inaccurate. In contrast to both sympathy and empathy stands **personal distress**, which entails one's own aversive feelings at perceiving another person's distress but not feeling what the other person is feeling. For example, one might be upset at seeing an unconscious accident victim, whereas the victim might be feeling nothing. Personal distress is self-oriented, whereas empathy and sympathy both are other-oriented.

**EVIDENCE**   Personal distress is empirically distinct from sympathy (and empathy): Distress leads to egoistic motivation, whereas sympathy leads to altruistic motivation. For example, the more personal distress people report *(alarmed, grieved, upset, worried, disturbed, distressed, troubled, perturbed)*, the less they help when they can escape the situation. In contrast, the more sympathy they report *(sympathetic, moved, compassionate, warm, soft-hearted, tender)*, the more they help, regardless of whether they can escape the situation or not (Batson, O'Quin, Fultz, Vanderplus, & Isen, 1983). Similarly, in both children and adults, sympathy and personal distress show distinct patterns of heart rate. Deceleration, which typically correlates with taking in information, interest, and an outward focus, correlates with sympathy. Acceleration, which typically correlates with cognitive problem-solving and active coping, correlates with distress (Eisenberg et al., 1989). A variety of indicators show the same distinction. In both children and adults, empathy and sympathy (as indicated by facial expressions, behavior, and heart rate) correlate with prosocial behavior and prosocial dispositions. In contrast, personal distress indicators correlate either negatively or not at all with prosocial behavior (Eisenberg, 2000). Given the mixed effects of negative mood on helping (covered earlier), perhaps this is not surprising.

Assorted evidence fits the motivating role of empathy (Hoffman, 1981). These findings indicate that empathic arousal (a) precedes helping, (b) increases with the severity of the victim's distress, and (c) correlates with helping. For example, one study (Coke, Batson, & McDavis, 1978) tested the hypothesis that taking the other's perspective leads to empathy, which in turn increases helping. Undergraduates heard a newscast about a fellow undergraduate whose parents had recently died in a car crash.

She was struggling to support her younger sibling while finishing college and needed help with childcare, transportation, and errands. Students listened to the newscast, trying either to imagine her feelings (empathy set) or to identify the media techniques (observation set). Further, they had been given a capsule just before the newscast and were told either that it would arouse them or that it would calm them. Participants in the empathy-arouse combination would think their distress was due to the pill and ignore it. In contrast, those in the empathy-calm combination would not be able to misattribute their arousal to the pill, and they should be especially likely to help if empathy motivates helping. Participants in the observe condition (whether in combination with the calming pill or arousing pill condition) should not especially help because they had failed to take the role of the other, so they would not feel empathy. Results supported the two-stage model of perspective taking and empathy leading to help. Altogether, a variety of evidence supports the role of empathy, consistent with the altruism hypothesis.

**CONTROVERSY**    However, the relationship between helping and sympathy (or empathy) still could result from egoistic or altruistic motivations (Batson, 1998; Piliavin & Charng, 1990). That is, empathy and sympathy could conceivably entail egoistic motives: reducing one's own empathic distress, avoiding empathy-specific punishments, gaining empathy-specific rewards, and self-other merging. Luckily for the empathy-altruism hypothesis, researchers have tackled each of these proposals and so far have found them wanting.

Reducing one's own **empathic distress** might seem to resemble the negative-state-relief model, discussed earlier as sadness, with the conclusion that much evidence fails to fit this idea. Most relevant here, sadness does not account for the effects of empathic concern on helping (Dovidio, Allen, & Schroeder, 1990). However, distinguish negative state relief, which refers to egoistic self-reward, from empathic distress. The latter creates a tension state and a drive to reduce that tension (recall drive reduction models from Chapter 6). As we have just seen, empathy does mediate helping, but the idea that acting on empathy reflects an egoistic motive to reduce distress seems unlikely, given the evidence showing that empathy and personal distress are distinct.

**Empathy-specific punishments** consist in one's experience that if one feels empathy and fails to help, then censure, embarrassment, shame, and guilt will follow as negative consequences (Tangney, Stuewig, & Mashek, 2007). **Empathy-specific rewards** include praise, gratitude, elevation, honor, and pride. In contrast to this punishment-reward view, recall that altruism entails helping purely in order to improve the other's welfare. In one set of studies that parallel one just described (Batson et al., 1988, Studies 2 & 5), students listened to an audiotaped interview of a fellow student whose parents and sister had recently been killed in a car crash, leaving her to struggle through her last year of school, as she attempted to support her two remaining siblings. When induced to feel empathy by focusing on how the target feels (as opposed to focusing on technical aspects of the audiotape), people helped more (Table 9.11, lines 1 and 2). As an indicator of the empathy process, the high-empathy helpers also were more distracted by victim-relevant words (*loss, needy, adopt, tragic*), as

**Table 9.11**    Empathy as a Predictor of Helping

|  | Low Empathy | High Empathy |
|---|---|---|
| Helping (percent) | 35% | 70% |
| Helping (amount) | .45 | 1.20 |
| Responsiveness to victim-related words |  |  |
|   Helpers | −29.11 | 47.32 |
|   Nonhelpers | −24.66 | −44.22 |
| Helping predicted by response to |  |  |
|   Victim-related words | −.06 | .62 |
|   Reward-relevant words | −.15 | −.30 |
|   Punishment-related words | −.29 | −.30 |

The first two lines come from Study 2; the remainder come from Study 5. For amount of helping, 0 = no help, 1 = 1 to 2 hours; 2 = 3 to 5 hours; 3 = 6 to 8 hours; 4 = 9 to 10 hours. Response to words was measured by the degree of **interference** (distraction, measured as **response latency** or time delay) that the words created when participants attempted to ignore their meaning and just name the font's color. Higher numbers indicate slower times to name the ink color and therefore greater interference (i.e., distraction) by the meaning of the words themselves.

*Source:* From Batson et al., 1988. Copyright © American Psychological Association. Adapted with permission.

shown (Table 9.11, lines 3 and 4). And they were less distracted by words that were reward-relevant *(nice, proud, honor, praise)* or punishment-relevant *(duty, guilt, shame, oblige)*. Also, the more participants were distracted by the victim-relevant (empathy) words, the more they helped, which was not true for reward and punishment-related words (last three lines of table). In short, the process was more consistent with empathy leading to victim-relevant thoughts, which in turn encourage helping, than with a process anchored in empathy-specific rewards and punishments.

A variant on the empathy-specific reward hypothesis relies on the notion of **empathic-joy** (Smith, Keating, & Stotland, 1989), defined as sensitivity to the emotional state of the victim, which causes relief, pleasure, and happiness when the victim feels those emotions, as a result of being helped. This differs from empathy-specific rewards because it focuses on experiencing what the other person experiences, the defining feature of empathy. It also differs from the negative-state-relief model because it emphasizes empathy per se and because it is an intrinsically positive experience, not just a contrast with a negative experience. But it resembles the negative-state-relief model in focusing on rewards to self. In this view, only empathic people will help and only when they can receive feedback that the victim feels better, which makes them experience empathic joy, the presumed goal of helping, in this model.

Indeed, in one study, participants had the opportunity to write advice to a first-year student (viewed on videotape) who felt so stressed and isolated that she considered dropping out. People high in self-reported empathy were far more likely to help (93%) when they knew they would receive feedback from her after she had read their advice, compared with high-empathy participants not expecting feedback (63%) or low-empathy participants in either feedback condition (53% in both cases). Similar effects occurred when instructions manipulated an empathy goal ("try to take the perspective of the person being interviewed"), compared with a detached observer goal ("watch all of this person's body movements ... try to be objective"). Consistent with the empathy-altruism hypothesis, all the empathy goal participants helped more than did the observer-goal participants. But suggestive of the empathic-joy hypothesis, the empathy-goal participants especially helped when feedback was expected. This study's results seem to fit the empathic-joy hypothesis because none of the other models predicts that feedback from the victim should differentially affect high-empathy witnesses.

Nevertheless, the empathy effect is bigger than the feedback effect, and subsequent studies (Batson et al., 1991) failed to replicate the empathic-joy effect. Moreover, researchers reasoned that high-empathy participants might be interested in feedback from the victim, to see how she was doing, regardless of whether she would in fact be better and reward them with their own experience of empathic joy. Recall that the empathy-altruism hypothesis predicts that empathy creates an interest in the victim's welfare, regardless of how well she is likely to be doing. In contrast, the empathic-joy hypothesis predicts that her probability of improvement should predict the chance of empathic joy. Consistent with the empathy-altruism hypothesis, level of empathy did in fact predict higher rates of wanting to see how the victim was doing, regardless of how likely it was that she would indeed be better. These results contradict the empathic-joy hypothesis and support the empathy-altruism hypothesis.

Despite all the evidence favoring altruism, efforts to find egoism in altruism continue. The **self-other merging** hypothesis goes beyond empathic joy to propose that, under empathy, one's representation of the other person merges with the self. Recall from Chapter 8 the theory of relationships that defines intimacy in terms of self-other overlap. Extending that idea, any situation in which people take the perspective of another could involve merging of self and other (Davis, Conklin, & Luce, 1996); empathy certainly takes the other's perspective. Participants instructed to imagine the perspective of a videotaped target or to imagine themselves as the target both contrasted with participants instructed to observe neutrally the target's nonverbal behavior. The two role-taking groups both ascribed positive traits to the target person that overlapped with their own prior self-descriptions. These results fit the idea that empathy generates self-other overlap.

There ensued a controversy regarding the meaning of self-other overlap in helping behavior. If empathic concern leads to self-other overlap, does that mean that helping the other really equals helping the self? Is that behavior therefore egoistic, not altruistic? From one perspective, **oneness** or self-other overlap constitutes a nonaltruistic explanation consistent with kin selection ideas (Cialdini, Brown, Lewis, Luce, & Neuberg, 1997). Measuring oneness as the inclusion of other in the self scale (Chapter 8) and as a self-reported usage of "we" to describe the relationship, researchers found that relationship closeness predicted both empathy and oneness but that only oneness, not empathy, predicted helping. Consistent with a kin selection idea, severity of need also predicted empathy and helping, but again helping was independent of empathy. (Note, however, that other studies have clearly linked empathy and helping, so this failure to replicate is puzzling.)

In response, defenders of the altruism hypothesis argued in part that the studies (a) did not manipulate empathy, only relationship closeness, and (b) used written scenarios and self-reports, not a real person and actual volunteering to help. Their own studies found that empathy did predict helping, without regard for group membership, and that self-other merging did not mediate (account for) the effect (Batson et al., 1997). The egoism camp replied that the offered helping was only superficial (letter-writing) and that severity of need was an empathy manipulation (Neuberg et al., 1997). Not surprisingly, the empathy theorist Batson (1997a, b) disagreed, leaving readers to decide.

One resolution to the egoism-altruism controversy is that some situations and some people do genuinely demonstrate helping for purely selfless reasons, and others do genuinely demonstrate help for selfish reasons. Such a resolution supports the altruism perspective, which contends only that empathic altruism can sometimes motivate helping, regardless of frequency or prevalence. However, this resolution would not equally support the egoism perspective, which contends that altruism can never constitute the primary motive for helping; an egoistic motive must always underlie all seemingly prosocial behavior. Regardless of one's view of the weight of the evidence in this ongoing controversy, however, manipulated empathy and measured empathy do predict helping. What's more, people do differ in levels of dispositional empathy, as the next section shows.

**INDIVIDUAL DIFFERENCES IN EMPATHY**   A variety of approaches demonstrate that people vary in their inclination to be concerned for the welfare of others. Concerning empathy per se, one of its dimensions involves ascription of responsibility, perspective-taking, social responsibility, and sympathy, whereas another dimension involves personal distress and emotional intensity (Carlo, Eisenberg, Troyer, Switzer, & Speer, 1991). Everyone is more likely to help under strong situational constraints (in this study, an evocative need and a situation difficult for the observer to escape, as compared to less evocative and easy-escape conditions). Dispositional differences emerge when the situation is weaker: When the situation is easy to escape but the portrayal is evocative, then dispositional empathy predicts sympathy in the moment (feeling *sympathetic, touched, soft-hearted, compassionate, sorrowful*, and *concerned for others*), as well as helping. In parallel with results noted earlier, dispositional empathy but not personal distress predicts helping (Eisenberg, 2000). These dispositional empathy results have replicated in Japan (Misumi & Peterson, 1990).

In real-world settings, certain dispositional variables reliably predict real-world helping, such as volunteering to help people with AIDS (Penner & Finkelstein, 1998). For example, other-oriented empathy (*concern for the welfare of others, satisfaction from being helpful, feeling responsible for others' welfare*) predicts time spent volunteering. Other individual differences that might seem relevant to prosocial behavior predict less well. Nevertheless, helpfulness does also relate somewhat to individual differences in dominance, self-efficacy, self-confidence, and competence. (The motive to help in these cases relates to the core social motive of controlling, not altruism and trust.) As further evidence related to real-world helping, dispositional pity and empathy also distinguished 231 gentiles who saved Jews during World War II from 126 nonrescuers matched on age, sex, education, and location (Oliner & Oliner, 1988). (See Table 9.1 for a variety of personality variables related and unrelated to helping.)

Children learn empathy and sympathy from parents who are sympathetic; such parents focus on understanding others' feelings, express little hostile emotion, and help children cope with their own negative feelings (Eisenberg, 2000). Cross-culturally, some results are similar. Hong Kong Chinese children's altruistic orientation results from families that are cohesive and harmonious, with little anger, aggression, and conflict (Ma & Leung, 1995). In the same setting, an orientation to work well with others (belonging) and to gain skill (controlling) predicts prosocial behavior, whereas a personal competence orientation (self-enhancement) does not (Cheung, Ma, & Shek, 1998).

In general, the tendency toward empathy correlates with the tendency to trust others (Piliavin & Charng, 1990), affirming the core social motive of trusting. Cooperators view cooperation (which entails trust) as good, whereas competitors view cooperation as weak. Cooperators especially expect cooperation more from honest (good) people, whereas competitors expect cooperation more from unintelligent (weak, stupid) people (Van Lange & Kuhlman, 1994). Although these results come from experimental games (noted earlier in this chapter), where cooperation often improves pay-off in the long run, their analogy to helping as another form of prosocial behavior is apt. Thus, those low on trust are likely to see trust as reflecting gullibility and not to appreciate its role in prosocial behavior. These individual differences in both trust and trustworthiness may have a biological basis in the hormone oxytocin, which, as the relationships chapter noted, also increases social bonding (Kosfeld, Heinrichs, Zak, Fischbacher, & Fehr, 2005; Zak, Kurzban, & Matzner, 2005).

## Summary of Altruism Hypotheses

Altruism begins when people avoid diffusion of responsibility to others (bystanders or the victim) and go through the steps toward felt responsibility for another's misfortune. Moreover, people are more likely to feel pity and to help victims seen as not responsible for their own plight, that is, when attributing responsibility to external, uncontrollable causes. Helping varies by attributed responsibility for both cause and cure, with varying models in different helping professions.

Empathy means feeling another person's feelings, and it results in either sympathy (apprehending the other person's feelings), which promotes helping, or personal distress, which does not. Ongoing controversy pits the empathy-altruism hypothesis against egoistic alternatives. If empathic people help merely to relieve personal distress, that would fit the egoistic negative-state-relief model, but the evidence does not support that view. If empathic people help merely to avoid empathy-specific punishment, that also would be egoistic, but evidence contradicts that view as well. Alternatively, empathic people could help in order to obtain empathy-specific rewards or to experience empathic joy, but empathic people seem to help even in the absence of those rewards. Finally, egoistic and altruistic theories differ regarding self-other merging and the feeling of oneness. If empathic people's self merges with the other they help, does that make empathy selfish or selfless? Regardless of one's endorsement of either the egoistic or altruistic model, people and situations do differ in empathy and perhaps therefore also in the motivations to help. Empathy develops from a family environment that models empathy.

## COLLECTIVISM: MAINTAINING GROUP BELONGING

Self-interest and other-interest, discussed so far, do not exhaust the possibilities for motives to explain prosocial behavior. **Collective interest** reflects a concern with the group's welfare. It not only differs from but can conflict with both self- and other-interest at the individual level (Batson et al., 1995). For example, in one study, students received 16 raffle tickets that they could distribute to themselves, to another individual group member, or to the group as a whole. Here's the catch: If they gave the tickets back to the group, their 16 tickets would become 24, which would then be divided equally among group members (see Figure 9.3). If everyone in the 4-person group donated their tickets back, the group resources would go from 64 to 96, and each group member would end up with 24. If the other 3 participants donated their tickets back, but the participant kept his or her own tickets, the participant would get the 16 original tickets plus 18, making 34 total, while other members would receive 18 each. But if the participant were the only one to donate tickets back, and other members kept theirs, the participant would get only 6 tickets and the others would get 22 each. These conditions set up a **social dilemma**, in which self-interest conflicts with group interest; they expand the two-person game dilemmas introduced earlier (see Figure 9.1 and Chapter 12).

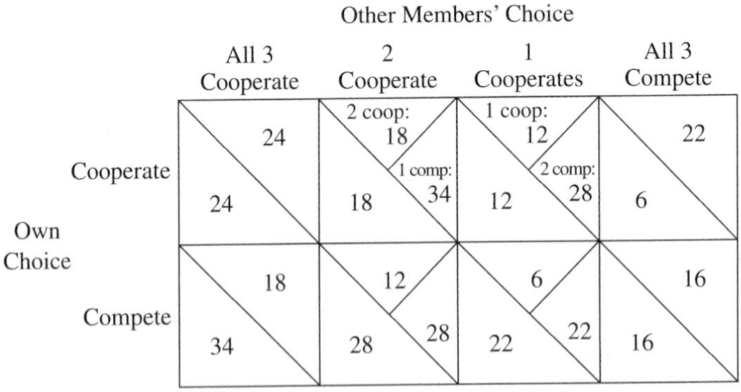

Within each cell, the lower left triangle represents own payoffs and the upper right triangle represents the rest of the group's payoff. Where the group is subdivided, the cooperators are the upper triangle and the competitors are the right triangle.

**Figure 9.3**    Payoff Matrix for a Four-Person Social Dilemma Involving Prosocial Cooperation and Individualistic Competition

The prosocial possibilities had still another level. The social dilemma allowed participants further to choose to give half their own original tickets to one other student, a victim of a recent break-up from a long-term relationship, who needed "something good to happen to cheer me up." Researchers predicted that empathy for this individual would undermine the group good, if empathic people donated some of their tickets directly to the victim, thereby leaving fewer for the group pot.

Researchers measured naturally occurring empathy after participants read the note, by self ratings on *feeling sympathetic, warm, compassionate, soft-hearted, tender,* and *moved*. (Another study obtained similar results by manipulating empathy.) As Table 9.12 shows, low-empathy participants were most likely to act in the collective interest, self-interest, or the two combined, while high-empathy participants were most likely to act in a combination of self- and other-interest, that is, to give half their tickets to the victim. Their other-oriented altruism at the individual level undermined the collective good (also see Batson et al., 1999).

Thus, the collective interest is separable from egoistic self- and altruistic other-interest. **Collectivism** reflects the motivation to benefit one's own group as a whole, and it is separate from individual-level empathy. For example, in a social dilemma such as the one just described, people have to balance the group good against individual good (both their own and other people's). When group members have a chance to discuss allocation, they are more likely to act for the collective welfare (Caporael, Dawes, Orbell, & van de Kragt, 1989). Although discussion could instill other egoistic motivations (social reinforcement, for example), the finding fits other data on collectivist motives. In Chapter 12, we see other examples that differentiate personal (self), interpersonal (other), and collective (group) phenomena as distinct, but this chapter for now addresses just three collective phenomena of prosocial behavior, focusing in turn on the role of similarity and group identity, group norms, and individual differences in group prosocial orientation.

**Table 9.12**   Allocation of Raffle Tickets in Self-Interest, Other-Interest, and Collective Interest

| | Self-Reported Empathy | |
| --- | --- | --- |
| Allocation of Tickets | Low | High |
| Both halves to self (self-interest) | 6 | 4 |
| Both halves to group (collective interest) | 9 | 5 |
| Half to self; half to group (collective and self-interest) | 7 | 5 |
| Half to self; half to victim (other- and self-interest) | 1 | 8 |
| Total number of participants | 23 | 22 |

*Source:* From Batson et al., 1995. Copyright © American Psychological Association. Adapted with permission.

## Similarity and Group Identity

Recall that when good moods specifically enhance people's social outlook—their positive feelings about other people—they are more likely to help. Consistent with the more specific idea that people can be motivated to help group welfare, people are more likely to help in a variety of circumstances that reinforce their sense of group identity. For example, people are more likely to help a stranger whose opinions are similar to their own. However, the effect seems to depend on developing a sense of **we-ness** (Flippen, Hornstein, Siegel, & Weitzman, 1996; Sole, Marton, & Hornstein, 1975; Wagner, Hornstein, & Holloway, 1982). Attraction seems to be less the issue than group identity, particularly under external threat, which increases group loyalty (Flippen et al., 1996; Sole et al., 1975). That is, people are more likely to help members of their own group when their group identity is salient.

In one indirect manipulation of groupiness, investigators found that reminding people of their own mortality caused them to be more helpful (Jonas, Schimel, Greenberg, & Pyszczynski, 2002). Typically, this kind of **mortality salience** (priming thoughts of one's own death) makes people affirm cultural values that will endure beyond their lifetimes. In the case of prosocial behavior, people reminded of their own mortality (thinking about their own death) are more helpful, but only to their own group, in this case, an American charity, not a foreign one.

People sometimes help those in their own group more than those in another group (Batson, 1998; Crosby, Bromley, & Saxe, 1980), particularly when they have an excuse (see Chapter 11; Frey & Gaertner, 1986; Gaertner & Dovidio, 1977; Gaertner, Dovidio, & Johnson, 1982). However, this bias toward one's own group vanishes when two previously separate groups merge to form a **one-group identity**. As Chapter 11 indicates, in one larger group, they start to help all group members equally (Dovidio et al., 1997). As a fictional example, perhaps Art helped Ruth's mother because he was, in translating his solitary "I" into "we," showing his identification of them as a family unit.

Group identity clearly facilitates helping. People differ in their degree of group-prosocial orientation, depending on group identification. For example, group empathy better predicts helping ingroup recipients, compared with outgroup ones, and perceived similarity among ingroup members strengthens the empathy → ingroup-helping relationship (Stürmer, Snyder, Kropp, & Siem, 2006; Stürmer, Snyder, & Omoto, 2005). The importance of identification on group-level helping also appears in evidence that neighborhood stability encourages community identification and pro-community behavior (Oishi et al., 2007).

People may vary in the size and type of group with which they identify. For example, men may tend to identify with the broad social matrix and help strangers more often, whereas women may identify more with close relationship and help intimate others more (Baumeister & Sommer, 1997). Both levels of identification can serve the social belonging motive, but the desire for connection may operate at different levels of group.

Scattered cultural comparisons suggest that Westerners may define a level of group that makes them appear more selfish with regard to helping their group than Easterners are. For example, Americans do not feel responsible even for siblings and colleagues if they don't happen to like them, whereas Asian Indians feel responsible regardless of liking (Miller & Bersoff, 1998). Similarly, Americans do not feel obligated to help either best friends or strangers even in cases of moderately serious need, whereas Indians feel obligated even to strangers (Miller, Bersoff, & Harwood, 1990). The exception, for Americans, comes with parents caring for their own children (regardless of liking) or anyone with a life-threatening need, whom they do feel obligated to help. Americans and independent cultures may view helping as best coming from internal sources, when it is spontaneous, but feel externally obligated when helping is forced on them by reciprocity, which seems too utilitarian (Miller & Bersoff, 1994). In contrast, Indians and interdependent cultures may view helping as a broadly applicable affirmative personal choice, whether driven by norms of reciprocity or not. In perhaps related findings, Japanese (interdependent) children gave equal say to a minority within their own classroom, whereas Australians (independent) followed self-interest and favored their own group (Mann, Radford, & Kanagawa, 1985). Again, the more collectivist culture shows a broader, less self-serving sense of their prosocial obligations. The relevant group to be helped depends on local definitions, but similarity and identity are important everywhere.

## Norms

However defined, groups develop **norms**, unwritten rules for who should help whom, and when. The reciprocity norm, discussed earlier, is one example. Another is **social responsibility**, the idea that people are responsible for one another's welfare. As we saw earlier, though, the social responsibility norm carries several exceptions. Based on attributional evidence, potential helpers must feel personally responsible, must feel that others are not, must attribute the victim's fate to uncontrollable or external factors, and must attribute responsibility for the cure to people like themselves.

The effects of norms on helping are surprisingly difficult to detect (Batson, 1998). One reason may be that the salience of prosocial norms varies across situations, and behavior follows the norm only when it is salient (Cialdini, Kallgren, & Reno, 1991). For example, not littering (arguably a prosocial behavior) is influenced by the situational salience of antilittering norms. Norms can be salient based on the behavior of other people (as in the modeling that is characteristic of social learning). For instance, people litter less in litter-free settings. The setting communicates a **descriptive norm** that says what people actually do, what is.

In addition, the setting can communicate an **injunctive norm** that says what ought to be. The development of social norms requires sanctions, and people will experience rewards and incur personal costs to sanction norm-violators, especially when the victim is an ingroup member; this might be termed altruistic punishment in support of moral norms (Bernhard, Fischbacher, & Fehr, 2006; de Quervain et al., 2004; Fehr & Fischbacher, 2004).

The impact of injunctive norms (e.g., moral norms) has been much less clear in research on prosocial behavior, as the chapter's final section on moral principles will show. However, injunctive norms can vary in salience as well. In one study, researchers (Cialdini et al., 1991) made antilittering injunctive norms salient by sweeping all the litter into a tidy pile. In another study, they primed the cognitive accessibility

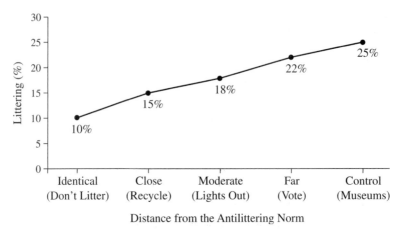

**Figure 9.4**    Littering as a Function of the Accessibility of Injunctive Antilittering Norms
*Source:* Cialdini et al., 1991. Copyright © American Psychological Association. Adapted with permission.

of the antilittering norm and other norms at varying proximity to it (e.g., recycling norms are close, but voting norms are far; see Figure 9.4); they did this by giving pedestrians a handbill promoting the relevant message. Littering the handbill increased linearly as the norm departed further from the littering issue.

Further evidence for the importance of cognitive accessibility comes from a study that also primed norms at varying proximity to helping norms (Harvey & Enzle, 1981). Participants read one of three stories: One story primed norms against harming another person (close to helping norms); another primed norms against property damage (farther from helping norms); and a third primed norms against speeding (farthest from helping norms). Participants then had an opportunity to help a professor by crossing out vowels on several pages of text. They were more likely to help, the closer the primed norm was to helping norms. Overall, the role of norms depends on their salience in the environment and hence their cognitive accessibility in people's minds.

The salience of norms varies not just with setting but also with age. As children develop, they become aware of prosocial norms. Some evidence fits the idea that children become increasingly aware of social expectations, which causes them to behave in a progressively more prosocial manner (Cialdini et al., 1981; Piliavin & Charng, 1990).

## Individual Differences in Group Prosocial Orientation

People's perceptions of social norms vary, depending on their own degree of prosocial orientation to others. Social value orientation, measured as indicated in Table 9.2, differentiates among people with cooperative (prosocial), competitive, and individualistic orientations to others. Prosocial value orientation emphasizes both equalizing outcomes and enhancing joint outcomes (Van Lange, 1999). Competitive and individualist orientations are proself, the former by maximizing the difference between self and other and the latter by maximizing own outcome, regardless of the other person's outcome.

In general, people expect consensus from others, that is, agreement on their own social values. The **false consensus effect** (Chapter 5) predicts this projecting of self onto others. Competitors expect a more competitive norm than cooperators do (Kelley & Stahelski, 1970). However, people's expectations of consensus with their own individual orientations decrease as the population goes from near (friends, classmates) to far (schoolmates, other peers) (Iedema & Poppe, 1999).

People with different prosocial orientations create different group dynamics for themselves, creating a self-fulfilling mirror-image world for themselves. A meta-analysis examined particularly difficult conflicts, in which negotiators highly resisted yielding to the other side. Prosocial negotiators were generally less contentious, engaged in more problem-solving, and (ironically) ended up with higher joint outcomes than more egoistic negotiators (De Dreu, Weingart, & Kwon, 2000). For example, in one study, prosocial dyads negotiated by restructuring the problem, supporting each other, and managing the negotiation process so both perceived it to be fair. Egoistic (individualistic and competitive) dyads similarly exchanged information and concessions and avoided arguing. Mixed dyads argued about distribution of outcomes (i.e., who gets what) (Olekalns & Smith, 1999). Prosocial people see the other person as more fair and considerate. They demand less and make concessions more. In contrast, noncooperative people elicit less cooperation from partners, as well as tendencies to withdraw to lower levels of interdependence (Van Lange & Visser, 1999). The prosocial orientation is not antiself but enhances the whole social experience for self and others.

Social value orientation moderates (i.e., influences the impact of) several situational variables already discussed. For example, a prosocial orientation facilitates reciprocity (Van Lange, 1999; Van Lange & Semin-Goossens, 1998). In contrast, an egoistic (proself) orientation facilitates perceived personal costs of helping (Cameron, Brown, & Chapman, 1998). And the impact of cooperative versus competitive value orientations is exaggerated by a focus on loss (De Dreu & McCusker, 1997). Thus, personality interacts with situation to predict prosocial behavior.

Another individual difference variable, less studied, is **prosocial self-schema**. (Recall from Chapter 5 that a self-schema is the most central aspect of one's self-concept.) Individual differences in prosocial self-schemas also predict prosocial behavior, but they again interact with the situation. That is, situational factors, including the salience of normative ideals (self-awareness) and salience of the opportunity to help, increase the impact of prosocial self-schemas (Froming, Nasby, & McManus, 1998). Over time, prosocial behaviors in childhood predict later popularity with peers and even academic achievement (Caprara, Barbaranelli, Pastorelli, Bandura, & Zimbardo, 2000). This fits the view that both social and academic goals at school determine learning (Covington, 2000).

People develop a prosocial orientation from different patterns of social interaction as they are growing up (Van Lange, DeBruin, Otten, & Joireman, 1997). Prosocial behavior results from secure attachment (introduced in Chapter 8 as one indicator of trusting), because it requires openness to others. Also, in keeping with the idea of building on past interaction patterns, people are more likely to be prosocial if they have had siblings (especially sisters!), presumably because they have had to cooperate with them. But, as just noted, people become more prosocial as they age, in any case.

This may stem from the experience that a positive social value orientation fosters more positive social processes and outcomes than a proself orientation, an experience supported by the self-fulfilling nature of a cooperative, prosocial orientation, noted earlier.

## Summary of Collectivism Hypotheses

Collective interest is distinct from both self-interest and individual other-interest. In social dilemmas, empathy for individual others may actually undermine collective interest. Prosocial behavior aimed at benefiting the group can result from group identity. A sense of we-ness or one-group identity encourages helping ingroup members. Group-oriented prosocial behavior also can result from salient norms. Norms can be descriptive (what people do) or injunctive (what people ought to do). Finally, people differ in their degree of group prosocial orientation. Prosocial, cooperative behavior (within limits) elicits like behavior from others, more constructive negotiating processes, and higher joint outcomes. Proself (competitive or individualistic) behavior elicits less constructive processes and outcomes.

## PRINCIPLISM: MORAL UNDERSTANDING

Theoretically, people might engage in prosocial behavior for neither personal, interpersonal, nor group interest but simply because it is the right thing to do. **Principlism** is the motivation to uphold a moral stand (Batson, 1994, 1998). Moral principles might include impartial justice, the greatest good for the greatest number, or love thy neighbor. Principlism goes beyond self, other, and group interest.

Because where you stand depends on where you sit, people might make the most impartial judgments when they do not know their own relative position. That is, people's understanding of universal moral values takes them "behind the veil of ignorance" (Rawls, 1971) to behavior deemed right, without knowing whether one might be victim, perpetrator, or helper and whether an ingroup or outgroup member. Judgments of fairness without knowing one's own position reveal principles uncontaminated by self-interest or other biases. The Rawls **veil of ignorance** proposed that people should make moral choices without knowing how they, specific others, and their groups would fare.

Indeed, research participants making ability-based task assignments were more willing to subscribe to the principle of meritocracy when they could not be seduced by specific interests. In effect, they were more likely to endorse inequality that trades one group of people against another when they did not know their own position (Brickman, 1977). This supports the idea of a principled (abstract, impartial, though not necessarily consensual) form of moral reasoning. Extending this type of logic, social psychologists have used two approaches to moral reasoning, both of which involve an abstract understanding and an effort to control outcomes and sometimes a group-belonging motive, all as possible prosocial motivations.

# Moral Reasoning

**Moral reasoning** reflects how people think about ethical dilemmas. In this view, opportunities for prosocial behavior are cognitive puzzles to be solved, and people can develop through several stages of sophistication in their type of moral reasoning. In the first well-known account (Colby & Kohlberg, 1987; Kohlberg, 1963), people can operate at three primary levels of moral reasoning (see Table 9.13). The pre-conventional level operates in an egoistic fashion, with concern only for short-term self-interest. For example, a person reasoning in this fashion would worry mainly about getting caught in a transgression; this fits the motive to control one's outcomes. The conventional level operates in a collectivist, belonging fashion, with concern for group standards. A person reasoning conventionally would worry about upholding the group's rules. The postconventional level operates according to abstract principles thought to be universal, consistent with the understanding motive. A person reasoning in a postconventional fashion would worry about equality, dignity, and justice, also consistent with an understanding motive.

The Kohlberg approach drew a lot of attention, both admiring and critical, primarily in developmental and educational psychology, so most of it lies beyond our scope. Some of the criticisms included disputes over the alleged universality of the scheme, its requirement of linear stages, its possible gender differences, and its exclusion of caring and altruism as moral bases of action (Batson, 1998; Eisenberg, 1991). In response, other partially overlapping schemes developed (e.g., Eisenberg, 1982; see Table 9.13).

**Table 9.13**  Levels of Moral Reasoning

| Kohlberg (1963) | | Eisenberg (1982) | |
|---|---|---|---|
| Level | Concerns | Level | Concerns |
| Preconventional | Immediate consequences for self; own needs; reward and punishment | (1) Hedonistic | Self |
| | | (2) Needs-oriented | Others' needs |
| Conventional | Obedience to social norms, rules, and laws; social order; approval and disapproval | (3) Stereotyped | Images of good and bad people; approval |
| | | (4a) Empathic | Other's humanity |
| | | (4b) Transitional | Larger society |
| Postconventional | Transcendent universal principles; generality beyond group | (5) Internalized | Values, norms, responsibility |

*Source:* From descriptions by Eisenberg, 1982; Kohlberg, 1963.

Another tactic was to downplay the stage idea and study people's **utilization** of various moral judgment processes (Thoma, Rest, & Davison, 1991). This recognizes the flexibility of people's moral understanding. For example, consider the classic moral dilemma, whether Heinz should steal a costly drug to save his sick wife (part of the original Kohlberg dilemma and also in the Defining Issues Test, Figure 9.5). People can come to the same conclusion by different levels' reasoning processes (don't steal the drug because of possibly getting caught versus because it's wrong). Or they could come to different conclusions, even at the same level. For example, someone at a conventional Kohlbergian level might define the Heinz dilemma in terms of family duty (steal the drug) or duty to society (don't steal). A four-step model of moral behavior (Rest, 1983) breaks moral reasoning down to include the following:

- Interpreting the situation as a moral problem (utilizing empathy and perspective-taking)
- Applying relevant standards to action plans (judging morally right and wrong action)
- Evaluating how actions serve moral values (decision making and trade-offs)
- Executing and implementing action (using self-regulatory processes)

Level of moral reasoning predicts prosocial behavior, according to one meta-analysis of varied studies (Underwood & Moore, 1982). "In many ways, the data for moral reasoning are the most compelling we have seen, not for the magnitude of the relationship but for the generality of that relationship" across participant populations, helping measures, and moral reasoning measures (p. 158). However, levels of moral reasoning can be confounded with age, education, and social class, so these other variables may account for the impressive effect. Nevertheless, as one important example of principlism, gentiles who rescued Jews had higher ethical values than those who did not (Oliner & Oliner, 1988), as noted earlier.

What predicts type of moral reasoning? As people's education increases, they use increasingly sophisticated forms of moral reasoning (Rest & Thoma, 1985). Moral reasoning also increases with age (Darley & Shultz, 1990; Eisenberg, 1991; Piliavin & Charng, 1990).

Moral reasoning cannot be reduced to equivalence with religious involvement because it depends on the type of religious motivation one has. For example, one could be motivated by religious beliefs about rewards and punishments, by social approval and disapproval from one's co-believers, or by impartial principles from one's religion (e.g., Batson, 1990). Similarly, moral reasoning cannot be reduced to cultural ideology (Narvaez, Getz, Rest, & Thoma, 1999). Finally, moral reasoning is distinct from empathy and may sometimes conflict with it (Batson, Klein, Highberger, & Shaw, 1995).

An argument for the adaptive universality of moral reasoning is that humans have always had to solve the problem of maximizing gains from living in groups but also resolving conflicts of interest (Krebs, 2008). Moral reasoning could be strategic in managing cooperation, deference, and altruism, generating impartial principles for group living.

## HEINZ AND THE DRUG

In Europe a woman was near death from a special kind of cancer. There was one drug that doctors thought might save her. It was a form of radium that a druggist in the same town had recently discovered. The drug was expensive to make, but the druggist was charging ten times what the drug cost to make. He paid $200 for the radium and charged $2000 for a small dose of the drug. The sick woman's husband, Heinz, went to everyone he knew to borrow the money, but he could only get together about $1000, which is half of what it cost. He told the druggist that his wife was dying, and asked him to sell it cheaper or let him pay later. But the druggist said, "No, I discovered the drug and I'm going to make money from it." So Heinz got desperate and began to think about breaking into the man's store to steal the drug for his wife.

Should Heinz steal the drug? (Check one)

____ Should steal it      ____ Can't decide      ____ Should not steal it

IMPORTANCE:

| Great | Much | Some | Little | No | |
|---|---|---|---|---|---|
| | | | | | 1. Whether a community's laws are going to be upheld. |
| | | | | | 2. Isn't it only natural for a loving husband to care so much for his wife that he'd steal? |
| | | | | | 3. Is Heinz willing to risk getting shot as a burglar or going to jail for the chance that stealing the drug might help? |
| | | | | | 4. Whether Heinz is a professional wrestler, or has considerable influence with professional wrestlers. |
| | | | | | 5. Whether Heinz is stealing for himself or doing this solely to help someone else. |
| | | | | | 6. Whether the druggist's rights to his invention have to be respected. |
| | | | | | 7. Whether the essence of living is more encompassing than the termination of dying, socially and individually. |
| | | | | | 8. What values are going to be the basis for governing how people act towards each other. |
| | | | | | 9. Whether the druggist is going to be allowed to hide behind a worthless law which only protects the rich anyhow. |
| | | | | | 10. Whether the law in this case is getting in the way of the most basic claim of any member of society. |
| | | | | | 11. Whether the druggist deserves to be robbed for being so greedy and cruel. |
| | | | | | 12. Would stealing in such a case bring about more total good for the whole society or not. |

From the list of questions above, select the four most important:

Most important ____      Second most important ____

Third most important ____      Fourth most important ____

**Figure 9.5**  The Heinz Moral Dilemma from the Defining Issues Test

*Source:* Thoma et al., 1991. Copyright © Elsevier. Adapted with permission.

## Reasoning or Rationale?

Whatever people's level of moral reasoning, people may deceive themselves about their own ethics. A series of studies demonstrates one version of **moral hypocrisy** (Batson, Thompson, & Chen, 2002; Batson, Thompson, Seuferling, Whitney, & Strongman, 1999). In the experiments, people were fully capable of convincing themselves that they had used a fair decision rule (coin flip) for allocating a more desirable task to themselves over another person. But in fact they could be observed falsifying the coin flip, despite clear instructions and labels, as well as salient social standards. In the real world, likewise, people can claim one moral rationale but act on another (Carlsmith, Darley, & Robinson, 2002). When people are asked the appropriate moral basis for punishment by society, as in the legal justice system, they frequently cite utilitarian (controlling) motives, such as deterrence or incapacitation, that aim to prevent further harm doing. However, their theory differs from their practice. Empirically, people make choices that reflect revenge or retribution. They apparently focus on what the harm doer supposedly deserves, that is, on just deserts. People heed the dimensions of offenses that reflect just deserts (seriousness, morality) and not those that would reflect deterrence (frequency, ease of detection). Their decisions about penalties do not reflect their high-minded ideals about the operations of society, but rather punishment in proportion to harm, or as Kant put it, the criminal's apparent "internal wickedness."

People's lack of moral self-insight suggests that moral reasoning may be a post hoc rationale, rather than a true underlying motive. Indeed, a growing set of evidence suggests that moral responses may often be relatively automatic and even more emotional or intuitive than rational and abstract. People's judgments about hypothetical dilemmas or their post hoc justifications for their moral decisions may not represent their actual, spontaneous moral decision-making. Several points argue for a more intuitive, less rational approach to moral responses (Haidt, 2001, 2007): (a) dual-processes in social cognition suggest a role for automatic as well as deliberate response (see Chapter 4); moral intuition is fast, automatic, and often affect-laden, preceding deliberate moral reasoning; (b) moral actions link more closely to emotions than to reasoning (see also Tangney, Stuewig, & Mashek, 2007). (c) The role of motivation is well-established elsewhere in social cognition; moral reasoning—much of it post hoc—often operates pragmatically to preserve one's reputation; and (d) moral communities preserve adaptive group solidarity, based on various norms: harm/care and fairness/reciprocity are most familiar to Americans, especially liberals, but ingroup/loyalty, authority/respect, and purity/sanctity also matter, for example, to conservative Americans and in more traditional societies. The intuitive, affective basis for moral reasoning questions not the presence but the origins of morality (Miller, 2008). In a provocative set of findings, some kinds of moral judgment clearly evoke emotional responses in the brain, rather than simply rational responses (Greene & Haidt, 2002; Greene, Sommerville, Nystrom, Darley, & Cohen, 2001). Moral reasoning may not be all it's cracked up to be.

## Personal Norms and Values

People sometimes operate on principles dictated by **personal norms:** self-expectations for specific action in particular situations (Schwartz, 1977). People construct personal norms themselves, so they are internalized, although socially learned. When activated, personal norms are experienced as moral obligations. In this view, particular situations generate a feeling of personal moral obligation, which guides helping, unless people neutralize those feelings by denying their relevance. Personal norms do predict altruistic behavior, but only for people who are aware that their behavior has consequences for others and who do not deny responsibility for those consequences.

**Personal values** are standards that cut across specific situations. They are general beliefs about desirable ends; they guide evaluations and behavior; and they are ordered by importance (Schwartz, 1992). One psychological structure of human values considers biological needs, interpersonal coordination, and group welfare, in order to derive eight motivational domains of values (Schwartz & Bilsky, 1987). The values appear to have a similar structure across cultures, as shown in Figure 9.6. The value of benevolence, closely linked to universalism, promotes concern for the welfare of others.

People from communal (roughly, collectivist) societies prioritize different values than do people from contractual (i.e., exchange-oriented; roughly, individualist) societies. For example, people from relatively communal Taiwan value conformity more, whereas people from relatively contractual New Zealand value stimulation more (Schwartz, 1992). As noted earlier, Asian Indian adults prioritize responsibility to help colleagues and siblings based on moral values, but Americans prioritize helping by personal liking and disliking (Miller & Bersoff, 1998). The role of affect in moral reasoning surfaces again.

A more specific type of personal value relates directly to prosocial behavior. **Belief in a just world** (Lerner & Miller, 1978; Rubin & Peplau, 1973, 1975) holds that people get what they deserve, that the world is fundamentally a fair place. If a person encounters bad outcomes, the person must have done something bad to merit it. Believers in a just world will blame and derogate a victim, allowing them to maintain their belief that the world is fair. Earlier (in this chapter and in Chapter 3), we described differing attributions for poverty, finding that people who attribute poverty to the dispositions of poor people (i.e., blame them) show more anger, but those who attribute poverty to the situation of the poor people show more pity and are more likely to help them (Zucker & Weiner, 1993).

Similarly, believers in a just world will help people with an isolated or a temporary problem—presumably because helping can restore justice to their world—but they will not try to help people with pervasive or long-term problems—presumably because helping one person at one time will still leave a lot of inexplicable suffering (Miller, 1977). Believers in a just world also help others in order to make themselves more deserving of good outcomes (luck on an upcoming exam, for example; Zuckerman, 1975), clearly an egoistic motive in this case. More generally, they are protecting their

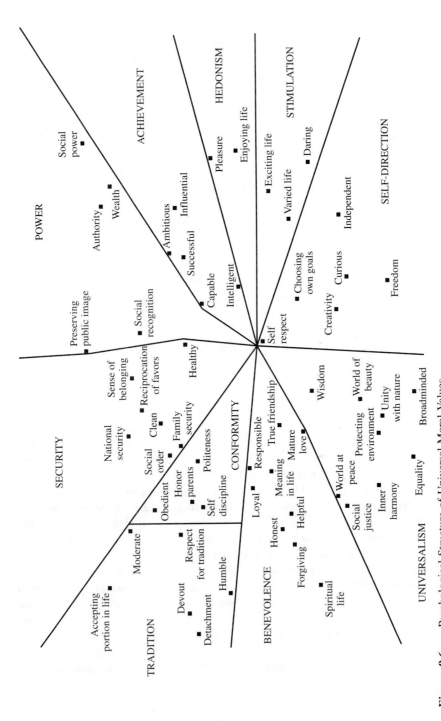

**Figure 9.6** Psychological Structure of Universal Moral Values

*Source:* Schwartz, 1992. Copyright © Elsevier. Reprinted with permission.

own understanding that the world is a just place and that they can control their own outcomes in it. Some cultural differences in just world beliefs suggest that they can help people justify the status quo in an unjust society, for instance, during apartheid in South Africa (Furnham, 1985).

Most people hold personal values that matter deeply. Even thinking about violating such sacred values (e.g., putting a monetary value on human life) makes people angry. Racial egalitarians refuse to consider certain kinds of racial statistics, and Christian fundamentalists refuse to consider everyday explanations for biblical events (Tetlock, Kristel, Elson, Green, & Lerner, 2000). Whatever they are, the violation of sacred values makes people angry and motivated to reaffirm their own beliefs.

Many people's personal values include religious beliefs, although social psychologists rarely study the role of religion in people's lives. Religious beliefs of some kinds (internal, intrinsic, secure) benefit people more than other kinds (imposed, unexamined, tenuous). Religion can improve the outlook of groups that are marginalized and individuals who are under stress (Pargament, 2002). But religion can also be a source of stress, confusion, and sadness (Exline, 2002). Although religious involvement links to mental and physical health, various correlated variables might account for it: social support, health practices, self-esteem, and self-efficacy, as well as beliefs such as a sense of coherence (George, Ellison, & Larson, 2002). So far, the evidence does not clearly indicate whether any of these variables accounts for the sometimes salutary effects of religious involvement. Ironically, none of the relevant research focuses on prosocial behavior as a beneficial outcome of religious involvement.

## Summary of Principlism Hypotheses

When people are motivated to help because of abstract moral principles that they perceive to be universal, this motivation can operate independently of egoism, altruism, and collectivism. Prosocial behavior can result from varying levels of moral reasoning, which range from controlling outcomes and promoting self-interest to more collective concerns to understanding abstract moral principles, although emotion and intuition may matter more. Specific personal norms can operate in a given situation, and more general moral values transcend situations.

## CHAPTER SUMMARY

Return to the example of the washerwoman who donated her life savings for college scholarships. If prosocial behavior includes behavior intended to benefit others, certainly her act qualifies as prosocial. Social psychologists have studied prosocial behavior in experimental games by examining personality differences in strategy choices that reveal social value orientations (cooperative, competitive, individualist). People differ in empathy and perspective-taking as well.

Social psychologists focus more often on situational causes of prosocial behavior. One approach uses the experimental games in which people can choose to cooperate or compete, and their combined behavior determines their respective payoffs. Researchers then vary situational factors. Another situational approach designs socially realistic, highly impactful, and personally involving situations in which participants witness an emergency and researchers measure helping. Alternatively, participants may encounter a person with an ongoing need. Finally, social psychologists also study real-world helping situations, such as volunteering and blood donation.

Washerwoman McCarty's gift could have stemmed from many motivational sources. Core social motives underlying prosocial behavior can include self-enhancement, trusting, belonging, or understanding. In helping research, a continuing controversy debates these motives respectively as egoism, altruism, collectivism, and principlism.

The egoism hypothesis starts from an evolutionary puzzle: Why would people help others when it apparently makes no contribution to their own genetic survival? From an evolutionary perspective, the primary explanation rests on kin selection, and people do indeed help genetic kin more readily than others. Necessary adaptive ingredients would include recognizing kin and detecting distress, both of which are present in people from an early age. However, the evolutionary explanation is silent on the psychological mediators, which may include emotional closeness, mere exposure, or other mechanisms compatible with a variety of explanations.

Social learning potentially supports the egoism hypothesis, as people aim to obtain social rewards and avoid social punishments. One of the most robust forms of social learning is reciprocity, in which people help others who help them in return. Equity holds that mutual help is proportional (each person's cost-to-benefit ratio is the same). Under exchange, helping is returned equally. In experimental games, a strategy of tit-for-tat works well to reward the other's cooperation and punish competing defections, which results in higher joint payoffs. It also deters cheaters and other free-riders, who try to exploit others. According to enlightened self-interest, people often learn that selfish behavior does not pay off in the long run. People do receive a variety of social rewards for helping (approval, praise) and try to avoid social punishments for not helping (disapproval, censure). People learn vicariously, by observation, and they imitate models.

The third major leg of the egoism hypothesis rests on mood protection. Maintaining good moods nicely predicts prosocial behavior: Cheerful people do indeed reliably help others more. The good mood is more effective when based on one's own happiness rather than someone else's good fortune. Especially important is the mood's connection to improving one's general social outlook. Good moods accentuate the positive in perceptions of self, other people, the helping situation, and society. In contrast stands the concomitance hypothesis, which maintains that the link between good moods and helping is a mere by-product but not psychologically meaningful.

In contrast to good moods, bad moods have more variable effects. Guilt does consistently encourage helping, perhaps through attention to one's own position relative to the other person. Sadness tends to undermine helping. The negative-state-relief hypothesis holds that people help in order to relieve their personal distress at another's misfortune or because they have learned that helping relieves sadness in general.

None of the egoism hypotheses particularly explain Ms. McCarty's scholarship donation. The altruism hypothesis proposes that the primary motivation of helping can indeed be the other person's welfare, and her case could fit this analysis. People must first attribute responsibility for the victim's predicament because people do not pity or help another person unless the causes of the troubles are external, uncontrollable, or both. Next, people must experience felt responsibility, interpreting the situation as an emergency and attributing responsibility to themselves. The presence of passive others can undermine both processes. Moreover, either victim or others can be held responsible for the problem or its cause, leading to different models of the helping situation.

Empathy would provide the clearest evidence for altruism. Empathy, feeling another person's distress, does reliably increase prosocial behavior. Empathy is distinct from sympathy, acknowledging the other person's situation, and personal distress, being upset by it regardless of how the other is actually feeling. Only the sympathetic aspect of empathy facilitates helping. The negative-state-relief model would predict helping from personal distress, but the effects are controversial. Empathy-specific rewards (including empathic-joy) and punishments constitute another egoistic explanation for empathy effects on helping. A final egoistic argument asserts that empathy causes people to merge self with other into oneness, so that helping the other becomes helping the self. Empathy theorists disagree and muster impressive evidence for the role of altruism. Regardless, people individually high on empathy (but not personal distress) do help others more. They learn empathy from secure trusting relationships and are more likely to engage in a series of real-world prosocial behaviors. Ms. McCarty's donations clearly could result from empathic motives.

Her donations to the local university could also result from collectivism, the motive to improve group welfare. People help similar others more, and they help more when they have a sense of we-ness or one-group identity. Social dilemmas pit individual interests against group interest, but sometimes the group interest comes out on top.

Group norms may be descriptive (what people do) or injunctive (what people ought to do). Norms prominently include reciprocity and social responsibility, discussed earlier. But other prosocial norms may be more specific (e.g., not to litter), and their effect depends on how salient they are. People also differ in their orientation to others, and prosocial (cooperative) people inhabit different worlds than proself (competitive or individualist) people. Prosocial orientation involves trust. It elicits trust and cooperation, more constructive group processes, and higher outcomes all around.

The final proposed motivation for prosocial behavior is principlism, upholding moral standards. Without knowing Ms. McCarty's personal beliefs, one cannot know; however, the newspaper interviews make principlism seem likely. Abstract levels of moral reasoning predict helping for different reasons than other forms of moral reasoning, which rely on egoistic or collectivist motives. People's personal norms and values also predict helping. People have a varied set of potential motives for helping others. As we will see, their motives for hurting others are equally varied.

## SUGGESTIONS FOR FURTHER READING

BATSON, C. D. (1998). Altruism and prosocial behavior. In D. T. GILBERT, S. T. FISKE, & G. LINDZEY (Eds.), *Handbook of social psychology* (4th ed., Vol. 2, pp. 283–316). New York: McGraw-Hill.

DE WAAL, F. B. M. (2008). Putting the altruism back into altruism: The evolution of empathy. *Annual Review of Psychology*, *59*, 279–300.

EISENBERG, N. (2000). Emotion, regulation, and moral development. *Annual Review of Psychology*, *51*, 665–697.

HAIDT, J., & KESEBIR, S. (2010). Morality. In S. T. FISKE, D. T. GILBERT, & G. LINDZEY (Eds.), *Handbook of social psychology* (5th ed.). New York: Wiley.

PENNER, L. A., DOVIDIO, J. F., PILIAVIN, J. A., & SCHROEDER, D. A. (2005). Prosocial behavior: Multi-level perspectives. *Annual Review of Psychology*, *56*, 365–392.

PYSZCZYNSKI, T., GREENBERG, J., KOOLE, S., & SOLOMON, S. (2010). Experimental existential psychology: Coping with the facts of life. In S. T. FISKE, D. T. GILBERT, & G. LINDZEY (Eds.), *Handbook of social psychology* (5th ed.). New York: Wiley.

TANGNEY, J. P., STUEWIG, J., & MASHEK, D. J. (2007). Moral emotions and moral behavior. *Annual Review of Psychology*, *58*, 345–372.

# Chapter **10**

# Aggression: Antisocial Behavior

Richard Russo's novel, *Empire Falls*, focuses on a small town in Maine. High school student John Voss—described earlier as comatose, unknowable, dressed in strange thrift-shop clothes, and without a single friend—walks into art class after an unexplained absence of several days.

> Without looking at anyone, John sets his folded grocery bag down with a dull thud.... Justin Dibble is the first to speak. "Hey, John," he says, as if this were a normal day, just another class. "What's in the bag?"
>
> At first he doesn't appear to hear. When he finally reaches into the bag and takes out the revolver, it seem to Tick that he may have done so in response not to Justin but to a voice in his own head. The revolver looks like an antique, or maybe a stage prop, with its wooden grip and a long barrel. He points it and pulls the trigger without hesitation, and then Justin Dibble vanishes in the roar. He simply isn't sitting there anymore. (Russo, 2001, pp. 446–447)[1]

John Voss proceeds deliberately to shoot the art teacher, another classmate, and the high school principal before trying to shoot himself. This scene, reminiscent of school shootings around the world, certainly depicts aggression, as most people and most social psychologists understand it.

Consider the behavior of another character in the book, Mrs. Francine Whiting, who has inherited from her late husband's family most of the small town's commercial property, and with it, the single most dominant hand in the town's finances. She has particular control over the finances of the middle-aged manager of the Empire Grill. And she has reason to resent him. As a boy decades before, he had witnessed his mother's brief affair with Mrs. Whiting's late husband. Her long-term strategy for revenge on his family is revealed as she says:

---

[1] Copyright © Richard Russo. Reprinted with permission.

"Payback is *how* we endure, dear boy. Now, before you say another word in anger, for which I shall have to punish you, you'll have to stop and consider not just your own future, but your daughter's. She may require assistance with her university expenses in a couple of years, much as *you* did." She paused to let this sink in. "And of course there are your brother and the others who depend on the Empire Grill for their admittedly slender livelihoods. In the end, though, it's up to you, just as it always has been."

"Power and control. Right, Francine?" . . .

"Ah," she said in mock delight, "you *were* paying attention to my little lessons, weren't you, dear boy!" (Russo, 2001, p. 435)[2]

Many social psychologists would call her behavior just as aggressive as more direct physical violence.

Within aggression, social psychologists study wide varieties, using techniques that run from laboratory experiments on cognitive structure to archival studies of homicide rates. These data matter, as this chapter shows, because aggression raises chronic social issues involving the roles of media violence, guns, and alcohol, which we describe in order to set the societal context. Fortunately, a substantial amount of theory-based research has examined the problem of aggression. Much research starts from the core social motive of understanding, targeting the surprisingly powerful role of antisocial cognitions (think of aggressors being suspicious and quick to take offense). Other core social motives that run through aggression include frustrated efforts at controlling others (think of road rage, when all the other drivers seem intent on blocking your way) and protecting one's self-esteem (think of people becoming angry when their feelings are hurt). Significant theories and research traditions reflect each of these motives: cognitive theories of aggression (understanding), conflict theories (controlling), and image protection theories (self-enhancement).

## WHAT IS AGGRESSION?

Conceptual and operational definitions, chronic social problems, and the core social motives all introduce the variety of ways that social researchers tackle aggression. Given the topic, we devote some space to the chronic social problems associated with aggression.

### Conceptual Definitions

**Aggression** entails any behavior whose proximate intent is harm to another person. Injury must be the *intent*, according to social psychologists (Anderson & Bushman, 2002a; Baron & Richardson, 1994; Berkowitz, 1993; Bushman & Huesmann, 2009; Geen, 1998) and laypeople (Lysak, Rule, & Dobbs, 1989). Otherwise, parents, surgeons, and drill sergeants, who sometimes inflict mental or physical pain in the line of duty, might be viewed as aggressive, when their proximate intent is helping the

---

[2] Copyright © Richard Russo. Reprinted with permission.

other. Similarly, accidents are not aggression because they do not intend harm. And many aggression theorists point out that sadomasochism is not aggression because the victim's masochistic pleasure, not harm, is the immediate goal.

The definition, then, focuses on *behavior* with a particular intent. Aggressive thoughts, without the behavior, are not aggression. Behavior that harms another person, without the intent, is not aggression. Thus, contrary to popular parlance, assertiveness is not aggression. One can assert one's needs, rights, or views without the primary intent being harm to others.

Focus on the **proximate** (closest and most immediate) intent is distinct from focusing on the **primary** (ultimate) intent (Bushman & Anderson, 2001a). Aggressors operate with multiple motives, and determining the primary one would be tricky. School shootings may have the primary intent of revenge, suicide, or fame. Terrorist attacks may have various primary intents: revenge, escalating tensions, genocide, political control, moral influence, personal salvation, or publicity. Domestic abuse may have a primary intent of control, self-enhancement, relief from tension, or fulfilling a role. In the fictional example, Mrs. Whiting's apparent charity had a major element of revenge ("payback ... dear boy ... power and control"). In sponsoring the college education of the son and granddaughter of the woman responsible for her husband's betrayal, one might at first assume her motive was forgiveness and prosocial charity. But her dialogue makes clear that she finds power and control over the other family to be a satisfying form of revenge. Because people's motives are often complex, focusing on the most immediate, closest, or proximate goal seems more fruitful than trying to decide the primary one.

A related distinction has endured for decades but may be passing from usefulness (Bushman & Anderson, 2001a). Researchers traditionally have distinguished between two forms of aggression: **instrumental aggression**, which seeks harm as a means to another end (control, money, status), and **hostile aggression**, which seeks harm as the primary goal (e.g., Baron & Richardson, 1994). Instrumental aggression, in this view, is premeditated and controlled, whereas hostile aggression is angry, impulsive, and automatic. However, in apparent contradiction, hostile aggression sometimes can be controlled, as when an angry person plots revenge over time, and instrumental aggression sometimes can be impulsive, as when a child hits another child to get a toy back. Moreover, some researchers consider all aggression to be instrumental, to have the goal of obtaining some kind of reward, so that all aggression is **coercive action** (Malamuth & Addison, 2001; Tedeschi & Felson, 1994). Either way, the distinction loses its utility.

Researchers also distinguish between proactive and reactive aggression (Dodge & Coie, 1987). **Proactive aggression** takes the initiative: uses physical force to dominate, gets others to gang up on a peer, or threatens and bullies others. **Reactive aggression** instead responds to a perceived threat: when teased, strikes back; blames others in fights; or overreacts angrily to accidents. Researchers find that both types of aggression elicit social rejection from others, but they differ in their basic mechanisms, as we shall see.

Another set of distinctions creates a taxonomy of aggression (Buss, 1961; see Table 10.1). Although not empirically based and not currently in use, it is worth

**Table 10.1** Conceptual Types of Aggression

| | Active | | Passive | |
|---|---|---|---|---|
| | Direct | Indirect | Direct | Indirect |
| Physical | Stabbing, punching or shooting another person | Setting a booby trap for another person; hiring an assassin to kill an enemy | Physically preventing another person from obtaining a desired goal or performing a desired act (as in a sit-in demonstration) | Refusing to perform necessary tasks (e.g., refusal to move during a sit-in) |
| Verbal | Insulting or derogating another person | Spreading malicious rumors or gossip about another individual | Refusing to speak to another person, to answer questions, etc. | Failing to make specific verbal comments (e.g., failing to speak up in another person's defense when he or she is unfairly criticized) |

*Source:* Taxonomy from Buss, 1961.

considering because it expands laypeople's assumptions about what can constitute aggression. The taxonomy points out three dimensions: **physical-verbal** (involving body versus words), **active-passive** (by doing versus not doing), and **direct-indirect** (targeted versus roundabout). Active, direct, physical aggression (face-to-face bodily harm) comes to everyone's mind as the prototype of aggression. More unusual examples involve passive aggression (not speaking to someone, failing to help) or indirect aggression (harm via a third party or after a delay). As we will see, verbal and physical types of aggression are highly correlated (e.g., Carlson, Marcus-Newhall, & Miller, 1989). Researchers rarely study passive aggression (a pity, as it's uncommonly irritating in a colleague or close relationship!). However, some work targets ostracism and the silent treatment, but more from the victim's responses than the perpetrator's intent (e.g., Sommer, Williams, Ciarocco, & Baumeister, 2001; Williams, 1997; Williams, Shore, & Graphe, 1998). Direct versus indirect aggression does receive some research attention, for example, in gender differences that we cover later.

## Operational Definitions

Social psychologists face a challenge in operationalizing the social contexts that give rise to aggression. More than any other topic, harm-doing presents ethical difficulties for researchers (Darley, 1999). Consider the Stanford prison study described in the first chapter (Haney, Banks, & Zimbardo, 1973). The actual degree of aggressive harm inflicted on role-playing prisoners by role-playing guards was severe enough that researchers terminated the study. Much of the fame of that study stems precisely from its extraordinary impact. The more impactful and realistic the setting, the more the ethical issues: One cannot inflict actual harm, merely in order to study it. Hence, most social psychological studies of aggression use laboratory studies in which people think they are harming another person, but they actually are not.

For example, one of the classic laboratory methods (Anderson & Bushman, 1997) entails physical aggression using an **aggression machine** (Buss, 1961), a method simultaneously and apparently independently pioneered as a **shock generator** in Milgram's famous obedience experiments (1963, footnote 3; see Chapter 13). The method goes like this: A participant and a confederate appear to be randomly assigned as teacher and learner, respectively, in a study allegedly focused on learning processes. The learner's wrong answers are allegedly punished by electric shocks (though no shocks are actually received by the confederate). The teacher-participant can choose among levels of shock by pushing buttons labeled as *barely perceptible* to *excruciatingly painful*. This continuum allows researchers to measure intensity, number, and duration of shocks delivered. Researchers have also used other noxious stimuli, such as blasts of white noise supposedly delivered through earphones.

Critics might wonder whether the Buss aggression machine properly operationalizes aggression because, for example, the participant plays a role that socially sanctions harming the learner, so harm might not be the immediate intent. However, in aggression studies, the learner (or the experimenter) typically provokes the teacher (participant) in some fashion, and the participant's aggression then rises above the minimal level necessary to fulfill the role. More recently, a popular paradigm for studying aggression has included a competitive reaction time task, in which the winner who reacts faster gets to punish the loser (Taylor, 1967; see Giancola & Zeichner, 1995). Both the Taylor and the Buss measures of physical aggression are valid (Bernstein, Richardson, & Hammock, 1987). Another clever method involves the amount of hot sauce given to a person who hates spicy food (e.g., Lieberman, Solomon, Greenberg, & McGregor, 1999). Where tested, these operationalizations of physical aggression correlate with other measures, such as verbal aggression.

Verbal aggression measures typically include oral or written responses to a confederate (Anderson & Bushman, 1997). Researchers record and code the severity of direct verbal attacks. Alternatively, researchers elicit written ratings of a confederate, in settings where the potential aggressor knows that negative comments and evaluations will harm the confederate's future outcomes.

A critic might argue that verbal and physical measures of aggression tap entirely different forms. For instance, some people might talk tough but not act; others might act tough but not talk much. However, the same people and situations indeed do elicit both kinds of aggression, according to meta-analysis (Carlson, Marcus-Newhall, & Miller, 1989). That is, when the same participants aggress in more than one way within a single study, the verbal and physical measures correlate highly. What's more, in studies that manipulate situational antecedents of aggression, the effects on physical and verbal aggression are the same.

Beyond verbal and physical expression of aggression, one might assume that physiological indicators would most objectively assess aggressive tendencies. Unfortunately, just as aggressive behavior is complex, so too are its neural correlates (Baskin, Edersheim, & Price, 2007) and its peripheral physiological correlates (e.g., heart rate, electro-dermal responses; Lorber, 2004). Although physiological indicators lend themselves to both laboratory and field studies of violence, neither setting clearly supports their use, yet. Nonetheless, the possibilities are intriguing (Carnagey, Anderson, & Bartholow, 2007).

Critics might also wonder whether the laboratory studies of aggression generalize to the real world. They do. In the real world, indicators of aggression range from horn-honking to violent crime (murder, assault, robbery, rape), all of which clearly reflect an intent to harm the victim. Researchers often use archival data (e.g., murder rate as a function of daily temperature) and observational methods (e.g., taunting or hitting in classrooms and summer camps, as a function of social status). Based on these data, clear and consistent evidence supports the external validity of conclusions from laboratory studies of aggression (according to meta-analyses; Anderson & Bushman, 1997). That is, the same kinds of individuals and situations elicit aggression both in the laboratory and in the field. Thus, the two types of evidence clearly converge. As in many other areas of social psychology, effects obtained in laboratory studies hold up quite well in the field. In any case, programmatic research that combines laboratory and field data strengthens the conclusions shared by both methods.

## Chronic Social Issues: Aggression and Social Artifacts

When people consider aggression as a social problem, various images come to mind, including media violence, guns, and alcohol. Certain social **artifacts** (human products) facilitate aggression, as researchers from a variety of theoretical traditions have shown. Unlike other topics, the study of aggression is grounded in a series of social problems that revolve around these cultural artifacts, so we will ground our examination of aggression in the societal context provided by these applied problems.

**MEDIA VIOLENCE**    American society is addicted to television. In average American households with children, the television is on 28 hours per week for preteens and 23 hours per week for teens (Donnerstein, Slaby, & Eron, 1994), accounting for half of children's leisure time. Prime time shows average 5 or 6 acts of violence per hour, and Saturday morning children's programs average 20 to 25 per hour. The most violent programming appears before school (6–9 a.m., 497 violent scenes) and after school (2–5 p.m., 609 violent scenes). If children watch 2 to 4 hours of television daily, they will have witnessed over 8,000 murders and over 100,000 other acts of violence by the time they leave elementary school (Donnerstein et al., 1994). These figures do not include cable, internet, video, or video games, which have even more graphic violence.

Research unequivocally demonstrates that media violence facilitates aggression. Although the public remains broadly isolated from this knowledge, review after review supports the conclusion: In 586 separate laboratory tests, exposure to media violence had a large effect on aggression; in 556 studies conducted outside the laboratory, with fewer controls, exposure to media violence had medium effects on aggression (Paik & Comstock, 1994). A more recent meta-analysis similarly found larger effects in laboratory than field studies (Anderson & Bushman, 2002b). Differences in the effect size could result from a host of factors, including the recency and concentration of exposure (higher in the laboratory) or precision of operationalization (also higher in the laboratory). For experimental designs, exposure typically consisted of viewing edited excerpts of violent programs, whereas in the field, exposure typically entailed reported frequency of watching television programs identified as violent.

Across both kinds of studies, the most frequent kinds of aggression measures involved self-reported behavioral intentions or actual actions on an aggression machine, but also interpersonal aggression during informal social interactions (e.g., hitting or pushing during play). Experimental studies in general show medium effects of media violence on aggression in the subset of settings that involve unstructured social interaction, again slightly larger in laboratory than field experiments (Wood, Wong, & Chachere, 1991). In all these reviews, only 6% to 10% of the tests show reversed effects—that is, media violence *decreasing* postexposure aggression—which could be interpreted as **catharsis** (i.e., letting off steam by watching violence instead of engaging in it; we will come back to this). The vast majority of studies show an effect significantly larger than zero, so media violence clearly facilitates aggression. The link of violent media to aggression is one of the most reliable findings in social psychology.

In one study typical of the laboratory paradigms (Meyer, 1972), undergraduate men participated in a study supposedly about grading each other's work by means of electric shocks. After writing an essay on the importance of a college education, participants received 8 shocks (representing a graded scale of 1 to 8); this presumably aroused hostility toward their partner (a confederate). While waiting for their partner to write an essay on the same topic, they participated in a supposedly unrelated study that entailed watching a 2- to 3-minute film segment. As Table 10.2 indicates, they watched either real violence (an execution with a knife during the Vietnam war), fictional violence (a movie knife fight), exciting nonviolence (a cowboy riding a half-broken

**Table 10.2**  Number of Shocks, as a Function of Exposure to Filmed Violence

| Type of Filmed Violence | Justification | | |
|---|---|---|---|
| | Justified | Neutral | Unjustified |
| Real | 7.36 | 4.96 | 4.96 |
| Fictional | 7.16 | 7.40 | 5.20 |
| No violence | | 5.20 | |
| No film | | 4.76 | |

*Source:* From Meyer, 1972.
Copyright © American Psychological Association. Adapted with permission.

wild horse), or nothing. For participants who viewed violent film segments, a voiceover either justified the violence, labeled it as unjustified, or was absent.

After the film, participants went back to the alleged main experiment and graded an essay by assigning 1 to 10 shocks to the confederate. As the table shows, a brief prior exposure to justified violence increased the number of shocks, compared with unjustified violence or no violence. Thus, when primed by justified violence, participants were more likely to aggress against the confederate in the service of revenge. (In the neutral condition, which lacked a voiceover, the fictional violence drew more aggression than the real violence did, probably because of baseline differences in how intrinsically justified the incident seemed.)

A noteworthy recent study examined the effects of television viewing on aggression in both childhood and adolescence, tracking 707 randomly sampled families over 17 years (Johnson, Cohen, Smailes, Kasen, & Brook, 2002). A clear relationship emerged between time spent watching television (in adolescence and early adulthood) and aggressive acts. The study is one of the longest and largest longitudinal datasets and takes the measures of violence into severe forms, including assault and robbery. And it still controls for possible confounds such as previous aggressive behavior, childhood neglect, family income, neighborhood violence, parental education, and psychiatric disorders. Although it measured television viewing in general and not exposure to television violence per se, over 60% of television programs contain violence, so this is not a fatal flaw (Anderson & Bushman, 2002a), especially given the staggering number of other studies isolating the effects of violent media.

How do violent media affect aggression? Watching media violence increases angry feelings, aggressive thoughts, physiological arousal, and aggressive behavior, but decreases helpful behavior and physiological sensitivity to violence (Anderson et al., 2004; Carnagey, Anderson, & Bushman, 2007). Identifying with video warriors makes gamers especially aggressive (Konijn, Nije Bijvank, & Bushman, 2007). Essentially, media violence primes short-term accessibility of aggression, creates long-term norms about its prevalence and acceptability, provides role models, desensitizes viewers, and in the case of video games, actively involves consumers in violence (Anderson & Bushman, 2002).

For decades, the weight of evidence from hundreds of studies clearly has shown that media violence facilitates viewer aggression in the short run and the long run. Violent video games have precisely the same effects as television and film violence (Anderson & Bushman, 2001; Anderson & Dill, 2000). Given the clarity of the evidence, a disjunction between scientific findings and media coverage is puzzling indeed (Bushman & Anderson, 2001b). The empirical correlations, in a cumulative meta-analysis, show larger and even more reliable media violence effects over time. At the exact same time, news reports have presented the relationship as ever more tenuous and moderate as the studies accumulate.

Conflict of interest (pleasing their advertisers) would seem a sufficient explanation for this neglect of the scientific evidence. But the media appear to be unaware of one crucial fact. Television violence does not necessarily help their advertisers. Television violence actually decreases memory for advertisements embedded in those segments (Bushman, 1998a, 2005; Bushman & Bonacci, 2002; Bushman & Phillips,

2001). Sex and violence in the ads themselves also impairs memory for the product (Bushman, 2007). Viewers of violence get into an angry mood, and anger impairs their memory—hardly the result desired by advertisers.

Nevertheless, oblivious to this business liability, media executives and advertisers apparently believe that violence attracts viewers (which it does, especially if accompanied by warning labels; Bushman & Stack, 1996). But if the advertisers knew that the viewers were not recalling their ads, they would be less interested in buying time on violent programming. Thus, despite clear and convincing evidence—evidence almost as strong as the smoking-cancer link and even stronger than links between such well-known health effects as condom use and HIV prevention or lead exposure and IQ damage (Bushman & Anderson, 2001b)—media violence continues as standard fare, with predictable results on aggression. These results occur in Europe as much as in the United States (Mummendey, 1996).

Various psychological processes contribute to violent media effects on aggression. Later in the chapter, we see how the mechanisms of violent media alter people's social motives, including how they understand aggression, how they control others, and how they enhance themselves.

**WEAPONS**    Another cultural artifact is the easy presence of aggressive weapons. Countries differ, for example, in the ease of gun ownership, with the United States having both the highest rate of gun ownership and the highest rate of firearm homicide among industrialized Western countries (Berkowitz, 1994). Across 16 countries in Europe, each country's availability of firearms correlates with its firearm homicide rate.

A more direct comparison is Seattle and Vancouver, two cities similar in location, size, income, education, unemployment, and, most important, rates of burglary and robbery. However, one has gun control and one does not. Over a six-year period, Seattle residents ran only a slightly higher risk of aggravated assault (1.16 to 1), but the rate of assault with firearms was fully seven times higher (Sloan et al., 1988). The risk of dying from homicide in Seattle was significantly higher than in Vancouver (1.6 times), a difference completely explained by a nearly fivefold increase in the risk of being murdered by a handgun. Rates of homicide by other means did not differ, evidence suggesting to the authors that "restricting access to handguns may reduce the rate of homicide in a community."

Advocates of unrestricted gun ownership argue that people need guns to protect themselves, but other studies suggest that gun owners are more likely to be hurt by their own guns than to hurt an intruder. For example, keeping a gun at home is associated with a nearly threefold increased risk of homicide, in virtually all cases involving a family member or an intimate (Kellermann et al., 1993). Households with recent purchasers of handguns are at greater risk for both homicide and suicide, a risk that endures for more than five years after purchase (Cummings, Koepsell, Grossman, Savarino, & Thompson, 1997; Wintemute, Parham, Beaumout, Wright, & Drake, 1999). Guns make aggression more lethal when it does occur, not a surprising effect. But (more surprising) guns also provoke aggression in their own right, simply by being there.

Social psychologists have shown one mechanism by which guns provoke aggression. Cultural learning imbues certain objects with aggressive associations (Berkowitz

& LaPage, 1967): "The presence of the aggressive objects should generally lead to more intense attacks upon an available target than would occur in the presence of a neutral object" (p. 203).

In a study allegedly involving shocks as evaluations for problem-solving performance, undergraduate men encountered a partner who delivered seven shocks, provoking the participant, or only one shock (control). When it was the participants' turn to deliver evaluative shocks, the table containing the shock key also contained either (a) a 12-gauge shotgun and a .38 caliber revolver, said to be associated with the partner's research project, (b) the same guns, said to be associated with someone else's research project, or (c) nothing. As an additional control, some of the provoked participants also saw badminton racquets said to be associated with the partner (see Table 10.3). The unprovoked (one-shock) participants gave the least shock in return, and the presence of weapons did not matter. For provoked participants, the mere presence of weapons, either associated or not, led to the most shocks, whereas the absence of weapons led to more moderate levels of shock. These classic results, soon known as the **weapons effect**, fit the idea that weapons cue more aggressive behavior than would otherwise occur (Berkowitz, 1993, 1994).

Meta-analysis (Carlson, Marcus-Newhall, & Miller, 1990) indicates that the weapons effect is most reliable for two kinds of participants who are least likely to monitor their own behavior in the experiment. First, being naïve (according to a postexperimental interview, unaware of the hypothesis) means not being suspicious and thus not monitoring their behavior as much. Second, being low on **evaluation apprehension** (not worried about making a favorable impression) again means not monitoring their behavior as much.

Aggressive cues need not be limited to weapons. The generality of the **aggressive cue** phenomenon (i.e., beyond the weapons effect) appears most reliably in work that essentially primes people. Some work uses the same name for an aggressor and a subsequent potential target of aggression, and other work exposes people to hostile verbal cues, such as bumper stickers. All in all, uncovering this phenomenon anticipated more recent interest in the unconscious activation of motives: "Situational stimuli can exert relatively 'automatic' control over socially relevant human actions" (Berkowitz & La Page, 1967, p. 203).

**Table 10.3**    Number of Shocks Delivered, as a Function of Aggressive Cues

|  | Shocks Received | |
| --- | --- | --- |
| Cue Condition | 1 | 7 |
| Associated weapon | 2.60 | 6.07 |
| Unassociated weapon | 2.30 | 5.67 |
| No object | 3.07 | 4.67 |
| Badminton racquet | — | 4.60 |

*Source:* From Berkowitz & LaPage, 1967.
Copyright © American Psychological Association. Adapted with permission.

Overall, the data clearly link the presence of guns with number of homicides, but this result is neutral about policy implications, and reasonable people can disagree. The solutions to this problem are many and beyond the scope of current scientific social psychology to determine. People favor solutions ranging from gun control to safety locks to training to increased punishment for crimes committed with firearms. The most important message, regardless of one's view of the appropriate solution, is the demonstrable link between guns and lethal aggression. What one does about it is another matter. Later, the bulk of the chapter examines the psychological mechanisms that predispose people to be violent by whatever means.

**ALCOHOL**    About 50% of violent crimes are committed while the assailant is intoxicated (Anderson & Bushman, 1997; Steele & Southwick, 1985). In controlled laboratory studies, likewise, intoxication facilitates aggression. Meta-analyses show a small to medium effect (Bushman & Cooper, 1990; Ito, Miller, & Pollock, 1996; Steele & Josephs, 1990; Steele & Southwick, 1985) that depends on dosage. Moderate to high doses appear to facilitate aggression, whereas low doses do not.

Moreover, the study's control condition matters to the effect size. Studies showing the largest effects compare alcohol to a **placebo** (an inactive substance indistinguishable from the active drug). For example, people might drink ginger ale and peppermint oil as a placebo or the same drink with alcohol added. This isolates the *physiological effect* of alcohol on aggression, and it is large. Comparing the placebo to a simple control, in which people correctly know they are not drinking alcohol, isolates the effects of *mere expectation*. That is, in both the placebo and control conditions, no one receives any alcohol, but the placebo participants think they are receiving it. Surprisingly, the sheer expectancy of having consumed alcohol causes no effect on aggression (Bushman & Cooper, 1990; Hull & Bond, 1986).

Alcohol affects aggression in part by **alcohol myopia** (Steele & Josephs, 1990), that is, by impairing cognitive processes (Hull & Bond, 1986; Steele & Southwick, 1985). According to Steele's **inhibitory conflict model**, many social behaviors occur under contradictory impulses, simultaneous desires to act and not to act. Aggressing constitutes a central example, but so can sexual adventuring, self-disclosing, gambling, and excessive drinking (see Table 10.4). When people drink, they undermine their ability to process conflicting responses, so they respond to only one of two conflicting impulses. This results in more extreme, less moderated behavior. Often, the inhibiting response is weaker and more complex, whereas the instigating response is powerful and simple, so it is easier to follow the original impulse when one is not thinking clearly.

Consistent with this idea are findings that **self-awareness** (getting people to think about themselves; see Chapter 9) eliminates the differences between drunk and sober people's aggression (Ito, Miller, & Pollock, 1996). Thus, when people are drinking, they cannot think as easily about their own internalized standards, which might otherwise inhibit their aggressive or other destructive impulses. If they are prompted to think about their own standards, they can indeed control their behavior, even when drunk. Alcohol myopia accounts for the rewarding features of drinking, in that it impairs stress-inducing thoughts, particularly when one is distracted (Steele, Southwick, & Pagano, 1986). Alcohol enables people to escape from self (Baumeister, 1991), which can be relaxing but also can facilitate aggression.

**Table 10.4**    Level of Conflict and Effects of Alcohol

| Behavior | Conflict Level | |
|---|---|---|
| | High | Low |
| Aggression | 1.32 | 0.17 |
| Drinking | 0.88 | −0.38 |
| Gambling | 0.38 | 0.05 |
| Self-disclosure | 1.34 | 0.07 |
| Sexual interest | 0.42 | −0.06 |

*Source:* From Steele & Josephs, 1990.
Copyright © American Psychological Association. Adapted with permission.

Further consistent with the alcohol myopia idea are findings from meta-analyses that the effects of alcohol on aggression are, oddly, even stronger when the partner may be able to retaliate (Bushman & Cooper, 1990). Thus, when people are sober, they notice when aggression will elicit retaliation—they see both sides of the response conflict—so they inhibit their aggressive impulses. But when they have been drinking, they ignore the possible ill effects of their own aggression. This explains how some of the worst fights occur when both parties are drunk and unable to consider the consequences.

Finally, alcohol myopia helps explain the effects of alcohol on marital violence (Murphy & O'Farrell, 1996). People with higher alcohol consumption are more likely to be physically violent toward their partners. But if they stop drinking, their violence drops to levels typical of the general population, a finding consistent with the short-term effects of alcohol on disinhibiting aggressive impulses.

Alcohol does not, by itself, create aggression. Alcohol's effect on aggression occurs when people are provoked, not distracted from it, and lack a nonaggressive alternative (Bushman & Cooper, 1990). Certain conditions exaggerate the effects of alcohol. Studies that involve fasting for at least four hours, consuming vodka, or consuming other distilled spirits show stronger effects than studies involving shorter fasts, beer, or pure alcohol. Unfortunately, experimenter expectancy effects (see Chapter 2) also seem to operate, making effects much bigger when experimenters are not blind to condition. This suggests using not only placebos but also **doubleblind trials** (in which neither experimenter nor participant knows whether alcohol or placebo is involved). Carefully designed experiments are crucial to document the role of alcohol in aggression (Pedersen, Aviles, Ito, Miller, & Pollock, 2002). Nevertheless, the facilitating effects of alcohol on aggression are already clear-cut.

**CONCLUSION**    The chronic social issues of media violence, weapons, and alcohol all concern social artifacts that facilitate aggression. Research shows that these cultural factors indeed contribute to real, persistent dangers to people's safety. However, people are still the aggressors, and the most frequently studied antecedents of aggression are interpersonal conflict (Geen, 1998, p. 318). Beyond social artifacts that may facilitate aggression, people themselves motivate aggression, and various social psychological theories account for it.

## Core Social Motives

Social psychological research on aggression primarily focuses on three motives: understanding, controlling, and self-enhancing. Surprisingly, understanding is the single motive most studied in the aggression field, a focus perhaps contrary to laypeople's perceptions of what should motivate aggression.

**UNDERSTANDING**    Even as people decry its effects, aggression often follows from shared social understandings. People learn the cultural cues for threat and retaliation. Thus, for example, people learn norms for acceptable and unacceptable aggression, in order to maintain group membership, as a later section shows. Aggression on behalf of the group cements belonging to the ingroup. Conversely, aggression in defiance of the group provokes rejection, incapacitation, or punishment. Therefore, as we will see, some aggressors are just following orderly norms regarding aggression: shared understandings of acceptable provocation, methods, sequences, and consequences. The chapter's next section takes up this kind of social learning and the resulting cognitive structures. If cognition seems like a dry approach to aggression, consider the horrifying role of education, indoctrination, and shared group understanding in teenage gangs and terrorist training camps.

Does shared understanding always shape aggression? What about people who are not socialized, who are aggressive toward others in general, even ingroup others? What about an isolate who turns on others? In most cases, such aggressors see their actions as justified retaliation for harm previously caused to them. As we will see, they are playing by the rules as they understand them. This may be viewed as a case of shared understanding gone awry. Perpetrators apply what they think are appropriate rules for aggression, a form perhaps of antisocial understanding that later sections will elaborate.

**CONTROLLING**    Remember Mrs. Francine Whiting's principles of "power and control" as she threatens revenge on the small-town grill owner whose family she hates? Although laypeople rarely consider aggression as control, think of a mugger holding a gun to someone's head. Sometimes aggression is clearly coercive, when people use aggression to control their outcomes or to obtain resources. As noted earlier, some researchers define aggression solely as a coercive influence tactic (Malamuth & Addison, 2001; Tedeschi & Felson, 1994). From this perspective, people have evolved instrumental **aggression modules** (or **mods**), defined as specific, inherited psychological mechanisms that potentiate aggression as a coercive response to certain environmental conditions. This is the strongest evolutionary stance for human aggression, which views aggression as a broadly applied type of social influence.

A more socially functional stance views aggression primarily as a response to perceived threat. In this view, aggression defends self, intimates, or ingroup as part of an adaptive impulse to protect. It thus entails controlling others, in this case, coercing the potential perpetrator to prevent or cease inflicting harm. This important view of aggression broadens its scope to include female aggression, more than otherwise, for example in defense of others. Given gender differences in who traditionally takes care of whom, the nature of aggression's sought-for control differs dramatically by gender. The operation of control in aggression becomes more evident upon a closer look at gender differences in patterns of aggression.

More than in any other topic within social psychology, men's and women's aggression differs, particularly their manner of aggression. According to meta-analyses, men are more aggressive than women, especially when inflicting physical, rather than psychological, harm (Eagly & Steffen, 1986) and especially when unprovoked (Bettencourt & Miller, 1996); these results occur across both laboratory and field studies (Anderson & Bushman, 1997). Women and girls are more likely to use verbal aggression, relative to men's and boy's emphasis on physical aggression (Geen, 1998). Again, Francine Whiting's tactics contrast with those of the high-school shooter John Voss.

Research suggests that both boys and girls engage in socially sanctioned forms of aggression, fitting their respective gender roles in elementary school. Girls are more involved in **relational aggression**, that is, behaviors intended to damage another child's friendships or sense of belonging to a peer ingroup (Crick, 1995, 1997; Crick, Casas, & Mosher, 1997; Crick & Grotpeter, 1995; Crick & Werner, 1998). Examples include exclusion, gossip, or manipulation, and it starts as early as preschool. Girls not only are more likely to engage in relational aggression but also are more provoked by it when it does occur. Boys more typically engage in physical aggression.

Note that, as always, gender differences do not specify psychological processes; they could be due to social roles or biology or some combination. A social role analysis is supported, for example, by meta-analysis of gender differences in perceived consequences of aggression: Women perceive more harm to the victim, danger to self, and guilt or anxiety, so they aggress less (Eagly & Steffen, 1986). Men whose social roles include belonging to all-male groups (e.g., fraternities, sports teams) are more likely to endorse and report sexual aggression against women, according to meta-analysis (Murnen & Kohlman, 2007). A more explicitly biological analysis is supported, for example, by meta-analyses finding that higher levels of the masculine hormone testosterone are associated with male aggressive behavior (Archer, 1991; 1994; Archer, Birring, & Wu, 1998; Archer, Graham-Kevan, & Davies, 2005). And testosterone varies with the social situation; for example, male winners of male-male competitions show increased testosterone levels (Gladue, Boechler, & McCaul, 1989). Other underlying gender differences could explain differential aggression by a combination of biological and social factors: Women develop social cognitive skills earlier than men, decreasing their need for blunt, physical forms of control (Bennett, Farrington, & Huesmann, 2005).

Regardless of its specifically biological or social origins, aggression may still be viewed as an effort to control others, but who and how differs by gender. An evolutionary account posits that men have to compete for mates more than women do. Recall the **parental investment theories** (Chapter 7; Trivers, 1971): Because of pregnancy and lactation, women have had to invest more resources in each child they produce than men do. An account based on **sexual selection** (the selection for male versus female reproductive success) would argue that men have a higher theoretical maximum number of progeny and therefore higher variance in number of progeny. Thus, the argument runs, men should compete for mates more vigorously (Daly & Wilson, 1988). Men can further their access to mates by aggression against other men. In this argument, men can also acquire status by a reputation for aggression, and women are supposed to seek high-status mates, to enhance the survival of their offspring. Finally, men are supposed to be more sexually jealous because paternity is more ambiguous than maternity, so they would have to guard against sexual infidelity of their mates.

These predictions have been supported in a number of evolutionary psychology studies. For example, consistent with male competition for mates, male-male aggression is more frequent than male-female aggression. Male-male aggression is directed to strangers, who might compete for mates, but male-female aggression, when it occurs, is directed toward sexual partners, presumably as a form of control (Hilton, Harris, & Rice, 2000; Kenrick & Sheets, 1993). Men report that their strategies to retain mates include threats of violence to other men and debasement of their own partners, especially the younger and more attractive their partner (Buss & Shackelford, 1997). Men who are violent against their spouses are also highly controlling, jealous, and debasing (Wilson & Daly, 1996). Also chillingly consistent with this line of argument, stepfathers are 500 times more likely than genetic fathers to kill their infants and toddlers (Daly & Wilson, 1996). Children of all ages are 70 times more at risk from stepfathers than from fathers (Daly & Wilson, 1988).

However, not all the datasets agree on this point (Temrin, Buchmayer, & Enquist, 2000). Moreover, these accounts of male violence can be explained in more social-cultural terms, as demands of male gender roles that define sole possession of women as a necessary form of honor. Evolutionary explanations can work through culture, but not all cultural practices necessarily result directly from evolutionary pressures. (We will come back to cultural differences in aggression.)

Female-male homicide occurs rarely, but when it does, it typically occurs in defense against male violence (Wilson, 1989). Women physically aggress against men more than against other women, but in both cases of female violence, the victims are more likely to be intimates than strangers (Hilton, Harris, & Rice, 2000; Kenrick & Sheets, 1993). The motives here may differ; such violence may be less an expression of control over possessions and more an effort to control (maintain) the family unit.

Whereas male responses to stress tend to focus on **fight-or-flight** (aggression or escape), female responses to stress focus more on nurturing and attachment activities newly termed **tend-and-befriend** (Taylor et al., 2000; see relationships chapter). Thus, viewing aggression as the core social motive of controlling, as in the coercive features of male aggression, finds a possible exception in female responses, which more often emphasize belonging motives. Note, however, that women protecting themselves or their offspring may be aggressive, but the underlying motive seems to differ. Of course, the evidence for relational aggression suggests that women aren't exactly heroines.

**SELF-ENHANCING**    Using aggression as a coercive influence tactic could follow from a motive to self-enhance almost as much as to control. Acquiring resources, status, and reputation partly occurs in the service of enhancing one's image. Rather than focusing on control over one's external outcomes, a self-enhancement explanation focuses on internal feelings of self-worth. For aggression as a coercive tactic, the explanation in terms of control is more direct, whereas the explanation in terms of self-enhancement constitutes an inference.

The related view of aggression as an effort to counteract perceived threat similarly could follow from a motivation to protect the self from damage, almost as much as from an effort to control. Here, the protection and promotion of self is more evident. What is less evident is the direction of the effect. One might think that people with low self-esteem would be the most aggressive, in an effort to repair their self-esteem, but the research says otherwise, as we see later.

### Summary of Definitions, Social Issues, and Motives

Aggression is behavior whose proximate intent is harm to another person. It may be more or less hostile, instrumental, or coercive. Aggression varies on how active-passive, direct-indirect, and physical-verbal it is. Operational definitions of aggression most often entail active, direct aggression. Physical aggression studies often provoke participants and then measure their reactions on the (fake) shock generator usually called the aggression machine. Verbal measures of aggression include negative ratings that can harm the other person. Verbal and physical measures of aggression do correlate with each other. More generally, laboratory measures correspond well to field measures (observations, archival records).

Aggression interacts with chronic social issues, such as media violence, guns, and alcohol. Social psychologists have shown that each facilitates aggression in people who have been provoked. Various theoretical approaches account for these effects, as we will see. The main motives identified in aggression theories are shared understanding of social norms, controlling others, and self-enhancing, which can make aggression seem adaptive for the perpetrator if not the victim.

## COGNITIVE THEORIES OF AGGRESSION: ANTISOCIAL UNDERSTANDING

A surprising amount of aggression research focuses on cognitive approaches, which may seem a cool approach to a hot topic, if ever there was one. On the other hand, consider the background that novelist Richard Russo gives to John Voss, the high school boy who shoots classmates and teachers. When he was noisy as an infant and toddler, his parents hung him in a laundry sack on a closet door to get him out of the way. And their abuse did not stop there. His warped understanding of the social world had deep roots. Similarly, Francine Whiting's idea that revenge should be visited on the descendants of the woman who wronged her is unusual in modern American culture but not so unusual an understanding in other times and places. Aggression clearly results from people's construction of social situations, and understanding (cognition) is how they get there. Social learning theories address understanding how and when to aggress, giving both actions and consequences. Attributional theories address people's understanding of why to aggress. And cognitive structure theories address what habits of aggression to acquire and why.

## Social Learning: Understanding How and When

Attitudes, as described in an earlier chapter, can develop via **modeling** (imitating the behavior of another person) and via **vicarious conditioning** or **observational learning** (watching someone else get rewarded or punished). Initial work in the social learning of aggression emerged from an effort to show "no-trial" learning in social settings (Bandura, 1965). Normally, learning operates through a series of trials, direct experiences with actions and consequences. For aggressive behavior, one's own, direct, trial-and-error learning could prove maladaptive to the point of fatality. Thus, a more indirect approach to understanding aggression would be safer. Such an approach requires cognitive representation. Counter to many of the original learning theorists, who did not believe in cognition, Bandura argued for the function of representational processes. Learning processes are mediated by "imaginal and verbal" symbols (p. 47), an early way of talking about cognitive structures. In this view, cognitive **matching processes** occur when people learn by first watching others, represent that scene in their minds, and then perform the same behavior. A cognitive representation needs to bridge the gap between one's observation and one's subsequent action.

Aggression clearly can develop by imitating aggressive models, whether real people, filmed people, or cartoon characters (Bandura, Ross, & Ross, 1963a). For example, nursery school children watched a model aggress against a Bobo doll (a large inflated tippy clown with a weighted bottom). The aggression included novel and unusual forms, such as kicking the doll in the air, saying "Sock him in the nose!" and "Pow!" Observers then frustrated the children (by not allowing them to play with some desirable toys) and then watched the children in a room with other toys, including a smaller Bobo doll. Aggression was coded as imitative, partially imitative, or nonimitative. **Imitative aggression** included the unusual forms of aggression clearly derived from the model's behavior. As Table 10.5 indicates in the last line, children were almost twice as aggressive overall when they had observed an aggressive

**Table 10.5**   Imitation of Novel Aggression from Models

| Type of Aggression | Type of Model | | | |
| --- | --- | --- | --- | --- |
| | Live Model | Filmed Human | Cartoon | Control |
| Imitative | 21.3 | 16.4 | 12.0 | 2.8 |
| Nonimitative | 34.1 | 34.2 | 49.6 | 29.1 |
| Total (including partially imitative and gun play) | 83.0 | 91.5 | 99.0 | 54.3 |

*Source:* Calculated from Bandura et al., 1963a.

model than when they had observed no model (about 91 versus 54 actions). Most relevant to Bandura's theory, the pattern was clearest for imitative aggression (16 versus 3 acts) and less so for nonimitative aggression (39 versus 29). Although the imitative aggression was less frequent overall, its appearance after only one exposure to the model speaks volumes. Children demonstrably learn novel forms of aggressive behavior through modeling, thereby arguably learning *how* to aggress.

In addition to modeling how, social learning teaches *when* to aggress: what effects aggression has. Nursery school children (in a paradigm similar to the previous example) observed an aggressor win control of toys and snacks, marching off with a sack of loot, singing "Hi ho, hi ho, it's off to play I go." Other children saw the aggressor lose control of the toys and get spanked by the child who had originally forfeited the toys. When children see aggression rewarded, they are more likely to imitate it (Bandura, 1965; Bandura, Ross, & Ross, 1963b).

Clearly, such modeling of observed aggression flies in the face of people's hunches that violent media might provide a **catharsis** or harmless outlet for aggressive impulses. (We will come back to catharsis shortly.) Social learning theory has illuminated the ill effects of violent media documented earlier (Donnerstein, Slaby, & Eron, 1994; Mummendey, 1996). Violent media have the most impact under the very circumstances predicted by social learning theory: when the media violence occurs with (a) efficacy as an instrument to reach one's goals; (b) omission of observable consequences to the victim; (c) similarity between viewer and perpetrator; and (d) entailing the viewer's frustration, emotional arousal, or aggressive predisposition (Comstock & Paik, 1991).

Social learning theory has also guided work on the long-term development of antisocial behavior patterns (Patterson, DeBaryshe, & Ramsey, 1989). In particular, it addresses self-regulatory mechanisms, treating them as **self-sanctions** (self-rewards and punishments). For example, if people normally inhibit their own aggression toward human targets by self-sanctions, then dehumanization of the targets disinhibits aggression because the self-sanctions no longer apply (Bandura, Underwood, & Fromson, 1975). Similarly, removing self-sanctions can disinhibit aggression by other routes, such as blaming victims, ignoring their harm, linking one's aggression to a worthy cause, or diffusing personal responsibility.

Such **moral disengagement** (believing that ethical standards do not apply to oneself in a particular context) reduces self-censure and eases aggression (Bandura, Barbaranelli, Caprara, & Pastorelli, 1996). In some of the most evil acts of aggression, such as terrorism, these mechanisms (worthy cause, vilification of victims) clearly operate (Bandura, 1999). Moral disengagement, moral exemption (Staub, 1990), moral hypocrisy (covered in Chapter 9; Batson et al., 1997; 1999), socially induced evil (Darley, 1992), and socially sanctioned violence (Jackman, 2002) all name forms of violence that seem prosocial to the perpetrators but aggressive from the perspective of victims or observers. Going back to Chapter 9's principlism, the moral principles that can motivate prosocial behavior, note that moral conviction has a darker side (Skitka & Mullen, 2002). Perceived moral mandates can lead people to excuse any means—ethical or not—in the service of their valued goals. People sometimes believe so utterly in their own righteousness that they ignore other human values and procedural safeguards. People learn cognitive representations, sanction themselves, and manage their moral self-regulation in the service of desired ends.

Because it addresses how aggression is acquired, instigated, and regulated, social learning theory addresses developmental issues more directly than much of social psychology (Bandura, 1973). Social learning theory focuses on well-learned patterns of voluntary response. It assumes that aggression has a substantially intentional component, as an instrumental activity in the service of acquiring rewards (adding a control motive to the more obvious understanding motive). However, other cognitive theories subscribe to a more automatic, less controlled view of aggression.

## Cognitive Structural Approaches: Understanding What Habits of Aggression to Acquire and Why

As noted, social learning theory early on advocated a role for mental representations. This stand flew in the face of the narrowest forms of learning theory available at the time, which viewed anything except stimulus and response as an unscientific fiction. Nevertheless, it remained for other theories to spell out the nature and function of the posited cognitive structures.

**AGGRESSION SCRIPTS**    Children learn complex sequences of behavior by observation and by doing. Cognitive representations called **scripts**—habitual programs of behavior (Chapter 4)—encode attended material, which can strengthen by **rehearsal** (mental repetition), and retrieved if accessible (Huesmann, 1988; Huesmann & Eron, 1989). Violent media contribute to this process (Huesmann, 1986), but so does the child's own behavior. According to a 22-year longitudinal study (Huesmann & Eron, 1984), children with intellectual deficits are more likely to behave aggressively then and later, perhaps because they are easily frustrated by ordinary problem-solving (see Figure 10.1). As patterns of aggression repeat, they are encoded and rehearsed, becoming more accessible in the future, a self-perpetuating process. Cognitive rehearsal of aggression—fantasizing—both predicts and is predicted by overt aggression. What's more, both rehearsal and aggression correlate with television viewing habits. A reciprocal model emerges, in which aggression, television violence, and scripts reinforce each other. Intellectual incompetence could affect several of the variables, abetting the cycle, as just noted.

Individual predispositions to aggress combine with specific learning experiences to produce stability in aggression. That is, intellectual incompetence combines with scripts learned from television and personal observation, creating persistent patterns of aggression. Aggression scripts suggest plausible behaviors, but these filter through **normative beliefs** about appropriate and acceptable behavior (Huesmann & Guerra, 1997). Normative beliefs about aggression and individual differences in aggression each predict the other. That is, people who aggress often believe their responses are appropriate, according to the norms.

Knowing this role of normative beliefs, the substantial gender differences in physical aggression make sense. In the Bandura social learning studies cited earlier, for

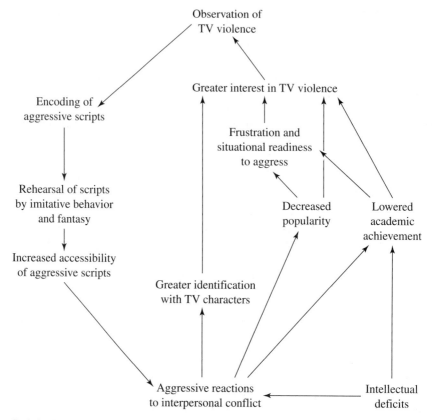

Cycle begins in lower right corner

**Figure 10.1** Model of Mass Media Effects on Violence

*Source:* Donnerstein et al., 1994. Copyright © American Psychological Association. Adapted with permission.

example, boys were typically twice as aggressive as girls. A meta-analysis of gender differences (Bettencourt & Miller, 1996) as noted demonstrates that unprovoked men are generally more aggressive than unprovoked women. When provoked, men are more likely to perceive the provocation as intense and to view retaliation as not dangerous. Maybe some of the same processes are operating in unprovoked situations. That is, maybe men are more likely than women to interpret an ambiguous situation as a provocation and to minimize the danger of retaliation, hence their higher baseline levels of aggression.

However, at high levels of provocation, the gender differences attenuate, perhaps because the norm against female aggression is trumped by the norm allowing for retaliatory aggression. In short, normative beliefs—one component of aggression scripts—can mediate effects of gender roles on aggression.

Given all these roles for script processes in aggression, the stability of aggression over the life cycle makes unfortunate sense. Aggression at age 8 years tends to predict criminal behavior, spouse abuse, traffic violations, and self-reported physical aggression in adults (Huesmann, Eron, Lefkowitz, & Walder, 1984). Aggression across generations within one family is *even more* stable than aggression within one individual. This stability within individuals and families can result from any number of factors—such as social class, parenting patterns, modeling, or inherited temperament—but the script analysis provides one viable account. That is, one learns aggressive scripts from one's family and continues acting on them throughout one's life.

**COGNITIVE NEO-ASSOCIATION THEORY**   If social learning theory explains the ways people develop an understanding of *how* and *when* to aggress, and if aggressive scripts explain *what* aggressive habits people acquire over time, the **cognitive neo-association theory** describes *why*, the immediate conditions that instigate aggression (Berkowitz, 1990, 1993). People's transitory situations can activate feelings and understandings that provoke impulsive aggression.

The model hinges on associations in memory. Start with ordinary, unpleasant situations that range from frustration and provocation to noise, heat, crowding, and smells. These all lead to unpleasant feelings, including rudimentary fear or anger (see Figure 10.2). The negative rudimentary affects in turn activate cognitions and behavior related to fight-or-flight responses: respective impulses toward aggression or escape. Either impulse can prevail, depending on person and situation. At the same time, situational cues can influence a chain of more complex emotional reactions to aversive situations: Anger, envy, anxiety, hurt, sadness, and depression can emerge as more complicated cognitive processing unfolds. Thus, these more complex emotions result from complex cognitions, such as interpretations, attributions, and explanations. (Recall from Chapter 3, Personology, and Chapter 9, Helping, that complex cognitions such as attributions of control over an aversive event, for example, lead to complex emotions such as anger and pity.) One main point here is that this model posits both rudimentary associations (unpleasant feelings, fight-or-flight impulses) and more complex associations (cognitive interpretation and complex emotions).

Discovery of the weapons effect, mentioned earlier, spurred this model. In an aversive situation (such as the provocation in those studies), situational cues (such as guns) instigate aggression. As noted, numerous studies have replicated this effect, at least when participants are not suspicious or self-conscious.

Recent research supports the outlines of the more general cognitive neo-association model. Automatic priming does result from exposure to a weapon (Anderson, Benjamin,

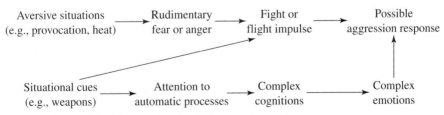

**Figure 10.2**   Model of Aggressive Cue Effects on Aggression

*Source:* As described by Berkowitz, 1993.

& Bartholow, 1998). For example, people can identify aggression-related words faster after they have just seen a weapon name or picture. This suggests that weapons make aggressive thoughts more accessible. Violent media also make aggressive thoughts more accessible (Bushman, 1998b): After seeing a violent video, people list more aggressive associations to both ambiguously aggressive and nonaggressive words, and they identify aggressive words faster. Aggressive cues do seem to activate aggressive associations, as the model would predict.

Individuals differ in their typical levels of aggressiveness, and the cognitive associations of chronically aggressive individuals contain, indeed, more aggression. Their associations among aggressive words are stronger, as are their associations between ambiguously and clearly aggressive words (Bushman, 1996). These richer associative links help explain why aggressive individuals respond more strongly to violent media: choosing to watch it more often, becoming more angry when they do watch it, and aggressing more afterward (as illustrated in Chapter 2, Bushman, 1995; Josephson, 1987).

Gender differences also provide indirect support for the cognitive association model of impulsive aggression. When people ruminate, mood-relevant thoughts remain accessible, and angry moods are no exception: Angry rumination primes angry thoughts and actions (Bushman, Bonacci, Pedersen, Vasquez, & Miller, 2005). Women are more likely to distract themselves from ruminating when they feel angry than when they are feeling neutral, but men do not (Rusting & Nolen-Hoeksema, 1998). This could contribute to gender differences in aggression.

Gender differences and individual differences combine. For some men, a constellation of associations links power motivation, sex, and aggression. For men identified as likely to sexually harass or attracted to sexual aggression, power is linked to sex (Bargh, Raymond, Pryor, & Stack, 1995). In these men, high levels of power motivation and strong power-sex associations predict typical forms of sexual aggression, which are direct (seeking younger or drunk women who could not resist sexual advances as easily, punishing sexual resistance with silence or changed feelings, or giving expensive gifts with the clear expectation of sexual favors in return). In women, power combines instead with strong intimacy-affiliation motives to predict sexual aggression, which tends to be more indirect (dressing seductively or playing hard to get, as deliberate seductions) (Zurbriggen, 2000). Although both men and women can link aggression and sex, priming with sex-related words facilitates aggression only for men (Mussweiler & Foerster, 2000). For women, priming sex facilitates perceptions of aggression in others. Overall, given different social learning, the genders differ in their associations among power, sex, and aggression. Demonstrating consistent clusters in the cognitive networks of associations among aggressive thoughts and feelings lends support to the cognitive neo-association theory.

**GENERAL AGGRESSION MODEL**    The similarities among the social learning and cognitive structural (script and neo-association) approaches led to the **general aggression model**. It relies on the idea of **knowledge structures** (expectations in Chapter 4), linked to affect, arousal, and behavior (Anderson & Bushman, 2002a). The model focuses on a single event or **episode**, involving a person-in-a-situation unit.

Within an episode, people make **automatic appraisals**, rapid evaluations of threat in the environment (after the appraisal idea in emotion theories; see Zajonc, 1998). Such automatic priming clearly cues aggression (Todorov & Bargh, 2002). People also make **controlled reappraisals**, more complex cognitive analyses. Aggressive inputs (personality and situation) are mediated via these processes to determine aggressive (or nonaggressive) responses. The model is entirely consistent with the other cognitive theories of aggression, so data that support them also support it, and vice versa (e.g., Anderson, 1997; Lindsay & Anderson, 2000). But it has a more up-to-date understanding of social cognitive processes.

Some of the model's original impetus came from observing the link between high temperatures and aggression, which is well-established in field settings (see Figure 10.3; Anderson, 1989; Anderson, Bushman, & Groom, 1997). In the laboratory, high temperatures sometimes cause aggression (Anderson, Anderson, Dorr, DeNeve, & Flanagan, 2000; Baron & Richardson, 1994), and low temperatures also increase hostility (Anderson, Anderson, & Deuser, 1996) and sometimes aggression (Anderson et al., 2000). Curiously, the low-temperature effect does not occur in the field; perhaps societies are better at counteracting the negative effects of cold by warming people than at counteracting the negative effects of heat by cooling them. In any case, when people are hot, they experience discomfort and hostility, so they are more easily provoked or cued to aggress. This provides indirect support for the general aggression model's predictions about automatic appraisals.

In one series of studies testing many parts of the model, participants were selected as falling into the top or bottom third of the trait hostility scale (from a mass pretest, including items such as "I easily fly off the handle with those who do not listen or understand." And "I often feel like a powder keg ready to explode."). Thus, trait hostility was one independent variable. As another independent variable, half the participants were randomly assigned to the pain condition, which consisted of holding their nondominant arm horizontally in the air for 2.5- to 3-minute intervals, with

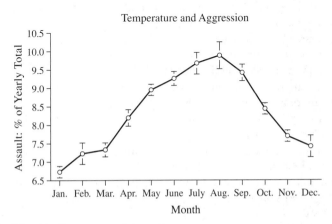

**Figure 10.3**   Monthly Occurrence of Assaults

*Source:* Anderson et al., 2000. Copyright © Elsevier. Adapted with permission.

30-second rests, throughout the experiment (try it); control participants did nothing. Pain participants rated their discomfort at 3.31 on a 5-point scale, not major pain, but twice as uncomfortable as the controls (1.65). Finally, as a third independent variable, some participants viewed pictures of weapons (aggressive cues) and some viewed pictures of nature.

The individual difference variable, trait hostility, had the most consistent results across measures, sometimes interacting with the situational variables (pain and aggressive cues). People who scored high on trait (chronic) hostility not surprisingly (a) also rated themselves as higher on state (temporary) hostility (e.g., outraged, burned up, discontented, not cooperative, not friendly), and (b) they wanted to escape. More interesting from the model's interactive predictions, trait hostility predicted (c) more accessible aggressive thoughts, mainly when provoked by pain and the aggressive cue, and (d) more aggressive punishment of an opponent during a reaction-time game, especially when already primed by the aggressive cues. These results are consistent with the general aggression model, but also its forebears, the cognitive neo-association model, the script approach, and the social learning approach.

## Attributional Approaches: Understanding Why

As noted at the outset, both laypeople and scientists define aggression as requiring intent. Interpreting one's own and another's intent thus commences a potentially aggressive encounter. Attribution theories (Chapter 3) describe how people understand intent, and two major cognitive theories have addressed the role of attributions in aggression. The first focuses on people's attributions about others' intent. The second focuses on people's attributions about their own aggressive feelings. Both fit the cognitive structural assumption that people mentally represent the social conditions for aggression, in this case aggressive intent.

**HOSTILE ATTRIBUTION BIAS**    All the cognitive theories discussed so far bear on the core social motive of understanding, but all produce an *anti*social understanding, a warped version of shared social understanding. The aggressive perceiver may view this understanding as shared, or at least as socially justified, but it is not. In fact, aggressive people have particular biases in their understandings, which encourage aggression, bad reputations, and a spiral of rejection.

Compared with other children, chronically aggressive children tend toward a **hostile attribution bias** (Nasby, Hayden, & DePaulo, 1979), interpreting ambiguous behavior as aggressive. In an early study (Dodge, 1980), peers and teachers nominated various boys as generally more or less aggressive. The boys then experienced a negative, frustrating outcome, portrayed as resulting from an anonymous peer's hostile, benign, or ambiguous intent. All boys accurately interpreted the clearly hostile or clearly benign intents, but aggressive boys saw *ambiguous* intent as more hostile than did the nonaggressive boys. These biases result in more aggressive responses (Dodge & Frame, 1982).

The cycle partly reflects the lived experience of aggressive boys, who are indeed frequent targets of peer aggression. However, aggressive boys act as perpetrators even more often than as targets of aggression. The hostile attribution bias thus seems to exaggerate a selective aspect of their experience. How does it do so? In one study (Dodge & Tomlin, 1987), children heard stories in which (for example) a peer spilled milk on them, and various eyewitnesses gave mixed testimony suggesting intent both hostile ("I saw him laughing at you") and benign ("He wasn't looking where he was going"). Participants then interpreted the peer's intent as hostile or benign and explained why. Their explanations mostly included the cues provided as well as other people's typical behavior toward themselves personally. As Table 10.6 shows, aggressive children were more likely to attribute hostile intent. In doing so, compared with nonaggressive children, they used less of the relevant evidence (second column of data). And they specifically weighted benign cues relatively less (third column) and self-schemas relatively more (last column).

Oddly, they did not weigh aggressive intent relatively more than other children do. The problem seems to be a failure to notice and credit benign explanations. In judging self-relevant social situations, aggressive boys respond faster, which causes them to attend and to recall less (Dodge & Frame, 1982; Dodge & Newman, 1981). These deficits and biases increase under social anxiety and personal threat (Dodge & Somberg, 1987).

The dynamics suggest that certain boys react defensively to others, partly based on bad experiences that become self-fulfilling prophecies. Aggressive children develop normative beliefs, akin to aggression scripts, about the permissibility of retaliation. Belief in retaliation predicts biased understanding of aggressive situations a year later, which also predicts aggressive behavior a year later (Zelli, Dodge, Lochman, Laird, & Conduct Problems Prevention Research Group, 1999). The problematic situations revolve around social interpretations of provocation. That is, the hostile attribution bias occurs in reactive (responsive) aggression, not proactive (initiated) aggression (Dodge & Coie, 1987), which are distinct patterns of antisocial behavior (Dodge, Lochman, Harnish, Bates, & Pettit, 1997).

The hostile attribution bias spotlights the **social construction** of aggression (Mummendey, 1996). Certain pairs of boys react aggressively to each other, beyond their own individual aggressiveness toward others (Hubbard, Dodge, Cillessen, Coie, & Schwartz, 2001). For example, initiators and responders both may view their own behavior as appropriate and the other's as inappropriate. Attributions of aggressive intent carry evaluative overtones, as forms of social understanding.

**Table 10.6**   Hostile Attribution Biases and Underuse of Social Cues

| Participant Group | Attributing Hostile Intent (Percent of Participants) | Use of Relevant Cues (Percent of Participants) | Breakdown of Cues Actually Used (of All Cues) | | |
|---|---|---|---|---|---|
| | | | Benign | Hostile | Self-Schema |
| Aggressive | 44% | 67% | .34 | .33 | .33 |
| Nonaggressive | 30% | 79% | .54 | .26 | .20 |

*Source:* Adapted from Dodge & Tomlin, 1987. Copyright © Guilford. Adapted with permission.

**EXCITATION TRANSFER, NOT CATHARSIS**    Arousal has surfaced in several contexts already, some specific to aggression and some related to other affect-laden behavior in this book. The rapid and incomplete attributions of aggressive children under perceived threat suggest a state of chronic arousal and vigilance that other people experience only sporadically. We saw a role for short-term arousal in the general aggression model as well. In discussing attribution previously (Chapter 3), we saw arousal combine with people's attributions to produce their feelings in general: Schachter's two-component theory defines experienced emotion as resulting from cognition (attribution) plus arousal. In that context and in discussing passion in close relationships (Chapter 8), we described studies in which people misattributed fear-based arousal (from a suspension bridge or a horror movie) to heterosexual attraction (Dutton & Aron, 1974; Zillmann, Weaver, Mundorf, & Aust, 1986).

The phenomenon of **excitation transfer** documents how arousal from an irrelevant prior source (e.g., the bridge or the movie) then persists and spills over to the next setting (e.g., attraction or provocation), to which it is then misattributed (Zillmann, 1988). Some surprising misattributional mix-ups occur. For example, exposing undergraduate men to explicit erotica (pornography) increased their aggression in response to provocation (Ramirez, Bryant, & Zillmann, 1982). That is, the students saw a short, sexually explicit film (or sexually suggestive photographs, or nonerotic snapshots of faces), with an experimenter who repeatedly accused them of not following instructions. When later given a chance to evaluate the experimenter to a university committee that would allocate research funding, they expressed more annoyance and delivered more hostile ratings after viewing the explicitly sexual film than in the two control conditions. The excitatory potential of the erotica continues afterward and then is misattributed to the provocation, so the combination particularly increases retaliation (Zillmann, Bryant, & Carveth, 1981). Women show the same aggressive response to explicitly erotic films as men do (Cantor, Zillmann, & Einsiedel, 1978). However, milder sexually oriented materials (which are not arousing) have, if anything, a dampening effect on people's retaliatory aggression (Zillmann & Sapolsky, 1977) because aggression and romantic affection are incompatible responses.

Other sources of arousal support the misattribution of arousal resulting in aggression. For example, the effects of extreme heat on aggression are consistent with the excitation-transfer idea (Anderson, 1989). For misattribution to occur, the actual source of arousal (excessive heat) must recede from awareness, so that arousal can be attributed instead to provocation. Noise also arouses people and makes them aggressive, but only in the context of provocation (Donnerstein & Wilson, 1976).

Violent media make people more aggressive, as we saw earlier, and arousal is one conduit for its effects. As noted earlier, the competing hypothesis has always been **catharsis:** the idea that aggressive feelings could be expressed vicariously and so diminished in actual encounters. Scientific evidence does not support the catharsis hypothesis (Bushman, Baumeister, & Stack, 1999; Geen & Quanty, 1977). For example, aggressive video games, as noted, do not help the player let off steam but instead increase aggression in both the short and long term (Anderson & Dill, 2000). Standard attempts at catharsis instead maintain the aggressive arousal and elaborate the cognitions that justify the aggression. Nevertheless, people continue to believe in catharsis, apparently holding the belief that venting anger will make them feel better, although it in fact makes them more aggressive and does not reduce negative affect (Berkowitz, 1962; Bushman, Baumeister, & Phillips, 2001; Bushman, Baumeister, & Stack, 1999). What's more, even if level of excitation holds constant, people who vent become more angry and aggressive (Bushman, 2002). Angry people may experience transitory pleasant feelings when they aggress and may sometimes deter the person who provoked them. But these positive experiences only reinforce future aggression (Baron & Richardson, 1994).

## Summary of Cognitive Theories

Antisocial understanding develops through the same routes as shared social understanding: learning, mental representation, and subsequent interpretation. The understandings promoted by some people and some situations encourage aggressive reactions. Social learning theory teaches people how and when to aggress, through modeling of imitative aggression and vicarious learning of sanctions. Cognitive structures such as aggression scripts develop through rehearsal of aggressive episodes, teaching normative beliefs that stabilize patterns of aggression. Cognitive neo-association theory links affect to the cognitive structures of aggression. The general aggression model, consistent with all the preceding ones, posits knowledge structures that aid automatic appraisals, which may be modified by controlled appraisals. All these kinds of prior knowledge about aggression affect people's attribution of aggressive intent to others and to self. Some people are biased toward hostile attributions about other people, underusing benign cues, especially when threatened. In attributing aggressive feelings to oneself, prior irrelevant arousal may be misattributed to provocations, encouraging aggression. All these types of understanding—learning, cognitive structures, and attributions—build on theories covered in earlier chapters but given new significance in this context.

## CONFLICT: CONTROLLING OTHERS

Whatever their basis of understanding, aggression serves people's efforts to control their outcomes by controlling other people's behavior. Some accounts of instrumental aggression, as noted, aim to express this kind of motive. Accounts of aggression as coercive influence, also described earlier, more explicitly express this viewpoint. Aggression as control especially emerges in the classic frustration-aggression hypothesis and in newer work on bullying and intimate abuse.

### Frustration-Aggression Hypothesis

According to the original **frustration-aggression hypothesis**, frustration typically leads to aggression in some form, and all aggression results from frustration of some kind (Dollard, Doob, Miller, Mowrer, & Sears, 1939). In this work, **frustration** is the blocking of any goal-directed sequence of behavior. Early evidence was often flawed by confounding frustration with other factors such as anger (Baron & Richardson, 1994). Although another interpretation would be that anger mediates the effects of frustration on aggression, that was not the original hypothesis.

People certainly do sometimes aggress as a response to other people thwarting their goals. In one study (Geen, 1968), some male undergraduates underwent initial instigation to aggression: rewards for shocking a peer in a teacher-learner paradigm; others shocked but received no rewards. They also either (a) worked on an unsolvable puzzle, (b) worked on a solvable puzzle but with constant interruptions, (c) worked on the solvable puzzle but with subsequent insults by a confederate, or (d) experienced neither frustration nor insults. Their aggression against the confederate (who acted as the learner) was low in the control condition (d), moderate in the two frustration conditions (a and b), and highest in the insult condition (c). Thus, both task frustration (unsolvable problems) and social frustration (interruptions) certainly can lead to aggression. (Rewards also increased aggression.)

Despite a few promising early studies, the frustration-aggression pattern has proved elusive and unreliable in the laboratory. At a minimum, some **moderators** (facilitating and inhibiting conditions) do predict when frustration does indeed provoke aggression (Baron & Richardson, 1994). In agreement with the cognitive approaches, all the moderators relate to the types of attributions frustrated people might make. For example, the magnitude of the frustration matters. Larger frustrations facilitate aggression perhaps because they are more likely to trigger a (perhaps biased) search for an explanation, which would favor dispositional attributions about the agent of frustration and so facilitate aggression. Similarly, arbitrary frustrations, lacking justification, can prime both hostile attributions and aggression. The presence of aggressive cues, as in the Geen study, also facilitates aggression. Here, too, aggressive cues may prime hostile attributions. So one **mediator** (mechanism) shared by all the moderators might be the attributions triggered.

The moderators—magnitude, arbitrariness/justification, and aggressive cues—all fit another mediator. Frustrations may provoke aggression only when they arouse negative affect (Berkowitz, 1962, 1989, 1993). The greater the frustration's magnitude, perhaps the greater the negative affect, all else being equal. As another example, if someone constantly interrupts for a justified reason (hearing difficulty), rather than for an arbitrary reason (whim), that could elicit pity rather than anger. People also examine justifications for their own negative situation and feel accordingly. The attributional models of helping (Chapter 9) address the role of justification regarding people's negative situations and the resulting feelings of anger or pity. Finally, in keeping with the cognitive neo-association model, frustration is an aversive event, and if interpreted as an aggressive cue, it can prime primitive anger and aggression.

Direct aggression constitutes only one prong of the frustration-aggression hypothesis, which specifies aggression in some form (not necessarily directed toward the agent of frustration). **Displaced aggression**—directed toward someone other than the instigator of frustration—also fits the frustration-aggression hypothesis. The results here are clearer than those for direct aggression. A meta-analysis of laboratory studies (Marcus-Newhall, Pedersen, Carlson, & Miller, 2000) finds a sizeable effect of provocation on aggression toward an innocent third party when retaliation against the provoking person is not possible. Frustrations on a task, for example, produce aggression, just as much as do various kinds of provocation (such as negative eval-uations, verbal attacks plus shocks) and irritants (such as odors and extreme tem-peratures). In accord with the affective mediators proposed by Berkowitz's cognitive neo-association model, feelings of displeasure likely mediate the effects of provocation and perhaps frustration on displaced aggression (Pedersen, Gonzales, & Miller, 2000).

In the field, evidence for displaced aggression has provided a real mystery. An early study found awful correlations between drops in the price of cotton in the U.S. South and white lynching of blacks (Hovland & Sears, 1940); this suggests displacement of aggression from economic frustrations onto an outgroup scapegoat. Some subsequent studies have corroborated these results (for reviews, see Berkowitz, 1993; Geen, 1998), showing community-level effects of job loss on violence, for example (Catalano, Novaco, & McConnnell, 1997). However, the group-level frustration-aggression results remain controversial and difficult to replicate (Green, Glaser, & Rich, 1998). Moreover, at these societal levels of analysis (i.e., macro), the mediating psychological processes (i.e., micro) remain unidentified.

Work on displaced aggression in the laboratory, however, remains convincing, so we know that at least sometimes it *can* occur. In any case, the frustration-aggression research fits other models of aversive situations or retaliation scripts, at least when mediated by hostile attributions or anger.

All the work inspired by the frustration-aggression hypothesis relates to the core social motive of control. When someone else thwarts one's goal-directed activity, the conflict is precisely about control. Aggressive responses that attempt to remove frustrating blockages obviously stem from direct efforts to control someone who is (in that respect at least) in a position of strength. Less obviously, displaced aggression also may result from indirect efforts to restore a sense of control. In other domains—for example, interpersonal perception—diminished control in one setting prompts efforts to create control in other, irrelevant settings (Pittman & Pittman, 1980).

## Controlling the Weak

Displaced aggression often focuses on a weaker, safer target than the frustrating agent. Related work on bullying and partner abuse shows aggression against others as a pure exercise of control over someone in a weaker position.

**BULLYING: PEER ABUSE**    Some people, **bullies**, consistently initiate aggression against weaker people, victims. Such proactive aggression is not unique to particular personal relationships but seems to be a function of particular actors likely to bully everyone they can and particular targets likely to be victims of several bullies (Hubbard et al., 2001).

On the bully side, some studies suggest that bullies are disagreeable, controlling people in general. Some children endorse beliefs that aggression (hitting, yelling, pushing, insulting) is okay, especially when they are angry. These children are disproportionately aggressors (Huesmann & Guerra, 1997), consistent with the script model emphasizing normative beliefs. Bullies tend to be impulsive, dominating, strong, and aggressive (Olweus, 1995). Among boys, they may seem to have high self-esteem, as viewed by self and peers, but it turns out to be the defensive sort: The bully always wants to be the center of attention, thinks too much of himself, and cannot take criticism (Salmivalli, Kaukiainen, Kaistaniemi, & Lagerspetz, 1999). (Adolescents with genuinely high self-esteem defend victims against bullies or avoid the situation.)

Chronic victims differ by gender. Victimized boys often have low self-esteem, across all measures, and victimized girls may show **humble pride**, having high self-esteem, though their peers rate them as having low self-esteem (Salmivalli et al., 1999). (The opposite combination, self-belittlers, who do have low self-esteem, though their peers think otherwise, tend to stay out of the situation.) In general, victims seem to be anxious, insecure, cautious, sensitive, quiet, and weaker (Olweus, 1995).

Teasing can be one form of verbal bullying. Although teasing contains ambiguous combinations of aggression and humor, and it may fail the aggression test by the actor's stated intent not to harm, it is often experienced by victims as hurtful. In general, teasers see their motives as benign and friendly (Keltner, Young, Heerey, Oemig, & Monarch, 1998; Shapiro, Baumeister, & Kessler, 1991), although victims may not, especially among children. And the victims may be onto something, given the personalities of teasers. For example, disagreeable, unreliable, extraverted people tease more (Georgesen, Harris, Milich, & Young, 1999). And disagreeable men tease in more hostile ways than do other men and all women (Keltner et al., 1998). They tend to threaten the other person's public image (**face**) more and not to **redress** (not to provide sufficient cues that the tease is playful, off-record, and not serious).

Although personality may differentiate who becomes bully (or teaser) and who becomes victim (or target), situations matter too. Sanctions from the environment determine whether or not bullies act on their aggressive impulses. For example, schools can cut down on bullying when adults are warm, interested, involved, and clear that bullying is unacceptable (Olweus, 1995, 1997). Schools are wise to prevent bullying, which correlates with depression and loneliness, predicting absenteeism, low GPA, social maladjustment (Juvonen, Nishina, & Graham, 2000), and even suicide (Sugimori, 1998). The control the bully exerts over the victim, who in turn feels helpless, can be vicious.

**WORKPLACE VIOLENCE**    We've all seen the tragic news story of someone "going postal," shooting coworkers and self, if the police do not arrive in time. This evokes images of a random, unpredictable, mentally ill shooter—previously known to be quiet and isolated—who tracks down a supervisor after being laid off, and meanwhile has been secretly abusing family members. In this view, workplace violence cannot be prevented because it is all too random.

On the contrary, according to accumulated research (Barling, Dupré, & Kelloway, 2009), workplace violence involves an angry, hostile shooter with a history of violence who kills because of perceived **interactional justice** (that is, interpersonal treatment). But **distributive justice** (actual outcomes such as layoffs) or **procedural** justice (unfair practices) do not in fact predict workplace aggression. Thus, it is control that aggressors seek, but interpersonal more than procedural or tangible control. Nor, by the way, is the Post Office the site of disproportionate workplace violence; on the contrary, it is actually much safer and more secure than other worksites.

Who are the targets of workplace violence? Targets of directed aggression are often specific, but displaced aggression may endanger others caught in the vicinity. More routine workplace violence—that is, peer bullying—targets those perceived to be weak but threatening, suggesting a role for control motives. For example, workers with low self-esteem but difficult personalities often are victims (Aquino & Thau, 2009). However, because the results are correlational, workplace bullying could lower a person's self-esteem and make the person seem demanding and difficult.

Situations that encourage workplace aggression also undermine people's sense of control. Role conflict, role ambiguity, and lack of control correlate with workplace victimization (Aquino & Thau, 2009). Being victimized is associated with a host of negative psychological effects, including depression, anxiety, stress, shame, and physical illness (Bowling & Beehr, 2006).

**BATTERING: PARTNER ABUSE**   The dynamics of domestic abuse, like those of peer abuse, partly reflect the dynamics of control. Aggression in close relationships, as we saw in Chapter 8, recruits some familiar mechanisms: hostile attribution, social insensitivity, and domineering personality. In another twist of misattribution, abusive men blame their partners for their own negative feelings and ruminate on this, resulting in anger (Dutton, 1995a). Blaming attributions, along with feeling emotionally out of control, can result in instrumental, coercive violence that seeks to eliminate those negative feelings.

Attachment styles of abusive men tend to be insecure, mostly anxious and fearful (Dutton, 1995b, 2000; Dutton, Saunders, Starzomski, & Bartholomew, 1994). Both styles involve a negative and unstable sense of self, which may result from many abusive men's recall of frequent public shaming by their parents (Dutton, 1995b, 2000; Dutton, van Ginkel, & Starzomski, 1995).

Finally, modeling enters into intimate violence; as is well known, exposure to parental violence, vicarious or personal, leads to own violent behavior later (Dutton, 2000), as social learning would predict. Outside the current scope lie some issues, both clinical (e.g., borderline personality disorder) and developmental (parent-child relations). Nevertheless, other aspects of intimate violence carry familiar themes of antisocial understanding, as well as attempts to restore felt lack of control.

## Controlling the Strong: Terrorism as Frustration-Aggression

As I drafted the first edition of this chapter, the events of September 11, 2001, had just transformed our nation and the world. No one would doubt that suicide hijacking and anthrax dissemination constitute aggression of the worst kind, targeted at large numbers of innocent people.

At first, social psychologists (and others) understandably focused on empirical analysis of the reactions of victims, not the dynamics of perpetrators, partly because of feasibility (Byron & Peterson, 2002; Fredrickson, Tugade, Waugh, & Larkin, 2003; Galea et al., 2002; Mehl & Pennebaker, 2003; Silver, Holman, McIntosh, Poulin, & Gil-Rivas, 2002). But this chapter, like most social psychology of aggression, focuses on the aggressor, not the victim, so what light can we shed on terrorism here? As social psychology, this chapter speaks mainly to interpersonal aggression and less to either intergroup hostility (but see the next chapter) or the interpersonal processes that allow individuals to participate in large-scale aggression against civilians.

Nevertheless, some social psychological analyses are beginning to explain how people become terrorist aggressors against noncombatant populations. First, terrorism is a political and combat tool, like any other tactic (e.g., aerial bombing of military bases). As a tool, it serves certain goals (Kruglanaski & Fishman, 2006). Terrorists, by this logic, view the techniques as furthering their objectives, better than comparable means, and not interfering with other important goals (e.g., ingroup long-term welfare). To discourage the use of terrorism requires undermining its perceived effectiveness, feasibility, and hindrance of other important goals. Easier to say than do, of course, but this analysis takes terrorism out of the realm of "senseless violence" and into a domain where one can begin to understand how to attempt averting it.

Another, compatible perspective describes how people can become terrorists, as a multi-step process, like climbing a staircase past multiple floors (Moghaddam, 2005). In the first place is **fraternal** or **group-level relative deprivation**, which is the perception that one's ingroup is suffering relative to other groups. Lacking individual mobility or out of strong ingroup identification, many people seek to improve their group's situation. If they perceive the deprivation to be unfair (i.e., attributing it to deliberate, illegitimate injury by others), then they are more likely to be angry and frustrated, the second floor on the staircase. Anger and frustration, as we have seen, can trigger displaced aggression, onto an enemy designated by leaders. At the third level, a minority of frustrated group members may begin to endorse gradually the morality of terrorist organizations as a solution (as in the means-ends analysis of terrorism as a tool). The more justified they see the terrorist strategy, the more receptive they are to terrorist recruiters on the fourth level. Within a terrorist organization, the enemy is viewed as categorically "them," not at all related to "us." Finally, an even smaller number of these deprived, frustrated, angry converts get to the last level, where they view civilians as part of the blameworthy enemy and distance themselves from the civilians, so they are willing to hurt others and themselves in what they see as a necessary, even heroic sacrifice for their cause. Prevention efforts would target each of these stages, the earlier the better, because more people inhabit the lower than the upper floors.

Other processes that generate terrorism and mass killing stem partly from the social psychology of intergroup biases, group dynamics, and social influence (so later chapters will touch on topics relevant to mass violence), but large-scale aggression also results from economic, political, and religious dynamics beyond the scope of this book (see Jackman, 2002; Newman & Erber, 2002; Staub, 1989). Terrorists always believe in the virtue of their cause, whether religious beliefs (Bushman, Ridge, Das, Key, & Busath, 2007) or secular ones prime and allegedly justify their aggression.

## Summary of Control Theories

Felt lack of control begets violence. Frustration, paired with other aggressive cues, often leads to aggression, either direct or displaced. Mediators include blaming attributions and angry affect. A similar effort to assert control may underlie bullying. Bullying of peers relates to defensive self-esteem and settings that permit bullying. Again implicating control, abuse of intimates relates to unstable, insecure attachment and sense of self. Intimate abuse also relates to antisocial understanding, given the roles of blaming attributions and parental modeling of abuse. Familiar social psychological processes explain even terrorists' psychology of aggression.

## PROTECTING ONE'S IMAGE: SELF-ENHANCEMENT

Conventional wisdom holds that people are aggressive because their low self-esteem limits their ability to express their needs in more constructive ways. However, social psychology suggests just the opposite. Two lines of social psychological work on aggression illustrate how high self-esteem—but of a defensive, inflated, fragile sort—can lead to aggression. This suggests a role for the core social motive of self-enhancement in aggression.

### Narcissistic Rage

Threatened egoism underlies a variety of aggression, according to a review of work on aggression, crime, and violence (Baumeister, Smart, & Boden, 1996). Some of the most aggressive people do not show low self-esteem. They are, instead: not depressed, but rather maniacally grandiose; psychopaths, who are narcissistic; men, who on average have higher self-esteem than women; or intoxicated, which inflates self-esteem. Insecure arrogance describes the narcissism of people most likely to aggress (Baumeister, 1997). As we saw among bullies, aggressors often have unstable self-esteem, and domestic abusers often have an insecure sense of self. High but unstable self-esteem remains vulnerable to threat and predicts both anger and hostility (Kernis, Grannermann, & Barclay, 1989).

For example, in one study (Bushman & Baumeister, 1998), laboratory aggression was irrelevant to conventional self-esteem (measured by items such as "I feel that I have a number of good qualities"; "I take a positive attitude toward myself"; and "I am able to do things as well as most people"; see Chapter 5). However, researchers also measured **narcissism** (that is, excessive self-love, measured as agreeing with items such as "If I ruled the world, it would be a much better place"; "I am going to be a great person"; and "I am more capable than other people"). The combination of high narcissism and insult predicted high aggression toward the source of the insult

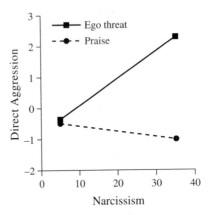

When people are praised, narcissism does not
relate to aggression (the dashed line is flat).
When people receive a blow to the ego, the
more narcissistic they are, the more
aggressive they become (the solid line
increases steeply).

**Figure 10.4**    Aggression as a Function of Narcissism and Threat

*Source:* Bushman & Baumeister, 1998. Copyright © American Psychological Association. Adapted with permission.

(see Figure 10.4). People who view themselves more favorably than other people
view them, having unrealistically high self-esteem, are likely to receive frequently
disappointing feedback as a matter of course.

Narcissism becomes narcissistic rage only when insult and shame are added.
**Shame** involves a public threat to the entire self. Individual differences in shame
proneness clearly predict maladaptive responses to anger (Tangney, Wagner,
Hill-Barlow, Marschall, & Gramzow, 1996), as do situations that invoke shame
(Tangney, 1992). Bullies and batterers also emerge from experiences of shame.
Shame is negatively related to empathy; that is, the more focused one is on one's
own shameful exposure, the less receptive one is to other people's experiences.

In a similar vein, **sensitivity to rejection**—a disposition to defensively expect,
readily perceive, and intensely react to social rejection—often predicts aggression
(Ayduk et al., 2000; Downey, Feldman, & Ayduk, 2000; Downey, Lebolt, Rincon, &
Freitas, 1998). Consistent with this idea, sexual aggressors discount and are suspicious
of the veridicality of women's communications (Malamuth & Brown, 1994), as if they
are vigilant to being shamed and humiliated by women's rejection.

Sexual aggression seems to be a particular case in point. Men who are self-centered,
rather than sensitive to the needs of others, are more likely to act on their aggressive
sexual fantasies (Dean & Malamuth, 1997). **Hostile masculinity** entails being insecure,
defensive, hypersensitive, hostile, and distrustful, as well as gratified from dominating
women. It predicts sexual aggression and conflictual relationships with women, even as
much as ten years later (Malamuth, 1986; Malamuth, Linz, Heavey, Barnes, & Acker,
1995). Hostile masculinity comes from attitudes supporting violence against women,

but more relevant here, also from **masculine role stress** (feeling stressed about failing at the traditional male role by being unemployed, subordinated to a woman, intellectually inferior, shorter than a woman, sexually inadequate, and so on). Similarly, hostile sexism (which includes the beliefs that some women are trying to control men; Glick & Fiske, 1996; see Chapter 11) predicts likelihood of sexual harassment (Begany & Milburn, 2002). Thus, aggression can result from particular insults to some men's masculine self-esteem.

Men with unrealistically inflated self-esteem may try to dominate others in an effort to confirm their fragile sense of superiority. Sexual aggressors link dominance to sexuality, as demonstrated by a variety of evidence, some noted earlier. For example, some men's needs for power and dominance, along with aggressiveness and anger, predict attitudes accepting of rape (Anderson, Cooper, & Okamura, 1997). At the automatic, unconscious level, power and dominance prime sexuality for men who are likely to sexually harass or aggress (Bargh, Raymond, Pryor, & Strack, 1995; Pryor & Stoller, 1994). Certain people and certain situations facilitate sexual harassment; again, a person-situation combination predicts better than either variable alone (Pryor, Giedd, & Williams, 1995). Men with a need to dominate women, coupled with harassment-accepting norms, may bolster their fragile self-esteem by sexual harassment and aggression. These patterns suggest general proclivities consistent with narcissism.

The pattern of **narcissistic rage**, shamed narcissism erupting in aggression, does not have to be always a matter of individual differences. Situational threats to the continuity of the self have similar effects on most people.

Interpersonal rejection can make almost anybody angry and aggressive. Several individual differences moderate the relationship between perceived rejection and aggression (Leary, Twenge, & Quinlivan, 2006). And several mechanisms may mediate this relationship; rejection may be experienced as pain, frustration, or self-esteem threat, and aggression may improve one's mood, influence others, reestablish control, or inflict revenge. Or people who feel rejected may simply feel relieved of the necessity to attend to social norms and control themselves, allowing expression of aggressive impulses. The rejection-aggression relationship would seem over-determined.

Some degree of rejection is inevitable, so is aggression also inevitable, beyond individual differences that dampen potential aggression? Even dispositional narcissists can reduce their normally aggressive responses to criticism if they perceive a prior unit relationship (i.e., a bond) between themselves and the other person (Konrath, Bushman, & Campbell, 2006). So perhaps anyone who is feeling ego-threat and therefore prone to aggression, can be soothed by inclusion and social bonds.

Consider also, as a situational threat, **mortality salience**—reminders that, like all living things, one ultimately will die—can provoke aggression (McGregor et al., 1998). Mortality salience (e.g., manipulated by writing about one's own death or a control topic) makes people cling to values (e.g., ethical, religious, political) that will endure beyond their own life span. Given the salience of their own mortality, then confronted with a person who disparages their world views (e.g., political beliefs), participants responded aggressively (assigned the person to consume more hot sauce). Derogation (verbal aggression) operates in the same way. One could view mortality salience as a threat to ordinary people's narcissism, in the sense of our unspoken belief that we will live forever. Wounded narcissism again lashes out.

## Culture of Honor

Moving up a level of analysis from individuals and situations to cultures, one might imagine an entire culture that is shame avoidant. The **culture of honor** hypothesis holds that, because of local norms, Southern males more often value their reputation for toughness and retaliation to insult. They more frequently endorse violence for the protection of self and possessions and respond with greater anger to insults (Nisbett, 1993). The United States South, and portions of the West originally settled by Southerners, have higher homicide rates than the North and East. These values and the correlated aggression might be linked historically to herding cultures, in which one's wealth can be easily stolen, and a reputation for aggressiveness may shield one's investments. In field experiments, Southern and Western employers were more forgiving of job applicants with a history of killing someone in an honor-related conflict, and Southern and Western newspapers crafted more sympathetic stories about a stabbing in response to a family insult (Cohen & Nisbett, 1997). Note that these results are specific to honor-related violence, for example, arguments, not to all forms of violence. In laboratory experiments, Southern men insulted by a confederate more often thought their masculine reputation threatened, felt upset, were primed for aggression cognitively and physiologically, and behaved aggressively and dominantly (Cohen, Nisbett, Bowdle, & Schwarz, 1996).

Consistent with the cultural transmission idea, greater social organization is associated in the South and West with greater violence on several levels: argument-related homicides; violence in choices of media, recreation, and vocation; and votes on gun control and national defense (Cohen, 1998). Similarly, Southern and Western states' laws reflect greater acceptance of violence as a form of self-protection: This appears in laws related to gun control, defense of self and family, and foreign policy (Cohen, 1996). In Southern former slave states, some laws also reflect greater acceptance of violence for coercion and punishment: This appears in laws related to spouse abuse, corporal punishment, capital punishment, and foreign policy.

In interpersonal interactions, the stuff of social psychology, Southerners are more polite and less sensitive to minor cues of hostility. Northerners were more likely to give and receive small doses of hostility (Cohen, Vandello, Puente, & Rantilla, 1999). Southerners were more likely to ignore annoyance until it accumulated but then to react more severely. Argument-related violence in Northern and Southern cities reflects similar patterns.

## Summary of Self-Enhancement Theories

Narcissistic rage appears in individuals with inflated but fragile self-esteem when they are threatened. Research on narcissism, shame proneness, rejection sensitivity, hostile masculinity, male dominance, and mortality salience all illustrate aggression in response to ego threats. On a cultural level, male Northerners may exchange hostilities at lower levels, being less polite, but male Southerners defend their honor when insults reach a serious level, endorsing aggression as a form of self and family protection.

## CHAPTER SUMMARY

We opened the chapter with one example of overt interpersonal physical aggression (a school shooting) and one example of subtle, relational, verbal aggression (revenge by power and control over an entire family for generations). Aggression is any behavior whose proximate intent is harm to another person. Proximate (immediate) intent may differ from the ultimate (primary) intent, as in instrumental aggression, which may be a means to an end. Although all aggression may contain elements of coercive influence, that is not a necessary component, as when someone reacts mainly out of anger. Proactive aggression takes the initiative, and reactive aggression responds to perceived threat. Aggression differs along several dimensions: physical-verbal, active-passive, and direct-indirect.

The most common operational definitions in the laboratory include physical responses (aggression machine, reaction-time competition with noise blasts or shocks, doses of hot sauce) and verbal responses, which show parallel results. Field studies include archival crime data, direct observation in schools, and public behavior such as horn-honking. Results from laboratory and field studies clearly converge.

Chronic social issues around cultural artifacts—media violence, guns, and alcohol—continue to raise controversy. In all three cases, according to decades of social psychological research, unrestricted access enhances aggression, when people are provoked. Media violence operates via various psychological processes, especially social learning. The presence of weapons operates by cuing aggressive associations. And alcohol myopia operates by making people less able to consider conflicting impulses not to aggress.

Core social motives prominent in aggression research include antisocial understanding, controlling resources via inherited mods, and self-enhancing for those with high but unstable self-esteem. In service of understanding, social learning teaches how and when to aggress, via modeling and vicarious conditioning. Its operation is particularly clear in imitative aggression (how), but people also learn self-sanctions (when). Observational learning suggests that catharsis does not result from observing aggression. Social learning posits cognitive representations that link observation of behavior and its imitation.

More recent accounts of cognitive representations include scripts, associations, and episodes. The script theory addresses how rehearsal of aggression facilitates stable patterns of aggression in individuals and family members. Scripts are accompanied by normative beliefs about appropriate behavior. Cognitive neo-association theory describes people's immediate associations to aggressive cues, including rudimentary emotions related to fight or flight, as well as more complex cognitive and emotional responses. The general aggression model relies on the broad idea of knowledge structures to integrate several previous theories. To these, it adds automatic appraisal and more controlled reappraisals. Further, cognitive theories focus on the what and why of aggression.

Attributional approaches include the hostile attribution bias, in which aggressors ignore benign cues in ambiguous settings and infer malignant intent. Excitation transfer focuses on attributions for the causes of arousal, including the misattribution from prior irrelevant sources to aggressive situations. This again undermines the notion of catharsis. Attribution tells people why to aggress.

Interpersonal conflicts focus on controlling others. Frustration often results in anger and displaced aggression and sometimes also aggression in the service of removing an obstacle. In a sense, it is an effort to control someone stronger. Efforts to control people in a weaker position include bullying and partner abuse. Both of these hinge on a combination of people prone to aggression and situations that permit it.

Aggression also results from efforts to shore up a weak or unstable sense of high self-esteem, resulting in narcissistic rage. The culture of honor's link to aggression may be seen as a cultural analog to narcissism. In the next chapter, we take up the cultural phenomenon of intergroup relations, which can result in aggression when people interact as representatives of conflicting groups.

## SUGGESTIONS FOR FURTHER READING

ANDERSON, C. A., & BUSHMAN, B. J. (2002). Human aggression. *Annual Review of Psychology*, *53*, 27–51.

AQUINO, K., & THAU, S. (2009). Workplace victimization: Aggression from the target's perspective. *Annual Review of Psychology*, *60*, 717–741.

BARLING, J., DUPRÉ, K. E., & KELLOWAY, E. K. (2009). Predicting workplace aggression and violence. *Annual Review of Psychology*, *60*, 671–692.

BUSHMAN, B. J., & HUESMANN, L. R. (2010). Aggression. In S. T. FISKE, D. T. GILBERT, & G LINDZEY (Eds.), *Handbook of social psychology* (5th ed.). New York: Wiley.

DE DREU, C. K. W. (2010). Social conflict: The emergence and consequences of struggle and negotiation. In S. T. FISKE, D. T. GILBERT, & G LINDZEY (Eds.), *Handbook of social psychology* (5th ed.). New York: Wiley.

FISKE, S. T. (2010). Interpersonal stratification: Status, power, and subordination. In S. T. FISKE, D. T. GILBERT, & G LINDZEY (Eds.), *Handbook of social psychology* (5th ed.). New York: Wiley.

MUMMENDEY, A. (1996). Aggressive behavior. In M. HEWSTONE, W. STROEBE & G. M. STEPHENSON (Eds.), *Introduction to social psychology* (2nd ed., pp. 403–435). Malden, MA: Blackwell.

PYSZCZYNSKI, T., GREENBERG, J., KOOLE, S., & SOLOMON, S. (2010). Experimental existential psychology: Coping with the facts of life. In S. T. FISKE, D. T. GILBERT, & G. LINDZEY (Eds.), *Handbook of social psychology* (5th ed.). New York: Wiley.

# Chapter 11

# Stereotyping, Prejudice, and Discrimination: Social Biases

In *Freedomland*, a white woman claims that an African-American man stole her car with her four-year-old son in the backseat. A manhunt focuses on the housing project near the scene of the crime. Media converge on the neighborhood. Cops surround the project.... Lorenzo Council is a black cop assigned to the case. Living in the community, he knows and cares about the people there. He spontaneously warns some students in the local public school:

> "*Excuse* me," Lorenzo stepped into the room and exploded, paralyzing his audience. "I got to *go*, but I would like to give you kids some *tips* on the next few nights out here. I'd like to give you some tips on survival. No theories, no speeches. *Facts.*" Prowling the room now, Lorenzo glared at them. "*Facts*. The police, is angry. The police, is scared. And the ones you're gonna see around here tonight? Tomorrow night? They don't *know* you. They don't know what's in your head, who your mother is, if you're a good kid, bad kid, all they know is they're living on the edge of their own nerves *just like you*." (Price, 1998, p. 484)[1]

Here, a black cop is trying to protect his own neighborhood kids (he knows what's in their heads, who their mothers are, who's a good kid or a bad kid). He is trying to protect them from police officers he knows to be "living on the edge of their own nerves" and likely to act on racial biases. Treating black kids as a category—as if they all were criminal and dangerous—constitutes stereotyping, prejudice, and discrimination. Moreover, in this case, the accusation is a fiction; there was no black male car-jacker, but everyone was all too ready to believe the white woman's (desperate but racist) story.

In this chapter, we address both blatant and subtle misunderstandings between groups of people, the effects of this bias on people's lives, and strategies for change.

---

[1] Copyright © Richard Price. Reprinted with permission.

Just as aggression research reveals the basic social psychology of processes that can prove deadly, the research on bias reveals processes that are demonstrably unhealthy and sometimes deadly for both agents and targets of bias.

Research on bias is a hot topic, in more ways than one. People have strong opinions about the fact of bias: Some think bias is a thing of the past—not really a problem any more—and others think it is a real and present danger to targeted social groups. As a result of these differences of opinion, people worry about discussing bias for fear of being misunderstood or from irritation about having to listen to the same old insulting, half-baked arguments. Bias is a taboo topic in many campus contexts. People are personally affected by bias, no matter what their category, so feelings run high.

Bias is a hot topic among researchers as well. In the last years, about a third of the talks at social psychology's national and international conferences have addressed bias and intergroup relations. Submissions to one of the field's leading journals were dominated by work on stereotyping, prejudice, and intergroup relations (Suls, 2001). Clearly this topic matters to people. Fortunately, social psychologists have studied it for decades (by some counts, 80 years) and have learned quite a lot about both subtle and blatant biases, their effects on targets, and strategies for change. The core social motives that move through all kinds of intergroup bias include belonging, understanding, controlling, and self-enhancing, as the research indicates. But first, some definitions.

## WHAT ARE PREJUDICE, STEREOTYPING, AND DISCRIMINATION?

### Conceptual Definitions

As social psychologists often separate cognition, affect, and behavior, so, too, intergroup bias researchers find it useful to distinguish among the legs of this tripod (Fiske, 1998b). All forms of bias involve **category-based** responses, reacting to another person as an interchangeable member of a social group. People have the clearest category-based responses to members of **outgroups**, that is, groups to which they do not personally belong. Category-based responses to outgroups typically are more negative than responses to the **ingroup**, one's own group. Category-based responses include stereotyping, prejudice, and discrimination.

**Stereotyping** entails applying to an individual one's cognitive expectancies and associations about the group. As such, stereotypes represent one kind of expectation (covered in Chapter 4, social cognition; also see Dovidio, Brigham, Johnson, & Gaertner, 1996; Stangor & Lange, 1994). Recall that an expectation is a coherent concept or naïve theory that renders the world manageable. A cognitive structure, it comprises the attributes of a concept and the relationships among the attributes. As a specific kind of expectation, stereotypes are beliefs about the characteristics of group members and theories about why those attributes go together (Hilton & von Hippel, 1996). Stereotypes are fixed ideas that accompany a category (Allport, 1954b). From a functional perspective, stereotypes justify (or rationalize) our affective and behavioral reactions to the category (Jost & Major, 2001). From a cultural perspective, they embody a societal consensus, a collective belief system (Stangor & Schaller, 1996). Modern definitions do not assume that stereotypes are either accurate or inaccurate, which is an empirical issue we will address.

**Prejudice** entails reacting emotionally to an individual on the basis of one's feeling about the group as a whole. "The net effect of prejudice ... is to place the object of prejudice at some disadvantage not merited by his [or her] own misconduct" (Allport, 1954b, p. 9). One wag defined prejudice as "A vagrant opinion without visible means of support" (Bierce, 1911, p. 264). Many researchers define prejudice as an overall attitude (including affect, cognition, and behavioral correlates; e.g., Dovidio et al., 1996). However, the core component of an attitude, as Chapter 6 showed, is the evaluation of the attitude object, in this case, outgroup members, so it is useful here to define prejudice by emphasizing the feelings component. Prejudices theoretically include both positive and negative affective reactions, but most research focuses on the negative. Nevertheless, even positive prejudices can place the target at a disadvantage, as we will see.

**Discrimination** entails acting on the basis of one's stereotypes and prejudices, denying equality of treatment that people wish to have. Allport (1954b) defined steps in the rejection of outgroups: verbal rejection, avoidance, segregation, physical attack, and extermination. Although verbal discrimination may not seem serious, stereotypical slurs, jokes, and put-downs create a hostile climate that enables even more serious forms of hostility to be enacted, not to mention offending the targets of such insults. Even if the people making the biased comments would not themselves dream of going further, the verbal disrespect creates norms that enable others with poorer judgment to feel that their own more overt forms of discrimination would be condoned. Avoidance also may not seem serious, but when people stay with their comfortable ingroup, they exclude members of other groups. And they certainly do not learn anything new. Segregation, attack, and group extermination are, without question, forms of discrimination. Later sections will address these complex issues in detail.

Conceptually separating stereotyping, prejudice, and discrimination proves useful because they are correlated, but not redundant, forms of bias. Consider all these plausible combinations: People can discriminate because of either hot prejudices or cold stereotypes. People can hold mental stereotypes but not act on them. People can have strong feelings but few supporting beliefs. Thoughts and feelings are not damaging until they are enacted.

One analysis across studies found the relationships shown in Figure 11.1, indicating that individual differences in emotional prejudice correlate with discrimination better than stereotypes do (Dovidio et al., 1996). A meta-analysis of experimental studies also found that affective reactions predict racial discrimination far better than stereotypic beliefs do (Talaska, Fiske, & Chaiken, 2009). Although the relationship between prejudice and discrimination is moderate, its size is comparable to the general attitude-behavior relationship. As in that domain, so too in the intergroup area: Many factors determine when people act on their thoughts and feelings (Mackie & Smith, 1998). For example, attitudes have to be activated to predict behavior, and, likewise, stereotypes and prejudice have to be activated to predict discrimination. Similarly, various motivations determine when people do and do not enact their stereotypes and prejudices, as we saw in the attitudes chapter. In any event, because they are not redundant, it is useful to separate them conceptually.

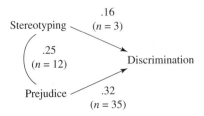

Number of studies are indicated in parentheses.

**Figure 11.1**    Relationships among Individual Differences in Stereotyping, Prejudice, and Discrimination
*Source:* From data reported by Dovidio et al., 1996.

Collectively, stereotyping, prejudice, and discrimination all are **biases** because treating the individual as an exact representation of the group is never accurate. The individual is never identical in all respects to one's image of the group, and no individual exactly represents in all respects the average of the group. Even if the judgment were treated as probabilistic, people rarely put odds on their statements about outgroup members' characteristics. A later section returns to issues of accuracy and error, but stereotypes, prejudice, and discrimination all are biases, in at least the sense of anchoring one's perceptions of an individual based on perceived group averages. That being said, group membership is relevant to behavior, as when it defines particular roles (e.g., police versus gang members) or helps distinguish people (Wegener & Klauer, 2004). Some theories, such as self-categorization theory, covered later, take this perspective.

In addition to biases against people as group members, society designates certain people as marked by an individual **stigma**, discredited and not fully human (Crocker, Major, & Steele, 1998; Goffman, 1963; Heatherton, Kleck, Hebl, & Hull, 2000; Jones et al., 1984). Physical and mental disabilities, for example, are stigmatizing. Stigma and category-based biases both entail prejudice, stereotyping, and discrimination.

## Operational Definitions

As this chapter shows, researchers operationalize bias in a number of ways (Fiske, 1998b). Laboratory measures of discrimination (e.g., in studies of interracial aggression) begin with varying combinations of verbal hostility: written ratings that disparage an outgroup individual or category, negative outgroup attitudes on questionnaires. At the subtle behavioral level, laboratory studies measure nonverbal indicators of hostility, such as seating distance or tone of voice. Related nonverbal measures include coding overt facial expressions, as well as measuring minute, nonvisible movements in the facial muscles that constitute the precursors of a frown (vs. a smile). Measurements of brain activity in emotion centers (such as the amygdala, for vigilance) are being used as well (Amodio, 2008). Equally subtle measures include speed of response to stereotypic associations, memory biases for stereotype-confirming information, stereotypic interpretations of ambiguous information, and stereotypic distortion in judgments.

**Table 11.1**  Old-fashioned and Modern (Symbolic) Racism Scales (Selected Items)

Old-Fashioned Racism Scale

It is a bad idea for blacks and whites to marry one another.

Black people are generally not as smart as whites.

If a black family with about the same income and education as I have moved next door, I would mind it a great deal.

It was wrong for the United States Supreme Court to outlaw segregation in its 1954 decision.

*Source:* From McConahay, 1986. Copyright © Elsevier. Adapted with permission.

Symbolic Racism Scale

Irish, Italian, Jewish, and many other minorities overcame prejudice and worked their way up. Blacks should do the same.

How much of the racial tension that exists in the United States today do you think blacks are responsible for creating? (1–4: *all of it* to *not much at all*)

How much discrimination against blacks do you feel there is in the United States today, limiting their chances to get ahead? (1–4: *a lot* to *none at all*)

Over the past few years, blacks have gotten more economically than they deserve.

(1–4: *strongly agree* to *strongly disagree*), except as shown
*Source:* From Henry & Sears, 2002. Copyright © Blackwell. Adapted with permission.

Moving up a level, measures of discriminatory avoidance include participants' choice to associate or work with an outgroup member, volunteer to help an organization, or directly aid an outgroup member who requests it. In a laboratory setting, segregation can be measured by how people constitute small groups or choose leaders for small groups. Finally, aggression against outgroups can be measured in laboratory settings by competitive games or teacher-learner scenarios in which one person is allowed to punish the other, an outgroup member, with low levels of shock, blasts of noise, or other aversive experiences (that is, measuring sanctioned forms of aggression, Chapter 10).

Surveys outside the laboratory measure racial attitudes by distinguishing old-fashioned bigotry from modern, subtler forms of bias. Table 11.1 shows one such scale; the items focusing on prejudice are typically hidden among a variety of other political attitudes. Other scales assess specific motivations regarding prejudice, as well as many specific kinds of racism, sexism, ageism, heterosexism, and more.

## Core Social Motives

**UNDERSTANDING**  People maintain biases toward other people partly in order to make sense of intergroup encounters. As Chapter 4 (social cognition) indicates, people understand other people in large part by reference to familiar categories, expectations, and concepts. Social categories defined by (e.g.) age, gender, ethnicity, class, and disability carry well-worn baggage that guides people's interactions. Because people are complex stimuli and because outgroups are less familiar than ingroups, people rely heavily on prior beliefs in intergroup encounters. This **cognitive miser** perspective (Fiske & Taylor, 2008; Chapter 4) emphasizes the role of stereotypes as resource-saving devices.

Research supports the understanding motive as one factor in stereotype usage. For example, people code other people by social categories, such as gender, race, and age, and this process can be useful for identifying them. However, it can go awry when people confuse two people within the same category (e.g., confusing two women with each other or two black people with each other). A paradigm that came to be known as "who-said-what" (Taylor, Fiske, Etcoff, & Ruderman, 1978) showed that people make more confusions *within* category than *between* categories. Although errors embarrass the perceiver and humiliate the target, this tendency to treat category members as equivalent appears across a range of social categories, including even religion (Weeks & Vincent, 2007; see Fiske, 1998b for a review and Klauer & Wegener, 1998, for methodological refinements); the range shows how useful it is to understanding other people.

Using stereotypes does simplify the processing of information about other people. In one study (Macrae, Hewstone, & Griffiths, 1993), people watched a videotape of a young woman discussing her lifestyle. Some observers learned that she was a hairdresser and some that she was a doctor, and then the video depicted her as engaging in a mix of behavior. Some behavior fit the hairdresser stereotype (enjoys discos; wears mini-skirts; has a chauvinistic boyfriend) but not the doctor stereotype, and some fit the doctor stereotype (interested in politics; attends opera; drives a fast car) but not the hairdresser stereotype. When people concentrated on the video without distraction, they recalled the inconsistent information, presumably because it was puzzling and they had thought about it (see Chapter 4). However, when people had to rehearse an eight-digit number while they watched the videotape—that is, when they were slightly distracted—they showed the opposite pattern of recall. When they were busy, they recalled more stereotype-consistent than inconsistent information. Thus, under the busy conditions of ordinary interaction, people can save cognitive resources by using stereotype-consistent information. Meta-analysis indicates that this stereotypic memory bias is a general phenomenon under the complex circumstances of normal interactions (Stangor & McMillan, 1992). This supports the role of the understanding motive for stereotype usage.

Several other studies indicate that people typically rely on stereotypes more when they are mentally busy or overloaded, making judgments on that basis (e.g., Bodenhausen & Wyer, 1985; Bodenhausen & Lichtenstein, 1987; van Knippenberg, Dijksterhuis, & Vermeulin, 1999). People demonstrably do have more online mental resources when they use stereotypes than when they do not (Macrae, Milne, & Bodenhausen, 1994).

What's more, some people have a chronic orientation to the social world as full of fixed entities, for instance, believing in people with essential traits (as opposed to malleable personalities that develop incrementally). **Entity theorists** focus not only on fixed personality traits (as described in Chapter 3), but also on stereotype-consistent information (Plaks, Stroessner, Dweck, & Sherman, 2001). Stereotypes can form when entity theorists view the social world as amenable to a fixed, stable kind of understanding. Cultures differ in how much they encourage entity theories and thus intergroup stereotyping (Levy, Plaks, Hong, Chiu, & Dweck, 2001) as a strategy for understanding.

**BELONGING**    People maintain biases toward outgroups partly to cement ties within their ingroups. As we will see, much of prejudice concerns ingroup preference more than outgroup derogation. For example, students often self-segregate in dining halls and cafeterias (Tatum, 1997); this most likely reflects ingroup comfort and favoritism, at least as much as outgroup discomfort, and not at all necessarily outgroup derogation (Brewer, 1979; Mummendey, 1995). This ingroup bias is especially strong among those who value their ingroups (Branscombe & Wann, 1994; Crocker & Luhtanen, 1990), which fits the role of the belonging motive in intergroup bias.

Even more in keeping with our analysis of core social motives, people apparently stigmatize others who threaten the effective functioning of their group (Neuberg, Smith, & Asher, 2000; see also Kurzban & Leary, 2001). That is, just as we have argued that the primary evolutionary context is social—the ingroup—so too should people both try to survive within the group and reject those who undermine that group. From this follows the idea that certain categories of people will be universally stigmatized: The **nonreciprocator** includes anyone who fails to exchange fully or share cooperatively within the ingroup; thieves and people with disabilities, respectively, do not and cannot reciprocate. The **treacherous** are those who break the bonds of ingroup trust: liars, cheaters, and traitors all thrive on ingroup deception. The **countersocializers** are those who undermine ingroup values; deviants threaten the mainstream socialization processes that transform newcomers into cooperative group members. Finally, of course, the **outgroup** lies beyond ingroup boundaries by definition. All of these threats to the ingroup are derogated, which fits with the importance of the belonging motive.

Groups are importantly defined by shared goals (see Chapter 12), so outgroups presumably have goals that differ from the ingroup's goals. If they do not share the ingroup's goals, the outgroup's goals may actively interfere with the ingroup's goals. At a minimum, they do not facilitate the ingroup's goals. Goal blockage leads to negative emotions (as we saw in Chapter 8, close relationships). By this argument (Fiske & Ruscher, 1993), then, outgroups, precisely because they are not the ingroup and do not share its goals, will elicit prejudice. Belonging—or not—lies at the core of anti-outgroup biases.

**CONTROLLING**    Avoiding threat also underlies responses to outgroups. Assuming that people typically are motivated to avoid danger and to have a sense of control over their outcomes, outgroups pose a problem in at least two respects. First, because they are novel, unfamiliar, and unpredictable, relative to the ingroup, they undermine one's sense of control (Fiske & Ruscher, 1993). Loss of control generates anger and resentment.

Second, people tend to pin danger on people who are different: People outside the ingroup represent a variety of tangible (concrete) or symbolic (abstract) threats (Stangor & Crandall, 2000). These include (a) resource conflict (with outgroups or with ingroup traitors), (b) dangers to physical health (from someone who is contagious), (c) symbolic threat to bodily integrity or mortality (from someone physically deformed or dying), (d) violations of a just and fair world (from apparent innocents who suffer), and (e) moral undermining (from deviants). Common kinds of stigma fit these descriptions: people with leprosy, facial damage, terminal illness, accidental disabilities, and homosexual orientations all face rejection, perhaps on the basis of tangible or symbolic threat. People want to preserve the ingroup or at least have the illusion of protecting themselves from these perceived threats.

Ingroups thus seem to control danger by differentiating outgroups from the ingroup and then communicating those differences to each other. This social sharing of stereotypes creates a sense of ingroup prediction and possibly control over external threats. Controlling via stereotypes also protects the ingroup's superior position, maintaining status and power; system justification makes up another important feature of this motive, as we will see.

**ENHANCING SELF**    The simple idea is that people make themselves feel better by derogating people from outgroups. The simple idea is wrong. First, people are more likely to favor the ingroup than disfavor the outgroup (Brewer & Brown, 1998), so the direction of the most frequent bias is ingroup favoritism, not outgroup derogation.

Second, even ingroup favoritism does not necessarily make people feel better (Brown, 1995; Fiske & Taylor, 2008). What appears true is nevertheless relevant to self-enhancing motives: Short-term threat to self does matter. In a given situation, people who have just experienced threat indeed do derogate outgroup members (Wills, 1981). Being insecure or anxious enhances stereotyping (Wilder & Shapiro, 1989b). Threats to self-image facilitate even the automatic activation of stereotypes (Spencer, Fein, Wolfe, Fong, & Dunn, 1998).

One class of threats to self-concept includes reminders of one's own ultimate death, that is, **mortality salience**. When people confront their own death they experience existential anxiety (Solomon, Greenberg, & Pyszczynski, 1991). One can bolster one's vulnerable self-image by subscribing to enduring cultural world views that will survive one's own limited existence. Recall from Chapters 9 and 10 that mortality salience bolsters prosocial and antisocial behaviors that fit enduring values. The social order, consisting of some groups dominating other groups, can also serve this function. And as we will see, mortality salience indeed intensifies both ingroup favoritism and outgroup derogation. But it is not clear that this actually does thereby enhance the self.

Finally, the direction of the hypothesized enhancement process may differ from people's intuitions. Rather than people with low self-esteem favoring the ingroup in order to feel better, it is people with already high (but threatened) self-esteem who favor the ingroup (Crocker, Major, & Steele, 1998). The relationship between self-enhancement and prejudice is not as simple as it seems, so we will come back to it later. The bottom line is that short-term threats to self matter in combination with chronic tendencies to self-enhancement.

## Summary of Definitions and Motives

Category-based biases include reactions in favor of one's own ingroup and against outgroups (members of groups not one's own). They take the form of stereotypes (cognitive biases), prejudice (affective biases), and discrimination (behavioral biases). All are biases because—at a minimum—the perceiver treats the other individual as an interchangeable member of the category. Stigma is a more specific term that addresses people who are individually marked for disfavor by society.

Operationally, biases have been measured by subtle means in the laboratory: verbal and nonverbal behavior, neural patterns, cognitive associations, and behavioral choices about whom to help, hurt, and befriend. Surveys tend to operationalize bias by a variety of measures getting at both old-fashioned bigotry and modern, subtle forms.

Several core social motives enter into bias. Understanding motives encourage simplified, efficient stereotypic understandings of others. Belonging emphasizes loyalty to the ingroup and, by extension, at least relative neglect of the outgroup. Belonging also singles out those who undermine ingroup cohesion, from outside or inside. Controlling focuses even more specifically on protecting the ingroup from a variety of threats. Enhancement increases the biases of those who have just experienced immediate threat to the self, especially if they have high self-esteem.

## SUBTLE BIAS: (MIS)UNDERSTANDING OTHERS BUT ENHANCING SELF

People's endorsement of stereotypes has decreased dramatically over the last 80 years. For example, students rating ten national and ethnic groups four times over the 20th century are producing ratings that are now more moderate (Bergsieker, Leslie, Constantine, & Fiske, 2008; see Figure 11.2); the most negatively rated groups in 1933 (non-Europeans, including "Negroes," Turks, Japanese, and Chinese) are now neutral and even slightly higher than the most positively rated group in 1933 (Americans), whose positive evaluation has also moderated; European outgroups on average have remained relatively neutral. What's more, the students have increasingly refused to report any stereotypes at all. Whether due to changing cohorts or contexts, overt endorsement has decreased.

Whites' overall understandings of racial issues, as reported on national surveys over 60 years, have also moved toward tolerance (Bobo, 2001). On items concerning principles of equality and integration, respondents have gone from 54 percent believing that public transportation should be segregated to virtually no one endorsing that view; similar trends occur for respondents believing that whites should receive preferences over blacks for jobs. So few people endorsed the intolerant sides of these items that they have been dropped altogether from national surveys. On the issue of school integration, the trend has been slower but clearly improving, with fully 68 percent endorsing school segregation in the early 1940s, down to a mere (but still shocking)

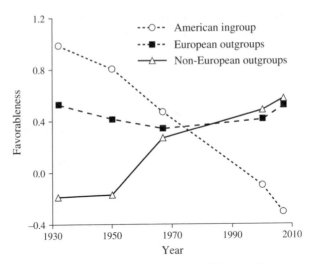

**Figure 11.2**   Moderation of Extreme Stereotypes in the Princeton Quartet

*Source:* Bergsieker, Leslie, Constantine, & Fiske, 2008. Copyright © Hilary Bergsieker. Adapted with permission.

4 percent in 1995. The more public the arena and the more abstract the principle, the more marked the improvement. For example, in the early 1960s, only a third of whites believed that blacks and whites should be allowed by law to marry each other; by 1995, four of every five whites believed in marital choice. But that means that a full fifth of whites still believe that blacks and whites should be actually prohibited by law from marrying each other.

On another question, however, only two-thirds of whites actively favored intermarriage. This begins to suggest that when racial matters get up close and personal, people are less egalitarian. Other survey evidence supports this white resistance to endorsing all the consequences of full implementation of equality as compared with abstract principles. For example, virtually all whites now report being willing to live next door to a black family, but roughly 70 percent report that they would move away if blacks came to their neighborhood in "great numbers." Fifty percent say they would object if their children went to a school where more than half of the children were black. Only about 15 percent believe that the government should help blacks improve their living standards, because of past discrimination. In short: Whites appear more supportive of equal rights in principle than of equal rights in practice, when they require commitment to specific steps involving their own lives and the status of their own group. This suggests layers of support and resistance.

Moreover, the disjunction in survey results fits people's individual behavior. When people have excuses, they will discriminate racially, but only in subtle ways. About the same time as the improved survey results, more unobtrusive and subtle measures of discrimination and prejudice showed that white bias was more prevalent than surveys indicated (Crosby, Bromley, & Saxe, 1980). At that time, a review of interracial helping, aggression, and nonverbal behavior indicated that (a) whites tended to help whites more often than they helped blacks, especially when they did not have to face directly the person in need of help; (b) under sanctioned conditions (e.g., in competitive games or administering punishment), whites aggressed against blacks more than against whites, but only when the consequences were low (under conditions of no retaliation, no censure, and anonymity); (c) studies of white nonverbal behavior indicated a discrepancy between verbal nondiscrimination and nonverbal hostility or discomfort, betrayed in tone of voice, seating distance, and the like. This early review sparked the realization that modern forms of discrimination have taken subtle, covert, and possibly unconscious forms. Current data support this insight.

Most estimates put 70 percent to 80 percent of the white population as relatively high on modern, subtle forms of racism. Most people hold prejudices that are subtler than the kinds of blatant prejudices we usually imagine. As the ensuing sections show, subtle prejudice is cool and indirect. It's automatic, unconscious, and unintentional; it's ambiguous; and it's ambivalent (Fiske, 2002). All of these factors make subtle prejudice hard to notice, but its effects are clear, as we shall see. The culture and its norms promote subtle prejudice, which is more cognitively cool and indirect than blatant bias, which is more emotionally hot and direct, covered later.

## Cool and Indirect Biases: Modern Racism and Subtle Prejudice

The possibility of something new, subtle, and covert appears in the latest results from scales designed to assess modern racial attitudes (see Table 11.1). If you have not already done so, take the scale before reading on. White students' scores on this modern racism scale are not related to direct, personal, negative experiences with blacks (Monteith & Spicer, 2000). Their attitudes do correlate with general antiegalitarian sentiments, as well as with negative themes in open-ended essays about their racial attitudes (e.g., negative stereotypes, denial of own personal responsibility for racism, and believing blacks are getting more than they deserve). Among adults, modern racism correlates with voting for white over black mayoral candidates, being opposed to busing of school children to achieve integration, having antiblack feelings, lacking sympathy for underdogs in general, and lacking education (McConahay, 1986). People high on modern racism construct intergroup relations as a zero-sum competition. This belief system fulfills an understanding motive.

Subtle prejudice is not a uniquely American, white-on-black phenomenon (Pettigrew, 1998b; Pettigrew & Meertens, 1995). In Europe, subtle forms of prejudice operate against various kinds of outgroups: French against North Africans, British against South Asians, Germans against Turks. In both Europe and the United States, people score higher on subtle prejudice, in general, than they score on blatant prejudice, so far more people would be classified as holding subtle (modern) than blatant (old-fashioned) prejudices. Let's examine subtle prejudice in some detail, precisely because it is so common, yet so unknown to most people.

Subtle prejudice is, first and foremost, indirect. When people hold subtle prejudices, they do not come out and say they are biased. The items measuring subtle bias all blame the outgroup. For example (Pettigrew & Meertens, 1995), some questionnaire items say that outgroups (e.g., for whites, African-Americans, Asians) should not push themselves where they are not wanted, but at the same time they should try harder. (Exactly how is an outgroup member supposed to do that—not be too pushy but, on the other hand, try harder? Contradictions are inherent in prejudice.) As another example of being indirect, another scale of discrimination and diversity issues (Wittenbrink, Judd, & Park, 1997, 2001a) includes items claiming that blacks do not take responsibility and that they blame the system too much, as well as faulting them for maintaining their own cultural identity (see Table 11.2). Such responses tend to correlate with stereotyping.

Subtle forms of racism also correlate with covert forms of aggression. In one study, white and black participants played a competitive game. The white participants delivered *lower-intensity* noise bursts to black than white losers, presumably for fear of appearing overly racist. But white people who scored high on modern racism delivered *longer* noise bursts to their black opponents than to comparable white opponents, a more covert form of aggression (Beal, O'Neal, Ong, & Ruscher, 2000).

Subtle prejudice also exaggerates cultural differences, viewing the outgroup's linguistic, religious, and sexual practices as completely and utterly different (Pettigrew & Meertens, 1995). Subtle prejudice tends to exaggerate differences between groups and compress differences within groups, as we will see. These kinds of distinctions come in the context of "us" and "them," ingroup and outgroup, however the culture constructs those dimensions: "The outgroup members are all the same and different from us." So prejudice against the outgroup is justified because they are not like us, and they are to blame for their problems.

**Table 11.2**    Discrimination and Diversity Scales (Illustrative Items)

Discrimination Items

Members of ethnic minorities have a tendency to blame whites too much for problems that are of their own doing.

These days, reverse discrimination against whites is as much a problem as discrimination against blacks.

A primary reason that ethnic minorities tend to stay in lower-paying jobs is that they lack the motivation required for moving up.

In the United States, people are no longer judged by their skin color.

Diversity Items

There is a real danger that too much emphasis on cultural diversity will tear the United States apart.

The desire of many ethnic minorities to maintain their cultural traditions impedes the achievement of racial equality.

The establishment and maintenance of all-black groups and coalitions prevent successful racial integration.

Items are used with 5-point Likert scales (endpoints are *strongly agree* and *strongly disagree*).
*Source:* From Wittenbrink et al., 1997. Copyright © American Psychological Association. Adapted with permission.

The perception that the outgroup differs fundamentally from the ingroup tends to reify (treat as if real) what are actually social constructions. That is, intergroup stereotypes depend on local custom. For example, different cultures and time periods define race and ethnicity differently, which belies perceptions that race and ethnicity are somehow objective. As noted, in the United States, the history of slavery gave rise to laws in many states that defined anyone with as little as 1/16 African heritage as black (Banks & Eberhardt, 1998). In Hannah Crafts's (2002) *The Bondswoman's Narrative*, one unscrupulous character becomes wealthy by exposing the distant African ancestors of apparently white women, who are then sold into slavery, abandoned by their humiliated (presumably purely white) husbands. Clearly, the racial definition is biologically arbitrary (why is someone with half-African and half-European heritage typically viewed as black, not white?).

Nevertheless, once people categorize other people into separate groups, they perceive the groups to possess **entitativity**, the property of being a coherent, unified, meaningful object (Campbell, 1958). As the groups chapter (Chapter 12) indicates, aggregates of people are perceived as groups to the extent that they seem similar and share a common fate, which makes them seem like a social entity to themselves and other people. When groups are viewed as entities, people believe in their **essentialism**, an underlying, deep core that makes their group membership seem real (Rothbart & Taylor, 1992; Yzerbyt, Corneille, & Estrada, 2001). This perceived essence often takes the form of a belief in unambiguous biological properties (genetics, "blood," or nature) that define the group. People do not typically recognize the extent to which group boundaries are not natural categories (like species) but instead social constructions such as race.

One implication of people's belief in a group essence is that they look for similarities among group members, overinterpreting them. Another implication is that they interpret the group's outcomes in terms of the group's own intrinsic characteristics, instead of, for example, their situation. This group-level analog to the fundamental attribution error or correspondence bias (Chapter 3) has been dubbed the **ultimate attribution error** (Pettigrew, 1979). People tend to view good actions as intrinsic to the ingroup's essence (or disposition) and bad actions as fundamental to the outgroup's essence; conversely, the ingroup's bad actions and the outgroup's good actions are viewed as meaningless products of the situation. For example, women's success at traditionally male tasks is often explained away as due to luck or unusual effort, whereas men's comparable success is often attributed to their intrinsic dispositions, such as ability or ambition (Deaux & Emswiller, 1974; Swim & Sanna, 1996). In interethnic attributions, people protect the ingroup, attributing success and high status to internal factors (our group's stable essence) but any failures to unstable or external factors (Hewstone, 1990). These attributional patterns of credit and blame do indirect damage to the outgroup, in the service of protecting the ingroup. Only the ingroup is given the benefit of the doubt.

If one blames a person or a group for their own bad outcomes, one tends to feel angry and resentful, but if one views the bad outcomes as beyond their control, one feels sympathy and pity (as discussed in Chapter 9, helping). This results in another way that subtle prejudice is cool and indirect: It withholds positive emotions from outgroup members—*not* being sympathetic, *not* admiring them. The ingroup/outgroup distinction means that one has positive associations to the ingroup and less-positive associations to the outgroup. The perceptions of the outgroup as negative are less clear, but perceptions of the outgroup are *relatively* negative because they are less good. These kinds of judgments tend to favor the ingroup so that one rewards the ingroup but not so much the outgroup. For example, one has a job; one gives it to the ingroup member. So, subtle prejudice is largely a matter of indirectly neglecting outgroup members.

Explicit measures of subtle racism on attitude surveys all correlate with each other and with overt forms of discrimination (Dovidio, Kawakami, Johnson, Johnson, & Howard, 1997). However, assessing indirect, cool, subtle forms of prejudice still presents a challenge. Although prejudices are often assessed with attitude scales such as those in Tables 11.1 and 11.2, whites' reactions to these scales can sometimes be **reactive**, that is, reflect people's motives to respond in socially desirable ways. For example, people score lower on the scale when administered by a black experimenter in a one-on-one setting, as opposed to a white experimenter or a mass-testing session (Fazio, Jackson, Dunton, & Williams, 1995). Ruling out such potential problems—by going beyond self-report—affords an opportunity to study even more subtle forms of subtle bias.

## Automatic Biases: Categorization and Associations

Automatic biases reflect what Richard Price, the author of *Freedomland*, calls "the American flu":

> I wanted to create a woman who—whose credentials as a "liberal" are four-star. . . . She works in the projects. She works with the children in the projects. She's got . . . a history of interracial dating. As much as it's possible, for somebody from her town to embrace the life of the other, she has done this. Her sense of being an outcast has probably made this very appealing for her.
>
> And yet again, she—when it hits the fan—that, you know, that kneejerk reaction "a black guy did it" just pops right out of her mouth. I mean, she's an American. It's an acculturated panic button. She knows people are going to buy it. And I went out of my way to create somebody whose got sort of superlative credentials, so to speak . . . as much as anybody could be, she's an honorary sister as far as everybody's concerned.
>
> Doesn't make a difference. It's the American flu.[2]

Automatic biases are not just the American flu; they are a universal virus. Indeed, even bacteria distinguish "us" from "them" (Gibbs, Urbanowski, & Greenberg, 2008)! Subtle prejudice relies on automatic categorization, activation, and application of associations. As Chapter 4 noted, responses are wholly **automatic** when they occur without intention, awareness, effort, or control. In the first moment of encountering someone,

---

[2] From Terry Gross's interview with Richard Price, author of *Freedomland*, May 21, 1998. Copyright © WHYY. Reproduced with permission.

one can see, automatically, some categories about that person. Subtle prejudice builds on this kind of automatic perception process. People are extremely good at categorizing, within a fraction of a second, people's race, sex, and age, based on visual cues that are highly practiced (Fiske, 1998b). People do not always categorize on these dimensions (Quinn & Macrae, 2005), but when they do, it can happen faster than an instant (Ito & Urland, 2003). These categories often activate stereotypic associations, which may then be applied to the individual. As Chapter 6 noted, many attitudes operate automatically or at least implicitly, especially in socially sensitive domains such as prejudice.

This kind of automatic bias appears for subliminal cues, that is, stimuli presented so rapidly that people are not aware of what they have seen. Nevertheless, these subliminal stimuli, presented at an unconscious level, affect people's perceptions, feelings, thoughts, and behavior. When people see a subliminal outgroup photograph, or a subliminal ethnic group name, or even "us" versus "them," people have distinctly positive associations to the ingroup. Their reactions occur within milliseconds (also see Chapter 6).

To demonstrate automaticity, psychologists frequently use priming methods, described earlier (Fazio & Olson, 2003). For example, some of the earliest studies (Dovidio, Evans, & Tyler, 1986; Gaertner & McLaughlin, 1983; Perdue, Dovidio, Gurtman, & Tyler, 1990) showed that white people read and identify positive attributes (such as "smart") faster just after seeing the word "whites" than after the word "blacks." The positive associations to "white" primed them for the positive words that followed. Similar effects occur for "us" and "them" as primes. The speed of these cognitive associations is a reliable measure over time (Kawakami & Dovidio, 2001).

Neuroimaging data also suggest automatic race-based reactions (Hart et al., 2000; Lieberman, Hariri, Jarcho, Eisenberger, & Bookheimer, 2005; Phelps et al., 2000; Wheeler & Fiske, 2005). In the United States, when white people look at faces of unfamiliar black Americans, but also sometimes when blacks look at faces of unfamiliar white Americans, researchers observe differential activation in the amygdala area of the brain, especially for people who score high on subtle prejudice. The amygdala is, among other things, associated with vigilance. This race effect also occurs for dark-skinned white targets (Ronquillo et al., 2007), a result consistent with greater bias against darker-skinned blacks (Maddox, 2004) but also whites with Afrocentric features (Blair, Judd, & Fallman, 2004). This bias operates automatically (Blair, Judd, Sadler, & Jenkins, 2002). More generally, the tight perceptual link between prototypic black male faces and crime (Eberhardt, Goff, Purdie, & Davies, 2004) helps explain the amygdala (vigilance) bias.

Race effects on early perceptual and neural activity have important consequences. Recall the shooter bias, whereby people, even police, fire faster on armed black than white male targets and are slower to avoid firing on unarmed blacks than whites (Correll, Park, Judd, Wittenbrink, Sadler, & Keesee, 2007; Payne, 2001, 2006); the shooter bias results directly from split-second neural responses (event-related brain potentials or ERPs; Correll, Urland, & Ito, 2006). Perhaps these automatic biases explain why having more Afrocentric features predicts death sentences, even controlling for features of the crime, for both black (Eberhardt, Davies, Purdie-Vaughns, & Johnson,

2006) and white defendants (Blair, Judd, & Chapleau, 2004). The automatic perceptual biases correspond to centuries of cultural images linking Africans to dehumanizing images such as apes (Goff, Eberhardt, Williams, & Jackson, 2008). Other severely derogated outgroups—for example, homeless or injection-drug-using people, regardless of race—also receive dehumanizing perceptions and neural responses (Harris & Fiske, 2006).

However, even these automatic, neural-level biases are amenable to early-onset efforts at control. For example, the race-amygdala effect depends on speed of exposure; at the briefest exposures (30 msec.), the amygdala activates, but at longer exposures (half a second), control-related neural components come into play (Cunningham et al., 2004). Similarly, instructions asking perceivers to individuate—that is, to attend to the individual preferences of the pictured person—also eliminate the race-amygdala effect (Wheeler & Fiske, 2005) and rehumanize the homeless and drug-addicted (Harris & Fiske, 2007). And perceivers habituate quickly, dampening the amygdala response to familiar black faces (Phelps et al., 2000). The point is that many, perhaps most, people have relatively automatic category-based responses that are unbelievably rapid, but of course, rapid does not mean inevitable, as Chapter 6 shows.

So far, we have seen automatic biases revealed by categorization and association, with subliminal cues, conscious priming, and neural responses, all of which avoid the self-report issues of deliberate responding. Like it or not, as the attitude chapter indicates, people make simultaneous associations between outgroup cues and positive or negative words (Fazio & Olson, 2003). As the Implicit Associations Test (IAT) shows (see Chapter 6), most people show automatic reactions on the basis of common social categories such as race, gender, and age (others include religion, ethnicity, and nationality; Rudman, Greenwald, Mellott, & Schwartz, 1999). After doing the IAT, students report that they can experience just how automatic subtle prejudice can be. Again, people have specifically positive associations to their own ingroup (and therefore less positive associations to outgroups). It follows from balance principles (attitudes, Chapter 6) that if people generally like themselves and identify with a particular group, they will also tend to favor that group (Greenwald, Banaji, Rudman, Farnham, Nosek, & Mellott, 2002). Even minimal, arbitrary ingroups, created within an experiment, can elicit automatically favorable ingroup biases and negative outgroup biases (Ashburn-Nardo, Voils, & Monteith, 2001).

The patterns of automatic associations include four types (Fiske, 1998b):

- *Ingroup advantage*, whereby the ingroup is more rapidly associated with positive attributes and feelings than the outgroup, and the ingroup is recognized and categorized faster than the outgroup.
- *Stereotype-matching advantage*, whereby outgroups are rapidly associated with stereotypic attributes, and those stereotypes rapidly prime other stereotypes for the same outgroup.
- *Marked disadvantage*, whereby groups that deviate from the cultural default (i.e., not white, male, 30–40 years of age, heterosexual, Protestant, able-bodied, etc.) acquire marked status; people are categorized most rapidly along whatever dimensions distinguish them from the default, so that black

men are categorized as black faster than as male, and white women are categorized faster as women than as white.

- *Categorization advantage*, whereby people respond to other people more rapidly when they can categorize them according to race, gender, and age, than when they cannot. Rapid categorization and automatic associations are cognitively useful, saving mental resources in reactions to other people.

One might well question the meaning of all these automatic reactions and whether they reflect merely cultural knowledge or actual personal beliefs (Devine, 1989). That is, if all people, regardless of overt bias, show automatic stereotypic associations to outgroups, perhaps it is because all people know the cultural stereotypes, but that does not inevitably translate to agreeing with them. People do develop implicit associations from exposure to evaluative pairings in the environment, but they may not necessarily endorse them (Karpinski & Hilton, 2001). Children develop implicit evaluative associations to race from as early as age six (Dunham, Baron, & Banaji, 2008), in Anglo American (Baron & Banaji, 2006), Hispanic American (Dunham, Baron, & Banaji, 2007), and Japanese samples (Dunham, Baron, & Banaji, 2006). Children's implicit racial attitudes correlate with parental attitudes (Sinclair, Dunn, & Lowery, 2005). Even infants as young as three months show a visual preference for own-race faces, but newborns do not, and the preference results from exposure to predominantly own-race faces (Bar-Haim, Ziv, Lamy, & Hodes, 2006; Kelly et al., 2005). The familiar face overgeneralization hypothesis can account for ingroup favoritism in adults (Zebrowitz, Bronstad, & Lee, 2007). Hence, even if the culture does create these relatively automatic associations and preferences, it may do so indirectly (through de facto racial segregation of daily experience), quite early (infants!), and as a relatively rapid learning process (e.g., as short as three months).

As we have seen (Chapter 6), people have some kinds of control over the effects of automatic processes. People's responses in fact go beyond the initial, automatic culturally based reactions. Nevertheless, these automatic or implicit responses form the starting point for our interactions with others, which at a minimum makes them into a millstone that handicaps spontaneous interaction. Even if people do not explicitly endorse ingroup preferences, they may still possess them as a foundation underlying more mature and explicit attitudes.

## Ambiguous Biases: Excuses

Subtle bias is not only indirect, cool, and automatic but also **ambiguous**, that is, concealed behind responses that are open to various interpretations. Subtle bias often occurs in nonverbal behavior and in the speed of responses, both of which are ambiguous—hard for ordinary people to decipher. What the work on ambiguous bias pinpoints is that subtle prejudice occurs in settings where people have other excuses for their discrimination. "It's not that he's black; it's just that the other candidate was better on what we value," where "what we value" turns out to be a moving target (Norton, Vandello, & Darley, 2003).

Consider some puzzling findings that demonstrate the ambiguity of whites' responses: When whites are not angry, they are actually more aggressive toward white than black targets, but when angry (providing an excuse), they are more aggressive toward blacks (Rogers & Prentice-Dunn, 1981). When whites witness an accident befalling a black victim, if they think they are the only bystander (so they have no excuse), they help the black person slightly more often than a white victim, but when other bystanders are present (providing an excuse for inaction), they help the black victim only half as often as the white one (Gaertner & Dovidio, 1977). When white college students are prejudiced, they are actually more likely to hire a well-qualified black than a well-qualified white, but if they have the excuse of poor qualifications, the prejudiced students are instead less likely to hire a black than a white applicant (McConahay, 1983).

One crucial feature in these ambiguity studies and dozens of others is that most white people find the thought of their own possible racism unpleasant, so they avoid behaving in overtly racist ways when the interpretation of their behavior would be obvious to them and to others. **Aversive racism** (Dovidio & Gaertner, 2004; Gaertner & Dovidio, 1986) refers to forms of racism that are unpleasant to the people who hold them. The research illustrates well-intentioned white people behaving in racist ways mainly when they have a nonracist excuse for their behavior, making it ambiguous. Indeed, when they cannot avoid the conflict between their stated attitudes and their own actual behavior, their prejudice reduces (Son Hing & Zanna, 2002). Implicit and explicit prejudice can operate independently, creating four combinations of low and high scores on each dimension (Son Hing, Chung-Yan, Hamilton, & Zanna, 2008). Aversive racists are high on implicit but low on explicit racism and express prejudice when the attribution for their negative evaluation is ambiguous.

A final, recently-identified ambiguous bias against outgroups highlights the importance of emotions in prejudice. **Infrahumanization** views the outgroup as less human than the ingroup. Specifically, it views the outgroup as less capable of experiencing complex, uniquely human emotions that result from secondary appraisals (Demoulin et al., 2005; Leyens et al., 2003). For example, outgroups and animals can show relatively simple and automatic fear, but only ingroups can show the more complex, thought-induced emotion of dread. People seem most motivated to view the ingroup as uniquely human in this way, independent of intergroup conflict (Demoulin et al., 2005). Infrahumanization operates automatically (Boccato, Cortes, Demoulin, & Leyens, 2007), and the link between uniquely human emotions and perceived humanity operates in both directions (Vaes, Paladino, & Leyens, 2006). Denying uniquely human emotions (e.g. anguish, mourning, remorse) to the outgroup makes them seem not to suffer as much when, for example, a natural disaster kills their family members; this undermines empathy and aid because while they suffer, they suffer like animals, not like humans (Cuddy, Rock, & Norton, 2007). Like other forms of ambiguous bias, infrahumanizing the outgroup by denying them uniquely human emotions seems harmless only on the surface.

## Ambivalent Biases: Mixed Feelings

A final feature of subtle bias is ambivalence. For example, well-intentioned whites sometimes respond more extremely to blacks than they would to comparable whites. **Response amplification** cuts both ways: responding more positively to a black person in a positive situation but responding more negatively in a negative situation. Other studies have shown these kinds of amplification effects: A positive outgroup member is liked over a comparably positive ingroup member, but a negative outgroup member is disliked more than a negative one. This type of response fits not only aversive racism but also **ambivalent racism** (Katz & Hass, 1988; Katz, Wackenhut, & Hass, 1986).

Racial ambivalence (another term for ambivalent racism) captures the idea that most whites possess both positive and negative feelings toward blacks (see Table 11.3). Reminiscent of modern racism, their antiblack attitudes blame black Americans for their relative disadvantage because they supposedly violate the Protestant work ethic (alleged lack of family responsibility, community leadership, personal values, drive). Their problack attitudes (which are "pro" in the paternalistic sense of pity) stress the obstacles African Americans face, ongoing discrimination, and other situational barriers, which correlate with whites' own belief in humanitarianism and egalitarianism. Precisely because racial ambivalence comprises simultaneously positive and negative attitudes, it is unstable, tipping in one direction or the other, overreacting to

**Table 11.3**  Racial Ambivalence Scale (Sample Items)

Pro-Black

Black people do not have the same employment opportunities that whites do.
It's surprising that black people do as well as they do, considering all the obstacles they face.
Too may blacks still lose out on jobs and promotions because of their skin color.

Anti-Black

Although there are exceptions, black urban neighborhoods don't seem to have strong community organization or leadership.
On the whole, black people don't stress education and training.
Many black teenagers don't respect themselves or anyone else.

Protestant Ethic

Our society would have fewer problems if people had less leisure time.
Money acquired easily is usually spent unwisely.
Most people who don't succeed in life are just plain lazy.

Humanitarianism-Egalitarianism

One should be kind to all people.
One should find ways to help others less fortunate than oneself.
There should be equality for everyone—because we are all human beings.

*Source:* From Katz & Hass, 1988. Copyright © American Psychological Association. Adapted with permission.

small cues in the situation. Ambivalent racism predicts precisely this kind of response amplification.

Other kinds of subtle prejudice also are ambivalent. Attitudes toward women reflect not only the **hostile sexism** normally considered but also **benevolent sexism**, a subjectively positive but paternalizing form of prejudice that belittles women (Glick & Fiske, 1996; 2001a). Hostile sexism is directed toward nontraditional women who violate narrow gender roles (female professionals, lesbians, feminists, and female athletes), and it tolerates sexual harassment (Begany & Milburn, 2002; Weiner, Hurt, Russell, Mannen, & Gasper, 1997) as well as spouse abuse (Glick, Sakalli-Ugurlu, Ferreira, & DeSouza, 2002). Benevolent sexism is directed toward traditional women who adhere to narrow gender roles: housewives, in particular (Glick, Diebold, Bailey-Warner, & Zhu, 1997). The Ambivalent Sexism Inventory (ASI; see Table 11.4) reflects two dimensions that together support the status quo for women, by rewarding subordinate women with male protection and appreciation for their alleged purity but threatening uppity women with dislike and exclusion (Glick & Fiske, 2001b). This dynamic—in traditional gender relationships—does not

**Table 11.4**  The Ambivalent Sexism Inventory (ASI)

Relationships between Men and Women

Below is a series of statements concerning men and women and their relationships in contemporary society. Please indicate the degree to which you agree or disagree with each statement, using the following scale: 0 = *disagree strongly;* 1 = *disagree somewhat;* 2 = *disagree slightly;* 3 = *agree slightly;* 4 = *agree somewhat;* 5 = *agree strongly.*

**Benevolent Sexism (sample items)**

No matter how accomplished he is, a man is not truly complete as a person unless he has the love of a woman.

Men should be willing to sacrifice their own well-being in order to provide financially for the women in their lives.

Many women have a quality of purity that few men possess.

A good woman should be set on a pedestal by her man.

Most women fail to appreciate fully all that men do for them.

**Hostile Sexism (sample items)**

Women exaggerate problems they have at work.

Once a woman gets a man to commit to her, she usually tries to put him on a tight leash.

When women lose to men in a fair competition, they typically complain about being discriminated against.

Women seek to gain power by getting control over men.

Most women fail to appreciate fully all that men do for them.

*Source:* From Glick & Fiske, 1996. Copyright © Peter Glick and Susan T. Fiske. Reprinted with permission.

result from political correctness or liberal good intentions. Instead, it reflects fairly universal gender dynamics across cultures (Glick et al., 2000; Glick & Fiske, 2001c). Societal power and intimate interdependence shape gender relations (Rudman & Glick, 2008).

Overall, then, prejudice is not just pure hatred; its dimensions include disrespecting groups for perceived incompetence and disliking groups for perceived lack of warmth. Logically, then, a bigot could dislike but respect certain outgroups (Asians) and disrespect but like others (old people). The **stereotype content model** (Cuddy, Fiske, & Glick, 2008; Fiske et al., 2002) hypothesizes that people want to know two things about outgroups (and in parallel, about other individuals in general):

a)   Are their intentions good or ill toward me and my group (i.e., are they warm or not)?

b)   Can they enact their intentions (i.e., are they competent or not)?

These turn out to be so-far universal dimensions of social perception, accounting for most of the variance in impressions (Fiske, Cuddy, & Glick, 2007). Groups then may be more threatening: for example, when they are respected as competent but disliked as not warm (e.g., feminists, successful immigrants, and minority professionals). Asians fit this category in the United States (Lin, Kwan, Cheung, & Fiske, 2005). Or groups may be less threatening: for example, when they are liked as warm but disrespected as incompetent (e.g., people with physical or mental disabilities; re older people: Cuddy, Norton, & Fiske, 2005). Many groups fall into these mixed quadrants of envy or pity, reflecting a kind of ambivalence consistent with the earlier analyses of ambivalent racism and ambivalent sexism. Of course, some outgroups are flat-out disliked and disrespected: undocumented immigrants (Lee & Fiske, 2006) as well as drug addicts and homeless people (Harris & Fiske, 2006). The warmth and competence attributions predict specific intergroup emotions, such as pride for the ingroup, envy for the competent but cold outgroups, pity for the warm but incompetent outgroups, and contempt for the low-low outgroups; distinct forms of discrimination follow from these prejudiced emotions (Cuddy, Fiske, & Glick, 2007).

In research (Fiske, Cuddy, Glick, & Xu, 2002), the model reveals different kinds of outgroups, many of which reflect this kind of ambivalent prejudice. In the United States, outgroups are differentiated by perceivers on the basis of their perceived competence, the horizontal axis, and their perceived warmth, the vertical axis in Figure 11.3. Take the figure counter-clockwise from the top left-hand corner. Elderly people, people with mental disabilities, and people with physical disabilities all are seen as relatively warm and nice but not competent; they are disrespected but can be liked; in short, they are pitied. Then, in the bottom left-hand corner, poor people, welfare recipients, and homeless people are neither liked nor respected; they're seen as incompetent and not warm. That is what people consider traditional, unambivalent prejudice, but it applies only to those groups, who receive contempt from prejudiced people. Then, the cluster to the lower right consists of rich people, men, Jews, Asians, professionals, and educated people; basically these are groups of people who are disliked but respected—in short, envied. They are seen as highly competent, having achieved a lot, but they're not nice—they allegedly gave up their humanity to get there. And

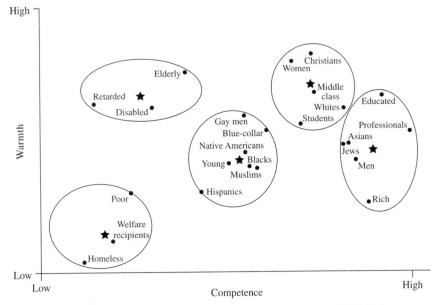

**Figure 11.3**    Stereotype Content Model Showing Different Clusters of United States Out-Groups

*Source:* From Fiske et al., 2002. Copyright © American Psychological Association. Adapted with permission.

consistent with ambivalent sexism, two subtypes of women, professional women and feminists, appear that category, too.

So who's allowed to be both warm and competent? "Us." The cultural default. And in this particular sample, that included Christians, women in general, middle-class people, whites, and students. Societal reference groups are up in that top right quadrant. Finally, the groups who are in the middle can be in the middle for different reasons. They can be in the middle because people do not have clear stereotypes, as was probably the case for Native Americans in this sample from the northeastern United States. Groups can also be in the middle because of conflicting stereotypes about them. For example, American blacks end up in the middle, but as soon as they are subtyped into poor blacks and black professionals, they move to the two opposite corners of contempt and pride (Fiske, Bergsiecker, Russell, & Williams, 2009).

This model of stereotype content holds up in other countries, for groups that are important in their societies (in over a dozen other nations, Cuddy et al., 2009). Figure 11.4 shows German views of the European Union (EU) community. Great Britain and Germany end up as envied, highly competent but supposedly not warm. Belgium and Austria are the poor cousins (perhaps due to economic and political scandals at the time). And then in the top left are the southern Europeans—the warm Mediterraneans—plus the Irish. These are places people want to go on vacation, in part because the people are stereotypically so nice. In the multination EU, no single nation ranks the most-admired EU ingroup or shared reference group, because of a strong EU ideology of equal status, though Sweden, Denmark, and Finland come closest across

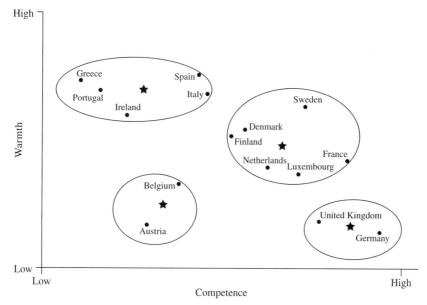

**Figure 11.4**   Stereotype Content Model, Showing Different Clusters of EU Nations

*Source:* Cuddy et al., 2009. Copyright © Amy J. C. Cuddy. Reproduced with permission.

countries. The ambivalent competence by-warmth structure of stereotype content is not just something about politically correct Americans.

A final comment about the ambivalence of stereotype contents: The specific contents, though not the ambivalence, of stereotypes change over time and place. In the stereotype content model, for example, the content of group stereotypes depends on the group's perceived status (which predicts perceived competence) and perceived competitiveness (which predicts perceived lack of warmth), at a particular historical juncture (Bergsieker, Leslie, Fiske, & Constantine, 2008; Durante, Volpato, & Fiske, 2009). For example, the first Chinese immigrants in the United States arrived in large numbers to build the railroads, and they were not perceived to be technically competent professionals, as are the current generations of Asian immigrants. Nevertheless, every time and place has its pitied, envied, and contempt-inducing outgroups.

Across all these models of ambivalent prejudice, the point holds: A lot of prejudices involve mixed feelings, and it is not just a phenomenon of political correctness or antiprejudice norms. The middle 70 percent to 80 percent of the population simply just does not hate outgroups. Many outgroups are given a little something; "they're nice, but they're stupid," or "they're smart, but you know, they're not so nice." These kinds of ambivalent reactions are typical.

All these cool and indirect aspects of subtle bias—being automatic, ambiguous, and ambivalent—reflect its origins in people's core social motive to understand their social worlds. Where does subtle prejudice come from? It comes from internal conflict in people's efforts to build an understanding that complies with contradictory information. People want to comply with their own antiprejudice ideals, their understanding that everyone is equal. But their understanding is also influenced at least unconsciously by information coming from the culture all around them. So a tension arises from wanting to comply with norms against bias, and even having personal values against bias, but not wanting to admit to oneself that one ever discriminates, prejudges, or stereotypes. Many people have automatic associations that come from the media, from other cultural influences, and from sheer inexperience with outgroups, just not having enough contact with people who are somehow different from themselves, and so they are left with associations that are relatively stereotypic. These automatic stereotypic thoughts conflict with antiprejudice norms and values, leading to an internal conflict that is resolved by these more subtle, ambiguous, ambivalent forms of bias.

## Summary of Subtle Biases: Automotic, Ambiguous, Ambivalent

As overt expressions of bias improved over the course of the 20th century, the concept of subtle bias emerged. The Modern Racism Scale and subsequent scales showed that people might have cool and indirect forms of bias, blaming outgroups for their situations, viewing outgroup disadvantage as an intrinsic feature of their essential make-up, and withholding sympathy and respect. An important and surprising set of insights came from work demonstrating that people's biased associations can be automatic; priming and simultaneous associations both reveal how rapidly people link group cues to thoughts, feelings, and behavior. Many of the associations reflect ingroup favoritism at least as much as outgroup derogation. Subtle bias is also ambiguous, in the sense that people discriminate when they have nonprejudiced excuses for their behavior, which fits the idea of aversive bias that is unacceptable to the people who possess it. And subtle bias is also ambivalent, involving a mix of hostile and subjectively positive feelings that combine, both to create extreme responses and to mask bias in paternalistic or envious guises. Various outgroups are viewed with emotions more complex than simple antipathy. Subtle forms of bias reflect both a motive for coherent (though often misguided) understanding and self-enhancing (protecting one's image as unbiased).

## SUBTLE BIAS IS SOCIALLY USEFUL: BELONGING AND CONTROLLING

Subtle forms of bias persist because they are socially pragmatic, whether or not morally acceptable. This section shows that subtle biases guide the perceiver's behavior, shape the reciprocal responses of outgroup members, guide ingroup communications about outgroup members, and create a circumscribed experience of accuracy. The social utility of bias serves motives of socially shared understanding, in part by smoothing interactions in which both people play according to stereotypic roles.

### Subtle Bias Predicts Deniable Discrimination

Recent, provocative evidence indicates that stereotype-related *behavior* is spontaneously primed by outgroup categories (Dijksterhuis & Bargh, 2001; Wheeler & Petty, 2001). Recall from Chapter 2 the Trivial Pursuits study (Dijksterhuis & van

Knippenberg, 1998) in which students primed with "professor" performed better on a factual knowledge test than students not so primed. Recall from Chapter 4 the automaticity study in which students primed with elderly stereotypes then walked to the elevator more slowly, and white people primed with black faces responded with more hostility when provoked (Bargh, Chen, & Burrows, 1996). Automatic evaluations result in predispositions to behave consistently with that evaluation (Chen & Bargh, 1999). Recall embodied cognition (Chapter 6), wherein people respond faster to negative cues when simultaneously pushing a lever away from themselves (enacting avoidance) and to positive cues when pulling a lever toward themselves (enacting approach).

Automatic associations most clearly predict subtle forms of behavior outside people's ordinary conscious control (Dovidio, Kawakami, & Gaertner, 2002; Dovidio, Kawakami, Johnson, Johnson, & Howard, 1997). For example, spontaneous nonverbal behavior follows from implicit forms of prejudice. Subtle forms of nonverbal bias reveal discomfort, avoidance, and anxiety: sitting farther away, ending interviews sooner, making less eye contact, and nervous blinking or speech errors (Dovidio et al., 1997; Word, Zanna, & Cooper, 1974). The relatively automatic forms of bias predict the relatively spontaneous forms of discrimination.

In contrast, more controlled, deliberate forms of behavior follow from more explicit measures of prejudice. As noted, scores on the Modern Racism Scale predict strategic but covert forms of interracial aggression (Beal et al., 2000). The dissociation between automatic processes and controlled processes is clear; whites may even bend over backward to be more pleasant to blacks than whites, but their subtle nonverbal cues indicate bias nonetheless (Vanman, Paul, Ito, & Miller, 1997). Perhaps because they feel uncomfortable together, people's subtle forms of bias also predict avoidance when people have discretion about spending time together, as at meals or parties.

Subtle forms of discrimination are socially useful precisely because they operate at the edge of awareness for both parties, so the target is unlikely to comprehend fully what is going on, and the perceiver can deny—to self and other alike—that the interaction was biased. Social utility is not necessarily moral justification, of course. Indeed, such hidden biases challenge the legal system's assumption that discrimination has to be consciously intended; legal scholarship is responding to the evidence of automatic, ambiguous, and ambivalent biases (Krieger & Fiske, 2006; Lane, Kang, & Banai, 2007).

## Self-fulfilling Prophecies Create Confirming Behavior

Subtle forms of discrimination affect the target. Besides creating negative outcomes (avoidance, neglect) or a hostile atmosphere, an even more insidious effect is bringing about the very behavior that the biased perceiver expects. For example, automatic priming effects have direct impact on the behavior of people's interaction partners. In one study already mentioned (Chen & Bargh, 1997), white participants subliminally primed with black male faces acted in a stereotype-consistent fashion (hostile). But the point here is that they also elicited hostile behavior from their white interaction partner, thereby causing the original participants to see their interaction partner as a hostile person. This implies that whites interacting with a black male (and therefore primed) would act hostilely, evoking hostile behavior in return. The process by which the perceiver's biases affect target behavior, in turn supporting the perceiver's original biases, is termed a **self-fulfilling prophecy** (Merton, 1948), **expectancy confirmation**, or **behavioral confirmation** (e.g., Darley & Fazio, 1980; Klein & Snyder, 2003; Miller & Turnbull, 1986; Snyder & Stukas, 1998).

The path goes by way of nonverbal communication and indirect verbal cues. That is, nonverbal behaviors such as smiling, nodding, eye contact, close distance, and greater length or frequency of interactions all communicate friendly attention versus hostile neglect (Harris & Rosenthal, 1985). In addition, verbal cues such as praise and criticism communicate expectancies (Harris & Rosenthal, 1985). Leading questions can confirm expectancies, and open-ended questions can allow targets to disconfirm expectancies (Leyens, 1989; Neuberg, 1989). People convey positive or negative climates, which lead targets to reciprocate, feeling more or less comfortable, resulting in the predicted behavior (Snyder, Tanke, & Berscheid, 1977; Word, Zanna, & Cooper, 1974). In a study Chapter 7 noted (Snyder et al., 1977), men speaking with women over the phone saw a photograph of an attractive or unattractive woman as their partner. Although the women were unaware of the randomly assigned photograph, they behaved in a more friendly, sociable way when their partners believed them to be attractive. Similarly (Word et al., 1974), when white interviewers treated naïve white interviewees with nonverbal behaviors typical of white behavior toward blacks (e.g., greater seating distance, more speech errors, shorter interview), the naïve white interviewees saw the interviewer as unfriendly and inadequate, and themselves performed less well in the interview.

Ironically, when perceivers and targets cooperatively confirm stereotypic expectancies, both may feel the interaction went smoothly (Leyens, Dardenne, & Fiske, 1998), but this depends on both subscribing to the same biases. Expectancy-confirming perceivers may behave in a warm, relaxed manner, even as they confirm a negative expectancy (Judice & Neuberg, 1998). People may even self-stereotype in expectancy-confirming ways, especially when they believe that close others think the stereotype applies to them (Sinclair, Hardin, & Lowery, 2006) or when affiliative (belonging) motives are high (Sinclair, Huntsinger, Skorinko, & Hardin, 2005). This kind of social tuning can affect even implicit responses (Lun, Sinclair, Whitchurch, & Glenn, 2007; Sinclair, Lowery, Hardin, & Colangelo, 2005). Overall, behavioral confirmation is socially useful because it makes interaction superficially easier for everyone, even if the longer-term consequences are disastrous.

## Socially Communicated Biases Build Ingroup Cohesion

Subtle bias also is socially useful because it fulfills the core social motive to belong: Shared stereotypes are easily communicated and enhance group cohesion (Ruscher, 2001). Prejudiced speech facilitates group interaction by being simple-minded and efficient, speaking in shorthand references to outgroup caricatures. Prejudiced speech facilitates group belonging motives, because it enhances ingroup superiority, dominance, and separation from the outgroup (see Table 11.5). For all these reasons,

**Table 11.5**    Functions of Prejudiced Speech

| Function | Examples | Elaboration |
|---|---|---|
| Economy of expression | Group labels such as "white trash" or "Jap" | Shorthand that evokes stereotype is efficient |
| Group enhancement | Hostile humor | Points out superiority of ingroup |
| Social functions | Delegitimization, rationalization | Keeps outgroup separate for reduced contact |
| Ingroup dominance | Control of media, controlling nonverbals | Perpetuates stereotypes and social structure to retain ingroup status |
| Impression management | Bifurcation, illusion of universality | Presents nonprejudiced image to the world |

*Source:* From Ruscher, 2001. Copyright © Guilford. Adapted with permission.

group interactions tend to focus on shared stereotypes. When people are motivated to form a consensus, their conversations focus on stereotypic information and encourage stereotypic impressions (Ruscher, Hammer, & Hammer, 1996). In general, discussion polarizes outgroup stereotypes, although one person with a strong supply of countersterotypic information—an ally—can counteract the consensus (Brauer, Judd, & Jacquelin, 2001; Thompson, Judd, & Park, 2000).

Social sharing among ingroup members—gossip, rumor, opinions, stories, media—contributes to consensus in stereotyped beliefs and related prejudices. The most easily communicated traits constitute the core of most stable stereotypes (Schaller & Conway, 2001). For example, people communicate some traits more frequently *(intelligent, athletic, sensitive, quick-tempered)* and others less frequently *(slovenly, pugnacious, stolid, mercenary, grasping).* The traits most often appearing in social discourse constitute the most frequent contents of stereotypes (Schaller, Conway, & Tanchuk, 2002). When people actually communicate stereotypes, they are more likely to endorse them than if they merely think and write about them (Schaller & Conway, 1999). This suggests the group-belonging aspect of stereotypic communication.

When people communicate a story containing both stereotypic and counterstereotypic information, the story becomes more and more stereotypic, after several people tell it (Kashima, 2000). Like other forms of rumor transmission (Allport & Postman, 1946), the story simplifies and sharpens the stereotypes as it passes from person to person. Moreover, as people infer other people's prejudices and stereotypes, that gives them social permission to respond in equally biased ways, reinforcing their own and other people's stereotypes and prejudice (Wittenbrink & Henly, 1996). Finding out about the stereotypes held by peers influences prejudiced people in particular, as a validation of their stereotypic beliefs.

Not all stereotype communication occurs by direct transmission of stereotype content. Indirect endorsement of stereotypes comes through the use of abstract terms—implying generality—instead of concrete terms—implying a single specific observation. For example, describing an interaction by labeling one person as "aggressive" differs from saying that person "pushed the other person away." The **linguistic intergroup bias** reflects people's tendency to describe expectancy-consistent events (positive ingroup behavior and negative outgroup behavior) more abstractly, because it is presumably stable and typical; they describe expectancy-inconsistent events (negative ingroup behavior and positive outgroup behavior) more concretely, as if it is an isolated incident (Maass, Salvi, Arcuri, & Semin, 1989). This makes cognitive sense: Expectancy-consistent information is more readily attributed to abstract dispositions (Maass, Milesi, Zabbini, & Stahlberg, 1995; Wigboldus, Semin, & Spears, 2000), so it serves an understanding motive. Recall that the ultimate attribution error noted earlier shows the same pattern. More prejudiced people describe stereotypic behaviors in more abstract terms, regardless of valence (positivity or negativity), so this linguistic bias subtly reveals their prejudice and reinforces everyone's stereotypes (Schnake & Ruscher, 1998). People can conversely undermine stereotypes by communicating expectancy-inconsistent information in abstract terms (Ruscher & Duval, 1998). Finally, people use this bias more when the ingroup is threatened (Maass, Ceccarelli, & Rudin, 1996). Protection of the cohesive ingroup serves multiple motives (belonging, controlling, and self-enhancing).

## Accuracy Would Make Stereotypes Useful

Most stereotyping research remains agnostic about the truth of stereotypes. Assessing how people perceive other people on the basis of perceived group membership remains an intrinsically important goal. Even if a stereotype were, in some sense, accurate, it would ignore the range of people within the group, including those for whom the stereotype is not at all true. More important, assessing stereotype accuracy poses far more considerable challenges than the casual observer imagines (e.g., Judd & Park, 1993).

First, most stereotypes consist of traits: hostile, dishonest, lazy, harmless, stupid, and so on. If stereotypes consisted solely of easily measured attributes, such as height and weight, the assessment issue would be simpler. However, even with objective physical measurements, stereotypes can distort laypeople's estimates (Biernat, Manis, & Nelson, 1991), and scientists' measurements are not immune (Gould, 1981). According to the **shifting standards model**, what laypeople mean by even physical descriptions is conditioned on group membership (*tall* for a woman is not *tall* for a man; Biernat & Manis, 1994; Biernat et al., 1991). When trait evaluations enter in, the situation becomes even more biased because the same trait carries different meanings for different groups: Different behavior is expected from a woman who is a *competent* parent than from a man who is; different performance is expected of a black person who is *competent* at math than of a white person who is (Kobrynowicz & Biernat, 1997). Lower performance is evaluated as *competent* for the group not typically expected to do well on the task ("competent parent, for a man"; "competent at math, for a black person"). This has implications for people's outcomes in situations where judges must choose between two candidates. A person from the group devalued on that dimension (e.g., women on athletics) may be told consistently that his or her performance is great (for a member of that outgroup, the message implies, though never says), but when forced to choose, judges will choose the member of the group stereotyped to be better (Biernat & Vescio, 2002).

Second, even if one can surmount the shifting standards issue, the critical question is, whose point of view constitutes the criterion for accuracy? Do we measure perceptions held by the stereotyped group? They are likely to be motivated to maintain a positive group identity, although they may sometimes adopt the stigmatized identity offered by society as a way to differentiate themselves from others (Ellemers, Spears, & Doosje, 2002). Do we measure the consensus of other groups about the targeted group? If they are the ones holding the stereotype, then we have hardly distinguished between the stereotype and the reality. Indeed, for people who believe that a stereotype validly applies to an individual, increased accuracy motivation and added attention merely strengthen their stereotyping (Madon, Guyll, Hilbert, Kyriakatos, & Vogel, 2006). Do we measure the consensus of experts? Even supposedly neutral parties are regarded with suspicion by groups on conflicting sides of the same question (Vallone, Ross, & Lepper, 1985), so who is truly qualified to judge?

What about objective measures? What one side views as objective, the other side may not; people's judgments of the quality of evidence are affected by their attitudes toward the relevant issue. People on one side of a social dispute tend to discount evidence for the other side of the dispute (Lord, Ross, & Lepper, 1979). And people tend to see their own perspective as less biased than other people's (Pronin, Lin, & Ross, 2002). How can we all be less biased than the average person?

Nevertheless, suppose that we could find a criterion (test or measurement) that both ingroup and outgroup could accept as fair. Suppose one group scores noticeably above zero on this criterion measure. What degree of the trait would mean that one group really does possess the trait? Would they have to score higher than the midpoint? Most tests do not have an absolute score that labels a person categorically as possessing the trait or not. All scores are relative to other people's scores.

Absolute scores aside, how much higher does the group have to be than a comparison group (and which comparison group)? How much of a difference matters? The standard statistical answer is to compare the average between-group difference, relative to the variability within each group. The distributions of group scores will matter here. In many instances of group differences, the actual differences are small, and the distributions overlap so substantially that drawing inferences about individuals is meaningless; differences are small relative to individual variation (e.g., Costa, Terracciano, & McCrae, 2001). As Figure 11.5(A) indicates, **overlapping normal distributions** acknowledge the possibility of average group differences but even greater variability within the group. In this case, would one really want to judge the individual by the group mean?

Other issues of distribution also matter. Supposing one set a cut-point for possessing the trait or not, how many of the group would have to have a particular attribute? Some characteristics or behaviors are prescribed as vital for virtually all members of the group (college professors having a Ph.D.). Allport described these as the **J-curve of conformity behavior** (see Figure 11.5[B]); he uses workers' arrival times at a

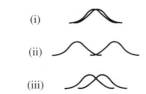

(A) Varying degrees of overlap in curves of normal distribution

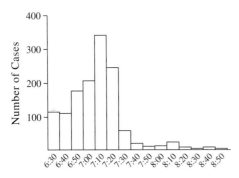

(B) (i)  Number of employees punching time clock at 10-minute intervals. A variant on the *J*-curve

(ii)  Hypothetical percentage of Americans who speak English— a conformity attribute

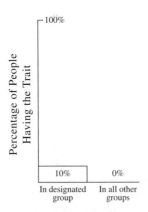

(C) Approximate situation in a rare-zero differential

**Figure 11.5**   Hypothetical Distributions of Actual Group Differences

*Source:* From Allport, 1954. Copyright © Perseus. Adapted with permission.

factory, but one could easily use students' arrival at class, Americans' ability to speak English, or little girls who play with dolls and little boys who play with trucks. The height of the peak (how many people conform exactly) and the length of the tail determine how characteristic the trait really is. In this kind of distribution, most people in the group behave as prescribed, but the pattern still ignores how much this conformity differentiates the group from others. (All people in one group might speak English, but so might all people in the other group.)

But sometimes the exceptional behavior of unusual group members can define perceptions of the group. If a few people's standings on the criterion tend to be extreme, but most group members do not possess the trait at all, and absolutely no one outside the group possesses the trait, Allport (1954b) calls this a **rare-zero differential** (see Figure 11.5[C]). For example, some Asian Indian women wear saris in public, and essentially no non-Indian women do so.

The point of examining criteria and distributions is that no single characteristic identifies every last member of a particular group. But even suppose one group is over-represented as geniuses or murderers; few members of the group are geniuses or murderers, but their group has more than other groups do, relative to their numbers. Does that make the group as a whole stereotypically geniuses or murderers?

Although some have argued that stereotypes generally are accurate (Jussim, McCauley, & Lee, 1995; Ottati & Lee, 1995), or at least that some are accurate (Hall & Carter, 1999), others have argued that this viewpoint is premature, pointless, and damaging (Allport, 1954b; Fiske, 1998b; Stangor, 1995). A compromise position holds that stereotypes result from the uneven distribution of group members into particular social roles, which leads people to infer that the behavior—which is role-based—actually characterizes the group's inherent dispositions. For example, stereotypes of men and women depend on their current social context. According to **social role theory**, the group's behavior in its most common social roles causes inferences about the group's enduring dispositions. Applied to men and women, this suggests that men will be stereotyped as agentic, because they are overrepresented in roles that require instrumental activity outside the home; women will be stereotyped as communal because they are overrepresented in roles that require nurturing behavior inside the home (Eagly, 1987; Eagly, Wood, & Diekman, 2000). This social role account suggests that as gender roles change, stereotypes will change. People do think sex differences are diminishing as social roles change, and this particularly holds true for women's roles, perceived to be changing more than men's are (Diekman & Eagly, 2000).

A parallel theory describes the evolution of **enemy images** in international relations (Alexander, Brewer, & Herrmann, 1999; Alexander, Brewer, & Livingston, 2005). Other countries are assessed on three dimensions: relative power, relative status, and degree of cooperation or competition. Varying combinations of these dimensions result in common stereotypes of other nations as allies, enemies, dependents, and barbarians. These images presumably function to justify one's own actions (as a country or as an individual). The content of the social stereotypes derives from the intergroup context in which they form. In that sense, they could be viewed as apparently accurate from the perspective of a particular side of the situation.

## Summary and Conclusion Regarding Functions of Subtle Bias

Subtle forms of bias not only serve cognitive functions of providing a biased understanding while protecting the self from knowledge of that bias but also serve social functions. They allow prejudiced people to (a) discriminate, when they have nonprejudiced excuses for doing so; (b) shape the behavior of others to confirm their own biases; and (c) communicate with each other, reinforcing group cohesion. Also, (d) they allow certain kinds of constrained accuracy, in the context of perceiving social role behavior to reflect intrinsic properties of the roles' occupants.

Is the "American flu" inevitable? Is the acculturated panic button universal? Given all the ramifications of subtle, automatic bias, people immediately wonder how controllable it is. After the initial shock of discovering how prejudiced we can be without even knowing it, most people hope to discover the routes to control, if any. Essentially, responding in an unbiased way requires both **capacity** (cognitive space) and **motivation** (a goal or intention to respond in a particular way). As Chapter 6 indicated, these two requirements appear in studies of individual differences in control over prejudice, situational goals controlling prejudice, and stimulus contexts controlling prejudice.

## BLATANT BIAS: BELONGING WITH THE INGROUP, CONTROLLING OUTGROUP THREATS, AND ENHANCING THE SELF

If subtle forms of bias result primarily from understanding motives, with a little self-enhancement thrown in, the more overt, explicit forms of bias operate somewhat differently: Blatant bias emphasizes belonging and controlling more than the other motives. Belonging surfaces via ingroup identity and status concerns, whereas controlling surfaces via concerns about resources held by the ingroup. In all of this, people strive to feel good about themselves as group members.

### Realistic Group Conflict Theory: Threat to Resources

The most obvious explanation for group prejudices, stereotypes, and discrimination is that group interests conflict, so of course groups harbor biases against each other. **Realistic group conflict theory** holds that threats to ingroup advantage result in negative intergroup reactions. Threats may be economic, political, military, or prestige-related, but the key idea is that they are, in some sense, real (Campbell, 1965). This obvious explanation is dramatically incomplete, however.

Early research on intergroup relations seemed to support the idea. The classic Sherif and Sherif (1953) Robbers Cave study took place in a boys' summer camp (Chapter 1 cited it as evidence for belonging). When researchers arranged for the boys to compete as two separate teams (Eagles versus Rattlers), they each formed ingroup friendships, favored their own group, and were hostile to the other group. When the researchers later forced the two teams to cooperate in their shared common interest, they became more amicable.

Some other research also seemed to fit (for reviews, see Brewer & Brown, 1998; Jackson, 1993). Intergroup competition increases hostility, and intergroup cooperation decreases hostility, not only for children, but also for adolescents (Rabbie &

Horowitz, 1969) and adults (Blake & Mouton, 1961, 1962). White voters living in areas experiencing or about to experience busing (which could be construed as realistic group conflict) show less racial tolerance (Bobo, 1983). Corroborating the field research, some laboratory studies have found that manipulated conflict increases hostility (Worchel, Axsom, Ferris, Samaha, & Schweitzer, 1978). Some of the work testing the frustration-aggression hypothesis (Chapter 10) at a societal level also seemed to fit. When people's own economic outcomes suffer, they turn hostile toward competing groups (Hepworth & West, 1988; Hovland & Sears, 1940).

Despite deserving to be true, realistic group conflict theory receives only limited and uneven support. Many other studies fail to support the core hypothesis and instead find that other variables matter more than sheer group self-interest. For example, links between macroeconomic fate and intergroup hostility prove elusive (Green, Glaser, & Rich, 1998; Green, Strolovitch, & Wong, 1998). Consistent with our earlier account of modern racism, the perceived symbolic threat to one's group matters more than the personal, tangible consequences (Kinder & Sears, 1981; Sears & Kinder, 1985).

What apparently matters most are people's perceptions of group relations: group threat, group identity, and symbolic threats, as we will see. While it is true that subjective perceptions of group threat fit some version of realistic group conflict theory (e.g., Bobo, 1983), then one might as well drop "realistic" from the theory's name and shift toward "perceived group conflict theory." *Perceived* conflict does predict negative attitudes toward the outgroup (Brown, Maras, Masser, Vivian, & Hewstone, 2001; Hennessy & West, 1999). For black South Africans, under competitive and threatening intergroup conditions, degree of ethnic group identification was associated with negative attitudes about nonblacks (Duckitt & Mphuthing, 1998). For white Anglos, perceived conflict with Latinos predicted opposition to bilingual education programs (Huddy & Sears, 1995). Under realistic group threat, Euro-Americans especially resent Asians (Maddux, Galinsky, Cuddy, & Polifroni, 2008).

Competition matters mainly when people identify with their ingroups. More important, ingroup identification by itself can account for intergroup hostility, even without competition (Brewer & Brown, 1998). Not only perceived threats but also another subjective perception, group identity, predicts intergroup responses. For African-Americans, the part of racial identity that includes perceived oppression does predict positive attitudes toward affirmative action, over and above personal benefit (Schmerund, Sellers, & Mueller, 2001). In short, social identity and perceived threat seem more impactful variables than realistic conflict of interest. Social psychologists therefore have energetically pursued investigations of group identity and perceived threats.

## Social Identity, Self-Categorization, and Related Theories: Threat to Group Identity

As we have just seen, groups fight over more than mere material outcomes; they fight over symbolic and identity issues. Intangible outcomes—such as group recognition, status, and prestige—create conflict far more often than do tangible resources. Even when the conflicts appear to concern resources, frequently the real payoffs are pride in one's identity in a valued group able to win such resources. Group conflict is an inherently social competition that goes beyond concrete self-interest. One result of the struggle for positive identity is bias against the outgroup.

This type of explanation contrasts with the flavor of the more purely cognitive explanations launched in the first several sections of this chapter. In this view, bias results from more social processes than just the inevitable cognitive processes, which the first part of this chapter documents. Conflict also emerges as a normal part of intergroup interaction (e.g., Oakes, 2001). People align themselves with a particular social perspective, which results from a fundamental part of their self-definition as a group member. According to social identity and self-categorization theories, as we will see, self-definition in a social context provides certain ingroup perspectives that naturally contrast with the perspectives of outgroup members.

**BASIC THEORIES**    **Social identity theory** (SIT) locates interactions along a continuum from interpersonal (based on individual characteristics) to intergroup (based on salient group memberships) (Tajfel, 1981; Tajfel & Turner, 1979). **Social identity** is the part of one's self-concept that derives from group membership; it includes evaluations of group attributes, as well as prescriptions about ideal group attributes. For example, people from California may view themselves as more informal and fit, whereas people from New York may view themselves as more driven and stylish. Social identity aims to base self-esteem on a positive evaluation of one's group in comparison with other groups. Thus, social identity requires at least one other group for contrast.

The relevant core social motives are belonging and self-enhancing. Social identity theorists argue that categorizing people into "us" and "them"—creating ingroups and outgroups—differentiates social categorization from other types of categorization. Because the self is directly implicated, self-enhancing motives are inherent to social identity theory. In this view, people need a positive social identity. Belonging motives determine the effort to find a positive and distinct group identity.

Categorization of any kind exaggerates differences between groups and minimizes differences within groups. This makes group members seem less variable than they would be as individuals. And, theorists argue, they may actually behave in less variable ways as self-identified group members because of conformity pressures that the next two chapters will discuss.

**Self-categorization theory** (SCT) builds on social identity theory, abandoning the self-esteem hypothesis and focusing on what categories people actually use in a given intergroup setting (Turner, 1985). The self is not fixed but depends on fitting categories salient in a given social context. Self-categorization depends on two kinds of fit. **Comparative fit** specifies that perceivers will compare between-group differences with within-group differences and use those distinctions that best differentiate the groups. This so-called meta-contrast determines the relevant social categories. In this view, self-categorization rests on actual group differences.

**Normative fit** specifies that the direction of the group differences must match the socially shared meaning of the two social categories. The emphasis on recognizing socially defined group differences as important aspects of people's self-concept emerges from the European context of social psychology, some of which has a more sociological and political orientation. It may also matter that Europeans, more than many North Americans, have contact with people of other national identities, many of whom affirm and value their own group membership. Thus, European group identities are more clearly acknowledged as socially accepted group differences. This contrasts with the American melting-pot ideology that traditionally seeks to assimilate all group differences into a single colorblind identity.

Self-categorization theory is less a theory of ethnocentrism and bias than a theory of psychological group membership (Turner & Reynolds, 2001). As such, we see in the next chapter that it illuminates various processes of psychological groups and social influence.

Theories related to SIT and SCT address specific aspects of social identity. For example, the balance between a unique identity and a group identity appears in **optimal distinctiveness theory** (Brewer, 1991). In this view, bias affirms the satisfaction of belonging to the right groups and differentiates the ingroup from outgroups at the optimal level of difference. People balance individual autonomy against group identity, and versions of this occur even in non-Western cultures (Vignoles, Chryssochoou, & Breakwell, 2000). Belonging motives underlie ingroup favoritism, but a need for distinctiveness (self-enhancement) predicts outgroup derogation (Vignoles & Moncaster, 2007).

As another example, **subjective uncertainty reduction theory** (Hogg & Abrams, 1993) proposes that people identify with groups in order to find group norms that reduce uncertainty. Ingroup favoritism results from attraction to a group that allays the tension of uncertainty (the next chapter returns to this phenomenon).

The core theory, SIT, sheds light on some critical processes related to intergroup bias: perceived homogeneity, ingroup favoritism, and group-based self-esteem. As we will see, all serve to reinforce the positive distinctiveness of people's social identity with their ingroup (Brewer, 2007a).

**GROUP HOMOGENEITY**   Categorizing people into a group implies seeing them as similar to each other. SIT suggests that people will accentuate the **homogeneity** within groups and the differences between groups. People often see the outgroup as more homogeneous than the ingroup ("they are all alike; we are more varied"). Although this perception sometimes occurs (Linville, Fischer, & Salovey, 1989; Messick & Mackie, 1989; Mullen & Hu, 1989), the picture is more complicated than intuition suggests. First, group variability might appear in three different components (Ostrom & Sedikides, 1992; Park & Judd, 1990):

- Perceived *stereotypicality* of each group (the degree to which they receive extremely high ratings on stereotypic attributes and extremely low ratings on counterstereotypic attributes)
- Perceived *dispersion* of each group (how much or how little group members seem to vary from others in the same group)
- Perceived *similarity* within each group (whether group members seem to resemble each other)

All three—stereotypicality, dispersion, and similarity—have appeared as higher for outgroup than ingroup, especially in natural settings.

The perceived homogeneity effect is common, although far from universal (Brewer & Brown, 1998; Brown, 2000; Devos, Comby, & Deschamps, 1996). Outgroup homogeneity is stronger for (a) groups that are unfamiliar (Linville et al., 1989), (b) real, as opposed to laboratory groups (Ostrom & Sedikides, 1992), and (c) organized in people's minds at more abstract, superordinate levels, often true for outgroups (Park, Ryan, & Judd, 1992). However, the effect weakens or reverses for (d) numerical minority perceivers (Mullen & Hu, 1989; Simon, 1992) and (e) dimensions important to ingroup identity (Kelly, 1989; Simon, 1992); under those conditions, an *ingroup* homogeneity bias occurs. Overall, when the intergroup context is salient—under group threat or competition—people highly identified with their group see both ingroups and outgroups as more homogeneous (Ellemers, Spears, & Doosje, 1997).

Perceived group homogeneity serves to justify and reify (make real) the designation of a group. Sometimes, the context emphasizes the social reality of the outgroup, as in a dominant group stereotyping a subordinate group. Sometimes, the context emphasizes the social reality of the ingroup, as when a minority pulls together for mutual support along common dimensions of identity. Sometimes, the context emphasizes the social reality of both groups, as when they compete. Social identity theory describes how the intergroup context emphasizes interpersonal (more variable) or intergroup (more homogeneous) perceptions.

**INGROUP FAVORITISM**    Prejudice consists largely in liking "us," more than disliking "them." People tend to think of prejudice against outgroups as the core phenomenon, but SIT suggests—and the data show—instead that prejudice favoring the ingroup is the foundation (Brewer, 1999, 2007b; Hewstone, Rubin, & Willis, 2002; Mullen, Brown & Smith, 1992). A positive social identity suggests benefiting the ingroup because they are part of the self and better than the outgroups (Otten & Wentura, 2001). Of course, ingroup favoritism in a zero-sum competition means depriving the outgroup. Therefore, much intergroup discrimination occurs by neglect rather than deliberate derogation.

Evidence of ingroup favoritism over outgroup derogation takes several forms (Hewstone et al., 2002). We saw earlier that ingroup favoritism occurs automatically, prior to awareness, and that the effect selectively associates positive attributes with the ingroup, rather than negative attributes with the outgroup (Dovidio, Evans, & Tyler, 1986; Gaertner & McLaughlin, 1983; Perdue, Dovidio, Gurtman, & Tyler, 1990). We also saw earlier that aversive and subtle forms of racism consist in the absence of positive feelings and reactions to racial outgroups, more than the presence of virulent negative reactions (Gaertner & Dovidio, 1986; Pettigrew & Meertens, 1995). People benefit the ingroup by giving rewards rather than withholding punishments (Mummendey & Otten, 1998). What's more, patriotism (national pride) does not mean nationalism (national belligerence) (Feshbach, 1994).

Ingroup favoritism is encouraged by several moderators (Hewstone et al., 2002) that all protect positive social identity: Strong ingroup identification (Branscombe &

Wann, 1994; Perreault & Bourhis, 1999) provides the most obvious case for ingroup bias protecting social identity. But minority status (Mullen et al., 1992; Otten et al., 1996) and moderate distinctiveness (Jetten, Spears, & Manstead, 1998) also suggest cases of vulnerable social identity in need of protection. Here, too, ingroup favoritism would bolster a positive identity. In the case of high power or status, which also enhances ingroup favoritism (Brown, 2000; Mullen et al., 1992), people still discriminate when they feel vulnerable (e.g., because their high status is perceived to be unstable, illegitimate, and permeable; Bettencourt, Charlton, Dorr, & Hume, 2001). Perhaps high-status people also discriminate sometimes because they feel entitled (Fiske, 1993, 2010; Richeson & Ambady, 2003; Sachdev & Bourhis, 1987, 1991).

Ingroup favoritism does not depend on personal advantage, nor does it even depend on absolute group advantage. That is, people will favor the ingroup over the outgroup, maximizing the *relative* difference, even at the expense of the ingroup's *absolute* outcome (Rabbie & Horwitz, 1969; Tajfel et al., 1971). The **minimal group paradigm** especially shows this by placing people into arbitrary, temporary groups in the laboratory and giving them points to allocate to ingroup and outgroup members (excluding themselves). SIT receives support from findings that intergroup differentiation (a) occurs only on dimensions that favor the ingroup and (b) increases when people need to differentiate the groups (given conflict, boundary breakdown, ingroup importance) (Hogg, 1995b). When group distinctiveness is under threat, high identifiers in particular will differentiate their group by ingroup favoritism, according to meta-analysis (Jetten, Spears, & Postmes, 2004). Ingroup favoritism can occur even on negative dimensions that help define the group and differentiate it from other groups; according to SCT, fit should matter most (Reynolds, Turner, & Haslam, 2000). Overall, ingroup favoritism is a key result of SIT and SCT.

**SELF-ESTEEM**   SIT makes two predictions about self-esteem and discrimination. As part of the search for a distinct, positive social identity, (a) intergroup differentiation should elevate self-esteem and, conversely, (b) low self-esteem should motivate people to discriminate, in order to raise their self-esteem (Hogg & Abrams, 1990). Regarding the first prediction: When people do show ingroup favoritism, they feel better about themselves afterward, in direct support of SIT (Lemyre & Smith, 1985; Oakes & Turner, 1980; for a review, see Rubin & Hewstone, 1998). Consistent with SIT, the kind of self-esteem that improves is **state self-esteem**, which responds to changes in the person's circumstances. As we noted earlier, SIT posits that identity changes, depending on context, and so would self-esteem. **Trait self-esteem**, which is more stable, does not change as a function of discrimination. It also does not matter whether self-esteem is measured on a personal or collective level, globally or specifically (Rubin & Hewstone, 1998). Higher state self-esteem thus is an outcome of discrimination.

The second prediction, that low self-esteem should motivate discrimination, has not received clear support. Some studies have shown support, but an equal number have failed to find support (Aberson, Healy, & Romero, 2000; Brewer, 2007a; Hewstone et al., 2002; Rubin & Hewstone, 1998). Instead, research needs to focus on temporary reductions in state self-esteem among people highly identified with their group and whether low state self-esteem can cause discrimination in the service of social change that aids group identity (Turner & Reynolds, 2001). What's more, people with *high* self-esteem actually may be those most likely to discriminate, at least in the most direct and self-serving way of discriminating in favor of a group in which they are active participants (Aberson et al., 2000). Although everyone tends to discriminate in favor of the ingroup, people with high self-esteem may feel less constrained about displaying their self-interested behavior.

**SUMMARY**    Partly in reaction to the emphasis of realistic group conflict theory on material, tangible resources as the basis for intergroup conflict, social identity theory and related approaches focus on people's need for a distinct, positive self-definition as a group member and the ensuing impact on intergroup reactions. Perceived group homogeneity follows from categorizing people into groups, and because the self is a member of one of those groups, ingroup favoritism follows. In the short-run, ingroup favoritism increases state self-esteem.

## Authoritarianism: Threat to Values

Yes or no?

- Obedience and respect for authority are the most important virtues children should learn.
- A person who has bad manners, habits, and breeding can hardly expect to get along with decent people.
- People can be divided into two distinct classes: the weak and the strong.
- Human nature being what it is, there will always be war and conflict.
- Homosexuals are hardly better than criminals and ought to be severely punished.

A whole series of "yes" responses to these and similar items would indicate conventionality, submission to authority, toughness, cynicism, and aggression on behalf of those values, according to the theory of **authoritarian personality** (Adorno et al., 1950). A slightly more bizarre set of items was also thought to correlate with this personality syndrome:

- The wild sex life of the Greeks and Romans was tame compared to some of the "goings-on" in this country, even in places where people might least expect it.
- Some day it will probably be shown that astrology can explain a lot of things.
- Most people don't realize how much our lives are controlled by plots hatched in secret places.
- Nowadays more and more people are prying into matters that should remain personal and private.

The authoritarian personality theory proposed a constellation of personality traits, brought about by strict and punitive child-rearing practices. This socialization theoretically resulted in idealizing one's parents and displacing aggressive impulses onto outgroups. The hypothesized result was widespread ethnocentrism.

The ethnocentrism part of the empirical foundation was solid: People prejudiced against one group tend to be prejudiced against other groups, a reliable observation. The authors of the original theory were grounded in the Holocaust, trying to explain Nazi genocide and to understand anti-Semitism elsewhere as well. Yet much of their theoretical background relied on Freudian interpretations of child-rearing and personality, and their assumptions about socialization and personality structure have not been well supported (e.g., Brown, 1965; Duckitt, 1992). Plus, some well-known methodological problems included unrepresentative samples, interviewer bias, failure to control for education or social class, and the focus on authoritarianism of the political right. Moreover, the scale failed to word some items in reverse, so that an acquiescence response bias (agreeability; see Chapter 2) would tend to be confounded with agreeing to items indicating authoritarianism (Hyman & Sheatsley, 1954). These critiques of both method and theory undermined the credibility of the scale.

However, some relationship between authoritarianism and prejudice remains. A modern version of this insight, the **Right-Wing Authoritarianism (RWA) Scale** (Altemeyer, 1981, 1988) proves to be more viable. This version of the scale focuses on three themes: conventionality (conformity to traditional values), authoritarian submission (obeying powerful leaders), and authoritarian aggression (inflicting harm on those who deviate from conventional beliefs, especially when harming is sanctioned by one's leaders). RWA consistently correlates with prejudice against a variety of outgroups (e.g., Duckitt, 1993; Meloen, Van der Linden, & De Witte, 1996). But why do these responses tend to correlate?

Intense but insecure identification with the ingroup may underlie all four aspects of RWA (conventionality, submission, aggression, prejudice) (Duckitt, 1989, 1992). Valuing the ingroup and perceiving it as threatened combine to demand cohesion for the ingroup and therefore conventional conformity to norms, obedient submission to authorities, and aggressive intolerance of deviance. RWA's underlying psychology rests on perceiving the world as a dangerous place, which arouses fear and hostility, as well as moral superiority, based on authority sanctions, which justifies aggression against perceived threats, namely outgroups. People high on RWA endorse harsh, punitive policies on a variety of social problems: AIDS, abortion, child abuse, drugs, homelessness, trade deficits, as well as the purpose of higher education (Peterson, Doty, & Winter, 1993), although they do not have much knowledge about these issues (Peterson, Duncan, & Pang, 2002). They also deny the reality of the Holocaust (Yelland & Stone, 1996). And they dislike feminists (Haddock & Zanna, 1994) and homosexuals (Haddock, Zanna, & Esses, 1993). All these RWA responses indicate a refusal to negotiate constructively with perceived threat to cherished conventional values, which is then one important predictor of prejudice.

A related perspective relies not on individual differences in personality but on situational factors. **Terror management theory** focuses on perceived threat not to the group but to the continuity of the self, as when people confront their own mortality (see Chapter 9 with regard to mortality salience and prosocial behavior, as well as Chapter 10 with regard to mortality salience and aggression). However, in contrast to RWA, mortality salience depends on context, not personality (Pyszczynski, Greenberg, & Solomon, 1997; 1999; Solomon, Greenberg, & Pyszczynski, 2000). The main idea is that people instinctively desire continued life and that death-related thoughts are threatening. People avoid death-related thoughts by trying to suppress them when they are conscious. When death-related thoughts are unconscious, people try to maintain self-esteem (see Chapter 5) and to defend their cultural worldview, including cherished values that will live beyond their own lifetimes.

Most relevant here are findings that when mortality is salient, people respond especially harshly to those who violate or criticize accepted values and those who are from outgroups (Greenberg et al., 1990; McGregor, Zanna, Holmes, & Spencer, 2001; Rosenblatt, Greenberg, Solomon, Pyszczynski, & Lyon, 1989; Schimel et al., 1999). Some of these findings hold especially for people high on authoritarianism, when it is measured. The link between reactions to mortality salience and authoritarianism makes sense: Authoritarianism, like mortality salience, sees the world as threatening and dangerous and sees conformity to cherished values as the first line of defense. Context determines how values are enacted; for example, liberals, when tolerance is salient, become more tolerant under mortality salience (Greenberg, Simon, Pyszczynski, Solomon, & Chatel, 1992). Similarly, authoritarians express prejudice as a function of their currently salient self-categorized social identity (Reynolds, Turner, Haslam, & Ryan, 2001). But all these variations on authoritarian responses depend on perceived threat to cherished values.

More generally, meta-analysis across cultures finds relationships between political conservatism and variables related to awareness and acknowledgement of threat: concern about threat, awareness of death, concern about system instability, avoidance of ambiguity, and motivation for order. Liberalism correlates with seeking experience, tolerating uncertainty, and integrating complexity (Jost, Glaser, Kruglanski, & Sulloway, 2003). Consistent with liberals' responsiveness to novelty, ambiguity, and complexity, they show greater activity in the brain's conflict-related anterior cingulate cortex; conservatives' more structured and persistent style makes them less responsive in this discrepancy-monitoring area (Amodio, Jost, Master, & Yee, 2007).

## Social Dominance Orientation: Threat to Group Status

Another personality variable related to prejudice is **social dominance orientation** (SDO) (Pratto, Sidanius, Stallworth, & Malle, 1994; Sidanius & Pratto, 1999), the degree to which one endorses a hierarchy in which some groups dominate other groups. SDO differs from authoritarianism and interpersonal dominance, but like them it does predict prejudice. People high on SDO support policies that maintain inequality (for example, opposing affirmative action; Sidanius, Pratto, & Bobo, 1996), and they choose careers that enhance existing hierarchies. For example, they are more likely to go into business, police work, or public prosecution (enhancing current hierarchies), rather than teaching, social work, or public defense (attenuating current hierarchies). High SDO people do well in hierarchy-enhancing roles: for example, students majoring in business and economics. Low SDO people excel in hierarchy-attenuating roles: for example, students majoring in anthropology, ethnic studies, sociology, social work, or nursing (Pratto, Stallworth, Sidanius, & Siers, 1997; van Laar, Sidanius, Rabinowitz, & Sinclair, 1999).

Men are more likely than women to be high on SDO, and it correlates with being tough-minded and viewing the world as a competitive place (Sidanius, Pratto, & Bobo, 1994). High SDO favors the powerful. For high-status groups, high SDO exaggerates ingroup favoritism. And even for low-status groups, if they view the hierarchy as legitimate, high SDO also predicts favoring the high-status groups (Levin, Federico, Sidanius, & Rabinowitz, 2002). According to both lab and field studies, having a high-status position leads to SDO, which in turn causes prejudice (Guimond, Dambrun, Michinov, & Duarte, 2003).

How does SDO relate to RWA? Although both relate to an inflexible defense of some group interests over others, their psychology differs. One way to understand the relationship between various individual differences and prejudice is according to the kind of threat posed to the ingroup. Authoritarianism focuses on perceived threat to ingroup values in a dangerous world, whereas social dominance orientation focuses on perceived threat to ingroup status in a competitive world (Duckitt, 2001; see Figure 11.6). In this **dual-process theory of ideology and prejudice**, one path goes from punitive socialization, to social conformity, to viewing the world as dangerous, to RWA, and thence to ingroup favoritism and outgroup prejudice. The other path goes from unaffectionate socialization, to tough-mindedness, to viewing the world

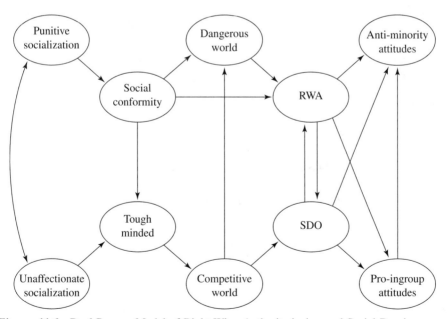

**Figure 11.6**    Dual-Process Model of Right-Wing Authoritarianism and Social Dominance Orientation

*Source:* From Duckitt, 2001. Copyright © Elsevier. Adapted with permission.

as competitive, to SDO, and thence to ingroup favoritism and outgroup prejudice. The links among socialization, personality, world view, and ideology receive strong research support in the United States, Europe, South Africa, and New Zealand (Duckitt, 2001). Different kinds of blatant prejudice result from different kinds of motivational dynamics.

## System Justification: Threats to the Status Quo

Blatant forms of bias operate to justify the current system of inequality. Several theories make related arguments. Among the first to make this argument in social psychology, Jost and Banaji (1994; Jost, Banaji, & Nosek, 2004; Jost, Burgess, & Mosso, 2001) proposed that stereotypes operate in the service of **system justification**, the psychology of legitimizing current social arrangements, even at personal and group cost. For high-status groups, supporting the self (ego justification), the group (group justification), and the system all are compatible processes. But for low-status groups, system justification operates at the expense of the other two. So, for example, women may buy into benevolent sexism as an ideology because it legitimates the stability of current arrangements between men and women (Glick & Fiske, 2001b); sexist women receive some benefits from believing that women are pure and need to be protected and cherished by men, in return for women being submissive. Women are prized for being nice, while men are prized for being competent, in this view. More generally, society's **status beliefs** (Ridgeway, 2001) are ways of understanding and organizing cooperation across unequal groups, such as traditional gender roles or black-white relations in the Old South. The **legitimating myths** of SDO (Sidanius, Levin, Federico, & Pratto, 2001) are ideologies that intellectually and morally justify the superiority of high-status groups in the existing social structure. For example, beliefs in the genetic superiority of whites or men or heterosexuals would be a legitimating myth; pseudoscience has often been used to justify the status quo.

## Summary of Blatant Bias

Blatant, overt forms of bias sometimes result from direct conflict over tangible resources, as suggested by realistic group conflict theory, but not as often as people suppose. More often, bias against outgroups results from favoring the ingroup, but seeing it as threatened in less tangible ways. Social identity theory, self-categorization theory, and optimal distinctiveness theory all address people's attempts to establish and maintain a positive and distinct social identity. This tends to result in seeing group members as relatively homogeneous, typically favoring the ingroup, and boosting state self-esteem. Individual differences in authoritarianism, viewing the world as a dangerous place where ingroup values are under threat, operate in parallel with social dominance orientation, viewing the world as a competitive hierarchy where the ingroup's status is under threat. Both sets of beliefs work to justify the existing social arrangements, with some groups on top and others subordinate. In all these theories, people's core social motives appear in people's need to belong to a group (identity); to control resources, status, and values (threats); and to enhance themselves (feeling good as a group member).

# EFFECTS OF BIAS ON TARGETS: BELONGING, CONTROLLING, AND SELF-ENHANCING

At first glance, Anglo whites often assume that members of racial and ethnic minorities in the United States must suffer from low self-esteem. Quite the contrary is true; blacks, for example, have self-esteem higher than whites (Crocker, Major, & Steele, 1998), at least in recent years (Twenge & Crocker, 2002). People from most groups subject to stereotyping, prejudice, and discrimination can still feel good about themselves and their groups, precisely as social identity theory would argue. In doing so, they face the challenge of affirming their identity as belonging to a group devalued by society. **Stigma** (devaluation due to a marked identity) adheres to their group and to themselves as a member of it. Nevertheless, a positive social identity buffers the effects of stigma. The processes are various and not simple, involving specific identity issues, stereotype threat, and attributional ambiguity, as we shall see.

## Collective Identity and Well-being

A person's **collective self-esteem** (CSE) (Crocker & Luhtanen, 1990; Luhtanen & Crocker, 1992) is the value one places on one's social groups, as a function of social identity, or perceived memberships in various social groups, including, for example, race, ethnicity, gender, age, weight, college, geographic region, and so on. As Table 11.6 indicates, CSE has four components. Two elements of CSE—(a) feelings about one's worth as a group member and (b) one's personal, private regard for one's group—predict psychological well-being (i.e., depression, life satisfaction,

**Table 11.6**  Collective Self-Esteem Scale

---

*Subscale* and Sample Items

---

*Membership*

　I am a worthy member of the social groups I belong to.

　I am a cooperative participant in the social groups I belong to.

*Private*

　In general, I'm glad to be a member of the social groups I belong to.

　I feel good about the social groups I belong to.

*Public*

　Overall, my social groups are considered good by others.

　In general, others respect the social groups that I am a member of.

*Identity*

　The social groups I belong to are an important reflection of who I am.

　In general, belonging to social groups is an important part of my self-image.

---

*Source:* From Luhtanen & Crocker, 1992. Copyright © Sage. Adapted with permission.

hopelessness), even controlling for personal self-esteem. Another component, (c) public regard for one's group, does not correlate with private regard for one's group among blacks, but the correlation is high among Asians (with whites in the middle; Crocker, Luhtanen, Blaine, & Broadnax, 1994). A fourth component, (d) strength of identity, does not relate directly to well-being.

The collective self-esteem of people from stigmatized groups depends on the situation, on which identity is salient, and on which social representation of that identity is salient (Crocker, 1999). In this view, self-worth is constructed, depending on the social context. Various dimensions of social identity vary with the situation. For African-Americans, for example, the centrality (importance) of their own racial group identity increases when race is salient (e.g., the participant is the only racial ingroup member among others watching a video of black-on-white violence) (Shelton & Sellers, 2000). Momentary salience of racial identity is an important component, according to the multidimensional model of racial identity (Sellers, Smith, Shelton, Rowley, & Chavous, 1998).

Many aspects of collective identity function as relatively stable individual differences. For example, the **Multidimensional Inventory of Black Identity** (MIBI) (Sellers, Rowley, Chavous, Shelton, & Smith, 1997) suggests that identity consists of centrality (sense of belonging), ideology (from assimilationist, to humanist, to oppressed, to nationalist), and private regard (own esteem for blacks and self as black). Individual differences on the MIBI predict frequency of interracial interactions and choosing black studies courses. Some individuals' identity configurations are notable—those for whom race is central to identity, ideology is (black) nationalist, and beliefs maintain that other groups have negative attitudes toward blacks. This identity configuration predicts experiences of discrimination but also buffers against their mental health consequences, such as depression, anxiety, and stress. Otherwise, people are bothered by experiences of discrimination, even at the level of micro-aggressions (hassles such as being followed around a store or being overlooked for service) (Sellers & Shelton, 2003).

The dilemma of belonging to a stigmatized group is real. Race- and ethnicity-based stressors can undermine physical and mental health (Allison, 1998; Clark, Anderson, Clark, & Williams, 1999; Contrada et al., 2000). Gender discrimination also undermines women's psychological well-being (Swim, Hyers, Cohen, & Ferguson, 2001). Nevertheless, stigmatized group members are not passive targets of discrimination; instead, they cope actively (Heatherton, Kleck, Hebl, & Hull, 2000; Swim & Stangor, 1998). When blacks interact with whites whom they expect to be prejudiced, they can counteract prejudice, making both people enjoy the interaction more, though the black participant may feel less true to self (Shelton, 2003).

Problems of racial bias require researchers to examine all sides of the interaction (Shelton, 2000). Ingroup dynamics, as well as outgroup dynamics, matter to intergroup encounters (Prentice & Miller, 2002). For example, ethnic identity makes people more aware of discrimination, especially when it is subtle or ambiguous (Operario & Fiske, 2001b; Shelton & Sellers, 2000). Perceiving discrimination cuts both ways: It adds stress, but it also allows coping.

As one negative example, exaggerated **stigma consciousness** (vigilance when interacting with outgroup members) can make one forego opportunities to invalidate stereotypes or even create a negative loop of expecting prejudice, reacting negatively, and eliciting negative behavior (Pinel, 1999; 2002). Even a momentary, role-played stigma can create a paranoid stance (Santuzzi & Ruscher, 2002). Nevertheless, being an oblivious victim is hardly healthy. For example, women believe it's best to respond to sexist jokes, though only a few do respond because of the social costs (Swim & Hyers, 1999). Women do not report sexual harassment nearly as often as people think they do; indeed, the most common response is to avoid the perpetrator (Fitzgerald, Swan, & Fischer, 1995). Perceiving prejudice has both costs and benefits, and people's degree of vigilance and overt responding depends on those factors (Barrett & Swim, 1998).

## Attributional Ambiguity

All negative life events cause people to appraise the degree of threat, which then motivates coping. One of the ways that people can cope with bad outcomes, if they have a stigmatized identity, is by attributing them to the other person's prejudice (Major, Quinton, & McCoy, 2002). When individuals from stigmatized groups have a negative encounter, they could attribute its cause either to something about themselves personally or to prejudice against their group membership; that dilemma is termed **attributional ambiguity** (Crocker & Major, 1989). In one study, women received negative feedback from a male evaluator whom they knew to be either prejudiced or not. When he was prejudiced, they attributed his feedback to that prejudice and reported feeling less depressed than women evaluated by an unprejudiced man. In a related study, black students received either negative or positive feedback from a white evaluator who could see them (and therefore their race) or not. Attributions to prejudice protected their self-esteem from the negative feedback but injured their self-esteem after positive feedback because they could not take credit for their own success (Crocker, Voelkl, Testa, & Major, 1991). According to correlational studies, people who consistently attribute their negative outcomes to discrimination have lower self-esteem than those who do not (Major, Quinton, & McCoy, 2002). Experimental studies show that when clues to prejudice are clear, attributions to it do enhance self-esteem. Perhaps in real life circumstances, clues to prejudice are most often ambiguous, and a negative outlook explains both perceived discrimination and low self-esteem.

People differ in the extent to which they use attributions to prejudice. For example, consider black conservatives such as Supreme Court Justice Clarence Thomas, who minimizes the role of prejudice in the lives of black Americans. People who believe in the ideology of individual opportunity are less likely to attribute any bad outcomes to discrimination (or any good ones to affirmative action) (Major, Gramzow, McCoy, Levin, Schmader, & Sidanius, 2002). Stigmatized groups also differ. For example, women who feel overweight blame negative evaluations on their weight, not on the evaluator's prejudice, and their self-esteem suffers (Crocker, Cornwell, &

Major, 1993). This is especially true if they subscribe to the Protestant ethic notion that their weight is due to moral failings of self-indulgence and laziness (Quinn & Crocker, 1999). But otherwise, when people from most stigmatized groups blame negative outcomes on prejudice, it buffers them against taking it personally.

Of course, one cannot take credit for positive feedback, if one attributes it to prejudice of the overcompensating, positivity bias sort. Affirmative action can cause this kind of dilemma if people think they were hired only because of their membership in a protected category. When women think they were picked solely on the basis of gender, they attribute their own outcome as less due to merit and see it as less important (Major, Feinstein, & Crocker, 1994).

By law, affirmative action requires that people meet a certain merit standard and then adds gender (or race) as an additional criterion (e.g., Plous, 1996). This framing tends to make affirmative action seem more reasonable to people: All else equal, pick the person from the underrepresented group, because diversity is important for the institution's effective functioning. (For more on the social psychology of affirmative action, see Skedsvold & Mann, 1996; Turner & Pratkanis, 1994.)

Two other mechanisms protect the stigmatized (Crocker & Major, 1989). One involves selective ingroup comparisons: comparing one's own outcomes with those of other ingroup members, thereby ignoring the outgroup (especially effective when they are doing better). People whose outcomes compare unfavorably with outgroup members (e.g., the dominant group) are unaffected emotionally, presumably because the advantaged outgroupers are seen as irrelevant. But people whose outcomes compare unfavorably with ingroup members feel depressed and attribute less ability to themselves (Major, Sciacchitano, & Crocker, 1993).

Another protective mechanism involves devaluing domains of disadvantage for one's own group and valuing domains that advantage one's group (Schmader & Major, 1999). People apparently do this when they view group status differences as legitimate and the other group ranks lower than theirs (Schmader, Major, Eccleston, & McCoy, 2001). This is presumably the case in which it is easiest to justify devaluing the domain. However, the devaluation hypothesis is most related to its cousin, recent research on stereotype threat.

## Stereotype Threat

Stereotypes impute a variety of ability differences to a variety of groups. Members of groups described as low ability face a predicament in any relevant achievement setting. If they fail, their failure reflects not only on themselves but also on their group, confirming the worst stereotypes about it. This predicament—called **stereotype threat** (Steele, 1997; Steele, Spencer, & Aronson, 2002)—actually lowers performance when group membership is salient in the testing situation, presumably because the threat directly interferes with the performance of stigmatized group members. Over time, stereotype threat may cause affected individuals to disidentify with the domain, that is, to dismiss it as unimportant and direct their energies elsewhere. In one study, for example, black students were unaffected by (bogus) failure on an intelligence test, due to both chronic and short-term disengagement of self-esteem from being contingent on that domain (Major, Spencer, Schmader, Wolfe, & Crocker, 1998).

The classic stereotype threat studies show the stigmatized group underperforming only when their group membership is made salient, for example, by requiring them to list their race at the beginning of a test or by telling them that the test is diagnostic of ability (the normal conditions for standardized tests). When these conditions are removed, the stigmatized group performs as well as the control group. Stereotype threat occurs for everyone under relevant circumstances: blacks on intellectual tests, Latinos and women on math tests, men on emotional sensitivity tests, whites on athletic performance, and people of lower socioeconomic status on intellectual ability tests (Croizet & Claire, 1998; Gonzales, Blanton, & Williams, 2002; Leyens, Désert, Croizet, & Darcis, 2000; Spencer, Steele, & Quinn, 1999; Steele & Aronson, 1995; Stone, Lynch, Sjomeling, & Darley, 1999). Members of any group can suffer stereotype threat, even if they are normally stereotyped as adept. Thus, under stereotype threat, white men outperform white women, but the white men underperform when tested alongside Asian men (Aronson et al., 1999). Similarly, Asian women underperform when their gender is salient but outperform when their ethnicity is salient (Shih, Pittinsky, & Ambady, 1999), and children as young as kindergarten show these effects (Ambady, Shih, & Pittinsky, 2001). Stereotype threat occurs outside the laboratory in thousands of college students (Massey & Fischer, 2006). The effects of stereotype threat are not trivial, even presenting a health risk. For blacks under stereotype threat, blood pressure reliably increases (Blascovich, Spencer, Quinn, & Steele, 2001), suggesting a stress response that, if chronic, could contribute to hypertension. And, of course, ability tests have widespread significance in people's lives.

The mechanisms, however, remain a mystery. Why should stereotype threat cause people to underperform when the evidence indicates stereotype-threatened people are trying even harder, not simply failing because it is expected (Steele et al., 2002)? Stereotype threat is not the self-fulfilling prophecy, described earlier, in which someone encounters a prejudiced person and subtle pressures to conform to a negative stereotype. Instead, the person must only be a member of a group stigmatized with regard to the particular achievement domain, care about the domain, and attempt to perform well but be undermined by the threat in the air. Attempts to uncover mediation of stereotype threat so far prove inconclusive, although some hints emerge. Probably, both motivation and cognition are involved (Steele et al., 2002; Wheeler & Petty, 2001). Some evidence, but not all, suggests anxiety. Some evidence, but not all, suggests stereotype activation. Some evidence, but not all, suggests lower expectations for performance (Kray, Galinsky, & Thompson, 2002; Stangor, Carr, & Kiang, 1998; but see Steele et al., 2002). Some suggestive evidence proposes that efforts to suppress the stereotype may have the ironic effect of keeping it activated and so interfering with performance (Steele et al., 2002). None of the most obvious contenders are supported unequivocally, but some combination of vigilance and stress seems likely.

Remedies for stereotype threat occur at the level of affected individuals, contexts, and institutions (Steele et al., 2002). For individuals, an understanding that intelligence is not a fixed entity, but malleable, may undermine stereotype threat. Just as entity theorists stereotype other people more (Plaks, Stroessner, Dweck, & Sherman, 2001), so they themselves may be more vulnerable to stereotype threat (Aronson, Fried, & Good, 2002). Individuals could also try to identify less with their own group (Schmader, 2002), but such a strategy is unlikely to have wide appeal. On the other hand, realizing that race is a social construction, as multiracial people do, can buffer against stereotype threat (Shih, Bonam, Sanchez, & Peck, 2007).

At the level of immediate context, presenting a test as insensitive to group differences or as fair to all groups can prevent stereotype threat. Similarly, presenting the setting's actual diversity or commitment to diverse groups can increase comfort and trust, which avert stereotype threat (Steele et al., 2002). Also, a temporary psychological disengagement from the immediate situation can bolster persistence and performance (Nussbaum & Steele, 2007).

At the level of longer-term institutional factors, mentors can advocate both high standards and the student's ability to meet them, thereby motivating trust and effort (Cohen, Steele, & Ross, 1999). Interventions that mitigate doubts about the minority belonging in the college can raise academic achievement (Walton & Cohen, 2007). The institution can also encourage opportunities for cross-race friendships, which the next section will show can prove helpful to all concerned.

### Summary of Target Responses to Bias

Belonging, controlling, and self-enhancing each motivate bias's effects on members of stigmatized groups. Collective self-esteem is the value one places on one's collective identity, belonging to a social group. Collective identity can make people more aware of subtle forms of prejudice but can also buffer them against its ill effects, protecting their well-being and enhancing the self. People's particular collective identity depends both on momentary situational factors and on stable individual differences. People's degree of vigilance depends on the costs and benefits of perceiving discrimination, including their ability to control it or not.

Attributional ambiguity, interpreting one's outcomes as due to prejudice or personal factors, presents a dilemma for targets of prejudice. Attributing outcomes to prejudice can enhance the self in the case of negative outcomes but deprive the self of credit for positive outcomes. People and groups differ in the extent to which they use this strategy, and the extent to which it works when they do.

Stereotype threat describes people's response to a threat in the air, in performance situations, when failure not only could be personal but also could confirm stereotypes about one's group. People deal with this predicament by increased vigilance, which ironically undermines their performance. However, understanding the malleability of intelligence, perceiving a test as unbiased, and trusting the setting all can contribute to averting stereotype threat.

### STRATEGIES FOR CHANGE: CONSTRUCTIVE INTERGROUP CONTACT CAN CONTROL BIAS

Friendship cures more than stereotype threat. **Intergroup contact**—that is, interactions between individual members of socially distinct groups—has proved tried and true, but only under specific circumstances. Gordon Allport (1954b) formalized the conditions of constructive intergroup contact:

- Equal status of the groups within the context
- Common goals

- Cooperation, or at least no competition
- Authority sanction for the contact

These conditions make complete sense, but they are not easy to meet; we are still learning what works (Paluck & Green, 2009).

In one well-known application, children in integrated classrooms are made to be fully interdependent (combining common goals and cooperation): In small groups, they need each other because each is responsible for teaching the others part of the day's lesson. This resulting **jigsaw classroom** (Aronson, 1990; Aronson & Bridgeman, 1979; Aronson & Osherow, 1980) improves their liking for each other across group lines and improves self-esteem, morale, and the academic performance of minorities, without undermining the performance of majority students.

Generally, if the groups do perceive that they are coming together as equal partners, on common ground, that they need each other, and that those in power want them to get along, contact works well to reduce prejudice. In a meta-analysis of 376 studies and more than 156,000 participants, Pettigrew and Tropp (2006) found clear support for the beneficial effects of intergroup contact and for the importance of meeting as many of the constructive conditions as possible. The listed conditions are not necessary, but instead each facilitates people's overcoming their hostility and discomfort.

Causal direction matters here: Do prejudiced people shun contact, and tolerant people seek it, so of course contact correlates with tolerance? Or does intergroup contact itself lower people's prejudice? No doubt both could be true, but the contact hypothesis needs to show the latter in isolation from the former. And, indeed, the more rigorously the study tests contact actually causing tolerance, the stronger the effect (experiments' effects are stronger than correlational studies). The more the study removes reverse causality, by allowing participants no choice about the contact, the stronger the effect. Nevertheless, both randomly assigned and voluntary contact generally reduces prejudice (van Laar, Levin, Sinclair, & Sidanius, 2005).

Emotional prejudices show bigger improvement as a result of contact than stereotypic beliefs do. As in other research on bias, emotions drive the process more than cognitions do (Dovidio et al., 1996; Talaska, Fiske, & Chaiken, 2009; Tropp & Pettigrew, 2005). People feel anxious and threatened in intergroup encounters, as attested both by self-reports (Stephan & Stephan, 2000) and by physiological indicators such as cardiovascular reactivity (Blascovich, Mendes, Hunter, Lickel, & Kowai-Bell, 2001). The emotional strain has consequences for people's ability to self-regulate during and after such encounters: Neuroimaging and cognitive performance both show that interracial contact depletes executive function, for minority and majority alike (Richeson et al., 2003; Richeson, & Shelton, 2003; Richeson, & Trawalter, 2005; Richeson, Trawalter, & Shelton, 2005). Overcoming automatic reactions—a necessary feature of constructive contact—requires executive function (Payne, 2005).

Much of the contact effect lies in the opportunity for intergroup friendships (Pettigrew, 1997, 1998a). The effects are the best for outgroups that present the best opportunity for friendship and the least opportunity for threat once comfort is established (Pettigrew & Tropp, 2006). For example, intergroup contact with homosexuals shows the most improvement; contact with ethnic and racial minorities shows average effects; and contact with physically and mentally disabled people shows the least. In contact settings that provide the most opportunity for friendship—such as workplaces over the long-term—effects are stronger than in short-term recreational or travel contact. What's more, even just knowing about other ingroup members' friendships with outgroup members can improve intergroup attitudes (Wright, Aron, McLaughlin-Volpe, & Ropp, 1997).

Moreover, contact's beneficial effects generalize to other members of the outgroup and to other outgroups (Pettigrew & Tropp, 2006). Contact diversifies people's friendships, which in turn generalizes to more positive feelings about a variety of outgroups (Pettigrew, 1997). Multicultural and multiracial friendships represent the intersection of interpersonal and intergroup relations (Gaines & Liu, 2000).

How does contact work? When people are interdependent, when they need each other to complete a joint task for a shared reward, they go to more trouble to learn about each other (Erber & Fiske, 1984; Fiske, 2000a; Neuberg & Fiske, 1987; Ruscher & Fiske, 1990). They selectively attend to the most diagnostic cues: information that disputes their stereotypes about the other person's group. They then use this counter-stereotypic information to make personalized dispositional inferences about the other person. As a result, they form more idiosyncratic, individuating impressions (based less on the other person's category membership and relatively more on their own interpretations of the other person's characteristics). All of this undercuts stereotypes and allows the possibility of individual friendship.

In intergroup contact, people do not necessarily ignore each other's group membership; indeed, if people remember each other's categories while getting to know them, they may be honoring that person's social identity. For example, immigrants may value their culture of origin as well as the culture of their host country (Berry, 2001). Thus, for the positive effects of intergroup contact to generalize beyond the immediate groups of people directly in contact, **mutual differentiation** may be important for two reasons. People need to retain some awareness of each other's social identity in the contact situation. Also, group members need to seem typical, in the sense of being representative of their group (Brown, 2000; Brown, Vivian, & Hewstone, 1999; Greenland & Brown, 1999; Hewstone & Brown, 1986; Hewstone, Rubin, & Willis, 2002).

This social identity perspective contrasts with various alternative ideas about optimal outcomes of intergroup contact. One perspective argues that people should **decategorize** altogether, minimizing their prior social categories (Brewer & Miller, 1986), but another perspective argues that people should **recategorize**, using a **common ingroup identity**, a new more-inclusive group that supercedes prior separate group memberships (Dovidio, Kawakami, & Gaertner, 2000). When groups are temporary, decategorization works well. But the common ingroup identity also works well, mediating changes for both temporary and longer-term groups (Dovidio, Gaertner, & Validzic, 1998; Dovidio, Gaertner, Validzic, Matoka, Johnson, & Frazier, 1997; Terry, Carey, & Callan, 2001). In the end, "we're different groups, but all on the same team," seems to be the key (Dovidio et al., 2000; Gaertner & Dovidio, 2000). A variant, the **cross-categorization** approach (Brewer, 2000; Marcus-Newhall, Miller, Holtz, & Brewer, 1993), maintains at least two separate but cross-cutting category systems (such as occupation and ethnicity, or gender and team), in which people represent all combinations. People who are outgroup on one dimension but ingroup on another fare better than people who are double outgroup members, though not as well as double ingroup members (Migdal, Hewstone, & Mullen, 1998; Mullen, Migdal, & Hewstone, 2001; Urban & Miller, 1998). Evidence supports a balance between maintaining one's various identities and finding identities in common with other individuals, under as many as possible of Allport's main criteria for constructive contact (Park & Judd, 2005).

Ultimately, contact works well when people are not merely tolerant of each other but enthusiastic about meeting people who differ from them on some dimensions. Approaching the outgroup member, rather than merely not avoiding, improves contact experiences (Kawakami, Phills, Steele, & Dovidio, 2007). Outgroup orientation includes liking to meet, get to know, and spend time with people from other ethnic groups (Wittig & Molina, 2000)—and it mediates the positive effects of intergroup climate on prejudice reduction.

## CHAPTER SUMMARY

Biases operate against both group members and individuals who are stigmatized. Such category-based responses to outgroups include emotional prejudices, cognitive stereotypes, and discriminatory behaviors. Discrimination ranges from verbal hostility and avoidance all the way to segregation, physical attack, and group extermination. Operationally, social psychologists study explicit, overt forms of bias on self-report questionnaires and blatant forms of aggression. The implicit, subtle forms of bias appear in millisecond stereotypic and prejudicial associations, as well as in nonverbal behavior, both of which are less controllable than verbal and other overt behaviors.

Various core social motives operate to sustain bias. Most important is belonging to one's own group, at the expense of the outgroup. Biases then further our efficient shared social understandings of those outgroups. Controlling the perceived unpredictability of the outgroup and controlling perceived threats to the ingroup both contribute to biases. Enhancing the self as having a positive, distinct ingroup identity also enters into the motivational mix.

Subtle forms of bias build understandings that protect the self. Whites' racial attitudes have changed over the century, but mostly in overt ways that protect the self-image as egalitarian. In more subtle ways, such as nonverbal behavior, bias persists. The new, implicit forms of bias include the cool and indirect forms reflected in modern racism and subtle prejudice scales that show patterns of policy preferences that all blame the outgroup, oppose support for minorities, exaggerate intergroup differences, and make ingroup-serving attributions. Automatic forms of bias appear in responses to subliminal intergroup cues and millisecond priming, all automatic associations that advantage the ingroup, match the stereotype, reinforce categorization, and disadvantage outgroups. The subtle forms of bias—besides being cool, indirect, automatic—also are ambiguous, providing excuses for discriminatory behavior by people who find the thought of their own racism to be aversive. Subtle bias is also ambivalent, with prime examples being racism and sexism, which include subjectively benevolent paternalistic responses as well as the more obvious hostile ones. Many outgroups are pitied (liked but disrespected) or envied (respected but disliked).

Subtle forms of bias are socially useful, facilitating both ingroup belonging and control over perceived threats. Automatic forms of subtle bias produce deniable discrimination in the unconscious nonverbal priming of stereotype-consistent behavior (e.g., walking more slowly after being primed with elderly stereotypes). Self-fulfilling prophecies elicit from targets the very behavior that confirms stereotypes, again operating largely via nonverbal cues and, ironically, smoothing the intergroup interactions. Ingroup communication about outgroup stereotypes helps to build ingroup cohesion, as people trade stories about *us* versus *them*, using easily communicated ideas and linguistic biases that make the outgroup's negative behaviors seem especially diagnostic of stable traits. People use the same term in different ways, depending on the group ("good parent" for a man implies different standards than "good parent" for a woman). Such issues complicate the question of how accurate stereotypes may or may not be. Some challenges to this line of work would include picking fair and unbiased criteria, dimensions, observers, cut-offs, and distributions. All this has to take account of the unequal distribution of social roles, whereby groups overrepresented in particular roles (housewife, welfare recipient, enemy) are attributed traits consistent with those roles. Subtle bias is controllable to the extent that people have the motivation and capacity to understand outgroups differently.

Blatant forms of bias focus even more on cementing ingroup belonging in the face of perceived outgroup threat, thereby enhancing the self. Realistic group conflict theory addresses actual conflicts over resources, although these matter less than perceived conflict and symbolic resources. Social identity theory and related efforts focus on the psychology of belonging to a group, in contrast with acting as an individual. People seek positive, distinct social identities, and they minimize within-group differences, while maximizing between-group differences, in direct comparisons and normative interpretations. Self-categorization, optimal distinctiveness, and uncertainty reduction all are served by ingroup belonging and favoritism, to the exclusion of the outgroup. State self-esteem is served by differentiating between ingroup and outgroup.

In addition to variations in social identity, other important personality differences are authoritarianism and social dominance orientation. Authoritarianism, in its revised form, right-wing authoritarianism, emerges from punitive socialization, which encourages social conformity, in the face of a world perceived to be dangerous; the resulting RWA endorses authoritarian submission to the powerful and aggression on their behalf, favors the threatened ingroup and harbors prejudice toward the dangerous outgroups. In parallel, social dominance orientation emerges from unaffectionate socialization, which encourages tough-mindedness, in the face of a world perceived to be relentlessly competitive; the resulting SDO endorses social hierarchy, ingroup favoritism, and outgroup prejudice. Both RWA and SDO result in some of the most virulent forms of blatant prejudice.

Both subtle and blatant biases affect their stigmatized targets, but not in the most obvious ways. Collective self-esteem can buffer individuals from the consequences of bias, depending on identity salience in the situation. Individual differences in racial identity's centrality, ideology, and regard similarly can buffer people against discrimination, although highly identified individuals are more aware of the discrimination in the first place. Hypervigilant stigma consciousness can be detrimental to people's well-being. Likewise, attributing negative outcomes to prejudice can buffer people's self-esteem, but it can also undermine the self-affirming effects of positive outcomes that are attributed to race. Other buffering strategies include comparing self to ingroup others, rather than the potentially threatening outgroup, and devaluing domains where the ingroup fares poorly.

Stereotype threat, the focus of a particularly active area of research, describes how members of any group can experience a threat in the air, based on the stereotype that their group performs poorly on some dimension. The mere reputation suffices to make people underperform; unlike a self-fulfilling prophecy, one need not meet a prejudiced individual. Identity salience, again, depends on context, and therefore so does stereotype threat. The most likely mechanisms of stereotype threat are probably vigilance and stress. Stereotype threat is remedied by knowing that intelligence is malleable and improvable, not fixed; by fair-minded contexts that minimize group differences; and by larger settings that demonstrate a commitment to diversity and trust.

Constructive intergroup contact can mitigate bias and its effects on both perceivers and targets. It requires conditions that provide the opportunity for intergroup friendship: equal status, common goals, cooperation, and authority sanctions. The jigsaw classroom exemplifies intergroup contact, but the concept has endured for decades, and the effects are strong. The mechanisms involve people's mutual attention to each other in the service of furthering their interdependent goals, which allows them to go beyond group membership, while not ignoring it. The salutary effects of contact generalize when people discover cross-cutting categories or a common ingroup identity. In the end, enthusiastic openness to people from other groups paves the way for improving intergroup relations.

## SUGGESTIONS FOR FURTHER READING

BREWER, M. B. (2007). The social psychology of intergroup relations: Social categorization, ingroup bias, and outgroup prejudice. In A. W. KRUGLANSKI & E. T. HIGGINS (Eds.), *Social psychology: Handbook of basic principles* (2nd ed., pp. 695–715). New York: Guilford.

BROWN, R. J. (1995). *Prejudice: Its social psychology*. Oxford, UK: Blackwell.

CROCKER, J., MAJOR, B., & STEELE, C. (1998). Social stigma. In D. T. GILBERT, S. T. FISKE, & G. LINDZEY (Eds.), *Handbook of social psychology* (4th ed., Vol. 2, pp. 504–553). New York: McGraw-Hill.

DE DREU, C. K. W. (2010). Social conflict: The emergence and consequences of struggle and negotiation. In S. T. FISKE, D. T. GILBERT, & G. LINDZEY (Eds.), *Handbook of social psychology* (5th ed.). New York: Wiley.

DOVIDIO, J. F., & GAERTNER, G. L. (2010). Intergroup bias. In S. T. FISKE, D. T. GILBERT, & G. LINDZEY (Eds.), *Handbook of social psychology* (5th ed.). New York: Wiley.

DOVIDIO, J. F., GLICK, P., & RUDMAN, L. A. (Eds.), (2005). *Reflecting on "The Nature of Prejudice."* Malden, MA: Blackwell.

EBERHARDT, J. L., & FISKE, S. T. (Eds.) (1998). *Confronting racism: The problem and the response*. Thousand Oaks, CA: Sage.

FAZIO, R. H., & OLSON, M. A. (2003). Implicit measures in social cognition research: Their meaning and use, *Annual Review of Psychology, 54*, 297–328.

FISKE, S. T. (2010). Stratification, status, and power. In S. T. FISKE, D. T. GILBERT, & G. LINDZEY (Eds.), *Handbook of social psychology* (5th ed.). New York: Wiley.

HOLTGRAVES, T. (2010). Social psychology and language: Words, utterances, and conversations. In S. T. FISKE, D. T. GILBERT, & G. LINDZEY (Eds.), *Handbook of social psychology* (5th ed.). New York: Wiley.

MACRAE, C. N., & BODENHAUSEN, G V. (2001). Social cognition: Categorical person perception. *British Journal of Psychology*, *92*, 239–255.

MAJOR, B., & O'BRIEN, L. T. (2005). The social psychology of stigma. *Annual Review of Psychology*, *56*, 393–421.

RUDMAN, L. A., & GLICK, P. (2008). *The social psychology of gender: How power and intimacy shape gender relations*. New York: Guilford.

SWIM, J. K., & STANGOR, C. (Eds.) (1998). *Prejudice: The target's perspective*. New York: Academic Press.

YZERBYT, V., & DEMOULIN, S. (2010). Intergroup relations: The context. In S. T. FISKE, D. T. GILBERT, & G. LINDZEY (Eds.), *Handbook of social psychology* (5th ed.). New York: Wiley.

# Chapter 12

# Small Groups: Ongoing Interactions

Two old school chums have a chance encounter as adults, and one—English, but raised at first in China—is left thinking about the other English fellow's casual remark that he had been "such an odd bird at school."

> In fact, it has always been a puzzle to me that Osbourne should have said such a thing of me that morning, since my own memory is that I blended perfectly into English school life. I do not believe that I did anything to cause myself embarrassment. On my very first day, for instance, I recall observing a mannerism many of the boys adopted when standing and talking—of tucking the right hand into a waistcoat pocket and moving the left shoulder up and down in a kind of shrug to underline certain of their remarks. I distinctly remember reproducing this mannerism on that same first day with sufficient expertise that not a single of my fellows noticed anything odd or thought to make fun.
>
> In much the same bold spirit, I rapidly absorbed other gestures, turns of phrase and exclamations popular among my peers, as well as grasping the deeper mores and etiquettes prevailing in my new surroundings. (Ishiguro, 2000, p. 7)[1]

Who has not, as the new kid in school, or newcomer at work, struggled to grasp the group's ways of talking and behaving, in order to fit in? And no wonder, because being branded as the odd duck bodes ill for one's continuing place in the group.

The group is the lynchpin of social situations. We began this book by describing people's core social motivation to belong as underlying all the other social motives. At the outset, we saw the evidence for people's well-being and even survival as enhanced by belonging to at least one group. The book so far has toured various forms of social being in that context, from within the individual to between pairs of people. The

---

last chapter started to move to the group level of analysis, examining how people's division of themselves and others into ingroups and outgroups can cause a variety of intergroup biases, even when only two people are involved, because they are seen as representing distinct groups. In this chapter, we turn to processes that operate within just one group, processes that motivate many intergroup, interpersonal, and intrapersonal processes we have seen before. We address both the individual in the group and the group itself. We begin by defining groups and some salient social motives and then move to the development of group membership—actual belonging—including the role of social identity, cohesion, diversity, and socialization. A focus on socially shared cognition—shared understanding—will frame the discussion of group structure, including norms, roles, leadership, and subgroups. Group performance—understanding group goals and controlling productivity—brings us to decision-making and performance. Finally, intragroup conflict results from people's attempt to control their own and other people's outcomes, when these are not identical, comprising a discussion of social dilemmas and negotiation. This chapter revisits some theories and concepts seen earlier in the book, but cast in a new light by the specifically group-oriented context and the special salience of belonging to a group, so as not to be an odd duck, a turkey, or any other kind of "odd bird."

## WHAT IS A GROUP?

Naturally interacting groups typically include two to six members, according to observational studies. People prefer these small groups when actual interaction is integral to the purpose of the group, whether accomplishing a task or enjoying each other socially (Levine & Moreland, 1998; Mullen, 1991). As total group size increases, people get unhappy; participation rate not only decreases but becomes more variable (some people dominate), and various indicators of commitment show dissatisfaction: Attrition, turnover, and conflict increase; cooperation and performance decrease. This chapter focuses on the small, face-to-face interacting groups.

### Conceptual Definitions

Social psychologists converge on three approaches to defining a group. Some definitions view a group as comprising individuals whose combined behavior simply summates into a group phenomenon. Others consider a group to have unique properties that go beyond merely interpersonal processes (for example, developing a social identity; Chapter 11). Others view groups as a major evolutionary transition within the biological hierarchy, like the transition whereby cells form organisms; groups represent the next level after individuals, when between-group selection dominates within-group selection (Wilson, Van Vugt, & O'Gorman, 2008). Still others abandon the effort at definition (Hogg, 1995a; Levine & Moreland, 1998). Based on what social psychologists have discovered about them, we argue that groups have unique, emergent properties that differentiate them from a mere aggregate of individuals on three counts: perceived entitativity, perceived volition, and actual behavior.

**PERCEIVED ENTITATIVITY**    For our purposes, we consider a **psychological group**—whom we can initially define as interacting people considered by themselves or others to belong together. What tends to make people define an aggregate of people as a group? Viewing the quality of groupiness as a continuum, not a dichotomy, will help. Half a century ago, Donald Campbell (1958) relied on the Gestalt properties of perceiving stimuli to be a single unit, an entity having real existence. Recall from Chapter 11 that **entitativity** entails being perceived as a coherent whole, based on similarity, common fate (interdependence), and perhaps proximity.

Several people in an elevator are proximate but do not fit any other definition of a group. They perceive themselves as more groupy, more of a psychological unit or entity, if the elevator stalls, because they develop a common fate. Safety depends on some degree of cooperation. Having a common goal creates interdependence, because they need each other to accomplish it. If they are similar in age, gender, ethnicity, or class, they may become still more of a group. Ongoing interaction (after the initial event, for example in a post-trauma therapy group) would make them even more of a group because it increases the sense of a common fate. Interdependence toward a common purpose is key in many definitions of groups (e.g., McGrath, Arrow, & Berdahl, 2000). All these factors—proximity, similarity, interdependence (common fate), and ongoing interaction—encourage cohesion and social integration, which foster among the individuals a sense of group membership, the topic of a later section. Essentially, cohesion results in developing a shared understanding of their situation and an emotional bond with each other. Psychological groupiness from the perspective of group members seems to follow Gestalt principles.

From the perspective of outsiders, what makes a group distinctive, as compared to an aggregate of individuals? Gestalt principles again apply (Asch, 1952). Observers expect groups to be more unitary and coherent than mere aggregates, although not as unified and coherent as an individual person (Hamilton & Sherman, 1996; Hamilton, Sherman, & Castelli, 2002). This makes sense: We expect individuals to have a coherent personality without too many internal contradictions, but we are not surprised when various members of a group show various attributes, including some that are inconsistent between members. Still, in accord with Gestalt principles, we expect the group members to be more similar (and less contradictory) then a random assortment of people.

To test this idea, researchers have to compare the same set of behaviors attributed to a single individual, a meaningful group, or a loose aggregate and see whether people's impression-formation processes differ with the degree of expected entitativity. In one such study (Susskind, Maurer, Thakkar, Hamilton, & Sherman, 1999), participants viewed clusters of four behaviors (for example, "did 100 sit-ups and 50 push-ups before bed"; "attended two parties with friends over the weekend"; "wrote a letter to congressman about the pending bill"; and "won a chess tournament against strong competition"). Each cluster represented either an individual doing four things, a group of four close friends each doing one thing, or an aggregate of four randomly selected people each doing one thing. People saw the very same four behaviors, when attributed to an individual, as fitting a pattern and being an organized, integrated unit (i.e., an entity), more so than when the same behaviors were attributed to four group members or a random sample of four students. Their confidence about and memory for an individual were stronger as well, and here the friendship group fared better than the mere aggregate, suggesting that the group was more of an entity than the aggregate. Although people do expect individuals to be more predictable and coherent than groups, when they encounter a group explicitly described as having members who know each other well and do a lot of things together, they form impressions of the group in ways that closely parallel their impressions of an individual and differ from an aggregate randomly selected from dorms at a large state university (McConnell, Sherman, & Hamilton, 1997).

In earlier studies (Srull, 1981; Srull, Lichtenstein, & Rothbart, 1985), people forming an impression from a series of behaviors had later recalled more when the behaviors were attributed to individuals and meaningful groups (e.g., a political caucus) than nonmeaningful groups (various people who all happen to be more conscientious than average). What's more, the pattern of memory shows that people puzzle over inconsistencies more for individuals and meaningful groups than for mere aggregates. Again, people expect more coherence from individuals and meaningful groups than from aggregates, so they struggle to resolve incongruence. This too is consistent with the idea that entitativity—being perceived as a meaningful unit—forms a continuum from an individual to a psychologically meaningful group to an aggregate.

Among groups, some specific types seem more entitative than others (Lickel et al., 2000): Intimacy groups (family, close friends) receive the highest marks on entitativity, followed by task groups (committee, project team), both of which differ from broad social categories (blacks, women), and loose associations (people in the same neighborhood, classical music lovers). Groups naturally perceived as having more entitativity are also those seen as having common goals, common outcomes, and similarity (all Gestalt principles), as well as being high in personal importance and degree of interaction.

People view highly entitative groups as having characteristic kinds (as well as amounts) of interaction. Recall from Chapter 8 the four **relational styles** identified in A. P. Fiske's (1992) relational models theory: communal sharing, equality matching, market pricing, and authority ranking. People expect intimacy groups to have communal-sharing relational styles, task groups to have authority ranking, loose associations to use market pricing, and social categories to have no particular interaction styles (Lickel, Hamilton, & Sherman, 2001). Moreover, people value their own groups the more they perceive them to be a distinct entity. The groups highest on entitativity (family and friends) also link most to people's social identity (Lickel et al., 2000).

The differences among intimacy groups, task groups, and social categories are validated by a study of memory confusion. Recall from Chapter 11 that people categorize each other by gender, race, and age, confusing people within category (i.e., confusing two black people with each other) more than between categories (confusing a black person and a white person). This who-said-what technique (Taylor et al., 1978) shows people's propensity to treat category members as interchangeable but distinct from other categories. In a study validating perceived differences among types of groups (e.g., intimacy versus task groups), people confused people within

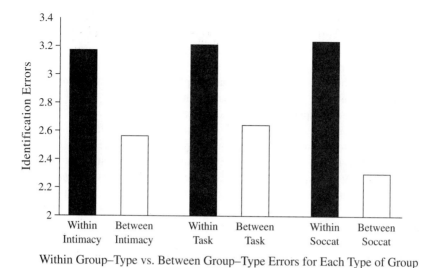

Within Group–Type vs. Between Group–Type Errors for Each Type of Group

**Figure 12.1** Memory Confusions *within* Types of Groups, More Than *between* Types

*Source:* Sherman et al., 2002. Copyright © American Psychological Association APA. Adapted with permission.

type of group. That is, they confused people within different intimacy groups, so they might confuse a family member with a friend, or they confused people within different task groups (a coworker with a jury member), but they did not confuse people across type of group (they did not confuse an intimacy group member with a task group member). Specifically (Sherman, Castelli, & Hamilton, 2002), participants saw 60 male faces, each paired with a group label (family, friend, coworker, juror, French, Presbyterian). In a subsequent recognition test (Figure 12.1), people made more errors within category than between categories—showing people's propensity to treat certain categories of groups (i.e., intimacy groups, such as friends and family) as interchangeable but distinct from others (social categories, such as French and Presbyterian). This further supports the idea of different types of groups, which vary in degree of entitativity.

Individuals do differ in the propensity to see groups (and other stimuli) as fixed entities; to the extent they do view groups as entities, they also tend to see groups as homogeneous (Levy, Plaks, Hong, Chiu, & Dweck, 2001). Similarly, cultural differences in the tendency to rely on group-level (versus individual) understandings are paralleled by memory for events that best fit the cultural schema (Ng & Zhu, 2001). Not only do groups vary in perceived entitativity, but individuals and cultures vary in the extent to which they tend to view groups that way.

**PERCEIVED VOLITION: GROUPS' HOSTILE INTENT** Besides perceived entitativity as defining a group, people perceive groups to differ from each other and from individuals in degree of volition or intent. That is, people assume that individuals are causal agents, origins of actions, as Chapter 3 demonstrated in discussing attributions of causality to individuals. If people view groups as they do individuals, people should view groups also as causal agents. If they view groups differently from individuals, they should not. As the entitativity research indicates, groups vary in how unitary and cohesive they seem, that is, in how much they resemble individuals who are unitary and cohesive. To the extent that people view the group as an entity, then, they might also view the group as a causal agent.

Research indeed supports this idea. Situational manipulations that increase the perceived similarity and proximity of group members (factors that increase entitativity) also increase perceived responsibility and intent. The catch is that people attribute not only intent to the group but also specifically hostile intent (Abelson, Dasgupta, Park, & Banaji, 1998). For example, priming the word *they* before an ambiguous story then makes collective actors more threatening, just as priming the word *he* makes a single actor more threatening. In both cases, a focus on the causal agent (protagonist) presumably increases perceived intent and (in this instance) perceived hostility. Similarly, manipulating the similarity and proximity of imaginary group members—making them more entitative—leads to more negative judgments about their likely intergroup behavior.

Besides manipulating the degree to which a group is an entity, researchers can draw on cultural tendencies to focus on individual or collective agency. That is, collectivist cultures see groups as having more impact than individualist cultures do. In East Asian newspapers, compared with American newspapers, accounts of trading scandals focus more on the organization than on the individuals (Menon, Morris, Chiu, & Hong, 1999). Similar results occur for team versus individual responsibility in a scenario study involving a maladjusted team member who is not well integrated into the group. Although the bad situation could be the fault of the individual or the group, East Asians tend to view it as more of a group responsibility, whereas Americans blame the individual.

Why do groups perceived to be entitative elicit not only attributed intent but specifically hostile intent? Part of the answer lies in perceptions of what makes a group a group. As noted in the previous chapter, people expect different groups to have incompatible goals. The same is not so markedly true of individuals. If part of what defines a group as a group is shared goals (as noted), then different groups will have different goals. To the extent they have differing goals, the goals are likely to be incompatible or competing. Hence, merely in pursuing its own goals, one group will interfere with another group and provoke negative emotions (Fiske & Ruscher, 1993). People seem to expect this, given the just-cited finding that perceived groupiness elicits perceived hostile intent (Abelson et al., 1998). What's more, people preferentially remember instances of intergroup competition, compared with interpersonal (interindividual) competition (Pemberton, Insko, & Schopler, 1996), thereby confirming their expectations that groups allegedly have hostile intent more than individuals do.

**ACTUAL BEHAVIOR: INTERPERSONAL-INTERGROUP DISCONTINU-ITY IN HOSTILITY**    People apparently are not wrong to expect hostile behavior from other people in groups. The **interpersonal-intergroup discontinuity effect** (Schopler & Insko, 1992) shows that people behave differently in interpersonal dyads than they do in intergroup interactions. The experimental paradigm for this work is a mixed-motive game, in which self-interest conflicts with the other side's self-interest and yields lower outcomes than mutual cooperation. In Chapters 8 and 9, we saw matrices like the one in Figure 12.2, in discussing relationship interdependence and cooperative helping. In the mixed-motive case depicted here, each side individually profits by making a competitive choice, but only if the other side simultaneously cooperates. Both sides lose if they both make a competitive choice. Thus, each side's outcomes are negatively correlated—**noncorrespondent**—on the whole; their interests are not the same. However, the negative correlation is not complete; people can make choices (both cooperate) that together serve them better than other choices (both compete).

In this case, individuals typically learn to cooperate over time (as we will see in a later section), but groups do not. Groups make more competitive choices on average than individuals do, as the top row of Table 12.1 indicates (Insko, Schopler, Hoyle, Dardis, & Graetz, 1990). Groups choose competition over cooperation roughly 10 out of 20 times, whereas individuals do so only 1 in 20 times (left two columns). Given the additional choice to withdraw, groups still choose to compete more than twice as often as individuals do (right two columns). The effect is reliable and substantial over studies and appears even in domains that do not use an explicit payoff matrix (Pemberton, Insko, & Schopler, 1996; Schopler et al., 2001). The more negatively correlated the outcomes of the two sides, the more groups (but not individuals) behave competitively. Counter to gender stereotypes, groups of women show this escalation under increased competition more than groups of men do (Schopler et al., 2001). One explanation is that they react with more anger to the unfairness of the other side's behavior (Mikolic, Parker, & Pruitt, 1997), perhaps because they tend to have a more interdependent self-construal (Chapter 5).

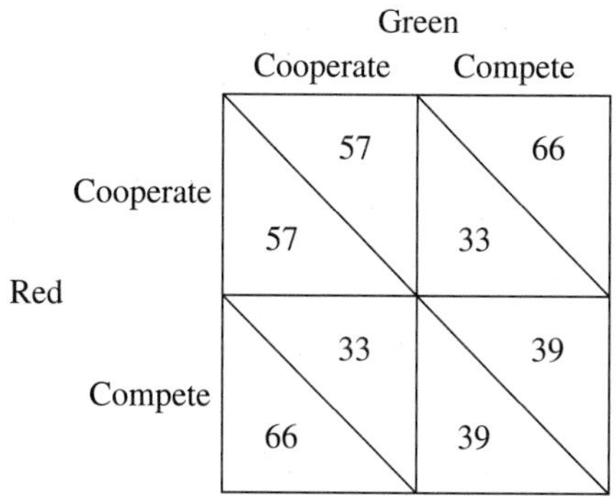

The red side receives the payoffs in the lower left half of each cell, and the green side receives those in the top right half of each cell.

**Figure 12.2**  Experimental Game Matrix of Outcomes, Given Each Side's Choice, in a Mixed-Motive Case

*Source:* From Schopler & Insko, 1992. Copyright © Wiley. Adapted with permission.

The interpersonal-intergroup discontinuity is driven by two processes: fear and greed. Fear appears in people's negative expectations that outgroups will be competitive and self-serving, which (some would argue) is just a rational response in experimental games of the kind shown in the figure. Evidence for the role of fear comes from studies showing a correlation between decreases in the number of cooperative choices and the extent to which the group on one side discusses their distrust of the other side (Insko et al., 1990). Groups are less trusting than individuals (Kugler, Bornstein, Kocher, & Sutter, 2007). Their fear fits the threat theories of intergroup bias (such as realistic group conflict, social dominance orientation, and right-wing authoritarianism, covered in Chapter 11). Fear thus fits our core social motive of controlling one's outcomes. It might also fit our understanding motive as a way to make sense of intergroup rivalry.

Greed, on the other hand, fits control and perhaps also self-enhancement. Even if the situation neutralizes fear (and competitive expectancies), apparent greed remains in the willingness to exploit the other side. Suppose one side has the opportunity to withdraw from competition (the middle choice in Figure 12.3). Groups do use this option (more than individuals do), and their cooperation increases when this self-protective choice is available, but they still cooperate less often than individuals do (see right side of Table 12.1; Insko et al., 1990; Schopler, et al., 1993). Greed increases with ingroup social support, in the form of group members arguing for the exploitation of the other side (Schopler et al., 1993; Wildschut, Insko, & Gaertner, 2002). Groups try to maximize their relative advantage over other groups, as predicted by social identity theory, introduced in Chapter 11. The locus of the effect also appears in maximizing own group outcomes, which fits the literature showing that much discrimination operates via ingroup favoritism more than outgroup derogation. Groups' greed apparently focuses on short-term advantage, because under long-term interactions, or even the anticipation of same, the effect dissipates (Insko et al., 2001; Insko et al., 1998).

The interpersonal-intergroup discontinuity effect emphasizes the intrinsic differences between individual and group behavior. Not only do people expect groups to

**Table 12.1**    Competitive Choices, Cooperative Choices, and Withdrawal Choices as a Function of Type or Number of Choices and Groups versus Individuals

| | Choices | | | |
|---|---|---|---|---|
| | Cooperative or Competitive Only | | Cooperative, Competitive, or Withdrawal | |
| Responses | Groups | Individuals | Groups | Individuals |
| Competitive | 10.14 | 1.00 | 4.50 | 1.75 |
| Cooperative | 9.86 | 19.00 | 10.43 | 17.36 |
| Withdrawal | – | – | 5.07 | 0.89 |

Each of the three choice totals has a possible range from 0 to 20.
*Source:* From Insko et al., 1990. Copyright © American Psychological Association. Adapted with permission.

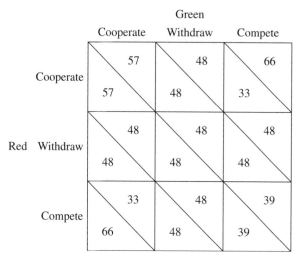

**Figure 12.3**  Experimental Game Matrix of Outcomes, with Addition of a Safe Withdrawal Option

*Source:* Schopler & Insko, 1992. Copyright © Wiley. Adapted with permission.

be more competitive and self-serving than individuals, as the previous section indicated, but also they are apparently right to do so, as this section indicates. Although entitativity helps define a group psychologically, competition forms an integral part of people's understanding of groups.

## Operational Definitions

As implied by some of the research just described, the groups studied by social psychologists most often (about 76% of the time) are short-term experimental groups formed by recruiting participants from psychology department subject pools (Moreland, Hogg, & Hains, 1994). These groups tend to meet for a short time, often only one session, to work on a task assigned by the experimenter.

Some of the typical experimental methods have already appeared in our discussion of the interpersonal-intergroup discontinuity; participants play experimental games (with tangible monetary outcomes) in the laboratory, to simulate groups in the outside world. We see more examples of this technique in the section on conflict in groups. Other methods include assigning the group a problem-solving task or a decision to make.

Problems with the laboratory approach include isolation from a larger context (e.g., a team exists within an organization), lack of a past or a future, assumptions that the behaviors of student participants generalize to a variety of other adults, and narrowly focusing on a particular cause-effect relationship (McGrath, Arrow, & Berdahl, 2000). These issues are not unique to the literature on groups (e.g., Chapters 9–11). To be fair, experiments are designed precisely to isolate and imply a particular cause-effect relationship, and they cannot necessarily claim generalizability to other participant populations and contexts. That is why social psychology typically replicates its most important findings in field studies, outside the laboratory. Contrary to the expectations of skeptics, most group phenomena are actually stronger in the field (real groups) than in the laboratory (artificial groups), according to meta-analyses of various group effects (Mullen, Brown, & Smith, 1992; Mullen & Copper, 1994; Mullen & Hu, 1989; Ostrom & Sedikides, 1992).

About 9% of group studies use surveys, presumably yielding correlational data on groups outside the laboratory (Moreland, Hogg, & Haines, 1994). This overall pattern reflects the methods of the rest of social psychology, so it is not surprising, except that many studies of groups reflect on phenomena such as organizational behavior. Indeed, compared with group studies appearing in social psychology journals, those appearing in organizational journals tend to report experiments less often (50%), field studies and field experiments more often (28%), and about the same number of surveys (10%) (Sanna & Parks, 1997). Field studies on "real" groups tend to take more account of the complexities of the groups' organizational context, for example, in examining airline cockpit crews, management teams, and quality improvement groups (McGrath, Arrow, & Berdahl, 2000).

Regardless of experimental or correlational technique, laboratory or field, studying groups is an inherently daunting enterprise, which has at times discouraged researchers from this topic (Hogg, 1995a; Levine & Moreland, 1998; Steiner, 1974). The biggest problem is that the unit of analysis becomes the group, instead of the individuals in the group. That is, to draw conclusions about group behavior, researchers need to observe enough separate, independent groups to be able to find statistically reliable results. So, for example, a phenomenon that might require 30 people in a study of individuals would require 3 to 5 times that number of people to study as a group phenomenon (assuming a minimum of 3 people to make a group makes the total 90; assuming a more complex group of 5 makes the total 150 individuals). The group level of analysis makes finding enough participants many times more inconvenient and expensive.

What's more, group data are inherently complex. Examining a single individual's reactions entails one single set of observations. Examining a dyad entails three kinds of observation: each person's perspective, as well as any interactions that are unique to particular combinations of people (e.g., individual males might react one way and individual females another, but the particular gender combination in a dyad might create still a third pattern). Now consider a three-person minimalist group. The researcher would have data from three individuals, as well as data from each of them reacting specifically to the other two (six more kinds of observations), as well as data resulting from the group as a whole, which might vary as a function of group composition. That's ten types of observation. Besides, interaction patterns may create coalitions. You see the problem.

Whatever the number and pattern of interactions, their content then has to be coded. One long-running system for coding the content of group interactions is **Interaction Process Analysis**, also known as SYMLOG (simultaneous multilevel analysis for groups; Bales, 1950, 1970, 1999). The coding scheme involves three dimensions. The first dimension, dominance-submission, is labeled *Upward-Downward* and is most reliably indicated by sheer talking time in the group. The second dimension, friendly-unfriendly, is labeled *Positive-Negative* and indicates the pleasantness of people's interaction. The third dimension, on-task-off-task, is labeled *Forward-Backward* and indicates the degree of instrumental control versus emotional expression. To give a sense about the combinations, consider how some famous people would appear in a group, along these dimensions (Isenberg & Ennis, 1981). Groucho Marx would be Upward (talkative), Positive (friendly), and Backward (expressive and off-task); Adolph Hitler would also be Upward (dominant) but Negative (unpleasant) and Forward (instrumental); Abraham Lincoln would be Upward, Positive, and Forward. Famous people are less likely to be submissive, but Charlie Chaplin would be Positive and Backward (like Groucho Marx, but more Downward than Upward). And Shakespeare's agonizing but inactive Hamlet would be Downward, Negative, and Backward (passive, gloomy, expressive, and off-task). In a real group, each comment can be coded, on-line, in real time, by observers (such as your author, in graduate school). The pattern of interactions across individuals reveals a three-dimensional space that describes the group structure. Content analysis techniques yield an abundance of rich data, challenging but ultimately satisfying. Indeed, "completing a major project on groups, especially one that involves extensive data on interaction patterns, seems to serve as a 'rite of passage'" for researchers new to the small-groups area (Levine & Moreland, 1998, p. 419).

Finally, the statistical challenges of analyzing group interactions are nontrivial, because all the members of a group influence each other, violating some basic statistical assumptions about independence of observations. Solutions often require the researcher to move outside the normal statistical procedures (Forsyth, 1998; Kenny, Mannetti, Pierro, Livi, & Kashy, 2002; Sadler & Judd, 2001). No wonder one commentator observed "the data from group research are rarely neat, tidy, and easily explained" (Hogg, 1995a, p. 270). Nevertheless, the efforts are extremely important and all the more amazing when the data come out.

One recent reaction to these methodological issues has been computational models of isolated features of group interactions. For example, modeling the mutual influences among interacting individuals, in **dynamical evolutionary psychology**, focuses on competition and cooperation (especially mating) within a web of mutual contingencies (Kenrick, Li, & Butner, 2003). This allows quantitative specification of individual decisions in a social context. Emergent properties characterize the group, norms being one example, and they are not predictable from simple rules about individual beliefs or even dyadic interaction, so **agent-based** computational models (i.e., comprising autonomous individuals) (Goldstone, Roberts, & Gureckis, 2008) represent an alternative method.

## Core Social Motives

Going back to the social psychology of the group itself, three main motives—belonging, understanding, and controlling—have formed the core of small group research and seem to capture people's main motives for participating in group interaction.

**BELONGING**    Earlier, in the context of definitions, we said that entitativity was one of the main features of a psychologically meaningful group. Now, in the context of motives, consider how the entitativity of the group allows it to meet people's need to belong (Yzerbyt, Castano, Leyens, & Paladino, 2000). Ingroup entitativity predicts degree of social identification with the group, it being easier to identify with a group that has clear definitions and boundaries. Seeing the ingroup as coherent enables people to see the group positively, as a whole, thereby increasing identification.

But more than that, high identifiers emphasize **ingroup homogeneity** (entitativity) especially when the group is threatened, for example by its having low status, unfavorable stereotypes, unfair outcomes, or even mortality salience (Castano, Yzerbyt, Paldini, & Sacchi, 2002; Yzerbyt et al., 2000). (Recall group homogeneity from Chapter 11 and mortality salience from Chapters 9–11.) When group members identify with their group, its coherence matters to them because it is motivationally easier to protect loyally a well-defined entity than a loosely-defined aggregate. Similarly, threat *from* an entitative outgroup, compared with a mere aggregate, increases identification with the ingroup (Dépret & Fiske, 1999). Consider the typical American emphasis on the diversity of the nation, but consider also how much Americans seemed to pull together as a cohesive unit after September 11, 2001, when the threat by a more clearly defined outgroup became unavoidable. Belonging together became a central motivation for most Americans under intergroup threat.

Two other lines of evidence implicate the motivational primacy of ingroup belonging. A phenomenon dubbed the **black sheep effect** shows that ingroup members firmly reject an ingroup deviant, often even more than an outgroup member who deviates from ingroup values (Marques, Abrams, Páez, & Hogg, 2001; Marques, Yzerbyt, & Leyens, 1988). Compared with ratings of outgroup members, judgments of ingroup members are more extremely positive if the person is likeable (an extension of ingroup favoritism) but also more extremely negative if the person is unlikable (the black sheep effect). Reactions to outgroup members are not as extreme, either positively or negatively, as reactions to ingroup members. In comparisons of ingroup and outgroup, correlations among perceived traits of the ingroup are higher, suggesting that people's implicit theory of the ingroup is more coherent, making it seem more entitative. Thus, ingroup deviants stand out more than outgroup deviants.

People seem to maintain ingroup boundaries with some care, rejecting those negative deviants unacceptable to social identity. The role of identity is specifically implicated because the black sheep effect occurs only on identity-relevant traits. Also, high identifiers show the effect more clearly than low identifiers and are willing to invest considerable cognitive resources to concentrate attention on the threatening negative ingroup member (Coull, Yzerbyt, Castano, Paladino, & Leemans, 2001). All this suggests the motivational importance of ingroup belonging.

If the black sheep effect reflects group members curing the already-contaminated ingroup, another phenomenon may be viewed as preventing potential contamination (Yzerbyt et al., 2000). The **ingroup overexclusion effect** refers to ingroup members' carefully guarding their own group's boundaries, more than other groups' (Leyens & Yzerbyt, 1992; Yzerbyt, Leyens, & Bellour, 1995). That is, group members are more cautious about inferring ingroup membership, compared with outgroup membership, for someone whose group membership is ambiguous. For example, people demand more information to admit the potential ingroup member, and especially when the cues are positive or stereotype-consistent (because negative or stereotype-inconsistent cues would allow them to reject the potential ingroup member immediately). Ingroup members must be judged more carefully than outgroup members because the stakes of inclusion are higher for one's own group than the stakes of allowing someone to be classified as belonging (or not) to someone else's group. Overall, the clear psychological entitativity and boundaries of ingroups support group belonging motives.

A complementary line of evidence even more dramatically indicates the motivational importance of belonging by showing what people do when they are excluded (e.g., rejected as an ingroup member). Two theories address the problem. A **model of ostracism** suggests that being socially rejected threatens people's need to belong. In one study, people reported their experiences of receiving the **silent treatment**, that is, other people avoiding eye contact and verbal communication. People specifically mentioned their damaged feelings of belonging (as well as self-esteem, control, and meaning; Williams, Shore, & Grahe, 1998). In another study, two confederate participants excluded a third real participant simply by tossing a ball back and forth to each other and leaving out the other person (Williams & Sommer, 1997). Excluded female participants worked especially hard on an ensuing group task, as apparent social compensation for their prior exclusion (males did not; we will come back to this). More direct evidence related to the belonging motive comes from a study that simulated the ball-tossing game and subsequent exclusion on an Internet Web site (Williams, Cheung, & Choi, 2000). Even with this minimal form of ostracism (a symbolic ball and excluders who were never encountered directly as real people), 1,486 participants from 62 countries reported losing a sense of belonging and self-esteem, which in turn made them feel bad. In a second study, participants ostracized in this way showed more conformity on a subsequent task, again an apparent social compensation for their exclusion. People apparently try harder at first, but high and persistent levels of ostracism eventually make them withdraw effort. Regardless of whether computer-mediated or face-to-face, ostracism has broadly similar negative effects (Williams, 2007; Williams et al., 2002).

Still another theoretical approach centers on the belonging motive and its role in social exclusion. Recall from Chapter 1 the Baumeister-Leary (1995) evidence for the centrality of the belonging motive. In general, people seek social attachments, benefit physically and psychologically from them, and resist their dissolution. Specifically with regard to social exclusion, recall from Chapter 5 that people's self-esteem depends on their assessment of their degree of personal acceptance by others, a phenomenon studied as the **sociometer hypothesis** (Leary, Tambor, Terdal, & Downs, 1995). Personal exclusion from important social groups correlates with anxiety and depression (Baumeister & Tice, 1990; Leary, 1990; Nezlek, Kowalski, Leary, Blevins, & Holgate, 1997). To illustrate people's efforts to belong, one might consider a study of 22 separate task groups, in which positive, pleasant acts outnumbered negative, unpleasant acts by a ratio of 3.4 to 1 (Bales & Strodtbeck, 1951). The baseline positivity of interaction suggests people's efforts to cooperate and get along in the service of continued belonging.

Finally, attachment theory (recall from Chapter 8)—which began by explaining infant-parent bonds and later moved into adult close relationships—also can apply to an individual's **attachment to social groups** (Smith, Murphy, & Coats, 1999). Just as people have mental working models of self and others in close relationships, so they have working models of self (as a group member) and the group (as a source of social support and identity). Just as with attachment styles in close relationships, so too some people are relatively avoidant, anxious, or secure in their attachment to groups, and this predicts their style of belonging to the group.

Other individual difference and person variables relate to group belonging, including possible gender differences. To the extent that women have more interdependent self-construals on average, compared with men, they may operate more in terms of relationships than in terms of autonomy (Cross & Madson, 1997). Consequently, women and men may view their group memberships differently (Gabriel & Gardner, 1999). In particular, women might focus more on the **relational** aspects of interdependence within groups, whereas men might focus relatively more on **collective** aspects of interdependence within groups. That is, women operate relatively more in terms of intimate relationships and interpersonal harmony within dyads and small groups and less often in terms of larger collectives, such as teams and social groups. Men within groups operate in relatively more collective and less relational ways than women. Relevant data include self-construals, important emotional events, memory for others, and behavior in experimental games. In one study, women were more attentive during the interaction, particularly in committed relationships, and men were less attentive (Stiles et al., 1997). Thus, the meaning of belonging to groups may differ on average by gender.

Cultural variation also shows that the meaning of belonging differs by such dimensions as **collectivism-individualism** (see previous chapters) and **power distance** (which differentiates more hierarchical cultures from more egalitarian ones) (M. H. Bond & Smith, 1996). For example, people in collectivist cultures are likely to define themselves and be motivated more in terms of their group memberships than are people in individualist cultures. On the other hand, people in individualist cultures belong to more groups, moving in and out of them more rapidly and easily, and are less attached to any one of them.

As another example of cultural variation, power distance strengthens the role expectations for leaders and followers; that is, it increases the difference between leaders and followers as a function of their respective roles. For example, high power distance demands more assertive and dominant behavior by leaders, whereas low power distance demands more ingratiation and exchange from leaders. Regardless of cultural and individual variation, however, belonging forms an important motivation for human group membership. Attempts to fortify belonging, in the face of exclusion, tend to make people think and behave prosocially (Williams, 2007), which helps maintain the group (Levine & Kerr, 2007).

**UNDERSTANDING**    So far in this book, we have seen that motives for a socially shared understanding matter for people making sense of others, the self, and various attitude objects, as well as entering into close relationships, helping, aggression, and intergroup bias. So, too, do groups serve an understanding motive. People have a stronger trust in a shared reality with a group than with an individual (Hardin & Higgins, 1996; Higgins, Echterhoff, Crespillo, & Kopietz, 2007).

A clear example of the understanding motive in groups comes from a motivational theory of social identity processes. The **subjective uncertainty reduction hypothesis** (Hogg, 2000, 2007; Hogg & Abrams, 1993) argues that, when people feel unsure about self-relevant matters, self-categorization as a group member reduces their uncertainty. For example, a student new on campus—full of self-doubt and ignorance about local norms—often gladly identifies with the first-year class, certain clubs or teams, and some areas of study rather than others. When people identify with a group, they **depersonalize**—become less oriented to their individual identity—and orient more toward being a prototypic member of the group. Assimilating self to the group's **prescriptive prototype**, that is, the group ideals, reduces feelings of uncertainty by providing guides for thoughts, feelings, and actions. Moreover, the group consensus validates individual group members' reactions when they assimilate to the group prototype. People are especially likely to identify with highly entitative groups when their self-certainty is low (Hogg, Sherman, Dierselhuis, Maitner, & Moffitt, 2007). The theory argues that people are motivated to join groups, precisely in order to reduce their own uncertainties: "People need to feel certain about their world and their place within it; certainty renders experience meaningful and gives one confidence in how to behave, and what to expect from one's physical and social environment" (Hogg, 2000, p. 227). The Ishiguro example that opened this chapter characterizes this experience.

Evidence for the uncertainty reduction hypothesis comes from several studies using the **minimal group paradigm** (recall from last chapter), in which people are divided into arbitrary groups and then allocate rewards to ingroup and outgroup. The typical finding is that people advantage the ingroup, which is interpreted as identifying with their own group. What is, of course, most surprising is how easily people do this, even with the most minimal of explicitly arbitrary groups. In this paradigm, Hogg argues, people show ingroup favoritism *only* when they are in a state of temporary uncertainty. For example, when people first encounter the unfamiliar, complex matrices they have to use to allocate rewards in this paradigm, they identify with the ingroup more than when they have already practiced with the matrices (Grieve & Hogg, 1999). The same occurs when people are uncertain about important attitudes (Mullin & Hogg, 1999). What's more, reminiscent of the importance of entitativity, people prefer homogeneous (entitative) groups for uncertainty reduction (Jetten, Hogg, & Mullin, 2000). All this evidence supports the importance of group membership as validating one's own responses under uncertainty. An entitative group provides a sense of consensus, socially shared understanding.

Socially shared cognition in ongoing groups results from common experience, social interaction, coordinated communication, and social comparison (Tindale, Meisenhelder, Dykema-Engblade, & Hogg, 2001), as a later section elaborates. And Chapter 13 elaborates on some classic studies noted in Chapter 1 (Asch's and Sherif's studies), which show how groups allow people to develop norms for appropriate judgments. Another classic example is people's tendency to affiliate with others when they are afraid, in order to make social comparisons of their ambiguous experience (Schachter, 1959). For present, the point is that motives for a socially shared understanding are satisfied by group identity.

When a sense of shared social understanding fails, people become uncomfortable (as argued in previous chapters). In the group context, people may become paranoid (irrationally distrustful and suspicious), when they do not share the group's understanding (Kramer, 1998). Uncertainty about one's social standing can result from being new or different, for example. These situational uncertainties can make people hyper-vigilant and make them ruminate, which together lead to perceived conspiracies, personal insults, and evil intent. These maladaptive forms of understanding occur only when people have not fulfilled their motive for shared understanding (and belonging) by fully secure group membership. Issues of socially shared understanding occur at early stages in the life history of a group, when many members are new and are all getting oriented to each other (Bales & Strodtbeck, 1951). At those stages, giving or requesting information, clarification, or confirmation each illustrates an effort to develop shared understanding.

**CONTROLLING**    Because groups, by definition, comprise people who are interdependent, motives for control matter in groups. Precisely because members' outcomes depend on each other, groups arouse, and often meet, people's needs for control. Commitment to the group results from its mutual reward value, as newcomers become socialized (Levine, Moreland, & Choi, 2001). Group negotiations (Thompson, Medvec, Seiden, & Kopelman, 2001), power relations (Lord, Brown, & Harvey, 2001), and social dilemmas, which pit individual against group interest (Kerr & Park, 2001), all especially raise issues of control, which later sections revisit. In addition, individuals and the group as a whole aim to control the group's outcomes and reach common goals.

Some people and some situations elicit a particularly strong need for control. When people are ostracized, if their control motives also are endangered, then they may respond in antisocial ways, further undermining the group and their place in it (Williams, 2007). But this is an extreme reaction to ostracism; in an ongoing group, control needs can facilitate certain kinds of group process. When people are dispositionally or situationally high in one kind of control motive, need for closure, the group becomes more business-like. Interaction focuses toward the task at hand and away from positive social interactions that do not directly advance the task (DeGrada, Kruglanski, Mannetti, & Pierro, 1999). At such junctures, group interactions are less egalitarian and demand more conformity from their members. Groups similarly may focus on issues of control at later stages in group development, when executing their tasks becomes critical (Bales & Strodtbeck, 1951). Giving and requesting suggestions, directions, or plans illustrate behaviors that reflect mutual control over each other and the group's outcomes. Clearly, this also implies a role for the core motive of trust, but the research has been framed more in terms of mutual control than mutual trust.

## Summary of Definitions and Motives

Psychological groups comprise interacting people who consider themselves or whom others consider to belong together. Groups differ in entitativity, the degree to which they make a coherent whole, through Gestalt principles of similarity, proximity, interdependence, and interaction. Intimacy groups, such as family and friends, are experienced as more coherent and cohesive than loose associations (such as neighborhoods) and social categories (such as women), with task groups falling in between. People value their own groups to the extent they view them as cohesive, coherent entities. In contrast, to the extent people view an outgroup as being an entitative group, they see it as having hostile intent. Because groups are typified by shared goals that operate in the group's own interest, and entitative groups appear as causal agents—that is, as originating action—outgroups are expected to act on their own interests, which will be hostile to other groups. And, indeed, groups are more competitive than individuals. Both fear of losing control over one's outcomes and greed to enhance self contribute to group competitiveness.

Social psychologists most often study groups by creating short-term, artificial, experimental groups that often play experimental games, all of which might seem to lack generalizability to the real world. Nonetheless, real-world effects are often stronger than laboratory demonstrations of the same phenomena. Researchers use survey and observational methods when they study real-world groups. People in both artificial and real groups satisfy a number of core social motives, including most obviously the need to belong but also to validate a shared social understanding and a sense of control. Each of the main sections of the chapter addresses one or two of the core motives, to discuss group membership (belonging), socially shared cognition (understanding and controlling), group performance (understanding and controlling), and intragroup conflict (controlling).

## GROUP MEMBERSHIP: BELONGING

This section addresses what happens when people belong to a group: how their identity changes, how their attraction to group members creates cohesion, and how they become socialized into the group. People readily affiliate with similar and proximate others, forming interdependent bonds that foster identity and attraction; groups deal with diversity in composition via socialization processes. All these processes occur because people are fundamentally motivated to belong to groups.

### Social Identity Operates in Context

In the last chapter, **social identity theory** (SIT) and **self-categorization theory** (SCT) appeared in their intergroup context as sources of bias. Self-definition in a given social context creates a useful and feasible particular group identity for a particular setting. Social identity is that part of the self-concept that derives from group membership. In the last chapter, we saw that merely categorizing self and others as group members increases each group's perceived homogeneity (and entitativity). Self-categorization and social (as opposed to interpersonal) identity increase ingroup favoritism and consequent outgroup disadvantage. This kind of intergroup differentiation increases at least short-term self-esteem, linking the belonging motive to self-enhancement.

In the current context of examining *intra*-group reactions, the experience of the individual becoming a group member is paramount. Why should people move from interpersonal to intergroup self-categorization? In some contexts, the individual self motivationally dominates the collective self (Gaertner, Sedikides, & Graetz, 1999). Relative to collective threat, Westerners consider individual threat more severe, react more negatively, and more severely derogate the source of the threat. These results hold up despite individual variations in individualism and collectivism. This might suggest the motivational primacy of the individual self, who might then not bother to join groups. Nevertheless, people demonstrably do want to join groups, and the very nature of their individual self depends on the groups that they actually join. The individual self (however important it may be) still varies as a function of context (as Chapter 5 showed). Social identity, whether individual or collective, is context-specific; that is, it depends on one's relevant groups and situations.

In one study, for example, targets were rated on five personality traits by people from three different groups, all of whom knew them well: family, friends, and coworkers (Malloy, Albright, Kenny, Agatstein, & Winquist, 1997). Each person was judged consensually *within* any given group but differently in *different* groups. Within-group consensus accounted for fully 30% of the variance in ratings, and consensus was statistically reliable in all 15 tests (5 traits in each of 3 groups). In contrast, between-group consensus accounted for much less variance (less than 10%) and was statistically reliable in only 5 of 15 tests (5 traits in each series of 3 paired comparisons). This difference in perceptions across groups (but not within groups) supports the idea that one's personality and identity depend on the context provided by a particular group. You might be one person to your family and quite another to your coworkers or friends. Contextual differences in your perceived personality could reflect either different groups' different perceptions or differences in your actual behavior, but both bear on group-specific identity.

Given the importance of social identity, it is critical to know when social identity matters more and when personal identity matters more. A taxonomy of situations predicts that group commitment and type of threat combine to raise distinct identity concerns and motives (Ellemers, Spears, & Doosje, 2002). Individual concerns and motives come to the fore when group commitment is low, as shown in Table 12.2, and as follows:

- Under no threat to self, low group commitment (cell 1) allows a focus on efficiency in relating to others, as in dual-process models of social cognition (Fiske et al., 1999; Brewer & Harasty Feinstein, 1999; see Chapter 4).

- However, when the individual self is threatened, and group commitment remains low (cell 3), individuals are concerned about self-affirmation (Steele, 1988; see Chapter 5). Cases of stereotype threat (Steele, Spencer, & Aronson, 2002; see Chapter 11) and outgroup derogation to protect damage to personal self-esteem (Fein & Spencer, 1997) exemplify this self-threat, low group-commitment context. Here, individuals' primary concern is having themselves categorized negatively.

- In the last low-commitment situation, but now under a group threat (cell 5), individuals orient toward individual mobility out of the group, being more

**Table 12.2**  Primary Concerns and Motives of the Social Self: A Taxonomy

| | Group Commitment | |
|---|---|---|
| | Low | High |
| No threat | 1. | 2. |
| Concern | Efficiency | Social meaning |
| Motive | Noninvolvement | Identity expression |
| Individual-directed threat | 3. | 4. |
| Concern | Negative categorization | Exclusion |
| Motive | Self-affirmation | Acceptance |
| Group-directed threat | 5. | 6. |
| Concern | Own value | Group distinctiveness, value |
| Motive | Individual mobility | Group-affirmation |

*Source:* From Ellemers et al., 2002. Copyright © Annual Reviews. Adapted with permission.

concerned about restoring the value of their own personal identity. Individuals become dissatisfied, distance themselves from the group, identify less with their group, see it as more heterogeneous, self-stereotype less as a group member, and are less willing to help the group, unless they can gain personally (Branscombe, Spears, Ellemers, & Doosje, 2002; Doosje, Spears, & Ellemers, 2002; Ellemers, 1993; Ellemers, Spears, & Doosje, 1997; Jackson, Sullivan, Harnish, & Hodge, 1996; Spears, Doosje, & Ellemers, 1997).

In contrast, this taxonomy proposes that high group commitment brings other identity concerns to the fore, given varying degrees of threat.

- Under no threat but high commitment (cell 2), group members' intragroup and intergroup reactions should follow social identity and self-categorization theory (Tajfel, 1974; Tajfel & Turner, 1979; Turner, 1985), expressing their identity as a member of a positive, distinct group. As the previous chapter indicates, high commitment and identification enhance perceived group homogeneity and ingroup favoritism.

- When self-threat intervenes in a high-commitment context (cell 4), group members become concerned about being excluded by the group and are motivated toward acceptance. This illustrates situations in which someone wants to be a member of a group that is reluctant to admit the person. Marginal group members become even more critical of other marginal group members (Marques & Paez, 1994) and of outgroup members, in public, where it might raise their status in the ingroup (Branscombe, Wann, Noel, & Coleman, 1993; Noel, Wann, & Branscombe, 1995).

- Finally, in the case of high group commitment but group threat (cell 6), group members are concerned about the value and distinctiveness of their group and move to affirm it, by self-stereotyping (Spears et al., 1997), emphasizing ingroup homogeneity and cohesiveness (Branscombe, Schmitt, & Harvey, 1999; Doosje, Ellemers, & Spears, 1995; Doosje, Spears, & Ellemers, 2002).

Determining individual commitment to the group is crucial to this taxonomy. Also, commitment overlaps conceptually and operationally with identification, and social identification with the group is both an independent variable and a dependent variable in this research. For example, people may apparently belong to one group but personally identify with another; this will affect their degree of identification, loyalty, and commitment (Barreto & Ellemers, 2002). Regardless of the challenge of specifying degrees of commitment, the distinction clearly matters to social identity, in interaction with threat. The context provided by group commitment, together with group threat or self-threat, determines loyalty to the ingroup.

## Attraction to the Group Fosters Cohesion

People join groups in part because they become attracted to groups at a social level that differs from attraction to the individual group members. The social attraction hypothesis (Hogg, 1992, 1993) proposes that attraction to the group is not simply the sum of individual members' attraction to each other. Rather, it reflects the forces that keep the group together. Theoretically, **social attraction** results from interdependence in the satisfaction or expected satisfaction of one's goals, and social attraction turns people into a psychologically meaningful group.

Empirically, social attraction results from identification, which itself reflects not only identifying with the group, but also having a clear sense of the group's prototype and seeing self as prototypical. Social attraction does not result from interpersonal attraction, which relates to similarity and personal friendship (as we saw in Chapter 7). In an intergroup context, depersonalized social attraction hinges on self-categorization as a group member, not interpersonal relations (Hogg & Hains, 1996). Perceived prototypicality as a group member itself is associated with social attraction, not personal attraction, in both enduring organizational groups and ad hoc student groups (Hogg, Cooper-Shaw, & Holzworth, 1993).

Social attraction predicts conformity to the group (Hogg, 2001; Hogg & Hains, 1998; Hogg & Hardie, 1992), so it is useful for group cohesion. When group members are attracted to the ideal of the group, its prototype, they adhere to its norms regardless of individual friendships. Social attraction is the glue that builds group cohesion.

Social attraction has theoretical origins in interdependence, that is, people being attracted to groups that meet goals they cannot meet as individuals. However, the attraction-interdependence link is less than clear from the social-identity/self-categorization theory (SIT/SCT) approaches, which have not pursued interdependence in detail. Indeed, a narrow interpretation of SIT/SCT would say that categorization, not interdependence, suffices for group membership and attraction. However, group-level interdependence by itself, rather than similarity (an interpersonal variable), does form the ingroup boundaries (Flippen, Hornstein, Siegel, & Weitzman, 1996). In a study of pedestrians encountering an allegedly lost envelope, neighborhood residents helped unknown other residents more when their common fate was stressed (their neighborhood was perceived to be under threat). Identification with the group goes hand-in-hand with interdependence in the service of group goals (Caporael & Dawes, 1991).

## Diversity Both Challenges and Facilitates the Group

Although we have just seen that interpersonal similarity does not affect attraction to the group as a whole, variability in composition of the group does matter to group identity. **Diversity** can reflect variety in visible demographic variables such as ethnicity, gender, and age, or it can reflect variety in nonobservable attributes such as values, skills, or experience (Mannix & Neale, 2005; Milliken & Martins, 1996; Williams & O'Reilly, 1998). Identifying with a diverse group is harder, perhaps because the group is a less clearly defined entity. As we saw, depersonalized attraction to a group fosters cohesion, so the diversity of group composition should matter to group members because it might undercut cohesion. As we noted at the outset (Levine & Moreland, 1998), naturally interacting groups typically comprise 2–6 members, and in practice they indeed are often homogeneous. Groups are more homogeneous on personal attributes than would be expected by chance. One common mechanism—recruitment from within the larger organization—encourages the trend toward homogeneity (e.g., Jackson et al., 1991). People are attracted to similar others, as we know from Chapter 7, which makes difficult people's interactions with people who differ from themselves, as we know from Chapter 11.

Primarily focusing on field settings, diversity's effects differ in the affective, cognitive, and behavioral domains. Affectively, as the previous chapter might suggest, many group members are uncomfortable with diversity (e.g., Pelled, Eisenhardt, & Xin, 1999). Members of the contextually minority category within any particular group are the most unhappy, perhaps because they stand out (Mullen, 1991). Indeed, dissatisfaction with being the minority particularly occurs for men and for whites, who may not be used to being in that position (Williams & O'Reilly, 1998). The minority subcategory often expresses lower satisfaction, commitment, and identification, as well as perceiving discrimination (a tendency that occurs regardless of the minority's own gender or ethnicity). The group as a whole experiences some coordination costs—friction and conflict—leading to lower social integration (e.g., Mannix & Neale, 2005; O'Reilly, Caldwell, & Barnett, 1989).

The behavioral results of these uncomfortable feelings (particularly for people who are different—the minority subgroups in a given setting) are absenteeism, deviant behavior, and increased turnover (e.g., Jackson et al., 1991; Wagner, Pfeffer, & O'Reilly, 1984). All these factors would tend to increase the homogeneity of the group, if attrition selects out the people who are different. Many of the conflict and turnover effects can improve over time, however, as people accept the diversity as inevitable and learn to work together (Pelled et al., 1999; Watson, Kumar, & Michaelsen, 1993). Also, if people feel affirmed as individuals, then they may feel free to identify with the group, and productivity improves (Swann, Kwan, Polzer, & Milton, 2003). And group diversity can measurably increase morale and cooperation when groups are proud of their own diversity (Cox, Lobel, & McLeod, 1991; Jehn, Northcraft, & Neale, 1999; van Knippenberg & Schippers, 2007).

On the cognitive side, the group clearly benefits from the range of perspectives, innovation, and quality of ideas introduced by diversity (e.g., Hoffman & Maier, 1961). The behavioral results of these creative cognitions are improved performance (Jehn et al., 1999) and communication with outsiders, probably because the group thinks in more complex ways and has more external resources (Milliken & Martins, 1996). Diversity of demographic or nonobservable attributes has enormous symbolic value for the organization, which may indirectly improve identification, commitment, and performance. Overall, some research supports the **value in diversity** hypothesis (Cox, Lobel, & McLeod, 1991), but the road is rocky and paved with conflict. Team-building activities may help (e.g., stressing interdependence and common goals), as may the group endorsing the intrinsic value of its diversity, and simply waiting for time to heal the tensions, as people get used to each other (van Knippenberg & Schippers, 2007).

## Joining a Group Occurs in Stages

Given a diversity of members, as well as variance in identity and attraction, how do a variety of people become members of the group? Consider the last group you joined (your academic concentration, a club). As Figure 12.4 indicates, joining a group is

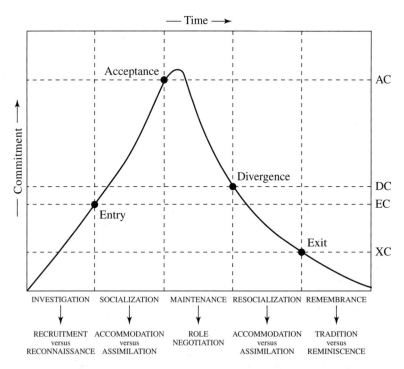

Decision criteria include the entry criterion (EC), acceptance criterion (AC), divergence criterion (DC), and exit criterion (XC).

**Figure 12.4**   Phases of Group Membership

*Source:* Levine et al., 2001. Copyright © Blackwell. Adapted with permission.

a process, not a single outcome (Levine & Moreland, 1994; Levine, Moreland, & Choi, 2001; Moreland & Levine, 1982; see also Bales & Strodtbeck, 1951). Even in formal groups with crisp calendars for initiating new recruits (e.g., colleges, the military), people go through a process of deciding to apply and being accepted, and then after joining, they spend time learning the ropes. For informal groups, joining is less cut-and-dried, but it still constitutes a process with certain typical characteristics. Individuals and groups move through as many as five potential stages that unfold over time and vary in degree of commitment:

- **Investigation**, when individual reconnaissance identifies groups that might meet that person's needs and, reciprocally, group recruitment identifies individuals who might meet the group's goals.
- Upon the individual's entry into the group, **socialization**, when the individual assimilates to the group and the group accommodates the individual.
- Upon mutual acceptance, **maintenance**, when both individual and group negotiate the person's role. If role negotiation succeeds, meeting both individual needs and group goals, mutual commitment remains high and maintains the membership.
- If role negotiation fails, interests diverge, and commitment falls, **resocialization** can attempt to accommodate the group and to assimilate the individual, which can prompt a return to maintenance.
- If interests continue to diverge, and commitment falls further, then the individual may exit the group, creating **remembrance**, when individuals reminiscence about the group and the individual becomes part of the group's history.

Research on the group socialization model has focused on the first, investigation stage (for some work on other stages, see Levine & Moreland, 1994). For example, prospective group members (college freshmen scouting for activities to join) were more optimistic about their own future experiences as group members than about the average other person (suggesting a self-enhancement motive for belonging; Brinthaupt, Moreland, & Levine, 1991). In general, college freshmen with good experiences in high school groups made more effort identifying and pursuing relevant groups (Pavelchak, Moreland, & Levine, 1986). Investigation is mutual, of course, and groups are particularly likely to be open to new members when their numbers (staffing levels) fall below what they need (Cini, Moreland, & Levine, 1993). But new members raise issues of trust, toward them and among existing group members (Moreland & Levine, 2002). Nevertheless, as with other kinds of diversity, new members bring the possibility of innovation (Levine et al., 2001).

## Summary of Group Belonging

Belonging to a group, becoming a member, revolves around one's identity as a group member, which depends on context, as social identity theory and self-categorization theory predict. Individual concerns matter most when group commitment is low, and in that case, threats to self or group simply motivate individual solutions (self-affirmation or individual mobility out of the group). When group commitment is high, group-level concerns matter more, especially under threat of personal exclusion or threat to group cohesion. Depersonalized social attraction to the group fosters cohesion, as members identify with the group prototype, based on their interdependence as group members. Diversity both challenges and benefits the group. Minuses include potential discomfort, friction, and turnover, but pluses include creativity, innovation, and performance. Joining a group is a process, not an outcome, as groups and group members move through mutual investigation, socialization, maintenance, resocialization, and remembrance.

## SOCIALLY SHARED COGNITION: UNDERSTANDING GROUP STRUCTURE

Having joined a group, members acquire an understanding of its norms, culture, roles, leadership, rankings, and coalitions. For groups to function, and especially for groups to function effectively, people have to have an understanding of what's in other people's minds: their positions, relations, norms, and values (Asch, 1952). Moreover, those representations must overlap if the group is to function. As a variant on the Chapter 4 comment derived from William James, namely, that thinking is for doing (S. T. Fiske, 1992), collective thinking is for collective doing (Levine, 1999). As noted in this chapter and last chapter's discussion of social identity and self-categorization, psychological membership in a group derives from linking oneself to the cognitive representation of the group as a whole, its prototype (Turner, Hogg, Oakes, Reicher, & Wetherell, 1987; Hogg, 2000, 2007). These must be socially shared cognitions for the group to function. That is, people's mutual understandings of the group prototype must be good enough for the group to operate effectively.

Social sharing constitutes one criterion for good-enough accuracy. Recall (from Chapter 4) that social consensus sometimes operationalizes accuracy. People's knowledge of each other's minds entails at least some accuracy in judging dispositions such as traits and attitudes, as well as emotions (Chapters 3 and 4). In ongoing interactions, another kind of psychological state also matters, namely people's transitory thoughts and feelings. Ability to judge another person's short-term state constitutes **empathic accuracy**, as distinct from judging more dispositional qualities of the individual (Ickes, 1993). This kind of socially shared understanding—of the other person's goals, thoughts, and feelings—emerges from a history of interaction and an expectation of future interaction, part of any ongoing, psychologically meaningful group.

What's more, this kind of **shared reality**, social verification through joint experience, acknowledged by others, enables people to feel that their subjective experiences (otherwise transitory and random) are objective (fixed and systematic). People create and maintain their experiences through a social process of understanding, in this view (Hardin & Higgins, 1996). SIT/SCT approaches argue that social reality *is* objective reality for group members (as we will see in Chapter 13).

At the group level, operationally, shared understanding comprises people's knowledge of each other's respective contributions (expertise), their representation of systematic links (who works with whom), and subordination (who's under whom) (Weick & Roberts, 1993). For example, as flight operation crews on aircraft carriers heed these collective understandings, errors decrease. Operational reliability results from reasonably accurate, workable, socially shared understandings.

People are encouraged to develop a socially shared reality by various motivations, namely, to define the situation, reduce uncertainty, reach common ground, and communicate effectively (Thompson & Fine, 1999). As Figure 12.5 shows, these motivations for understanding drive goals for social interaction and group interdependence, which result in **shared meaning**. Although socially shared meaning includes affect-laden outcomes, such as group identification and self-enhancement through group membership, these issues were already discussed in this and the previous chapter. Socially shared meaning that results in more overt behavior (such as performance effects) appear in a later section.

A third class of shared meaning is cognitive, including shared mental representations, transactive memory, and shared mental models. These cognitive forms of social meaning lie at the heart of this section. Shared mental representations include **social representations** (Moscovici, 1988), which are everyday, collective ways of explaining strange, new, cultural trends as something more familiar (a current dictator as Hitler, Internet messages as a form of mail, portable computers as notebooks). Social representations emerge from group processes to create commonsense knowledge, framed by the social position of the group vis-à-vis other groups. For example, some types of religious groups, observing that AIDS was at first overrepresented among gay men, spontaneously framed AIDS as divine retribution, whereas anti-American groups framed it as a CIA plot, and racist groups framed it as an African problem (Lorenzi-Cioldi & Clémence, 2001).

Shared mental representations also include **transactive memory** (Wegner, 1986), in which group members delegate different domains of memory expertise to different

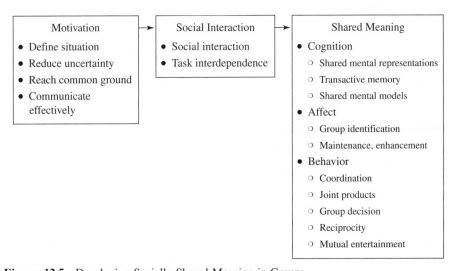

**Figure 12.5** Developing Socially Shared Meaning in Groups

*Source:* From Thompson & Fine, 1999. Copyright © Wiley. Adapted with permission.

people and perform better as a result (Hollingshead, 1998; Wegner, Erber, & Raymond, 1991). For example, one group member might become the informal historian, remembering precedents; one might become the informal ambassador, remembering outside contacts; another might become the organizer, remembering deadlines. Also relevant to group performance are **shared mental models**, which reflect a group's need to hold common representations of task requirements (goals, roles, processes; Klimoski & Mohammed, 1994). A mental model is essentially equivalent to an expectation (Chapter 4). The remainder of this section focuses on various kinds of mental models, focusing in turn on how people develop a shared understanding of group norms, roles including leadership, and structure including subgroups.

## All Norms Are Local

Why do concertgoers sometimes get crushed? Why do victorious sports fans sometimes rampage through downtown, breaking windows and overturning cars? Why do race riots occur? Older ideas had explained the sometimes violent and destructive behavior of mobs as a loss of individual responsibility and autonomy. One of the original social psychology theories, LeBon's (1895) theory of crowd behavior, held that the **collective mind** took over when people in a crowd become anonymous, highly suggestible (easily influenced), and subject to contagion (mindless adoption of others' behavior). In more scientific terms, Festinger, Pepitone, and Newcomb (1952) described a state of **deindividuation** in which people do not act as individuals, and inner restraints against counter-normative behavior fall away, leading to classic mob behavior. A later version of the theory (Zimbardo, 1969) proposed that even individuals could become deindividuated (disinhibited), given such conditions as anonymity, low individual responsibility, arousal, mind-altering substances, sensory overload, or ill-defined situations. Another account focused on lack of **self-awareness** (recall from Chapter 6), leading to deindividuation (Diener, 1980). Typical studies manipulated group size, anonymity, or self-awareness to induce deindividuation. They then measured disinhibition, stealing, cheating, aggression, or failure to help (Postmes & Spears, 1998). Although these are classic social psychology accounts, they may be wrong according to more recent evidence, evidence instead consistent with groups developing a shared social understanding of local norms that guide behavior. Instead of disinhibited behavior in response to deindividuation, crowd behavior may better fit conformity to perceived group norms.

**Norms** are behaviors of group members that act as implicit rules, considered to be both **descriptive** of what group members are and **prescriptive** of how they should be (Levine & Moreland, 1998; Miller & Prentice, 1996). Norms emerge as groups become coherent, developing socially shared understandings. In one view, mere aggregates of people—crowds—become coherent groups as people mill around, exchanging rumors, information, interpretations, and norms, which become the basis for action. Crowds become groups by information exchange, according to **emergent norm theory** (Turner & Killian, 1987). But this theory does not account for rapid changes in understanding, those that occur too quickly to have followed a process of milling around, all people communicating with all others.

Self-categorization and social identity theory (SCT/SIT, cited earlier) do better. If people identify as members of a particular group, then its norms follow. For example, a speaker at a rally will often evoke particular group identities (American citizenship, oppressed ethnicity, neighborhood residence) in order to evoke particular norms (thus, shared ideas about what the present group should do) and therefore shared actions. Meta-analysis of 60 studies fails to support predictions from the older deindividuation theories but instead indicates that **situation-specific norms** predict collective behavior (Postmes & Spears, 1998). For example, although a crowd's behavior may be counternormative with respect to society at large, the crowd as a group expresses its own norms for appropriate behavior in that particular situation, which may include smashing store windows or even attacking certain (outgroup) categories of people.

In particular, one SIT model of crowds, the **social identity model of deindividuation** (Reicher, Spears, & Postmes, 1995), argues that as a particular group identity becomes salient, people strategically express that identity by contextually evoked behavior. Under an elaborated social identity model (Reicher, 2001), people's identity in crowds develops as part of the intergroup interaction. An observational research example: Crowds in various protest movements often initially represent both moderate and extreme factions, but an external group (the police or an opposing protest movement) may treat them all alike as equally extreme and illegitimate. The outgroup (police) defining the ingroup (protesters) as a homogeneous category causes the outgroup to move against the ingroup crowd, unifying the heterogeneous factions in the face of such treatment. As political activists know, police action can radicalize the moderates.

Group behavior may look irrational from the outside but may instead be driven by the contingencies of the particular situation, which include the behavior of powerful outgroups. Shared social norms define what behavior the ingroup members view as contextually appropriate, according to their potentially changing definition of their own identities in the intergroup context. Deindividuation, in this view, depersonalizes the individual and makes ingroup identity cognitively salient, enhancing the importance of ingroup norms. At the same time, deindividuation makes it strategically possible for group members to express their identity if they are identifiable to the ingroup but not to the outgroup, thereby freeing them to act on their own group's norms with fewer concerns for consequences from an opposing outgroup. Clearly, this view of norms is highly sensitive to the context.

More generally, defining norms as local is far more effective than expecting group members to act on abstract societal norms. For every abstract norm, some subgroup defines itself in part by acting against it. (Try thinking of a societal norm that does not get contradicted by at least one social group, as we have defined it.) Like politics, all norms are local. According to Miller and Prentice (1996), norms are a function of context, which is inherently local. For example, research shows that people's global self-esteem and judgments of their own ability depend entirely on their standard of comparison, which tends to be local. That is, students in a high-caliber school actually view themselves less favorably than do students of the same ability level in a low-caliber school (Marsh & Parker, 1984), because of their frame of reference. Also, recall from Chapter 7 the importance of physical attractiveness to initial liking: Even standards for attractiveness can change, depending on the attractiveness of others in context—presumably a kind of social norm—changing evaluations of one's potential romantic partner (Kenrick & Gutierres, 1980; Kenrick, Gutierres, & Goldberg, 1989). Local norms and standards guide perceptions and behavior.

As implicit rules, norms are not given. People must infer norms (Miller & Prentice, 1996), and they do so by direct communication ("this is how we do things here"), observing behavior (everyone walking around in orange and black jackets), and extrapolating from self-knowledge (if I am willing to do it, then everyone in my ingroup must be). Direct communication might seem the least ambiguous method of socializing people to norms, but in practice, socialization involves both what is said and what is unsaid. What is said depends on a host of factors, all reflecting the norm's apparent support, on the basis of social desirability, perceived trends, and known traditions. What is unsaid depends paradoxically on what people assume is so obvious or normal that it does not have to be said. For example, people explain the gender gap in voting behavior (e.g., whereby women tend to show less support for war) by explaining the nonnormative group (in this case, women, as I did here; Miller, Taylor, & Buck, 1991). This implies that the standard, normative voter is male, so women need to be explained, just as the standard, normative parent is female, so the fathers' behavior has to be explained.

Inferring norms is not the only process in constructing them. People also pick certain others to observe. As noted in Chapter 5, social comparison serves functions of understanding and self-enhancement by evaluating self in comparison to norms represented by particular others one chooses to heed. Several principles apply. In making comparisons, first, people heavily weight others who are similar on characteristics relevant to the judgment, according to **related attributes theory** (Goethals & Darley, 1977). Second, when people do construct comparisons by relevant attributes, those are relatively universalistic assessments, but people often prefer to weight ingroup others, those relevant according to shared identity, and make **particularistic evaluations**, rather than general ones (Miller, Turnbull, & McFarland, 1988). People may specifically seek comparisons on attributes relevant to performance in that particular group, because esteem derives from group feedback (Darley, 2001). For example, the relevant standards differ considerably in task groups and affinity (social) groups. Third, people may compare to groups that are not their own membership groups, that is, **reference groups** they admire and want to emulate (or derogate and want to avoid), even if those are not their ingroups. Not all membership groups are reference groups and vice versa. Finally, as noted in Chapter 5, people sometimes prefer esteem-enhancing downward comparisons that promote comfort and reduce threat, but sometimes they do seek self-improving upward comparisons. All forms of comparison appraise the self vis-à-vis norms perceived to be relevant in a given context, so those norms often are quite specific.

Moreover, the salience of norms will differ, as will their importance in guiding behavior. Both the salience of norms and accountability to the ingroup will increase the importance of enforcing ingroup norms (Marques, Abrams, Paez, & Martinez-Taboada, 1998). Norms matter because people who do not conform to the local group norms pay a substantial price, if the group matters to people and if the deviance occurs on a dimension relevant to the group's purpose. Group members first try persuading ingroup deviants to change and then reject deviants, as classic social psychology has shown (Schachter, 1951). Deviants who consistently maintain an opinion that differs from modal group opinion are rejected, especially if their subgroup size is substantial, according to meta-analysis (Tanford & Penrod, 1984; Tata et al., 1996).

Group members enforce ingroup norms by several techniques. One way is by derogating deviant ingroup members and modal outgroup members (both of whom challenge ingroup norms and support outgroup norms) (Marques et al., 1998). Another way is by enhancing those who conform (ingroup modal and outgroup deviant). Group members bolster their social identity by enforcing ingroup norms, as we saw earlier in arguing for the primacy of the ingroup, and the resulting black sheep effect that penalizes ingroup deviants even more than typical outgroup members. Another piece of evidence argues for the importance of defending ingroup norms, as a route to a legitimate and distinctive ingroup identity. When ingroup norms are especially uncertain, group members particularly derogate an ingroup deviant (Marques, Abrams, & Serodio, 2001). Finally, it is not deviance from the ingroup average that matters, so much as counternormative deviance; ingroup members who deviate in favor of the group norm—but more extremely than the modal ingroup member—are valued. Pronorm deviance is preferred (Abrams, Marques, Bown, & Henson, 2000). It's not the deviance the group rejects, it's the norm that the group protects.

According to a theory of **subjective group dynamics** (Marques et al., 2001; see Figure 12.6), descriptive ingroup norms often operate automatically, as in categorizing "us versus them" by salient physical features (see top *inter*group half of figure). The automaticity of social categorization (e.g., by gender, race, and age), as well as social categorization theory's meta-contrast principle (both described in Chapter 11), point to this type of rapidly assessed descriptive ingroup norm. People automatically classify self and others, making ingroup deviants salient.

However, ingroup deviants make salient the prescriptive, *intra*group norms (lower half of figure): Why doesn't this person fit in? This question matters, as noted, more for ingroup than outgroup, due to needs for positive identity. This two-process model is analogous to others we have seen, whereby the default is rapid and automatic, whereas the troubleshooting deliberative mode intervenes in the event of problems. The subjective group dynamics bring to people's minds the interdependence between self and ingroup, as well as renewed awareness of and commitment to ingroup prescriptive norms, with consequent derogation of outgroup deviants, as in the black sheep effect. Although complex, the model shows both inter- and intragroup dynamics.

When ingroup deviants make prescriptive norms salient, people try to explain the deviant, reasoning backward to consider the standard the person has violated. **Norm theory** (Kahneman & Miller, 1986) describes this kind of backward processing. When people encounter an unexpected event, they reason backward to generate a context-specific frame of reference (i.e., a norm) to understand why the event feels counterintuitive. The reasoning process creates a **counterfactual** (what could have been); Chapter 4 described this process of mentally undoing a unfortunate event, but the theory applies to any unexpected event, such as an ingroup member who deviates from ingroup norms. Constructing what-should-have-been makes people aware (in

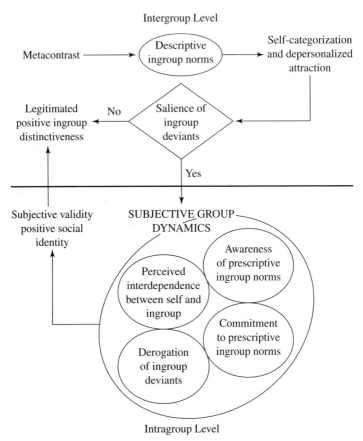

**Figure 12.6**   A Model of Subjective Group Dynamics, Separating Automatic Intergroup and Deliberative Intragroup Levels

*Source:* Marques et al., 2001. Copyright © Blackwell. Adapted with permission.

retrospect) of the norm that has been violated, fixing the prescriptive norm that is otherwise taken for granted (Forsyth, 1995).

Norms depend on the immediate group context and one's social identity. Norms matter, expressing group members' social identity. Norms matter because group members influence each other (Tanford & Penrod, 1984). Norms matter because they predict attitudes (Cooper, Kelly, & Weaver, 2001) and behavior (Ajzen, 1996; Terry & Hogg, 1996) that basically conform to the group. Norms also matter because they show how motivated people are to belong to the group and understand its implicit rules, to avoid rejection, as well as to express social identity.

## Roles Include Leadership and Much More

People typically conform to group norms, for reasons of both expressing group identity and avoiding group censure. Nevertheless, people also need to balance the self and the group. Social roles serve this function. Social **roles**—expectations for the behavior of a person in a particular position—differ from norms because they pertain to a single person or set of people occupying that position (e.g., Levine & Moreland, 1998). Because of this mix of individual and group, social roles meet needs both for connectedness to the group (belonging) and for autonomy of the self (controlling), as viewed through the lens of need satisfaction (Bettencourt & Sheldon, 2001). Students in both ongoing and ad hoc social groups rated roles that fostered their own authentic self-expression as also being those that best met their needs for group relatedness. Autonomy and relatedness each separately predicted subjective well-being. This principle also supports Brewer's optimal distinctiveness theory (Chapter 11). Thus, understanding and fulfilling one's social role can combine what might otherwise seem to be conflicting motives for group belonging and individual controlling.

Roles also function well for the group (Levine & Moreland, 1998), developing as the group needs them, rewarding those who fulfill those group functions, and improving group dynamics. Group roles that come immediately to laypeople's minds are leader and follower, but the range of potential roles is far more complex: task facilitator, socio-emotional facilitator, idea person, recorder, scapegoat, devil's advocate, entertainer, ambassador, realist, and more. Ironically, the functional contribution of roles has been studied less than their dysfunctional qualities. Role dysfunctions include conflict over who should have what role, failed consensus over what the role entails, ambiguity for enacting the role, strain in playing the role, conflict between simultaneous roles, and transitions into and out of roles.

One reason most roles may escape research attention could be the difficulty of feasibly operationalizing them. Some work manipulates roles by defining and then assigning them to ad hoc groups (Bettencourt & Sheldon, 2001). Other work defines roles by their place in the SYMLOG dimensions introduced earlier: upward/downward, forward/backward, and positive/negative (Isenberg & Ennis, 1981). Using only the upward/downward dimension, a specific operationalization of the leadership role could be sheer talking time (Mullen, Salas, & Driskell, 1989; Stein & Heller, 1979); according to meta-analysis, this holds regardless of whether group members or observers identify the leader and whether the group is real or artificial.

Nevertheless, leaders are something more than the biggest talkers. Leaders do tend to be extraverted, open to experience, and conscientious (Hogg, 2007). According to meta-analyses, they are close to others, central to group communication, satisfied with the group, and esteemed (Bass, 1954; Mullen, 1991). How does this happen? Leadership depends less on individual personality characteristics than people—including social psychologists—think at first (Chemers, 2000; Hogg, 2007; Hollander, 1985; Levine & Moreland, 1998). People who are leaders in one group are not necessarily leaders in another group, in part because group tasks may require a variety of expertise (motor, artistic, mathematical, literary, social, spatial; Barlund, 1962). Nevertheless, consistent leaders do emerge, averaging as much as 64% of ratings being due to something about the individual, perhaps adaptability to different contexts (Kenny & Zaccaro, 1983). Four major types of theory address contextual factors, stressing the leaders' responsiveness to a particular group.

First, **contingency theories** (e.g., Fiedler, 1964, 1978) hold that effective leaders emerge as a function of the interaction between person and situation. In this theory, the leader's own personal style (relative task or social emphasis) interacts with the group's degree of situational control (degree of authority, task clarity, quality of relationships). When situational control is moderate, a social style should work well. But a task emphasis should work well when control is either very low (structure is needed) or very high (efficiency is fine). Leadership style is operationalized by a test of the leader's regard for the **least preferred coworker** (less dislike for one's least favorite person indicating greater tolerance and more social orientation). The original datasets analyzed to produce this curvilinear theory supported it better than subsequent studies did, but the overall support is not bad (Graen, Alvares, Orris, & Martella, 1970; Peters, Hartke, & Pohlmann, 1985; Strube & Garcia, 1981), and subsequent theories picked up the idea of leadership interacting with the group's situation (Chemers, 2000; Howell, Dorfman, & Kerr, 1986). This type of theory echoes core social motives of group effectiveness and control over outcomes, as well as shared understandings of who's in charge and what that means.

A second wave of leadership theory, **transactional leadership theories**, emphasize leader and follower exchange of valued resources (praise, esteem, loyalty, as well as tangible rewards). In this view (Burns, 1978), ordinary people as followers need not reach consensus with each other or their political and ideological leaders. Instead, conflicts create a dynamic reciprocal exchange that in turn creates leaders. That is, the leader is the one who can distribute resources the most effectively and receive resources in turn from each other group member. This theory, which emphasizes motives of control over resources and self-enhancement, also relies on shared understanding of and compliance with group norms.

Leadership theory based on contingency or transaction did not, however, sufficiently explain cultural and demographic differences, so it returned to some of the personality ideas that started this line of work. A third wave of leadership research, cognitive theories emphasizing **leadership prototypes**, makes some inroads here, clearly demonstrating the motive for shared understanding constrained by a particular context (Lord, Brown, & Harvey, 2001; Lord & Maher, 1991). Leader prototypes specify intelligence, masculinity, and dominance, according to meta-analysis (Lord, de Vader, & Alliger, 1986). Moreover, across cultures (62 nations; Den Hartog et al., 1999), people's implicit theory of leadership tends to agree on ideal leaders being visionary, inspirational, team-integrating, trustworthy, diplomatic, and not self-centered, malevolent, inexplicit, or autocratic. Cultures differ the most on whether leaders are supposed to be harmony-oriented (conflict-avoidant, subdued, sensitive). A leader can be both dominant and insist on avoiding conflict (some collectivist cultures) or dominant and tolerate conflict (some individualist cultures). Whatever the cultural expectation, people unconsciously evaluate potential leaders on their fit to salient leadership prototypes (Emrich, 1999), make attributions on that basis (Phillips & Lord, 1981), and remember accordingly (Lord, Foti, & De Vader, 1984; Phillips & Lord, 1982).

To the extent that cultures expect leaders to be masculine, people view women as being poor candidates for leadership. According to this **lack-of-fit model** (Heilman, 1983, 2001), people's expectations for good managers and for typical women do not mesh—indeed, prototypical managers have masculine characteristics—so people tend to be biased against the idea of women as leaders. Meta-analyses indicate a small overall tendency to evaluate female leaders less favorably, but this is particularly true when the female leader behaves in a stereotypically masculine style, that is, outside the gender role, though inside the leader role (Eagly, Makhijani, & Klonsky, 1992). This is unfortunate, given that actual leaders in organizations do not differ by gender in their leadership styles (Eagly & Johnson, 1990), so quite a few task-oriented women leaders are likely to end up being devalued. Men and women leaders are equally effective, according to meta-analysis, but not surprisingly, men fare better when leadership is defined in more masculine terms (Eagly, Karau, & Makhijani, 1995). All these results tend to support a **social role theory** of leadership, emphasizing perceived lack of fit for women in certain kinds of leadership roles. Bias in evaluating women leaders is global (Schein, 2001), resting on the assumption that men will be more legitimate and competent leaders, according to **expectation states theory** (Ridgeway, 2001). Certain ascribed status characteristics (e.g., being male, white, older) lead to assumptions about who will (and will not) top the hierarchy. Women do disproportionately hold roles incompatible with enhancing hierarchies and themselves leading them. That is, women instead hold hierarchy-attenuating roles (e.g., helpers and caretakers, rather than enforcers and competitors), as predicted by social dominance theory (Pratto, Stallworth, Sidanius, & Siers, 1997; introduced in Chapter 11). The dearth of women in hierarchy-enhancing positions seems to be due not only to hiring biases, as lack-of-fit would predict, but also to self-selection (women opt out) and to value-matching (hierarchy-enhancing values tend to favor men).

Social identity theories, the fourth and new wave of leadership theories, take the concept of leader prototype one step further (Hogg, 2001, 2007). In this view, group members differ in how much they fit the prototype of the group. Recall that depersonalized social attraction to the group encourages cohesion, because group members identify with the group prototype, based on their interdependence in the service of shared goals. Because of members' attraction to the prototype, the person who best fits the group prototype will have the most influence and therefore be the leader. Consensual social attraction also confers apparent status, which leads to power relations in which followers depend on leaders and attend to them as unique individuals (Fiske, 1993; Fiske & Dépret, 1996). Correspondence bias or the fundamental attribution error (Chapter 3) assigns the leader's influence to allegedly special features of that individual's personality. All this results in a leader being seen as the one who best represents the group's identity. Group membership has to be salient for this process to occur, creating a frame of reference in which group members see themselves as similar to each other (Hogg, Hains, & Mason, 1998). When people do identify with the group (i.e., it is salient to them), they endorse leaders prototypical of the ingroup (Platow & van Knippenberg, 2001), as the social identity theory of leadership would suggest.

Regardless of which leadership theory one endorses, leaders' behavior affects people in the reciprocal role, that is, followers. Declaring someone a leader can make others work *less* hard, for example (Kerr & Stanfel, 1993), but generally, people like to have a leader. To the extent the leader leads (by initiating structure or considering others), followers are more satisfied, according to meta-analyses (Lowe, Kroeck, & Sivisubramaniam, 1996; Mullen, Symons, Hu, & Salas, 1989; Wofford & Liska, 1993). Groups need leaders to coordinate effectively, but leader-follower ambivalence is perhaps inevitable, due to possible exploitation (Van Vugt, Hogan, & Kaiser, 2008; also see next chapter's discussion of power).

According to meta-analysis, people prefer democratic leadership, especially when it is authentically democratic, and this is more true as group size increases (presumably because smaller groups have more cohesion and less need of explicit democracy) (Foels, Driskell, Mullen, & Salas, 2000; Gastil, 1994). Legitimate authority in groups rests on **procedural justice**—that is, on having fair processes—not just on people's own personal outcomes (Tyler & Lind, 1992). People want to feel that, in being treated fairly, they are respected by the group and can feel proud of the group (Tyler, Degoey, & Smith, 1996); in other words, their belonging is affirmed. Democracy doubtless ranks high as a fair process because it respects everyone's opinions as an equally valued member of the group.

Many of the leadership theories address a shared understanding motive, specifying who and what the leader is to be. In addition (Chemers, 2000, 2001), leaders function to meet people's other core social motives by establishing credibility (trusting), relationship (belonging), and effectiveness (controlling). The leadership role is, by definition, the most influential role, but all roles embody the shared understanding of group structure.

## Subgroups: Minorities and Majorities

So far, we have examined mutually understood group structure in the form of norms as implicit rules and individual roles emphasizing leadership. Now we turn to structures of member relationships within groups. The patterns of member relations represent various networks of liking, status, influence, and communication. As Figure 12.7 indicates, people may like each other reciprocally or not, as revealed by various networks of **sociometric choice** (Moreno, 1953; introduced in Chapter 7). People's communication patterns (frequency of who-to-whom) constitute part of the SYMLOG record already mentioned. And influence hierarchies appear in members' judging each other and self on (e.g.) influence, contributions, and popularity (Arrow, 1997). By these measures, small groups show a fair degree of equilibrium in structure over time, readjusting after disruptions such as member turnover. Status hierarchies are communicated by repeated enactment of deference (hesitant, unconfident, unassertive behavior); they quickly result in consensus judgments of members' status and competence (Ridgeway & Erickson, 2000).

Subgroups inevitably result from patterns of influence, status, communication, and liking. **Social impact theory** (Latané, 1981; to be addressed in more detail next chapter), a dynamical social computational model, argues that four features of group dynamics result from spatially adjacent individuals influencing each other. These features are the relevant point here: (a) consolidation of the group, (b) clustering of subgroup opinions, (c) correlations of opinions within subgroup clusters, and (d) continuing diversity by protecting minorities within subgroups (Latané & Bourgeois,

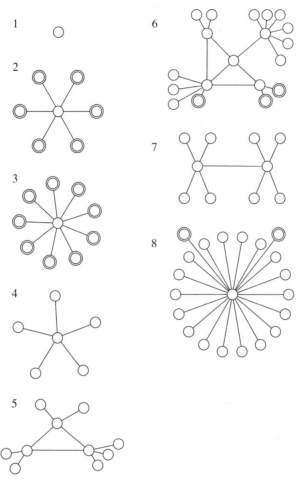

**Figure 12.7** Patterns of Sociometric Choice Typical in an Early Field Study
*Source:* Moreno, 1953.

2001). Because people most often interact with and influence those adjacent to them-selves, even if the group started out with randomly distributed opinions, subgroup opinion clusters would eventually result, as Latané and colleagues have shown via computer models simulating social impact on attitude change. For current purposes, the point is that the existence of subgroups within an overall group is likely. And recognizing this inevitability may even maintain group harmony (Hornsey & Hogg, 2000; Kameda & Sugimori, 1995; see Chapter 11 on subgroups).

Whenever subgroups occur, some will be larger and some smaller. As our dis-cussion of group norms has implied (and as the topic of conformity in the next chapter will develop), people typically conform to the larger group. The 1940 Asch line-perception conformity study, introduced in Chapter 1, nicely illustrates that idea and has had substantial impact. In reaction to all that emphasis on conformity to majority group norms, Moscovici (1976, 1980, 1985) argued that **minority influence** is important to innovation. It results from the conflict that minorities create (Levine & Russo, 1987; Martin & Hewstone, 2001). In this view, minorities are a force for innovation because they advocate their positions with consistency, confidence, and conviction, so they disrupt the existing norm, creating uncertainty. Because they will not budge, they demand attention for their alternative position, and the majority is forced to accommodate and consider their understanding of the issues. As originally conceived, minorities provide **informational influence**, pressuring group members to validate their position and convert by virtue of the merit of the information available (thus, the understanding motive). In contrast, people conform to majorities by **normative influence**, whereby they compare themselves to other group members and do what they do (thus, the belonging motive). As the next chapter will show, these two forms of influence are applied more broadly than minority and minority influence (but appear here for the first time in this chapter.) A related two-process idea proposed different kinds of thinking engendered by majorities—**convergent thinking** (unreflective acceptance of conventional wisdom)—and minorities—**divergent thinking** (attending to a wider range of information and re-examining premises to come to more creative decisions) (Nemeth, 1986).

Research supports some, but not all, aspects of the theory (Wood, 2000). Minority impact results from a consistent but flexible ingroup minority whose deviant opinions otherwise fit the group's values (Mugny, Perez, & Lamongie, 1991). Ingroup minorities are influential when their stands do not threaten the group's existence (Crano, 2000). The unexpected distinctiveness of the ingroup minority's message encourages careful consideration of their viewpoint, with a **leniency contract** (benefit of the doubt) accorded to them because of their ingroup status (Alvaro & Crano, 1997; Crano & Chen, 1998). Minority influence can be persistent precisely because it is information-based, especially if the topic is not central to the group and the minority is active (Kerr, 2002). Individualistic cultures are especially likely to show higher decision quality under minority influence, but collectivistic cultures do also, if the minority influence agent is high status (Ng & Van Dyne, 2001).

In an odd twist, minority influence is most often indirect, according to meta-analysis (Wood, Lungren, Ouellette, Busceme, & Blackstone, 1994). That is, minorities have an influence on topics that are related to, but not equivalent to, their focal arguments, as if majority members do not want to admit that the minority changed the majority's mind. Consistent with this form of indirect influence is a stronger minority effect on measures that are private, concealed from the source. People's self-esteem suffers when they find themselves aligned with derogated minorities (Pool, Wood, & Leck, 1998), so they shift accordingly (Wood, Pool, Leck, & Purvis, 1996).

Identification with the ingroup is a necessary condition for minority influence (Leonardelli, 2001). This fits much of the other work we have seen that emphasizes the importance of social identity and the primacy of the ingroup. Outgroup minorities have little influence.

Some of the dynamics of subgroups depend on sheer impact of numbers on cognition. The proportionate sizes of different groups affect who captures attention; small numbers attract attention because they stand out (Taylor, 1981; Taylor & Fiske, 1978). As noted in Chapter 4, salience has social cognitive consequences. The smaller perceptual unit (minority) appears as a figure against the larger group as a background. A series of meta-analyses focused on salience, as a function of groups' proportionate size (Mullen, 1991), indicated that people in the minority have more self-focused attention, overestimate their own consensus, exaggerate their own ingroup bias, see themselves as more alike, and see group differences as larger. Reciprocally, majorities do over-attend to minorities, overestimate their consensus, and view them as all alike. So the cognitive effects of proportionate subgroup sizes are a two-way street.

What are the consequences for members of smaller subgroups to have more self-focused attention (Mullen, 1983)? **Solos** or **tokens** (who are the only members of their social categories) can be distracted by the experience of other people attending to them and their own self-consciousness as a result. Consequently, they may not remember as much as uninvolved observers do (Lord & Saenz, 1985); the memory deficit appears to result from being worried about the scrutiny of others and the impression one is making (Lord, Saenz, & Godfrey, 1987). Indeed, if tokens mentally restructure their role so that they are the ones judging others, instead of focusing on being judged, the effect completely evaporates (Saenz & Lord, 1989).

Whether single individuals or small subgroups, minorities within groups are critical to understanding the group's structure, even if much of the influence they exert is indirect. Some of the consistency and conviction of opinion minorities may result from the cognitive factors that increase their ingroup focus.

## Summary of Group Cognition

Group structure results from socially shared understandings of the group. Norms specify implicit local rules for group members' behavior. Specific individuals fill roles that specify the behavior expected of them, and leaders fill a particularly important role. Subgroups within the group emerge as a function of differing opinions, and ingroup minorities can elicit thoughtful but indirect forms of opinion change.

## PERFORMANCE: UNDERSTANDING AND CONTROLLING

Shared group understanding determines group performance. To the extent that cognitions, identities, and preferences of group members are shared, those socially shared ideas will have a greater impact on group outcomes (Tindale & Kameda, 2000). Social sharedness is crucial to group decision making and performance, in keeping with the core social motive of understanding. Not only are group members motivated to have socially shared understandings, but they also are motivated to obtain favorable outcomes; that is, they show the core motive for controlling what happens to them. Typically following both the understanding and controlling motives, social psychologists' research on group performance focuses on decision making and productivity.

## Decision Making

Conventional wisdom promotes group decisions as more considered and balanced than individual decisions, resulting in better quality decisions overall. However, fifty years ago, two group phenomena proved conventional wisdom to be wrong. First, groups make more polarized (extreme) decisions than the aggregation of individual decisions. Second, they pressure group members to agree and not to consider deviant viewpoints. These two decision phenomena have shaped the study of group decision making ever since.

**GROUP POLARIZATION**   Early research indicated that group discussion surprisingly leads to more risky decisions than the original preferences of any of the group members as individuals (Wallach, Kogan, & Bem, 1964; for an early review, see Myers & Lamm, 1976). Although originally dubbed the **risky shift**, it turns out that groups go to extremes in *either* a more risky or a more cautious direction, so the effect more accurately became **group polarization**. Meta-analyses (Isenberg, 1986) initially supported either of two processes: (a) Merely knowing other people's views creates a normative influence process of social comparison, whereby group discussion reveals cultural values more extreme than those of individuals, so members shift to gain approval. (b) Hearing other people's arguments creates an informational influence process of persuasive arguments, whereby group discussion highlights novel arguments that favor its initial tendency, causing group members to become more extreme (Burnstein & Sentis, 1981). Later work also supported (c) a social-identity/self-categorization theory approach, whereby group members construct a group prototype, to which they conform (Turner, Wetherell, & Hogg, 1989). This ideal prototype may serve identity by being more extreme than the average group member's opinion, so conformity leads to polarization (McGarty, Turner, Hogg, Davidson, & Wetherell, 1992). As a variant on this process, priming the ingroup leads to attitude assimilation, whereas priming the outgroup leads to contrast, creating attitude polarization depending on context and group identity (Ledgerwood & Chaiken, 2007). Still another possibility does not depend on the individual feeling connected to the group: (d) people become more convinced, the more they repeat their own arguments (Brauer, Judd, & Gliner, 1995), consistent with mere exposure, availability, or self-enhancement.

**GROUPTHINK**   Groupthink illustrates the failure of groups to consider all available and relevant information in making a decision (Janis, 1972). First observed in policy-making groups responsible for some incredible international fiascos (e.g., the United States 1961 Bay of Pigs invasion of Cuba), **groupthink** theoretically results from a "psychological drive for consensus at any cost that suppresses dissent and appraisal of alternatives in cohesive decision-making groups." Groupthink theoretically occurs when the group is cohesive and isolated, the leader is biased, procedures are unclear, and members are homogeneous. Provocative situations include high stress from external threats with no good solution, and a temporary drop in self-esteem because of recent failures, current difficulties, and moral dilemmas.

Although an appealing theory that deserves to be true, and although evidence from descriptive studies seemed supportive, nonetheless groupthink experiments failed to pin it down clearly (Aldag & Fuller, 1993; Kerr & Tindale, 2004; Mullen, Anthony, Salas, & Driskell, 1994). General models of group problem solving currently seem more useful.

**GROUP PROBLEM SOLVING**    Decision-making groups are trying to solve a problem, and clearly both task and social dimensions matter. For example, information sharing is key to task performance. Individuals often prefer information that supports their initial attitudes over information that conflicts, as Chapter 6 indicated. Groups prefer supportive information as well (Schulz-Hardt, Frey, Luethgens, & Moscovici, 2000; Stasser & Titus, 1985). Group members also prefer to discuss information that is already shared, rather than unshared, so shared information has more influence on group decisions (Kerr & Tindale, 2004; Stasser & Titus, 1985; introduced in Chapter 1, Table 1). The **common knowledge effect**—the influence of previously shared information—could result either from sheer likelihood of being brought up in the discussion, from people's preference for shared information, from carrying more weight in individual judgments, or from premature closure, the sheer press to decide (Gigone & Hastie, 1997; Kerr & Tindale, 2004; Stasser & Titus, 1987). Groups do show this less-than-optimal tendency to neglect unshared information, especially under cognitive load and time pressure, consistent with groupthink predictions. They do, however, get to unshared information eventually, over time (Larson, Foster-Fishman, & Keys, 1994; Stasser & Titus, 1987). And knowing who knows what—that is, assigning certain people to be experts—facilitates the mentioning of unshared information (Stewart & Stasser, 1995).

Social cohesiveness is also key, in keeping with social identity approaches. Depersonalized social attraction promotes groupthink, whereas personal friendships undermine it (Hogg & Hains, 1998). When other antecedents (e.g., overly directive leadership) promote groupthink, cohesiveness exaggerates the detrimental effect on group decision making (Mullen, Anthony, Salas, & Driskell, 1994). This holds true especially for cohesiveness operationalized as attraction.

A series of such results shows how complicated group decision making really is. No single broad-brush model will make sense of all the important factors. Parts of the process are indicated in Figure 12.8 (Aldag & Fuller, 1993). Various antecedent conditions include characteristics of the decision (e.g., its importance, time pressure), the group structure (e.g., cohesiveness, homogeneity), and the context (goals, political realities). Emergent group characteristics result from this combination of a particular group making a particular decision in a particular context. For example, a group's perceived vulnerability might affect its openness to processing negative feedback. The decision process itself then entails a variety of information processing and decision stages, resulting in not only the decision, but also political implications for leaders and group, as well as their satisfaction. All these factors influence how groups go about solving the problem of making their decision.

**PREDICTING GROUP DECISIONS**    If groups' bias equals individuals' bias, how do group decisions result from those individuals (Kerr, MacCoun, & Kramer, 1996)? **Social decision rules** (consistent patterns in the group's rules for its decisions) use less cognitive effort than weighing all the pros and cons of each individual

Antecedents

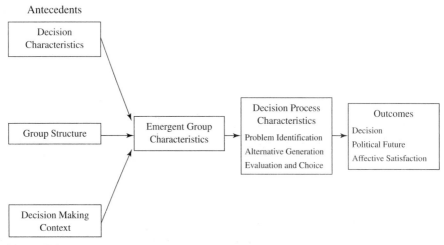

**Figure 12.8**    General Group Problem-Solving Model

*Source:* Aldag & Fuller, 1993. Copyright © American Psychological Association. Adapted with permission.

person's preferences. For example, many groups use "majorities or pluralities win" to make binary choices (Davis, 1973), especially when no clearly correct alternative emerges. This decision rule may be explicit in group decision procedures; even if not, the final result fits a formal model (mathematical equation) in which the group behaves as if using this rule. "Majority rules" is an adaptive policy (Kerr & Tindale, 2004). If choices require decisions along a continuum, then the rule is "median wins" (Crott, Szilvas, & Zuber, 1991; Davis, Hulbert, Au, Chen, & Zarnoth, 1997); note that the group mean (arithmetic average) does less well than the median (middle value). Again, this is a formal mathematical representation of how to predict the outcome, not the psychological process of group members' decision. If choices require an active consensus building for a decision along a continuum, then the group follows a weighted linear combination, where members' opinions receive more weight if their position is closer to the group's center (Davis et al., 1997).

This last model fits the social sharedness perspective, whereby group members are influential in direct proportion to their representing the group. As the person becomes more cognitively central, the person's influence increases because of perceived expertise resulting from the group agreement (Kameda, Ohtsubo, & Takezawa, 1997). This would contrast with a social-identity/self-categorization model, in which a more extreme (but idealized prototype) group member might carry more weight. All three of the formal models predict the idea of group polarization, in the sense of exaggerating the majority position among individual preferences because members closer to the group median carry more weight (Tindale & Kameda, 2000). The potentially moderating influence of people who disagree is apparently lost in most group decisions, consistent with the findings of group polarization.

Other kinds of decision rules operate when the group must decide on a demonstrably correct answer. In that case, "truth wins," if members share beliefs about how to establish what is true (Laughlin & Ellis, 1986). Groups develop mental models of the problem, just as they develop the previously introduced mental models of norms, roles, and subgroups, functioning better when those understandings are shared (Tindale, 1993).

## Productivity

Groups make decisions in order to be productive, to further their goals, and to obtain desired outcomes. All these goals entail the core social motive to control individual and group outcomes. Depending on its type of work, a group's productivity concretely may include various records of output: revenues, publications, recordings, performances, demand met, and work remaining unfinished. Records of production quality also may include inspector or manager-assigned evaluations (Sundstrom, McIntyre, Halfhill, & Richards, 2000). To the extent that group productivity involves processing information, group motivations explicitly involve the core motive of understanding. Here, cognitive commonality matters to productivity: shared information, as noted earlier; overlap of ideas; depth of cognitive processes; and experience of belonging (Hinsz, Tindale, & Vollrath, 1997). Both understanding and controlling run through productivity, along with the core motive of belonging.

In attempting to understand information, control outcomes, and belong, people often think they will be more productive in groups than alone. Indeed, people do work faster in the presence of others when they have a well-practiced or dominant response, a classic phenomenon termed **social facilitation** (Zajonc, 1965). Even cockroaches show social facilitation, and people show social facilitation to their favorite TV characters (Gardner & Knowles, 2008). Nevertheless, people assume they will be more productive in groups, regardless of task and practice. For example, people think they will generate more ideas brainstorming in groups than alone (Paulus, Dzindolet, Poletes, & Camacho, 1993). In fact, they do not, according to meta-analysis (Mullen, Johnson, & Salas, 1991). But the illusion results from people forgetting who thought of what idea and (through self-enhancement) taking credit for other people's ideas (Paulus et al., 1993; Stroebe, Diehl, & Abakoumkin, 1992). The principle of getting less done in a genuinely interactive group than in a merely **nominal group** (performance aggregated across individuals) is termed **productivity loss**, the most frequent group performance outcome (Kerr & Tindale, 2004), as compared with the few occasions of **productivity gain**.

**PRODUCTIVITY LOSS**    In brainstorming groups, productivity loss partly results from people matching the performance of the least productive member (Paulus & Dzindolet, 1993); people who are individually inhibited about expressing their ideas thus tend to dampen the group's overall production of ideas (Camacho & Paulus, 1995). Inhibited people particularly worry about what others will think of them (**evaluation apprehension**), so social anxiety undermines their motivation to contribute to the group, according to a variety of group studies (Geen, 1991). This fits the pattern of brainstorming groups, where productivity loss is greater under those circumstances especially likely to inhibit shy people: larger groups, experimenter presence, tape-recording oral contributions, and the physical presence of fellow group members (Mullen et al., 1991). Even without shy group members, another explanation for productivity loss in brainstorming groups is sheer access to talking time, whereby more productive members block less productive ones (Paulus, Dugosh, Dzindolet, Coskun, & Putman, 2002; Stroebe & Diehl, 1994).

Beyond brainstorming, research on group productivity indicates the pervasive problem variously called **social loafing** (loss of motivation and effort in group tasks; Latané, Williams, & Harkins, 1979), **free riding** (enjoying group benefits without having to make the effort to contribute; Kerr, 1983; Olson, 1965), and the **sucker effect** (wanting to avoid the risk of being the only one to invest in contributing to benefit the group; Kerr, 1983; Orbell & Dawes, 1981). In keeping with the core social motive of controlling one's outcomes, a key mechanism in all these cases of productivity loss is decreased motivation, when people individually (a) lack incentive to contribute, (b) see contributing as costly, and (c) view their own perspective as dispensable (Shepperd, 1993). In a meta-analysis, social loafing fits this kind of individual incentives perspective: Social loafing is more likely when people are not accountable for their individual inputs to the group, when their inputs are redundant, when expectations of coworker performance are high or moderate, and when the task or group is unpleasant (Karau & Williams, 1993). Also in line with individual incentives, Westerners and men (more individualist, on average) show stronger social loafing effects than Easterners and women.

**PRODUCTIVITY GAIN**    Groups do work better than individuals when they counteract all the processes that lead to productivity loss. For example, providing people with higher standards, comparable to individual performance, eliminates productivity loss that otherwise results from members conforming to the least productive member (Paulus & Dzindolet, 1993). To the extent that the group makes people accountable for their individual inputs to the group, and to the extent that people compete to contribute unique perspectives, rather than feeling dispensable and redundant, they may contribute more (Paulus et al., 2002).

Group cohesiveness also correlates with group performance, according to meta-analyses (Evans & Dion, 1991; Gully, Devine, & Whitney, 1995; Mullen & Copper, 1994). Performance increases cohesiveness more than vice versa, although both are true. The causal factor may be commitment to the task. When people are committed to the task, they attend more to each other's input and stimulate each other (Dugosh, Paulus, Roland, & Yang, 2000; Paulus et al., 2002). Such groups are both more cohesive and more productive. Similarly, when group members are able to get others to see them as they see themselves (i.e., attend to their self-presentations), members feel more connected to their groups and group grades improve on creative tasks (Swann, Milton, & Polzer, 2000). Friendship groups perform better than acquaintance groups (Jehn & Shah, 1997). And Latinos, who prefer groups with a strong interpersonal orientation, may be especially sensitive to the relationships between cohesion and performance (Sanchez-Burks, Nisbett, & Ybarra, 2000). When people feel good in organizations, they are creative, helpful, and persistent (Brief & Weiss, 2002). As noted, they help coworkers, protect the organization, make constructive suggestions, and spread goodwill (George & Brief, 1992). People work better when they are rewarded in various ways (Shepperd, 1995). All this seems obvious, but it is surprising how much these basic ideas are neglected in many organizations. In all these settings, an appreciation for one's individual role in the group enhances productivity and cohesiveness.

General principles of group productivity include more than the factors already mentioned: individual accountability, individual standards, cohesiveness, feeling appreciated, and commitment to the task. A feeling of group efficacy ("we think we can") also helps (e.g., Hecht, Allen, Klammer, & Kelly, 2002). As mentioned earlier, diversity in composition can also boost performance. And a variety of other factors matter: average ability, training, tenure, interdependence, rewards, and external communication (Guzzo & Dickson, 1996; Sundstrom et al., 2000). As one example, in a wide variety of college science, math, and technology courses, small-group learning reliably enhances performance (achievement, persistence, and attitudes) (Springer, Stanne, & Donovan, 1999). And cultural variations in motives, goals, feedback, rewards, and satisfaction all moderate group performance (Gelfand, Erez, & Aycan, 2007). Overall, although groups do not outperform individuals as much as people think they do, under the right circumstances groups can be highly productive.

## Summary of Group Performance

Group performance draws on motivations to form a shared understanding and to control individual and group outcomes. Group decision making can polarize individual attitudes, as people learn about other people's attitudes, as well as express their own, and conform to the group prototype. Although groupthink per se occurs less than first thought, groups do tend to focus on already shared common knowledge, and cohesiveness can undermine optimal decision making. Groups actually make decisions using a variety of decision rules that predict group judgment better than any single principle. Groups can be less productive than individuals when incentives are low, costs are high, and individuals feel dispensable. One salient cost is evaluation apprehension, which can drag group contributions down to the least productive group member. Social loafing is a salient example of this. On the other hand, groups can be highly productive when people are individually accountable to appropriate standards, when the group is performing well or thinks it can, and when the group is cohesive.

## CONFLICT WITHIN GROUPS: CONTROLLING

We have seen that group membership provides people with a sense of belonging (identity and attraction), even in diverse groups and over the stages of joining a group. Group members develop socially shared understandings of group structures such as norms, roles, and subgroups. And we have just seen that they can be productive under the right circumstances. But groups are composed of individuals whose agendas sometimes contradict each other. For example, one evolutionary viewpoint would hold that people individually want to protect self, form coalitions, gain status, choose mates, maintain relationships, and care for offspring (Kenrick et al., 2002); these goals predict certain trade-offs between cooperation and competition, which computer simulation can model (Kenrick, Li, & Butner, 2003; cf. Cosmides & Tooby, 1989). Our core social motives framework suggests that people's individual goals include enhancing self and controlling own outcomes, which could introduce conflict within a group, whereas the others (belonging, understanding, and trusting) would tend to reduce conflict within the group.

Regardless of the source, conflict within groups highlights two topics we will cover here: both the social dilemma of when to strive for individual or group gain, as well as more explicit negotiation and bargaining within the group (e.g., Pruitt, 1998; Levine & Thompson, 1996).

## Social Dilemmas

Group members by definition are interdependent, that is, their outcomes depend on each other. In this circumstance, people may discover the advantages to cooperation over repeated interactions (Kelley, Thibaut, Radloff, & Mundy, 1962). But in a **social dilemma**, self-interest and collective interest conflict: Each person can receive a higher individual outcome for defecting than cooperating, but everyone loses if everyone else defects (Pruitt, 1998). All are better off if all cooperate consistently. One kind of social dilemma is a **commons dilemma**, in which people all harvest from a shared resource, but if everyone partakes too much, it will be depleted. Originally named for the practice of grazing private flocks on the shared village green, it persists today in roommates sharing from a common larder, colleagues sharing laboratory space, or people using public parks. Another kind is a **public goods dilemma**, in which people contribute resources to keep something going that they (and others) can use. Everyday examples include public radio and club dues. People can benefit individually from overharvesting or failing to contribute, but if everyone does so, then the commons are destroyed, the public goods are no longer available, and no one benefits. In general, social dilemmas often appear as **mixed motive** (self vs. collective) experimental games that use the payoff matrix format described earlier.

Given the structure of payoff matrices in cases where self-interest and collective interest conflict, and given some (mis)interpretations of individualistically oriented evolutionary survival motives, it might seem surprising that people ever cooperate at all. Indeed, conflict among group members for individual outcomes is assumed in mixed-motive settings (Deutsch, 1949, 1973). Rational economic models classically assume individual self-interest. As one test of a completely rational actor, computer simulations can vary strategies, modeling the behavior of individuals who play tit-for-tat (reciprocating the partner's previous move); win-stay and lose-change (repeat a winning strategy, change a losing one); or win-cooperate and lose-defect (self-explanatory). Computer simulations that vary strategies, incentives, and social comparisons often produce patterns that mimic data from laboratory experiments (Messick & Liebrand, 1995, 1997).

People's tendency to follow narrow self-interest may be less frequent than many observers assume. First, groups can handle conflicts over outcome distributions in a variety of ways, not all of which pit people against each other: (a) conflict avoidance (inaction, withdrawal, or preemptive solutions), (b) conflict reduction (unilateralism, voting, negotiation), or (c) conflict exacerbation (highlighting or exaggerating differences) (Levine & Thompson, 1996). Second, when conflict does occur, many people demonstrably do sacrifice their own preferences for others, accommodate instead of retaliate, and forgive betrayals (Rusbult & Van Lange, 2003).

Third, individual differences in social value orientation, covered in Chapter 9, demonstrate that only some people take chronically individualist orientations (max own), whereas others hold orientations that are competitive (max difference), cooperative (max joint), egalitarian (max equality), or even generous (max other) (Van Lange, 2000). The last three kinds of motivation often operate in concert, displayed by the same individuals. Prosocial orientations result from experiences growing up (e.g., having siblings, especially sisters) and in adult life (e.g., the long-term gain in outcomes from cooperation). Even tit-for-tat, the typical strategy designed to elicit cooperation over repeated encounters (Chapter 9) may yield to a more flexible process that allows for **noise** (random error that interferes with communication). When generosity occurs along with reciprocity, joint outcomes are higher (Van Lange, Ouwerkerk, & Tazelaar, 2002). That is, a partner who does not just exactly reciprocate good for good and bad for bad but reciprocates and adds a little extra indeed does elicit more cooperation—even in a noisy situation that better approximates real life (Figure 12.9).

Finally, people who have a choice about playing the game may be more cooperatively inclined than people without choice (Orbell & Dawes, 1993). People who intend to cooperate may be more likely to enter willingly into interdependent relationships. Cooperatively oriented participants are sensitive to issues of resource depletion (Kramer, McClintock, & Messick, 1986). Perhaps trust is underrated in comparing individual and collective interest.

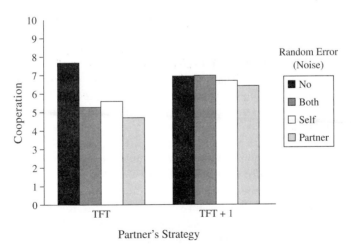

**Figure 12.9**    Cooperation, as a Function of Tit-for-Tat (TFT) or the More Generous Tit-for-Tat Plus a Bonus (TFT+1), as Well as Kind of Noise

*Source:* Van Lange et al., 2002. Copyright © American Psychological Association. Adapted with permission.

At another level, though, people are less generous outside the ingroup. As Chapter 11 shows, intergroup trust is low, and ingroup identity is key here. As one indicator of the importance of identity, dilemmas between groups (i.e., outgroups) represent the biggest challenge (Dawes & Messick, 2000). Moreover, although large groups typically elicit less cooperation than small groups, perhaps because of identity issues, people might cooperate with smaller factions within larger groups. A computer simulation can model this as a function not necessarily of identity, but of sheer payoff matrix to the individual (Parks & Komorita, 1997) or perhaps to the subgroup (de Heus, 2000). Besides identity and sheer payoff issues, cooperation under conflicting motives may be a function of self-efficacy or collective efficacy (Kerr, 1996). That is, feelings of **efficacy** or personal control (does my contribution really matter?) can enhance cooperation either directly or as a mediator for other antecedents such as group size. Moreover, communication among all concerned can dramatically increase cooperation. Consistent with the importance of collective communication, when people identify with the group, they have a collective sense of self, so their goals transform such that individual goals become group goals (De Cremer, Van Knippenberg, Van Dijk, & Van Leeuwen, 2008). Thus, a variety of factors determine when people compromise individual short-term self-interest for the collective good.

## Negotiation

When group members have conflicting individual interests, sometimes they can act unilaterally and sometimes they use another type of social decision rule, such as voting. But sometimes interdependent group members must problem-solve to make joint decisions about allocating scarce resources, that is, engage in **negotiation** (Bazerman, Curhan, & Moore, 2001; Bazerman, Mannix, & Thompson, 1988; Levine & Thompson, 1996; Thompson, 1990). Negotiation reduces conflict when it is **binding:** All must abide by the consensus. To reduce conflict, consensus must be possible and better than alternatives outside the group. Just as in close relationships (Chapter 8), comparison level for alternatives can undermine people's motivation for negotiating.

On the bright side, **integrative negotiation** can uncover ways in which all participants' interests can mesh. That is, additional resources may improve everyone's outcomes, or some people may care more about some issues, while others care about others, and trade-offs can leave everyone satisfied. People often fail to understand the ways that their interests can be compatible, partly because people fail to provide the necessary information (Thompson, 1991). Participants often think they know what other people want, tending to be biased toward perceiving the possible outcomes as a **fixed pie** (diametrically opposed) and believing that differences are irreconcilable. Indeed, opposing parties often exaggerate the conflict, the extremity of their opponent's position, and their opponent's biases (Keltner & Robinson, 1996).

Revealing actual priorities is more constructive than making assumptions and often results in better outcomes (Thompson, 1991). Accuracy motivation helps negotiators revise their fixed-pie perceptions to reflect the possibilities of integrative solutions (de Dreu, Koole, & Steinel, 2000). In collectivist cultures, negotiators may be more sensitive to the types of relationship they have with the other party, trying to preserve the relationships (Carnevale & Leung, 2001). Concerns with relationships can enhance accuracy in perceiving the position of the other party in collectivist settings, undermining the fixed-pie error (Gelfand & Christakopoulou, 1999).

Accuracy can be undermined or promoted by individual differences. According to a classic **theory of cooperation and competition** (Deutsch, 1949), egoistic (self-interested, individualistic) negotiators show distrust, hostility, and negative perceptions; as a result, they argue, bluff, threaten, and manipulate to get their way. Prosocial negotiators show trust, openness, and positive perceptions, and consequently they listen, inform, and understand, in order to reach integrative solutions, which they often do. According to meta-analysis, participants with a prosocial orientation do indeed contend less, problem solve more, and achieve higher joint outcomes (de Dreu, Weingart, & Kwon, 2000), but only under one additional condition, high resistance to yielding (i.e., negotiators' intransigence).

To understand the role of resistance, consider another theory of integrative negotiation. The **dual concerns theory** (Pruitt, 1998; Pruitt & Rubin, 1986) also holds that negotiators vary in their social motives, but it separates self-concern (low to high) from other-concern (low to high). For example, individualist motives reflect high self-concern and low other-concern, whereas prosocial motives reflect high concern for both; thus, other-concern best differentiates the two.

Egoistic and prosocial motives relate to valued outcomes. In contrast, resistance relates to feasible means (behaviors), that is, willingness to make concessions. Independent of other-concern is negotiators' **resistance to yielding**, that is, their intransigence and commitment to their own position. Resistance is operationalized as lack of external boundaries: low time pressure, high bottom-line limits, high accountability to third parties, low importance of reaching agreement, and high concern for self (de Dreu et al., 2000). Prosocial motives facilitate constructive motivation only when resistance is high. That is, negotiators have to respect their own constraints and concerns, as well as the other person's concerns, for negotiations to be successful.

## CHAPTER SUMMARY

Psychological groups comprise interacting people who consider themselves or whom others consider to belong together. Groups differ in entitativity, the degree to which they make a coherent whole, through Gestalt principles of similarity, proximity, interdependence, and interaction. Intimacy groups, such as family and friends, are experienced as more coherent and cohesive than loose associations (e.g., neighborhoods) and social categories (e.g., women), with task groups falling in between. People value their own groups to the extent they view them as cohesive, coherent entities. In contrast, to the extent people view an outgroup as being an entitative group, they see it as having hostile intent. Because groups are typified by shared goals that operate in the group's own interest, and entitative groups are seen as causal agents, that is, as originating action, outgroups are expected to act on their own interests, which will be hostile to other groups. And indeed groups are more competitive than individuals. Both fear of losing control over one's outcomes and greed to enhance self contribute to group competitiveness.

Social psychologists most often study groups by creating short-term, artificial, experimental groups, often playing experimental games, all which might seem to lack generalizability to the real world. Nonetheless, real-world effects are often stronger than laboratory demonstrations of the same phenomena. Researchers use survey and observational methods when they study real-world groups. People in both artificial and real groups satisfy a number of core social motives, including most obviously the need to belong, but also to validate a shared social understanding and a sense of control. Each of the main sections of the chapter addresses one or two of the core motives, to discuss group membership (belonging), socially shared cognition (understanding and controlling), group performance (understanding and controlling), and intragroup conflict (controlling).

Belonging to a group, becoming a member, revolves around one's identity as a group member, which depends on context, as social identity theory and self-categorization theory predict. Individual concerns matter most when group commitment is low, and threats to self or group simply motivate individual solutions (self-affirmation or individual mobility out of the group). When group commitment is high, group-level concerns matter more, especially under threat of personal exclusion or threat to group cohesion. Depersonalized social attraction to the group fosters cohesion, as members identify with the group prototype, based on their interdependence as group members. Diversity both challenges and benefits the group. Minuses include potential discomfort, friction, and turnover, but pluses include creativity, innovation, and performance. Joining a group is a process, not an outcome, as groups and group members move through mutual investigation, socialization, maintenance, resocialization, and remembrance.

Group structure results from socially shared understandings of the group. Norms specify implicit local rules for group members' behavior. Specific individuals fill roles that specify the behavior expected of them, and leaders fill a particularly important role. Subgroups within the group emerge as a function of differing opinions, and ingroup minorities can elicit thoughtful but indirect forms of opinion change.

Group performance results from decision making and productivity. Group decision making is less rational than originally expected. Groups tend to polarize in their decisions, compared with the starting positions of members as individuals. Groupthink, conformity to the opinions of a leader with a particular agenda within a highly cohesive and isolated group, occurs only under particular circumstances. More useful are general models that acknowledge the range of antecedents, processes, and consequences in group decision making, as well as social decision schemes that predict the outcome of group decisions. Group productivity occurs when people are individually accountable to appropriate standards, the group is already performing well (or thinks it can), and people are committed to the task. Individual incentives matter.

Group members conflict over controlling resources. In social dilemmas, individual self-interest conflicts with collective interest, creating mixed motives. In a commons dilemma, the conflict occurs over taking resources from a common pool, and in a public goods dilemma, conflict occurs over contributing to the maintenance of a shared benefit. Sometimes groups avoid, reduce, or accommodate conflict, but sometimes they exacerbate it. Individual differences in social value orientation matter a lot here.

Generosity creates higher joint payoffs, and it is especially likely when people have a choice, interact with their ingroup, or feel efficacious.

When cooperation fails and conflicting interests endure, group members must negotiate over scarce resources. Negotiation works well when it is binding and when people reach integrative solutions that go beyond a fixed pie. Accurate information about the others' preferences and priorities, as well as a prosocial orientation and high concern for the others, all facilitate negotiations. But successful negotiators must also stand firm with their own concerns and resist too-rapid yielding to the influence of others. Chapter 13 takes us into our final exploration in this book, namely, how people do and do not influence each other.

## SUGGESTIONS FOR FURTHER READING

BROWN, R. (2000). *Group processes* (2nd ed). Oxford, UK: Blackwell.

DE DREU, C. K. W. (2009). Social conflict: The emergence and consequences of struggle and negotiation. In S. T. FISKE, D. T. GILBERT, & G. LINDZEY (Eds.), *Handbook of social psychology* (5th ed.). New York: Wiley.

GRUENFELD, D. H., & TIEDENS, L. Z. (2010). On the social psychology of organizing. In S. T. FISKE, D. T. GILBERT, & G. LINDZEY (Eds.), *Handbook of social psychology* (5th ed.). New York: Wiley.

HACKMAN, R., & KATZ, N. (2010). Group performance and behavior. In S. T. FISKE, D. T. GILBERT, & G. LINDZEY (Eds.), *Handbook of social psychology* (5th ed.). New York: Wiley.

HOGG, M. A. (2010). Influence and leadership. In S. T. FISKE, D. T. GILBERT, & G. LINDZEY (Eds.), *Handbook of social psychology* (5th ed.). New York: Wiley.

KERR, N. L. & TINDALE, R. S. (2004). Group performance and decision making. *Annual Review of Psychology*, 55, 623–655.

LEVINE, J. M., & KERR, N. L. (2007). Inclusion and exclusion: Consequences for group process. In A. W. KRUGLANSKI & E. T. HIGGINS (Eds.), *Social psychology: Handbook of basic principles* (2nd ed., pp. 759–784). New York: Guilford.

WILLIAMS, K. D. (2007). Ostracism. *Annual Review of Psychology*, 58, 425–452.

# Chapter **13**

# Social Influence: Doing What Others Do and Say

- Rob a bank.
- Run naked in public.
- Cheat on an exam.
- Voice some of my weirder thoughts to strangers.
- Not pay my bills.
- Scream in a crowded place.
- Kill someone.
- Stop working.
- Rescue children from parents who yell at them in public.

What would you do if you could do anything at all and get away with it, with no social repercussions? My students over the years have offered various answers, some of which I've just paraphrased. Some forbidden impulses are aggressive, immoral, or illegal; some are harmless but weird; and some are even prosocial in intent. What they all have in common is the chance to deviate from social norms, to ignore social conventions. In actual practice, when my colleagues and I have assigned social psychology students actually to do something deviant (excluding the dangerous, harmful, or illegal), they decided to:

- Face the back of a crowded elevator.
- Stage a screaming personal argument in the middle of class.
- Wear their clothes backward.
- Drape themselves with holiday lights (plugged-in) during class.

Professors fantasize about doing counternormative behavior also. One professor (Meiss, 1997) suggested activities for teaching the first day of class:

- Wear a hood with one eyehole. Periodically make strange gurgling sounds.
- Bring a CPR dummy to class and announce that it will be the teaching assistant for the semester. Assign it an office and office hours.

- Jog into class, rip the textbook in half, and scream, "Are you pumped? ARE YOU PUMPED? I CAN'T HEEEEAR YOU!"
- After confirming everyone's names on the roll, thank the class for attending Advanced Astrodynamics 690, and mention that yesterday was the last day to drop the class.
- Wear a feather boa, and ask the students to call you "Snuggles."

Most of the time, of course, professors do not wear feather boas, scream at their students, or make gurgling noises, and students do not wear holiday lights to class. Why? For the same reasons that explain the example in Chapter 1, when students in my classes make their syllabus into a paper airplane on the first day: simply because an authority asks and peers comply.

In the first chapter, we defined social psychology essentially as the influence of people on other people. As such, social influence research is the hallmark of social psychology. Not surprisingly, all the core social motives enter prominently into social influence. Nevertheless, we will see that social influence research has been more specific than that. After defining social influence conceptually and operationally, we will address how the core motives relate to social influence. The main part of the chapter examines classic topics in social influence: conformity with peers, obedience to authorities, and compliance with requests. But each area brings in more recent approaches, such as the roles of group identity and minority influence in conformity, the role of power in obedience, and the role of ingroups in compliance. In every case, as well, culture matters to who influences whom, when, and how. The focus, however, is always on social relationships and social context, and we will see that group identity most often provides the relevant context, which is why this chapter comes after the groups chapter. You will also see that this chapter on social influence recaps many ideas covered in previous chapters, precisely because social influence caps the study of social psychology, serving as our penultimate chapter in this journey.

## WHAT IS SOCIAL INFLUENCE?

### Conceptual Definitions

**Social influence** broadly encompasses any changes in beliefs, attitudes, or behavior that result from interpersonal interaction. More narrowly, social influence focuses on changes mainly in behavior resulting directly from interpersonal interaction. Social influence typically refers to these interpersonal processes that change other people's behavior (Chaiken, Wood, & Eagly, 1996; Cialdini & Goldstein, 2004; Turner, 1995). As such, social influence processes focus on norms and roles in rich, interactive settings.

In contrast to attitude change via persuasion, the influence agent may or may not intend to influence the other. Notice also the emphasis on behavior and on direct interaction, which sets social influence apart from attitude change. This type of influence focuses more on behavior than on private thoughts and feelings. In contrast, persuasion theories of attitude change (Chapter 6) focus on deliberate advocacy to change opinions, focusing on intentional messages.

Some key concepts aid our analysis of social influence. First is **norms**, which we've encountered in many previous chapters, as the unwritten rules for behavior. Second, the sections of this chapter separately address **conformity**, the influence of the majority on individual behavior; **obedience**, the influence of authority demands on subordinates; and **compliance**, the influence of a peer's request.

## Operational Definitions

**CONFORMITY**   In studying conformity, social psychologists build on work by Muzafer Sherif (1936) on the autokinetic effect and Solomon Asch (1955) on line judgments. Recall from Chapter 1 that Sherif's groups developed norms to interpret the optical illusion of an isolated point of light seeming to move in a dark space. Recall also from Chapter 1 that Asch's participants sometimes went along with the group's erroneous judgment of line lengths, despite the evidence of their eyes.

Subsequent conformity research has also used group settings, sometimes with confederates giving prearranged answers. It typically has measured agreement with an erroneous or arbitrary norm (e.g., Abrams, Wetherell, Cochrane, Hogg, & Turner, 1990). Clearly, conformity is more obvious when people under group pressure answer in ways they would not ordinarily. Control groups demonstrate this difference, the effect of group pressure, by having confederates absent or not giving wrong answers. In some field studies, the confederates are absent, but evidence of other people's behavior appears, for example, in the amount of litter left behind (recall Cialdini et al.'s studies from Chapter 9). This stretches the conceptual definition of social influence as behavior change resulting from social interaction, until you remember the actual, imagined, or implied presence of others defined as "social."

**OBEDIENCE**   How much do you agree with this statement, attributed to Karl Marx? "Those who hold and those who are without property have ever formed two distinct classes." Early research on the influence of authorities began with the work on **prestige suggestion**, in which the same statement is judged differently, depending on whether it is attributed to a derogated authority (for Americans in the 1940s, Karl Marx) or to its rightful author, John Adams (Asch, 1948).

Research on reactions to authorities as obedience per se began with Milgram's classic (1964) study, probably the most famous study in social psychology. As Chapter 10 implied, the aggression machine that participants use in their role as teachers to punish the errors of the student (confederate) originated simultaneously in aggression and obedience research. We will describe the Milgram study in more detail later.

**COMPLIANCE**   Compliance research focuses on people's attempt to get someone else to do something, and an early example includes the Freedman and Fraser (1966) **foot-in-the-door** technique. In this case, some people were asked to comply with a trivial request (place a tiny be-a-safe-driver sign in their front window). These people later complied with a large unreasonable request (install a DRIVE CAREFULLY billboard on their front lawn), more than people who had not acceded to the seemingly harmless initial request. In dozens of subsequent studies, the key ingredient was face-to-face interaction and a small initial request.

All told, the operational definitions of social influence rank as some of people's favorite studies in social psychology because they involve realistic interpersonal situations, apparently tiny manipulations of social context, and meaningful changes in behavior.

## Core Social Motives: Belonging, Understanding, Controlling, Self-enhancing, and Trusting

Much of social influence fits a framework of maintaining one's group identity and harmony within the group. As such, social influence results significantly from the core social motive of belonging. However, this is a relatively new approach to social influence.

For many years, social psychologists assumed that the primary impetus for social influence was to avoid the uncertainty brought about by one's apparent disagreement with others. Researchers differentiated two kinds of uncertainty-reducing motivation for social influence. **Informational influence** was described as trying to get at objective reality (Deutsch & Gerard, 1955). As such, it would fit the core motive to develop a shared understanding. The other traditional kind of motivation was **normative influence**, sometimes described as trying to elicit approval from others (Turner, 1995). As such, it could fit the idea of gaining social rewards and avoiding social punishments, consistent with the core social motive to control one's outcomes. But normative influence could be broader; it could also fit the need to enhance the self, maintain self-esteem, and avoid anxiety or guilt (Chaiken et al., 1996). Or it could be viewed as a version of belonging, when people go along with the group norms in order to fit in. As we will see, the mix of motives probably is no longer so usefully split between informational and normative influences, but the background is useful to understand the framing of the original research problems as "objective reality" versus "social reality."

Finally, I would argue for the importance of the core social motive to trust others in the ingroup as benevolent. Allowing oneself to be influenced by others in the ingroup, assuming their influence to be benign, is separate from merely trying to maintain harmony through belonging. Instead, it implies that others are a trustworthy source of influence.

Sometimes social influence is broken down into three motives that overlap with the ones noted: mere **compliance** in the service of gaining rewards and avoiding punishments (like controlling); **conformity** with valued reference groups (like belonging); and **internalization** of valid information about reality (like understanding) (Kelman, 1958; note that the use of compliance and conformity retains the flavor of our earlier definitions but uses the terms more narrowly). Mentioning this social influence triad serves to remind us that social psychologists have long been aware of people's varied motivations for going along with social influence.

## Summary of Definitions and Motives

Social influence could be all of social psychology (as we defined it: how the thoughts, feelings, and behaviors of individuals are influenced by the actual, imagined, or implied presence of others). More often, it is changes in behavior that result from social interaction. Operationally, the research tends to fall into methods for studying conformity with peers, obedience to authorities, and compliance with direct requests. All the core social motives are relevant to social influence, as we will see.

## CONFORMITY: BELONGING AND UNDERSTANDING BY DOING WHAT OTHERS DO

Conformity, going along with others, reflects adhering to group norms for behavior. We start with the classic studies, some already described, address more recent research on the processes involved, and end the section by taking seriously the role of group belonging in social influence. We also discuss contemporary myths and legends, in the context of conformity to shared understanding of group norms.

### Classic Studies: Sherif and Asch

Participants sat in a darkened room, along with others, voicing their judgments about an apparently moving point of light. Sherif (1935) wanted to demonstrate the impact of norms on individual judgment, so he used an ambiguous task in which all answers (other than zero) were arbitrary and wrong. In later research, other participants reacted to statements such as the one about social classes and property, noted earlier, or this one about rebellion, attributed to Lenin or Jefferson: "I hold that a little rebellion, now and then, is a good thing, and as necessary in the political world as storms are in the physical." Asch (1948) found that readers changed the meaning of "rebellion" to "agitation" when the author was Jefferson and "rebellion" to "revolution" when the alleged author was Lenin. They then rated their agreement with the statement accordingly. In keeping with his Gestalt approach (see Chapter 4), Asch (1940, p. 458) famously noted that the difference was a "change in the object of judgment" (agitation or revolution), rather than a "change in the judgment of the object" (rebellion as intrinsically good or bad).

Subsequently, still other participants sat, along with others, voicing their judgments about the comparative length of three lines to one standard line (see Figure 1.1). Asch (1956) wanted to show the limitations on conformity, so he chose a less ambiguous judgment task than either illusory movement or ambiguous words, expecting little or no social influence. Nevertheless, participants made errors about a third of the time (compared with controls judging alone, who made practically no errors).

This simple task set up a cottage industry of replications and extensions (R. Bond & Smith, 1996). As of 1994, about 40 years later, 94 studies had used Asch's paradigm and another 39 had used a modified paradigm in which participants sit in booths, hearing false feedback about others' unanimous but wrong responses (Crutchfield, 1955).

That's an impressive rate of more than three new studies per year for four decades. In 133 studies, the average participant conformed 29% of the time, according to the meta-analysis. Conformity was greater when researchers (a) most closely replicated Asch's original paradigm, (b) used ambiguous stimuli (as reflected by a high error rate), and (c) used ingroup members as the influential minority, all for obvious reasons. Furthermore, although conformity occurs across all 17 cultures in which it has been tested, it does occur (d) more strongly in relatively collectivist cultures. This seems to be a function of individualist cultures' emphasis on individual autonomy, both affective and intellectual, which fits other patterns of cultural variation. For example, East Asians tend to encounter social influence attempts that focus on conformity, portrayed as harmony and connectedness, in advertising and consumer preferences. Americans, in contrast, tend to encounter social influence attempts that focus on independence, freedom, and uniqueness, again as reflected in advertising and consumer preferences (Kim & Markus, 1999). These cultural tendencies for social influence make sense, given everything we have seen so far.

Less obvious are the reasons for larger conformity effects according to two unrelated factors (R. Bond & Smith, 1996): The first anomaly is more conformity in studies that included women as participants. Other research has found that both women and men each are more open to social influence in judgments that do not reflect their own gender's expertise (Eagly & Carli, 1981); perhaps the female participants in the Asch paradigm were more likely to mistrust their own perception of comparative line measurement because they viewed it as outside their own expertise. Own perceived competence does correlate with resisting conformity (Allen, 1965).

The second anomaly is more conformity in those studies that took place at an earlier date. Apart from stereotypes about the conforming 1950s, the nonconforming 1960s to 1970s, and the individualistic 1980s, it is hard to know how to interpret this result. The more important point is how robust the fundamental conformity effect really is across a variety of settings.

Arguably, Asch's work focused on a stripped-down form of social influence without real interaction. His method took an individualist view of groups, rather than a more social interactionist view of groups. That is, he focused on the participants as individuals within a group rather than on group process per se. None of his groups actually interacted, and he focused on individual independence rather than group members' interdependence (Leyens & Corneille, 1999). Asch believed that people maintain independence mainly because they want the group to achieve a correct consensus, so they cooperatively abandon their own position if they personally seem to be wrong (Levine, 1999). One of the reasons for viewing the conformity studies as the proper topic of this chapter on social influence, rather than the previous one on groups, is that Asch's groups were not very groupy.

Nevertheless, Asch (1940) recognized the difference between the influence of a congenial group (which people accept) and an antagonistic group (which people reject). Note also, for future reference, how much the conformity effect depends on ingroup members as the influential majority. What's more, this holds in all cultures (M. H. Bond & Smith, 1996). An early review of the conformity studies noted that the participant's attraction and similarity to, as well as interdependence with, the erroneous majority readily predicted how much people conformed (Allen, 1965). This hints at the crucial role of group identity.

Asch believed that groups help people to construe the meaning of ambiguous phenomena, and then they conform accordingly (Levine, 1999). This suggests a causal sequence whereby groups affect initial perception. However, sometimes people conform and then change the meaning of the object in order to justify their conformity (Buehler & Griffin, 1994; Griffin & Buehler, 1993). This suggests a causal sequence whereby groups affect judgment, which then affects reinterpretation of the stimulus. What's the evidence: Does influence occur during initial perception, automatically, or only post hoc, after conformity, perhaps with more thought?

## Conformity Processes: Fairly Automatic

Both processes of conformity apparently occur. In a distinction reminiscent of dual process models of social cognition (Chapter 4), persuasion (Chapter 6), and bias (Chapter 11), one process is relatively automatic and the other more controlled kinds of processes. Consider the following example of automatic conformity to social norms.

Participants viewed photographs of a library reading room or a train station interior after learning they would have to visit the setting afterward (Aarts & Dijksterhuis, 2003). Still other participants viewed the library without the goal of going there. Presumably, when the goal of going to a social environment is active, the relevant norms are activated to cue conformity. And, indeed, only those people primed with the goal to visit the library did more rapidly recognize words related to silence (silent, quiet, still, whisper) than unrelated control words. In a subsequent study, participants primed in the same way also spoke more softly, even on an unrelated task. Parallel effects occurred for participants primed with the goal of visiting an exclusive restaurant and behaving in a well-mannered way. Primed participants ate crackers during unrelated experimental tasks and actually tidied up more often if they had been primed. This was especially true for people who personally had demonstrated a previously strong associative strength between the exclusive restaurant and being well mannered.

Relying on norms may be a rapid (if not exactly automatic) heuristic strategy that people use when they do not have time, capacity, or inclination to use more effortful processes (Wood, 2000). Otherwise unmotivated participants conform to the consensus indicated by opinion poll results, regardless of the poll's reliability, demonstrating a heuristic form of conformity (Darke, Chaiken, Bohner, Einwiller, Erb, & Hazlewood, 1998). Similarly, people will conform to match the positivity of another person's self-presentation, apparently unaware that they have done so (Vorauer & Miller, 1997), consistent with a relatively automatic process. Even if participants are motivated (by incentives for accuracy), they still use heuristic processing when the task becomes too difficult. In this case, people conform at high levels (i.e., even more than when the task is not difficult; Baron, Vandello, & Brunsman, 1996). People can be automatically influenced, too, simply by the friends they keep; the interdependence of two friends' experiences means that if one person likes, for example, a restaurant, then the other person will come along to try it as well, creating a spillover of the first person's preference, even apart from persuasion processes, simply because we over-sample our friends' favorite experiences (Denrell & Le Mens, 2007).

Indirectly, people's relatively automatic tendency to think others agree with them may reflect a kind of unthinking conformity. That is, the **false consensus effect** (Ross, Greene, & House, 1977) shows that people tend to think that other people would do as they have done. The most famous example is the original study in which some students agreed to walk around campus wearing a sandwich board that said "Eat at Joe's." Students who agreed thought that others also would agree, whereas students who declined thought others would decline. Many years earlier, students who admitted to cheating on exams similarly expected others to cheat (Katz & Allport, 1931). The false consensus effect is well established, according to meta-analysis (Mullen et al., 1985). Most people think they are in the majority (Kreuger & Clement, 1997), so even minorities overestimate the degree of consensus with their position. Although mostly believing they are in the majority, majorities sometimes underestimate the degree of consensus (Gross & Miller, 1997). People in general assume that most others share their opinions, a phenomenon also called **social projection**, which appears to be an unthinking or even automatic process (Kreuger, 1998). The false consensus and social projection effects do have limits: People rapidly infer that only the ingroup will agree with them, not that the outgroup will. This reinforces the importance of conformity to ingroups.

## Minority Influence: Another Process

As suggested here and in Chapter 12, people conform to the ingroup and assume that the ingroup agrees with them. Moscovici viewed the emphasis on conformity to the ingroup as a tyranny of the majority (Martin & Hewstone, 2001; Wood, 2000). In good contrarian fashion, he set out to demonstrate the conditions under which people actually do conform to an outgroup. He emphasized not only an outgroup but a minority outgroup (Moscovici, 1980, 1985). As introduced in Chapter 12, **minority influence**—the impact of a smaller subgroup that disagrees with the majority—comes through conflict. The minority's opposing viewpoint confronts the majority viewpoint and creates conflict within the individual and between individuals in the two subgroups.

Minority viewpoints create influence by becoming salient and demanding attention because of conflict. Recall that persistent minorities provoke others to think more creatively about their positions (Nemeth, 1986), a process called **divergent thinking**. Majority influence (conformity) may be relatively automatic and unthinking, as suggested earlier, but minority influence in contrast may require more thought and even a reflective conversion.

Minorities influence only when they behave consistently, according to meta-analysis (as noted in Chapter 12; Wood, Lundgren, Ouellette, Busceme, & Blackstone, 1994). The importance of consistency stems from the Kelley attribution theory (Chapter 3). When someone consistently adopts a unique response, that indicates low consensus. The response focuses on a specific attitude object (high distinctiveness).

And when the person does so consistently, observers infer a dispositional cause, that is, a sincere belief.

A sincere minority belief that opposes the norm requires some creative thought in order to resolve its contradiction of prevailing views (Maass, West, & Cialdini, 1987). Some would argue that minority and extreme positions will be more thoughtful and sophisticated because people have to defend them more often (Sidanius, 1988; Zdaniuk & Levine, 1996). Others argue that ingroup minorities in particular receive more attention. For example, in one study (Alvaro & Crano, 1996), participants read an antigay message attributed to an obscure group at their own university (ingroup minority), the same group at another university (outgroup minority), or their own student body (ingroup majority). Of these three sources, when the message was counterattitudinal for a particular recipient, the ingroup minority's message received the most positive thoughts, the most accurate memory, and the least negative evaluations (see Table 13.1). In effect, the ingroup minority receives the benefit of the doubt—a **leniency** advantage (Crano, 2000), as noted in Chapter 12—but one that entails thoughtful consideration of the ingroup minority position.

In contrast to the dual-process idea that conformity to the majority happens unreflectively, but that minority influence requires creative thinking, some theorists have proposed a single mechanism for both kinds of social influence. For example, **social impact theory** (Latané, 1981; introduced in Chapter 12) argues that any kind of influence, whether majority conformity or minority influence, results from the same factors. In the immediate social **force field** (a concept borrowed from field founder Kurt Lewin; Chapter 1), influence results from the number, strength, and immediacy of influence sources. Whereas the majority may have greater numbers, they may not have greater strength of opinion or immediacy. A related **social influence model** (Tanford & Penrod, 1984) argues that influence results similarly from the number of influence sources but adds source consistency, as well as the number of influence *targets*, to predict conformity and minority influence.

A third single-mode approach, the **judgmental process model** (Kruglanski & Mackie, 1990), argues for one process, based on minorities and majorities showing many similar moderators of influence. Both increase their influence in similar ways, with increases in, for example: credible sources, ingroup sources, consistent sources, target bias toward compatible conclusions, similarity to target position, and focus on source versus message. But the model also notes that minority and majority influence

**Table 13.1**  Leniency for Ingroup Minority Opinion in Counterattitudinal Communications

| Measure | Majority | Ingroup Minority | Outgroup Minority |
|---|---|---|---|
| Positive thoughts | 1.16 | 2.18 | .82 |
| Memory errors | 2.05 | .89 | 2.13 |
| Negative evaluations of source | 16.90 | 13.61 | 13.83 |

*Source:* From Alvaro & Crano, 1996. Copyright © British Psychological Society.

processes typically differ by extremity of position, target's need for closure, congruence with the prevailing view, status rebellion, respectability, salience, accessibility, and conflict. All these typical differences in minority and majority influence suggest that, while they share some common features of social influence, they also often operate by different processes.

Minority influence occurs most in private, that is, on measures that protect the converted majority individuals from appearing publicly to abandon their majority position (Wood et al., 1994). For the same reason, influence is often indirect, emerging on issues merely related to the contentious issues, or delayed beyond the immediate context (Crano, 2000). Thus, majorities can be converted by minorities, but majority individuals do not admit it to others, and perhaps not to themselves, thereby avoiding public identification with the unpopular minority position. And indeed, when people lose majority status in a group, they are less attracted to the group and expect less positive interaction (Prislin, Limbert, & Bauer, 2000), as Chapter 12 noted.

Group identity is key. When people identify strongly with the majority, they do indeed conform to it and resist minority influence. But when they identify with the minority, they will shift to align with them instead (Wood, Pool, Leck, & Purvis, 1996).

## Self-categorization Theory: Conforming to Social Reality

We have already seen several instances of group identification shaping social influence by both minorities and majorities (i.e., conformity). The importance of the ingroup in social influence reaches its apex in the **self-categorization theory** interpretations of social influence. Implied in the traditional work on conformity is relatively automatic, mindless error. However, people may thoughtfully conform to the social reality that is accurate, at least from the most relevant perspective, namely, their ingroup.

Instead of automatically doing what others do, perhaps people know what to do by knowing who they are (Abrams, Wetherell, Cochrane, Hogg, & Turner, 1990). In three studies, each used an established paradigm but also manipulated ingroup identity. Ingroup identity mattered every time. In the Sherif autokinetic paradigm, the impact of the confederates on norm formation decreased as their outgroup membership became more salient. In the Asch conformity paradigm, ingroup (but not outgroup) confederates increased conformity pressures. In a group polarization paradigm, distinct subgroups (i.e., mutual outgroups) inhibited opinion convergence. In each case, the ingroup defined reality, whether in perceiving the movement of light, the length of lines, or the shift in opinions. As we saw in Chapter 12, groups punish deviance from the ingroup norm. But groups also reward pronorm deviance from the modal group opinion—that is, someone who conforms to the ideal group prototype, which is not necessarily the actual group average (Abrams, Marques, Bown, & Henson, 2000; Hogg, 2001).

Self-categorization theory defines social influence this way: the processes by which people agree about appropriate behavior, as defined by ingroup norms (Turner, 1991). Given that social norms guide people's actual behavior, then in this view, social influence phenomena such as conformity and minority influence entail changing behavior to fit ingroup consensus about what is appropriate. As such, error is an irrelevant concept because norms describe actual similarities among ingroup members. Norms reduce subjective uncertainty about ambiguous situations, creating **subjective validity**—confidence in what is appropriate, correct, and desirable. Subjective validity clearly applies to conditions described earlier as normative influence.

But does subjective validity describe informational influence? How can social reality be objective reality? Informational influence researchers always assumed objective, physical reality testing as the gold standard. Gradations in accuracy presumably involved valid arguments about objective reality, assessed via in-depth processing (as in the central, systematic, deliberate processing of dual-mode attitude theories, Chapter 6). In contrast, a social identity approach argues that normative versus informational influence constitutes a false dichotomy. Individuals test reality by validating cognitive, perceptual, and behavioral information. This reality testing provides subjectivity validity only if the individual believes that relevant others would have achieved the same results of the reality test. If the individual is the only one who can obtain the test result, then the individual is unique, deviant, and idiosyncratic, and the person's social standing is threatened. Moreover, the person's sense of self is threatened (why am I the only one who can see that six-foot hairy spider coming down the street?). Information is intrinsically social, in the social identity theory (SIT)/self-categorization theory (SCT) view. This interpretation also fits our use of the core motive for a socially shared understanding, as an offshoot of the basic motive to belong.

In this view, people will be more open to influence the more they identify with and see themselves as similar to the group. Correspondingly, the group will have more influence the more it is cohesive, consensual, consistent, and distinctive. As noted, ingroups are more influential, as are members who exemplify its prototype (Abrams et al., 1990, 2000; Allen, 1965; Clark & Maass, 1988a, 1988b; Mackie, 1986, 1987; Mackie & Cooper, 1984; Martin, 1988a, 1988b, 1988c; van Knippenberg & Wilke, 1988; Wood et al., 1996). When people identify with the ingroup, they especially conform to norms that define the group (Reicher, 1984a, b; Spears, Lea, & Lee, 1990; Wilder & Shapiro, 1984). What's more, the group identity as a context and the individual behavior influence each other, so it's a two-way street (Postmes, Haslam, & Swaab, 2005). All these principles fit an SCT/SIT account of conformity processes, and they broaden the context for interpreting these effects. The framework provides new vitality to this classic area of research.

## Memes, Modern Myths, Rumors, and Gossip

The research covered in this conformity section all pertains to norms, but a closely related term has surfaced recently. Some researchers have adopted the term **meme** (Dawkins, 1976), which is supposed to be a social analog to the gene but instead pertains to units of culture. For example, urban legends (**modern myths**) such as disgusting stories about pets in microwaves or razor blades in Halloween candy—never shown to have actually occurred—nonetheless circulate, and the more disgusting, the more popular the legend (Heath, Bell, & Sternberg, 2001). Rumor and gossip both reflect similar transmission of social information, important to group identity. But they both tend to be verbal, whereas norms tend to be behavioral, at least as most often studied so far. Still, contemporary legends can control behavior, as when parents either forbid their children to go trick-or-treating or scrutinize the candy they bring home.

A **rumor**—defined as a word-of-mouth belief without secure evidence—shows an important form of peer social influence. Older research on the psychology of rumor (Allport & Postman, 1946; Festinger et al., 1948; Knapp, 1944) noted that rumors surface under ambiguous circumstances when people seek meaning to explain emotionally important topics. Later work more precisely indicated that rumors are generated and transmitted when people are anxious, uncertain, credulous, and involved (Rosnow, 1980; 1991). As rumors spread, Allport and Postman posited that they **level** (eliminating some details), **sharpen** (emphasizing others), and assimilate. As anyone knows who has played "telephone," distortions occur at each stage of verbal transmission, and phonetic research supports this experience (Tiffany & Bennett, 1968). Initial tellers of information make less extreme judgments than listeners who receive the information second-hand (Gilovich, 1987; Inman, Reichl, & Baron, 1993), suggesting a process similar to Allport and Postman's leveling and sharpening. This seems to occur in part when listeners do not pay careful attention, so they miss important mitigating information (Baron, David, Brunsman, & Inman, 1997). As we saw in Chapter 3, when people first judge another person's behavior, without correcting for mitigating circumstances, they are more likely to make an extreme dispositional attribution. Rumors and **gossip** (rumors specifically describing people) are justifiably notorious for being merciless with regard to other people's reputations.

### Summary of Conformity

Conformity, the influence of the majority on individual behavior, began with studies of perceptual suggestion, group norms, and group pressure. Although people show much independence, it was the degree of conformity in the face of apparently objective reality that captured the attention of researchers. People do conform to the ingroup fairly automatically, to the extent that they identify with it, feel similar, and are attracted to it. This occurs in all cultures, although more so in collectivist ones. When minorities do influence people, they do it by being persistent and consistent, and the influence appears most on private or indirect responses. People are open to minority influence—as with majority influence—when they identify with the minority. Self-categorization and social identity theories explain conformity as a process of reducing uncertainty with the aid of appropriate social reality. Some of the more unusual cases of reducing uncertainty occur in the social transmission of urban legends or rumors. The joint roles of understanding and belonging are clear throughout this work.

### OBEDIENCE: BELONGING, CONTROLLING, TRUSTING, AND UNDERSTANDING BY DOING WHAT OTHERS SAY

Earlier, we defined obedience as the influence of authority demands on subordinates. In discussing obedience, we examine the notorious Milgram studies, which illustrate social forces influencing the individual, and power in general, which especially illustrates controlling resources and maintaining relationships as methods of influence.

## Social Forces: Milgram

The single most famous study of obedience—and arguably the best-known study in social psychology—remains hugely impactful. Following his mentor, Solomon Asch, Milgram designed a simple but elegant paradigm for studying obedience to malevolent authority (Elms, 1995; Milgram, 1963; 1965). He used the very structure of the experiment to create an authority who could demand obedience. The experimenter welcomed two community participants to a laboratory at Yale University. The experimenter described a learning experiment in which the teacher would punish the learner for errors by using an electric shock machine (described earlier as the Buss aggression machine, Chapter 10). The participants, typically both middle-aged men, drew slips of paper to determine their roles, and the teacher's first job was to strap the learner's wrists to the chair arms, so the electrodes would not accidentally fall off. The teacher received a sample shock—an unpleasant 45 volts—and then went to the adjoining room to begin teaching the learner a series of word pairs. The learner started out well but progressively made more mistakes, each one requiring the teacher progressively to administer 15 volts more shock. From his room, the learner began to protest the shocks, kicking the wall in apparently intolerable pain and eventually ceasing to answer. In response to any hesitation on the teacher's part, the experimenter, dressed in a gray technician's coat and holding an authoritative clip board, insisted as follows, in an escalating series of commands, at each succeeding sign of resistance:

- "Please continue." *or* "Please go on."
- "The experiment requires that you continue."
- "It is absolutely essential that you continue."
- "You have no other choice; you *must* go on."

In that elaborate context, participants obeyed. The core findings showed that 65% of participants progressed up the shock generator past *Danger: Severe Shock* to 450 volts labeled simply *XXX*. Only 35% resisted.

Participants clearly suffered in the process of obeying, displaying their tension by nervous laughter, hand-wringing, and facial distress. They reported moderate to extreme tension and nervousness, when asked. Fortunately, they were debriefed carefully about the matters on which they were not fully informed: The study concerned obedience, not learning and memory; the learner was a confederate; no shocks were ever delivered, except the sample to the teacher; and the experimenter's prods, as well as the learner's protests, were carefully scripted.

The results were appalling, of course. Most variations of the original paradigm (silent, remote learner) failed to depress obedience by much (Milgram, 1974); people still obeyed if the learner screamed and protested a heart condition (screaming, remote learner; 62%). But fewer people did obey when the learner sat in the same room as the teacher (proximate; 40%) or when they personally had to place the learner's hand on the shock plate (touching; 30%). The maximum shock decreased steadily from the farthest to most immediate conditions: from silent remote to screaming remote to proximate to touching. Besides the victim's immediacy, the authority's immediacy also mattered. Obedience dropped sharply as the experimenter moved from a few feet away to a telephoned intercom to a mere tape recording. And conducting the experiment in a rundown commercial suite decreased obedience to 48%. When teachers were supported by disobedient peers, only 10% obeyed.

Milgram explicitly understood the conditions of obedience to reflect the social force field operating on the participant. Going back again to Kurt Lewin's concept of life space (Chapter 1), people operate in a social force field, influenced by social pressures that vary in strength, which is determined by their number, direction, and proximity. Social impact theory, described earlier in this chapter, adopts a similar framework. When the authority is proximate, the authority's commands carry more force. When the victim is immediate, the victim's suffering carries more force. Disobedient peers and a less impressive setting also weaken the experimenter's force field.

Social forces know no cultural or temporal boundaries. Subsequent research has demonstrated the robustness of the obedience effects (Blass, 1999; Miller, Collins, & Brief, 1995). Men and women show the same rates of obedience, although women react with greater tension and nervousness. Over the decades since the original studies, obedience rates have stayed the same. Similar rates of obedience occur in Europe, Jordan, South Africa, and Australia.

In one conceptual replication—that is, obedience to authority using a different paradigm—participants had to criticize and derogate a job applicant, disturbing him so that he failed the test and remained unemployed (Meeus & Raaijmakers, 1986; 1995). Although the consequences for the applicant getting the job were allegedly real, the experimenter supposedly wanted to disrupt the applicant in order to study stress. Despite their discomfort with the task, 90% obeyed. However, in numerous variations, as with the original Milgram studies, experimenter absence and peer rebellion both reduced obedience, as did information indicating the participant's own legal liability.

The obedience effects are robust, across a variety of people and many situations, but individual differences nonetheless do matter (Blass, 1991). Sometimes authoritarianism matters; this fits its definition (Chapter 11) as the tendency toward conventionality (conformity to traditional values), authoritarian submission (obeying powerful leaders), and authoritarian aggression (sanctioned aggression against deviants). All these factors relate to obedience. Other factors sometimes matter: Dispositional hostility, trust in authorities, moral judgment, external locus of control, and belief in divine control can predict obedience.

In general, personality variables for ceding control tend to predict obedience, which makes sense. Our core motive of control emerges here. The control contingency appears to take this form: If I do this, I will not be punished. Also relevant are a core motive for shared understanding. To understand the situation the way the authority defines it ("the experiment requires that you continue"), participants apparently resist having to contradict the authority's assertion that they have no choice. Disobedience would disrupt a powerful, socially shared understanding. Finally, some researchers have proposed that trusting the authority's expertise and legitimacy is also relevant, although the evidence for this core social motive is mixed.

In keeping with the control motive interpretation, when obedience does occur, lay observers tend to view the participants as having relinquished control to a legitimate, expert authority (Blass, 1995, 1996a; Blass & Schmitt, 2001). The more authoritarian the observers, the more they absolve the participant of responsibility, probably because they endorse authoritarian submission. Also, the more observers view obedience as common, the more they absolve the participant (Blass, 1996b; Tyler & Devinitz, 1981).

Ultimately, responsibility rests with the researcher for the participant's suffering. Replications of the Milgram studies have ceased in the United States because of regulations protecting human research participants from procedures now viewed as harmful. Nevertheless, some important questions remain for conceptual replications of obedience studies. First, the exact features of the situational variants that maintain or reduce obedience are not well specified (Blass, 1991). That is, what exactly is it about the experimenter's presence or absence that might matter? What is it about Yale versus the storefront that might matter?

Second, some other situational findings (victim proximity) also might not be reliable (Blass, 1991); boundary conditions need to be clarified. One likely candidate for boundary condition is the victim's response. A meta-analysis of the original Milgram studies shows a critical decision point at 150 volts, the point at which the victim first asks to be released (Packer, 2008). The maximum disobedience occurred here and predicts the overall rate of disobedience. Apparently, participants disobeyed when they saw the victim's rights as over-riding the experimenter's commands.

Third, participants are not always assigned randomly to condition, so the original Milgram studies and some follow-ups are not true experiments, and confounding, for example, time with condition, is possible. As noted in Chapter 2, other famous studies (the Zimbardo prison study, the Langer-Rodin nursing home study) were not true experiments but still have had enormous impact as demonstrations of the power of the situation. What's more, the "control group" in this case is people's expectations about what would happen, and observers consistently underestimate the amount of obedience that will occur.

Milgram explicitly undertook his research to explain the obedience of seemingly ordinary people following Nazi orders to destroy millions of Jewish people during the Holocaust. He certainly succeeded in demonstrating the extent of obedience to one form of destructive authority. But does this fully capture the potential evils of social influence? **Evil** is defined as action that constitutes an intentional, egregious violation of moral norms, especially when the actor is fully responsible but gains little, compared with the suffering of the victims (Baumeister, 1997; Berkowitz, 1999; Darley, 1992). The Milgram studies are a paradigm for understanding evil, but opinions differ as to whether the actual participants were necessarily behaving in an evil manner.

## Power: Control Resources and Maintain Belonging

To jaywalk or not to jaywalk? Stand at a stoplight and watch who follows whom to cross against the light. Meta-analysis indicates that people normally jaywalk about 24% of the time, but if someone else obeys the light, they jaywalk only 16%, whereas if someone else jaywalks, they do too, about 44% of the time. A high-status model (i.e., a middle-aged white male in a business suit) produces more obedience to the light by obeying than does a high-status model who jaywalks (Mullen, Copper, & Driskell, 1990). **Status** is defined by having a high position in a hierarchy, and it often correlates with power. The jaywalking example illustrates the everyday roles of status and power in social influence.

Classic definitions of power rely on the role of social influence. According to this view, **power** is the ability to exert influence. In field theory terms, Lewin (1941, 1944) defined power as the amount of force one person can induce on another. Force does not necessarily imply change, for the target can resist. "Power is potential influence, and influence is power in action" (Ng, 1980, p. 157). Social psychologists realized early that power comes in many forms (French & Raven, 1959):

- **Reward power** = target's perception that the other person controls benefits
- **Coercive power** = target's perception that the other controls punishments
- **Referent power** = target identifying with the other
- **Expert power** = target perceiving the other to be knowledgeable
- **Legitimate power** = target's perception of the other's right to influence

Notice that all these forms of power presuppose that the target perceives the powerful other in certain ways. Thus, if one person actually controls resources, is appointed leader, or possesses relevant knowledge, that is not necessarily power. Power operates via perception. In this view, power thus is ceded by the powerless, an irony that researchers often ignore (Dépret & Fiske, 1993, 1996).

An alternative definition that both recognizes the role of the powerless and relies less on the success of influence but more on the potential for influence would say that **power** is control over valued resources (Fiske, 1993a; Fiske, 2010; Fiske & Berdahl, 2007; Keltner, Gruenfeld, & Anderson, 2003), which may include rewards, punishments, status, identity, and knowledge. In this **power-as-control** view, control is central to understanding power, although other motives are relevant, as we shall see.

We address research on each basis of power, in turn. In reviewing the French-Raven bases of power, we return to many of the leadership principles described in Chapter 12, but the emphasis here contrasts the different sources of influence, rather than the role of the leader in the group.

**CONTROLLING REWARDS**   Leaders who offer rewards contingent upon performance are indeed effective, according to meta-analysis (Lowe, Kroeck, & Sivisubramaniam, 1996). This kind of contingency motivates subordinates to perform because they thereby know how they can control their outcomes. This text has argued that control is a core social motive; people do want to know the contingency between their own behavior and their outcomes. From this, it follows that those who lack control over their outcomes (the powerless) will attend to those who do control those outcomes (the powerful). The less powerful attend upward, seeking understanding and potential control (e.g., Fiske, 1993a). Those who hold control will be less motivated to attend to their subordinates, who retain less control over resources (Fiske, 2010). A series of studies have found precisely those complementary patterns: People attend to others on whom their outcomes depend and interpret their behavior in dispositional terms, in an effort to predict their behavior (Dépret & Fiske, 1999; Erber & Fiske, 1984; Guinote, Brown, & Fiske, 2006; Neuberg & Fiske, 1987; Ruscher & Fiske, 1990; Stevens & Fiske, 2000). Attention to diagnostic information allows individuated impressions of the powerful. People expect the powerful to be free of constraint, so they attribute their behavior to more dispositional causes (Overbeck, Tiedens, & Brion, 2006). All this careful interpretive processing comes at a cost: Being powerless impairs executive function that allows people to maintain a focus on their main goals (Smith, Jostmann, Galinsky, & van Dijk, 2008).

Conversely, powerful people attend less to those who depend on them (Goodwin, Gubin, Fiske, & Yzerbyt, 2000; Operario & Fiske, 2001a) and in general the powerful are free to prioritize central, goal-consistent, focal features of any given situation—expectancies, goals, sensations—making them more goal directed but also changeable and unpredictable (Guinote, 2007a, 2007b, 2008; Guinote, Judd, & Brauer, 2002; Weick & Guinote, 2008). Their attentional neglect of seemingly peripheral features (and people) allows stereotyping of subordinates, as we saw in Chapter 11. Powerful parties to a conflict do indeed judge their opponents less accurately, whereas they are judged accurately by others (Ebenbach & Keltner, 1998; Keltner & Robinson, 1996, 1997). Powerful people are not good at taking others' perspectives (Galinsky, Magee, Inesi, & Gruenfeld, 2006). Powerful people's focus on the crucial features relevant to pursuing their goals means that they can view others in instrumental ways, that is, approaching them only if they are useful, thereby objectifying them (Gruenfeld, Inesi, Magee, & Galinsky, 2008).

This neglect-of-useless-subordinates effect occurs mainly for powerful people who are exchange-oriented and focused on organizational, rather than relational and interpersonal concerns (Chen, Lee-Chai, & Bargh, 2001; Overbeck & Park, 2001). When powerful people feel interdependent with an opponent, they are more generous, but if they are an interdependent team, they are less generous toward an opponent team (Howard, Gardner, & Thompson, 2007). Powerful people, who already control rewards, by definition, also are free to follow the rewards in the situation.

A related view of power (Keltner, Gruenfeld, & Anderson, 2003) associates power with rewards and freedom for the powerful person. Because of this, people in positions of power should be more oriented toward approach tendencies: cheerful, focused on rewards, behaviorally unconstrained, and cognitively automatic. People with less relative power should orient more toward inhibition tendencies: emotionally negative, focused on threat and on others' interests, behaviorally constrained, and cognitively controlled (see Table 13.2). This **approach-inhibition theory of power** integrates a variety of responses (affect, cognition, behavior) by analyzing the interpersonal power of people who control rewards (and punishments). For example, being powerful sparks positive emotions and behavioral approach; being powerless creates negative emotions and behavioral inhibition (Anderson & Berdahl, 2002; Langner & Keltner, 2008). Powerful people are more likely to take risks (Anderson & Galinsky, 2006), to fix an unpleasant situation (Galinsky, Gruenfeld, & Magee, 2003), and to move first to gain a competitive advantage (Magee, Galinsky, & Gruenfeld, 2007). But all this holds only when both sides perceive their power to be legitimate (Lammers, Galinsky, Gordijn, & Otten, 2008). If legitimate, power is clearly a preferable state because one can act on one's goals. But power is not without its costs.

A more cynical **metamorphic effects theory** suggests that power corrupts relationships (Kipnis, 1976). In this view, people choose influence strategies based on their

**Table 13.2**  Power, Approach, and Inhibition

| Reaction | Power | |
| --- | --- | --- |
| | High | Low |
| Affect | Positive | Negative |
| Attentional focus | Rewards | Threat, punishment |
| | Others as means to own ends | Self as means to others' ends |
| Information-processing | Automatic | Controlled |
| Social behavior | Disinhibited | Inhibited |

*Source:* From description by Keltner et al., 2003.

degree of dominance over others, their expectations of compliance, and their goals (Kipnis, 1984). Powerful people use rewards to influence subordinates who ingratiate (present themselves as likable and flatter the powerholder) (Kipnis & Vanderveer, 1971). Dominant people do like ingratiators, but they may not respect them (Operario & Fiske, 2001a). Powerful people in general devalue their subordinates because they believe that they themselves controlled their subordinate's performance, so therefore the subordinate does not deserve any credit (Kipnis, 1972; Kipnis, Castell, Gergen, & Mauch, 1976; Kipnis, Schmidt, Price, & Stitt, 1981). Ironically, this does not enhance the powerholder's own self-esteem. A cynical view would argue the adaptive value of the potentially powerful developing strategies for exploiting the potentially powerless through "deception, manipulation, coercion, intimidation, terrorization, and force"; evidence includes perceiving who's muggable, cheatable, abusable, assaultable, or killable (Buss & Duntley, 2008). Grim thoughts.

On the other hand, reward power does have beneficial effects, as noted, on performance. In one study (Figure 13.1), reward power apparently encouraged perceiving the powerholder as having both expert and referent power. These perceptions in turn led to more constructive behavior and improved performance (Rahim, Antonioni, & Psenicka, 2001). And to be fair, powerful-subordinate relations function best when each expects the other to behave in complementary fashion (Tiedens, Unzueta, & Young, 2007). The more people care about a task, the more they perceive their partner to behave in the complementary power position (Tiedens & Fragale, 2003). Organizations arguably function better as hierarchies (Gruenfeld & Tiedens, 2010).

**CONTROLLING PUNISHMENTS**    In many frameworks, whether the powerholder can dispense benefits or punishments would seem like flip sides of the same coin. But controlling punishments is more coercive than controlling rewards, as the French and Raven label implies. Power does carry overtones of control, more than mere influence does, and coercive power in particular carries those negative overtones (Hollander, 1985).

Coercive power works in the short run but not the long run. Subordinates may comply under coercion, but they disrespect and dislike the supervisor. They also become avoidant (withdrawn) and not happy, open, problem-solving, or obliging

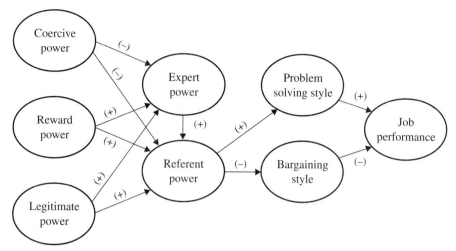

**Figure 13.1**   Relationships among Different Kinds of Power, Conflict Styles, and Job Performance

*Source:* From Rahim et al., 2001. Copyright © Information Age Publishing. Adapted with permission.

(Carson, Carson, Roe, Birkenmeir, & Phillips, 1999; Rahim, Antonioni, & Psenicka,
2001; Shaw & Condelli, 1986). Reciprocally, the more a powerholder uses coercive
power, the less favorably the powerholder views the subordinate and the whole process
(O'Neal, Kipnis, & Craig, 1994). Discipline problems evoke the use of punishments
(Goodstadt & Kipnis, 1970), so maybe coercive power (punishment) operates in a
power relationship already contaminated by poor authority relations. Being in the role
of an authority may give people the perceived right to punish, but the effects soon
evaporate, and continued obedience requires surveillance.

**REFERENT POWER**   When people identify with the authority, the source of
power is relational or referent. According to meta-analyses, people like leaders who
show them consideration (Lowe, Knoeck, & Sivasubramaniam, 1996; Wofford &
Liska, 1993) and establish good relations (Gerstner & Day, 1997). Often, they are more
productive as well under good leader-subordinate relationships. Chapter 12 noted that
perceptions of just treatment depend in part on feeling respected by the group (Tyler
& Lind, 1992). Referent power predicts a constructive, problem-solving orientation by
subordinates and avoids a difficult, dominating, unobliging orientation (Rahim, Antonioni, & Psenicka, 2001; see Figure 13.1). Not surprisingly, referent power predicts
commitment, attitudinal compliance, behavioral compliance, and satisfaction, according to meta-analysis (Carson, Carson, & Roe, 1993; e.g., Rahim, 1989; Rahim & Afza,
1993).

Perceived expertise and legitimacy help to confer referent power (Rahim et
al., 2001). We saw in Chapter 12 that leaders who embody the group prototype
elicit social identification (i.e., referent power), in keeping with social identity and
self-categorization theory. Indeed, members who leave the group and return, although

they may be highly involved, creative, knowledgeable, and apparent candidates for leader, instead are viewed as less loyal and valuable; therefore, they have less influence, because their identity is questioned (Gruenfeld, Martorana, & Fan, 2000).

Leaders oriented toward the group's social relationships are most effective in settings of mid-range difficulty for the group, defined in terms of control over task, authority, and morale (Peters, Hartke, & Pohlmann, 1985; Schriesheim, Tepper, & Tetrault, 1994; Strube & Garcia, 1981; see Richard, Bond, & Stokes 2001a, 2003, report of these meta-analytic effects). This tends to fit Fiedler's (1964) contingency theory of leadership, introduced in Chapter 12, which says that the effectiveness of a task versus social leadership style depends on the favorability of the situation, although the support is uneven.

**EXPERT POWER**    Expert power, authority stemming from knowledge, also tends to fit with contingency theory, namely, the effectiveness of task-oriented leaders when situational control is either very low (structure is needed; Graen, Alvres, Orris, & Martella, 1970; Peters, Hartke, & Pohlmann, 1985; Schriesheim et al., 1994; Strube & Garcia, 1981) or very high (efficiency is fine; Peters, Hartke, & Pohlmann, 1985; Schriesheim, Tepper, & Tetrault, 1994; Strube & Garcia, 1981). Being task-oriented under these circumstances apparently confers credibility on the leader.

The role of intelligence in anointing authorities also suggests the importance of expert power (Lord, de Vader, & Alliger, 1986; Mann, 1959; Stogdill, 1948). When subordinates are inept, expert power intervenes to correct poor performance (Goodstadt & Kipnis, 1970). Expert power builds subordinate commitment, compliance, satisfaction, and attitude change (Rahim, 1989; Rahim & Mainuddin, 1993). These effects on persuasion also fit the discussion in Chapter 6 on source credibility effects. What's more, high status confers perceived competence, especially for perceivers high on belief in a just world or social dominance orientation (Oldmeadow & Fiske, 2007), so perceived power and expertise reinforce each other.

Expert power might seem to rely on the difference between self and the powerful expert (Ng, 1980). But SIT/SCT interprets expertise as the person who most represents the group consensus and therefore its prototype (Turner, 1991). The powerful expert differs from self only in better expressing the group's shared identity. Thus, any difference occurs in a pronormative direction. This interpretation ties expert power to referent power and to legitimacy.

**LEGITIMATE POWER**    Being in the role of an authority gives the opportunity for exercising various kinds of power (Rahim, Antonioni, & Psenicka, 2001). So, who then is viewed as an appropriate leader? In Chapter 12, we saw that leaders have good relationships with others (essentially referent power), being close, central, satisfied, and respected, according to meta-analysis (Bass, 1954; Mullen, 1991). Legitimacy and referent power indeed are closely linked (Rahim, Antonioni, & Psenicka, 2001).

Certain individual characteristics predict who is perceived to be a legitimate leader: Authorities are typically expected to be male, as we saw in Chapter 12, but also older (Stogdill, 1948). **Expectation states theory**, introduced in Chapter 12 (Berger, Webster, Ridgeway, & Rosenholtz, 1986; Ridgeway, 2001), predicts that people develop expectations about the competence of other group members through status characteristics (such as gender, age) and culturally valued abilities that may or may not be relevant to the task at hand. Given the traditional divisions of labor between men and women, according to **social role theory**, women are expected to be less competent leaders (Eagly & Karau, 2002). Although a masculine style predicts leadership (Lord, de Vader, & Alliger, 1986), women are penalized for behaving in a masculine fashion, so they are less likely to be viewed as authorities in traditionally masculine settings (Eagly, Makhijani, & Klonsky, 1992), as noted in the last chapter.

Other personality characteristics predict who will be perceived as having legitimate power, that is, the right to be a leader or an authority: intelligence and dominance (Lord et al., 1986; Mann, 1959; Stogdill, 1948). As noted in the last chapter, a benign view of leader personality holds across cultures (Den Hartog et al., 1999), and it is consistent with notions of charisma: visionary, inspirational, team-integrating, trustworthy, diplomatic, and not self-centered, malevolent, inexplicit, or autocratic. Consistent with this interpretation of charisma, charismatic leaders indeed are effective, according to meta-analyses (Fuller, Patterson, Hester, & Stringer, 1996; Lowe, Kroeck, & Sivasubramanian, 1996).

And of course, legitimate power is conferred by culturally accepted means: election, moral mandate, or appointment. People may even seek power to resolve injustice (Foster & Rusbult, 1999). Democratically elected leaders, for example, like and respect their subordinates (Kipnis, Schmidt, Price, & Stitt, 1981), and their subordinates like them as well, according to meta-analysis (Gastil, 1994). The importance of the processes that select leaders and determine group decisions can hardly be overstated. Process sometimes matters more than the outcomes, a point in Chapter 12 introduced as **procedural justice** (Tyler & Lind, 1992; Tyler & Smith, 1998). **Legitimacy** is the subjective sense that an authority (or institution) is appropriate, proper, and just (Tyler, 2006). Legitimacy has a strong relational component, whereby legitimate leaders elicit voluntary deference to the extent people feel valued in the group and authorities maintain good relations (Tyler, 1997; Tyler, Degoey, & Smith, 1996). Powerholders who are more relationship-oriented—as opposed to more instrumental and exchange-oriented—behave in more socially responsible ways (Chen, Lee-Chai, & Bargh, 2001), and powerholders can be constrained to behave in more interpersonally concerned ways (Overbeck & Park, 2001). Obtaining voluntary acquiescence creates the most effective leadership, even when times are hard (Tyler, 2006).

People prefer democratic, elected, internal leaders, especially when they identify strongly with the group (Foels, Driskell, Mullen, & Salas, 2000; Gastil, 1994; Van Vugt & De Cremer, 1999). Legitimacy may be conferred by best representing the group ideal or consensus (Hogg, Hains, & Mason, 1998). People talk in terms of "leaders" when they identify with the otherwise legitimate authority as having referent power, but they tend to talk in terms of "power" per se when the authority controls resources (rewards and punishments), especially if they do not identify with the authority (Turner, 1991). Belonging motives thus are critical to legitimate leadership.

## Summary of Obedience

Obedience—the social influence of an authority or a powerholder on a subordinate—operates by social forces, coming from the authority, peers, and potential victims. Milgram showed that people are surprisingly obedient to destructive but otherwise legitimate authority, and the obedience effect holds up over time, culture, gender, personality, and many situations. Some people (low authoritarians) and some situations (rebellious peers, authority distance, victim proximity) do undermine obedience, but the role of obedience is surprisingly strong compared to common sense. On the other hand, people could not survive long in groups if the members did not typically obey the authorities. A motive for socially shared understanding between authority and subordinate matters here, as does trust, to some extent.

Authority stems from various bases of power: instrumental, controlling rewards and punishments; relational, conferring referent power through identification; expertise, through knowledge or consensus; and legitimacy through normative beliefs. Control motives (resources) and belonging motives (relational identity) are relevant here.

## COMPLIANCE: STRATEGIES TO UNDERSTAND SELF, MAINTAIN BELONGING, AND CONTROL RESOURCES

We defined compliance as social influence from a peer's request. Several strategies are used by real-world influence agents (Cialdini, 1987, 1993). The core motives of the targets make these strategies effective, as they variously promote the target's motives for socially shared understanding, belonging, and controlling outcomes.

### Understanding Self as Consistent

A single consistency explanation for compliance appears in various guises. **Consistency** (introduced in Chapters 5 and 6) refers to people's strong tendency to view themselves as behaving in ways that fit their earlier behavior. **Self-perception** (introduced in Chapters 3, 5, and 6) refers to Bem's theory that people learn about themselves by observing their own behavior. **Learning by doing** refers to steps along the continuum of social influence, starting with a small, innocuous step and culminating in a major step, sometimes along a path of destructive behavior (Staub, 1989, 1999). What they all share in common is a person behaving in ways consistent with earlier, related behavior but ending up in ways that might otherwise be undesirable when considered in isolation. That is, they describe the slippery slope to behavior people normally want to avoid. Compliance works in many of the same ways.

The **foot-in-the-door technique** (FITD; Freedman & Fraser, 1966) describes this phenomenon as a strategy for eliciting compliance: A small favor (sure to be granted) is followed by a large, related favor. In one of the original studies, housewives agreed to a short phone survey about household products, followed a few days later by agreeing to have several men search their home for two hours. Similarly, as noted earlier, placing a small "drive carefully" sign in one's window increases compliance with a request to erect an enormous lawn sign several days later. Normally, the FITD strategy requires a delay between the initial small request and the later large one. If the requests come too close together, people feel exploited, and they refuse, perhaps due to **reactance**, that is, an unwillingness to let other people control them (Brehm, 1966; Brehm & Cole, 1966; Brehm & Sensenig, 1966). Otherwise, as we will see, the FITD effect depends on how it's done (Beaman, Cole, Preston, Klentz, & Steblay, 1983), but it works under the right circumstances.

The self-perception explanation for FITD is that people infer their attitude based on their response to the first request and then act on the larger request in response to their newly inferred attitude. This process suggests three hypotheses, all supported by meta-analysis (Burger, 1999):

- A stronger FITD effect when people are *involved* in the initial request, because then they will recall it when they encounter the second one
- A stronger FITD effect when people *actually perform* the first request, rather then merely agreeing to it, because action creates more commitment
- A weaker FITD effect when the initial request is so *big* that people refuse

All these results also fit the consistency notion. But consistency goes one step farther. In keeping with the consistency explanation, people with a high individual need for consistency show bigger FITD effects (Cialdini, Trost, & Newsom, 1995). Individual differences in need for consistency can override even the normal requirement for a delay between the initial small request and the subsequent large one, if the person's prior compliance is salient (Guadagno, Asher, Demaine, & Cialdini, 2001).

Closely related to the idea of consistency is commitment. As long as people commit themselves to the initial request, many of the same compliance processes are set in motion. For example, if people answer "just a few questions" and then are requested to answer continued questions (i.e., continuing same request; Burger, 1999), they are more likely to comply.

Also, in processes similar to self-perception, attributions can be key in compliance processes. One's attribution for agreeing to the initial request, for why one did it, encourages similar future behavior. If the initially compliant person is labeled as cooperative or helpful, compliance with the second request is more likely because it fits the new self-attribution (Burger, 1999). In a similar vein, attributions of intrinsic motivation—and continued compliance—are more likely if the requester avoids extrinsic rewards, also in line with self-perception theory.

Using the FITD technique has negative consequences for the person using it. Influence agents who use the FITD strategy enjoy it less and like the target less (O'Neal, Kipnis, & Craig, 1994). Perhaps their own self-perception changes, as they learn by doing to manipulate or exploit another person.

All these processes hinge on people's motivation to understand themselves as maintaining a consistent and coherent self. Learning about their own history of compliance (that is, invoking the consistency-commitment principles) especially affects

Americans or those with a highly individualist orientation. In contrast, a more belonging type of motivation—**social proof** (their peers' history of compliance)—can affect Poles and those with more collectivist orientation (Cialdini, Wosinska, Barrett, Butner, & Gornik-Durose, 1999). This brings us to the second core motive underlying compliance.

## Belonging via Reciprocity, Liking, and Approval

People feel obligated to comply, in return for a favor, gift, invitation, and so on. This, of course, is the principle of "free gifts" used in marketing and fund-raising. People feel more obligated than they otherwise would. Survey researchers have discovered that attaching to their mailed questionnaires a small incentive, monetary or not, increases the return rate by nearly 20%. Payment contingent on completing the survey does not have the same effect. It's the unsolicited gift that does the trick (Tourangeau, 2004).

Reciprocity, the exchange of benefits for like benefits, appears in relationships (Chapter 8), helping (Chapter 9), and groups (Chapter 12). Meta-analysis (Burger, 1999) supports reciprocity as a compliance principle for FITD. Reciprocity requires that each person avoid making repeated requests, which break the rules of fair exchange. When the same person makes both the small and large request with no intervening delay, people refuse to comply, as apart from all other combinations of delay (short/long) and requestor (same/different). This supports the idea that people react to perceived exploitation: Why is this person asking so much and giving so little? It also fits reactance, as noted earlier. For people to maintain their relationships, they must abide by the rules of reciprocity (Cialdini & Trost, 1998).

Sometimes, the reciprocity norm allows influence agents to obtain compliance by starting big and then moderating to a more reasonable request. The **door-in-the-face** technique trades on the influence agent appearing to step back, which makes the target feel guilty and perhaps need to reciprocate by agreeing to the more moderate request. Whatever the mechanism, it works (O'Keefe & Hale, 2001).

People also comply to maintain mutual liking. Influence agents often try to appear likeable, and we saw in Chapter 6 that persuasion occurs in part when sources are likeable and attractive. Liked friends sell more Tupperware. Their likeability and social ties, viewed as degree of **social capital**, are measured by the strength of the buyer-seller tie and buyer indebtedness to the seller (reciprocity again). Social capital significantly predicts the likelihood of purchasing little plastic food storage dishes and other Tupperware products (Frenzen & Davis, 1990).

As we know, attractive people receive favorable attributions of being successful, socially skilled, and somewhat more competent (Eagly, Ashmore, Makhijani, & Longo, 1991; Feingold, 1992b). Accordingly, they sell products, win votes, raise funds, and shorten their jail sentences, all reflecting their success as compliance agents. This builds on the belonging principle of people going along with those they like.

Perceived similarity also predicts compliance, further reinforcing the belonging motive. A fundamental principle of attraction is perceived similarity (Chapters 7, 11, and 12). People comply more often when similar others have complied, which maintains their sense of social identity. People compare themselves with similar others to see how they are doing (Chapter 5), which functions to help them understand, enhance, and improve themselves. But it also reflects their sense of belonging with similar others.

From belonging with similar others also follows people's need for social approval. People comply with implied group norms, as we have seen in conformity. But norms also reinforce compliance with direct requests. For example, the FITD effect increases with relevant norms (Burger, 1999). In one study (DeJong, 1981), people who signed a petition (small initial request) were told that almost everyone else also agreed or that they were the only one so far. When told their behavior fit the norm, they were much more likely to help a second person, as befits complying with the perceived norm to be helpful.

Thus, a number of compliance principles fit the belonging motive: reciprocity, liking, attraction, social comparison, and adhering to norms. We turn now to another core social motive, control over one's outcomes.

## Controlling Resources by Valuing Freedom and Scarcity

People also comply to control their own outcomes, attaining valued resources. We have already touched on reactance, which is the clearest indicator of this motive. People will comply in order to maintain their sense of freedom to choose. The principle of **scarcity** reflects people's tendency to value rare commodities, so they will try to obtain items that are going out of stock, about to become unavailable, or otherwise almost out of reach (Cialdini & Trost, 1998). College students valued even their cafeteria food when they learned that it was no longer available because of a fire in the building (West, 1975).

Items or information that are exclusive or hard to obtain are viewed as more valuable, so people use scarcity as a heuristic for value (Cialdini, 1993). Information, too, is more persuasive when it is a rare commodity (Brock & Brannon, 1992); censorship increases the value of banned communications (Worchel, 1992). And even love affairs are more appealing when they are secret (Wegner, Lane, & Dimitri, 1994). We saw earlier that obstacles can increase passion for another person (Chapter 8). Apparent scarcity can increase the value of an object. Hence, scarcity is an effective compliance technique that relies on people's motive to control valued resources.

## Summary of Compliance

People comply with direct requests partly in order to maintain a view of themselves as consistent. The foot-in-the-door technique describes people's compliance with a big request, because it fits their previous compliance with a related, though smaller, request. Consistency, commitment, self-perception, and learning-by-doing all explain related compliance phenomena that maintain coherent self-understanding.

People also comply in order to maintain their belonging with valued others. People adhere to the rules of reciprocity, returning benefit for benefit received. They comply with people who are likeable and attractive. And they comply with the norms of their groups in order to maintain social approval.

People attempt to control scarce resources because rarity often indicates value. But also people want to maintain their freedom to choose. Reactance names people's resistance to restrictions on their own freedom.

## CHAPTER SUMMARY

Social influence is change in behavior as a result of interpersonal interaction. Because it focuses on actual behavior change and on social interaction, the research and theory remain distinct from persuasion and attitude change. Moreover, not all social influence is deliberate, whereas persuasion is. Operationally, social influence paradigms include (a) conformity to group norms that are arbitrary or erroneous (thereby showing the effects of group pressure); (b) obedience to destructive authority, enacted with the framework of the experimenter as authority over a participant; and (c) compliance with direct requests, mostly in field studies.

All five core social motives bear on social influence, which makes sense given its central role in social psychology. Early descriptions of social influence discussed its role in reducing uncertainty. Researchers differentiated between informational influence (about seemingly objective reality) and normative influence (about supposedly subjective social reality). Similarly, researchers described compliance in the service of controlling outcomes, identification in the service of group belonging, and internalization in the service of objective understanding.

However, these distinctions break down because informational and normative influence both depend on social consensus and multiple motives. The same is true of their respective parallels as internalization (due to information) and identification (due to social ties). The overlap between social and objective reality is clear, upon reflection. People would not, for example, assume that they would be the only ones to see objective reality but instead assume that the social consensus would agree with them because others would see what they see. Similarly, people rarely admit that their social reality is not objectively true. Belonging and understanding thus intermingle here. Controlling resources, trusting ingroup others, and enhancing self also matter.

The first conformity studies used ambiguous stimuli (Sherif's point of light, Asch's abstract words) to show conformity. Seeking to show independence, Asch introduced a perceptual task on which the majority was clearly in error; still, people conformed a surprising amount (one-third of the time). Scores of replications have shown stronger conformity under conditions that replicate the original studies, use ambiguous stimuli, and employ ingroup confederates as the majority viewpoint. Collectivist cultures, people operating outside their own spheres of expertise, and earlier eras also show stronger conformity effects.

Conformity can be relatively automatic, or at least heuristic, as when people assume that others share their opinions (false consensus effect) and assume they are conforming with what would be the prevailing norm. Majority influence, in particular, conveys this kind of unthinking agreement. In contrast, a consistently disagreeing minority viewpoint creates conflict, potentially resulting in divergent, creative thinking and attitude change on private or indirect dimensions, as a result of having to think about the minority perspective. Social impact theories describe the number, strength, and immediacy of influence agents as producing change, by whatever process, automatic or controlled.

Social categorization clearly matters, as people are open to social influence by ingroup others. People conform because their ingroup provides subjective validity, especially given the more similar and attracted they feel to the ingroup. People view the most representative perspective as the prototype of the group and conform to it as a function of identity. The more cohesive, consistent, and coherent the group perspective, the more people conform, all in keeping with social identity approaches.

Salient forms of conformity include memes (units of culture that get passed along), rumors (verbally conveyed beliefs, without benefit of evidence), and gossip (rumors about people). People's belief in these intangible cultural artifacts reflects compliance as a result of group belonging and socially shared understanding.

Obedience to authority was most dramatically demonstrated by Milgram's original studies, reflecting the operation of social forces. The high rates of destructive obedience replicate across gender, place, and decade, although personality differences do matter somewhat. And contextual manipulations that reflect the proximity of social forces (the authority, the victim, peers) also matter a lot.

Power is the potential to influence others, through control over resources and relationships. Coercive power (punishment) often backfires, whereas reward power leads to more constructive results, although it requires surveillance. Referent power extends our understanding to the arena of group belonging, as leaders represent the prototypic ideal or group consensus and have power that way. This kind of power depends on maintaining group relationships. Expert power depends on perceived knowledge, but can also represent the group's consensus. From all sources of power and contributing to all of them is legitimacy, that is, the authority having the perceived right to lead and to demand obedience. Control over resources and belonging to group relationships both are important motives, along with the socially shared understanding of the situation and trust in ingroup authorities.

Compliance results from strategies that allow people to understand the self as consistent and committed. People also seek to maintain belonging through reciprocity, liking, and social approval. They attempt to control resources by complying with requests that protect their freedom and allow them to obtain scarce commodities.

## SUGGESTIONS FOR FURTHER READING

CIALDINI, R. B. & GOLDSTEIN, N. J. (2004). Social influence: Compliance and conformity. *Annual Review of Psychology*, 55, 591–621.

CRANO, W. D. (2000). Milestones in the psychological analysis of social influence. *Group Dynamics*, 4, 68–80.

FISKE, S. T. (2010). Interpersonal stratification: Status, power, and subordination. In S. T. FISKE, D. T., GILBERT, & G. LINDZEY (Eds.), *Handbook of social psychology* (5th ed.). New York: Wiley.

HOGG, M. A. (2001). Social categorization, depersonalization, and group behavior. In M. A. HOGG & R. S. TINDALE (Eds.), *Blackwell handbook of social psychology: Group processes* (pp. 56–85). Malden, MA: Blackwell.

HOGG, M. (2010). Influence and leadership. In S. T. FISKE, D. T., GILBERT, & G. LINDZEY (Eds.), *Handbook of social psychology* (5th ed.). New York: Wiley.

MARTIN, R., & HEWSTONE, M. (2001). Conformity and independence in groups: Majorities and minorities. In M. A. HOGG & R. S. TINDALE (Eds.), *Blackwell handbook of social psychology: Group processes* (pp. 209–210). Malden, MA: Blackwell.

TURNER, J. C. (1991). *Social influence*. Pacific Grove, CA: Brooks/Cole.

WOOD, W. (2000). Attitude change: Persuasion and social influence. *Annual Review of Psychology, 51,* 539–570.

# Chapter 14

# Conclusion: Social Beings

We have come on a long journey together, and now it is time to look back on where we have been. People as social beings are complex, nuanced, and fascinating. I have aimed to describe social psychology's insights in terms of a few themes that unify this rich field. For a straight review, you can reread each end-of-chapter summary. I don't want to repeat those, and you don't want to reread them in another form. In this conclusion, I will instead take a different approach.

Let's consider social psychology's intellectual landscape from the perspective of the core social motives and see how they fit with more traditional broad-brush theoretical ways of dividing up ideas in social psychology. As you read through this account of by-now-familiar material, I hope you will be impressed by how much you have learned, as well as develop a fresh understanding of how it all fits into psychology's classic ideas (and everyday life) as a whole.

## SOCIAL TO THE CORE: SITUATIONS, ADAPTATION, CULTURE, AND CORE MOTIVES

This book makes an argument that other people are the most important niche for human adaptation over evolutionary time and across cultures. Chapter 1 argued that the importance of other people to our sheer survival has made us especially sensitive to the social situation, including our own particular culture. The consequent power of the social situation over us—called *situationism*—is the stock-in-trade of social psychologists. The motive for *belonging* with other people drives much of our social behavior. In order to function well in interactions with others, people are motivated to develop a socially shared *understanding*, as well as a sense of *controlling* their interpersonal outcomes. And in order to motivate participation in our various groups and relationships, people need to be *enhancing self*, in the sense of seeing the self as better, improvable, or at least sympathetic. *Trusting* ingroup others also allows people to function socially. Social psychological research and theory have addressed each of these motives, as we have seen across the book's substantive chapters (3–13). In reviewing material relevant to each motive, we parse the material the way the book is broadly parsed: within the individual, between individuals, and within groups.

## BELONGING: FOCUS ON NORMS, ROLES, AND IDENTITY

This has been the workhorse motive in a century of social psychology. People's need to participate in group life has generated a wide variety of contributions that emphasize the place of the individual in the group. Social psychology concerns the whole person reacting to the actual, imagined, or implied presence of others, so people's motive to belong with those others naturally carries a lot of weight in this field. And with good reason. As we have seen, people connected to other people live longer, healthier, happier lives than people who are isolated. As a result, people attune themselves to social *norms* and to *roles* within groups, as well as their *identity* with the group. These three central concepts therefore figure prominently in research inspired by the belonging motive. They lie intellectually at the sociological end of social psychology, best characterized by Goffman's *dramaturgical* metaphor for all of us as players on the stage of social life, adhering to defined roles and normative scripts.

### Within Individuals

Role theories describe the impact of group norms and roles on how people understand and present themselves. Examples (Chapter 5) include *reflected self-appraisals*, the *looking-glass self* and *symbolic interaction*, all theories that take seriously people viewing themselves through the eyes of an audience, primarily ingroup others. *Self-presentation, impression management, self-monitoring*, and *self-regulation* all show people positioning their overt behavior to fit with ingroup others.

Not just people's self-presentation but also their attitudes can result from their motive to belong (Chapter 6). People's *social identity*, their *self-categorization* as a group member, shapes their attitudes, as reflected in the *value expressive function* of attitudes. The attitudes' *social adjustive function* even more directly reflects people's desire to get along with others. People's occasional neglect of their attitudes' logical implications for behavior often reflects the influence of situational norms on the *attitude-behavior correlation*. And people's belief in *memes, rumors, gossip*, and *modern myths* (Chapter 13) also shows how belonging motives socially influence processes within the individual.

### Between Individuals

People *conform* to the social reality conveyed by their interactions with others, that is, they match behavior of people with whom they share *social identity* (Chapter 13). Social influence as a result of such *identification*, also known as *normative influence* from *reference groups*, specifically reflects this idea of ingroup interactions affecting beliefs and behavior. Social influence strategies that rely on *liking, reciprocity*, or *approval* also show the importance of belonging.

To facilitate belonging within their ongoing relationships, people abide by the relevant norms of *exchange, communal sharing*, and other models (authority ranking, market pricing), in accord with the *relational models theory* (Chapters 7 and 8). The *social support* that people receive from their relationships is good for their health (Chapters 1 and 8). Maintaining relationships requires going beyond one's own specific outcomes: Negotiation works better when people keep in mind *dual concerns* and abide by fair procedures, demonstrating *procedural justice* (Chapter 12).

Belonging also facilitates prosocial behavior, when helping results from *collectivist* motives (Chapter 9). These belonging-type motives operate on the basis of perceived *similarity, group identity*, and *prosocial norms*, all of which facilitate individuals' maintenance of their relationships and group identity via their prosocial interactions with others. In social psychology experiments (Chapter 2), the belonging motive can go awry, creating an *artifact* called an *expectancy effect*, when participants too anxious to please the experimenter comply with the experimenter's hypothesis instead of reacting spontaneously.

## Groups

Belonging motives appear even more clearly in ongoing group interactions. People follow prescribed norms and roles within the group structure, the better to fit in. Within the group structure of power relations, subordinates show surprising levels of *obedience to authority* (Chapter 13). Perhaps this is not surprising, given that many leaders operate by maintaining relationships with their subordinates, as suggested by the *contingency theory of leadership*, whereby socially oriented leadership works well under moderate conditions (Chapter 12). The *relational theories of leadership* focus on leader-subordinate relationships, which emphasize the importance of group belonging, and the SIT/SCT depiction of the *leader as the group prototype* also emphasizes belonging. The relational role of leaders similarly appears in *legitimate* and *referent power*, which respectively depend on group members' *status expectations* and *identification*. In general, social influence within groups fits Lewin's *field theory*, as updated in *social impact* approaches that describe *social forces* as a function of proximity, numbers, and strength.

Belonging motives at the group level (Chapter 12) also are expressed in *group cohesion* and *depersonalized social attraction*, which provide the glue for group members. They can encourage *groupthink*, the failure to consider counternormative perspectives. And *attitude polarization* results from group identity and interaction. As individuals join groups and go through group *socialization*, and as groups themselves develop *emergent norms*, people become depersonalized group members, adhering to local group norms. When this occurs at the cost of societal norms, people appear to be disinhibited and *deindividuated* in anonymous groups and crowds.

Group belonging predicts both benefits and costs to performance. General models of group problem-solving note that they operate by systematic procedural rules, *social decision schemes*, which can be more or less constructive (Chapter 12). *Social facilitation* makes people work faster, which can be constructive if their dominant response is correct. *Productivity gains* can result under the right circumstances, but so can *productivity losses*, such as *social loafing*. Similarly, *diversity* within the group produces both gains and losses, depending on how it is handled. Competition between groups can cause *realistic group conflict*, but *group identity* can also promote individual well-being and enrich the group.

## Belonging: Key to Life

People act as if they have a strong motive to belong with other people. Across a wide variety of behavior at a range of levels (from within and between people to within and between groups), belonging drives much of social behavior. Can we point to a particular behavior or spot in the brain that "proves" belonging? No. But social (and personality) psychologists over the past century have achieved considerable conceptual mileage out of manipulating and measuring belonging-related constructs that all apparently tap a similar underlying impetus for social inclusion. The belonging motive ties together a lot of evidence, makes adaptational sense, builds culture, and underlies the remaining motives.

## UNDERSTANDING: FOCUS ON GESTALTS AND COGNITION

The understanding motive made its first major scientific appearance in German *Gestalt* approaches imported to the United States in the 1940s. The understanding motive has enjoyed a major resurgence in the last couple of decades, as a result of the *cognitive revolution* (Chapters 3 and 4). Both Gestalt and cognitive principles emphasize *consistency*, shortcuts, and structured knowledge, such as *schemas, categories, expectations*, and *heuristics*. Much current work emphasizes *dual processes* that contrast relatively *automatic* use of such prior knowledge structures with alternatively more *deliberate, controlled*, and therefore detailed *individuated* or *piecemeal* processes of understanding.

Whether automatic or controlled, category-based or piecemeal, a coherent, *socially shared understanding* facilitates interactions with others. Consequently, the understanding motive is ubiquitous in social psychology, especially since the advent of social cognition approaches.

## Within Individuals

The understanding motive stars in all four kinds of theories and research within individuals: attribution, impressions, self, and attitudes. In attribution theory (Chapter 3), Heider's view of the social perceiver as *naïve psychologist* framed attributional processes as a search for behavioral *invariances* that prompt *dispositional attributions*. Building on this base, *correspondent inference theory* specified when a single behavior would be interpreted as reflecting an underlying disposition; the related *covariation model* specified patterns of behavior over time that encourage dispositional or other kinds of attributions. Recent *stage models* describe the initial, relatively automatic *identification* and *categorization* of behavior, resulting in dispositional *anchoring* or *characterization*, followed by situational *correction* or *adjustment*.

Other dual-process models emerged in research on impression formation (Chapter 4). Asch initially proposed a Gestalt-based holistic, configural process, contrasted with a hypothetical elemental process, later realized in algebraic *information integration theory*. This contrast reappeared, updated in a *continuum model* and a *dual process model* of impression formation. *Expectancy* theories relied heavily on the related ideas of *schemas, categories*, and *prototypes*, to explain how people make rapid, initial sense of each other. Although people originally came across as *cognitive misers*, focusing on automatic and error-prone *heuristics* and other shortcuts, as *motivated tacticians* people's goals and needs more pragmatically determine which strategy they follow. Impression *accuracy* results in good-enough, socially shared impressions.

Motivations themselves can activate *automatically*. Key concepts here include the contextual *salience* or cognitive *accessibility* of concepts, schemas, motives, exemplars, or any other mental representation. *Accessibility* or the *availability heuristic* underlies several rapid ways of understanding, through *representativeness, simulation*, or *anchoring and adjustment*, along with other quick-and-dirty forms of thinking prone to errors and biases. Some can attenuate under *counterfactual* thinking, according to *norm theory*. In social psychology research (Chapter 2), researchers must anticipate the participants' *construal* of the situation, whether automatic or deliberate, configural or elemental.

One form of heuristic self-understanding (Chapter 5) relies on organized prior knowledge of self, described as *self-schemas*, in the spirit of the Gestalt tradition, updated by the cognitive revolution. *Self-complexity* varies, partly as a function of how people acquire self-knowledge. People evaluate themselves by *social comparison, reflected appraisals*, and *self-perception*. Always, the tension arises between understanding via *self-verification* versus *self-enhancement* in developing and maintaining the long-term self-concept. In the short term, people assess their attitudes by *self-perception* of behavior and situational constraints, and people infer their emotions by observing the social context, as it affects *arousal and cognition*.

Going back to the Gestalt theme, note that *consistency theories* of attitudes describe people's tendency toward coherent, congruent understanding (Chapter 6). *Balance theory*, the most explicitly Gestalt approach, emphasizes consistent feelings among two people and a shared attitude object. *Dissonance theory* emphasizes the consistency that is relevant to an attitude object, especially consistency among cognitions regarding one's self and one's behavior.

Other attitude theories downplay consistency but focus on the dual-process theme. The *elaboration likelihood model* and the *heuristic-systematic model* each contrast a respectively peripheral or heuristic mode with, respectively, a central or a systematic mode, depending on motivation and capacity. Focusing solely on the more deliberate side of understanding, the Yale approach concentrated on how people understand *persuasive communications*. And the *theory of reasoned action* and the *theory of planned behavior* both assess attitudes toward a behavior and subjective norms (and the latter theory adds perceived control as a predictor, in addition to attitudes and norms).

## Between Individuals

Theories of socially shared understanding between individuals split along the dual-process lines just reviewed. Some focus on efficient prior knowledge, and others focus on more deliberate, controlled processing. Starting with prepackaged prior information, many theories of attraction (Chapter 7) follow the principle *of familiarity* and liking. What is familiar is easily understood. The *mere exposure* phenomenon is a prime example (frequency of exposure → liking). *Proximity* works in similar ways because those who are nearby are likely to become familiar. *Similarity* might also work by attraction to what resembles the most familiar person (i.e., self). In Chapter 13, we also saw that similar others exert social influence, according to *compliance principles*.

Conversely, dissimilar, unfamiliar others elicit repulsion (Chapter 11). Individuals with a *stigma* elicit dislike, partly because they are hard to understand. More broadly, *category-based impressions* can attach to individuals as a function of their social group membership. When perceivers think they understand the social category, they use it to understand the individual, even *automatically*, and their *interpersonal expectancies* can create *self-fulfilling prophecies* or *behavioral confirmation* through dyadic expectancy confirmation processes, mostly nonverbal. A target's merely knowing other people's negative expectancies can create *stereotype threat*. Perceiver motivations to understand another person, using socially shared understandings, can have positive or negative effects on interpersonal interactions. Some motivations, goals, and situations allow *control* over seemingly automatic processes of understanding.

Nevertheless, people do receive new information during their interactions with each other in several ways. For example, people understand each other's feelings through nonverbal behavior, via nonverbal leakage cues to *deception* and nonverbal *immediacy* cues to attraction (Chapter 3). As another example, prosocial behavior (Chapter 9) often results from an analysis of social cues, as people develop a sense of personally *felt responsibility* or *make responsibility attributions* to others. And as people develop *moral reasoning*, that also guides their tendencies to help or not. Through *social learning*, people understand new information about how and when to aggress, especially when they make *attributions of hostile intent* to others (Chapter 10).

## Groups

Socially shared understandings enable groups to function. Small groups can provide *informational influence*, and people are open to social influence attempts that manipulate their perceived *self-consistency and commitment* (Chapter 13). Leaders who hold power by virtue of being *expert* or socially *legitimate* evoke *internalized* influence. People operate on the basis of their shared understanding of group structures, such as *norms, roles*, and *subgroups* (Chapter 12). Decision making and productivity are more efficient, fair, and effective when group members agree on basic structure. The down-side is that groups tend to focus on *shared information* and may *polarize* based on exposure to norms and to *persuasive arguments*. Moreover, the *common knowledge effect*, whereby groups tend to focus on socially shared information, especially implicates *socially communicated stereotypes and prejudices* (Chapter 11). But *minority influence* can convert people by making them think harder about counternormative perspectives. Socially shared understanding is best captured by *self-categorization* and *social identity* processes. The leader represents the *group prototype,* and *pronorm deviance* is valued. At a societal level, *social representations* reflect the search for socially shared understanding, by making the new into something familiar.

## Understanding: Thinking Is for Doing

People develop socially shared understanding for pragmatic reasons. They need to understand each other—and to understand each other's understandings—in order to function. Coordination in social settings requires a good-enough understanding of socially defined reality. People want to know the social consensus because then they know how to behave, which in turn predicts their outcomes.

## CONTROLLING: FOCUS ON OUTCOMES

People are highly motivated to know the contingencies in their environment—how their actions will affect their outcomes. The intellectual origins of this motive lie in theories of *effectance*, or *control*, and learning theories' *reinforcements*. In economic models, these constitute *rewards and costs*. People try to maximize, or at least improve, their outcomes, in this tradition. Social psychologists know that the reality is more complex than the simple theory that people maximize self-interest.

## Within Individuals

People perceiving other people tend to overestimate people's control over their own outcomes, making overly dispositional attributions, partly to impute human agency (Chapter 3). *The fundamental attribution error, correspondence bias*, and the *actor-observer effect* all name this phenomenon of believing that people control their actions, underestimating the power of the situation. When people lack perceived control, their *control motivation* causes them to seek information and reassert control through attributions.

People also like to feel personally in control, starting with their own thoughts, which turn out to reflect more *automaticity* than they suspect (Chapter 4). People's processes are more automatic when they do not have the motivation or capacity to bother with control. Turning to actions, people resist limits on their own behavioral control, showing *reactance* (Chapter 6) and being socially influenced by *scarcity* (Chapter 13). In experimental settings, researchers have to disguise their hypotheses so that participants do not assert control by resisting or acceding to the situation's *demand characteristics* (Chapter 2).

If people do feel controlled by external factors, inside the laboratory or out, they show less *intrinsic motivation* because their effort is *overjustified by* the external reward (Chapter 3). Too high *a need for control* leads to overly rigid thinking and stereotyping (Chapter 11).

Control over one's outcomes underlies some interpretations of attitudes as resulting from *social learning* (Chapter 6). Even the *Yale communication and persuasion* approach—though oriented toward message-learning and thus a form of understanding—begins with incentives.

## Between Individuals

*Exchange* theories focus on people controlling the costs and benefits of interaction with others. Examples include *equity theory*, emphasizing the ratio of benefits to costs (Chapter 8). But socially understood norms differ in different kinds of relationships. In ongoing relationships, the most developed theory of socially shared outcomes is *interdependence theory*, which catalogs the varieties of ways that people in relationships depend on one another. Patterns of mutual outcome control explain the *development* of close relationships, *emotions* because of them, *commitment* within them, *and accommodation* to disruption.

Interdependence can have positive effects on the motivated *continuum of impression formation*, thereby undercutting people's tendencies toward bias (Chapters 4 and 11). When people need each other, they pay more detailed attention, in order to predict and possibly control their outcomes. People also control their *cost-reward* balance when deciding whether to help another person (Chapter 9). From a social learning perspective, people consider the explicitly *social rewards and costs* of helping, *modeling* helpful others and observing *vicarious reinforcement*. Rewards and costs of prosocial behavior include beneficial impact on one's *genetic kin. Moral values* and norms in a different way reflect a sense of reliable, structured control over prosocial behavior.

The negative side of control in interdependence shows up in relationship conflict and abuse that results from excessive desire to control: failure to *accommodate, attributions of negative intent*, and general *negative tracking* in a *conflict spiral* (Chapter 8). Outside ongoing relationships, aggression also results from *attributions of hostile intent* (Chapter 10). The *frustration-aggression* link results from people's reaction to losing control over their outcomes. *Bullying* of the weak by the strong similarly reflects control issues. *Environmental stressors* also increase aggression through lost *control*. All aggression is a form of *instrumental* control over one's outcomes, in these varied senses.

## Groups

In joining groups, just as in starting any relationship, people weigh the costs and benefits at each stage during *group socialization* (Chapter 12). *Interdependence* is a defining feature of group life. The group often works to enhance its *own productivity gains* and avoid *productivity losses*, which otherwise can result from *social loafing* and *diffusion of responsibility*. Control over individual and group resources underlies many *social dilemmas*, and two-party *negotiations* work to maximize joint outcomes. Those who control resources have *reward power* and *coercive power*. An incentive orientation is not the most effective form of leadership, eliciting only short-term *compliance*. *Social forces*, based on valued goals, can exert considerable social influence, including *obedience to authority*. In social hierarchies, *evolutionary psychology* posits that individuals, especially men, strive to dominate others, in order to enhance their reproductive outcomes.

Moving to the intergroup level (Chapter 11), note that perceived control over actual resources defined the *realistic group conflict theory*, but even more mileage has come from examining perceived intergroup threats to ingroup status *(social dominance theory)* and ingroup values *(right-wing authoritarianism)*. Both serve the function of status quo *system justification. Just world beliefs* serve the same function, asserting that people control and therefore are responsible for their own fate (Chapter 9). Attempts to control one's own outcomes as a member of a stigmatized group result in *attributional ambiguity* and *stereotype threat*.

## Controlling: Contingencies of Cost and Benefit

People doubtless do care about their outcomes, rewards, and costs from an economic or reinforcement theory perspective. What social psychology has added to this, however, is knowing that people are neither literal-minded nor narrowly self-interested nor completely rational. People value explicitly social outcomes, including the possibility of maximizing someone else's outcomes rather than merely their own because of interdependence. And they are not always so good at calculating or adhering to raw self-interest. Nevertheless, some powerful principles emerge from an incentive analysis: People act to control their outcomes.

## ENHANCING SELF: FOCUS ON DEFENSE AND IMPROVEMENT

People's own selves do hold a special place, even if people are not invariably oriented toward blatant self-interest. Though it takes varied forms, from inflated self-esteem to self-sympathy to self-improvement, the self's special place guides people's social responses. The common thread is the special status of the self, anticipated intellectually by Freudian psychoanalytic theories that do not, however, appear much in modern social psychology. Just about the sole holdover has been a simple emphasis on self-esteem. And from a social-adaptation perspective, a special role for the self suggests why people are motivated to get up in the morning, struggle to get along with others, and work at belonging, understanding, and controlling, as we have seen.

## Within Individuals

The only explicitly psychoanalytic theory surviving in social psychology is the *authoritarian personality* approach to prejudice (Chapter 11), based as it is in punitive childrearing practices, which result in people's theoretical motivation to defend the conscious self from unacceptable impulses. A simpler version, absent the Freudian perspective, is *right-wing authoritarianism*, also correlated with prejudice. The broader theme of self-enhancement appears in attributional biases: *defensive, self-serving*, and *self-centered*, especially attributed responsibility for success and failure (Chapter 3).

*Positive illusions* about the self underlie certain indicators of health and well-being in Western settings (Chapter 5). When threatened in one domain, people *self-affirm* in others. With threat from their own *mortality salience*, people especially endorse their comforting and enduring worldviews, including prosocial values and ingroup favoritism (Chapters 9, 11, and 12). Some attitudes serve explicitly *ego-defensive functions* or at least *value-expressive functions* (Chapter 6). *Self-discrepancy theory* describes the emotions that people feel when their actual selves fall short of their ideals (depression) or obligations (anxiety) (Chapter 5). People show poor *affective forecasting* because they ignore various self-protective mechanisms that help them maintain their equilibrium.

## Between Individuals

People protect themselves in the ways they form and maintain relationships. People are attracted to others who enhance them, liking *physically attractive* people, who reflect well on their own public worth. People also like those who like them *(direct reciprocity)*, as well as those they associate with *good moods* and *rewards*, such as *resources, status*, or *sex* (Chapter 7). Similarly, people help people likely to help them, in keeping with *kin selection* and *social learning* (Chapter 9). And they sometimes help in order to improve or protect their moods, according to a *negative state relief* perspective. People may represent the *self-in-relationship* as substantially overlapping their partner (Chapter 8). In ongoing relationships, *self evaluation maintenance* shows how people balance their own areas of competence against those of related others, to protect their self-esteem (Chapter 5). People also protect their self-esteem by presenting themselves in *socially desirable* ways, in psychology experiments as in life (Chapter 2). All this reflects self-enhancing processes.

Self-enhancing has a negative side, as well. *Inflated self-esteem* can underlie aggression, as wounded narcissists attempt to protect the seemingly injured self (Chapter 10). Perceived threats to self underlie what used to be called *affective (angry) aggression*, based on pervasive perceptions showing *attributions of hostile intent*. People from a *culture of honor* seem especially vulnerable to aggression in response to perceived insults.

## Groups

*Sociometer theory* maintains that people use their self-esteem as a measure of their standing in their group, so the belonging and self-enhancing motives show some interplay here (Chapters 11 and 12). People incorporate the *self-in-the-group* in an effort to maintain a positive view of self as a member of a positive group. This fits *social identity theory's* premise that people derive personal self-esteem from group identity. People balance individual and group identities to achieve *optimal distinctiveness* for a positive self-view. In *interdependent* and *collectivist cultures*, the role of the self in the group outflanks the *independent* or *individualist* self (Chapter 5).

Threats to group identity increase ingroup favoritism, consistent also with *self-categorization theory* (Chapter 12). People conceal their own prejudices from themselves, displaying *aversive prejudice, ambivalent prejudice*, and *subtle prejudice*, all of which escape their notice and enhance their view of themselves as unprejudiced.

## Enhancing Self: Varieties of Ways to Keep Going

Maintaining a sense of self as socially viable helps to keep people productive, healthy, and cooperative. Lacking any sense of self as worthy, or at least improvable, robs people of their motivation to function socially. Enhancing the self can be maladaptive, but on the whole and in moderation it seems to facilitate social life.

## TRUSTING: FOCUS ON POSITIVITY AND ATTACHMENT

Like all the other core social motives, trust shows variability across people, though everyone reveals at least some version of it. Trusting at least ingroup others and close others facilitates social life. As an intellectual tradition in social psychology, this motive's roots are less obvious, but *attachment theory* provides one grounding for it. People's special feelings for ingroup others (parallel to people's special feelings for self) appear in attachment throughout the life cycle and in a generalized default *positivity bias* in making sense of others.

## Within Individuals

The default positivity bias appears in the *Pollyanna effect* and the *person-positivity effect* (Chapter 4), which also show up in people's rating of other people in social psychological research (Chapter 2). People's baseline expectancies of other people and of their own social outcomes are generally positive. Against this rosy backdrop, negative information and outcomes stand out, by virtue of *salience, diagnosticity*, and *motivated vigilance*. Negativity carries more weight, and it triggers a *mobilization-minimization* process that protects people. When bad things do happen, people struggle to maintain *trust in a benevolent world*.

## Between Individuals

Relationships are impossible without trust (Chapter 8). From early *attachment* processes onward, secure relationships combine a reasonably positive *working model* of self and other, indicating both enhancing self and trusting the other. Although people differ in their *relationship orientation*, the secure pattern underlies most lasting relationships. In different kinds of relationships, trust may entail responding to each other's needs (*communal sharing*) or reciprocating like for like (*exchange*).

    *Sympathy* (apprehending another person's feelings) and *empathy* (actually feeling another person's feelings) both contribute to *altruistic motivation* and encourage helping (Chapter 9). In *experimental games*, trust encourages cooperation.

## Groups

Americans tend to trust people in general, whereas East Asians tend to trust mainly the ingroup, according to a cultural *theory of trust*. Within groups, *interdependence* and shared *social identity* both contribute to trust (Chapter 12). Superordinate goals encourage trust between groups, as the *contact hypotheses* would suggest (Chapter 11). Distinct groups can even come to view themselves as *one group*.

## Trusting: Keeping the World Benevolent

Not every reader will appreciate the role of trust in a benevolent (local) world, but the argument rests clearly on the adaptability of basic trust in close and ingroup others. People who are reasonably trusting fare better socially and emotionally than do people who are overly guarded. Groups work better when members trust each other. On the whole, trust is an underrated core social motive.

## CONCLUSION: THE SOCIAL PSYCHOLOGY ENTERPRISE

By one count, social psychology boasts several hundred theories (Fiske, 2002a), not to mention famous phenomena and fascinating findings that do not really count as formal theories. The enterprise is rich but may be overwhelming without an intellectual framework. In this book, I have focused on theories and major phenomena, tracing them to their deeper intellectual roots, sustaining the five core social motives that aim to capture the big picture in social psychology.

# References

Aarts, H., & Dijksterhuis, A. (2000). Habits as knowledge structures: Automaticity in goal-directed behavior. *Journal of Personality and Social Psychology, 78*, 53–63.

Aarts, H., & Dijksterhuis, A. (2003). The silence of the library: Environment, situational norm, and social behavior. *Journal of Personality and Social Psychology, 84*, 18–28.

Abbey, A. (1982). Sex differences in attributions for friendly behavior: Do males misperceive females' friendliness? *Journal of Personality and Social Psychology, 42*, 830–838.

Abele, A. E., & Wojciszke, B. (2007). Agency and communion from the perspective of self versus others. *Journal of Personality and Social Psychology, 93*, 751–763.

Abelson, R. P. (1986). Beliefs are like possessions. *Journal for the Theory of Social Behaviour, 16*, 222–250.

Abelson, R. P., Aronson, E., McGuire, W. J., Newcomb, T. M., Rosenberg, M. J., & Tannebaum, P. H. (Eds.) (1968). *Theories of cognitive consistency: A sourcebook*. Chicago: Rand McNally.

Abelson, R. P., Dasgupta, N., Park, J., & Banaji, M. R. (1998). Perceptions of the collective other. *Personality and Social Psychology Review, 2*, 243–250.

Abelson, R. P., Kinder, D. R., Peters, M. D., & Fiske, S. T. (1982). Affective and semantic components in political person perception. *Journal of Personality and Social Psychology, 42*, 619–630.

Aberson, C. L., Healy, M., & Romero, V. (2000). Ingroup bias and self-esteem: A meta-analysis. *Personality and Social Psychology Review, 4*, 157–173.

Abrams, D., Marques, J. M., Bown, N., & Henson, M. (2000). Pro-norm and anti-norm deviance within and between groups. *Journal of Personality and Social Psychology, 78*, 906–912.

Abrams, D., Wetherell, M. S., Cochrane, S., Hogg, M. A., & Turner, J. C. (1990). Knowing what to think by knowing who you are: Self-categorization and the nature of norm formation, conformity and group polarization. *British Journal of Social Psychology, 29*, 97–119.

Adams Jr., R. B., Ambady, N., Macrae, C. N., & Kleck, R. E. (2006). Emotional expressions forecast approach-avoidance behavior. *Motivation and Emotion, 30*, 179–188.

Adams Jr., R. B., & Kleck, R. E. (2005). Effects of direct and averted gaze on the perception of facially communicated emotion. *Emotion, 5*, 3–11.

Adolphs, R. (2009). The social brain: Neural bases of social knowledge. *Annual Review of Psychology, 60*.

Adorno, T. W., Frenkel-Brunswik, E., Levinson, D. J., & Sanford, R. N. (1950). *The authoritarian personality*. New York: Harper.

Agnew, C. R., Van Lange, P. A. M., Rusbult, C. E., & Langston, C. A. (1998). Cognitive interdependence: Commitment and the mental representation of close relationships. *Journal of Personality and Social Psychology, 74*, 939–954.

Aguinis, H., & Handelsman, M. M. (1997). Ethical issues in the use of the bogus pipeline. *Journal of Applied Social Psychology, 27*, 557–573.

Ainsworth, M., Blehar, M. C., Waters, E., & Wall, S. (1978). *Patterns of attachment: A psychological study of the strange situation*. Hillsdale, NJ: Erlbaum.

Ajzen, I. (1987). Attitudes, traits and actions: Dispositional prediction of behavior in personality and social psychology. In L. Berkowitz (Ed.), *Advances in experimental social psychology* (Vol. 20, pp. 1–63). New York: Academic Press.

Ajzen, I. (1991). The theory of planned behavior. *Organizational Behavior and Human Decision Processes, 50*, 179–211.

Ajzen, I. (2001). Nature and operation of attitudes. *Annual Review of Psychology, 52*, 27–58.

Ajzen, I., & Fishbein, M. (1973). Attitudinal and normative variables as predictors of specific behaviors. *Journal of Personality and Social Psychology, 27*, 41–57.

Ajzen, I., & Fishbein, M. (2005). The influence of attitudes on behavior. In D. Albarracín, B. T. Johnson, & M. P. Zanna (Eds.), *The handbook of attitudes* (pp. 173–221). Mahwah, NJ: Erlbaum.

Albarracín, D., & Kumkale, G. T. (2003). Affect as information in persuasion: A model of affect identification and discounting. *Journal of Personality and Social Psychology, 84*, 453–469.

Albarracín, D., & Vargas, P. (2010). Attitude formation and change: From biology to social responses to persuasive intent. In S. T. Fiske, D. T. Gilbert, & G. Lindzey (Eds.), *Handbook of social psychology* (5th ed., in press). New York: Wiley.

Albright, L., & Malloy, T. E. (1999). Self-observation of social behavior and metaperception. *Journal of Personality and Social Psychology, 77*, 724–726.

Albright, L., Malloy, T. E., Dong, Q., Kenny, D. A., Fang, X., Winquist, L., & Yu, D. (1997). Cross-cultural consensus in personality judgments. *Journal of Personality and Social Psychology, 72*, 558–569.

Aldag, R. J., & Fuller, S. R. (1993). Beyond fiasco: A reappraisal of the groupthink phenomenon and a new model of group decision processes. *Psychological Bulletin, 113*, 533–552.

Alexander, M. G., Brewer, M. B., & Hermann, R. K. (1999). Images and affect: A functional analysis of out-group stereotypes. *Journal of Personality and Social Psychology, 77*, 78–93.

Alexander, M. G., Brewer, M. B., & Livingston, R. W. (2005). Putting stereotype content in context: Image theory and interethnic stereotypes. *Personality and Social Psychology Bulletin, 31*, 781–794.

Algoe, S. B., Haidt, J., & Gable, S. L. (2008). Beyond reciprocity: Gratitude and relationships in everyday life. *Emotion, 8*, 425–429.

Allen, V. L. (1965). Situational factors in conformity. In L. Berkowitz (Ed.), *Advances in experimental social psychology* (Vol 2, pp. 133–175). New York: Academic Press.

Allison, K. W. (1998). Stress and oppressed social category membership. In J. K. Swim & C. Stangor (Eds.), *Prejudice: The target's perspective* (pp. 145–170). New York: Academic Press.

Allport, G. W. (1954a). The historical background of modern social psychology. In G. Lindzey (Ed.), *Handbook of social psychology* (Vol. 1, pp. 3–56). Reading, MA: Addison-Wesley.

Allport, G. W. (1954b). *The nature of prejudice*. Reading, MA: Addison-Wesley.

Allport, G. W., & Postman, L. (1946). An analysis of rumor. *Public Opinion Quarterly, 10*, 501–517.

Altemeyer, B. (1981). *Right-wing authoritarianism*. Winnipeg, Canada: University of Manitoba Press.

Altemeyer, B. (1988). *Enemies of freedom: Understanding right-wing authoritarianism*. San Francisco, CA: Jossey-Bass.

Alter, A. L., & Oppenheimer, D. M. (2006). Predicting short-term stock fluctuations by using processing fluency. *Proceedings of the National Academy of Sciences, 103*, 9369–9372.

Alter, A. L., Oppenheimer, D. M., Epley, N., & Eyre, R. N. (2007). Overcoming intuition: Metacognitive difficulty activates analytic reasoning. *Journal of Experimental Psychology: General, 136*, 569–576.

Alvaro, E. M., & Crano, W. D. (1996). Cognitive responses to minority or majority-based communications: Factors that underlie minority influence. *British Journal of Social Psychology, 35*, 105–121.

Alvaro, E. M., & Crano, W. D. (1997). Indirect minority influence: Evidence for leniency in source evaluation and counterargumentation. *Journal of Personality and Social Psychology, 72*, 949–964.

Ambady, N., Bernieri, F. J., & Richeson, J. A. (2000). Toward a histology of social behavior: Judgmental accuracy from thin slices of the behavioral stream. In M. P. Zanna (Ed.), *Advances in experimental social psychology* (Vol. 32, pp. 201–271). New York: Academic Press.

Ambady, N., Hallahan, M., & Rosenthal, R. (1995). On judging and being judged accurately in zero acquaintance situations. *Journal of Personality and Social Psychology, 69*, 518–529.

Ambady, N., Krabbenhoft, M. A., & Hogan, D. (2006). The 30-sec sale: Using thin-slice judgments to evaluate sales effectiveness. *Journal of Consumer Psychology, 16*, 4–13.

Ambady, N., & Rosenthal, R. (1992). Thin slices of expressive behavior as predictors of interpersonal consequences: A meta-analysis. *Psychological Bulletin, 111*, 256–274.

Ambady, N., Shih, M., Kim, A., & Pittinsky, T. L. (2001). Stereotype susceptibility in children: Effects of identity activation on quantitative performance. *Psychological Science, 12*, 385–390.

Ambady, N., & Weisbuch, M. (2010). Nonverbal behavior. In S. T. Fiske, D. T. Gilbert, & G. Lindzey (Eds.), *Handbook of social psychology* (5th ed.). New York: Wiley.

Amodio, D. M. (2008). Contributions of the social neuroscience approach to research on intergroup bias. *European Review of Social Psychology, 19*, 1–54.

Amodio, D. M., Devine, P. G., & Harmon-Jones, E. (2007). A dynamic model of guilt: Implications for motivation and self-regulation in the context of prejudice. *Psychological Science, 18*, 524–530.

Amodio, D. M., Devine, P. G., & Harmon-Jones, E. (2008). Individual differences in the regulation of intergroup bias: The role of conflict monitoring and neural signals for control. *Journal of Personality and Social Psychology, 94*, 60–74.

Amodio, D. M., & Frith, C. D. (2006). Meeting of minds: The medial frontal cortex and social cognition. *Nature Review Neuroscience, 7*, 268–277.

Amodio, D. M., Harmon-Jones, E., Devine, P. G., Curtin, J. J., Hartley, S. L., & Covert, A. E. (2004). Neural signals for the detection of unintentional race bias. *Psychological Science*, *15*, 88–93.

Amodio, D. M., Jost, J. T., Master, S. L., & Yee, C. M. (2007). Neurocognitive correlates of liberalism and conservatism. *Nature Neuroscience*, *10*, 1246–1247.

Amodio, D. M., Kubota, J. T., Harmon-Jones, E., & Devine, P. G. (2006). Alternative mechanisms for regulating racial responses according to internal vs. external cures. *Social Cognitive and Affective Neuroscience*, *1*, 26–36.

Andersen, S. M. (1984). Self-knowledge and social inference: II. The diagnosticity of cognitive/ affective and behavioral data. *Journal of Personality and Social Psychology*, *46*, 294–307.

Andersen, S. M., & Bem, S. L. (1981). Sex typing and androgyny in dyadic interaction: Individual differences in responsiveness to physical attractiveness. *Journal of Personality and Social Psychology*, *41*, 74–86.

Andersen, S. M., & Chen, S. (2002). The relational self: An interpersonal social-cognitive theory. *Psychological Review*, *109*, 619–645.

Andersen, S. M., & Ross, L. (1984). Self-knowledge and social inference: I. The impact of cognitive/ affective and behavioral data. *Journal of Personality and Social Psychology*, *46*, 280–293.

Anderson, C., & Berdahl, J. L. (2002). The experience of power: Examining the effects of power on approach and inhibition tendencies. *Journal of Personality and Social Psychology*, *83*, 1362–1377.

Anderson, C. A. (1989). Temperature and aggression: Ubiquitous effects of heat on occurrence of human violence. *Psychological Bulletin*, *106*, 74–96.

Anderson, C. A. (1997). Effects of violent movies and trait hostility on hostile feelings and aggressive thoughts. *Aggressive Behavior*, 23, 161–178.

Anderson, C. A., Anderson, K. B., & Deuser, W. E. (1996). Examining an affective aggression framework: Weapon and temperature effects on aggressive thoughts, affect, and attitudes. *Personality and Social Psychology Bulletin*, *22*, 366–376.

Anderson, C. A., Anderson K. B., Dorr, N., DeNeve, K. M., & Flanagan, M. (2000). Temperature and aggression. In M P. Zanna (Ed.), *Advances in experimental social psychology* (Vol. 32, pp. 63–133). San Diego, CA: Academic Press.

Anderson, C. A., Benjamin, A. J., & Bartholow, B. D. (1998). Does the gun pull the trigger? Automatic priming effects of weapon pictures and weapon names. *Psychological Science*, *9*, 308–314.

Anderson, C. A., & Bushman, B. J. (1997). External validity of "trivial" experiments: The case of laboratory aggression. *Review of General Psychology*, *1*, 19–41.

Anderson, C. A., & Bushman, B. J. (2001). Effects of violent video games on aggressive behavior, aggressive cognition, aggressive affect, physiological arousal, and prosocial behavior: A meta-analytic review of the scientific literature. *Psychological Science*, *12*, 353–359.

Anderson, C. A., & Bushman, B. J. (2002a). Human aggression. *Annual Review of Psychology*, *53*, 27–51.

Anderson, C. A., & Bushman, B. J. (2002b). The effects of media violence on society. *Science*, *295*, 2377–2379.

Anderson, C. A., Bushman, B. J., & Groom, R. W. (1997). Hot years and serious and deadly assault: Empirical tests of the heat hypothesis. *Journal of Personality and Social Psychology*, *73*, 1213–1223.

Anderson, C. A., Carnagey, N. L., Flanagan, M., Benjamin, A. J., Eubanks, J., & Valentine, J. C. (2004). Violent video games: Specific effects of violent content on aggressive thoughts and behavior. In M. P. Zauna (Ed.), *Advances in experimental social psychology*, (Vol. *36*, pp. 199–249). San Diego, CA: Academic Press.

Anderson, C. A., & Dill, K. E. (2000). Video games and aggressive thoughts, feelings, and behavior in the laboratory and in life. *Journal of Personality and Social Psychology*, *78*, 772–790.

Anderson, C. A., & Lindsay, J. J. (1998). The development, perseverance, and change of naive theories. *Social Cognition*, *16*, 8–30.

Anderson, C. A., & Galinsky, A. D. (2006). Power, optimism, and risk-taking. *European Journal of Social Psychology*, *36*, 511–536.

Anderson, K. B., Cooper, H., & Okamura, L. (1997). Individual differences and attitudes toward rape: A meta-analytic review. *Personality and Social Psychology Bulletin*, *23*, 295–315.

Anderson, N. H. (1974). Information integration: A brief survey. In D. H. Krantz, R. C. Atkinson, R. D. Luce, & P. Suppes (Eds.), *Contemporary developments in mathematical psychology* (pp. 236–305). San Francisco: Freeman.

Aquino, K., & Thau, S. (2009). Workplace victimization: Aggression from the target's perspective. *Annual Review of Psychology*, *60*, 717–741.

Archer, J. (1991). The influence of testosterone on human aggression. *British Journal of Psychology*, *82*, 1–28.

Archer, J. (1994). Testosterone and aggression. *Journal of Offender Rehabilitation*, *21*, 3–39.

Archer, J., Birring, S. S., & Wu, F. C. W. (1998). The association between testosterone and aggression in young men: Empirical findings and a meta-analysis. *Aggressive Behavior, 24*, 411–420.

Archer, J., Graham-Kevan, N., & Davies, M. (2005). Testosterone and aggression: A reanalysis of Book, Starzyk, and Quinsey's (2001) study. *Aggression and Violent Behavior, 10*, 241–261.

Are music and movies killing America's soul? (1995, June 12). *Time.*

Ariely, D., & Norton, M. I. (2009). Conceptual consumption. *Annual Review of Psychology, 60*, 475–499.

Armor, D. A., & Taylor, S. E. (1998). Situated optimism: Specific outcome expectancies and self-regulation. In M. P. Zanna (Ed.), *Advances in experimental social psychology* (Vol. 30, pp. 309–379). New York: Academic Press.

Aron, A., Aron, E. N., & Smollan, D. (1992). Inclusion of other in the self scale and the structure of interpersonal closeness. *Journal of Personality and Social Psychology, 63*, 596–612.

Aron, A., Aron, E. N., Tudor, M., & Nelson, G. (1991). Close relationships as including other in the self. *Journal of Personality and Social Psychology, 60*, 241–253.

Aron, A., Norman, C. C., Aron, E. N., McKenna, C., & Heyman, R. E. (2000). Couples' shared participation in novel and arousing activities and experiences relationship quality. *Journal of Personality and Social Psychology, 78*, 273–284.

Aron, A., Paris, M., & Aron, E. N. (1995). Falling in love: Prospective studies of self-concept change. *Journal of Personality and Social Psychology, 6*, 1102–1112.

Aron, A., & Westbay, L. (1996). Dimensions of the prototype of love. *Journal of Personality and Social Psychology, 70*, 535–551.

Aronson, E. (1968). Dissonance theory: Progress and problems. In R. P. Abelson, E. Aronson, W. J. McGuire, T. M. Newcomb, M. J. Rosenberg, & P. H. Tannebaum (Eds.), *Theories of cognitive consistency: A sourcebook* (pp. 5–27). Chicago: Rand McNally.

Aronson, E. (1990). Applying social psychology to desegregation and energy conservation. *Personality and Social Psychology Bulletin, 16*, 118–132.

Aronson, E. (1992). The return of the repressed: Dissonance theory makes a comeback. *Psychological Inquiry, 3*, 303–311.

Aronson, E., & Bridgeman, D. (1979). Jigsaw groups and the desegregated classroom: In pursuit of common goals. *Personality and Social Psychology Bulletin, 5*, 438–446.

Aronson, E., & Mills, J. (1959). The effect of severity of initiation on liking for a group. *Journal of Abnormal and Social Psychology, 59*, 177–181.

Aronson, E., & Osherow, N. (1980). Cooperation, prosocial behavior, and academic performance: Experiments in the desegregated classroom. *Applied Social Psychology Annual, 1*, 163–196.

Aronson, J., Fried, C. B., & Good, C. (2002). Reducing the effects of stereotype threat on African American college students by shaping theories of intelligence. *Journal of Experimental Social Psychology, 38*, 113–125.

Aronson, J., Lustina, M. J., Good, C., Keough, K., Steele, C. M., & Brown, J. (1999). When white men can't do math: Necessary and sufficient factors in stereotype threat. *Journal of Experimental Social Psychology, 35*, 29–46.

Arriaga, X. B., & Rusbult, C. E. (1998). Standing in my partner's shoes: Partner perspective taking and reactions to accommodative dilemmas. *Personality and Social Psychology Bulletin, 24*, 927–948.

Arrow, H. (1997). Stability, bistability, and instability in small group influence patterns. *Journal of Personality and Social Psychology, 72*, 75–85.

Asch, S. E. (1940). Studies in the principles of judgments and attitudes: II. Determination of judgments by group and by ego standards. *Journal of Social Psychology, 12*, 433–465.

Asch, S. E. (1946). Forming impressions of personality. *Journal of Abnormal and Social Psychology, 41*, 1230–1240.

Asch, S. E. (1948). The doctrine of suggestion, prestige and imitation in social psychology. *Psychological Review, 55*, 250–276.

Asch, S. E. (1952). *Social psychology.* Oxford, UK: Prentice-Hall.

Asch, S. E. (1955). Opinions and social pressure. *Scientific American, 193*, 31–35.

Asch, S. E. (1956). Studies of independence and conformity: A minority of one against a unanimous majority. *Psychological Monographs: General and Applied, 70*, 1–70.

Asch, S. E., & Zukier, H. (1984). Thinking about persons. *Journal of Personality and Social Psychology, 46*, 1230–1240.

Ashburn-Nardo, L., Voils, C. I., & Monteith, M. J. (2001). Implicit associations as the seeds of intergroup bias: How easily do they take root? *Journal of Personality and Social Psychology, 81*, 789–799.

Associated Press. (1992, Summer). Killing the golden goose: Hollywood's death wish. *Beverly Hills Bar Journal.*

Augoustinos, M. (2001). Social categorization: Towards theoretical integration. In K. Deaux & G. Philogène (Eds.), *Representations of the social:*

*Bridging theoretical traditions* (pp. 201–216). Malden, MA: Blackwell.

Augoustinos, M., Walker, I., & Donaghue, N. (2006). *Social cognition: An integrated introduction* (2nd ed.). Thousand Oaks, CA: Sage.

Axelrod, R., & Hamilton, W. D. (1981). The evolution of cooperation. *Science, 211*, 1390–1396.

Ayduk, O., Mendoza-Denton, R., Mischel, W., Downey, G., Peake, P. K., & Rodriguez, M. (2000). Regulating the interpersonal self: Strategic self-regulation for coping with rejection sensitivity. *Journal of Personality and Social Psychology, 79*, 776–792.

Back, M. D., Schmukle, S. C., & Egloff, B. (2008). Becoming friends by chance. *Psychological Science, 19*, 439–440.

Balcetis, E., & Dunning, D. (2006). See what you want to see: Motivational influences on visual perception. *Journal of Personality and Social Psychology, 91*, 612–625.

Balcetis, E., & Dunning, D. (2007). Cognitive dissonance and the perception of natural environments, *Psychological Science, 18*, 917–921.

Baldwin, M. W. (1992). Relational schemas and the processing of social information. *Psychological Bulletin, 112*, 461–484.

Baldwin, M. W., & Sinclair, L. (1996). Self-esteem and "if ... then" contingencies of interpersonal acceptance. *Journal of Personality and Social Psychology, 71*, 1130–1141.

Bales, R. F. (1950). A set of categories for the analysis of small group interaction. *American Sociological Review, 15*, 257–263.

Bales, R. F. (1970). *Personality and interpersonal behavior*. New York: Holt, Rinehart and Winston.

Bales, R. F. (1999). *Social interaction systems: Theory and measurement*. New Brunswick, NJ: Transaction.

Bales, R. F., & Strodtbeck, F L. (1951). Phases in group problem-solving. *Journal of Abnormal and Social Psychology, 46*, 485–495.

Banaji, M. R., & Prentice, D. A. (1994). The self in social contexts. *Annual Review of Psychology, 45*, 297–332.

Bandura, A. (1965). Influence of models' reinforcement contingencies on the acquisition of imitative responses. *Journal of Personality and Social Psychology, 1*, 589–595.

Bandura, A. (1973). *Aggression: A social learning analysis*. New York: Prentice-Hall.

Bandura, A. (1999). Moral disengagement in the perpetration of inhumanities. *Personality and Social Psychology Review, 3*, 193–209.

Bandura, A., Barbaranelli, C., Caprara, G. V., & Pastorelli, C. (1996). Mechanisms of moral disengagement in the exercise of moral agency.

*Journal of Personality and Social Psychology, 71*, 364–374.

Bandura, A., Ross, D., & Ross, S. A. (1963a). Imitation of film-mediated aggressive models. *Journal of Abnormal and Social Psychology, 66*, 3–11.

Bandura, A., Ross, D., & Ross, S. A. (1963b). Vicarious reinforcement and imitative learning. *Journal of Abnormal and Social Psychology, 67*, 601–607.

Bandura, A., Underwood, B., & Fromson, M. E. (1975). Disinhibition of aggression through diffusion of responsibility and dehumanization of victims. *Journal of Research in Personality, 9*, 253–269.

Banks, R. R., & Eberhardt, J. L. (1998). Social psychological processes and the legal bases of racial categorization. In J. L. Eberhardt & S. T. Fiske (Eds.), *Racism: The problem and the response* (pp. 54–75). Thousand Oaks, CA: Sage.

Bargh, J. A. (1984). Automatic and conscious processing of social information. In R. S. Wyer Jr., & T. K. Srull (Eds.), *Handbook of social cognition* (Vol. 3, pp. 1–44). Hillsdale, NJ: Erlbaum.

Bargh, J. A. (1996). Automaticity in social psychology. In E. T. Higgins & A. W. Kruglanski (Eds.), *Social psychology: Handbook of basic principles* (pp. 169–183). New York: Guilford.

Bargh, J. A. (1997). The automaticity of everyday life. In R. S. Wyer Jr. (Ed.), *The automaticity of everyday life: Advances in social cognition* (Vol. 10, pp. 1–61). Mahwah, NJ: Erlbaum.

Bargh, J. A., & Chartrand, T. L. (1999). The unbearable automaticity of being. *American Psychologist, 54*, 462–479.

Bargh, J. A., Chen, M., & Burrows, L. (1996). Automaticity of social behavior: Direct effects of trait construct and stereotype activation on action. *Journal of Personality and Social Psychology, 71*, 230–244.

Bargh, J. A., & McKenna, K. Y. A. (2004). The Internet and social life. *Annual Review of Psychology, 55*, 573–590.

Bargh, J. A., Raymond P., Pryor, J. B., & Stack, F. (1995). Attractiveness of the underling: An automatic power → sex association and its consequences for sexual harassment and aggression. *Journal of Personality and Social Psychology, 68*, 768–781.

Bar-Haim, Y., Ziv, T., Lamy, D., & Hodes, R. M. (2006). Nature and nurture in own-race face processing. *Psychological Science, 17*, 159–163.

Barling, J., Dupré, K. E., & Kelloway, E. K. (2009). Predicting workplace aggression and violence. *Annual Review of Psychology, 60*, 671–692.

Barlund, D. C. (1962). Consistency of emergent leadership in groups with changing tasks and members. *Speech Monographs, 29*, 45–52.

Baron, A. S., & Banaji, M. R. (2006). The development of implicit attitudes: Evidence of race evaluations from ages 6 and 10 and adulthood. *Psychological Science, 17*, 53–58.

Baron, J. (1997). The illusion of morality as self-interest: A reason to cooperate in social dilemmas. *Psychological Science, 8*, 330–335.

Baron, R. A., & Richardson, D. R. (1994). *Human aggression*. New York: Plenum Press.

Baron, R. S., David, J. P., Brunsman, B. M., & Inman, M. L. (1997). Why listeners hear less than they are told: Attentional load and the teller-listener extremity effect. *Journal of Personality and Social Psychology, 72*, 826–838.

Baron, R. S., Vandello, J. A., & Brunsman, B. (1996). The forgotten variable in conformity research: Impact of task importance on social influence. *Journal of Personality and Social Psychology, 71*, 915–927.

Barreto, M., & Ellemers, N. (2002). The impact of respect versus neglect of self-identities on identification and group loyalty. *Personality and Social Psychology Bulletin, 28*, 629–639.

Barrett, L., & Henzi, P. (2005). The social nature of primate cognition. *Proceedings: Biological Sciences, 272*, 1865–1875.

Barrett, L. F., & Swim, J. K. (1998). Appraisals of prejudice and discrimination. In J. K. Swim & C. Stangor (Eds.), *Prejudice: The target's perspective* (pp. 11–36). New York: Academic Press.

Barsalou, L. W. (1987). The instability of graded structure: Implications for the nature of concepts. In U. Neisser (Ed.), *Concepts and conceptual development* (pp. 101–140). Cambridge: Cambridge University Press.

Barsalou, L. W. (2008). Grounded cognition. *Annual Review of Psychology, 59*, 617–645.

Bartholomew, K., & Horowitz, L. M. (1991). Attachment styles among young adults: A test of a four category model. *Journal of Personality and Social Psychology, 61*, 226–244.

Bartholow, B. D., Dickter, C. L., & Sestir, M. A. (2006). Stereotype activation and control of race bias: Cognitive control of inhibition and its impairment by alcohol. *Journal of Personality and Social Psychology, 90*, 272–287.

Bartlett, F A. (1932). *Remembering: A study in experimental and social psychology*. New York: Cambridge University Press.

Baskin, J. H., Edersheim, J. G., & Price, B. H. (2007). Is a picture worth a thousand words? Neuroimaging in the courtroom. *American Journal of Law and Medicine, 33*, 239–269.

Bass, B. M. (1954). The leaderless group discussion. *Psychological Bulletin, 51*, 465–492.

Batson, C. D. (1987). Prosocial motivation: Is it ever truly altruistic? In L. Berkowitz (Ed.), *Advances in experimental social psychology* (Vol. 20, pp. 65–122). New York: Academic Press.

Batson, C. D. (1990). Good Samaritans—or priests and Levites? Using William James as a guide in the study of religious prosocial motivation. *Personality and Social Psychology Bulletin, 16*, 758–768.

Batson, C. D. (1994). Why act for the public good? Four answers. *Personality and Social Psychology Bulletin, 20*, 603–610.

Batson, C. D. (1997a). Is empathy-induced helping due to self-other merging? *Journal of Personality and Social Psychology, 73*, 495–509.

Batson, C. D. (1997b). Self-other merging and the empathy-altruism hypothesis: Reply to Neuberg et al. *Journal of Personality and Social Psychology, 73*, 517–522.

Batson, C. D. (1998). Altruism and prosocial behavior. In D. T. Gilbert, S. T. Fiske, & G. Lindzey (Eds.), *Handbook of social psychology* (4th ed., Vol. 2, pp. 282–316). New York: McGraw-Hill.

Batson, C. D., Ahmad, N., Yin, J., Bedell, S. J., Johnson, J. W., Templin, C. M., & Whiteside, A. (1999). Two threats to the common good: Self-interested egoism and empathy and empathy–induced altruism. *Personality and Social Psychology Bulletin, 25*, 3–16.

Batson, C. D., Batson, J. G., Griffitt, C. A., Barrientos, S., Brandt, J. R., Sprengelmeyer, P., & Bayly, M. J. (1989). Negative-state relief and the empathy-altruism hypothesis. *Journal of Personality and Social Psychology, 56*, 922–933.

Batson, C. D., Batson, J. G., Slingsby, J. K., Harrell, K. K., Peekna, H. M., & Todd, R. M. (1991). Empathic joy and the empathy-altruism hypothesis. *Journal of Personality and Social Psychology, 61*, 413–426.

Batson, C. D., Batson, J. G., Todd, R. M., Brummett, B. H., Shaw, L. L., & Aldequer, C. M. R. (1995). Empathy and the collective good: Caring for one of the others in a social dilemma. *Journal of Personality and Social Psychology, 68*, 619–631.

Batson, C. D., Dyck, J. L., Brandt, J. R., Batson, J. G., Powell, A. K., McMaster, R., & Griffitt, C. (1988). Five studies testing two egoistic alternatives to the empathy-altruism hypothesis. *Journal of Personality and Social Psychology, 55*, 52–77.

Batson, C. D., Klein, T. R., Highberger, L., & Shaw L. L. (1995). Immorality from empathy-induced altruism: When compassion and justice conflict. *Journal of Personality and Social Psychology, 68*, 1042–1054.

Batson, C. D., Kobrynowicz, D., Dinnerstein, J. L., Kampf, H. C., & Wilson, A. D. (1997). In a very different voice: Unmasking moral hypocrisy. *Journal of Personality and Social Psychology, 72*, 1335–1348.

Batson, C. D., O'Quin, K., Fultz, J., Vanderplas, M., & Isen, A. M. (1983). Influence of self-reported distress and empathy on egoistic versus altruistic motivation to help. *Journal of Personality and Social Psychology, 45*, 706–718.

Batson, C. D., Sager, K., Garst, E., Kang, M., Rubchinsky, K., & Dawson, K. (1997). Is empathy-induced helping due to self-other merging? *Journal of Personality and Social Psychology, 73*, 495–509.

Batson, C. D., Thompson, E. R., & Chen, H. (2002). Moral hypocrisy: Addressing some alternatives. *Journal of Personality and Social Psychology, 83*, 330–339.

Batson, C. D., Thompson, E. R., Seuferling, G., Whitney, H., & Strongman, J. A. (1999). Moral hypocrisy: Appearing moral to oneself without being so. *Journal of Personality and Social Psychology, 77*, 525–537.

Batson, C. D., & Weeks, J. K. (1996). Mood effects of unsuccessful helping: Another test of the empathyaltruism hypothesis. *Personality and Social Psychology Bulletin, 22*, 148–157.

Baum, A., & Valins, S. (1979). Architectural mediation of residential density and control: Crowding and the regulation of social contact. In L. Berkowitz (Ed.), *Advances in experimental social psychology* (Vol. 12, pp. 131–175). New York: Academic Press.

Baumeister, R. F. (1982). A self-presentational view of social phenomena. *Psychological Bulletin, 91*, 3–26.

Baumeister, R. F. (1991a). *Escaping the self*. New York: Basic Books.

Baumeister, R. F. (1991b). *Meanings of life*. New York: Guilford Press.

Baumeister, R. F. (1995). Self. In A. S. R. Manstead & M. Hewstone (Eds.), *Blackwell encyclopedia of social psychology*. (pp. 496–501). Cambridge: Blackwell.

Baumeister, R. F. (1997). *Evil: Inside human cruelty and violence*. New York: W. H. Freeman.

Baumeister, R. F. (1998). The self. In D. T. Gilbert, S. T. Fiske, & G. Lindzey (Eds.), *Handbook of social psychology* (4th ed., Vol. 1, pp. 680–740). New York: McGraw-Hill.

Baumeister, R. F., & Bratslavsky, E. (1999). Passion, intimacy and time: Passionate love as a function of change in intimacy. *Personality and Social Psychology Review, 3*, 49–67.

Baumeister, R. F., Bratslavsky, E., Muraven, M., & Tice, D. M. (1998). Ego depletion: Is the active

self a limited resource? *Journal of Personality and Social Psychology, 74*, 1252–1265.

Baumeister, R. F., & Leary, M. R. (1995). The need to belong: Desire for interpersonal attachments as a fundamental human motivation. *Psychological Bulletin, 117*, 497–529.

Baumeister, R. F., Smart, L., & Boden, J. M. (1996). Relation of threatened egotism to violence and aggression: The dark side of high self-esteem. *Psychological Review, 103*, 5–33.

Baumeister, R. F., & Sommer, K. L. (1997). What do men want? Gender differences and two spheres of belongingness. *Psychological Bulletin, 22*, 38–44.

Baumeister, R. F., & Tice, D. M. (1990). Anxiety and social exclusion. *Journal of Social and Clinical Psychology, 9*, 165–195.

Bayliss, A. P., & Tipper, S. P. (2006). Predictive gaze cues and personality judgments: Should eye trust you? *Psychological Science, 17*, 514–520.

Bazerman, M. H., Curhan, J. R., & Moore, D. A. (2001). The death and rebirth of the social psychology of negotiation. In G. J. O. Fletcher & M. S. Clark (Eds.), *Blackwell handbook of social psychology: Interpersonal processes* (pp. 196–228). Malden, MA: Blackwell.

Bazerman, M. H., Mannix, E., & Thompson, L. (1988). Groups as mixed-motive negotiations. In E. J. Lawler & B. Markovsky (Eds.), *Advances in group processes: A research annual* (Vol. 5, pp. 195–216). Greenwich, CT: JAI Press.

Beal, D. J., O'Neal, E. C., Ong, J., & Ruscher, J. B. (2000). The ways and means of interracial aggression: Modern racists' use of covert retaliation. *Personality and Social Psychology Bulletin, 26*, 1225–1238.

Beaman, A. L., Cole, C. M., Preston, M., Kleutz, B., & Steblay, N. M. (1983). Fifteen years of foot-in-the-door research: A meta-analysis. *Personality and Social Psychology Bulletin, 9*, 181–196.

Begany, J. J., & Milburn, M. A. (2002). Psychological predictors of sexual harassment: Authoritarianism, hostile sexism, and rape myths. *Psychology of Men and Masculinity, 3*, 119–126.

Bem, D. J. (1967). Self-perception: An alternative interpretation of cognitive dissonance phenomena. *Psychological Review, 74*, 183–200.

Bem, D. J. (1972). Self-perception theory. In L. Berkowitz (Ed.), *Advances in experimental social psychology* (Vol. 6, pp. 1–62). New York: Academic Press.

Bem, D. J. (1996). Exotic becomes erotic: A developmental theory of sexual orientation. *Psychological Review, 103*, 320–335.

Bem, D. J. (1998). Is EBE theory supported by the evidence? Is it androcentric? A reply to Peplau et al. (1998). *Psychological Review, 105*, 395–398.

Bem, D. J. (2000). Exotic becomes erotic: Interpreting the biological correlates of sexual orientation. *Archives of Sexual Behavior*, *29*, 531–548.

Bennett, S., Farrington, D. P., & Huesmann, L. R. (2005). Explaining gender differences in crime and violence: The importance of social cognitive skills. *Aggression and Violent Behavior*, *10*, 263–288.

Berger, J., Webster, M. Jr., Ridgeway, C. L., & Rosenholtz, S. J. (1986). Status cues, expectations, and behavior. In E. J. Lawler (Ed.), *Advances in group processes* (Vol. 3, pp. 1–22). Greenwich, CT: JAI Press.

Berger, S. M., & Lambert, W. W. (1968). Stimulus response theory in contemporary social psychology. In G. Lindzey & E. Aronson (Eds.), *The handbook of social psychology* (2nd ed., Vol. 1, pp. 81–178). Reading, MA: Addison-Wesley.

Bergsieker, H., Leslie, L. M., Fiske, S. T., & Constantine, V. S. (2008). *Stereotyping by omission: Accentuate the positive, eliminate the negative*. Unpublished manuscript, Princeton University.

Berkman, L. F. (1995). The role of social relations in health promotion. *Psychosomatic Medicine*, *57*, 245–254.

Berkman, L. F., Glass, T., Brissette, I., & Seeman, T. E. (2000). From social integration to health: Durkheim in the new millennium. *Social Science and Medicine*, *51*, 843–857.

Berkman, L. F., & Syme, S. L. (1979). Social networks, host resistance, and mortality. *American Journal of Epidemiology*, *109*, 186–204.

Berkowitz, L. (1962). *Aggression: A social psychological analysis*. New York: McGraw-Hill.

Berkowitz, L. (1989). Frustration-aggression hypothesis: Examination and reformulation. *Psychological Bulletin*, *106*, 59–73.

Berkowitz, L. (1990). On the formation and regulation of anger and aggression. *American Psychologist*, *45*, 494–503.

Berkowitz, L. (1993). *Aggression: Its causes, consequences and control*. New York: McGraw-Hill.

Berkowitz, L. (1994). Guns and youth. In L. D. Eron, J. H. Gentry, & P. Schlegel (Eds.), *Reason to hope: A psychosocial perspective on violence and youth*. Washington, DC: American Psychological Association.

Berkowitz, L. (1999). Evil is more than banal: Situationism and the concept of evil. *Personality and Social Psychology Bulletin*, *3*, 246–253.

Berkowitz, L, & LePage, A. (1967). Weapons as aggression-eliciting stimuli. *Journal of Personality and Social Psychology*, *7*, 202–207.

Bernhard, H., Fischbacher, U., & Fehr, E. (2006). Parochial altruism in humans. *Nature*, *442*, 912–915.

Bernieri, F. J., Reznick, J. S., & Rosenthal, R. (1988). Synchrony, pseudosynchrony, and dissynchrony: Measuring the entrainment process in mother–infant interactions. *Journal of Personality and Social Psychology*, *54*, 243–253.

Bernieri, F. J., & Rosenthal, R. (1991). Interpersonal coordination: Behavior matching and interactional synchrony. In R. S. Feldman, & B. Rimé (Eds.), *Fundamentals of nonverbal behavior* (pp. 401–432). New York: Cambridge University Press.

Bernstein, S., Richardson, D., & Hammock, G. (1987). Convergent and discriminant validity of the Taylor and Buss measures of physical aggression. *Aggressive Behavior*, *13*, 15–24.

Berry, D. S. (2000). Attractiveness, attraction, and sexual selection: Evolutionary perspectives on the form and function of physical attractiveness. In M. P. Zanna (Ed.), *Advances in experimental social psychology* (Vol. 32, pp. 273–342). New York: Academic Press.

Berry, J. W. (2001). A psychology of immigration. *Journal of Social Issues*, *57*, 615–631.

Berscheid, E. (1983). Emotion. In H. H. Kelley, E. Berscheid, A. Christensen, J. H. Harvey, T. L. Huston, G. Levinger, E. McClintock, L. A. Peplau, & D. R. Peterson (Eds.), *Close relationships* (pp. 110–168). New York: W. H. Freeman.

Berscheid, E. (1985). Interpersonal attraction. In G. Lindzey & E. Aronson (Eds.), *Handbook of social psychology* (3rd ed., Vol. 2, pp. 413–484). New York: Random House.

Berscheid, E. (1994). Interpersonal relationships. *Annual Review of Psychology*, *45*, 79–129.

Berscheid, E., Dion, K. K., Walster, E. M., & Walster, G. W. (1971). Physical attractiveness and dating choice: A test of the matching hypothesis. *Journal of Experimental Social Psychology*, *7*, 173–189.

Berscheid, E., & Reis, H. T. (1998). Attraction and close relationships. In D. T. Gilbert, S. T. Fiske, & G. Lindzey (Eds.), *Handbook of social psychology* (4th ed., Vol. 2, pp. 193–281). New York: McGraw-Hill.

Berscheid, E., Snyder, M., & Omoto, A. M. (1989). The relationship closeness inventory: Assessing the closeness of interpersonal relationships. *Journal of Personality and Social Psychology*, *57*, 792–807.

Bersoff, D. M. (1999). Why good people sometimes do bad things: Motivated reasoning and unethical behavior. *Personality and Social Psychology Bulletin*, *25*, 28–39.

Bettencourt, B. A., Charlton, K., Dorr, N., & Hume, D. L. (2001). Status differences and in-group bias: A meta-analytic examination of the effects of status stability, status legitimacy, and group permeability. *Psychological Bulletin*, *127*, 520–542.

Bettencourt, B. A., & Miller, N. (1996). Gender differences in aggression as a function of provocation: A meta-analysis. *Psychological Bulletin*, *119*, 422–447.

Bettencourt, B. A., & Sheldon, K. (2001). Social roles as mechanism for psychological need satisfaction within social groups. *Journal of Personality and Social Psychology*, *81*, 1131–1143.

Bickman, L., & Rosenbaum, D. P. (1977). Crime reporting as a function of bystander encouragement, surveillance, and credibility. *Journal of Personality and Social Psychology*, *35*, 577–586.

Bierce, A. (1911). *The devil's dictionary*. Cleveland, OH: World Publishing.

Biernat, M., & Eidelman, S. (2007). Standards. In A. W. Kruglanski & E. T. Higgins (Eds.), *Social psychology: Handbook of basic principles* (2nd ed., pp. 308–333). New York: Guilford

Biernat, M., & Manis, M. (1994). Shifting standards and stereotype-based judgment. *Journal of Personality and Social Psychology*, *66*, 5–20.

Biernat, M., Manis, M., & Nelson, T. E. (1991). Stereotypes and standards of judgment. *Journal of Personality and Social Psychology*, *60*, 485–499.

Biernat, M., & Vescio, T. K. (2002). She swings, she hits, she's great, she's benched: Implications of gender-based shifting standards for judgment and behavior. *Personality and Social Psychology Bulletin*, *28*, 66–77.

Biernat, M., & Wortman, C. B. (1991). Sharing of home responsibilities between professionally employed women and their husbands. *Journal of Personality and Social Psychology*, *60*, 844–860.

Biesanz, J. C., Neuberg, S. L., Judice, T. N., & Smith, D. M. (1999). When interviewers desire accurate impressions: The effects of notetaking on the influence of expectations. *Journal of Applied Social Psychology*, *29*, 2529–2549.

Biesanz, J. C., Neuberg, S. L., Smith, D. M., Asher, T., & Judice, T. N. (2001). When accuracy-motivated perceivers fail: Limited attentional resources and the reemerging self-fulfilling prophecy. *Personality and Social Psychology Bulletin*, *27*, 621–629.

Blair, I. V., & Banaji, M. R. (1996). Automatic and controlled processes in stereotype priming. *Journal of Personality and Social Psychology*, *70*, 1142–1163.

Blair, I. V., Judd, C. M., & Chapleau, K. M. (2004). The influence of Afrocentric facial features in criminal sentencing. *Psychological Science*, *15*, 674–679.

Blair, I. V., Judd, C. M., & Fallman, J. L. (2004). The automaticity of race and Afrocentric facial

features in social judgments. *Journal of Personality and Social Psychology*, *87*, 763–778.

Blair, I. V., Judd, C. M., Sadler, M. S., & Jenkins, C. (2002). The role of Afrocentric features in person perception: Judging by features and categories. *Journal of Personality and Social Psychology*, *83*, 5–25.

Blair, I. V., Ma, J. E., & Lenton, A. P. (2001). Imagining stereotypes away: The moderation of implicit stereotypes through mental imagery. *Journal of Personality and Social Psychology*, *81*, 828–841.

Blake, R. R., & Mouton, J. S. (1961). Reactions to intergroup competition under win-lose conditions. *Management Science*, *7*, 420–435.

Blake, R. R., & Mouton, J. S. (1962). The intergroup dynamics of win-loss conflict and problem-solving collaboration in union-management relations. In M. Sherif (Ed.), *International relations and leadership* (pp. 94–141). New York: Wiley.

Blaney, P. H. (1986). Affect and memory: A review. *Psychological Bulletin*, *99*, 229–246.

Blanton, H., Buunk, B. P., Gibbons, F. X., & Kuyper, H. (1999). When better-than-others compare upward: Choice of comparison and comparative evaluation as independent predictors of academic performance. *Journal of Personality and Social Psychology*, *76*, 420–430.

Blanton, H., & Stapel, D. A. (2008). Unconscious and spontaneous and . . . Complex: The three selves model of social comparison assimilation and contrast. *Journal of Personality and Social Psychology*, *94*, 1018–1032.

Blascovich, J., & Mendes, W. B. (2010). Social psychophysiology and embodiment. In S. T. Fiske, D. T. Gilbert, & G. Lindzey (Eds.), *Handbook of social psychology* (5th ed., in press). New York: Wiley.

Blascovich, J., Mendes, W. B., Hunter, S. B., Lickel, B., & Kowai-Bell, N. (2001). Perceiver threat in social interactions with stigmatized others. *Journal of Personality and Social Psychology*, *80*, 253–267.

Blascovich, J., Spencer, S. J., Quinn, D., & Steele, C. M. (2001). African Americans and high blood pressure: The role of stereotype threat. *Psychological Science*, *12*, 225–229.

Blass, T. (1991). Understanding behavior in the Milgram obedience experiment: The role of personality, situations, and their interactions. *Journal of Personality and Social Psychology*, *60*, 398–413.

Blass, T. (1995). Right-wing authoritarianism and role as predictors of attributions about obedience to authority. *Personality and Individual Differences*, *19*, 99–100.

Blass, T. (1996a). Attribution of responsibility and trust in the Milgram obedience experiment. *Journal of Applied Social Psychology, 26*, 1529–1535.

Blass, T. (1996b). The Milgram obedience experiment: Support for a cognitive view of defensive attribution. *Journal of Social Psychology, 136*, 407–410.

Blass, T. (1999). The Milgram paradigm after 35 years: Some things we now know about obedience to authority. *Journal of Applied Social Psychology, 29*, 955–978.

Blass, T., & Schmitt, C. (2001). The nature of perceived authority in the Milgram paradigm: Two replications. *Current Psychology, 20*, 115–121.

Blieszner, R., & Adams, R. G. (1992). *Adult friendship*. Newbury Park, CA: Sage.

Bobo, L. D. (1983). Whites' opposition to busing: Symbolic racism or realistic group conflict? *Journal of Personality and Social Psychology, 45*, 1196–1210.

Bobo, L. D. (2001). Racial attitudes and relations at the close of the twentieth century. In N. J. Smelser, W. J. Wilson, & F. Mitchell (Eds.), *American becoming: Racial trends and their consequences*. (pp. 264–301). Washington, DC: National Academy Press.

Boccato, G., Cortes, B. P., Demoulin, S., & Leyens, J.-Ph. (2007). The automaticity of infra-humanization. *European Journal of Social Psychology, 37*, 987–999.

Bodenhausen, G. V., Gabriel, S., & Lineberger, M. (2000). Sadness and susceptibility to judgmental bias: The case of anchoring. *Psychological Science, 11*, 320–323.

Bodenhausen, G. V., Kramer, G. P., & Suesser, K. (1994). Happiness and stereotypic thinking in social judgment. *Journal of Personality and Social Psychology, 66*, 621–632.

Bodenhausen, G. V., & Lichtenstein, M. (1987). Social stereotypes and information processing strategies: The impact of task complexity. *Journal of Personality and Social Psychology, 52*, 871–880.

Bodenhausen, G. V., Sheppard, L. A., & Kramer, G. P. (1994). Negative affect and social judgment: The differential impact of anger and sadness. *European Journal of Social Psychology, 24*, 45–62.

Bodenhausen, G. V., & Wyer, R. S, Jr. (1985). Effects of stereotypes on decision making and information processing strategies. *Journal of Personality and Social Psychology, 48*, 267–282.

Bond, M. H., & Smith, P. B. (1996). Cross-cultural social and organizational psychology. *Annual Review of Psychology, 47*, 205–235.

Bond, R., & Smith, P. B. (1996). Culture and conformity: A meta-analysis of studies using Asch's (1952b, 1956) line judgment task. *Psychological Bulletin, 119*, 111–137.

Bono, J. E., & Ilies, R. (2006). Charisma, positive emotions and mood contagion. *Leadership Quarterly, 17*, 317–334.

Boon, S. D. (1995). Trust. In A. S. R. Manstead & M. Hewstone (Eds.), *Blackwell encyclopedia of social psychology* (pp. 656–657). Oxford: Blackwell.

Boring, E. G. (1950). *A history of experimental psychology* (2nd ed.). Englewood Cliffs, NJ: Prentice-Hall.

Bornstein, R. F. (1989). Exposure and affect: Overview and meta-analysis of research, 1968–1987. *Psychological Bulletin, 106*, 265–289.

Bornstein, R. F. (1994). Dependency as a social cue: A meta-analytic review of research on the dependency-helping relationship. *Journal of Research in Personality, 28*, 182–213.

Bornstein, R. F., Leone, D. R., & Galley, D. J. (1987). The generalizability of subliminal mere exposure effects: Influence of stimuli perceived without awareness on social behavior. *Journal of Personality and Social Psychology, 53*, 1070–1079.

Botvinick, M. M., Cohen, J. D., & Carter, C. S. (2004). Conflict monitoring and anterior cingulate cortex: An update. *Trends in Cognitive Sciences, 8*, 539–546.

Bovet, D., Vauclair, J., & Blaye, A. (2005). Categorization and abstraction abilities in 3-year-old children: A comparison with monkey data. *Animal Cognition, 8*, 53–59.

Bowen, E. S. (1954). *Return to laughter*. London: Gollancz.

Bowlby, J. (1969). *Attachment and loss*, Vol. 1, *Attachment*. New York: Basic Books.

Bowlby, J. (1973). *Attachment and loss*, Vol. 2, *Separation: Anxiety and anger*. New York: Basic Books.

Bowlby, J. (1980). *Attachment and loss*, Vol. 3, *Loss*. New York: Basic Books.

Bowlby, J. (1982). Attachment and loss: Retrospect and prospect. *American Journal of Orthopsychiatry, 52*, 664–678.

Bowling, N. A., & Beehr, T. A. (2006). Workplace harassment from the victim's perspective: A theoretical model and meta-analysis. *Journal of Applied Psychology, 91*, 998–1012.

Bradbury, T. N., & Fincham, F. D. (1990). Attributions in marriage: Review and critique. *Psychological Bulletin, 107*, 3–33.

Bragg, R. (1996, November 12). She opened world to others: Her world has opened, too. *New York Times*, pp. A1, A22.

Branscombe, N. R., Schmitt, M. T., & Harvey, R. D. (1999). Perceiving pervasive discrimination among African Americans: Implications for group identification and well-being. *Journal of Personality and Social Psychology, 77*, 135–149.

Branscombe, N. R., Spears, R., Ellemers, N., & Doosje, B. (2002). Intragroup and intergroup evaluation effects on group behavior. *Personality and Social Psychology Bulletin, 28*, 744–753.

Branscombe, N. R., & Wann, D. L. (1994). Collective self-esteem consequences of outgroup derogation when a valued social identity is on trial. *European Journal of Social Psychology, 24*, 641–657.

Branscombe, N. R., Wann, D. L., Noel, J. G., & Coleman, J. (1993). In-group or outgroup extremity: Importance of the threatened social identity. *Personality and Social Psychology Bulletin, 19*, 381–388.

Bransford, J. D., & Johnson, M. K. (1972). Contextual prerequisites for understanding: Some investigations of comprehension and recall, *Journal of Verbal Learning and Verbal Behavior, 11*, 717–726.

Brauer, M., Judd, C. M., & Gliner, M. D. (1995). The effects of repeated expressions on attitude polarization during group discussions. *Journal of Personality and Social Psychology, 68*, 1014–1029.

Brauer, M., Judd, C. M., & Jacquelin, V. (2001). The communication of social stereotypes: The effects of group discussion and information distribution on stereotypic appraisals. *Journal of Personality and Social Psychology, 81*, 463–475.

Brauer, M., Wasel, W., & Niedenthal, P. (2000). Implicit and explicit components of prejudice. *Review of General Psychology, 4*, 79–101.

Breckler, S. J., & Wiggins, E. C. (1989). Scales for the measurement of attitudes toward blood donation. *Transfusion, 29*, 401–404.

Brehm, J. W. (1956). Postdecision changes in the desirability of alternatives. *Journal of Abnormal and Social Psychology, 52*, 384–389.

Brehm, J. W. (1966). *A theory of psychological reactance*. Oxford, England: Academic Press.

Brehm, J. W., & Cole, A. H. (1966). Effect of a favor which reduces freedom. *Journal of Personality and Social Psychology, 3*, 420–426.

Brehm, J. W., & Sensenig, J. (1966). Social influence as a function of attempted and implied usurpation of choice. *Journal of Personality and Social Psychology, 4*, 703–707.

Brehm, S. S. (1992). *Intimate relationships*. New York: McGraw-Hill.

Brennan, K. A., Clark, C. L., & Shaver, P. R. (1998). Self-report measurement of adult attachment: An integrative view. In J. Simpson & W. S. Rholes (Eds.), *Attachment theory and close relationships* (pp. 46–76). New York: Guilford.

Bressler, E. R., Martin, R. A., & Balshine, S. (2006). Production and appreciation of humor as sexually selected traits. *Evolution and Human Behavior, 27*, 121–130.

Brewer, M. B. (1979). Ingroup bias in the minimal intergroup situation: A cognitive-motivational analysis. *Psychological Bulletin, 86*, 307–324.

Brewer, M. B. (1991). The social self: On being the same and different at the same time. *Personality and Social Psychology Bulletin, 17*, 475–482.

Brewer, M. B. (1999). The psychology of prejudice: Ingroup love or outgroup hate? *Journal of Social Issues, 55*, 429–444.

Brewer, M. B. (2000). Reducing prejudice through cross-categorization: Effects of multiple social identities. In S. Oskamp (Ed.), *Reducing prejudice and discrimination*. Mahwah, NJ: Erlbaum.

Brewer, M. B. (2007a). The importance of being we: Human nature and intergroup relations. *American Psychologist, 62*, 728–738.

Brewer, M. B. (2007b). The social psychology of intergroup relations: Social categorization, ingroup bias, and outgroup prejudice. In A. W. Kruglanski & E. T. Higgins (Eds.), *Social psychology: Handbook of basic principles* (2nd ed., pp. 695–715). New York: Guilford Press.

Brewer, M. B., & Brown, R. J. (1998). Intergroup relations. In D. T. Gilbert, S. T. Fiske, & G. Lindzey (Eds.), *Handbook of social psychology* (4th ed., Vol. 2, pp. 554–594). New York: McGraw Hill.

Brewer, M. B., & Chen, Y. (2007). Where (who) are collectives in collectivism? Toward conceptual clarification of individualism and collectivism. *Psychological Review, 114*, 133–151.

Brewer, M. B., & Gardner, W. L. (1996). Who is this "we"? Levels of collective identity and self representation. *Journal of Personality and Social Psychology, 71*, 83–93.

Brewer, M. B., & Harasty Feinstein, A. S. (1999). Dual processes in the cognitive representation of persons and social categories. In S. Chaiken & Y. Trope (Eds.), *Dual-process theories in social psychology* (pp. 255–270). New York: Guilford.

Brickman, P. (1977). Preference for inequality. *Social Psychology Quarterly, 40*, 303–310.

Brickman, P. (1980). A social psychology of human concerns. In R. Gilmour & S. Duck (Eds.), *The development of social psychology* (pp. 5–28). New York: Academic Press.

Brickman, P., Rabinowitz, V. C., Karuza, J. Jr., Coates, D., Cohn, E., & Kidder, L. (1982). Models of helping and coping. *American Psychologist, 37*, 368–384.

Brief, A. P., & Weiss, H. M. (2002). Organizational behavior: Affect in the workplace. *Annual Review of Psychology, 53*, 279–307.

Briñol, P., & Petty, R. E. (2003). Overt head movements and persuasion: A self-validation analysis. *Journal of Personality and Social Psychology, 84*, 1123–1139.

Brinthaupt, T. M., Moreland, R. L., & Levine, J. M. (1991). Sources of optimism among prospective group members. *Personality and Social Psychology Bulletin, 17*, 36–43.

Britt, T. W., Boniecki, K. A., Vescio, T. K., Biernat, M., & Brown, L. M. (1996). Intergroup anxiety: A person x situation approach. *Personality and Social Psychology Bulletin, 22*, 1177–1188.

Brock, T. C., & Brannon, L. A. (1992). Liberalization of commodity theory. *Basic and Applied Social Psychology, 13*, 135–144.

Brockner, J., & Chen, Y. R. (1996). The moderating roles of self-esteem and self-construal in reaction to a threat to the self: Evidence from the People's Republic of China and the United States. *Journal of Personality and Social Psychology, 71*, 603–615.

Brockner, J., & Swap, W. C. (1976). Effects of repeated exposure and attitudinal similarity on self-disclosure and interpersonal attraction. *Journal of Personality and Social Psychology, 33*, 531–540.

Brontë, C. (1847). *Jane Eyre*. New York: Penguin.

Brown, J. D. (1998). *The self*. New York: McGraw-Hill.

Brown, R. (1965). *Social psychology*. New York: Free Press.

Brown, R. J. (1995). *Prejudice: Its social psychology*. Oxford, UK: Blackwell.

Brown, R. J. (2000). Social identity theory: Past achievements, current problems and future challenges. *European Journal of Social Psychology, 30*, 745–778.

Brown, R. J., Maras, P., Massar, B., Vivian, J., & Hewstone, M. (2001). Life on the ocean wave: Testing some intergroup hypotheses in a naturalistic setting. *Group Processes and Intergroup Relations, 4*, 81–97.

Brown, R. J., & Smith, A. (1989). Perceptions of and by minority groups: The case of women in academia. *European Journal of Social Psychology, 19*, 61–75.

Brown, R. J., Vivian, J., & Hewstone, M. (1999). Changing attitudes through intergroup contact: The effects of group membership salience. *European Journal of Social Psychology, 29*, 741–764.

Brown, S. L., Nesse, R. M., Vinokur, A. D., & Smith, D. M. (2003). Providing social support may be more beneficial than receiving it: Results from a prospective study of mortality. *Psychological Science, 14*, 320–327.

Bruner, J. S. (1957a). Going beyond the information given. In H. Gruber, K. R. Hammond, & R. Jessor (Eds.), *Contemporary approaches to cognition*. Cambridge, MA: Harvard University Press.

Bruner, J. S. (1957b). On perceptual readiness. *Psychological Review, 64*, 123–152.

Brunswik, E. (1952). The conceptual framework of psychology. In *International Encyclopedia of Unified Science* (Vol. 1, No. 10). Chicago: University of Chicago Press.

Bryan, J. H., & Test, M. A. (1967). Models and helping: Naturalistic studies in aiding behavior. *Journal of Personality and Social Psychology, 6*, 400–407.

Buchanan, D. A. (2008). You stab my back, I'll stab yours: Management experience and perceptions of organization political behaviour. *British Journal of Management, 19*, 49–64.

Buck, R., & Ginsburg, B. (1991). Spontaneous communication as altruism. In M. S. Clark (Ed.), *Review of personality and social psychology: Prosocial behavior* (Vol. 12, pp. 149–175). Newbury Park, CA: Sage.

Buehler, R., & Griffin, D. W. (1994). Change-of-meaning effects in conformity and dissent: Observing construal processes over time. *Journal of Personality and Social Psychology, 67*, 984–996.

Bulcroft, K., & O'Connor, M. (1986). The importance of dating relationships on quality of life for older persons. *Family Relations, 35*, 397–401.

Burdein, I., Lodge, M., & Taber, C. (2006). Experiments on the automaticity of political beliefs and attitudes. *Political Psychology, 27*, 359–371.

Burger, J. M. (1981). Motivational biases in the attribution of responsibility for an accident: A meta-analysis of the defensive-attribution hypothesis. *Psychological Bulletin, 90*, 496–512.

Burger, J. M. (1999). The foot-in-the door compliance procedure: A multiple process analysis and review. *Personality and Social Psychology Review, 3*, 303–325.

Burns, J. M. (1978). *Leadership*. New York: Harper & Row.

Burnstein, E., Crandall, C. S., & Kitayama, S. (1994). Some neo-Darwinian decision rules for altruism: Weighing cues for inclusive fitness as a function of the biological importance of the decision. *Journal of Personality and Social Psychology, 67*, 773–789.

Burnstein, E., & Sentis, K. P. (1981). Attitude polarization in groups. In R. E. Petty, T. M. Ostrom, & T. C. Brock (Eds.), *Cognitive responses in persuasion* (pp. 197–216). Mahwah, NJ: Erlbaum.

Bushman, B. J. (1995). Moderating role of trait aggressiveness in the effects of violent media on aggression. *Journal of Personality and Social Psychology, 69*, 950–960.

Bushman, B. J. (1996). Individual differences in the extent and development of aggressive cognitive-associative networks. *Personality and Social Psychology Bulletin, 22*, 811–819.

Bushman, B. J. (1997). Effects of alcohol on human aggression: Validity of proposed explanations. In D. Fuller, R. Dietrich, & E. Gottheil (Eds.), *Recent developments in alcoholism: Alcohol and violence* (Vol. 13, pp. 227–243). New York: Plenum.

Bushman, B. J. (1998a). Effects of television violence on memory for commercial messages. *Journal of Experimental Psychology: Applied, 4*, 291–307.

Bushman, B. J. (1998b). Priming effects of media violence on the accessibility of aggressive constructs in memory. *Personality and Social Psychology Bulletin, 24*, 537–545.

Bushman, B. J. (2002). Does venting anger feed or extinguish the flame? Catharsis, rumination, distraction, anger, and aggressive responding. *Personality and Social Psychology Bulletin, 28*, 724–731.

Bushman, B. J. (2005). Violence and sex in television programs do not sell products in advertisements. *Psychological Science, 16*, 702–708.

Bushman, B. J. (2007). That was a great commercial, but what were they selling? Effects of violence and sex on memory for products in television commercials. *Journal of Applied Social Psychology, 37*, 1784–1796.

Bushman, B. J., & Anderson, C. A. (2001a). Is it time to pull the plug on the hostile versus instrumental aggression dichotomy? *Psychological Review, 108*, 273–279.

Bushman, B. J., & Anderson, C. A. (2001b). Media violence and the American public. *American Psychologist, 56*, 477–489.

Bushman, B. J., & Anderson, C. A. (2002). Violent video games and hostile expectations: A test of the general aggression model. *Personality and Social Psychology Bulletin, 28*, 1679–1686.

Bushman, B. J., & Baumeister, R. F. (1998). Threatened egotism: Narcissism, self-esteem, and direct and displaced aggression: Does self-love or self-hate lead to violence? *Journal of Personality and Social Psychology, 75*, 219–229.

Bushman, B. J., Baumeister, R. F., & Phillips, C. M. (2001). Do people aggress to improve their mood? Catharsis beliefs, affect regulation opportunity, and aggressive responding. *Journal of Personality and Social Psychology, 81*, 17–32.

Bushman, B. J., Baumeister, R. F., & Stack, A. D. (1999). Catharsis, aggression, and persuasive influence: Self-fulfilling or self-defeating prophecies? *Journal of Personality and Social Psychology, 76*, 367–376.

Bushman, B. J., & Bonacci, A. M. (2002). Violence and sex impair memory for television ads. *Journal of Applied Psychology, 87*, 557–564.

Bushman, B. J., Bonacci, A. M., Pedersen, W. C., Vasquez, E. A., & Miller, N. (2005). Chewing on it can chew you up: Effects of rumination on triggered displaced aggression. *Journal of Personality and Social Psychology, 88*, 969–983.

Bushman, B. J., & Cooper, H. M. (1990). Effects of alcohol on human aggression: An integrative research review. *Psychological Bulletin, 107*, 341–354.

Bushman, B. J., & Phillips, C. M. (2001). If the television program bleeds, memory for the advertisement recedes. *Current Directions in Psychological Science, 10*, 44–47.

Bushman, B. J., Ridge, R. D., Das, E., Key, C. W., & Busath, G. L. (2007). When God sanctions killing: Effect of scriptural violence on aggression. *Psychological Science, 18*, 204–207.

Bushman, B. J., & Stack, A. D. (1996). Forbidden fruit versus tainted fruit: Effects of warning labels on attraction to television violence. *Journal of Experimental Psychology: Applied, 2*, 207–226.

Buss, A. H. (1961). *The psychology of aggression*. New York: Wiley.

Buss, D. M. (1989). Sex differences in human mate preferences: Evolutionary hypothesis tested in 37 cultures. *Behavioral and Brain Sciences, 12*, 1–49.

Buss, D. M. (Ed.) (2005). *The handbook of evolutionary psychology*. Hoboken, NJ: Wiley.

Buss, D. M., & Barnes, M. (1986). Preferences in human mate selection. *Journal of Personality and Social Psychology, 50*, 559–570.

Buss, D. M., & Duntley, J. D. (2008). Adaptations for exploitation. *Group Dynamics: Theory, Research, and Practice, 12*, 53–62.

Buss, D. M., & Kenrick, D. T. (1998). Evolutionary social psychology. In D. T. Gilbert, S. T. Fiske, & G. Lindzey (Eds.), *Handbook of social psychology* (4th ed., Vol. 2, pp. 982–1026). New York: McGraw-Hill.

Buss, D. M., & Schmitt, D. P. (1993). Sexual strategies theory: An evolutionary perspective on human mating. *Psychological Review, 100*, 204–232.

Buss, D. M., & Shackelford, T. K. (1997). From vigilance to violence: Mate retention tactics in married couples. *Journal of Personality and Social Psychology, 72*, 346–361.

Buunk, B. P., Collins, R. L., Taylor, S. E., VanYperen, N. W., & Dakof, G. A. (1990). The affective consequences of social comparison: Either direction has its ups and downs. *Journal of Personality and Social Psychology, 59*, 1238–1249.

Byrne, D. (1971). *The attraction paradigm*. New York: Academic Press.

Byron, K., & Peterson, S. (2002). The impact of a large scale traumatic event on individual and organizational outcomes: Exploring employee and company reactions to September 11, 2001. *Journal of Organizational Behavior, 23*, 895–910.

Cacioppo, J. T., & Berntson, G. G. (1994). Relationship between attitudes and evaluative space: A critical review, with emphasis on the separability of positive and negative substrates. *Psychological Bulletin, 115*, 401–423.

Cacioppo, J. T., & Berntson, G. G. (1999). The affect system: Architecture and operating characteristics. *Current Directions in Psychological Science, 8*, 133–137.

Cacioppo, J. T., Berntson, G. G., & Crites, S. L., Jr. (1996). Social neuroscience: Principles of physiological arousal and response. In E. T. Higgins & A. W. Kruglanski (Eds.), *Social psychology: Handbook of basic principles* (pp. 72–101). New York: Guilford.

Cacioppo, J. T., Crites S. L., Jr., Gardner, W. L., & Berntson, G. G. (1994). Bioelectrical echoes from evaluative categorizations: A late positive brain potential that varies as a function of trait negativity and extremity. *Journal of Personality and Social Psychology, 67*, 115–125.

Cacioppo, J. T., Marshall-Goodell, B. S., Tassinary, L. G., & Petty, R. E. (1992). Rudimentary determinants of attitudes: Classical conditioning is more effective when prior knowledge about the attitude stimulus is low than high. *Journal of Experimental Social Psychology, 28*, 207–233.

Cacioppo, J. T., Petty, R. E., Feinstein, J. A., & Jarvis, W. B. G. (1996). Dispositional differences in cognitive motivation: The life and times of individuals varying in need for cognition. *Psychological Bulletin, 119*, 197–253.

Cacioppo, J. T., Petty, R. E., Kao, C. F., & Rodriguez, R. (1986). Central and peripheral routes to persuasion: An individual difference perspective. *Journal of Personality and Social Psychology, 51*, 1032–1043.

Camacho, L. M., & Paulus, P. B. (1995). The role of social anxiousness in group brainstorming. *Journal of Personality and Social Psychology, 68*, 1071–1080.

Cameron, L. D., Brown, P. M., & Chapman, J. G. (1998). Social value orientations and decisions to take proenvironmental action. *Journal of Applied Social Psychology, 28*, 675–697.

Campbell, D. T. (1958). Common fate, similarity, and other indices of the status of aggregates of persons as social entities. *Behavioral Science, 3*, 14–25.

Campbell, D. T. (1965). Ethnocentric and other altruistic motives. In D. Levine (Ed.), *Nebraska Symposium on Motivation* (pp. 283–311). Lincoln: University of Nebraska Press.

Campbell, D. T. (1969). Reforms as experiments. *American Psychologist, 24*, 409–429.

Cantor, J. R., Zillmann, D., & Einsiedel, E. F. (1978). Female responses to provocation after exposure to aggressive and erotic films. *Communication Research, 5*, 395–412.

Cantor, N., & Mischel, W. (1977). Traits as prototypes: Effects on recognition memory. *Journal of Personality and Social Psychology, 35*, 38–48.

Cantor, N., & Mischel, W. (1979). Prototypes in person perception. In L. Berkowitz (Ed.), *Advances in experimental social psychology* (Vol. 12, pp. 3–52). New York: Academic Press.

Cantor, N., Mischel, W., & Schwartz, J. (1982). Social knowledge: Structure, content, use, and abuse. In A. H. Hastorf & A. M. Isen (Eds.), *Cognitive social psychology* (pp. 33–68). New York: Elsevier.

Caporael, L. R. (1989). Mechanisms matter: The difference between sociobiology and evolutionary psychology. *Behavioral and Brain Sciences, 100*, 204–232.

Caporael, L. R. (1997). The evolution of truly social cognition: The core configurations model. *Review of Personality and Social Psychology, 1*, 276–298.

Caporael, L. R. (2001). Evolutionary psychology: Toward a unifying theory and a hybrid science. *Annual Review of Psychology, 52*, 607–628.

Caporael, L. R., & Dawes, R. M. (1991). Altruism: Docility or group identification? *Science, 252*, 192.

Caporael, L. R., Dawes, R. M., Orbell, J. M., & van de Kragt, A. (1989). Selfishness examined: Cooperation in the absence of egoistic incentives. *Behavioral and Brain Sciences, 12*, 683–739.

Caprara, G. V., Barbaranelli, C., Pastorelli, C., Bandura, A., & Zimbardo, P. G. (2000). Prosocial foundations of children's academic achievement. *Psychological Science, 11*, 302–306.

Caprara, G. V., Vecchione, M., Barbaranelli, C., & Fraley, R. C. (2007). When likeness goes with liking: The case of political preference. *Political Psychology, 28*, 609–632.

Carlo, G., Eisenberg, N., Troyer, D., Switzer, G., & Speer A. K. (1991). The altruistic personality: In what contexts is it apparent? *Journal of Personality and Social Psychology*, *61*, 450–458.

Carlsmith, K. M., Darley, J. M., & Robinson, P. H. (2002). Why do we punish? Deterrence and just deserts as motives for punishment. *Journal of Personality and Social Psychology*, *83*, 284–299.

Carlson, M., Charlin, V., & Miller, N. (1988). Positive mood and helping behavior: A test of six hypothesis. *Journal of Personality and Social Psychology*, *55*, 211–229.

Carlson, M., Marcus-Newhall, A., & Miller, N. (1989). Evidence for a general construct of aggression. *Personality and Social Psychology Bulletin*, *15*, 377–389.

Carlson, M., Marcus-Newhall, A., & Miller, N. (1990). Effects of situational aggression cues: A quantitative review. *Journal of Personality and Social Psychology*, *58*, 622–633.

Carlson, M., & Miller, N. (1987). Explanation of the relation between negative mood and helping. *Psychological Bulletin*, *102*, 91–108.

Carlson, M., & Miller, N. (1988). Bad experiences and aggression. *Sociology and Social Research*, *72*, 155–157.

Carnagey, N. L., Anderson, C. A., & Bartholow, B. D. (2007). Media violence and social neuroscience: New questions and new opportunities. *Current Directions in Psychological Science*, *16*, 178–182.

Carnagey, N. L., Anderson, C. A., & Bushman, B. J. (2007). The effect of video game violence on physiological desensitization to real-life violence. *Journal of Experimental Social Psychology*, *43*, 489–496.

Carnegie, D. (1936). *How to win friends and influence people*. New York: Simon & Schuster.

Carnevale, P. J., & Leung, K. (2001). Cultural dimensions of negotiation. In M. A. Hogg & R. S. Tindale (Eds.), *Blackwell handbook of social psychology: Group processes* (pp. 482–496). Malden, MA: Blackwell.

Carroll, J. M., & Russell, J. A. (1996). Do facial expressions signal specific emotions?: Judging emotion from the face in context. *Journal of Personality and Social Psychology*, *70*, 205–218.

Carson, K. D., Carson, P. P., Roe, C. W., Birkenmeir, B. J., & Phillips, J. S. (1999). Four commitment profiles and their relationships to empowerment, service recovery, and work attitudes. *Public Personnel Management*, *28*, 1–13.

Carson, P. P., Carson, K. D., & Roe, C. W. (1993). Social power bases: A meta-analytic examination of interrelationships and outcomes. *Journal of Applied Social Psychology*, *23*, 1150–1169.

Castano, E., Yzerbyt, V., Paladino, M. P., & Sacchi, S. (2002). I belong, therefore, I exist: Ingroup identification, ingroup entitativity, and ingroup

bias. *Personality and Social Psychology Bulletin*, *28*, 135–143.

Catalano, R., Novaco, R., & McConnell, W. (1997). A model of the net effect of job loss on violence. *Journal of Personality and Social Psychology*, *72*, 1440–1447.

Centerbar, D. B., & Clore, G. L. (2006). Do approach-avoidance actions create attitudes? *Psychological Science*, *17*, 22–29.

Cervone, D. (2005). Personality architecture: Within-person structures and processes. *Annual Review of Psychology*, *56*, 423–452.

Cesario, J., & Higgins, E. T. (2008). Making message recipients "feel right": How nonverbal cues can increase persuasion. *Psychological Science*, *19*, 415–420.

Cesario, J., Plaks, J. E., & Higgins, E. T. (2006). Automatic social behavior as motivated preparation to interact. *Journal of Personality and Social Psychology*, *90*, 893–910.

Chaiken, S. (1980). Heuristic versus systematic information processing and the use of source versus message cues in persuasion. *Journal of Personality and Social Psychology*, *39*, 752–766.

Chaiken, S., & Trope, Y. (Eds.). (1999). *Dual-process theories in social psychology*. New York: Guilford.

Chaiken, S., Wood, W., & Eagly, A. H. (1996). Principles of persuasion. In E. T. Higgins & A. W. Kruglanski (Eds.), *Social psychology: Handbook of basic principles* (pp. 702–742). New York: Guilford.

Chaiken, S., & Yates, S. (1985). Affective-cognitive consistency and thought-induced attitude polarization. *Journal of Personality and Social Psychology*, *49*, 1470–1481.

Chartrand, T. L., & Bargh, J. A. (1999). The chameleon effect: The perception-behavior link and social interaction. *Journal of Personality and Social Psychology*, *76*, 893–910.

Chartrand, T. L., Fitzsimons, G. M., & Fitzsimons, G. J. (2008). Automatic effects of anthropo-morphized objects on behavior. *Social Cognition*, *26*, 198–209.

Chemers, M. M. (2000). Leadership research and theory: A functional integration. *Group Dynamics*, *4*, 27–43.

Chemers, M. M. (2001). Leadership effectiveness: An integrative review. In M. A. Hogg & S. Tindale (Eds.), *Blackwell handbook of social psychology: Group processes* (pp. 376–399). Malden, MA: Blackwell.

Chen, M., & Bargh, J. A. (1997). Nonconscious behavioral confirmation processes. The self-fulfilling consequences of automatic stereotype activation. *Journal of Experimental Social Psychology*, *33*, 541–560.

Chen, M., & Bargh, J. A. (1999). Consequences of automatic evaluation: Immediate behavioral predispositions to approach or avoid the stimulus. *Personality and Social Psychology Bulletin, 25*, 215–224.

Chen, N. Y., Shaffer, D. R., & Wu, C. (1997). On physical attractiveness stereotyping in Taiwan: A revised sociocultural perspective. *Journal of Social Psychology, 137*, 117–124.

Chen, S., Boucher, H. C., & Tapias, M. P. (2006). The relational self revealed: Integrative conceptualization and implications for interpersonal life. *Psychological Bulletin, 132*, 151–179.

Chen, S., & Chaiken, S. (1999). The heuristic-systematic model in its broader context. In S. Chaiken & Y. Trope (Eds.), *Dual-process theories in social psychology* (pp. 73–96). New York: Guilford.

Chen, S., Chen, K. Y., & Shaw, L. (2004). Self-verification motives at the collective level of self-definition. *Journal of Personality and Social Psychology, 86*, 77–94.

Chen, S., Lee-Chai, A. Y., & Bargh, J. A. (2001). Relationship orientation as a moderator of the effects of social power. *Journal of Personality and Social Psychology, 80*, 173–187.

Chen, S., Shechter, D., & Chaiken, S. (1996). Getting at the truth or getting along: Accuracy– versus impression-motivated heuristic and systematic processing. *Journal of Personality and Social Psychology, 71*, 262–275.

Chen, Z., Fiske, S. T., & Lee, T. L. (2009). Ambivalent sexism and power-related gender-role ideology in marriage. *Sex Roles, 60*, 765–778.

Cheng, C., Bond, M. H., & Chan, S. C. (1995). The perception of ideal best friends by Chinese adolescents. *International Journal of Psychology, 30*, 91–108.

Cheng, C. M., & Chartrand, T. L. (2003). Self-monitoring without awareness: Using mimicry as a nonconscious affiliation strategy. *Journal of Personality and Social Psychology, 85*, 1170–1179.

Cheung, P. C., Ma, H. K., & Shek, D. T. K. (1998). Conceptions of success: Their correlates with prosocial orientation and behavior in Chinese adolescents. *Journal of Adolescence, 21*, 31–42.

Chiu, C., Hong, Y., & Dweck, C. S. (1997). Lay dispositionism and implicit theories of personality. *Journal of Personality and Social Psychology, 73*, 19–30.

Chiu, C., Morris, M. W., Hong, Y., & Menon, T. (2000). Motivated cultural cognition: The impact of implicit cultural theories on dispositional attribution varies as a function of need for closure. *Journal of Personality and Social Psychology, 78*, 247–259.

Choi, I., Nisbett, R. E., & Norenzayan, A. (1999). Causal attribution across cultures: Variation and universality. *Psychological Bulletin, 125*, 47–63.

Christensen, A., & Heavey, C. L. (1993). Gender differences in marital conflict: The demand/withdraw interaction pattern. In S. Oskamp & M. Costanzo (Eds.), *Gender issues in contemporary society* (pp. 113–141). Newbury Park, CA: Sage.

Cialdini, R. B. (1987). Compliance principles of compliance professionals: Psychologists of necessity. In M. P. Zanna, J. M. Olson, & C. P. Herman (Eds.), *Social influence: The Ontario symposium* (Vol. 5, pp. 165–184). Mahwah, NJ: Erlbaum.

Cialdini, R. B. (1993). *Influence: Science and practice* (3rd ed.). New York: Harper Collins.

Cialdini, R. B., Baumann, D. J., & Kenrick, D. T. (1981). Insights from sadness: A three-step model of the development of altruism as hedonism. *Developmental Review, 3*, 207–223.

Cialdini, R. B., Brown, S. L., Lewis, B. P., Luce, C., & Neuberg, S. L. (1997). Reinterpreting the empathy-altruism relationship. When one into one equals oneness. *Journal of Personality and Social Psychology, 73*, 481–494.

Cialdini, R. B., Darby, B. L., & Vincent, J. E. (1973). Transgression and altruism: A case for hedonism. *Journal of Experimental Social Psychology, 9*, 502–516.

Cialdini, R. B., & Fultz, J. (1990). Interpreting the negative mood-helping literature via "mega"-analysis: A contrary view. *Psychological Bulletin, 107*, 481–494.

Cialdini, R. B., & Goldstein, N. J. (2004). Social influence: Compliance and conformity. *Annual Review of Psychology, 55*, 591–621.

Cialdini, R. B., Kallgren, C. A., & Reno, R. R. (1991). A focus theory of normative conduct: A theoretical refinement and reevaluation of the role of norms in human behavior. In M. P. Zanna (Ed.), *Advances in experimental social psychology* (Vol. 24, pp. 201–234). New York: Academic Press.

Cialdini, R. B., & Trost, M. R. (1998). Social influence: Social norms, conformity, and compliance. In D. T. Gilbert, S. T. Fiske, & G. Lindzey (Eds.), *Handbook of social psychology* (4th ed., Vol. 2, pp. 151–192). New York: McGraw-Hill.

Cialdini, R. B., Trost, M. R., & Newsom, J. T. (1995). Preference for consistency: The development of a valid measure and the discovery of surprising behavioral implications. *Journal of Personality and Social Psychology, 69*, 318–328.

Cialdini, R. B., Wosinska, W., Barrett, D. W., Butner, J., & Gornick-Durose, M. (1999). Compliance with a request in two cultures: The differential influence of social proof and commitment/consistency on collectivists and individualists. *Personality and Social Psychology Bulletin*, *25*, 1242–1253.

Cini, M. A., Moreland, R. L., & Levine, J. M. (1993). Group staffing levels and responses to prospective and new group members. *Journal of Personality and Social Psychology*, *65*, 723–734.

Clark, M. (1984). Record keeping in two types of relationships. *Journal of Personality and Social Psychology*, *47*, 549–557.

Clark, M. S., & Finkel, E. J. (2005). Willingness to express emotion: The impact of relationship type, communal orientation, and their interaction. *Personal Relationships*, *12*, 169–180.

Clark, M. S., & Grote, N. K. (1998). Why aren't indices of relationship costs always negatively related to indices of relationship quality? *Personality and Social Psychology Review*, *2*, 2–17.

Clark, M. S., & Mills, J. (1979). Interpersonal attraction in exchange and communal relationships. *Journal of Personality and Social Psychology*, *37*, 12–24.

Clark, M. S., & Mills, J. (1993). The difference between communal and exchange relationships: What it is and is not. *Personality and Social Psychology Bulletin*, *19*, 684–691.

Clark, M. S., Mills, J., & Powell, M. C. (1986). Keeping track of needs in communal and exchange relationships. *Journal of Personality and Social Psychology*, *51*, 333–338.

Clark, M. S., & Waddell, B. A. (1983). Effects of moods on thoughts about helping, attraction and information acquisition. *Social Psychology Quarterly*, *46*, 31–35.

Clark, R., Anderson, N. B., Clark, V. R., & Williams, D. R. (1999). Racism as a stressor for African Americans: A biopsychosocial model. *American Psychologist*, *54*, 805–816.

Clark, R., & Maass, A. (1988a). Social categorization in minority influence: The case of homosexuality. *European Journal of Social Psychology*, *18*, 347–364.

Clark, R., & Maass, A. (1988b). The role of social categorization and perceived source credibility in minority influence. *European Journal of Social Psychology*, *18*, 381–394.

Cloutier, J., Heatherton, T. F., Whalen, P. J., & Kelley, W. M. (2008). Are attractive people rewarding? Sex differences in the neural substrates of facial attractiveness. *Journal of Cognitive Neuroscience*, *20*, 941–951.

Cohen, D. (1996). Law, social policy, and violence: The impact of regional cultures. *Journal of Personality and Social Psychology*, *70*, 961–978.

Cohen, D. (1998). Culture, social organization, and patterns of violence. *Journal of Personality and Social Psychology*, *75*, 408–419.

Cohen, D. (2001). Cultural variation: Considerations and impressions. *Psychological Bulletin*, *127*, 451–471.

Cohen, D., & Nisbett, R. E. (1997). Field experiments examining the culture of honor: The role of institutions in perpetuating norms about violence. *Personality and Social Psychology Bulletin*, *23*, 1188–1199.

Cohen, D., Nisbett, R. E., Bowdle, B. F., & Schwarz, N. (1996). Insult, aggression, and the Southern culture of honor: An "experimental ethnography." *Journal of Personality and Social Psychology*, *70*, 945–960.

Cohen, D., Vandello, J. A., Puente, S., & Rantilla, A. (1999). "When you call me that, smile!" How norms for politeness, interaction styles, and aggression work together in Southern culture. *Social Psychology Quarterly*, *62*, 257–275.

Cohen, G. L., Steele, C. M., & Ross, L. D. (1999). The mentor's dilemma: Providing critical feedback across the racial divide. *Personality and Social Psychology Bulletin*, *25*, 1302–1318.

Cohen, J. (1992). A power primer. *Psychological Bulletin*, *112*, 155–159.

Cohn, E. G., & Rotton, J. (1997). Assault as a function of time and temperature: A moderator-variable time-series analysis. *Journal of Personality and Social Psychology*, *72*, 1322–1334.

Coke, J. S., Batson, C. D., & McDavis, K. (1978). Empathic mediation of helping: A two-stage model. *Journal of Personality and Social Psychology*, *36*, 752–766.

Colby, A., & Kohlberg, L. (1987). *The measurement of moral judgment*, Vol. 1: *Theoretical foundations and research validation*; Vol 2: *Standard issue scoring manual*. New York: Cambridge University Press.

Coleman, A. M. (1982). *Game theory and experimental games*. Oxford, UK: Pergamon.

Collins, N. L. (1996). Working models of attachment: Implications for explanation, emotion, and behavior. *Journal of Personality and Social Psychology*, *71*, 810–832.

Collins, N. L., & Feeney, B. C. (2004). Working models of attachment shape perceptions of social support: Evidence from experimental and observational studies. *Journal of Personality and Social Psychology*, *87*, 363–383.

Collins, N. L., Ford, M. B., Guichard, A. C., & Allard, L. M. (2006). Working models of attachment and attribution processes in intimate relationships. *Personality and Social Psychology Bulletin*, *32*, 201–219.

Collins, N. L., & Miller, L. C. (1994). Self-disclosure and liking: A meta-analytic review. *Psychological Bulletin, 116*, 457–475.

Collins, R. L. (1996). For better or worse: The impact of upward social comparison on self-evaluations. *Psychological Bulletin, 119*, 51–69.

Comstock, G., & Paik, H. (1991). *Television and the American child*. San Diego, CA: Academic Press.

Condon, J. W., & Crano, W D. (1988). Inferred evaluation and the relation between attitude similarity and interpersonal attraction. *Journal of Personality and Social Psychology, 54*, 789–797.

Contrada, R. J., Ashmore, R. D., Gary, M. L., Coups, E., Egeth, J. D., Sewell, A., Ewell, K., Goyal, T. M., & Chasse, V. (2000). Ethnicity-related sources of stress and their effects on well-being. *Current Directions in Psychological Science, 9*, 136–139.

Cook, K. S., Yamagishi, T., Cheshire, C., Cooper, R., Matsuda, M., & Mashima, R. (2005). Trust building via risk taking: A cross-societal experiment. *Social Psychology Quarterly, 68*, 121–142.

Cooley, C. H. (1902). *Human nature and the social order*. New York: Scribner.

Cooper, J. (1995). Cognitive dissonance theory. In A. S. R. Manstead & M. Hewstone (Eds.), *Blackwell encyclopedia of social psychology* (pp. 99–109). Oxford, UK: Blackwell.

Cooper, J., & Cooper, G. (2002). Subliminal motivation: A story revisited. *Journal of Applied Social Psychology, 32*, 2213–2227.

Cooper, J., & Fazio, R. H. (1984). A new look at dissonance theory. In L. Berkowitz (Ed.), *Advances in experimental social psychology* (Vol. 17, pp. 229–266). New York: Academic Press.

Cooper, J., Kelly, K. A., & Weaver, K. (2001). Attitudes, norms, and social groups. In M. A. Hogg & R. S. Tindale (Eds.), *Blackwell handbook of social psychology: Group Processes* (pp. 259–282). Malden, MA: Blackwell.

Correll, J., Park, B., Judd, C. M., Wittenbrink, B., Sadler, M. S., & Keesee, T. (2007). Across the thin blue line: Police officers and racial bias in the decision to shoot. *Journal of Personality and Social Psychology, 92*, 1006–1023.

Correll, J., Urland, G. R., & Ito, T. A. (2006). Event-related potentials and the decision to shoot: The role of threat perception and cognitive control. *Journal of Experimental Social Psychology, 42*, 120–128.

Cosmides, L. (1989). The logic of social exchange: Has natural selection shaped how humans reason? Studies with the Wason selection task. *Cognition, 31*, 187–276.

Cosmides, L., & Tooby, J. (1996). Are humans good intuitive statisticians after all? Rethinking some conclusions from the literature on judgment under uncertainty. *Cognition, 58*, 1–73.

Costa, P. Jr., Terracciano, A., & McCrae, R. R. (2001). Gender differences in personality traits across cultures: Robust and surprising findings. *Journal of Personality and Social Psychology, 81*, 322–331.

Coull, A., Yzerbyt, V. Y., Castano, E., Paladino, M. P., & Leemans, V. (2001). Protecting the ingroup: Motivated allocation of cognitive resources in the presence of threatening ingroup members. *Group Processes and Intergroup Relations, 4*, 327–339.

Cousins, S. D. (1989). Culture and self-perception in Japan and the United States. *Journal of Personality and Social Psychology, 56*, 124–131.

Covington, M. V. (2000). Goal theory, motivation, and school achievement: An integrative review. *Annual Review of Psychology, 51*, 171–200.

Cox, T. H., Lobel, S. A., & McLeod, P. L. (1991). Effects of ethnic group cultural differences on cooperative and competitive behavior on a group task. *Academy of Management Journal, 34*, 827–847.

Craft, H. (2002). Gates, H. L. Jr. (Ed.). (2002). *The bondswoman's narrative*. New York: AOL Time Warner.

Crano, W. D. (2000). Milestones in the psychological analysis of social influence. *Group Dynamics, 4*, 68–80.

Crano, W. D., & Chen, X. (1998). The leniency contract and persistence of majority and minority influence. *Journal of Personality and Social Psychology, 74*, 1437–1450.

Crano, W. D., & Prislin, R. (2006). Attitudes and persuasion. *Annual Review of Psychology, 57*, 345–374.

Crick, N. R. (1995). Relational aggression: The role of intent attributions, feelings of distress, and provocation type. *Development and Psychopathology, 7*, 313–322.

Crick, N. R. (1997). Engagement in gender normative versus non-normative forms of aggression: Links to social-psychological adjustment. *Developmental Psychology, 33*, 610–617.

Crick, N. R., Casas, J. F., & Mosher, M. (1997). Relational and overt aggression in preschool. *Developmental Psychology, 33*, 579–588.

Crick, N. R., & Grotpeter, J. K. (1995). Relational aggression, gender, and social-psychological adjustment. *Child Development, 66*, 710–722.

Crick, N. R., & Werner, N. E. (1998). Response direction processes in relational and overt aggression. *Child Development, 69*, 1630–1639.

Crisp, R. J., Stone, C. H., & Hall, N. R. (2006). Recategorization and subgroup identification: Predicting and preventing threats from common ingroups. *Personality and Social Psychology Bulletin*, *32*, 230–243.

Crocker, J. (1981). Judgment of covariation by social perceivers. *Psychological Bulletin*, *90*, 272–292.

Crocker, J. (1999). Social stigma and self-esteem: Situational construction of self-worth. *Journal of Experimental Social Psychology*, *35*, 89–107.

Crocker, J., Cornwell, B., & Major, B. (1993). The stigma of overweight: Affective consequences of attributional ambiguity. *Journal of Personality and Social Psychology*, *64*, 60–70.

Crocker, J., & Knight, K. M. (2005). Contingencies of self-worth. *Current Directions in Psychological Science*, *14*, 200–203.

Crocker, J., & Luhtanen, R. (1990). Collective self-esteem and ingroup bias. *Journal of Personality and Social Psychology*, *58*, 60–67.

Crocker, J., Luhtanen, R., Blaine, B., & Broadnax, S. (1994). Collective self-esteem and psychological well-being among White, Black, and Asian college students. *Personality and Social Psychology Bulletin*, *20*, 503–513.

Crocker, J., & Major, B. (1989). Social stigma and self-esteem: The self-protective properties of stigma. *Psychological Review*, *96*, 608–630.

Crocker, J., Major, B., & Steele, C. M. (1998). Social stigma. In D. T. Gilbert, S. T. Fiske, & G. Lindzey (Eds.), *Handbook of social psychology* (4th ed., Vol. 2, pp. 504–553). New York: McGraw-Hill.

Crocker, J., Thompson, L., McGraw, K. M., & Ingerman, C. (1987). Downward comparison, prejudice, and evaluations of others: Effects of self-esteem and threat. *Journal of Personality and Social Psychology*, *52*, 907–916.

Crocker, J., Voelkl, K., Testa, M., & Major, B. (1991). Social stigma: The affective consequences of attributional ambiguity. *Journal of Personality and Social Psychology*, *60*, 218–228.

Croizet, J. C., & Claire, T. (1998). Extending the concept of stereotype threat to social class: The intellectual underperformance of students from low socioeconomic backgrounds. *Personality and Social Psychology Bulletin*, *24*, 588–594.

Crosby, F. J. (1991). *Juggling: The unexpected advantages of balancing career and home for women and their families*. New York: Free Press.

Crosby, F. J., Bromley, S., & Saxe, L. (1980). Recent unobtrusive studies of Black and White discrimination and prejudice: A literature review. *Psychological Bulletin*, *87*, 546–563.

Cross, S. E., Bacon, P. L., & Morris, M. L. (2000). The relational-interdependent self-construal and relationships. *Journal of Personality and Social Psychology*, *78*, 791–808.

Cross, S. E., & Madson, L. (1997). Models of the self: Self-construals and gender. *Psychological Bulletin*, *122*, 5–37.

Crott, H. W., Szilvas, K., & Zuber, J. A. (1991). Group decision, choice shift, and polarization in consulting, political, and local political scenarios: An experimental investigation and theoretical analysis. *Organizational Behavior and Human Decision Processes*, *49*, 22–41.

Crutchfield, R. S. (1955). Conformity and character. *American Psychologist*, *10*, 191–198.

Cuddy, A. J. C., Fiske, S. T., & Glick, P. (2007). The BIAS map: Behaviors from intergroup affect and stereotypes. *Journal of Personality and Social Psychology*, *92*, 631–648.

Cuddy, A. J. C., Fiske, S. T., & Glick, P. (2008). Competence and warmth as universal trait dimensions of interpersonal and intergroup perception: The Stereotype Content Model and the BIAS Map. In M. P. Zanna (Ed.), *Advances in Experimental Social Psychology* (Vol. 40, pp. 61–149). New York: Academic.

Cuddy, A. J. C., Fiske, S. T., Kwan, V. S. Y., Glick, P., Demoulin, S., Leyens, J-Ph., Bond, M. H., Croizet, J-C., Ellemers, N., Sleebos, E., Htun, T. T., Yamamoto, M., Kim, H-J., Maio, G., Perry, J., Petkova, K., Todorov, V., Rodríguez-Bailón, R., Morales, E., Moya, M., Palacios, M., Smith, V., Perez, R., Vala, J., & Ziegler, R. (2009). Is the stereotype content model culture-bound? A cross-cultural comparison reveals systematic similarities and differences. *British Journal of Social Psychology*, *48*, 1–33.

Cuddy, A. J. C., Norton, M. I., & Fiske, S. T. (2005). This old stereotype: The pervasiveness and persistence of the elderly stereotype. *Journal of Social Issues*, *61*, 267–285.

Cuddy, A. J. C., Rock, M. S., & Norton, M. I. (2007). Aid in the aftermath of Hurricane Katrina: Inferences of secondary emotions and intergroup helping. *Group Processes and Intergroup Relations*, *10*, 107–118.

Cummings, P., Koepsell, T. D., Grossman, D. C., Savarino, J., & Thompson, R. S. (1997). The association between the purchase of a handgun and homicide or suicide. *American Journal of Public Health*, *87*, 974–978.

Cunningham, M. R. (1985–1986). Levites and brother's keepers: A sociobiological perspective on prosocial behavior. *Humboldt Journal of Social Relations*, *13*, 35–67.

Cunningham, M. R. (1986). Measuring the physical in physical attractiveness: Quasi-experiments on the sociobiology of female facial beauty. *Journal of Personality and Social Psychology*, *50*, 925–935.

Cunningham, M. R., Roberts, A. R., Barbee, A. P., Druen, P. B., & Wu, C. (1995). "Their ideas of beauty are, on the whole, the same as ours": Consistency and variability in the cross-cultural perception of female physical attractiveness.

*Journal of Personality and Social Psychology, 68*, 261–279.

Cunningham, M. R., Shaffer, D. R., Barbee, A. P., Wolff, P. L., & Kelley, D. J. (1990). Separate processes in the relation of elation and depression to helping: Social versus personal concerns. *Journal of Experimental Social Psychology, 26*, 13–33.

Cunningham, M. R., Steinberg, J., & Grev, R. (1980). Wanting to and having to help: Separate motivations for positive mood and guilt-induced helping. *Journal of Personality and Social Psychology, 38*, 181–192.

Cunningham, W. A., Johnson, M. K., Raye, C. L., Gatenby, J. C., Gore, J. C., & Banaji, M. R. (2004). Separable neural components in the processing of black and white faces. *Psychological Science, 15*, 806–813.

Cunningham, W. A., Raye, C. L., & Johnson, M. K. (2004). Implicit and explicit evaluation: fMRI correlates of valence, emotional intensity, and control in the processing of attitudes. *Journal of Cognitive Neuroscience, 16*, 1717–1729.

Cunningham, W. A., Van Bavel, J. J., & Johnsen, I. R. (2008). Affective flexibility: Evaluative processing goals shape amygdala activity. *Psychological Science, 19*, 152–160.

Daly, M., & Wilson, M. I. (1988). *Homicide*. New York: Aldine De Gruyter.

Daly, M., & Wilson, M. I. (1996). Violence against stepchildren. *Current Directions in Psychological Science, 5*, 77–90.

Darke, P. R., Chaiken, S., Bohner, G., Einwiller, S., Erb, H. P., & Hazlewood, J. D. (1998). Accuracy motivation, consensus information, and the law of large numbers: Effects on attitude judgment in the absence of argumentation. *Personality and Social Psychology Bulletin, 24*, 1205–1215.

Darley, J. M. (1992). Social organization for the production of evil. *Psychological Inquiry, 3*, 199–218.

Darley, J. M. (1999). Methods for the study of evil-doing actions. *Personality and Social Psychology Review, 3*, 269–275.

Darley, J. M. (2001). The dynamics of authority in organizations. In J. M. Darley, D. M. Messick, & T. R. Tyler (Eds.), *Social influences on ethical behavior in organizations* (pp. 37–52). Mahwah, NJ: Erlbaum.

Darley, J. M., & Berscheid, E. (1967). Increased liking as a result of the anticipation of personal contact. *Human Relations, 20*, 29–40.

Darley, J. M., Carlsmith, K. M., & Robinson, P. H. (2000). Incapacitation and just deserts as motives for punishment. *Law and Human Behavior, 24*, 659–683.

Darley, J. M., & Fazio, R. H. (1980). Expectancy confirmation processes arising in the social interaction sequence. *American Psychologist, 35*, 867–881.

Darley, J. M., & Latané, B. (1968). Bystander intervention in emergencies: Diffusion of responsibility. *Journal of Personality and Social Psychology, 8*, 377–383.

Darley, J. M., & Shultz, T. R. (1990). Moral rules: Their content and acquisition. *Annual Review of Psychology, 41*, 525–556.

Dasgupta, N., & Greenwald, A. G. (2001). On the malleability of automatic attitudes: Combating automatic prejudice with images of admired and disliked individuals. *Journal of Personality and Social Psychology, 81*, 800–814.

Dasgupta, N., McGhee, D. E., Greenwald, A. G., & Banaji, M. R. (2000). Automatic preference for white Americans: Eliminating the familiarity explanation. *Journal of Experimental Social Psychology, 36*, 316–328.

Davis, J. H. (1973). Group decision and social interaction: A theory of social decision schemes. *Psychological Review, 80*, 97–125.

Davis, J. H., Hulbert, L., Au, W T., Chen, X. P., & Zarnoth, P. (1997). Effects of group size and procedural influence on consensual judgments of quantity: The examples of damage awards and mock civil juries. *Journal of Personality and Social Psychology, 73*, 703–718.

Davis, J. H., Zarnoth, P., Hulbert, L., Chen, X. P., Parks, C., & Nam, K. (1997). The committee charge, framing interpersonal agreement, and consensus models of group quantitative judgment. *Organizational Behavior and Human Decision Processes, 72*, 137–157.

Davis, J. L., & Rusbult, C. E. (2001). Attitude alignment in close relationships. *Journal of Personality and Social Psychology, 81*, 65–84.

Davis, M. H., Conklin, L., Smith, A., & Luce, C. (1996). Effect of perspective taking on the cognitive representation of persons: A merging of self and other. *Journal of Personality and Social Psychology, 70*, 713–726.

Dawes, R. M. (1998). Behavioral decision making and judgment. In D. T. Gilbert, S. T. Fiske, & G. Lindzey (Eds.), *Handbook of social psychology* (4th ed., Vol. 1, pp. 497–548). New York: McGraw-Hill.

Dawes, R. M., Faust, D., & Meehl, P. E. (1989). Clinical versus actuarial judgment. *Science, 243*, 1668–1674.

Dawes, R. M., & Messick, D. M. (2000). Social dilemmas. *International Journal of Psychology, 35*, 111–116.

Dawkins, R. (1976). *The selfish gene*. New York: Oxford University Press.

Dean, K. E., & Malamuth, N. M. (1997). Characteristics of men who aggress sexually and of men who imagine aggressing: Risk and moderating variables. *Journal of Personality and Social Psychology, 72,* 449–455.

Deaux, K. (1993). Reconstructing social identity. *Personality and Social Psychology Bulletin, 19,* 4–12.

Deaux, K., & Emswiller, T. (1974). Explanations of successful performance on sex-linked tasks: What is skill for the male is luck for the female. *Journal of Personality and Social Psychology, 29,* 80–85.

DeCarlo, T. E. (2005). The effects of sales message and suspicion of ulterior motives on salesperson evaluation. *Journal of Consumer Psychology, 15,* 238–249.

Decety, J., & Jackson, P. L. (2006). A social-neuroscience perspective on empathy. *Current Directions in Psychological Science, 15,* 54–58.

Deci, E. L., Koestner, R., & Ryan, R. M. (1999). A meta-analytic review of experiments examining the effects of extrinsic rewards on intrinsic motivation. *Psychological Bulletin, 125,* 627–668.

De Cremer, D., Van Knippenberg, D., Van Dijk, E., & Van Leeuwen, E. (2008). Cooperating if one's goals are collective-based: Social identification effects in social dilemmas as a function of goal transformation. *Journal of Applied Social Psychology, 38,* 1562–1579.

De Dreu, C. K. W., Koole, S. L., & Steinel, W. (2000). Unfixing the fixed pie: A motivated information processing approach to integrative negotiation. *Journal of Personality and Social Psychology, 79,* 975–987.

De Dreu, C. K. W., & McCusker, C. (1997). Gain-loss frames and cooperation in two-person social dilemmas: A transformation analysis. *Journal of Personality and Social Psychology, 72,* 1093–1106.

De Dreu, C. K. W., & Van Lange, P. A. M. (1995). The impact of social value orientations on negotiator cognition and behavior. *Personality and Social Psychology Bulletin, 21,* 1178–1188.

De Dreu, C. K. W., Weingart, L. R., & Kwon, S. (2000). Influence of social motives on integrative negotiation: A meta-analytic review and test of two theories. *Journal of Personality and Social Psychology, 78,* 889–905.

DeGrada, E., Kruglanski, A. W., Mannetti, L., & Pierro, A. (1999). Motivated cognition and group interaction: Need for closure affects the contents and processes of collective negotiations. *Journal of Experimental Social Psychology, 35,* 346–365.

de Heus, P. (2000). Do reciprocal strategies work in social dilemmas? *Personality and Social Psychology Review, 4,* 278–288.

de Hoog, N., Stroebe, W., & de Wit, J. B. F. (2007). The impact of vulnerability to and severity of a health risk on processing and acceptance of fear-arousing communications: A meta-analysis. *Review of General Psychology, 11,* 258–285.

DeJong, W. (1981). Consensus information and the foot-in-the-door effect. *Personality and Social Psychology Bulletin, 7,* 423–430.

de la Haye, A. M. (1975). Recherches sur l'interaction anticipee. [Research on anticipated interaction.] *Année Psychologie, 75,* 153–168.

de la Haye, A. M. (1991). Problems and procedures: A typology of paradigms in interpersonal cognition. *European Bulletin of Cognitive Psychology, 11,* 279–304.

Demo, D. H. (1992). The self-concept over time: Research issues and directions. *Annual Review of Sociology, 18,* 303–326.

Demoulin, S., Leyens, J.-Ph., Rodríguez-Torres, R., Rodríguez-Pérez, A., Paladino, P. M., & Fiske, S. T. (2005). Motivation to support a desired conclusion versus motivation to avoid an undesirable conclusion: The case of infra-humanization. *International Journal of Psychology, 40,* 416–428.

Demoulin, S., Torres, R. R., Perez, A. R., Vaes, J., Paladino, M. P., Gaunt, R., Pozo, B. C., & Leyens, J.-Ph. (2005). Emotional prejudice can lead to infra-humanisation. *European Review of Social Psychology, 15,* 259–296.

Den Hartog, D. N., House, R. J., Hanges, P. J., Ruiz-Quintanilla, S. A., Dorfman, P. W., et al. (1999). Culture specific and cross-culturally generalizability implicit leadership theories: Are attributes of charismatic/transformational leadership universally endorsed? *Leadership Quarterly, 10,* 219–256.

Denrell, J. (2003). Vicarious learning, undersampling of failure, and the myths of management. *Organization Science, 14,* 227–243.

Denrell, J. (2005). Why most people disapprove of me: Experience sampling in impression formation. *Psychological Review, 112,* 951–978.

Denrell, J., & Le Mens, G. (2007). Interdependent sampling and social influence. *Psychological Review, 114,* 398–422.

DePaulo, B. M. (1992). Nonverbal behavior and self presentation. *Psychological Bulletin, 111,* 203–243.

DePaulo, B. M., Charlton, K., Cooper, H., Lindsay, J. J., & Muhlenbruck, L. (1997). The accuracy-confidence correlation in the detection of deception. *Personality and Social Psychology Review, 1,* 346–357.

DePaulo, B. M., & Friedman, H. S. (1998). Nonverbal communication. In D. T. Gilbert, S. T. Fiske, & G. Lindzey (Eds.), *Handbook of social psychology*

(4th ed., Vol. 2, pp. 3–41). New York: McGraw-Hill.

DePaulo, B. M., & Kashy, D. A. (1998). Everyday lies in close and casual relationships. *Journal of Personality and Social Psychology, 74*, 63–79.

Dépret, E. F., & Fiske, S. T. (1993). Social cognition and power: Some cognitive consequences of social structure as a source of control deprivation. In G. Weary, F. Gleicher, & K. Marsh (Eds.), *Control motivation and social cognition* (pp. 176–202). New York: Springer-Verlag.

Dépret, E. F., & Fiske, S. T. (1999). Perceiving the powerful: Intriguing individuals versus threatening groups. *Journal of Experimental Social Psychology, 35*, 461–480.

de Quervain, D. J.-F., Fischbacher, U., Treyer, V., Schellhammer, M., Schnyder, U., Buck, A., & Fehr, E. (2004). The neural basis of altruistic punishment. *Science, 305*, 1254–1258.

Derlega, V. J., Metts, S., Petronio, S., & Margulis, S. T. (1993). *Self disclosure*. Newbury Park, CA: Sage.

DeSteno, D. A., Bartlett, M. Y., Braverman, J., & Salovey, P. (2002). Sex differences in jealousy: Evolutionary mechanism or artifact of measurement? *Journal of Personality and Social Psychology, 83*, 1103–1116.

DeSteno, D. A., Dasgupta, N., Bartlett, M. Y., & Cajdric, A. (2004). Prejudice from thin air: The effect of emotion on automatic intergroup attitudes. *Psychological Science, 15*, 319–324.

DeSteno, D. A., & Salovey, P. (1996). Evolutionary origins of sex difference in jealousy? Questioning the "fitness" of the model. *Psychological Science, 7*, 367–372.

Deutsch, F. M. (1999). *Halving it all: How equally shared parenting works*. Cambridge: Harvard.

Deutsch, F. M. (2001). Equally shared parenting. *Current Directions in Psychological Science, 10*, 25–28.

Deutsch, F. M., & Saxon, S. E. (1998). The double standard of praise and criticism for mothers and fathers. *Psychology of Women Quarterly, 22*, 665–683.

Deutsch, M. (1949). A theory of cooperation and competition. *Human Relations, 2*, 199–231.

Deutsch, M. (1973). *The resolution of conflict: Constructive and destructive processes*. New Haven, CT: Yale University Press.

Deutsch, M., & Gerard, H. B. (1955). A study of normative and informational social influences upon individual judgment. *Journal of Abnormal and Social Psychology, 51*, 629–636.

Devine, P. G. (1989). Stereotypes and prejudice: Their automatic and controlled components. *Journal of Personality and Social Psychology, 56*, 5–18.

Devine, P. G., Monteith, M. J., Zuwerink, J. R., & Elliot, A. J. (1991). Prejudice with and without compunction. *Journal of Personality and Social Psychology, 60*, 817–830.

Devine, P. G., Plant, E. A., & Buswell, B. N. (2000). Breaking the prejudice habit: Progress and obstacles. In S. Oskamp (Ed.), *Reducing prejudice and discriminaton*. Mahwah, NJ: Erlbaum.

Devos, T., Comby, L., & Deschamps, J. C. (1996). Asymmetries in judgments of ingroup and outgroup variability. In W. Stroebe & M. Hewstone (Eds.), *European review of social psychology* (Vol. 7, pp. 95–104). Chichester: Wiley.

de Waal, F. B. M. (2008). Putting the altruism back into altruism: The evolution of empathy. *Annual Review of Psychology, 59*, 279–300.

Diamond, W. D., & Kashyap, R. K. (1997). Extending models of prosocial behavior to explain university alumni contributions. *Journal of Applied Social Psychology, 27*, 915–928.

Diekman, A. B., & Eagly, A. H. (2000). Stereotypes as dynamic constructs: Women and men of the past, present, and future. *Personality and Social Psychology Bulletin, 26*, 1171–1188.

Diener, E. (1980). Deindividuation: The absence of self-awareness and self-regulation in group members. In P. B. Paulus (Ed.), *Psychology of group influence* (pp. 209–242). Hillside, NJ: Erlbaum.

Dijksterhuis, A., Aarts, H., Bargh, J. A., & van Knippenberg, A. (2000). On the relation between associative strength and automatic behavior. *Journal of Experimental Social Psychology, 36*, 531–544.

Dijksterhuis, A., & Bargh, J. A. (2001). The perception behavior expressway: Automatic effects of social perception on social behavior. In M. P. Zanna (Ed.), *Advances in experimental social psychology* (Vol. 33, pp. 1–40). New York: Academic Press.

Dijksterhuis, A., Bos, M. W., Nordgren, L. F., & van Baaren, R. B. (2006). On making the right choice: The deliberation-without-attention effect. *Science, 311*, 1005–1007.

Dijksterhuis, A., Preston, J., Wegner, D. M., & Aarts, H. (2008). Effects of subliminal priming of self and God on self-attribution of authorship for events. *Journal of Experimental Social Psychology, 44*, 2–9.

Dijksterhuis, A., Spears, R., & Lépinasse, V. (2001). Reflecting and deflecting stereotypes: Assimilation and contrast in impression formation and automatic behavior. *Journal of Experimental and Social Psychology, 37*, 286–299.

Dijksterhuis, A., Spears, R., Postmes, T., Stapel, D., Koomen, W., van Knippenberg, A., & Scheepers,

D. (1998). Seeing one thing and doing another: Contrast effects in automatic behavior. *Journal of Personality and Social Psychology, 75*, 862–871.

Dijksterhuis, A., & van Knippenberg, A. (1998). The relation between perception and behavior, or how to win a game of Trivial Pursuit. *Journal of Personality and Social Psychology, 74*, 865–877.

Dijksterhuis, A., & van Knippenberg, A. V. (1999). On the parameters of associative strength: Central tendency and variability as determinants of stereotype accessibility. *Personality and Social Psychology Bulletin, 25*, 527–536.

Dijksterhuis, A., & van Knippenberg, A. V. (2000). Behavioral indecision: Effects of self-focus on automatic behavior. *Social Cognition, 18*, 55–74.

Dion, K. K., Pak, A. W., & Dion, K. L. (1990). Stereotyping physical attractiveness: A sociocultural perspective. *Journal of Cross-Cultural Psychology, 21*, 158–179.

Dodge, K. A. (1980). Social cognition and children's aggressive behavior. *Child Development, 51*, 162–170.

Dodge, K. A., & Coie, J. D. (1987). Social-information-processing factors in reactive and proactive aggression in children's peer groups. *Journal of Personality and Social Psychology, 53*, 1146–1158.

Dodge, K. A., & Frame, C. L. (1982). Social cognitive biases and deficits in aggressive boys. *Child Development, 53*, 620–635.

Dodge, K. A., Lochman, J. E., Harnish, J. D., Bates, J. E., & Pettit, G. S. (1997). Reactive and proactive aggression in school children and psychiatrically impaired chronically assaultive youth. *Journal of Abnormal Psychology, 106*, 37–51.

Dodge, K. A., & Newman, J. P. (1981). Biased decision-making processes in aggressive boys. *Journal of Abnormal Psychology, 90*, 375–379.

Dodge, K. A., & Somberg, D. R. (1987). Hostile attributional biases among aggressive boys are exacerbated under conditions of threats to the self. *Child Development, 58*, 213–224.

Dodge, K. A., & Tomlin, A. M. (1987). Utilization of self-schemas as a mechanism of interpretational bias in aggressive children. *Social Cognition, 5*, 280–300.

Doise, W., & Moscovici, S. (1983). *Current issues in European social psychology*. Cambridge, UK: Cambridge University Press.

Dollard, J., Doob, L. W., Miller, N. E., Mowrer, O. H., & Sears, R. R. (1939). *Frustration and aggression*. New Haven, CT: Yale University Press.

Donnerstein, E., Slaby, R. G., & Eron, L. D. (1994). The mass media and youth aggression. In L. D. Eron, J. H. Gentry, & P. Schlegel (Eds.), *Reason*

*to hope: A psychosocial perspective on violence and youth* (pp. 219–250). Washington, DC: American Psychological Association.

Donnerstein, E., & Wilson, D. W. (1976). Effects of noise and perceived control on ongoing and subsequent aggressive behavior. *Journal of Personality and Social Psychology, 34*, 774–781.

Doosje, B., Ellemers, N., & Spears, R. (1995). Perceived intragroup variability as a function of group status and identification. *Journal of Personality and Social Psychology, 31*, 410–436.

Doosje, B., Spears, R., de Redelijkheid, H., & van Onna, J. (2007). Memory for stereotype (in)consistent information: The role of in-group identification. *British Journal of Social Psychology, 46*, 115–128.

Doosje, B., Spears, R., & Ellemers, N. (2002). Social identity as both cause and effect: The development of group identification in response to anticipated and actual changes in the intergroup status hierarchy. *British Journal of Social Psychology, 41*, 57–76.

Dornbusch, S. M., Hastorf, A. H., Richardson, S. A., Muzzy, R. E., & Vreeland, R. S. (1965). The perceiver and perceived: Their relative influence on categories of interpersonal perception. *Journal of Personality and Social Psychology, 1*, 434–440.

Dovidio, J. F. (1984). Helping behavior and altruism: An empirical and conceptual overview. In L. Berkowitz (Ed.), *Advances in experimental social psychology* (Vol. 17, pp. 361–427). New York: Academic Press.

Dovidio, J. F., Allen, J. L., & Schroeder, D. A. (1990). Specificity of empathy-induced helping: Evidence for the altruistic motivation. *Journal of Personality and Social Psychology, 59*, 249–260.

Dovidio, J. F., Brigham, J. C., Johnson, B. T., & Gaertner, S. L. (1996). Stereotyping, prejudice, and discrimination: Another look. In C. N. Macrae, C. Stangor, & M. Hewstone (Eds.), *Stereotypes and stereotyping* (pp. 276–322). New York: Guilford.

Dovidio, J. F., Evans, N., & Tyler, R. B. (1986). Racial stereotypes: The contents of their cognitive representations. *Journal of Experimental Social Psychology, 22*, 22–37.

Dovidio, J. F., & Gaertner, S. L. (2004). Aversive racism. In M. P. Zanna (Ed.), *Advances in experimental social psychology* (Vol. 36, pp. 1–52). San Diego, CA: Elsevier Academic Press.

Dovidio, J. F., Gaertner, S. L., & Validzic, A. (1998). Intergroup bias: Status, differentiation, and a common in-group identity. *Journal of Personality and Social Psychology, 75*, 109–120.

Dovidio, J. F., Gaertner, S. L., Validzic, A., Matoka, K., Johnson, B., & Frazier, S. (1997). Extending the benefits of recategorization: Evaluations, self-disclosure, and helping. *Journal of Experimental Social Psychology*, *33*, 401–420.

Dovidio, J. F., Kawakami, K., & Gaertner, S. L. (2000). Reducing contemporary prejudice: Combating explicit and implicit bias at the individual and intergroup level. In S. Oskamp (Ed.), *Reducing prejudice and discrimination* (pp. 137–164). Mahwah, NJ: Erlbaum.

Dovidio, J. F., Kawakami, K., & Gaertner, S. L. (2002). Implicit and explicit prejudice and interracial interaction. *Journal of Personality and Social Psychology*, *82*, 62–68.

Dovidio, J. F., Kawakami, K., Johnson, C., Johnson, B., & Howard, A. (1997). On the nature of prejudice: Automatic and controlled processes. *Journal of Experimental Social Psychology*, *33*, 510–540.

Dovidio, J. F., Piliavin, J. A., Gaertner, S. L., Schroeder, D. A., & Clark, R. D. III (1991). The arousal: cost-reward model and the process of intervention. In M. S. Clark (Ed.), *Review of personality and social psychology: Prosocial behavior* (Vol. 12, pp. 86–118). Newbury, CA: Sage.

Dovidio, J. F., ten Vergert, M., Stewart, T. L., Gaertner, S. L., Johnson, J. D., Esses, V. M., Riek, B. M., & Pearson, A. R. (2004). Perspective and prejudice: Antecedents and mediating mechanisms. *Personality and Social Psychology Bulletin*, *30*, 1537–1549.

Downey, G., Feldman, S., & Oyduk, O. (2000). Rejection sensitivity and male violence in romantic relationships. *Personal Relationships*, *7*, 45–61.

Downey, G., Lebolt, A., Rincon, C., & Freitas, A. L. (1998). Rejection sensitivity and children's interpersonal difficulties. *Child Development*, *69*, 1074–1091.

Doyle, A. C. (1892–1927). *The complete Sherlock Holmes*. New York: Doubleday.

Drabman, R. S., & Thomas, M. H. (1974). Exposure to filmed violence and children's tolerance of real life aggression. *Personality and Social Psychology Bulletin*, *1*, 198–199.

Drigotas, S. M., & Rusbult, C. E. (1992). Should I stay or should I go? A dependence model of breakups. *Journal of Personality and Social Psychology*, *62*, 62–87.

Drigotas, S. M., Whitney, G. A., & Rusbult, C. E. (1995). On the peculiarities of loyalty: A diary study of responses to dissatisfaction in everyday life. *Personality and Social Psychology Bulletin*, *21*, 596–609.

Duck, S. (1988). *Relating to others*. Chicago: Dorsey.

Duckitt, J. (1989). Authoritarianism and group identification: A new view of an old construct. *Political Psychology*, *10*, 63–84.

Duckitt, J. (1992). *The social psychology of prejudice*. Westport, CT: Praeger.

Duckitt, J. (1993). Right-wing authoritarianism among white South American students: Its measurement and correlates. *Journal of Social Psychology*, *133*, 553–563.

Duckitt, J. (2001). A dual-process cognitive-motivational theory of ideology and prejudice. In M. P. Zanna (Ed.), *Advances in experimental social psychology* (Vol. 33, pp. 41–113). New York: Academic Press.

Duckitt, J., & Mphuthing, T. (1998). Group identification and intergroup attitudes: A longitudinal analysis in South Africa. *Journal of Personality and Social Psychology*, *74*, 80–85.

Dugan, E., & Kivett, V R. (1998). Implementing the Adams and Blieszner conceptual model: Predicting interactive friendship processes of older adults. *Journal of Social and Personal Relationships*, *15*, 607–622.

Dugosh, K. L., Paulus, P. B., Roland, E. J., & Yang, H. C. (2000). Cognitive stimulation in brainstorming. *Journal of Personality and Social Psychology*, *79*, 722–735.

Dunbar, R., & Schultz, S. (2007). Evolution in the social brain. *Science*, *317*, 1344–1347.

Duncan, S. Jr., & Fiske, D. W. (1977). *Face-to-face interaction: Research, methods, and theory*. Hillsdale, NJ: Erlbaum.

Dunham, Y., Baron, A. S., & Banaji, M. R. (2006). From American city to Japanese village: A cross-cultural investigation of implicit race attitudes. *Child Development*, *77*, 1268–1281.

Dunham, Y., Baron, A. S., & Banaji, M. R. (2007). Children and social groups: A developmental analysis of implicit consistency in Hispanic Americans. *Self and Identity*, *6*, 238—255.

Dunham, Y., Baron, A. S., & Banaji, M. R. (2008). The development of social cognition. *Trends in Cognitive Science*, *12*, 248–253.

Dunton, B. C., & Fazio, R. H. (1997). An individual difference measure of motivation to control prejudiced reactions. *Personality and Social Psychology Bulletin*, *23*, 316–326.

Durante, F., Volpato, C., & Fiske, S. T. (2009). Using the Stereotype Content Model to examine group depictions in Fascism: An archival approach. *European Journal of Social Psychology*, *39*, 1–19.

Durkheim, E. (1951). *Suicide*. New York: Free Press.

Dutton, D. G. (1995a). Intimate abusiveness. *Clinical Psychology: Science and Practice*, *2*, 207–224.

Dutton, D. G. (1995b). Male abusiveness in intimate relationships. *Clinical Psychology Review*, *15*, 567–581.

Dutton, D. G. (2000). Witnessing parental violence as a traumatic experience shaping the abusive personality. *Journal of Aggression, Maltreatment and Trauma*, *3*, 59–67.

Dutton, D. G., & Aron, A. P. (1974). Some evidence for heightened sexual attraction under conditions of high anxiety. *Journal of Personality and Social Psychology*, *30*, 510–517.

Dutton, D. G., Saunders, K., Starzomski, A., & Bartholomew, K. (1994). Intimacy-anger and insecure attachment as precursors of abuse in intimate relationships. *Journal of Applied Social Psychology*, *24*, 1367–1386.

Dutton, D. G., van Ginkel, C., & Starzomski, A. (1995). The role of shame and guilt in the intergenerational transmission of abusiveness. *Violence and Victims*, *10*, 121–131.

Duval, S., Duval, V. H., & Neely, R. (1979). Self-focus, felt responsibility, and helping behavior. *Journal of Personality and Social Psychology*, *37*, 1769–1778.

Duval, S., & Wicklund, R. A. (1972). *A theory of objective self awareness*. New York: Academic Press.

Eagly, A. H. (1987). *Sex differences in social behavior: A social-role interpretation*. Mahwah, NJ: Erlbaum.

Eagly, A. H., Ashmore, R. D., Makhijani, M. G., & Longo, L. C. (1991). What is beautiful is good, but . . . : A meta-analytic review of research on the physical attractiveness stereotype. *Psychological Bulletin*, *110*, 109–128.

Eagly, A. H., & Carli, L. L. (1981). Sex of researchers and sex-typed communications as determinants of sex differences in influenceability: A meta-analysis of social influence studies. *Psychological Bulletin*, *90*, 1–20.

Eagly, A. H., & Chaiken, S. (1993). *The psychology of attitudes*. Orlando, FL: Harcourt Brace Jovanovich.

Eagly, A. H., & Chaiken, S. (1998). Attitude structure and function. In D. T. Gilbert, S. T. Fiske, & G. Lindzey (Eds.), *Handbook of social psychology* (4th ed., Vol. 1, pp. 269–322). New York: McGraw-Hill.

Eagly, A. H., & Chaiken, S. (2007). The advantages of an inclusive definition of attitude. *Social Cognition*, *25*, 582–602.

Eagly, A. H., Chen, S., Chaiken, S., & Shaw-Barnes, K. (1999). The impact of attitudes on memory: An affair to remember. *Psychological Bulletin*, *125*, 64–89.

Eagly, A. H., & Johnson, B. T. (1990). Gender and leadership style: A meta-analysis. *Psychological Bulletin*, *108*, 233–256.

Eagly, A. H., & Karau, S. J. (2002). Role congruity theory of prejudice toward female leaders. *Psychological Review*, *109*, 573–598.

Eagly, A. H., Karau, S. J., & Makhijani, M. G. (1995). Gender and the effectiveness of leaders: A meta-analysis. *Psychological Bulletin*, *117*, 125–145.

Eagly, A. H., Makhijani, M. G., & Klonsky, B. G. (1992). Gender and the evaluation of leaders: A meta-analysis. *Psychological Bulletin*, *111*, 3–22.

Eagly, A. H., & Steffen, V. J. (1986). Gender and aggressive behavior: A meta-analytic review of the social psychological literature. *Psychological Bulletin*, *100*, 309–330.

Eagly, A. H., & Wood, W. (1999). The origins of sex differences in human behavior: Evolved dispositions versus social roles. *American Psychologist*, *54*, 408–423.

Eagly, A. H., Wood, W., & Diekman, A. B. (2000). Social role theory of sex differences and similarities: A current appraisal. In T. Eckes & H. M. Trautner (Eds.), *The developmental social psychology of gender* (pp. 123–174). Mahwah, NJ: Erlbaum.

Eastwick, P. W., Eagly, A. H., Glick, P., Johannesen-Schmidt, M. C., Fiske, S. T., Blum, A. M. B., Eckes, T., Freiburger, P., Huavg, L., Fernandez, M. L., Manganelli, A. M., Pek, J. C. X., Castro, Y. R., Sakalli Ugurlu, N., Six-Materna, I., & Volpato, C. (2006). Is traditional gender ideology associated with sex-typed mate preference? A test in nine nations. *Sex Roles*, *54*, 603–614.

Eastwick, P. W., & Finkel, E. J. (2008). Sex differences in mate preferences revisited: Do people know what they initially desire in a romantic partner? *Journal of Personality and Social Psychology*, *94*, 245–264.

Ebbinghaus, H. (1964). [Memory: A contribution to experimental psychology] (H. A. Ruger & C. E. Bussenius, trans.). New York: Dover. (Originally published, 1885).

Ebenbach, D. H., & Keltner, D. (1998). Power, emotion, and judgmental accuracy in social conflict: Motivating the cognitive miser. *Basic and Applied Social Psychology*, *20*, 7–21.

Eberhardt, J. L., Davies, P. G., Purdie-Vaughns, V. J., & Johnson, S. L. (2006). Looking deathworthy: Perceived stereotypicality of black defendants predicts capital-sentencing outcomes. *Psychological Science*, *17*, 383–386.

Eberhardt, J. L., Goff, P. A., Purdie, V. J., & Davies, P. G. (2004). Seeing black: Race, crime, and visual processing. *Journal of Personality and Social Psychology*, *87*, 876–893.

Edmondson, C. B., & Conger, J. C. (1995). The impact of mode of presentation on gender differences in social perception. *Sex Roles*, *32*, 169–183.

Edwards, J. A., & Weary, G. (1993). Depression and the impression-formation continuum: Piecemeal processing despite the availability of category information. *Journal of Personality and Social Psychology*, *64*, 636–645.

Edwards, K. (1990). The interplay of affect and cognition in attitude formation and change. *Journal of Personality and Social Psychology*, *59*, 202–216.

Ehrlinger, J., & Dunning, D. (2003). How chronic self–views influence (and potentially mislead) estimates of performance. *Journal of Personality and Social Psychology*, *84*, 5–17.

Eisenberg, N. (1982). The development of reasoning regarding prosocial behavior. In N. Eisenberg (Ed.), *The development of prosocial behavior* (pp. 219–249). New York: Academic Press.

Eisenberg, N. (1991). Meta-analytic contributions to the literature on prosocial behavior. *Personality and Social Psychology Bulletin*, *17*, 273–282.

Eisenberg, N. (2000). Emotion, regulation and moral development. *Annual Review of Psychology*, *51*, 665–697.

Eisenberg, N., Fabes, R. A., Miller, P. A., Fultz, J., Shell, R., Mathy, R. M., & Reno, R. R. (1989). Relation of sympathy and personal distress to prosocial behavior: A multi-method study. *Journal of Personality and Social Psychology*, *57*, 55–66.

Eisenberger, N. I., Lieberman, M. D., & Williams, K. D. (2003). Does rejection hurt? An fMRI study of social exclusion. *Science*, *302*, 290–292.

Ekman, P. (1993). Facial expression and emotion. *American Psychologist*, *48*, 384–392.

Ekman, P., & O'Sullivan, M. (1991). Who can catch a liar? *American Psychologist*, *46*, 913–920.

Elfenbein, H. A., & Ambady, N. (2003). When familiarity breeds accuracy: Cultural exposure and facial emotion recognition. *Journal of Personality and Social Psychology*, *85*, 276–290.

Ellemers, N. (1993). The influence of socio-structural variables on identity management strategies. In W. Stroebe & M. Hewstone (Eds.), *European review of social psychology* (Vol. 4, pp. 27–58). New York: Wiley.

Ellemers, N., Spears, R., & Doosje, B. (1997). Sticking together or falling apart: Ingroup identification as a psychological determinant of group commitment. *Journal of Personality and Social Psychology*, *72*, 617–626.

Ellemers, N., Spears, R., & Doosje, B. (2002). Self and social identity. *Annual Review of Psychology* *53*, 161–186.

Ellsworth, P. C., & Scherer, K. R. (2003). Appraisal processes in emotion. In R. J. Davidson, K. R. Scherer, & H. H. Goldsmith (Eds.), *Handbook of affective sciences* (pp. 572–595). New York: Oxford University Press.

Elms, A. C. (1995). Obedience in retrospect. *Journal of Social Issues*, *51*, 21–32.

Emrich, C. G. (1999). Context effects in leadership perception. *Personality and Social Psychology Bulletin*, *25*, 991–1006.

Endo, Y., Heine, S., & Lehman, D. R. (2000). Culture and positive illusions in close relationships: How my relationships are better than yours. *Personality and Social Psychology Bulletin*, *26*, 1571–1586.

Engell, A. D., Haxby, J. V., & Todorov, A. (2007). Implicit trustworthiness decisions: Automatic coding of face properties in the human amygdala. *Journal of Cognitive Neuroscience*, *19*, 1508–1519.

English, T., & Chen, S. (2007). Culture and self-concept stability: Consistency across and within contexts among Asian Americans and European Americans. *Journal of Personality and Social Psychology*, *93*, 478–490.

Epley, N. (2008). Solving the (real) other minds problem. *Personality and Social Psychology Compass*, *2*, 1455–1474.

Epley, N., Akalis, S., Waytz, A., & Cacioppo, J. T. (2008). Creating social connection through inferential reproduction: Loneliness and perceived agency in gadgets, gods, and greyhounds. *Psychological Science*, *19*, 114–120.

Epley, N., & Dunning, D. (2000). Feeling "holier than thou": Are self-serving assessments produced by errors in self or social prediction? *Journal of Personality and Social Psychology*, *79*, 861–875.

Epley, N., & Gilovich, T. (2006). The anchoring-and-adjustment heuristic: Why the adjustments are insufficient. *Psychological Science*, *17*, 311–318.

Epley, N., Keysar, B., Van Boven, L., & Gilovich, T. (2004). Perspective taking as egocentric anchoring and adjustment. *Journal of Personality and Social Psychology*, *87*, 327–339.

Epley, N., Savitsky, K., & Gilovich, T. (2002). Empathy neglect: Reconciling the spotlight effect and the correspondence bias. *Journal of Personality and Social Psychology*, *83*, 300–312.

Epley, N., Waytz, A., Akalis, S., & Cacioppo, J. T. (2009). When we need a human: Motivational determinants of anthropomorphism. *Social Cognition*, *26*, 143–155.

Epley, N., Waytz, A., & Cacioppo, J. T. (2007). On seeing human: A three-factor theory of anthropomorphism. *Psychological Review*, *114*, 864–886.

Epstein, C. F. (2007). Great divides: The cultural, cognitive, and social bases of the global subordination of women. *American Sociological Review*, *72*, 1–22.

Epstein, S. (1980). The stability of behavior: II. Implications for psychological research. *American Psychologist*, *35*, 790–807.

Epstein, S. (1984). Controversial issues in emotion theory. In P. Shaver (Ed.), *Review of personality and social psychology:* Volume 5: *Emotions, relationships, and health* (pp. 64–88). Beverly Hills CA: Sage.

Erber, R., & Fiske, S. T. (1984). Outcome dependency and attention to inconsistent information. *Journal of Personality and Social Psychology*, *47*, 709–726.

Ermer, E., Guerin, S. A., Cosmides, L., Tooby, J., & Miller, M. B. (2006). Theory of mind broad and narrow: Reasoning about social exchange engages ToM areas, precautionary reasoning does not. *Social Neuroscience*, *1*, 196–219.

Esses, V M., & Zanna, M. P. (1995). Mood and the expression of ethnic stereotypes. *Journal of Personality and Social Psychology*, *69*, 1052–1068.

Essock-Vitale, S. M., & McGuire, M. T. (1985). Women's lives viewed from an evolutionary perspective: II. Patterns of helping. *Ethology and Sociobiology* *6*, 155–173.

Evans, C. R., & Dion, K. L. (1991). Group cohesion and performance: A meta-analysis. *Small Group Research*, *22*, 175–186.

Evans, J. St. B. T. (2008). Dual-processing accounts of reasoning, judgment, and social cognition. *Annual Review of Psychology*, *59*, 255–278.

Evans-Pritchard, E. E. (1972). *Witchcraft, oracles and magic among the Azande*. London: Oxford University Press.

Exline, J. J. (2002). Stumbling blocks on the religious road: Fractured relationships, nagging vices, and the inner struggle to believe. *Psychological Inquiry*, *13*, 182–189.

Exline, J. J., Baumeister, R. F., Bushman, B. J., Campbell, W. K., & Finkel, E. J. (2004). Too proud to let go: Narcissistic entitlement as a barrier to forgiveness. *Journal of Personality and Social Psychology*, *87*, 894–912.

Fabes, R. A., Fultz, J., Eisenberg, N., May-Plumlee, T., & Christopher, F. S. (1989). Effects of rewards on children's prosocial motivation: A socialization study. *Developmental Psychology*, *25*, 509–515.

Fazio, R. H. (1989). On the power and functionality of attitudes: The role of attitude accessibility. In A. R. Pratkanis, S. J. Breckler, & A. G.

Greenwald (Eds.), *Attitude structure and function* (pp. 153–179). Hillsdale, NJ: Erlbaum.

Fazio, R. H. (1990). Multiple processes by which attitudes guide behavior: The MODE model as an integrative framework. In M. P. Zanna (Ed.), *Advances in experimental social psychology* (Vol. 23, pp. 75–109). San Diego, CA: Academic Press.

Fazio, R. H. (2001). On the automatic activation of associated evaluations: An overview. *Cognition and Emotion*, *15*, 115–141.

Fazio, R. H., & Dunton, B. C. (1997). Categorization by race: The impact of automatic and controlled components of racial prejudice. *Journal of Experimental Social Psychology*, *33*, 451–470.

Fazio, R. H., Jackson, J. R., Dunton, B. C., & Williams C. J. (1995). Variability in automatic activation as an unobtrusive measure of racial attitudes: A bona fide pipeline? *Journal of Personality and Social Psychology*, *69*, 1013–1027.

Fazio, R. H., & Olson, M. A. (2003). Implicit measures in social cognition research: Their meaning and use. *Annual Review of Psychology*, *54*, 297–327.

Fazio, R. H., & Powell, M. C. (1997). On the value of knowing one's likes and dislikes: Attitude accessibility, stress, and health in college. *Psychological Science*, *8*, 430–436.

Feather, N. T. (1996). Reactions to penalties for an offense in relation to authoritarianism, values, perceived responsibility, perceived seriousness, and deservingness. *Journal of Personality and Social Psychology*, *71*, 571–587.

Federal Bureau of Investigation. (1996). *Uniform crime reports for the United States 1996*. Washington, DC: Government Printing Office.

Fehr, B. (1996). *Friendship processes*. Thousand Oaks, CA: Sage.

Fehr, B., Baldwin, M., Collins, L., Patterson, S., & Benditt, R. (1999). Anger in close relationships: An interpersonal script analysis. *Personality and Social Psychology Bulletin*, *25*, 299–312.

Fehr, B., & Harasymchuk, C. (2005). The experience of emotion in close relationships: Toward an integration of the emotion-in-relationships and interpersonal script models. *Personal Relationships*, *12*, 181–196.

Fehr, E., & Fischbacher, U. (2004). Social norms and human cooperation. *Trends in Cognitive Sciences*, *8*, 187–190.

Fein, S., & Spencer, S. J. (1997). Prejudice as self-image maintenance: Affirming the self through derogating others. *Journal of Personality and Social Psychology*, *73*, 31–44.

Feingold, A. (1988). Matching for attractiveness in romantic partners and same-sex friends: A meta-analysis and theoretical critique. *Psychological Bulletin, 104*, 226–235.

Feingold, A. (1992a). Gender differences in mate selection preferences: A test of the parental investment model. *Psychological Bulletin, 112*, 125–139.

Feingold, A. (1992b). Good-looking people are not what we think. *Psychological Bulletin, 111*, 304–341.

Feldman, K. A. (1987). Research productivity and scholarly accomplishment of college teachers as related to their instructional effectiveness: A review and exploration. *Research in Higher Education, 26*, 227–298.

Feldman, R. S., Forrest, J. A., & Happ, B. R. (2002). Self-presentation and verbal deception: Do self-presenters lie more? *Basic and Applied Social Psychology, 24*, 163–170.

Feldman, R. S., Tomasian, J. C., & Coats, E. C. (1999). Nonverbal deception abilities and adolescents' social competence: Adolescents with higher social skills are better liars. *Journal of Nonverbal Behavior, 23*, 237–250.

Felmlee, D. H. (1998). "Be careful what you wish for....": A quantitative and qualitative investigation of "fatal attractions." *Personal Relationships, 5*, 235–253.

Ferrin, D. L., Bligh, M. C., & Kohles, J. C. (2007). Can I trust you to trust me?: A theory of trust, monitoring, and cooperation in interpersonal and intergroup relationships. *Group and Organization Management, 32*, 465–499.

Feshbach, S. (1994). Nationalism, patriotism, and aggression: A clarification of functional differences. In L. R. Huesmann (Ed.), *Aggressive behavior: Current perspectives* (pp. 275–291). New York: Plenum.

Festinger, L. (1954). A theory of social comparison processes. *Human Relations, 7*, 117–140.

Festinger, L. (1957). *A theory of cognitive dissonance*. Evanston, IL: Row, Peterson.

Festinger, L., & Carlsmith, J. M. (1959). Cognitive consequences of forced compliance. *Journal of Abnormal and Social Psychology, 58*, 203–210.

Festinger, L., Cartwright, D., Barber, K., Fleischl, J., Gottsdanker, J., Keysen, A., & Leavitt, G. (1948). A study of a rumor: Its origin and spread. *Human Relations, 1*, 464–485.

Festinger, L., Pepitone, A., & Newcomb, T. (1952). Some consequences of de-individuation in a group. *Journal of Abnormal and Social Psychology, 47*, 382–389.

Festinger, L., Riecken, H. W., & Schachter, S. (1956). *When prophecy fails: A social and psychological study of a modern group that predicted the destruction of the world*. New York: Harper.

Festinger, L., Schachter, S., & Back, K. (1950). *Social pressures in informal groups: A study of a housing community*. Palo Alto, CA: Stanford University Press.

Fiedler, F. E. (1964). A contingency model of leadership effectiveness. In L. Berkowitz (Ed.), *Advances in experimental social psychology* (Vol. 1, pp. 149–190). New York: Academic Press.

Fiedler, F. E. (1978). The contingency model and the dynamics of the leadership process. In L. Berkowitz (Ed.), *Advances in experimental social psychology* (Vol. 11, pp. 59–112). New York: Academic Press.

Fischer, P., Greitemeyer, T., & Frey, D. (2007). Ego depletion and positive illusions: Does the construction of positivity require regulatory resources? *Personality and Social Psychology Bulletin, 33*, 1306–1321.

Fischhoff, B., Lichtenstein, S., Slovic, P., Derby, S. L., & Keeney, R. L. (1981). *Acceptable risk*. New York: Cambridge University Press.

Fishbach, A., & Ferguson, M. J. (2007). The goal construct in social psychology. In A. W. Kruglanski & E. T. Higgins (Eds.), *Social psychology: Handbook of basic principles* (pp. 490–515). New York: Guilford.

Fishbein, M., & Ajzen, I. (1975). *Belief attitude, intention, and behavior: An introduction to theory and research*. Reading, MA: Addison-Wesley.

Fiske, A. P. (1992). The four elementary forms of sociality: Framework for a unified theory of social relations. *Psychological Review, 99*, 689–723.

Fiske, A. P. (1993). Social errors in four cultures: Evidence about universal forms of social relations. *Journal of Cross-Cultural Psychology, 24*, 463–494.

Fiske, A. P., & Haslam, N. (1996). Social cognition is thinking about relationships. *Current Directions in Psychological Science, 5*, 149–155.

Fiske, A. P., Haslam, N., & Fiske, S. T. (1991). Confusing one person with another: What errors reveal about the elementary forms of social relations. *Journal of Personality and Social Psychology, 60*, 656–674.

Fiske, A. P., Kitayama, S, Markus, H. R., & Nisbett, R. E. (1998). The cultural matrix of social psychology. In D. T. Gilbert, S. T. Fiske, & G. Lindzey (Eds.), *Handbook of social psychology* (4th ed., Vol. 2, pp. 915–981). New York: McGraw-Hill.

Fiske, S. T. (1980). Attention and weight in person perception: The impact of negative and extreme behavior. *Journal of Personality and Social Psychology, 38*, 889–906.

Fiske, S. T. (1989). Examining the role of intent: Toward understanding its role in stereotyping and prejudice. In J. S. Uleman & J. A. Bargh (Eds.),

*Unintended thought* (pp. 253–283). New York: Guilford Press.

Fiske, S. T. (1992). Thinking is for doing: Portraits of social cognition from daguerreotype to laserphoto. *Journal of Personality and Social Psychology, 63*, 877–889.

Fiske, S. T. (1993a). Controlling other people: The impact of power on stereotyping. *American Psychologist, 48*, 621–628.

Fiske, S. T. (1993b). Social cognition and social perception. *Annual Review of Psychology, 44*, 155–194.

Fiske, S. T. (1995). Social cognition. In A. Tesser (Ed.), *Advanced social psychology* (pp. 149–193). New York: McGraw-Hill.

Fiske, S. T. (1998a). Goal taxonomies, then and now. In J. Darley & J. Cooper (Eds.), *Attribution and social interaction: The legacy of Edward E. Jones* (pp. 153–161). Washington, DC: American Psychological Association.

Fiske, S. T. (1998b). Stereotyping, prejudice, and discrimination. In D. T. Gilbert, S. T. Fiske, & G. Lindzey (Eds.), *Handbook of social psychology* (4th ed., Vol. 2, pp. 357–411). New York: McGraw-Hill.

Fiske, S. T. (2000a). Interdependence and the reduction of prejudice. In S. Oskamp (Ed.), *Reducing prejudice and discrimination* (pp. 115–135). Mahwah, NJ: Erlbaum.

Fiske, S. T. (2000b). Schema. In A. E. Kazdin (Ed.), *Encyclopedia of psychology* (Vol. 7, pp. 158–160). Washington, DC: American Psychological Association.

Fiske, S. T. (2002). What we know now about bias and intergroup conflict, problem of the century. *Current Directions in Psychological Science, 11*, 123–128.

Fiske, S. T. (2004). Developing a program of research. In C. Sansone, C. C. Morf, & A. T. Panter (Eds.), *Handbook of methods in social psychology* (pp. 71–90). Thousand Oaks, CA: Sage.

Fiske, S. T. (2008). Core social motivations, a historical perspective: Views from the couch, consciousness, classroom, computers, and collectives. In J. Y. Shah & W. L. Gardner (Eds.), *Handbook of motivation science* (pp. 3–22). New York: Guilford.

Fiske, S. T. (2010). Interpersonal stratification: Status, power, and subordination. In S. T. Fiske, D. T. Gilbert, & G. Lindzey (Eds.), *Handbook of social psychology* (5th ed.). New York: Wiley.

Fiske, S. T., Bergsieker, H., Russell, A. M., & Williams, L. (2009). Images of black Americans: Then, "them" and now, "Obama!" *DuBois Review: Social Science Research on Race, 6*, 1–19.

Fiske, S. T., Cuddy, A. J. C., & Glick, P. (2007). Universal dimensions of social perception:

Warmth and competence. *Trends in Cognitive Science, 11*, 77–83.

Fiske, S. T., Cuddy, A. J. C., Glick, P., & Xu, J. (2002). A model of (often mixed) stereotype content: Competence and warmth respectively follow from perceived status and competition. *Journal of Personality and Social Psychology, 82*, 878–902.

Fiske, S. T., & Dépret, E. (1996). Control, interdependence, and power: Understanding social cognition in its social context. In W. Stroebe & M. Hewstone (Eds.), *European review of social psychology* (Vol. 7, pp. 31–61). New York: Wiley.

Fiske, S. T., Harris, L. T., & Cuddy, A. J. C. (2004). Policy Forum: Why ordinary people torture enemy prisoners. *Science, 306*, 1482–1483.

Fiske, S. T., Lin, M. H., & Neuberg, S. L. (1999). The Continuum Model: Ten years later. In S. Chaiken & Y. Trope (Eds.), *Dual process theories in social psychology* (pp. 231–254). New York: Guilford.

Fiske, S. T., & Neuberg, S. L. (1990). A continuum of impression formation, from category-based to individuating processes: Influences of information and motivation on attention and interpretation. In M. P. Zanna (Ed.), *Advances in experimental social psychology* (Vol. 23, pp 1–74). New York: Academic Press.

Fiske, S. T., Neuberg, S. L., Beattie, A. E., & Milberg, S. J. (1987). Category-based and attribute-based reactions to others: Some informational conditions of stereotyping and individuating processes. *Journal of Experimental Social Psychology, 23*, 399–427.

Fiske, S. T., & Ruscher, J. B. (1993). Negative interdependence and prejudice: Whence the affect? In D. M. Mackie & D. L. Hamilton (Eds.), *Affect, cognition, and stereotyping: Interactive processes in group perception* (pp. 239–268). San Diego CA: Academic Press.

Fiske, S. T., & Taylor, S. E. (1984). *Social cognition*. New York: Random House.

Fiske, S. T., & Taylor, S. E. (1991). *Social cognition* (2nd ed.). New York: McGraw-Hill.

Fiske, S. T., & Taylor, S. E. (2008). *Social cognition: From brains to culture*. New York: McGraw-Hill.

Fiske, S. T., & Von Hendy, H. M. (1992). Personality feedback and situational norms can control stereotyping processes. *Journal of Personality and Social Psychology, 62*, 577–596.

Fitzgerald, L. F., Swan, S., & Fischer, K. (1995). Why didn't she just report him? The psychological and legal implications of women's responses to sexual harassment. *Journal of Social Issues, 51*, 117–138.

Fletcher, G. J. O., & Clark, M. S. (Eds.) (2001). *Blackwell handbook of social psychology: Interpersonal processes*. Malden, MA: Blackwell.

Flippen, A. R., Hornstein, H. A., Siegal, W. E., & Weitzman, E. A. (1996). A comparison of similarity and interdependence as triggers for in-group formation. *Personality and Social Psychology Bulletin*, *22*, 882–893.

Florian, V., Mikulincer, M., & Hirschberger, G. (2002). The anxiety-buffering function of close relationships: Evidence that relationship commitment acts as a terror management mechanism. *Journal of Personality and Social Psychology*, *82*, 527–542.

Foels, R., Driskell, J. E., Mullen, B., & Salas, E. (2000). The effects of democratic leadership on group member satisfaction: An integration. *Small Group Research*, *31*, 676–701.

Forest, D., Clark, M. S., Mills, J., & Isen, A. M. (1979). Helping as a function of feeling state and nature of the helping. *Motivation and Emotion*, *3*, 161–169.

Forgas, J. P. (1998). Asking nicely? The effects of mood on responding to more or less polite requests. *Personality and Social Psychology Bulletin*, *24*, 173–185.

Forgas, J. P., & Fiedler, K. (1996). Us and them: Mood effects on intergroup discrimination. *Journal of Personality and Social Psychology*, *70*, 28–40.

Förster, J., & Liberman, N. (2007). Knowledge activation. In A. W. Kruglanski & E. T. Higgins (Eds.), *Social psychology: Handbook of basic principles* (2nd ed., pp. 201–231). New York: Guilford.

Forsyth, D. R. (1995). Norms. In A. S. R. Manstead & M. Hewstone (Eds.), *Blackwell encyclopedia of social psychology* (pp. 412–417). Malden, MA: Blackwell.

Forsyth, D. R. (1998). Methodological advances in the study of group dynamics. *Group Dynamics*, *2*, 211–212.

Foster, C. A., & Rusbult, C. E. (1999). Injustice and powerseeking. *Personality and Social Psychology Bulletin*, *25*, 834–849.

Frable, D. E. S. (1997). Gender, racial, ethnic, sexual, and class identities. *Annual Review of Psychology*, *48*, 130–162.

Franco, F. M., & Maass, A. (1996). Implicit versus explicit strategies of out-group discrimination: The role of intentional control in biased language use and reward allocation. *Journal of Language and Social Psychology*, *15*, 335–359.

Franco, F. M., & Maass, A. (1999). Intentional control over prejudice: When the choice of the measure matters. *European Journal of Social Psychology*, *29*, 469–477.

Franklin, K. M., Janoff-Bulman, R., & Roberts, J. E. (1990). Long-term impact of parental divorce on optimism and trust: Changes in general assumptions or narrow beliefs? *Journal of Personality and Social Psychology*, *59*, 743–755.

Frazier, C. (1997). *Cold mountain*. New York: Atlantic Monthly Press.

Fredrickson, B. L., Tugade, M. M., Waugh, C. E., & Larkin, G. R. (2003). What good are positive emotions in crisis? A prospective study of resilience and emotions following the terrorist attacks on the United States on September 11th, 2001. *Journal of Personality and Social Psychology*, *84*, 365–376.

Freedman, J. L., & Fraser, S. C. (1966). Compliance without pressure: The foot-in-the-door technique. *Journal of Personality and Social Psychology*, *4*, 195–202.

Freedman, J. L., & Sears, D. O. (1965). Selective exposure. In L. Berkowitz (Ed.), *Advances in experimental social psychology* (Vol. 2, pp. 57–97). San Diego, CA: Academic Press.

Freitas, A. L., Liberman, N., & Higgins, E. T. (2002). Regulatory fit and resisting temptation during goal pursuit. *Journal of Experimental Social Psychology*, *38*, 291–298.

Freitas, A. L., Liberman, N., Salovey, P., & Higgins, E. T. (2002). When to begin? Regulatory focus and initiating goal pursuit. *Personality and Social Psychology Bulletin*, *28*, 121–130.

French, J. R. P. Jr., & Raven, B. H. (1959). The bases of power. In D. Cartwright (Ed.), *Studies in social power* (pp. 150–167). Ann Arbor, MI: Institute for Social Research.

Frenzen, J. K., & Davis, H. L. (1990). Purchasing behavior in embedded markets. *Journal of Consumer Research*, *17*, 1–12.

Frey, D. L. (1986). Recent research on selective exposure to information. In L. Berkowitz (Ed.), *Advances in experimental social psychology* (Vol. 19, pp. 41–80). New York: Academic Press.

Frey, D. L., & Gaertner, S. L. (1986). Helping and the avoidance of inappropriate interracial behavior. A strategy that perpetuates a nonprejudiced self-image. *Journal of Personality and Social Psychology*, *50*, 1083–1090.

Friedman, J. N. W., Oltmanns, T. F., Gleason, M. E. J., & Turkheimer, E. (2006). Mixed impressions: Reactions of strangers to people with pathological personality traits. *Journal of Research in Personality*, *40*, 395–410.

Frischen, A., Bayliss, A. P., & Tipper, S. P. (2007). Gaze cueing of attention: Visual attention, social cognition, and individual differences. *Psychological Bulletin*, *133*, 694–724.

Froming, W. J., Nasby, W. J., & McManus, J. (1998). Prosocial self-schemas, self-awareness, and children's prosocial behavior. *Journal of Personality and Social Psychology, 75*, 766–777.

Fujino, D. C. (1997). The rates, patterns and reasons for forming heterosexual interracial dating relationships among Asian Americans. *Journal of Social and Personal Relationships, 14*, 809–828.

Fujita, K., Eyal, T., Chaiken, S., Trope, Y., & Liberman, N. (2008). Influencing attitudes toward near and distant objects. *Journal of Experimental Social Psychology, 44*, 562–572.

Fuller, J. B., Patterson, C. E. P., Hester, K., & Stringer, D. Y. (1996). A quantitative review of research on charismatic leadership. *Psychological Reports, 78*, 271–287.

Funder, D. C. (1987). Errors and mistakes: Evaluating the accuracy of social judgment. *Psychological Bulletin, 101*, 75–90.

Funder, D. C. (2001). Personality. *Annual Review of Psychology, 52*, 197–221.

Furnham, A. (1985). Just world beliefs in an unjust society: A cross cultural comparison. *European Journal of Social Psychology, 15*, 363–366.

Fussell, S. R., & Krauss, R. M. (1989). The effects of intended audience on message production and comprehension: Reference in a common ground framework. *Journal of Experimental Social Psychology, 25*, 203–219.

Gable, S. L. (2006). Approach and avoidance social motives and goals. *Journal of Personality, 74*, 175–222.

Gable, S. L., Reis, H. T., Impett, E. A., & Asher, E. R. (2004). What do you do when things go right? The intrapersonal and interpersonal benefits of sharing positive events. *Journal of Personality and Social Psychology, 87*, 228–245.

Gabriel, S., & Gardner, W. L. (1999). Are there "his" and "hers" types of interdependence? The implications of gender differences in collective versus relational interdependence for affect, behavior, and cognition. *Journal of Personality and Social Psychology, 77*, 642–655.

Gaertner, S. L., & Dovidio, J. F. (1977). The subtlety of white racism, arousal, and helping behavior. *Journal of Personality and Social Psychology, 35*, 691–707.

Gaertner, S. L., & Dovidio, J. F. (1986). The aversive form of racism. In J. F. Dovidio & S. L. Gaertner (Eds.), *Prejudice, discrimination, and racism* (pp. 61–88). Thousand Oaks, CA: Academic Press.

Gaertner, S. L., & Dovidio, J. F. (2000). *Reducing intergroup bias: The common ingroup identity model*. Philadelphia: Psychology Press.

Gaertner, S. L., Dovidio, J. F., & Johnson, G. (1982). Race of victim, nonresponsive bystanders, and helping behavior. *Journal of Social Psychology, 117*, 69–77.

Gaertner, S. L., & McLaughlin, J. P. (1983). Racial stereotypes: Associations and ascriptions of positive and negative characteristics. *Social Psychology Quarterly, 46*, 23–30.

Gaertner, S. L., Sedikides, C., & Graetz, K. (1999). In search of self-definition: Motivational primacy of the individual self, motivational primacy of the collective self, or contextual primacy? *Journal of Personality and Social Psychology, 76*, 5–18.

Gailliot, M. T., Baumeister, R. F., DeWall, C. N., Maner, J. K., Plant, E. A., Tice, D. M., Brewer, L. E., & Schmeichel, B. J. (2007). Self-control relies on glucose as a limited energy source: Willpower is more than a metaphor. *Journal of Personality and Social Psychology, 92*, 325–336.

Gaines, S. O., Jr., & Liu, J. H. (2000). Multicultural/multiracial relationships. In C. Hendrick & S. S. Henrick (Eds.), *Close relationships: A sourcebook* (pp. 97–108). Thousand Oaks, CA: Sage.

Galea, S., Ahern, J., Resnick, H., Kilpatrick, D., Buccuvalas, M., Gold, J., & Vlahov, D. (2002). Psychological sequelae of September 11, 2001 terrorist attacks in New York City. *New England Journal of Medicine, 346*, 982–987.

Galinsky, A. D., Gruenfeld, D. H., & Magee, J. C. (2003). From power to action. *Journal of Personality and Social Psychology, 85*, 453–466.

Galinsky, A. D., Magee, J. C., Inesi, M. E., & Gruenfeld, D. H. (2006). Power and perspectives not taken. *Psychological Science, 17*, 1068–1074.

Galinsky, A. D., & Moskowitz, G. B. (2000). Perspective-taking: Decreasing stereotype expression, stereotype accessibility, and in-group favoritism. *Journal of Personality and Social Psychology, 78*, 708–724.

Galinsky, A. D., Stone, J., & Cooper, J. (2000). The reinstatement of dissonance and psychological discomfort following failed affirmations. *European Journal of Social Psychology, 30*, 123–147.

Gangestad, S. W. (1993). Sexual selection and physical attractiveness: Implications for mating dynamics. *Human Nature, 4*, 205–235.

Gangestad, S. W., & Snyder, M. (2000). Self-monitoring: Appraisal and reappraisal. *Psychological Bulletin, 126*, 530–555.

Garcia, S., Stonson, L., Ickes, W., Bissonnette, V., & Briggs, S. R. (1991). Shyness and physical attractiveness in mixed-sex dyads. *Journal of Personality and Social Psychology, 61*, 35–49.

Gardner, W. L., & Knowles, M. L. (2008). Love makes you real: Favorite television characters are perceived as "real" in a social facilitation paradigm. *Social Cognition, 26*, 156–168.

Gardner, W. L., Pickett, C. L., Jefferis, V., & Knowles, M. (2005). On the outside looking in:

Loneliness and social monitoring. *Personality and Social Psychology Bulletin*, *31*, 1549–1560.

Gastil, J. (1994). A meta-analytic review of the productivity and satisfaction of democratic and autocratic leadership. *Small Group Research*, *25*, 384–410.

Gawronski, B. (2004). Theory-based bias correction in dispositional inference: The fundamental attribution error is dead, long live the correspondence bias. *European Review of Social Psychology*, *15*, 83–217.

Gawronski, B., & Bodenhausen, G. V. (2006). Associative and propositional processes in evaluation: An integrative review of implicit and explicit attitude change. *Psychological Bulletin*, *132*, 692–731.

Geen, R. G. (1968). Effects of frustration, attack, and prior training in aggressiveness upon aggressive behavior. *Journal of Personality and Social Psychology*, *9*, 316–321.

Geen, R. G. (1991). Social motivation. *Annual Review of Psychology*, *42*, 377–399.

Geen, R. G. (1998). Aggression and antisocial behavior. In D. T. Gilbert, S. T. Fiske, & G. Lindzey (Eds.)., *The handbook of social psychology* (4th ed., Vol. 2, pp. 317–356). New York: McGraw-Hill.

Geen, R. G., & Quanty, M. B. (1977). The catharsis of aggression: An evaluation of a hypothesis. In L. Berkowitz (Ed.), *Advances in experimental social psychology* (Vol. 10, pp. 1–37). New York: Academic Press.

Geertz, C. (1975). On the nature of anthropological understanding. *American Scientist*, *63*, 47–53.

Gelfand, M. J., & Christakopoulou, S. (1999). Culture and negotiator cognition: Judgment accuracy and negotiation processes in individualistic and collectivistic cultures. *Organizational Behavior and Human Decision Processes*, *79*, 248–269.

Gelfand, M. J., Erez, M., & Aycan, Z. (2007). Cross-cultural organizational behavior. *Annual Review of Psychology*, *58*, 479–514.

George, J. M., & Brief, A. P. (1992). Feeling good–doing good: A conceptual analysis of the mood at work–organizational spontaneity relationship. *Psychological Bulletin*, *112*, 310–329.

George, L. K., Ellison, C. G., & Larson, D. B. (2002). Explaining the relationships between religious involvement and health. *Psychological Inquiry*, *13*, 190–200.

Georgesen, J. C., Harris, M. J., & Milich, R. (1999). "Just teasing ... ": Personality effects on perceptions and life narratives of childhood teasing. *Personality and Social Psychology Bulletin*, *25*, 1254–1267.

Gerstner, C. R., & Day, D. V. (1997). Meta-analytic review of leader-member exchange theory: Correlates and construct issues. *Journal of Applied Psychology*, *82*, 827–844.

Giancola, P. R., & Zeichner, A. (1995). Construct validity of a competitive reaction time aggression paradigm. *Aggressive Behavior*, *21*, 199–204.

Gibbons, F. X., Eggleston, T. J., & Benthin, A. C. (1997). Cognitive reactions to smoking relapse: The reciprocal relation between dissonance and self-esteem. *Journal of Personality and Social Psychology*, *72*, 184–195.

Gibbs, K. A., Urbanowski, L. A., & Greenberg, E. P. (2008). Genetic determinants of self identity and social recognition in bacteria. *Science*, *321*, 256–259.

Gigone, D., & Hastie, R. (1997). The impact of information on small group choice. *Journal of Personality and Social Psychology*, *72*, 132–140.

Gilbert, D. T. (1998). Ordinary personology. In D. T. Gilbert, S. T. Fiske, & G. Lindzey (Eds.), *The handbook of social psychology* (4th ed., Vol. 2, pp. 89–150). New York: McGraw-Hill.

Gilbert, D. T., Brown, R. P., Pinel, E. C., & Wilson, T. D. (2000). The illusion of external agency. *Journal of Personality and Social Psychology*, *79*, 690–700.

Gilbert, D. T., & Hixon, J. G. (1991). The trouble of thinking: Activation and application of stereotypic beliefs. *Journal of Personality and Social Psychology*, *60*, 509–517.

Gilbert, D. T., & Malone, P. S. (1995). The correspondence bias. *Psychological Bulletin*, *117*, 21–38.

Gilbert, D. T., Pelham, B. W., & Krull, D. S. (1988). On cognitive busyness: When person perceivers meet persons perceived. *Journal of Personality and Social Psychology*, *54*, 733–740.

Gilbert, D. T., Pinel, E. C. C., Wilson, T. D., Blumberg, S. J., & Wheatley, T. P. (1998). Immune neglect: A source of durability bias in affective forecasting. *Journal of Personality and Social Psychology*, *75*, 617–638.

Gilbert, D. T., & Wilson, T. D. (2001). Prospection: Experiencing the future. *Science*, *317*, 1351–1354.

Gilovich, T. (1987). Secondhand information and social judgment. *Journal of Experimental Social Psychology*, *23*, 59–74.

Gilovich, T., & Savitsky, K. (1999). The spotlight effect and the illusion of transparency: Egocentric assessments of how we are seen by others. *Current Directions in Psychological Science*, *8*, 165–168.

Gilovich, T., Savitsky, K., & Medvec, V. H. (1998). The illusion of transparency: Biased assessments of others' ability to read one's emotional states.

*Journal of Personality and Social Psychology*, *75*, 332–346.

Giner-Sorolla, R. (2004). Is affective material in attitudes more accessible than cognitive material? The moderating role of attitude basis. *European Journal of Social Psychology*, *34*, 761–780.

Gladue, B. A., Boechler, M., & McCaul, K. D. (1989). Hormonal response to competition in human males. *Aggressive Behavior*, *15*, 409–422.

Gleicher, F., & Weary, G. (1995). Control motivation. In A. S. R. Manstead & M. Hewstone (Eds.), *Blackwell encyclopedia of social psychology* (pp. 132–136). Oxford, UK: Blackwell.

Glick, P., Diebold, J., Bailey-Werner, B., & Zhu, L. (1997). The two faces of Adam: Ambivalent sexism and polarized attitudes toward women. *Personality and Social Psychology Bulletin*, *23*, 1323–1334.

Glick, P., & Fiske, S. T. (1996). The Ambivalent Sexism Inventory: Differentiating hostile and benevolent sexism. *Journal of Personality and Social Psychology*, *70*, 491–512.

Glick, P., & Fiske, S. T. (2001a). Ambivalent sexism. In M. P. Zanna (Ed.), *Advances in experimental social psychology* (Vol. 33, pp. 115–188). Thousand Oaks, CA: Academic Press.

Glick, P., & Fiske, S. T. (2001b). Ambivalent stereotypes as legitimizing ideologies: Differentiating paternalistic and envious prejudice. In J. T. Jost & B. Major (Eds.), *The psychology of legitimacy* (pp. 278–306). New York: Cambridge University Press.

Glick, P., & Fiske, S. T. (2001c). An ambivalent alliance: Hostile and benevolent sexism as complementary justifications of gender inequality. *American Psychologist*, *56*, 109–118.

Glick, P., Fiske, S. T., Mladinic, A., Saiz, J. L., Abrams, D., Masser, B., Adetoun, B., Osagie, J. E., Akande, A., Alao, A., Brunner, A., Willemsen, T. M., Chipeta, K., Dardenne, B., Dijksterhuis, A., Wigboldus, D., Eckes, T., Six-Materna, I., Expósito, F., Moya, M., Foddy, M., Kim, H. J., Lameiras, M., Sotelo, M. J., Mucchi-Faina, A., Romani, M., Sakalli, N., Udegbe, B., Yamamoto, M., Ui, M., Ferreira, M. C., & López López, W. (2000). Beyond prejudice as simple antipathy: Hostile and benevolent sexism across cultures. *Journal of Personality and Social Psychology*, *79*, 763–775.

Glick, P., Sakalli Ugurlu, N., Feffeira, M. C., & Aguiar de Souza, M. (2002). Ambivalent sexism and attitudes toward wife abuse in Turkey and Brazil. *Psychology of Women Quarterly*, *26*, 291–296.

Godfrey, D. K., Jones, E. E., & Lord, C. G. (1986). Self-promotion is not ingratiating. *Journal of Personality and Social Psychology*, *50*, 106–115.

Goethals, G. R., & Darley, J. M. (1977). Social comparison theory: An attributional approach. In J. M. Suls & R. L. Miller (Eds.), *Social comparison processes: Theoretical and empirical perspectives* (pp. 55–77). Washington, DC: Hemisphere/Halsted.

Goff, P. A., Eberhardt, J. L., Williams, M. J., & Jackson, M. C. (2008). Not yet human: Implicit knowledge, historical dehumanization, and contemporary consequences. *Journal of Personality and Social Psychology*, *94*, 292–306.

Goffman, E. (1963). *Stigma: Notes on the management of spoiled identity*. Englewood Cliffs, NJ: Prentice-Hall.

Goffman, E. (1967). *Interaction ritual: Essays on face-to-face behavior*. Garden City, NY: Doubleday.

Goldberg, S. (1973). *The inevitability of patriarchy*. New York: Morrow.

Golden, A. (1998). *Memoirs of a geisha*. New York: Knopf.

Goldstone, R. L., Roberts, M. E., & Gureckis, T. M. (2008). Emergent processes in group behavior. *Current Directions in Psychological Science*, *17*, 10–15.

Gollwitzer, P. M., & Brandstatter, V. (1997). Implementation intentions and effective goal pursuit. *Journal of Personality and Social Psychology*, *73*, 186–199.

Gollwitzer, P. M., Heckhausen, H., & Steller, B. (1990). Deliberative vs. implemental mind-sets: Cognitive tuning toward congruous thoughts and information. *Journal of Personality and Social Psychology*, *59*, 1119–1127.

Gollwitzer, P. M., & Sheeran, P. (2006). Implementation intentions and goal achievement: A meta-analysis of effects and processes. In M. P. Zanna (Ed.), *Advances in experimental social psychology* (Vol. 38, pp. 69–119). San Diego: Elsevier Academic Press.

Gonzales, P. M., Blanton, H., & Williams, K. J. (2002). The effects of stereotype threat and double-minority status on the test performance of Latino women. *Personality and Social Psychology Bulletin*, *28*, 659–670.

Goodstadt, B., & Kipnis, D. (1970). Situational influences on the use of power. *Journal of Applied Psychology*, *54*, 201–207.

Goodwin, R., & Tang, D. (1991). Preferences for friends and close relationships partners: A cross-cultural comparison. *Journal of Social Psychology*, *131*, 579–581.

Goodwin, S. A., Fiske, S. T., Rosen, L. D., & Rosenthal, A. M. (2002). The eye of the beholder: Romantic goals and impression biases. *Journal of Experimental Social Psychology*, *38*, 232–241.

Goodwin, S. A., Gubin, A., Fiske, S. T., & Yzerbyt, V. (2000). Power can bias impression formation: Stereotyping subordinates by default and by design. *Group Processes and Intergroup Relations*, *3*, 227–256.

Gosling, S. D., Ko, S. J., Mannarelli, T., & Morris, M. E. (2002). A room with a cue: Personality judgments based on offices and bedrooms. *Journal of Personality and Social Psychology*, *82*, 379–398.

Gottman, J. M., & Levenson, R. W. (1992). Marital processes predictive of later dissolution: Behavior, physiology, and health. *Journal of Personality and Social Psychology*, *63*, 221–233.

Gould, S. J. *The mismeasure of man*. New York: Norton.

Gouldner, A. W. (1960). The norm of reciprocity: A preliminary statement. *American Sociological Review*, *25*, 161–179.

Graen, G., Alvares, K., Orris, J. B., & Martella, J. A. (1970). Contingency model of leadership effectiveness: Antecedent and evidential results. *Psychological Bulletin*, *74*, 285–296.

Gray, H. M., & Ambady, N. (2006). Methods for the study of nonverbal communication. In V. Manusov & M. L. Patterson (Eds.), *The Sage handbook of nonverbal communication* (pp. 41–58). Thousand Oaks, CA: Sage.

Gray, H. M., Gray, K., & Wegner, D. M. (2007). Dimensions of mind perception. *Science*, *315*, 619.

Green, D. P., Glaser, J., & Rich, A. (1998). From lynching to gay bashing: The elusive connection between economic conditions and hate crime. *Journal of Personality and Social Psychology*, *75*, 82–92.

Green, D. P., Strolovitch, D. Z., & Wong, J. S. (1998). Defended neighborhoods, integration, and racially motivated crime. *American Journal of Sociology*, *104*, 372–403.

Greenberg, J., Pyszczynski, T., Solomon, S., Rosenblatt, A., Veeder, M., Kirkland, S., & Lyon, D. (1990). Evidence for terror management theory II: The effects of mortality salience on reactions to those who threaten or bolster the cultural worldview. *Journal of Personality and Social Psychology*, *58*, 308–318.

Greenberg, J., Simon, L., Pyszczynski, T., Shelton, S., & Chatel, D. (1992). Terror management and tolerance: Does mortality salience always intensify negative reactions to others who threaten one's worldview? *Journal of Personality and Social Psychology*, *63*, 212–220.

Greenberg, J., Williams, K. D., & O'Brien, M. K. (1986). Considering the harshest verdict first: Biasing effects on mock juror verdicts. *Personality and Social Psychology Bulletin*, *12*, 41–50.

Greene, J. D., & Haidt, J. (2002). How (and where) does moral judgment work? *Trends in Cognitive Sciences*, *6*, 517–523.

Greene, J. D., Sommerville, R. B., Nystrom, L. E., Darley, J. M., & Cohen, J. D. (2001). An fMRI investigation of emotional engagement in moral judgment. *Science*, *293*, 2105–2108.

Greenland, K., & Brown, R. J. (1999). Categorization and intergroup anxiety in contact between British and Japanese nationals. *European Journal of Social Psychology*, *29*, 503–521.

Greenwald, A. G., Banaji, M. R., Rudman, L. A., Farnham, S. D., Nosek, B. A., & Mellott, D. S. (2002). A unified theory of implicit attitudes, stereotypes, self-esteem, and self-concept. *Psychological Review*, *109*, 3–25.

Greenwald, A. G., McGhee, D. E., & Schwartz, J. L. K. (1998). Measuring individual differences in implicit cognition: The implicit association test. *Journal of Personality and Social Psychology Bulletin*, *74*, 1464–1480.

Greenwald, A. G., Nosek, B. A., & Banaji, M. R. (2003). Understanding and using the Implicit Association Test: I. An improved scoring algorithm. *Journal of Personality and Social Psychology*, *85*, 197–216.

Greenwald, A. G., Poehlman, T. A., Uhlmann, E., & Banaji, M. R. (2009). Understanding and using the Implicit Association Test: III. Meta-analysis of predictive validity. *Journal of Personality and Social Psychology*, *97*, 17–41.

Grieve, P. G., & Hogg, M. A. (1999). Subjective uncertainty and intergroup discrimination in the minimal group situation. *Personality and Social Psychology Bulletin*, *25*, 926–940.

Griffin, D. W., & Buehler, R. (1993). Role of construal processes in conformity and dissent. *Journal of Personality and Social Psychology*, *65*, 657–669.

Griffitt, W. (1968). Attraction toward a stranger as a function of direct and associated reinforcement. *Psychonomic Science*, *11*, 147–148.

Griffitt, W., & Veitch, R. (1971). Hot and crowded: Influence of population density and temperature on interpersonal affective behavior. *Journal of Personality and Social Psychology*, *17*, 92–98.

Gross, S. R., & Miller, N. (1997). The "golden section" and bias in perceptions of social consensus. *Personality and Social Psychology Bulletin*, *1*, 241–271.

Gruenfeld, D. H., Inesi, M. E., Magee, J. C., & Galinsky, A. D. (2008). Power and the objectification of social targets. *Journal of Personality and Social Psychology*, *95*, 111–127.

Gruenfeld, D. H., Martorana, P. V., & Fan, E. T. (2000). What do groups learn from their worldliest members? Direct and indirect influence in dynamic teams. *Organizational Behavior and Human Decision Processes*, *82*, 45–59.

Grusec, J. E. (1991). The socialization of altruism. In M. S. Clark (Ed.), *Review of personality and social psychology: Prosocial behavior* (Vol. 12, pp. 9–13). Newburg Park, CA: Sage.

Guadagno, R. E., Asher, T., Demaine, L. J., & Cialdini, R. B. (2001). When saying yes leads to saying no: Preference for consistency and the reverse foot-in-the door effect. *Personality and Social Psychology Bulletin*, *27*, 859–867.

Guenther, C. L., & Alicke, M. D. (2008). Self-enhancement and belief perseverance. *Journal of Experimental Social Psychology*, *44*, 706–712.

Guimond, S. (Ed.) (2006). *Social comparison and social psychology: Understanding cognition, intergroup relations, and culture*. New York: Cambridge.

Guimond, S., Dambrun, M., Michinov, N., & Duarte, S. (2003). Does social dominance generate prejudice? Integrating individual and contextual determinants of intergroup cognitions. *Journal of Personality and Social Psychology*, *84*, 697–721.

Guinote, A. (2007a). Power affects basic cognition: Increased attentional inhibition and flexibility. *Journal of Experimental Social Psychology*, *43*, 685–697.

Guinote, A. (2007b). Power and goal pursuit. *Personality and Social Psychology Bulletin*, *33*, 1076–1087.

Guinote, A. (2008). Power and affordances: When the situation has more power over powerful than powerless individuals. *Journal of Personality and Social Psychology*, *95*, 237–252.

Guinote, A., Brown, M., & Fiske, S. T. (2006). Minority status decreases sense of control and increases interpretive processing. *Social Cognition*, *24*, 169–186.

Guinote, A., Judd, C. M., & Brauer, M. (2002). Effects of power on perceived and objective group variability: Evidence that more powerful groups are more variable. *Journal of Personality and Social Psychology*, *82*, 708–721.

Gully, S. M., Devine, D. J., & Whitney, D. J. (1995). A meta-analysis of cohesion and performance: Effects of levels of analysis and task interdependence. *Small Group Research*, *26*, 497–520.

Gurtman, M. B. (1992). Trust, distrust, and interpersonal problems: A circumplex analysis. *Journal of Personality and Social Psychology*, *62*, 989–1002.

Guzzo, R. A., & Dickson, M. W. (1996). Teams in organizations: Recent research on performance and effectiveness. *Annual Review of Psychology*, *47*, 307–338.

Haddock, G., & Zanna, M. P. (1994). Preferring "housewives" to "feminists": Categorization and the favorability of attitudes toward women. *Psychology of Women Quarterly*, *18*, 25–52.

Haddock, G., & Zanna, M. P. (1998). Assessing the impact of affective and cognitive information in predicting attitudes toward capital punishment. *Law and Human Behavior*, *22*, 325–339.

Haddock, G., Zanna, M. P., & Esses, V. M. (1993). Assessing the structure of prejudicial attitudes: The case of attitudes toward homosexuals. *Journal of Personality and Social Psychology*, *65*, 1105–1118.

Haidt, J. (2001). The emotional dog and its rational tail: A social intuitionist approach to moral judgment. *Psychological Review*, *108*, 814–834.

Haidt, J. (2007). The new synthesis in moral psychology. *Science*, *316*, 998–1002.

Hall, J. A. (1978). Gender effects in decoding nonverbal cues. *Psychological Bulletin*, *85*, 845–857.

Hall, J. A. (1984). *Nonverbal sex differences*. Baltimore: Johns Hopkins.

Hall, J. A., & Carter, J. D. (1999). Gender-stereotype accuracy as an individual difference. *Journal of Personality and Social Psychology*, *77*, 350–359.

Hamill, R., Wilson, T. D., & Nisbett, R. E. (1980). Insensitivity to sample bias: Generalizing from atypical cases. *Journal of Personality and Social Psychology*, *39*, 578–589.

Hamilton, D. L., Katz, L. B., & Leirer, V. O. (1980). Cognitive representation of personality impressions: Organizational processes in first impression formation. *Journal of Personality and Social Psychology*, *39*, 1050–1063.

Hamilton, D. L., & Rose, T. L. (1980). Illusory correlation and the maintenance of stereotypic beliefs. *Journal of Personality and Social Psychology*, *39*, 832–845.

Hamilton, D. L., & Sherman, S. J. (1996). Perceiving persons and groups. *Psychological Review*, *103*, 336–355.

Hamilton, D. L., Sherman, S. J., & Castelli, L. (2002). A group by any other name: The role of entitativity in group perception. In W. Stroebe & M. Hewstone (Eds.), *European review of social psychology* (Vol. 12, pp. 139–166). New York: Wiley.

Hamilton, W. D. (1964). The genetical evolution of social behavior: I & II. *Journal of Theoretical Biology*, *7*, 1–32.

Haney, C., Banks, C., & Zimbardo, P. G. (1973). Interpersonal dynamics in a simulated prison. *International Journal of Criminology and Penology*, *1*, 69–97.

Hardin, C. D., & Higgins, E. T. (1996). Shared reality: How social verification makes the subjective objective. In R. M. Sorrentino & E. T. Higgins (Eds.), *Handbook of motivation and cognition* (Vol. 3, pp. 28–34). New York: Guilford.

Harker, L. A., & Keltner, D. (2001). Expressions of positive emotion in women's college yearbook pictures and their relationship to personality and life outcomes across adulthood. *Journal of Personality and Social Psychology, 80*, 112–124.

Harlow, H. F. (1962). The heterosexual affectional system in monkeys. *American Psychologist, 17*, 1–9.

Harmon-Jones, E., Harmon-Jones, C., Fearn, M., Sigelman, J. D., & Johnson, P. (2008). Left frontal cortical activation and spreading of alternatives: Tests of the action-based model of dissonance. *Journal of Personality and Social Psychology, 94*, 1–15.

Harmon-Jones, E., & Mills, J. (Eds.) (1999). *Cognitive dissonance: Progress on a pivotal theory in social psychology*. Washington, DC: American Psychological Association.

Harris, K. J., Kacmar, K. M., Zivnuska, S., & Shaw, J. D. (2007). The impact of political skill on impression management effectiveness. *Journal of Applied Psychology, 92*, 278–285.

Harris, L. T., & Fiske, S. T. (2006). Dehumanizing the lowest of the low: Neuroimaging responses to extreme out-groups. *Psychological Science, 17*, 847–853.

Harris, L. T., & Fiske, S. T. (2007). Social groups that elicit disgust are differentially processed in mPFC. *Social Cognitive and Affective Neuroscience, 2*, 45–51.

Harris, L. T., Todorov, A., & Fiske, S. T. (2005). Attributions on the brain: Neuro-imaging dispositional inferences, beyond theory of mind. *NeuroImage, 28*, 763–769.

Harris, M. J., & Rosenthal, R. (1985). Mediation of interpersonal expectancy effects: 31 meta-analyses. *Psychological Bulletin, 97*, 363–386.

Hart, A. J., Whalen, P. J., Shin, L. M., McInerney, S. C., Fischer, H., & Rauch, S. L. (2000). Differential response in the human amygdala to racial outgroup vs ingroup face stimuli. *Neuroreport: For Rapid Communication of Neuroscience Research, 11*, 2351–2355.

Hart, K. (2008). The rise of alter egos in everybody's space. *Washington Post, 131* (158).

Hartup, W. W., & Stevens, N. (1999). Friendship and adaptation across the life span. *Current Directions in Psychological Science, 8*, 76–79.

Harvey, J. H., & Omarzu, J. (1997). Minding the close relationship. *Personality and Social Psychology Review, 1*, 224–240.

Harvey, J. H., & Pauwels, B. G. (1999). Recent developments in close-relationships theory.

*Current Directions in Psychological Science, 8*, 93–95.

Harvey, M. D., & Enzle, M E. (1981). A cognitive model of social norms for understanding the transgression-helping effect. *Journal of Personality and Social Psychology, 41*, 866–875.

Hass, R. G., Katz, I., Rizzo, N., Bailey, J., & Eisenstadt, D. (1991). Cross-racial appraisal as related to attitude ambivalence and cognitive complexity. *Personality and Social Psychology Bulletin, 17*, 83–92.

Hastie, R., & Park, B. (1986). The relationship between memory and judgment depends on whether the judgment task is memory-based or on-line. *Psychological Review, 93*, 258–268.

Hastorf, A. H., & Cantril, H. (1954). They saw a game: A case study. *Journal of Abnormal and Social Psychology, 49*, 129–134.

Hatfield, E., Cacioppo, J. T., & Rapson, R. L. (1993). Emotional contagion. *Current Directions in Psychological Science, 2*, 96–99.

Hattie, J., & Marsh, H. W. (1996). The relationship between research and teaching: A meta-analysis. *Review of Educational Research, 66*, 507–542.

Haxby, J. V., Hoffman, E. A., & Gobbini, M. I. (2002). Human neural systems for face recognition and social communication. *Biological Psychiatry, 51*, 59–67.

Hazan, C., & Shaver, P. R. (1987). Romantic love conceptualized as an attachment process. *Journal of Personality and Social Psychology, 52*, 511–524.

Hazan, C., & Shaver, P. R. (1994). Attachment as an organizational framework for research on close relationships. *Psychological Inquiry, 5*, 1–22.

Head, B. (1971). *Maru*. Exeter, NH: Heinemann.

Heath, C., Bell, C., & Sternberg, E. (2001). Emotional selection in memes: The case of urban legends. *Journal of Personality and Social Psychology, 81*, 1028–1041.

Heatherton, T. F., & Baumeister, R. F. (1991). Binge eating as escape from self-awareness. *Psychological Bulletin, 110*, 86–108.

Heatherton, T. F., Kleck, R. E., Hebl, M. R., & Hull, J. G. (Eds.) (2000). *The social psychology of stigma*. New York: Guilford.

Heatherton, T. F., & Polivy, J. (1991). Development and validation of a scale for measuring state self-esteem. *Journal of Personality and Social Psychology, 60*, 895–910.

Heatherton, T. F., Striepe, M., & Wittenberg, L. (1998). Emotional distress and disinhibited eating: The role of self. *Personality and Social Psychology Bulletin, 24*, 301–313.

Heatherton, T. F., & Vohs, K. D. (2000). Interpersonal evaluations following threats to self: Role of self-esteem. *Journal of Personality and Social Psychology*, *78*, 725–736.

Heatherton, T. F., Wyland, C. L., Macrae, C. N., Demos, K. E., Denny, B. T., & Kelley, W. M. (2006). Medial prefrontal activity differentiates self from close others. *Social Cognitive and Affective Neuroscience*, *1*, 18–25.

Hecht, T. D., Allen, N. J., Klammer, J. D., & Kelly, E. C. (2002). Group beliefs, ability, and performance. *Group Dynamics*, *6*, 143–152.

Heider, F. (1958). *The psychology of interpersonal relations*. New York: Wiley.

Heider, J. D., Scherer, C. R., Skowronski, J. J., Wood, S. E., Edlund, J. E., & Hartnett, J. L. (2007). Trait expectancies and stereotype expectancies have the same effect on person memory. *Journal of Experimental Social Psychology*, *43*, 265–272.

Heilman, M. E. (1983). Sex bias in work settings: The lack of fit model. *Research in Organizational Behavior*, *5*, 269–298.

Heilman, M. E. (2001). Description and prescription: How gender stereotypes prevent women's ascent up the organizational ladder. *Journal of Social Issues*, *57*, 657–674.

Heine, S. J., & Buchtel, E. E. (2009). Personality: The universal and the culturally specific. *Annual Review of Psychology*, *60*, 369–394.

Heine, S. J., Lehman, D. R., Markus, H. R., & Kitayama, S. (1999). Is there a universal need for positive self-regard? *Psychological Review*, *106*, 766–794.

Helgeson, V. S., & Mickelson, K. D. (1995). Motives for social comparison. *Personality and Social Psychology Bulletin*, *21*, 1200–1209.

Helms, J. E. (1992). *A race is a nice thing to have*. Topeka, KS: Content Communications.

Henderson, A. J. Z., Bartholomew, K., & Dutton, D. G. (1997). He loves me; he loves me not: Attachment and separation resolution of abused women. *Journal of Family Violence*, *12*, 169–191.

Henderson, M. D., Fujita, K., Trope, Y., & Liberman, N. (2006). Transcending the "here": The effect of spatial distance on social judgment. *Journal of Personality and Social Psychology*, *91*, 845–856.

Hennessy, J., & West, M. A. (1999). Intergroup behavior in organizations: A field test of social identity theory. *Small Group Research*, *30*, 361–382.

Henry, P. J. (2008). College sophomores in the laboratory redux: Influences of a narrow data base on social psychology's view of the nature of prejudice. *Psychological Inquiry*, *19*, 49–71.

Henry, P. J., & Reyna, C. (2007). Value judgments: The impact of perceived value violations on American political attitudes. *Political Psychology*, *28*, 273–298.

Henry, P. J., & Sears, D. O. (2002). The symbolic racism 2000 scale. *Political Psychology*, *23*, 253–283.

Hepworth, J. T., & West, J. G. (1988). Lynchings and the economy: A time-series reanalysis of Hovland and Sears (1940). *Journal of Personality and Social Psychology*, *55*, 239–247.

Hewstone, M. (1990). The "ultimate attribution error"? A review of the literature on intergroup causal attribution. *European Journal of Social Psychology*, *20*, 311–335.

Hewstone, M., & Brown, R. J. (1986). *Contact is not enough: An intergroup perspective on the "contact hypothesis."* Cambridge, MA: Blackwell.

Hewstone, M., Rubin, M., & Willis, H. (2002). Intergroup bias. *Annual Review of Psychology*, *53*, 575–604.

Higgins, E. T. (1987). Self-discrepancy: A theory relating self and affect. *Psychological Review*, *94*, 319–340.

Higgins, E. T. (1997). Beyond pleasure and pain. *American Psychologist*, *52*, 1280–1300.

Higgins, E. T. (1998). Promotion and prevention: Regulatory focus as a motivational principle. In M. P. Zanna (Ed.), *Advances in experimental social psychology* (Vol. 30, pp. 1–46). New York: Academic Press.

Higgins, E. T. (2006). Value from hedonic experience and engagement. *Psychological Review*, *113*, 439–460.

Higgins, E. T. (2007). Value. In A. W. Kruglanski & E. T. Higgins (Eds.), *Social Psychology: Handbook of basic principles* (2nd ed., pp. 454–472). New York: Guilford.

Higgins, E. T., Bond, R. N., Klein, R., & Strauman, T. (1986). Self-discrepancies and emotional vulnerability: How magnitude, accessibility, and type of discrepancy influence affect. *Journal of Personality and Social Psychology*, *51*, 5–15.

Higgins, E. T., Echterhoff, G., Crespillo, R., & Kopietz, R. (2007). Effects of communication on social knowledge: Sharing reality with individual versus group audiences. *Japanese Psychological Research*, *49*, 89–99.

Higgins, E. T., King, G. A., & Mavin, G. H. (1982). Individual construct accessibility and subjective impressions and recall. *Journal of Personality and Social Psychology*, *43*, 35–47.

Higgins, E. T., Rholes, W. S., & Jones, C. R. (1977). Category accessibility and impression formation. *Journal of Experimental Social Psychology*, *13*, 141–154.

Higgins, E. T., Shah, J., & Friedman, R. (1997). Emotional responses to goal attainment: strength of regulatory focus as moderator. *Journal of Personality and Social Psychology*, *72*, 515–525.

Hilton, D. J. (1990). Conversational processes and causal explanation. *Psychological Bulletin, 107,* 65–81.

Hilton, J. L., & Fein, S. (1989). The role of typical diagnosticity in stereotype-based judgments. *Journal of Personality and Social Psychology, 57,* 201–211.

Hilton, J. L., & von Hippel, W. (1996). Stereotypes. *Annual Review of Psychology, 47,* 237–271.

Hilton, N. Z., Harris, G. T., & Rice, M. E. (2000). The functions of aggression by male teenagers. *Journal of Personality and Social Psychology, 79,* 988–994.

Himmelfarb, S. (1993). The measurement of attitudes. In A. H. Eagly & S. Chaiken (Eds.), *The psychology of attitudes* (pp. 23–87). Orlando, FL: Harcourt Brace Jovanovich.

Hinsz, V. B., Tindale, R. S., & Vollrath, D. A. (1997). The emerging conceptualization of groups as information processers. *Psychological Bulletin, 121,* 43–64.

Ho, D. Y. F. (1998). Interpersonal relationships and relationship dominance: An analysis based on methodological relationalism. *Asian Journal of Social Psychology, 1,* 1–16.

Hoffman, L. R., & Maier, N. R. F. (1961). Quality and acceptance of problem solutions by members of homogeneous and heterogeneous groups. *Journal of Abnormal and Social Psychology, 62,* 401–407.

Hoffman, M. L. (1981). Is altruism part of human nature? *Journal of Personality and Social Psychology, 40,* 121–137.

Hogg, M. A. (1992). *The social psychology of group cohesiveness: From attraction to social identity.* London, UK: Harvester Wheatsheaf.

Hogg, M. A. (1993). Group cohesiveness: A critical review and some new directions. In M. Hewstone & W. Stroebe (Eds.), *European review of social psychology* (Vol. 4, pp. 85–111). New York: Wiley.

Hogg, M. A. (1995a). Group processes. In A. S. R. Manstead & M. Hewstone (Eds.), *Blackwell encyclopedia of social psychology* (pp. 269–274). Oxford, UK: Blackwell.

Hogg, M. A. (1995b). Social identity theory. In A. S. R. Manstead, & M. Hewstone (Eds.), *Blackwell encyclopedia of social psychology* (pp. 555–560). Oxford, UK: Blackwell.

Hogg, M A. (2000). Subjective uncertainty reduction through self-categorization: A motivational theory of social identity process. In W. Stroebe & M. Hewstone (Eds.), *European review of social psychology* (Vol. 11, pp. 223–255). New York: Wiley.

Hogg, M. A. (2001). Social categorization, depersonalization, and group behavior. In M. A. Hogg & R. S. Tindale (Eds.), *Blackwell handbook of social psychology: Group processes* (pp. 56–85). Malden, MA: Blackwell.

Hogg, M. A. (2007a). Social psychology of leadership. In A. W. Kruglanski & E. T. Higgins (Eds.), *Social psychology: Handbook of basic principles* (2nd ed., pp. 716–733). New York: Guilford.

Hogg, M. A. (2007b). Uncertainty-identity theory. In M. P. Zanna (Ed.), *Advances in experimental social psychology* (Vol. 39, pp. 69–126). San Diego: Elsevier Academic Press.

Hogg, M. A., & Abrams, D. (1990). Social motivation, self-esteem and social identity. In M. A. Hogg & D. Abrams (Eds.), *Social identity theory: Constructive and critical advances.* London, UK: Harvester Wheatsheaf.

Hogg, M. A., & Abrams, D. (1993). Towards a single process uncertainty-reduction model of social motivation in groups. In M. A. Hogg & D. Abrams (Eds.), *Group motivation: Social psychological perspectives.* London, UK: Harvester Wheatsheaf.

Hogg, M. A., Cooper-Shaw, L., & Holzworth, D. W. (1993). Group prototypicality and depersonalized attraction in small interactive groups. *Personality and Social Psychology Bulletin, 19,* 452–465.

Hogg, M. A., & Hains, S. C. (1996). Intergroup relations and group solidarity: Effects of group identification and social beliefs on depersonalized attraction. *Journal of Personality and Social Psychology, 70,* 295–309.

Hogg, M. A., & Hains, S. C. (1998). Friendship and group identification: A new look at the role of cohesiveness in groupthink. *European Journal of Social Psychology, 28,* 323–341.

Hogg, M. A., Hains, S. C., & Mason, I. (1998). Identification and leadership in small groups: Salience, frame of reference, and leader stereotypicality effects on leader evaluations. *Journal of Personality and Social Psychology, 75,* 1248–1263.

Hogg, M. A., & Hardie, E. A. (1992). Prototypicality, conformity and depersonalized attraction: A self-categorization analysis of group cohesiveness. *British Journal of Social Psychology, 31,* 41–56.

Hogg, M. A., Sherman, D. K., Dierselhuis, J., Maitner, A. T., & Moffitt, G. (2007). Uncertainty, entitativity, and group identification. *Journal of Experimental Social Psychology, 43,* 135–142.

Hollander, E. P. (1985). Leadership and power. In G. Lindzey & E. Aronson (Eds.), *Handbook of social psychology* (3rd ed., Vol. 2, pp. 485–537). New York: Random House.

Hollingshead, A. B. (1998). Retrieval processes in transactive memory systems. *Journal of Personality and Social Psychology, 74,* 659–671.

Holloway, S., Tucker, L., & Hornstein, H. A. (1977). The effects of social and nonsocial information on interpersonal behavior of males: The news makes news. *Journal of Personality and Social Psychology*, *35*, 514–522.

Holtzworth-Munroe, A., & Hutchinson, G. (1993). Attributing negative intent to wife behavior: The attributions of maritally violent versus nonviolent men. *Journal of Abnormal Psychology*, *102*, 206–211.

Holtzworth-Munroe, A., & Jacobson, N. S. (1985). Causal attributions of married couples: When do they search for causes? What do they conclude when they do? *Journal of Personality and Social Psychology*, *48*, 1398–1412.

Holtzworth-Munroe, A., Smutzler, N., & Stuart, G. L. (1998). Demand and withdraw communication among couples experiencing husband violence. *Journal of Consulting and Clinical Psychology*, *66*, 731–743.

Holtzworth-Munroe, A., & Stuart, G. L. (1994). Typologies of male batterers: Three subtypes and the differences among them. *Psychological Bulletin*, *116*, 476–497.

Holtzworth-Munroe, A., Stuart, G. L., Sandin, E., Smutzler, N., & McLaughlin, W (1997). Comparing the social support behaviors of violent and nonviolent husbands during discussions of wife personal problems. *Personal Relationships*, *4*, 395–412.

Holyoak, K. J., & Gordon, P. C. (1984). Information processing and social cognition. In R. Wyer & T. K. Srull (Eds.), *Handbook of social cognition* (Vol. 1, pp. 39–70). Hillsdale, NJ: Erlbaum.

Hood, B. M., Macrae, C. N., Cole-Davies, V., & Dias, M. (2003). Eye remember you: The effects of gaze direction on face recognition in children and adults. *Developmental Science*, *6*, 67–71.

Hornsey, M. J., & Hogg, M. A. (2000). Assimilation and diversity: An integrative model of subgroup relations. *Personality and Social Psychology Review*, *4*, 143–156.

Hornstein, H. A., Fisch, E., & Holmes, M. (1968). Influence of model's feeling about his behavior and his relevance as a comparison other on observers' helping behavior. *Journal of Personality and Social Psychology*, *10*, 222–226.

Hornstein, H. A., LaKind, E., Frankel, G., & Manne, S. (1975). Effects of knowledge about remote social events on prosocial behavior, social conception, and mood. *Journal of Personality and Social Psychology*, *32*, 1038–1046.

House, J. S., Landis, K. R., & Umberson, D. (1988). Social relationships and health. *Science*, *241*, 540–545.

Hovland, C. I., & Sears, R. R. (1940). Minor studies of aggression: VI. Correlation of lynchings with economic indices. *Journal of Psychology*, *9*, 301–310.

Howard, E. S., Gardner, W. L., & Thompson, L. (2007). The role of the self-concept and the social context in determining the behavior of power holders: Self-construal in intergroup versus dyadic dispute resolution negotiations. *Journal of Personality and Social Psychology*, *93*, 614–631.

Howell, J. P., Dorfman, P. W., & Kerr, S. (1986). Moderator variables in leadership research. *Academy of Management Review*, *11*, 88–102.

Hsee, C. K. (1996). Elastic justification: How unjustifiable factors influence judgments. *Organizational Behavior and Human Decision Processes*, *66*, 122–129.

Hubbard, J. A., Dodge, K. A., Cillessen, A. H. N., Coie, J. D., & Schwartz, D. (2001). The dyadic nature of social information processing in boys' reactive and proactive aggression. *Journal of Personality and Social Psychology*, *80*, 268–280.

Huddy, L., & Sears, D. O. (1995). Opposition to bilingual education: Prejudice or the defense of realistic interests? *Social Psychology Quarterly*, *58*, 133–143.

Huesmann, L. R. (1986). Psychological processes promoting the relation between exposure to media violence and aggressive behavior by the viewer. *Journal of Social Issues*, *42*, 125–139.

Huesmann, L. R. (1988). An information processing model for the development of aggression. *Aggressive Behavior*, *14*, 13–24.

Huesmann, L. R., & Eron, L. D. (1984). Cognitive processes and the persistence of aggressive behavior. *Aggressive Behavior*, *10*, 243–251.

Huesmann, L. R., & Eron, L. D. (1989). Individual differences and the trait of aggression. *European Journal of Personality 3*, 95–106.

Huesmann, L. R., Eron, L. D., Lefkowitz, M. M., & Walder, L. O. (1984). Stability of aggression over time and generations. *Developmental Psychology*, *20*, 1120–1134.

Huesmann, L. R., & Guerra, N. G. (1997). Children's normative beliefs about aggression and aggressive behavior. *Journal of Personality and Social Psychology*, *72*, 409–419.

Hull, J. G., & Bond, C. F., Jr. (1986). Social and behavioral consequences of alcohol consumption and expectancy: A meta-analysis. *Psychological Bulletin*, *99*, 347–360.

Huston, T. L., & Levinger, G. (1978). Interpersonal attraction and relationships. *Annual Review of Psychology*, *29*, 115–156.

Hyman, H. H., & Sheatsley, P. B. (1954). The authoritarian personality: A methodological critique. In R. Christie & M. Jahoda (Eds.), *Studies in the scope and method of "the authoritarian personality"* (pp. 50–122). Glencoe, IL: Free Press.

Iacoboni, M. (2009). Imitation, empathy, and mirror neurons. *Annual Review of Psychology, 60,* 653–670.

Iacoboni, M., Lieberman, M. D., Knowlton, B. J., Molnar-Szakacs, I., Moritz, M., Throop, C. J., & Fiske, A. P. (2004). Watching social interactions produces dorsomedial prefrontal and medial parietal BOLD fMRI signal increases compared to a resting baseline. *Neuroimage, 21,* 1167–1173.

Ibrahim, Y. M. (1999, May 26). Importance of being persuasive: Daimler-Chrysler merger made an art of making a case. *New York Times,* pp. C1, C7.

Ickes, W. (1993). Empathic accuracy. *Journal of Personality, 61,* 587–610.

Ickes, W., Stinson, L., Bissonette, V., & Garcia, S. (1990). Naturalistic social cognition: Empathic accuracy in mixed-sex dyads. *Journal of Personality and Social Psychology, 59,* 730–742.

Idson, L. C., Liberman, N., & Higgins, E. T. (2000). Distinguishing gains from nonlosses and losses from nongains: A regulatory focus perspective on hedonic intensity. *Journal of Experimental Social Psychology, 36,* 252–274.

Iedema, J., & Poppe, M. (1999). Expectations of others' social value orientations in specific and general populations. *Personality and Social Psychology Bulletin, 25,* 1443–1450.

Impett, E. A., Gable, S. L., & Peplau, L. A. (2005). Giving up and giving in: The costs and benefits of daily sacrifice in intimate relationships. *Journal of Personality and Social Psychology, 89,* 327–344.

Impett, E. A., Strachman, A., Finkel, E. J., & Gable, S. L. (2008). Maintaining sexual desire in intimate relationships: The importance of approach goals. *Journal of Personality and Social Psychology, 94,* 808–823.

Inman, M. L., Reichl, A. J., & Baron, R. S. (1993). Do we tell less than we know or hear less than we are told? Exploring the teller-listener extremity effect. *Journal of Experimental Social Psychology, 29,* 528–550.

Insko, C. A. (1965). Verbal reinforcement of attitude. *Journal of Personality and Social Psychology, 2,* 621–623.

Insko, C. A., Schopler, J., Gaertner, L., Wildschut, T., Kozar, R., Pinter, B., Finkel, E. J., Brazil, D. M., Cecil, C. L., & Montoya, M. R. (2001). Interindividual-intergroup discontinuity reduction through the anticipation of future interaction. *Journal of Personality and Social Psychology, 80,* 95–111.

Insko, C. A., Schopler, J., Hoyle, R. H., Dardis, G. J., & Graetz, K. A. (1990). Individual-group discontinuity as a function of fear and greed.

*Journal of Personality and Social Psychology, 58,* 68–79.

Insko, C. A., Schopler, J., Pemberton, M. B., Wieselquist, J., McIlraith, S. A., Currey, D. P., & Gaertner, L. (1998). Long-term outcome maximization and the reduction of interindividual-intergroup discontinuity. *Journal of Personality and Social Psychology, 75,* 695–711.

Isen, A. M. (1987). Positive affect, cognitive processes, and social behavior. In L. Berkowitz (Ed.), *Advances in experimental social psychology* (Vol. 20, pp. 203–253). New York: Academic Press.

Isen, A. M., & Levin, P. F. (1972). Effect of feeling good on helping: Cookies and kindness. *Journal of Personality and Social Psychology, 21,* 384–388.

Isen, A. M., Shalker, T. E., Clark, M. S., & Karp, L. (1978). Affect, accessibility of material in memory, and behavior: A cognitive loop? *Journal of Personality and Social Psychology, 36,* 1–13.

Isen, A. M., & Simmonds, S. F. (1978). The effect of feeling good on a helping task that is incompatible with good mood. *Social Psychology, 41,* 346–349.

Isenberg, D. J. (1986). Group polarization: A critical review and meta-analysis. *Journal of Personality and Social Psychology, 50,* 1141–1151.

Isenberg, D. J., & Ennis, J. G. (1981). Perceiving group members: A comparison of derived and imposed dimensions. *Journal of Personality and Social Psychology, 41,* 293–305.

Ishiguro, K. (2000). *When we were orphans.* New York: Knopf.

Ito, T. A., Miller, N., & Pollock, V E. (1996). Alcohol and aggression: A meta-analysis on the moderating effects of inhibitory cues, triggering events, and self-focused attention. *Psychological Bulletin, 120,* 60–82.

Ito, T. A., & Urland, G. R. (2003). Race and gender on the brain: Electrocortical measures of attention to the race and gender of multiply categorizable individuals. *Journal of Personality and Social Psychology, 85,* 616–626.

Iyengar, S. S., & Lepper, M. R. (1999). Rethinking the value of choice: A cultural perspective on intrinsic motivation. *Journal of Personality and Social Psychology, 76,* 349–366.

Iyengar, S. S., & Lepper, M. R. (2000). When choice is demotivating: Can one desire too much of a good thing? *Journal of Personality and Social Psychology, 79,* 995–1006.

Jackman, M. R. (2002). Violence in social life. *Annual Review of Sociology, 28,* 387–415.

Jackson, J. W. (1993). Realistic group conflict theory: A review and evaluation of the theoretical and empirical literature. *Psychological Record, 43,* 395–414.

Jackson, L. A., Hunter, J. E., & Hodge, C. N. (1995). Physical attractiveness and intellectual competence: A meta-analytic review. *Social Psychology Quarterly*, *58*, 108–122.

Jackson, L. A., Sullivan, L. A., Harnish, R., & Hodge, C. N. (1996). Achieving positive social identity: Social mobility, social creativity, and permeability of group boundaries. *Journal of Personality and Social Psychology*, *70*, 241–254.

Jackson, L. M., & Esses, V. M. (1997). Of scripture and ascription: The relation between religious fundamentalism and intergroup helping. *Personality and Social Psychology Bulletin*, *23*, 893–906.

Jackson, S. E., Brett, J. F., Sessa, V. I., Cooper, D. M., Julia, J. A., & Peyronnin, K. (1991). Some differences make a difference: Individual dissimilarity and group heterogeneity as correlates of recruitment, promotions, and turnover. *Journal of Applied Psychology*, *76*, 675–689.

Jacobs, R. C., & Campbell, D. T. (1961). The perpetuation of an arbitrary tradition through several generations of a laboratory microculture. *Journal of Abnormal and Social Psychology*, *62*, 649–658.

James, B. (1986). *The Bill James historical baseball abstract*. New York: Villard.

James, H. (1877). *The American*. New York: Penguin.

James, H. (1881). *The portrait of a lady*. New York: Bantam.

James, W. (1890). *The principles of psychology*. New York: Holt.

Jamieson, D. W., Lydon, J. E., & Zanna, M. P. (1987). Attitude and activity preference similarity: Differential bases of interpersonal attraction for low and high self-monitors. *Journal of Personality and Social Psychology*, *53*, 1052–1060.

Jamieson, D. W., & Zanna, M. P. (1989). Need for structure in attitude formation and expression. In A. R. Pratkanis, S. J. Breckler, & A. G. Greenwald (Eds.), *Attitude structure and function* (pp. 383–406). Hillsdale, NJ: Erlbaum.

Janis, I. L. (1972). *Victims of groupthink: A psychological study of foreign-policy decisions and fiascoes*. Boston: Houghton-Mifflin.

Janis, I. L., & Feshbach, S. (1953). Effects of fear-arousing communications. *Journal of Abnormal and Social Psychology*, *48*, 78–92.

Janoff-Bulman, R. (1992). *Shattered assumptions: Towards a new psychology of trauma*. New York: Free Press.

Jarvis, W. B. G., & Petty, R. E. (1996). The need to evaluate. *Journal of Personality and Social Psychology*, *70*, 172–194.

Jehn, K. A., Northcraft, G. B., & Neale, M. A. (1999). Why differences make a difference: A field study of diversity, conflict, and performance in workgroups. *Administrative Science Quarterly*, *44*, 741–763.

Jehn, K. A., & Shah, P. P. (1997). Interpersonal relationships and task performance: An examination of mediating processes in friendship and acquaintance groups. *Journal of Personality and Social Psychology*, *72*, 775–790.

Jennings, D., Amabile, T. M., & Ross, L. (1982). Informal covariation assessment: Data-based vs. theory-based judgments. In A. Tversky, D. Kahneman, & P. Slovic (Eds.), *Judgment under uncertainty: Heuristics and biases* (pp. 211–230). New York: Cambridge University Press.

Jensen-Campbell, L. A., Graziano, W. G., & West, S. G. (1995). Dominance, prosocial orientation, and female preferences: Do nice guys really finish last? *Journal of Personality and Social Psychology*, *68*, 427–440.

Jetten, J., Hogg, M. A., & Mullin, B. A. (2000). In-group variability and motivation to reduce subjective uncertainty. *Group Dynamics*, *4*, 184–198.

Jetten, J., Spears, R., & Manstead, A. S. R. (1998). Defining dimensions of distinctiveness: Group variability makes a difference to differentiation. *Journal of Personality and Social Psychology*, *74*, 1481–1492.

Jetten, J., Spears, R., & Postmes, T. (2004). Intergroup distinctiveness and differentiation: A meta-analytic integration. *Journal of Personality and Social Psychology*, *86*, 862–879.

Ji, L. J., Peng, K., & Nisbett, R. E. (2000). Culture, control, and perception of relationships in the environment. *Journal of Personality and Social Psychology*, *78*, 943–955.

John, O. P. (1990). The "big five" factor taxonomy: Dimensions of personality in the natural language and in questionnaires. In L. A. Pervin (Ed.), *Handbook of personality: Theory and research* (pp. 66–100). New York: Guilford.

Johnson, B. T., & Eagly, A. H. (1989). Effects of involvement on persuasion: A meta-analysis. *Psychological Bulletin*, *106*, 290–314.

Johnson, C. S., & Stapel, D. A. (2007). No pain, no gain: The conditions under which upward comparisons lead to better performance. *Journal of Personality and Social Psychology*, *92*, 1051–1067.

Johnson, E. J., & Tversky, A. (1983). Affect generalization and the perception of risk. *Journal of Personality and Social Psychology*, *45*, 20–31.

Johnson, J. G., Cohen, P., Smailes, E. M., Kasen, S., & Brook, J. S. (2002). Television viewing and aggressive behavior during adolescence and adulthood. *Science*, *295*, 2468–2471.

Jonas, E., Schimel, J., Greenberg, J., & Pyszczynski, T. (2002). The Scrooge effect: Evidence that mortality salience increases prosocial attitudes and behavior. *Journal of Personality and Social Psychology*, *28*, 1342–1353.

Jones, B. C., DeBruine, L. M., Little, A. C., Conway, C. A., & Feinberg, D. R. (2006). Integrating gaze direction and expression in preferences for attractive faces. *Psychological Science*, *17*, 588–591.

Jones, E. E. (1979). The rocky road from acts to dispositions. *American Psychologist*, *34*, 107–117.

Jones, E. E. (1990). *Interpersonal perception*. New York: Freeman.

Jones, E. E., & Davis, K. E. (1965). From acts to dispositions: The attribution process in person perception. In L. Berkowitz (Ed.), *Advances in experimental social psychology* (Vol. 2, pp. 220–266). New York: Academic Press.

Jones, E. E., Farina, A., Hastorf, A. H., Markus, H., Miller, D. T., & Scott, R. A. (1984). *Social stigma: The psychology of marked relationships*. New York: Freeman.

Jones, E. E., & Harris, V. A. (1967). The attribution of attitudes. *Journal of Experimental Social Psychology*, *3*, 1–24.

Jones, E. E., & Nisbett, R. E. (1972). The actor and the observer: Divergent perceptions of the causes of behavior. In E. E. Jones, D. E. Kanouse, H. H. Kelley, R. E. Nisbett, S. Valins, & B. Weiner (Eds.), *Attribution: Perceiving the causes of behavior* (pp. 79–94). Morristown, NJ: General Learning Press.

Jones, E. E., & Pittman, T. S. (1982). Toward a general theory of strategic self-presentation. In J. Suls (Ed.), *Psychological perspectives on the self* (Vol. 1, pp. 231–262). Hillsdale, NJ: Erlbaum.

Jones, E. E., & Sigall, H. (1971). The bogus pipeline: A new paradigm for measuring affect and attitude. *Psychological Bulletin*, *76*, 349–364.

Jones, E. E., & Thibaut, J. W. (1958). Interaction goals as bases of inference in interpersonal perception. In R. Tagiuri & L. Petrullo (Eds.), *Person perception and interpersonal behavior* (pp. 151–178). Stanford, CA: Stanford University Press.

Josephson, W. L. (1987). Television violence and children's aggression: Testing the priming, social script, and disinhibition predictions. *Journal of Personality and Social Psychology*, *53*, 882–890.

Jost, J. T., & Banaji, M. R. (1994). The role of stereotyping in system-justification and the production of false consciousness. *British Journal of Social Psychology*, *33*, 1–27.

Jost, J. T., Banaji, M. R., & Nosek, B. A. (2004). A decade of system justification theory: Accumulated evidence of conscious and unconscious bolstering of the status quo. *Political Psychology*, *25*, 881–920.

Jost, J. T., Burgess, D., & Mosso, C. O. (2001). Conflicts of legitimacy among self, group and system: The integrative potential of system justification theory. In J. T. Jost & B. Major (Eds.), *The psychology of legitimacy* (pp. 363–388). New York: Cambridge University Press.

Jost, J. T., Federico, C. M., & Napier, J. L. (2009). Political ideology: Its structure, functions, and elective affinities. *Annual Review of Psychology*, *60*, 307–337.

Jost, J. T., Glaser, J., Kruglanski, A. W., & Sulloway, F. J. (2003). Political conservatism as motivated social cognition. *Psychological Bulletin*, *129*, 339–375.

Jost, J. T., & Major, B. (Eds.) (2001). *The psychology of legitimacy*. New York: Cambridge University Press.

Judd, C. M., Drake, R. A., Downing, J. W., & Krosnick, J. A. (1991). Some dynamic properties of attitude structures: Context-induced response faciliation and polarization. *Journal of Personality and Social Psychology*, *60*, 193–202.

Judd, C. M., James-Hawkins, L., Yzerbyt, V., & Kashima, Y. (2005). Fundamental dimensions of social judgment: Understanding the relations between judgments of competence and warmth. *Journal of Personality and Social Psychology*, *89*, 899–913.

Judd, C. M., & Park, B. (1993). Definition and assessment of accuracy in social stereotypes. *Psychological Review*, *100*, 109–128.

Judice, T. N., & Neuberg, S. L. (1998). When interviewers desire to confirm negative expectations: Self-fulfilling prophecies and inflated applicant self-perceptions. *Basic and Applied Social Psychology*, *20*, 175–190.

Jussim, L., McCauley, C. R., & Lee, Y. (1995). Why study stereotype accuracy and inaccuracy? In Y. Lee, L. Jussim, & C. R. McCauley (Eds.), *Stereotype accuracy*. Washington, DC: American Psychological Association.

Juvonen, J., Nishina, A., & Graham, S. (2000). Peer harassment, psychological adjustment, and school functioning in early adolescence. *Journal of Educational Psychology*, *92*, 349–359.

Kahneman, D., & Miller, D. T. (1986). Norm theory: Comparing reality to its alternatives. *Psychological Review*, *93*, 136–153.

Kahneman, D., & Tversky, A. (1982). The simulation heuristic. In D. Kahneman, P. Slovic, & A. Tversky (Eds.), *Judgment under uncertainty: Heuristics and biases* (pp. 201–208). New York: Cambridge University Press.

Kalick, S. M., Zebrowitz, L. A., Langlois, J. H., & Johnson, R. M. (1998). Does human facial attractiveness honestly advertise health? Longitudinal data on an evolutionary question. *Psychological Science*, *9*, 8–13.

Kameda, T., Ohtsubo, Y., & Takezawa, M. (1997). Centrality in sociocognitive networks and social influence: An illustration in a group decision-making context. *Journal of Personality and Social Psychology*, *73*, 296–309.

Kameda, T., & Sugimori, S. (1995). Procedural influence in two-step group decision making: Power of local majorities in consensus formation. *Journal of Personality and Social Psychology*, *69*, 865–876.

Kanouse, D. E., & Hanson, L. R. Jr. (1972). Negativity in evaluations. In E. E. Jones, D. E. Kanouse, H. H. Kelley, R. E. Nisbett, S. Valins, & B. Weiner (Eds.), *Attribution: Perceiving the causes of behavior* (pp. 47–62). Morristown, NJ: General Learning Press.

Karau, S. J., & Williams, K. D. (1993). Social loafing: A meta-analytic review and theoretical integration. *Journal of Personality and Social Psychology*, *65*, 681–706.

Karney, B. R., & Bradbury, T. N. (2000). Attributions in marriage: State or trait? A growth curve analysis. *Journal of Personality and Social Psychology*, *78*, 295–309.

Karpinski, A., & Hilton, J. L. (2001). Attitudes and the implicit associations test. *Journal of Personality and Social Psychology*, *81*, 774–788.

Karremans, J. C., Van Lange, P. A. M., Ouwerkerk, J. W., & Kluwer, E. (2003). When forgiving enhances psychological well-being: The role of interpersonal commitment. *Journal of Personality and Social Psychology*, *84*, 1011–1026.

Kashima, Y. (2000). Maintaining cultural stereotypes in the serial reproduction of narratives. *Personality and Social Psychology Bulletin*, *26*, 594–604.

Kashima, Y., Siegal, M., Tanaka, K., & Kashima, E. S. (1992). Do people believe behaviours are consistent with attitudes? Towards a cultural psychology of attribution processes. *British Journal of Social Psychology*, *31*, 111–124.

Kashima, Y., & Yamaguchi, S. (1999). Introduction to the special issue on self. *Asian Journal of Social Psychology*, *2*, 283–287.

Kassin, S. M. (1979). Consensus information, prediction, and causal attribution: A review of the literature and issues. *Journal of Personality and Social Psychology*, *37*, 1966–1981.

Katz, D. (1960). The functional approach to the study of attitudes. *Public Opinion Quarterly*, *24*, 163–204.

Katz, D., & Allport, F. (1931). *Students' attitudes*. Syracuse, NY: Craftsman Press.

Katz, I., & Hass, R. G. (1988). Racial ambivalence and American value conflict: Correlational and priming studies of dual cognitive structures. *Journal of Personality and Social Psychology*, *55*, 893–905.

Katz, I., Wackenhut, J., & Hass, R. G. (1986). Racial ambivalence, value duality, and behavior. In J. F. Dovidio & S. L. Gaertner (Eds.), *Prejudice, discrimination, and racism* (pp. 35–59). San Diego, CA: Academic Press.

Katzev, R., Edelsach, L., Steinmetz, G., Walker, T., & Wright, R. (1978). The effect of reprimanding transgressions on subsequent helping behavior: Two field experiments. *Personality and Social Psychology Bulletin*, *4*, 326–329.

Kawakami, K., Dion, K. L., & Dovidio, J. F. (1998). Racial prejudice and stereotype activation. *Personality and Social Psychology Bulletin*, *24*, 407–416.

Kawakami, K., & Dovidio, J. F. (2001). The reliability of implicit stereotyping. *Personality and Social Psychology Bulletin*, *27*, 212–225.

Kawakami, K., Dovidio, J. F., Moll, J., Hermsen, S., & Russin, A. (2000). Just say no (to stereotyping): Effects of training in the negation of stereotypic associations on stereotype activation. *Journal of Personality and Social Psychology*, *78*, 871–888.

Kawakami, K., Dovidio, J. F., & van Kamp, S. (2005). Kicking the habit: Effects of nonstereotypic association training and correction processes on hiring decisions. *Journal of Experimental Social Psychology*, *41*, 68–75.

Kawakami, K., Phills, C. E., Steele, J. R., & Dovidio, J. F. (2007). (Close) distance makes the heart grow fonder: Improving implicit racial attitudes and interracial interactions through approach behaviors. *Journal of Personality and Social Psychology*, *92*, 957–971.

Kellerman, J., Lewis, J., & Laird, J. D. (1989). Looking and loving: The effects of mutual gaze on feelings of romantic love. *Journal of Research in Personality*, *23*, 145–161.

Kellermann, A. L., Rivara, F. P., Rushforth, N. B., Banton, J. G., Reay, D. T., Francisco, J. T., Locci, A. B., Prodzinski, J., Hackman, B. B., & Somes, G. (1993). Gun ownership as a risk factor for homicide in the home. *New England Journal of Medicine*, *329*, 1084–1091.

Kelley, H. H. (1950). The warm-cold variable in first impressions of persons. *Journal of Personality*, *18*, 431–439.

Kelley, H. H. (1967). Attribution theory in social psychology. In D. Levine (Ed.), *Nebraska symposium on motivation* (Vol. 15, pp. 192–238). Lincoln: University of Nebraska Press.

Kelley, H. H. (1972). Attribution in social interaction. In E. E. Jones, D. E. Kanouse, H. H. Kelley, R. E.

Nisbett, S. Valins, & B. Weiner (Eds.), *Attribution: Perceiving the cause of behavior* (pp. 1–26). Morristown, NJ: General Learning Press.

Kelley, H. H. (1979). *Personal relationships*. Hillsdale, NJ: Erlbaum.

Kelley, H. H., Berscheid, E., Christensen, A., Harvey, J. H., Huston, T. L., Levinger, G., McClintock, E., Peplau, L. A., & Peterson, D. R. (1983). *Close relationships*. New York: Freeman.

Kelley, H. H., & Stahelski, A. J. (1970). Social interaction basis of cooperators' and competitors' beliefs about others. *Journal of Personality and Social Psychology*, *16*, 66–91.

Kelley, H. H., Thibaut, J. W., Radloff, R., & Mundy, D. (1962). The development of cooperation in the "minimal social situation." *Psychological Monographs: General and Applied*, *76*, Whole No. 538.

Kelly, C. (1989). Political identity and perceived intragroup homogeneity. *British Journal of Social Psychology*, *28*, 239–250.

Kelly, D. J., Quinn, P. C., Slater, A. M., Lee, K., Gibson, A., Smith, M., Ge, L., & Pascalis, O. (2005). Three-month-olds, but not newborns, prefer own-race faces. *Developmental Science*, *8*, F31–F36.

Kelman, H. C. (1958). Compliance, identification, and internalization: Three processes of attitude change. *Journal of Conflict Resolution*, *2*, 51–60.

Keltner, D., Gruenfeld, D. H., & Anderson, C. (2003). Power, approach, and inhibition. *Psychological Revew*, *110*, 265–284.

Keltner, D., & Lerner, J. (2010). Emotion. In S. T. Fiske, D. T. Gilbert, & G. Lindzey (Eds.), *Handbook of social psychology* (5th ed., in press). New York: Wiley.

Keltner, D., & Robinson, R. J. (1996). Extremism, power, and the imagined basis of social conflict. *Current Directions in Psychological Science*, *5*, 101–105.

Keltner, D., & Robinson, R. J. (1997). Defending the status quo: Power and bias in social conflict. *Personality and Social Psychology Bulletin*, *23*, 1066–1077.

Keltner, D., Young, R. C., Heerey, E. A., Oemig, C., & Monarch, N. D. (1998). Teasing in hierarchical and intimate relations. *Journal of Personality and Social Psychology*, *75*, 1231–1247.

Kennedy, B. P., Kawachi, I., Prothrow-Stith, D., Lochner, K., & Gupta, V. (1998). Social capital, income inequality, and firearm violent crime. *Social Science and Medicine*, *47*, 7–17.

Kenny, D. A. (1991). A general model of consensus and accuracy in interpersonal perception. *Psychological Review*, *98*, 155–163.

Kenny, D. A. (1994). *Interpersonal perception: A social relations analysis*. New York: Guilford.

Kenny, D. A., & Acitelli, L. K. (2001). Accuracy and bias in the perception of the partner in a close relationship. *Journal of Personality and Social Psychology 80*, 439–448.

Kenny, D. A., & Albright, L. (1987). Accuracy in interpersonal perception: A social relations analysis. *Psychological Bulletin*, *102*, 390–402.

Kenny, D. A., Albright, L., Malloy, T. E., & Kashy, D. A. (1994). Consensus in interpersonal perception: Acquaintance and the big five. *Psychological Bulletin*, *116*, 245–258.

Kenny, D. A., & DePaulo, B. M. (1993). Do people know how others view them? An empirical and theoretical account. *Psychological Bulletin*, *114*, 145–161.

Kenny, D. A., & La Voie, L. (1984). The social relations model. In L. Berkowitz (Ed.), *Advances in experimental social psychology* (Vol. 18, pp. 141–182). New York: Academic Press.

Kenny, D. A., Mannetti, L., Pierro, A., Livi, S., & Kashy, D. A. (2002). The statistical analysis of data from small groups. *Journal of Personality and Social Psychology*, *83*, 126–137.

Kenny, D. A., West, T. V., Cillessen, A. H. N., Coie, J. D., Dodge, K. A., Hubbard, J. A., & Schwartz, D. (2007). Accuracy in judgments of aggressiveness. *Personality and Social Psychology Bulletin*, *33*, 1225–1236.

Kenny, D. A., & Zaccaro, S. J. (1983). An estimate of variance due to traits in leadership. *Journal of Applied Psychology*, *68*, 678–685.

Kenrick, D. T., Groth, G. E., Trost, M. R., & Sadalla, E. K. (1993). Integrating evolutionary and social exchange perspectives on relationships: Effects of gender, self-appraisal, and involvement level on mate selection criteria. *Journal of Personality and Social Psychology*, *64*, 951–969.

Kenrick, D. T., & Gutierres, S. E. (1980). Contrast effects and judgments of physical attractiveness: When beauty becomes a social problem. *Journal of Personality and Social Psychology*, *38*, 131–140.

Kenrick, D. T., Gutierres, S. E., & Goldberg, L. L. (1989). Influence of popular erotica on judgments of strangers and mates. *Journal of Experimental Social Psychology*, *25*, 159–167.

Kenrick, D. T., & Keefe, R. C. (1992). Age preferences in mates reflect sex differences in reproductive strategies. *Behavioral and Brain Sciences*, *15*, 97–116.

Kenrick, D. T., Li, N. P., & Butner, J. (2003). Dynamical evolutionary psychology: Individual decision rules and emergent social norms. *Psychological Review*, *110*, 3–28.

Kenrick, D. T., Maner, J. K., Butner, J., Li, N. P., Becker, D. V., & Schaller, M. (2002). Dynamical evolutionary psychology: Mapping the domains of the new interactionist paradigm. *Personality and Social Psychology Review*, *6*, 347–356.

Kenrick, D. T., & Sheets, V. (1993). Homicidal fantasies. *Ethology and Sociobiology 14*, 231–246.

Kernis, M. H., Grannemann, B. D., & Barclay, L. C. (1989). Stability and level of self-esteem as predictors of anger arousal and hostility. *Journal of Personality and Social Psychology*, *56*, 1013–1022.

Kerr, N. L. (1983). Motivation losses in small groups: A social dilemma analysis. *Journal of Personality and Social Psychology*, *45*, 819–828.

Kerr, N. L. (1996). "Does my contribution really matter?": Efficacy in social dilemmas. In W. Stroebe & M. Hewstone (Eds.), *European review of social psychology* (Vol. 7, pp. 209–240). New York: Wiley.

Kerr, N. L. (2002). When is a minority a minority?: Active versus passive minority advocacy and social influence. *European Journal of Social Psychology*, *32*, 471–483.

Kerr, N. L., MacCoun, R. J., & Kramer, G. P. (1996). Bias in judgment: Comparing individuals and groups. *Psychological Review*, *103*, 687–719.

Kerr, N. L., & Park, E. S. (2001). Group performance in collaborative and social dilemma tasks: Progress and prospects. In M. A. Hogg & R. S. Tindale (Eds.), *Blackwell handbook of social psychology: Group processes* (pp. 107–138). Malden, MA: Blackwell.

Kerr, N. L., & Stanfel, J. A. (1993). Role schemata and member motivation in task groups. *Personality and Social Psychology Bulletin*, *19*, 432–442.

Kerr, N. L., & Tindale, R. S. (2004). Group performance and decision making. *Annual Review of Psychology*, *55*, 623–655.

Khanna, N. (2004). The role of reflected appraisals in racial identity: The case of multiracial Asians. *Social Psychology Quarterly*, *67*, 115–131.

Kidd, R. F., & Berkowitz, L. (1976). Effect of dissonance arousal on helpfulness. *Journal of Personality and Social Psychology*, *33*, 613–622.

Kiecolt-Glaser, J. K., McGuire, L., Robles, T. F., & Glaser, R. (2002). Emotions, morbidity, and mortality: New perspectives from psychoneuroimmunology. *Annual Review of Psychology 53*, 83–107.

Kiesler, S., Powers, A., Fussell, S. R., & Torrey, C. (2008). Anthropomorphic interactions with a robot and robot-like agent. *Social Cognition*, *26*, 169–181.

Kim, H., & Markus, H. R. (1999). Deviance or uniqueness, harmony or conformity? A cultural analysis. *Journal of Personality and Social Psychology*, *77*, 785–800.

Kim, H. S., Sherman, D. K., Ko, D., & Taylor, S. E. (2006). Pursuit of comfort and pursuit of harmony: Culture, relationships, and social support seeking. *Personality and Social Psychology Bulletin*, *32*, 1595–1607.

Kim, J., Lim, J., & Bhargava, M. (1998). The role of affect in attitude formation: A classical conditioning approach. *Journal of the Academy of Marketing Science*, *26*, 143–152.

Kinder, D. R. (1998). Communication and opinion. *Annual Review of Political Science*, *1*, 167–197.

Kinder, D. R., & Sears, D. O. (1981). Prejudice and politics: Symbolic racism versus racial threats to the good life. *Journal of Personality and Social Psychology*, *40*, 414–431.

King, L. A., & Hicks, J. A. (2007). Whatever happened to "What might have been?" Regrets, happiness, and maturity. *American Psychologist*, *62*, 625–636.

Kipnis, D. (1972). Does power corrupt? *Journal of Personality and Social Psychology*, *24*, 33–41.

Kipnis, D. (1976). *The powerholders*. Oxford, England: University of Chicago Press.

Kipnis, D. (1984). The use of power in organizations and in interpersonal settings. *Applied Social Psychology Annual*, *5*, 179–210.

Kipnis, D., Castell, J., Gergen, M., & Mauch, D. (1976). Metamorphic effects of power. *Journal of Applied Psychology*, *61*, 127–135.

Kipnis, D., Schmidt, S., Price, K., & Stitt, C. (1981). Why do I like thee: Is it your performance or my order? *Journal of Applied Psychology*, *66*, 324–328.

Kipnis, D., & Vanderveer, R. (1971). Ingratiation and the use of power. *Journal of Personality and Social Psychology*, *17*, 280–286.

Kitayama, S., & Markus, H. R. (1999). Yin and yang of the Japanese self: The cultural psychology of personality coherence. In D. Cervone & Y. Shoda (Eds.), *The coherence of personality: Social cognitive bases of personality consistency, variability and organization* (pp. 242–302). New York: Guilford.

Kitayama, S., Markus, H. R., Matsumoto, H., & Norasakkunkit, V. (1997). Individual and collective processes in the construction of the self: Self-enhancement in the United States and self-criticism in Japan. *Journal of Personality and Social Psychology*, *72*, 1245–1267.

Klauer, K. C., & Wegener, I. (1998). Unraveling social categorization in the "Who said what?" paradigm. *Journal of Personality and Social Psychology*, *75*, 1155–1178.

Klein, O., & Snyder, M. (2003). Stereotypes and behavioral confirmation: From interpersonal to intergroup perspectives. In M. P. Zanna (Ed.), *Advances in experimental social psychology* (Vol. 35, pp. 153–233). New York: Academic Press.

Klein, S. B., Cosmides, L., Tooby, J., & Chance, S. (2002). Decisions and the evolution of memory: Multiple systems, multiple functions. *Psychological Review, 109*, 306–329.

Klimoski, R., & Mohammed, S. (1994). Team mental model: Construct or metaphor? *Journal of Management, 20*, 403–437.

Kluegel, J. R., & Smith, E. R. (1986). *Beliefs about inequality: Americans' beliefs about what is and what ought to be.* New York: Aldine de Gruyter.

Knapp, R. H. (1944). A psychology of rumor. *Public Opinion Quarterly, 8*, 22–37.

Knutson, K. M., Wood, J. N., Spampinato, M. V., & Grafman, J. (2006). Politics on the brain: An fMRI investigation. *Social Neuroscience, 1*, 25–40.

Kobrynowicz, D., & Biernat, M. (1997). Decoding subjective evaluations: How stereotypes provide shifting standards. *Journal of Experimental Social Psychology, 33*, 579–601.

Kohlberg, L. (1963). The development of children's orientations toward a moral order: I. Sequence in the development of moral thought. *Vita Humana, 6*, 11–33.

Konijn, E. A., Nije Bijvank, M., & Bushman, B. J. (2007). I wish I were a warrior: The role of wishful identification in the effects of violent video games on aggression in adolescent boys. *Developmental Psychology, 43*, 1038–1044.

Konrath, S., Bushman, B. J., & Campbell, W. K. (2006). Attenuating the link between threatened egotism and aggression. *Psychological Science, 17*, 995–1001.

Korchmaros, J. D., & Kenny, D. A. (2001). Emotional closeness as a mediator of the effect of genetic relatedness on altruism. *Psychological Science, 12*, 262–265.

Kosfeld, M., Heinrichs, M., Zak, P. J., Fischbacher, U., & Fehr, E. (2005). Oxytocin increases trust in humans. *Nature, 435*, 673–676.

Kramer, R. M. (1998). Paranoid cognition in social systems: Thinking and acting in the shadow of doubt. *Personality and Social Psychology Review, 2*, 251–275.

Kramer, R. M., McClintock, C. G., & Messick, D. M. (1986). Social values and cooperative response to a simulated resource conservation crisis. *Journal of Personality 54*, 576–592.

Kraus, S. J. (1995). Attitudes and the prediction of behavior: A meta-analysis of the empirical literature. *Personality and Social Psychology Bulletin, 21*, 58–75.

Krauss, R. M., & Fussell, S. R. (1991). Perspective taking in communication: Representations of others' knowledge in reference. *Social Cognition, 9*, 2–24.

Kray, L. J., Galinsky, A. D., & Thompson, L. (2002). Reversing the gender gap in negotiations: An exploration of stereotype regeneration. *Organizational Behavior and Human Decision Processes, 87*, 386–409.

Krebs, D. L. (2008). Morality: An evolutionary account. *Perspectives on Psychological Science, 3*, 149–243.

Krieger, L. H., & Fiske, S. T. (2006). Behavioral realism in employment discrimination law: Implicit bias and disparate treatment. *California Law Review, 94*, 997–1062.

Krosnick, J. A., Boninger, D. S., Chuang, Y. C., Berent, M. K., & Carnot, C. G. (1993). Attitude strength: One construct or many related constructs? *Journal of Personality and Social Psychology, 65*, 1132–1151.

Krosnick, J. A., Miller, J. M., & Tichy, M. P. (2004). An unrecognized need for ballot reform: Effects of candidate name order. In A. N. Crigler, M. R. Just, & E. J. McCaffery (Eds.), *Rethinking the vote: The politics and prospects of American election reform* (pp. 51–74). New York: Oxford University Press.

Krosnick, J. A., & Visser, P. S. (2010). Political psychology. In S. T. Fiske, D. T. Gilbert, & G. Lindzey (Eds.), *Handbook of social psychology* (5th ed., in press). New York: Wiley.

Krueger, F., McCabe, K., Moll, J., Kriegeskorte, N., Zahn, R., Strenziok, M., Heinecke, A., & Grafman, J. (2007). Neural correlates of trust. *PNAS: Proceedings of the National Academy of Sciences of the United States of America, 104*, 20084–20089.

Krueger, J. (1998). On the perception of social consensus. In M. P. Zanna (Ed.), *Advances in experimental social psychology* (Vol. 30, pp. 16–24). New York: Academic Press.

Krueger, J., & Clement, R. W. (1997). Estimates of social consensus by majorities and minorities: The case for social projection. *Personality and Social Psychology Review, 1*, 299–313.

Kruger, J., & Dunning, D. (1999). Unskilled and unaware of it: How difficulties in recognizing one's own incompetence lead to inflated self-assessments. *Journal of Personality and Social Psychology, 77*, 1121–1134.

Kruglanski, A. W. (1989). The psychology of being "right": On the problem of accuracy in social perception and cognition. *Psychological Bulletin, 106*, 395–409.

Kruglanski, A. W., & Fishman, S. (2006). Terrorism between "syndrome" and "tool." *Current Directions in Psychological Science, 15*, 45–48.

Kruglanski, A. W., & Mackie, D. M. (1990). Majority and minority influence: A judgmental process analysis. In W. Stroebe & M. Hewstone (Eds.), *European review of social psychology* (Vol. 1, pp. 229–262). New York: Wiley.

Kruglanski, A. W., & Orehek, E. (2007). Partitioning the domain of social inference: Dual mode and systems models and their alternatives. *Annual Review of Psychology, 58*, 291–316.

Kruglanski, A. W., & Webster, D. M. (1991). Group members' reactions to opinion deviates and conformists at varying degrees of proximity to decision deadline and of environmental noise. *Journal of Personality and Social Psychology, 61*, 212–225.

Kruglanski, A. W., & Webster, D. M. (1996). Motivated closing of the mind: "Seizing" and "freezing." *Psychological Review, 103*, 263–283.

Krumhuber, E., Manstead, A. S. R., Cosker, D., Marshall, D., Rosin, P. L., & Kappas, A. (2007). Facial dynamics as indicators of trustworthiness and cooperative behavior. *Emotion, 7*, 730–735.

Kubitschek, W. N., & Hallinan, M. T. (1998). Tracking and students' friendships. *Social Psychology Quarterly, 61*, 1–15.

Kugler, T., Bornstein, G., Kocher, M. G., & Sutter, M. (2007). Trust between individuals and groups: Groups are less trusting than individuals but just as trustworthy. *Journal of Economic Psychology, 28*, 646–657.

Kuiper, N. A., & Rogers, T. B. (1979). Encoding of personal information: Self-other differences. *Journal of Personality and Social Psychology, 37*, 499–514.

Kumashiro, M., Rusbult, C. E., Finkenauer, C., & Stocker, S. L. (2007). To think or to do: The impact of assessment and locomotion orientation on the Michelangelo phenomenon. *Journal of Social and Personal Relationships, 24*, 591–611.

Kunce, L., & Shaver, P. R. (1994). An attachment-theoretical approach to caregiving in romantic relationships. In D. Perlman & K. Bartholomew (Eds.), *Advances in personal relationships:* Vol. 5, *Attachment processes in adulthood* (pp. 205–238). London: Jessica Kingsley.

Kunda, Z. (1987). Motivated inference: Self-serving generation and evaluation of causal theories. *Journal of Personality and Social Psychology, 53*, 636–647.

Kunda, Z. (1990). The case for motivated reasoning. *Psychological Bulletin, 108*, 480–498.

Kunda, Z. (1999). *Social cognition: Making sense of people*. Cambridge: MIT Press.

Kunda, Z, & Sinclair, L. (1999). Motivated reasoning with stereotypes: Activation, application, and inhibition. *Psychological Inquiry, 10*, 12–22.

Kurzban, R., & Leary, M. R. (2001). Evolutionary origins of stigmatization: The functions of social exclusion. *Psychological Bulletin, 127*, 187–208.

Kwan, V. S. Y., Bond, M. H., & Singelis, T. S. (1997). Pancultural explanations for life satisfaction: Adding relationship harmony to self-esteem. *Journal of Personality and Social Psychology, 73*, 1038–1051.

Kwan, V. S. Y., & Fiske, S. T. (2008). Missing links in social cognition: The continuum from nonhuman agents to dehumanized humans. *Social Cognition, 26*, 125–128.

Kwan, V. S. Y., Gosling, S. D., & John, O. P. (2008). Anthropomorphism as a special case of social perception: A cross-species Social Relations Model analysis of humans and dogs. *Social Cognition, 26*, 129–142.

Kwan, V. S. Y., John, O. P., Kenny, D. A., Bond, M. H., & Robins, R. W. (2004). Reconceptualizing individual differences in self enhancement bias: An interpersonal approach. *Psychological Review, 111*, 94–110.

Kwan, V. S. Y., John, O. P., Robins, R. W., & Kuang, L. L. (2008). Conceptualizing and assessing self-enhancement bias: A componential approach. *Journal of Personality and Social Psychology, 94*, 1062–1077.

Lakin, J. L., & Chartrand, T. L. (2003). Using nonconscious behavioral mimicry to create affiliation and rapport. *Psychological Science, 14*, 334–339.

Lambert, A. J., Khan, S. R., Lickel, B. A., & Fricke, K. (1997). Mood and the correction of positive versus negative stereotypes. *Journal of Personality and Social Psychology, 72*, 1002–1016.

Lamm, H., & Wiesmann, U. (1997). Subjective attributes of attraction: How people characterize their liking, their love, and their being in love. *Personal Relationships, 4*, 271–284.

Lammers, J., Galinsky, A. D., Gordijn, E. H., & Otten, S. (2008). Illegitimacy moderates the effects of power on approach. *Psychological Science, 19*, 558–564.

Lane, K. A., Kang, J., & Banaji, M. R. (2007). Implicit social cognition and law. *Annual Review of Law and Social Science, 3*, 427–451.

Langer, E. J., & Rodin, J. (1976). The effects of choice and enhanced personal responsibility for the aged: A field experiment in an institutional setting. *Journal of Personality and Social Psychology, 34*, 191–198.

Langlois, J. H., & Roggman, L. A. (1990). Attractive faces are only average. *Psychological Science, 1*, 115–121.

Langner, C. A., & Keltner, D. (2008). Social power and emotional experience: Actor and partner effects within dyadic interactions. *Journal of Experimental Social Psychology*, *44*, 848–856.

LaPiere, R. T. (1934). Attitudes vs. actions. *Social Forces*, *13*, 230–237.

Larson, J. R., Christensen, C., Franz, T. M., & Abbott, A. S. (1998). Diagnosing groups: The pooling, management, and impact of shared and unshared case information in team-based medical decision making. *Journal of Personality and Social Psychology*, *75*, 93–108.

Larson, J. R., Foster-Fishman, P. G., & Keys, C. B. (1994). Discussion of shared and unshared information in decision-making groups. *Journal of Personality and Social Psychology*, *67*, 446–461.

Lassiter, D. G., & Briggs, M. A. (1990). Effect of anticipated interaction on liking: An individual difference analysis. *Journal of Social Behavior & Personality* 5, 357–367.

Lasswell, H. D. (1948). The structure and function of communication in society. In L. Bryson (Ed.), *The communication of ideas: Religion and civilization series* (pp. 37–51). New York: Harper & Row.

Latané, B. (1981). The psychology of social impact. *American Psychologist*, *36*, 343–356.

Latané, B., & Bourgeois, M. J. (2001). Dynamic social impact and the consolidation, clustering, correlation, and continuing diversity of culture. In M. A. Hogg & R. S. Tindale (Eds.), *Blackwell handbook of social psychology: Group processes* (pp. 235–258). Malden, MA: Blackwell.

Latané, B., & Darley, J. M. (1968). Group inhibition of bystander intervention in emergencies. *Journal of Personality and Social Psychology*, *10*, 215–221.

Latané, B., & Darley, J. M. (1970). *The unresponsive bystander: Why doesn't he help?* Englewood Cliffs, NJ.: Prentice-Hall.

Latané, B., Williams, K. D., & Harkins, S. (1979). Many hands make light the work: The causes and consequences of social loafing. *Journal of Personality and Social Psychology*, *37*, 822–832.

Laughlin, P. R., & Ellis, A. L. (1986). Demonstrability and social combination processes on mathematical intellective tasks. *Journal of Experimental Social Psychology*, *22*, 177–189.

Lavine, H., Lodge, M., & Freitas, K. (2005). Threat, authoritarianism, and selective exposure to information. *Political Psychology*, *26*, 219–244.

Lavine, H., Thomsen, C. J., Zanna, M. P., & Borgida, E. (1998). On the primacy of affect in the determination of attitudes and behavior: The moderating role of affective-cognitive ambivalence. *Journal of Experimental Social Psychology*, *34*, 398–421.

Laye, C. (1954). *The dark child*. New York: Farrar, Straus, & Giroux.

Lazarus, R. S. (1982). Thoughts on the relations between emotion and cognition. *American Psychologist*, *39*, 124–129.

Leary, M. R. (1990). Responses to social exclusion: Social anxiety, jealousy, loneliness, depression, and low self-esteem. *Journal of Social and Clinical Psychology*, *9*, 221–229.

Leary, M. R. (2005). Sociometer theory and the pursuit of relational value: Getting to the root of self-esteem. *European Review of Social Psychology*, *16*, 75–111.

Leary, M. R. (2007). Motivational and emotional aspects of the self. *Annual Review of Psychology*, *58*, 317–344.

Leary, M. R., & Baumeister, R. F. (2000). The nature and function of self-esteem: Sociometer theory. In M. P. Zanna (Ed.), *Advances in experimental social psychology* (Vol. 32, pp. 1–62). New York: Academic Press.

Leary, M. R., & Kowalski, R. M. (1990). Impression management: A literature review and two-component model. *Psychological Bulletin*, *107*, 34–47.

Leary, M. R., Tambor, E. S., Terdal, S. K., & Downs, D. L. (1995). Self-esteem as an interpersonal monitor: The sociometer hypothesis. *Journal of Personality and Social Psychology*, *68*, 518–530.

Leary, M. R., Tate, E. B., Adams, C. E., Batts-Allen, A., & Hancock, J. (2007). Self-compassion and reactions to unpleasant self-relevant events: The implications of treating oneself kindly. *Journal of Personality and Social Psychology*, *92*, 887–904.

Leary, M. R., Twenge, J. M., & Quinlivan, E. (2006). Interpersonal rejection as a determinant of anger and aggression. *Personality and Social Psychology Review*, *10*, 111–132.

LeBon, G. (1895/1995). *The crowd: A study of the popular mind*. London: Transaction. (Original work published in French in 1895.)

Leddo, J., Abelson, R. P., & Gross, P. H. (1984). Conjunctive explanations: When two reasons are better than one. *Journal of Personality and Social Psychology*, *47*, 933–943.

Ledgerwood, A., & Chaiken, S. (2007). Priming us and them: Automatic assimilation and contrast in group attitudes. *Journal of Personality and Social Psychology*, *93*, 940–956.

Lee, A. Y., Aaker, J. L., & Gardner, W. L. (2000). The pleasures and pains of distinct self-construals: The role of interdependence in regulatory focus. *Journal of Personality and Social Psychology*, *78*, 1122–1134.

Lee, T. L., & Fiske, S. T. (2006). Not an outgroup, but not yet an ingroup: Immigrants in the stereotype content model. *International Journal of Intercultural Relations*, *30*, 751–768.

Lee, T. L., Fiske, S. T., & Glick, P. (in press). Ambivalent sexism in close relationships: (Hostile) power and (benevolent) romance shape relationship ideals. *Sex Roles*.

Lehman, D. R., Lempert, R. O., & Nisbett, R. E. (1988). The effects of graduate training on reasoning: Formal discipline and thinking about everyday-life events. *American Psychologist*, *43*, 431–442.

Lemay E. P., Jr., & Clark, M. S. (2008). How the head liberates the heart: Projection of communal responsiveness guides relationship promotion. *Journal of Personality and Social Psychology*, *94*, 647–671.

Lemay E. P., Jr., Clark, M. S., & Feeney, B. C. (2007). Projection of responsiveness to needs and the construction of satisfying communal relationships. *Journal of Personality and Social Psychology*, *92*, 834–853.

Lemyre, L., & Smith, P. M. (1985). Intergroup discrimination and self-esteem in the minimal group paradigm. *Journal of Personality and Social Psychology*, *49*, 660–670.

Lench, H. C., & Ditto, P. H. (2008). Automatic optimism: Biased use of base rate information for positive and negative events. *Journal of Experimental Social Psychology*, *44*, 631–639.

Leonardelli, G. J. (2001). Minority and majority discrimination: When and why. *Journal of Experimental Social Psychology*, *37*, 468–485.

Lepore, L., & Brown, R. J. (1997). Category and stereotype activation: Is prejudice inevitable? *Journal of Personality and Social Psychology*, *72*, 275–287.

Lepper, M. R., Greene, D., & Nisbett, R. E. (1973). Undermining children's intrinsic interest with extrinsic reward: A test of the "overjustification" hypothesis. *Journal of Personality and Social Psychology*, *28*, 129–137.

Lerner, J. S., & Keltner, D. (2000). Beyond valence: A model of emotion-specific influences on judgment and choice. *Cognition and Emotion*, *14*, 473–493.

Lerner, M. J., & Miller, D. T. (1978). Just world research and the attribution process: Looking back and looking ahead. *Psychological Bulletin*, *85*, 1030–1051.

Lett, H. S., Blumenthal, J. A., Babyak, M. A., Catellier, D. J., Carney, R. M., Berkman, L. F., Burg, M. M., Mitchell, P., Jaffe, A. S., & Schneiderman, N. (2007). Social support and prognosis in patients at increased psychosocial risk recovering from myocardial infarction. *Health Psychology*, *26*, 418–427.

Levenson, R. W., Carstensen, L. L., & Gottman, J. M. (1994). Influence of age and gender on affect, physiology, and their interrelations: A study of long-term marriages. *Journal of Personality and Social Psychology*, *67*, 56–68.

Leventhal, H., Weinman, J., Leventhal, E. A., & Phillips, L. A. (2008). Health psychology: The search for pathways between behavior and health. *Annual Review of Psychology*, *59*, 477–505.

Levin, S., Federico, C. M., Sidanius, J., & Rabinowitz, J. L. (2002). Social dominance orientation and intergroup bias: The legitimation of favoritism for high-status groups. *Personality and Social Psychology Bulletin*, *28*, 144–157.

Levine, J. M. (1999). Solomon Asch's legacy for group research. *Personality and Social Psychology Review*, *3*, 358–364.

Levine, J. M., & Kerr, N. L. (2007). Inclusion and exclusion: Consequences for group process. In A. W. Kruglanski & E. T. Higgins (Eds.), *Social psychology: Handbook of basic principles* (2nd ed., pp. 759–784). New York: Guilford.

Levine, J. M., & Kerr, N. L. (2007). Inclusion and exclusion: Implications for group processes. In A. W. Kruglanski & E. T. Higgins (Eds.), *Social psychology: Handbook of basic principles* (2nd ed., pp. 759–784). New York: Guilford.

Levine, J. M., & Moreland, R. L. (1994). Group socialization: Theory and research. In W. Stroebe & M. Hewstone (Eds.), *European review of social psychology* (Vol. 5, pp. 305–336). New York: Wiley.

Levine, J. M., & Moreland, R. L. (1998). Small groups. In D. T. Gilbert, S. T. Fiske, & G. Lindzey (Eds.), *Handbook of social psychology* (4th ed., pp. 415–469). New York: McGraw-Hill.

Levine, J. M., Moreland, R. L., & Choi, H. S. (2001). Group socialization and newcomer innovation. In M. A. Hogg & R. S. Tindale (Eds.), *Blackwell handbook of social psychology: Group processes* (pp. 86–106). Malden, MA: Blackwell.

Levine, J. M., & Russo, E. M. (1987). Majority and minority influence. In C. Hendrick (Ed.), *Review of personality and social psychology: Group processes*. Newbury Park, CA: Sage.

Levine, J. M., & Thompson, L. (1996). Conflict in groups. In E. T. Higgins & A. W. Kruglanski (Eds.), *Social psychology: Handbook of basic principles* (pp. 745–776). New York: Guilford.

Levinger, G. (1980). Toward the analysis of close relationships. *Journal of Experimental Social Psychology*, *16*, 510–544.

Levinger, G., & Breedlove, J. (1966). Interpersonal attraction and agreement. *Journal of Personality and Social Psychology*, *3*, 367–372.

Levy, S. R., Freitas, A. L., Mendoza-Denton, R., & Kugelmass, H. (2006). Hurricane Katrina's impact on African Americans' and European Americans' endorsement of the Protestant Work Ethic.

*Analyses of Social Issues and Public Policy (ASAP), 6*, 75–85.

Levy, S. R., Plaks, J. E., Hong, Y., Chiu, C., & Dweck, C. S. (2001). Static versus dynamic theories and the perception of groups: Different routes to different destinations. *Personality and Social Psychology Review, 5*, 156–168.

Lewin, K. (1941). Analysis of the concepts whole, differentiation, and unity. *University of Iowa Studies in Child Welfare, 18*, 226–261. Reprinted in D. Cartwright (Ed.), *Field theory in social science* (pp. 305–338). London: Tavistock.

Lewin, K. (1944). Constructs in psychology and psychological ecology. *University of Iowa Studies in Child Welfare, 20*, 1–29. Reprinted under the title of Constructs in field theory. In D. Cartwright (Ed.), *Field theory in social science* (pp. 30–42). London: Tavistock.

Lewin, K. (1951/1997). Behavior and development as a function of the total situation. In D. Cartwright (Ed.), *Field theory in social psychology* (pp. 337–381). Washington, DC: American Psychological Association.

Lewin, K. (1952). Group decision and social change. In G. E. Swanson, T. M. Newcomb, E. L. Hartley, & others (Eds.), *Readings in social psychology* (pp. 459–473). New York: Holt.

Leyens, J.-Ph. (1989). Another look at confirmatory strategies during a real interview. *European Journal of Social Psychology, 19*, 55–62.

Leyens, J.-Ph., & Corneille, O. (1999). Asch's social psychology: Not as social as you may think. *Personality and Social Psychology Review, 3*, 345–357.

Leyens, J.-Ph., Cortes, B., Demoulin, S., Dovidio, J. F., Fiske, S. T., Gaunt, R., Paladino, M., Rodriguez-Perez, A., Rodriguez-Torres, R., & Vaes, J. (2003). Emotional prejudice, essentialism, and nationalism: The 2002 Tajfel Lecture. *European Journal of Social Psychology, 33*, 703–717.

Leyens, J.-Ph., Dardenne, B., & Fiske, S. T. (1998). Why and under what circumstances is a hypothesis-consistent testing strategy preferred in interviews? *British Journal of Social Psychology, 37*, 259–274.

Leyens, J.-Ph., Désert, M., Croizet, J. C., & Darcis, C. (2000). Stereotype threat: Are lower status and history of stigmatization preconditions of stereotype threat? *Personality and Social Psychology Bulletin, 26*, 1189–1199.

Leyens, J.-Ph., Herman, G., & Dunand, M. (1982). The influence of an audience upon the reactions to filmed violence. *European Journal of Social Psychology, 12*, 131–142.

Leyens, J.-Ph., & Yzerbyt, V. Y. (1992). The ingroup overexclusion effect: Impact of valence and confirmation on stereotypical information search. *European Journal of Social Psychology, 22*, 549–569.

Leyens, J.-Ph., Yzerbyt, V. Y., & Schadron, G. (1992). The social judgeablity approach to stereotypes. In W Stroebe & M. Hewstone (Eds.), *European Review of Social Psychology* (Vol. 3, pp. 91–120). London: Wiley.

Li, N. P., Bailey, J. M., Kenrick, D. T., & Linsenmeier, J. A. (2002). The necessities and luxuries of mate preference. *Journal of Personality and Social Psychology, 82*, 947–955.

Liberman, N., Molden, D. C., Idson, L. C., & Higgins, E. T. (2001). Promotion and prevention focus on alternative hypothesis: Implications for attributional functions. *Journal of Personality and Social Psychology, 80*, 5–18.

Lickel, B., Hamilton, D. L., & Sherman, S. J. (2001). Elements of a lay theory of groups: Types of groups, relational styles, and the perception of group entitativity. *Personality and Social Psychology Review, 5*, 129–140.

Lickel, B., Hamilton, D. L., Wieczorkowska, G., Lewis, A., Sherman, S. J., & Uhles, A. N. (2000). Varieties of groups and the perception of group entitativity. *Journal of Personality and Social Psychology, 78*, 223–246.

Lieberman, J. D., Solomon, S, Greenberg, J., & McGregor, H. A. (1999). A hot new measure of aggression: Hot sauce allocation. *Aggression Behavior, 25*, 331–348.

Lieberman, M. D. (2007). Social cognitive neuroscience: A review of core processes. *Annual Review of Psychology, 58*, 259–290.

Lieberman, M. D. (2010). Social cognitive neuroscience. In S. T. Fiske, D. T. Gilbert, & G. Lindzey (Eds.), *The handbook of social psychology* (5th ed.). New York: Wiley.

Lieberman, M. D., Gaunt, R., Gilbert, D. T., & Trope, Y. (2002). Reflexion and reflection: A social cognitive neuroscience approach to attributional inference. In M. P. Zanna (Ed.), *Advances in Experimental Social Psychology* (Vol. 34, 199–249). New York: Academic Press.

Lieberman, M. D., Hariri, A., Jarcho, J. M., Eisenberger, N. I., & Bookheimer, S. Y. (2005). An fMRI investigation of race-related amygdala activity in African-American and Caucasian-American individuals. *Nature Neuroscience, 8*, 720–722.

Lieberman, M. D., Jarcho, J. M., & Satpute, A. B. (2004). Evidence-based and intuition-based self-knowledge: An fMRI study. *Journal of Personality and Social Psychology, 87*, 421–435.

Lieberman, M. D., Ochsner, K. N., Gilbert, D. T., & Schacter, D. L. (2001). Do amnesics exhibit cognitive dissonance reduction? The role of explicit memory and attention in attitude change. *Psychological Science, 12*, 135–140.

Lin, M. H., Kwan, V. S. Y., Cheung, A., & Fiske, S. T. (2005). Stereotype content model explains prejudice for an envied outgroup: Scale of Anti-Asian American Stereotypes. *Personality and Social Psychology Bulletin, 31*, 34–47.

Lin, Y W., & Rusbult, C. E. (1995). Commitment to dating relationships and cross-sex friendships in America and China. *Journal of Social and Personality Relationships, 12*, 7–26.

Lindsay, J. J., & Anderson, C. A. (2000). From antecedent conditions to violent actions: A general affective aggression model. *Personality and Social Psychology Bulletin, 26*, 533–547.

Linville, P. W. (1982). The complexity-extremity effect and age-based stereotyping. *Journal of Personality and Social Psychology, 42*, 193–211.

Linville, P. W. (1985). Self-complexity and affective extremity: Don't put all of your eggs in one cognitive basket. *Social Cognition, 3*, 94–120.

Linville, P. W. (1987). Self-complexity as a cognitive buffer against stress-related depression and illness. *Journal of Personality and Social Psychology, 52*, 663–676.

Linville, P. W., Fischer, G. W., & Salovey, P. (1989). Perceived distributions of the characteristics of ingroup and outgroup members: Empirical evidence and a computer simulation. *Journal of Personality and Social Psychology, 38*, 689–703.

Lipkus, I. M., McBride, C. M., Pollak, K. I., Lyna, P., & Bepler, G. (2004). Interpretation of genetic risk feedback among African American smokers with low socioeconomic status. *Health Psychology, 23*, 178–188.

London, P. (1970). The rescuers: Motivational hypothesis about Christians who saved Jews from the Nazi. In J. Macaulay, & L. Berkowitz (Eds.), *Altruism and helping behavior* (pp. 241–250). New York: Academic Press.

Lorber, M. F. (2004). Psychophysiology of aggression, psychopathy, and conduct problems: A meta-analysis. *Psychological Bulletin, 130*, 531–552.

Lord, C. G., Ross, L., & Lepper, M. R. (1979). Biased assimilation and attitude polarization: The effects of prior theories on subsequently considered evidence. *Journal of Personality and Social Psychology, 37*, 2098–2109.

Lord, C. G., & Saenz, D. S. (1985). Memory deficits and memory surfeits: Differential cognitive consequences of tokenism for tokens and observers. *Journal of Personality and Social Psychology, 49*, 918–926.

Lord, C. G., Saenz, D. S., & Godfrey, D. K. (1987). Effects of perceived scrutiny on participant

memory for social interactions. *Journal of Experimental Social Psychology, 23*, 498–517.

Lord, R. G., Brown, D. J., & Harvey, J. L. (2001). System constraints on leadership perceptions, behavior, and influence: An example of connectionist level processes. In M A. Hogg & R. S. Tindale (Eds.), *Blackwell handbook of social psychology: Group processes* (pp. 283–310). Malden, MA: Blackwell.

Lord, R. G., de Vader, C. L., & Alliger, G. M. (1986). A meta-analysis of the relation between personality traits and leadership perceptions: An application of validity generalization procedures. *Journal of Applied Psychology*, 402–410.

Lord, R. G., Foti, R. J., & de Vader, C. L. (1984). A test of leadership categorization theory: Internal structure, information processing, and leader perceptions. *Organizational Behavior and Human Performance, 34*, 343–378.

Lord, R. G., & Maher, K. J. (1991). *Leadership and information processing: Linking perceptions and performance*. New York: Routledge.

Lorenzi-Cioldi, F., & Clémence, A. (2001). Group processes and the construction of social representations. In M. A. Hogg & R. S. Tindale (Eds.), *Blackwell handbook of social psychology: Group processes* (pp. 311–333). Malden, MA: Blackwell.

Lott, B. E., & Lott, A. J. (1960). The formation of positive attitudes toward group members. *Journal of Abnormal and Social Psychology, 61*, 297–300.

Lott, B. E., & Lott, A. (1972). The power of liking: Consequences of interpersonal attitudes derived from a liberalized view of secondary reinforcement. In L. Berkowitz (Ed.), *Advances in experimental social psychology* (Vol. 6, pp. 109–149). New York: Academic Press.

Lott, B. E., & Lott, A. J. (1985). Learning theory in contemporary social psychology. In G. Lindzey & E. Aronson (Eds.), *Handbook of social psychology* (3rd ed., Vol. 1, pp. 109–135). New York: Random House.

Lowe, K. B., Kroeck, K. G., & Sivasubramaniam, N. (1996). Effectiveness correlates of transformation and transactional leadership: A meta-analytic review of the MLQ literature. *Leadership Quarterly, 7*, 385–425.

Lowery, B. S., Hardin, C. D., & Sinclair, S. (2001). Social influence effects on automatic racial prejudice. *Journal of Personality and Social Psychology, 81*, 842–855.

Luce, R. D., & Raiffa, H. (1957). *Games and decision: Introduction and critical survey*. New York: Wiley.

Luhtanen, R., & Crocker, J. (1992). A collective self-esteem scale: Self-evaluation of one's social identity. *Personality and Social Psychology Bulletin*, *18*, 302–318.

Lun, J., Sinclair, S., Whitchurch, E. R., & Glenn, C. (2007). (Why) do I think what you think? Epistemic social tuning and implicit prejudice. *Journal of Personality and Social Psychology*, *93*, 957–972.

Lysak, H., Rule, B. G., & Dobbs, A. R. (1989). Conceptions of aggression: Prototype or defining features? *Personality and Social Psychology Bulletin*, *15*, 233–243.

Ma, H. K. (1985). Cross-cultural study of altruism. *Psychological Reports*, *57*, 337–338.

Ma, H. K., & Leung, M. C. (1995). The relation of altruistic orientation to family social environment in Chinese children. *Psychologia: An International Journal of Psychology in the Orient*, *38*, 109–115.

Maass, A., Ceccarelli, R., & Rubin, S. (1996). Linguistic intergroup bias: Evidence for in-group protective motivation. *Journal of Personality and Social Psychology*, *71*, 512–526.

Maass, A., Milesi, A., Zabbini, S., & Stahlberg, D. (1995). Linguistic intergroup bias: Differential expectancies or in-group protection? *Journal of Personality and Social Psychology*, *68*, 116–126.

Maass, A., Salvi, D., Arcuri, L., & Semin, G. R. (1989). Language use in intergroup contexts: The linguistic intergroup bias. *Journal of Personality and Social Psychology*, *57*, 981–993.

Maass, A., West, S. G., & Cialdini, R. B. (1987). Minority influence and conversion. In C. Hendrick (Ed.), *Review of personality and social psychology: Group processes* (pp. 55–79). Newbury Park, CA: Sage.

Maccoby, E. E. (1973). Sex in the social order. *Science*, *182*, 469–471.

Maccoby, E. E. (2000). Parenting and its effects on children: On reading and misreading behavior genetics. *Annual Review of Psychology*, *51*, 1–27.

Mackie, D. M. (1986). Social identification effects in group polarization. *Journal of Personality and Social Psychology*, *50*, 720–728.

Mackie, D. M. (1987). Systematic and nonsystematic processing of majority and minority persuasive communications. *Journal of Personality and Social Psychology*, *53*, 41–52.

Mackie, D. M., & Cooper, J. (1984). Attitude polarization: Effects of group membership. *Journal of Personality and Social Psychology*, *46*, 575–585.

Mackie, D. M., & Smith, E. R. (1998). Intergroup relations: Insights from a theoretically integrative approach. *Psychological Review*, *105*, 499–529.

Macrae, C. N., & Bodenhausen, G. V. (2001). Social cognition: Categorical person perception. *British Journal of Psychology*, *92*, 239–255.

Macrae, C. N., Bodenhausen, G. V., & Milne, A. B. (1998). Saying no to unwanted thoughts: Self-focus and the regulation of mental life. *Journal of Personality and Social Psychology*, *74*, 578–589.

Macrae, C. N., Bodenhausen, G. V., Milne, A. B., & Ford, R. L. (1997). On the regulation of recollection: The intentional forgetting of stereotypical memories. *Journal of Personality and Social Psychology*, *72*, 709–719.

Macrae, C. N., Bodenhausen, G. V., Milne, A. B., & Jetten, J. (1994). Out of mind but back in sight: Stereotypes on the rebound. *Journal of Personality and Social Psychology*, *67*, 808–817.

Macrae, C. N., Bodenhausen, G. V., Milne, A. B., Thorn, T. M. J., & Castelli, L. (1997). On the activation of social stereotypes: The moderating role of processing objectives. *Journal of Experimental Social Psychology*, *33*, 471–489.

Macrae, C. N., Hewstone, M., & Griffiths, R. J. (1993). Processing load and memory for stereotype-based information. *European Journal of Social Psychology*, *23*, 77–87.

Macrae, C. N., Hood, B. M., Milne, A. B., Rowe, A. C., & Mason, M. F. (2002). Are you looking at me? Eye gaze and person perception. *Psychological Science*, *13*, 460–464.

Macrae, C. N., Milne, A. B., & Bodenhausen, G. V. (1994). Stereotypes as energy-saving devices: A peek inside the cognitive toolbox. *Journal of Personality and Social Psychology*, *66*, 37–47.

Madden, T. J., Ellen, P. S., & Ajzen, I. (1992). A comparison of the theory of planned behavior and the theory of reasoned action. *Personality and Social Psychology Bulletin*, *18*, 39.

Maddox, K. B. (2004). Perspectives on racial phenotypicality bias. *Personality and Social Psychology Review*, *8*, 383–401.

Maddux, W. W., Galinsky, A. D., Cuddy, A. J. C., & Polifroni, M. (2008). When being a model minority is good . . . and bad: Realistic threat explains negativity toward Asian Americans. *Personality and Social Psychology Bulletin*, *34*, 74–89.

Madon, S., Guyll, M., Hilbert, S. J., Kyriakatos, E., & Vogel, D. L. (2006). Stereotyping the stereotypic: When individuals match social stereotypes. *Journal of Applied Social Psychology*, *36*, 178–205.

Magee, J. C., Galinsky, A. D., & Gruenfeld, D. H. (2007). Power, propensity to negotiate, and moving first in competitive interactions. *Personality and Social Psychology Bulletin*, *33*, 200–212.

Maio, G. R., & Olson, J. M. (1995). Relations between values, attitudes, and behavioral intentions: The moderating role of attitude function. *Journal of Experimental Social Psychology, 31*, 266–285.

Major, B. (1980). Information acquisition and attribution processes. *Journal of Personality and Social Psychology, 39*, 1010–1023.

Major, B., Feinstein, J., & Crocker, J. (1994). Attributional ambiguity of affirmative action. *Basic and Applied Social Psychology, 15*, 113–141.

Major, B., Gramzow, R. H., McCoy, S. K., Levin, S., Schmader, T., & Sidanius, J. (2002). Perceiving personal discrimination: The role of group status and legitimizing ideology. *Journal of Personality and Social Psychology, 82*, 269–282.

Major, B., Quinton, W. J., & McCoy, S. K. (2002). Antecedents and consequences of attributions to discrimination: Theoretical and empirical advances. In M. P. Zanna (Ed.), *Advances in experimental social psychology* (Vol. 34, pp. 251–330). New York: Academic Press.

Major, B., Sciacchitano, A. M., & Crocker, J. (1993). In-group versus out-group comparisons and self-esteem. *Personality and Social Psychology Bulletin, 19*, 711–721.

Major, B., Spencer, S. J., Schmader, T., Wolfe, C., & Crocker, J. (1998). Coping with negative stereotypes about intellectual performance: The role of psychological disengagement. *Personality and Social Psychology Bulletin, 24*, 34–50.

Malamuth, N. M. (1986). Predictors of naturalistic sexual aggression. *Journal of Personality and Social Psychology, 50*, 953–962.

Malamuth, N. M., & Addison, T. (2001). Integrating social psychological research on aggression within an evolutionary-based framework. In G. J. O. Fletcher & M. S. Clark (Eds.), *Blackwell handbook of social psychology: Interpersonal processes*. Malden, MA: Blackwell.

Malamuth, N. M., & Brown, L. M. (1994). Sexually aggressive men's perceptions of women's communications: Testing three explanations. *Journal of Personality and Social Psychology 67*, 699–712.

Malamuth, N. M., Linz, D., Heavey, C. L., Barnes, G., & Acker, M. (1995). Using the confluence model of sexual aggression to predict men's conflict with women: A 10-year follow-up study. *Journal of Personality and Social Psychology 69*, 353–369.

Malle, B. F. (2006). The actor-observer asymmetry in attribution: A (surprising) meta-analysis. *Psychological Bulletin, 132*, 895–919.

Malloy, T. E., Albright, L., Kenny, D. A., Agatstein, F., & Winquist, L. (1997). Interpersonal perception and metaperception in nonoverlapping social groups. *Journal of Personality and Social Psychology 72*, 390–398.

Malloy, T. E., Albright, L., & Scarpati, S. (2007). Awareness of peers' judgments of oneself: Accuracy and process of metaperception. *International Journal of Behavioral Development, 31*, 603–610.

Malt, B. C., & Smith, E. E. (1984). Correlated properties in natural categories. *Journal of Verbal Learning and Verbal Behavior, 23*, 250–269.

Mandler, G. (1975). *Mind and emotion*. New York: Wiley.

Maner, J. K., DeWall, C. N., & Gailliot, M. T. (2008). Selective attention to signs of success: Social dominance and early stage interpersonal perception. *Personality and Social Psychology Bulletin, 34*, 488–501.

Mann, L., Radford, M., & Kanagawa, C. (1985). Cross-cultural differences in children's use of decision rules: A comparison between Japan and Australia. *Journal of Personality and Social Psychology, 49*, 1557–1564.

Mann, R. D. (1959). A review of the relationships between personality and performance in small groups. *Psychological Bulletin, 56*, 241–270.

Mannix, E., & Neale, M. A. (2005). What differences make a difference? The promise and reality of diverse teams in organizations. *Psychological Science in the Public Interest, 6*, 31–55.

Manucia, G. K., Baumann, D. J., & Cialdini, R. B. (1984). Mood influences on helping: Direct effects or side effects? *Journal of Personality and Social Psychology, 46*, 357–364.

Mar, R. A., & Oatley, K. (2008). The function of fiction is the abstraction and simulation of social experience. *Perspectives on Psychological Science, 3*, 173–192.

Marcus-Newhall, A., Miller, N., Holtz, R., & Brewer, M. B. (1993). Cross-cutting category membership with role assignment: A means of reducing intergroup bias. *British Journal of Social Psychology, 32*, 125–146.

Marcus-Newhall, A., Pedersen, W. C., Carlson, M., & Miller, N. (2000). Displaced aggression is alive and well: A meta-analytic review. *Journal of Personality and Social Psychology, 78*, 670–689.

Margolin, G., Talovic, S., & Weinstein, C. D. (1983). Areas of change questionnaire: A practical approach to marital assessment. *Journal of Consulting and Clinical Psychology, 51*, 944–955.

Markus, H. R. (1977). Self-schemata and processing information about the self. *Journal of Personality and Social Psychology, 35*, 63–78.

Markus, H. R., & Kitayama, S. (1991). Culture and the self: Implications for cognition, emotion, and motivation. *Psychological Review, 98*, 224–253.

Markus, H. R., & Nurius, P. (1986). Possible selves. *American Psychologist, 41*, 954–969.

Markus, H. R., & Wurf, E. (1987). The dynamic self-concept: A social psychological perspective. *Annual Review of Psychology, 38*, 299–337.

Marques, J. M., Abrams, D., Páez, D., & Hogg, M. A. (2001). Social categorization, social identification, and rejection of deviant group members. In M. A. Hogg & R. S. Tindale (Eds.), *Blackwell handbook of social psychology: Group processes* (pp. 400–424). Malden, MA: Blackwell.

Marques, J. M., Abrams, D., Páez, D., & Martinez-Taboada, C. (2001). The role of categorization and in-group norms in judgments of groups and their members. *Journal of Personality and Social Psychology, 75*, 976–988.

Marques, J. M., Abrams, D., & Serodio, R. G. (2001). Being better by being right: Subjective group dynamics and derogation of in-group deviants when generic norms are undermined. *Journal of Personality and Social Psychology, 81*, 436–447.

Marques, J. M., & Páez, D. (1994). The "black sheep effect": Social categorization, rejection of ingroup deviates, and perception of group variability. In W. Stroebe & M. Hewstone (Eds.), *European review of socal psychology* (Vol. 5, pp. 37–68). New York: Wiley.

Marques, J. M., Yzerbyt, V. Y., & Leyens, J.-Ph. (1988). The "black sheep effect": Extremity of judgments towards ingroup members as a function of group identification. *European Journal of Social Psychology, 18*, 1–16.

Marsh, A. A., Elfenbein, H. A., & Ambady, N. (2003). Nonverbal "accents": Cultural differences in facial expressions of emotion. *Psychological Science, 14*, 373–376.

Marsh, H. W., & Parker, J. W. (1984). Determinants of student self-concept: Is it better to be a relatively large fish in a small pond even if you don't learn to swim as well? *Journal of Personality and Social Psychology, 47*, 213–231.

Marshall, T. C. (2008). Cultural differences in intimacy: The influence of gender-role ideology and individualism-collectivism. *Journal of Social and Personal Relationships, 25*, 143–168.

Martin, L. L., & Tesser, A. (1989). Toward a motivational and structural theory of ruminative thought. In J. S. Uleman & J. A. Bargh (Eds.), *Unintended thought* (pp. 306–326). New York: Guilford.

Martin, R. (1988a). Ingroup and outgroup minorities: Differential impact upon public and private responses. *European Journal of Social Psychology, 18*, 39–52.

Martin, R. (1988b). Minority influence and social categorization: A replication. *European Journal of Social Psychology, 18*, 369–373.

Martin, R. (1988c). Minority influence and "trivial" social categorization. *European Journal of Social Psychology, 18*, 465–470.

Martin, R., & Hewstone, M. (2001). Conformity and independence in groups: Majorities and minorities. In M. A. Hogg & R. S. Tindale (Eds.), *Blackwell handbook of social psychology: Group processes* (pp. 209–234). Malden, MA: Blackwell.

Martz, J. M., Verette, J., Arriaga, X. B., Slocik, L. F., Cox, C. L., & Rusbult, C. E. (1998). Positive illusion in close relationships. *Personal Relationships, 5*, 159–181.

Mason, M. F., Hood, B. M., & Macrae, C. N. (2004). Look into my eyes: Gaze direction and person memory. *Memory, 12*, 637–643.

Mason, M. F., Norton, M. I., Van Horn, J. D., Wegner, D. M., Grafton, S. T., & Macrae, C. N. (2007). Wandering minds: The default network and stimulus-independent thought. *Science, 315*, 393–395.

Mason, M. F., Tatkow, E. P., & Macrae, C. N. (2005). The look of love: Gaze shifts and person perception. *Psychological Science, 16*, 236–239.

Masor, H. N., Hornstein, H. A., & Tobin, T. A. (1973). Modeling, motivational interdependence, and helping. *Journal of Personality and Social Psychology, 28*, 236–248.

Massey, D. S. (2005). *Strangers in a strange land: Humans in an urbanizing world.* New York: Norton.

Massey, D. S. (2007). *Categorically unequal: The American stratification system.* New York: Russell Sage.

Massey, D. S., & Fischer, M. J. (2006). The effect of childhood segregation on minority academic performance at selective colleges. *Ethnic and Racial Studies, 29*, 1–26.

Matlin, M. W., & Stang, D. J. (1978). *The Pollyanna principle.* Cambridge, MA: Schenkman.

Mayer, J. D., Gaschke, Y. N., Braverman, D. L., & Evans, T. W. (1992). Mood-congruent judgment is a general effect. *Journal of Personality and Social Psychology, 63*, 119–132.

Mayer, J. D., & Salovey, P. (1988). Personality moderates the interaction of mood and cognition. In K. Fiedler & J. Forgas (Eds.), *Affect, cognition, and social behavior* (pp. 87–99). Toronto: Hogrefe.

McArthur, L. A. (1972). The how and what of why: Some determinants and consequences of causal attribution. *Journal of Personality and Social Psychology, 22*, 171–193.

McConahay, J. B. (1983). Modern racism and modern discrimination: The effects of race, racial attitudes, and context on simulated hiring decisions. *Personality and Social Psychology Bulletin, 9*, 551–558.

McConahay, J. B. (1986). Modern racism, ambivalence, and the modern racism scale. In J. F. Dovidio & S. L. Gaertner (Eds.), *Prejudice, discrimination, and racism* (pp. 91–125). Thousand Oaks, CA: Academic Press.

McConahay, J. B., Hardee, B. B., & Batts, V. (1981). Has racism declined in America? It depends on who is asking and what is asked. *Journal of Conflict Resolution, 25*, 563–579.

McConahay, J. B., & Hough, J. C. (1976). Symbolic racism. *Journal of Social Issues, 32*, 23–45.

McConnell, A. R., Renaud, J. M., Dean, K. K., Green, S. P., Lamoreaux, M. J., Hall, C. E., & Rydell, R. J. (2005). Whose self is it anyway? Self-aspect control moderates the relation between self-complexity and well-being. *Journal of Experimental Social Psychology, 41*, 1–18.

McConnell, A. R., Rydell, R. J., Strain, L. M., & Mackie, D. M. (2008). Forming implicit and explicit attitudes toward individuals: Social group association cues. *Journal of Personality and Social Psychology, 94*, 792–807.

McConnell, A. R., Sherman, S. J., & Hamilton, D. L. (1997). Target entitativity: Implications for information processing about individual and group targets. *Journal of Personality and Social Psychology, 72*, 750–762.

McCoy, S. K., & Major, B. (2007). Priming meritocracy and the psychological justification of inequality. *Journal of Experimental Social Psychology, 43*, 341–351.

McCullough, M. E., Worthington, E. L., & Rachal, K. C. (1997). Interpersonal forgiving in close relationships. *Journal of Personality and Social Psychology, 73*, 321–336.

McDougall, W. (1908). *An introduction to social psychology*. London: Methuen.

McElroy, T., & Seta, J. J. (2003). Framing effects: An analytic-holistic perspective. *Journal of Experimental Social Psychology, 39*, 610–617.

McFarland, C., & Alvaro, C. (2000). The impact of motivation on temporal comparisons: Coping with traumatic events by perceiving personal growth. *Journal of Personality and Social Psychology, 79*, 327–343.

McGarty, C., Turner, J. C., Hogg, M. A., Davidson, B., & Wetherell. M. S. (1992). Group polarization as conformity to the prototypical group member. *British Journal of Social Psychology, 31*, 1–19.

McGrath, J. E., Arrow, H., & Berdahl, J. L. (2000). The study of groups: Past, present and future. *Personality and Social Psychology Review, 4*, 95–105.

McGregor, H. A., Lieberman, J. D., Greenberg, J., Solomon, S., Arndt, J., Simon, L., & Pyszczynski, T. (1998). Terror management and aggression: Evidence that mortality salience motivates aggression against worldview-threatening others. *Journal of Personality and Social Psychology, 74*, 590–605.

McGregor, I., Zanna, M. P., Holmes, J. G., & Spencer, S. J. (2001). Compensatory conviction in the face of personal uncertainty: Going to extremes and being oneself. *Journal of Personality and Social Psychology, 80*, 472–488.

McGuire, W. J. (1969). The nature of attitudes and attitude change. In G. Lindzey & E. Aronson (Eds.), *The handbook of social psychology* (2nd ed., Vol. 3, pp. 136–314). Reading, MA: Addison-Wesley.

McGuire, W. J., & McGuire, C. V. (1988). Content and process in the experience of self. In L. Berkowitz (Ed.), *Advances in experimental social psychology* (Vol. 21, pp. 97–144). New York: Academic Press.

McHugo, G. J., Lanzetta, J. T., Sullivan, D. G., Masters, R. D., & Englis, B. G. (1985). Emotional reactions to a political leader's expressive displays. *Journal of Personality and Social Psychology, 49*, 1513–1529.

Mead, G. H. (1934). *Mind, self, and society*. Chicago: University of Chicago Press.

Medina, J. (2008, March 5). Next question: Can students be paid to excel? *New York Times*, p. 1.

Medvec, V H., Madey, S. F., & Gilovich, T. (1995). When less is more: Counterfactual thinking and satisfaction among Olympic medalists. *Journal of Personality and Social Psychology, 69*, 603–610.

Meeus, W. H. J., & Raaijmakers, Q. A. (1986). Administrative obedience: Carrying out orders to use psychological-administrative violence. *European Journal of Social Psychology, 16*, 311–324.

Meeus, W. H. J., & Raaijmakers, Q. A. W. (1995). Obedience in modern society: The Utrecht studies. *Journal of Social Issues, 51*, 155–175.

Mehl, M. R., & Pennebaker, J. W. (2003). The social dynamics of cultural upheaval: Social interactions surrounding September 11, 2001. *Psychological Science, 14*, 579–585.

Meiss, A. (1997). Fun things for professors to do on the first day of class. http://www.aaaugh.com/meiss/humor/profs.htm.

Meloen, J. D., Van der Linden, G., & De Witte, H. (1996). A test of the approaches of Adorno et al., Lederer, and Altemeyer of authoritarianism in Belgian Flanders: A research note. *Political Psychology, 17*, 643–656.

Mendoza-Denton, R., Ayduk, O., Mischel, W., Shoda, Y., & Testa, A. (2001). Person × situation interactionism in self-encoding (I am . . . when . . . ): Implications for affect regulation and social information processing. *Journal of Personality and Social Psychology, 80*, 533–544.

Menon, T., Morris, M. W., Chiu, C. Y., & Hong, Y. Y. (1999). Culture and the construal of agency: Attribution to individual versus group dispositions. *Journal of Personality and Social Psychology, 76*, 701–717.

Merton, R. K. (1948). The self-fulfilling prophecy. *Antioch Review, 8*, 193–210.

Mesquita, B., & Karasawa, M. (2002). Different emotional lives. *Cognition and Emotion, 16*, 127–141.

Messick, D. M., & Liebrand, W. B. G. (1995). Individual heuristics and the dynamics of cooperation in large groups. *Psychological Review, 102*, 131–145.

Messick, D. M., & Liebrand, W. B. G. (1997). Levels of analysis and the explanation of the costs and benefits of cooperation. *Personality and Social Psychology Review, 1*, 129–139.

Messick, D. M., & Mackie, D. M. (1989). Intergroup relations. *Annual Review of Psychology, 40*, 45–81.

Messick, D. M., & McClintock, C. G. (1968). Motivational bases of choice in experimental games. *Journal of Experimental Social Psychology, 4*, 1–25.

Meyer, T. P. (1972). Effects of viewing justified and unjustified real film violence on aggressive behavior. *Journal of Personality and Social Psychology, 23*, 21–29.

Migdal, M. J., Hewstone, M., & Mullen, B. (1998). The effects of crossed categorization on intergroup evaluations: A meta-analysis. *British Journal of Social Psychology, 37*, 303–324.

Mikolic, J. M., Parker, J. C., & Pruitt, D. G. (1997). Escalation in response to persistent annoyance: Groups versus individuals and gender effects. *Journal of Personality and Social Psychology, 72*, 151–163.

Milgram, S. (1963). Behavioral study of obedience. *Journal of Abnormal and Social Psychology, 67*, 371–378.

Milgram, S. (1964). Group pressure and action against a person. *Journal of Abnormal and Social Psychology, 69*, 137–143.

Milgram, S. (1965). Some conditions of obedience and disobedience to authority. *Human Relations, 18*, 57–75.

Milgram, S. (1974). *Obedience to authority*. New York: Harper and Row.

Miller, A. G., Collins, B. E., & Brief, D. E. (1995). Perspectives on obedience to authority: The legacy of the Milgram experiments. *Journal of Social Issues, 51*, 1–19.

Miller, D. T. (1976). Ego involvement and attributions for success and failure. *Journal of Personality and Social Psychology, 34*, 901–906.

Miller, D. T. (1977). Altruism and threat to a belief in a just world. *Journal of Experimental Social Psychology, 13*, 113–124.

Miller, D. T., Norman, S. A., & Wright, E. (1978). Distortion in person perception as a consequence of the need for effective control. *Journal of Personality and Social Psychology, 36*, 598–607.

Miller, D. T., & Prentice, D. A. (1996). The construction of social norms and standards. In E. T. Higgins & A. W. Kruglanski (Eds.), *Social psychology: Handbook of basic principles* (pp. 799–829). New York: Guilford.

Miller, D. T., & Ratner, R. K. (1998). The disparity between the actual and assumed power of self-interest. *Journal of Personality and Social Psychology, 74*, 53–62.

Miller, D. T., & Ross, M (1975). Self-serving biases in attribution of causality: Fact or fiction? *Psychological Bulletin, 82*, 213–225.

Miller, D. T., Taylor, B., & Buck, M. L. (1991). Gender gaps: Who needs to be explained? *Journal of Personality and Social Psychology, 61*, 5–12.

Miller, D. T., & Turnbull, W. (1986). Expectancies and interpersonal processes. *Annual Review of Psychology, 37*, 233–256.

Miller, D. T., Turnbull, W., & McFarland, C. (1988). Particularistic and universalistic evaluation in the social comparison process. *Journal of Personality and Social Psychology, 55*, 908–917.

Miller, G. (2008). The roots of morality. *Science, 320*, 734–737.

Miller, J. G. (1984). Culture and the development of everyday social explanation. *Journal of Personality and Social Psychology, 46*, 961–978.

Miller, J. G. (1987). Cultural influences on the development of conceptual differentiation in person description. *British Journal of Developmental Psychology, 5*, 309–319.

Miller, J. G., & Bersoff, D. M. (1994). Cultural influences on the moral status of reciprocity and the discounting of endogenous motivation. *Journal of Personality and Social Psychology, 20*, 592–602.

Miller, J. G., & Bersoff, D. M. (1998). The role of liking in perceptions of the moral responsibility to help: A cultural perspective. *Journal of Experimental Social Psychology, 34*, 443–469.

Miller, J. G., Bersoff, D. M., & Harwood, R. L. (1990). Perceptions of social responsibilities in India and in the United States: Moral imperatives or personal decisions? *Journal of Personality and Social Psychology, 58*, 33–47.

Miller, N., & Brewer, M. B. (1986). Categorization effects on ingroup and outgroup perception. In J. F. Dovidio & S. L. Gaertner (Eds.), *Prejudice, discrimination, and racism* (pp. 209–230). San Diego, CA: Academic Press.

Milliken, F. J., & Martins, L. L. (1996). Searching for common threads: Understanding the multiple effects of diversity in organizational groups. *Academy of Management Review*, *21*, 402–433.

Mills, J., Clark, M. S., Ford, T. E., & Johnson, M. (2004). Measurement of communal strength. *Personal Relationships*, *11*, 213–230.

Mischel, W. (2004). Toward an integrative science of the person. *Annual Review of Psychology*, *55*, 1–22.

Misumi, J., & Peterson, M. F. (1990). Psychology in Japan. *Annual Review of Psychology*, *41*, 231–241.

Mitchell, J. P. (2008). Contributions of functional neuroimaging to the study of social cognition. *Current Directions in Psychological Science*, *17*, 142–146.

Moghaddam, F. M. (2005). The staircase to terrorism: A psychological exploration. *American Psychologist*, *60*, 161–169.

Molm, L. D., Collett, J. L., & Schaefer, D. R. (2007). Building solidarity through generalized exchange: A theory of reciprocity. *American Journal of Sociology*, *113*, 205–242.

Molm, L. D., Schaefer, D. R., & Collett, J. L. (2007). The value of reciprocity. *Social Psychology Quarterly*, *70*, 199–217.

Monteith, M. J. (1993). Self-regulation of prejudiced responses: Implications for progress in prejudice reduction efforts. *Journal of Personality and Social Psychology*, *65*, 469–485.

Monteith, M. J. (1996). Contemporary forms of prejudice-related conflict: In search of a nutshell. *Personality and Social Psychology Bulletin*, *22*, 461–473.

Monteith, M. J., Devine, P. G., & Zuwerink, J. R. (1993). Self-directed versus other-directed affect as a consequence of prejudice-related discrepancies. *Journal of Personality and Social Psychology*, *64*, 198–210.

Monteith, M. J., & Mark, A. Y. (2005). Changing one's prejudiced ways: Awareness, affect, and self-regulation. *European Review of Social Psychology*, *16*, 113–154.

Monteith, M. J., Sherman, J. W., & Devine, P. G. (1998). Suppression as a stereotype control strategy. *Personality and Social Psychology Review*, *2*, 63–82.

Monteith, M. J., & Spicer, C. V. (2000). Contents and correlates of whites' and blacks' racial attitudes. *Journal of Experimental Social Psychology*, *36*, 125–154.

Monteith, M. J., Spicer, C. V., & Tooman, G. D. (1998). Consequences of stereotype suppression: Stereotypes on and not on the rebound. *Journal of Experimental Social Psychology*, *34*, 355–377.

Monteith, M. J., & Voils, C. I. (1998). Proneness to prejudiced responses: Toward understanding the authenticity of self-reported discrepancies. *Journal of Personality and Social Psychology*, *75*, 901–916.

Monteith, M. J., & Walters, G. L. (1998). Egalitarianism, moral obligation, and prejudice-related personal standards. *Personality and Social Psychology Bulletin*, *24*, 186–199.

Montgomery, K. J., Isenberg, N., & Haxby, J. V. (2007). Communicative hand gestures and object-directed hand movements activated the mirror neuron system. *Social Cognitive and Affective Neuroscience*, *2*, 114–122.

Moreland, R. L., & Beach, S. R. (1992). Exposure effects in the classroom: The development of affinity among students. *Journal of Experimental Social Psychology*, *28*, 255–276.

Moreland, R. L., Hogg, M. A., & Hains, S. C. (1994). Back to the future: Social psychological research on groups. *Journal of Experimental Social Psychology*, *30*, 527–555.

Moreland, R. L., & Levine, J. M. (1982). Socialization in small groups: Temporal changes in individual-group relations. In L. Berkowitz (Ed.), *Advances in experimental social psychology* (Vol. 15, pp. 137–192). New York: Academic Press.

Moreland, R. L., & Levine, J. M. (2002). Socialization and trust in work groups. *Group Processes and Intergroup Relations*, *5*, 185–201.

Moreland, R. L., & Zajonc, R. B. (1977). Is stimulus recognition a necessary condition for the occurrence of exposure effects? *Journal of Personality and Social Psychology*, *35*, 191–199.

Moreno, J. L. (1953). *Who shall survive? Foundations of sociometry group psychotherapy and sociodrama*. Beacon, NY: Beacon House.

Morewedge, C. K., & Clear, M. E., (2008). Anthropomorphic God concepts engender moral judgment. *Social Cognition, 26*, 182–189.

Morf, C. C. (2006). Personality reflected in a coherent idiosyncratic interplay of intra- and interpersonal self-regulatory processes. *Journal of Personality*, *74*, 1527–1556.

Morf, C. C., & Rhodewalt, F. (2001). Unraveling the paradoxes of narcissism: A dynamic self-regulatory processing model. *Psychological Inquiry*, *12*, 177–196.

Morling, B., & Fiske, S. T. (1999). Defining and measuring harmony control. *Journal of Research in Personality 33*, 379–414.

Morris, M. W., Menon, T., & Ames, D. R. (2001). Culturally conferred conceptions of agency: A key to social perceptions of persons, groups, and other actors. *Personality and Social Psychology Review*, *5*, 169–182.

Morris, M. W., & Peng, K. (1994). Culture and cause: American and Chinese attributions for social and physical events. *Journal of Personality and Social Psychology, 67*, 949–971.

Morrison, K. R., Wheeler, S. C., & Smeesters, D. (2007). Significant other primes and behavior: Motivation to respond to social cues moderates pursuit of prime-induced goals. *Personality and Social Psychology Bulletin, 33*, 1661–1674.

Morrison, T. (1993). *The bluest eye*. New York: Knopf.

Morry, M. M. (2007). The attraction-similarity hypothesis among cross-sex friends: Relationship satisfaction, perceived similarities, and self-serving perceptions. *Journal of Social and Personal Relationships, 24*, 117–138.

Moscovici, S. (1976). *Social influence and social change*. London: Academic Press.

Moscovici, S. (1980). Toward a theory of conversion behavior. In L. Berkowitz (Ed.), *Advances in experimental social psychology* (Vol. 13, pp. 209–239). New York: Academic Press.

Moscovici, S. (1984). The phenomenon of social representations. In R. M. Farr & S. Moscovici (Eds.), *Social representations* (pp. 1–35). Cambridge, UK: Cambridge University Press.

Moscovici, S. (1985). Social influence and conformity. In G. Lindzey & E. Aronson (Eds.), *Handbook of social psychology* (3rd ed., Vol. 2, pp. 347–412). New York: Random House.

Moscovici, S. (1988). Notes toward a description of social representations. *European Journal of Social Psychology, 18*, 211–250.

Moscovici, S., & Faucheux, C. (1972). Social influence, conformity bias, and the study of active minorities. In L. Berkowitz (Ed.), *Advances in experimental social psychology* (Vol. 6, pp. 149–202). New York: Academic Press.

Moskowitz, G. B. (2004). *Social cognition: Understanding self and others*. New York: Guilford.

Moskowitz, G. B., Gollwitzer, P. M., Wasel, W., & Schaal, B. (1999). Preconscious control of stereotype activation through chronic egalitarian goals. *Journal of Personality and Social Psychology, 77*, 167–184.

Moskowitz, G. B., Salomon, A. R., & Taylor, C. M. (2000). Preconsciously controlling stereotyping: Implicitly activated egalitarian goals prevent the activation of stereotypes. *Social Cognition, 18*, 151–177.

Mugny, G., Perez, J. A., & Lamongie, V. W. (1991). *The social psychology of minority influence*. New York: Cambridge University Press.

Mullen, B. (1983). Operationalizing the effect of the group on the individual: A self-attention perspective. *Journal of Experimental Social Psychology, 19*, 295–322.

Mullen, B. (1991). Group composition, salience, and cognitive representations: The phenomenology of being in a group. *Journal of Experimental Social Psychology, 27*, 297–323.

Mullen, B., Anthony, S., Salas, E., & Driskell, J. E. (1994). Group cohesiveness and quality of decision making: An integration of tests of the group-think hypothesis. *Small Group Research, 25*, 189–204.

Mullen, B., Atkins, J. L., Champion, D. S., Edwards, C., Hardy, D., Story, J. E., & Vanderklok, M. (1985). The false consensus effect: A meta-analysis of 115 hypothesis tests. *Journal of Experimental Social Psychology, 21*, 262–283.

Mullen, B., Brown, R. J., & Smith, C. (1992). Ingroup bias as a function of salience, relevance, and status: An integration. *European Journal of Social Psychology, 22*, 103–122.

Mullen, B., & Copper, C. (1994). The relation between group cohesiveness and performance: An integration. *Psychological Bulletin, 115*, 210–227.

Mullen, B., Copper, C., & Driskell, J. E. (1990). Jaywalking as a function of model behavior. *Personality and Social Psychology Bulletin, 16*, 320–330.

Mullen, B., & Hu, L. (1989). Perceptions of ingroup and outgroup variability: A meta-analytic integration. *Basic and Applied Social Psychology, 10*, 233–252.

Mullen, B., Johnson, C., & Salas, E. (1991). Productivity loss in brainstorming groups? A meta-analytic integration. *Basic and Applied Social Psychology, 12*, 3–23.

Mullen, B., Migdal, M. J., & Hewstone, M. (2001). Crossed categorization versus simple categorization and intergroup evaluations: A meta-analysis. *European Journal of Social Psychology, 31*, 721–736.

Mullen, B., & Riordan, C. A. (1988). Self-serving attributions for performance in naturalistic settings: A meta-analytic review. *Journal of Applied Social Psychology, 18*, 3–22.

Mullen, B., Salas, E., & Driskell, J. E. (1989). Salience, motivation, and artifact as contributions to the relation between participation rate and leadership. *Journal of Experimental Social Psychology, 25*, 545–559.

Mullen, B., Symons, C., Hu, L. T., & Salas, E. (1989). Group size, leadership behavior, and subordinate satisfaction. *Journal of General Psychology, 116*, 155–170.

Mulligan, E. J., & Hastie, R. (2005). Explanations determine the impact of information on financial investment judgments. *Journal of Behavioral Decision Making, 18*, 145–156.

Mullin, B. A., & Hogg, M. A. (1999). Motivations for group membership: The role of subjective importance and uncertainty reduction. *Basic and Applied Social Psychology, 21*, 91–102.

Mummendey, A. (1995). Positive distinctiveness and social discrimination: An old couple living in divorce. *European Journal of Social Psychology, 25*, 657–670.

Mummendey, A. (1996). Aggressive behaviour. In M. Hewstone, W. Stroebe, J. P., Forgas, & G. M. Stephenson (Eds.), *Introduction to social psychology* (pp. 404–435). Oxford, England: Blackwell.

Mummendey, A., & Otten, S. (1998). Positive-negative asymmetry in social discrimination. In W. Stroebe & M. Hewstone (Eds.), *European review of social psychology* (Vol. 9, pp 108–143). New York: Wiley.

Murnen, S. K., & Kohlman, M. H. (2007). Athletic participation, fraternity membership, and sexual aggression among college men: A meta-analytic review. *Sex Roles, 57*, 145–157.

Murphy, C. M., & O'Farrell, T. J. (1996). Marital violence among alcoholics. *Current Directions, 5*, 183–186.

Murphy, S. T., Monahan, J. L., & Zajonc, R. B. (1995). Additivity of nonconscious affect: Combined effects of priming and exposure. *Journal of Personality and Social Psychology, 69*, 589–602.

Murray, S. L., Bellavia, G. M., Rose, P., & Griffin, D. W. (2003). Once hurt, twice hurtful: How perceived regard regulates daily marital interactions. *Journal of Personality and Social Psychology, 84*, 126–147.

Murray, S. L., & Holmes, J. G. (1993). Seeing virtues as faults: Negativity and the transformation of interpersonal narratives in close relationships. *Journal of Personality and Social Psychology, 65*, 707–722.

Murray, S. L., Holmes, J. G., Bellavia, G., Griffin, D. W., & Dolderman, D. (2002). Kindred spirits? The benefits of egocentrism in close relationships. *Journal of Personality and Social Psychology, 82*, 563–581.

Murray, S. L., Holmes, J. G., & Collins, N. L. (2006). Optimizing assurance: The risk regulation system in relationships. *Psychological Bulletin, 132*, 641–666.

Murray, S. L., Holmes, J. G., & Griffin, D. W. (1996). The benefits of positive illusions: Idealization and construction of satisfaction in close relationships. *Journal of Personality and Social Psychology, 70*, 79–98.

Murray, S. L., Holmes, J. G., & Griffin, D. W. (2000). Self-esteem and the quest for felt security: How perceived regard regulates attachment processes. *Journal of Personality and Social Psychology, 78*, 478–498.

Murray, S. L., Holmes, J. G., Griffin, D. W., Bellavia, G., & Rose, P. (2001). The mismeasure of love: How self-doubt contaminates relationship beliefs. *Personality and Social Psychology Bulletin, 27*, 423–436.

Murray, S. L., Rose, P., Bellavia, G. M., Holmes, J. G., & Kusche, A. G. (2002). When rejection stings: How self-esteem constrains relationship-enhancement processes. *Journal of Personality and Social Psychology, 83*, 556–573.

Mussweiler, T., & Förster, J. (2000). The sex → aggression link: A perception-behavior dissociation. *Journal of Personality and Social Psychology, 79*, 507–520.

Myers, D. G., & Lamm, H. (1976). The group polarization phenomenon. *Psychological Bulletin, 83*, 602–627.

Nadler, A. (1993). Deviance in primary groups: The social negotiation of personal change. In W. Stroebe & M. Hewstone (Eds.), *European review of social psychology* (Vol. 4, pp. 187–222). New York: Wiley.

Narvaez, D., Getz, I., Rest, J. R., & Thoma, S. J. (1999). Individual moral judgment and cultural ideologies. *Developmental Psychology, 35*, 478–488.

Nasby, W., Hayden, B., & DePaulo, B. M. (1979). Attributional bias among aggressive boys to interpret unambiguous social stimuli as displays of hostility. *Journal of Abnormal Psychology, 89*, 459–468.

National survey (1995, June 9–11). *Los Angeles Times*.

Nemeth, C. J. (1986). Differential contributions of majority and minority influence. *Psychological Review, 93*, 23–32.

Neuberg, S. L. (1989). The goal of forming accurate impressions during social interactions: Attenuating the impact of negative expectancies. *Journal of Personality and Social Psychology, 56*, 374–386.

Neuberg, S. L., Cialdini, R. B., Brown, S. L., Luce, C., Sagarin, B. J., & Lewis, B. P. (1997). Does empathy lead to anything more than superficial helping? *Journal of Personality and Social Psychology, 73*, 510–516.

Neuberg, S. L., & Fiske, S. T. (1987). Motivational influences on impression formation: Outcome dependency, accuracy-driven attention, and individuating processes. *Journal of Personality and Social Psychology, 53*, 431–444.

Neuberg, S. L., & Newsom, J. T. (1993). Personal need for structure: Individual differences in the desire for simple structure. *Journal of Personality and Social Psychology*, *65*, 113–131.

Neuberg, S. L., Smith, D. M., & Asher, T. (2000). Why people stigmatize: Toward a biocultural framework. In T. F. Heatherton, R. E. Kleck, M. R. Hebl, & J. G. Hull (Eds.), *The social psychology of stigma* (pp. 31–61). New York: Guilford.

Newcomb, A. F., & Bagwell, C. L. (1995). Children's friendship relations: A meta-analytic review. *Psychological Bulletin*, *117*, 306–347.

Newcomb, T. M. (1961). *The acquaintance process*. New York: Holt, Rinehart & Winston.

Newman, L. S., & Erber, R. (Eds.) (2002). *Understanding genocide*. Oxford, UK: Oxford University Press.

Nezlek, J. B., Kowalski, R. M., Leary, M. R., Blevins, T., & Holgate, S. (1997). Personality moderators of reactions to interpersonal rejection: Depression and trait self-esteem. *Personality and Social Psychology Bulletin*, *23*, 1235–1244.

Ng, K. Y., & Van Dyne, L. (2001). Individualism-collectivism as a boundary condition for effectiveness of minority influence in decision making. *Organizational Behavior and Human Decision Processes*, *84*, 198–225.

Ng, S. H. (1980). Psychological views of social power. In S. H. Ng (Ed.), *The social psychology of power* (pp. 155–185). New York: Academic Press.

Ng, S. H., & Zhu, Y. (2001). Attributing causality and remembering events in individual and group-acting situations: A Beijing, Hong Kong, and Wellington comparison. *Asian Journal of Social Psychology*, *4*, 39–52.

Nickerson, R. S. (1998). Confirmation bias: A ubiquitous phenomenon in many guises. *Review of General Psychology*, *2*, 175–220.

Nicks, S. D., Korn, J. H., & Maineiri, T. (1997). The rise and fall of deception in social psychology and personality research, 1921 to 1994. *Ethics and Behavior*, *7*, 69–77.

Niedenthal, P. M., Barsalou, L. W., Winkielman, P., Krauth-Gruber, S., & Ric, F. (2005). Embodiment in attitudes, social perception, and emotion. *Personality and Social Psychology Review*, *9*, 184–211.

Niedenthal, P. M., & Beike, D. R. (1997). Interrelated and isolated self-concepts. *Personality and Social Psychology Review*, *1*, 106–128.

1994's most bizarre suicide. Retrieved May 22, 2008 from www.cybertown.com/suicide.html.

Nisbett, R. E. (1993). Violence and U.S. regional culture. *American Psychologist*, *48*, 441–449.

Nisbett, R. E., Caputo, C., Legant, P., & Marecek, J. (1973). Behavior as seen by the actor and as seen by the observer. *Journal of Personality and Social Psychology*, *27*, 154–164.

Nisbett, R. E., Peng, K., Choi, I., & Norenzayan, A. (2001). Culture and systems of thought: Holistic versus analytic cognition. *Psychological Review*, *108*, 291–310.

Nisbett, R. E., & Ross, L. (1980). *Human inference: Strategies and shortcomings of social judgment*. Englewood Cliffs, NJ: Prentice-Hall.

Nisbett, R. E., & Wilson, T. D. (1977a). Telling more than we can know: Verbal reports on mental processes. *Psychological Review*, *84*, 231–259.

Nisbett, R. E., & Wilson, T. D. (1977b). The halo effect: Evidence for unconscious alteration of judgments. *Journal of Personality and Social Psychology*, *35*, 250–256.

Nisbett, R. E., Zukier, H., & Lemley, R. E. (1981). The dilution effect: Non-diagnostic information weakens the implications of diagnostic information. *Cognitive Psychology*, *13*, 248–277.

Noel, J. G., Wann, D. L., & Branscombe, N. R. (1995). Peripheral group membership status and public negativity toward outgroups. *Journal of Personality and Social Psychology*, *68*, 127–137.

Norenzayan, A., Hansen, I. G., & Cady, J. (2008). An angry volcano? Reminders of death and anthropomorphizing nature. *Social Cognition*, *26*, 190–197.

Norton, M. I., Sommers, S. R., & Brauner, S. (2007). Bias in jury selection: Justifying prohibited peremptory challenges. *Journal of Behavioral Decision Making*, *20*, 467–479.

Norton, M. I., Vandello, J. A., & Darley, J. M. (2004). Casuistry and social category bias. *Journal of Personality and Social Psychology*, *87*, 817–831.

Nosek, B. A., Greenwald, A. G., & Banaji, M. R. (2005). Understanding and using the Implicit Association Test: II. Method variables and construct validity. *Personality and Social Psychology Bulletin*, *31*, 166–180.

Nowak, M. 2006. Five rules for the evolution of cooperation. *Science*, *314*, 1560–1563.

Nussbaum, A. D., & Steele, C. M. (2007). Situational disengagement and persistence in the face of adversity. *Journal of Experimental Social Psychology*, *43*, 127–134.

Oakes, P. J. (2001). The root of all evil in intergroup relations? Unearthing the categorization process. In R. Brown & S. L. Gaertner (Eds.), *Blackwell handbook of social psychology: Intergroup processes* (pp. 4–21). London: Blackwell.

Oakes, P. J., Haslam, S. A., & Turner, J. C. (1994). *Stereotyping and social reality*. Oxford: Blackwell.

Oakes, P. J., & Turner, J. C. (1980). Social categorization and intergroup behaviour: Does minimal intergroup discrimination make social identity more positive? *European Journal of Social Psychology*, *10*, 295–301.

Ochsner, K. N., Knierim, K., Ludlow, D. H., Hanelin, J., Ramachandran, T., Glover, G., & Mackey, S. C. (2004). Reflecting upon feelings: An fMRI study of neural systems supporting the attribution of emotion to self and other. *Journal of Cognitive Neuroscience, 16*, 1746–1772.

Ochsner, K. N., & Lieberman, M. D. (2001). The emergence of social cognitive neuroscience. *American Psychologist, 56*, 717–734.

O'Doherty, J., Kringelbach, M. L., Rolls, E. T., Hornak, J., & Andrews, C. (2001). Abstract reward and punishment representations in the human orbitofrontal cortex. *Nature Neuroscience, 4*, 95–102.

Oishi, S., Rothman, A. J., Snyder, M., Su, J., Zehm, K., Hertel, A. W., Gonzales, M. H., & Sherman, G. D. (2007). The socioecological model of procommunity action: The benefits of residential stability. *Journal of Personality and Social Psychology, 93*, 831–844.

O'Keefe, D. J., & Hale, S. L. (2001). An odds-ratio-based meta-analysis of research on the door-in-the-face influence strategy. *Communication Reports, 14*, 31–38.

Oldmeadow, J., & Fiske, S. T. (2007). System-justifying ideologies moderate status = competence stereotypes: Roles for belief in a just world and social dominance orientation. *European Journal of Social Psychology, 37*, 1135–1148.

Olekalns, M., & Smith, P. L. (1999). Social value orientations and strategy choices in competitive negotiations. *Personality and Social Psychology Bulletin, 25*, 657–668.

Oliner, S. P., & Oliner, P. M. (1988). *The altruistic personality: Rescuers of Jews in Nazi Europe.* New York: Free Press.

Olson, J. M., Roese, N. J., & Zanna, M. P. (1996). Expectancies. In E. T. Higgins & A. W. Kruglanski (Eds.), *Social psychology: Handbook of basic principles* (pp. 211–238). New York: Guilford.

Olson, J. M., & Zanna, M. P. (1993). Attitudes and attitude change. *Annual Review of Psychology, 44*, 117–154.

Olson, M. (1965). *The logic of collective action: Public goods and the theory of groups.* Cambridge, MA: Harvard University Press.

Olson, M. A., & Fazio, R. H. (2001). Implicit attitude formation through classical conditioning. *Psychological Science, 12*, 413–417.

Olson, M. A., & Fazio, R. H. (2006). Reducing automatically activated racial prejudice through implicit evaluating conditioning. *Personality and Social Psychology Bulletin, 32*, 421–433.

Olsson, A., Nearing, K. I., & Phelps, E. A. (2007). Learning fears by observing others: The neural systems of social fear transmission. *Social Cognitive and Affective Neuroscience, 2*, 3–11.

Olweus, D. (1995). Bullying or peer abuse at school: Facts and interventions. *Current Directions in Psychological Science, 4*, 196–200.

Olweus, D. (1997). Bully/victim problems in school: Facts and intervention. *European Journal of Psychology of Education, 12*, 495–510.

O'Neal, E. C., Kipnis, D., & Craig, K. M. (1994). Effects on the persuader of employing a coercive influence technique. *Basic and Applied Social Psychology, 15*, 225–238.

O'Neill, P., & Petrinovich, L. (1998). A preliminary cross-cultural study of moral intuitions. *Evolution and Human Behavior, 19*, 349–367.

Oosterhof, N. N., & Todorov, A. (2008). The functional basis of face evaluation. *Proceedings of the National Academy of Sciences of the United States of America, 105*, 11087–11092.

Operario, D., & Fiske, S. T. (2001a). Effects of trait dominance on powerholders' judgments of subordinates. *Social Cognition, 19*, 161–180.

Operario, D., & Fiske, S. T. (2001b). Ethnic identity moderates perceptions of prejudice: Judgments of personal versus group discrimination and subtle versus blatant bias. *Personality and Social Psychology Bulletin, 27*, 550–561.

Oppenheimer, D. M., & Frank, M. C. (2008). A rose in any other font would not smell as sweet: Effects of perceptual fluency on categorization. *Cognition, 106*, 1178–1194.

Orbell, J. M., & Dawes, R. M. (1981). Social dilemmas. In G. Stephenson & H. H. Davis (Eds.), *Progress in applied social psychology* (Vol. 1, pp. 37–65). New York: Wiley.

Orbell, J. M., & Dawes, R. M. (1993). Social welfare, cooperators' advantage, and the option of not playing the game. *American Sociological Review, 58*, 787–800.

O'Reilly, C. A., Caldwell, D. F., & Barnett, W. P. (1989). Work group demography, social integration, and turnover. *Administrative Science Quarterly, 34*, 21–37.

Orne, M. T. (1962). On the social psychology of the psychological experiment: With particular reference to demand characteristics and their implications. *American Psychologist, 17*, 776–783.

Osgood, C. E., Suci, G. J., & Tannenbaum, P. H. (1957). *The measurement of meaning.* Urbana: University of Illinois Press.

Ostrom, T. M., & Sedikides, C. (1992). Outgroup homogeneity effect in natural and minimal groups. *Psychological Bulletin, 112*, 536–552.

Ottati, V., & Lee, Y. (1995). Accuracy: A neglected component of stereotype research. In Y. Lee, L. J. Jussim, & C. R. McCauley (Eds.), *Stereotype accuracy: Toward appreciating group differences*. Washington, DC: American Psychological Association.

Otten, S., Mummendey, A., & Blanz, M. (1996). Intergroup discrimination in positive and negative outcome allocations: Impact of stimulus valence, relative group status, and relative group size. *Personality and Social Psychology Bulletin, 22*, 568–581.

Otten, S., & Wentura, D. (2001). Self-anchoring and in-group favoritism: An individual profiles analysis. *Journal of Experimental Social Psychology, 37*, 525–532.

Overbeck, J. R., & Park, B. (2001). When power does not corrupt: Superior individuation processes among powerful perceivers. *Journal of Personality and Social Psychology, 81*, 549–565.

Overbeck, J. R., Tiedens, L. Z., & Brion, S. (2006). The powerful want to, the powerless have to: Perceived constraint moderates causal attributions. *European Journal of Social Psychology, 36*, 479–496.

Oyserman, D., Bybee, D., & Terry, K. (2006). Possible selves and academic outcomes: How and when possible selves impel action. *Journal of Personality and Social Psychology, 91*, 188–204.

Oyserman, D., Coon, H. M., & Kemmelmeier, M. (2002). Rethinking individualism and collectivism: Evaluation of theoretical assumptions and meta-analysis. *Psychological Bulletin, 128*, 3–72.

Oyserman, D., & Lee, S. W. S. (2008). Does culture influence what and how we think? Effects of priming individualism and collectivism. *Psychological Bulletin, 134*, 311–342.

Ozer, D. J., & Benet-Martínez, V. (2006). Personality and the prediction of consequential outcomes. *Annual Review of Psychology, 57*, 401–421.

Packer, D. J. (2008). Identifying systematic disobedience in Milgram's obedience experiments: A meta-analytic review. *Perspectives on Psychological Science, 3*, 301–304.

Paik, H., & Comstock, G. (1994). The effects of television violence on antisocial behavior: A meta-analysis. *Communication Research, 21*, 516–546.

Paluck, E. L., & Green, D. P. (2009). Prejudice reduction: What works? A review and assessment of research and practice. *Annual Review of Psychology, 60*, 339–367.

Parducci, A. (1964). Sequential effects in judgment. *Psychological Bulletin, 61*, 163–167.

Parducci, A. (1968). The relativism of absolute judgments. *Scientific American, 219*, 84–90.

Pargament, K. I. (2002). The bitter and the sweet: An evaluation of the costs and benefits of religiousness. *Psychological Inquiry, 13*, 168–181.

Park, B., & Judd, C. M. (1989). Agreement on initial impressions: Differences due to perceivers, trait dimensions, and target behaviors. *Journal of Personality and Social Psychology, 56*, 493–505.

Park, B., & Judd, C. M. (1990). Measures and models of perceived group variability. *Journal of Personality and Social Psychology, 5*, 73–91.

Park, B., & Judd, C. M. (2005). Rethinking the link between categorization and prejudice within the social cognition perspective. *Personality and Social Psychology Review, 9*, 108–130.

Park, B., Ryan, C. S., & Judd, C. M. (1992). Role of meaningful subgroups in explaining differences in perceived variability in ingroups and outgroups. *Journal of Personality and Social Psychology, 63*, 553–567.

Park, J., & Banaji, M. R. (2000). Mood and heuristics: The influence of happy and sad states on sensitivity and bias in stereotyping. *Journal of Personality and Social Psychology, 78*, 1005–1023.

Parks, C. D., & Komorita, S. S. (1997). Reciprocal strategies for large groups. *Personality and Social Psychology Review, 1*, 314–322.

Patterson, G. R., DeBaryshe, B. D., & Ramsey, E. (1989). A developmental perspective on antisocial behavior. *American Psychologist, 44*, 329–335.

Patterson, M. L., Iizuka, Y., Tubbs, M. E., Ansel, J., Tsutsumi, M., & Anson, J. (2007). Passing encounters east and west: Comparing Japanese and American pedestrian interactions. *Journal of Nonverbal Behavior, 31*, 155–166.

Paulus, P. B., Dugosh, K. L., Dzindolet, M. T., Coskun, H., & Putman, V. L. (2002). Social and cognitive influences in group brainstorming: Predicting production gains and losses. In W. Stroebe & M. Hewstone (Eds.), *European review of social psychology* (Vol. 12, pp. 299–325). Chichester: John Wiley.

Paulus, P. B., & Dzindolet, M. T. (1993). Social influence processes in group brainstorming. *Journal of Personality and Social Psychology, 64*, 575–586.

Paulus, P. B., Dzindolet, M. T., Poletes, G., & Camacho, L. M. (1993). Perception of performance in group brainstorming: The illusion of group productivity. *Personality and Social Psychology Bulletin, 19*, 78–89.

Paunonen, S. V. (1989). Consensus in personality judgments: Moderating effects of target-rater acquaintanceship and behavior observability. *Journal of Personality and Social Psychology, 56*, 823–833.

Pavelchak, M. A. (1989). Piecemeal and category-based evaluation: An idiographic analysis. *Journal of Personality and Social Psychology, 56*, 354–363.

Pavelchak, M. A., Moreland, R. L., & Levine, J. M. (1986). Effects of prior group memberships on subsequent reconnaissance activities. *Journal of Personality and Social Psychology, 50*, 56–66.

Payne, B. K. (2001). Prejudice and perception: The role of automatic and controlled processes in misperceiving a weapon. *Journal of Personality and Social Psychology, 81*, 181–192.

Payne, B. K. (2005). Conceptualizing control in social cognition: How executive functioning modulates the expression of automatic stereotyping. *Journal of Personality and Social Psychology, 89*, 488–503.

Payne, B. K. (2006). Weapon bias: Split-second decisions and unintended stereotyping. *Current Directions in Psychological Science, 15*, 287–291.

Payne, J. W., Burkley, M. A., & Stokes, M. B. (2008). Why do implicit and explicit attitude tests diverge? The role of structural fit. *Journal of Personality and Social Psychology, 94*, 16–31.

Pedersen, W. C., Aviles, F. E., Ito, T. A., Miller, N., & Pollock, V. E. (2002). Psychological experimentation on alcohol-induced human aggression. *Aggression and Violent Behavior, 7*, 293–312.

Pedersen, W. C., Gonzales, C., & Miller, N. (2000). The moderating effect of trivial triggering provocation on displaced aggression. *Journal of Personality and Social Psychology, 78*, 913–927.

Peeters, G., & Czapinski, J. (1990). Positive-negative asymmetry in evaluations: The distinction between affective and informational negativity effects. In W. Stroebe & M. Hewstone (Eds.), *European review of social psychology* (Vol. 1, pp. 33–60). New York: Wiley.

Pelled, L. H., Eisenhardt, K. M., & Xin, K. R. (1999). Exploring the black box: An analysis of work group diversity, conflict, and performance. *Administrative Science Quarterly, 44*, 1–28.

Pemberton, M. B., Insko, C. A., & Schopler, J. (1996). Memory for an experience of differential competitive behavior of individuals and groups. *Journal of Personality and Social Psychology, 5*, 953–966.

Pennebaker, J. W., Rimé, B., & Blankenship, V. E. (1996). Stereotypes of emotional expressiveness of Northerners and Southerners: A cross-cultural test of Montesquieu's hypotheses. *Journal of Personality and Social Psychology, 70*, 372–380.

Penner, L. A., & Finkelstein, M. A. (1998). Dispositional and structural determinants of volunteerism. *Journal of Personality and Social Psychology, 74*, 525–537.

Pennington, N., & Hastie, R. (1991). A cognitive theory of juror decision making: The story model. *Cardozo Law Review, 13*, 519–557.

Peplau, L. A., & Fingerhut, A. W. (2007). The close relationships of lesbians and gay men. *Annual Review of Psychology, 58*, 405–424.

Peplau, L. A., Garnets, L. D., Spalding, L. R., Conley, T. D., & Veniegas, R. C. (1998). A critique of Bem's "exotic becomes erotic" theory of sexual orientation. *Psychological Review, 105*, 387–394.

Perdue, C. W., Dovidio, J. F., Gurtman, M. B., & Tyler, R. B. (1990). Us and them: Social categorization and the process of intergroup bias. *Journal of Personality and Social Psychology, 59*, 475–486.

Perreault, S., & Bourhis, R. Y. (1999). Ethnocentrism, social identification, and discrimination. *Personality and Social Psychology Bulletin, 25*, 92–103.

Peters, K., & Kashima, Y. (2007). From social talk to social action: Shaping the social triad with emotion sharing. *Journal of Personality and Social Psychology, 93*, 780–797.

Peters, L. H., Hartke, D. D., & Pohlmann, J. T. (1985). Fiedler's contingency theory of leadership: An application of the meta-analysis procedures of Schmidt and Hunter. *Psychological Bulletin, 97*, 274–285.

Peterson, B. E., Doty, R. M., & Winter, D. G. (1993). Authoritarianism and attitudes toward contemporary social issues. *Personality and Social Psychology Bulletin, 19*, 174–184.

Peterson, B. E., Duncan, L. E., & Pang, J. S. (2002). Authoritarianism and political impoverishment: Deficits in knowledge and civic disinterest. *Political Psychology, 23*, 97–112.

Petrinovich, L., O'Neill, P., & Jorgensen, M. (1993). An empirical study of moral intuitions: Toward an evolutionary ethics. *Journal of Personality and Social Psychology, 64*, 467–478.

Pettigrew, T. F. (1979). The ultimate attribution error: Extending Allport's cognitive analysis of prejudice. *Personality and Social Psychology Bulletin, 5*, 461–476.

Pettigrew, T. F. (1996). *How to think like a social scientist*. New York: Harper Collins.

Pettigrew, T. F. (1997). Generalized intergroup contact effects of prejudice. *Personality and Social Psychology Bulletin, 23*, 173–185.

Pettigrew, T. F. (1998a). Intergroup contact theory. *Annual Review of Psychology, 49*, 65–85.

Pettigrew, T. F. (1998b). Reactions toward the new minorities of Western Europe. *Annual Review of Sociology, 24*, 77–103.

Pettigrew, T. F., & Meertens, R. W. (1995). Subtle and blatant prejudice in western Europe. *European Journal of Social Psychology, 25*, 57–75.

Pettigrew, T. F., & Tropp, L. R. (2006). A meta-analytic test of intergroup contact theory.

*Journal of Personality and Social Psychology, 90*, 751–783.

Petty, R. E., & Briñol, P. (2008). Persuasion: From single to multiple to metacognitive processes. *Perspectives on Psychological Science, 3*, 137–147.

Petty, R. E., & Cacioppo, J. T. (1981). *Attitudes and persuasion: Classic and contemporary approaches*. Dubuque, IA: Brown.

Petty, R. E., & Krosnick, J. A. (Eds.) (1995). *Attitude strength: Antecedents and consequences*. Mahwah, NJ: Erlbaum.

Petty, R. E., & Wegener, D. T. (1998). Attitude change: Multiple roles for persuasion variables. In D. T. Gilbert, S. T. Fiske, & G. Lindzey (Eds.), *Handbook of social psychology* (4th ed., Vol. 1, pp. 323–390). New York: McGraw-Hill.

Pfeifer, J. H., Iacoboni, M., Mazziotta, J. C., & Dapretto, M. (2008). Mirroring others' emotions relates to empathy and interpersonal competence in children. *NeuroImage, 39*, 2076–2085.

Phelps, E. A., O'Connor, K. J., Cunningham, W. A., Funayama, E. S., Gatenby, J. C., Gore, J. C., & Banaji, M. R. (2000). Performance on indirect measures of race evaluation predicts amygdala activation. *Journal of Cognitive Neuroscience, 12*, 729–738.

Phillips, J. S., & Lord, R. G. (1981). Causal attributions and perceptions of leadership. *Organizational Behavior and Human Decision Processes, 28*, 143–163.

Phillips, J. S., & Lord, R. G. (1982). Schematic information processing and perceptions of leadership in problem-solving groups. *Journal of Applied Psychology, 67*, 486–492.

Piaget, J. (1952). *The origins of intelligence in children* ( M. Cook, Trans.). New York: Norton.

Pickett, C. L., Gardner, W. L., & Knowles, M. (2004). Getting a cue: The need to belong and enhanced sensitivity to social cues. *Personality and Social Psychology Bulletin, 30*, 1095–1107.

Piliavin, I. M., Rodin, J., & Piliavin, J. A. (1969). Good Samaritanism: An underground phenomenon? *Journal of Personality and Social Psychology, 13*, 289–299.

Piliavin, J. A., & Callero, P. L. (1991). *Giving blood: The development of an altruistic identity*. Baltimore, MD: Johns Hopkins University Press.

Piliavin, J. A., & Charng, H. W. (1990). Altruism: A review of recent theory and research. *Annual Review of Sociology, 16*, 27–65.

Pinel, E. C. (1999). Stigma consciousness: The psychological legacy of social stereotypes. *Journal of Personality and Social Psychology, 76*, 114–128.

Pinel, E. C. (2002). Stigma consciousness in intergroup contexts: The power of conviction.

*Journal of Experimental Social Psychology, 38*, 178–185.

Pinker, S. (1997). *How the mind works*. New York: Norton.

Pittman, T. S. (1998). Motivation. In D. T. Gilbert, S. T. Fiske, & G. Lindzey (Eds.), *Handbook of social psychology* (4th ed., Vol. 1, pp. 549–590). New York: McGraw-Hill.

Pittman, T. S., & Pittman, N. L. (1980). Deprivation of control and the attribution process. *Journal of Personality and Social Psychology, 39*, 377–389.

Plaks, J. E., Stroessner, S. J., Dweck, C. S., & Sherman, J. W. (2001). Person theories and attention allocation: Preferences for stereotypic versus counterstereotypic information. *Journal of Personality and Social Psychology, 80*, 876–893.

Platow, M. J., & van Knippenberg, D. (2001). A social identity analysis of leadership endorsement: The effects of leader ingroup prototypicality and distributive intergroup fairness. *Personality and Social Psychology Bulletin, 27*, 1508–1519.

Plous, S. (1996). Ten myths about affirmative action. *Journal of Social Issues, 52*, 25–31.

Pöhlmann, C., Carranza, E., Hannover, B., & Iyengar, S. S. (2007). Repercussions of self-construal for self-relevant and other-relevant choice. *Social Cognition, 25*, 284–305.

Pomerantz, E. M., Chaiken, S., & Tordesillas, R. S. (1995). Attitude strength and resistance processes. *Journal of Personality and Social Psychology, 69*, 408–419.

Pool, G. J., Wood, W., & Leck, K. (1998). The self-esteem motive in social influence: Agreement with valued majorities and disagreement with derogated minorities. *Journal of Personality and Social Psychology, 75*, 967–975.

Porter, R. H. (1987). Kin recognition: Functions and mediating mechanisms. *Annual Review of Sociology, 16*, 175–204.

Porter, S., & ten Brinke, L. (2008). Reading between the lies: Identifying concealed and falsified emotions in universal facial expressions. *Psychological Science, 19*, 508–514.

Postmes, T., Haslam, S. A., & Swaab, R. I. (2005). Social influence in small groups: An interactive model of social identity formation. *European Review of Social Psychology, 16*, 1–42.

Postmes, T., & Spears, R. (1998). Deindividuation and antinormative behavior: A meta-analysis. *Psychological Bulletin, 123*, 238–259.

Pratkanis, A. R. (1989). The cognitive representations of attitudes. In A. R. Pratkanis, S. J. Breckler, & A. G. Greenwald (Eds.), *Attitude structure and function* (pp. 71–98). Hillsdale, NJ: Erlbaum.

Pratto, F., & John, O. P. (1991). Automatic vigilance: The attention-grabbing power of negative social information. *Journal of Personality and Social Psychology*, *61*, 380–391.

Pratto, F., Sidanius, J., & Stallworth, L. M. (1993). Sexual selection and the sexual and ethnic basis of social hierarchy. In L. Ellis (Ed.), *Social stratification and socioeconomic inequality: A comparative biosocial analysis* (Vol. 1, pp. 111–137). Westport, CT: Praeger/Greenwood.

Pratto, F., Sidanius, J., Stallworth, L. M., & Malle, B. F. (1994). Social dominance orientation: A personality variable predicting social and political attitudes. *Journal of Personality and Social Psychology*, *67*, 741–763.

Pratto, F., Stallworth, L. M., Sidanius, J., & Siers, B. (1997). The gender gap in occupational role attainment: A social dominance approach. *Journal of Personality and Social Psychology*, *72*, 37–53.

Prentice, D. A. (1987). Psychological correspondence of possessions, attitudes, and values. *Journal of Personality and Social Psychology*, *53*, 993–1003.

Prentice, D. A., & Miller, D. T. (1993). Pluralistic ignorance and alcohol use on campus: Some consequences of misperceiving the social norm. *Journal of Personality and Social Psychology*, *64*, 243–256.

Prentice, D. A., & Miller, D. T. (2002). The emergence of homegrown stereotypes. *American Psychologist*, *5*, 353–359.

Preston, J., & Wegner, D. M. (2007). The eureka error: Inadvertent plagiarism by misattributions of effort. *Journal of Personality and Social Psychology*, *92*, 575–584.

Price, K. O., Harburg, E., & Newcomb, T. M. (1966). Psychological balance in situations of negative interpersonal attitudes. *Journal of Personality and Social Psychology*, *3*, 265–270.

Price, R. (1998). *Freedomland*. New York: Broadway.

Prislin, R. (1996). Attitude stability and attitude strength: One is enough to make it stable. *European Journal of Social Psychology*, *26*, 447–477.

Prislin, R., Limbert, W. M., & Bauer, E. (2000). From majority to minority and vice versa: The asymmetrical effects of losing and gaining majority position within a group. *Journal of Personality and Social Psychology*, *79*, 385–397.

Pronin, E., Gilovich, T., & Ross, L. (2004). Objectivity in the eye of the beholder: Divergent perceptions of bias in self versus others. *Psychological Review*, *111*, 781–799.

Pronin, E., Kruger, J., Savitsky, K., & Ross, L. (2001). You don't know me, but I know you: The illusion of asymmetric insight. *Journal of Personality and Social Psychology*, *81*, 639–656.

Pronin, E., & Kugler, M. B. (2007). Valuing thoughts, ignoring behavior: The introspection illusion as a source of the bias blind spot. *Journal of Experimental Social Psychology*, *43*, 565–578.

Pronin, E., Lin, D. Y., & Ross, L. (2002). The bias blind spot: Perceptions of bias in self versus others. *Personality and Social Psychology Bulletin*, *28*, 369–381.

Pronin, E., & Ross, L. (2006). Temporal differences in trait self-ascription: When the self is seen as an other. *Journal of Personality and Social Psychology*, *90*, 197–209.

Pronin, E., Wegner, D. M., McCarthy, K., & Rodriguez, S. (2006). Everyday magical powers: The role of apparent mental causation in the overestimation of personal influence. *Journal of Personality and Social Psychology*, *91*, 218–231.

Pruitt, D. G. (1998). Social conflict. In D. T. Gilbert, S. T. Fiske, & G. Lindzey (Eds.), *Handbook of social psychology* (4th ed., Vol. 2, pp. 470–503). New York: McGraw-Hill.

Pruitt, D. G., & Rubin, J. Z. (1986). *Social conflict: Escalation, stalemate, and settlement*. New York: Random House.

Pryor, J. B., Giedd, J. L., & Williams, K. B. (1995). A social psychological model for predicting sexual harassment. *Journal of Social Issues*, *51*, 69–84.

Pryor, J. B., Reeder, G. D., & McManus, J. A. (1991). Fear and loathing in the workplace: Reactions to AIDS-infected co-workers. *Personality and Social Psychology Bulletin*, *17*, 133–139.

Pryor, J. B., & Stoller, L. M. (1994). Sexual cognition processes in men high in the likelihood to sexually harass. *Personality and Social Psychology Bulletin*, *20*, 163–169.

Pyszczynski, T., Greenberg, J., & Solomon, S. (1997). Why do we need what we need? A terror management perspective on the roots of human social motivation. *Psychological Inquiry*, *8*, 1–20.

Pyszczynski, T., Greenberg, J., & Solomon, S. (1999). A dual-process model of defense against conscious and unconscious death-related thoughts: An extension of terror management theory. *Psychological Review*, *106*, 835–845.

Quadflieg, S., Mason, M. F., & Macrae, C. N. (2004). The owl and the pussycat: Gaze cues and visuospatial orienting. *Psychonomic Bulletin & Review*, *11*, 826–831.

Quattrone, G. A. (1982). Overattribution and unit formation: When behavior engulfs the person. *Journal of Personality and Social Psychology*, *42*, 93–607.

Quinn, D. M., & Crocker, J. (1999). When ideology hurts: Effects of belief in the Protestant ethic and feeling overweight on the psychological wellbeing of women. *Journal of Personality and Social Psychology*, *77*, 402–414.

Quinn, K. A., & Macrae, C. N. (2005). Categorizing others: The dynamics of person construal. *Journal of Personality and Social Psychology, 88*, 467–479.

Rabbie, J., & Horowitz, M. (1969). Arousal of ingroup-outgroup bias by a chance win or loss. *Journal of Personality and Social Psychology, 13*, 269–277.

Rabinovitz, J. (1996, November 15). College idealism was fertile soil for fringe group. *New York Times*, pp. A1, B4.

Rabow, J., Newcomb, M. D., Monto, M. A., & Hernandez, A. C. (1990). Altruism in drunk driving situations: Personal and situational factors in intervention. *Social Psychology Quarterly, 53*, 199–213.

Radke-Yarrow, M., & Zahn-Waxler, C. (1986). The role of familial factors in the development of prosocial behavior: Research findings and questions. In D. Olweus, J. Block, & M. Radke-Yarrow (Eds.), *Development of antisocial and prosocial behavior: Research, theories, and issues* (pp. 207–233). New York: Academic Press.

Rahim, M. A. (1989). Relationships of leader power to compliance and satisfaction with supervision: Evidence from a national sample of managers. *Journal of Management, 15*, 545–556.

Rahim, M. A., Antonioni, D., & Psenicka, C. (2001). A structural equations model of leader power, subordinates' styles of handling conflict, and job performance. *International Journal of Conflict Management, 12*, 191–211.

Rahim, M. A., & Mainudden, A. (1993). Leader power, commitment, satisfaction, compliance, and propensity to leave a job among U.S. accountants. *Journal of Social Psychology, 133*, 611–625.

Rai, S. N., & Rathmore, J. (1988). Attraction as a function of cultural similarity and proportion of similar attitudes related to different areas of life. *Psycho-Lingua, 29*, 123–131.

Rajecki, D. W., Rasmussen, J. L., & Conner, T. J. (2007). Punish and forgive: Causal attribution and positivity bias in response to cat and dog misbehavior. *Society and Animals, 15*, 311–328.

Ramirez, J., Bryant, J., & Zillmann, D. (1982). Effects of erotica on retaliatory behavior as a function of level of prior provocation. *Journal of Personality and Social Psychology, 43*, 971–978.

Rasmussen, H. N., Wrosch, C., Scheier, M. F., & Carver, C. S. (2006). Self-regulation processes and health: The importance of optimism and goal adjustment. *Journal of Personality, 74*, 1721–1747.

Rawls, J. (1971). *A theory of justice*. Cambridge, MA: Harvard University Press.

Reber, R., Schwarz, N., & Winkielman, P. (2004). Processing fluency and aesthetic pleasure: Is beauty in the perceiver's processing experience? *Personality and Social Psychology Review, 8*, 364–382.

Reeder, G. D., & Brewer, M. B. (1979). A schematic model of dispositional attribution in interpersonal perception. *Psychological Review, 86*, 61–79.

Regan, D. T., & Fazio, R. (1977). On the consistency between attitudes and behavior: Look to the method of attitude formation. *Journal of Experimental Social Psychology, 13*, 28–45.

Reicher, S. (2001). The psychology of crowd dynamics. In M. A. Hogg & R. S. Tindale (Eds.), *Blackwell handbook of social psychology: Group processes* (pp. 182–208). Malden, MA: Blackwell.

Reicher, S., Spears, R., & Postmes, T. (1995). A social identity model of deindividuation phenomena. In W. Stroebe & M. Hewstone (Eds.), *European review of social psychology* (Vol. 6, pp. 161–198). New York: Wiley.

Reicher, S. D. (1984a). Social influence in the crowd: Attitudinal and behavioural effects of de-individuation in conditions of high and low group salience. *British Journal of Social Psychology, 23*, 341–350.

Reicher, S. D. (1984b). The St. Paul's riot: An explanation of the limits of crowd action in terms of a social identity model. *European Journal of Social Psychology, 14*, 1–21.

Reis, H. T., & Patrick, B. C. (1996). Attachment and intimacy: Component processes. In E. T. Higgins & A. W. Kruglanski (Eds.), *Social psychology: Handbook of basic principles* (pp. 523–563). New York: Guilford.

Reis, H. T., Senchak, M., & Solomon, B. (1985). Sex differences in the intimacy of social interaction: Further examination of potential explanations. *Journal of Personality and Social Psychology, 48*, 1204–1217.

Reis, H. T., & Shaver, P. R. (1988). Intimacy as an interpersonal process. In S. W. Duck (Ed.), *Handbook of personal relationships* (pp. 367–389). Chichester, UK: John Wiley.

Reis, H. T., Wilson, I. M., Monestere, C., Berstein, S., Clark, K., Seidl, E., Franco, M., Gioioso, E., Freeman, L., & Radoane, K. (1990). What is smiling is beautiful and good. *European Journal of Social Psychology, 20*, 259–267.

Rempel, J. K., Holmes, J. G., & Zanna, M. P. (1985). Trust in close relationships. *Journal of Personality and Social Psychology, 49*, 95–112.

Rempel, J. K., Ross, M., & Holmes, J. G. (2001). Trust and communicated attributions in close relationships. *Journal of Personality and Social Psychology, 81*, 57–64.

Rest, J. R. (1983). Morality. In P. Mussen (Ed.), *Manual of child psychology* (4th ed., Vol. 3, pp. 556–629). New York: Wiley.

Rest, J. R., & Thoma, S. J. (1985). Relation of moral judgment development to formal education. *Developmental Psychology, 21*, 709–714.

Reynolds, K. J., Turner, J. C., & Haslam, S. A. (2000). When are we better than them and they worse than us? A closer look at social discrimination in positive and negative domains. *Journal of Personality and Social Psychology, 78*, 64–80.

Reynolds, K. J., Turner, J. C., Haslam, S. A., & Ryan, M. K. (2001). The role of personality and group factors in explaining prejudice. *Journal of Experimental Social Psychology, 37*, 427–434.

Rhodes, G. (2006). The evolutionary psychology of facial beauty. *Annual Review of Psychology, 57*, 199–226.

Rhodes, N., & Wood, W (1992). Self-esteem and intelligence affect influenceability: The mediating role of message reception. *Psychological Bulletin, 111*, 156–171.

Richard, F. D., Bond Jr., C. F., & Stokes-Zoota, J. J. (2003). One hundred years of social psychology quantitatively described. *Review of General Psychology, 7*, 331–363.

Richeson, J. A., & Ambady, N. (2003). Effects of situational power on automatic racial prejudice. *Journal of Experimental Social Psychology, 39*, 177–183.

Richeson, J. A., Baird, A. A., Gordon, H. L., Heatherton, T. F., Wyland, C. L., Trawalter, S., & Shelton, J. N. (2003). An MRI investigation of the impact of interracial contact on executive function. *Nature Neuroscience, 6*, 1323–1328.

Richeson, J. A., & Shelton, J. N. (2003). When prejudice does not pay: Effects of interracial contact on executive function. *Psychological Science, 14*, 287–290.

Richeson, J. A., & Trawalter, S. (2005). Why do interracial interactions impair executive function? A resource depletion account. *Journal of Personality and Social Psychology, 88*, 934–947.

Richeson, J. A., Trawalter, S., & Shelton, J. N. (2005). African Americans' implicit racial attitudes and the depletion of executive function after interracial interactions. *Social Cognition, 23*, 336–352.

Rickabaugh, C. A., & Tomlinson-Keasey, C. (1997). Social and temporal comparisons in adjustment to aging. *Basic and Applied Social Psychology, 19*, 307–328.

Ridgeway, C. L. (2001). The emergence of status beliefs: From structural inequality to legitimizing ideology. In J. T. Jost & B. Major (Eds.), *The psychology of legitimacy* (pp. 257–277). New York: Cambridge University Press.

Ridgeway, C. L., & Erickson, K. G. (2000). Creating and spreading status beliefs. *American Journal of Sociology, 106*, 579–615.

Rilling, J. K., Gutman, D. A., Zeh, T. R., Pagnoni, G., Berns, G. S., & Kilts, C. D. (2002). A neural basis for social cooperation. *Neuron, 35*, 395–405.

Riordan, C. A., Dunaway, F. A., Haas, P., James, M. K., & Kruger, D. (1984). Prosocial behavior following transgression: Evidence for intrapsychic and interpersonal motives. *Journal of Social Psychology, 124*, 51–55.

Rizzolatti, G., & Craighero, L. (2004). The mirror-neuron system. *Annual Review of Neuroscience, 27*, 169–192.

Robins, R. W., & Beer, J. S. (2001). Positive illusions about the self: Short-term benefits and long-term costs. *Journal of Personality and Social Psychology, 80*, 340–352.

Robinson, D. T., & Smith-Lovin, L. (2001). Getting a laugh: Gender, status, and humor in task discussions. *Social Forces, 80*, 123–158.

Roccas, S., & Brewer, M. (2002). Social identity complexity. *Personality and Social Psychology Review, 6*, 88–106.

Rodin, J., & Langer, E. J. (1977). Long-term effects of a control-relevant intervention with the institutionalized aged. *Journal of Personality and Social Psychology, 35*, 897–902.

Roese, N. J., & Jamieson, D. W. (1993). Twenty years of bogus pipeline research: A critical review and meta-analysis. *Psychological Bulletin, 114*, 363–375.

Rogers, R. W., & Prentice-Dunn, S. (1981). Deindividuation and anger-mediated interracial aggression: Unmasking regressive racism. *Journal of Personality and Social Psychology, 41*, 63–73.

Ronquillo, J., Denson, T. F., Lickel, B., Lu, Z., Nandy, A., & Maddox, K. B. (2007). The effects of skin tone on race-related amygdala activity: An fMRI investigation. *Social Cognitive and Affective Neuroscience, 2*, 39–44.

Rook, K. S., Pietromonaco, P. R., & Lewis, M. (1994). When are depressives distressing to others and vice-versa? Effects of friendship, similarity, and interaction task. *Journal of Personality and Social Psychology, 67*, 548–559.

Rosch, E., Mervis, C. B., Gray, W., Johnson, D., & Boyes-Braem, P. (1976). Basic objects in natural categories. *Cognitive Psychology, 8*, 382–439.

Rosenberg, M. (1965). *Society and the adolescent self-image*. Princeton, NJ: Princeton University Press.

Rosenberg, S., & Sedlak, A. (1972). Structural representations of implicit personality theory. In L. Berkowitz (Ed.), *Advances in experimental social psychology* (Vol. 6, pp. 235–297). New York: Academic Press.

Rosenblatt, A., Greenberg, J., Solomon, S., Pyszczynski, T., & Lyon, D. (1989). Evidence for terror management theory: I. The effects of mortality salience on reactions to those who violate or uphold cultural values. *Journal of Personality and Social Psychology*, *57*, 681–690.

Rosenhan, D. L. (1970). The natural socialization of altruistic autonomy. In J. Macaulay & L. Berkowitz (Eds.), *Altruism and helping behavior* (pp. 251–268). New York: Academic Press.

Rosenhan, D. L., Salovey, P., & Hargis, K. (1981). The joys of helping: Focus of attention mediates the impact of positive effect on altruism. *Journal of Personality and Social Psychology*, *40*, 899–905.

Rosenthal, R. (1994). Interpersonal expectancy effects: A 30-year perspective. *Current Directions in Psychological Science*, *3*, 176–179.

Rosenthal, R. (1995). Methodology. In A. Tesser (Ed.), *Advanced social psychology* (pp. 17–49). New York: McGraw-Hill.

Rosenthal, R., & Rosnow, R. L. (1975). *The volunteer subject*. New York: Wiley.

Rosnow, R. L. (1980). Psychology of rumor reconsidered. *Psychological Bulletin*, *87*, 578–591.

Rosnow, R. L. (1991). Inside rumor: A personal journey. *American Psychologist*, *46*, 484–496.

Ross, L. Greene, D., & House, P. (1977). The false consensus effect: An egocentric bias in social perception and attribution processes. *Journal of Experimental Social Psychology*, *13*, 279–301.

Ross, L. & Nisbett, R. E. (1991). *The person and the situation: Perspectives of social psychology*. New York: McGraw-Hill.

Ross, M. (1989). Relation of implicit theories to the construction of personal histories. *Psychological Review*, *96*, 341–57.

Ross, M., & Newby-Clark, I. R. (1998). Construing the past and future. *Social Cognition*, *16*, 133–150.

Ross, M., & Sicoly, F. (1979). Egocentric biases in availability and attribution. *Journal of Personality and Social Psychology*, *37*, 322–336.

Rotenberg, K. J. (1994). Loneliness and interpersonal trust. *Journal of Social and Clinical Psychology*, *13*, 152–173.

Rothbart, M., & Park, B. (1986). On the confirmability and disconfirmability of trait concepts. *Journal of Personality and Social Psychology*, *50*, 131–142.

Rothbart, M., & Taylor, M. (1992). Category labels and social reality: Do we view social categories as natural kinds? In G. Semin & K. Fiedler (Eds.), *Language, interaction and social cognition* (pp. 11–36). London: Sage.

Rothbaum, F., Pott, M., Azuma, H., Miyake, K., & Weisz, J. (2000). The development of close relationships in Japan and the United States: Paths of symbiotic harmony and generative tension. *Child Development*, *71*, 1121–1142.

Rothbaum, F., Weisz, J., Pott, M., Miyake, K., & Morelli, G. (2000). Attachment and culture: Security in the United States and Japan. *American Psychologist*, *55*, 1093–1104.

Rotter, J. B. (1980). Interpersonal trust, trustworthiness, and gullibility. *American Psychologist*, *35*, 17.

Rotton, J., & Cohn, E. G. (2000). Violence is a curvi-linear function of temperature in Dallas: A replication. *Journal of Personality and Social Psychology*, *78*, 1074–1081.

Rubin, M., & Hewstone, M. (1998). Social identity theory's self-esteem hypothesis: A review and some suggestions for clarification. *Personality and Social Psychology Review*, *2*, 40–62.

Rubin, Z. (1973). *Liking and loving: An invitation to social psychology*. New York: Holt, Rinehart, & Winston.

Rubin, Z., & Peplau, L. A. (1973). Belief in a just world and reactions to another's lot: A study of participants in the national draft lottery. *Journal of Social Issues*, *29*, 73–93.

Rubin, Z., & Peplau, L. A. (1975). Who believes in a just world? *Journal of Social Issues*, *31*, 65–89.

Rudman, L. A., Ashmore, R. D., & Gary, M. L. (2001). "Unlearning" automatic biases: The malleability of implicit prejudice and stereotypes. *Journal of Personality and Social Psychology*, *81*, 856–868.

Rudman, L. A., & Glick, P. (2008). *The social psychology of gender: How power and intimacy shape gender relations*. New York: Guilford.

Rudman, L. A., Greenwald, A. G., Mellott, D. S., Schwartz, J. L. K. (1999). Measuring the automatic components of prejudice: Flexibility and generality of the Implicit Association Test. *Social Cognition*, *17*, 437–465.

Rusbult, C. E. (1980). Commitment and satisfaction in romantic associations: A test of the investment model. *Journal of Experimental Social Psychology*, *16*, 172–186.

Rusbult, C. E., & Buunk, B. P. (1993). Commitment processes in close relationships: An interdependence analysis. *Journal of Social and Personal Relationships*, *10*, 175–204.

Rusbult, C. E., & Martz, J. M. (1995). Remaining in an abusive relationship: An investment model analysis of nonvoluntary dependence. *Personality and Social Psychology Bulletin*, *21*, 558–571.

Rusbult, C. E., Martz, J. M., & Agnew, C. R. (1998). The investment model scale: Measuring commitment level, satisfaction level, quality of alternatives, and investment size. *Personal Relationships*, *5*, 357–391.

Rusbult, C. E., Onizuka, R. K., & Lipkus, I. (1993). What do we really want? Mental models of ideal romantic involvement explored through multidimensional scaling. *Journal of Experimental Social Psychology, 29*, 493–527.

Rusbult, C. E., & Van Lange, P. A. M. (1996). Interdependence processes. In E. T. Higgins & A. W. Kruglanski (Eds.), *Social psychology: Handbook of basic principles* (pp. 564–596). New York: Guilford.

Rusbult, C. E., & Van Lange, P. A. M. (2003). Interdependence, interaction, and relationships. *Annual Review of Psychology, 54*, 351–375.

Rusbult, C. E., Verette, J., Whitney, G. A., Slovik, L. F., & Lipkus, I. (1991). Accommodation processes in close relationships: Theory and preliminary empirical evidence. *Journal of Personality and Social Psychology, 60*, 53–78.

Ruscher, J. B. (2001). *Prejudiced communication*. New York: Guilford.

Ruscher, J. B., & Duval, L. L. (1998). Multiple communicators with unique target information transmit less stereotypical impressions. *Journal of Personality and Social Psychology, 74*, 329–344.

Ruscher, J. B., & Fiske, S. T. (1990). Interpersonal competition can cause individuating processes. *Journal of Personality and Social Psychology, 58*, 832–843.

Ruscher, J. B., Hammer, E. Y., & Hammer, E. D. (1996). Forming shared impressions through conversation: An adaptation of the continuum model. *Personality and Social Psychology Bulletin, 22*, 705–720.

Rushton, J. P. (1992). Evolutionary biology and heritable traits (with reference to oriental-white-black differences): The 1989 AAAS paper. *Psychological Reports, 71*, 811–822.

Russell, J. A. (1994). Is there universal recognition of emotion from facial expressions? A review of the cross-cultural studies. *Psychological Bulletin, 115*, 102–141.

Russo, J. E., Staelin, R., Nolan, C. A., Russell, G. J., & Metcalf, B. L. (1986). Nutrition information in the supermarket. *Journal of Consumer Research, 13*, 48–70.

Russo, R. (2001). *Empire falls*. New York: Knopf.

Rusting, C. L., & Nolen-Hoeksema, S. (1998). Regulating responses to anger: Effects of rumination and distraction on angry mood. *Journal of Personality and Social Psychology, 74*, 790–803.

Sachdev, I., & Bourhis, R. Y. (1987). Status differentials and intergroup behaviour. *European Journal of Social Psychology, 17*, 277–293.

Sachdev, I., & Bourhis, R. Y. (1991). Power and status differentials in minority and majority group relations. *European Journal of Social Psychology, 21*, 1–24.

Sadler, M. S., & Judd, C. M. (2001). Overcoming dependent data: A guide to the analysis of group data. In M. A. Hogg & R. S. Tindale (Eds.), *Blackwell handbook of social psychology: Group processes* (pp. 497–524). Malden, MA: Blackwell.

Saenz, D. S., & Lord, C. G. (1989). Reversing roles: A cognitive strategy for undoing memory deficits associated with token status. *Journal of Personality and Social Psychology, 56*, 698–708.

Salmivalli, C., Kaukiainen, A., Kaistaniemi, L., & Lagerspetz, K. M. J. (1999). Self-evaluated self-esteem, peer-evaluated self-esteem, and defensive egotism as predictors of adolescents' participation in bullying situations. *Personality and Social Psychology Bulletin, 25*, 1268–1278.

Salovey, P., Mayer, J. D., & Rosenhan, D. L. (1991). Mood and helping. In M. S. Clark (Ed.), *Review of personality and social psychology: Prosocial behavior* (Vol. 12, pp. 215–237). Newbury Park, CA: Sage.

Sanchez-Burks, J., Nisbett, R. E., & Ybarra, O. (2000). Cultural styles, relationship schemas, and prejudice against outgroups. *Journal of Personality and Social Psychology, 79*, 174–189.

Sande, G. N., Goethals, G. R., & Radloff, C. E. (1988). Perceiving one's own traits and others': The multifaceted self. *Journal of Personality and Social Psychology, 54*, 13–20.

Sanfey, A., & Hastie, R. (1998). Does evidence presentation format affect judgment? An experimental evaluation of displays of data for judgments. *Psychological Science, 9*, 99–103.

Sanna, L. J., & Parks, C. D. (1997). Group research trends in social and organizational psychology: Whatever happened to intragroup research. *Psychological Science, 8*, 261–267.

Santuzzi, A. M., & Ruscher, J. B. (2002). Stigma salience and paranoid social cognition: Understanding variability in metaperceptions among individuals with recently-acquired stigma. *Social Cognition, 20*, 171–198.

Sapadin, L. A. (1988). Friendship and gender: Perspectives of professional men and women. *Journal of Social and Personal Relationships, 5*, 387–403.

Saxe, R., Carey, S., & Kanwisher, N. (2004). Understanding other minds: Linking developmental psychology and functional neuroimaging. *Annual Review of Psychology, 55*, 87–124.

Schachter, S. (1951). Deviation, rejection, and communication. *Journal of Abnormal and Social Psychology, 46*, 190–207.

Schachter, S. (1959). *The psychology of affiliation: Experimental studies of the sources of gregariousness*. Oxford, UK: Stanford University Press.

Schachter, S. (1964). The interaction of cognitive and physiological determinants of emotional state. In L. Berkowitz (Ed.), *Advances in experimental social psychology* (Vol. 1, pp. 49–80). New York: Academic Press.

Schachter, S., & Singer, J. (1962). Cognitive, social, and physiological determinants of emotional state. *Psychological Review*, *69*, 378–399.

Schaller, M., & Cialdini, R. B. (1988). The economics of empathic helping: Support for a mood management motive. *Journal of Experimental Social Psychology*, *24*, 163–181.

Schaller, M., & Conway, L. G. (1999). Influence of impression-management goals on the emerging contents of group stereotypes: Support for a social-evolutionary process. *Personality and Social Psychology Bulletin*, *25*, 819–833.

Schaller, M., & Conway, L. G. (2001). From cognition to culture: The origins of stereotypes that really matter. In G. B. Moskowitz (Ed.), *Cognitive social psychology: The Princeton symposium on the legacy and future of social cognition* (pp. 163–176). Mahwah, NJ: Erlbaum.

Schaller, M., Conway, L. G., & Tanchuk, T. L. (2002). Selective pressures on the once and future contents of ethnic stereotypes: Effects of the "communicability" of traits. *Journal of Personality and Social Psychology*, *82*, 861–877.

Schaller, M., Simpson, J. A., & Kenrick, D. T. (Eds.) (2006). *Evolution and social psychology*. Madison, CT: Psychosocial Press.

Schank, R. C., & Abelson, R. P. (1977). *Scripts, plans, goals, and understanding: An inquiry into human knowledge structures*. Hillsdale, NJ: Erlbaum.

Scheibe, K. E. (1985). Historical perspectives on the presented self. In B. R. Schlenker (Ed.), *The self and social life* (pp. 33–64). New York: McGraw-Hill.

Scheier, M. F., & Carver, C. S. (1983). Self-directed attention and the comparison of self with standards. *Journal of Experimental Social Psychology*, *19*, 205–222.

Schein, V. E. (2001). A global look at psychological barriers to women's progress in management. *Journal of Social Issues*, *57*, 675–688.

Scher, S., & Cooper, J. (1989). Motivational basis of dissonance: The singular role of behavioral consequences. *Journal of Personality and Social Psychology*, *56*, 899–906.

Schimel, J., Simon, L., Greenberg, J., Pyszczynski, T., Solomon, S., Waxmonsky, J., & Arndt, J. (1999). Stereotypes and terror management: Evidence that mortality salience enhances stereotypic thinking

and preferences. *Journal of Personality and Social Psychology*, *77*, 905–926.

Schlenker, B. R., & Weigold, M. F. (1992). Interpersonal processes involving impression regulation and management. *Annual Review of Psychology*, *43*, 133–168.

Schmader, T. (2002). Gender identification moderates stereotype threat effects on women's math performance. *Journal of Experimental Social Psychology*, *38*, 194–201.

Schmader, T., & Major, B. (1999). The impact of ingroup vs. outgroup performance on personal values. *Journal of Experimental Social Psychology*, *35*, 47–67.

Schmader, T., Major, B., Eccleston, C. P., & McCoy, S. K. (2001). Devaluing domains in response to threatening intergroup comparisons: Perceived legitimacy and the status value asymmetry. *Journal of Personality and Social Psychology*, *80*, 782–796.

Schmerund, A., Sellers, R., & Mueller, B. (2001). Attitudes toward affirmative action as a function of racial identity among African American college students. *Political Psychology*, *22*, 759–774.

Schmidt, G., & Weiner, B. (1988). An attribution-affect-action theory of behavior: Replications of judgments of help-giving. *Personality and Social Psychology Bulletin*, *14*, 610–621.

Schnake, S. B., & Ruscher, J. B. (1998). Modern racism as a predictor of the linguistic intergroup bias. *Journal of Language and Social Psychology*, *17*, 484–491.

Schneider, D. J., Hastorf, A. H., & Ellsworth, P. C. (1979). *Person perception* (2nd ed.). Menlo Park, CA: Addison-Wesley.

Schopler, J., & Insko, C. A. (1992). The discontinuity effect in interpersonal and intergroup relations: Generality and mediation. In W. Stroebe & M. Hewstone (Eds.), *European review of social psychology* (Vol. 3, pp. 121–151). New York: Wiley.

Schopler, J., Insko, C. A., Graetz, K. A., Drigotas, S., Smith, V A., & Dahl, K. (1993). Individual group discontinuity: Further evidence for mediation by fear and greed. *Personality and Social Psychology Bulletin*, *19*, 419–431.

Schopler, J., Insko, C. A., Wieselquist, J., Pemberton, M., Witcher, B., Kozar, R., Roddenberry, C., & Wildschut, T. (2001). When groups are more competitive than individuals: The domain of the discontinuity effect. *Journal of Personality and Social Psychology*, *80*, 632–644.

Schriesheim, C. A., Tepper, B. J., & Tetrault, L. A. (1994). Least preferred co-worker score, situational control, and leadership effectiveness: A meta-analysis of contingency model performance predictions. *Journal of Applied Psychology*, *79*, 561–573.

Schroeder, D. A., Penner, L. A., Dovidio, J. F., & Piliavin, J. A. (1995). *Psychology of helping and altruism: Problems and puzzles*. New York: McGraw-Hill.

Schulz-Hardt, S., Frey, D., Luethgens, C., & Moscovici, S. (2000). Biased information search in group decision making. *Journal of Personality and Social Psychology*, *78*, 655–669.

Schwartz, S. H. (1977). Normative influences on altruism. In L. Berkowitz (Ed.), *Advances in experimental social psychology* (Vol. 10, pp. 221–282). New York: Academic Press.

Schwartz, S. H. (1992). Universals in the content and structure of values: Theoretical advances and empirical tests in 20 countries. In M. P. Zanna (Ed.), *Advances in experimental social psychology* (Vol. 25, pp. 1–65). San Diego, CA: Academic Press.

Schwartz, S. H., & Bilsky, W. (1987). Toward a universal structure of human values. *Journal of Personality and Social Psychology*, *53*, 550–562.

Schwartz, S. H., & Bilsky, W. (1990). Toward theory of the universal content and structure of values: Extensions and cross-cultural replications. *Journal of Personality and Social Psychology*, *58*, 878–891.

Schwartz, S. H., & Clausen, G. T. (1970). Responsibility, norms, and helping in an emergency. *Journal of Personality and Social Psychology*, *16*, 299–310.

Schwarz, N. (2004). Metacognitive experiences in consumer judgment and decision making. *Journal of Consumer Psychology*, *14*, 332–348.

Schwarz, N., & Clore, G. L. (1983). Mood, misattribution, and judgments of well-being: Informative and directive functions of affective states. *Journal of Personality and Social Psychology*, *45*, 513–523.

Schwarz, N., & Clore, G. L. (2007). Feelings and phenomenal experiences. In A. W. Kruglanski & E. T. Higgins (Eds.), *Social psychology: Handbook of basic principles* (2nd ed., pp. 385–407). New York: Guilford.

Sears, D. O. (1983). The person-positivity bias. *Journal of Personality and Social Psychology*, *44*, 233–250.

Sears, D. O. (1986). College sophomores in the laboratory: Influences of a narrow data base on social psychology's view of human nature. *Journal of Personality and Social Psychology*, *51*, 515–530.

Sears, D. O., & Kinder, D. R. (1985). Whites' opposition to busing: On conceptualizing and operationalizing group conflict. *Journal of Personality and Social Psychology*, *48*, 1148–1161.

Seay, B., Hansen, E., & Harlow, H. F. (1962). Mother-infant separation in monkeys. *Journal of Child Psychology and Psychiatry*, *3*, 123–132.

Seay, B., & Harlow, H. F. (1965). Maternal separation in the rhesus monkey. *Journal of Nervous and Mental Disease*, *140*, 434–441.

Sedikides, C., Gaertner, L., & Toguchi, Y. (2003). Pancultural self-enhancement. *Journal of Personality and Social Psychology*, *84*, 60–79.

Sedikides, C., & Skowronski, J. J. (1997). The symbolic self in evolutionary context. *Personality and Social Psychology Review*, *1*, 80–102.

Sedikides, C., & Strube, M. J. (1997). Self-evaluation: To thine own self be good, to thine own self be sure, to thine own self be true, and to thine own self be better. In M. P. Zanna (Ed.), *Advances in experimental social psychology* (Vol. 29, pp. 209–269). New York: Academic Press.

Sellers, R. M., Rowley, S. A. J., Chavous, T. M., Shelton, J. N., & Smith, M. A. (1997). Multidimensional Inventory of Black Identity: A preliminary investigation of reliability and construct validity. *Journal of Personality and Social Psychology*, *73*, 805–815.

Sellers, R. M., & Shelton, J. N. (2003). The role of racial identity in perceived racial discrimination. *Journal of Personality and Social Psychology*, *84*, 1079–1092.

Sellers, R. M., Smith, M. A., Shelton, J. N., Rowley, S. A. J., & Chavous, T. M. (1998). Multidimensional model of racial identity: A reconceptualization of African American racial identity. *Personality and Social Psychology Review*, *2*, 18–39.

Semmann, D., Krambeck, H., & Milinski, M. (2004). Strategic investment in reputation. *Behavioral Ecology and Sociobiology*, *56*, 248–252.

Sentis, K. P., & Burnstein, E. (1979). Remembering schema-consistent information: Effects of a balance schema on recognition memory. *Journal of Personality and Social Psychology*, *37*, 2200–2211.

Shaffer, D. R., Crepaz, N. & Sun, C. R. (2000). Physical attractiveness stereotyping in cross-cultural perspective: Similarities and differences between Americans and Taiwanese. *Journal of Cross-Cultural Psychology*, *31*, 557–582.

Shaffer, D. R., Rogel, M., & Hendrick, C. (1975). Intervention in the library: The effect of increased responsibility on bystanders' willingness to prevent a theft. *Journal of Applied Social Psychology*, *5*, 303–319.

Shah, J., & Higgins, E. T. (1997). Expectancy-value effects: Regulatory focus as determinant of magnitude and direction. *Journal of Personality and Social Psychology*, *73*, 447–458.

Shah, J., & Higgins, E. T. (2001). Regulatory concerns and appraisal efficiency: The general impact of promotion and prevention. *Journal of Personality and Social Psychology*, *80*, 693–705.

Shah, J., Higgins, E. T., & Friedman, R. S. (1998). Performance incentives and means: How regulatory focus influences goal attainment. *Journal of Personality and Social Psychology*, *74*, 285–293.

Shah, J. Y., & Gardner, W. L. (Eds.) (2008). *Handbook of motivation science*. New York: Guilford Press.

Shapiro, J. P., Baumeister, R. F., & Kessler, J. W. (1991). A three-component model of children's teasing: Aggression, humor, and ambiguity. *Journal of Social and Clinical Psychology*, *10*, 459–472.

Shaver, K. G. (1970). Defensive attribution: Effects of severity and relevance on the responsibility assigned for an accident. *Journal of Personality and Social Psychology*, *14*, 101–113.

Shavitt, S. (1990). The role of attitude objects in attitude functions. *Journal of Experimental Social Psychology*, *26*, 124–148.

Shaw, J. I., & Condelli, L. (1986). Effects of compliance outcome and basis of power on the powerholder-target relationship. *Personality and Social Psychology Bulletin*, *12*, 236–246.

Shelton, J. N. (2000). A reconceptualization of how we study issues of racial prejudice. *Personality and Social Psychology Review*, *4*, 374–390.

Shelton, J. N. (2003). Interpersonal concerns in social encounters between majority and minority group members. *Group Processes and Intergroup Relations*, *6*, 171–185.

Shelton, J. N., & Sellers, R. M. (2000). Situational stability and variability in African American racial identity. *Journal of Black Psychology*, *26*, 27–50.

Sheppard, J. A. (1993). Productivity loss in performance groups: A motivation analysis. *Psychological Bulletin*, *113*, 67–81.

Sheppard, J. A. (1995). Remedying motivation and productivity loss in collective settings. *Current Directions in Psychological Science*, *4*, 131–134.

Sherif, M. (1935). A study of some social factors in perception. *Archives of Psychology*, *27*, 1–60.

Sherif, M. (1936). *The psychology of social norms*. Oxford, England: Harper.

Sherif, M. (1966). *Group conflict and co-operation: Their social psychology*. London: Routledge & Kegan Paul.

Sherif, M., Harvey, O. J., White, B. J., Hood, W. R., & Sherif, C. W. (1961/1988). *The Robbers Cave experiment: Intergroup conflict and cooperation*. Middletown, CT: Wesleyan University Press.

Sherif, M., & Sherif, C. W. (1953). *Groups in harmony and tension: An integration of studies on intergroup relations*. Oxford, England: Harper & Brothers.

Sherman, J. W., Lee, A. Y., Bessenoff, G. R., & Frost, L. A. (1998). Stereotype efficiency reconsidered: Encoding flexibility under cognitive load. *Journal of Personality and Social Psychology*, *75*, 589–606.

Sherman, S. J., Castelli, L., & Hamilton, D. L. (2002). The spontaneous use of a group typology as an organizing principle in memory. *Journal of Personality and Social Psychology*, *82*, 328–342.

Shih, M., Bonam, C., Sanchez, D., & Peck, C. (2007). The social construction of race: Biracial identity and vulnerability to stereotypes. *Cultural Diversity and Ethnic Minority Psychology*, *13*, 125–133.

Shih, M., Pittinsky, T. L., & Ambady, N. (1999). Stereotype susceptibility: Identity salience and shifts in quantitative performance. *Psychological Science*, *10*, 80–83.

Shira, G., & Gardner, W. L. (1999). Are there "his" and "hers" types of interdependence? The implications of gender differences in collective versus relational interdependence for affect, behavior, and cognition. *Journal of Personality and Social Psychology*, *77*, 642–655.

Shoda, Y., Mischel, W., & Wright, J. C. (1994). Intraindividual stability in the organization and patterning of behavior: Incorporating psychological situations into the idiographic analysis of personality. *Journal of Personality and Social Psychology*, *67*, 674–687.

Shrauger, J. S., & Schoeneman, T. J. (1979). Symbolic interactionist view of self-concept: Through the looking glass darkly. *Psychological Bulletin*, *86*, 549–573.

Shweder, R. A., & Bourne, E. J. (1982). Does the concept of the person vary cross-culturally? In A. J. Marsella & G. M. White (Eds.), *Cultural conceptions of mental health and therapy* (pp. 97–137). Dordrecht: D Reidel.

Sia, T. L., Lord, C. G., Blessum, K. A., Ratcliff, C. D., & Lepper, M. R. (1997). Is a rose always a rose? The role of social category exemplar change in attitude stability and attitude-behavior consistency. *Journal of Personality and Social Psychology*, *72*, 501–514.

Sidanius, J. (1988). Political sophistication and political deviance: A structural equation examination of context theory. *Journal of Personality and Social Psychology*, *55*, 37–51.

Sidanius, J., Levin, S., Federico, C. M., & Pratto, F. (2001). Legitimizing ideologies: The social dominance approach. In J. T. Jost & B. Major (Eds.), *The psychology of legitimacy* (pp. 307–331). New York: Cambridge University Press.

Sidanius, J., & Pratto, F. (1999). *Social dominance: An intergroup theory of social hierarchy and oppression*. New York: Cambridge University Press.

Sidanius, J., Pratto, F., & Bobo, L. (1994). Social dominance orientation and the political psychology of gender: A case of invariance? *Journal of Personality and Social Psychology, 67*, 998–1011.

Sidanius, J., Pratto, F., & Bobo, L. (1996). Racism, conservation, affirmative action, and intellectual sophistication: A matter of principled conservatism or group dominance? *Journal of Personality and Social Psychology, 70*, 476–490.

Sigall, H. (1997). Ethical considerations in social psychological research: Is the bogus pipeline a special case? *Journal of Applied Social Psychology, 27*, 574–581.

Silver, R. C., Holman, E. A., McIntosh, D. N., Poulin, M., & Gil-Rivas, V. (2002). Nationwide longitudinal study of psychological responses to September 11. *Journal of the American Medical Association, 288*, 1235–1244.

Simon, B. (1992). Intragroup differentiation in terms of ingroup and outgroup attributes. *European Journal of Social Psychology, 22*, 407–413.

Simpson, B., & Willer, R. (2008). Altruism and indirect reciprocity: The interaction of person and situation in prosocial behavior. *Social Psychology Quarterly, 71*, 37–52.

Simpson, J. A. (1987). The dissolution of romantic relationships: Factors involved in relationship stability and emotional distress. *Journal of Personality and Social Psychology, 53*, 683–692.

Simpson, J. A., Gangestad, S. W., & Lerma, M. (2000). Perception of physical attractiveness: Mechanisms involved in the maintenance of romantic relationships. *Journal of Personality and Social Psychology, 59*, 1192–1201.

Simpson, J. A., Oriña, M. M., & Ickes, W. (2003). When accuracy hurts, and when it helps: A test of the empathic accuracy model in marital interactions. *Journal of Personality and Social Psychology, 85*, 881–893.

Simpson, J. A., & Rholes, W. S. (1998). *Attachment theory and close relationships*. New York: Guilford.

Sinclair, L., & Fehr, B. (2005). Voice versus loyalty: Self-construals and responses to dissatisfaction in romantic relationships. *Journal of Experimental Social Psychology, 41*, 298–304.

Sinclair, L., & Kunda, Z. (1999). Reactions to a black professional: Motivated inhibition and activation of conflicting stereotypes. *Journal of Personality and Social Psychology, 77*, 885–904.

Sinclair, L., & Kunda, Z. (2000). Motivated stereotyping of women: She's fine if she praised me but incompetent if she criticized me. *Personality and Social Psychology Bulletin, 26*, 1329–1342.

Sinclair, S., Dunn, E., & Lowery, B. S. (2005). The relationship between parental racial attitudes and children's implicit prejudice. *Journal of Experimental Social Psychology, 41*, 283–289.

Sinclair, S., Hardin, C. D., & Lowery, B. S. (2006). Self-stereotyping in the context of multiple social identities. *Journal of Personality and Social Psychology, 90*, 529–542.

Sinclair, S., Huntsinger, J., Skorinko, J., & Hardin, C. D. (2005). Social tuning of the self: Consequences for the self-evaluations of stereotype targets. *Journal of Personality and Social Psychology, 89*, 160–175.

Sinclair, S., Lowery, B. S., Hardin, C. D., & Colangelo, A. (2005). Social tuning of automatic racial attitudes: The role of affiliative motivation. *Journal of Personality and Social Psychology, 89*, 583–592.

Skedsvold, P. R., & Mann, T. L. (1996). Affirmative action: Linking research, policy and implementation. *Journal of Social Issues, 52*, 3–18.

Skitka, L. J. (1999). Ideological and attributional boundaries on public compassion: Reactions to individuals and communities affected by natural disaster. *Personality and Social Psychology Bulletin, 25*, 793–808.

Skitka, L. J., & Mullen, E. (2002). The dark side of moral conviction. *Analyses of Social Issues and Public Policy 30*, 35–41.

Skitka, L. J., & Tetlock, P. E. (1993). Providing public assistance: Cognitive and motivational processes underlying liberal and conservative policy preferences. *Journal of Personality and Social Psychology, 65*, 1205–1223.

Skowronski, J. J., & Carlston, D. E. (1989). Negativity and extremity biases in impression formation: A review of explanations. *Psychological Bulletin, 105*, 131–142.

Sloan, J. H., Kellermann, A. L., Reay, D. T., Ferris, J. A., Koepsell, T., Rivara, F. P., Rice, C., Gray, L., & LoGerfo, J. (1988). Handgun regulations, crime, assaults, and homicide: A tale of two cities. *New England Journal of Medicine, 319*, 1256–1262.

Small, D. A., & Lerner, J. S. (2008). Emotional policy: Personal sadness and anger shape judgments about a welfare case. *Political Psychology, 29*, 149–168.

Small, D. A., Lerner, J. S., & Fischhoff, B. (2006). Emotion priming and attributions for terrorism:

Americans' reactions in a national field experiment. *Political Psychology, 27*, 289–298.

Smith, B. (1992). Intragroup differentiation in terms of ingroup and outgroup attributes. *European Journal of Social Psychology, 22*, 407–413.

Smith, E. R. (1998). Mental representation and memory. In D. T. Gilbert, S. T. Fiske, & G. Lindzey (Eds.), *Handbook of social psychology* (4th ed., Vol. 1, pp. 391–445). Boston: McGraw-Hill.

Smith, E. R., Fazio, R. H., & Cejka, M. A. (1996). Accessible attitudes influence categorization of multiply categorizable objects. *Journal of Personality and Social Psychology, 71*, 888–898.

Smith, E. R., Murphy, J., & Coats, S. (1999). Attachment to groups: Theory and measurement. *Journal of Personality and Social Psychology, 77*, 94–110.

Smith, K. D., Keating, J. P., & Stotland, E. (1989). Altruism reconsidered: The effect of denying feedback on a victim's status to empathic witnesses. *Journal of Personality and Social Psychology, 57*, 641–650.

Smith, M. B. (1947). The personal setting of public opinions: A study of attitudes toward Russia. *Public Opinion Quarterly, 11*, 507–523.

Smith, P. B., & Bond, M. H. (1994). *Social psychology across cultures: Analysis and perspective*. Needham Heights, MA: Allyn and Bacon.

Smith, P. K., Jostmann, N. B., Galinsky, A. D., & van Dijk, W. W. (2008). Lacking power impairs executive functions. *Psychological Science, 19*, 441–447.

Smith, S. M., & Petty, R. E. (1996). Message framing and persuasion: A message processing analysis. *Personality and Social Psychology Bulletin, 22*, 257–268.

Snell, J., Gibbs, B. J., & Varey, C. (1995). Intuitive hedonics: Consumer beliefs about the dynamics of liking. *Journal of Consumer Psychology, 4*, 33–60.

Snyder, M. (1974). Self-monitoring of expressive behavior. *Journal of Personality and Social Psychology, 30*, 526–537.

Snyder, M. (1987). *Public appearances, private realities: The psychology of self monitoring*. New York: Freeman.

Snyder, M. (2006). Building bridges between personality and social psychology: Understanding the ties that bind persons and situations. In P. A. M. Van Lange (Ed.), *Bridging social psychology: Benefits of transdisciplinary approaches* (pp. 187–191). Mahwah, NJ: Erlbaum.

Snyder, M., Berscheid, E., & Glick, P. (1985). Focusing on the exterior and the interior: Two

investigations of the initiation of personal relationships. *Journal of Personality and Social Psychology, 48*, 1427–1439.

Snyder, M., & Cantor, N. (1998). Personality and social behavior. In D. T. Gilbert, S. T. Fiske, & G. Lindzey (Eds.), *Handbook of social psychology* (4th ed., Vol. 1, pp. 635–679). New York: McGraw-Hill.

Snyder, M., & DeBono, K. G. (1989). Understanding the functions of attitudes: Lessons from personality and social behavior. In A. R. Pratkanis, S. J. Breckler, & A. G. Greenwald (Eds.), *Attitude structure and function* (pp. 339–359). Hillsdale, NJ: Erlbaum.

Snyder, M., & Omoto, A. M. (1992). Volunteerism and society's response to the HIV epidemic. *Current Directions in Psychological Science, 1*, 113–116.

Snyder, M. & Stukas, A. A., Jr. (1998). Interpersonal processes: The interplay of cognitive, motivational, and behavioral activities in social interaction. *Annual Review of Psychology, 50*, 273–303.

Snyder, M., & Swann, W. B, Jr. (1976). When actions reflect attitudes: The politics of impression management. *Journal of Personality and Social Psychology, 34*, 1034–1042.

Snyder, M., Tanke, E. D., & Berscheid, E. (1977). Social perception and interpersonal behavior: On the self-fulfilling nature of social stereotypes. *Journal of Personality and Social Psychology, 35*, 656–666.

Sole, K., Marton, J., & Hornstein, H. A. (1975). Opinion similarity and helping: Three field experiments investigating the bases of promotive tension. *Journal of Experimental Social Psychology, 11*, 1–13.

Solomon, S., Greenberg, J., & Pyszczynski, T. (1991). A terror management theory of social behavior: The psychological functions of self-esteem and cultural world views. In M. P. Zanna (Ed.), *Advances in experimental social psychology* (Vol. 24, pp. 93–159). San Diego, CA: Academic Press.

Solomon, S., Greenberg, J., & Pyszczynski, T. (2000). Pride and prejudice: Fear of death and social behavior. *Current Directions in Psychological Science, 9*, 200–204.

Sommer, K. L., Williams, K. D., Ciarocco, N. J., & Baumeister, R. F. (2001). When silence speaks louder than words: Explorations into the intrapsychic and interpersonal consequences of social ostracism. *Basic and Applied Social Psychology, 23*, 225–243.

Son Hing, L. S., Chung-Yan, G. A., Hamilton, L. K., & Zanna, M. P. (2008). A two-dimensional model that employs explicit and implicit attitudes to characterize prejudice. *Journal of Personality and Social Psychology*, *94*, 971–987.

Son Hing, L. S., Li, W., & Zanna, M. P. (2002). Inducing hypocrisy to reduce prejudicial responses among aversive racists. *Journal of Experimental Social Psychology*, *38*, 71–78.

Spears, R., Doosje, B., & Ellemers, N. (1997). Self-stereotyping in the face of threats to group status and distinctiveness: The role of group identification. *Personality and Social Psychology Bulletin*, *23*, 538–553.

Spears, R., Lea, M., & Lee, S. (1990). De-individuation and group polarization in computer-mediated communication. *British Journal of Social Psychology*, *29*, 121–134.

Spencer, S. J., Fein, S., Wolfe, C. T., Fong, C., & Dunn, M. A. (1998). Automatic activation of stereotypes: The role of self-image threat. *Personality and Social Psychology Bulletin*, *24*, 1139–1152.

Spencer, S. J., Steele, C. M., & Quinn, D. M. (1999). Stereotype threat and women's math performance. *Journal of Experimental Social Psychology*, *35*, 4–28.

Sporer, S. L., & Schwandt, B. (2007). Moderators of nonverbal indicators of deception: A meta-analytic synthesis. *Psychology, Public Policy, and Law*, *13*, 1–34.

Springer, L., Stanne, M. E., & Donovan, S. S. (1999). Effects of small-group learning on undergraduates in science, mathematics, engineering, and technology: A meta-analysis. *Review of Educational Research*, *69*, 21–51.

Srull, T. K. (1981). Person memory: Some tests of associative storage and retrieval models. *Journal of Experimental Psychology: Human Learning and Memory*, *7*, 440–446.

Srull, T. K., Lichtenstein, M., & Rothbart, M. (1985). Associative storage and retrieval processes in person memory. *Journal of Experimental Psychology: Learning, Memory, and Cognition*, *11*, 316–345.

Staats, A. W., & Staats, C. K. (1958). Attitudes established by classical conditioning. *Journal of Abnormal and Social Psychology*, *57*, 37–40.

Stangor, C. (1995). Content and application inaccuracy in social stereotyping. In Y. Lee, L. Jussim, & C. R. McCauley (Eds.), *Stereotype accuracy: Toward appreciating group differences* (pp. 275–292). Washington, DC: American Psychological Association.

Stangor, C. (1998). *Research methods for the behavioral sciences*. New York: Houghton Mifflin.

Stangor, C., Carr, C., & Kiang, L. (1998). Activating stereotypes undermines task performance expectations. *Journal of Personality and Social Psychology*, *75*, 1191–1197.

Stangor, C., & Crandall, C. S. (2000). Threat and the social construction of stigma. In T. F. Heatherton, R. E. Kleck, M. R. Hebl, & J. G. Hull (Eds.), *The social psychology of stigma* (pp. 62–87). New York: Guilford.

Stangor, C., & Lange, J. E. (1994). Mental representations of social groups: Advances in understanding stereotypes and stereotyping. In M. P. Zanna (Ed.), *Advances in experimental social psychology* (Vol. 26, pp. 357–416). New York: Academic Press.

Stangor, C., & McMillan, D. (1992). Memory for expectancy-congruent and expectancy-incongruent social information: A meta-analytic review of the social psychological and social developmental literatures. *Psychological Bulletin*, *111*, 42–61.

Stangor, C., & Schaller, M. (1996). Stereotypes as individual and collective representations. In C. N. Macrae, C. Stangor, & M. Hewstone (Ed.), *Stereotypes and stereotyping* (pp. 3–37). New York: Guilford.

Stansfeld, S. A., Bosma, H., Hemingway, H., & Marmot, M. G. (1998). Psychosocial work characteristics and social support as predictors of SF-36 health functioning: The Whitehall II study. *Psychosomatic Medicine*, *60*, 247–255.

Stapel, D. A., & Koomen, W. (2006). The flexible unconscious: Investigating the judgmental impact of varieties of unaware perception. *Journal of Experimental Social Psychology*, *42*, 112–119.

Stasser, G., & Titus, W. (1985). Pooling of unshared information in group decision making: Biased information sampling during discussion. *Journal of Personality and Social Psychology*, *48*, 1467–1478.

Stasser, G., & Titus, W. (1987). Effects of information load and percentage of shared information on the dissemination of unshared information during group discussion. *Journal of Personality and Social Psychology*, *53*, 81–93.

Staub, E. (1974). Helping a distressed person: Social, personality, and stimulus determinants. In L. Berkowitz (Ed.), *Advances in experimental social psychology* (Vol. 7, pp. 293–341). London, UK: Academic Press.

Staub, E. (1989). *The roots of evil: The origins of genocide and other group violence*. New York: Cambridge University Press.

Staub, E. (1990). Moral exclusion, personal goal theory, and extreme destructiveness. *Journal of Social Issues*, *46*, 47–64.

Staub, E. (1999). The roots of evil: Social conditions, culture, personality, and basic human needs. *Personality and Social Psychology Review*, *3*, 179–192.

Steele, C. M. (1988). The psychology of self-affirmation: Sustaining the integrity of the self. In L. Berkowitz (Ed.), *Advances in experimental social psychology* (Vol. 21, pp. 261–302). New York: Academic Press.

Steele, C. M. (1997). A threat in the air: How stereotypes shape intellectual identity and performance. *American Psychologist, 52,* 613–629.

Steele, C. M., & Aronson, J. (1995). Stereotype threat and the intellectual test performance of African Americans. *Journal of Personality and Social Psychology, 69,* 797–811.

Steele, C. M., & Josephs, R. A. (1990). Alcohol myopia: Its prized and dangerous effects. *American Psychologist, 45,* 921–933.

Steele, C. M., & Southwick, L. (1985). Alcohol and social behavior I: The psychology of drunken excess. *Journal of Personality and Social Psychology, 48,* 18–34.

Steele, C. M., Southwick, L., & Pagano, R. (1986). Drinking your troubles away: The role of activity in mediating alcohol's reduction of psychological stress. *Journal of Abnormal Psychology, 95,* 173–180.

Steele, C. M., Spencer, S. J., & Aronson, J. (2002). Contending with group image: The psychology of stereotype and social identity threat. In M. P. Zanna (Ed.), *Advances in experimental social psychology* (Vol. 34, pp. 379–440). San Diego, CA: Academic Press.

Stein, R. T., & Heller, T. (1979). An empirical analysis of the correlations between leadership status and participation rates reported in the literature. *Journal of Personality and Social Psychology, 37,* 1993–2002.

Steiner, I. D. (1974). Whatever happened to the group in social psychology? *Journal of Experimental Social Psychology, 10,* 94–108.

Stephan, W G., & Stephan, C. W. (2000). An integrated threat theory of prejudice. In S. Oskamp (Ed.), *Reducing prejudice and discrimination* (pp. 23–45). Mahwah, NJ: Erlbaum.

Sternberg, R. J. (1986). A triangular theory of love. *Psychological Review, 93,* 119–135.

Stevens, L. E., & Fiske, S. T. (2000). Motivated impressions of a powerholder: Accuracy under task dependency and misperception under evaluation dependency. *Personality and Social Psychology Bulletin, 26,* 907–922.

Stewart, D. D., & Stasser, G. (1995). Expert role assignment and information sampling during collective recall and decision making. *Journal of Personality and Social Psychology, 69,* 619–628.

Stewart, T. L., Doan, K. A., Gingrich, B. E., & Smith, E. R. (1998). The actor as context for social judgments: Effects of prior impressions and

stereotypes. *Journal of Personality and Social Psychology, 75,* 1132–1154.

Stiles, W B., Lyall, L. M., Knight, D. P., Ickes, W., Waung, M., Hall, C. L., & Primeau, B. E. (1997). Gender differences in verbal presumptuousness and attentiveness. *Personality and Social Psychology Bulletin, 23,* 759–772.

Stinson, D. A., Logel, C., Zanna, M. P., Holmes, J. G., Cameron, J. J., Wood, J. V., & Spencer, S. J. (2008). The cost of lower self-esteem: Testing a self- and social-bonds model of health *Journal of Personality and Social Psychology, 94,* 412–428.

Stinson, L., & Ickes, W. (1992). Empathic accuracy in the interactions of male friends versus male strangers. *Journal of Personality and Social Psychology, 62,* 787–797.

Stogdill, R. M. (1948). Personal factors associated with leadership: A survey of the literature. *Journal of Psychology, 25,* 35–71.

Stone, J., & Cooper, J. (2001). A self-standards model of cognitive dissonance. *Journal of Experimental Social Psychology, 37,* 228–243.

Stone, J., & Fernandez, N. C. (2008). To practice what we preach: The use of hypocrisy and cognitive dissonance to motivate behavior change. *Social and Personality Psychology Compass, 2,* 1024–1051.

Stone, J., Lynch, C. I., Sjomeling, M., & Darley, J. M. (1999). Stereotype threat effects on black and white athletic performance. *Journal of Personality and Social Psychology, 77,* 1213–1227.

Storbeck, J., & Clore, G. L. (2007). On the interdependence of cognition and emotion. *Cognition & Emotion, 21,* 1212–1237.

Strack, F., & Deutsch, R. (2004). Reflective and impulsive determinants of social behavior. *Personality and Social Psychology Review, 8,* 220–247.

Strickland, B. R. (1989). Internal-external control expectancies: From contingency to creativity. *American Psychologist, 44,* 1–12.

Stroebe, W., & Diehl, M. (1994). Why groups are less effective than their members: On productivity losses in idea-generating groups. In W. Stroebe & M. Hewstone (Eds.), *European Review of Social Psychology* (Vol. 5, pp. 272–303). New York: Wiley.

Stroebe, W., Diehl, M., & Abakoumkin, G. (1992). The illusion of group effectivity. *Personality and Social Psychology Bulletin, 18,* 643–650.

Strube, M. J., & Garcia, J. E. (1981). A meta-analytic investigation of Fiedler's contingency model of leadership effectiveness. *Psychological Bulletin, 90,* 307–321.

Struthers, C. W., Eaton, J., Czyznielewski, A., & Dupuis, R. (2005). Judging up the corporate ladder: Understanding the social conduct of workers. *Journal of Applied Social Psychology*, *35*, 1223–1245.

Stürmer, S., Snyder, M., Kropp, A., & Siem, B. (2006). Empathy-motivated helping: The moderating role of group membership. *Personality and Social Psychology Bulletin*, *32*, 943–956.

Stürmer, S., Snyder, M., & Omoto, A. M. (2005). Prosocial emotions and helping: The moderating role of group membership. *Journal of Personality and Social Psychology*, *88*, 532–546.

Sugimori, S. (1998). Bullying in Japanese schools: Cultural and social psychological perspectives. In M. W. Watts (Ed.), *Cross-cultural perspectives on youth and violence* (pp. 175–186). Stamford, CT: JAI Press.

Suls, J. (2001). Report from the Editor of PSPB: Turning the corner! *Dialogue*, *16(4)*, 28.

Sundstrom, E., McIntyre, M., Halfhill, T., & Richards, H. (2000). Work groups: From the Hawthorne studies to work teams of the 1990s and beyond. *Group Dynamics*, *4*, 44–67.

Suomi, S. J., Collins, M. L., & Harlow, H. F. (1973). Effects of permanent separation from mother on infant monkeys. *Developmental Psychology*, *9*, 376–384.

Susskind, J., Maurer, K., Thakkar, V., Hamilton, D. L., & Sherman, J. W. (1999). Perceiving individuals and groups: Expectancies, dispositional inferences, and causal attributions. *Journal of Personality and Social Psychology*, *76*, 181–191.

Sutherland, A. E., & Insko, C. A. (1973). Attraction and interestingness of anticipated interaction. *Journal of Personality 41*, 234–243.

Sutton, S. (1998). Predicting and explaining intentions and behavior: How well are we doing? *Journal of Applied Social Psychology*, *28*, 1317–1338.

Swann, W. B., Jr. (1984). Quest for accuracy in person perception: A matter of pragmatics. *Psychological Review*, *91*, 457–477.

Swann, W. B., Jr. (1990). To be known or to be adored? The interplay of self-enhancement and self-verification. In R. M. Sorrentino & E. T. Higgins (Eds.), *Handbook of motivation and cognition: Foundations of social behavior* (Vol. 2, pp. 408–448). New York: Guilford.

Swann, W. B., Jr., Hixon, J. G., De La Ronde, C. (1992). Embracing the bitter truth: Negative self-concepts and marital commitment. *Psychological Science*, *3*, 118–121.

Swann, W. B., Jr., Hixon, J. G., Stein-Seroussi, A., & Gilbert, D. T. (1990). The fleeting gleam of praise: Cognitive processes underlying behavioral reactions to self-relevant feedback. *Journal of Personality and Social Psychology*, *59*, 17–26.

Swann, W. B., Jr., Kwan, V. S. Y., Polzer, J. T., & Milton, L. P. (2003). Fostering harmony and productivity in diverse groups: The role of

individuation and self-verification. *Personality and Social Psychology Bulletin*, *29*, 1396–1409.

Swann, W. B., Jr., Milton, L. P., & Polzer, J. T. (2000). Should we create a niche or fall in line? Identity negotiation and small group effectiveness. *Journal of Personality and Social Psychology*, *79*, 238–250.

Swim, J. K., & Hyers, L. L. (1999). Excuse me—What did you just say?!: Women's public and private responses to sexist remarks. *Journal of Experimental Social Psychology*, *35*, 68–88.

Swim, J. K., Hyers, L. L., Cohen, L. L., & Ferguson, M. J. (2001). Everyday sexism: Evidence for its incidence, nature, and psychological impact from three daily diary studies. *Journal of Social Issues*, *57*, 31–53.

Swim, J. K., & Sanna, L. J. (1996). He's skilled, she's lucky: A meta-analysis of observers' attributions for women's and men's successes and failures. *Personality and Social Psychology Bulletin*, *22*, 507–519.

Swim, J. K., & Stangor, C. (Eds.) (1998). *Prejudice: The target's perspective*. New York: Academic Press.

Symons, C. S., & Johnson, B. T. (1997). The self-reference effect in memory: A meta-analysis. *Psychological Bulletin*, *121*, 371–394.

Tagiuri, R., & Petrullo, L. (1958). Introduction. In R. Tagiuri, & L. Petrullo (Eds.), *Person perception and interpersonal behavior* (pp. ix–xvii). Stanford, CA: Stanford University Press.

Tajfel, H. (1974). Social identity and intergroup behaviour. *Social Science Information/Sur les Sciences Socials*, *13*, 65–93.

Tajfel, H. (1981). *Human groups and social categories*. New York: Cambridge University Press.

Tajfel, H., Flament, C., Billing, M. G., & Bundy, R. P. (1971). Social categorization and intergroup behavior. *European Journal of Social Psychology*, *1*, 149–178.

Tajfel, H., & Turner, J. C. (1979). The social identity theory of intergroup behavior. In W. G. Austin & S. Worchel (Eds.), *The social psychology of intergroup relations* (pp. 7–24). Chicago, IL: Nelson-Hall.

Takahashi, K., Ohara, N., Antonucci, T. C., & Akiyama, H. (2002). Commonalities and differences in close relationships among the Americans and Japanese: A comparison by the individualism/collectivism concept. *International Journal of Behavioral Development*, *26*, 453–465.

Talaska, C. A., Fiske, S. T., & Chaiken, S. (2008). Legitimating racial discrimination: A meta-analysis of the racial attitude-behavior literature shows that emotions, not beliefs, best predict discrimination. *Social Justice Research: Social Power in Action, 21*, 263–296.

Tan, A. (2001). *The bonesetter's daughter*. New York: Putnam.

Tancredi, L. R., & Brodie, J. D. (2007). The brain and behavior: Limitations in the legal use of functional magnetic resonance imaging. *American Journal of Law and Medicine, 33*, 271–294.

Tanford, S., & Penrod, S. (1984). Social influence model: A formal integration of research on majority and minority influence processes. *Psychological Bulletin, 95*, 189–225.

Tangney, J. P. (1992). Situational determinants of shame and guilt in young adulthood. *Personality and Social Psychology Bulletin, 18*, 199–206.

Tangney, J. P., Stuewig, J., & Mashek, D. J. (2007). Moral emotions and moral behavior. *Annual Review of Psychology, 58*, 345–372.

Tangney, J. P., Wagner, P. E., Hill-Barlow, D., Marschall, D. E., & Gramzow, R. (1996). Relation of shame and guilt to constructive versus destructive responses to anger across the lifespan. *Journal of Personality and Social Psychology, 70*, 797–809.

Tata, J., Anthony, T., Lin, H., Newman, B., Millson, M., Sivakumar, K., & Tang, S. (1996). Proportionate group size and rejection of the deviate: A meta-analytic integration. *Journal of Social Behavior and Personality 11*, 739–752.

Tatum, B. D. (1997). *Why are all the black kids sitting together in the cafeteria?* New York: Basic Books.

Taylor, S. E. (1981). A categorization approach to stereotyping. In D. L. Hamilton (Ed.), *Cognitive processes in stereotyping and intergroup behavior* (pp. 83–114). Mahwah, NJ: Erlbaum.

Taylor, S. E. (1983). Adjustment to threatening events: A theory of cognitive adaptation. *American Psychologist, 38*, 1161–1173.

Taylor, S. E. (1991). Asymmetrical effects of positive and negative events: The mobilization -minimiza-tion hypothesis. *Psychological Bulletin, 110*, 67–85.

Taylor, S. E. (2006). Tend and befriend: Biobehavioral bases of affiliation under stress. *Current Directions in Psychological Science, 15*, 273–277.

Taylor, S. E., & Brown, J. D. (1988). Illusion and well-being: A social psychological perspective on mental health. *Psychological Bulletin, 103*, 193–210.

Taylor, S. E., & Fiske, S. T. (1975). Point-of-view and perceptions of causality. *Journal of Personality and Social Psychology, 32*, 439–445.

Taylor, S. E., & Fiske, S. T. (1978). Salience, attention, and attribution: Top of the head phenomena. In L. Berkowitz (Ed.), *Advances in experimental social psychology* (Vol. 11, pp. 249–288). New York: Academic Press.

Taylor, S. E., Fiske, S. T., Etcoff, N. L., & Ruderman, A. J. (1978). Categorical and contextual bases of person memory and stereotyping. *Journal of Personality and Social Psychology, 36*, 778–793.

Taylor, S. E., Klein, L. C., Lewis, B. P., Gruenewald, T. L., Gurung, R. A. R., & Updegraff, J. A. (2000). Biobehavioral responses to stress in females: Tend-and-befriend, not fight-or-flight. *Psychological Review, 107*, 411–429.

Taylor, S. E., Lerner, J. S., Sage, R. M., Lehman, B. J., & Seeman, T. E. (2004). Early environment, emotions, responses to stress, and health. *Journal of Personality, 72*, 1365–1393.

Taylor, S. P. (1967). Aggressive behavior and physiological arousal as a function of provocation and the tendency to inhibit aggression. *Journal of Personality, 35*, 297–310.

Tedeschi, J. T., & Felson, R. B. (1994). *Violence, aggression, and coercive actions*. Washington, DC: American Psychological Association.

Tedeschi, J. T., Schlenker, B. R., & Bonoma, T. V. (1971). Cognitive dissonance: Private ratiocination or public spectacle? *American Psychologist, 26*, 685–695.

Television sex and violence. (1989, September 19). *Los Angeles Times*, poll 196.

Temrin, H., Buchmayer, S., & Enquist, M. (2000). Step-parents and infanticide: New data contradict evolutionary predictions. *Proceedings: Biological Sciences (The Royal Society), 267*, 943–945.

Tennen, H., & Affleck, G. (1990). Blaming others for threatening events. *Psychological Bulletin, 108*, 209–232.

Terry, D. J., Carey, C. J., & Callan, V J. (2001). Employee adjustment to an organizational merger: An intergroup perspective. *Personality and Social Psychology Bulletin, 27*, 267–280.

Terry, D. J., & Hogg, M. A. (1996). Group norms and the attitude-behavior relationship: A role for group identification. *Personality and Social Psychology Bulletin, 22*, 776–793.

Tesser, A. (1978). Self-generated attitude change. In L. Berkowitz (Ed.), *Advances in experimental social psychology* (Vol. 11, pp. 289–338). New York: Academic Press.

Tesser, A. (1988). Toward a self-evaluation maintenance model of social behavior. In L. Berkowitz (Ed.), *Advances in experimental social psychology* (Vol. 21, pp. 181–227). New York: Academic Press.

Tesser, A., Millar, M., & Moore, J. (1988). Some affective consequences of social comparison and reflection processes: The pain and pleasure of being close. *Journal of Personality and Social Psychology, 54*, 49–61.

Tesser, A., & Shaffer, D. R. (1990). Attitudes and attitude change. *Annual Review of Psychology, 41*, 479–523.

Tetlock, P. E. (1992). The impact of accountability on judgment and choice. In M. P. Zanna (Ed.), *Advances in experimental social psychology* (Vol. 23, pp. 331–376). New York: Academic Press.

Tetlock, P. E., Kristel, O. V., Elson, S. B., Green, M., & Lerner, J. S. (2000). The psychological of the unthinkable: Taboo trade-offs, forbidden base rates, and heretical counterfactuals. *Journal of Personality and Social Psychology, 78*, 853–870.

Thibaut, J. W., & Kelley, H. H. (1959). *The social psychology of groups*. New Brunswick, NJ: Transaction.

Thoma, S. J., Rest, J. R., & Davison, M. L. (1991). Describing and testing a moderator of the moral judgment and action relationship. *Journal of Personality and Social Psychology, 61*, 659–669.

Thomas, G., Fletcher, G. J. O., & Lange, C. (1997). On-line empathic accuracy in marital interaction. *Journal of Personality and Social Psychology, 72*, 839–850.

Thomas, M. H., Horton, R. W., Lippincott, E. C., & Drabman, R. S. (1977). Desensitization to portrayals of real–life aggression as a function of television violence. *Journal of Personality and Social Psychology, 35*, 450–458.

Thompson, L. (1990). Negotiation behavior and outcomes: Empirical evidence and theoretical issues. *Psychological Bulletin, 108*, 515–532.

Thompson, L. (1991). Information exchange in negotiation. *Journal of Experimental Social Psychology, 27*, 161–179.

Thompson, L. (1995). "They saw a negotiation": Partisanship and involvement. *Journal of Personality and Social Psychology, 68*, 839–853.

Thompson, L., & Fine, G. A. (1999). Socially shared cognition, affect, and behavior: A review and integration. *Personality and Social Psychology Review, 3*, 278–302.

Thompson, L., Medvec, V. H., Seiden, V., & Kopelman, S. (2001). Poker face, smiley face, and rant 'n' rave: Myths and realities about emotion in negotiation. In M. A. Hogg & R. S. Tindale (Eds.), *Blackwell handbook of social psychology: Group processes* (pp. 139–163). Malden, MA: Blackwell.

Thompson, M., Judd, C. M., & Park, B. (2000). The consequences of communicating social stereotypes. *Journal of Personality and Social Psychology, 36*, 567–599.

Thompson, W. C., Cowan, C. L., & Rosenhan, D. L. (1980). Focus of attention mediates the impact of negative affect on altruism. *Journal of Personality and Social Psychology, 38*, 291–300.

Tickle-Degnen, L., & Rosenthal, R. (1990). The nature of rapport and its nonverbal correlates. *Psychological Inquiry, 1*, 285–293.

Tidwell, M. O., Reis, H. T., & Shaver, P. R. (1996). Attachment, attractiveness, and social interaction: A diary study. *Journal of Personality and Social Psychology, 71*, 729–745.

Tiedens, L. Z. (2001). Anger and advancement versus sadness and subjugation: The effect of negative emotion expressions on social status conferral. *Journal of Personality and Social Psychology, 80*, 86–94.

Tiedens, L. Z., & Fragale, A. R. (2003). Power moves: Complementarity in dominant and submissive nonverbal behavior. *Journal of Personality and Social Psychology, 84*, 558–568.

Tiedens, L. Z., Unzueta, M. M., & Young, M. J. (2007). An unconscious desire for hierarchy? The motivated perception of dominance complementarity in task partners. *Journal of Personality and Social Psychology, 93*, 402–414.

Tiffany, W. R., & Bennett, D. N. (1968). Phonetic distortions in the serial transmission of short speech samples. *Journal of Speech and Hearing Research, 11*, 33–48.

Tindale, R. S. (1993). Decision errors made by individuals and groups. In N. J. Castellan, Jr. (Ed.), *Individual and group decision making: Current issues* (pp. 109–124). Hillsdale, NJ: Erlbaum.

Tindale, R. S., & Kameda, T. (2000). "Social sharedness" as a unifying theme for information processing in groups. *Group Processes and Intergroup Relations, 3*, 123–140.

Tindale, R. S., Meisenhelder, H. M., Dykema-Engblade, A. A., & Hogg, M. A. (2001). Shared cognition in small groups. In M. A. Hogg & R. S. Tindale (Eds.), *Blackwell handbook of social psychology: Group processes* (pp. 1–30). Malden, MA: Blackwell.

Tindale, R. S., Sheffey, S., & Scott, L. A. (1993). Framing and group decision-making: Do cognitive changes parallel preference changes? *Organizational Behavior and Human Decision Processes, 55*, 470–485.

Todorov, A. (2008). Evaluating faces on trustworthiness: An extension of systems for recognition of emotions signaling approach/avoidance behaviors. *Annals of New York Academy of Science, 1124*, 208–224.

Todorov, A., & Bargh, J. A. (2002). Automatic sources of aggression. *Aggression and Violent Behavior, 7*, 53–68.

Todorov, A., Baron, S. G., & Oosterhof, N. N. (2008). Evaluating face trustworthiness: A model based approach. *Social Cognitive and Affective Neuroscience, 3*, 119–127.

Todorov, A., & Engell, A. D. (2008). The role of the amygdala in implicit evaluation of emotionally neutral faces. *Social Cognitive and Affective Neuroscience*, *3*, 303–312.

Todorov, A., Gobbini, M. I., Evans, K. K., & Haxby, J. V. (2007). Spontaneous retrieval of affective person knowledge in face perception. *Neuropsychologia*, *45*, 163–173.

Todorov, A., Mandisodza, A. N., Goren, A., & Hall, C. C. (2005). Inferences of competence from faces predict election outcomes. *Science*, *308*, 1623–1626.

Todorov, A., & Uleman, J. S. (2004). The person reference process in spontaneous trait inferences. *Journal of Personality and Social Psychology*, *87*, 482–493.

Tourangeau, R. (2004). Survey research and societal change. *Annual Review of Psychology*, 55, 775–801.

Tourangeau, R., Smith, T. W., & Rasinski, K. A. (1997). Motivation to report sensitive behaviors on surveys: Evidence from a bogus pipeline experiment. *Journal of Applied Social Psychology*, *27*, 209–222.

Towles-Schwen, T., & Fazio, R. H. (2001). On the origins of racial attitudes: Correlates of childhood experiences. *Personality and Social Psychology Bulletin*, *27*, 162–175.

Triandis, H. C. (1990). Cross-cultural studies of individualism and collectivism. In J. Berman (Ed.), *Nebraska symposium on motivation* (pp. 41–133). Lincoln: University of Nebraska Press.

Triandis, H. C. (1994). *Culture and social behavior*. New York: McGraw-Hill.

Triandis, H. C., Marin, G., Lisansky, J., & Betancourt, H. (1984). Simpatia as a cultural script of Hispanics. *Journal of Personality and Social Psychology*, *47*, 1363–1375.

Triandis, H. C., & Suh, E. M. (2002). Cultural influences on personality. *Annual Review of Psychology*, *53*, 133–160.

Trivers, R. L. (1971). The evolution of reciprocal altruism. *Quarterly Review of Biology*, *46*, 35–57.

Trivers, R. L. (1985). *Social evolution*. Menlo Park, CA: Benjamin/Cummings.

Trope, Y. (1986). Identification and inferential processes in dispositional attribution. *Psychological Review*, *93*, 239–257.

Trope, Y., & Liberman, N. (2003). Temporal construal. *Psychological Review*, *110*, 403–421.

Trzesniewski, K. H., Donnellan, M. B., & Robins, R. W. (2003). Stability of self-esteem across the life span. *Journal of Personality and Social Psychology*, *84*, 205–220.

Turner, J. C. (1985). Social categorization and the self-concept: A social cognitive theory of group

behaviour. In E. J. Lawler (Ed.), *Advances in group processes* (Vol. 2, pp. 77–122). Greenwich, CT: JAI Press.

Turner, J. C. (1991). *Social influence*. Pacific Grove, CA: Brooks/Cole Publishing.

Turner, J. C. (1995). Social influence. In A. S. R. Manstead & M. Hewstone (Eds.), *Blackwell encyclopedia of social psychology* (pp. 562–567). Cambridge, MA: Blackwell.

Turner, J. C., Hogg, M. A., Oakes, P. J., Reicher, S. D., & Wetherell, M. S. (1987). *Rediscovering the social group: A self-categorization theory*. Cambridge, MA: Blackwell.

Turner, J. C., & Reynolds, K. J. (2001). The social identity perspective in intergroup relations: Theories, themes, and controversies. In R. Brown & S. L. Gaertner (Eds.), *Blackwell handbook of social psychology: Intergroup processes* (pp. 133–152). London: Blackwell.

Turner, J. C., Wetherell, M. S., & Hogg, M. A. (1989). Referent informational influence and group polarization. *British Journal of Social Psychology*, *28*, 135–147.

Turner, M. E., & Pratkanis, A. R. (1994). Social psychological perspectives on affirmative action. [Special Issue] *Basic and Applied Social Psychology*, *15* (1 and 2).

Turner, R. H., & Killian, L. M. (1987). *Collective behavior* (3rd ed.). Upper Saddle River, NJ: Prentice-Hall.

TV violence: More objectionable in entertainment than in newscasts. (1993, March 24). *Times Mirror Media Monitor*.

Tversky, A., & Kahneman, D. (1974). Judgment under uncertainty: Heuristics and biases. *Science*, *185*, 1124–1131.

Tversky, A., & Kahneman, D. (1983). Extensional versus intuitive reasoning: The conjunction fallacy in probability judgment. *Psychological Review*, *90*, 293–315.

Twenge, J. M., & Crocker, J. (2002). Race and self-esteem: Meta-analyses comparing whites, blacks, Hispanics, Asians, and American Indians and comment on Gray-Little and Hafdahl (2000). *Psychological Bulletin*, *128*, 371–408.

Tyler, A. (1995). *Ladder of years*. New York: Ballentine.

Tyler, T. R. (1997). The psychology of legitimacy: A relational perspective on voluntary deference to authorities. *Personality and Social Psychology Review*, *1*, 323–345.

Tyler, T. R. (2006). Psychological perspectives on legitimacy and legitimation. *Annual Review of Psychology*, *57*, 375–400.

Tyler, T. R., Degoey, P., & Smith, H. (1996). Understanding why the justice of group procedures matters: A test of the psychological dynamics of the group-value model. *Journal of Personality and Social Psychology*, *70*, 913–930.

Tyler, T. R., & Devinitz, V. (1981). Self-serving bias in the attribution of responsibility: Cognitive versus motivational explanations. *Journal of Experimental Social Psychology*, *17*, 408–416.

Tyler, T. R., & Lind, E. A. (1992). A relational model of authority in groups. In M. P. Zanna (Ed.), *Advances in experimental social psychology* (Vol. 25, pp. 115–192). New York: Academic Press.

Tyler, T. R., & Smith, H. J. (1998). Social justice and social movements. In D. T. Gilbert, S. T. Fiske, & G. Lindzey (Eds.), *Handbook of social psychology* (4th ed., Vol. 2, pp. 595–629). New York: McGraw-Hill.

Uleman, J. S., Saribay, S. A., & Gonzalez, C. M. (2008). Spontaneous inferences, implicit impressions, and implicit theories. *Annual Review of Psychology*, *59*, 329–360.

Underwood, B., & Moore, B. (1982). Perspective-taking and altruism. *Psychological Bulletin*, *91*, 143–173.

United States Bureau of the Census. (1997). *Statistical abstract of the United States*. Washington, DC: U.S. Government Printing Office.

Urban, L. M., & Miller, N. (1998). A theoretical analysis of crossed categorization effects: A meta-analysis. *Journal of Personality and Social Psychology*, *74*, 894–908.

Utz, S., Ouwerkerk, J. W., & Van Lange, P. A. M. (2004). What is smart in a social dilemma? Differential effects of priming competence on cooperation. *European Journal of Social Psychology*, *34*, 317–332.

Vaes, J., Paladino, M. P., & Leyens, J-Ph. (2006). Priming uniquely human emotions and the in-group (but not the outgroup) activates humanity concepts. *European Journal of Social Psychology*, *36*, 169–181.

Vallone, R. P., Ross, L., & Lepper, M. R. (1985). The hostile media phenomenon: Biased perception and perceptions of media bias in coverage of the Beirut massacre. *Journal of Personality and Social Psychology*, *49*, 577–585.

Van Boven, L., Kamada, A., & Gilovich, T. (1999). The perceiver as perceived: Everyday intuitions about the correspondence bias. *Journal of Personality and Social Psychology*, *77*, 1188–1199.

Vandello, J. A., & Cohen, D. (1999). Patterns of individualism and collectivism across the United States. *Journal of Personality and Social Psychology*, *77*, 279–292.

Van IJzendoorn, M. H. (1995). Adult attachment representations, parental responsiveness, and infant attachment: A meta-analysis on the predictive validity of the adult attachment interview. *Psychological Bulletin*, *117*, 387–403.

Van Kleef, G. A., De Dreu, C. K. W., & Manstead, A. S. R. (2006). Supplication and appeasement in conflict and negotiation: The interpersonal effects of disappointment, worry, guilt, and regret. *Journal of Personality and Social Psychology*, *91*, 124–142.

van Knippenberg, A., Dijksterhuis, A., & Vermeulen, D. (1999). Judgment and memory of a criminal act: The effects of stereotypes and cognitive load. *European Journal of Social Psychology*, *29*, 191–201.

van Knippenberg, A., & Wilke, H. (1988). Social categorization and attitude change. *European Journal of Social Psychology*, *18*, 395–406.

van Knippenberg, D., & Schippers, M. C. (2007). Work group diversity. *Annual Review of Psychology*, *58*, 515–541.

Van Laar, C., Levin, S., Sinclair, S., & Sidanius, J. (2005). The effect of university roommate contact on ethnic attitudes and behavior. *Journal of Experimental Social Psychology*, *41*, 329–345.

Van Laar, C., Sidanius, J., Rabinowitz, J. L., & Sinclair, S. (1999). The three Rs of academic achievement: Reading, 'riting, and racism. *Personality and Social Psychology Bulletin*, *25*, 139–151.

Van Lange, P. A. M. (1999). The pursuit of joint outcomes and equality in outcomes. An integrative mode of social value orientation. *Journal of Personality and Social Psychology*, *77*, 337–359.

Van Lange, P. A. M. (2000). Beyond self-interest: A set of propositions relevant to interpersonal orientations. In W. Stroebe & M. Hewstone (Eds.), *European review of social psychology* (Vol. 11, pp. 297–331). New York: Wiley.

Van Lange, P. A. M., Agnew, C. R., Harinick, F., & Steemers, G. E. M. (1997). From game theory to real life: How social value orientation affects willingness to sacrifices in ongoing close relationship. *Journal of Personality and Social Psychology*, *73*, 1330–1344..

Van Lange, P. A. M., DeBruin, E. M. N., Otten, W., & Joireman, J. A. (1997). Development of prosocial, individualistic, and competitive orientations: Theory and preliminary evidence. *Journal of Personality and Social Psychology*, *73*, 733–746.

Van Lange, P. A. M., & Kuhlman, D. M. (1994). Social value orientations and impressions of partner's honesty and intelligence: A test of the might versus morality effect. *Journal of Personality and Social Psychology*, *67*, 126–141.

Van Lange, P. A. M., Ouwerkerk, J. W., & Tazelaar, M. J. A. (2002). How to overcome the detrimental effects of noise in social interaction: The benefits of generosity. *Journal of Personality and Social Psychology, 82*, 768–780.

Van Lange, P. A. M., & Rusbult, C. E. (1995). My relationship is better than—and not as bad as—yours is: The perception of superiority in close relationships. *Personality and Social Psychology Bulletin, 21*, 32–44.

Van Lange, P. A. M., Rusbult, C. E., Drigotas, S. M., Arriaga, X. B., Witcher, B. S., & Cox, C. L. (1997). Willingness to sacrifice in close relationship. *Journal of Personality and Social Psychology, 72*, 1373–1395.

Van Lange, P. A. M., & Semin-Goossens, A. (1998). The boundaries of reciprocal cooperation. *European Journal of Social Psychology, 28*, 847–854.

Van Lange, P. A. M., & Visser, K. (1999). Locomotion in social dilemmas: How people adapt to cooperative, tit-for-tat and noncooperative partners. *Journal of Personality and Social Psychology, 77*, 762–773.

Vanman, E. J., Paul, B. Y., Ito, T. A., & Miller, N. (1997). The modern face of prejudice and structural features that moderate the effect of cooperation on affect. *Journal of Personality and Social Psychology, 73*, 941–959.

Van Vugt, M., & De Cremer, D. (1999). Leadership in social dilemmas: The effects of group identification on collective actions to provide public goods. *Journal of Personality and Social Psychology, 76*, 587–599.

Van Vugt, M., Hogan, R., & Kaiser, R. B. (2008). Leadership, followership, and evolution: Some lessons from the past. *American Psychologist, 63*, 182–196.

Van Yperen, N. W., & Buunk, B. P. (1990). A longitudinal study of equity and satisfaction in intimate relationships. *European Journal of Social Psychology, 20*, 287–309.

V-chip backed with much vigor by Americans. (1996, August 8). *Hollywood Reporter*.

Verkuyten, M., & Masson, K. (1996). Culture and gender differences in the perception of friendship by adolescents. *International Journal of Psychology, 31*, 207–217.

Verplanken, B., Friborg, O., Wang, C. E., Trafimow, D., & Woolf, K. (2007). Mental habits: Metacognitive reflection on negative self-thinking. *Journal of Personality and Social Psychology, 92*, 526–541.

Verplanken, B., Hofstee, G., & Janssen, H. J. W. (1998). Accessibility of affective versus cognitive components of attitudes. *European Journal of Social Psychology, 28*, 23–35.

Vescio, T. K., Sechrist, G. B., & Paolucci, M. P. (2003). Perspective taking and prejudice reduction: The meditational role of empathy arousal and situational attributions. *European Journal of Social Psychology, 33*, 455–472.

Vignoles, V. L., Chryssochoou, X., & Breakwell, G. M. (2000). The distinctiveness principle: Identity, meaning, and the bounds of cultural relativity. *Personality and Social Psychology Review, 4*, 337–354.

Vignoles, V. L., & Moncaster, N. J. (2007). Identity motives and in-group favouritism: A new approach to individual differences in intergroup discrimination. *British Journal of Social Psychology, 46*, 91–113.

Vignoles, V. L., Regalia, C., Manzi, C., Golledge, J., & Scabini, E. (2006). Beyond self-esteem: Influence of multiple motives on identity construction. *Journal of Personality and Social Psychology, 90*, 308–333.

Visser, P. S., & Krosnick, J. A. (1998). Development of attitude strength over the life cycle: Surge and decline. *Journal of Personality and Social Psychology, 75*, 1389–1410.

Vohs, K. D., & Heatherton, T. F. (2000). Self-regulatory failure: A resource-depletion approach. *Psychological Science, 11*, 249–254.

Vohs, K. D., Mead, N. L., & Goode, M. R. (2006). The psychological consequences of money. *Science, 314*, 1154–1156.

von Goethe, J. W. (1808/1994). ( J. A. Froude, trans.) *Elective affinities*. Oxford: Oxford University Press.

von Hippel, W., Sekaquaptewa, D., & Vargas, P. (1995). On the role of encoding processes in stereotype maintenance. In M. P. Zanna (Ed.), *Advances in experimental social psychology* (Vol. 27, pp. 177–254). San Diego, CA: Academic Press.

von Hippel, W., Sekaquaptewa, D., & Vargas, P. (1997). The linguistic intergroup bias as an implicit indicator of prejudice. *Journal of Experimental Social Psychology, 33*, 490–509.

von Hippel, W., Silver, L. A., & Lynch, M. E. (2000). Stereotyping against your will: The role of inhibitory ability in stereotyping and prejudice among the elderly. *Personality and Social Psychology Bulletin, 26*, 523–532.

Vonk, R. (1993). The negativity effect in trait ratings and in open-ended descriptions of persons. *Personality and Social Psychology Bulletin, 19*, 269–278.

Vonk, R. (1998). The slime effect: Suspicion and dislike of likeable behavior toward superiors. *Journal of Personality and Social Psychology, 74*, 849–864.

Vorauer, J. D., Hunter, A. J., Main, K. J., & Roy, S. A. (2000). Meta-stereotype activation: Evidence from indirect measures for specific evaluative concerns experienced by members of dominant groups in intergroup interaction. *Journal of Personality and Social Psychology, 78*, 690–707.

Vorauer, J. D., Main, K. J., & O'Connell, G. B. (1998). How do individuals expect to be viewed by members of lower status groups? Content and implications of meta-stereotypes. *Journal of Personality and Social Psychology, 75*, 917–937.

Vorauer, J. D., & Miller, D. T. (1997). Failure to recognize the effect of implicit social influence on the presentation of self. *Journal of Personality and Social Psychology, 73*, 281–295.

Vormbrock, J. K. (1993). Attachment theory as applied to wartime and job-related marital separation. *Psychological Bulletin, 114*, 122–144.

Wagner, S., Hornstein, H. A., & Holloway, S. (1982). Willingness to help a stranger: The effects of social context and opinion similarity. *Journal of Applied Social Psychology, 12*, 429–443.

Wagner, W. G., Pfeffer, J., & O'Reilly, C. A. (1984). Organizational demography and turnover in top management groups. *Administrative Science Quarterly, 29*, 74–92.

Wallach, M. A., Kogan, N., & Bem, D. J. (1964). Diffusion of responsibility and level of risk taking in groups. *Journal of Abnormal and Social Psychology, 68*, 263–274.

Walster, E. M., Berscheid, E., & Walster, G. W. (1973). New directions in equity research. *Journal of Personality and Social Psychology, 25*, 151–176.

Walster, E. M., Walster, G. W., & Berscheid, E. (1978). *Equity: Theory and research*. Boston: Allyn and Bacon.

Walster, E. M., Walster, G. W., Piliavin, J., & Schmidt, L. (1973). "Playing hard to get": Understanding an elusive phenomenon. *Journal of Personality and Social Psychology, 26*, 113–121.

Walter, F., & Bruch, H. (2008). The positive group affect spiral: A dynamic model of the emergence of positive affective similarity in work groups. *Journal of Organizational Behavior, 29*, 239–261.

Walther, E. (2002). Guilty by mere association: Evaluative conditioning and the spreading attitude effect. *Journal of Personality and Social Psychology, 82*, 919–934.

Walther, E., Nagengast, B., & Trasselli, C. (2005). Evaluative conditioning in social psychology: Facts and speculations. *Cognition and Emotion, 19*, 175–196.

Walton, G. M., & Cohen, G. L. (2007). A question of belonging: Race, social fit, and achievement. *Journal of Personality and Social Psychology, 92*, 82–96.

Wang, Q. (2001). Culture effects on adults' earliest childhood recollection and self-description: Implications for the relation between memory and the self. *Journal of Personality and Social Psychology, 81*, 220–233.

Wason, P. C. (1968). Reasoning about a rule. *Quarterly Journal of Experimental Psychology, 20*, 273–281.

Watson, W. E., Kumar, K., & Michaelsen, L. K. (1993). Cultural diversity's impact on interaction process and performance: Comparing homogeneous and diverse task groups. *Academy of Management Journal, 36*, 590–602.

Weary, G., & Edwards, J. A. (1994). Individual differences in causal uncertainty. *Journal of Personality and Social Psychology, 67*, 308–318.

Weary, G., Jacobson, J. A., Edwards, J. A., & Tobin, S. J. (2001). Chronic and temporarily activated causal uncertainty beliefs and stereotype usage. *Journal of Personality and Social Psychology, 81*, 206–219.

Webb, E. J., Campbell, D. T., Schwartz, R. D., Sechrest, L., & Grove, J. B. (1981). *Nonreactive measures in the social sciences* (2nd ed.). Boston, MA: Houghton Mifflin.

Weber, E. U., & Johnson, E. J. (2009). Mindful judgment and decision making. *Annual Review of Psychology, 60*, 53–85.

Webster, D. M., & Kruglanski, A. W. (1994). Individual differences in need for cognitive closure. *Journal of Personality and Social Psychology, 67*, 1049–1062.

Weeks, M., & Vincent, M. A. (2007). Using religious affiliation to spontaneously categorize others. *International Journal for the Psychology of Religion, 17*, 317–331.

Wegener, D. T., & Petty, R. E. (1994). Mood management across affective states: The hedonic contingency hypothesis. *Journal of Personality and Social Psychology, 66*, 1034–1048.

Wegener, I., & Klauer, K. C. (2004). Inter-category versus intra-category fit: When social categories match social context. *European Journal of Social Psychology, 34*, 567–593.

Wegner, D. M. (1986). Transactive memory: A contemporary analysis of the group mind. In B. Mullen & G. R. Goethals (Eds.), *Theories of group behavior* (pp. 185–208). New York: Springer-Verlag.

Wegner, D. M. (1994). Ironic processes of mental control. *Psychological Review, 101*, 34–52.

Wegner, D. M. (2003). The mind's best trick: How we experience conscious will. *Trends in Cognitive Sciences, 7*, 65–69.

Wegner, D. M., Erber, R., & Raymond, P. (1991). Transactive memory in close relationships. *Journal of Personality and Social Psychology, 61*, 923–929.

Wegner, D. M., Lane, J. D., & Dimitri, S. (1994). The allure of secret relationships. *Journal of Personality and Social Psychology, 66*, 287–300.

Weick, K. E., & Roberts, K. H. (1993). Collective mind in organizations: Heedful interrelating on flight decks. *Administrative Science Quarterly, 38*, 357–381.

Weick, M., & Guinote, A. (2008). When subjective experiences matter: Power increases reliance on the ease of retrieval. *Journal of Personality and Social Psychology, 94*, 956–970.

Weiner, B. (1980). A cognitive (attribution)-emotion-action model of motivated behavior: An analysis of judgments of help-giving. *Journal of Personality and Social Psychology, 39*, 186–200.

Weiner, B. (1985). An attributional theory of achievement motivation and emotion. *Psychological Review, 92*, 548–573.

Weiner, B., Perry, R. P., & Magnusson, J. (1988). An attributional analysis of reactions to stigmas. *Journal of Personality and Social Psychology, 55*, 738–748.

Weise, D. R., Pyszczynski, T., Cox, C. R., Arndt, J., Greenberg, J., Solomon, S., & Kosloff, S. (2008). Interpersonal politics: The role of terror management and attachment processes in shaping political preferences. *Psychological Science, 19*, 448–455.

Weiss, B., & Feldman, R. S. (2006). Looking good and lying to do it: Deception as an impression management strategy in job interviews. *Journal of Applied Social Psychology, 36*, 1070–1086.

Weiss, R. F., Boyer, J. L., Lombardo, J. P., & Stich, M. H. (1973). Altruistic drive and altruistic reinforcement. *Journal of Personality and Social Psychology, 25*, 390–400.

Welfare stereotype said far from fact. (1996, September 9). *Hampshire Gazette*, pp. 1, 4.

Wells, A. J. (1988). Variations in mothers' self-esteem in daily life. *Journal of Personality and Social Psychology, 55*, 661–668.

West, S. G. (1975). Increasing the attractiveness of college cafeteria food: A reactance theory perspective. *Journal of Applied Psychology, 60*, 656–658.

Weyant, J. M. (1978). Effects of mood states, costs, and benefits on helping. *Journal of Personality and Social Psychology, 36*, 1169–1176.

Wheeler, L., & Kim, Y. (1997). What is beautiful is culturally good: The physical attractiveness stereotype has different content in collectivistic cultures. *Personality and Social Psychology Bulletin, 23*, 795–800.

Wheeler, L., Martin, R., & Suls, J. (1997). The proxy model of social comparison for self-assessment of ability. *Personality and Social Psychology Review, 1*, 54–61.

Wheeler, L., Reis, H. T., & Bond, M. H. (1989). Collectivism-individualism in everyday social life: The middle kingdom and the melting pot. *Journal of Personality and Social Psychology, 57*, 79–86.

Wheeler, M. E., & Fiske, S. T. (2005). Controlling racial prejudice: Social-cognitive goals affect amygdala and stereotype activation. *Psychological Science, 16*, 56–63.

Wheeler, S. C., & Petty, R. E. (2001). The effects of stereotype activation on behavior: A review of possible mechanisms. *Psychological Bulletin, 127*, 797–826.

White, R. W. (1959). Motivation reconsidered: The concepts of competence. *Psychological Review, 66*, 297–333.

Whitley, B. E., & Frieze, I. H. (1985). Children's causal attributions for success and failure in achievement settings: A meta-analysis. *Journal of Educational Psychology, 77*, 608–616.

Whitley, B. E., & Frieze, I. H. (1986). Measuring causal attributions for success and failure: A meta-analysis of the effects of question-wording style. *Basic and Applied Social Psychology, 7*, 35–51.

Wicker, A. W. (1969). Attitudes versus actions: The relationship of verbal and overt behavioral responses to attitude objects. *Journal of Social Issues, 25*, 41–79.

Wiener, R. L., Hurt, L., Russell, B., Mannen, K., & Gasper, C. (1997). Perceptions of sexual harassment: The effects of gender, legal standard, and ambivalent sexism. *Law and Human Behavior, 21*, 71–93.

Wigboldus, D. H. J., Semin, G. R., & Spears, R. (2000). How do we communicate stereotypes? Linguistic bases and inferential consequences. *Journal of Personality and Social Psychology, 78*, 5–18.

Wilder, D. A., & Shapiro, P. N. (1984). Role of outgroup cues in determining social identity. *Journal of Personality and Social Psychology, 47*, 342–348.

Wilder, D. A., & Shapiro, P. N. (1989). The role of competition-induced anxiety in limiting the beneficial impact of positive behavior by an outgroup member. *Journal of Personality and Social Psychology, 56*, 60–69.

Wildschut, T., Insko, C. A., & Gaertner, L. (2002). Intragroup social influence and intergroup competition. *Journal of Personality and Social Psychology, 82*, 975–992.

Williams, G. C. (1966). *Adaptation and natural selection: A critique of some current evolutionary thought*. Princeton, NJ: Princeton University Press.

Williams, K. D. (1997). Social ostracism. In R. Kowalski (Ed.), *Aversive interpersonal behaviors* (pp. 130–170). New York: Plenum.

Williams, K. D. (2007). Ostracism. *Annual Review of Psychology, 58*, 425–452.

Williams, K. D., Cheung, C. K. T., & Choi, W. (2000). Cyberostracism: Effects of being ignored over the internet. *Journal of Personality and Social Psychology, 79*, 748–762.

Williams, K. D., Govan, C. L., Croker, V., Tynan, D., Cruickshank, M., & Lam, A. (2002). Investigations into differences between social and cyberostracism. *Group Dynamics, 6*, 65–77.

Williams, K. D., Shore, W J., & Graphe, J. E. (1998). The silent treatment: Perceptions of its behaviors and associated feelings. *Group Processes and Intergroup Relations, 1*, 117–141.

Williams, K. D., & Sommer, K. L. (1997). Social ostracism by coworkers: Does rejection lead to loafing or compensation? *Personality and Social Psychology Bulletin, 23*, 693–706.

Williams, K. Y., & O'Reilly, C. A. (1998). Demography and diversity in organizations: A review of 40 years of research. In B. Staw & R. Sutton (Eds.), *Research in organizational behavior* (Vol. 20, pp. 77–140). Greenwich, CT: JAI Press.

Williams, L. E., & Bargh, J. A. (2008). Keeping one's distance: The influence of spatial distance cues on affect and evaluation. *Psychological Science, 19*, 302–308.

Wills, T. A. (1981). Downward comparison principles in social psychology. *Psychological Bulletin, 90*, 245–271.

Wilson, D. S., & Sober, E. (1994). Reintroducing group selection to the human behavioral sciences. *Behavioral and Brain Sciences, 17*, 585–654.

Wilson, D. S., Van Vugt, M., & O'Gorman, R. (2008). Multilevel selection theory and major evolutionary transitions: Implications for psychological science. *Current Directions in Psychological Science, 17*, 6–9.

Wilson, M. I. (1989). Marital conflict and homicide in evolutionary perspective. In R. W. Bell & N. J. Bell (Eds.), *Sociobiology and the social sciences*. Lubbock: Texas Tech University Press.

Wilson, M. I., & Daly, M. (1996). Male sexual proprietariness and violence against wives. *Current Directions in Psychological Science, 5*, 2–7.

Wilson, T. D., Aronson, E., & Carlsmith, K. (2010). The art of laboratory experimentation. In S. T. Fiske, D. T. Gilbert, & G. Lindzey (Eds.), *The handbook of social psychology* (5th ed.). New York: Wiley.

Wilson, T. D., & Brekke, N. (1994). Mental contamination and mental correction: Unwanted influences on judgments and evaluations. *Psychological Bulletin, 116*, 117–142.

Wilson, T. D., Dunn, D. S., Kraft, D., & Lisle, D. J. (1989). Introspection, attitude change, and attitude-behavior consistency: The disruptive effects of explaining why we feel the way we do. In L. Berkowitz (Ed.), *Advances in experimental social psychology* (pp. 287–343). San Diego, CA: Academic Press.

Wilson, T. D., & Gilbert, D. T. (2005). Affective forecasting: Knowing what to want. *Current Directions in Psychological Science, 14*, 131–134.

Wilson, T. D., Hodges, S. D., & La Fleur, S. J. (1995). Effects of introspecting about reasons: Inferring attitudes from accessible thoughts. *Journal of Personality and Social Psychology, 69*, 16–28.

Wilson, T. D., Houston, C. E., & Meyers, J. M. (1998). Choose your poison: Effects of lay beliefs about mental processes on attitude change. *Social Cognition, 16*, 114–132.

Wilson, T. D., & Schooler, J. W. (1991). Thinking too much: Introspection can reduce the quality of preferences and decisions. *Journal of Personality & Social Psychology, 60*, 181–192.

Wilson, T. D., Wheatley, T., Meyers, J. M., Gilbert, D. T., & Axsom, D. (2000). Focalism: A source of durability bias in affective forecasting. *Journal of Personality and Social Psychology, 78*, 821–836.

Winkielman, P., & Cacioppo, J. T. (2001). Mind at ease puts a smile on the face: Psychophysiological evidence that processing facilitation elicits positive affect. *Journal of Personality and Social Psychology, 81*, 989–1000.

Wintemute, G. J., Parham, C. A., Beaumont, J. J., Wright, M., & Drake, C. (1999). Mortality among recent purchasers of handguns. *New England Journal of Medicine, 341*, 1583–1589.

Winter, L., & Uleman, J. S. (1984). When are social judgments made? Evidence for the spontaneousness of trait inferences. *Journal of Personality and Social Psychology, 47*, 237–252.

Witte, K., & Allen, M. (2000). A meta-analysis of fear appeals: Implications for effective public health campaigns. *Health Education and Behavior, 27*, 591–615.

Wittenbrink, B., & Henly, J. R. (1996). Creating social reality: Informational social influence and the content of stereotypic beliefs. *Personality and Social Psychology Bulletin, 22*, 598–610.

Wittenbrink, B., Judd, C. M., & Park, B. (1997). Evidence for racial prejudice at the implicit level and its relationship with questionnaire measures. *Journal of Personality and Social Psychology, 72*, 262–274.

Wittenbrink, B., Judd, C. M., & Park, B. (2001a). Evaluative versus conceptual judgments in automatic stereotyping and prejudice. *Journal of*

*Experimental and Social Psychology, 37*, 244–252.

Wittenbrink, B., Judd, C. M., & Park, B. (2001b). Spontaneous prejudice in context: Variability in automatically activated attitudes. *Journal of Personality and Social Psychology, 81*, 815–827.

Wittig, M. A., & Molina, L. (2000). Moderators and mediators of prejudice reduction in multicultural education. In S. Oskamp (Ed.), *Reducing prejudice and discrimination*. Mahwah, NJ: Erlbaum.

Wofford, J. C., & Liska, L. Z. (1993). Path-goal theories of leadership: A meta-analysis. *Journal of Management, 19*, 857–876.

Wolsko, C., Park, B., Judd, C. M., & Wittenbrink, B. (2000). Framing interethnic ideology: Effects of multicultural and color-blind perspectives on judgments of groups and individuals. *Journal of Personality and Social Psychology, 78*, 635–654.

Wood, J. V. (1989). Theory and research concerning social comparisons of personal attributes. *Psychological Bulletin, 106*, 231–248.

Wood, W. (2000). Attitude change: Persuasion and social influence. *Annual Review of Psychology, 51*, 539–570.

Wood, W., & Eagly, A. H. (2002). A cross-cultural analysis of the behavior of women and men: Implications for the origins of sex differences. *Psychological Bulletin, 128*, 699–727.

Wood, W., Lundgren, S., Ouellette, J. A., Busceme, S., & Blackstone, T. (1994). Minority influence: A meta-analytic review of social influence processes. *Psychological Bulletin, 115*, 323–345.

Wood, W., Pool, G. J., Leck, K., & Purvis, D. (1996). Self-definition, defensive processing, and influence: The normative impact of majority and minority groups. *Journal of Personality and Social Psychology, 71*, 1181–1193.

Wood, W., Wong, F. Y., & Chachere, J. G. (1991). Effects of media violence on viewers' aggression in unconstrained social interaction. *Psychological Bulletin, 109*, 371–383.

Worchel, S. (1992). Beyond a commodity theory analysis of censorship: When abundance and personalism enhance scarcity effects. *Basic and Applied Social Psychology, 13*, 79–92.

Worchel, S., Axsom, D., Ferris, S., Samaha, C., & Schweitzer, S. (1978). Determinants of the effect of intergroup cooperation on intergroup attraction. *Journal of Conflict Resolution, 22*, 429–439.

Word, C. O., Zanna, M. P., & Cooper J. (1974). The nonverbal mediation of self-fulfilling prophecies in interracial interaction. *Journal of Experimental Social Psychology, 10*, 109–120.

Wright, S. C., Aron, A., McLaughlin-Volpe, T., & Ropp, S. A. (1997). The extended contact effect: Knowledge of cross-group friendships and

prejudice. *Journal of Personality and Social Psychology, 73*, 73–90.

Wundt, W. (1897). *Outlines of psychology*. New York: Stechert. (Translated 1907).

Wyer, N. A., Sherman, J. W., & Stroessner, S. J. (1998). The spontaneous suppression of racial stereotypes. *Social Cognition, 16*, 340–352.

Wyer, N. A., Sherman, J. W., & Stroessner, S. J. (2000). The roles of motivation and ability in controlling the consequences of stereotype suppression. *Personality and Social Psychology Bulletin, 26*, 13–25.

Wyer, R. S., Jr. (2007). Principles of mental representation. In A. W. Kruglanski & E. T. Higgins (Eds.), *Social psychology: Handbook of basic principles* (2nd ed., pp. 285–307). New York: Guilford.

Wynne-Edwards, V. C. (1965). Self-regulating systems in populations of animals. *Science, 147* (Whole No. 3665), 1543–1548.

Yamagishi, T. (1998). *Trust: The evolutionary game of mind and society*. Tokyo, Japan: Tokyo University Press.

Yamagishi, T. (2002). The structure of trust: An evolutionary game of mind and society. *Hokkaido Behavioral Science Report*, No. SP-13.

Yamagishi, T., Cook, K. S., & Watanabe, M. (1998). Uncertainty, trust, and commitment in the United States and Japan. *American Journal of Sociology 104*, 165–194.

Yamagishi, T., & Yamagishi, M. (1994). Trust and commitment in the United States and Japan. *Motivation and Emotion, 18*, 129–166.

Ybarra, O., & Stephan, W. G. (1999). Attributional orientations and the prediction of behavior: The attribution-prediction bias. *Journal of Personality and Social Psychology, 76*, 718–727.

Yelland, L. M., & Stone, W. F. (1996). Belief in the Holocaust: Effects of personality and propaganda. *Political Psychology, 17*, 551–562.

Yu, A. B., & Yang, K. S. (1994). The nature of achievement motivation in collectivist societies. In U. Kim, H. C. Triandis, C. Kâitcibasi, S. C. Choi, & G. Yoon (Eds.), *Individualism and collectivism: Theory, method, and applications* (pp. 239–256). Thousand Oaks, CA: Sage.

Yzerbyt, V., Castano, E., Leyens, J.-Ph., & Paladino, M. P. (2000). The primacy of the ingroup: The interplay of entitativity and identification. *European Journal of Social Psychology, 11*, 257–295.

Yzerbyt, V., Corneille, O., & Estrada, C. (2001). The interplay of subjective essentialism and entitativity in the formation of stereotypes. *Personality and Social Psychology Review, 5*, 141–155.

Yzerbyt, V. Y., Leyens, J.-Ph., & Bellour, F. (1995). The ingroup overexclusion effect: Identity concerns in decisions about group membership. *European Journal of Social Psychology*, *25*, 1–16.

Zajonc, R. B. (1965). Social facilitation. *Science*, *149* (Whole No. 3681), 269–274.

Zajonc, R. B. (1968). Attitudinal effects of mere exposure. *Journal of Personality and Social Psychology*, *9*, 1–27.

Zajonc, R. B. (1980). Feeling and thinking: Preferences need no inferences. *American Psychologist*, *35*, 151–175.

Zajonc, R. B. (1984). On the primacy of affect. *American Psychologist*, *39*, 117–123.

Zajonc, R. B. (1998). Emotions. In D. T. Gilbert, S. T. Fiske, & G. Lindzey (Eds.), *Handbook of social psychology* (4th ed., Vol. 1, pp. 591–634). New York: McGraw-Hill.

Zajonc, R. B., & Adelmann, P. K. (1987). Cognition and communication: A story of missed opportunities. *Social Science Information*, *26*, 3–30.

Zajonc, R. B., Adelmann, P. K., Murphy, S. T., & Niedenthal, P. M. (1987). Convergence in the physical appearance of spouses. *Motivation and Emotion*, *11*, 335–346.

Zak, P. J., Kurzban, R., & Matzner, W. T. (2005). Oxytocin is associated with human trustworthiness. *Hormones and Behavior*, *48*, 522–527.

Zdaniuk, B., & Levine, J. M. (1996). Anticipated interaction and thought generation: The role of faction size. *British Journal of Social Psychology*, *35*, 201–218.

Zebrowitz, L. A., Bronstad, P. M., & Lee, H. K. (2007). The contribution of face familiarity to ingroup favoritism and stereotyping. *Social Cognition*, *25*, 306–338.

Zebrowitz, L. A., & Collins, M. A. (1997). Accurate social perception at zero acquaintance: The affordances of a Gibsonian approach. *Personality and Social Psychology Review*, *1*, 204–223.

Zeifman, D., & Hazan, C. (1997). Attachment: The bond in pair-bonds. In J. A. Simpson & D. T. Kenrick (Eds.), *Evolutionary social psychology* (pp. 237–263). Mahwah, NJ: Erlbaum.

Zelli, A., Dodge, K. A., Lochman, J. E., Laird, R. D., & Conduct Problems Prevention Research Group (1999). The distinction between beliefs legitimizing aggression and deviant processing of social cues: Testing measurement validity and the hypothesis that biased processing mediates the effects of beliefs on aggression. *Journal of Personality and Social Psychology*, *77*, 150–166.

Zillmann, D. (1988). Cognition-excitation interdependencies in aggressive behavior. *Aggressive Behavior*, *14*, 51–64.

Zillmann, D., Bryant, J., & Carveth, R. A. (1981). The effect of erotica featuring sadomasochism and bestiality on motivated intermale aggression. *Personality and Social Psychology Bulletin*, *7*, 153–159.

Zillmann, D., Bryant, J., Comisky, P. W., & Medoff, N. J. (1981). Excitation and hedonic valence in the effect of erotica on motivated intermale aggression. *European Journal of Social Psychology*, *11*, 233–252.

Zillmann, D., & Sapolsky, B. S. (1977). What mediates the effects of mild erotica on annoyance and hostile behavior in males? *Journal of Personality and Social Psychology*, *35*, 587–596.

Zillmann, D., Weaver, J. B., Mundorf, N., & Aust, C. F. (1986). Effects of an opposite-gender companion's affect to horror on distress, delight, and attraction. *Journal of Personality and Social Psychology*, *51*, 586–594.

Zimbardo, P. G. (1969). The human choice: Individuation, reason, and order vs. deindividuation, impulse, and chaos. In W. J. Arnold & D. Levine (Eds.), *Nebraska Symposium on Motivation* (pp. 237–307). Lincoln: University of Nebraska Press.

Zucker, G. S., & Weiner, B. (1993). Conservatism and perceptions of poverty: An attributional analysis. *Journal of Applied Social Psychology*, *23*, 925–943.

Zuckerman, M. (1975). Belief in a just world and altruistic behavior. *Journal of Personality and Social Psychology*, *31*, 972–976.

Zuckerman, M., DePaulo, B. M., & Rosenthal, R. (1981). Verbal and nonverbal communication of deception. In L. Berkowitz (Ed.), *Advances in experimental social psychology* (Vol. 14, pp. 1–59). New York: Academic Press.

Zurbriggen, E. L. (2000). Social motives and cognitive power-sex associations: Predictors of aggressive sexual behavior. *Journal of Personality and Social Psychology*, *78*, 559–581.

# Author Index

# Subject Index

abuse in relationships, 327–328
accessibility, coherent self and, 190–191
accommodation
    in close relationships, 308, 323–326
    in commitment, 325
    defined, 325
accountable, 173
accuracy
    acquaintance and, 136–138
    circumscribed, 138–139
    defined, 135
    in different contexts, 138–139
    on different dimensions, 138
    of impressions, 135–149
    in inferences and heuristics, 139–148
    in social cognition, 134–149
    in subtle biases, 454–457
achieved status, physical attractiveness and, 286
acquaintance, 136–138
activated negative categories, 231
active-passive aggression, 392
actor-observer effect, 115–116
actual-ideal discrepancy, 209
actual-ought discrepancy, 209
actual self, 208
affect
    defined, 5
    primacy of, 241
affective disharmony, 304–305
affective forecasting, 213
affect-laden attitudes, controlling, 242–251
    individual differences in, 243–246
    situational context as, 250–251
    situational goals used in, 246–250
affiliation, 278
agency, defined, 123
agent-based computational model, 491
agentic roles of men, 300
agent self, 180
aggression, 389–426
    as coercive action, 391
    cognitive theories of (*See* cognitive theories of
        aggression)
    conceptual definitions of, 390–392
    conflict and (*See* conflict)
    core social motives of, 401–404
    displaced, 416–417
    fight-or-flight response and, 403
    imitative, 405–406
    instrumental *vs.* hostile, 391

measures of, 393–394
    moderators/mediators in, 416
    operational definitions of, 392–394
    proactive *vs.* reactive, 391
    proximate intent *vs.* primary intent in, 391
    relational, 402
    self-enhancement and, 421–424
    social artifacts facilitating (*See* social artifacts
        of aggression)
    social construction of, 413
    taxonomy of, 391–392
    tend-and-befriend response and, 403
aggression machine, Buss's, 393
aggression modules, 401
aggressive cue phenomenon, 398
alcohol myopia, 399
alcohol, social issues of, 399–400
algebraic model, Anderson's, 152–153
alternatives in commitment, 324
altruism
    defined, 342, 347, 361
    evidence for, 361–362
    reciprocal, 351–353
altruism hypotheses, 361–372
    attributions of responsibility and, 362–365
    empathy/sympathy and, 365–371
ambiguity
    attributional, 471–472
    in racism, 445–446
    in subtle biases, 443–444
ambivalence, 305
Ambivalent Sexism Inventory (ASI), 446
amygdala, 441–442
analytic decision-making, 148
anchor, 145
anchoring-and-adjustment heuristic, 145
anger scripts, 322
anthropomorphism, 123–124
anxious-ambivalent people, 330
appraisals, automatic, 411
approach-inhibition theory of power, 547
approval, compliance and, 554–555
artifacts, defined, 73, 394. *See also* social artifacts
    of aggression
ascribed status, physical attractiveness as, 286
assimilation, 169
association
    in classical conditioning, 236
    in inferring causality, 62
associative memory model, 160